International Conference on Recent Advances in Natural Language Processing 2015 (RANLP 2015)

Hissar, Bulgaria
7 – 9 September 2015

Editors:

Galia Angelova
Kalina Bontcheva
Ruslan Mitkov

ISBN: 978-1-5108-1328-1

Printed from e-media with permission by:

Curran Associates, Inc.
57 Morehouse Lane
Red Hook, NY 12571

Some format issues inherent in the e-media version may also appear in this print version.

Printed by Curran Associates, Inc. (2015)

Association for Computational Linguistics
209 N. Eighth Street
Stroudsburg, Pennsylvania 18360

Phone: 1-570-476-8006
Fax: 1-570-476-0860

acl@aclweb.org

Additional copies of this publication are available from:

Curran Associates, Inc.
57 Morehouse Lane
Red Hook, NY 12571 USA
Phone: 845-758-0400
Fax: 845-758-2634
Email: curran@proceedings.com
Web: www.proceedings.com

INTERNATIONAL CONFERENCE

RECENT ADVANCES IN

NATURAL LANGUAGE PROCESSING

PROCEEDINGS

Edited by
Galia Angelova, Kalina Bontcheva, Ruslan Mitkov

Hissar, Bulgaria

7–9 September, 2015

INTERNATIONAL CONFERENCE
RECENT ADVANCES IN
NATURAL LANGUAGE PROCESSING'2015

PROCEEDINGS

Hissar, Bulgaria
7–9 September 2015

ISSN 1313-8502

Designed and Printed by INCOMA Ltd.
Shoumen, BULGARIA

Preface

Welcome to the 10th International Conference on "Recent Advances in Natural Language Processing" (RANLP 2015) in Hissar, Bulgaria, 7–9 September 2015. The main objective of the conference is to give researchers the opportunity to present new results in Natural Language Processing (NLP) based on modern theories and methodologies.

The conference is preceded by two days of tutorials (5–6 September 2015) and the lecturers are:

- Leon Derczynski (University of Sheffield, UK)
- Constantin Orasan (University of Wolverhampton, UK)
- Paolo Rosso (University of Valencia, Spain)
- Hiracio Saggion (Universitat Pompeu Fabra, Spain)

The conference keynote speakers are:

- Marcello Federico (Fondazione Bruno Kessler, Italy)
- Khalil Sima'an (University of Amsterdam, the Netherlands)
- Idan Szpektor (Yahoo! Research, Israel)
- Piek Vossen (VU University Amsterdam, The Netherlands)
- Bonnie Webber (University of Edinburgh, UK)
- Michael Zock (CNRS-LIF, France)

This year 14 regular papers, 43 short papers, and 38 posters have been accepted for presentation at the conference. In 2015 RANLP hosts 5 workshops on influential NLP topics, such as Linked Open Data (LOD) for NLP, Balto-Slavic NLP, NLP for the legal domain, NLP for translation memories, and LT for closely related languages.

The proceedings cover a wide variety of NLP topics, including but not limited to: opinion mining and sentiment analysis; textual entailment, NLP for e-learning and healthcare; machine translation; part-of-speech tagging; lexicons and ontologies; named entity recognition; NLP for social media; temporal and semantic processing; word sense disambiguation; parsing.

We would like to thank all members of the Programme Committee and all reviewers. Together they have ensured that the best papers were included in the proceedings and have provided invaluable comments for the authors.

Finally, special thanks go to the University of Wolverhampton, the Bulgarian Academy of Sciences, the AComIn European project, and Ontotext for their generous support for RANLP.

Welcome to Hissar and we hope that you enjoy the conference!

The RANLP 2015 Organisers

The International Conference RANLP–2015 is organised by:

Research Group in Computational Linguistics,
University of Wolverhampton, UK

Linguistic Modelling and Knowledge Processing Department,
Institute of Information and Communication Technologies,
Bulgarian Academy of Sciences, Bulgaria

RANLP–2015 is partially supported by:

AComIn (Advanced Computing for Innovation, FP7 Capacity grant 316087)

Ontotext AD

Programme Committee Chair:

Ruslan Mitkov, University of Wolverhampton, UK

Organising Committee Chair:

Galia Angelova, Bulgarian Academy of Sciences, Bulgaria

Workshop Coordinator:

Kiril Simov, Bulgarian Academy of Sciences, Bulgaria

Publication Chair:

Kalina Bontcheva, University of Sheffield, UK

Tutorial Coordinator:

Preslav Nakov, Qatar Computing Research Institute, Qatar Foundation, Qatar

Proceedings Printing:

Nikolai Nikolov, INCOMA Ltd., Shoumen, Bulgaria

Programme Committee Coordinators:

Ivelina Nikolova, Bulgarian Academy of Sciences
Irina Temnikova, Qatar Computing Research Institute, Qatar Foundation, Qatar

Program Committee:

Guadalupe Aguado de Cea (Polytechnic University of Madrid)
Wilker Aziz (University of Amsterdam)
Jerome Bellegarda (Apple Inc.)
Chris Biemann (Technical University Darmstadt)
Kalina Bontcheva (University of Sheffield)
Svetla Boytcheva (Bulgarian Academy of Sciences)
António Branco (University of Lisbon)
Chris Brew (Thomson Reuters Corporate Research)
Nicoletta Calzolari (Institute of Computational Linguistics "Antonio Zampolli", Pisa)
Kevin Cohen (University of Colorado School of Medicine)
Gloria Corpas (University of Malaga)
Dan Cristea ("Alexandru Ioan Cuza" University of Iasi)
Richard Evans (University of Wolverhampton)
Antonio Ferrández Rodríguez (University of Alicante)
Fumiyo Fukumoto (University of Yamanashi)
Josef van Genabith (University of Saarland)
Ralph Grishman (New York University)
Tracy Holloway King (Ebay INC)
Veronique Hoste (Ghent University)
Mans Hulden (University of Colorado Boulder)
Diana Inkpen (University of Ottawa)
Hitoshi Isahara (Toyohashi University of Technology)
Alma Kharrat (Microsoft)
Milen Kouylekov (University of Oslo)
Udo Kruschwitz (University of Essex)
Hristo Krushkov (University of Plovdiv)
Sandra Kübler (University of Indiana)
Qun Liu (Dublin City University)
Bernardo Magnini (Foundation Bruno Kessler)
Suresh Manandhar (University of York)
Johanna Monti (University of Sassari)
Andres Montoyo (University of Alicante)
Alessandro Moschitti (Qatar Computing Research Institute, HBKU and University of Trento)
Rafael Muñoz-Guillena (University of Alicante)
Preslav Nakov (Qatar Computing Research Institute, HBKU)
Roberto Navigli (Sapienza University of Rome)
Mark-Jan Nederhof (University of St Andrews)
Vincent Ng (University of Texas at Dallas)
Michael Oakes (University of Wolverhampton)
Kemal Oflazer (Carnegie Mellon University - Qatar)
Constantin Orasan (University of Wolverhampton)
Petya Osenova (Bulgarian Academy of Sciences)
Pavel Pecina (Charles University in Prague)
Stelios Piperidis (Athena RC/ILSP)
Massimo Poesio (University of Essex)
Gábor Prószéky (Pázmány Péter Catholic University)

Allan Ramsay (University of Manchester)
Horacio Rodriguez (Polytechnic University of Catalonia)
Paolo Rosso (Polytechnic University of Valencia)
Vasile Rus (The University of Memphis)
Fatiha Sadat (University of Quebec in Montreal)
Horacio Saggion (University Pompeu Fabra)
Patrick Saint-Dizier (IRIT-CNRS)
Satoshi Sekine (New York University)
Violeta Seretan (University of Geneva)
Khaled Shaalan (The British University in Dubai)
Kiril Simov (Bulgarian Academy of Sciences)
Jan Šnajder (University of Zagreb)
Mark Stevenson (University of Sheffield)
Keh-Yih Su (Academia Sinica)
Stan Szpakowicz (University of Ottawa)
Marko Tadić (University of Zagreb)
Dan Tufis (Romanian Academy of Sciences)
Paola Velardi (Sapienza University of Rome)
Suzan Verberne (Radboud University Nijmegen)
Karin Verspoor (The University of Melbourne)
Aline Villavicencio (Federal University of Rio Grande do Sul)
Piek Vossen (VU University Amsterdam)
L. Alfonso Urena Lopez (University of Jaen)
Yorick Wilks (Florida Institute of Human and Machine Cognition)
Roman Yangarber (University of Helsinki)
Min Zhang (SooChow University)
Michael Zock (CNRS-LIF)

Reviewers:

Ahmet Aker (University of Sheffield)
Najah Albaqawi (University of Wolverhampton)
Itziar Aldabe (University of the Basque Country)
Ahmed Ali (Qatar Computing Research Institute, HBKU)
Hassina Aliane (Cerist)
Fahd Alotaibi (Faculty of Computing, King Abdulaziz University, KSA)
Le An Ha (University of Wolverhampton)
Eduard Barbu (Translated.net)
Alberto Barrón-Cedeño (Qatar Computing Research Institute, HBKU)
Leonor Becerra (University Jean Monnet)
Hannah Bechara (University of Wolverhampton)
Cosmin Bejan (Vanderbilt University)
Victoria Bobicev (Technical University of Moldova)
Houda Bouamor (Carnegie Mellon University in Qatar)
Boryana Bratanova (St Cyril and St Methodius University of Veliko Turnovo)
Erik Cambria (Nanyang Technological University)
Hernani Costa (University of Coimbra)
Giovanni Da San Martino (Qatar Computing Research Institute, HBKU)

Orphee De Clercq (Ghent University)
Leon Derczynski (University of Sheffield)
Isabel Duran (University of Málaga)
Ismail El Maarouf (University of Wolverhampton)
Rui Fang (Thomson Reuters R & D)
Mariano Felice (University of Cambridge)
Darja Fišer (University of Ljubljana)
Wei Gao (Qatar Computing Research Institute, HBKU)
Georgi Georgiev (Ontotext AD)
Goran Glavaš (University of Zagreb)
Rohit Gupta (University of Wolverhampton)
Ales Horak (Masaryk University)
Adrian Iftene ("Alexandru Ioan Cuza" University of Iasi)
Ruben Izquierdo Bevia (Vrije University of Amsterdam)
Ali Jaoua (Qatar University)
Junyi Jessy Li (University of Pennsylvania)
Héctor Jiménez-Salazar (Intersel)
Kristiina Jokinen (University of Cambridge)
Mijail Kabadjov (University of Essex)
David Kauchak (Pomona College)
Natalia Konstantinova (First Utility and University of Wolverhampton)
Ioannis Korkontzelos (University of Manchester)
Sujay Kumar Jauhar (Carnegie Mellon University)
Laska Laskova (University of Bologna)
Maria Liakata (University of Warwick)
Elena Lloret (University of Alicante)
Oier Lopez de Lacalle (University of the Basque Country)
Annie Louis (University of Edinburgh)
Wolfgang Maier (University of Düsseldorf)
Mireille Makary (University of Wolverhampton)
Shervin Malmasi (Macquarie University)
Manuel Maña López (University of Huelva)
Eugenio Martínez-Cámara (University of Jaén)
Irina Matveeva (NexLP LLC and Illinois Institute of Technology)
Georgiana Marsic (University of Wolverhampton)
Petar Mitankin (Sofia University)
Makoto Miwa (Toyota Technological Institute)
Behrang Mohit (Carnegie Mellon University in Qatar)
Arturo Montejo-Ráez (University of Jaén)
Johanna Monti (University of Sassari)
Paloma Moreda Pozo (University of Alicante)
Hamdy Mubarak (Qatar Computing Research Institute, HBKU)
Vinita Nahar (University of Wolverhampton)
Ivelina Nikolova (Bulgarian Academy of Sciences)
Maciej Ogrodniczuk (Polish Academy of Sciences)
Liviu P. Dinu (University of Bucharest)
Noa P. Cruz Diaz (University of Huelva)
Alexander Panchenko (Digital Society Laboratory)

Paul Piwek (The Open University)
Natalia Ponomareva (University of Wolverhampton)
Victoria Porro (University of Geneva)
Vinodkumar Prabhakaran (Columbia University)
John Prager (IBM)
Prokopis Prokopidis (Athena RC/ILSP)
Marta R. Costa-Jussà (Polytechnic University of Catalonia)
Carlos Ramisch (Aix-Marseille University)
Miguel Rios (University of Leeds)
Raphael Rubino (Prompsit Language Engineering)
Pavel Rychlý (Masaryk University)
Federico Sangati (Foundation Bruno Kessler, Trento)
Estela Saquete (University of Alicante)
Gerold Schneider (University of Zurich)
Nasredine Semmar (French Alternative Energies and Atomic Energy Commission (CEA))
Samira Shaikh (University at Albany)
Thamar Solorio (University of Houston)
Sanja Štajner (University of Lisbon)
Ekaterina Stambolieva (University of Lisbon)
Sebastian Stüker (Karlsruhe Institute of Technology)
Yoshimi Suzuki (University of Yamanashi)
Shiva Taslimipoor (University of Wolverhampton)
Irina Temnikova (Qatar Computing Research Institute, HBKU)
Marco Turchi (Foundation Bruno Kessler)
Cristina Vertan (Uiversity of Hamburg)
Manuel Vilares Ferro (University of Vigo)
Veronika Vincze (University of Szeged)
Yaqin Yang (Brandeis University)
Wajdi Zaghouani (Carnegie Mellon University in Qatar)

Table of Contents

POS Tagging for Arabic Tweets

Fahad Albogamy
School of Computer Science,
University of Manchester,
Manchester, M13 9PL, UK
albogamf@cs.man.ac.uk

Allan Ramsay
School of Computer Science,
University of Manchester,
Manchester, M13 9PL, UK
allan.ramsay@cs.man.ac.uk

Abstract

Part-of-Speech (POS) tagging is a key step in many NLP algorithms. However, tweets are difficult to POS tag because there are many phenomena that frequently appear in Twitter that are not as common, or are entirely absent, in other domains: tweets are short, are not always written maintaining formal grammar and proper spelling, and abbreviations are often used to overcome their restricted lengths. Arabic tweets also show a further range of linguistic phenomena such as usage of different dialects, romanised Arabic and borrowing foreign words. In this paper, we present an evaluation and a detailed error analysis of state-of-the-art POS taggers for Arabic when applied to Arabic tweets. The accuracy of standard Arabic taggers is typically excellent (96-97%) on Modern Standard Arabic (MSA) text; however, their accuracy declines to 49-65% on Arabic tweets. Further, we present our initial approach to improve the taggers' performance. By doing some improvements based on observed errors, we are able to reach 79% tagging accuracy.

1 Introduction

The last few years have seen an enormous growth in the use of social networking platforms such as Twitter in the Arab World. A study prepared and published by Semiocast in 2012 has revealed that Arabic was the fastest growing language on Twitter in 2011. People post about their lives, share opinions on a variety of topics and discuss current issues. There are millions of tweets daily, yielding a corpus which is noisy and informal, but which is sometimes informative. As a result, Twitter has become one of the most important social information mutual platforms. The nature of the text content of microblogs differs from traditional blogs. In Twitter, for example, a tweet is short and contains a maximum of 140 characters. Tweets also are not always written maintaining formal grammar and proper spelling. They are ambiguous and rich in acronyms. Slang and abbreviations are often used to overcome their restricted lengths (Java et al., 2007).

POS tagging is an essential processing step in a wide range of high level text processing applications such as information extraction, machine translation and sentiment analysis (Barbosa and Feng, 2010). However, people working on Arabic tweets have tended to concentrate on low level lexical relations which were used for shallow parsing and sentiment analysis such as (Mourad and Darwish, 2013; El-Fishawy et al., 2014). They do not use the standard linguistic pipeline tools such as POS tagging which might enable a richer linguistic analysis (Gimpel et al., 2011). The properties listed above of the microblogging domain make POS tagging on Twitter very different from their counterparts in more formal texts. It is an open question how well the features and techniques of NLP used on more well-formed data (e.g. in newswire domain) will transfer to Twitter in order to understand and exploit tweets. Therefore, we experimentally evaluate the performance of state-of-the-art POS taggers for MSA on Arabic tweets. POS tagging accuracy drops from about 97% on MSA to 49-65% on Arabic tweets. We also analyse their limitations and errors they made. Finally, we propose an approach to boost their performance and we are able to reach 79% tagging accuracy.

Our contributions in this paper are as follows:

1. Evaluating how robust state-of-the-art POS taggers for MSA are on Arabic tweets.
2. Identifying problem areas in tagging Arabic tweets and what caused the majority of er-

Proceedings of Recent Advances in Natural Language Processing, pages 1–8,
Hissar, Bulgaria, Sep 7–9 2015.

rors.

3. Boosting the taggers' performance on Arabic tweets by using pre- and post-processing techniques to address Arabic tweets' noisiness.

2 Related Work

POS tagging is a well-studied problem in computational linguistics and NLP over the past decades. This can be inferred from high accuracy of state-of-the-art POS tagging not only for English, but also most other languages such as Arabic, which reaches 97% for Arabic and English being at 97.32% (Gadde et al., 2011). However, the performance of standard POS taggers for English is severely degraded on Tweets due to their noisiness and sparseness (Ritter et al., 2011). Therefore, POS taggers for English tweets have been developed such as ARK, T-Pos and GATE TwitIE which reaches 92.8%, 88.4% and 89.37% accuracy respectively (Derczynski et al., 2013).

People working on Arabic tweets have tended to concentrate on lexical relations because a tagger that can actually work on this domain with an acceptance degree of accuracy, is yet to be developed (Elsahar and El-Beltagy, 2014). There has been relatively little work on building POS tools for Arabic tweets or similar text styles. (Al-Sabbagh and Girju, 2012; Abdul-Mageed et al., 2012) are strictly supervised approaches for tagging Arabic social media and they have assumed labelled training data. Their weakness is that they need a high quantity and quality of training data and this labelled data quickly becomes unrepresentative of what people post on Twitter. They also have been built specifically for dialectal Arabic and subjectivity and sentiment analysis.

Our work is, to best of our knowledge, the first step towards developing a POS tagger for Arabic tweets which can benefit a wide range of downstream NLP applications such as information extraction and machine translation. We evaluate the existing state-of-the-art POS tagging tools on Arabic tweets, with an intention of developing a POS tagger for Arabic tweets by utilising the existing standard POS taggers for MSA instead of building a separate tagger. We use pre- and post-processing modules to improve their accuracy. Then, we will use agreement-based bootstrapping on unlabelled data to create a sufficient amount of labelled training tweets that we can retrain our augmented version of Stanford on it.

3 Data Collection

There is a growing interest within the NLP community to build Arabic social media corpora by harvesting the web such as (Refaee and Rieser, 2014; Abdul-Mageed et al., 2012). However, none of these resources are publicly available yet. They also do not contain all phenomena of tweets as they appear in their original forms in Twitter and they have been built to be used mainly in sentiment analysis. Hence, we built our own corpus which preserves all phenomena of Arabic tweets. We used Twitter Stream API to crawl Twitter by setting a query to retrieve tweets from the Arabian Peninsula and Egypt by using latitude and longitude coordinates of these regions since Arabic dialects in these regions share similar characteristics and they are the closest Arabic dialects to MSA. We did not restrict tweets language to "Arabic" in the query since users may use other character sets such as English to write their Arabic tweets (Romanisation) or they may mix Arabic script with another language in the same tweets. Next, we excluded all tweets which were written completely in English. Then, we sampled 390 tweets (5454 words) from the collected set to be used in our experiments (similar studies for English tweets use a few hundred of tweets e.g. (Gimpel et al., 2011)).

4 Evaluating Existing POS Taggers

We evaluate three state-of-the-art publicly available POS taggers for Arabic, namely AMIRA (Diab, 2009), MADA (Habash et al., 2009) and Stanford Log-linear (Toutanova et al., 2003).

4.1 Gold Standard

A set of correctly annotated tweets (gold standard) is required in order to be able to appraise the outputs of POS taggers. Once we have this, we can compare the outputs of the POS taggers with this gold standard. Since there is no publicly available annotated corpus for Arabic tweets, we have created POS tags for Twitter phenomena (i.e. REP, MEN, HASH, LINK, USERN and RET for replies, mentions, hashtags, links, usernames and retweets respectively) and we manually annotated our dataset. To speed up manual annotation, we tagged tweets by using the taggers, and then we corrected the output of the taggers to construct a gold standard.

4.2 POS Tagging Performance Comparison

We compare three taggers on 390 tweets (5454 words) from our corpus. The performance of these taggers are computed by comparing the output of each tagger against the manually corrected gold standard. We use standard precision, recall and F-score as evaluation measures. The results for the AMIRA, MADA and Stanford which were trained on newswire text present poor success rates, for example, the precision (P) for AMIRA, MADA and Stanford on Arabic tweets are 60.2%, 65.8% and 49.0% respectively (see Table 1). These figures are far below the performance of the same taggers on well-formed genres such as PATB, where accuracy is around 96% for AMIRA and Stanford whereas MADA achieves over 97% accuracy. This huge drop in the accuracy of these taggers when applied to Arabic tweets warrants some analysis of the problem and of mistagged cases.

Tagger	Newswire	Arabic Tweets
AMIRA	96.0%	**60.2%**
MADA	97.0%	**65.8%**
Stanford	96.5%	**49.0%**

Table 1: POS tagging performance comparison

4.3 Error Analysis

We noticed that most of the mistagged tokens are unknown words. In this case, the taggers rely on contextual clues such as the word's morphology and its sentential context to assign them the most appropriate POS tags (Foster et al., 2011). We identified the unknown words that were mistagged and classified them into two groups: Arabic words and non-Arabic tokens (see Table 2 for more details).

Arabic words These are words which are written in Arabic, but which were assigned incorrect POS tags by the taggers. This category represents 73.5%, 68.1% and 79.2% of the total of mistagged items by AMIRA, MADA and Stanford respectively. We observed that words in this category have different characteristics and most of them are twitter phenomena. So, we classify them into subcategories as follows:

MSA words These are proper words which are used in well-formed text and part of MSA vocabulary, but which were assigned incorrect POS tags by the taggers. We observed that the accuracy of MSA words which are not noisy dropped from 96% for AMIRA, 96.5% for Stanford and 97% for MADA on newswire domain to 71.8%, 55% and 79.3% respectively on Arabic tweets. There are three possible reasons for that: 1) the context of MSA words being noisy, 2) text structure has been changed, for example, many function words are omitted in tweets and 3) the domain change between the Arabic Treebank corpus on which they were trained and tested and the Arabic tweets. For example, the word "عصينا" (disobey) was tagged *NN* by AMIRA,*noun* by MADA and *NNP* by Stanford but, in fact, it is a verb.

Concatenation In this classification, two or more words were connected to each other to form one token. So, the taggers struggled to label them. Users may connect words deliberately to overcome tweets restricted length or accidentally. In this experiment, the taggers mistagged all connected words in the subset. For example, the word "تأكدأن" was labelled *NN* by AMIRA, labelled *noun* by MADA and tagged *NNP* by Stanford. But, in fact, it is two words "تأكد" and "أن" connected together which are a verb and a conjunction respectively.

Repeated letters Words in this classification have one or more letters repeated. Users repeat letters deliberately to express subjectivity and sentiment. For example, the word "واااااااااااقفيييييييين" (standing) was labelled *NNS* by AMIRA and Stanford and *noun* by MADA but , in fact, it is an adjective.

Named entities All of these words should be labelled proper noun by the taggers because they refer to person, place or organization, but they mistagged them since these words were not part of their training data. For example, the proper noun "مسلم" was tagged *NN* by AMIRA and Stanford and labelled *noun* by MADA.

Spelling mistakes It is not easy to know the intent of the user, but some words seem likely to have been accidentally misspelled. Most words belonging to this category were mistagged by the taggers. For example, the word "كثرة" was misspelled and it should be written as "كثرت" (abounded). AMIRA and Stanford tagged it *NN* and MADA labelled it *noun* but , in fact, it is a verb.

Slang It is one of Twitter phenomena. The words in this category are regarded as informal and are typically restricted to a particular context or group of people. They are often mistagged by

Tagger	Types of mistagged items	Arabic Words								Non-Arabic Tokens				
		MSA words	Concatenation	Repeated letters	Named Entities	Spelling mistakes	Slang	Characters deletion	Transliteration	Romanisation	Emoticons	Emoji	Foreign words	Twitter specific
AMIRA	% of Errors	53.3%	1.8%	0.8%	8.7%	0.6%	6.2%	0.9%	1.2%	1.0%	0.5%	2.8%	2.6%	19.6%
	Accuracy	71.8%	0.0%	40.0%	49.2%	35.0%	30.4%	16.7%	61.8%	21.4%	0.0%	0.0%	35.6%	0.0%
MADA	% of Errors	45.5%	2.1%	0.8%	8.5%	0.6%	7.1%	1.0%	2.4%	1.4%	0.5%	3.3%	3.9%	22.8%
	Accuracy	79.3%	0.0%	50.0%	57.0%	40.0%	32.0%	20.8%	35.3%	7.1%	0.0%	0.0%	17.2%	0.0%
Stanford	% of Errors	65.5%	1.4%	0.9%	3.2%	0.6%	6.4%	0.5%	0.8%	0.7%	0.4%	2.2%	2.4%	15.1%
	Accuracy	55.0%	0.0%	20.0%	75.7%	20.0%	7.2%	45.8%	67.6%	25.0%	0.0%	0.0%	21.8%	0.0%

Table 2: Errors percentage of each mistagged class and its accuracy

the taggers. For example, the slang word "شوف" is the counterpart of MSA word "انظر" which means *look!*.

Characters deletion Arabic users delete letters from words deliberately to overcome tweets restricted length or because they do not have enough time to write complete words. For example, the word "في" (at) was shorten to only one letter "ف". This word was tagged *PUNC* by AMIRA, *conj* by MADA and *CC* by Stanford but , in fact, it is a preposition.

Transliteration Arabic users borrow some words and multiwords abbreviations from English. They use their Arabic transliteration in Arabic tweets. For example, LOL in English (Laugh Out Loud) is written in Arabic as "لول" and "mix" in English is written in Arabic as "مكس" . AMIRA and Stanford tagged the translated form of mix as *NN* whereas MADA labelled them all as *noun* but, in fact, it is a verb.

Twitter-specific They are elements that are unique to Twitter such as reply, mention, retweet, hashtag and url. They represent 19.6%, 22.8% and 15.1% of the total of mistagged items by AMIRA, MADA and Stanford respectively. In fact, taggers mistagged all Twitter-specific elements in the experiment and they tokenised them in different ways. AMIRA uses punctuation as an indicator for a new token so replies, mentions, retweets and hashtags in tweets are broken into the indicator part (@ for replies, mentions and retweets and # for hashtags) and the remainder of them. Moreover, if the remainder part contains punctuation marks, AMIRA will split it further into parts. AMIRA also breaks urls into parts since they contain punctuation marks. In contrast, MADA and Stanford do not break all Twitter-specific elements into parts since they use the space as an indicator for a new token. MADA has one exception to this rule. If a hashtag started with an Arabic letter, then MADA breaks it into parts when punctuation is found. We notice that MADA always labels unsplitted Twitter-specific elements as nouns *noun* (see Table 3).

	AMIRA		MADA/Stanford	
Twitter element	Token	Tag	Token	Tag
@Moh_Ali	@	PUNC	@Moh_Ali	noun
	Moh	NN		
	_	PUNC		
	Ali	NN		

Table 3: Twitter element tokenised and tagged by taggers

Non-Arabic tokens This group contains the remaining twitter phenomena which are appear in Arabic tweets, but which are not written by using the Arabic alphabet. They represent 6.9%, 9.1% and 5.7% of the total of mistagged items by AMIRA, MADA and Stanford respectively. We classify them into subcategories based on their shared characteristics as follows:

Romanisation Arabic users tend to use Latin letters and Arabic numerals to write Arabic tweets because the actual Arabic alphabet is unavailable for technical reasons, difficult to use or they speak Arabic but they cannot write Arabic script. For example, the word 3ala which is the Romanised form of the Arabic word "على" was tagged *NN* by AMIRA, labelled *noun* by MADA and *CD* by Stanford but, in fact, it is a preposition.

Emoticons They are constructed by using traditional alphabetics or punctuation, usually a face expression. They are used by users to express their feelings or emotions in tweets. AMIRA and MADA break emoticons into parts during tokenisation processes and they deal with each part as punctuation so all emoticons lost their meaning.

For example, the emoticon (= was broken into two parts: "(" (labelled *PUNC*) and "=" (labelled *PUNC*). In contrast, Stanford does not break them into parts but it mistagged all of them.

Untagged emoji Emoji means symbols provided in software as small pictures in line with the text which are used by users to express their feelings or emotions in tweets. AMIRA and MADA omitted these symbols in the tokenisation stage and they did not tag them. For example, the heart symbol ♡ was omitted when tweets were tokenised by the taggers. In contrast, Stanford does not omit them but it mistagged all of them.

Foreign words Some Arabic tweets contain foreign words especially from English. These words may refer to events, locations, English hashtags or retweet of English tweets with comments written in Arabic. "I'm at Arab Bank البنك العربي" this tweet is an example of this category. AMIRA and Stanford tagged foreign words in this tweet as 'I'm' is a *VBD*, 'at' is a *PUNC*, 'Arab' is a *NN* and 'Bank' as *NN* whereas MADA labelled them all as *noun*.

5 Improving POS Tagging Performance

Our experiments show that the taggers present poor success rates since they were trained on newswire text and designed to deal with MSA text. They fail to deal with Twitter phenomena. As a result, their outcomes are not useful to be used in linguistics downstream processing applications such as information extraction and machine translation in microblogging domain. Therefore, there is a need for a POS tagger which should take into consideration the characteristics of Arabic tweets and yield acceptable results.

Our goal is not to build a new POS tagger for Arabic tweets. The goal is to make existing POS taggers for MSA robust towards noise. There are two ways to do so, one is to retrain POS taggers on Arabic tweets and alter their implementation if needed, the other is to overcome noise through pre- and post-processing to the tagging. Our approach is based on both approaches. We combine normalisation and external knowledge to boost the taggers' performance. Then, we will retrain Stanford tagger on Arabic tweets since its speed is ideal for tweets domain and it is only the retrainable tagger. However, we do not have suitable labelled training data to do so. Therefore, we will use bootstrapping on unlabelled data to create a sufficient amount of labelled training tweets.

5.1 Pre- and Post-processing

As seen in error analysis, unknown words (out-of-vocabulary tokens or OOV) represent a large proportion of mistagged tokens. We argue that normalisation and external knowledge will reduce this proportion which will improve the performance of the proposed tagger. Normalisation is the process of providing in-vocabulary (IV) versions of OOV words (Han and Baldwin, 2011). We create a mapping from OOV tokens to their IV equivalents by using suitable dictionaries and the original token is replaced with its equivalent IV token. External sources of knowledge such as regular expression rules, gazetteer lists and an output of English tagger are also used. The combination of normalisation and external knowledge is applied to text as pre- and post-processing steps.

Handling Concatenation Users may connect words deliberately to overcome tweets restricted length or accidentally. This forms tokens which all taggers struggle to tag them correctly. One approach to deal with these cases is to use a MSA dictionary. We constructed a MSA dictionary from 250k Arabic words which were extracted from news website[1]. We handle concatenation for a word in the corpus W as follows:

1. If the length of W is <= 5, then it is left as it is, since the average length of Arabic words is five letters (Mustafa, 2012).
2. Else, if W exists in the MSA dictionary, then it is left as it is, since it is a valid MSA word.
3. Else, if a part P of W exists in the MSA dictionary, then W is split into two parts P and the remainder and the same steps are applied to the remainder.

We apply the above algorithm on "تأكدأن". The length of this token is six characters, it is larger than the average length of Arabic words, so we check if it exists in the MSA dictionary, but it does not exist in the dictionary. Then we check if any part of it exists in the dictionary, we find "تأكد" in the dictionary so we split the token into two parts "تأكد" and the remaining characters and then we apply the algorithm on the second part. Because the length of the second part "أن" is two characters, it is left as it is and the algorithm stops.

Handling Elongated Words We handle these

[1] http://sourceforge.net/projects/ar-text-mining/files/Arabic-Corpora/

cases by using the same MSA dictionary mentioned above. Given a word in the corpus W, we do the following steps:

1. If a word W exists in the MSA dictionary, then it is left as it is, even it contains repeated letters.
2. Else, a compressed form of it is constructed by removing any repetition in letters.

Handling Characters Deletion We have noticed that users tend to shorten closed-class lexical items more than other speech classes to overcome tweets restricted length since it is easy for recipients of tweets to recognise them. We handle these cases by detecting and replacing them by their IV equivalents.

Handling Slang We handle these cases by mapping slangs to their IV equivalents, but slang is an open class and it is difficult to detect all slangs in tweets domain. Therefore, we select the most frequent twenty slang words from 17k types in our corpus (10 million tokens) and map them to their IV equivalents.

Handling Twitter-specific Items We use regular expression rules to detect and tag Twitter-specific elements such as mentions, hashtags, urls and etc. by doing some pre-processing and then tagging and finally doing post-processing. Due to the space limit, we present the way we deal with hashtags: all the remaining Twitter elements are tagged in similar ways. First, we detected hashtags by using regular expression rules. Then, we removed the hashtag signs and underscores from raw tweets. Next, we tagged them by using AMIRA, MADA and Satnford. Finally, we inserted hashtag signs in their original place in tweets to indicate the beginning and the end of hashtags content as shown in Table 4.

Raw Tweet	حياتي فالبيت بقضيهاجنب الشاحن!! #جالاكسي _لا _تكلمني
MADA	... !,punc !,punc #,punc jAlAksy,noun _, noun **lA,verb**_,noun tklmny,verb
Preprocessing	حياتي فالبيت بقضيها جنب الشاحن !! جالاكسي لا تكلمني
MADA	... punc !,punc jAlAksy,noun **lA,part_neg** tklmny,verb
Postprocessing	... punc !,punc <**hash**> jAlAksy,noun lA,part_neg tklmny,verb </**hash**>

Table 4: Pre- and post-processing (tag hashtag's words)

In fact, the taggers not just mistagged Twitter elements, but they also mistagged some MSA words in the same tweets because the text is noisy and the taggers rely on contextual clues. By using the above approach, we are not just able to tag Twitter elements correctly but we also make the context less noisy so the taggers are more likely to tag MSA words correctly as "IA" word in Table 4.

Handling Named Entities These can be recognised by using gazetteer lists. We use ANERGazet[2] which a collection of three Gazetteers, (i) Locations: it contains names of continents, countries, cities, etc.; (ii) People: it has names of people recollected manually from different Arabic websites; and finally (iii) Organizations: it contains names of organizations like companies, football teams, etc..

Handling English Words Our focus is on Arabic tweets, but some of them contain English words. These words may refer to events, locations, English hashtags or retweet of English tweets with comments written in Arabic and they are part of the syntactic structure of Arabic tweets. So, they need to be tagged correctly. In this case, we use Stanford for English (Toutanova et al., 2003) to tag English words as a post-processing step.

5.2 Agreement-based Bootstrapping

Bootstrapping is used to create a labelled training data from large amounts of unlabelled data (Cucerzan and Yarowsky, 2002; Zavrel and Daelemans, 2000). There are different ways to select the labelled data from the taggers' outputs. We will follow (Clark et al., 2003) in using agreement-based training method. We will use the augmented versions of AMIRA, MADA and Stanford taggers to tag a large amount of Arabic tweets and add the tokens which they are agreed on to the training data. The taggers use different tagsets. Therefore, we will map these tagsets to a unified tagset consisting of main POS tags. Finally, we will retrain Stanford tagger on the selected labelled data.

Results for Pre- and Post-processing

In our experiments, the taggers were adapted to handle Twitter phenomena. The experiments were run using three off-the-shelf taggers trained on PATB and our augmented approach to address Arabic tweets noisiness as described in Section 5. Table 5 shows the overall performance of the augmented versions of the taggers compared with their baseline performance in Table 1. By combining normalisation and external knowledge,

[2]http://users.dsic.upv.es/grupos/nle/?file=kop4.php

we are able to reduce unknown tokens in each category which boosts the taggers' performance. The overall performance of the three taggers increases by absolute twelve percent accuracy for AMIRA, by absolute thirteen percent for MADA and by absolute sixteen percent for Stanford. This improvement in accuracy will reduce the propagation of POS tagging errors to downstream applications on Arabic tweets such as information extraction.

Tagger	Tweets	Processed Tweets
AMIRA	60.2%	**72.6%**
MADA	65.8%	**79.0%**
Stanford	49.0%	**65.2%**

Table 5: Impact of applying pre- and post-processing on POS tagging accuracy

6 Conclusion and Future Work

We have examined the consequences of applying MSA-trained POS tagging to Arabic tweets. The combination of normalisation and external knowledge was applied to text as pre- and post-processing steps. These steps go some of the way towards improving the taggers' accuracy over the MSA baseline. Our next step is to use bootstrapping and taggers agreement on unlabelled data to create a sufficient amount of labelled training tweets in order to retrain Stanford on it since it is only the retrainable tagger.

Acknowledgments

The authors would like to thank the anonymous reviewers for their encouraging feedback and insights. Fahad would also like to thank King Saud University for their financial support. Allan Ramsay's contribution to this work was partially supported by Qatar National Research Foundation (grant NPRP-7-1334-6 -039).

References

Muhammad Abdul-Mageed, Sandra Kübler, and Mona Diab. 2012. SAMAR: A system for subjectivity and sentiment analysis of Arabic social media. In *Proceedings of WASSA*.

Rania Al-Sabbagh and Roxana Girju. 2012. A supervised POS tagger for written Arabic social networking corpora. In *Proceedings of KONVENS*.

Fahad Albogamy and Allan Ramsay. 2015. Towards POS tagging for Arabic tweets. In *Proceedings of ACL Workshop on Noisy User-generated Text*.

Luciano Barbosa and Junlan Feng. 2010. Robust sentiment detection on twitter from biased and noisy data. In *Proceedings of ACL*.

Eric Brill. 1995. Transformation-based error-driven learning and natural language processing: A case study in part-of-speech tagging. *Computational Linguistics*.

Stephen Clark, James R. Curran, and Miles Osborne. 2003. Bootstrapping POS taggers using unlabelled data. In *Proceedings of NAACL*. ACL.

Silviu Cucerzan and David Yarowsky. 2002. Bootstrapping a multilingual part-of-speech tagger in one person-day. In *Proceedings of NLL*. ACL.

Leon Derczynski, Alan Ritter, Sam Clark, and Kalina Bontcheva. 2013. Twitter part-of-speech tagging for all: Overcoming sparse and noisy data. In *Proceedings of RANLP*.

Mona Diab. 2009. Second generation AMIRA tools for Arabic processing: Fast and robust tokenization, POS tagging, and base phrase chunking. In *2nd International Conference on Arabic Language Resources and Tools*.

Nawal El-Fishawy, Alaa Hamouda, Gamal M. Attiya, and Mohammed Atef. 2014. Arabic summarization in twitter social network. *Ain Shams Engineering Journal*.

Hady Elsahar and Samhaa R. El-Beltagy. 2014. A fully automated approach for Arabic slang lexicon extraction from microblogs. In *Proceedings of CICLing*.

Jennifer Foster, Özlem Çetinoglu, Joachim Wagner, Joseph Le Roux, Stephen Hogan, Joakim Nivre, Deirdre Hogan, Josef Van Genabith, et al. 2011. # hardtoparse: POS tagging and parsing the twitterverse. In *Proceedings of AAAI*.

Phani Gadde, L. V. Subramaniam, and Tanveer A. Faruquie. 2011. Adapting a WSJ trained part-of-speech tagger to noisy text: Preliminary results. In *Proceedings of MOCR*.

Kevin Gimpel, Nathan Schneider, Brendan O'Connor, Dipanjan Das, Daniel Mills, Jacob Eisenstein, Michael Heilman, Dani Yogatama, Jeffrey Flanigan, and Noah A. Smith. 2011. Part-of-speech tagging for Twitter: Annotation, features, and experiments. In *Proceedings of ACL: HLT*.

Nizar Habash, Owen Rambow, and Ryan Roth. 2009. Mada+ tokan: A toolkit for Arabic tokenization, diacritization, morphological disambiguation, POS tagging, stemming and lemmatization.

Bo Han and Timothy Baldwin. 2011. Lexical normalisation of short text messages: Makn sens a #twitter. In *Proceedings of ACL: HLT*.

Akshay Java, Xiaodan Song, Tim Finin, and Belle Tseng. 2007. Why we Twitter: Understanding microblogging usage and communities. In *Proceedings of WebKDD*. ACM.

Ahmed Mourad and Kareem Darwish. 2013. Subjectivity and sentiment analysis of modern standard Arabic and Arabic microblogs. In *Proceedings of WASSA*. ACL.

Suleiman H Mustafa. 2012. Word stemming for Arabic information retrieval: The case for simple light stemming.

Eshrag Refaee and Verena Rieser. 2014. An Arabic Twitter corpus for subjectivity and sentiment analysis. In *Proceedings of LREC*.

Alan Ritter, Sam Clark, Mausam, and Oren Etzioni. 2011. Named entity recognition in tweets: An experimental study. In *Proceedings of EMNLP*.

Kristina Toutanova, Dan Klein, Christopher D. Manning, and Yoram Singer. 2003. Feature-rich part-of-speech tagging with a cyclic dependency network. In *Proceedings of NAACL*.

Jakub Zavrel and Walter Daelemans. 2000. Bootstrapping a tagged corpus through combination of existing heterogeneous taggers. In *Proceedings of LREC*.

Lexicon-based Sentiment Analysis for Persian Text

Fatemeh Amiri[1], **Simon Scerri**[2] **and Mohammad H. Khodashahi**[3]
[1]Media Informatics, RWTH Aachen University, Germany
[2]Fraunhofer IAIS, Sankt Augustin, NRW, Germany
[3]Institute of Computer Science, University of Bonn, Germany
amirii.fatemeh@gmail.com
simon.scerri@iais.fraunhofer.de
mh.khodashahi@gmail.com

Abstract

The vast information related to products and services available online, of both objective and subjective nature, can be used to provide contextualized suggestions and guidance to possible new customers. User feedback and comments left on different shopping websites, portals and social media have become a valuable resource, and text analysis methods have become an invaluable tool to process this kind of data. A lot of business use-cases have applied sentiment analysis in order to gauge people's response to a service or product, or to support customers with reaching a decision when choosing such a product. Although methods and techniques in this area abound, the majority only address a handful of natural languages at best. In this paper, we describe a lexicon-based sentiment analysis method designed around the Persian language. An evaluation of the developed GATE pipeline shows an encouraging overall accuracy of up to 69%.

1 Introduction

In comparison to other more popular and widespread language, few research efforts have sought to provide text analytics services targeting Persian text documents on the Web. As the official language of Iran, Afghanistan, and Tajikistan and an estimated 110 million people, we feel that the Persian language has not been given the attention it deserves. Besides attaining merit from a purely linguistic point of view, providing technologies for Persian text analysis has also business implications in the regions where the language remains a preferred working language. In particular, sentiment analysis has a high potential in providing insights for several Persian online communities and social media. Most of the limited available techniques have employed Machine Learning (ML) algorithms, such as Support Vector Machine-based (SVM) methods. In contrast, our approach is based on a manually-created lexicon enriched with sentiment scores; coupled with hand-coded grammar rules. In tackling our objective, we are faced with language-specific challenges and constraints. In the Persian language there is typically a large difference between formal and informal writing styles. There is also a high level of complexity due to the frequent morphological operations. Besides a complex morphology, Persian has some other distinctive features, such as lexicon intricacy, a high context sensitivity of the script, and a free words order due to independent case-marking (Hajmohammadi and Ibrahim, 2013). Therefore models used in approaches behind other languages, or even aspects of which, can hardly be used in Persian text analytics methods.

In this paper, we describe how we approached the language-specific challenges when designing and implementing a lexicon-based sentiment analysis method for Persian text. An evaluation of this method is also presented. But before we provide an overview of related work in this area.

2 Related Work

As a technique, sentiment analysis has improved significantly in recent years, especially for mainstream languages such as English. The technique has an especially important role in business and financial circles. Efforts such as (Feldman et al., 2011) have specifically focused on stock markets and market predictions, whereas others focused on deriving changing opinions and perceptions from subjective information shared on social networks (Pak and Paroubek, 2010). Many studies have been performed to try and identify a

Proceedings of Recent Advances in Natural Language Processing, pages 9–16,
Hissar, Bulgaria, Sep 7–9 2015.

superior approach in the many techniques available (Feldman, 2013), in order to attain better results and higher accuracies. Different surveys have been carried out, with different viewpoints and results (Liu, 2012) (Liu, 2010). A large share of sentiment analysis techniques employ learning-based approaches (Pang et al., 2002) (Jo and Oh, 2011). Of these the most promising are SVM- and Nave Bayes-based methods. Using a supervised classification task, these methods attain up to 82.9% accuracy (Hajmohammadi and Ibrahim, 2013). However, various drawbacks have been noted, such as their strict reliance on a corpus of human-coded texts for training, and their domain dependency (Basiri et al., 2014) (Taboada et al., 2011).

A contrasting approach is the use of lexicon-based methods (Ding et al., 2008) (Thelwall et al., 2010), which calculate a documents orientation from the semantic orientation of words or phrases within that document (Turney, 2002). Sentiment-bearing words and phrases forming a sentiment lexicon (Liu, 2012) can be derived from different resources. Some have employed seed words to expand the final list of words (Hatzivassiloglou and McKeown, 1997), or use existing linguistic resources like the ANEW words (Bradley and Lang, 1999), SentiWordNet (Baccianella et al., 2010) and WordNet Affect (Strapparava et al., 2004).

Some research efforts have satisfactorily mixed the two above approaches to gain a better response (Mudinas et al., 2012). Although future work will consider extending our method with aspects from the first of the two approaches, for the moment we have opted to investigate a technique based solely on the second approach. Other surveyed research efforts, including the ones cited above, have already provided similar techniques that identify the orientation of a document based on the polarity of adjectives in a dictionary. However, they addressed either English (Hatzivassiloglou and McKeown, 1997) or other languages such as Urdu (Syed et al., 2010), Chinese (Zagibalov and Carroll, 2008), French (Ghorbel and Jacot, 2011) or Arabic (Abdul-Mageed et al., 2011).

Of the surveyed efforts which tackle the Persian language, a majority also utilized machine learning approaches. Bagheri and Saraee (Saraee and Bagheri, 2013) devised a learning-based approach that employs Nave-Bayes text classification. They proposed a new feature selected method (MMI) and reported a performance of 70%. Hajmohammadi and Ibrahim (Hajmohammadi and Ibrahim, 2013) used standard machine learning techniques incorporated into the domain of online Persian-written movie reviews to automatically classify reviews as either positive or negative. They also combined Nave-Bayes and SVM, in conjunction with six feature presentations concerning n-gram presence/frequency in order to examine the effects of the classifiers and the feature options on Persian sentiment classification.

More recently, a lexicon-based unsupervised approach (Basiri et al., 2014) addressed specific Persian text processing difficulties, such as different forms of writing styles and ignoring short spaces between words in texts. The approach utilises the SentiStrength library, which applies a combined method to detect the polarity and strength of short informal social texts. However, as this library was designed around the English language, the authors rely on the translation of the core resulting list to Persian. The reported results indicate an F-measure of around 90%.

The major difference between our approach and the above-mentioned effort is that we use an own-constructed lexicon and involve a number of human annotators to provide multiple sentiment scores. In resolving any resulting conflicts, we also address the issue of subjectivity. Therefore, our approach is in theory more appropriate as the generated lexicon and polarity pairs are Persian language-specific, whereas language translations such as the method used in the above-mentioned approach are problematic since languages are intrinsically different.

Our final aim is to outperform existing ML-based methods and achieve an acceptable F-measure. The evaluation results of this approach will then indicate whether our approach has any value, so that a more comprehensive effort at collecting key-word/phrase and polarity pairs will result in an improved approach that has the potential to rival the results reported by Basiri et. al.

3 Approach

3.1 Data Collection

For our lexicon-based sentiment analysis technique we needed a wide range of Persian vocabulary entries, and their sentiment. As no Persian API was available for achieving this requirement, we opted to manually gather a number of Persian adjectives, words and expressions (7179) from two online Persian language resources[1] . The criteria for selecting these gazetteer entries, as followed by the two native speakers authoring this paper, were the following:

- Terms (words or multi-word expressions) that can alter or influence the sentiment of a given statement in any conceivable context.
- Gathered lexicons are used in either formal or informal communication between Persian people.
- Gathered lexicons correspond to either standard Persian or obsolete Persian as used by certain sections of native speakers.

As already mentioned the formal and informal styles of Persian writing has a huge impact on the semantics. In many cases one cannot understand the meaning of an informal textual comment unless they are a native speaker. So the need to enrich the lexicon with as many informal expressions and comments was as necessary, if not more pressing than, gathering all the formal forms. In addition, some of the collected words and adjectives correspond to the old usage of the language among older native speakers. Although these are not used regularly in daily speech or text, they are still important to make our gazetteer as varied and as broad as possible. The resulting terms have been saved in a personal database in preparation for the sentiment annotation phase described below.

3.2 Sentiment Annotation

The results of the collection process were stored in a database, and in order to achieve the required lexicon we then required to annotate each entry with a sentiment score. To support with this task, we set up a Web interface[2] that enables native Speakers to manually assign a score to random entries. At each click, the interface presented a new adjective which could then be voted either as having either a positive, negative or neutral sentiment expression. A five-tier scoring spectrum was considered but eventually discarded in favour of the three-tier option above, for the sole reason that it was cognitively easier for the volunteers to decide on an outcome, and as a result, more votes were expected.

The exercise was shared between a number of volunteers , following requests via own and extended social networks of a personal and academic nature. Half of the targeted volunteers were Persian students. As a result, the annotation was performed by people having different levels of education, age groups and sectors corresponding to the Persian society. For the 7179 adjectives in the database, we received a total of 8278 votes. This discrepancy is intended and is due to the decision to allow multiple voting by different volunteers. In cases where the opinion expressed contrasted, manual conflict resolution was performed following a discussion, or the inconclusive entry was marked as neutral. Future work can focus on these entries and flag their polarity as highly contextual.

3.3 A lexicon-based Sentiment Analysis Pipeline

Following the establishment of an annotated Persian sentiment lexicon, we designed and developed a linguistic pipeline based on the GATE framework (Cunningham et al., 2002). The pipeline utilizes existing components that were already available[3], namely a Persian tokenizer, sentence splitter and POS tagger. In addition, our lexicon was provided as the basis for the gazetteer, and JAPE (Cunningham et al., 1999) grammar rules were then manually coded to address the most general features of the Persian language in its written form. The pipeline and its components is depicted in Fig. 1. A breakdown of all these components is provided below.

3.3.1 Tokenizer

The imported tokenizer splits the text into very simple tokens like words, numbers, spaces and punctuation. As the Persian script is not case-sensitive like most Latin scripts, the employed tokenizer excludes similar checks.

3.3.2 Sentence Splitter

The imported sentence splitter fragments the text into sentences. It uses a list of abbreviations to

[1] We collected Persian adjectives from the Wiktionary open source dictionary: http://goo.gl/o0J8K0 and from a reference database for the Persian lanaguage at: http://dadegan.ir/

[2] http://www.computerssl.com/sentiment/

[3] Although the library and components imported in our pipeline have not been made available online, they were kindly supplied by the author: http://sazvar.student.um.ac.ir/

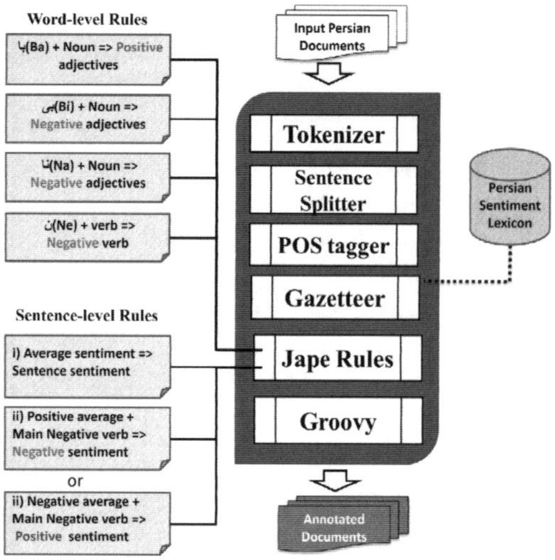

Figure 1: The Sentiment Analysis Pipeline

help distinguish sentence-marking full stops from other kind of splits.

3.3.3 POS Tagger

The imported tagger produces a part-of-speech tag as an annotation for each word or symbol. It uses a default lexicon and rule set which can be manually modied.

3.3.4 Gazetteer

The gazetteer includes all information resulting from the data collection and sentiment analysis exercises. In short, the employed gazetter is the basis for our lexicon-based approach. Whenever a gazetteer entry appears in the text, it is marked and assigned a sentiment score accordingly.

3.3.5 Hand-coded Persian grammar patterns

JAPE provides finite state transduction over annotations based on regular expressions. In our pipeline, we utilize JAPE rules to identify regular expressions we have formulated as a grammar base for Persian. Therefore, together with the gazetteer, this is one of the main contributions presented in this paper. We designed rules in two phases:

1. Phase I: patterns are focussed on and around each individual text-based token (i.e. words) in an input text segment.

2. Phase II: we address the sentiment of the entire text segment, based on the computed sentiment of each individual word.

Both phases are also depicted in Fig. 1. To identify the sentiment at the word-level, we created rules to consider an alternate sentiment to that otherwise identified by the gazetteer due to a special prefix and postfix. For example, in Persian, in a majority of cases a "Ba" prefix before a noun alters the polarity to positive, whereas a "Bi" or "Na" prefix alters it to negative. Some examples of the above alterations are shown in the table below. Similarly, we have catered for the linguistic alternative of verbs. Most notably, in Persian the verbs can be given a negative connotation by using "n" as a prefix (equivalent to the effect of having a do not before a verb in English). Examples are also shown in the below table.

Persian (before)	Persian (after)	English (before)	English (after)
اخلاق	بی اخلاق	Moral	Immoral
ادب	بی ادب	Politeness	Impolite
معرفت	بامعرفت	Wisdom	Wise
درست	نادرست	Correct	Incorrect
ندارد		Don't understand	
نمیفهمد		Don't have	

In many cases, in order to calculate the sentiment of an entire sentence or text segment it is not simply a case of averaging or combining the sentiment of each word as identified in Phase I. Some adjectives or phrases have a direct effect on the entire sentence, e.g., the presence of just one special negative verb in a sentence that otherwise consists of mostly positive words, alters the entire polarity of the sentence to negative (irony). Therefore, in this second phase the JAPE rules follow this sequence:

1. Step 1: the number of positive and negative words in a sentence are counted and the average is used to identify the polarity of the sentence

2. Step 2: the main verb of the sentence is identified, and if it matches one of the known exceptional negative verbs, the polarity of the pre-computed sentence is reversed

Examples of cases which are addressed by step 2 above are in the table below, with their English language equivalent.

Persian	English Equivalent
"این فیلم بازیگران معروف زیادی داشت ولی نتوانست نظر مردم را جلب کند"	"That film had a lot of famous actors but it couldn't attract people's attention."
"فیلم خوبی نبود"	"It wasn't a good film!"
"آدم دروغگویی نیست"	"He is not a liar"

3.3.6 Groovy scripting processing resource

The result of the two JAPE phases are then forwarded to the Groovy scripting processing resource, for which GATE also provides support. The Groovy plugin is used to count the number of positive and negative annotations in a given piece of text and determine an overall polarity score. Therefore, this can also be considered a third phase in the sentiment analysis, which takes place at the paragraph or entire document level. It must be noted that at the moment, the final sentiment score determined is either positive, negative or neutral.

4 Evaluation

In order to evaluate the performance of our approach, we performed two experiments. In the initial one, we relied on a pre-existing corpus of annotated text, based on the availability of reviews related to accommodation online. However, the information available here was not in a form to enable us to confidently reach conclusive results. Therefore, in a second experiment, we again instructed native speakers to rate a large amount of Persian news items and compared their judgment against the ones determined by our pipeline. Details and results are presented below.

4.1 Corpus-based Evaluation

In this experiment we choose customer reviews that are available online for a website[4] specializing in hotel reservation and accommodation in different cities of Iran. Although its popularity has recently seen a downturn[5], the site has been used for 15 years and therefore there are a lot of valuable reviews that can be used for this kind of experiment. Website visitors are able to leave their opinions about their previous experience in a hotel (including references to price, quality and local sightseeing) by filling verifiable identification fields, thus meaning that the expressed opinions are probably genuine and reliable. The main problem with this corpus is that the reviews are star base, on a scale of 1 (poor) to 5 (excellent) stars. Therefore, in order to be able to compare to the results generated by the developed pipeline we were required to map this expression of sentiment as follows:

- 1 and 2 stars: Negative
- 3 stars: Neutral
- 4 and 5 stars: Positive

From the above, we generated a corpus of test and evaluation data. The reviews were each passed on to the pipeline, and the calculated sentiment score was directly compared to the ones derived from the rating system. Based on this comparison, we calculated two measures:

1. Class-specific accuracy
2. Multi-class F-measure

We first calculated the accuracy for positive and negative sentiment, i.e., the proportion of positive and negative reviews rated correctly to all positive and negative reviews respectively. The results, grouped by rating, is shown in Fig. 2. At a value of between 50 - 80%, this result indicated that there was potential in our approach. Given that the classes are only three, it can be argued that a tool that randomly assigns one of the three classes can achieve up to 33.33% accuracy. For this purpose, we include a baseline for a better interpretation of the result. Also, accuracy calculated in this manner is not ideal and does not provide a reliable result since each calculation only factors in true positives and true negatives per class.

In a second experiment, we calculated the multi-class F-measure (weighing precision and recall equally), with equal weighting for precision and recall. Thus, recall identified the proportion of neutral, positive and negative reviews correctly identified against respectively all the neutral, positive and negative reviews, whereas precision identified the proportion of correctly classified (neutral, positive, negative) reviews against all reviews.

[4]www.iran-booking.com

[5]At the time of submission, Alexa lists the website as only the 7,063rd most popular in the country: http://www.alexa.com/siteinfo/www.iran-booking.com

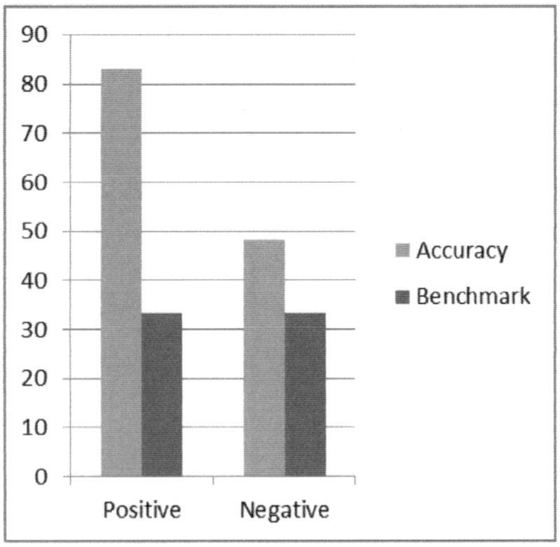

Figure 2: Overall accuracy for each rating

The resulting confusion matrix contained comparisons for the three classes and precision and recall was computed for each. The result of the three f-measures is shown in Fig. 3, again compared to the baseline. In this result, we note that although the top-performing class (positive) has gone down to just under 70%, the other two classes are not far from the 60% mark. Averaging the f-measures for the two most important classes (positive and negative), yields an average score of 68.5%.

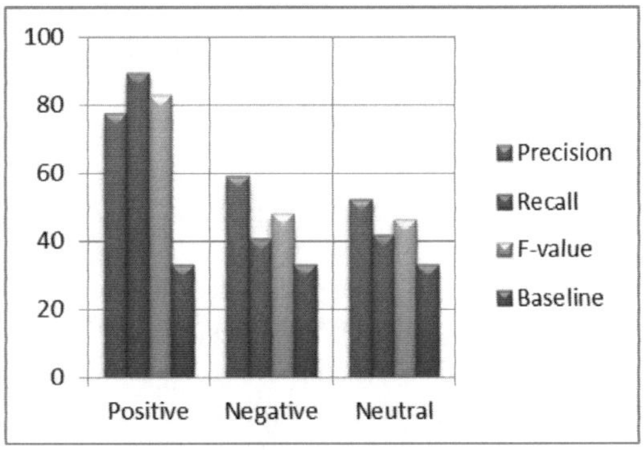

Figure 3: Multi-class F-measure

4.2 User-based Evaluation

Due to the limitations discussed above, we performed a second evaluation. In this experiment, we considered around 5100 news items from the four most popular Persian news portals (www.farsnews.com, www.tabnak.ir, www.yjc.ir www.varzesh3.com). The news items were obtained from different categories, including sport, social, politics, economic and international. For the user-based evaluation, we randomly retrieved 1170 of these items and copied them on to our website[6]. In a similar effort to the sentiment annotation phase, we circulated a request for volunteers to rate each news item. Although for the same reason as explained earlier, an exact count of volunteers is not available, website visitor IP tracking during the two weeks when the experiment was run suggests that a total of between 35-50 people have participated. This is also consistent with the appeal to rate at least 20 news items. The exercise resulted in 1116 votes for a total of 897 distinct news items. Once again, conflicting results for items with more than one vote were either resolved upon discussion (majority rule) or set to neutral. The results of manual user rating were then compared to the automatic ratings. In this case, we only focused on accuracy, starting with the user-based evaluation as the authoritative score. The results, shown in Fig. 4, show the following accuracy levels:

- positives: 67%,
- negatives: 61.8%
- neutrals: 52.5%
- overall accuracy: 60.4%
- overall accuracy (exc. neutrals): 64.4%

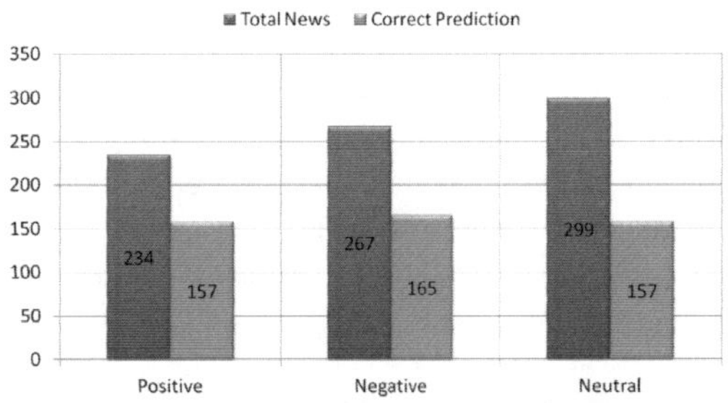

Figure 4: Performance in User-based Evaluation

5 Conclusions and Future Work

The presented approach is unique for the Persian language, since it relies on a list of entries (lexicon) paired with sentiment scores that was generated by a large number of native speakers. The approach addresses subjectivity by marking entries

[6]http://www.computerssl.com/sentiment/news.php

with conflicting scores and attempting to manually resolve said conflicts. Our experiments yield between 60-69% accuracy rates for the initial version of the lexicon-based Persian Sentiment Analysis API. Although it is still not as precise as the ML-based approach described in (Basiri et al., 2014), this compares fairly well with related work and the experiments confirm that there is value in our approach. In particular, an acceptably accurate lexicon-based approach can be used to bootstrap an ML-based system that does not require a large training set to start achieving results. Alternatively, the gazetteer could also be semi-automatically enhanced through the correction of incorrectly rated entries in a process involving human supervision. The combination of our lexicon-based approach with the most promising Persian-language ML approach to achieve a hybrid system is therefore one of the top priorities for future work. A Persian sentiment analysis API that can effectively avoid the cold-start problem when applied to a new domain can be of great value to future business use-cases. Sentiment analysis is still a highly-challenging requirement at the core of many attempts to gauge people's response or opinion about a service or product, with many use-cases in the stock market, marketing and customer care domains, as well as online customer advice. By addressing the lack of diversity in Persian sentiment analysis approaches, we want to contribute to the advancement of techniques bound to a language which remains the working language of a relatively large population. As in other languages, written Persian also faces high ambiguity in terms of context and polarity, with a high complexity also arising from mixed use of formal and informal text. In the presented research we have tried to cover both formal and informal cases in our lexicon. The evaluation indicates that there is value in our language-specific lexicon driven approach. However, a lot more remains to be done to outperform ML-based techniques and rival the list-translation (English to Persian) approach introduced by Basiri et. al. Primarily, we intend to encourage more native speakers to add and rate adjectives and phrases for the construction of a more flexible and comprehensive lexicon. In addition we also intend to improve the grammar rules to cover more of the exceptions and characteristics of the Persian language. In particular, we want to address rules centered around notorious Persian conjunctions, such as 'but and 'although. Last but not least, we also want to address abbreviated forms of writing, which is also rather common-place and which has not been addressed by the literature so far.

Acknowledgements

We would like to thank Majid Sazvar for providing us with the three own-developed linguistic components incorporated in our pipeline.

References

Muhammad Abdul-Mageed, Mona T Diab, and Mohammed Korayem. 2011. Subjectivity and sentiment analysis of modern standard arabic. In *Proceedings of the 49th Annual Meeting of the Association for Computational Linguistics: Human Language Technologies: short papers-Volume 2*, pages 587–591. Association for Computational Linguistics.

Stefano Baccianella, Andrea Esuli, and Fabrizio Sebastiani. 2010. Sentiwordnet 3.0: An enhanced lexical resource for sentiment analysis and opinion mining. In *LREC*, volume 10, pages 2200–2204.

Mohammad Ehsan Basiri, Ahmad Reza Naghsh-Nilchi, and Nasser Ghassem-Aghaee. 2014. A framework for sentiment analysis in persian.

Margaret M Bradley and Peter J Lang. 1999. Affective norms for english words (anew): Instruction manual and affective ratings. Technical report, Technical Report C-1, The Center for Research in Psychophysiology, University of Florida.

Hamish Cunningham, Diana Maynard, and Valentin Tablan. 1999. Jape: a java annotation patterns engine.

Hamish Cunningham, Diana Maynard, Kalina Bontcheva, and Valentin Tablan. 2002. A framework and graphical development environment for robust nlp tools and applications. In *ACL*, pages 168–175.

Xiaowen Ding, Bing Liu, and Philip S Yu. 2008. A holistic lexicon-based approach to opinion mining. In *Proceedings of the 2008 International Conference on Web Search and Data Mining*, pages 231–240. ACM.

Ronen Feldman, Benjamin Rosenfeld, Roy Bar-Haim, and Moshe Fresko. 2011. The stock sonarsentiment analysis of stocks based on a hybrid approach. In *Twenty-Third IAAI Conference*.

Ronen Feldman. 2013. Techniques and applications for sentiment analysis. *Communications of the ACM*, 56(4):82–89.

Hatem Ghorbel and David Jacot. 2011. Sentiment analysis of french movie reviews. In *Advances in Distributed Agent-Based Retrieval Tools*, pages 97–108. Springer.

Mohammad Sadegh Hajmohammadi and Roliana Ibrahim. 2013. A svm-based method for sentiment analysis in persian language. In *2012 International Conference on Graphic and Image Processing*, pages 876838–876838. International Society for Optics and Photonics.

Vasileios Hatzivassiloglou and Kathleen R McKeown. 1997. Predicting the semantic orientation of adjectives. In *Proceedings of the 35th annual meeting of the association for computational linguistics and eighth conference of the european chapter of the association for computational linguistics*, pages 174–181. Association for Computational Linguistics.

Yohan Jo and Alice H Oh. 2011. Aspect and sentiment unification model for online review analysis. In *Proceedings of the fourth ACM international conference on Web search and data mining*, pages 815–824. ACM.

Bing Liu. 2010. Sentiment analysis: A multi-faceted problem. *IEEE Intelligent Systems*, 25(3):76–80.

Bing Liu. 2012. Sentiment analysis and opinion mining. *Synthesis Lectures on Human Language Technologies*, 5(1):1–167.

Andrius Mudinas, Dell Zhang, and Mark Levene. 2012. Combining lexicon and learning based approaches for concept-level sentiment analysis. In *Proceedings of the First International Workshop on Issues of Sentiment Discovery and Opinion Mining*, page 5. ACM.

Alexander Pak and Patrick Paroubek. 2010. Twitter as a corpus for sentiment analysis and opinion mining. In *LREC*, volume 10, pages 1320–1326.

Bo Pang, Lillian Lee, and Shivakumar Vaithyanathan. 2002. Thumbs up?: sentiment classification using machine learning techniques. In *Proceedings of the ACL-02 conference on Empirical methods in natural language processing-Volume 10*, pages 79–86. Association for Computational Linguistics.

Mohamad Saraee and Ayoub Bagheri. 2013. Feature selection methods in persian sentiment analysis. In *Natural Language Processing and Information Systems*, pages 303–308. Springer.

Carlo Strapparava, Alessandro Valitutti, et al. 2004. Wordnet affect: an affective extension of wordnet. In *LREC*, volume 4, pages 1083–1086.

Afraz Z Syed, Muhammad Aslam, and Ana Maria Martinez-Enriquez. 2010. Lexicon based sentiment analysis of urdu text using sentiunits. In *Advances in Artificial Intelligence*, pages 32–43. Springer.

Maite Taboada, Julian Brooke, Milan Tofiloski, Kimberly Voll, and Manfred Stede. 2011. Lexicon-based methods for sentiment analysis. *Computational linguistics*, 37(2):267–307.

Mike Thelwall, Kevan Buckley, Georgios Paltoglou, Di Cai, and Arvid Kappas. 2010. Sentiment strength detection in short informal text. *Journal of the American Society for Information Science and Technology*, 61(12):2544–2558.

Peter D Turney. 2002. Thumbs up or thumbs down?: semantic orientation applied to unsupervised classification of reviews. In *Proceedings of the 40th annual meeting on association for computational linguistics*, pages 417–424. Association for Computational Linguistics.

Taras Zagibalov and John Carroll. 2008. Automatic seed word selection for unsupervised sentiment classification of chinese text. In *Proceedings of the 22nd International Conference on Computational Linguistics-Volume 1*, pages 1073–1080. Association for Computational Linguistics.

Automatic Construction of a TMF Terminological Database Using a Transducer Cascade

Chihebeddine Ammar
MIRACL & Sfax University
Sfax, Tunisia
chihebeddine.ammar@fss.rnu.tn

Kais Haddar
MIRACL & Sfax University
Sfax, Tunisia
kais.haddar@fss.rnu.tn

Laurent Romary
INRIA & Humboldt University
Berlin, Germany
laurent.romary@inria.fr

Abstract

The automatic development of terminological databases, especially in a standardized format, has a crucial aspect for multiple applications related to technical and scientific knowledge that requires semantic and terminological descriptions covering multiple domains. In this context, we have, in this paper, two challenges: the first is the automatic extraction of terms in order to build a terminological database, and the second challenge is their normalization into a standardized format. To deal with these challenges, we propose an approach based on a cascade of transducers performed using CasSys tool of the Unitex linguistic platform that benefits from both: the success of the rule-based approach for the extraction of terms, and the performance of the TMF standard for the representation of terms. We have tested and evaluated our approach on an Arabic scientific and technical corpus for the Elevator domain and the results are very encouraging.

1 Introduction

The automation of terminology will reduce the time and cost that usually takes terminological database construction. It will also help us to construct terminological databases with broad coverage, especially for recent concepts and poor language coverage (Arabic for example). On the other side, the representation of terminological data in a standard format allows the integration and merging of terminological data from multiple source systems, while improving terminological data quality and maintaining maximum interoperability between different applications.

One of the very rich in terminology working area are the scientific and technical documents. They cover several scientific and technical fields, so, we will need several terminological databases, one for each field. For this reason, we decided to work on a specific domain: the elevators.

To automate any process, we need a framework. The choice of this framework is not an easy task. In fact, many frameworks exist, based on: formal grammars, logical formalism, discrete mathematics, etc. The rule-based approach requires: a thorough study of the characteristics of terms and construction of necessary resources such as dictionaries, trigger words and extraction rules.

Finite automata and in particularly transducers are often used in the Natural Language Processing (NLP). The general idea is to replace the rules of formal grammars with representation forms. Transducers offer a particularly nice and simple formulation, and prove their capability of representing complex grammars due to their graphic representation. They have a success for the extraction of named entities (NE) and terms. In fact, precision is more important for rule-based systems.

Another issue is to decide which standard will we choose to model our terminological databases, which standard will best represent scientific and technical terms and which model to use, onomasiological or semasiological?

Our main objective is to create a standardized terminological resource from a corpus of Arabic scientific and technical documents (patents, manuals, scientific papers) able to support automatic text processing applications. Our approach is based on a cascade of transducers performed using CasSys tool of Unitex. It aims to extract and annotate under standardized TMF (Terminological Markup Framework) form technical terms of elevator field. The first step is a pre-treatment to resolve some problems of the Arabic language (e.g. agglutination). The second step is to extract and annotate terms. And the final one is a post-treatment consisting of cleaning documents.

Proceedings of Recent Advances in Natural Language Processing, pages 17–23,
Hissar, Bulgaria, Sep 7–9 2015.

This paper is organized as follows. Section 2 is devoted to the presentation of the previous work. We present, in section 3, the characteristics of Arabic scientific and technical terms. In section 4, we argue the choice of terminology model. In section 5, we present our approach. Section 6 is devoted to experimentation and evaluation and we conclude and enunciate some perspectives in section 7.

2 Previous Work

Three methods for building a terminological knowledge base exist: manual, semi-automatic and automatic. In the literature, there are some terminological databases for scientific and technical fields, most of them were constructed manually or semi-automatically.

For instance, the multilingual terminology of the European Union, IATE[1], contains 8,4 million terms in 23 languages covering EU specific terminology as well as multiple fields such as agriculture or information technology. The multilingual terminology portal of the World Intellectual Property Office, WIPO Pearl[2], gives access to scientific and technical terms in ten languages, including Arabic, derived from patent documents. It contains 15,000 concepts and 90,000 terms. Since WIPO has not a collection of Arabic patents, Arabic terms are often translations from the WIPO translation service. In (Lopez and Romary, 2010b), the authors developed a multilingual terminological database called GRISP covering multiple technical and scientific fields from various open resources.

Three main approaches are generally followed for extraction: rule-based (or linguistic) approach, training based (or statistic) approach and hybrid approach. What distinguishes the approaches mentioned, is not the type of information considered, but their acquisition and handling. The linguistic approach is based on human intuition, with the manual construction of analysis models, usually in the form of contextual rules. It requires a thorough study of the types of terms, but it has a success for the extraction of NE and terms. In fact, precision is more important for symbolic systems.

In previous work on non scientific and technical documents, there are those who used linguistic methods based on syntactic analysis (see for instance (Bourigault, 1992) and (Bourigault, 1994)). But the most used approach is the hybrid approach combining statistical and linguistic techniques (Dagan and Church, 1994).

The most recent work on scientific and technical documents were mainly based on purely statistical approaches. They used standard techniques of information retrieval and data extraction. Some of them use machine learning tools to extract header metadata using support vector machines (SVM) (Do et al., 2013), hidden markov models (HMM) (Binge, 2009), or conditional random fields (CRF) (Lopez, 2009). Others use machine learning tools to extract metadata of citations (Hetzner, 2008), tables (Liu et al., 2007), figures (Choudhury et al., 2013) or to identify concepts (Rao et al., 2013). All these approaches rely on previous training and natural language processing.

The need to allow exchanges between reference formats (Geneter, DXLT, etc.) has brought to the birth of the standard ISO 16642, TMF, specifying the minimum structural requirements to be met by every TML (terminological Markup Language).

3 Characteristics of Arabic Scientific and Technical Terms

Our study corpus contains 60 Arabic documents: 50 patents, 5 scientific papers and 5 manuals and installation documents of elevators collected from multiple resources: manuals from the websites of elevator manufacturers, patents from multiple Arabic intellectual property offices and scientific papers from some Arabic journals. All of these documents are text files and contain a total number of 619k tokens.

This corpus will allow us to construct the necessary resources such as dictionaries, trigger words and extraction rules and to study the characteristics of Arabic terms. Indeed, we noted the existence of some semantic relationships among terms of our collection, such as synonymy.

In fact, some terms have the same signified and different signifiers. For example, مصعد بدون وزن عكسي signifies مصعد بدون وزن معادل "elevator without counterweight". Here, the two terms have the same part (مصعد بدون وزن "elevator without weight") and two synonymous words (معادل "equivalent" and عكسي "reverse"). Another type of semantic relationships is the hierarchical relationship in two ways. Firstly, from the generic term to the specific term(s) (from hy-

[1]http://iate.europa.eu

[2]http://www.wipo.int/wipopearl/search/home.html

peronym to hyponym). For example, hyperonym: مركبة "vehicle", hyponyms: مصعد "elevator", عربة "car". Secondly, from the all to the different parts (from holonym to meronyms). For example, holonym: مصعد "elevator", meronyms: عربة "car", باب "door", زر "button", etc.

Some factors make the automatic analysis of Arabic texts a painful task, such as: the agglutination of Arabic terms. In fact, the Arabic language is a highly agglutinative language from the fact that clitics stick to nouns, verbs, adjectives which they relate. Therefore, we find particles that stick to the radicals, preventing their detection. Indeed, textual forms are made up of the agglutination of prefixes (articles: definite articleال "the", prepositions:ل "for", conjunctions: و "and"), and suffixes (linked pronouns) to the stems (inflected forms: أبوابه "its doors", أبواب "doors" + ه "its").

Another problem is the ambiguity which may be caused by several factors. For example, Arabic language is one of the Semitic languages that is defined as a diacritized language. Unfortunately, diacritics are rarely used in current Arabic writing conventions. So two or more words in Arabic can be homographic. Such as the word يعد (without diacritics) that could be (if we add diacritics): يعُد "return", يُعِدّ "prepare" or يَعُدّ "count".

Despite documents of our corpus are in Arabic language, some of them have a literal translation of key terms and technical words. These translations can be in English or French and are usually of a very high quality because they are made by professional human translators. They facilitate the task of our terminological database implementation (Language Section and Term Section of the TMF model) and make it multilingual.

4 TMF Terminological Model

The terminology is interested in what the terms mean: notions, concepts, and words or phrases that they nominate. This is the notional or conceptual approach. Motivated from the terminology industrial practice, the Terminological Markup Framework (TMF[3]) (Romary, 2001) was developed as a standard for onomasiological (sense to term) resources. In this paper, we need a generic model able to cover a variety of terminological resources. That is why we consider that the standard TMF is the most appropriate for our terminological database. The meta-model of the standard TMF is defined by logical hierarchical levels. It thus represents a structural hierarchy of the relevant nodes in a linguistic description. The meta-model describes the main structural elements and their internal connections.

It is combined with data categories (ISO 12620[4]) from a data category selection (DCS). Using the data model based on ISO 16642 allows us to fulfill the requirements of standardization and to exploit Data Category Registry (DCR) following the ISO 12620 standard for facilitating the implementation of filters and converters between different terminology instances and to produce a Generic Mapping Tool (GMT) representation, i.e. a canonical XML representation. The main role of our terminological extractor is to automatically generate terms in GMT format and create a normalized terminological database of scientific and technical terms.

Figure 1 shows an example of scientific terminological entry (Multi-car elevator) in the form of an XML document conforming GMT in three languages (Arabic, French and English).

5 Proposed Approach

The extraction method of Arabic terms that we advocate is rule-based. In fact, the rules that are manually built, express the structure of the information to extract and take the form of transducers. These transducers generally operate morphosyntactic information, as well as those contained in the resources (lexicons or dictionaries). Moreover, they allow the description of possible sequences of constituents of Arabic terms belonging to the field of elevators. The approach that we propose to extract terms for the field of elevators is composed of two steps (Figure. 2): (i) identifying the neces-

[3]ISO 16642:2003. Computer Applications in Terminology: Terminological Markup Framework

[4]ISO 12620:2009. Terminology and Other Language and Content Resources – Specification of Data Categories and Management of a Data Category Registry for Language Resources

```
<?xml version="1.0" encoding="utf-8"?>
<tmf>
    <struct type="TE">
        <feat type="EntryIdentifier">32</feat>
        <feat type="SubjectField">Elevator</feat>
        <feat type="Definition">مصعد بسيارات تعلق معا</feat>
        <struct type="LS">
            <feat type="Lang">Anglais</feat>
            <struct type="TS">
                <feat type="Term">multi-car elevator</feat>
                <feat type="Synonym">multi-deck elevator</feat>
            </struct>
        </struct>
        <struct type="LS">
            <feat type="Lang">Arabe</feat>
            <struct type="TS">
                <feat type="Term">مصعد متعدد المقصورات</feat>
                <feat type="Synonym">مصعد متعدد العربات</feat>
            </struct>
        </struct>
        <struct type="LS">
            <feat type="Lang">Francais</feat>
            <struct type="TS">
                <feat type="Term">ascenseur multi-voiture</feat>
            </struct>
        </struct>
    </struct>
</tmf>
```

Figure 1: Terminological entry conforming GMT

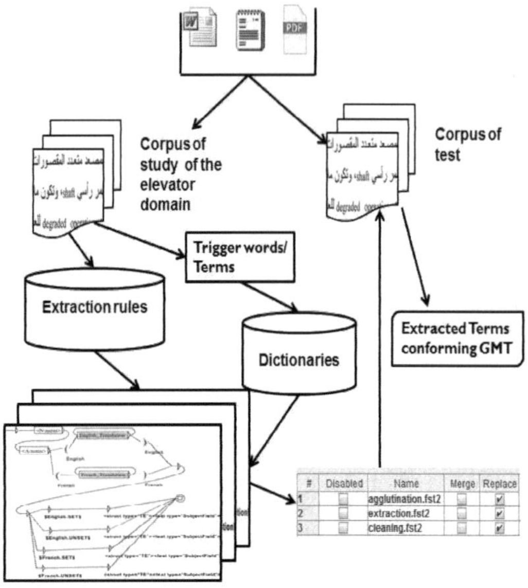

Figure 2: Proposed approach

sary resources to identify terms to extract, (ii) the creation of a cascade of transducer each of which has its own role.

In the following, we detail the different resources and steps of our approach.

5.1 Necessary Linguistic Resources

For our approach, we construct linguistic resouces from our study corpus, such as dictionaries, trigger words and extraction rules (syntactic patterns). In the following, we present these resources.

5.1.1 Dictionaries

For the domain of elevator, subject of our study, we identified the following dictionaries: a dictionary of inflected nouns and their canonical forms, a dictionary of inflected verbs, a dictionary for adjectives, a dictionary for trigger words of the domain and dictionaries of particles, possessive pronouns, demonstrative pronouns and relative pronouns. The structure of the various dictionary entries is not the same. It can vary from one dictionary to another. It must contain the grammatical category of the entry (noun, adjective), but, according to the dictionary, it may contain also: gender (masculine, feminine or neutral) and number (singular, dual, plural or broken plural), definition (defined or undefined), case (accusative, nominative or genitive) or mode (indicative, subjunctive or jussive), person (1st person, 2nd person or 3rd person) and voice (active or passive).

5.1.2 Trigger Words

The extraction rules generally use morphosyntactic information such as trigger words for the detection of the beginning of a term. We opted for increasing the number of rules and triggers in order to have as efficient as possible extraction system. We identified 162 trigger words, some of them can trigger the recognition of up to 5 terms. For this reason we classified them in classes.

5.1.3 Extraction Rules

To facilitate the identification of the necessary transducers for the extraction of terms, we have built a set of extraction rules. Indeed, they give the arrangement of the various constituents of terms in a linear manner easily transferable as graphs. We identified 12 extraction rules. Table 1 shows some of them. Four grammatical features are attribuated here: gender (masculine (m) or feminine (f)), number (singular (s), dual (d) or plural (p)), definition (defined (r) or undefined (n)) and case (accusative (a), nominative (u) or genitive (i)).

Examples of trigger words are: تحريك "mobilization" for the rules **R1** and **R5**, صيانة "mainte-

Rule number	Extraction rules
R1	<Pattern 1>:=<Trigger word> <N:nums><PREP>(<N:nums>)$^+$
R2	<Pattern 2>:=<N:nums> <PREP><N:nufs>[<Adj:nufs>]
R3	<Pattern 3>:=<Trigger word> <N:nums><Adj:nums>
R4	<Pattern 4>:= <Trigger word> <N:nufs><N:rums>
R5	<Pattern 5>:= <Trigger word> <N:nufp><N:rums>

Table 1: Some extraction rules of Arabic patent terms

nance" for the rule **R3** and رفع "lifting" for the rule **R4**. Table 2 shows some extracted terms due to the precedent extraction rules (here identified by their number in Table 1).

Rule number	Extracted terms
R1	مصعد بدون وزن عكسي "elevator without counterweight"
R2	مصعد ببكرة محزوزة "elevator with splined roller"
R3	مصعد آلي "automatic elevator"
R4	عربة المصعد "elevator car" لوحة التحكم "contor panel"
R5	أحبال الرفع "hoisting ropes"

Table 2: Terms extracted due to extraction rules

5.2 Implementation of Extraction Rules

We created three types of transducers. The first one is the transducer of pre-treatment solving Arabic prefixes and suffixes agglutination. To recognize the agglutinative character, we should enter inside the token. As Unitex works on a tokenized version of the text, it is not possible to make queries entering within the tokens, except with morphological filters or the morphological mode which is more appropriate in our case. To do this, we must define the whole portion of grammar using the symbols $<$ and $>$ as presented in Figure. 3). The transducer annotate every part of the agglutinated token with appropriate grammatical category.

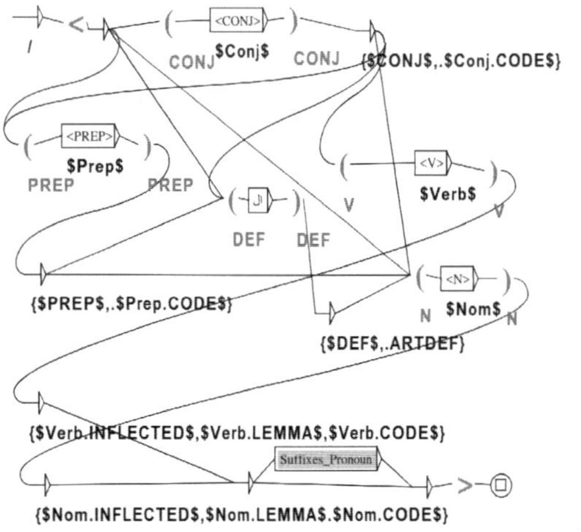

Figure 3: Transducer of resolution of agglutination

The second transducer, as shown in Figure. 4, includes all subgraphs of term extraction and annotation under the GMT format ("extraction_trasducers" box). In order to improve terms extraction, trigger words are regrouped into the "trigger_words" box.

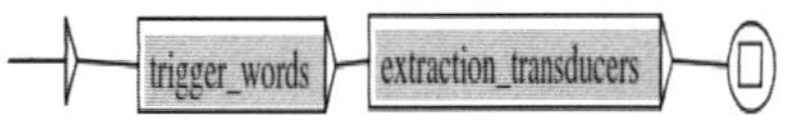

Figure 4: The main extraction transducer

Figure. 5 shows one of the transducers that extract and annotate terms. It also recognizes the French or English translation of terms (if available) thanks to the "French_Translation" and "English_Translation" subgraphs and annotate them in a new Language Section (LS) in the GMT format as shown in Figure. 1.

The final transducer is a post-treatment transducer consisting on document cleaning: its role is to delete all text remains (which is not XML). Figure. 6 is an overview of this transducer. The subgraph "XML" recognize all the XML element that could be contained by the <struct type="TE"> GMT element.

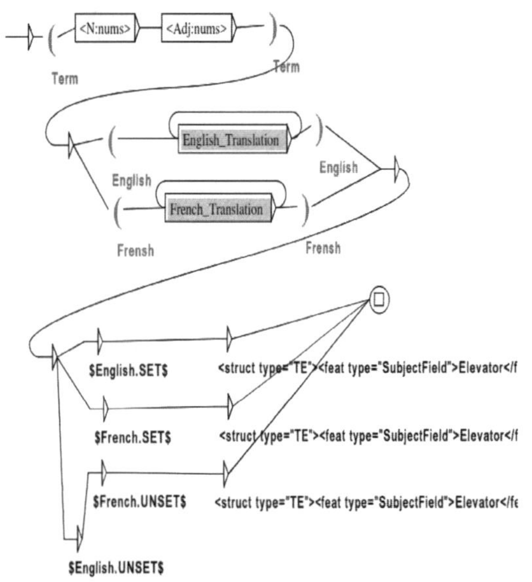

Figure 5: Example of extraction subgraph

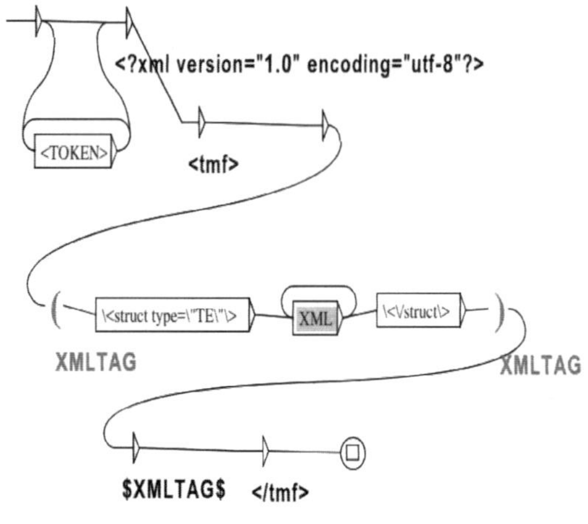

Figure 6: Post-treatment transducer

6 Experimentation and Evaluation

Our test corpus contains 160 Arabic documents from multiple resources: 100 patents, 50 scientific papers and 10 manuals and installation documents of elevators, with a total number of 1.6m tokens. Our transducers are called in a specific order in a transducer cascade which is directly implemented in the linguistic platform Unitex[5] using the CasSys tool (Friburger and Maurel, 2004). Each graph adds its own annotations due to the mode "Replace". This mode provides, as output, a recognized term surrounded by a GMT annotation defined in the transducers.

In order to conduct an evaluation, we applied the cascade implemented on the test corpus. We manually evaluated the quality of our work on the test corpus. The total number of terms is 852. Table 3 gives an overview of the obtained results.

Terms	Extracted terms	Erroneous terms
852	827	59

Table 3: Overview of the obtained results

The obtained results are satisfactory, the transducers were able to cover the majority of terms with a precision of 0.95 and a recall of 0.97 with a F-score of 0.95. We therefore find that the proposed method is effective.

[5]Unitex: http://www-igm.univ-mlv.fr/ unitex/

The noise can be caused by the absence of diacritics in our corpus and dictionaries, which could create ambiguity problem. It may also be caused by the absance of high granularity features of our dictionary entries. For this reason, we will try to add other semantic and grammatical features to our dictionary entries to improve our results. Despite the good results, we were forced to spend our terminological database to a terminologist to correct erroneous terms and their definitions. We believe that the automatic integration and merging of our database with other existing databases can help us to automatically correct errors.

7 Conclusion

In this paper, we built a set of transducers. Then we generated a cascade allowing extraction of scientific and technical terms. Extracted terms were represented in a standardized format (GMT). The generation of this cascade is performed using the CasSys tool, built-in Unitex linguistic platform. The operation of the transducer cascade required the construction of resources such as dictionaries.

In the immediate future, we will create a transducer cascade to extract bibliographic data and metadata of citations, tables, formulas and figures from scientific and technical documents and patents. We will also extract terms using a satatistic approach. Finally, we will try to combine the two approaches in a hybrid one.

Acknowledgments

We would like to thank Alexis Neme and Denis Maurel for helpful discussion and advice.

References

Cui Binge. 2009. Scientific literature metadata extraction based on HMM. *CDVE 2009*, pages 64-68. Luxembourg, Luxembourg.

Didier Bourigault. 1992. Surface Grammatical Analysis for the Extraction of Terminological Noun Phrases. In *Proceedings of the 14th International Conference on Computational Linguistics COLING'92*, volume 3, pages 977-981. Nantes, France.

Didier Bourigault. 1994. LEXTER, Un Logiciel d'Extraction de TERminologie. Application à l'Acquisition de Connaissances à Partir de Textes. *Doctoral thesis*. Ecole des hautes Etudes en Sciences Sociales.

Erik Hetzner. 2008. A simple method for citation metadata extraction using hidden markov models. *JCDL 2008*, pages 280-284. New York, USA.

Huy H.N. Do, Muthu K. Chandrasekaran, Philip S. Cho and Min Y. Kan. 2013. Extracting and Matching Authors and Affiliations in Scholarly Documents. *JCDL 2013*. Indianapolis, Indiana, USA.

Ido Dagan and Ken Church. 1994. Termight: Identifying and Translating Technical Terminology. In *Proceedings of the 4th Applied Natural Language Processing Conference ANLP'94*, pages 34-40. Stuttgart, Germany.

Laurent Romary. 2001. An Abstract Model for the Representation of Multilingual Terminological Data: TMF Terminological Markup Framework. *TAMA 2001*. Antwerp, Belgium.

Nathalie Friburger, Denis Maurel. 2004. Finite-state transducer cascades to extract named entities in texts. In *Theoretical Computer Science*,volume 313, pages 93-104.

Patrice Lopez. 2009. GROBID: Combining Automatic Bibliographic Data Recognition and Term Extraction for Scholarship Publications. *ECDL 2009*. Corfu, Greece.

Patrice Lopez and Laurent Romary. 2010b. GRISP: A Massive Multilingual Terminological Database for Scientific and Technical Domains. *LREC 2010*. La Valette, Malta.

Pattabhi R.K. Rao, Sobha L. Devi, Paolo Rosso. 2013. Automatic Identification of Concepts and Conceptual relations from Patents Using Machine Learning Methods. *ICON 2013*, pages 18-20. Noida, India.

Sagnik R. Choudhury, Prasenjit Mitra, Andi Kirk, Silvia Szep, Donald Pellegrino, Sue Jones and C Lee Giles. 2013. Figure Metadata Extraction from Digital Documents. *ICDAR 2013*, pages 135 - 139. Washington, USA.

Ying Liu, Kun Bai, Prasenjit Mitra and C. Lee Giles. 2007. Tableseer: automatic table metadata extraction and searching in digital libraries. *JCDL 2007*, pages 91-100. Vancouver, Canada.

A Statistical Model for Measuring Structural Similarity between Webpages

Zhenisbek Assylbekov, Assulan Nurkas, Inês Russinho Mouga
School of Science and Technology
Nazarbayev University
53 Kabanbay batyr ave., Astana, Kazakhstan
{zhassylbekov, anurkas, ines.russinho}@nu.edu.kz

Abstract

This paper presents a statistical model for measuring structural similarity between webpages from bilingual websites. Starting from basic assumptions we derive the model and propose an algorithm to estimate its parameters in unsupervised manner. Statistical approach appears to benefit the structural similarity measure: in the task of distinguishing parallel webpages from bilingual websites our language-independent model demonstrates an F-score of 0.94–0.99 which is comparable to the results of language-dependent methods involving content similarity measures.

1 Introduction

A parallel corpus is a collection of text with translations into another language. Such corpora plays an important role in machine translation and multilingual language retrieval. Unfortunately, they are not readily available in the necessary quantities: some of them are subject to subscription or license fee and thus are not freely available, while others are domain-specific. However, there is the World Wide Web, which can be considered as one of the largest sources of parallel corpora, since there are many websites which are available in two or more languages. Many approaches have been therefore proposed for trying to exploit the Web as a parallel corpus: STRAND (Resnik and Smith, 2003), PT-Miner (Chen and Nie, 2000), BITS (Ma and Liberman, 1999), WPDE (Zhang et al., 2006), Bitextor (Esplà-Gomis and Forcada, 2010), ILSP-FC (Papavassiliou et al., 2013), etc. For most of these mining systems, there is a typical strategy for mining parallel texts: (1) locate bilingual websites; (2) identify parallel web pages; (3) extract bitexts. For the step (2) three main strategies can be found in the literature – they exploit:

- similarities in URLs;
- structural similarity of HTML files;
- content-similarity of texts.

Measuring structural similarity of HTML files, which is the "heart of STRAND" architecture (Resnik and Smith, 2003), involves calculating some quantitative features of candidate webpages and then comparing them to manually chosen threshold values or embedding those features into machine learning algorithms. Such approaches do not take into account the intrinsic stochastic nature of the mentioned features, and they require supervised learning of the parameters for each given website/language. In this paper we develop a more refined language-independent technique for measuring structural similarity between HTML pages, which uses the same amount of information as previous approaches, but is more accurate in distinguishing parallelism of webpages and can be applied in unsupervised manner.

2 Related Work

Measuring structural similarity between HTML files was first introduced in (Resnik, 1998), where a linearized HTML structure of candidate pairs was used to confirm parallelism of texts. Shi et al. (2006) used a file length ratio, an HTML tag similarity and a sentence alignment score to verify translational equivalence of candidate pages. Zhang et al. (2006) used file length ratio, HTML structure and content translation to train k-nearest-neighbors classifier for parallel pairs verification. Esplà-Gomis and Forcada (2010) used text-language comparison, file size ratio, total text length difference for preliminary filtering and then HTML tag structure and text block length were used for deeper filtering. In (San Vicente and Manterola, 2012) the bitext detection module runs

Proceedings of Recent Advances in Natural Language Processing, pages 24–31,
Hissar, Bulgaria, Sep 7–9 2015.

three major filters: link follower filter, URL pattern search, and a combination of an HTML structure filter and a content filter. In (Papavassiliou et al., 2013) structural filtering is based on length ratios and edit distances between linearized versions of candidate pairs. Liu et al. (2014) proposed a link-based approach in conjuction with content-based similarity and page structural similarity to distinguish parallel web pages from bi-lingual web sites.

To explain the essence of our work let us assume that candidate pairs are linearized as in STRAND and linearized sequences are aligned using a standard dynamic programming technique (Hunt and MacIlroy, 1976). For example, consider two documents that begin as follows:

```
<HTML>
<TITLE>The Republic of Kazakhstan</TITLE>
<BODY>
<H1>The Republic of Kazakhstan</H1>
The Republic of Kazakhstan is a unitary state with a presidential form of government.
⋮
```

```
<HTML>
<TITLE>Қазақстан Республикасы</TITLE>
<BODY>
Қазақстан Республикасы – президенттік басқару нысанындағы біртұтас мемлекет.
⋮
```

The aligned linearized sequences would be as follows:

[START: HTML]	[START: HTML]
[START: TITLE]	[START: TITLE]
[Chunk: 23]	[Chunk: 21]
[END: TITLE]	[END: TITLE]
[START: BODY]	[START: BODY]
[START: H1]	
[Chunk: 23]	
[END: H1]	
[Chunk: 72]	[Chunk: 69]

Let W denote the alignment cost, i.e. the total number of alignment tokens that are in one linearized file but not the other, M denote the total number of alignment tokens in one linearized file and N denote the total number of alignment tokens in the other linearized file (in the example above, $W = 3$, $M = 9$, $N = 6$). In all of the above-mentioned works the behavior of $W/(M+N)$ (or of W itself) is a crucial factor in making decision on parallelism of candidate pairs. However, the intrinsic stochastic nature of these quantities was never adressed before. In this paper we develop a statistical model for W, M and N, whose parameters can be estimated in unsupervised manner, and we show how structural filtering benefits from such model.

3 Statistical Model

3.1 Assumptions

Let random variables (r.v.) W, M, and N have the same meaning as in Section 2. Suppose that we are observing a pair of webpages for which $M = m$ and $N = n$. Then W is equal to the number of alignment tokens out of total $(m + n)$ tokens that are missing in either of the linearized sequences, which means that the r.v. W can be modeled by the binomial distribution with parameters $(m+n)$ and q, i.e.

$$\Pr(W = w|M = m, N = n) = \\ = \binom{m+n}{w} q^w (1-q)^{m+n-w}. \quad (1)$$

It is important to notice here that the parameter $q = \Pr(\text{token is removed})$ should be different for parallel and non-parallel pairs, since we expect significantly higher proportion of misalignments in non-parallel case than in parallel case. Thus, observing a small value of $W/(M + N)$ is one of the indicators in favor of parallelism of two pages. Another indicator is the similarity of M and N, which can be formalized in the following way:

$$N \begin{cases} = kM + b + \epsilon & \text{for a parallel pair,} \\ \text{indep. of } M & \text{for a non-parallel pair,} \end{cases} \quad (2)$$

where k, b are constants and the r.v. ϵ represents an error term of linear regression model, and is assumed to be independent from M and N. Our investigation shows that a Gaussian mixture model (GMM) fits well the distribution of ϵ (See Appendix A). Therefore we assume that ϵ is distributed according to the pdf

$$f_\epsilon(x; \lambda, \mu_{1,2}, \sigma_{1,2}) \\ = \frac{1}{\sqrt{2\pi}} \left(\frac{\lambda}{\sigma_1} e^{-\frac{(x-\mu_1)^2}{2\sigma_1^2}} + \frac{1-\lambda}{\sigma_2} e^{-\frac{(x-\mu_2)^2}{2\sigma_2^2}} \right). \quad (3)$$

The third indicator of parallelism that we are going to exploit is the similarity between text lengths: if L_1 and L_2 denote total lengths of text chunks in a candidate pair of webpages, then we assume that

$$L_2 \begin{cases} = aL_1 + c + z\sigma\sqrt{L_1} & \text{for a par. pair,} \\ \text{indep. of } L_1 & \text{for a non-par. pair,} \end{cases} \tag{4}$$

where a, c, σ are constants, z is a standard normal random variable and the variance of the difference $(L_2 - aL_1 - c)$ is modeled proportional to the length L_1 as in (Gale and Church, 1993). We notice here, that the assumptions (1) and (2) were made regardless of the text lengths L_1 and L_2: thus knowing the values of L_1 and L_2 does not affect the distribution of W (when M and N are given) or the joint distribution of (M, N).

Hereinafter we use the following notation: $\hat{p}_X(x)$ denotes an empirical pdf for a r.v. X, calculated from a set of observations $\{x_i\}$; the symbol "$\|$" is used to denote that "pages under consideration are parallel"; and the symbol "$\nparallel$" is used to denote that "pages under consideration are not parallel". When there is no possibility for confusion, we write Pr(x) for Pr$(X = x)$, and use similar shorthands throughout.

3.2 Derivation

Let us denote $\boldsymbol{x} = (w, m, n, l_1, l_2)$. Our ultimate goal is to be able to calculate Pr$(\| \, |\boldsymbol{x})$ and Pr$(\nparallel |\boldsymbol{x})$, and then to compare them in order to select the most probable case. These probabilities can be rewritten using Bayes' rule:

$$\begin{aligned} \Pr(\| \, |\boldsymbol{x}) &= \frac{\Pr(\boldsymbol{x}| \, \|) \Pr(\|)}{\Pr(\boldsymbol{x})} \\ \Pr(\nparallel |\boldsymbol{x}) &= \frac{\Pr(\boldsymbol{x}| \nparallel) \Pr(\nparallel)}{\Pr(\boldsymbol{x})} \end{aligned} \tag{5}$$

Since the denominators in (5) are same, it is sufficient to compare the numerators. Now, let us derive a model for the distribution of W, M, N, L_1 and L_2 in case of a parallel pair:

$$\begin{aligned} A_{\|} := &\Pr(w, m, n, l_1, l_2| \, \|) = \\ &= \Pr(w, m, n|l_1, l_2, \|) \Pr(l_1, l_2| \, \|) = \\ &= \Pr(w|m, n, l_1, l_2, \|) \Pr(m, n|l_1, l_2, \|) \times \\ &\quad \times \Pr(l_1, l_2| \, \|) = \\ &= \{\text{independence assumptions}\} = \\ &= \underbrace{\Pr(w|m, n, \|)}_{B_{\|}} \underbrace{\Pr(m, n| \, \|)}_{C_{\|}} \underbrace{\Pr(l_1, l_2| \, \|)}_{D_{\|}}. \end{aligned} \tag{6}$$

From (1) and the remark after it, we can say that

$$B_{\|} = \binom{m+n}{w} q_{\|}^{w} (1 - q_{\|})^{m+n-w}, \tag{7}$$

where $q_{\|} = \Pr(\text{token is removed}| \, \|)$. Also, from the assumption (2) we get

$$\begin{aligned} C_{\|} &= \Pr(M = m, kM + b + \epsilon = n) \\ &= \Pr(M = m) \cdot \Pr(kM + b + \epsilon = n|M = m) \\ &\approx \{\text{continuity correction for } \epsilon\} \\ &\approx \hat{p}_M(m) \Pr(\epsilon \in n - km - b \pm .5|M = m) \\ &= \{\text{independence of } M \text{ and } \epsilon\} \\ &= \hat{p}_M(m) \cdot \Pr(\epsilon \in n - km - b \pm .5) \\ &= \hat{p}_M(m) \cdot \int_{n-km-b-.5}^{n-km-b+.5} f_\epsilon(x; \lambda, \mu_{1,2}, \sigma_{1,2}) dx, \end{aligned} \tag{8}$$

where $f_\epsilon(x; \lambda, \mu_{1,2}, \sigma_{1,2})$ is defined by (3). From the assumption (4) we obtain

$$\begin{aligned} D_{\|} &= \Pr\left(L_1 = l_1, aL_1 + c + z\sigma\sqrt{L_1} = l_2\right) \\ &= \Pr(L_1 = l_1) \\ &\quad \times \Pr\left(aL_1 + c + z\sigma\sqrt{L_1} = l_2|L_1 = l_1\right) \\ &\approx \{\text{continuity correction for } z\} \\ &\approx \hat{p}_{L_1}(l_1) \cdot \Pr\left(z \in \frac{l_2 - al_1 - c \pm .5}{\sigma\sqrt{l_1}}\right) \\ &= \hat{p}_{L_1}(l_1) \cdot \frac{1}{\sqrt{2\pi l_1}\sigma} \int_{l_2-al_1-c-.5}^{l_2-al_1-c+.5} e^{\frac{-x^2}{2l_1\sigma^2}} dx. \end{aligned} \tag{9}$$

Combining (6), (7), (8) and (9) we obtain

$$\begin{aligned} A_{\|} &\approx \binom{m+n}{w} q_{\|}^{w} (1 - q_{\|})^{m+n-w} \\ &\times \hat{p}_M(m) \cdot \int_{n-km-b-.5}^{n-km-b+.5} f_\epsilon(x; \lambda, \mu_{1,2}, \sigma_{1,2}) dx \\ &\times \hat{p}_{L_1}(l_1) \cdot \frac{1}{\sqrt{2\pi l_1}\sigma} \int_{l_2-al_1-c-.5}^{l_2-al_1-c+.5} e^{\frac{-x^2}{2l_1\sigma^2}} dx. \end{aligned} \tag{10}$$

Similarly, let us derive a model for the distribution of W, M, N, L_1 and L_2 in case of a non-parallel pair:

$$\begin{aligned}A_{\nparallel} &:= \Pr(w, m, n, l_1, l_2 | \nparallel) \\ &= \Pr(w, m, n | l_1, l_2, \nparallel) \Pr(l_1, l_2 | \nparallel) = \\ &= \Pr(w | m, n, l_1, l_2, \nparallel) \Pr(m, n | l_1, l_2, \nparallel) \times \\ &\quad \times \Pr(l_1, l_2 | \nparallel) = \\ &= \{\text{independence assumptions}\} = \\ &= \underbrace{\Pr(w | m, n \nparallel)}_{B_{\nparallel}} \underbrace{\Pr(m, n | \nparallel)}_{C_{\nparallel}} \underbrace{\Pr(l_1, l_2 | \nparallel)}_{D_{\nparallel}}.\end{aligned} \tag{11}$$

As discussed earlier, under non-parallelism we should assume probability of an alignment token to be removed $q_{\nparallel}$ to be different from $q_{\parallel}$ and thus:

$$B_{\nparallel} = \binom{m+n}{w} q_{\nparallel}^{w} (1 - q_{\nparallel})^{m+n-w}. \tag{12}$$

Due to independence assumption between M and N (2) under non-parallelism we have:

$$\begin{aligned}C_{\nparallel} &= \Pr(M = m | \nparallel) \cdot \Pr(N = n | \nparallel) \\ &\approx \{\text{marginal pdf's do not depend on } \nparallel\} \\ &\approx \hat{p}_M(m) \cdot \hat{p}_N(n).\end{aligned} \tag{13}$$

And, similarly, from (4) we have

$$\begin{aligned}D_{\nparallel} &= \Pr(L_1 = l_1 | \nparallel) \cdot \Pr(L_2 = l_2 | \nparallel) \\ &\approx \hat{p}_{L_1}(l_1) \cdot \hat{p}_{L_2}(l_2).\end{aligned} \tag{14}$$

Now, from (11), (12), (13) and (14) we obtain

$$\begin{aligned}A_{\nparallel} \approx &\binom{m+n}{w} q_{\nparallel}^{w} (1 - q_{\nparallel})^{m+n-w} \\ &\times \hat{p}_M(m) \cdot \hat{p}_N(n) \cdot \hat{p}_{L_1}(l_1) \cdot \hat{p}_{L_2}(l_2).\end{aligned} \tag{15}$$

Our model $A_{\parallel}(w, m, n, l_1, l_2; q_{\parallel}, k, b, \lambda, \mu_{1,2}, \sigma_{1,2}, a, c, \sigma)$ has 11 parameters ($q_{\parallel}$, k, b, λ, $\mu_{1,2}$, $\sigma_{1,2}$, a, c, σ), it receives the values of w, m, n, l_1, l_2 as input, and outputs the probability to observe such values under *parallelism*. The model $A_{\nparallel}(w, m, n, l_1, l_2; q_{\nparallel})$ has one parameter ($q_{\nparallel}$), it also receives the values of w, m, n, l_1 and l_2 as input, and outputs the probability to observe such values under *non-parallelism*. For the sake of simplicity we will denote

$$\begin{aligned}\boldsymbol{\theta}_{\parallel} &= (q_{\parallel}, k, b, \lambda, \mu_{1,2}, \sigma_{1,2}, a, c, \sigma), \\ p_{\parallel} &= \Pr(\parallel).\end{aligned}$$

3.3 Parameters Estimation

In order to show how expectation maximization (EM) algorithm (Dempster et al., 1977) can be used to estimate the parameters of our models let us assume that the set of candidate pairs consists of s pairs. Let us introduce the variables (for $i = \overline{1, s}$)

$$\alpha_i = \begin{cases} 1, & \text{if i}^{\text{th}} \text{ pair is parallel} \\ 0, & \text{otherwise.} \end{cases}$$

Then the likelihood function for our data is given by

$$\begin{aligned}L(q_{\parallel,\nparallel}, &k, b, \lambda, \mu_{1,2}, \sigma_{1,2}, \sigma, p_{\parallel}) = \\ &= C \prod_{i=1}^{s} [A_{\parallel}(\boldsymbol{x}_i; \boldsymbol{\theta}_{\parallel}) p_{\parallel}]^{\alpha_i} \times \\ &\quad \times [A_{\nparallel}(\boldsymbol{x}_i; q_{\nparallel})(1 - p_{\parallel})]^{1-\alpha_i},\end{aligned} \tag{16}$$

where $C = \prod_{i=1}^{s} [\Pr(\boldsymbol{x}_i)^{-1}]$ is a constant w.r.t. parameters $\boldsymbol{\theta}$, $q_{\nparallel}$, and $p_{\parallel}$. According to Lemma B.1, the likelihood (16) is maximized w.r.t $\{\alpha_i\}$ if

$$\alpha_i = \begin{cases} 1, & \text{if } A_{\parallel}(\boldsymbol{x}_i; \boldsymbol{\theta}_{\parallel}) p_{\parallel} > \\ & \quad > A_{\nparallel}(\boldsymbol{x}_i; q_{\nparallel})(1 - p_{\parallel}), \\ 0, & \text{otherwise.} \end{cases} \tag{17}$$

The formula (17) is basically the decision rule for our task of binary classification of candidate pairs into parallel or non-parallel ones (assuming that we know the parameters of $A_{\parallel}$ and $A_{\nparallel}$). Now the essence of the EM algorithm (Algorithm 1) can be described as follows.

We first initilize parameters on line 1 using the following reasoning: $q_{\parallel}$ should be less than $q_{\nparallel}$ due to the comment after (1); N should be approximately equal to M for parallel pairs, therefore we take $k = 1$ and $b = 0$ as initial guesses; since we know almost nothing about the components of the Gaussian mixture in (3), we set $\lambda = 0.5$ and $\mu_{1,2} = 0$, however we can expect that one of the components should be responsible for larger deviations from the mean (i.e. for heavy tails), and thus we set $\sigma_2 > \sigma_1$; we choose initial values for $a = 1$, $c = 0$ and $\sigma = \sqrt{6.8}$ based on the suggestion in (Gale and Church, 1993), and for $p_{\parallel} = 2/3$ based on the experiments in (Resnik and Smith, 2003).

After such initial guesses on parameters, we perform an E-step on lines 3–10, i.e. the models $A_{\parallel}$ and $A_{\nparallel}$ are applied to the data, and as a result we obtain two sets of indexes: I keeps the indexes

Algorithm 1 EM algorithm for $A_{\parallel}$ and $A_{\nparallel}$

Input: set of values $\{(w_i, m_i, n_i, l_{1,i}, l_{2,i})\}_{i=1}^{s}$

Output: indexes $I \subset \{1, \ldots, s\}$ of parallel pairs, indexes $J \subset \{1, \ldots, s\}$ of non-parallel pairs, estimates for $q_{\parallel}$, $q_{\nparallel}$, k, b, λ, $\mu_{1,2}$, $\sigma_{1,2}$, a, c, σ, $p_{\parallel}$

1: Initialize $q_{\parallel} \leftarrow 0.2$, $q_{\nparallel} \leftarrow 0.5$, $k \leftarrow 1$, $b \leftarrow 0$, $\lambda \leftarrow 0.5$, $\mu_1 \leftarrow 0$, $\mu_2 \leftarrow 0$, $\sigma_1 \leftarrow 1$, $\sigma_2 \leftarrow 10$, $a \leftarrow 1$, $c \leftarrow 0$, $\sigma \leftarrow \sqrt{6.8}$, $p_{\parallel} = 2/3$.

2: **while** not converged **do**

3:     **for** $i \in \{1, \ldots, s\}$ **do**

4:         **if** $\frac{A_{\parallel}(\boldsymbol{x}_i;\boldsymbol{\theta}_{\parallel})}{1-p_{\parallel}} > \frac{A_{\nparallel}(\boldsymbol{x}_i;q_{\nparallel})}{p_{\parallel}}$ **then**

5:             $\alpha_i \leftarrow 1$

6:         **else**

7:             $\alpha_i \leftarrow 0$

8:         **end if**

9:     **end for**

10:     $I \leftarrow \{i | \alpha_i = 1\}$, $J \leftarrow \{j | \alpha_j = 0\}$

11:     $q_{\parallel} \leftarrow \frac{\sum_{i \in I} w_i}{\sum_{i \in I}(m_i + n_i)}$

12:     $q_{\nparallel} \leftarrow \frac{\sum_{j \in J} w_j}{\sum_{j \in J}(m_j + n_j)}$

13:     $(k, b) \leftarrow \arg\min_{(k,b)} \sum_{i \in I} \rho(n_i - k m_i - b)$

14:     **for** $i \in I$ **do**

15:         $\epsilon_i = n_i - k m_i - b$

16:     **end for**

17:     $(\lambda, \mu_{1,2}, \sigma_{1,2}) \leftarrow$ $\leftarrow \arg\max_{(\lambda,\mu_{1,2},\sigma_{1,2})} \prod_{i \in I} f_{\epsilon}(\epsilon_i; \lambda, \mu_{1,2}, \sigma_{1,2})$

18:     $(a, c) \leftarrow \arg\min_{(a,c)} \sum_{i \in I} \rho(l_{2,i} - a l_{1,i} - c)$

19:     **for** $i \in I$ **do**

20:         $\delta_i = l_{2,i} - a l_{1,i} - c$

21:     **end for**

22:     $\sigma \leftarrow \arg\min_{\sigma} \sum_{i \in I} \rho(\delta_i^2 - \sigma l_{1,i})$

23:     $p_{\parallel} \leftarrow |I|/s$

24: **end while**

of parallel pairs, and J keeps the indexes of non-parallel pairs. Then the M-step is performed on lines 11–23, where we update the parameters as follows: MLE for $q_{\parallel}$ and $q_{\nparallel}$ are given by Lemma B.2; the method of iteratively reweighted least squares is used to estimate k and b on line 13 where ρ is an Huber function (Huber, 2011). The obtained values for (k, b) are then used to calculate residuals $\{\epsilon_i\}_{i \in I}$; then, the parameters of GMM, $\lambda, \mu_{1,2}, \sigma_{1,2}$, are updated based on MLE (an additional EM-procedure is usually needed for this task); σ is estimated using robust linear regression (Huber, 2011) as suggested in (Gale and Church, 1993); finally, $p_{\parallel}$ is estimated as the proportion of parallel pairs.

An R-script, which implements the Algorithm 1, is available at `https://svn.code.sf.net/p/apertium/svn/branches/zaan/`.

4 Experiments

We selected five different websites to test our model: official site of the President of the Republic of Kazakhstan (`http://akorda.kz`), official site of the Ministry of Foreign Affairs of the Republic of Kazakhstan (`http://mfa.kz`), electronic government of the Repuplic of Kazakhstan (`http://egov.kz`), official site of the Presidency of the Portuguese Republic (`http://presidencia.pt`), and official site of the Prime Minister of Canada (`http://pm.gc.ca`). We downloaded all candidate pairs with the help of *wget* tool, and then removed boilerplates, i.e. navigational elements, templates, and advertisements which are not related to the main content, using simple Python scripts[1]. The details on the number of mined pairs are given in Table 1. We applied Algorithm 1 to all five websites (values of w, m, n, l_1, and l_2 were obtained using a modified version[2] of an open-source implementation of STRAND algorithm[3]). Then for each website we extracted a representative sample of candidate pairs and manually checked them (sample sizes were calculated based on Cochran's formula (Cochran, 2007) for

Website	Lang's	# of pairs	Sample size
`akorda.kz`	kk-en	4135	352
`mfa.kz`	kk-en	180	180
`egov.kz`	kk-en	1641	312
`presidencia.pt`	pt-en	960	275
`pm.gc.ca`	fr-en	1397	302

Table 1: Websites for experiments

[1]the scripts as well as archives of the mined webpages are available at `https://svn.code.sf.net/p/apertium/svn/branches/kaz-eng-corpora`

[2]`https://github.com/assulan/STRANDAligner`

[3]`https://github.com/jrs026/STRANDAligner`

all websites except `mfa.kz`, for which we checked all pairs due to small amount of them). The metrics used to evaluate our model have been precision ($prec$), recall (rec), and F-score (F). The results of the experiments are given in Table 2.

Website	$prec$	rec	F
akorda.kz	0.941	0.971	0.956
mfa.kz	0.944	1.000	0.971
egov.kz	0.915	0.969	0.941
presidencia.pt	0.991	0.950	0.970
pm.gc.ca	0.990	1.000	0.995

Table 2: Results of the experiments

5 Discussion and Future Work

The experiments have shown that statistical modeling of misalignments in linearized HTML files allows us to get better results in the task of measuring structural similarity between webpages from bilingual websites. The previous approaches for measuring structural similarity were based on finding threshold values for the number of misalignments (W) or the misalignments ratio ($\frac{W}{M+N}$), or using these characterisics as features in machine learning algorithms. Those approaches either led to high precision but low recall, or required supervised learning of underlying models, or both. Our approach has good recall and acceptable precision rates; it is language-independent and the parameters of our model are estimated in unsupervised manner through EM algorithm.

We have noticed that the suggested algorithm demonstrates higher precision for websites, which have good quality of translated texts in general (e.g. `presidencia.pt`), than for websites, which have worse quality of translation (e.g. `egov.kz`); but it keeps recall at good level in all cases. This means that the model tries not to throw away parallel pairs, but it sometimes fails to recognize non-parallelism for the websites with substantial amount of medium or low quality of translated texts.

We now address the typical errors made by the model as well as possible directions for the future work. Type II errors (false negatives) are mainly caused by the pairs which have the same (or almost the same) content in two languages but there is significant difference in HTML-formatting of two pages (e.g. when *<p>* and *</p>* tags are used in one version to surround paragraphs, while the other version uses a sequence of *

* tags to separate paragraphs). This problem could be handled by an appropriate pre-processing (normalizing) of the HTML files before applying the Algorithm 1. Type I errors (false positives) are primarily caused by the pairs which are consistent in HTML-formatting but have some differences in content (e.g. when one or few sentences/short paragraphs are missing in one version but are present in the other version). This problem could be tackled by better alignment of text-chunks and better exploitation of the similarity in text lengths if we want to stay in a language-independent framework, or by embedding content-similarity measures, if we decide to switch to language-dependent techniques. In the latter case we could also use morphological segmentation as in (Assylbekov and Nurkas, 2014) for preprocessing texts in morphologically rich languages (like Kazakh), in order to improve the existing methods of measuring content-similarity.

Acknowledgments

We would like to thank Dr. Igor Melnykov for the useful discussions of the EM algorithm.

A Goodness-of-fit Tests for ϵ

Let r.v.'s W, M, and N be defined as in Section 2, and let w, m, and n denote values of these r.v.'s. We downloaded candidate pairs from the official website of the President of the Republic of Kazakhstan located at `http://akorda.kz` and then from each webpage we removed the boilerplate, i.e. navigational elements, templates, and advertisements which are not related to the main content[4]. For each candidate pair we obtained values of w, m, and n using a modified version[5] of an open-source implementation of STRAND algorithm[6]. The following heuristic rule was used to keep seemingly parallel pairs:

$$\{\text{pages are parallel}\} \approx \left\{\frac{W}{M+N} \in (0, 0.2]\right\} \cap \cap \{M \in [19, 200]\} \cap \{N \in [19, 200]\}. \quad (18)$$

A threshold value of 0.2 for $W/(M+N)$ is recommended by the authors of STRAND. Boundaries for M and N are selected based on 1st and

[4] the scripts as well as the candidate pairs are available at `https://svn.code.sf.net/p/apertium/svn/branches/kaz-eng-corpora/akorda/`

[5] `https://github.com/assulan/STRANDAligner`

[6] `https://github.com/jrs026/STRANDAligner`

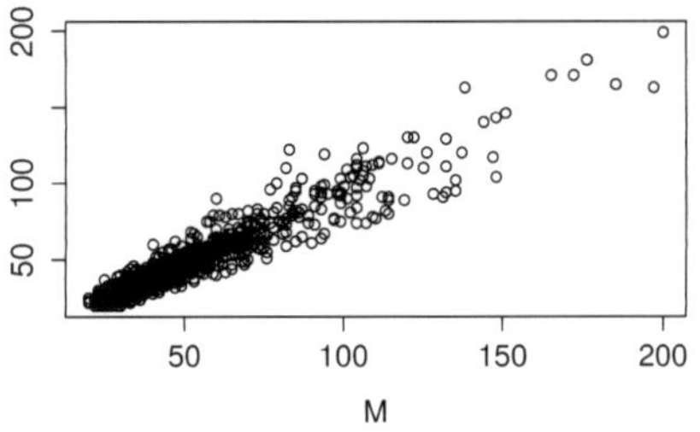

Figure 1: Scatter-plot of $\{(m_i, n_i)\}$ for seemingly parallel pairs.

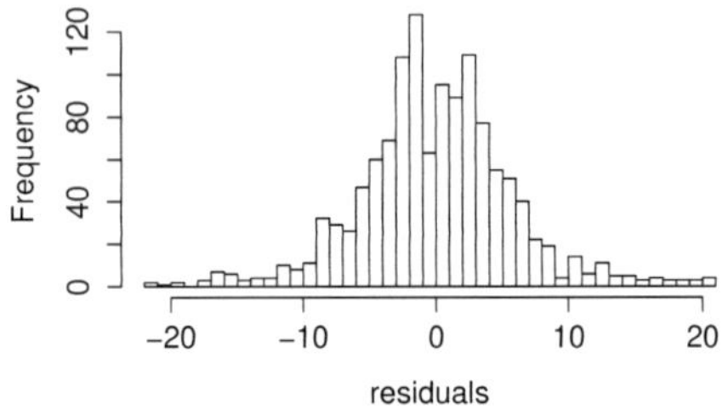

Figure 2: Distribution of the residuals $\{\epsilon_i\}$

99th percentiles and they are used to remove outliers. Application of the rule (18) resulted in 1271 seemingly parallel pairs. We stress here that the rule (18) *is not* used in our paper as the decision rule regarding parallelism of pages. Instead, it allows us to quickly identify pages which *seem* to be parallel and to look at the behavior of their M and N values. Figure 1 provides a scatter-plot of $\{(m_i, n_i)\}_{i=1}^{1271}$ for the filtered set of pages and it shows that the rule (18) supports our assumption on the linear relationship between M and N for parallel pages (2).

Next, we fit a linear regression model $N = kM + b + \epsilon$ to the data (m_i, n_i), and look at the residuals $\epsilon_i = n_i - km_i - b$ (Figure 2). Outliers among $\{\epsilon_i\}$ are dropped based on 1st and 99th percentiles, which resulted in 1245 observations (instead of 1271).

Further on we show that ϵ can be modeled using a Gaussian mixture model. A two-component mixture of Gaussian distributions has a pdf

$$f_{GMM}(x; \lambda, \mu_1, \sigma_1, \mu_2, \sigma_2) = \\ = \frac{1}{\sqrt{2\pi}} \left(\frac{\lambda}{\sigma_1} e^{-\frac{(x-\mu_1)^2}{\sigma_1^2}} + \frac{1-\lambda}{\sigma_2} e^{-\frac{(x-\mu_2)^2}{\sigma_2^2}} \right) \tag{19}$$

We first find MLE $\lambda^e, \mu_1^e, \sigma_1^e, \mu_2^e, \sigma_2^e$ for the parameters in (19) using EM-algorithm (Dempster et al., 1977), and then test a hypothesis

$$H_0: \ f_\epsilon(x) = f_{GMM}(x; \mu_1^e, \sigma_1^e, \mu_2^e, \sigma_2^e) \\ H_1: \ f_\epsilon(x) \neq f_{GMM}(x; \mu_1^e, \sigma_1^e, \mu_2^e, \sigma_2^e),$$

using the chi-square goodness-of-fit test. The details are provided in the Table 3, from where we decide not to reject H_0, i.e. there is no evidence that the residuals are not distributed according to (19). In other words, *a Gaussian mixture model does a good job in modelling* $\{\epsilon_i\}$.

Interval	Obs. Freq.	Exp. Freq.
$(-\infty, -19]$	5	5.26
$(-19, -16]$	10	6.92
$(-16, -14]$	9	8.03
$(-14, -12]$	8	12.38
⋮	⋮	⋮
$(12, 14]$	16	12.97
$(14, 16]$	8	8.62
$(16, 19]$	10	7.55
$(19, +\infty)$	7	5.88
$\chi^2 = 19.023$, df = 19, p-value = 0.4554		

Table 3: Fitting a Gaussian mixture model to $\{\epsilon_i\}$

B Auxiliary Lemmas

Lemma B.1. *Let* $f(\alpha_1, \ldots, \alpha_n) = \prod_{i=1}^n p_i^{\alpha_i} q_i^{1-\alpha_i}$, *where* $\alpha_i \in \{0, 1\}$ *and* $p_i, q_i \in [0, 1]$, $i = \overline{1, n}$. *Then* f *reaches its maximum at*

$$\alpha_i = \begin{cases} 1, & \text{if } p_i > q_i \\ 0, & \text{otherwise} \end{cases} \tag{20}$$

Proof. The proof is left as an excercise. □

Lemma B.2. *Let* $X_1, X_2, \ldots, X_m$ *be independent binomial random variables with parameters* (n_1, q), (n_2, q), ..., (n_m, q) *correspondingly. Then the maximum likelihood estimator for* q *is*

$$\hat{q} = \frac{\sum_{i=1}^m X_i}{\sum_{i=1}^m n_i} \tag{21}$$

Proof. The proof is left as an excercise. □

References

Zhenisbek Assylbekov and Assulan Nurkas. Initial explorations in kazakh to english statistical machine translation. In *The First Italian Conference on Computational Linguistics CLiC-it 2014*, page 12, 2014.

Jiang Chen and Jian-Yun Nie. Automatic construction of parallel english-chinese corpus for cross-language information retrieval. In *Proceedings of the sixth conference on Applied natural language processing*, pages 21–28. Association for Computational Linguistics, 2000.

William G Cochran. *Sampling techniques*. John Wiley & Sons, 2007.

Arthur P Dempster, Nan M Laird, and Donald B Rubin. Maximum likelihood from incomplete data via the em algorithm. *Journal of the royal statistical society. Series B (methodological)*, pages 1–38, 1977.

Miquel Esplà-Gomis and Mikel Forcada. Combining content-based and url-based heuristics to harvest aligned bitexts from multilingual sites with bitextor. *The Prague Bulletin of Mathematical Linguistics*, 93:77–86, 2010.

William A Gale and Kenneth W Church. A program for aligning sentences in bilingual corpora. *Computational linguistics*, 19(1):75–102, 1993.

Peter J Huber. *Robust statistics*. Springer, 2011.

James Wayne Hunt and MD MacIlroy. *An algorithm for differential file comparison*. Bell Laboratories, 1976.

Le Liu, Yu Hong, Jun Lu, Jun Lang, Heng Ji, and Jianmin Yao. An iterative link-based method for parallel web page mining. *Proceedings of EMNLP*, pages 1216–1224, 2014.

Xiaoyi Ma and Mark Liberman. Bits: A method for bilingual text search over the web. In *Machine Translation Summit VII*, pages 538–542, 1999.

Vassilis Papavassiliou, Prokopis Prokopidis, and Gregor Thurmair. A modular open-source focused crawler for mining monolingual and bilingual corpora from the web. In *Proceedings of the Sixth Workshop on Building and Using Comparable Corpora*, pages 43–51, 2013.

Philip Resnik. *Parallel strands: A preliminary investigation into mining the web for bilingual text.* Springer, 1998.

Philip Resnik and Noah A Smith. The web as a parallel corpus. *Computational Linguistics*, 29(3): 349–380, 2003.

Inaki San Vicente and Iker Manterola. Paco2: A fully automated tool for gathering parallel corpora from the web. In *LREC*, pages 1–6, 2012.

Lei Shi, Cheng Niu, Ming Zhou, and Jianfeng Gao. A dom tree alignment model for mining parallel data from the web. In *Proceedings of the 21st International Conference on Computational Linguistics and the 44th annual meeting of the Association for Computational Linguistics*, pages 489–496. Association for Computational Linguistics, 2006.

Ying Zhang, Ke Wu, Jianfeng Gao, and Phil Vines. Automatic acquisition of chinese–english parallel corpus from the web. In *Advances in Information Retrieval*, pages 420–431. Springer, 2006.

Predicting the Quality of Questions on Stackoverflow

Antoaneta Baltadzhieva
Tilburg University
a_baltadzhieva@yahoo.de

Grzegorz Chrupała
Tilburg University
g.a.chrupala@uvt.nl

Abstract

Community Question Answering websites (CQA) have a growing popularity as a way of providing and searching of information. CQA attract users as they provide a direct and rapid way to find the desired information. As recognizing good questions can improve the CQA services and the user's experience, the current study focuses on question quality instead. Specifically, we predict question quality and investigate the features which influence it. The influence of the question tags, length of the question title and body, presence of a code snippet, the user reputation and terms used to formulate the question are tested. For each set of dependent variables, Ridge regression models are estimated. The results indicate that the inclusion of terms in the models improves their predictive power. Additionally, we investigate which lexical terms determine high and low quality questions. The terms with the highest and lowest coefficients are semantically analyzed. The analysis shows that terms predicting high quality are terms expressing, among others, excitement, negative experience or terms regarding exceptions. Terms predicting low quality questions are terms containing spelling errors or indicating off-topic questions and interjections.

1 Introduction

CQA websites provide an interface for users to exchange and share knowledge. The user asking a question lacks knowledge of a specific topic and searches for an expert to provide the desired knowledge. In this way, the asker is querying a topic and the experts are the source of information, replacing other sources like documents or databases. However, the search results may not provide an exact solution to the user's problem. Although the idea of receiving a direct response to an information need sounds very appealing, CQA websites also involve risk as the quality of the provided information is not guaranteed. An important difference between user-generated content and traditional content is the range of the content quality: user-generated content shows a higher variance in quality (Agichtein et al., 2008) than traditional content (Anderson, 2006).

Stack Overflow (SO) is a CQA website in the field of computer programming. Access is free and answers are voted according to the asker's satisfaction[1]. The asker can tag a question to indicate a specific subject. Users can vote questions, answers and edits to indicate how helpful they were. The votes determine the user's reputation. In order to create a high-quality library of questions and their answers, SO allows users not only to post questions or answers but also to edit them.

Despite the encouragement of SO and the offered opportunities to maintain the content quality, a lot of questions on SO are not answered. With the increase in popularity of SO, not only the number of questions and the number of new members increased, but also the number of unanswered questions. According to statistics from 2012, approximately 45 questions per month remained unanswered (Asaduzzaman et al., 2013). By March 20, 2014, the number of unanswered questions was 752,533 out of 6,912,743 (approximately 10.9%). Interestingly, the fact that those questions are not answered is not caused by users not having seen them. In fact, unanswered questions are seen 139 times on average (Asaduzzaman et al., 2013). It is not obvious why a certain question receives more answers than others. Also, it is not clear whether the question characteristics

[1] http://stackoverflow.com/

Proceedings of Recent Advances in Natural Language Processing, pages 32–40,
Hissar, Bulgaria, Sep 7–9 2015.

that determine the number of answers a question receives also influence the question score. In this paper, we evaluate the features of questions in SO, how they influence the two above mentioned indicators of question quality, and attempt to predict these outcome measures for newly posted questions. Our main contributions are twofold. First, unlike previous work, we study the influence of specific individual terms, i.e. the words used to construct the question title and body. More specifically, we analyze the terms used in the posted questions and explore to what extent they can predict the question score and the probability of receiving an answer. The results indicate that the models have the best predictive power when the terms are included. Second, we study their influence on **two** measures of question quality: *the number of answers* and *the question score*.

1.1 Reserach Overview

In the current study, we investigate which features influence question quality, as measured by the number of answers and the question score a question receives, in a programming CQA. Also, we predict which lexical terms determine high and low quality questions. We test the influence of question tags, length of the question title and body, presence of a code snippet and the user reputation on question quality. In addition, we test the influence of terms used to formulate the question. For each of the two dependent variables, we estimate Ridge regression models with an increasing number of independent variables on a dataset of over 1.7 million questions posted on Stack Overflow, dividing them into a training, validation and test set. The results indicate that the inclusion of terms in the models improves their predictive power. To the best of my knowledge, this research is the first to analyze the terms used in the posted questions and to explore to what extent they can predict the probability of receiving an answer. We rank the significant terms based on their coefficient value. The terms with the highest and lowest coefficients were semantically analyzed and divided in subgroups to gain a better understanding of the semantic nature of the terms. We find that terms predicting high quality are terms expressing excitement, negative experience or frustration, and terms regarding exceptions, or indicate that the questions are posted by new members. The largest groups of terms predicting low quality questions is the group containing spelling errors. Also words that mark off-topic questions and interjections are an indication of low quality questions. The better understanding of the terms used in low and high quality questions would help to improve the question formulation and herewith the content if CQA websites.

2 Related Work

2.1 Question Quality

Due to the large number of CQA websites, the importance of high-quality content in CQA websites has been recognized and investigated in several studies. Agichtein et al. (2008) found that there is a correlation between the question quality and answer quality, i.e. question quality will influence CQA service quality. According to Li et al. (2012), high quality questions are expected to draw greater user attention and will make users feel more compelling to answer the question within a shorter period of time.

Different studies employ different definitions of question quality. As measures of question quality we consider *the number of answers* and *the question score* as those are the response of the community to the usefulness of the question (Anderson et al., 2012). The number of answers is a direct feedback on the usefulness of the question. Research has shown it is the most significant feature to predict the long term value of a question together with its answers set (Anderson et al., 2012). Also the question score reflects the question quality. A question can be voted up or down by using the up or respectively down arrow on the left side of the question. In general, answered questions on SO have higher scores compared to unanswered questions (Saha et al., 2013).

Although the question score and the number of answers are considered quality determinants, they are not necessarily correlated. A question that addresses a new development which is interesting to the community but difficult to answer may receive no answers but a lot of upvotes. If however a question was too easy or posted previously it may receive answers, but may not be evaluated high as it does not contribute to the CQA. A number of other measures of question quality have been used in the literature. For a detailed overview of the existing literature, see (Baltadzhieva and Chrupala, 2015).

2.2 Features Determining Question Quality

The features determining question quality are divided in a question-related and an asker-related group. The former is represented by the features *tags, terms, question title and question body length*, and *the presence of a code snippet*. Regarding asker-related features, the reputation of the user is taken into consideration. This researches focus on features that are available at the moment a question is posted, because features which are not available at the moment of the posting cannot help the asker to improve her question (Cheng et al., 2013; Correa and Sureka, 2014).

2.2.1 Question-related Features

In SO, askers can add tags to a question to indicate which topic(s) they address. Saha *et al.* (2013) analyzed the tags as topics and concluded that the large number of unanswered questions cannot be explained by a lack of sufficient experts for certain topics. Furthermore, Correa and Sureka (2014) observed that a high percentage of author-deleted questions are marked as too localized and off-topic, and that a high percentage of moderator-deleted questions are marked as subjective and not a real question. Asaduzzaman *et al.* (2013), state that incorrect tagging is one of the characteristics of unanswered questions. These results indicate that question topics, i.e. tags, may either be incorrect and/or may not be fully informative of the likelihood of receiving an answer, the number of answers, or question score. Therefore, a number of recent studies tried to infer question topics from the natural language used to formulate the questions. The current study uses both *tags*, as well as information from the questions' natural language formulation, the *terms*. In the term extraction process, terms are analyzed as the number of occurrences in the question title or question body where a term receives a value of 0 if it does not occur and otherwise the value of the number of occurrences.

Yang *et al.* (2011) found that the shortest and longest questions have the highest probability of obtaining an answer - short questions can be read and answered in a very short time, and long questions are mostly expertise-related, need more explanation and are therefore appealing for users with the same interest. In contrast, Asaduzzaman *et al.* (2013) found that too short questions are very likely to remain unanswered as they may miss important information; and too time-consuming questions are not very attractive for answerers. According to Saha *et al.* (2013) both classes have the same probability of receiving an answer. Correa and Sureka (2014), finally, found that compared to closed questions, deleted questions had a slightly higher number of characters in the question body. The existing literature is thus inconsistent regarding whether and to what extent question length influences question quality. Further, question length and question body length are never analyzed separately. Therefore, we explore the effects of both *question title* and *question body length* to see if the results point in the same direction.

Several studies have found that question categories that contain a code snippet have a high answer ratio and may have more than one possible good answer (Treude et al., 2011; Asaduzzaman et al., 2013). Also deleted questions have a lower percentage of code blocks than closed questions (Correa and Sureka, 2014). However, the presence of a code snippet may also have adverse effects as well if the code is hard to follow or if other users cannot see the problem (Asaduzzaman et al., 2013). Hence, it is unclear what the effect of *the presence of a code snippet* is on question quality.

2.2.2 Asker-related Features

Regarding asker-related features, we consider the asker's reputation as a feature that influences question quality metrics. The reputation scores are built on users' participation on the CQA website. Users with high reputations do not only provide an essential contribution to CQA websites in general, but they also provide the most helpful answers (Welser et al., 2007; Pal et al., 2012). SO rewards upvotes on answers more than on questions and assigns high reputation users more privileges in site management and bonuses than regular users. The most reputation points are scored when a user's answer is accepted as the best answer, when it is upvoted or when the answer has received a bounty. Anderson *et al.* (2012) show that users build their reputation mainly by receiving upvotes for their answers and not by asking questions themselves. Saha *et al.* (2013) found the asker's reputation to be one of the most dominant attributes to distinguish between answered and unanswered questions, the former having a max score of twice as much as unanswered questions. For a detailed overview, see (Baltadzhieva and Chrupala, 2015).

3 Dataset Description

Our dataset consists of JSON files extracted from SO using the Stack Exchange API (Application Programming Interface). The dataset contains questions in the period between 31 July 2008 and 9 June 2011. Within this time period, 1,713,400 questions were posted. Out of the total number of questions, 126,227 remained unanswered (7.37%). Each question contains information about the question itself, such as title, body, upvotes, downvotes etc., and about the question owner, e.g. registration status, reputation, name, id etc. In this research we are only interested in the variables as described below.

3.1 Data Overview

Tables 1 and 2 provide an overview of the data and descriptive statistics of the key variables normalized.

Data item	Count
Questions total	1,713,400
Questions unanswered	126,227
Code snippet 1/0	792,822/920,578
Terms	36,865
Tags	12 11,613

Table 1: Data overview

	Mean	SD	Median
Nr. of answers	2.242	1.869	2
Q. score	1.331	2.446	1.00
Q. title length	8.27	3.71	8.00
Q. body length	91.74	87.43	72.00
User rep.	1600.40	5552.40	301.00

Table 2: Descriptive statistics

The independent variables *title length, body length* and *user reputation* are normalized by the logarithmic transformation using the natural logarithm, and for *question score* and *number of answers* we use percentile normalization. Most questions receive a small number of answers. On average a question receives a relatively low score. Question titles and bodies consisting of only one word may be questions where only a code snippet was posted. The high mean value of the user reputation suggests that many SO users have a high user reputation. As it has been shown that there is a positive relationship between the user reputation and how fast the user replies to a question (Anderson et al., 2012), it can be concluded that SO askers are active community users.

To predict the number of answers and question score, the independent variables are defined as follows: the tags and the presence of a code snippet are represented as a Boolean value; the question title and body length are measured by the number of words; the user reputation is the user reputation score; the terms are a count variable of how often a term occurs in the question title or body. In order to extract numerical information from text content, first a tokenization process takes place (Manning et al., 2008). Stop words are filtered out from the vocabulary prior to natural language processing, because they are of little value in finding documents matching a user's information need (Manning et al., 2008).

Only the tags are included that appear in at least 20 questions and terms that appear at least in 50 questions. Results based on tags and terms that occur seldom are likely to be spurious and are not expected to have strong predictive power.

3.2 Method of Analysis

For the prediction task we use multiple linear regression models. The expected relationship is a linear function of the independent variables (Field, 2009):

$$y_i = \beta_0 + \sum_{j=1}^{J} \beta_j x_{ij} + \epsilon_i$$

Here, for question i, y_i represents the dependent variable *question score* or *number of answers* received, β represents the coefficients of the predictor variables x and ϵ is the difference between the predicted and the observed value of the outcome variable, which is assumed normally distributed.

When predicting future responses and investigating the relationship between the response variable and the predictor variables regularized regression models are preferred, because they solve highly variable estimates of the regression coefficients when there is multicollinearity or when the number of predictors is very large in connection to the number of observations (Hartmann et al., 2009). In programming languages a lot of terms appear together what can lead to multicollinearity. As the number of terms used in this study is extremely large (36,865) and in order to avoid overfitting, a regularized regression model, Ridge regression (Hoerl and Kennard, 1970b; Hoerl and

Kennard, 1970a), is used. Ridge regression applies a penalty to the sum of the squared values of the regression coefficients which shrink the coefficients towards zero, but never become zero, which means that all predictors remain in the model. Applying a penalty results in lower expected prediction error because it reduces the estimation variance (Hartmann et al., 2009).

We split the dataset in three subsets: a training set - the first 60%, a validation set - the next 20%, and a test set - the rest 20%. The sets are chronologically partioned as the goal of this study is to predict the quality of new questions. The validation set is used to optimize the regularization parameter for each model. To find the optimal ridge parameters, several values are tried in increasing order. The value that reduces the Mean Squared Error of the validation set the most is chosen as the optimal parameter. Finally, the obtained coefficients, given the optimal regularization parameter, are applied on the test set to assess the predictive validity of the models.

To investigate the question quality, two sets of multiple linear regression models are applied – one to predict the question score and the second one to predict the number of answers. For each set, four different regression models are applied and compared in order to discover which independent variables have the most predictive power. Model 0 is the baseline intercept-only model. In Model 1 only the tags are included, Model 2 contains question title and body length, code snippet and tags, Model 3 - the variables of Model 2 plus user reputation, and Model 4 - the variables of Model 3 plus terms. Each set uses the same dependent variable and a different set of independent variables. To compare the performance of the models in each set, the R-squared, Mean Squared Error (MSE) and Mean Absolute Error (MAE) are reported.

3.3 Results

As Model 4 has the best performance on the *test set* as presented in Table 3 and Table 4, only the coefficients of Model 4 are discussed in this section.

The results show that Model 1 performs better than the baseline model for both question score and number of answers, as the MSE has lower values. Compared to Model 2 however the performance does not change drastically. The MSE of Model 2 for predicting question score decreases with only 0.075 and for number of answers with only 0.031. These results indicate that the tags do influence the question quality, whereas the inclusion of the title length, body length and the presence of a code snippet gives a minor improvement.

	MSE	**MAE**	**R^2**	**F-statistic**
Model 0	5.675	1.482		
Model 1	5.138	1.375	0.088	3.768
Model 2	5.063	1.363	0.102	4.396
Model 3	4.869	1.323	0.136	6.124
Model 4	4.622	1.286	0.180	1.897

Table 3: Ridge regression *question score*

	MSE	**MAE**	**R^2**	**F-statistic**
Model 0	3.199	1.353		
Model 1	2.769	1.228	0.109	4.771
Model 2	2.738	1.219	0.119	5.257
Model 3	2.630	1.192	0.154	7.079
Model 4	2.514	1.163	0.191	2.048

Table 4: Ridge regression *number of answers*

For both model sets it applies that the more complex the model is, the better it performs on the training and test set: MSE and MAE decrease with the increase of the number of independent variables and all models outperform the baseline Model 0. This implies that Model 4 for both question score and number of answers fits the data best. The same conclusion can be drawn from the R-squared values. For number of answers, the R-squared for the test set increases from 0.102 for Model 2 to 0.180 for Model 4, meaning that Model 2 explains 10.2% of the variance in the question score in the test set while Model 4 explains 18.0%. Similarly, with regard to number of answers, the R-squared values for Models 1 and 3 for the test set are 0.119 and 0.191, respectively.

3.4 Coefficient Analysis

As Model 4 has the best performance, only the coefficients of Model 4 are presented and discussed. The *question title and body length* and *the presence of a code snippet* have a significant negative effect on the outcome variables, while reputation has a positive effect. To better understand the effect size, we calculate the effect of a 10% increase in body length, title length and user reputation, while taking the natural logarithm into account. A 10% increase in *title length, body length* and *user reputation* results in a change in the questions score of -0.010, -0.019 and 0.015, respectively. Including a code snippet reduces the question score by -0.155. Hence, the effect of all variables is fairly small. In Model 4, for *number of answers*, the *title length* effect is $\beta_t l$ = -0.058, which implies that, taking the mean title length as baseline and accounting for the logarithmic transformation, a 10% increase in *title length* results in a 0.006 reduction in the number of answers. Similarly, a 10% increase in *body length*, $\beta_b l$ = -0.132, and *user reputation*, $\beta_u r = 0.122$, gives an increase in the number of answers of -0.013 and 0.012 respectively. Including a code snippet reduces the expected number of answers by -0.050. The effects of the predictors are again fairly small.

3.4.1 Parts of Speech

Excessive use of (only) one part of speech might also influence the question quality. For example, too many verbs in a sentence can make it sound heavy and wordy (Weber, 2007) and therefore unpleasant to read. The number of nouns, verbs and adjectives are calculated using the Natural Language Toolkit (NLTK)[2]. Most of the terms that predict question score are nouns - 53.55%. This is not surprising as nouns are used most frequently in natural language. For number of answers, a Chi-square test is used to show that the counts of parts of speech differ significantly between high and low quality questions (χ^2 = 37.362, *df* = 3, $p = 0.01$). Particularly, the percentage of nouns is higher in the groups of terms predicting low question quality – 65.04%. At the same time the percentage of used adjectives is higher for high question quality – 13.55% vs. 8.98% for low questions quality. As adjectives are words that have a descriptive character and are used to assign a noun a specific property, it may be concluded, that questions with a low number of answers are less descriptive and maybe do not explain the information need clearly enough. For question score, the counts of parts of speech do not significantly differ between the high and low quality groups ($\chi^2 = 1.190$, *df* = 3, $p = 0.755$).

3.4.2 Semantic Analysis

In the term analysis only terms were included that have a statistically significant influence on the question quality. Due to the large number of such terms, we analyze only 10% of the terms with the highest coefficient values as they contribute to high question score and number of answers and 10% of the terms with lowest coefficient values that determine questions with low score and low number of answers. We assume that this percentage provides enough terms to discover patterns.

The extracted terms are analyzed and first divided into two groups – professional/expertise terms and generic terms. We assume that the question subject is expressed by the tags and that professional/expertise terms would overlap often with the tags. Furthermore, the goal of the study is not to explore the question topics, but the lexical terms. Therefore, only the generic terms will be considered and subdivided into several semantic groups. To be able to make a distinction between the two groups, in the programming/expertise term set, we include strict programming/expertise terms such as *resig, dataframe*, and words that are considered expertise words, not commonly used in natural language conversation such as *deprecate, indention* etc. We use the SO website for additional reference to recognize expertise terms, such as *mythical* that refers to the Software Engineering book The Mythical Man-Month by Fred Brooks (1975) or *girlfriend* that refers to the programming website Cocoa is my Girlfriend[3]. As proper nouns are mostly used as a reference and link to a new information source, they are considered too general and added to the group of generic terms.

The analysis shows that, for both high and low quality questions, the generic terms dominate. The terms having the most predictive power for *number of answers* are: *pricey, tolerable, fascinated, aspiring, believer, addicted, contenders, advocates, argues, laughing, praise, religious, corey, sniffed, motivations, analogies, techie, geeky, internationally, misconceptions*. The twenty most predictive terms for question score are: *fascinated, addicted, praise, mentality, camps, rage, lippert, misconceptions, blatant, contenders, mandated, analogies, coolest, speculate, thoughtful, newcomers, picturing, stackers, replays, darned*. For both dependent variables, we test whether there is a significant difference in the counts of generic and professional/expertise terms between high and low quality questions. Chi-square tests indicate that the differences are significant: χ^2 = 6.833, *df* = 1, $p < 0.01$ for question score and χ^2 = 24.189, *df* = 1, $p < 0.01$ for number of answers. For both de-

[2]www.nltk.org

[3]http://www.cimgf.com/

pendent variables we see the same pattern: in the term group that contributes to low question quality, the number of programming/expertise terms is larger. To have a better understanding of the nature of the generic terms, a further distinction was made based on the semantic nature of the terms.

The terms predicting a high question quality, can be divided in subgroups where the following subgroups are very similar across the two dependent variables:

Category	Examples
Excitement	praise, compelling, thrilled
Neg. Experience	blatant, miserable, horrific
Discussion	speculate, agree, misguided

Table 5: Semantic categories

The group of Excitement consists of terms which describe a passionate attitude towards a programming problem. These terms are assumed to be used by users who express emotional commitment to the subject in question. Terms of excitement that predict high question score are *fascinated, compelling, praise, remarkably, aspiring* etc. Similarly, terms such as *thrilled, believing, passion, amazed, enjoyed* account for a higher number of answers. The group of Negative experience/Frustration group consists of terms which express a negative emotion, mostly caused by lack of success when trying to solve a specific problem, i.e. *blatant, miserable, darned, disastrous, insanity, dread etc.* which, according to the model results, indicate high question score. Examples of terms of negative experience or frustration that account for high number of answers are *horrific, miserable, torn, scare, evil* etc. Such high degree of frustration may be the results of multiple attempts to solve the problem which indicates that the user is providing a serious question. The third group lists terms that are used to start a discussions or explanations of a particular problem: *speculate, agree, disagree, advocate, argumentative* suggest an attempt to discussion, and *beware, misguided, unambiguous* assume that a user is trying to explain a specific issue. Although the words in this group seem related, they are less distinct and further research should perform a more in-depth analysis of this group.

We found two more subgroups that account for a high question score:

Category	Examples
New members	newbies, newcomers, freshman
Exceptions	peculiarity, obscurity, surprises

Table 6: Semantic categories

The former determines questions posted by new members. Apparently, when users admit that they are new in the programming world, their question is appreciated by other new users or welcomed by experienced users who remember their first programming steps; or they are just easy to answer. The terms in the Exceptions group are used to discuss exceptional programming issues - *peculiarity, obscurity, surprises, counterintuitive, unintentional, nontrivial, contradicting, unintuitive*. Such cases seem to be intriguing and challenging for the community and are therefore more likely to be appreciated and highly graded.

The following categories have negative effect on the question quality:

Category	Examples
Spelling errors	workin, acessing, specifc
interjections	hmmm, hay, aha
Off-topic terms	hiring, graduate, bosses

Table 7: Semantic categories

The terms that have a negative effect on the question score and the number of answers have one subgroup in common - the group of the misspelled words. In the group of terms predicting a low number of answers 8.31% is not spelled correctly. It can be assumed that questions containing typos are not considered professional and worthy for the community. Such questions may not be taken seriously and users may refuse to spend time giving an answer. More importantly, terms containing typos would not appear in the search results. Apparently, SO users often ignore the integrated spelling checker. In the group of terms having a negative effect on the number of answers, also off-topic terms and interjections that express sounds normally used in daily conversations and more common in speaking than in writing were found. To the off-topic group belong terms that are used mostly in questions related to people searching for or offering a job, students searching for answers to problems for their bachelor thesis. Such questions may be considered as off-topic and not worthy to community users.

4 Discussion

The aim of this study is to investigate to what extent the discussed features influence the number of answers and the question score a question receives, and whether it is possible to predict these measures of question quality. The results from both sets of models showed that the inclusion of linguistic information improves the prediction accuracy of the models. An analysis of the extracted terms shows that they can be classified in subgroups based on their semantic nature. First, certain groups of generic terms have greater impact on question quality. Second, questions that contain terms regarding newcomers, attempts at discussion or explanation of a problem or strong commitment to the problem are more likely to receive a high question score and a large number of answers. Finally, the questions that are considered not worthy of a positive evaluation or receiving an answer are questions that include typos or that are found to be off-topic.

These findings are in line with Correa and Sureka (2014) and Saha *et al.* (2013) who find that deleted questions in SO are questions that are considered poor quality and off-topic. Also Saha *et al.* (2013) found that homework and job-hunting belong to the tags in deleted questions.

Another clear characteristic of low quality questions are misspellings and typos. Online social media sources are often characterized by not following common writing rules (Agichtein et al., 2008). Not taking them into account seems not appreciated and considered unprofessional.

With regard to the terms predicting high quality questions, the results of the current research revealed more similarities. Nasehi *et al.* (2012) considered the following question types groups: debug/corrective, need to know, how-to-do-it, seeking different solution. Truede *et al.* (2011) distinguish similar groups – decision help, error, how-to, discrepancy, review. All of these questions can be seen as seeking an explanation. To present their information need, askers use terms like *speculate, agree, disagree, argues* which were found to have a significant positive effect on the question quality.

Existing literature does not provide a consistent explanation of whether a code snippet increases the question score or the number of answers. Our study showed that the effect of a code snippet is negative which is in line with the statement of Asaduzzaman *et al.* (2013) who explained that a code snippet may have a negative effect on the number of answers if the code is hard to follow or the problem is not clear.

There also is disagreement in previous work about the influence of the question title and question body length. Where some researchers stated that very short and very long question are more likely to obtain an answer (Yang et al., 2011), others found that too short questions may miss important information and may therefore remain unanswered (Asaduzzaman et al., 2013). Our study indicates that the length variables negatively affect question quality. The current results thus are mostly in line with the findings of Correa and Sureka (2014) who found that deleted questions have a higher number of characters in the question body than closed questions. Although, title length, body length and the inclusion of a code snippet all have significant negative effects on the question quality, it must be noted, that all effects are rather small.

Regarding the quality measure user reputation, our results are in line with previous work. As Yang *et al.* (2011) also showed, users with a high reputation are more likely to receive an answer than new users who logically have a lower reputation. For both, question score and number of answers, it was found that the higher the reputation, the higher the value of the quality measure.

5 Future Research

In the current study lexical entities, the terms, are included to predict question quality above the level of the assigned tags. However, the terms were analyzed manually, based on human judgment. This is rather subjective and may result in a somewhat arbitrary assessment. An automated way to analyze the extracted terms would be an improvement and a good suggestion for future research. Another matter for a future work is to include the part-of-speech tagging in the predicting models and to use the parts of speech as features to improve the predictive power of the models.

References

Eugene Agichtein, Carlos Castillo, Debora Donato, Aristides Gionis, and Gilad Mishne. 2008. Finding high-quality content in social media. In *Proceedings of the 2008 International Conference on Web Search and Data Mining*, pages 183–194. ACM.

Ashton Anderson, Daniel Huttenlocher, Jon Kleinberg,

and Jure Leskovec. 2012. Discovering value from community activity on focused question answering sites: a case study of stack overflow. In *Proceedings of the 18th ACM SIGKDD international conference on Knowledge discovery and data mining*, pages 850–858. ACM.

Chris Anderson. 2006. *The long tail: Why the future of business is selling less of more*. Hyperion.

Muhammad Asaduzzaman, Ahmed Shah Mashiyat, Chanchal K Roy, and Kevin A Schneider. 2013. Answering questions about unanswered questions of stack overflow. In *Proceedings of the 10th Working Conference on Mining Software Repositories*, pages 97–100. IEEE Press.

Antoaneta Baltadzhieva and Grzegorz Chrupala. 2015. Predicting question quality in question answering forums.

Frederick P Brooks. 1975. *The mythical man-month*, volume 1995. Addison-Wesley Reading, MA.

Derrick Cheng, Michael Schiff, and Wei Wu. 2013. Eliciting answers on stackoverflow.

Denzil Correa and Ashish Sureka. 2014. Chaff from the wheat: characterization and modeling of deleted questions on stack overflow. In *Proceedings of the 23rd international conference on World wide web*, pages 631–642. International World Wide Web Conferences Steering Committee.

Andy Field. 2009. *Discovering statistics using SPSS*. Sage publications.

Armin Hartmann, Anita J Van Der Kooij, and Almut Zeeck. 2009. Exploring nonlinear relations: models of clinical decision making by regression with optimal scaling. *Psychotherapy Research*, 19(4-5):482–492.

Arthur E Hoerl and Robert W Kennard. 1970a. Ridge regression: applications to nonorthogonal problems. *Technometrics*, 12(1):69–82.

Arthur E Hoerl and Robert W Kennard. 1970b. Ridge regression: Biased estimation for nonorthogonal problems. *Technometrics*, 12(1):55–67.

Baichuan Li, Tan Jin, Michael R Lyu, Irwin King, and Barley Mak. 2012. Analyzing and predicting question quality in community question answering services. In *Proceedings of the 21st international conference companion on World Wide Web*, pages 775–782. ACM.

Christopher D Manning, Prabhakar Raghavan, Hinrich Schütze, et al. 2008. *Introduction to information retrieval*, volume 1. Cambridge university press Cambridge.

Seyed Mehdi Nasehi, Jonathan Sillito, Frank Maurer, and Chris Burns. 2012. What makes a good code example?: A study of programming q&a in stackoverflow. In *Software Maintenance (ICSM), 2012 28th IEEE International Conference on*, pages 25–34. IEEE.

Aditya Pal, F Maxwell Harper, and Joseph A Konstan. 2012. Exploring question selection bias to identify experts and potential experts in community question answering. *ACM Transactions on Information Systems (TOIS)*, 30(2):10.

Ripon K Saha, Avigit K Saha, and Dewayne E Perry. 2013. Toward understanding the causes of unanswered questions in software information sites: a case study of stack overflow. In *Proceedings of the 2013 9th Joint Meeting on Foundations of Software Engineering*, pages 663–666. ACM.

Christoph Treude, Ohad Barzilay, and Margaret-Anne Storey. 2011. How do programmers ask and answer questions on the web?: Nier track. In *Software Engineering (ICSE), 2011 33rd International Conference on*, pages 804–807. IEEE.

Wibke Weber. 2007. Text visualization-what colors tell about a text. In *Information Visualization, 2007. IV'07. 11th International Conference*, pages 354–362. IEEE.

Howard T Welser, Eric Gleave, Danyel Fisher, and Marc Smith. 2007. Visualizing the signatures of social roles in online discussion groups. *Journal of social structure*, 8(2):1–32.

Lichun Yang, Shenghua Bao, Qingliang Lin, Xian Wu, Dingyi Han, Zhong Su, and Yong Yu. 2011. Analyzing and predicting not-answered questions in community-based question answering services. In *AAAI*.

How Topic Biases Your Results?
A Case Study of Sentiment Analysis and Irony Detection in Italian

Francesco Barbieri, Francesco Ronzano, Horacio Saggion
Universitat Pompeu Fabra, DTIC, Barcelona, Spain
name.surname@upf.edu

Abstract

In this paper we present our approach to automatically identify the subjectivity, polarity and irony of Italian Tweets. Our system which reaches and outperforms the state of the art in Italian is well adapted for different domains since it uses abstract word features instead of bag of words. We also present experiments carried out to study how Italian Sentiment Analysis systems react to domain changes. We show that bag of words approaches commonly used in Sentiment Analysis do not adapt well to domain changes.

1 Introduction

The automatic identification of sentiments and opinions expressed by users online is a significant and challenging research trend. The task becomes even more difficult when dealing with short and informal texts like Tweets and other microblog texts. Sentiment Analysis of Tweets has been already investigated by several research studies (Jansen et al., 2009; Barbosa and Feng, 2010). Moreover, during the last few years, many evaluation campaigns have been organised to discuss and compare Sentiment Analysis systems tailored to Tweets. Among these campaigns, since 2013, in the context of SemEval (Nakov et al., 2013), several tasks targeting Sentiment Analysis of English Short Texts took place. In 2014, SENTIPOLC (Basile et al., 2014), the SENTIment POLarity Classification Task of Italian Tweets, was organized in the context of EVALITA 2014, the fourth evaluation campaign of Natural Language Processing and Speech tools for Italian. SENTIPOLC distributed a dataset of Italian Tweets annotated with respect to subjectivity, polarity and irony. This dataset enabled training, evaluation and comparison of the systems that participated to the three tasks of SENTIPOLC, respectively dealing with Subjectivity, Polarity and Irony detection. In the Subjectivity task participants were asked to recognise whether a Tweet is objective or subjective, in the Polarity Task they were asked to classify Tweets as positive or negative, and finally, in the Irony Task to detect whether the content of a Tweet is ironic. The following Tweets include an example of each SENTIPOLC class:

- **Objective Tweet:**
  RT @user: Fine primo tempo: #Fiorentina-Juve 0-2 (Tevez, Pogba). Quali sono i vostri commenti sui primi 45 minuti?#ForzaJuve
  (RT @user: First half: #FiorentinaJuve 0-2 (Tevez, Pogba). What are your comments on the first 45 minutes? #GOJUVE)

- **Subjective / Positive / Non-Ironic Tweet:**
  io vorrei andare a votare, ma non penso sia il momento di perder altro tempo e soprattutto denaro.Un governo Monti potrebbe andare. E x voi?
  (I would like to vote, but I do not think it is the moment to waste time and money. Monti's government might work. What do you think?)

- **Subjective / Negative / Ironic Tweet:**
  Brunetta sostiene di tornare a fare l'economista, Mario Monti terrorizzato progetta di mollare tutto ed aprire un negozio di pescheria
  (Brunetta states he will work as an economist again, a terrified Mario Monti plans to leave everything and open a fish shop)

The first example is an objective Tweet as the user only asks what are the opinions on the football match Fiorentina against Juventus. The second Tweet is subjective, positive and non-ironic as the user is giving his positive opinion on

Proceedings of Recent Advances in Natural Language Processing, pages 41–47,
Hissar, Bulgaria, Sep 7–9 2015.

the new government ("Monti's government might work"). The last Tweet is subjective, negative and ironic since the user is making fun of the politician Brunetta (who stated he would work as an economist again), saying that the prime minister Monti is so worried that he is considering to open a fish shop instead of working with Brunetta as an economist.

In this paper we introduce an extended version of the system reported in Barbieri et. al (2014) adding new features that improve our previous results and outperform the best systems presented at SENTIPOLC 2014. We explore the combination of domain independent features (like usage frequency in a reference corpus, number of associated synsets, etc.) and word-based features (like lemmas and bigrams). We employed the supervised algorithm Support Vector Machine (Platt, 1999). Additionally we describe the experiments performed in order to analyse the influence of the topic (politic vs non-politic Tweets) on the results.

The paper is structured in six sections. In the next Section we review the state of the art, in Section 3 we describe dataset and tools used to process Tweet contents, while in Section 4 we introduce the features of our model. In Section 5 we describe our experiments and the performances of our model. In the last two Sections we discuss our results and conclude the paper with future work.

2 Literature Review

The area of Sentiment Analysis includes all those studies that aim to automatically mine opinions and sentiments of the people. Sentiment Analysis became recently the subject of several works, many of them focused on short text (Jansen et al., 2009; Barbosa and Feng, 2010; Bifet et al., 2011; Tumasjan et al., 2010). Some of the best systems for Sentiment Analysis in English also participated to the SemEval shared task (Nakov et al., 2013; Rosenthal et al., 2014). The system that obtained the best performance in the Sentiment Analysis at message level task of Semeval 2013 (Nakov et al., 2013) and 2014 (Rosenthal et al., 2014) mined Twitter to build big sentiment (Mohammad et al., 2013) and emotion lexicons (Mohammad, 2012). Regarding Sentiment Analysis in Italian, the best system (Basile and Novielli, 2014) presented at the 2014 SENTIPOLC shared task used Distributional Semantics. This system took advantage of ten million Tweets split into four classes: subjective, objective, positive and negative ones. Word vectors were created by modelling the contents of the Tweets of each class and exploited to support the classification of new Tweets as belonging to one of these classes.

Since 2010 researchers have been proposing several models to detect irony automatically. Veale and Hao (2010) suggested an algorithm for separating ironic from non-ironic similes in English, detecting common terms used in this ironic comparison, Reyes et. al (Reyes et al., 2013) proposed a model to detect irony in English Tweets, pointing out the relevance of skip-grams (word sequences that contain arbitrary gap) to carry out this task. Barbieri and Saggion (2014) designed an irony detection system that avoided the use of word-based features, employing features like frequency imbalance (rare words in a context of common words) and ambiguity (number of senses of a word). However, irony has not been studied intensively in languages other than English. A few researches have been carried out on irony detection on other languages like Portuguese (Carvalho et al., 2009; de Freitas et al., 2014), Dutch (Liebrecht et al., 2013), Spanish (Barbieri et al., 2015), and Italian (Barbieri et al., 2014). Bosco et. al (2013) collected and annotated tweets in Italian for Sentiment Analysis and Irony detection (the corpus was used for EVALITA 2014).

3 Text Analysis and Tools

In order to process the text of Tweets so as to enable the feature extraction process, we used the same methodology and tools as Barbieri et al. (2014), the reader can find all the details on the tools used in the said paper.

In our experiments we used the dataset employed in SENTIPOLC – the combination SENTITUT (Bosco et al., 2013) and TWITA (Basile and Nissim, 2013)). Each Tweet was annotated over four dimensions: subjectivity/objectivity, positivity/negativity, irony/non-irony, and political/non-political topic. SENTIPOLC dataset is made of a collection of Tweet IDs, since the privacy policy of Twitter does not allow to share the text of Tweets. As a consequence we were able to retrieve by the Twitter API the text of only a subset of the Tweets included in the original SENTIPOLC dataset. In particular, our training set included 3998 Tweets (while the original dataset included 4513).

		Our system	Best of SENTIPOLC
Subjectivity	subjective	0.866	0.828
	objective	0.564	0.601
	avg	**0.715**	0.714
Polarity (POS)	positive	0.554	0.823
	other	0.839	0.527
	avg	**0.697**	0.675
Polarity (NEG)	negative	0.619	0.717
	other	0.741	0.641
	avg	**0.680**	0.679
Irony	ironic	0.260	0.355
	non-ironic	0.916	0.796
	avg	**0.588**	0.576

Table 1: Results of our system and best system of SENTIPOLC in the three Tasks subjectivity, polarity, and irony. We show F-Measures scores for each class and the arithmetic average too.

4 The Model

We extract two kind of features from the Tweets: domain dependent (Section 4.1 and 4.2) and domain independent which are the features proposed in Barbieri et al. (2014). The domain dependent group includes Word-Based and Synsets features described in Section 4.1 and 4.2 often used in text classifications and topic recognition tasks. On the other hand, the domain independent features are not strictly related to the topic of the message. These features are five: Synonyms, Ambiguity, Part Of Speech, Sentiments, Characters.

4.1 Word-Based

We designed this group of features to detect common word-patterns. With these features we are able to capture common phrases used in certain type of Tweet and grasp the common topics that are more frequent in certain type of Tweet (positive/negative/ironic). We computed three word-based features: *lemma* (lemmas of the Tweet), *bigrams* (combination of two lemmas in a sequence) and *skip one gram* (combination of three lemmas in a row, excluding the one in the middle).

4.2 Synsets

This group of features included features related to WordNet Synsets. After removing stop words, we disambiguated each word against Wordnet (UKB), thus obtaining the most likely sense (Synset) associated to the same word.

5 Experiments and Results

In this Section we show the performance of our system with respect to the three Tasks of SENTIPOLC 2014 (see Table 1). In order to compare our system with the best ones of SENTIPOLC, beside using the same dataset, we adopted the same experimental framework. Since each task was a binary decision (e.g. subjective vs objective), SENTIPOLC organisers computed the arithmetic average of the F-measures of the two classes (e.g. mean of F-Measures of subjective and objective).

We carried out a study of the features contribution to the classification process performing six classification experiments. In each experiment we added to the baseline (domain dependent features) one of the feature groups described in the previous Section. Thus we were able to measure the effect that the addition of the features has on the F-measure.

In Section 5.4 we present an experiment useful to check if our classification features are effective across different domains.

5.1 Task 1: Subjectivity Classification

SENTIPOL 2014 Task 1 was as follows: *given a message, decide whether the message is subjective or objective.*

As we can see in Table 1, in the subjectivity Task our system scored a very similar F-Measure score to the best of SENTIPOLC (0.715 vs 0.714). However, the two systems behave in different ways: our system scored less in the detection of the objective class (0.564 vs 0.601), but it is more accurate in subjective detection (0.866 vs 0.828).

		Subjectivity	Polarity (pos)	Polarity (neg)	Irony
BL	class 1	0.842	0.507	0.509	0.2
	class 2	0.335	0.829	0.720	0.913
	avg	0.589	0.668	0.6145	0.5565
BL + Ambig.	class 1	0.843	0.515	0.529	0.196
	class 2	0.327	0.833	0.716	0.914
	avg	0.585	0.674	0.623	0.555
	improvement	-0.004	0.006	0.008	-0.002
BL + Synset	class 1	0.835	0.514	0.520	0.239
	class 2	0.542	0.82	0.716	0.903
	avg	0.689	0.667	0.618	0.571
	improvement	**0.1**	-0.001	0.004	**0.015**
BL + Senti.	class 1	0.847	0.522	0.578	0.192
	class 2	0.520	0.833	0.731	0.911
	avg	0.684	0.678	0.655	0.552
	improvement	**0.095**	0.010	**0.040**	-0.005
BL + POS	class 1	0.847	0.513	0.542	0.192
	class 2	0.447	0.831	0.717	0.911
	avg	0.647	0.672	0.630	0.552
	improvement	**0.059**	0.004	**0.015**	-0.005
BL + Syno.	class 1	0.843	0.506	0.515	0.195
	class 2	0.322	0.828	0.718	0.913
	avg	0.583	0.667	0.617	0.554
	improvement	-0.006	-0.001	0.002	-0.0025
BL + Char.	class 1	0.832	0.532	0.559	0.212
	class 2	0.463	0.834	0.722	0.914
	avg	0.648	0.683	0.641	0.563
	improvement	**0.059**	0.015	**0.026**	0.007

Table 2: Features Analysis of our system. We add to the baseline (BL) one feature group of our domain independent model per time. We do it for all the four SENTIPOLC Tasks (Subj, Pol(pos), Pol(neg) and irony). In each task, class 1 and 2 are respectively: subjective/objective, positive/non-positive, negative/non-negative and ironic/non-ironic.

In Table 2 we can examine the F-Measure improvement of each feature group. We can note that the greatest improvement is given by Synset and Sentiment features (adding respectively 0.1 and 0.95 points to the baseline); POS and Characters produce an increasing of 0.059, hence can be considered rich features as well. The groups Ambiguity and Synonym do not increase the accuracy of the classification.

5.2 Task 2: Polarity Classification

SENTIPOL 2014 task 2 required *given a message, to decide whether the message is of positive, negative, neutral or mixed sentiment (i.e. conveying both a positive and negative sentiment).*
SENTIPOLC annotators tagged each Tweet with four tags related to polarity: positive, negative, mixed polarity, unspecified. As in SENTIPOLC we split up the Polarity classification in two subclassifications. The first one is the binary classification of positive and mixed-polarity Tweets versus negative and unspecified ones. The second one is focused on the recognition of negative Tweets being the binary decision between negative and mixed polarity versus positive and unspecified tags.

In the positive classification, our system reached a F-Measure of 0.697, while the F-Measure of the best SENTIPOLC system was 0.675 (see Table 1). As previously, the systems behaved differently: ours lacked in detection of the Positive + Mixed-polarity class but it was able to achieve a good F1 in the negative + unspecified class. In the negative classification we out-

Subjectivity	Polarity	Irony
monti	**syn (no, non, neanche)**	governo
syn (no, non, neanche)	**grazie**	passera
governo	monti	politico
syn (avere, costituire, rimanere)	grillo	bersani_non
syn (essere, fare, mettere)	governo	monti
mi	**piacere**	se_governo
paese	**syn (avere, costituire, rimanere)**	grillo
prince	**syn (essere, fare, mettere)**	bersani
essere_dire	paese	capello
of_Persia	**syn (migliaio, mille)**	cavallo

Table 3: For each test set topic the Ten Word-based and Synset features with higher information gain are shown. The domain independent words are in bold. "Syn(word1, word2)" is the synset associated to word1 and word2.

performed the SENTIPOLC system with a score of 0.680 (versus a 0.675). Again, the best SENTIPOLC system got a better score in negative + mixed-polarity and ours reached a better F1 in positive + unspecified.

In the feature analysis (Table 2) we can see that the most important groups of features for the negative classification were Sentiments (giving an improvement of 0.040 points), Characters (0.026) and POS (0.015). On the other hand, in the Positive classification, the word-base features seem to be the most important suggesting that word-patterns were very relevant for this task.

5.3 Task 3: Irony Detection

SENTIPOL 2014 Task 1 asked *given a message, to decide whether the message was ironic or not.* Our system scored a F1 of 0.059 (0.26 in the irony class, and 0.916 in non-irony) while best SENTIPOLC system a F1 of 0.5759 (0.3554 in the irony class and 0.7963 in non-irony). In this Task the use of the words and domain dependent features is very relevant. None of the other domain independent features increase the F1. The only feature that gives a F1 increase is Synset, which can be considered domain dependent. With the help of Table 3 we can note that the ten most important textual features in the irony task are related to a specific topic, and 4 out of 10 words are names of politicians (Passera, Bersani, Monti, Grillo) and the 4 are related to politics (with words like "politics" or "government"). Of course a name of a Politician can not be a good feature for irony detection in general.

5.4 Cross-Domain Experiments

In this section we show the results of the cross-domain experiments. We trained our classifier with the Tweets of one topic (politics related Tweets) and tested the same classifier with the Tweets related to the other topic (non-politics related Tweets). In this way, we can examine whether the model is robust with respect to domain-switches. We were able to run these experiments as SENTIPOLC Tweets provided a topic flag that points out if a Tweet is political or not. We obtained two different systems dividing our features in two groups: domain dependent (word-based and synset group) and domain independent (Sentiment, Synonyms, Character, Ambiguity). We run the cross-domain experiments over the Subjectivity and Polarity datasets with these two systems, and also with our model ("all"). Unfortunately, we were not able to run cross-domain experiments on irony as there were not enough data to effectively train a classifier (e.g. non-political ironic Tweets were only 39 in the test set).

We can see in Table 4 that in the cross-domain experiments domain independent features are five out of six times outperforming the domain dependent system. Moreover an interesting result is that in five out of six combinations the domain independent system outperforms the respective "all" features system, suggesting that when the domain changes, domain dependent features introduce noise.

6 Discussion

Our system outperformed the best SENTIPOLC systems in all the tasks. However, as showed in

		political / non-political	non-political / political
Subjectivity	dom. dependent	0.734	0.672
	dom. indepentent	**0.767**	**0.746**
	all	0.747	0.689
Polarity (POS)	dom. dependent	0.555	0.631
	dom. indepentent	0.443	**0.736**
	all	**0.583**	0.728
Polarity (NEG)	dom. dependent	0.614	0.554
	dom. indepentent	**0.671**	**0.624**
	all	0.663	0.567

Table 4: Cross-domain experiments, where "political / non-political" means training in politics dataset and testing in non-political dataset, "non-political / political" vice-versa. For these two domain combinations we report the results of three models: "domain dependent" (word-based + synset), "domain independent" (Sentiment, Synonyms, Character, Ambiguity), and the model "all" with all the features of our model.

the previous section, not all of our features are effective for the SENTIPOLC Tasks. Specifically, in Polarity and Irony Tasks the features with biggest impact on the classification accuracy resulted to be the domain dependent ones. We can identify two possible explanations. The first one is that for these Tasks is very important to model pattern that are representative of the different classes (for example common phrases used in negative Tweets to detect this class). The second hypothesis is that word-based features, that are often used to model a domain, worked well because training and test set of the dataset shared the same topics. Hence, word-based features worked well because there was a topic bias. For example, in the case of the Polarity Task, a word-based system could detect that often the name of a certain politician is present in the negative Tweets, then using this name as feature to model negative Tweets. With cross-domain experiments we confirmed the second hypothesis, showing that word-based features are not robust when the topic of training and test set are different. On the other hand domain independent features do not decrease their performance when training and test do not share the same topics.

However, in the SENTIPOLC task domain dependent features were relevant, and detecting the topic of a specific class was important. We show (Table 3) that the ten best word-based features are often related to a specific topic (politics in this particular case, see Table 3) rather than to typical expression (e.g. "worst", "don't like" to mean something negative), meaning that our word-based features modelled a specific domain. For example, using words like "Monti" and "Grillo" who are two Italian politicians is important to detect negative Tweets. These features may be in some cases important but they narrow the use of the system to the domain of the training set (and eventually to Tweets generated in the same time-frame).

In the light of these results, we suggest that if a Sentiment Analysis system has to recognise polarity cross-domain should avoid word-based features and focus more on features that are not influenced by the content. On the other hand, if the a Sentiment Analysis system is used in a specific domain, words may have an important role to play.

7 Conclusions

We presented a model for the automatic classification of subjectivity, polarity and recognition of irony in Twitter that outperform the best systems of SENTIPOLC, a shared Task of the EVALITA. Our model included two type of features: domain dependent and domain independent features. We showed with cross-domain experiments that the use of domain dependent feature may constrain a system to work only on a specific domain, while using domain independent features achieved domain independence and a greater robustness when the topic of the Tweet changes.

We are planning to combine the model used in this paper with new distributional semantics based approaches such Basile and Novielli (2014), and to explore new classification techniques like cascade classifiers to combine different classes (e.g. detecting if the Tweet is subjective before deciding if it is ironic, as irony implies subjectivity).

References

Francesco Barbieri and Horacio Saggion. 2014. Modelling Irony in Twitter. In *Proceedings of the EACL Student Research Workshop*, pages 56–64, Gothenburg, Sweden, April. ACL.

Francesco Barbieri, Francesco Ronzano, and Horacio Saggion. 2014. Italian Irony Detection in Twitter: a First Approach. *The First Italian Conference on Computational Linguistics CLiC-it 2014*, page 28.

Francesco Barbieri, Francesco Ronzano, and Horacio Saggion. 2015. Is this tweet satirical? a computational approach for satire detection in spanish. In *Spanish Society for Natural Language Processing*. Alicante, SEPLN.

Luciano Barbosa and Junlan Feng. 2010. Robust Sentiment Detection on Twitter from Biased and Noisy Data. In *Proceedings of the 23rd International Conference on Computational Linguistics*, pages 36–44. Association for Computational Linguistics.

Valerio Basile and Malvina Nissim. 2013. Sentiment Analysis on Italian Tweets. In *Proceedings of the 4th WASSA Workshop*, pages 100–107.

Pierpaolo Basile and Nicole Novielli. 2014. UNIBA at EVALITA 2014-SENTIPOLC Task: Predicting tweet Sentiment Polarity Combining Micro-Blogging, Lexicon and Semantic Features.

Valerio Basile, Andrea Bolioli, Malvina Nissim, Viviana Patti, and Paolo Rosso. 2014. Overview of the Evalita 2014 SENTIment POLarity Classification Task. In *Proceedings of the 4th evaluation campaign of Natural Language Processing and Speech tools for Italian (EVALITA'14)*, Pisa, Italy, December.

Albert Bifet, Geoff Holmes, Bernhard Pfahringer, and Ricard Gavalda. 2011. Detecting Sentiment Change in Twitter Streaming Data.

Cristina Bosco, Viviana Patti, and Andrea Bolioli. 2013. Developing Corpora for Sentiment Analysis and Opinion Mining: the Case of Irony and SENTI-TUT. *Intelligent Systems, IEEE*.

Paula Carvalho, Luís Sarmento, Mário J Silva, and Eugénio de Oliveira. 2009. Clues for Detecting Irony in User-Generated Contents: oh...!! it's so easy;-). In *Proceedings of the 1st international CIKM workshop on Topic-sentiment analysis for mass opinion*, pages 53–56. ACM.

Larissa A de Freitas, Aline A Vanin, Denise N Hogetop, Marco N Bochernitsan, and Renata Vieira. 2014. Pathways for Irony Detection in Tweets. In *Proceedings of the 29th Annual ACM Symposium on Applied Computing*, pages 628–633. ACM.

Andrea Gianti, Cristina Bosco, Viviana Patti, Andrea Bolioli, and Luigi Di Caro. 2012. Annotating Irony in a Novel Italian Corpus for Sentiment Analysis. In *Proceedings of the 4th Workshop on Corpora for Research on Emotion Sentiment and Social Signals, Istanbul, Turkey*, pages 1–7.

Bernard J Jansen, Mimi Zhang, Kate Sobel, and Abdur Chowdury. 2009. Twitter power: Tweets as electronic word of mouth. *Journal of the American society for information science and technology*, 60(11):2169–2188.

Christine Liebrecht, Florian Kunneman, and Antal van den Bosch. 2013. The Perfect Solution for Detecting Sarcasm in tweets# not. *WASSA 2013*, page 29.

Saif M. Mohammad, Svetlana Kiritchenko, and Xiaodan Zhu. 2013. NRC-Canada: Building the State-of-the-Art in Sentiment Analysis of Tweets. In *Proceedings of the seventh international workshop on Semantic Evaluation Exercises (SemEval-2013)*, Atlanta, Georgia, USA, June.

Saif Mohammad. 2012. #Emotional Tweets. In **SEM 2012: The First Joint Conference on Lexical and Computational Semantics – Volume 1: Proceedings of the main conference and the shared task, and Volume 2: Proceedings of the Sixth International Workshop on Semantic Evaluation (SemEval 2012)*, pages 246–255, Montréal, Canada, 7-8 June. Association for Computational Linguistics.

Preslav Nakov, Zornitsa Kozareva, Alan Ritter, Sara Rosenthal, Veselin Stoyanov, and Theresa Wilson. 2013. Semeval-2013 Task 2: Sentiment Analysis in Twitter.

John Platt. 1999. Fast Training of Support Vector Machines Using Sequential Minimal Optimization. *Advances in kernel methodssupport vector learning*, 3.

Antonio Reyes, Paolo Rosso, and Tony Veale. 2013. A multidimensional Approach for Detecting Irony in Twitter. *Language Resources and Evaluation*, pages 1–30.

Sara Rosenthal, Preslav Nakov, Alan Ritter, and Veselin Stoyanov. 2014. Semeval-2014 Task 9: Sentiment Analysis in Twitter. *Proc. SemEval*.

Andranik Tumasjan, Timm Oliver Sprenger, Philipp G Sandner, and Isabell M Welpe. 2010. Predicting Elections with Twitter: What 140 Characters Reveal about Political Sentiment. *ICWSM*, 10:178–185.

Tony Veale and Yanfen Hao. 2010. Detecting Ironic Intent in Creative Comparisons. In *ECAI*, volume 215, pages 765–770.

Arabic Named Entity Recognition Process using Transducer Cascade and Arabic Wikipedia

Fatma Ben Mesmia
University of Sfax,
Laboratory MIRACL, Multimedia, InfoRmation Systems and Advanced Computing Laboratory,
fatmabm@ymail.com

Nathalie Friburger
University François Rabelais of Tours,
LI, Computer laboratory,
nathalie.friburger@univ-tours.fr

Kais Haddar
University of Sfax,
Laboratory MIRACL, Multimedia, InfoRmation Systems and Advanced Computing Laboratory,
Kais.Haddar@fss.rnu.tn

Denis Maurel
University François Rabelais of Tours,
LI, Computer laboratory,
denis.maurel@univ-tours.fr

Abstract

Transducers namely transducer cascades are used in several NLP-applications such as Arabic named entity recognition (ANER). To experiment and evaluate an ANER process, a weight coverage corpus is necessary. In this paper, we propose an ANER method based on transducer cascade. The proposed transducer cascade is generated with the CasSys tool integrated in Unitex linguistic platform. The experimentation of our method is done on a Wikipedia corpus. The Wikipedia text format is obtained with Kiwix tool. The experiment results are satisfactory based on calculated measures.

Keywords: Cascade of transducers, Wikipedia, Arabic named entities, Unitex, CasSys

1. Introduction

Transducers can play an important role in the Information Extraction (IE) namely in the Named Entity Recognition (NER). At the same time, transducers can extract and classify the Arabic Named Entity (ANE). Generally, the use of transducers is realized in well defined succession that is called cascade (Friburger and Maurel, 2004).

In fact, the identification of necessary transducers is not an easy task because several linguistic phenomenacan interact (Shaalan, 2014; Ben Mesmia and al, 2015).

The free resource Wikipedia is an important information source. Indeed, several text processing applications based on transducer cascade can benefit from Wikipedia articles. Therefore, names of people, which are part of proper nouns, appear frequently in the Arabic Wikipedia. More efforts by NLP-researchers are concentrated on this type. Person names are considered as the most challenging task for Arabic.

In this context, our objective is to propose, using the rule-based approach, a transducer cascade for the recognition of personality's names. In this approach, we benefit from the robustness of transducers and exploit the free resource, Wikipedia. The recognition requires the identification of dictionaries, a list of trigger words and extraction rules allowing the development of a set of transducers acting on the corpus with a certain logic.

The present paper is composed of six sections. The second section presents previous work describing the developed systems for the recognizing of the personality names. The third section is dedicated to describing the categorization of person's names. The fourth section devoted to detail the proposed method that is implemented by using CasSys system. The experiment is presented and evaluated in section five. Finally, we give a conclusion and some perspectives.

2. Previous Work

There are several work treating the ANER based on several approaches among which we cite the work of (Shaalan and Raza, 2007). In this work, the authors proposed an ANER system based on the rule-based approach. This system called

Proceedings of Recent Advances in Natural Language Processing, pages 48–54,
Hissar, Bulgaria, Sep 7–9 2015.

PERA is composed of three components: gazetteers, local grammars and a filtration mechanism. PERA is applied to the ACE and ATB datasets.

In (Mesfar, 2007), the author developed a system identifying ANE of many types such as person names. This system consists of a tokenizer, a morphological analyzer and a NE finder. The system is evaluated by using the of news corpus extracted from le journal "Le monde diplomatique".

In (Elsebai et al, 2009), the authors proposed a rule-based system that integrates pattern matching with morphological analysis to extract Arabic person names. This system is evaluated by using news articles extracted from Aljazeera website.

In (Fehri and al., 2011), authors developed a rule-based system to recognize ANE for sport's domain such as place names and player's names. This system is composed of a set of dictionaries, syntactic patterns and transducers implemented with the linguistic platform NooJ.

In (Aboaoga and Aziz, 2013), the authors introduced a rule-based system that extracts Arabic person names. The system is composed of three steps: the preprocessing (tokenization, data cleaning and sentence splitting), the automatic ANE tagging and the application of rules to the Arabic texts in order to extract ANEs that do not exist in the built dictionaries. The domains covered by this system are sports, politics and economics.

In (Elsebai, 2008), the author developed a system adopting statistical approach for ANER. This system allows the recognition of Arabic proper names using heuristics. Heuristics based on a set of key-words rather than complex grammars and statistical techniques. The system is evaluated by using news articles extracted from the Aljazeera television website.

In (Shaalan and Oudah, 2014), the authors proposed a system based on hybrid approach. This system, which is capable of recognizing 11 types of Arabic named entities such as person names, is applied to ANERcorp standard dataset. According the study made by Shaalan (2014), systems which are developed for the ANER, are essentially based on restraint domains.

Namely in the NER, the use of transducer cascade is very frequent. A cascade is defined as a succession of transducers applied to text in a specific order to convert or extract patterns. Each transducer of the cascade uses the results of the previous transducer (Maurel and al., 2009).

Several systems based on cascades were developed in NLP that touch essentially the following domains: parsing, information extraction and translation. Among the systems constracted for the IE task, we cite the following work.

In EU project FACILE, (Ciravegna and Lavelli, 1999) implemented a module based on three transducers cascades. These cascades contain transducers representing respectively empirical, regular and default rules.

CasEN, the system developed by (Maurel and al., 2011) uses lexical resources and transducers acting together on texts by insertions, deletions or substitutions.

For Arabic, (Ben Mesmia and al, 2015) developed a transducer cascade allowing the recognition of ANE more precisely the dates. This cascade is generated by the CasSys that is module available under the Unitex platform.

3. Typology of Arabic Person's Names

The Arabic names may have variations related to origin of country, religion, culture, level of formality and even personal preference. In this section, we present firstly our study corpus. Secondly, we give the categorization of person names. We explain also phenomena that are related to their recognition.

3.1 Corpus of Study

The corpus of study was collected from Arabic Wikipedia through Arabic kiwix[1] tool. It regroups a number of texts from 19 Arabic countries and contains text files for a cumulative 79 659 tokens. This corpus allows us to identify the forms that will be transformed into extraction rules and transformed later in transducers.

3.2 Categorization of Person's Names

In general, an Arabic name can contain five parts, which follow no particular order: the ism, kunya, nasab, laqab, and nisba (Shaalan, 2014).

The ism is the first name. These are the names given to children at their birth. Male isms are such names as "*`bd allah*[2] / Abdullah", "*`aadl* / Adel", "*Hsyn* / Hussein". Men's isms are sometimes preceded by one of the attributes of Allah such as "*'aaHmd* / Ahmed", "*mHmwd* / Mahmoud" but this practice is declining, especially in areas influenced by Western practices, such as Lebanon,

[1] http://www.kiwix.org/wiki/Main_Page/fr

[2] Transliteration system : Al-Qalam : http://www.cs.bu.edu/ftp/amass/Arabic/qalam.txt

Morocco, and other North African countries. Female isms include "*`aa'sht* / Ayisha" and "*smyrt* / Samira". The "*t*" sound is a feminine ending.

The kunya is an honorific name. It is not part of a person's formal name. The kunya is used as an informal form of address and respect, much as we use "aunt" and "uncle". It indicates that the man or woman is the father or mother of a particular person, the birth of a child being considered praiseworthy and deserving of recognition. For example, "*'aam klthwm* / Oum Kultthum" means "mother of Kulthum", and "*'aabw klthwm* / Abu kulthum" means "father of Kulthum".

The nasab is the patronymic and starts with "*bn* /bin" or "*aabn*/ ibn", which means "son of", or "*bnt* / bint", which means "daughter of". It acknowledges the father of the child. The nasab often follows the ism, so that you have, for example, "*fHd bn `bd aal`zyz* / Fahad ibn Abdul Aziz", which means "Fahad, son of Abdul Aziz". A daughter would be "*mrym bnt `bd alla`zyz* / Maryam bint Abdul Aziz". If someone wishes to acknowledge the grandfather and great-grandfather as well, these names may be added. So one could have "khaald bn fySl bn `bd aal`zyz / Khalid ibn Faisal ibn Abdul Aziz". The use of bin and ibn varies greatly.

The laqab is defined as an epithet, usually a religious or descriptive one. For example, "*aalrshyd* / Al-Rashid" means "the rightly guided" and "*aalfZl* / Al-fadl" means "the prominent".

The nisba is similar to what people in the West call the surname. Again, the use of this term varies in Egypt and Lebanon, such as nisba is not used at all. Instead, laqab incorporates its meaning. The nisba is often used as the last name, although its use has decreased in some areas.

3.3 Difficulties of Extraction

In Arabic, several causes make the NER difficult. In the following, we mention some of them.

Absence of capitalization. In Arabic, capitalization does not exist.

Nature of proper nouns. Proper noun can belong to the adjective category or to the temporal expression. For example, "*jmyla*" can be a girl name or an adjective and "*jm`t*" can be a day (Friday) or a boy name.

Agglutination. An Arabic word can be a whole sentence. In fact, several particles can be attached to a root such as prepositions. For example, "لكتابته" means in English for writing it

Typographic variants. The drop of Hamza sign. For example, the proper name "*Aahmd*" can be written with or without the Hamza sign.

Nested ANE. To find the limit of ANE is not easy. A personality name can be a part of an event NE. For example, "*frHaat Hshaad*" is a personality name which it a part of the event "*laastshhaad aalmnaaDl frHaat Hshaad*". This event is also a part in "*Dhkrae stt w styn laastshhaad aalmnaaDl frHaat Hshaad*".

3.4 Relationship between Personality's Names with other ANE

The relationship between ANE can be binary (involving two entities) or more complex to be an imbrication of ANE. The ANE describing events and place names can have a compositional relationship with ANE of the type names of personality. In (1) and (2), "*aalTyb aalmhyry* / Al-Taieb al-Mhiri" and "*mHmd aalkhaams* / Mohamed Al-Khames" are two names of personality integrated in two ANE of the type name places preceded respectively by "*ml`b*" and "*shaar`*".

(1) ملعب الطيب المهيري بصفاقس
ml`b aalTyb aalmhyry b Sfaaqs

(2) شارع محمد الخامس
Shaar` mHmd aalkhaams

The organization name can contain famous name of personality such as in (3), "*aal`nwd*" is a first name of a princess.

(3) مؤسسة العنود الخيرية
M'wsst aal`nwd aalkhyryt

Arabic names of personalities can appear also in Events such as in (4), "*mraasm tnSyb*" are the two trigger words recognizing this type and the rest of the entity is the name of personality.

(4) مراسم تنصيب الملك عبد الله بن عبد العزيز آل سعود
mraasm tnSyb aalmlk `bd alllh bn `bd aal`zyz aal s`wd

4. Proposed Method Recognizing Personality Names

The proposed method is based on three steps: the construction of necessary dictionaries, the identification of extraction rules to recognize ANE and the establishment of the corresponding transducers. In the following, we detail these steps.

4.1 Construction of Dictionaries

For our method, we construct two dictionaries with several features. One contains the first names. The second dictionary contains the last names. Therefore, these dictionaries treat different variations of Arabic person's names

4.2 Identification of Extraction Rules

According to our study, we identify 14 extractions rules. Each rule describes an alternative form of personality name. These extraction rules are detected through trigger words. We identified 180 trigger words that are classified in eight classes. They are distributed as in Table 1.

Class names	Number of trigger words
Artistic function	47
Civilities	21
Military function	7
Nobiliare function	22
Political function	27
Profession	14
Religious	17
Sportive function	25

Table 1. Distribution of the trigger words by class

In the following, we give trigger word grammar for the identified classes.

Trigger Word → *Artistic function* | *Civilities* | *Military function* | *Nobiliare function* | *Political function* | *Profession* | *Religious* | *Sportive function*

Artistic function → *aalma'lf* | *aalmw'lft* | *aalmbd`* | *aalmbd`t* | *aalktb* | *aalktbt* | ...

Civility → *aalsydt* | *aalsyd* | *aalaa'nst* | ...

Military function → *aaljysh* | *aalraaae'd* | *aalz`ym* | *aalmqdm* | *aal`qyd* | ...

Nobiliare function → *aalaa'myr* | *aalaa'myrt* | *aalslTan* | *aalslTant* | ...

Political function → *rae'ys aaljmhwryt* | *aalwzyr* | *wzyr aaldwlt* | *rae'ys aaldwlt* | ...

Profession → *aalm`lm* | *aalmdyr* | *aalaa'staadh* | *aalm`lmt* | ...

Religious → *aalaa'maam* | *aalmw'dhn* | ...

Sportive function → *aallaa`b* | *aallaa`bt* | ...

Concerning the established extraction rules, we propose a classification based on three classes. The first class contains recognition paths depending on trigger words; the second class describes the recognition of independent paths. The third class concerns rules that appear in exceptional cases encountered during the study. Table 2 shows an example of extraction rules.

Extraction rules
<Trigger Word> < first name>$^+$ <last name>
(< first name> ben <first name>)$^+$ <last name>
(< first name> ben <first name>)$^+$ <Nisba>
<Trigger Word> <last name>
<Trigger Word> < Country name> <first name>
< first name> <Kunya> (ben <first name>)$^+$

Table 2. A set of extraction rules extracted from the study corpus

4.3 Establishment of Transducers

The extraction rules are translated in transducers. Each transducer regroups similar forms. Most of them are based on trigger words, which facilitate the recognition process. Even the trigger words are grouped into sub-transducers because they will be called by other graphs.

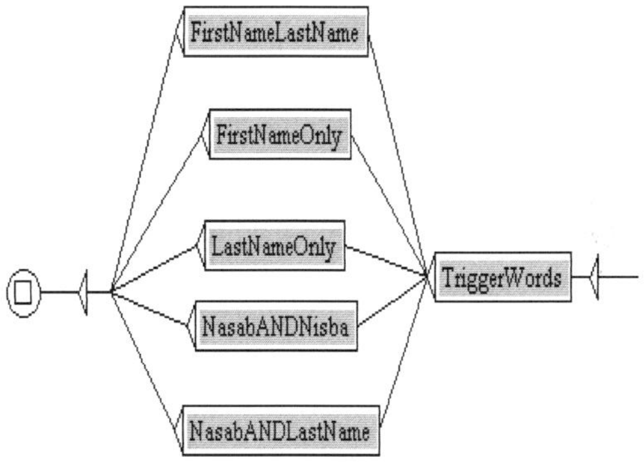

Figure 1. A transducer that call sub-transducers using the trigger words

Figure 1 shows the implementation of many extraction rules, which use triggers words, allowing the personality's names recognition. The sub-graph entitled "NasabANDNisba" describes the path allowing the recognition of an Nsab followed by a Nisba. This sub-graph is described in the following figure.

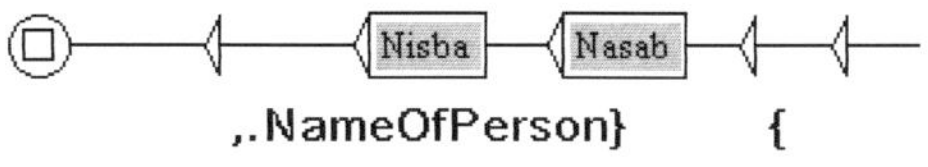

Figure 2. The path allowing the recognition of a Nasab followed by a Nisba

In Figure 2, there is two sub-graphs, which are respectively "Nasab" and "Nisba". These subsgraphs are surrounded by two-box containing the annotation that will appear in the corpus on which the transducer will be passed. The graphs "Nasab" and "Nisba" are presented in Figure 4 and 5.

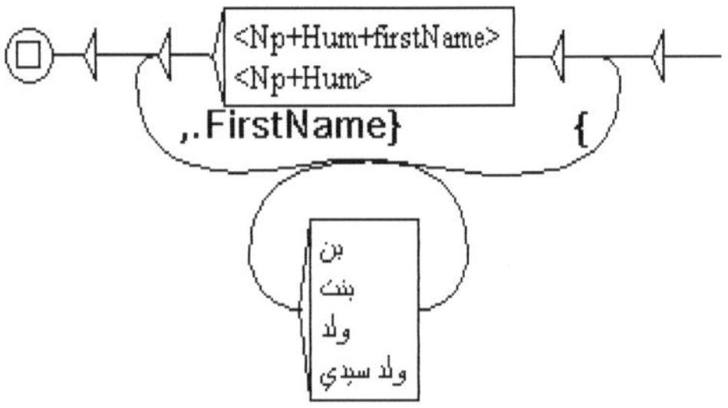

Figure 4. Transducer recognizing the Nasab

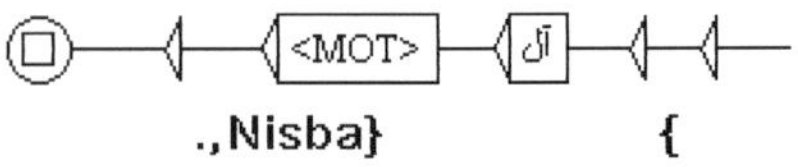

Figure 5. Transducer recognizing the Nisba

The sub-graph "Nasab" can also be called in another transducer that recognize a new form of appearance of personality's name.

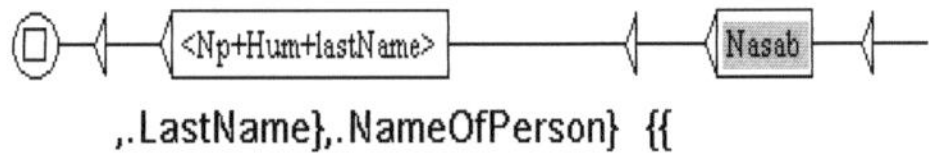

Figure 6. Transducer recognizing the Nasab followed by a last name

Figure 6 shows that the Nasab can be followed by a last name.

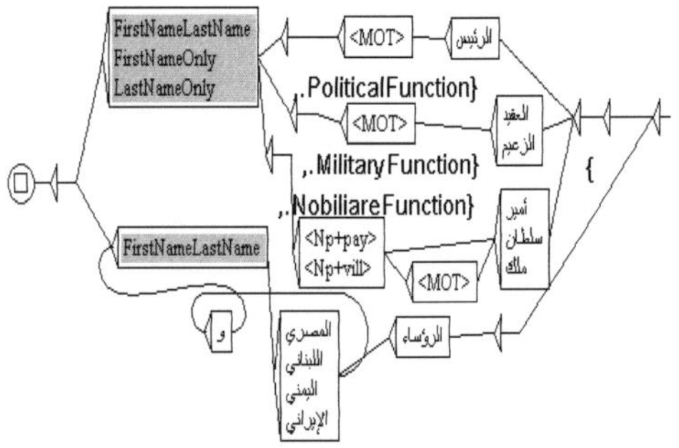

Figure 7. Transducer recognizing exceptional cases

In Figure 7, the transducer treat exceptional cases in the corpus of study. Knowing that those cases are dependent on trigger words.

4.4 Construction of Transducer Cascade

The constructed transducer cascade is based on the following principle: the passage of the main transducers is done in a specific order; labels in output files would enrich the recognized ANE with markup defined into the transducers.

5. Experimentation and Evaluation

As discussed, our prototype is based on the transducer cascade that we have proposed. The general architecture prototype is illustrated in Figure 8.

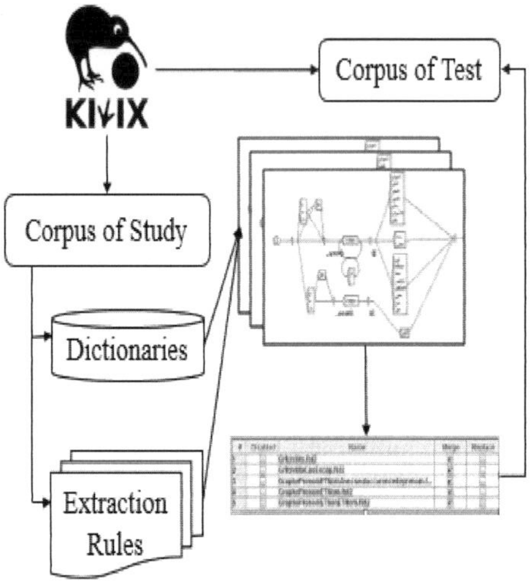

Figure 8. System architecture

Figure 8 shows the system architecture, which describes the steps of our proposed method for the recognition of Arabic personality names. The transducer cascade is applied on the test corpus. The collection of the test corpus is made in the same way as the study corpus presented in Section 3.1. It regroups a number of texts from 19 Arabic countries and contains text files for a cumulative 454 959 tokens.

As an output, we get an annotated corpus. Figure 9 illustrates an Arabic personality name that contains a trigger word. This entity will be annotated as follow: this entity contain a nobiliare trigger word, a Nasab; two first name related by the word "ben" and a Nisba.

```
{NobiliareFunction.,الأمير}
{\FirstName.\,\سلطان }\}
{\FirstName.\,\عبد العزيز }\بن
.{NameOfPerson.,{\Nisba,\.\آل سعود }\
```

Figure 9. Annotation of an Arabic personality's name

In addition to our dictionaries, we use the dictionary of proper names elaborated by (Doumi et al., 2013) available under Unitex platform. Table 3 shows the coverage of dictionaries exploited in our recognition process.

Dictionary	Coverage
Proper names	8 353
First names	1 152
Last names	895

Table 3. Coverage of dictionaries

#	Disabled	Name	Merge	Replace
1	☐	GraphsWithTriggerWords.fst2	☑	☐
2	☐	FirstNameLastName.fst2	☑	☐
3	☐	NasabANDNisba.fst2	☑	☐
4	☐	NasabANDLastName.fst2	☑	☐
5	☐	ExceptionalCases.fst2	☑	☐
6	☐	NasabANDFirstname.fst2	☑	☐

Figure 10. Transducer cascade recognizing names of personalities

Figure 10 shows the form of this cascade. The cascade call the six transducers with certain logic. It is generated through the CasSys tool that is integrated in Unitex the free linguistic platform. Moreover, the choice of passing the transducers is not random. First, the cascade must recognize personality's names having trigger words to add certain certitude (transducer 2). Then, we move to the recognition of personality names which contains first name and last name with one occurrence of the first name (transducer 2) and the recognition of Nasab followed by Nisba (transducer 3) or Last name (transducer 4). Afterward, exceptional cases must be recognized (transducer 5). Finally, we finish the recognition process by the recognition Nasab followed by a first name when the word "ben" is omitted (transducer number 6).

Every graph adds annotations to the text using the mode "Merge". This mode provides, as output, a recognized NE surrounded by a tag defined in defined in the boxes output in the transducer.

Recall	Precision	F-measure
0.98	0.94	0.95

Table 4. Table summarizing the measure values

We manually evaluated the quality of our work on the Wikipedia corpus. This evaluation is performed by evaluation metrics that are the precision, recall and F-measure. These measures are illustrated in Table 4.

The precision is the number of correct ANE for personality names recognized on the total of recognized ANE for personality names. Applying this formula, we get the value 0.94.

The recall is the total correct ANE for personality names recognized on the total ANE for personality names. Applying the formula, we get the value 0.98.

The F-measure is a combination of Precision and Recall for penalizing the large inequalities between these two measures. It is 2*P*R/(P+R). Applying this formula, we get the value 0.95. Therefore, we find that the results for the proposed method are motivating.

	Our system	(Shaalan and Raza, 2007)	(Elsebai and al., 2009)
Precision	94 %	85 %	93 %
Recall	98 %	89 %	86 %
F-measure	95 %	87.5 %	89 %

Table 5. Evaluation between Systems recognizing the type name of person

Table 5 shows an evaluation between our system and those developed by (Shaalan and Raza, 2007) and (Elsebai and al., 2009). We can remark that the results obtained by our system are efficient measures as those of the other two systems.

6. Conclusion and Perspectives

In this paper, we presented a method for recognizing ANE based on transducer cascade. We established a set of dictionaries, a list of extraction rules depending essentially on trigger words and a set of transducers allowing the recognition of several ANE categories. We gave also an experimentation on Wikipedia test corpus fitted with kiwix tool. The obtained results are satisfactory because the calculated measure values are encouraged.

As perspectives, we will improve our dictionaries by adding other features. Then, we will experiment the generated cascade on other types of ENA having relationship with personality's name. Finally, we are going to take advantage of our annotated corpus to develop an enrichment process to establish links to free resources such as Wikipedia and Geonames and to disambiguate them if needed.

References

Aboaoga M. and Aziz MJA. 2013. Arabic person names recognition by using a rule based approach. Journal of Computer Science, 922–927.

Ciravegna F. and Lavelli A. 1999. « Full text parsing using cascades of rules: An information extraction perspective », In Proceedings of EACL'99, Bergen, Norway, 102-109.

Elsebai A., Meziane F. and BelKredim FZ. 2009. A rule based Persons names Arabic extraction system. Communications of the IBIMA, 11: 53–59.

Elsebai A. 2008. Arabic Proper Names Recognition Using Heuristics. Proceeding of the 9th Annual Post Graduate Symposium on the Convergence of Telecommunications, Networking and Broadcasting (PGNET), ISBN: 978-1-902560-19-9.

Ben Mesmia F., Friburger N., Haddar K. and Maurel D. 2015. Transducer cascade for an automatic recognition of Arabic Named Entities in order to establish links to free resources. Will appear in IEEE-proceedings issue from CICLING'15.

Ben Mesmia F., Friburger N., Haddar K. and Maurel D. 2015. Construction d'une cascade de transducteurs pour la reconnaissance des dates à partir d'un corpus Wikipédia. Colloque pour les Étudiants Chercheurs en Traitement Automatique du Langage naturel et ses applications, 8-11.

Fehri H., Haddar K., Hamadou A. B. 2011. Recognition and Translation of Arabic Named Entities with NooJ Using a New Representation Model, in M. Constant, A. Maletti, A. Savary (eds), FSMNLP, 9th International Workshop, ACL, Blois, France, 134-142.

Friburger N., Maurel D. 2004. Finite-state transducer cascades to extract named entities in texts, Theoretical Computer Science, volume 313, 94-104.

Doumi, N., Lehireche, A., Maurel, D., and Ali Cherif, M. (2013a). La conception d'un jeu de ressources libres pour le TAL arabe sous Unitex.Paper presented at the TRADETAL2013, Colloque international en Traductologie et TAL, Oran - Algeria, 5-6 may.

Maurel D., Friburger N., Eshkol I. 2009. « Who are you, you who speak? Transducer cascades for information retrieval ». In Proceedings of 4th Language & Technology Conference: Human Language Technologies as a Challenge for Computer Science and Linguistics, Poznan, Poland, 220-223.

Maurel D., Friburger N., Antoine J.-Y., Eshkol-Taravella I. and Nouvel D. 2011. Cascades de transducteurs autour de la reconnaissance des entités nommées. Traitement automatique des langues, 52(1) : 69-961.

Mesfar S. 2007. Named Entity Recognition for Arabic Using Syntactic Grammars. Proceedings of the 12th International Conference on Application of Natural Language to Information Systems. Berlin, Heidelberg, 305-316.

Shaalan K. and Raza H. 2007. Person name entity recognition for Arabic. In: Proceedings of the 5th workshop on important unresolved matters, 17-24.

Shaalan K. and Oudah M. 2014. A hybrid approach to Arabic named entity recognition. Journal of Information Science, 40(1): 67–87.

Shaalan K. 2014. A Survey of Arabic Named Entity Recognition and Classification. Computational Linguistics, 40 (2) 469-510.

DanProof: Pedagogical Spell and Grammar Checking for Danish

Eckhard Bick
University of Southern Denmark
eckhard.bick@mail.dk

Abstract

This paper presents a Constraint Grammar-based pedagogical proofing tool for Danish. The system recognizes not only spelling errors, but also grammatical errors in otherwise correctly spelled words, and categorizes errors for WORD-integrated pedagogical comments. Possible spelling corrections are prioritized from context, and grammatical corrections generated by a morphological module. The system uses both phonetic similarity measures and traditional Levenshtein-distances, and has a special focus on compounding/splitting errors common in modern Danish. As a classical spell-checker DanProof achieves F-Scores over 95, and F=88 if compounding correction is included. With the maximal set of error types, 2/3 of all errors are found in school essays, and precision is 91.7%.

1 Introduction

Spell- and grammar-checking is not a new task, and is integrated in many standard text editors for the major languages. However, smaller languages are not so well covered, and the technology is very much inspired by what works for English where simple list checking will identify non-words, and correction suggestions can be found with the editing distance measure using the same list. However, the task is more difficult for morphologically rich languages, where word formation is too productive to allow lists with good coverage. A special problem for Danish is compounding, and standard, English-style spell checkers tempt users to (wrongly) split compounds into their parts just to satisfy their spell-checker. This phenomenon can now lead to a general tendency towards compounding errors in especially informal writing in Danish. Two other problems also deserve special attention: First, many errors are grammatical in nature rather than misspellings, and will lead to words that do exist in the spelling lexicon, an example being the confusion of finite and non-finite verb endings in Danish (*købe - køber*), which is considered a stigmatizing marker of low-level education. Detecting this error is only possible with context and true sentence analysis. Second, depending on the user group, it is not enough to come up with a loose list of similar words as correction suggestions - only good spellers will immediately see what the correct form is. Bad spellers need a well-prioritized list, or - if possible - just one suggestion, which is also desirable for tasks in automatic tool pipes, such as pre- and postprocessing of machine translation (Stymne & Ahrenberg 2010) or as an OCR module. To achieve such prioritization, simple editing distance is not enough. Rather, other factors, like phonetic similarity, compound-part similarity, frequency and not least context analysis, must be considered.

While initiatives like *hunspell* and the use of finite state transducers (Pirinen & Lindén 2014; Antonsen 2014), have addressed the variability of morphologically rich languages, the use of full-scale grammatical and sentence analysis is rare. For the Scandinavian languages, the Constraint Grammar (CG) approach (Karlsson et al. 1995) has been used for this task (Arppe 2000; Birn 2000; Carlberger et al. 2004 for Swedish; Hagen et al. 2001 for Norwegian), and working systems are distributed by the Finnish company Lingsoft Oy (www.lingsoft.fi). For Danish, a CG-based spell- and grammar-checker for developed with a special focus on dyslexics (Bick 2006), and it is this system, that is the point of departure for our current work. In the following we will show how our own approach makes use of morphological and syntactic analysis for both the task of detecting errors and the task of weighting correction suggestions.

Proceedings of Recent Advances in Natural Language Processing, pages 55–62,
Hissar, Bulgaria, Sep 7–9 2015.

2 System description

DanProof can be used as (a) a command-line tool for corpus work, research or automatic spell-checking of e.g. texts for machine translation, or (b) an end user application with Word-integration and pedagogical comments. The linguistic core consists of four modules, (1) word based spell checking and similarity matching, (2) morphological analysis of words, compounding and correction suggestions, (3) syntax-based disambiguation of all possible readings, and (4) context-based mapping of error types and correction suggestions. In the current version, levels (3) and (4) are actually run several times, first safe error mapping followed by loose morphological disambiguation, then full error mapping followed by strict morphosyntactic disambiguation, and finally a last round of error mapping exploiting syntactic function tags and (implicit) dependencies. Gender or number agreement errors between determiners, adjectives and nouns in an np are a good example for why this is useful: If no error mapping is performed before disambiguation, the latter may have removed an agreement-conflicting noun reading in favor of a verb reading already once the rule is run. On the other hand, disambiguated context may be necessary to decide which word, out of a string of conflicting words, should be tagged as wrong. Finally, long distance agreement, as between subject and subject complement, can only be safely resolved once syntactic relations are established.

2.1 Classical spell-checking and similarity matching

After tokenization, this is the first module of our pipe and represents a classical spell-checker. The error finder appends weighted lists of correction suggestions to tokens that either figure in a manually compiled error substitution list (5,800 entries), or that cannot be verified in the fullform lexicon (1,100,000 word forms). The substitution list allows both single- and multi-word forms, as well as variable word parts, and provides ready-made, similarity/likelihood-weighted corrections. To find correction matches from the fullform database, a special matching algorithm was developed, using partial-match databases rather than the full list (which would mean a prohibitive time consumption). The process is then repeated with a phonetically trans-scribed version of the database. Common permutations, gemination and mute letters are taken into account, and in a novel approach, consonant and vowel "phoneme skeletons" are matched (e.g. *'straden' – stdn/áè*). Next, the Comparator computes grapheme (w=written), phoneme (s=spoken) and frequency (f) weights for each correction candidate, using, among other criteria, word-length normalized Levenshtein distances. The different weights are combined into a single similarity value (with 40% below maximum as a cut-off for the correction list), but a marking is retained individually for the highest graphical, phonetic and frequency match value.

2.2 Tagger/parser-based word ranking

It is a core feature of our methodology that the ordinary rule body of a CG parser is used to choose the contextually most acceptable word from a list of correction suggestions. Thus, the best correction candidates are submitted to morphological analysis on par with the original word form, an the result used as input for the tagging stage[1] of the DanGram parser[2] (Bick 2001), whose about 6,000 rules, with their implicit contextual and semantic knowledge, will hopefully sort out the added ambiguity and single out the correct suggestion[3]. Too much ambiguity, however, can overwhelm the system, and with multiple errors in the same sentence, contexts become as ambiguous as the to-be-disambiguated word itself and may prevent the CG rules from working properly. Therefore, only the top-ranking correction suggestions are used and the most heuristic (= least safe) rules are excluded at this stage. For DanProof, we also added disambiguation rules specifically targeting spell-checker-suggested forms, and to be run *before* DanGram proper.

Unlike the original version of the spell-checker (called OrdRet, www.ordret.com), we are targeting not dyslexics' text, but ordinary text, or even pre-spellchecked text, with a lower error ratio, and expect edit distances between error and correction to be lower than for dyslexics.

[1] This stage disambiguates part of speech and morphology, but uses syntax only implicitly, avoiding the stricter disambiguation forced by the subsequent function-assigning syntax module.

[2] A public version of the tagger is accessible for teaching and research through SDU's VISL project [visl.sdu.dk/visl/da/parsing/automatic/]

[3] In the correction menu shown to the user, this will then be the number-one suggestion. The other readings will be "resurrected" and appended in the order of their original spellchecker ratings.

Therefore, we were able to use stricter similarity thresholds, resulting in shorter suggestion lists, less ambiguity for the tagger, and more cases with the correct suggestion as first alternative. Fig. 1 illustrates the interplay between the core spell-checker module, DanGram's morphological analysis and disambiguation and the error mapping CG module. Simplified output examples for the individual modules are shown in rectangular text boxes[4].

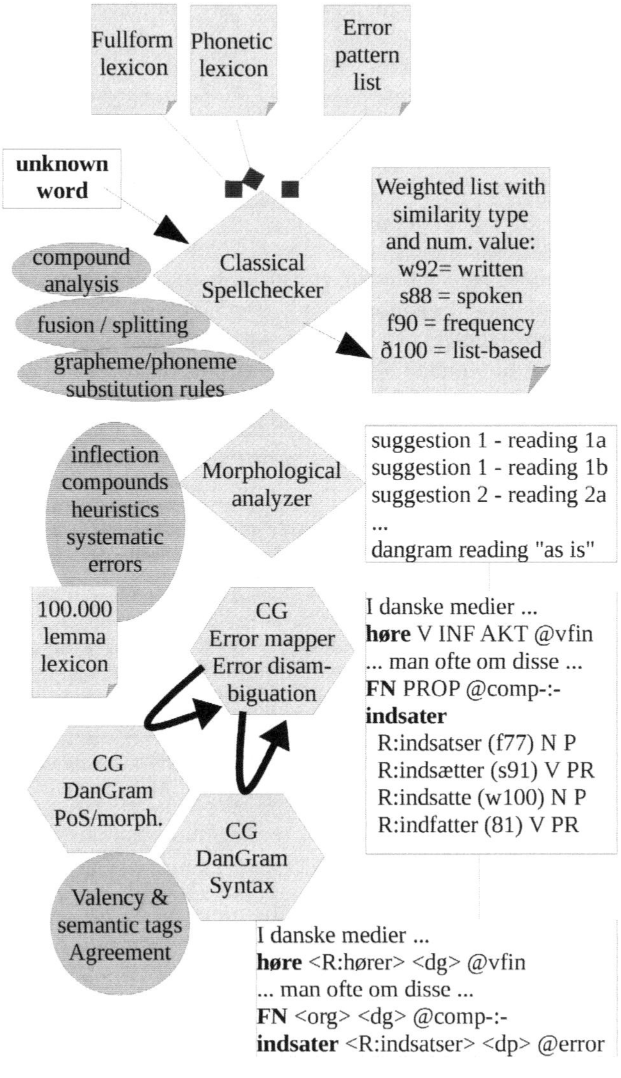

Fig. 1: System architecture

[4] The literal translation of the Danish example sentence is "In Danish media **hears** one often about these **UN initiatives.**" R:... -expressions contain (ambiguous) correction suggestions. V=verb, INF=infinitive, AKT=active, PROP=name, N=noun, P=plural, @vfin=finite verb, @comp=compound error

2.3 Morphological recognition

An important difference between our target data and dyslectics texts is lexical variation and word complexity. Thus, we found a much higher percentage of long words and compounds, and there was a higher risk of an "unknown" word in fact being correct rather than an error. Therefore, we extended the compound analysis module of DanGram as well as its heuristic, endings-based morphological word guesser. We also added a confidence tag for "good compounds", based on length and frequency of the compound parts. In the current version, these alternative analyses compete with possible error corrections and their tags are used to make CG rules more cautious, avoiding false positive classification of compounds or rare technical terms as errors.

Finally, we also wished to accommodate systematical errors made by immigrants or foreign language learners in Denmark, in particular endings errors due to category confusions[5] (e.g. noun gender, regular past tense inflection) or special orthographic rules, such as e-elision for inflected -el/er/en-words ('minist**ere**' -> 'minist**re**', plural of 'minister'). We therefore modified DanGram's analysis module to recognize and mark this kind of error. Together with the phonological and grapheme confusion tables used by the word similarity module, these cases cover many of the non-semantic L2 learner error types described by Hammarberg and Grigonytė (2014) for Swedish[6], though obviously not code switching or compounding loans. In order to effectively address the latter, L1-specific rule modules or substitution lists would have to be added.

2.4 Context-based error mapping

The next stage of the system is a dedicated error-driven Constraint Grammar (ca. 1450 rules) that maps grammatical errors on otherwise correctly spelled words. While DanGram is basically reductionist and removes (focuses) ambiguity, the error-CG *adds* information. For instance, the common Danish '-e/-er' verb-error (infinitive vs.

[5] Unlike English, Danish has 2 grammatical genders and two regular past tense endings, which do not follow strict patterns, and have to be learned together with the word.

[6] This study uses the ASU learner corpus. No corresponding data exist for Danish, but since the two languages are closely related, the inventory of error *types* can be assumed to be the same or at least very similar.

present tense, cf. example (b)) can often be resolved by checking local and global left context (infinitive marker, auxiliaries, subject candidates). Likewise, gender and number errors can be checked by noun phrase context (examples a,d). Suggestions are mapped[7] as @-tags in the style of CG syntactic tags, e.g. @pl (plural), @vfin (finite verb) or @utr (common gender). In the examples below, rule conditions are paraphrased in parentheses. DanProof's last stage generates corrected wordforms <R:....> from these inflectional tags, and in Word's graphical user interface, the tags are "translated" into error types and expanded with explanations and examples (see footnote[8] for translations).

(a) Det er også disse **menneske** (@pl <R:mennesker>) der mener ... *(noun phrase agreement: plural determiner)*

(b) 25 procent af alle voksne danskere **leve** (@vfin <R:lever>) i en **kerne** (@comp-) familie. *(subject candidate to the left, absence of infinitive-triggering contexts such as auxiliaries)*[9]

(c) Hun besøgte **barndoms** (@comp-) veninden. *(indefinite singular noun in the genitive, immediately preceding definite noun)*

(d) Det var en **stort** (@utr <R:stor>) oplevelse. *(noun phrase agreement)*

(e) Bægeret var fuld (@sc-neu <R:fuldt>). *(long-distance agreement between subject and subject complement)*

(f) Det har **vært** (@error <R:været>). *('været' V wins over 'vært' N after auxiliary.*

(g) Hun ønsker ikke **og** (@:at) hjælpe. *(infinitive to the right, infinitive-triggering verb to the left)*

Of course, not all errors are based on wrong inflection. Thus, the rules also mark casing, sentence separation, apostrophe and hyphenation errors, as well as word insertion and deletion, and fusion/splitting errors (cf. @comp- in example (b-c), all of which are not normally treated - or not treated well - by commercial spell-checkers. Finally, individual word substitution rules are added in a contextual way, where general, list based suggestions would have been too risky. While OrdRet only used tags for this (e.g. @:at in example (g)), we are also using APPEND rules for the same purpose in DanProof. APPEND rules are a relatively new feature in CG, implemented in the CG-3 compiler (Bick & Didriksen 2015), and add complete new reading lines *after* morphological analysis. Thus, we can include new tags, such as PoS and inflection, for the correction word and allow the disambiguation rules to compare the suggested form to the original one with regard to context compatibility.

One problem with inflectional error mapping is DanGram's disambiguation, which may well discard correct forms for the sake of erroneous ones if the context also contains erroneous forms. Thus, it may not be possible to re-map a finite verb as infinitive, because the same context that would allow the error-CG to do this, may have led DanGram to discard the verb-reading altogether if the word form as such (or any of its correction suggestions) was, say, a noun or adjective. Therefore, the safest error-mapping rules are run twice – both before and after DanGram. As "before"-rules they may apply while the necessary context is still in place, avoiding disambiguation interference. Run again as "after"-rules, the same rules may capture other necessary contexts that have been made safe by DanGram in the meantime, allowing the rules find and mark further errors.

Finally, there is a second, syntactic run (5,000 rules) of DanGram and a third round of error-mapping exploiting the syntactic tags, as does the subject complement rule in example (e) - as opposed to the "easier" noun phrase agreement error (d).

2.5 Pedagogical comments on error types

A major difference between OrdRet and DanProof, besides the target group adaptations, is the fact that the latter makes use of its error classification for pedagogical purposes. Each error that is not just a simple spelling error comes with a (short) definition and a (longer) explanation, as well as examples and links to

---

[7] Possible multiple mappings will be sorted out by subsequent contextual disambiguation rules.

[8] (a) It is also these **people** that think ..., (b) 25 percent of all adult Danes **live** in a **nucleus** family, (c) She visited [the/her] **childhood** friend, (d) It was *a* **great** experience, (e) [The] cup was full, (f) It has **been** ..., (g) She does not want **to** help

[9] In the real rule, there are 5 different negative contexts, for safety, as well as various other conditions.

external material such as on-line exercises and text book excerpts. All in all, about 35 error types are covered.

Error type	@inf
Definition	infinitiv (navnemåde)
Explanation	Du har sandsynligvis tilføjet et overflødigt -r til en infinitiv, der dermed bliver til er finit verbum. En vigtig regel er at et verbum (udsagnsord) er en ubøjet infinitiv (uden -r), hvis der til venstre står *'at'* eller *vil/ville, kan/kunne, skal/skulle, bør/burde.* Omvendt ...
Examples	De begynder <u>at</u> **danser** [danse] 'Han <u>forstår</u> engelsk' - 'Han <u>kan</u> **forstå** engelsk'
Links	En mulig øvelse er *R-problemer - verber,* samt VISL's grammatikspil *Balloon Ride.*

Table 1: Pedagogical comment fields (see footnote[10] for translations)

An added advantage from making error types transparent to the user, rather than just marking words as "wrong", is that the user can actively switch certain error types on or off. For a good speller with a good grasp of grammar, for instance, a high proportion of grammatical error markings will be false positive, while a lone false positive may be a fair price for a bad speller to pay for ridding himself of a dozen errors on the same page. Having an on/off setting for grammatical errors on a whole, or individual ones, remedies this problem. Similarly, some users employ uppercasing for emphasis, or prefer English-inspired apostrophes for names, and if this is a conscious decision, marking it only antagonizes the user.

A known problem with Danish orthography is that erstwhile errors often become allowed forms, and may even become the only allowed form, if sufficiently many people make the error. On the other hand, many individuals stick to the originally learned spelling over a life time. Therefore, DanProof adds markers (<frequent>, @green) for "wrong but widely used" forms, making possible an on/off-switch for "strict" spelling errors only.

2.6 The graphical user interface

DanProof has a graphical user interface integrated into Microsoft Word, with side bar fields for error-marked paragraphs and dynamic comment fields. In the main text window, optional colored underline marking can be activated, mimicking Word's own "correct spelling while writing" mode.

3 Evaluation

To evaluate the performance of DanProof, we looked for texts that would have some errors but not as many as dyslectics' texts, and not as few as published texts. High school exam texts seemed to be a good compromise and we decided to use Danish high school exam essays by Greenlandic speakers (Bæk et al. 2009). The essays (6632 words) were analyzed with DanProof and error markings inspected and corrected manually. In a second round of inspection false negatives were added, i.e. errors the system hadn't found. The texts did contain both ordinary spelling errors[11] and grammatical errors, but also many confusion spelling errors, i.e. errors where a word is replaced by another (wrong) word, but with the correct spelling (e.g. 'det' -> 'de'). We therefore computed performance at four different levels:

- All error markings
- Spell: Only spelling errors, excluding grammatical errors, but including compounding errors (fusion/splitting), hyphen and case
- Lex: Same as Spell, but not counting false positives if the word is not listed in *Retskrivningsordbogen* (e.g. 'fucked', 'adj') and not counting false negatives if the word does exist in *Retskrivningsordbogen* (e.g. 'da' [dag], 'single' in compounding errors)
- Classic: Same as Lex, but words are counted as error-marked, if DanProof marked them as unknown, yet feasible compounds

[10] Explanation: You have probably add a superfluous -r to an infinitive, thereby turning it into a finite verb. An important rule is that a verb is a non-inflected infinitive (without -r), if the words 'to' or 'will/would', 'can/could', 'shall/should' can be found to the left. Conversely, ..., Examples: The begin <u>to</u> **dances** [dance]; He <u>understands</u> English - He <u>can</u> **understand** English; Links: A possible exercise is *R-problems - verbs*, and VISL's grammar game *Balloon Ride*

[11] This is not always the case nowadays because students use Word's list-based spell checker while writing, so students will change an un-accepted word until it matches an existing word - leaving only confusion errors, compounding errors and grammatical errors.

	Recall	Precision	F-score
All	65.1	91.7	76.1
Spell	86.8	90.8	88.6
Lex	93.7	96.7	95.2
Classic	100.0	98.3	99.1

Table 2: Error detection performance, school essays

As can be seen from the table, DanProof is very reliable if used as a traditional spell-checker (Classic and Lex), even when the more difficult task of compounding correction is added for otherwise correctly spelled words (Spell). With the full range of error types, precision is still acceptable (even a little higher than for "Spell"), but recall is lower - DanProof misses out on about 1/3 of all errors of the addressed type.

Qualitative error analysis of false negatives showed that particularly difficult error types, recall-wise, are @insertion (i.e. missing words) and deletion (@nil). Confusion without grammatical motivation (@:...) was rarely spotted, but this is probably data-specific for the Greenland setting. Thus, 1/3 of the cases were confusion of the subject pronouns 'det' and 'de' which are hard to distinguish contextually, plus cases outside of DanProof's current scope, e.g. idioms and choice of preposition.

	Recall	Precision	F-score
@error (47)	83.0	95.1	88.6
@upper (28)	100.0	96.6	98.3
@comp- (25)	76.0	100.0	86.4
@comp-:- (22)	90.9	95.2	93.0
@nil (14)	28.6	100.0	44.5
@insert (12)	8.3	100.0	15.3
@vfin (9)	66.7	85.7	75.0
@: (35)	5.7	50.0	10.23
e.g. @:de (10)			
@pl (8)	62.5	83.3	71.4
@utr (7)	100.0	87.5	93.3
@def (4)	75.0	60.0	66.7
@new (3)	100.0	60.0	75.0
@neu (6)	16.7	100.0	28.6
@idf (4)	25.0	50.0	33.3
@lower (4)	75.0	100.0	85.7
@inf (4)	100.0	100.0	100.0

Table 3: Error type-specific performance

A direct comparison with OrdRet is difficult because of the different target domains, and because the OrdRet evaluation by Bick (2006) evaluated correction suggestion priority lists, rather than simple matches, and weighted correction suggestions with their inverse rank in the list. If a weighted score is approximated by assigning a weight of zero to all cases where the correct form was not matched, DanProof does get better scores for its essay texts than OrdRet had for its dyslectics texts[12], although OrdRet has a "performance reserve" because of the presence of correct suggestions at lower list ranks.

	R	P	F-score
All-weighted (DanProof)	61.6	86.7	72.0
All-weighted (OrdRet)	43.0	58.0	49.4

Table 4: Comparison OrdRet - DanProof

As a real-life control, we used MicrosoftWord 2007 on the same essays, and found considerable differences, both in scope and performance. First of all, Word does not find compounding errors and can't recognize names, the former creating false negatives, the latter false positives. It does even worse than DanProof on deletion and insertion, and it marks relatively few grammatical errors, albeit almost without false positives. In a direct comparison, this leads to very low - and unfair - scores[13] for the "all"-evaluation due to low recall. For "spell" and "lex", however, Word still finds considerably fewer errors than DanProof. Precision is better without counting names, but is still hampered by the missing compound analysis (e.g. *kønstradition* [gender tradition], *boginteresse* [book interest], *livsrygsæk* [life backpack], *middagsræs* [noon rush]).

	Recall	Precision	F-score
All	20.8	54.6	30.1
All-nonprop	20.8	71.6	33.1
Spell	75.0	51.1	60.8
Spell-nonprop	75.0	70.3	72.6
Lex	81.8	54.9	65.7
Lex-nonprop	81.8	77.6	79.6

Table 5: Word2007 performance

Once DanProof recognizes a word as wrong, the assigned error type is usually reliable (95.7% for "all", 96.6% with "spell" settings). For the

[12] A more direct comparison by running both systems on the same data was not possible because the original OrdRet setup could not be reconstructed.

[13] On the other hand, Word marked some simple spacing and punctuation errors that were not in the scope of our DanProof test.

correct error type markings, the suggested new word form was correctly chosen in 95.8% of cases, independently of "all" or "spell" settings. Word had a correct suggestion in 84.4%, and this was offered as the first choice in 68.9%, indicating that DanProof's context-based prioritization does make a difference.

Since the density of errors to be found is very much dependent on genre and text authors, an alternative measure of "experienced performance" is the number of false positives or false negatives *per page*[14]. Thus, for our essays, DanProof had 0.7 false positives per page with the 'all'-settings, and 0.4 false positives per page with 'spell' settings. For false negatives, the numbers were 4 and 0.4, respectively.

DanProof uses the tag @new, if it deems a word correct, but has done so using productive compound analysis. Conversely, @check! is used for words that are not "safely wrong" because no correction alternative was found, but that are more likely to be wrong than @new, because no productive analysis was found either. In a 178,000 word newspaper corpus chunk from Korpus2000 (...), @new was used 347 times, and was wrong on only 2 occasions (99.4% accuracy). Confronted with the same word list , Word2007 had false positives in 54.2%, evidently due to not having a compound analysis module. @check! was used 120 times and proved to be a very mixed category, with 23.3% spelling errors, 17.5% foreign words and 8.4% names (mostly lowercase brands, pharmaceuticals etc.), i.e. less about half were ordinary Danish words. Word2007 accepted 1/3 of the latter as correct, indicating DanProof would profit from a larger lexicon to supplement its compound analysis. Still, in a hybrid setup, given that the @new category is safe and 3 times bigger than the @check category, and that Word rejected half of the former, Word would probably benefit more from DanProof input than vice versa. In any case, the two systems' strengths seem to be in different areas, which would make hybridization, maybe with an arbiter system, a good idea.

[14] Lingsoft, for instance, claims less than 1% false positives per page for their products [http://www.lingsoft.fi/en/506, 19 Apr 2015]

4 Conclusion and outlook

We have described how a Constraint Grammar environment can be used to enhance a classical spell-checker module in a number of ways:

- weighting of correction suggestions for non-words and dubious words
- reduce the number of false positives through compound analysis and name recognition
- mapping and classification of grammatical errors
- syntactic validation of split compound recognition

For its target domain, the system achieved better recall and precision than its predecessor system (OrdRet) and outperformed MicrosoftWord's standard spell-checker, not least with regard to false positive non-word marking, split compounds and grammatical error-typing. For correctly typed errors, the right correction alternative was chosen in over 95% of cases. However, performance for grammatical, conditioned errors is not on par with the system's accuracy for classical spell-checking, and should be improved.

Transparent error-typing and confidence grading (@error, @new and @check!) allowed us to add pedagogical comments, but at the time of writing graphical integration into MicrosoftWord was not finished, and should be followed up by classroom testing and teacher feed-back, possibly integrated with existing didactical tools.

While word-based grammatical errors such as agreement errors and the so-called -r errors are well-covered, further syntactical error types should be added, such as word order errors and comma-checking. The latter is a sensitive, almost political, issue in Denmark, and should definitely be part of a Danish proofing suit, but is being addressed by a parallel R&D project, and therefore not evaluated here.

References

Antonsen, Lene. 2014. Evaluation of a North-Saami FST-Based Spellchecker Program. Presentation at SLTC 2014 [http://divvun.no/workshops/NorWEST2014/presentations/Antonsen.pdf]

Bick, Eckhard. 2001. En Constraint Grammar Parser for Dansk. In Widell, Peter & Kunøe, Mette (eds.), *8. Møde om Udforskningen af Dansk Sprog, 12.-13. oktober 2000*, p. 40-50. Århus: Århus University.

Bick, Eckhard. 2006. A Constraint Grammar Based Spellchecker for Danish with a Special Focus on Dyslexics". In: Suominen, Mickael et.al. (ed.) *A Man of Measure: Festschrift in Honour of Fred Karlsson on his 60th Birthday*. Special Supplement to SKY Jounal of Linguistics, Vol. 19. pp. 387-396. Turku: The Linguistic Association of Finland

Bick, Eckhard & Didriksen, Tino. 2015. CG-3 - Beyond Classical Constraint Grammar. In: Beáta Megyesi: Proceedings of NoDaLiDa 2015, Vilnius. pp. 31-39. Linköping: LiU Electronic Press

Birn, Jussi. 2000. Detecting grammar errors with Lingsoft's Swedish grammar checker. In Nordgård, Torbjørn (ed.) *NODALIDA '99 Proceedings from the 12th Nordiske datalingvistikkdager*, p. 28-40. Trondheim: Department of Linguistics, University of Trondheim.

Bæk, Jan & Elmose, Agnete & Olesen, Claus & Hartmann, Peter. 2009. Evaluering af skriftlig eksamen for Dansk i Grønland [http://www.uvm.dk/Uddannelser-og-dagtilbud/Gymnasiale-uddannelser/ Information-til-censorer-paa-de-gymnasiale-uddannelser/~/media/UVM/Filer/Udd/Gym/PDF11/Proever_og_eksamen/Censorvejledninger_dansk_maj_2011/110504_14.ashx] and [http://www.iserasuaat.gl/fileadmin/user_upload/Test_files/Raad_og_vink_Groenland_2009.doc]

Carlberger, Johan & Domeij, Rickard & Kann, Viggo & Knutsson, Ola. 2004. The development and performance of a grammar checker for Swedish: A language-engineering perspective. Natural Language Engineering, 1 (1).

Hagen, Kristin & Lane, Pia & Trosterud, Trond. 2001. En grammatikkontrol for bokmål. In Vannebo, Kjell Ivar & Helge Sandøy (eds.) *Språkknyt 3-2001*, p. 6-9, 47. Oslo: Norsk Språkråd

Hammarberg, Björn & Grigonytė, Gintarė. 2014. Non-Native Writers' Errors - a Challenge to a Spell-Checker. Presentation at SLTC 2014. [http://divvun.no/workshops/NorWEST2014/abstracts/Hammarberg_Grigonyte.pdf]

Karlsson, Fred & Voutilainen, Atro & Heikkilä, Jukka & Anttila, Arto. 1995. *Constraint Grammar: A language-independent system for parsing unrestricted text*, pp. 1-88. Berlin: Mouton de Gruyter.

Pirinen, Tommi A. & Lindén, Krister. 2014. State-of-the-Art in Weighted Finite-State Spell-Checking. In: Proceedings of CICLing 2014.

Stymne, Sara & Ahrenberg, Lars. 2010. Using a Grammar Checker for Evaluation and Postprocessing of Statistical Machine Translation. In: Proceedings of LREC 2010.

Maximal Repeats Enhance Substring-based Authorship Attribution

Romain Brixtel
Department of Organizational Behavior, Faculty of Business and Economics
University of Lausanne, Quartier Dorigny, 1015 Lausanne, Switzerland
romain.brixtel@unil.ch

Abstract

This article tackles the Authorship Attribution task according to the language independence issue. We propose an alternative of variable length character n-grams features in supervised methods: *maximal repeats* in strings. When character n-grams are by essence redundant, maximal repeats are a condensed way to represent any substring of a corpus. Our experiments show that the redundant aspect of n-grams contributes to the efficiency of character-based techniques. Therefore, we introduce a new way to weight features in vector based classifier by introducing n-th *order maximal repeats* (maximal repeats detected in a set of maximal repeats). The experimental results show higher performance with maximal repeats, with less data than n-grams based approach (approximately divided by a factor of 10).

1 Introduction

Internet makes it easy to let anyone share his opinion, to communicate news or to disseminate his literary production. A main feature of textual traces on the web is that they are mostly anonymous. Textual data mining is used to characterise authors, by categories (*e.g.* gender, age, political opinion) or as individuals. The latter case is called the Authorship Attribution (AA) issue. It consists of predicting the author of a text given a predefined set of candidates, thus falling in the supervised machine learning subdomain. This problem is often expressed as the ultimate objective, finding the author. Technically the task is to predict a new pair, considering given pairs linking text and author. It is also known as *writeprint*, in reference of *fingerprint* in written productions. For a survey, see (Koppel et al., 2009; Stamatatos, 2009; El Bouanani and Kassou, 2014).

For AA, stylometry is most often used. The assumption is that a writer leaves unintended clues that lead to his identification. Bouanani *et al.* (2014) define a set of numerical features that remains relatively constant for a given author and sufficiently contrasts his writing style against any author's style. In the previous studies, numerical data such as word-length, and literal data such as words or character strings were used to capture personal style features (Koppel et al., 2011). Unlike words or lemmas that belong to *a priori* resources, character strings are in compliance with a language independent objective. Supervised machine learning techniques are used to learn author's profile, from a training set where text and author pairs are known. Eventually, results are used to attribute new texts to the right author. This is a multi-variate classification problem. Support Vector Machine (SVM) is one of the favorite approaches to handle such complex tasks (Sun et al., 2012). This is the chosen solution here.

AA therefore consists of predicting the author of a textual message given a predefined set of candidates. The difficulty of the task depends on its scope and the choice of the training set. It increases when the objects of study come from the web, with different textual genres, styles or languages. Research on AA can focus on several issues. Item scalability addresses matching text with a huge number of authors. Language independence requires techniques that are efficient irrespective of language resources such as lexica.

In this study, the language independence issue is addressed, with character-based methods. However, computation of all the character subtrings in a text is costly. The major contribution of this paper is a new way to handle character substrings, to reduce the training data and therefore the training time and cost, without loosing accuracy in AA. The well-known variable length character n-grams approach is compared to a *variable length max-*

Proceedings of Recent Advances in Natural Language Processing, pages 63–71,
Hissar, Bulgaria, Sep 7–9 2015.

imal repeats approach. As a controversial statement, experiments conducted in this article highlight that the redundancy of features based on n-grams is beneficial in a classification task as AA. This introduces a new way to weight features that takes into account this redundancy with n-*th order maximal repeats* (maximal repeats in a set of maximal repeats). Experiments are conducted on three corpora: one in English, one in French and the concatenation of those two corpora.

The remainder of this article is organized as follows. Section 2 describes related work and commonly used features. Section 3 introduces the experimental settings, the characteristics of the corpora and the experimental pipeline. Section 4 describes features, detailing the maximal repeats algorithm. Section 5 details experimental results. Section 6 concludes.

2 Related Work

AA is a single-label multi-class categorisation task. Three characteristics have to be defined (Sun et al., 2012): single feature, set of features representing a text and the way to handle those sets to match a text with an author.

2.1 Features Definition

AA features exploited in the literature can be separated in different groups as advocated by Abbasi *et al.* (2008): numerical values associated with words (total number of words, number of character per word, number of character bi/tri-grams), hence called lexical; mixed values associated with syntax at sentence level (frequency of function words, n-grams of Part-Of-Speech tags); numerical values associated with bigger units (number of paragraphs, average length of paragraphs), called structural; values associated with content (bag-of-words, word bi-grams/tri-grams); and a last group called idiosyncratic related with individual use (misspellings, use of Leet speak).

Among those features, some are specific to some types of language and writing systems. For instance, tokenizing a text in words is common in word separating cases, but is a non-trivial task in Chinese or Japanese. Part-Of-Speech (POS) tagging requires specific tools that might lack in some languages. Approaches based on character n-grams appear to be the simplest and the most accurate methods when the aim is to handle *any* language (Grieve, 2007; Stamatatos, 2006).

But, as advocated by Bender *et al.* (2009), a language independent method should not be a *language naive* method. If the extraction of n-grams is done whatever the language, the n parameter has to be chosen according to the properties of the processed language. The same results cannot be expected for the same parameter on different languages according to their morphological typology (*e.g.* inflected or agglutinative languages).

Sun *et al.* (2012) argue that using a fixed value of n can only capture lexical informations (for small values of n), contextual or thematic informations (for larger values), but do not explain why or whether this is valid for Chinese or all languages. The authors argue that this issue is avoided by exploiting variable length n-grams (substrings of length in $[1, n]$). Variable length substrings are exploited in this study to see how this parameter impacts the results in French and English.

2.2 Feature-based Text/Author Representation

A single feature can be allocated to several text and author pairs. Each text and author does not systematically share the same set of features. Different sets of features can be defined to represent texts (and by extension, to represent authors). From existing methods, two main categories of set of features can be defined for AA:

- *off-line* set of features: features a priori considered relevant with prior knowledge, as those deeply described by Chaski *et al.* (2001). They are defined without the knowledge of the corpus to be processed.
- *on-line* set of features: features defined according to the current analysis (according to the training and test corpora for supervised methods, as the character language models described by Peng *et al.* (2003)). They can only be defined when the corpora to be processed (test and training) are fully collected.

On-line sets of features naturally match with the language-independence aim. The characteristics of the corpora are exploited without any external resource. The method described hereafter follows this principle.

2.3 Feature-based Text Categorisation

Different techniques for handling features extracted from texts have been proposed. SVM and Neural Network are established ways to conduct AA in the supervised machine-learning paradigm (Kacmarcik and Gamon, 2006; Tweedie et al.,

1996). When the set of authorship candidates is large or incomplete, thus not including the correct author, some approaches compare sets of features with specific similarity functions (Koppel et al., 2011). Individual level sets of features are used with machine-learning techniques to build a classifier per author. Each classifier acts as an expert dedicated to process a subarea of the features space (*i.e.* each classifier is specialised on detecting some specific authors). The experiments described in this article use an SVM classifier, keeping the same parameters for each experiment, to analyse the impact of the features.

3 Experimental Pipeline and Corpora

A classical AA pipeline is drawn in Figure 1. This pipeline contains two main elements: a Features selector (features are extracted from the training and the test corpus) and a Classifier (using the features extracted in the training corpora, each message of the test corpus is classified).

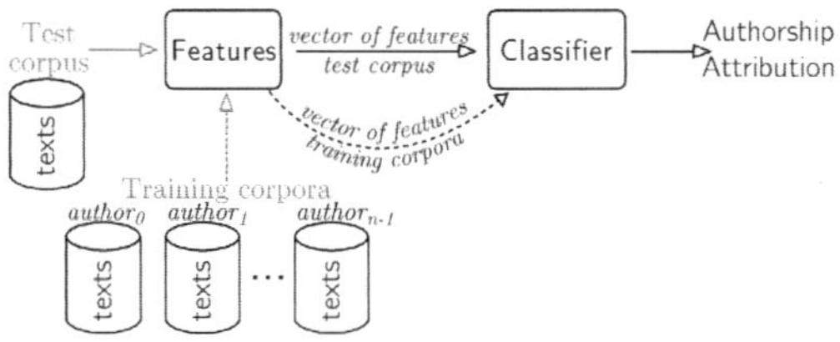

Figure 1: Pipeline processing for supervised AA.

Experiments are conducted to highlight characteristics of substring-based AA methods. SVM is used as the classifier of the pipeline for all experiments, following Sun *et al.* (2012) and Brennan *et al.* (2012). The features selection step is meant to extract the right features from corpora irrespective of language. The experimental pipeline is kept as simple as possible to avoid interferences in the analysis of the features selection.

3.1 Definitions

D is a dataset for stylometric analysis containing I texts and K authors. t_i is the i-th text and a_k the k-th author. F is the set of all the features in the dataset D, F_i the set of features of t_i. Each text t_i is represented as a vector of features. Considering $o_{(i,j)}$ the occurrence frequency of the jth feature f_j of the ith text t_i containing n features, the text is represented as $t_i = \{o_{(i,0)}, \ldots, o_{(i,n-1)}\}$. A weight function w can be applied on each feature of a text, $w(t_i) = \{w(f_0).o_{(i,0)}, \ldots, w(f_{n-1}).o_{(i,n-1)}\}$. A classifier C is therefore trained on a subsample of texts written by preselected authors (training corpora). The set of features used is the intersection of each set of features from the test and training corpora. During experiments, similar results have been obtained with features occurring only in the training corpus, but with a much larger search space to explore.

3.2 Corpora

Two corpora are exploited for experiments: a French one, the LIB corpus and an English one, the EBG corpus. Those two languages are chosen because they have many characters and linguistic characteristics in common. A third corpus, MIXT, is constituted from the merge of EBG and LIB.

A subcorpus of 40 authors, EBG, is extracted from the EXTENDED BRENNAN GREENSTADT adversarial corpus (Brennan et al., 2012). The EBG corpus is constituted of texts exclusively in English (Table 1).

	#characters	#texts	#authors
corpus	1.9×10^6	631	40
authors ($mean \pm stdv$)	$4.6 \times 10^4 \pm 8075$	15.8 ± 2.6	
texts ($mean \pm stdv$)	2945.1 ± 178.5		

Table 1: Overall characteristics of EBG.

The second corpus is extracted from the website of the French newspaper LIBÉRATION. The LIB corpus contains texts from 40 different authors who have written in more than one journalistic categorie, such as sports or health. This is intended to minor subgenre impact, *i.e.* characteristics that might blur the personal style. The corpus main characteristics are drawn in Table 2.

	#characters	#texts	#authors
corpus	5.1×10^6	1247	40
authors ($mean \pm stdv$)	1.3×10^5 $\pm 2.6 \times 10^4$	31.2 ± 4.2	
texts ($mean \pm stdv$)	4070.6 ± 1524.2		

Table 2: Overall characteristics of LIB.

LIB contains the same number of authors as EBG, but the number of texts bounded to each author is higher (31.2 ± 4.2 texts per author in LIB, 15.8 ± 2.6 in EBG). All texts in LIB and EBG are longer than the 250 words limit ($\approx$ 1500 characters), the minimum length considered effective for authorship analysis seen as a text classification task (Forsyth and Holmes, 1996).

The MIXT corpus, 80 authors with texts in both English and French, is obtained from the merge of EBG and LIB. It is built to erase language distinctions. During experiments, tests are also driven on different subcorpora of EBG, LIB and MIXT. We denote EBG-10 (respectively LIB-10 and MIXT-10) a sample of 10 authors from the EBG corpus (respectively LIB and MIXT). Note that the MIXT-20, ..., 80 are the merge of LIB-10 + EBG-10, ..., LIB-40 + EBG-40. Experiments using these corpora are described hereafter to highlight the characteristics of the features and their differences, used in the experimental pipeline.

4 Features

Maximal repeats, *motifs* in (Ukkonen, 2009), are based on the work of Ukkonen (2009) and Kärkkäinen (2006). The algorithm is described in Section 4.1 to explain the improvements discussed in Section 4.2. Motifs are a way to represent each substring of a corpus in a condensed manner. For the detection of *hapax legomena* inside a set of strings from their motifs, see the work of Ilie and Smyth (2011).

4.1 Maximal Repeats in Strings

Maximal repeats are substring patterns of text with the following characteristics: they are *repeated* (motifs occur twice or more) and *maximal* (motifs cannot be expanded to the left *–left maximality–* nor to the right *–right maximality–* without lowering the frequency).

For instance, the motifs found in the string $\mathcal{S} =$ HATTIVATTIAA are T, A and ATTI. TT is not a motif because it always occurs inside an occurrence of ATTI. In other words, its right-context is always I and its left-context A. All the motifs in a list of strings can be enumerated using an Augmented Suffix Array (Kärkkäinen et al., 2006).

Given two strings $\mathcal{S}_0 =$ HATTIV and $\mathcal{S}_1 =$ ATTIAA, Table 3 shows the Augmented Suffix Array of $\mathcal{S} = \mathcal{S}_0.\$_1.\mathcal{S}_1.\$_0$, where $\$_0$ and $\$_1$ are lexicographically lower than any character in the alphabet Σ and $\$_0 < \$_1$. The Augmented Suffix Array consists in the Suffix Array (SA), suffixes of $\mathcal{S}$ sorted lexicographically, with the Longest Common Prefix (LCP) between each two suffixes that are contiguous in SA. With, n the size of $\mathcal{S}$, $\mathcal{S}[i]$ the ith character of $\mathcal{S}$, $\mathcal{S}[n,m]$ a sample of $\mathcal{S}$ from the nth character to the mth, SA_i the starting offset of the suffix of $\mathcal{S}$ at the ith position in the lexicographical order and $lcp(str_1, str_2)$ the longest common prefix between two strings str_1 and str_2 :

$$\begin{aligned} LCP_i &= lcp(\mathcal{S}[SA_i, n-1], \mathcal{S}[SA_{i+1}, n-1]) \\ LCP_{n-1} &= 0 \end{aligned}$$

The LCP allows the detection of all the repeats inside a set of text. The maximal criterion is still not valid because the LCP only inquires on the *left maximality* between repeated prefixes in SA.

i	LCP_i	SA_i	$\mathcal{S}[SA_i]...\mathcal{S}[n]$
0	0	13	$\$_0$
1	0	6	$\$_1$ATTIAA$\$_0$
2	1	12	A$\$_0$
3	1	11	AA$\$_0$
4	4	7	ATTIAA$\$_0$
5	0	1	ATTIV$\$_1$ATTIAA$\$_0$
6	0	0	HATTIV$\$_1$ATTIAA$\$_0$
7	1	10	IAA$\$_0$
8	0	4	IV$\$_1$ATTIAA$\$_0$
9	2	9	TIAA$\$_0$
10	1	3	TIV$\$_1$ATTIAA$\$_0$
11	3	8	TTIAA$\$_0$
12	0	2	TTIV$\$_1$ATTIAA$\$_0$
13	0	5	V$\$_1$ATTIAA$\$_0$

Table 3: Augmented Suffix Array (SA and LCP) of $\mathcal{S} =$ HATTIV$\$_1$ATTIAA$\$_0$.

The substring ATTI occurs for example in $\mathcal{S}$ at the offsets $(1, 7)$, according to LCP_4 in Table 3. The process enumerates all the motifs by reading through LCP. The detection of those motifs is triggered according to the difference between a LCP and the next one in the way SA is ordered.

For example, TTI is equivalent to ATTI because the last characters of these two motifs occur at the offsets $(4, 10)$. They are said to be in a relation of *occurrence-equivalence* (Ukkonen, 2009). In that case, ATTI is kept as a motif because it is the longest of its equivalents. The others motifs A and T are maximal because their contexts differ in different occurrences. All motifs across different strings are detected at the end of the enumeration by mapping the offsets in $\mathcal{S}$ with those in $\mathcal{S}_0$ and $\mathcal{S}_1$. This way, any motif detected in $\mathcal{S}$ can be located in any of the strings $\mathcal{S}_i$. SA and LCP are constructed in time-complexity $O(n)$ (Kärkkäinen et al., 2006), while the enumeration process is done in $O(k)$, with k defined as the number of motifs and $k < n$ (Ukkonen, 2009). This corroborate the statement done by Umemura and Church (2009): there are too many substrings to work with in corpus $O(n^2)$, but they can be grouped into a manageable number of interesting classes $O(n)$.

4.2 *n*-th Order Motifs

Let $\mathcal{R}$ be the set of motifs detected in the n strings $\mathcal{S} = \{\mathcal{S}_0, \ldots, \mathcal{S}_{n-1}\}$, with $|\mathcal{S}| = \sum_{i=1}^{n} size(\mathcal{S}_i)$. The set of motifs $\mathcal{R}$ is computed on the concatenation of all strings $\mathcal{S}_i$: $c(\mathcal{S}) = \mathcal{S}_0\$_{n-1} \ldots \mathcal{S}_{n-1}\$_0$. Second order motifs $\mathcal{R}^2$ in $\mathcal{S}$ are computed from the concatenation of the set of m strings of $\mathcal{R}$ ($c(\mathcal{R}) = \mathcal{R}_0\$_{m-1} \ldots \mathcal{R}_{m-1}\$_0$ with $m < |\mathcal{S}|$, and each $\mathcal{R}_i$ a motif in $\mathcal{S}$). The set of n-th order motifs is noted $\mathcal{R}^n$. For instance, let $c(\mathcal{S})$ be HATTIV$\$_1$ATTIAA$\$_0$. The set of motifs $\mathcal{R}$ from $c(\mathcal{S})$ is a compound of the following motifs: $\mathcal{R} = \{\texttt{ATTI}, \texttt{A}, \texttt{T}\}$. The set of repeats $\mathcal{R}^2$ consists of the motifs T (twice in ATTI and once in T) and A (once in ATTI and once in A).

FACT — The set of motifs $\mathcal{R}^n$ is a subset of $\mathcal{R}^{n-1}$.
REDUCTIO AD ABSURDUM — Let assume that $\mathcal{R}^n \not\subset \mathcal{R}^{n-1}$. In other words, $\exists m$ a motif with $m \in \mathcal{R}^n$ and $m \notin \mathcal{R}^{n-1}$. m is maximal, so it occurs with different left-contexts (denoted a and b) and different right-contexts (c and d) with $a \neq b$, $c \neq d$ and a, b, c and d being any character of $c(\mathcal{R}^{n-1})$ – including the special character £ if m starts $c(\mathcal{R}^{n-1})$. $\mathcal{R}^n$ is computed from $c(\mathcal{R}^{n-1}) = ...amc...bmd...$ with $\mathcal{R}^{n-1} = \{amc, bmd, ...\}$ and $m \notin \mathcal{R}^{n-1}$. So, amc and bmd are two motifs detected in $\mathcal{R}^{n-2}$. Because m is repeated and have two differents contexts, it is a motif and should have been detected in $\mathcal{R}^{n-2}$ thus in $\mathcal{R}^{n-1}$ as well, so $m \in \mathcal{R}^{n-1}$ — a contradiction

Figure 2 draws the number of different motifs according to their order. Because $\mathcal{R}^n \subset \mathcal{R}^{n-1}$, the number of different motifs decreases steadily whatever the corpus. The number of motifs in $\mathcal{R}^n$ drops to 0 for $n = 26$ (LIB-40, EBG-40 and MIXT-80) and $n = 25$ (MIXT-40).

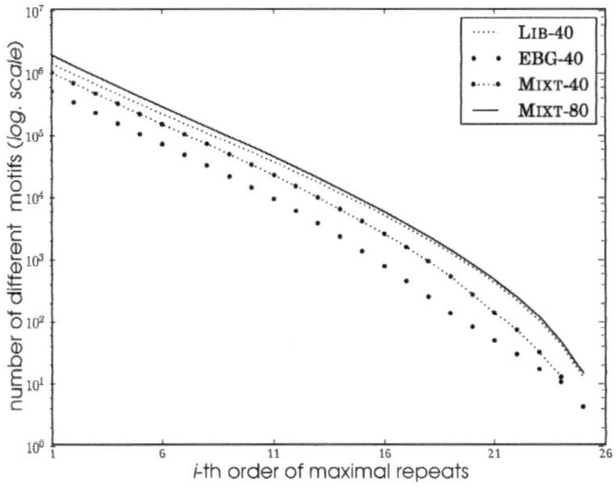

Figure 2: Evolution of the number of motifs (log. scale) according to the i-th order (LIB-40, EBG-40, MIXT-40 and MIXT-80)

The computation of 2nd order motifs is based on the same algorithm than the one used to extract motifs. The enumeration of all the 2nd order motifs is done in $O(n)$ as well. Those motifs are used to detect the repetitions encapsulated in a set of maximal repeats.

4.3 Exploiting the Differences between Character *n*-grams and Motifs

Experiments have emphasize that redundancy in n-grams have a positive impact in AA (Subsection 5.1). To explain the effect of this redundancy, this section deals with the main differences between character n-grams and motifs, and how to exploit them when dealing with vector-based representation of texts. As defined before, motifs are a condensed way to represent all substrings of a corpus. In other words, for a fixed value of n, the set of motifs of size n is a subset of all the character n-grams of a corpus (as well with variable length substrings: motifs with length in $[min, max]$ or character $[min, max]$-grams). The substrings that are not motifs are those that are only left-maximal, right-maximal (*i.e.* repeated but not maximal) or *hapax legomena*. In a supervised classification process, *hapax* have no impact because they only appear once in the training corpus or once in the test corpus.

If n-grams can catch different types of features according to n (lexical, contextual or thematic (Sun et al., 2012)), they also catch features that can be represented by substrings of size superior to n. For instance, let *abcdef* be a motif, occurring k times and none of its characters occurring elsewhere in the corpus. Because *abcdef* is maximal, each substring of *abcdef* has the same occurrence frequency k. Figure 3 shows how the use of 3-grams in a string containing the *abcdef* motif affects the vector representation of this substring. Indeed, n-grams "represent" motifs of size superior to n by adding features in the vector representation of the texts according to the frequency of those motifs.

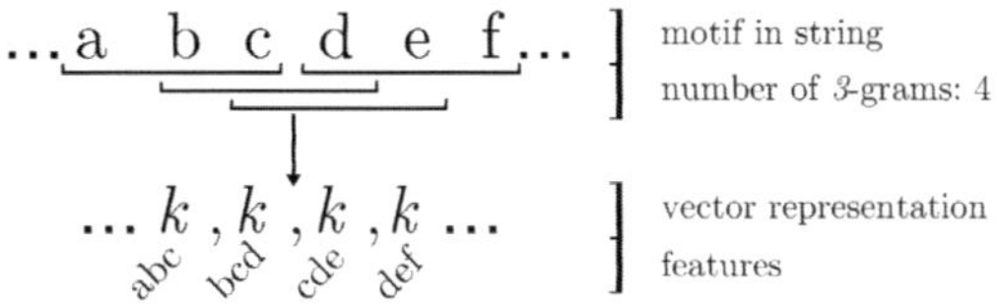

Figure 3: Substrings of a motif in a string.

Exploiting only motifs of size *3* will not allow to catch any substring of this motif with the same occurrence frequency than *abcdef* (according to the definition of a motif). Considering only some specific lengths affect the representation based on occurrence frequency, and *vise versa* according to the interdependency between frequency and length (Zipf, 1949).

2nd order motifs are used to exploit this characteristic with this assumption: a substring is more relevant than an other of same size if it encapsulates less repeated substrings. The weight function $w_{2^{nd}}(feat)$ is defined as the difference between the number of substrings of a feature and the number of motifs occurring in this feature $w_{2^{nd}}(feat) = pot(feat) - sub(feat)$. $pot(feat)$ is the potential number of substrings occurring inside a feature. $sub(feat)$ is the number of motifs occurring inside a feature and elsewhere in the corpus. $w_{2^{nd}}(feat)$ is linked to the length of the feature and two features with the same length can be weight differently. If there is only one different character between two motifs (*e.g. thing* and *things*), the weight function minimises this add: the products of the weight function and the frequency are close together. Conversely, a feature that is more than a small variation of any other motif has more importance.

With $\mathcal{S} = \{\mathcal{S}_0, \ldots, \mathcal{S}_{n-1}\}$, $\mathcal{R}$ the set of motifs from $\mathcal{S}$ and $\mathcal{R}^2$ the set of motifs from $\mathcal{R}$, each motif in $\mathcal{R}$ can be weighted according to the set of repeats $\mathcal{R}^2$. $\mathcal{R}_i$ is a motif used as a feature and $\mathcal{S}$ is the set each text of all authors. The number of different substrings in any string of size n, $pot(feat)$, is calculated with the formula $\frac{n(n+1)}{2}$ (*eq.* to the triangular number, the whole string is considered as a potential substring). The number of occurrences of each sub-repeat in $\mathcal{R}^2$ occurring in a feature $\mathcal{R}$, $sub(feat)$, is done by enumerating all the occurrences of all the motifs in a set of strings as described in Section 4.1. If each potential substring in a feature is a motif as well, then $w_{2^{nd}}(feat) = 1$. During our experiments, this weight function is compared with $w_{length}(feat) = \frac{n(n+1)}{2}$ (with n the length of the feature). Note that w_{length} cannot be easily applied to n-grams because the overlaps between contiguous n-grams make each potential substring of each n-gram appears elsewhere in the corpus.

5 Experiments

The experiments in this section examine the prediction accuracy of the proposed approach. Two sets of features with variable length are examined: n-grams and motifs. Three different ways to consider motifs are analysed: motifs with no weight, weighted by their length (using w_{length}) and weighted by 2nd order repeats (using $w_{2^{nd}}$).

A stratified 10-fold cross validation is used to validate the performances. Corpora are randomly partitioned into 10 equal size folds containing the same proportion of authors. To measure the performance of the systems, the prediction score is computed as follows: the number of correctly classified texts divided by the number of texts classified overall. SVM is used with linear kernels (adapted when the set of features is larger than the set of elements to be classified) and with the regularisation parameter $C = 1$. The aim of those experiments is to highlight the differences between motifs and n-grams. The same settings are therefore set whatever the feature, assuming that their impacts are similar on both n-grams and motifs.

5.1 Impact of the Length of Variable Substrings and Maximal Repeats

The prediction score of AA is computed in three corpora: EBG-40 (Figure 4), LIB-40 (Figure 5) and MIXT-80 (Figure 6). Each figure is constituted of 4 matrices using different sets of features: maximal repeats (*motif*), n-grams, maximal repeats weighted by length ($motif_{length}$) and maximal repeats weighted by 2nd order repeats ($motif_{2^{nd}}$). The prediction written in the coordinates (i, j) of each matrix is sourced from the use of features with length in the range $[i, j]$.

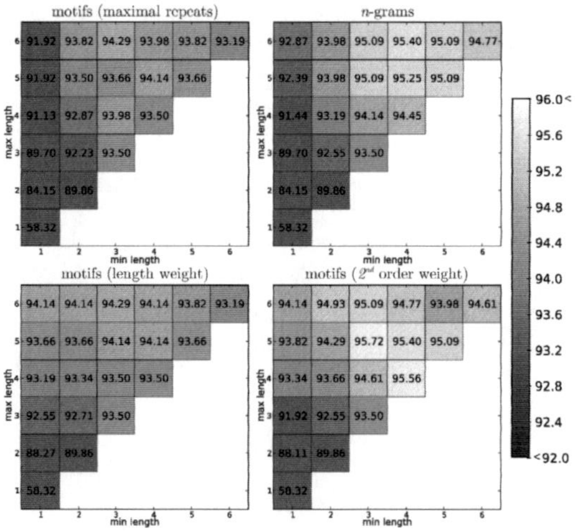

Figure 4: Prediction accuracy in EBG-40.

Whatever the corpus, the features can be ordered following their ability to correctly predict the author of a text: $motif \leq motif_{length} < n$-grams $< motif_{2^{nd}}$. The fact that $motifs < n$-grams shows the positive effect of feature redundancy. The diagonals of the matrix using $motif$ and $motif_{length}$ have the same values because a single factor affects every feature on the vector

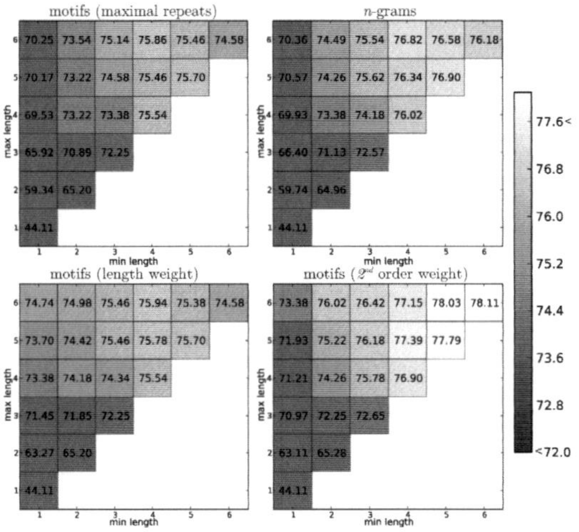

Figure 5: Prediction accuracy in LIB-40.

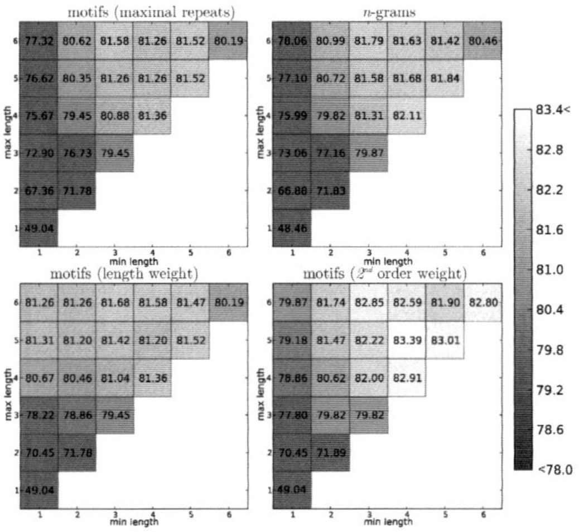

Figure 6: Prediction accuracy in MIXT-80.

representation of the texts. The overall high prediction score on the EBG corpus is explained by the bind between author and the thematic content of his written productions (for a given author, almost each of his texts is related to a single topic as sport or arts). For comparison, the systems tested by Brennan et al. (2012) obtain a prediction accuracy of approximately 80% in a sample of texts written by 40 authors in EBG as well ($\approx -15\%$). The task is more difficult on LIB because, contrary to EBG, each selected author has written texts in different thematic areas. Similar observations have been given by Stamatatos (2012) as well. The prediction on the three corpora has also been computed using $motif_{2nd}$ whatever their length, obtaining the following scores: 66.40% on EBG-40, 48.20% on LIB-40 and 54.21% MIXT-80. This emphasizes the necessity of selecting a subspace of *motifs* in AA. From these experiments, the best parameters for the length of the features are selected by computing the average of each prediction score on each matrix for each couple of parameters $[min, max]$ length (Table 4).

	best length parameter $[min, max]$	average prediction
n-grams	[4, 6]	84.61%
motifs	[4, 6]	83.69%
motifs (length)	[4, 6]	83.88%
motifs (2nd order)	[4, 5]	**85.39%**

Table 4: Best parameters on LIB-40, EBG-40 and MIXT-80.

$motif_{2nd}$ features obtain the smallest range of values among the set of parameters computed. Note that the best length parameter extracted for all the corpora is not necessarily the best parameters for each corpus (*i.e.* $motif_{2nd}$ have better results with parameters $[6, 6]$ in LIB than with $[4, 5]$). Aside from offering a condensed representation of substrings, motifs need less elements to perform better than other methods. The experiments show better results with variable length features than with fixed length ones. Using a large range of size in substring selection is not systematically the best option according to the results. For instance, a 4.01% discrepancy is observable between the range $[1, 6]$ and the optimal range $[4, 5]$ on the results on LIB using $motif_{2nd}$ features (Figure 5).

5.2 Influence of the Number of Authors on the Prediction and the Number of Features

Given the best parameters for each type of features (Table 4), the following experiments draw the evolution of the prediction based upon the number of authors (Figure 7).

Whatever the corpus and the type of features, the prediction score decreases steadily as the number of author increases. The corpus with the worst results is still LIB where the prediction score decreases from 92.04% to 77.38% (89.60% to 76.82% with *n*-grams). The prediction using $motif_{2nd}$ is higher than with the others methods. Moreover, weighting features by a factor of their length ($motif_{length}$) does not enhance significantly *motif*-based representations of text. The numbers of features used for the prediction is given on Figure 8. This number of features is the average of the length of the vector representing texts in each fold of the cross-validation.

Considering the motifs of length $[4, 5]$ reduce

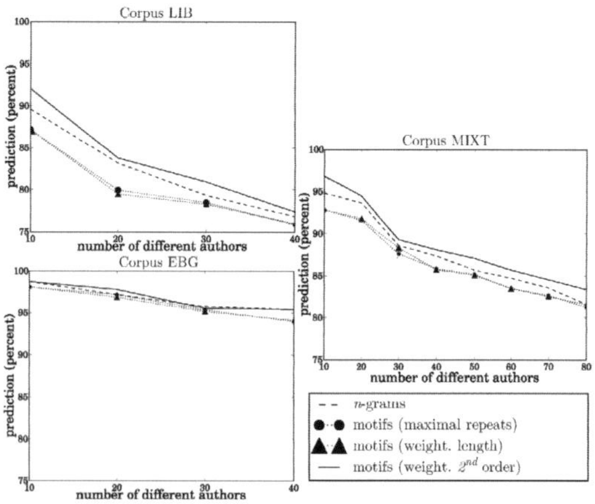

Figure 7: Evolution of the prediction accuracy according to the number of authors.

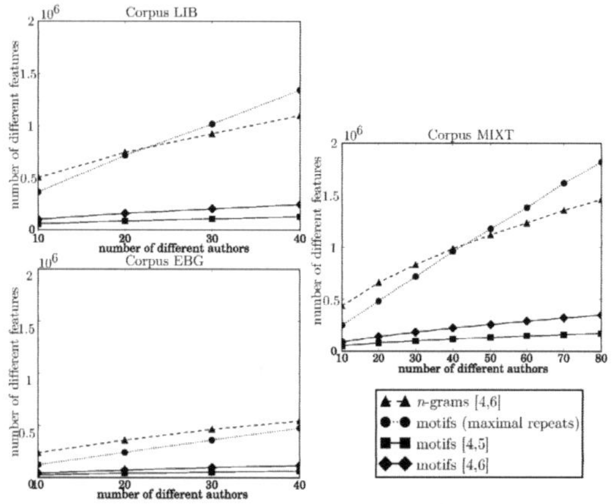

Figure 8: Evolution of the number of features according to the number of authors.

considerably the number of features with regards to the number of substrings with size $[4, 6]$ or the number of motifs of any size. The number of motifs grows linearly with the number of authors (*i.e.* with the size of the corpus). The number of substrings with length $[4, 6]$ is higher than the number of motifs at the beginning of the curve, but is lower after a certain amount of data due to its sublinear distribution. The number of motifs of size $[4, 5]$ seems to scale with the increase of data processed.

5.3 Monolingual Evaluation from Multilingual Corpora

The corpus MIXT is composed of the LIB corpus in French and the EBG corpus in English, both languages share pattern substrings because of their common origin. The use of two similar languages is well adapted to analyse the effects of the features in multilingual corpora. Table 5 shows the prediction accuracy on the two monolingual corpora, LIB and EBG, after applying the above methods on the multilingual corpus MIXT. The aim is to analyse how the features behave when different languages are processed at the same time.

Substrings with length in the range $[4, 6]$

nb. of authors	EBG	EBG from MIXT	LIB	LIB from MIXT
10	**98.75%**	**98.75%**	89.60%	**91.13%**
20	**97.20%**	96.89%	**83.15%**	82.69%
30	**95.79%**	94.85%	**79.34%**	78.65%
40	**95.40%**	94.10%	**76.82%**	75.03%

Motifs weighted by 2nd order motifs with length in $[4, 5]$

nb. of authors	EBG	EBG from MIXT	LIB	LIB from MIXT
10	**98.75%**	**98.75%**	92.01%	**92.35%**
20	**97.83%**	97.52%	**83.77%**	83.46%
30	95.59%	**96.84%**	**80.93%**	80.08%
40	**95.40%**	95.09%	77.38%	**77.47%**

Table 5: Predictions on LIB and EBG from the MIXT corpus using substrings with length in $[4, 6]$ and motifs weighted by 2nd order motifs with length in $[4, 5]$.

The results with the two settings, the multilingual corpus and each corpus processed independently, are close to each other. However, some improvements can be seen with the use of $motif_{2^{nd}}$, where in more cases the results are better when EBG and LIB are handled together. Using *n*-grams, the difference of results grows when the number of authors increases. On the contrary, using *motifs* seem to be adapted to this issue.

6 Conclusion

We proposed an efficient alternative to variable length *n*-grams approaches for AA with the use of maximal repeats in strings. They improve classical substring approaches in two major ways. First, maximal repeats are, in essence, non-redundant features compared with *n*-grams. Their maximality characteristic avoids the use of redundant occurrence equivalent substrings in corpora. This considerably reduces the feature space size and we advocate that they are a best breeding ground for variable subset selection (as Genetic Algorithm, Simulated Annealing, or Information Gain). Second, with the second order maximal repeats, the feature search space is condensed efficiently and propose a new way to enhance the prediction accuracy in AA. We have emphasize the positive effect of redundancy in features, and by doing so we validated the assumption that a long repeated substring is more important if it does not contain too many sub-repeats, thus guaranteeing consistency. We hope this research will herald more improvements in substring-based Authorship Attribution.

References

Ahmed Abbasi and Hsinchun Chen. 2008. Writeprints: A stylometric approach to identity-level identification and similarity detection in cyberspace. *ACM Transactions on Information Systems (TOIS)*, 26(2):7.

Emily M. Bender. 2009. Linguistically naïve != language independent: Why NLP needs linguistic typology. In *Proceedings of the EACL 2009 Workshop on the Interaction Between Linguistics and Computational Linguistics: Virtuous, Vicious or Vacuous?*, ILCL '09, pages 26–32. ACL.

Michael Brennan, Sadia Afroz, and Rachel Greenstadt. 2012. Adversarial stylometry: Circumventing authorship recognition to preserve privacy and anonymity. *ACM Transactions on Information and System Security (TISSEC)*, 15(3):12.

Carole E Chaski. 2001. Empirical evaluations of language-based author identification techniques. *Forensic Linguistics*, 8:1–65.

Sara El Manar El Bouanani and Ismail Kassou. 2014. Authorship analysis studies: A survey. *International Journal of Computer Applications*, 86:22–29.

Richard S Forsyth and David I Holmes. 1996. Feature-finding for text classification. *Literary and Linguistic Computing*, 11(4):163–174.

Jack Grieve. 2007. Quantitative authorship attribution: An evaluation of techniques. *Literary and linguistic computing*, 22(3):251–270.

Lucian Ilie and William F Smyth. 2011. Minimum unique substrings and maximum repeats. *Fundamenta Informaticae*, 110(1):183–195.

Gary Kacmarcik and Michael Gamon. 2006. Obfuscating document stylometry to preserve author anonymity. In *Proceedings of the COLING/ACL on Main conference poster sessions*, pages 444–451. Association for Computational Linguistics.

Juha Kärkkäinen, Peter Sanders, and Stefan Burkhardt. 2006. Linear work suffix array construction. *Journal of the ACM*, 53(6):918–936.

Moshe Koppel, Jonathan Schler, and Shlomo Argamon. 2009. Computational methods in authorship attribution. *Journal of the American Society for information Science and Technology*, 60(1):9–26.

Moshe Koppel, Jonathan Schler, and Shlomo Argamon. 2011. Authorship attribution in the wild. *Language Resources and Evaluation*, 45(1):83–94.

Fuchun Peng, Dale Schuurmans, Shaojun Wang, and Vlado Keselj. 2003. Language independent authorship attribution using character level language models. In *Proceedings of the tenth conference on European chapter of the Association for Computational Linguistics-Volume 1*, pages 267–274. Association for Computational Linguistics.

Efstathios Stamatatos. 2006. Ensemble-based author identification using character n-grams. In *Proceedings of the 3rd International Workshop on Text-based Information Retrieval*, pages 41–46.

Efstathios Stamatatos. 2009. A survey of modern authorship attribution methods. *Journal of the American Society for Information Science and Technology*, 60(3):538–556.

Efstathios Stamatatos. 2012. On the robustness of authorship attribution based on character n-gram features. *JL & Pol'y*, 21:421.

Jianwen Sun, Zongkai Yang, Sanya Liu, and Pei Wang. 2012. Applying stylometric analysis techniques to counter anonymity in cyberspace. *Journal of Networks*, 7(2).

Fiona J Tweedie, Sameer Singh, and David I Holmes. 1996. Neural network applications in stylometry: The Federalist papers. *Computers and the Humanities*, 30(1):1–10.

Esko Ukkonen. 2009. Maximal and minimal representations of gapped and non-gapped motifs of a string. *Theoretical Computer Science*, 410(43):4341–4349.

Kyoji Umemura and Kenneth Church. 2009. Substring statistics. In *Computational Linguistics and Intelligent Text Processing*, pages 53–71. Springer.

George Kingsley Zipf. 1949. *Human Behaviour and the Principle of Least-Effort : an Introduction to Human Ecology*. Addison-Wesley.

Improving Event Detection with Active Learning

Kai Cao Xiang Li Miao Fan Ralph Grishman
Computer Science Department
New York University
719 Broadway, New York, NY, 10003
{kcao, xiangli, grishman}@cs.nyu.edu
fanmiao.cslt.thu@gmail.com

Abstract

Event Detection (ED), one aspect of Information Extraction, involves identifying instances of specified types of events in text. Much of the research on ED has been based on the specifications of the 2005 ACE [Automatic Content Extraction] event task[1], and the associated annotated corpus. However, as the event instances in the ACE corpus are not evenly distributed, some frequent expressions involving ACE events do not appear in the training data, adversely affecting performance. In this paper, we demonstrate the effectiveness of a *Pattern Expansion* technique to import frequent patterns extracted from external corpora to boost ED performance. The experimental results show that our pattern-based system with the expanded patterns can achieve 70.4% (with 1.6% absolute improvement) F-measure over the baseline, an advance over current state-of-the-art systems.

1 Introduction

Event Extraction involves the extraction of particular types of events along with their arguments. In this paper we shall focus on a subproblem, that of Event Detection (ED) – identifying instances of specified types of events in text. In keeping with the design of the ACE [Automatic Content Extraction] Event task, we will associate each event mention with a *trigger*, which is a word or a sequence of words (most often a single verb or nominalization) that expresses that event. More precisely, our task involves identifying event triggers and classifying them into specific types. For instance, according to the ACE 2005 annotation guidelines[2], in the sentence "*She was **killed** in an automobile accident yesterday*", an event detection system should be able to recognize the word "*killed*" as a trigger for the event DIE. This task is quite challenging, as the same event might appear in the form of various trigger expressions and an expression might represent different events in different contexts. ED is a crucial component in the overall Event Extraction task, which also requires event argument identification and argument role labeling.

Most recent research work on the ACE Event Detection task relies on pattern-based or feature-based approaches, creating classifiers for trigger labeling. Since the distribution of ACE event types in the corpus is skewed, the test data includes some relatively common event expressions that do not occur in the training data. To overcome this problem, we propose to use active learning to help include more patterns for boosting ED performance. These patterns will be extracted from external corpora, such as the *EnglishGigaWord* corpus, labeled, and added to the training data. The experimental results demonstrate that our pattern-based system with the expanded patterns can achieve 70.4% (with 1.6% absolute improvement) F-measure over the baseline, an advance over the state-of-the-art systems.

The paper is organized as follows: In Section 2, we will introduce how to apply pattern expansion inside an active learning framework to improve ED performance. We will describe our ED systems including the baseline and enhanced system utilizing pattern expansion in Section 3, and experimental results as well as detailed discussion and comparison will be presented in Section 4. We will compare our approach with related work in

[1] http://www.itl.nist.gov/iad/mig/tests/ace/

[2] https://www.ldc.upenn.edu/sites/www.ldc.upenn.edu/files/english-events-guidelines-v5.4.3.pdf

Proceedings of Recent Advances in Natural Language Processing, pages 72–77,
Hissar, Bulgaria, Sep 7–9 2015.

Section 5, and Section 6 will conclude this work and list our future research directions.

2 Pattern Expansion

Supervised training can be moderately effective in creating an Event Detection system, but the process of annotating the large corpus required for good performance can be very expensive and time-consuming. The ACE 2005 corpus, with about 300,000 words, is one of the largest such corpora, with detailed event annotations covering 33 event types. Nonetheless, many expressions of these event types are not included, limiting performance of the trained system.

To significantly improve coverage through supervised training would require annotation of a corpus several times larger, which would be prohibitively expensive. Instead we used an active learning approach, in which we identified common constructs which were not represented in the original training corpus, selected examples of these constructs and presented these examples to the user for event annotation. In more detail:

1. Computing the frequency of dependency relations: Since our pattern-based framework is based on syntactic patterns taken from dependency parses, we select examples to be labeled based on their dependency relations. We use a large general news corpus to compute frequencies and select particular types of dependency relations (direct object and prepositional object).

2. Filtering Step: Select dependency relations for which the governor (verb) has appeared as a trigger in the training corpus but the dependency relation as a whole has not appeared in the training corpus.

3. For each high-frequency dependency relation, pick the sentence with at least 5 tokens whose dependency tree contains this dependency relation and maximizes the following ranking score function:

$$score(s) = \begin{cases} 0 & len(s) < 5 \\ \dfrac{\prod_{1 \leq i \leq n} freq(w_i)}{len(s)} & len(s) \geq 5 \end{cases} \quad (1)$$

   where w_i is the ith word in the sentence s, $freq(w_i)$ is the frequency probability of word w_i in the corpus, and $len(s)$ is the number of tokens of the sentence s[3]. This metric favors short sentences with common words, which should be easy to label.

   With this function, the most representative instance matching a pattern would be extracted. For example, if we try to find an instance containing the pattern "`take office`", the following sentence would be extracted:

   He is to take office today.

   This sentence is an instance of the event *Start-Position*.

4. Add the selected sentences: Annotate the selected instances with respect to the presence of event triggers and incorporate the annotated instances into the training data set.

5. Compare the results: Compare the performance of event detection applying pattern expansion with the AceJet baseline (without pattern expansion)

3 System Description

Jet, the Java Extraction Toolkit[4], provides a set of NLP components which can be combined to create information extraction systems. AceJet[5] is a subsystem of Jet to extract the types of information (entities, relations, and events) annotated on the ACE corpora. The AceJet Event Extraction framework is a combination of a pattern-based system and feature-based system.

Training proceeds in three passes over the annotated training corpus. Pass 1 collects all the event patterns, where a pattern cosists of a trigger and a set of arguments along with the path from the trigger to each argument; both the dependency path and the linear sequence path (a series of noun chunks and words) are recorded. Pass 2 records the frequency with which each pattern is associated with an event type – the 'event score'. Pass 3 treats the event score as a feature, combines it with a small number of other features and trains a maximum entropy model.

[3]The stop words are not counted here.

[4]`http://cs.nyu.edu/grishman/jet/jet.html`

[5]`http://cs.nyu.edu/grishman/jet/guide/ACEutilities.html`

At test time, to classify a candidate trigger (any word which has appearred at least once as a trigger in the training corpus) the tagger finds the best match between an event pattern and the input sentence and computes an event score. This score, along with other features, serves as input to the maximum entropy model to make the final ED prediction. (This brief description omits the classifiers for event arguments and argument roles.)

We can see from Table 1 that the resulting system performance is competitive with other recent system results, such as the joint beam search described in (Li et al., 2013).

4 Experiments

In this section, we will introduce the evaluation dataset, compare the performance of applying pattern expansion with other state-of-the-art systems, and discuss the contribution of pattern expansion.

4.1 Data

We used the ACE 2005 corpus as our testbed. For comparison, we used the same test set with 40 newswire articles (672 sentences) as in (Ji and Grishman, 2008; Liao and Grishman, 2010) for the experiments, and randomly selected 30 other documents (863 sentences) from different genres as the development set. The remaining 529 documents (14,840 sentences) are used for training.

Regarding the correctness criteria, following the previous work (Ji and Grishman, 2008; Liao and Grishman, 2010; Ji and Grishman, 2011; Li et al., 2013), a trigger candidate is counted as correct if its event subtype and offsets match those of a reference trigger. The ACE 2005 corpus has 33 event subtypes that, along with one class "*None*" for the non-trigger tokens, constitutes a 34-class classification problem in this work.

Finally we use *Precision* (*P*), *Recall* (*R*), and *F-measure* (*F1*) to evaluate the overall performance.

4.2 Performance Comparison

Table 1 presents the overall performance of the systems with gold-standard entity mention and type information. We can see that our system with active learning can improve the performance over our baseline, and also advances the current state-of-the-art systems. In the test sentence, "*The president is to **take office** tomorrow*", for instance, the system with expanded patterns can correctly identify the *Personnel:Start-Position* event, whereas the AceJet baseline even failed to recognize it as an event instance. Another example is, "*... the anti-communist Gen. Suharto **seized power** in 1965*", where the expanded pattern successfully detects the event trigger with the correct type *Personnel:Start-Position*.

4.3 Discussion

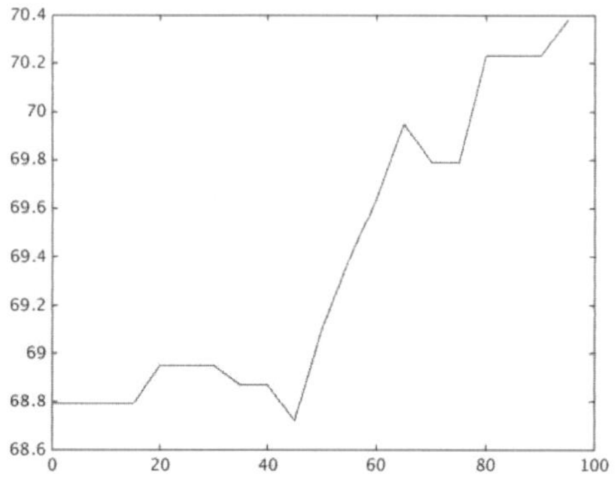

Figure 1: Semi-supervised pattern expansion performance (% in *F-Measure*)

In Figure 1, the x-axis is the number of instances added to the training data, while the y-axis is the corresponding F-measure. We can see from Figure 1 that the pattern expansion helps improve the performance; however the improvement is only modest. This is mainly because the frequent dependency pairs may not be closely related to events and not all dependency pairs align with ACE event patterns very well. Since the pattern-based framework is based on matching dependency relation types and named entity types, noun groups play a central role to identify the events. Therefore, we focus on two types of frequent dependency relations:

- **direct object**
  The object of a verb plays a significant role in understanding the phrase. For example, the phrase "*take office*" means that a duty or title is assumed while other phrases like "*take an apple*" would not trigger an ACE event.

- **preposition and object**
  The noun in the prepositional phrase sometimes conveys as much or more information than the verb. For example, "*fight for independence*" is generally a *Demonstrate* event.

Methods	*P*	*R*	*F1*
Sentence-level in (Ji and Grishman, 2011)	67.6	53.5	59.7
MaxEnt classifier with local features in (Li et al., 2013)	74.5	59.1	65.9
Joint beam search with local features in (Li et al., 2013)	73.7	59.3	65.7
Joint beam search with local and global features in (Li et al., 2013)	73.7	62.3	67.5
Cross-entity in (Ji and Grishman, 2011) †	72.9	64.3	68.3
MaxEnt classifier with local features	70.8	61.4	65.7
AceJet baseline	66.4	71.4	68.8
AceJet system with pattern expansion	68.9	72.0	**70.4**

Table 1: Performance comparison (%) with the state-of-the-art systems. † beyond sentence level.

In contrast, there are three main classes of dependency relations which generally are not helpful in improving ED peerformance::

1. **Time Patterns**
   Time expressions generally do not help identify the event type. For example, the phrase "*tell Michael on Tuesday*' contains a time-modifying prepositional phrase "*on Tuesday*", but this time modifier plays little role in determining the type of the event. The verb "*tell*" is by itself a strong indicator of a *Contact* event, with the object also playing some role in the classification.

2. **Sports Patterns**
   Since ACE events are mainly about commercial and security-related news, patterns related to sports should be removed. For example, "*win a title*" is one of the top 5 high-frequency dependency pairs in the *EnglishGigaWord* copus. This pattern appears mostly in a sports-related sentence or article. To remove the sports-related patterns, we plan to build a text classifier and exclude articles classified as sports-related from our frequency counts and as sources of examples.

3. **Redundant Patterns**
   Some verbs strongly favor a single event type. For example, "*die in hospital*" is a high-frequency pattern in *EnglishGigaWord*, however the verb "*die*" is sufficient to identify the *Die* event, whether a man dies in hospital, a room or on the road. Even if this pattern did not appear in the training data, adding it during pattern expansion will do little to improve event classifier accuracy because there are many *Die* events in the training data whose trigger is the verb "*die*". Other information from context will have minimal effect compared to the contribution of the verb "*die*" itself. We believe that such cases can be identified as patterns with triggers a large fraction of whose training examples represent the same event type.

Of the 100 examples tagged, 28 were positive (event triggers); of the 28, we considered 14 to be redundant (not helpful).

5 Related Work

Although there have been quite a few distinct designs for event extraction systems, most are loosely based on using patterns to detect instances of events, where the patterns consist of a predicate, *event trigger*, and constraints on its local syntactic context. The constraints may involve specific lexical items or semantic classes.

Efforts to improve event extraction performance have focused largely on either improving the pattern-matching kernel or adding new reasonable features. Most event extraction frameworks are feature-based systems. Some of the feature-based systems are based on phrase or sentence level extraction. Several recent studies use high-level information to aid local event extraction systems. For example, (Finkel et al., 2005), (Maslennikov and seng Chua, 2007), (Ji and Grishman, 2008) and (Patwardhan and Riloff, 2007) tried to use discourse, document, or cross-document information to improve information extraction. Other research extends these approaches by introducing cross-event information to enhance the performance of multi-event-type extraction systems. (Liao and Grishman, 2010) use information about other types of events to make predictions or resolve ambiguities regarding a given event. (Li et al., 2013) implements a joint model via structured prediction with cross-event features.

There have been several efforts over the past decade to develop semi-supervised methods for learning such pattern sets. One thread began with Riloff's observation that patterns occurring with substantially higher frequency in relevant documents than in irrelevant documents are likely to be good extraction patterns (Riloff, 1996). (Sudo et al., 2003) sorted relevant from irrelevant documents using a topic description and information retrieval engine. (Yangarber et al., 2000; Yangarber, 2003) developed a bootstrapping approach, starting with some seed patterns, using these patterns to identify some relevant documents, using these documents to identify additional patterns, etc. This approach was further refined in (Surdeanu et al., 2006), which explored alternative pattern ranking strategies. An alternative approach was adopted in (Stevenson and Greenwood, 2005), which used Wordnet-based similarity to expand an initial set of event patterns. (Huang and Riloff, 2012) developed a bootstrapping system to discover new triggers with selected roles. For example, the word "*sniper*" is very likely to be the *agent* of a *Die* event.

There has been growing interest over the last few years in applying active learning methods to reduce the annotation burden involved in developing corpus-trained NLP modules. Active learning has been applied to a variety of Information Extraction tasks, including name tagging, parsing, partial parsing, relation extraction, etc. (Majidi and Crane, 2013). We have previously investigated active learning methods based on co-testing for training relation extractors for ACE relations (Fu and Grishman, 2013). We have also applied such methods for the active learning of ACE event extractors, although with a very different approach (based on the distribution of event triggers across sentences) from that proposed here (Liao and Grishman, 2011).

6 Conclusion and Future Work

To date, the use of supervised methods for creating event extractors has been limited by their poor performance even using large annotated training corpora.

In this paper, we demonstrate the effectiveness of active learning to import more patterns extracted from external corpora to boost Event Detection performance. Since these newly added patterns may never appear in the training data, they can complement the patterns generated from the original training data to enhance ED performance. The experimental results show that our pattern-based system with the expanded patterns can achieve 70.4% (with 1.6% absolute improvement) F-measure over the baseline, an advance over current state-of-the-art systems.

These results were obtained using relatively simple criteria for selecting examples to label: new high-frequency dependency relations involving known triggers. We intend to explore several richer criteria which have have been used for semi-supervised ED, such as similarity measures derived from WordNet, as well as newer methods such as word embeddings using neural network models. This should allow us to improve the efficiency of our active learning by avoiding less promising examples and to improve final ED perfomance by including triggers not present in the training set.

References

Jenny Rose Finkel, Trond Grenager, and Christopher Manning. 2005. Incorporating non-local information into information extraction systems by gibbs sampling. In *Proceedings of ACL*.

Lisheng Fu and Ralph Grishman. 2013. An efficient active learning framework for new relation types. In *Proceedings of the Sixth International Joint Conference on Natural Language Processing*.

Ruihong Huang and Ellen Riloff. 2012. Bootstrapped training of event extraction classifiers. In *Proceedings of EACL*.

Heng Ji and Ralph Grishman. 2008. Refining event extraction through cross-document inference. In *Proceedings of ACL*.

Heng Ji and Ralph Grishman. 2011. Using cross-entity inference to improve event extraction. In *Proceedings of ACL*.

Qi Li, Heng Ji, and Liang Huang. 2013. Joint event extraction via structured prediction with global features. In *Proceedings of ACL*.

Shasha Liao and Ralph Grishman. 2010. Using document level cross-event inference to improve event extraction. In *Proceedings of ACL*.

Shasha Liao and Ralph Grishman. 2011. Using prediction from sentential scope to build a pseudo co-testing learner for event extraction. In *Proceedings of 5th International Joint Conference on Natural Language Processing*.

Saeed Majidi and Gregory Crane. 2013. Active learning for dependency parsing by a committee of parsers. *IWPT-2013*.

Mstislav Maslennikov and Tat seng Chua. 2007. A multi-resolution framework for information extraction from free text. In *Proceedings of ACL*.

Siddharth Patwardhan and Ellen Riloff. 2007. Effective information extraction with semantic affinity patterns and relevant regions. In *Proceedings of EMNLP*.

Ellen Riloff. 1996. Automatically generating extraction patterns from untagged text. In *Proceedings of AAAI*.

Mark Stevenson and Mark Greenwood. 2005. A semantic approach to ie pattern induction. In *Proceedings of ACL*.

Kiyoshi Sudo, Satoshi Sekine, and Ralph Grishman. 2003. An improved extraction pattern representation model for automatic ie pattern acquisition. In *Proceedings of ACL*.

Mihai Surdeanu, Jordi Turmo, and Alicia Ageno. 2006. Counter-training in discovery of semantic pattern. In *Proceedings of EACL 2006 Workshop on Adaptive Text Extraction and Mining (ATEM 2006)*.

Roman Yangarber, Ralph Grishman, Pasi Tapanainen, and Silja Huttunen. 2000. Automatic acquisition of domain knowledge for information extraction. In *Proceedings of Coling*.

Roman Yangarber. 2003. Counter-training in discovery of semantic pattern. In *Proceedings of ACL*.

Improving Event Detection with Dependency Regularization

Kai Cao **Xiang Li** **Ralph Grishman**
Computer Science Department
New York University
719 Broadway, New York, NY, 10003
{kcao, xiangli, grishman}@cs.nyu.edu

Abstract

Event Detection (ED) is an Information Extraction task which involves identifying instances of specified types of events in text. Most recent research on Event Detection relies on pattern-based or feature-based approaches, trained on annotated corpora, to recognize combinations of event *triggers*, arguments, and other contextual information. These combinations may each appear in a variety of linguistic forms. Not all of these event expressions will have appeared in the training data, thus adversely affecting ED performance. In this paper, we demonstrate the effectiveness of *Dependency Regularization* techniques to generalize the patterns extracted from the training data to boost ED performance. The experimental results on the ACE 2005 corpus show that our pattern-based system with the expanded patterns can achieve 70.49% (with 2.57% absolute improvement) F-measure over the baseline, which advances the state-of-the-art for such systems.

1 Introduction

Event Detection (ED) involves identifying instances of specified types of events in text, which is an important but difficult Information Extraction (IE) task. Associated with each event mention is a phrase, the event trigger (most often a single verb or nominalization), which evokes that event. More precisely, our task involves identifying event triggers and classifying them into specific types. For instance, according to the ACE 2005 annotation guidelines[1], in the sentence "*She was* ***killed*** *in an automobile accident yesterday*", an event detection system should be able to recognize the word "*killed*" as a trigger for the event DIE. This task is quite challenging, as the same event might appear in the form of various trigger expressions and an expression might represent different events in different contexts. ED is a crucial component in the overall Event Extraction task, which also requires event argument identification and argument role labeling.

Most recent research on Automatic Content Extraction (ACE) Event Detection task relies on pattern-based or feature-based approaches to building classifiers for event trigger labeling. Although the training corpus is quite large (300,000 words), the test data will inevitably contain some event expressions that never occur in the training data. To address this problem, we propose several *Dependency Regularization* methods to help generalize the syntactic patterns extracted from the training data in order to boost ED performance. Among the syntactic representations, dependency relations serve as important features or part of a pattern-based framework in IE systems, and play a significant role in IE approaches. These proposed regularization rules will be applied either to the dependency parse outputs of the candidate sentences or to the patterns themselves to facilitate detecting the event instances. The experimental results demonstrate that our pattern-based system with the expanded patterns can achieve 70.49% (with 2.57% absolute improvement) F-measure over the baseline, which is an advance over the state-of-the-art systems.

The paper is organized as follows: In Section 2, we will describe the role of dependency analysis in event detection and how dependency regularization methods can improve ED performance. We will describe our ED systems including the baseline and enhanced system utilizing dependency regularization in Section 3, and present experi-

[1] https://www.ldc.upenn.edu/sites/www.ldc.upenn.edu/files/english-events-guidelines-v5.4.3.pdf

Proceedings of Recent Advances in Natural Language Processing, pages 78–83,
Hissar, Bulgaria, Sep 7–9 2015.

mental results in Section 4. We will discuss related work in Section 5, and Section 6 will conclude this work and list our research directions.

2 Dependency Regularization

The ACE 2005 Event Guidelines specify a set of 33 types of events; these have been widely used for research on event extracton over the past decade.

Some trigger words are unambiguous indicators of particular types of events. For example, the word *murder* indicates an event of type *Die*. However, most words have multiple senses and so may be associated with multiple types of events. Many of these cases can be disambiguated based on the semantic types of the trigger arguments:

- *fire* can be either an ATTACK event ("fire a weapon") or and END-POSITION event ("fire a person"), with the cases distinguashable by the semantic type of the direct object. *discharge* has the same ambiguity and the same disambiguation rule.
- *leave* can be either a TRANSPORT event ("he left the building") or an END-POSITION event ("he left the administration"), again generally distinguishable by the type of the direct object.

Given a training corpus annotated with triggers and event arguments we can assemble a set of frames and link them to particular event types. Each frame will record the event arguments and their syntactic (dependency) relation to the trigger. When decoding new text, we will parse it with a dependency parser, look for a matching frame, and tag the trigger candidate with the corresponding event type.

One complication is that the frames may be embedded in different syntactic structures: verbal and nominal forms, relative clauses, active and passive voice, etc. Because of the limited size of the training corpus, some triggers will appear with frames not seen in the training corpus. To fill these gaps, we will adopt a dual approach using a set of *dependency regularization* rules: in some cases we will transform the syntactic structure of the input to reduce variation; in other cases we will expand the patterns to handle a wider variety of input.

We describe here three of the regulaization rules we use:

1. verb chain regularization
2. transparent word regularization
3. nominalization regularization

2.1 Verb Chain Regularization

We use a fast dependency parser (Tratz and Hovy, 2011) that analyzes multi-word verb groups (with auxiliaries) into chains with the first word at the head of the chain. *Verb Chain (vch) Regularization* reverses the verb chains to place the main (final) verb at the top of the dependency parse tree. This reduces the variation in the dependency paths from trigger to arguments due to differences in tense, aspect, and modality. Here is an example sentence containing a verb chain:

Kobe has defeated Michael . (1)

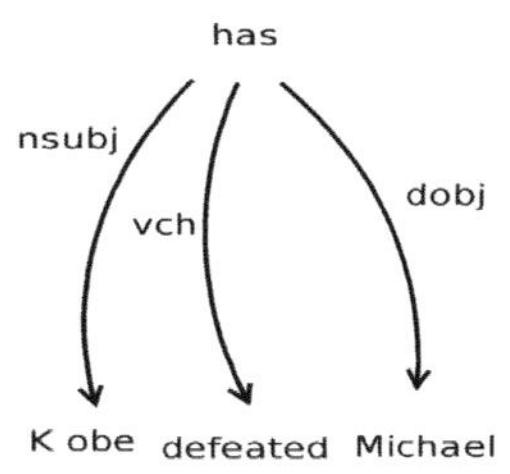

Figure 1: Original Dependency Tree

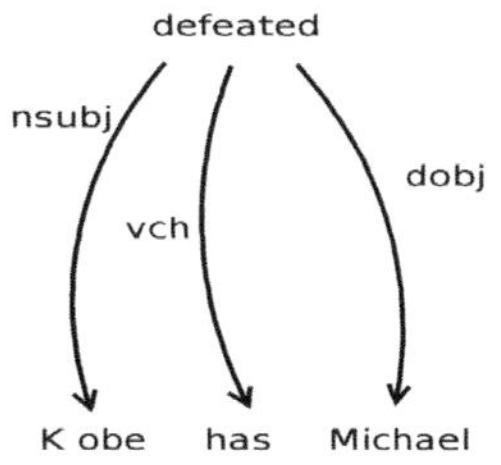

Figure 2: Dependency Tree with *Verb Chain Regularization*

In the above sentence, *"has"* is originally recognized as the root of the dependency parse tree, while *"defeated"* is the dependent of the word *"has"*. The dependency label of `(has, defeated)` is *vch*. However, the semantic head of the sequence (the word which determines the event type) is the last word in the verb chain. To bring the trigger and its arguments closer, we regularize the dependency structure by making the last verb in this chain the head of the whole verb chain. A further example:

You must come to school tomorrow . (2)

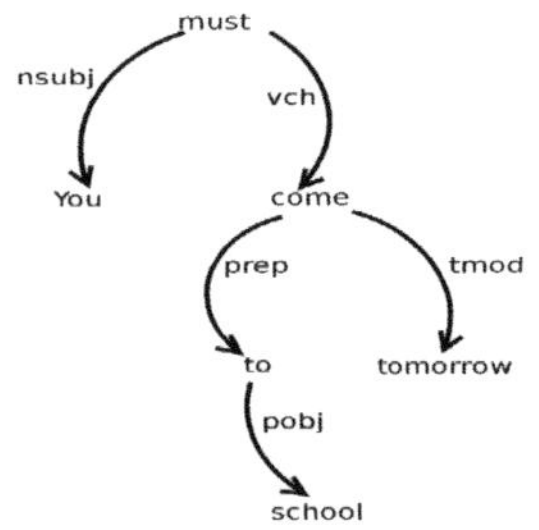

Figure 3: Original Dependency Tree

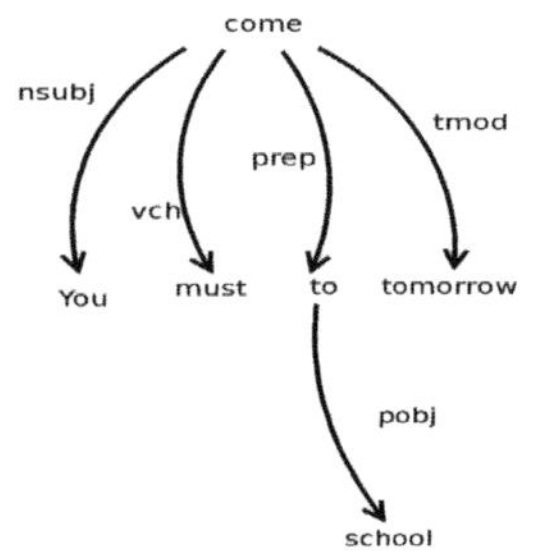

Figure 4: Dependency Tree with *Verb Chain Regularization*

2.2 Transparent Word Regularization

Some words, such as those expressing quantities, are semantically 'transparent': they take on the semantic type of their object. For purposes of determining event types, we want to 'look through' such words in the dependency parse. We do so by restructuring the tree. This is one of the most useful dependency regularization rules, since the dependency path is shortened and the head should reach the "real" dependent directly.

The army killed thousands of people . (3)

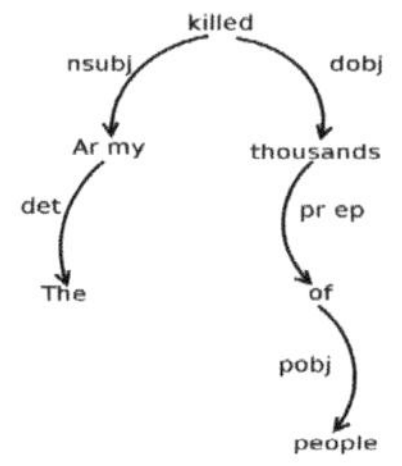

Figure 5: Original Dependency Tree

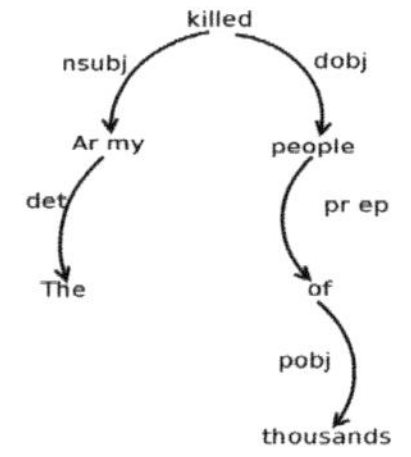

Figure 6: Dependency Tree with *Transparent Regularization*

In this case the semantic type of the object of the verb "*kill*" is determined by the word "*people*" instead of the word "*thousands*". Especially in the pattern-based framework, this kind of improvement helps substantially in finding the roles of the events.

2.3 Nominalization Regularization

Most types of events can be expressed by verbal or nominal constructions. However, in a number of cases the ACE training corpus includes the verbal construction but not the corresponding nominal one. We addressed this problem by automatically generating the nominal pattern from the verbal one. (The reverse case, with only a nominal pattern, was less frequent.)

Nomlex (NOMinalization LEXicon) is a dictionary of English nominalizations developed at New York University under the direction of Catherine Macleod. NOMLEX seeks not only to describe the allowed complements for a nominalization, but also to relate the nominal complements to the arguments of the corresponding verb. Therefore with Nomlex we can expand the patterns evoked

Methods	P	R	F
Sentence-level in (Ji and Grishman, 2011)	67.6	53.5	59.7
MaxEnt classifier with local features in (Li et al., 2013)	74.5	59.1	65.9
Joint beam search with local features in (Li et al., 2013)	73.7	59.3	65.7
Joint beam search with local and global features in (Li et al., 2013)	73.7	62.3	67.5
Cross-entity in (Ji and Grishman, 2011) †	72.9	64.3	68.3
AceJet baseline system	65.4	70.6	67.9
AceJet with dependency regularization	**68.2**	**72.8**	**70.4**

Table 1: Performance comparison (%) with the state-of-the-art systems. † beyond sentence level.

by verb triggers to patterns evoked by noun triggers. This translation is based on the correspondence between a verb with its arguments and a nominalization with its arguments.

For example, the sentence "*Microsoft acquired Nokia yesterday*" is an instance of the *Transfer-Ownership* event. "*The acquisition of Nokia from Microsoft was successful yesterday*" is also an event instance of the same type. However, they do not share the same event pattern. Our heuristic methods of dependency regularization transform one pattern into the other.

There are three types of pattern transformations, assigning different roles to the object of the verb. Let us suppose the original sentence is:

IBM appointed Alice Smith as vice president. (4)

Then we would automatically generate additional patterns for:

1. DET-POSS: a possessive determiner.

   Alice Smith's appointment as vice president (5)

2. N-N-MOD: a nominal modifier

   the Alice Smith appointment as vice president (6)

3. PP-OF: object of the preposition

   the appointment of Alice Smith as vice president (7)

In the sentences above , "*Alice Smith*" is the person who gets the job, and the phrase "*vice president*" is Alice's position. Thus the sentences share the same arguments, although the syntactic patterns are different.

3 System Description

Jet, the Java Extraction Toolkit[2], provides a set of NLP components which can be combined to create information extraction systems. AceJet[3] is a subsystem of Jet to extract the types of information (entities, relations, and events) annotated on the ACE corpora. The AceJet Event Extraction framework is a combination of a pattern-based system and feature-based system.

Training proceeds in three passes over the annotated training corpus. Pass 1 collects all the event patterns, where a pattern cosists of a trigger and a set of arguments along with the path from the trigger to each argument; both the dependency path and the linear sequence path (a series of noun chunks and words) are recorded. Pass 2 records the frequency with which each pattern is associated with an event type – the 'event score'. Pass 3 treats the event score as a feature, combines it with a small number of other features and trains a maximum entropy model.

At test time, to classify a candidate trigger (any word which has appearred at least once as a trigger in the training corpus) the tagger finds the best match between an event pattern and the input sentence and computes an event score. This score, along with other features, serves as input to the maximum entropy model to make the final ED prediction.

We incorporate the proposed *Dependency Regularization* techniques based on the AceJet baseline system to improve the system performance.

Regularization	Recall	Precision	F-measure
original	65.45	70.59	67.92
vch	66.82	70.84	68.77
transp	65.68	71.18	68.32
vch & transp	67.27	71.50	69.32
vch & transp & Nomlex	**68.18**	**72.82**	**70.42**

Table 2: Trigger identification performance (%) with different dependency regularizations, where original – original dependency parse output without regularization, *vch* – verb chain regularization, *transp* – transparent regularization, and *Nomlex* – Nomlex regularization.

4 Experiment

In this section, we will introduce the evaluation dataset, compare the performance of applying dependency regularization with other state-of-the-art systems, and discuss the contributions of these different dependency regularization rules.

4.1 Data set

We used the ACE 2005 corpus as our testbed. For comparison, we used the same test set with 40 newswire articles (672 sentences) as in (Ji and Grishman, 2008; Liao and Grishman, 2010) for the experiments, and randomly selected 30 other documents (863 sentences) from different genres as the development set. The remaining 529 documents (14,840 sentences) are used for training.

Regarding the correctness criteria: following previous work (Ji and Grishman, 2008; Liao and Grishman, 2010; Ji and Grishman, 2011; Li et al., 2013), a trigger candidate is counted as correct if its event subtype and offsets match those of a reference trigger. The ACE 2005 corpus has 33 event subtypes that, along with one class "*None*" for the non-trigger tokens, constitutes a 34-class classification problem in this work. Finally we use Precision (P), Recall (R), and F-measure (F1) to evaluate the overall performance.

Table 1 presents the overall performance of the systems with gold-standard entity mention and type information. We can see that our system with dependency regularizations can improve the performance over our baseline setting, and also advances the current state-of-the-art systems.

[2] http://cs.nyu.edu/grishman/jet/jet.html

[3] http://cs.nyu.edu/grishman/jet/guide/ACEutilities.html

4.2 Contributions of different dependency regularizations

Table 2 lists the system performance applying the different dependency regularization rules. The last line shows the performance with the combination of three types of Nomlex pattern expansion.

Dependency Regularization could help match patterns that failed in the original framework. For example,

1. With *Verb Chain Regularization*, the sentence "*Taco ball is* ***appealing***." is detected as an APPEAL event, which was ignored in the original framework.

2. With *Transparent Regularization*, the sentence "*The army* ***killed*** *thousands of people.*" is detected as a DIE event, which was ignored in the original framework.

3. With *Nomlex Regularization*, the sentence "*The* ***acquisition*** *of Banco Zaragozano...*" is detected as a TRANSFER-OWNERSHIP event, which was ignored in the original framework. This is because all the relevant sentences in the training data use the same trigger "*acquire*".

5 Related Work

Although there have been quite a few distinct designs for event extraction systems, most are loosely based on using patterns to detect instances of events, where the patterns consist of a predicate, *event trigger*, and constraints on its local syntactic context. The constraints may involve specific lexical items or semantic classes. Some recent studies use high-level information to aid local event extraction systems. For example, Finkel et al. (2005), Maslennikov and seng Chua (2007), Ji and Grishman (2008) and Patwardhan and Riloff (2007) tried to use discourse, document, or cross-document information to improve information extraction. Other research extends these approaches by introducing cross-event information to enhance the performance of multi-event-type extraction systems. Liao and Grishman (2010) use information about other types of events to make predictions or resolve ambiguities regarding a given event. Li et al. (2013) implements a joint model via structured prediction with cross-event features.

Event extraction systems have used patterns and features based on a range of linguistic representations. For example, Miwa et al. (2014) used both a deep analysis and a dependency parse. The original NYU system for the 2005 ACE evaluation (Grishman et al., 2005) incorporated GLARF, a representation which captured both notions of transparency and verb-nominalization correspondences.[4] However, assessment of the impact of individual regularizations has been limited; this prompted the investigation reported here.

6 Conclusion and Future Work

In this paper we have proposed several *Dependency Regularization* steps to improve the performance of the *Event Detection* framework, including *Verb Chain Regularization*, *Transparent Regularization*, and *Nomlex Regularization*. The experimental results have demonstrated the effectiveness of these techniques, which has helped our pattern-based system achieve 70.49% (with 2.57% absolute improvement) F-measure over the baseline, which significantly advances the state-of-the-art systems.

Dependency regularization is only one of the measures we can take to improve peformance. The training corpus cannot include all possible trigger words or all the senses of the triggers it does include. Simply enlarging the training corpus by sequential annotation would yield small gain at a large cost. In parallel work we have shown that carefully targeted active learning of new triggers and senses can produce significant improvement in event detection at modest cost.

References

Jenny Rose Finkel, Trond Grenager, and Christopher Manning. 2005. Incorporating non-local information into information extraction systems by gibbs sampling. In *Proceedings of ACL*.

Ralph Grishman, David Westbrook, and Adam Meyers. 2005. NYU's English ACE 2005 system description. In *Proceedings of the ACE 2005 Evaluation Workshop*.

Heng Ji and Ralph Grishman. 2008. Refining event extraction through cross-document inference. In *Proceedings of ACL*.

Heng Ji and Ralph Grishman. 2011. Using cross-entity inference to improve event extraction. In *Proceedings of ACL*.

Qi Li, Heng Ji, and Liang Huang. 2013. Joint event extraction via structured prediction with global features. In *Proceedings of ACL*.

Shasha Liao and Ralph Grishman. 2010. Using document level cross-event inference to improve event extraction. In *Proceedings of ACL*.

Mstislav Maslennikov and Tat seng Chua. 2007. A multi-resolution framework for information extraction from free text. In *Proceedings of ACL*.

Makoto Miwa, Paul Thompson, Ioannis Korkontzelos, and Sophia Ananiadou. 2014. Comparable study of event extraction in newswire and biomedical domains. In *Proceedings of COLING 2014, the 25th International Conference on Computational Linguistics: Technical Papers*.

Siddharth Patwardhan and Ellen Riloff. 2007. Effective information extraction with semantic affinity patterns and relevant regions. In *Proceedings of EMNLP*.

Stephen Tratz and Eduard Hovy. 2011. Fast, effective, non-projective, semantically-enriched parser. In *Proceedings of EMNLP*.

[4] The official evaluations were made with a complex *value* metric and so are hard to compare with more recent results.

Authorship Verification, Average Similarity Analysis

Daniel Castro Castro
CERPAMID, Cuba
daniel.castro@cerpamid.co.cu

Yaritza Adame Arcia
DATYS, Cuba
yaritza.adame@datys.cu

María Pelaez Brioso
DATYS, Cuba
maria.pelaez@datys.cu

Rafael Muñoz Guillena
Universidad de Alicante, España
rafael@dlsi.ua.es

Abstract

Authorship analysis is an important task for different text applications, for example in the field of digital forensic text analysis. Hence, we propose an authorship analysis method that compares the average similarity of a text of unknown authorship with all the text of an author. Using this idea, a text that was not written by an author, would not exceed the average of similarity with known texts and only the text of unknown authorship would be considered as written by the author, if it exceeds the average of similarity obtained between texts written by him. The experiments were realized using the data provided in PAN 2014 competition for Spanish articles for the task of authorship verification. We realize experiments using different similarity functions and 17 linguistics features. We analyze the results obtained with each pair function-features against the baseline of the competition. Additionally, we introduce a text filtering phase that delete all the sample text of an author that are more similar to the samples of other author, with the idea to reduce confusion or non-representative text, and finally we analyze new experiments to compare the results with the data obtained without filtering.

Keywords: Authorship detection, Author identification, similarity measures, linguistic features.

1 Authorship Analysis

Determine the true author of a document has been a task of social interest from the moment it was possible to attribute the authorship of words. Questions about the authorship of a document may be of interest not only to specialists in the field (forensics specialist, linguistics researchers, etc.), but also in a much more convenient sense for politicians, journalists, lawyers. Recently, with the development of statistical techniques and because of the wide availability of accessible data from computers, the authorship analysis automatically has become a very practical option.

There are many practical examples where the authorship analysis becomes the key to solve them. Suppose a malicious mail is sent using an email account belonging to someone else, which subsequently are accused of this fact, who is the author of the mail? It may happen that a person dies and there is a note that makes it seem that the person committed suicide, it really was a suicide note or was used to cover up a murder? It may be a document, say a digital newspaper that is altered so it cannot be used as evidence in a trial, was it or not altered this newspaper?

The authorship analysis task confronts the problem of determining the author of an anonymous document or one whose author is in doubt. For this it is necessary to try to infer linguistic characteristics (features) of the author through documents written by him, features that will allow us to create a model of the writing style of this author and measure how similar may be any unknown document to documents written by that author.

One of the principal evaluation labs for the dissemination, experimentation and collaboration in the development of methods for the authorship analysis is found in the PAN[1] lab associated to CLEF. It is important to notice, that most of the papers presented in different editions of this evaluation forum (Joula and Stamatatos, 2013; Stamatatos et al., 2014) used Natural Language Processing tools, in order to obtain the linguistic features which identify an author and differentiate it from the rest.

[1]http://pan.webis.de

Proceedings of Recent Advances in Natural Language Processing, pages 84–90,
Hissar, Bulgaria, Sep 7–9 2015.

In PAN editions, 2013 and 2014, specifically it was tested the task of authorship verification, where authors samples are formed by known author documents and an unknown document to check whether it was written by that author. No restrictions is imposed on the use of samples of others for support in finding a decision, or just use the samples of single author, the latter idea would be challenging and difficult because we need to capture the writing style of the author only with his samples.

The basic properties of the papers presented in the PAN 2014 authorship verification task (Stamatatos et al., 2014) are:

1. By the use of known documents samples of authors: intrinsic (only the documents of the author in analysis) or extrinsic (using samples of others authors).
2. Type of machine learning algorithms or approximation used: lazy or hard-working approaches (more training computational costs).
3. Type of linguistic features used: low-level features (characters, phonetic and lexical) and/or syntactic.

1.1 Linguistic Features

The *linguistic features* are the core of the authorship analysis task (regardless of the subtask or approach used in the analysis, such as author verification, author detection, plagiarism detection, etc.), they can be used to coded documents with any mathematical model, traditionally being the vector space model the approximation most used. The purpose lies in trying to identify a writing style of each author to distinguish it from the rest (Juola, 2008).

There are several number of features that have been taken into account in the authorship analysis task, in the majority is used a distribution of features grouped by linguistic layers (we call them also features obtained from the content writing) (Ruseti and Rebedea, 2012; Halvani et all., 2013; Castillo et all., 2014; Khonji and Iraqi, 2014).

Five linguistic feature layers are identified in (Stamatatos, 2009): phonetic, character, lexical, syntactic and semantic layer:

1. Phonetic layer: This layer includes features based on phonemes and can be extracted from the documents through dictionaries. Example: the International Phonetic Alphabet (IPA).
2. Character layer: This layer includes character-based features as prefixes, suffixes or n-grams of letters.
3. Lexical layer: This layer includes features based on terms such as auxiliary words.
4. Syntactic layer: This layer includes syntax based features such as sentences components.
5. Semantic layer: This layer includes semantic-based features as homonyms or synonyms.

Based on this structure feature layers, in our present work we use features of the 2,3 and 4 layers, which we illustrate in more detail in next sections.

In Section 2 we present the characteristics of our method and in section 3 the experimental results using the data of Authorship Verification PAN 2014 competition. Finally conclusions and future work.

2 Average Similarity Proposal

There are various aspects that need to be analyzed in order to implement a method that allows us to assess whether a text of unknown or disputed authorship, was written by an author from which we have written sample texts. It should be considered whether samples of the author belong to the same genre, theme, were written with a considerable time difference, are written in the same language or have sections written in other languages, or if the samples have been revised and corrected by someone else.

From a practical point of view in software application (real scenario) for the algorithms we also do not have the assurance that all documents given as examples of an author, have actually been written by the author in question. That is, it is possible that some samples were drafted by someone else.

Our method is based on the analysis of the average similarity (AS_{Unk}) of an unknown authorship text with the closeness to each of the samples of an author, comparing it to the Average Group Similarity (AGS) between samples of an author.

We performed experiments with a total of 17 types of linguistic features (we will illustrate the features in the following section) and used six similarity functions.

We identified three key steps in our method, these are:

1. Representation of all documents by one feature type. This must be done for all the features.

2. Average similarity between the documents samples of an author (AGS).
3. Average similarity between the document of unknown authorship and the known samples of one author (AS_{Unk}).

2.1 Linguistic Features used to Represent the Documents

We use the vector representation to store the values of the linguistic features extracted form one document, so each sample (document) with known or unknown author is represented by 17 vectors corresponding to each of the types of features with which experiments were performed.

The features evaluated and calculated are grouped in three layers: character, word and syntactic (lemma and Part of Speech)

1. Character
   a. Tri-grams of characters
   b. Quad-grams of characters
   c. Uni-grams of prefixes of size 2
   d. Uni-grams of suffixes of size 2
   e. Bi-grams of prefixes of size 2
   f. Bi-grams of suffixes of size 2
2. Words
   a. Uni-grams of words
   b. Tri-grams of words
   c. Bi-grams of words at the beginning of sentence
   d. Punctuations marks
3. Lemma and Part of Speech
   a. Uni-grams of lemmas
   b. Uni-grams of Part of Speech
   c. Tri-grams of lemmas
   d. Tri-grams of Part of Speech
   e. Bi-grams of lemmas at the beginning of sentence
   f. Bi-grams of Part of Speech at the beginning of sentence

The features of the third layer of analysis are obtained using tools of Natural Language Processing implemented in the *Xinetica*[2] platform.

2.2 Average Similarity

To illustrate the performance of our method, we show in the Figure 1 the process to calculate the average similarity from the documents of the known author and the average similarity of these samples with the unknown text. Initially we have several samples of documents (Doc) by an author and a document of unknown authorship (Unk). The first task is to represent each of these documents in a vector space model, analyzing one type of feature. Subsequently, for the samples documents of the author we analyze the average similarity of each document with the rest, using the following formula:

$$AS_j = \frac{\sum_{O_j \in K_j} Sim(O, O_j)}{|K_j| - 1}$$

Where "O" would be a document of the author and "O_j" the rest of the documents of the same author, K_j represents the author and $|K_j|$ the number of documents of the author. By $Sim(O, O_j)$, it's represented the similarity between two documents.

Therefore, for each document of known author their average similarity with the other is calculated and finally, the average similarity of all samples is calculated or what we call the average group similarity (AGS):

$$AGS = \frac{\sum_{O_j \in K_j} AS_j}{|K_j|}$$

Given document of unknown authorship, initially must be represented by the type of feature in which samples of known author are represented with which are to be compared. Then the AS_{Unk} is calculated using the known samples. The decision is made by comparing the AGS with unknown calculated AS_{Unk}. If $AS_{Unk} < AGS$, then the unknown sample is not considered written by this author. To determine if the response is positive (that is, that the document of unknown author was written by the author of the given samples), then the $AS_{Unk} \geq AGS$.

We have implemented 6 similarity functions in order to perform experiments with each of them, these are: Cosine, Dice, Jaccard, Tanimoto, Euclidean and MinMax (Gomaa and Fahmy, 2013).

One element to prove that we incorporate is related to the analysis of samples of each author, in order to filter out those that do not represent or characterize the writing style of the author. We incorporated a filtering stage prior to the calculation of AGS.

For each sample, the AS was calculated for each group of samples of the authors and eliminates those samples of documents that had an AS value greater with samples of different authors to his corresponding author. This filtering variant we will call "Non typical" and the variant without

[2] http://www.cerpamid.co.cu/xinetica/index.htm

filtering its call "No reduction". This reduction variant for not typical documents would be good in the future to test the effect or impact it would have on different collections of texts of the authors. For example, how it would affect the analysis of authorship if the authors samples correspond to the same topic or even an author's samples were not of the same length or a single topic.

We focus then our study in analyzing three aspects:

1. The idea of the AGS measure as a limit to determine when an unknown document was written by an author. We see this as an intrinsic approximation to the task.
2. Non typical known documents eliminated don't affect the purpose of correct identification the author of an unknown one, or incorrect assigning to an author a text that was not written by him.
3. How far are the results of each pair function-features in correspondence with the best and baseline of the experiments reported in PAN 2014 competition for Spanish dataset, in order to evaluate if the AGS measure could be used.

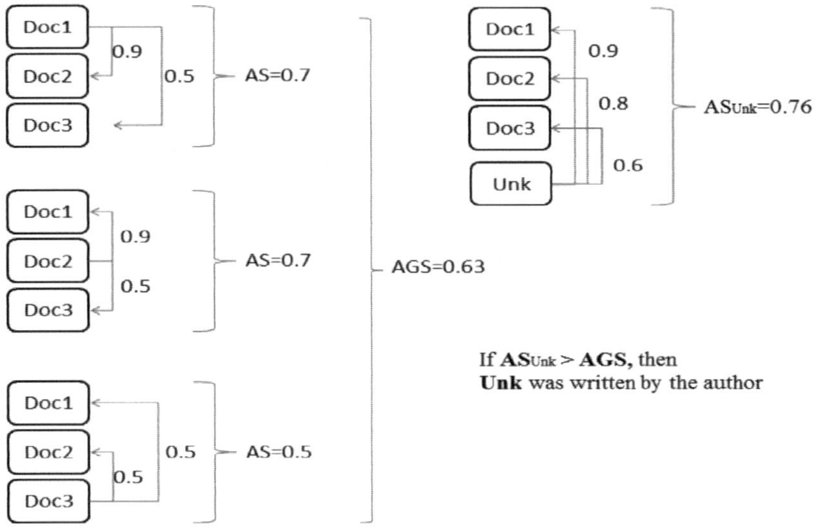

Figure 1: Average Group Similarity (AGS) analysis of an author documents samples and Average Similarity (AS_{Unk}) of an unknown authorship document

3 Experimental Results

With each pair function-feature we would evaluate the authorship verification method we propose. This section shows the results of evaluating the training and test dataset offered in the task of authorship verification of the PAN 2014 edition for the Spanish language using the *accuracy* measure. We present the results for each pair function-feature without reducing known documents samples of the authors and using a filtering phase where *Non typical* documents are eliminated.

In train and test dataset there are a maximum of 5 documents samples for each author and one unknown text, and the purpose is to determine if this unknown sample was written by this author. The train data has 100 authors and the test data 50.

The evaluation measure we use is *accuracy c@1* (Peñas and Rodrigo, 2011). This is the measure used in the competition:

$$c@1 = (1/n)*(nc+(nu*nc/n))$$

where n is the number of problems that correspond to the number of authors, nc is the number of correct answers (i.e. say **not** written by the author when the unknown text was indeed not written by him and **yes** when it was written)

and *nu* is the number of unanswered problems. In our method we answer all the problems so the *nu* value would be 0 and then we would evaluate *accuracy = nc/n*.
In (Stamatatos et al., 2014) are presented all the details of the dataset for the languages evaluated in the competition. In the overview is presented a baseline *accuracy* value that allows us to evaluate and compare the results of the participants, the *accuracy* value is 0.53 for the Spanish data. The best value of accuracy obtained in the competition was 0.79 using a META-CLASSIFIER developed with the combination of all the results of the participants. The best accuracy of a participant method was of 0.77 achieved by (Khonji and Iraqi, 2014).
Figures 2, 3 and 4 show the results with the test data with and without reduction, that is, in Figure 2 the results for all features of the character layer of are shown with and without reduction and likewise for 3 and 4. For most pair function-feature and both variants reducing samples or not, the values obtained with the test data are greater than the values obtained with the training, but its observed a uniform behavior with respect to those achieved with the test data.
As a general rule, with the features of the Character layer, the best results are appreciated for representations based on n-grams of characters for n 3 and 4; as well as the bi-grams of prefixes and suffixes of words. With regard to the similarity functions, highlight the values obtained using Dice and Jaccard, being quite similar.
If we analyze the results according to filtering variant of the samples, it is observed that the values of accuracy are slightly higher with the analysis of *Non typical*, the difference would lie in the need for a greater effort in the previous stage in which the non-typical samples are filtered, but for classification of unknown texts it would need less computing time.
In Figure 3 are appreciated the results without reducing samples and non-typical samples reduction for features of the layer Words.
We evaluate as positive the values achieved with representations of n-grams of words with *n* 1 and 3, noting that for uni-grams of words with the functions Dice and Jaccard are achieved the best values (0.78 and 0.8 of accuracy in that order) in all tests with any of the features from the three layers and close to the best obtained in the PAN 2014 competition for the Spanish dataset which was accuracy 0.79 from a meta-classifier (Stamatatos et al., 2014).

The Euclidean and MinMax functions (dissimilarity functions), in most cases have the lowest values.

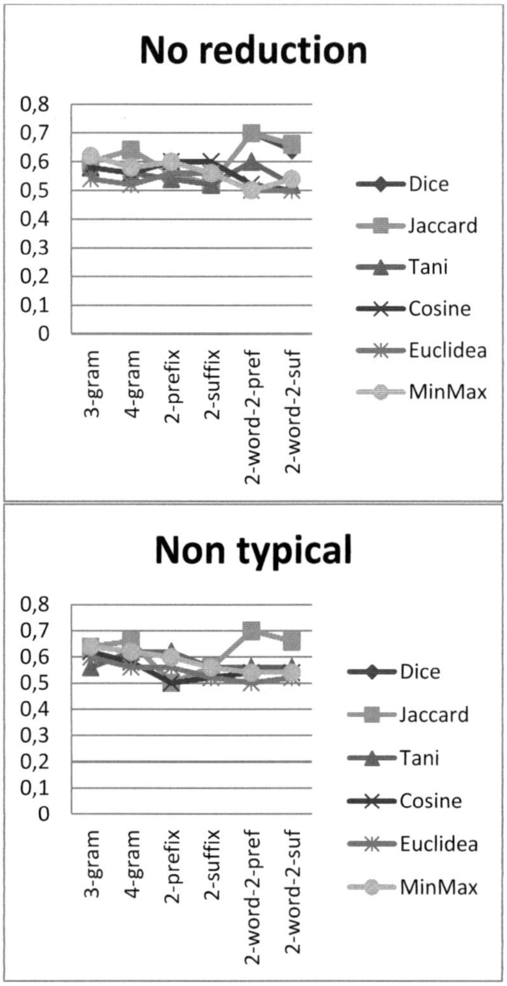

Figure 2: Results for the Character layer of features and all the similarity functions. No reduction filtering and Non typical reduction.

Figure 4 shows the results for the features of the Lemma and Part of Speech (PoS) layer.
There are illustrated good values with the representations of lemmas and PoS n-grams for *n* 1 and 3, primarily working with lemmas. It can be noted that to each word correspond a lemma and for one lemma may be associated more than one word, taking this into account we can analyze the results using the lemma n-grams and word n-gram representations.
For example, we see that for the variant without reduction of the samples, the results with the representation of words (terms) are higher

compared to the use of lemmas, and very similar if we use the feature representations 3-grams of words or lemmas. For variant with non-typical reduced samples, the results were quite similar for any of the representations.

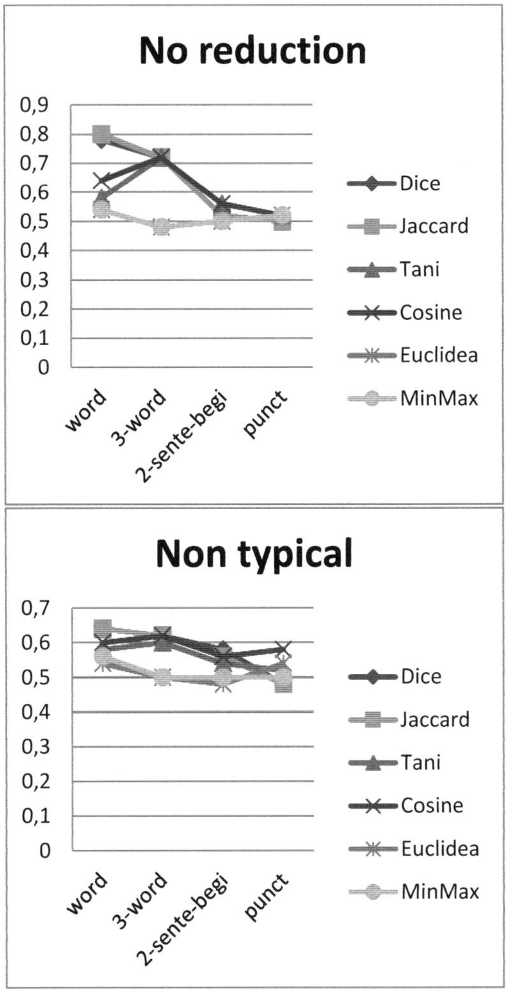

Figure 3: Results for the Word layer of features and all the similarity functions. No reduction filtering and Non typical reduction.

To summarize, the best results over the baseline value is obtained using the functions Dice, Jaccard, Tanimoto and Cosine, from these Dice and Jaccard are highlighted.

Analyzing the features representations used, good values are obtained with several features and especially those in which are achieved accuracy values close to 0.7 or higher.

Regarding to the reduction variants of samples texts of the author's, with some pair's function-features, are obtained better results without reducing samples and in other cases by non-typical filtering.

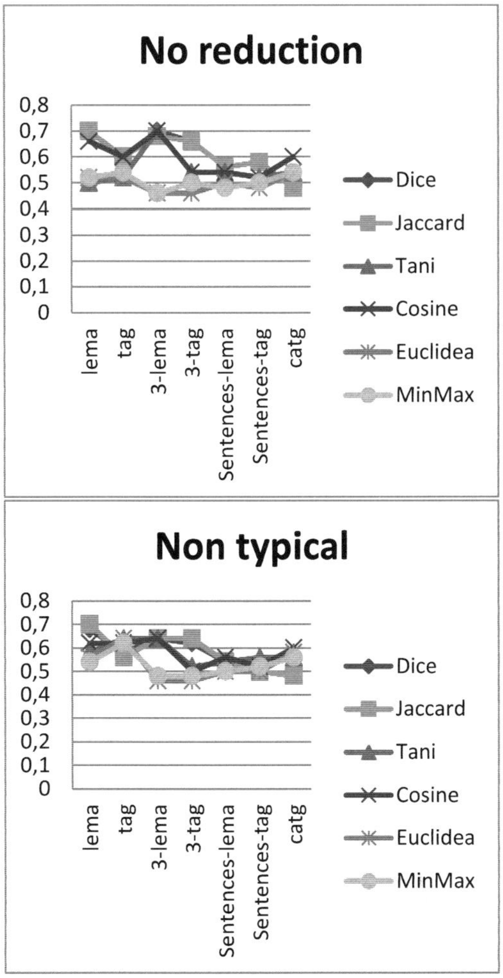

Figure 4: Results for the Lemma and Part of Speech layer of features and all the similarity functions. No reduction filtering and Non typical reduction.

4 Conclusions and Future Work

We have presented the implementation of a method for authorship analysis that compares the average similarity calculated between a document of unknown authorship and documents written by an author, with the average similarity of the samples of this author.

Using this idea, a text that was not written by an author, would not exceed the average of similarity with known texts and only the text of unknown authorship would be considered as

written by the author, if it exceeds the average of similarity obtained between texts written by him.
To prove the idea, we use 17 types of linguistic features to represent the documents and evaluate the similarity between two vector representations of documents using one of six's similarity functions implemented. We tested the method with each pair function-feature, evaluating the results between each execution and taking into account the baseline and best results exposed in the authorship verification task with training and test data of the PAN 2014 for the Spanish edition.
We also include a preliminary phase for reducing samples texts of each author, with the intention that the samples of the authors were representative of his style of writing and little similar to the samples of other authors, calling these *Non typical* reduction.
We evaluate the results of each pair function-feature without reducing samples and for *Non typical* reducing. This allowed us to assess whether occurred a drastic reduction in test results when samples of texts written by an author are eliminated, ensuring that the results do not differ much and in some cases increase.
We obtained several results above the baseline value reported in competition and in some cases near to the best.
We propose as future work, the implementation of a method that allows us to combine several function-feature pair's in order to give a final conclusion with some voting mechanism.

Acknowledgements

This research has been partially funded by the Spanish Ministry of Science and Innovation (TIN2012-38536-C03-03)

References

Castillo, E. Vilariño, D. Pinto, D. León, S. Cervantes, O. *Unsupervised method for the authorship identification task*. Notebook for PAN at CLEF 2014.

Gomaa, W. and A. Fahmy. 2013. *A Survey of Text Similarity Approaches*. International Journal of Computer Applications (0975 – 8887) Volume 68– No.13.

Halvani, O. Steinebach, M and Zimmermann, R. *Authorship Verification via k-Nearest Neighbor Estimation*. Notebook for PAN at CLEF 2013.

Juola, P. 2008. *Authorship Attribution*. Foundations and Trends in Information Retrieval Vol. 1, No. 3 (2006) 233–334

Juola, P. and E. Stamatatos. 2013. *Overview of the Author Identification Task at PAN 2013*. CLEF 2013.

Khonji, M and Iraqi, Y. *A Slightly-modified GI-based Author-verifier with Lots of Features (ASGALF)*. Notebook for PAN at CLEF 2014.

Peñas. A. and Rodrigo. A. 2011. *A Simple Measure to Assess Non response*. In Proc. of the 49th Annual Meeting of the Association for Computational Linguistics, Vol. 1, pages 1415-1424.

Ruseti, S and Rebedea, T. 2012. *Authorship Identification Using a Reduced Set of Linguistic Features*. Notebook for PAN at CLEF 2012.

Stamatatos, E., W. Daelemans, B. Verhoeven, M. Potthast, B. Stein, P. Juola and M. Sanchez-Perez. 2014. *Overview of the Author Identification Task at PAN 2014*. CLEF 2014.

Stamatatos, E. 2009. *A Survey of Modern Authorship Attribution Methods*. Journal of the American Society for Information Science and Technology, 60(3), pp. 538-556, 2009, Wiley.

Coreference Resolution to Support IE from Indian Classical Music Forums

Joe Cheri Ross **Pushpak Bhattacharyya**
Department of Computer Science and Engineering
Indian Institute of Technology Bombay
{joe,pb}@cse.iitb.ac.in

Abstract

Efficient music information retrieval (MIR) require to have meta information about music along with content based information in the knowledge base. Discussion forums on music are rich sources of information gathered from a wider audience. Taking into consideration the nature of text in these web resources, the yield of relation extraction is quite dependent on resolving the entity references in the document. Among the few music forums dealing with Indian classical music, *rasikas.org* (rasikas, 2015) having rich information about artistes, raga and other music concepts is taken for our study. The forum posts generally contain anaphoric references to the main topic of the thread or any other entity in the discourse. In this paper we focus on coreference resolution for short discourse noisy text like that of forum posts. Since grammatical roles capture relation between mentions in a discourse, those features extracted from dependency parsing are widely explored along with semantic compatibility feature. On investigation of issues, the need for integrating known dependencies between features emerged. A Bayesian network with predefined network structure is evaluated, since a Bayesian belief network enacts a probabilistic rule based system. To the extent possible the superior behaviour of Bayesian network over SVM is analysed.

1 Introduction

Information extraction from music repositories involves analysis of music audio. Efficient extraction of music information require meta-data along with content based information. The need for metadata led to information extraction from blogs and forums related to music. This should contain information about artistes, performances, music concepts etc. Apart from the available literature about Indian classical music, there are a few forums and blogs having rich metadata. Extracting information from these sources help to augment music ontology for Indian classical music with meta information along with content based information. Among the two main divisions in Indian classical music, Carnatic music community is more involved in web based discussions and information dissemination. *Rasikas.org* (rasikas, 2015) is one among the prominent discussion forums where they have discussions pertaining to Carnatic music topics comprising ragas, talas, artistes etc.

Extracting information from unstructured noisy text in websites of this kind is quite challenging. Efficient extraction of relations also require resolution of entities in the documents. Apart from resolving the entities with the real world entities, the intra-relations between the entities within the discourse have to be resolved. Identification of entities is a critical step in information extraction followed by identification of relations between them.

Posts in most forums are written in informal language with pronominal and alias mentions referring to the main topic of discussion or to another related entity mentioned in the discourse. Effecient extraction of relation is dependent on finding the exact antecedent of pronominal and nominal mentions, when it refers to another entity. It is commonly observed that the main topic of a post is referred by pronominal or alias mention. Following is a post from the forum. Coreferent mentions are marked with the same color.

```
Sri Ragam is
the asampoorna mela equivalent
of K Priya acc to MD's school.
Thyagaraja gave life to K.Priya
```


Proceedings of Recent Advances in Natural Language Processing, pages 91–96,
Hissar, Bulgaria, Sep 7–9 2015.

with his excellent compos, where as MD never touched this raga. In Sri ragam we have plenty of compos by the trinity incl the famous Endaro Sri Ranjani is a lovely janya of K Priya with plenty of compos by both T & MD.

The presence of a large number of such sentences containing potential relations present, make coreference resolution unavoidable for information extraction from these forums. The process of checking whether two expressions are coreferent to each other is termed as coreference resolution (Soon et al., 2001). The well-known discussion forum on Carnatic music *Rasikas.org*, is taken for our study. Enrolled with a good number of music loving users, the forum discusses many relevant topics on Carnatic music providing valued information. Sordo et al. evaluated information extraction from the same forum using contextual information (Sordo et al., 2012). Integration of natural language processing methods yields better coverage for the extracted relations. Largely the entities are mentioned using pronominal and nominal mentions in this forum. Resolution of these coreferences is crucial in increasing recall of relation extraction from forums. Coreference resolution identifies the real world entity, an expression is referring to (Cherry and Bergsma, 2005).

Though a widely researched area, coreference resolution will have to be applied differently considering the characteristics of the text in these forums. Forum posts are generally short discourse of text where the entities mentioned are limited to the scope of a few sentences. Supervised approach has been widely used in coreference resolution (Rahman and Ng, 2009; Soon et al., 2001; Aone and Bennett, 1995; McCarthy and Lehnert, 1995). We examine the commonly used conventional features and its variants that suits this domain of text. Soon et al. and Vincent et al. have investigated an exhaustive list of features for coreference resolution. Most of these methods model this problem as classification of mention-pair as coreferent or non-coreferent. Research on coreference resolution for similar domains of text are reported. Ding et al. has discussed features for supervised approach to coreference resolution for opinion mining where the discourse of text is short as in forum posts (Ding and Liu, 2010). Hendrickx et al. experimented their coreference resolution with unstructured text in news paper articles, user comments and blog data targeting opinion mining (Hendrickx and Hoste, 2009). Coreference resolution in this domain is restricted to resolve coreferential relations between entities within a discourse of a post. We follow a supervised approach with mention-pair model, learning to identify two mentions are coreferent or not. Mention pairs are constructed from the annotated mentions from the posts. Along with standard set of proven features, grammatical role features and its proposed variants are found to contribute to increase in accuracy. Grammatical role features (Kong et al., 2010; Ng, 2007; Uryupina, 2006) extracted from the dependency parse are intended to capture the characteristics of the human process of coreference resolution, getting the grammatical role of a mention in the corresponding sentence and thus obtaining the relation between the mentions in the pair. Semantic compatibility is a crucial feature in coreference resolution, exploiting named entity (NE) class of mentions. To satisfy the requirements of our domain, NE classes are extended to raga, music concept, music instrument, song.

We have analyzed the importance of dependency parse based grammatical role features, its variants and other features with the limited annotated music forum data available. A rule based chunking implementation is deployed for mention detection. To deal with data insufficiency we have also tried the performance of Bayesian network against SVM in the mention pair classification. This is evaluated with a defined network structure designed to capture some basic known dependencies between features. In this paper we employ a simple network structure with the intention to improve, based on the observations. In our experiments, we observe that Bayesian network has better performance compared to SVM with most of the evaluation metrics.

2 Knowledge Source for Coreference Resolution

Features are computed for a mention pair comprising of potential antecedent mention and anaphoric mention. We make use of a subset of conventional features including the features described in (Soon et al., 2001). String matching (STR_MATCH) and alias (ALIAS) features check for compatibility between the mention with regard to string similarity. These features depend on fuzzy string matching to bypass spelling differences. Same sentence (SAME_SENT) feature checks if both the mentions are in the same sentence and sentence distance gets the number of sentences in between the mentions(SENT_NO). The check for proper noun and pronoun is done for second mention in the pair (PRPN2, PRN2). Features include check for whether a mention is definite (DEF_NP) or demonstrative (DEM_NP).

2.1 Grammatical Role Features

Though the discussed features are significant for showing the coreferent characteristics of a mention pair, the grammatical role of a mention in a discourse and its relation with other mentions are prime features in coreference identification. In a short discourse where the mentions lie in close vicinity, the grammatical role is an important player in deciding coreference when compared to long discourse having coreferent mentions far apart. Apart from analyzing whether a mention in the pair is a subject or object of a sentence, we also analyze the role of other mentions coming in between the mentions of the pair under consideration. This helps to figure out the existence of any other potential antecedent for the anaphora in the mention pair (m_i,m_j). The existence of a potential antecedent should decrease the probability of the mention pair considered, to be coreferent. The grammatical role of a mention is determined with the help of dependency parse of a sentence obtained from Stanford dependency parser (De Marneffe and Manning, 2008)

These features take into consideration the relevance of a mention with respect to the grammatical role. The coreferent relation between two mentions is dependent on other mentions occurring around the mentions under consideration. So we designed a few other features to capture the behavior of other mentions around, inorder to supplement or weaken the coreferent relation between the mentions in the pair.

Subject mention between(SUBJ_BET): This feature is true when there is another mention in between m_i and m_j, having subject dependency relation to a verb in the occurring sentence. This feature is intended to reduce the probability of a mention pair becoming coreferent when there is a potential candidate present in between.

Subject mention associated with root verb between (ROOT_SUBJ_BET): This feature is a complement to the previous one, checking for existence of a mention between m_i and m_j having subject dependency relation with the root verb of the sentence. Such a mention has higher probability of being antecedent to the current anaphoric mention.

First mention subject of root verb (MEN1_ROOT_SUBJ): This feature checks for whether the first mention in the pair is associated with the root verb in the occurring sentence. This increases the chance of this mention being referred in the subsequent sentences.

2.2 Named Entity (NE) Class Feature

Semantic compatibility between the mentions is a critical feature while resolving coreferences (Ng, 2007), making other syntactic features irrelevant on semantic incompatibility. While commonly used NE classes are restricted to person, location, organization etc., in Indian classical music domain it is important to have NE classes like raga, music instrument, music concept, song along with the existing ones.

We follow a dictionary based approach for identification of mention's NE class with the help of entities from Musicbrainz[1]. The mentions are compared against the entities in the dictionary using fuzzy string matching to alleviate the impact of spelling discrepancies. Apart from this, certain heuristics are incorporated (ex. mentions starting with 'Shri' or 'Smt' are person names). Named entity class identification is made offline inorder to support manual curation.

3 Modeling

Since mention-pair model is followed training and testing requires mentions pairs to be formed from the corpus. In a supervised approach training requires positive instances created from mention pairs formed from within a coreferent cluster and negative mention pair instances contain mentions from different clusters. These instances are taken from annotated corpus. While forming mention pairs, the first mention in the pair is chosen to be a non-pronominal mention. An anaphoric mention can never be coreferent with a pronominal mention considering the nature of this corpus. Since the number of negative mention pair far exceeds the number of positive mention pair instances, negative instances are randomly selected from a forum

[1] https://musicbrainz.org/

Feature	Description
First mention subject (SUBJ1)	True, when m_i is a subject of any verb in the sentence
Second mention subject (SUBJ2)	True, when m_j is a subject of any verb in the sentence
First mention object (OBJ1)	True, when m_i is an object of any verb in the sentence
Second mention object (OBJ2)	True, when m_j is an object of any verb in the sentence

Table 1: Basic grammatical role features

post to cap the margin between positive and negative instances.

Test instances are formed from the test file having automatically detected mentions. The accuracy of the system is also dependent on the accuracy of mention detection.

4 Experiment Setup

4.1 Database

Forum	#Posts	#Sent.	#M	#P	#N
Raga & Alapana	143	893	2091	642	1829
Vidwans & Vidushis	180	1219	2749	1247	2742

Table 2: Details of annotated posts. (#Posts= No. of posts #Sent= No. of sentences in the forum. #M= No. of annotated mentions #P= positive mention pairs formed #N= negative mention pairs formed)

The corpus contains coreference annotated forum posts from 2 forums in *rasikas.org*. *Raga & Alapana* has discussions about Carnatic ragas and related concepts and *Vidwans & Vidushis* discusses about Carnatic artistes. Each thread has a title and the posts in the thread discuss the title of the thread. Table 2 shows statistics of annotated forum posts. The annotated data is made available in CoNLL format. Test CoNLL files for validation are also created from the same content by automating mention detection.

4.2 Mention Detection

Mention detection identifies entity boundaries. A rule based chunker is deployed to extract mentions limiting the extraction to predefined part-of-speech tag patterns which are identified from observations on annotated mentions. We depend on Stanford POS tagger for getting POS tags of the corpus(Toutanova et al., 2003). But the POS tagging produced is inaccurate due to noisy text which demands post processing to extract more relevant mentions. Certain proper nouns which are Indian names or Indian classical music terms categorized as nouns by the POS tagger are identified through a dictionary check. Possessive endings marked with different tags are also identified in this step.

Identification of accurate boundaries is challenging due to noisy text with grammatical issues. Making use of knowledge base from web can help in better identification of mention boundaries.

4.3 Evaluation

As explained before training instances are generated from annotated corpus and testing instances from corpus having mentions detected automatically. Experiments are carried out with SVM linear classifier and Bayesian network with predefined network structure. In these domains where the annotated data is scarce and the text is noisy, a Bayesian network with defined structure can work better(Antal et al., 2004). The network structure can incorporate the knowledge available along with the statistical information. Here the Bayesian network will integrate the benefits of both rule based and statistical approaches. A basic network structure is made use as described in fig 1.

We conducted 5-fold cross validation. As the mentions identified through automated mention detection are different from the annotated mentions, the train and test CoNLL content are different in terms of mention boundaries. Still during cross validation the posts considered for training are not included in the testing fold. During 5-fold validation the test mention pairs are classified as coreferent/not coreferent, which are then clustered to form the resultant CoNLL output. We applied best-first clustering(Ng, 2005), where the mention with highest likelihood value is selected as antecedent for an anaphoric mention.

Ablation testing is employed to find weakly per-

Experiments	MUC			B^3			CEAF-M		
	P	R	F	P	R	F	P	R	F
A	33.61	37.44	35.37	42.72	50.82	46.36	36.65	52.58	43.18
B	35.77	54.78	43.19	39.14	58.78	46.98	41.86	60.16	49.35
C	38.16	52.9	44.0	40.02	58.38	47.44	40.84	58.73	48.16

Table 3: Results (P:precision R:recall F:F-measure)
Experiments A: SVM without grammatical role features B: SVM with all features C: Bayes network with all features.

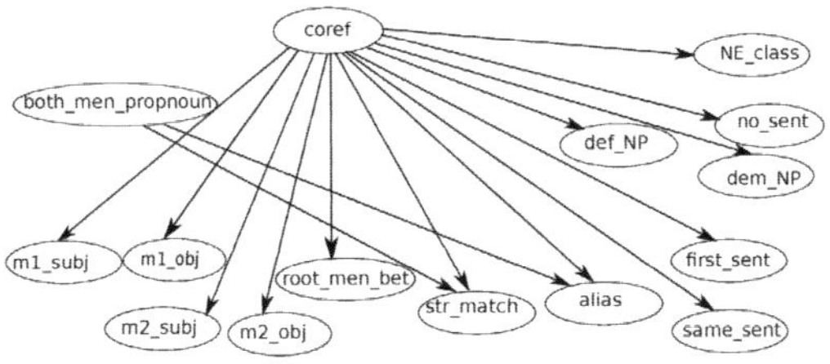

Figure 1: Bayesian network structure depicting dependencies between features

forming features and the most weakly performing 3 features are removed.

5 Results and Discussion

Results are reported in coreference evaluation metrics MUC, B^3 and CEAF-M. Experiment A is without grammatical role features and exp. B clearly indicates the improvement with the grammatical features. Experiment B and C uses all the selected features, using classifiers SVM and Bayes net respectively. As mentioned in section 4.3 the weakly performing features are removed using ablation testing and the results using these features are shown in table 3. The problems with mention detection is one major cause for low accuracy. Even among identified mentions, the mismatch in boundaries is a concern. Analysis of the errors bring forth the major shortcomings and advantages of evaluated classification methods. The problem of semantic incompatible mentions are coreferent with SVM as classifier is almost absent with Bayesian network. Though it contributes well to precision, the recall is seen low compared to SVM because of the relative low importance given to the string matching and alias features.

There are common problems observed with both the classifiers. Despite the hypothesis we had about MEN1_ROOT_SUBJ feature, it is observed that the introduction of this feature reduces accuracy. There are instances of deictic phrases, where the phrase refers to an entity outside the scope of mentions defined in the discourse(Pinkal, 1986). Isolation of deictic phrases can alleviate many false alarms. Certain misclassification occurs at the clustering phase, where the wrong antecedent get selected instead of the correct one even when mention pair with the correct mention is classified as coreferent. Some mentions which are supposed to be singleton are clustered with other clusters because of their linkage with one of the mentions in the cluster.

6 Conclusion and Future Work

This paper focuses on coreference resolution in short discourse of text in Indian classical music. The evaluated mention pair features are expected to capture the specificities of coreferent mentions in short discourses. The devised methods are expected to work well with similar nature forum texts.

Lack of annotated data poses serious problem to classification inspite of the prominent features. Bayesian network exhibits significant improvement in precision despite the small reduction in recall. Bayesian network assures the dominance required for the NE class feature, even though it leads to a few false alarms. The present network structure encodes limited dependencies. A more accurate network structure is evolving based on observations.

Given the fact that semantic/NE class feature has high precedence, accurate extraction of NE class is vital. Even though gender is an important feature, it is not computed due to lack of knowledge sources and methods for computing gender for Indian names. Considering the details of information Freebase posses about each entity, Freebase can aid both these subtasks. Coreference clustering can be further improved incorporating methods to compare belongingness of a mention to different cluster based on likelihood values between the mention and all the mentions in a cluster, instead of a single mention in the cluster.

References

Peter Antal, Geert Fannes, Dirk Timmerman, Yves Moreau, and Bart De Moor. 2004. Using literature and data to learn Bayesian networks as clinical models of ovarian tumors. *Artificial Intelligence in Medicine*, 30:257–281.

Chinatsu Aone and Scott William Bennett. 1995. Evaluating automated and manual acquisition of anaphora resolution strategies. In *Proceedings of the 33rd annual meeting on Association for Computational Linguistics*, pages 122–129. Association for Computational Linguistics.

Colin Cherry and Shane Bergsma. 2005. An expectation maximization approach to pronoun resolution. In *Proceedings of the Ninth Conference on Computational Natural Language Learning*, pages 88–95. Association for Computational Linguistics.

Marie-Catherine De Marneffe and Christopher D Manning. 2008. The stanford typed dependencies representation. In *Coling 2008: Proceedings of the workshop on Cross-Framework and Cross-Domain Parser Evaluation*, pages 1–8. Association for Computational Linguistics.

Xiaowen Ding and Bing Liu. 2010. Resolving object and attribute coreference in opinion mining. In *Proceedings of the 23rd International Conference on Computational Linguistics*, pages 268–276. Association for Computational Linguistics.

Iris Hendrickx and Veronique Hoste. 2009. Coreference resolution on blogs and commented news. In *Anaphora Processing and Applications*, pages 43–53. Springer.

Fang Kong, Guodong Zhou, Longhua Qian, and Qiaoming Zhu. 2010. Dependency-driven anaphoricity determination for coreference resolution. In *Proceedings of the 23rd International Conference on Computational Linguistics*, pages 599–607. Association for Computational Linguistics.

Joseph F McCarthy and Wendy G Lehnert. 1995. Using decision trees for coreference resolution. *arXiv preprint cmp-lg/9505043*.

Vincent Ng. 2005. Machine learning for coreference resolution: From local classification to global ranking. In *Proceedings of the 43rd Annual Meeting on Association for Computational Linguistics*, pages 157–164. Association for Computational Linguistics.

Vincent Ng. 2007. Semantic class induction and coreference resolution. In *ACL*, pages 536–543.

Manfred Pinkal. 1986. Definite noun phrases and the semantics of discourse. In *Proceedings of the 11th coference on Computational linguistics*, pages 368–373. Association for Computational Linguistics.

Altaf Rahman and Vincent Ng. 2009. Supervised models for coreference resolution. In *Proceedings of the 2009 Conference on Empirical Methods in Natural Language Processing: Volume 2-Volume 2*, pages 968–977. Association for Computational Linguistics.

rasikas. 2015. Rasikas.org. `http://www.rasikas.org`.

Wee Meng Soon, Hwee Tou Ng, and Daniel Chung Yong Lim. 2001. A machine learning approach to coreference resolution of noun phrases. *Computational linguistics*, 27(4):521–544.

Mohamed Sordo, Joan Serrà Julià, Gopala Krishna Koduri, and Xavier Serra. 2012. Extracting semantic information from an online carnatic music forum. In *Gouyon F, Herrera P, Martins LG, Müller M. ISMIR 2012: Proceedings of the 13th International Society for Music Information Retrieval Conference; 2012 Oct 8-12; Porto, Portugal. Porto: FEUP Ediçoes; 2012*. International Society for Music Information Retrieval (ISMIR).

Kristina Toutanova, Dan Klein, Christopher D. Manning, and Yoram Singer. 2003. Feature-rich part-of-speech tagging with a cyclic dependency network. In *Proceedings of the 2003 Conference of the North American Chapter of the Association for Computational Linguistics on Human Language Technology - Volume 1*, NAACL '03, pages 173–180, Stroudsburg, PA, USA. Association for Computational Linguistics.

Olga Uryupina. 2006. Coreference resolution with and without linguistic knowledge. In *Proceedings of LREC*, pages 893–898.

Readability Assessment of Translated Texts

Alina Maria Ciobanu[1,2], Liviu P. Dinu[1,2], Flaviu Ioan Pepelea[3]
[1]Faculty of Mathematics and Computer Science, University of Bucharest
[2]Center for Computational Linguistics, University of Bucharest
[3]Twitter
alina.ciobanu@my.fmi.unibuc.ro,
liviu.p.dinu@gmail.com, flaviupepelea@gmail.com

Abstract

In this paper we investigate how readability varies between texts originally written in English and texts translated into English. For quantification, we analyze several factors that are relevant in assessing readability – shallow, lexical and morpho-syntactic features – and we employ the widely used Flesch-Kincaid formula to measure the variation of the readability level between original English texts and texts translated into English. Finally, we analyze whether the readability features have enough discriminative power to distinguish between originals and translations.

1 Introduction and Related Work

The products of translation generally differ from original, non-translated texts. According to Koppel and Ordan (2011), two main aspects that lead to differences between the two categories have been identified: 1) effects of the translation process that are independent of the source language; 2) effects of the source language on the translation product, also known as source language interference. According to Sun (2012), the reception of a translated text is related to cross-cultural readability. Translators need to understand the particularities of both the source and the target language in order to transfer the meaning of the text from one language to another. While rendering the source language text into the target language, it is also important to maintain the style of the document. Various genres of text might be translated for different purposes, which influence the choice of the translation strategy. For example, for political speeches the purpose is to report exactly what is communicated in a given text (Trosborg, 1997). In this paper we investigate how readability features differ between original and translated texts.

Systems for automatic readability assessment have received an increasing attention during the last decade. While research focused initially on English, further studies have shown a growing interest in other languages, such as Spanish (Huerta, 1959), French (Kandel and Moles, 1958) or Italian (Franchina and Vacca, 1986; François and Miltsakaki, 2012). Readability assessment systems have a wide variety of applications. We mention here only a few: 1) they provide assistance in selecting reading material with an appropriate level of complexity from a large collection of documents, for second language learners and people with disabilities or low literacy skills (Collins-Thompson, 2011); 2) they help adapting the technical documents to various levels of medical expertise, within the medical domain (Elhadad and Sutaria, 2007); 3) they assist the processes of machine translation, text simplification, or speech recognition and evaluate their effectiveness, in the research area of NLP (Aluisio et al., 2010; Stymne et al., 2013).

Most of the traditional readability approaches investigate shallow text properties to determine the complexity of a text, based on assumptions which correlate surface features with the linguistic factors which influence readability. For example, the average number of characters or syllables per word, the average number of words per sentence and the percentage of words not occurring among the most frequent n words in a language are correlated with the lexical, syntactic and, respectively, the semantic complexity of the text. The Flesch-Kincaid measure (Kincaid et al., 1975) employs the average number of syllables per word and the average number of words per sentence to assess readability, while the Automated Readability Index (Smith and Senter, 1967) and the Coleman-Liau metric (Coleman and Liau, 1975) measure word length based on character count rather than syllable count; they are func-

Proceedings of Recent Advances in Natural Language Processing, pages 97–103,
Hissar, Bulgaria, Sep 7–9 2015.

tions of both the average number of characters per word and the average number of words per sentence. Gunning Fog (Gunning, 1952) and SMOG (McLaughlin, 1969) account also for the percentage of polysyllabic words and the Dale-Chall formula (Dale and Chall, 1995) relies on lists of most frequent words to assess readability.

2 Our Approach

The problem that we investigate in this paper is how the readability level varies across original and translated texts (from various source languages). We identify utterances from *Europarl* in a wide variety of languages, we identify their translations into English, and on these English translations we conduct a quantitative analysis of the readability features. As most research on readability focused on English so far, there are several formulas, features and tools available for quantifying the differences in the level of readability.

In this paper we complement our previous analysis (Ciobanu and Dinu, 2014) on the readability features for the original texts and their translations. Here we focus on the target language, analyzing whether different source languages lead to differences in the readability level for the translated texts.

Lang.	# speakers	# sentences
EN	62	1,262
SV	292	80,171
NL	226	156,836
DA	151	37,045
FI	99	36,768
DE	539	300,672
ET	22	4,284
MT	15	2,790
PL	175	62,479
FR	691	264,460
LV	30	4,652
SL	41	8,576
HU	89	23,129
CS	67	20,637
BG	33	5,432
SK	35	13,873
LT	48	14,834
ES	378	116,834
RO	75	24,586
IT	389	109,297
PT	166	98,653

Table 1: Number of speakers and sentences for each language in our *Europarl* subset.

2.1 Data

We run our experiments on *Europarl* (Koehn, 2005), a multilingual parallel corpus extracted from the proceedings of the European Parliament. Its main intended use is as aid for statistical machine translation research (Tiedemann, 2012). The corpus is tokenized and aligned in 21 languages. In Table 1 we report statistics extracted from our dataset. Given the fact that the Flesch-Kincaid formula is based on the average number of words per sentence and on the average number of syllables per word, the differences between the languages (in terms of the number of speakers and sentences) do not affect the results.

According to van Halteren (2008), translations in the European Parliament are generally made by native speakers of the target language. Translation is an inherent part of the political activity (Schäffner and Bassnett, 2010) and has a high influence on the way the political speeches are perceived. The question posed by Schäffner and Bassnett (2010) *"What exactly happens in the complex processes of recontextualisation across linguistic, cultural and ideological boundaries?"* summarizes the complexity of the process of translating political documents. Political texts might contain complex technical terms and elaborated sentences. Therefore, the results of our experiments are probably domain-specific and cannot be generalized to other types of text. Although parliamentary documents probably have a low readability level, our investigation is not negatively influenced by the choice of corpus because we are consistent across all experiments in terms of text gender and we report results obtained solely by comparison between source and target languages.

2.2 Pre-processing

To obtain the dataset for our experiments, we follow the pre-processing steps described by Ciobanu and Dinu (2014). We extract segments of text written in English, we identify their source languages, and we group them based on the language of the speaker. We compute the Flesch-Kicaid formula for each collection of segments of text T_i having the source language L_i and the target language English. The files contain annotations for marking the document (<*chapter*>), the speaker (<*speaker*>) and the paragraph (<*p*>). Some documents have the attribute *language* for the *speaker* tag, which indicates the language used by the original speaker. Another way of annotating the original language is by having the language abbreviation written between parentheses at the beginning of each segment of text. However, there are segments where the language is not marked in either of the two ways. We account only for sentences for which the original language could be determined.

We handle inconsistent encodings and values generated by the automatic extraction of the information from the website of the European Parliament, such as the occurrence of more than one speaker names in the <*speaker*> tag, separated either by a comma or by the *and* conjunction, or the occurrence of a speaker's affiliation in the <*speaker*> tag, e.g., *Ana Maria Gomes (PSE).* We discard the transcribers' descriptions of the parliamentary sessions (such as *"Applause"* or *"The President interrupted the speaker"*).

3 Experiments

In this section we describe our experiments on the variability of the readability feature values for original English texts and texts translated into English from various source languages.

3.1 Flesch-Kincaid

We employ the Flesch-Kincaid measure (Kincaid et al., 1975), which assesses readability based on the average number of syllables per word and the average number of words per sentence. The Flesch-Kincaid formula is one of the most widely used readability metrics developed for English. It assesses the level of readability accounting for the number of syllables per word (as an approximation of the difficulty of a word) and for the number of words per sentence (as estimation of the syntactic difficulty of a text). The metric is computed as follows:

$$0.39\frac{\#words}{\#sentences} + 11.8\frac{\#syllables}{\#words} - 15.59.$$

The Flesch-Kincaid formula produces values which correspond with U.S. grade levels. We apply this measure on English texts, either originally written in English or translated from other languages. To determine the number of syllable for English words, we employ CMU Pronouncing Dictionary[1], a machine-readable dictionary that contains over 125,000 words and provides information regarding their syllabication.

In order to investigate and compare the readability level for original English texts and texts translated from other languages, we complete the following experiments. In a first phase, we compute the Flesh-Kincaid metric for each language, for all the concatenated files in our Europarl subcorpus.

3.1.1 Outliers Removal

The readability of a text depends, among other things, on its author. We investigate whether the readability level characterizes certain speakers, if it varies across different utterances of the same speaker and if the readability level for a language is influenced by speakers having odd readability levels associated. For this purpose, we designed three experiments based on the same idea – identification of outliers in our dataset. Further, in order to eliminate a confounding factor, namely the individuality of the speakers, to focus on the source language of the text, we perform three stages of pruning for our dataset.

- **S1:** For each language, we account for the overall readability score computed for all documents of each speaker; based on these computed values, we determine outliers and remove them from the dataset; then, we rerun the experiments based on Flesch-Kincaid measure for the remaining speakers. In order to achieve this, we divide the dataset based on the source language of the segments of text and for each language we divide the segments of text based on the speaker. We compute the overall readability score for the utterances of each speaker and, after dividing the segments of text from the dataset based on the speakers, we compute the standard quartiles *Q1*, *Q2* and *Q3* with regard to the overall level of readability for each speaker. We use the interquartile range $IQR = Q3 - Q1$ to find outliers in data. For our experiments, we consider outliers the observations that fall below $Q1 - 1.5(IQR)$ (lower fence - LF) or above

[1] http://www.speech.cs.cmu.edu/cgi-bin/cmudict

$Q3 + 1.5(IQR)$ (upper fence - UF) (Sheskin, 2003). We compute the Flesch-Kincaid formula again accounting only for the speakers having the individual level of readability in $[LF, UF]$ range.

- **S2:** We repeat the previous experiment introducing a further level of granularity: we investigate outliers for each speaker by computing the Flesch-Kincaid metric individually for each document belonging to a speaker. We discard documents whose levels of readability are outliers and we compute the Flesch-Kincaid formula again accounting only for the documents having the individual level of readability in the $[LF, UF]$ range.

- **S3:** In the last experiment we consider, for each language, the readability scores of each document belonging to each speaker. We apply the same strategy as before: we detect outliers among documents and remove them from the dataset. Then we compute the Flesch-Kincaid measure again, for the concatenation of all the remaining documents after outliers removal, for each language.

3.1.2 Results

In Table 2, column 2, we report the Flesch-Kincaid values for all 21 languages. One can notice that the lowest Flesh-Kincaid value belongs to the collection of texts having English as the source language, followed by texts having Germanic source languages, texts having Slavic source languages and, finally, texts translated from Romance languages. Finno-Ugric languages represent the only family that doesn't form a cluster with regard to the Flesch-Kincaid metric value. Among the Romance languages, French is the only one that sets apart from the group, being closer to the Germanic cluster. For the outliers removal experiment we report the results in Table 2, columns 3-5. The results are very similar to those of the initial experiment, suggesting that although there are outliers in the data (in Figure 1 we represent the boxplot for the Flesch-Kincaid values for each speaker's utterances), their presence does not impact significantly the overall readability values.

	Flesch-Kincaid			
Lang.	**before removing outliers**	**after pruning**		
		S1	**S2**	**S3**
EN	11.45	11.50	11.47	11.51
SV	11.50	11.49	11.45	11.44
NL	11.56	11.55	11.51	11.50
DA	11.95	11.94	11.90	11.89
FI	11.99	12.01	11.95	11.94
DE	12.45	12.44	12.38	12.37
ET	12.71	12.71	12.66	12.62
MT	12.79	12.79	12.73	12.74
PL	12.81	12.81	12.75	12.73
FR	13.29	13.30	13.25	13.24
LV	13.34	13.34	13.25	13.26
SL	13.35	13.31	13.34	13.32
HU	13.46	13.41	13.42	13.41
CS	13.75	13.76	13.70	13.66
BG	13.90	13.73	13.80	13.84
SK	13.91	13.91	13.86	13.84
LT	14.69	14.72	14.60	14.59
ES	14.72	14.70	14.61	14.59
RO	15.01	15.00	14.91	14.88
IT	15.54	15.54	15.46	15.46
PT	15.60	15.60	15.47	15.44

Table 2: Flesch-Kincaid values for our *Europarl* subset before (column 2) and after (columns 3-5) removing outliers.

3.2 Classification

In this section we investigate the readability of translation as a classification problem. Taking as input original English sentences and sentences translated from other languages, our goal is to see whether the readability features have enough discriminative power to distinguish original from translated text. Thus, we train a logistic regression classifier[2] for a binary decision problem: original versus translation. We extract randomly from our dataset 1,000 English original sentences and 1,000 sentences translated into English[3]. We split this dataset into train and test subsets with a 3:1 ratio. We choose the optimal value for the logistic regression regularization parameter performing 3-fold cross-validation on the training set (we search over $\{10^{-3}, ..., 10^{3}\}$). Finally, we evaluate the model on the test set.

[2]We use the *scikit-learn* library (Pedregosa et al., 2011).

[3]We work with only 1,000 sentences in order to have a stratified dataset, since for English the number of sentences we identified is 1,262. The subset of translated sentences is also stratified: 50 from each of the 20 languages that we investigate, besides English.

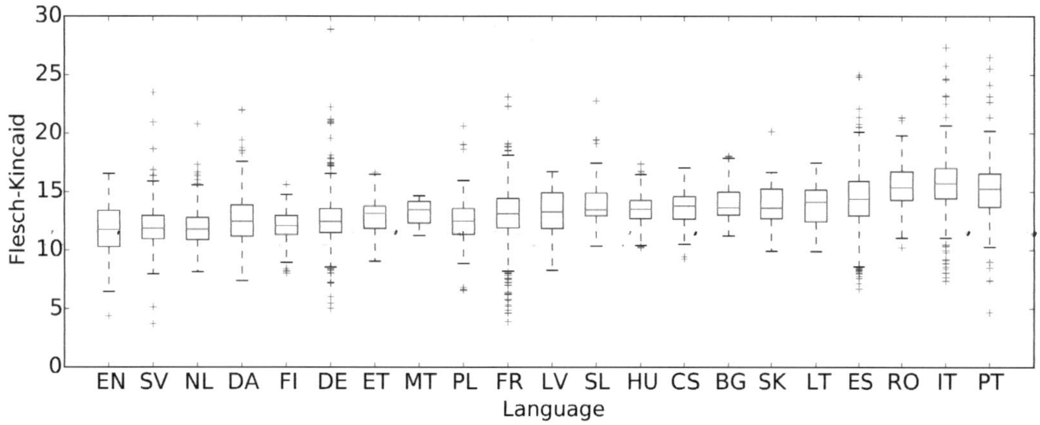

Figure 1: Boxplot for the Flesch-Kincaid values for each speaker's utterances, grouped by the language of the speaker.

3.2.1 Features

We use several shallow, lexical and morpho-syntactic features that were traditionally used for assessing readability and have proven high discriminative power within readability metrics:

- **Shallow Features**
  - **Average number of words per sentence.** The average sentence length is one of the most widely used metrics for determining readability level and was employed in numerous readability formulas, proving to be most meaningful in combined evidence with average word frequency. Feng et al. (2010) find the average sentence length to have higher predictive power than the other lexical and syllable-based features they used.
  - **Average number of characters (or syllables) per word.** It is generally considered that frequently occurring words are usually short, so the average number of characters per word was broadly used for measuring readability in a robust manner. Many readability formulas measure word length in syllables rather than letters.
- **Lexical Features**
  - **Type/Token Ratio.** The proportion between the number of lexical types and the number of tokens indicates the range of use of vocabulary. The higher the value of this feature, the higher the variability of the vocabulary used in the text.
- **Morpho-Syntactic Features**
  - **Relative frequency of POS unigrams.** The ratio for 5 POS (verbs, nouns, pronouns, adjectives and adverbs), computed individually on a per-token basis[4].
  - **Lexical density.** The proportion of content words (verbs, nouns, adjectives and adverbs), computed on a per-token basis. Grammatical features were shown to be useful in readability prediction (Heilman et al., 2007).

3.2.2 Results

The optimal value for the logistic regression regularization parameter is found to be 1. We obtain 0.59 F-score on the test set, on average, in deciding whether a sentence was translated into English or is an original English sentence. In Table 3 we report the precision, recall and F-score for the prediction task. We also report 95% confidence intervals (CI) measured on 1,000 iterations of bootstrap resampling with replacement (Koehn, 2004). The most informative features are morphological features, more specifically the POS ratios, as shown in Table 4. These results are significantly lower than state-of-the-art performance

[4]For tokenization, lemmatization and part of speech tagging we use the Stanford CoreNLP Natural Language Processing Toolkit (Manning et al., 2014).

Class	Precision	Recall	F-score
Original EN	0.60 [0.55, 0.65]	0.56 [0.51, 0.61]	0.58 [0.54, 0.62]
Translated	0.58 [0.53, 0.63]	0.62 [0.56, 0.67]	0.60 [0.56, 0.64]

Table 3: Classification results and 95% bootstrapped confidence intervals for a 2-class prediction problem — original vs. translated text — using readability features.

in translation identification, suggesting that readability features do not have enough discriminative power for the prediction task[5]. Adding n-grams of tokens and POS tags as features improves the performance of the model, leading to 0.75 average F-score ([0.71, 0.78] 95% CI) in discriminating between English sentences and translations.

4 Conclusions

In this paper we investigate the impact of translation on readability as a two-fold problem. Firstly, we investigate how the Flesch-Kincaid values vary for original English texts and for translations form different languages into English. We notice that the values form clusters for the investigated language families. Secondly, we use a set of shallow, lexical and morpho-syntactic readability features to investigate whether readability features have enough discriminative power to distinguish original English texts from translations. We obtain 0.59 F-score, on average, using only readability features, and an improvement to 0.75 when we add n-grams of tokens and POS tags as features. Our results show that, although the readability level of translated texts is similar for texts having the source language in the same language families, readability features do not have enough discriminative power to obtain high performance on distinguishing original texts from translations. However, using only readability features the prediction F-score is significantly better than chance ($p < 0.05$).

In our future work, we intend to enrich the variety of the texts, beginning with an analysis of translations of literary works. As far as resources are available, we plan to investigate other readability metrics as well. We believe our method can provide useful information regarding the difficulty of translation from one language into another in terms of readability.

[5]Repeating the classification experiment for each source language (that is, considering translations from each source language L_i, except for English, one at a time) shows that the differences in performance are not statistically significant ($p < 0.05$). Thus, we conclude that readability features cannot discriminate between original texts and translations significantly better for some of the source languages than for the others.

Feature	Coefficient
Verb ratio	–1.59
Adverb ratio	1.49
Adjective ratio	1.35
Pronoun ratio	–1.21
Noun ratio	–0.88
Lexical density	–0.83
Type/token ratio	0.49
Average number of syllables	0.49
Average number of characters	0.04
Average number of words	–0.01

Table 4: Logistic regression coefficients for readability features (the higher the absolute value of the coefficient, the more informative the feature).

Acknowledgements

We thank the anonymous reviewers for their helpful and constructive comments. The contribution of the authors to this paper is equal. Liviu P. Dinu was supported by UEFISCDI, PNII-ID-PCE-2011-3-0959.

References

Sandra Aluisio, Lucia Specia, Caroline Gasperin, and Carolina Scarton. 2010. Readability Assessment for Text Simplification. In *Proceedings of the NAACL HLT 2010 Fifth Workshop on Innovative Use of NLP for Building Educational Applications, IUNLPBEA 2010*, pages 1–9.

Alina Maria Ciobanu and Liviu Dinu. 2014. A Quantitative Insight into the Impact of Translation on Readability. In *Proceedings of the 3rd Workshop on Predicting and Improving Text Readability for Target Reader Populations, PITR 2014*, pages 104–113.

Meri Coleman and T. L. Liau. 1975. A Computer Readability Formula Designed for Machine Scoring. *Journal of Applied Psychology*, 60(2):283–284.

Kevyn Collins-Thompson. 2011. Enriching Information Retrieval with Reading Level Prediction. In *SIGIR 2011 Workshop on Enriching Information Retrieval*.

Edgar Dale and Jeanne Chall. 1995. *Readability Revisited: The New Dale-Chall Readability Formula*. Brookline Books, Cambridge.

Noemie Elhadad and Komal Sutaria. 2007. Mining a Lexicon of Technical Terms and Lay Equivalents. In *Proceedings of the Workshop on BioNLP 2007: Biological, Translational, and Clinical Language Processing, BioNLP 2007*, pages 49–56.

Lijun Feng, Martin Jansche, Matt Huenerfauth, and Noémie Elhadad. 2010. A Comparison of Features for Automatic Readability Assessment. In *Proceedings of the 23rd International Conference on Computational Linguistics: Posters, COLING 2010*, pages 276–284.

Thomas François and Eleni Miltsakaki. 2012. Do NLP and Machine Learning Improve Traditional Readability Formulas? In *Proceedings of the First Workshop on Predicting and Improving Text Readability for Target Reader Populations, PITR 2012*, pages 49–57.

Valerio Franchina and Roberto Vacca. 1986. Adaptation of Flesch Readability Index on a Bilingual Text Written by the Same Author both in Italian and English Languages. *Linguaggi*, 3:47–49.

Robert Gunning. 1952. *The Technique of Clear Writing*. McGraw-Hill.

Michael Heilman, Kevyn Collins-Thompson, Jamie Callan, and Maxine Eskenazi. 2007. Combining Lexical and Grammatical Features to Improve Readability Measures for First and Second Language Texts. In *Proceedings of the Human Language Technology Conference of the North American Chapter of the Association of Computational Linguistics, HLT-NAACL 2007*, pages 460–467.

Fernandez Huerta. 1959. Medida Sencillas de Lecturabilidad. *Consigna*, 214:29–32.

Lilian Kandel and Abraham Moles. 1958. Application de l'Indice de Flesch a la Langue Française. *Cahiers Etudes de Radio-Television*, 19:253–274.

Peter Kincaid, Robert P. Fishburne Jr., Richard L. Rogers, and Brad S. Chissom. 1975. *Derivation of New Readability Formulas (Automated Readability Index, Fog Count and Flesch Reading Ease Formula) for Navy Enlisted Personnel*. Research Branch Report, Millington, TN: Chief of Naval Training.

Philipp Koehn. 2004. Statistical Significance Tests for Machine Translation Evaluation. In *Proceedings of the 2004 Conference on Empirical Methods in Natural Language Processing, EMNLP 2004*, pages 388–395.

Philipp Koehn. 2005. Europarl: A Parallel Corpus for Statistical Machine Translation. In *Proceedings of the 10th Machine Translation Summit*, pages 79–86.

Moshe Koppel and Noam Ordan. 2011. Translationese and Its Dialects. In *Proceedings of the 49th Annual Meeting of the Association for Computational Linguistics: Human Language Technologies, ACL 2011*, pages 1318–1326.

Christopher D. Manning, Mihai Surdeanu, John Bauer, Jenny Finkel, Steven J. Bethard, and David McClosky. 2014. The Stanford CoreNLP Natural Language Processing Toolkit. In *Proceedings of 52nd Annual Meeting of the Association for Computational Linguistics: System Demonstrations*, pages 55–60.

Harry McLaughlin. 1969. SMOG Grading: a New Readability Formula. *Journal of Reading*, 12(8):639–646.

Fabian Pedregosa, Gaël Varoquaux, Alexandre Gramfort, Vincent Michel, Bertrand Thirion, Olivier Grisel, Mathieu Blondel, Peter Prettenhofer, Ron Weiss, Vincent Dubourg, Jake Vanderplas, Alexandre Passos, David Cournapeau, Matthieu Brucher, Matthieu Perrot, and Édouard Duchesnay. 2011. Scikit-learn: Machine Learning in Python. *Journal of Machine Learning Research*, 12:2825–2830.

Christina Schäffner and Susan Bassnett. 2010. Politics, Media and Translation - Exploring Synergies. In *Political Discourse, Media and Translation*, pages 1–29. Newcastle upon Tyne: Cambridge Scholars Publishing.

David J. Sheskin. 2003. *Handbook of Parametric and Nonparametric Statistical Procedures*. CRC Press.

Edgar A. Smith and R. J. Senter. 1967. Automated Readability Index. *Wright-Patterson Air Force Base. AMRL-TR-6620.*

Sara Stymne, Jörg Tiedemann, Christian Hardmeier, and Joakim Nivre. 2013. Statistical Machine Translation with Readability Constraints. In *Proceedings of the 19th Nordic Conference on Computational Linguistics, NODALIDA 2013*, pages 375–386.

Yifeng Sun. 2012. Translation and Strategies for Cross-Cultural Communication. *Chinese Translators Journal*, 33(1):16–23.

Jörg Tiedemann. 2012. Parallel Data, Tools and Interfaces in OPUS. In *Proceedings of the 8th International Conference on Language Resources and Evaluation, LREC 2012*, pages 2214–2218.

Anna Trosborg, editor. 1997. *Text Typology and Translation*. Benjamins Translation Library.

Hans van Halteren. 2008. Source Language Markers in EUROPARL Translations. In *Proceedings of the 22nd International Conference on Computational Linguistics, COLING 2008*, pages 937–944.

Processing and Normalizing Hashtags

Thierry Declerck
Dept. of Computational Linguistics,
Saarland University, Saarbrücken,
Germany
declerck@dfki.de

Piroska Lendvai
Dept. of Computational Linguistics,
Saarland University, Saarbrücken,
Germany
piroska.r@gmail.com

Abstract

We present ongoing work in linguistic processing of hashtags in Twitter text, with the goal of supplying normalized hashtag content to be used in more complex natural language processing (NLP) tasks. Hashtags represent collectively shared topic designators with considerable surface variation that can hamper semantic interpretation. Our normalization scripts allow for the lexical consolidation and segmentation of hashtags, potentially leading to improved semantic classification.

1 Introduction

The relevance of hashtags used in social media text, and more specifically in Twitter messages, has been recognized after some studies focused on the semantics that can be derived by such text constructs. For example, Laniado & Mika (2010) discussed whether hashtags behave as identifiers for Semantic Web applications. But the authors do not raise the issue of processing the hashtags in order to harmonize them, which would be necessary for gaining information on the specific semantics carried by hashtags.

Our observations are based on a large Twitter corpus dedicated to riots in the UK in the summer of 2011[1].Variants for hashtags that refer to the same topic abound, e.g. "#LondonRiots", "#londonriots", "#RiotsInLondon", "londonriot", "#LONDONRIOTS", and so on. We hypothesize that consolidating variants to a preferred hashtag form would benefit further tasks that draw on semantic similarity, such as the recently organized Semantic Textual Similarity Shared Task on Twitter data[2]. We have implemented a set of scripts in order to normalize the surface forms of hashtags. This includes case normalization, lemmatization and syntactic segmentation. We first describe related work, then our approach, and finally display some of our current results.

2 Related Work and Task Specification

(Pöschko, 2011) focuses on the detection of similar hashtags on the basis of their co-occurrences in a tweet. While the detection of co-occurrences is also present in our pipeline, we are additionally interested in detecting variants in order to reduce the amount of topics that hashtags designate. The expectation is that hashtag variants would all together represent only one topic.

(Antenucci et al., 2011) discuss an algorithm to learn the relationships between the literal content of a tweet and the types of hashtags that describe that content, which is one of our goals as well. Contrary to us, (Antenucci et al., 2011) do not suggest the harmonization (or reduction to a preferred form) of hashtags, but use similarity measurements between hashtags and words, while we implement patterns for explicitly relating variants of hashtags to a preferred form. We will use the results of their study for comparison with our approach.

(Costa et al., 2013) propose an approach that defines meta-hashtags by grouping the most used hashtags and their related hashtags into a meta-class, in order to improve the classification of

[1] This corpus was built on behalf of the newspaper „The Guardian", and its first objective was to gather data for tracking the emergence of rumours in social media. See http://www.theguardian.com/news/datablog/2011/dec/08/twitter-riots-interactive . An example usage of this corpus with NLP approaches for argumentation research is given in (Llewellyn et al., 2014).

[2] http://www.cis.upenn.edu/~xwe/semeval2015pit/

Proceedings of Recent Advances in Natural Language Processing, pages 104–109,
Hissar, Bulgaria, Sep 7–9 2015.

tweets. We aim at a reduced set of hashtag classes as well, but keeping normalization at the surface form level, without reaching a more abstract level. We promote the most frequent, lowercased hashtag variant to be the preferred form.

(Krokos and Samet, 2014) generate hashtags for tweets to be used as identifiers for NLP and Semantic Web applications, for which the preferred hashtag variant that we create would be directly of use.

Closely related work is presented by (Bansal et al., 2015). The authors seek to improve entity linking in tweets via semantic information provided by segmenting and linking entities that are present in a hashtag. Our approach is not limited to entities, but aims at covering the full lexical content of hashtags and targets general NLP scenarios.

Next to the normalization step that we mentioned above, syntactic parsing of hashtags would benefit retrieval tasks. A tweet could be more easily linked to other documents (e.g. documents from other genres that do not include hashtags, such as news articles). The query "#RiotsInLondon" would be less successful than the free-text query "Riots in London" or keyword query "Riots" and "London". Journalists, for example, need to establish verification links between a tweet and other sources in order to corroborate information in user-generated texts. Segmenting the text of the hashtag will allow using the derived components as search terms. The strong semantic and dependency relations between lexical components of the hashtag are typically not taken into account by search engines; this is why we aim to make these explicit.

(Bansal et al., 2015) discusses various algorithms for the segmentation of hashtags, like the Variable Length Sliding Window technique. We plan to investigate the application of this technique is the next steps of our work, but will use a simpler approach in the current study.

3 Harmonizing Hashtags

There are different ways of using hashtags in different languages: Spanish tweets are reported to contain much fewer hashtags than e.g. German tweets[3], while the use of CamelCase[4] notation seems to be much more popular in English tweets than in Spanish tweets[5].

Our first experiment is performed on a subset of the UK Riots corpus, selecting tweets between time stamps *2011-08-08/16:56:58* and *2011-08-08/17:18:53*. The subcorpus comprises 11,898 tweets. In this subcorpus 9,289 tweets are hapaxes. This yields a type-token ratio (TTR) of 78.07[6]. The subcorpus includes 16,716 hashtags tokens[7], but only 1,330 hashtags types, giving us a TTR of 7.95. We have 3,837 hashtags tokens and 188 hashtags types in CamelCase notation, yielding a TTR of 4.89.

Applying the simplest normalisation step – lowercasing all hashtags – leaves 1,156 hashtag types (TTR = 6.91). Lowercasing was applied 6,832 times. The number of matching between lowercased and original hashtags (in lowercase) is 5,921. From this figures we can see that this simple step is already reducing considerably the number of variants.

3.1 #LondonRiots

In order to show the relevance of lowercasing, the distribution of candidate variants of "#londonriots" in our subcorpus is displayed below in Figure 1.

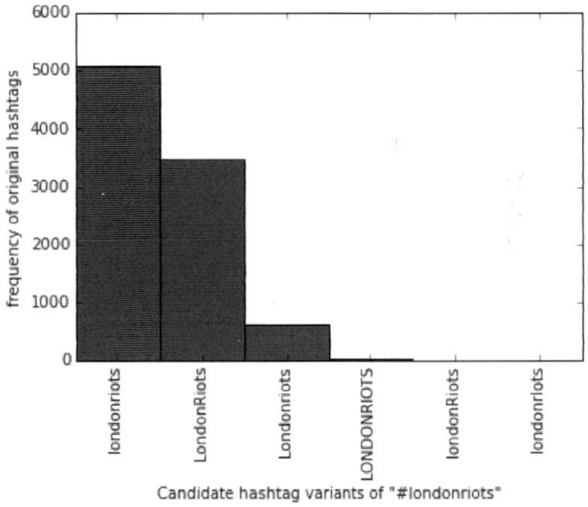

Figure 1: Distribution of candidate variants of #londonriots.

This gives us for those candidate variants a total of 9,218 harmonized hashtags (all original hashtags to be lowercased). We can see that this

[3] See (Weerkamp et al., 2011) on a cross-language study of the use of hashtags.

[4] An example of a CamelCased hashtag is „#LondonRiots". See https://en.wikipedia.org/wiki/CamelCase for more details on CamelCase.

[5] We still have to quantify this observation.

[6] TTR can be important for estimating the amount of noise in the corpus.

[7] The high number of hashtags might be collection-specific, the figures reported in (Weerkamp et al., 2011) for the use of hashtags in English tweets are lower.

harmonization step is considerably increasing the initial number of #londonriots hashtags (5,085). The tag "#londonriots" is promoted as the preferred form of these variants.8 Since the singular forms #londonriot, #LondonRiot (occurring respectively only six and one times in the subcorpus) and others are less frequent, we also replace these with the canonical plural form.

4 Segmenting Hashtags

Most of the English hashtags reflect a trend to use space-free compounding, e.g. "#LondonRiots", similar to e.g. German compounding. We also observe that the order of words in binary compounding follows the NE + N syntactical pattern, "#LondonRiots", while more complex compounding takes place via e.g. N + PP pattern "#RiotsInLondon". The dependency structure of this pattern makes it easier to determine the semantic head of the hashtag. In our example, the semantic head of the compound "#RiotsInLondon" is 'Riots'. Establishing a paraphrase relation to "#LondonRiots" allows us to state that also in the latter case the semantic head is "Riots" (although not being in the first position of the compound).

This approach for detecting paraphrases of compound terms has been investigated first in (Mihaela Vela, 2011). In a large corpus of German texts on financial topics, all detected binary compound words have been segmented. Then a search in the corpus was started in order to find within a small window of words the segments of the original compounds (in the reversed order) separated by either a preposition or a determiner in genitive case. This approach was effectively supporting the building of taxonomic structures from German compounds, since the paraphrases were offering additional semantics on relations between the components, marked by the preposition or by the genitive determiners. We apply a derived version of this approach to the (English) complex hashtags present in our UK Riots corpus.

First, we process hashtags that feature CamelCase notation: "RiotsInLondon" is segmented in 'Riots', 'In', and 'London'. We perform part-of-speech (POS) tagging[9] on the segments to check if they are part of the English vocabulary. This step is done in order to validate the segmentation. For our example, the NLTK default tagger delivers:

```
[('Riots', 'NNS'), ('In',
'IN'), ('London', 'NNP')]
```

And in this case, we are also lucky that no ambiguity is present in this tagged example, but the main purpose of tagging the resulting segments is to verify that there are no unknown words among the segments.

On the top of the results of the tagger, we are applying our SCHUG constituency and dependency parser[10]:

```
<NP
   TYPE="gen/5-attach_en/16"
   STRUCT="1_23_25"
   STRING="Riots In London"
   NP_HEAD_STEM="riot"
   NP_HEAD="Riots"
   NP_RULE="NP-PP"
   NP_MOD="[In London]">
   <TOKEN ORD="1" POS="1"
   TC="22"     STTS_POS="NNS"
   STEM="riot">Riots</TOKEN>
   <TOKEN STEM="in"
   STTS_POS="IN" TC="21"
   POS="23"
   ORD="2">In</TOKEN>
   <TOKEN ORD="3" POS="1"
   TC="22" STEM="London"
   STTS_POS="NNP">London</TO
   KEN>
</NP>
```

The main information for us is in this result the fact that the word "Riots" has been identified as the head of the segment, and "London" as part of the modifier.

Following strategies consisting in extracting semantic relations from dependency structures[11], we can infer that the sequence "RiotsInLondon" is a subclass of the class "Riots". Or that "RiotsInLondon" are an instance of "Riots". Another possibility consists in stating that the class "Riots" is equipped with a property "hasLocation".

While we are not now generating an ontological structure out of those segmented hashtags, we

[8] We are working on encoding all information in the emerging W3C standard 'Ontolex', cf. https://www.w3.org/community/ontolex/

[9] We use for this the part-of-speech tagger included in NLTK. See section 1 of http://www.nltk.org/book/ch05.html

[10] See (Thierry Declerck, 2002) for more details.

[11] See (Buitelaar et. al, 2004) and (Mihaela Vela, 2011).

are linking those with existing semantic resources in the Linked Open Data cloud[12]. We applied for this the sparqlwrapper module for Python[13], an example of which given just below:

```
from SPARQLWrapper import
SPARQLWrapper, JSON

sparql = SPARQLWrap-
per("http://dbpedia.org/sparql")

sparql.setQuery("""
PREFIX rdfs:
<http://www.w3.org/2000/01/rdf-
schema#>
PREFIX owl:
<http://www.w3.org/2002/07/owl#>
PREFIX dbpedia-owl:
<http://dbpedia.org/ontology/>
PREFIX dct:
<http://purl.org/dc/terms/>
   SELECT ?var
   WHERE
{<http://dbpedia.org/resource/Riot>
dct:subject  ?var }
   """)
sparql.setReturnFormat(JSON)
results = sparql.query().convert()
for result in re-
sults["results"]["bindings"]:
   print(result["label"]["value"])
```

In the example above the reader can see that we linked the hashtags "#riots", "#Riots", "#riot" and "#Riot" to a DBpedia entry, which is named "Riot". Since we segmented hashtags like "#LondonRiots" or "#TottenhamRiots", we can also link their "Riots" segments to this DBpedia entry, while the segments "London" and "Tottenham" can be linked to the corresponding DBpedia entries. At the end, we can compute the information that we are dealing with riots in UK cities.

The process is the same for both hashtag types "#LondonRiots" and "#RiotsInLondon", since we established that both hashtags are paraphrases of each other[14]. The process of segmentation helps gaining evidence that the main topic of the corpus is riots; while specific locations can be designated by specific hashtags, e.g. "#hackney-riots". Next, the components extracted from camel notation hashtags are used for supporting the segmentation of similar hashtags that are not written in camel case notation. For example "#londonriots" could be segmented into "london" and "riots" (as a reminder, the hashtag "#londonriots" is occurring 5,085 times in the corpus used in our experiment), or "#riotpolice" into "riot" and "police" (this hashtag in this form occurring only twice, and also twice in the CamelCase form).

The segmentation step can provide information about the number of semantic units located in the hashtagged text; this has been found in previous studies[15] indicative about the level of factuality expressed by a hashtag. Below we see two examples of segmented hashtags. The counts represent the position and frequency of the components of a compound hashtag.

```
'#LondonRiots' => {
        '0' => {'London' => 3461},
        '1' => { 'Riots' => 3461},
        'freq' => 3461},

'#SouthernFairiesCantHandleTheirWineGums' => {
    '0' => { 'Southern' = 1 },
    '1' => { 'Fairies' => 1 },
    '2' => { 'Cant' => 1 },
    '3' => {'Handle' => 1 },
    '4' => {'Their' => 1 },
    '5' => {'Wine' => 1 },
    '6' => {'Gums' => 1 },
    'freq' => 1
    },
```

#LondonRiots occurs 3,461 times. We then just add this frequency to the components of the compound. We can add this figure to the number of occurrences of the single hashtags "#Riots" and "#riots" (originally with a total of 1,096 occurrences, now with a total of 9778 occurrences), giving more evidence that a major topic of the corpus is "riots". This evidence is increasing still when we consider the cases of "#HackneyRiots" and the like. The increase of frequency of the from our algorithm partly generated hashtag candidates "#riots" and "#Riots" is show in **Figure 2** and **Figure 3**. Looking at the values for "#riots" we see a dramatic increase of frequency for the terms "riots" and "Riots", but also significant changes for the names of locations.

Additionally, we observed that both of the components of "#londonriots" and similar are often co-occurring in tweets in a non- or only a

[12] See http://lod-cloud.net/ for more details.

[13] See https://rdflib.github.io/sparqlwrapper/

[14] As mentioned earlier, we adapted for this a method used for German, consisting in searching for paraphrases of compounds. See (Mihaela Vela, 2011).

[15] Kotsakos et al. (2014) suggest that the length of a hashtagged text as one of the features that help in differentiating meme tweets from event reporting tweets: the longer the hashtagged text, the higher the probability that the tweet is a meme.

partly hashtagged form (like "London #riots"). This fact can give supplementary evidence that the segmentation of the hashtags was well motivated.

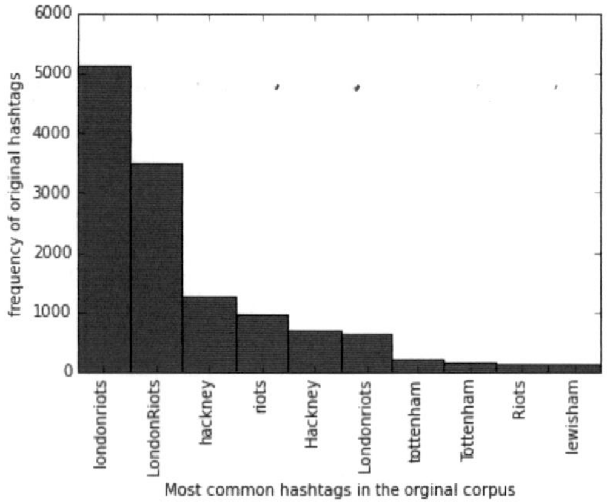

Figure 2: Most common hashtags in the original corpus.

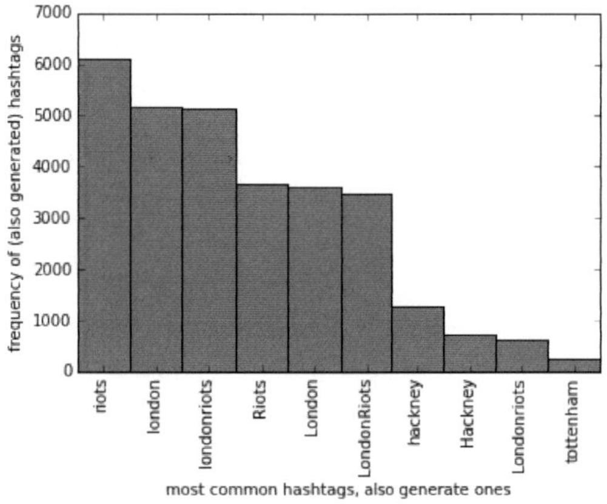

Figure 3: Increased frequency of certain hashtags, after segmentation of complex hashtags.

Related to this, we displayed above the example of the segmentation of the longer hashtag string "SouthernFairiesCantHandleTheirWineGums". We observed that none of the components are co-occurring in any relevant way in the tweets of our corpus. This can lead to the classification of such hashtags as spam or as not factual. This would be in accordance with the findings by (Kotsakos et al. 2014), stating that longer hashtags tend to not represent facts.

Finally we computed the frequency of usage of each word in different compound hashtags. We display below the example for "Riots". In this representation we also provide for information on the position of the components of the compounds: the word Riots is in the first position within the compound hashtag "#RiotsAffectOthers" ("0 =>"), etc. The representation provides thus contextual information of the word "Riots" when used in distinct hashtags.

```
'Riots' => {
        '0' => {
                '#RiotsAffectOthers' => 1
        },
        '1' => {
                '#BirminghamRiots' => 2,
                '#CroydonRiots' => 1,
                '#EnfieldRiots' => 1,
                '#HackneyRiots' => 9,
                '#LondonRiots' => 3461,
                '#StopRiots' => 1,
                '#StopRiotsInLondon' => 1,
                '#TottenhamRiots' => 9
        },
        '2' => {
            '#Hackney#LondonRiots'=> 1,
                '#NorthLondonRiots' => 1,
                '#StopTheRiots' => 1
        },
        'freq' => 3489
    },
```

5 Current Work

We are currently investigating if our approach can help in concrete applications. In one scenario, hashtag normalization is used to preprocess tweets in a tweet-vs-document similarity task. Similarity is computed by means of string alignment (across a tweet and each of the sentences of a document), and we hypothesize that hashtag normalization would allow for more matching.

In a second application we are aiming at improving the output of cluster algorithms applied to our data. In a preprocessing phase we normalized hashtags and we could already observe that the behavior of the used clustering algorithm (included in the NLTK package) was sensitive to this kind of lexical variation.

Finally, we started to investigate if and how Textual Entailment can be applied to social media text. We are using for this the Excitement Open Platform (EOP)[16]. Since one algorithm deployed in EOP is making strong use of detection of paraphrases, in order to support the system in recognizing similar statements, it is important to either add unifying semantic information to the text segments under entailment judgement and/or

[16] See http://hltfbk.github.io/Excitement-Open-Platform for more details.

to apply methods for reducing the lexical variety of the text segments (supporting the detection of longer matching segments between two text snippets). Our work on the segmentation and harmonization of hashtags is the first step for the investigation on the use of TE for Twitter text. An evaluation of our approach is currently on the way and will be reported soon.

Acknowledgments

The work described in this paper is partly funded by the European FP7 project PHEME ("Computing Veracity across Media, Languages, and Social Networks"), under agreement no: 611233.

References

D. Antenucci, G. Handy, A. Modi, and M. Tinkerhess. 2011. Classification of tweets via clustering of hashtags". EECS 545 FINAL PROJECT, FALL 2011.

Piyush Bansal, Romil Bansal and Vasudeva Varma. 2015. Towards Deep Semantic Analysis of Hashtags. In Proceedings of the 37th European Conference on Information Retrieval (ECIR 2015), Vienna, Austria.

Paul Buitelaar, Daniel Olejnik, Mihaela Hutanu, Alexander Schutz, Thierry Declerck, Michael Sintek. (2004). Towards Ontology Engineering Based on Linguistic Analysis. Proceedings of International Conference on Language Resources and Evaluation

Joana Costa, Catarina Silva, Mário Antunes and Bernardete Ribeiro. 2013. Defining Semantic Meta-Hashtags for Twitter Classification. In Proceedings of the 11th International Conference on Adaptive and Natural Computing Algorithms, ICANNGA 2013, Lausanne, Switzerland, April 4-6, 2013. Proceedings

Thierry Declerck. (2002). A set of tools for integrating linguistic and non-linguistic information. In Proceedings of SAAKM (ECAI Workshop).

Genevieve Gorrell, Johann Petrak, Kalina Bontcheva 2015. LOD-based Disambiguation of Named Entities in @tweets through Context #enrichment. In *Proceedings of ESWC 2015*, Portoroz, Slovenia.

Dimitrios Kotsakos, Panos Sakkos, Ioannis Katakis and Dimitrios Gunopulos, 2014. "#tag: Meme or Event?" In *Proceedings of ASONAM 2014*, Beijing, China

Eric Krokos Hanan Samet. 2014. A Look into Twitter Hashtag Discovery and Generation. In *Proceedings of the 7th ACM SIGSPATIAL Workshop on Location-Based Social Networks (LBSN'14)*, Dallas, TX, November 2014

David Laniado and Peter Mika. 2010. Making sense of Twitter. In *Proceedings of the 9th International Semantic Web Conference*. Shanghai, China, November 2010.

Clare Llewellyn, Claire Grover, Jon Oberlander and Ewan Klein. 2014. Re-using an Argument Corpus to Aid in the Curation of Social Media. In *Proceedings of the 9th Language Resources and Evaluation Conference*, 26-31 May, Reykjavik, Iceland

Jan Pöschko. 2011. Exploring Twitter Hashtags. CoRR abs/1111.6553.

Mihaela Vela, Extraction of Ontology Schema Components from Financial News. (2011). PhD Thesis, Saarbrücken

Xiaolong Wang, Furu Wei, Xiaohua Liu, Ming Zhou and Ming Zhang. 2011. Topic sentiment analysis in twitter: a graph-based hashtag sentiment classification approach. In *Proceedings of the 20th ACM international conference on Information and knowledge management*, Pages 1031-1040

Wouter Weerkamp, Simon Carter and Manos Tsagkias. 2011. How People use Twitter in Different Languages. *In Proceedings of Web Science.*

Tune Your Brown Clustering, Please

Leon Derczynski
University of Sheffield
leon@dcs.shef.ac.uk

Sean Chester
Aarhus University
schester@cs.au.dk

Kenneth S. Bøgh
Aarhus University
ksb@cs.au.dk

Abstract

Brown clustering, an unsupervised hierarchical clustering technique based on n-gram mutual information, has proven useful in many NLP applications. However, most uses of Brown clustering employ the same default configuration; the appropriateness of this configuration has gone predominantly unexplored. Accordingly, we present information for practitioners on the behaviour of Brown clustering in order to assist hyper-parametre tuning, in the form of a theoretical model of Brown clustering utility. This model is then evaluated empirically in two sequence labelling tasks over two text types. We explore the dynamic between the input corpus size, chosen number of classes, and quality of the resulting clusters, which has an impact for any approach using Brown clustering. In every scenario that we examine, our results reveal that the values most commonly used for the clustering are sub-optimal.

1 Introduction

Brown clustering (Brown et al., 1992) uses distributional information to group similar words. Unsupervised, it induces a hierarchical clustering over words to form a binary tree (e.g. Figure 1). This hierarchical clustering has recently been used in thousands of computational linguistics papers, often for feature generation. However, no work exists describing the behaviour and hyper-parametre tuning effects of Brown clustering; even the original paper concentrates on implementation rather than its behaviour.

Except for a few forays off the beaten track (e.g. Christodoulopoulos et al. (2010), Owoputi et al. (2012), Derczynski et al. (2015a)), default parametres dominate; either 800 or 1000 Brown clusters are generated in nearly every published use. Few experiments use other configurations, and we are not aware of any prior work on hyper-parametre tuning for Brown clustering.

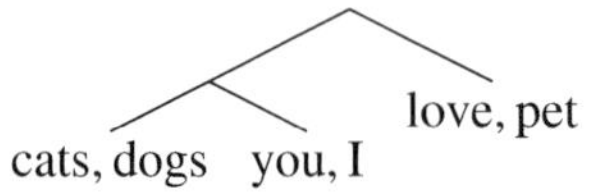

Figure 1: A binary, hierarchical clustering of semantically similar entries. Each leaf corresponds to a cluster of words (i.e., a "class") and leaves near to their common ancestors correspond to clusters that are similar to each other.

This paper addresses this information gap, providing practitioners with principled insights into the algorithm. We provide an analysis of how Brown clustering adds information over input, and, based on this, describe models for the effect that corpus size and cluster count have on the quality of results. These models are then tested in two sequence labeling tasks, cf. Qu et al. (2015). Finally, we compare the initial analysis to observations, leading to concrete advice for practitioners.

2 Background

Brown clustering uses mutual information to determine distributional similarity, placing similar words in the same cluster and similar clusters nearby in the binary tree. This is an unsupervised learned representation of language from the input corpus (Bengio et al., 2013). In the main implementation of Brown clustering (Liang, 2005), mutual information is measured at the bigram level. The resulting structure of word types can be used as feature representations in many NLP tasks, leading to quick, solid performance increases (Turian et al., 2010). In fact, as well as producing effective discriminative features, unsupervised hierarchical clusterings like Brown often lead to better taggers than models developed 20 years later (Blunsom and Cohn (2011), Owoputi et al. (2013)).

Proceedings of Recent Advances in Natural Language Processing, pages 110–117,
Hissar, Bulgaria, Sep 7–9 2015.

Bit path	Word types
00111001	can cn cann caan cannn ckan shalll ccan caaan cannnn caaaan
001011111001	ii id ion iv ll iii ud wd uma ul idnt provoking hed 1+1 ididnt hast ine 2+2 idw #thingsblackpeopledo iiii #onlywhitepeople dost doan uon apt-get

Table 1: Sample Brown clusters over English tweets.[1] Each set of terms is a leaf in the hierarchy.

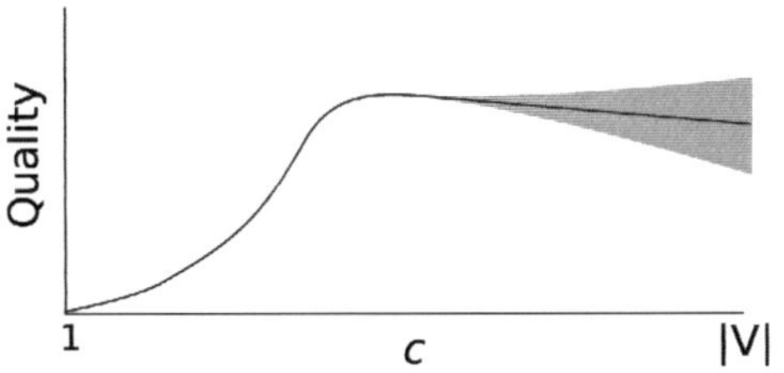

Figure 2: Expected cluster quality as c increases, given a hypothetical ideal cluster quality function.

In practice, Brown clustering takes an input corpus T and number of classes c, and uses mutual information to assign each term in the corpus vocabulary V to one of the c classes. Ideally, each class contains highly semantically-related words, by virtue of words being distributed according to their meaning (Wittgenstein, 1953). Each class is a leaf on an unbalanced binary tree. The path from the root to each leaf can be described as a bit string, where the i'th bit is 0 iff the path branches left at depth i (e.g., *you,I* is on the path `01` in Figure 1). Brown clustering posits that leaves with longer common path prefices are more semantically related. For example, in Figure 1, the *cats,dog* and *you,I* classes are more similar than either is to the *love,pet* class.

3 A Model for Brown Clustering

Here we outline our model for the behaviour of Brown clustering under various situations. Our goal is to describe how the number of classes, c, affects the quality of the resulting clustering.

Initial values for c might not be appropriate for a given task or data set. Large values of c risk forcing similar words into different classes, underrepresenting their similarity. Conversely, a small c may cluster too coarsely, thereby reducing the discriminative power of resulting representations.

Brown clustering adds two forms of information: *the agglomeration* of terms into similar groups and *the hierarchy* connecting semantically similar groups of terms. At extreme values of c, little is added: if $c = |V|$, each word has its own class and only the hierarchy is added; if $c = 1$, one cluster contains all terms and information is gained from neither clustering nor a hierarchy. So, the information added by clustering increases with $c > 1$, peaks, and then declines towards $|V|$.

However, the information added solely by the hierarchy increases with c and peaks when every word type has its own cluster, i.e., when $c = |V|$, as this gives the maximum number to the tree; we cannot add more leaves than there are word types (given a single root).

Also, a too-small c may produce classes of unequal quality. Table 1 lists two classes derived in Owoputi et al. (2012), with $c = 1000$, on a large social media corpus. The first cluster agglomerates a set of semantically close lexemes, but the second cluster is internally semantically disparate, conflating many different concepts. This could indicate an inadequate value for c that forces many concepts into a too-confined number of classes.

A c exceeding the number of word types is also problematic: each word type should have only one class. This can arise in small datasets and when the vocabulary is particularly formalised (e.g., in a controlled natural language) (Wyner et al., 2010). Indeed, the size of the input dataset not only affects the number of eventual word types (Montemurro, 2001), but also quality of the classes.

For a fixed task and corpus genre, we hypothesise that each corpus size has an optimal c and each c has an optimal corpus size. When increasing a corpus size, new word types and further distributional information is revealed. The new distributional information leads to better-informed assignment of terms to classes, thereby improving the cluster quality. Eventually, however, the profusion of word types outgrows c and semantically dissimilar words will be placed in the same class. Overall, we expect clustering performance to scale as shown in Figure 2: quality increases with c to an optimal value, then dips slightly and levels off with some stochastic variance.

In fact, this behaviour has been observed (but not explained nor analysed) before. Owoputi et al. (2012) comment on the performance of a PoS tagger that for *"different amounts of unlabeled tweets, keeping the number of clusters constant at* 800 [...] *initially there was a logarithmic rela-*

[1] `http://www.ark.cs.cmu.edu/TweetNLP/cluster_viewer.html`

tion between number of tweets and accuracy, but from from 750 thousand to 56 million tweets, the tagging accuracy remained relatively constant."

4 Method

Datasets We evaluate Brown tuning using two text types. For newswire, we use the Reuters RCV1 dataset (Rose et al., 2002). For social media, we draw randomly from a 10% sampling of tweets collected from 2009–2015, filtered for English using *langid.py* (Lui and Baldwin, 2012).

Preprocessing Drawing upon previous work (Turian et al., 2009; Owoputi et al., 2012), input data is preprocessed:

- Newswire data is *cleaned* per Liang (2005);
- Tabs, newlines and carriage returns are replaced with spaces;
- URLs are replaced with a <*URL*> marker;
- @Mentions are replaced by <*Mention*>; and
- Social media data has end-of-sequence markers <*EOS*> between tweets (see below).

Social media text was tokenised using the twokenize tool (O'Connor et al., 2010); newswire, with the Stanford tokenizer (Manning et al., 2014). The *cleaning* is the removal of any sentence where less than 90% of the characters are lowercase letters (excluding whitespace). This was not applied to tweets, as non-alphabet characters are markedly more frequent in social media text and an equivalent threshold is unclear. Cleaning has a notable effect on the RCV1 dataset, which has much potentially misleading non-text data such as numeric tables. Ultimately, $|T| = 1\,008.6$c for 72.1M social media tweets. For newswire, $|T| = 114.8$M.

Terminals We note that Brown et al. (1992) assume a corpus long enough ($T \rightarrow \infty$) that the final term in Equation 1 tends to 1, and so $Pr(c_1|c_2)$ tends to the relative frequency of consecutive classes c_1c_2.

$$Pr(c_1|c_2) = \frac{C(c_1c_2)}{T} \times \frac{C(c_1)}{\sum_c C(c_1c)} \quad (1)$$

When corpora are composed of long, structured documents, bigrams are unlikely to cross the boundaries of unrelated sentences. However, in social media corpora there is little running discourse: each document is ≤ 140 characters and usually just one sentence. Running discourse only occurs when consecutive messages are from the same user and temporally ordered (or perhaps relate to a hashtag or conversation, which may be non-linear). Given the uniformity of Twitter sampling (Kergl et al., 2014), this continuity is unlikely. Therefore, we introduce an <*EOS*> marker after each tweet to break bigrams. This also captures some sentence position information.

5 Evaluation

The effect of class count (c) and corpus size (number of tokens, $|T|$) is measured extrinsically in two scenarios. Firstly, the generated clusters are used as a plug-in to the CMU Twitter part-of-speech tagger, replacing the supplied clusters and paths. This evaluation only covers social media. Secondly, the clusters are used to support feature generation in named entity recognition. This covers newswire and social media. The scenarios and corresponding evaluation measures are described below. Clusters are generated from all word types, even those that occur only once in the corpus.

Note critically that we aim to observe the performance sensitivity to input parametres, and to gain insights for tuning Brown clustering. Achieving new top scores in any task is *not* the goal.

5.1 Part of Speech Tagging

Owoputi et al. (2013) present a PoS tagger for tweets which relies on (among other features) Brown clusters. A reference clustering (and two evaluation datasets) is provided with the tagger, which we substitute with newly generated clusters. To observe the impact of tuning Brown clustering, we vary input parametres to produce new clusters and measure the tagger's resultant tagging accuracy at token level. The "oct27" training and test splits are used.

5.2 Named Entity Recognition

We simplify NER to isolate the impact of c and $|T|$. A CRF (Okazaki, 2007) is used to train and classify NER models. The only features are Brown cluster path prefices of length [4,6,10,20] for newswire, as per Ratinov and Roth (2009), and [2,4,8,16] for newswire, as per Plank et al. (2014).

For newswire, we train and evaluate on the CoNLL data (Tjong Kim Sang and De Meulder, 2003) taking RCV clusters as input. For social media, we use the CRF with passive-aggressive updates to overcome some social media noise (Derczynski and Bontcheva, 2014), and train and eval-

	$T = 1M$	$T = 8M$		$T = 62.5k$
c	**SM F1**	**SM F1**	**NW F1**	**NW F1**
10	19.5	19.5	12.1	16.73
20	19.5	19.5	16.0	16.65
40	19.5	19.5	18.3	17.51
80	19.8	20.6	24.7	22.19
160	21.6	28.7	34.2	23.71
320	23.5	31.9	38.3	26.10
640	34.2	40.7	42.1	28.36
1000	*37.0*	*48.4*	*43.0*	*29.84*
1280	34.9	48.5	44.2	30.51
2560	41.2	49.2	44.5	31.57
5120	37.7	51.1	46.1	33.20
9229		-	-	33.23
10240	37.8	47.3	45.8	n/a

Table 2: NER accuracy, varying the number of classes c and corpus size $|T|$. For $T = 62.5\text{k}$, $|V| = 9\,229$.

T	**NW F1**	**SM F1**	T	**NW F1**	**SM F1**
8K	21.5	23.5	2M	39.1	38.6
16K	24.4	24.8	4M	41.4	45.0
32K	28.5	26.2	8M	43.0	48.4
62.5K	29.9	27.5	16M	44.2	50.2
125K	30.6	25.9	32M	45.6	54.2
250K	31.8	31.2	64M	46.9	51.7
500K	35.5	34.9	125M	n/a	51.7
1M	36.5	37.0	250M	n/a	53.6

Table 3: NER accuracy, varying corpus size $|T|$; $c = 1000$.

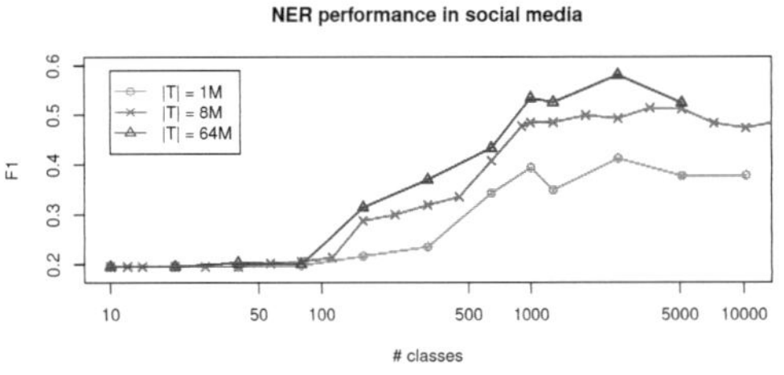

Figure 3: Social media NER F1.

uate on the Ritter et al. (2011) data, converted to PER / LOC / ORG / MISC and using the splits given by Derczynski et al. (2015b).

Additionally, we investigate feature representations. As we know that Brown clustering adds two kinds of information – the grouping of word types into classes and the hierarchy between classes (Section 3) – we isolate these two and analyse their individual performance. We evaluate performance of class-only and path-only features over the RCV1 data, due to its larger evaluation partition. Path-only features are extracted by truncating at $[1 : bits - 2]$, e.g., the cluster path 1100101 yields features (1,11,110,1100,11001).

6 Analysis

As expected, extrinsic performance increases as number of classes c rises for a given corpus size $|T|$, and also as $|T|$ rises for a given c, supporting our hypothesis that performance improves as c grows from 1. As c continues rising, word types are distributed more thinly across classes. Results show that performance levels off, and even begins to decrease (Table 2). In this experiment, we used an 8M token corpus and up to 10240 classes.

While this shows the effect of cluster quality decreasing when there are both too many and too few clusters, it does not approach the extreme value of c where there is one class for each word type. Thus, we ran another experiment varying cluster size but on a smaller corpus, which allowed examination of performance nearer to $c = |V|$. For this, we took 62500 tokens of cleaned RCV1, which contained 9229 word types, and kept the same range of c values. The news genre (NW) was selected for two reasons: the larger evaluation set provides better resolution in results, and the reduced lexical variation means lower word type proliferation, giving more distributional information for the same data. Results are given in Table 2. The plateauing behaviour matches the predicted idealised performance curve in Figure 2 reasonably well. Note that the NER extrinsic evaluation relies more on hierarchical information than clustering, and so the drop in quality may be less pronounced than in other tasks.

For the social media data (SM), we observe unstable quality for large $|T|$ (Table 3). This shows the point where too much data has been added and the classes have become noisy. Additional data for some $|T|$ values is shown in Figure 3. As the noise is balanced by the addition of distributional information, we do not expect cluster quality to plummet rapidly, but rather hover; the data reflects this.

For PoS tagging, we see that there is a peak performance with $c = 640$, after which accuracy drops unstably (Table 4). This matches our expectations. In fact, the performance for $c = 1000$ (the value used to generate the original clusters for the CMU tagger) is a local minimum in our test. The PoS task involves a lot of other factors, and so is not as close an estimate of clustering quality as the NER task is, but it does make use of both the clusters and the hierarchy. No clear result came from varying $|T|$ with a fixed c (Table 5), unlike in NER, where increasing $|T|$ had a strong impact.

Some low values of c are particularly bad, espe-

Classes c	Oct27 TA	Classes c	Oct27 TA
10	62.9	640	80.0
20	66.3	*1 000*	*76.9*
40	66.3	1 280	78.2
80	76.7	2 560	75.0
160	76.4	5 120	76.5
320	72.3	10 240	79.4

Table 4: PoS token accuracy (TA), varying c (8M tokens).

# tokens (T)	Oct27 TA	# tokens (T)	Oct27 TA
8K	78.7	2M	77.1
16K	80.6	4M	79.1
32K	76.9	8M	76.9
62.5K	79.5	16M	68.7
125K	79.5	32M	74.6
250K	76.4	64M	77.0
500K	76.1	125M	73.8
1M	72.6	250M	74.2

Table 5: PoS token accuracy, varying corpus size ($c = 1000$).

cially in the social media NER task, as in Table 2: with 40 or fewer classes, performance was consistently very low. This may be due to the smaller size of the SM evaluation set and high lexical variation in tweets, compared to newswire, where performance is also low but increases (sluggishly). As expected, we see (for SM) that larger input corpora benefit from higher c.[2] The default value gave sub-optimal results in every case.

The separation of cluster-path and class information (Tables 6, 7; Figures 4, 5) was revealing. In both cases, low values of c give not static but worsening performance as $|T|$ rises (see e.g. the

[2] During this we did in fact out-perform the leading system in a large study of Twitter NER systems; performance with $|T| = 32M, m = 1000$ (Table 3) was better than the best overall F1 in Table 3 of Derczynski et al. (2015b), despite using solely Brown cluster features.

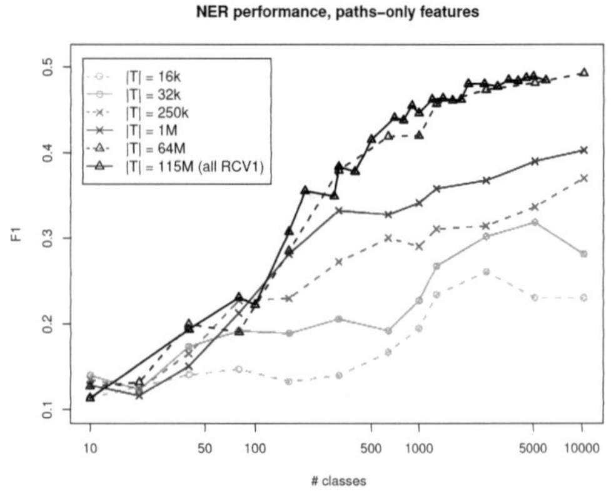

Figure 4: Using decomposed class prefices, without cluster ID, for paths-only features.

$c \downarrow; \lvert T\rvert$:	8K	16K	32K	250K	1M	8M	64M
10	11.9	11.3	14.0	13.5	12.8	12.7	12.7
40	12.6	14.1	17.4	16.5	15.1	16.8	20.0
80	13.2	14.7	19.2	22.7	21.3	22.3	19.0
160	12.8	13.3	18.9	23.0	28.1	30.4	28.5
320	18.8	14.0	20.6	27.2	33.3	36.0	38.0
640	19.6	16.7	19.2	30.0	32.8	40.3	41.9
1280	18.9	23.4	26.7	31.1	35.8	42.0	45.7
2560	21.7	**26.1**	30.2	31.4	36.8	42.8	47.4
5120	**24.0**	23.0	**31.9**	33.7	39.0	43.6	48.2
10240	-	-	28.1	**37.0**	**40.3**	**45.2**	**49.3**

Table 6: NER accuracy (F1); path-only (nonterminal) features; newswire. Bold indicates best c for a given $|T|$.

$c \downarrow; \lvert T\rvert$:	8K	16K	32K	250K	1M	8M	64M
10	12.6	14.1	17.4	15.3	14.7	12.1	11.7
40	12.7	14.2	17.6	16.6	16.9	18.4	22.3
80	13.9	15.5	19.5	23.1	22.7	24.8	29.1
160	14.3	16.8	20.2	25.7	29.3	34.3	32.7
320	16.2	17.7	19.7	28.1	33.9	38.3	40.4
640	18.4	20.2	23.1	30.2	35.6	41.8	46.5
1280	21.5	23.4	26.5	31.7	36.9	**44.1**	46.5
2560	22.2	24.5	28.9	33.4	**39.2**	44.1	**48.2**
5120	**22.2**	**25.1**	30.4	**34.5**	38.5	43.6	46.8
10240	-	-	**30.5**	34.1	37.7	41.7	45.3

Table 7: NER accuracy (F1); class-only feature; newswire. Bold indicates best c for T.

low-performance region in the lower back right of Figure 6). This is likely due to the effect c has on determining the number of items considered for a merge at any point; as the input corpus grows, this "window" comprises an ever-decreasing proportion of available word types. Also, performance is more sensitive to increases in c when $|T|$ is large, whereas increases under smaller $|T|$ are milder.

With the class-only experiment, performance peaks and then declines as $c \rightarrow |V|$, as expected (Section 3). The extreme class-only case, $c = |V|$, is one class per word, equivalent to a one-hot representation.[3] In the path-only experiment, perfor-

[3] We do not use a minimum token frequency cutoff; if one

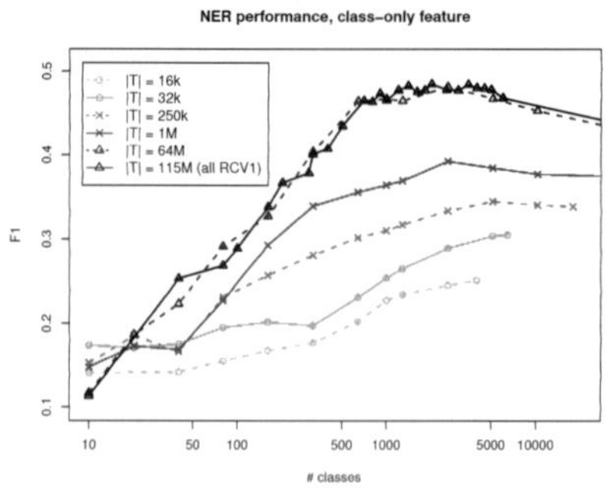

Figure 5: Using Brown class / cluster ID as sole feature. A 3D plot of these data points and others is shown in Figure 6.

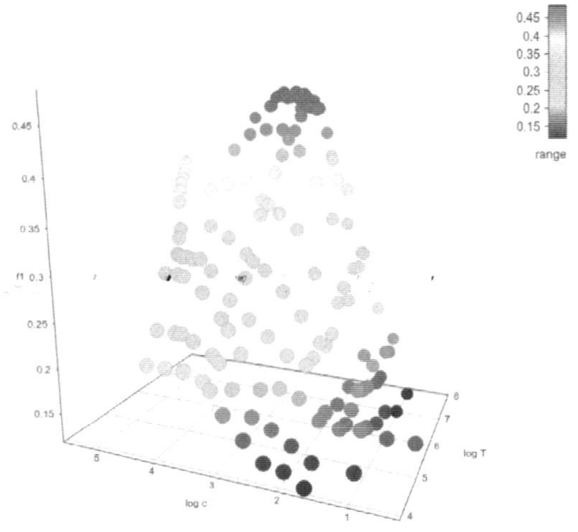

Figure 6: 3D plot of F1 using only cluster information, varying T and c. Interactive version at `http://derczynski.com/sheffield/brown-tuning/`.

mance increases with both $|T|$ and c. The advice here is that if $|T|$ is easier to increase than waiting for a large c, then get the big corpus first.

The best possible c behaves oppositely with class-only and path-only information. For class-only, with small corpora, c should be high (or set to $|V|$); as the corpora grow, so the best c levels off (Table 7). Conversely, for path-only, small corpora benefit from lower c, whereas larger corpora do better with high values of c (Table 6). This is because as $c \rightarrow |V|$, more path information is added, whereas clustering information decreases, as suggested in Section 3.

To exploit high values of c when $|T|$ is substantial, path features are required. Further, it may be more efficient to try a lower c and a larger $|T|$. In scenarios where the clusters are more important than hierarchical information, choosing too high a value for c is both expensive and risky.

Default values of c are unlikely to perform well, and are often even local minima in performance. Note that performance does not increase monotonically with either $|T|$ or c; this is likely due to poor decisions being made by the algorithm based on the information available at the time under those parameters. As a different tree is generated for every different corpus and class count, and these tree vary almost chaotically across text types and corpus sizes, and also as performance depends on how features are extracted, it is unlikely that a universal formula for selecting c exists. Ceteris paribus, it is reasonable to start finding c through random search (Bergstra and Bengio, 2012) beta-weighted against high c to reduce computation costs (Micenková et al., 2015) and against very low c where extrinsic performance is poor; e.g., something like $c \sim B(\alpha = 1.5, \beta = 5)c_{max}$, with c_{max} in the order of 10^{5+}, based on $|T|$ and our results in both text types.

Supplementary to this paper, we provide many clusters and paths for the two common text types investigated, to help researchers start exploring Brown parametre space for their problem for some values of c, thus deferring the initial large computational costs of running this algorithm.

is used, this equivalency no longer applies.

7 Conclusion

As a community, if Brown clustering is to continue its adoption in so many NLP tasks, we need methods to choose appropriate values for its hyper-parametres. We presented our model of how Brown clustering quality changes depending on its input and tuning. This model was supported in an empirical evaluation.

The target number of classes c has an impact on the utility of the classes. The corpus size $|T|$ also has an impact.

Setting c too low clusters too coarsely; setting it too high forces similar words to be split across clusters. Similarly, a preset c will not be optimal for ever-increasing corpus sizes: just adding more data will eventually make no difference or even reduce cluster quality. We therefore strongly recommend *avoiding* the default value of $c = 1000$, and instead finding values which fully activate this powerful hierarchical clustering technique.

Acknowledgments

This research has received funding from the EU's seventh Framework Programme for research, technological development and demonstration under grant agreement No. 611233, PHEME,[4] and from the WALLVIZ project,[5] supported by the Danish Council for Strategic Research, grant 10-092316.

References

Yoshua Bengio, Aaron Courville, and Pierre Vincent. 2013. Representation learning: A review and new perspectives. *IEEE Transactions on Pattern Analysis and Machine Intelligence*, 35(8):1798–1828.

[4] `http://www.pheme.eu/`

[5] `http://wallviz.dk/`

James Bergstra and Yoshua Bengio. 2012. Random search for hyper-parameter optimization. *Journal of Machine Learning Research*, 13(1):281–305.

Phil Blunsom and Trevor Cohn. 2011. A hierarchical Pitman-Yor process HMM for unsupervised part of speech induction. In *Proc. ACL*, pages 865–874.

Peter F Brown, Peter V Desouza, Robert L Mercer, Vincent J Della Pietra, and Jenifer C Lai. 1992. Class-based n-gram models of natural language. *Computational Linguistics*, 18(4):467–479.

Christos Christodoulopoulos, Sharon Goldwater, and Mark Steedman. 2010. Two Decades of Unsupervised POS induction: How far have we come? In *Proc. EMNLP*, pages 575–584. ACL.

Leon Derczynski and Kalina Bontcheva. 2014. Passive-aggressive sequence labeling with discriminative post-editing for recognising person entities in tweets. In *Proc. EACL*, volume 2, pages 69–73.

Leon Derczynski, Isabelle Augenstein, and Kalina Bontcheva. 2015a. USFD: Twitter NER with Drift Compensation and Linked Data. In *Proc. W-NUT workshop, ACL*.

Leon Derczynski, Diana Maynard, Giuseppe Rizzo, Marieke van Erp, Genevieve Gorrell, Raphaël Troncy, Johann Petrak, and Kalina Bontcheva. 2015b. Analysis of named entity recognition and linking for tweets. *Information Processing & Management*, 51(2):32–49.

Dennis Kergl, Robert Roedler, and Sebastian Seeber. 2014. On the endogenesis of Twitter's Spritzer and Gardenhose sample streams. In *Proc. ASONAM*, pages 357–364. IEEE.

Percy Liang. 2005. Semi-supervised learning for natural language. Master's thesis, Massachusetts Institute of Technology.

Marco Lui and Timothy Baldwin. 2012. langid.py: An off-the-shelf language identification tool. In *Proc. ACL*, pages 25–30.

Christopher Manning, Mihai Surdeanu, John Bauer, Jenny Finkel, Steven Bethard, and David McClosky. 2014. The Stanford CoreNLP natural language processing toolkit. In *Proc. ACL*, pages 55–60.

Barbora Micenková, Brian McWilliams, and Ira Assent. 2015. Learning representations for outlier detection on a budget. *arXiv:cs.LG/1507.08104*.

Marcelo A Montemurro. 2001. Beyond the Zipf–Mandelbrot law in quantitative linguistics. *Physica A: Statistical Mechanics and its Applications*, 300(3):567–578.

Brendan O'Connor, Michel Krieger, and David Ahn. 2010. TweetMotif: Exploratory Search and Topic Summarization for Twitter. In *Proc. ICWSM*, pages 384–385.

Naoaki Okazaki. 2007. CRFsuite: a fast implementation of conditional random fields (CRFs). *URL http://www. chokkan. org/software/crfsuite*.

Olutobi Owoputi, Brendan O'Connor, Chris Dyer, Kevin Gimpel, and Nathan Schneider. 2012. Part-of-speech tagging for Twitter: Word clusters and other advances. Technical Report CMU-ML-12-107, School of Computer Science, Carnegie Mellon University.

Olutobi Owoputi, Brendan O'Connor, Chris Dyer, Kevin Gimpel, Nathan Schneider, and Noah A Smith. 2013. Improved part-of-speech tagging for online conversational text with word clusters. In *Proc. NAACL*, pages 380–390.

Barbara Plank, Dirk Hovy, Ryan McDonald, and Anders Søgaard. 2014. Adapting taggers to Twitter with not-so-distant supervision. In *Proc. COLING*, pages 1783–1792.

Lizhen Qu, Gabriela Ferraro, Liyuan Zhou, Weiwei Hou, Nathan Schneider, and Timothy Baldwin. 2015. Big data small data, in domain out-of domain, known word unknown word: The impact of word representation on sequence labelling tasks. In *Proc. CoNLL*.

Lev Ratinov and Dan Roth. 2009. Design challenges and misconceptions in named entity recognition. In *Proc. CoNLL*, pages 147–155.

Alan Ritter, Sam Clark, Oren Etzioni, et al. 2011. Named entity recognition in tweets: an experimental study. In *Proc. EMNLP*, pages 1524–1534.

Tony Rose, Mark Stevenson, and Miles Whitehead. 2002. The Reuters Corpus Volume 1 - from yesterday's news to tomorrow's language resources. In *Proc. LREC*, volume 2, pages 827–832.

Karl Stratos, Do-kyum Kim, Michael Collins, and Daniel Hsu. 2014. A spectral algorithm for learning class-based n-gram models of natural language. *Proc. UAI*.

Erik F Tjong Kim Sang and Fien De Meulder. 2003. Introduction to the CoNLL-2003 shared task: Language-independent named entity recognition. In *Proc. NAACL*, volume 4, pages 142–147.

Joseph Turian, Lev Ratinov, Yoshua Bengio, and Dan Roth. 2009. A preliminary evaluation of word representations for named-entity recognition. In *Proc. NIPS ws. on Grammar Induction, Representation of Language & Language Learning*, pages 1–8.

Joseph Turian, Lev Ratinov, and Yoshua Bengio. 2010. Word representations: a simple and general method for semi-supervised learning. In *Proc. ACL*, pages 384–394.

Ludwig Wittgenstein. 1953. *Philosophical Investigations*. Basic Blackwell, London.

Adam Wyner, Krasimir Angelov, Guntis Barzdins, Danica Damljanovic, Brian Davis, Norbert Fuchs, Stefan Hoefler, Ken Jones, Kaarel Kaljurand, Tobias Kuhn, et al. 2010. On controlled natural languages: Properties and prospects. In *Controlled Natural Language*, pages 281–289. Springer.

Temporal Relation Classification using a Model of Tense and Aspect

Leon Derczynski
University of Sheffield
leon@dcs.shef.ac.uk

Robert Gaizauskas
University of Sheffield
robertg@dcs.shef.ac.uk

Abstract

Determining the temporal order of events in a text is difficult. However, it is crucial to the extraction of narratives, plans, and context. We suggest that a simple, established framework of tense and aspect provides a viable model for ordering a subset of events and times in a given text. Using this framework, we investigate extracting features that represent temporal information and integrate these in a machine learning approach. These features improve event-event ordering.

1 Introduction

It is important to understand time in language. The ability to express and comprehend expressions of time enables us to plan, to tell stories, and to discuss change in the world around us.

When we automatically extract temporal information, we are often concerned with events and times – referred to collectively as temporal **intervals**. We might ask, for example, *"Who is the current President of the USA?."* In order to extract a single contemporary answer to this question, we need to identify events related to persons becoming president and the times of those events. Crucially, however, we also need to identify the ordering between these events and times, by assigning a temporal relation type (from e.g. Allen (1983)). This last task, **temporal relation typing**, is challenging (UzZaman et al., 2013; Bethard et al., 2015), and is the focus of this paper.

When events are expressed as verbs, tense and aspect are used to convey temporal features of these events. Thus, it is intuitive that tense and aspect will be of value in determining the type of temporal relation that holds between two verb events, and evidence in human-annotated corpora supports this intuition.

Event-event relations are often the hardest to label (Derczynski, 2015). Around 45% of links in TempEval-3 (UzZaman et al., 2013) event-event ordering tasks cannot reliably be labelled automatically.

Temporal relations involving at least one argument with tense or aspect information are prevalent. Verb-verb links make up around a third of TimeBank's temporal relations,[1] and tensed verb-verb links the largest share of that set, so of all verb-verb relations, the majority are between two tensed verbs.

Data-driven approaches to the relation typing task are hampered in two ways. Firstly, there is a shortage of ground truth training data. This leads to low volumes of instances for many combinations of tense and aspect values for pairs of events, hampering automatic hypothesis learning (Lapata and Lascarides, 2006). Secondly, the range of tense and aspect expression in TimeML is relatively limited, describing three "tenses"[2] (past and past participle, present and present participle, and future) and three "aspects" (none, perfective and progressive). This markup language may be insufficiently descriptive to capture relations implied by variations in linguistic use of tense and aspect.

Reichenbach (1947) offers a theoretical framework for analysis of tense and aspect that can be used to predict constraints on temporal orderings between verb events based on their tense and aspect, and also between times and tensed verbs. Applying Reichenbach's framework requires tense and aspect information, which may yet be usefully available in existing corpora.

In this paper, we describe an approach to using Reichenbachs model to generate features for

[1]TimeBank is a corpus semantically annotated for temporal information in TimeML (Pustejovsky et al., 2003; Pustejovsky et al., 2004)

[2]In TimeML v1.2, the tense attribute of events has values that are conflated with verb form. This conflation is deprecated in newer versions of TimeML, post-TimeBank.

Proceedings of Recent Advances in Natural Language Processing, pages 118–122,
Hissar, Bulgaria, Sep 7–9 2015.

a machine learning approach to temporal relation typing and report an experiment showing it brings modest improvement.

2 Reichenbachian Tenses

Reichenbach details nine tenses (see Table 1). The tenses detailed by Reichenbach are past, present or future, and may take a simple, anterior or posterior form. In English, these apply to single finite verbs and to verbal groups consisting of head verb and auxiliaries. The tense system describes abstract time points for each tensed verb – event time E, speech/utterance time S, and reference time R – and how they may interact, both for a single verb and with other events.

In Reichenbach's view, different tenses specify different relations between E, R and S. Table 1 shows the six tenses conventionally distinguished in English. As there are more than six possible ordering arrangements of S, E and R, some English tenses might suggest more than one arrangement. Reichenbach's tenses also suffer from this ambiguity when converted to $S/E/R$ structures, albeit to a lesser degree. When following Reichenbach's tense names, it is the case that for past tenses, R always occurs before S; in the future, R is always after S; and in the present, S and R are simultaneous. Further, "anterior" suggests E before R, "simple" that R and E are simultaneous, and "posterior" that E is after R. The flexibility of this framework is sufficient to allow it to account for a very wide set of tenses, including all those described by Song and Cohen (1988), and this is sufficient to account for the observed tenses in many languages. Past, present and future tenses imply $R < S$, $R = S$ and $S < R$ respectively. Anterior, simple and posterior tenses imply $E < R$, $E = R$ and $R < E$ respectively.

2.1 Verb Interactions

While each tensed verb involves a speech, event and reference time, multiple verbs may share one or more of these points. For example, all narrative in a news article usually has the same speech time (that of document creation). Further, two events linked by a temporal conjunction (e.g. *after*) are very likely to share the same reference time. Basic methods of linking between verb events or linking verbs to fixed points on a time scale are described below.

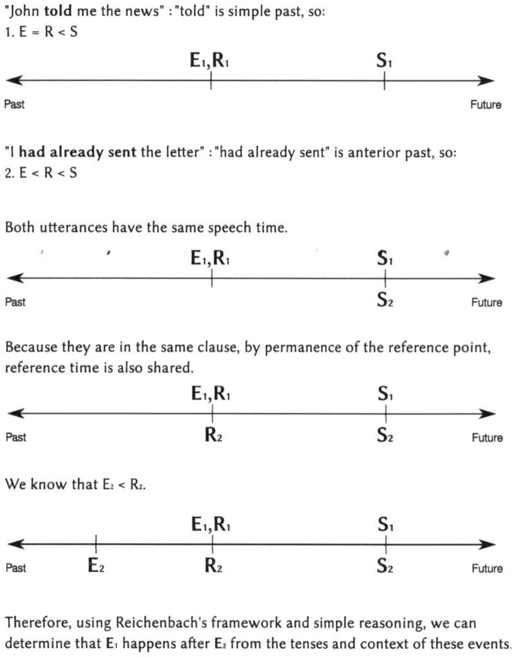

Figure 1: An example of permanence of the reference point.

2.2 Special Properties of the Reference Point

The reference point R has two special uses. These relate to verbs in the same *temporal context* and to the effect of time expressions on verbs. Reichenbach relies on a notion of "same temporal context" without ever defining it precisely. It could be similar to the concept put forward by Dowty (1986) with **temporal discourse interpretation principle** (TDIP). Below we operationalise the concept in several ways to mean either "same sentence" or "adjacent sentence pairs", though other interpretations are also possible.

Permanence Firstly, when sentences are combined to form a compound sentence, tensed main verbs interact, and implicit grammatical rules require tenses to be adjusted. These rules operate such that R is the same in all cases in the sequence. Reichenbach names this principle *permanence* of the reference point. Figure 1 contains an example of this principle.

Positional Secondly, when temporal expressions (such as a TimeML TIMEX3 of type DATE, but not DURATION) occur in the same clause as a verbal event, the temporal expression does not (as one might expect) specify event time E, but instead is used to position reference time R. This is named *positional* use of the reference point.

Relation	*Reichenbach's Tense Name*	*English Tense Name*	*Example*
E<R<S	Anterior past	Past perfect	*I had slept*
E=R<S	Simple past	Simple past	*I slept*
R<E<S R<S=E R<S<E	Posterior past		*I expected that I would sleep*
E<S=R	Anterior present	Present perfect	*I have slept*
S=R=E	Simple present	Simple present	*I sleep*
S=R<E	Posterior present	Simple future	*I will sleep (Je vais dormir)*
S<E<R S=E<R E<S<R	Anterior future	Future perfect	*I will have slept*
S<R=E	Simple future	Simple future	*I will sleep (Je dormirai)*
S<R<E	Posterior future		*I shall be going to sleep*

Table 1: Reichenbach's tenses; from Mani et al. (2005)

e1 ↓; e2 →	**Sim Past**	**Pos Past**	**Ant Pres**	**Sim Pres**	**Ant Fut**	**Sim Fut**
Sim Past	vague	after	vague	after	after	after
Pos Past	before	vague	vague	vague	after	after
Ant Pres	vague	vague	vague	after	vague	after
Sim Pres	before	vague	vague	overlap	vague	after
Ant Fut	before	before	vague	vague	vague	after
Sim Fut	before	before	before	before	before	vague

Table 2: Verb-verb event orderings based on the Reichenbachian tenses that map directly to those in TimeML. Cell values describe the `e1` $[rel]$ `e2` relationship.

In Example 1, the reference point is determined positionally with an explicit time (*10 o'clock*).

(1) *It was 10 o'clock, and Sarah had brushed her teeth.*

The verb group *had brushed* is anterior past tense; that is, $E < R < S$. The event is complete before the reference time – that is, at any point until *10 o'clock* – and so the relation between the event and timex can be determined (*brushed* BEFORE *10 o'clock*).

2.3 Feature Extraction

Two interpretations of the model are used in feature extraction. Firstly, a simple view is taken assuming permanence of the reference point. This provides a constraint dependent on the pairing of Reichenbachian tenses used, and is detailed in Table 2. Secondly, an advanced interpretation is used, following Derczynski and Gaizauskas (2013). This approach fully populates all Reichenbachian tense combinations using Freksa's temporal semi-interval algebra (Freksa, 1992) to derive a (large) temporal constraint table, which for space reasons is omitted here.

In all cases, the gold standard tense and aspect features annotated on the events in TimeBank are used as the basis for Reichenbachian representations.

3 The Framework in TLINK Typing

TimeML provides some of the information that Reichenbach's framework alone does not cater for and vice versa. A combination of the two may lead to better labelling performance, but relying on Reichenbach's framework alone for rule-based temporal relation label constraint is insufficient. However, the framework has shown to inform prior systems effectively (Chambers et al., 2014). The situations we examine are those where two verb events occur in the same temporal context, where a timex directly influences a verb event, and also verb events that report other verb events.

Reichenbach's framework is used as a linguistic model that generates temporal ordering features, which are added to a base feature set. The base features are those as in Mani et al. (2007), i.e.:

For each event: text; TimeML tense and aspect; modality; cardinality; polarity; event class; part-of-speech tag.

For each event pair: booleans for: are events in the same sentence; are events in adjacent sentences; do events have the same TimeML aspect, and again for tense; does event 1 textually precede event 2.

	Base features		Extended features	
Classifier	**Acc**	**Err. red.**	**Acc**	**Err. red.**
MCC	48.04%	-	48.04%	-
Maxent	57.47%	22.86%	**57.65%**	23.19%
ID3	56.52%	21.14%	**57.47%**	22.86%
N.Bayes	58.31%	24.37%	**58.72%**	25.12%

Table 3: Using Reichenbach-suggested event ordering features representing permanence of the reference point, considering only same-sentence TLINKs, using the advanced interpretation. 562 instances.

	Base features		Extended features	
Classifier	**Acc**	**Err. red.**	**Acc**	**Err. red.**
MCC	44.87%	-	44.87%	-
Maxent	62.28%	31.58%	**62.55%**	32.07%
ID3	**59.21%**	26.01%	58.74%	25.16%
N.Bayes	56.96%	21.92%	**57.58%**	23.05%

Table 4: Reichenbach-suggested event ordering feature representing permanence of the reference point, same-sentence and adjacent-sentence TLINKs. 858 instances.

3.1 Same Context Event-Event Links

Reichenbach's framework provides information for ordering events in the same temporal context (same context event-event relations, SCEE). This applies to any two verb events that have a shared reference point.

Verb events are those in TimeML that have a POS attribute of VERB. We exclude those with a TENSE of NONE or INFINITIVE. Shared reference points are assumed for event-event links having both arguments in the same or adjacent sentences.

4 Experimental Results

We conducted an experiment to test the utility of the Reichenbach-motivated temporal ordering features in a supervised learning approach to the temporal relation typing task. The goal is to find a way to incorporate Reichenbach's framework into a machine learning model. The experiment was conducted with 10-fold cross validation, using from TimeBank v1.2. Links in each document were never shared across a split (i.e., splits were made at document level). Experiments were conducted with relation folding, where the set of temporal relation types is reduced; e.g. AFTER and BEFORE can be switched between by flipping their argument order – A BEFORE B and B AFTER A are equivalent. The impact of Reichenbach's framework is measured by comparing classifier performance on SCEE links using the basic feature set and using the basic feature set plus the new feature. Features representing the text (i.e. lexical form) of events were removed as they consistently harmed performance, likely due to the sparsity of their values. Results are shown in Table 3. In this instance, the extended features provide a performance boost regardless of classifier choice. This shows that the framework can be integrated into a machine learning model for temporal relation typing. However, the improvements are modest. This can be attributed to a variety of factors salient to the relation typing task.

Firstly, the sizes of datasets, while not tiny, are still small. More temporally-annotated data will help here, though larger corpora using the same annotation standard are hard to come by. Next, Reichenbach can be applied with full accuracy to a tiny number of cases (where it makes an unambiguous suggestion) (Chambers et al., 2014), but this is only the first attempt to use it for constraining (rather than specifying) the target temporal relation type. Last, temporal context is not defined precisely but rather approximated. This is likely to affect results, and so we investigate further.

In the next case, the scope of temporal context is broadened to include cases where events are in adjacent sentences. Results are shown in Table 4. Here, classifiers with inductive biases toward the independence assumption do better with the extended feature set.

In both cases, there was a consistent performance increase from almost all classifiers with the introduction of the feature derived from the advanced interpretation of Reichenbach's framework. The performance increase was consistent when assuming that event-event relations in the same sentence are also in the same temporal context. The increase is smaller when context is stretched to adjacent sentences. We attribute this to weaknesses in modelling context, a task that others have also tackles (Miller et al., 2013) that remains an open and interesting research problem.

5 Conclusion

Reichenbach's framework for tense and aspect is intuitive, and of utility in typing temporal relations. Automatic identification of where the framework applies remains difficult. One question is how to formally define and annotate temporal context.We investigate two approximations for temporal context, both of which are useful. The other question is how to map Reichenbach's framework to features based on a common semantic annotation standard. We proposed two ways of using Reichenbach's framework to generate features for machine learning of temporal relations, which improved relation typing performance in this difficult task. The framework suggests helpful constraint of relation types in cases where verbs are in the same context, helping in the difficult task of automatic temporal relation typing.

References

J. Allen. 1983. Maintaining knowledge about temporal intervals. *Communications of the ACM*, 26(11):832–843.

S. Bethard, L. Derczynski, J. Pustejovsky, and M. Verhagen. 2015. Semeval-2015 task 6: Clinical TempEval. In *Proc. SemEval*.

N. Chambers, T. Cassidy, B. McDowell, and S. Bethard. 2014. Dense event ordering with a multi-pass architecture. *Transactions of the Association for Computational Linguistics*, 2:273–284.

L. Derczynski and R. Gaizauskas. 2013. Empirical Validation of Reichenbach's Tense Framework. In *Proceedings of the 10th Conference on Computational Semantics*, pages 71–82. ACL.

L. Derczynski. 2015. *Automatically Ordering Events and Times in Text*. Studies in Computational Intelligence. Springer.

D. Dowty. 1986. The effects of aspectual class on the temporal structure of discourse: semantics or pragmatics? *Linguistics and philosophy*, 9(1):37–61.

C. Freksa. 1992. Temporal reasoning based on semi-intervals. *Artificial intelligence*, 54(1):199–227.

M. Lapata and A. Lascarides. 2006. Learning sentence-internal temporal relations. *Journal of Artificial Intelligence Research*, 27(1):85–117.

I. Mani, J. Pustejovsky, and R. Gaizauskas. 2005. *The Language of Time: A Reader*. Oxford University Press.

I. Mani, B. Wellner, M. Verhagen, and J. Pustejovsky. 2007. Three approaches to learning TLINKS in TimeML. Technical Report CS-07-268, Brandeis University, Waltham, MA, USA.

T. A. Miller, S. Bethard, D. Dligach, S. Pradhan, C. Lin, and G. K. Savova. 2013. Discovering narrative containers in clinical text. *Proc. ACL*, page 18.

J. Pustejovsky, P. Hanks, R. Sauri, A. See, R. Gaizauskas, A. Setzer, D. Radev, B. Sundheim, D. Day, L. Ferro, et al. 2003. The Timebank Corpus. In *Corpus Linguistics*, pages 647–656.

J. Pustejovsky, B. Ingria, R. Sauri, J. Castano, J. Littman, and R. Gaizauskas. 2004. The Specification Language TimeML. In *The Language of Time: A Reader*, pages 545–557. Oxford University Press.

H. Reichenbach. 1947. The tenses of verbs. In *Elements of Symbolic Logic*. Dover Publications.

F. Song and R. Cohen. 1988. The interpretation of temporal relations in narrative. In *Proceedings of the 7th National Conference of AAAI*.

N. UzZaman, H. Llorens, L. Derczynski, J. Allen, M. Verhagen, and J. Pustejovsky. 2013. SemEval-2013 Task 1: TempEval-3: Evaluating Time Expressions, Events, and Temporal Relations. In *Proc. SemEval*, pages 1–9. Association for Computational Linguistics.

Efficient Named Entity Annotation through Pre-empting

Leon Derczynski
University of Sheffield
S1 4DP, UK
leon@dcs.shef.ac.uk

Kalina Bontcheva
University of Sheffield
S1 4DP, UK
kalina@dcs.shef.ac.uk

Abstract

Linguistic annotation is time-consuming and expensive. One common annotation task is to mark entities – such as names of people, places and organisations – in text. In a document, many segments of text often contain no entities at all. We show that these segments are worth skipping, and demonstrate a technique for reducing the amount of entity-less text examined by annotators, which we call "pre-empting". This technique is evaluated in a crowdsourcing scenario, where it provides downstream performance improvements for the same size corpus.

1 Introduction

Annotating documents is expensive. Given the dominant position of statistical machine learning for many NLP tasks, annotation is unavoidable. It typically requires an expert, but even non-expert annotation work (cf. crowdsourcing) has an associated cost. This makes it important to get the maximum value out of annotation.

However, in entity annotation tasks, annotators sometimes are faced with passage of text which bear no entities. These blank examples are especially common outside of the newswire genre, in e.g. social media text (Hu et al., 2013). While finding good examples to annotate next is a problem that has been tackled before, these systems often require a tight feedback loop and great control over which document is presented next. This is not possible in a crowdsourcing scenario, where large volumes of documents need to be presented for annotation simultaneously in order to leverage crowdsourcing's scalability advantages. The loosened feedback loop, and requirement to issue documents in large batches, differentiate the problem scenario from classical active learning.

We hypothesise that these blank examples are of limited value as training data for statistical entity annotation systems, and that it is preferable to annotate texts containing entities over texts without them. This proposition can be evaluated directly, in the context of named entity recognition (NER). If correct, it offers a new pre-annotation task: predicting whether an excerpt of text will contain an entity we are interested in annotating.

The goal is to reduce the cost of annotation, or alternatively, to increase the performance of a system that uses a fixed amount of data. As this pre-annotation task tries to acquire information about entity annotations before they are actually created – specifically, whether or not they exist – we call the task "pre-empting".

Unlike many modern approaches to optimising annotated data, which focus on how to best leverage annotations (perhaps by making inferences over those annotations, or by using unlabelled data), we examine the step before this – selecting what to annotate in order to boost later system performance.

In this paper, we:

- demonstrate that entity-bearing text results in better NER systems;
- introduce an entity pre-empting technique;
- examine how pre-empting entities optimises corpus creation, in a crowdsourcing scenario.

2 Validating The Approach

The premise of entity pre-empting is that entity-bearing text is better NER training data than entity-less text. To check this, we compare performance with entity-bearing vs. entity-less and also unsorted text. Our scenario has a base set of 2 000 sentences annotated for named entities. We add different kinds of sentences to this base set, and see how an NER system performs when trained on them. This mimics the situation where one has a

Proceedings of Recent Advances in Natural Language Processing, pages 123–130,
Hissar, Bulgaria, Sep 7–9 2015.

Dataset	P	R	F1
Base: 2k sentences	76.55	70.65	73.48
2k sents + 2k without entities	78.03	66.12	71.58
2k sents + 2k random	79.29	76.36	77.80
2k sents + 2k with entities	79.80	77.78	**78.77**

Table 1: Adding entity-less vs. entity-bearing data to a 2 000-sentence base training set

Dataset	P	R	F1	Δ F1
Base: All sentences	85.70	84.08	84.88	-
- 2k without entities	84.89	84.41	84.65	-0.23
- 2k with entities	85.43	83.17	84.29	-0.59

Table 2: Removing data from our training set

base corpus of quality annotated data and intends to expand this corpus.

2.1 Experimental Setup

For English newswire, we use the CoNLL 2003 dataset (Tjong Kim Sang and Meulder, 2003). The training part of this dataset has 14 040 sentences; of these, 11 131 contain at least one entity and so 2 909 have no entities. We evaluate against the more challenging `testb` part of this corpus, which contains 5 652 entity annotations. We use Finkel et al. (2005)'s statistical machine learning-based NER system.

2.2 Validation Results

Results are shown in Table 1. Adding 2 000 entity-bearing sentences gives the largest improvement in F1, and is better than adding 2 000 randomly chosen sentences – the case without pre-empting. Adding only entity-free text decreases overall performance, especially recall.

To double check, we try removing training data instead of adding it. In this case, removing content *without* entities should hurt performance less than removing content *with* entities. From all 14k sentences of English training data, we remove either 2 000 entity-beering sentences or 2 000 sentences with no entities. Results are given in Table 2.

Although the performance drop is small with this much training data, the drop from removing entity-bearing data is over twice the size of that from removing the same amount of entity-free data. So, examples containing entities are often the best ones to add to an initial corpus, and have a larger negative impact on performance when removed. Being able to pre-empt entities is valuable, and can improve corpus effectiveness.

3 Pre-empting Entity Presence

Having defined the pre-empting task, we take two approaches to investigate the practicality of pre-empting named entities in English newswire text. The first is discriminative learning. We use maximum entropy and SVM classifiers (Daumé III, 2004; Joachims, 1999); we experiment with cost-weighted SVM in order to achieve high recall (Morik et al., 1999). The second is to declare sentences containing proper nouns as entity-bearing. We use a random baseline that predicts NE presence based on the prior proportion of entity-bearing to entity-free sentences (≈4.8:1, entity-bearing is the dominant class, for any entity type).

For the machine learning approach, we use the following feature representations: character 1,2,3-grams; compressed word shape 1,2,3 grams;[1] and token 1,2,3 grams.

For the proper noun-based approach, we use the Stanford tagger (Toutanova et al., 2003) to label sentences. This is trained on Wall Street Journal data which does not overlap with the Reuters data in our NER corpus.

As data we use a base set of sentences as training examples, which are a mixture of entity-bearing and entity-free. We experiment with various sizes of base set. Evaluation is performed over a separate 4 000-sentence set, labelled as either having or not having any entities.

3.1 English Newswire, Any Entity

Intrinsic evaluation of these pre-empting approaches is made in terms of classification accuracy, precision, recall and F1. Results are given in Table 3. They indicate that our approach to pre-empting over all entity types in English newswire performs well. For SVM, few entity-bearing sentences were excluded by not being pre-empted (false negatives), and we achieved high precision. Maximum entropy achieved similar results, with the highest overall F-scores. We obtain close to oracle performance with little training data – a set of one hundred sentences affords a high overall performance. Repeating the experiment on the separate CoNLL evaluation set (gathered months after the training data, and so over some different entity

[1]Word shape reflects the capitalisations and classes of letters within a word; for example, "you" becomes "xxx" and "Free!" becomes "Xxxx." Compression turns runs of the same character into one, like an inverse + regex operator; this gives word shape representations "x" and "Xx." respectively.

Training sents.	Accuracy	P	R	F1
	Random baseline			
	68.77	78.90	82.28	80.55
	Proper nouns			
WSJ	72.43	92.29	92.14	92.22
	MaxEnt			
10*	75	85	83	84
100*	83.3	83.9	97.5	90.1
1000	90.38	93.04	94.85	93.94
5000	94.25	96.25	96.44	96.35
10000	95.08	96.56	97.20	**96.88**
	Plain SVM			
10*	79	79	100	88
100*	78.6	78.6	100	88.0
1000	90.58	92.12	96.25	91.34
5000	93.28	96.06	95.36	94.65
10000	94.22	96.46	96.18	**95.33**
	SVM + Cost, $j = 5$			
10*	79	79	100	88
100*	78.6	78.6	100	88.0
1000	86.33	86.53	97.84	86.43
5000	92.12	92.36	98.09	92.24
10000	94.15	94.25	98.57	**94.20**

Table 3: Evaluating entity pre-empting on English newswire. *We report figures at 2s.f. and 3s.f. for results with 10 and 100 examples respectively, as the training set is small enough to make higher precision inappropriate.

Training data	P	R	F1
500 base + 500 random	74.33	68.56	71.33
500 base + 500 pre-empted	74.80	69.43	**72.01**

Table 4: Entity recognition performance with random vs. pre-empted sentences

names) gives similar results; for example the pre-empting SVM trained on 100 examples from the training set performs with 79.81% precision and full recall, and with 1000 examples, 87.92% precision and near-full recall (99.53%). Even though entity-bearing sentences are the dominant class, we can still increase entity presence in a notable proportion of the training corpus.

3.2 Extrinsic Evaluation

It is important to measure the real impact of pre-empting on the resulting NER training data. To this end, we use 500 hand-labelled sentences as base data to train a pre-empting SVM, and add a further 500 sentences to this. We compare NER performance of a system trained on the base 500 + 500 random sentences, to that of one using 500 + 500 pre-empted entity-bearing sentences. As before, evaluation is against the `testb` set. Table 4 show results. Performance is better with pre-empted annotations, though so many sentences bear entities that the change in training data – and resultant effect – is small.

Language	Accuracy	P	R	F1
	Random baseline			
Dutch	49.0	46.7	46.4	46.5
Spanish	63.2	76.1	75.4	75.8
Hungarian	57.1	69.3	68.5	68.9
	SVM			
Dutch	92.9	89.9	98.2	93.9
Spanish	76.2	76.2	100	86.5
Hungarian	70.7	70.4	99.9	82.6

Table 5: Pre-empting performance for Dutch, Spanish and Hungarian

Training data	P	R	F1
Dutch, 3 926 entities			
100 base + 500 random	63.57	48.80	**55.22**
100 base + 500 pre-empted	62.46	44.93	52.27
Spanish, 3 551 entities			
100 base + 500 random	68.38	61.71	64.90
100 base + 500 pre-empted	73.00	66.91	**69.82**
Hungarian, 2 432 entities			
100 base + 500 random	76.55	67.52	**71.75**
100 base + 500 pre-empted	72.84	61.43	66.65

Table 6: Entity recognition performance with random vs. pre-empted sentences for Dutch, Spanish and Hungarian

3.3 Other Languages

Pre-empting is not restricted to just English. Similar NER datasets are available for Dutch, Spanish and Hungarian (Tjong Kim Sang, 2002; Szarvas et al., 2006). Results regarding the effectiveness of an SVM pre-empter for these languages are presented in Table 5. In each case, we train with 1 000 sentences and evaluate against a 4 000-sentence evaluation partition.

Strong above-baseline performance was achieved for each language. For Dutch and Spanish, this pre-empting approach performs in the same class as for English, with a low error rate. The error rate is markedly higher in Hungarian, a morphologically-rich language. This could be attributed to the use of token n-gram features; one would expect these to be sparser in a language with rich morphology, and therefore being harder to build decision boundaries over.

For extrinsic evaluation, we use a pre-empter trained with 100 sentences and then compare the performance benefits of adding either 500 randomly-selected sentences or 500 pre-empted sentences to this training data. The same NER system is used to learn to recognise entities. Results are given in Table 6. Pre-empting did not help in Hungarian and Dutch, though was useful for Spanish. This indicates that the pre-empting hypothesis may not hold for every language, or every genre. But as far as we can see, it certainly holds for English, and also for Spanish.

4 Crowdsourced Corpus Annotation

As pre-empting entities is useful during corpus creation, in this section we examine how to apply it with an increasingly popular new annotation method: crowdsourcing. Crowdsourcing annotation works by presenting a many *microtasks* to non-expert workers. They typically make their judgements over short texts, after reading a short set of instructions (Sabou et al., 2014). Such judgments are often simpler than those in linguistic annotation by experts; for example, workers might be asked to annotate only a single class of entity at a time. Through crowdsourcing, quality annotations can be gathered quickly and at scale (Aker et al., 2012).

There also tends to be a larger variance in reliability over crowd workers than in expert annotators (Hovy et al., 2013). For this reason, crowdsourced annotation microtasks are often all performed by at least two different workers. E.g., every sentence would be examined for each entity type by at least two different non-expert workers.

We investigate entity pre-empting of crowdsourced corpora for a challenging genre: social media. Newswire corpora are not too hard to come by, especially for English, and the genre is somewhat biased in style, mostly being written or created by working-age middle-class men (Eisenstein, 2013), and in topic, being related to major events around unique entities that one might refer to by a special name. In contrast, social media text has broad stylistic variance (Hu et al., 2013) while also being difficult for existing NER tools to achieve good accuracy on (Derczynski et al., 2013; Derczynski et al., 2015) and having no large NE annotated corpora.

In our setup, we subdivide the annotation task according to entity type. Workers perform best with light cognitive loads, so asking them to annotate one kind of thing at a time increases their agreement and accuracy (Krug, 2009; Khanna et al., 2010). Person, location and organisation entities are annotated, giving three annotation sub-tasks, following Bontcheva et al. (2015). Jobs were created automatically using the GATE crowdsourcing plugin (Bontcheva et al., 2014). An example sub-task is shown in Figure 1. This means that we must pre-empt according to entity type, instead of just pre-empting whether or not an excerpt contains any entities at all, which has the additional effect of changing entity-bearing/entity-free class distributions.

Entity type	Messages with	Messages without
Any	45.95%	54.05%
Location	9.52%	90.48%
Organisation	11.16%	88.84%
Person	32.49%	67.51%

Table 7: Entity distribution over twitter messages

Dataset	P	R	F1
Base: 500 messages	70.39	31.66	43.67
500 msgs + 1k without entities	85.00	25.15	38.81
500 msgs + 1k random	76.14	44.38	56.07
500 msgs + 1k with entities	71.21	54.14	**61.51**

Table 8: Adding entity-less vs. entity-bearing data to a 500-message base training set

We use two sources that share entity classification schemas: the UMBC twitter NE annotations (Finin et al., 2010), and the MSM2013 twitter annotations (Rowe et al., 2013). We also add the Ritter et al. (2011) dataset, mapping its geo-location and facility classes to location, and company, sports team and band to organisation. Mixing datasets reduces the impact of any single corpus' sampling bias on final results. In total, this gives 3 854 twitter messages (tweets). Table 7 shows the entity distribution over this corpus. From this we separated a 500 tweet training set, used as base NER training data and pre-empting training data, and another set of 500 tweets for evalution. Note that each message can contain more than one type of entity, and that names of people are the most common class of entity.

4.1 Re-validating the Hypothesis

As we now have a new dataset with potentially much greater diversity than newswire, our first step is to re-check our initial hypothesis – that entity-bearing text contributes more to the performance of a statistical NER system than entity-free or random text. Results are shown in Table 8.

The effect of entity-bearing training data is clear here. Only data without annotations to the base is harmful (-4.8 F1), adding randomly chosen messages is helpful (+14.4 F1), and adding only messages containing entities is the most helpful (+17.8 F1). The corpus is small; in this case, the evaluation data has only 338 entities. Even so, the difference between random and entity-only F1 is signif-

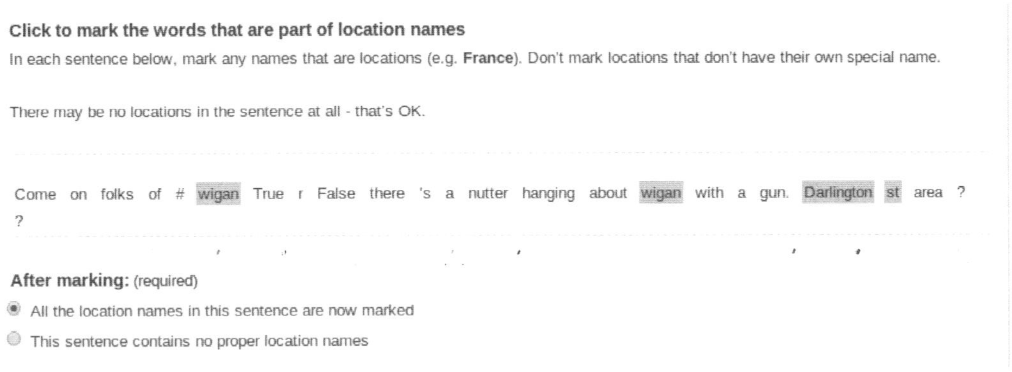

Figure 1: An example crowdsourced entity labelling microtask.

Training sents.	Accuracy	P	R	F1
	Random baseline			
	51.6	47.1	48.2	47.6
	Proper nouns			
From WSJ	54.0	49.8	85.4	62.9
	SVM + Cost, $j = 5$			
10	46	46	100	63
100	69.5	63.0	80.3	70.6
200	72.4	66.9	78.4	72.2
500	71.4	64.8	81.7	72.3
1000	47.7	68.0	83.6	75.1

Table 9: Evaluating any-entity tweet pre-empting.

Entity type	Acc.	P	R	F1
	Random baseline			
Person	56.63	33.33	33.87	33.60
Location	83.17	10.91	11.32	11.11
Organisation	80.08	8.86	9.09	8.97
	SVM + Cost, $j = 5$			
Person	74.87	65.69	70.10	67.77
Location	91.27	64.81	13.21	21.95
Organisation	89.55	60.42	9.42	16.30
	Maximum entropy			
Person	80.15	60.67	73.39	66.43
Location	90.85	7.92	55.26	13.86
Organisation	89.38	7.79	55.81	13.68

Table 10: Per-entity pre-empting on tweets.

icant at $p<0.00050$, using compute-intensive χ^2 testing following Yeh (2000).

4.2 Pre-empting Entities in Social Media

We construct a similar pre-empting classifier to that for newswire (Section 3.1). We continue using the base 500 messages as a source of training data, and evaluate pre-empting using the remainder of the data. The random baseline follows the class distribution in the base set, where 47.2% of messages have at least one entity of any kind.

We also evaluate pre-empting performance per entity class. The same training and evaluation sets are used, but a classifier is learned to pre-empt each entity class (person, location and organisation), as in Derczynski and Bontcheva (2014). This may greatly impact annotation, due to the one-class-at-a-time nature of the crowdsourced task and low occurrence of individual entity types in the corpus (see Table 7). We took 300 of the base set's sentences and used these for our training data, with the same evaluation set as before.

4.3 Results

Results for any-entity pre-empting on tweets are given in Table 9. Although performance is lower than on newswire, pre-empting is still possible in this genre. Only results for cost-weighted SVM are given.

We were able to learn accurate per-entity classifiers despite having a fairly small amount of data. Results are shown in Table 10. A good reduction is achieved over the baseline in all cases, though specifically predicting locations and organisations is hard. However, we do achieve high precision, meaning that a good amount of less-useful entity-free data is rejected. The SVM figures are with a reasonably high weighting in favour of recall. Conversely, while achieving similar F-scores to SVM, the maximum entropy pre-empter scores much better in terms of recall than precision.

These results are encouraging in terms of cost reduction. In this case, once we have annotated the first few hundred examples, we can avoid a lot of un-needed annotation by only paying crowd workers to complete microtasks on texts we suspect (with great accuracy) bear entities. From the observed entity occurrence rates in Table 7, given our pre-empting precision, we can avoid 41% of person microtasks, 59% of location microtasks and

Removed features	Acc.	P	R
Baseline			
None	90.58	92.12	96.25
-gram shortening			
3-grams	90.50	92.29	95.93
2-grams	90.15	91.62	96.28
1-grams	89.09	90.13	96.69
Removed feature classes			
Char-grams	87.47	89.46	95.29
Shape-grams	87.20	87.73	97.33
Token-grams	90.33	92.56	95.36

Table 11: Pre-empting feature ablation results.

58% of organisation microtasks where no entities occur – excluding a large amount material in preference for content that will give better NER performance later.

5 Analysis

5.1 Feature Ablation

The SVM system we have developed for pre-empting named entities is effective. To investigate further, we performed feature ablation along two dimensions. Firstly, we hid certain feature n-gram lengths (which are 1, 2 or 3 entries long). Secondly, we removed groups of features i.e. word n-grams, character n-grams or compressed word shape n-grams. We experimented using 1 000 training examples, on the newswire all-entities task, evaluating against the same 4 000-sentence evaluation set, with an SVM pre-empter. This makes figures comparable to those in Table 3.

Ablation results are given in Table 11. Shape grams, that is, subsequences of word characters, have the least overall impact on performance. Unigram features (across all character, shape and token groups) have the second-largest impact. This suggests that morphological information is useful in this task, and that the presence of certain words in a sentence acts as a pre-empting signal.

5.2 Informative Features

When pre-empting certain features are more helpful than others. The maximum entropy classifier implementation used allows output of the most informative features. These are reported – for newswire – in Table 12. In this case, the model was trained on 10 000 examples, and is the one for which results were given in Table 3, that achieved an F-score of 96.88.

Word shape features are the strongest indicators of named entity presence, and the strongest indicators of entity absence are all character grams.

Feature type	Feature value	Weight
shape	X_.	0.99558
char-gram	K	1.06190
shape	._	1.10804
shape	Xx_Xx_x	1.17046
shape	X	1.39189
shape	x_Xx_x	1.40092
shape	Xx_Xx	1.56733
shape	x_Xx	1.77390
shape	._.	-1.40075
char-gram	”	-1.03842
shape	x	-0.96047
char-gram	G_	-0.85378
char-gram	T_	-0.80422
char-gram	H_e_	-0.77069
n-gram	He	-0.77069
char-gram	I_	-0.75819

Table 12: Strongest features for pre-empting in English newswire.

Many shapes that indicate entity presence have one or more capitalised words in sequence, or linked to all-lower case words surrounding them. Apparently, sentences containing quote marks are less likely to contain named entities. Also, the characters sequence “He” suggests that a sentence does not contain an entity, perhaps because the target is being referred to pronomially.

5.3 Observations

Our experiments have begun with a base set of annotated sentences, mixing entity-bearing and entity-free. This not only serves a practical purpose of providing the pre-empter with training data and negative examples. It is also important to include some entity-free text in the NER training data so that systems based on it can observe that some sentences may have no entities. Without this observation, there is a risk that they will handle entity-free sentences poorly when labelling previously-unseen data.

It should be noted that segmenting into sentences risks the removal of long-range dependencies important in NER (Ratinov and Roth, 2009). However, overall performance in newswire – on longer documents – is not harmed by our approach. In the social media context we examined, entity co-reference is rare, due to its short texts.

6 Related Work

Avoiding needless annotation is a constant theme in NLP, and of interest to researchers, who often go to great lengths to avoid it. For example, recently, Garrette and Baldridge (2013) demonstrated the impressive construction of a part-of-speech tagger based on just two hours' annotation.

Similar to our work, Shen et al. (2004) proposed active learning for named entity recognition annotation, reducing annotation load without hurting NER performance, based on three metrics for each text batch and an iterative process. We differ from Shen et al. by giving a one-shot approach which does not need iterative re-training and is simple to implement in an annotation workflow, although we do not reduce annotation load as much. Our simplification means that pre-empting is easy to integrate into an annotation process, especially important for e.g. crowdsourced annotation, which is cheap and effective but gives a lot less control over the annotation process.

Laws et al. (2011) experiment with combining active learning and crowdsourcing. They find that not only does active learning generate better quality than randomly selecting crowd workers, it can be used to filter out miscreant workers. The goal in this work was to improve annotation quality and reduce cost that way. Recent advances in crowdsourcing technology offer much better quality than at the time of this paper. Rather than focusing on finding good workers, we aim for the extrinsic goal improving system performance by choosing which annotations to perform in the first place.

7 Conclusion

Entity pre-empting makes corpus creation quicker and more cost-effective. Though demonstrated with named entity annotation, it can apply to other annotation tasks, especially when for corpora used in information extraction, for e.g. relation extraction and event recognition.

This paper presents the pre-empting task, shows that it is worthwhile, and demonstrates an example approach in two application scenarios. We demonstrate that choosing to annotate texts that are rich in target entity mentions is more efficient than annotating randomly selected text. The example approach is shown to successfully pre-empt entity presencce classic named entity recognition. Applying pre-empting to the social media genre, where annotated corpora are lacking and NER is difficult, also offers improvement – but is harder.

Further analysis of the effect of pre-empting in different languages is also warranted, after the mixed results in Table 6. Larger samples can be used for training social media pre-empting; though we only outline an approach using 1 000 examples, up to 15 000 have been annotated and made publicly available for some entity types. For future work, the pre-empting feature set could be first adapted to morphologically rich languages, and then also to languages that do not necessarily compose tokens from individual letters, such as Mi'kmaq or Chinese.

Acknowledgments

This work is part of the uComp project (http://www.ucomp.eu//), which receives the funding support of EPSRC EP/K017896/1, FWF 1097-N23, and ANR-12-CHRI-0003-03, in the framework of the CHIST-ERA ERA-NET.

References

A. Aker, M. El-Haj, M.-D. Albakour, and U. Kruschwitz. 2012. Assessing crowdsourcing quality through objective tasks. In *Proceedings of the Conference on Language Resources and Evaluation*, pages 1456–1461.

K. Bontcheva, I. Roberts, L. Derczynski, and D. Rout. 2014. The GATE Crowdsourcing Plugin: Crowdsourcing Annotated Corpora Made Easy. In *Proceedings of the 14th Conference of the European Chapter of the Association for Computational Linguistics (EACL)*. Association for Computational Linguistics.

K. Bontcheva, L. Derczynski, and I. Roberts. 2015. Crowdsourcing named entity recognition and entity linking corpora. In N. Ide and J. Pustejovsky, editors, *The Handbook of Linguistic Annotation (to appear)*. Springer.

H. Daumé III. 2004. Notes on CG and LM-BFGS optimization of logistic regression. Paper available at `http://pub.hal3.name#daume04cg-bfgs`, implementation available at `http://hal3.name/megam/`, August.

L. Derczynski and K. Bontcheva. 2014. Passive-aggressive sequence labeling with discriminative post-editing for recognising person entities in tweets. In *Proceedings of the 14th Conference of the European Chapter of the Association for Computational Linguistics*, volume 2, pages 69–73.

L. Derczynski, D. Maynard, N. Aswani, and K. Bontcheva. 2013. Microblog-Genre Noise and Impact on Semantic Annotation Accuracy. In *Proceedings of the 24th ACM Conference on Hypertext and Social Media*. ACM.

L. Derczynski, D. Maynard, G. Rizzo, M. van Erp, G. Gorrell, R. Troncy, and K. Bontcheva. 2015. Analysis of named entity recognition and linking for tweets. *Information Processing and Management*, 51:32–49.

J. Eisenstein. 2013. What to do about bad language on the internet. In *Proceedings of the 2013 Conference of the North American Chapter of the Association for Computational Linguistics: Human Language Technologies*, pages 359–369. Association for Computational Linguistics.

T. Finin, W. Murnane, A. Karandikar, N. Keller, J. Martineau, and M. Dredze. 2010. Annotating named entities in Twitter data with crowdsourcing. In *Proceedings of the NAACL HLT 2010 Workshop on Creating Speech and Language Data with Amazon's Mechanical Turk*, pages 80–88.

J. Finkel, T. Grenager, and C. Manning. 2005. Incorporating non-local information into information extraction systems by Gibbs sampling. In *Proceedings of the 43rd Annual Meeting of the Association for Computational Linguistics*, pages 363–370. Association for Computational Linguistics.

D. Garrette and J. Baldridge. 2013. Learning a part-of-speech tagger from two hours of annotation. In *Proceedings of NAACL-HLT*, pages 138–147.

D. Hovy, T. Berg-Kirkpatrick, A. Vaswani, and E. Hovy. 2013. Learning Whom to trust with MACE. In *Proceedings of NAACL-HLT*, pages 1120–1130.

Y. Hu, K. Talamadupula, S. Kambhampati, et al. 2013. Dude, srsly?: The surprisingly formal nature of Twitter's language. *Proceedings of ICWSM*.

T. Joachims. 1999. Svmlight: Support vector machine. *SVM-Light Support Vector Machine http://svmlight. joachims. org/, University of Dortmund*, 19(4).

S. Khanna, A. Ratan, J. Davis, and W. Thies. 2010. Evaluating and improving the usability of Mechanical Turk for low-income workers in India. In *Proceedings of the first ACM symposium on computing for development*. ACM.

S. Krug. 2009. *Don't make me think: A common sense approach to web usability*. Pearson Education.

F. Laws, C. Scheible, and H. Schütze. 2011. Active learning with amazon mechanical turk. In *Proceedings of the conference on empirical methods in natural language processing*, pages 1546–1556. Association for Computational Linguistics.

K. Morik, P. Brockhausen, and T. Joachims. 1999. Combining statistical learning with a knowledge-based approach - a case study in intensive care monitoring. In *Proceedings of the 16th International Conference on Machine Learning (ICML-99)*, pages 268–277, San Francisco.

L. Ratinov and D. Roth. 2009. Design challenges and misconceptions in named entity recognition. In *Proceedings of the Thirteenth Conference on Computational Natural Language Learning*, pages 147–155. Association for Computational Linguistics.

A. Ritter, S. Clark, Mausam, and O. Etzioni. 2011. Named entity recognition in tweets: An experimental study. In *Proc. of Empirical Methods for Natural Language Processing (EMNLP)*, Edinburgh, UK.

M. Rowe, M. Stankovic, A. Dadzie, B. Nunes, and A. Cano. 2013. Making sense of microposts (#msm2013): Big things come in small packages. In *Proceedings of the WWW Conference - Workshops*.

M. Sabou, K. Bontcheva, L. Derczynski, and A. Scharl. 2014. Corpus annotation through crowdsourcing: Towards best practice guidelines. In *Proceedings of the 9th international conference on language resources and evaluation (LREC14)*, pages 859–866.

D. Shen, J. Zhang, J. Su, G. Zhou, and C.-L. Tan. 2004. Multi-criteria-based active learning for named entity recognition. In *Proceedings of the Annual Meeting on Association for Computational Linguistics*. Association for Computational Linguistics.

G. Szarvas, R. Farkas, L. Felföldi, A. Kocsor, and J. Csirik. 2006. A highly accurate named entity corpus for hungarian. In *Proceedings of International Conference on Language Resources and Evaluation*.

E. F. Tjong Kim Sang and F. D. Meulder. 2003. Introduction to the CoNLL-2003 Shared Task: Language-Independent Named Entity Recognition. In *Proceedings of CoNLL-2003*, pages 142–147. Edmonton, Canada.

E. F. Tjong Kim Sang. 2002. Introduction to the CoNLL-2002 shared task: Language-independent named entity recognition. In *Proceedings of CoNLL-2002*, pages 155–158. Taipei, Taiwan.

K. Toutanova, D. Klein, C. D. Manning, and Y. Singer. 2003. Feature-rich part-of-speech tagging with a cyclic dependency network. In *Proceedings of the 2003 Conference of the North American Chapter of the Association for Computational Linguistics on Human Language Technology*, NAACL '03, pages 173–180.

A. Yeh. 2000. More accurate tests for the statistical significance of result differences. In *Proceedings of the conference on Computational linguistics*, pages 947–953. Association for Computational Linguistics.

A Joint Model of Product Properties, Aspects and Ratings for Online Reviews

Ying Ding
School of Information Systems
Singapore Management University
ying.ding.2011@smu.edu.sg

Jing Jiang
School of Information Systems
Singapore Management University
jingjiang@smu.edu.sg

Abstract

Product review mining is an important task that can benefit both businesses and consumers. Lately a number of models combining collaborative filtering and content analysis to model reviews have been proposed, among which the Hidden Factors as Topics (HFT) model is a notable one. In this work, we propose a new model on top of HFT to separate product properties and aspects. Product properties are intrinsic to certain products (e.g. types of cuisines of restaurants) whereas aspects are dimensions along which products in the same category can be compared (e.g. service quality of restaurants). Our proposed model explicitly separates the two types of latent factors but links both to product ratings. Experiments show that our proposed model is effective in separating product properties from aspects.

1 Introduction

Online product reviews and the numerical ratings that come with them have attracted much attention in recent years. During the early years of research on product review mining, there were two separate lines of work. One focused on content analysis using review texts but ignored users, and the other focused on collaborative filtering-based rating prediction using user-item matrices but ignored texts. However, these studies do not consider the identifies of reviewers, and thus cannot incorporate user preferences into the models. In contrast, the objective of collaborative filtering-based rating prediction is to predict a target user's overall rating on a target product without referring to any review text (e.g. Salakhutdinov and Mnih (2007)). Collaborative filtering makes use of past ratings of the target user, the target item and other user-item ratings to predict the target user's rating on the target item.

Presumably if review texts, numerical ratings, user identities and product identities are analyzed together, we may achieve better results in rating prediction and feature/aspect identification. This is the idea explored in a recent work by McAuley and Leskovec (2013), where they proposed a model called Hidden Factors as Topics (HFT) to combine collaborative filtering with content analysis. HFT combines latent factor models for recommendation with Latent Dirichlet Allocation (LDA). In the joint model, the latent factors play dual roles: They contribute to the overall ratings, and they control the topic distributions of individual reviews.

While HFT is shown to be effective in both predicting ratings and discovering meaningful latent factors, we observe that the discovered latent factors are oftentimes not "aspects" in which products can be evaluated and compared. In fact, the authors themselves also pointed out that the topics discovered by HFT "are not similar to aspects" (McAuley and Leskovec, 2013). Here we use "aspects" to refer to criteria that can be used to compare all or most products in the same category. For example, we can compare restaurants by how well they serve customers, so *service* is an aspect. But we cannot compare restaurants by how well they serve Italian food if they are not all Italian restaurants to begin with, so *Italian food* cannot be considered an aspect; It is more like a feature or property that a restaurant either possesses or does not possess.

Identifying aspects would help businesses see where they lose out to their competitors and consumers to directly compare different products under the same criteria. In this work, we study how we can modify the HFT model to discover both properties and aspects. We use the term "product properties" or simply "properties" to refer to latent

Proceedings of Recent Advances in Natural Language Processing, pages 131–137,
Hissar, Bulgaria, Sep 7–9 2015.

factors that can explain user preferences but are intrinsic to only certain products. Besides types of cuisines, other examples of properties include brands of products, locations of restaurants or hotels, etc. Since a product's rating is related to both the properties it possesses and how well it scores in different aspects, we propose a joint model that separates product properties and aspects but links both of them to the numerical ratings of reviews.

We evaluate our model on three data sets of product reviews. Based on human judgment, we find that our model can well separate product properties and aspects while at the same time maintaining similar rating prediction accuracies as HFT. In summary, the major contribution of our work is a new model that can identify and separate two different kinds of latent factors, namely product properties and aspects.

2 Related Work

Research on modeling review texts and the associated ratings or sentiments has attracted much attention. In the pioneering work by Hu and Liu (2004), the authors extracted product aspects and predicted sentiment orientations. While this work was mainly based on frequent pattern mining, recent work in this direction pays more attention to modeling texts with principled probabilistic models like LDA. Wang et al. (2011a) modeled review documents using LDA and treated ratings as a linear combination of topic-word-specific sentiment scores. Sauper et al. (2011) modeled word sentiment under different topics with a topic-sentiment word distribution. While these studies simultaneously model review documents and associated ratings, they do not consider user identity and item identity, which makes them unable to discover user preference and item quality. There have been many studies on the extraction of product aspects (Qiu et al., 2011; Titov and McDonald, 2008b; Mukherjee and Liu, 2012). These studies use either linguistic patterns or a topic modeling approach, or a combination of both, to identify product features or aspects. However, they do not distinguish between aspects and properties.

More recent work has started paying attention to taking user and product identity into consideration. McAuley and Leskovec (2013) used a principled model similar to that of Wang and Blei (2011) to map each latent factor to a topic learned by LDA from review documents. Two variations of this model were proposed by Bao et al. (2014), which also took each review's helpfulness score into consideration. The latest work in this direction is a model proposed by Diao et al. (2014). This work further modeled the generation of sentiment words in review text, which was controlled by the estimated sentiment score of the corresponding aspect. However, in all the work discussed above, there was no separation and joint modeling of product properties and aspects.

3 Model

In this section, we will describe our join model for product properties, aspects and ratings.

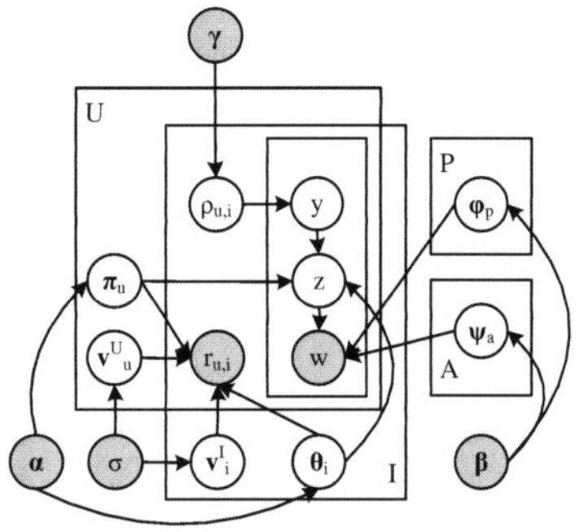

Figure 1: Plate notation of our PAR model. Circles in gray indicate hyperparameters and observations.

3.1 Our Model

3.1.1 Generation of Ratings

As we have pointed out in Section 1, many of the latent factors learned by HFT are product properties such as brands, which cannot be used to compare all products in the same category. In order to explicitly model both product properties and aspects, we first assume that there are two different sets of latent factors: There is a set of P product properties, and there is another set of A product aspects. Both are latent factors that will influence ratings.

Next, we assume that each product has a distribution over product properties and each user has a real-valued vector over product properties. Because properties generally model features that a product either possesses or does not possess, it makes sense to associate a distribution over properties with a product. For example, if each type of cuisines corresponds to a property, then a Mexican restaurant should have a high probability for the property *Mexican food* but low or zero probabilities for properties such as *Japanese food*, *Italian food*, etc. On the other hand, a user may like and dislike certain product properties, so it makes sense to use real numbers that can be positive or negative to indicate a user's preferences over different properties. For example, if a user does not like Japanese food, she is likely to give low ratings to Japanese restaurants, and therefore it makes sense to model this as a negative value associated with the property *Japanese food* in her latent vector.

Analogically, it makes sense to assume that a product has a real-valued latent vector over aspects, where a positive value means the product is doing well in that aspect and a negative value means the product is poor in that aspect. For example, a restaurant may get a negative score for the aspect *service* but a positive score for the aspect *price*. On the other hand, we assume that a user has a distribution over aspects to indicate their relative weight when the user rates a product. For example, if service is not important to a user but price is, she will have a low or zero probability for the aspect *service* in her vector but a high probability for the aspect *price*.

Formally, let $\boldsymbol{\theta}_i$ denote the property distribution of product i, $\boldsymbol{v}^U_u$ denote the property vector of user u, $\boldsymbol{\pi}_u$ denote the aspect distribution of user u and $\boldsymbol{v}^I_i$ denote the aspect vector of item i. Based on the assumptions above, it makes sense to model the rating of user u given to item i to be close to $(\boldsymbol{\theta}_i \cdot \boldsymbol{v}^U_u + \boldsymbol{\pi}_u \cdot \boldsymbol{v}^I_i)$. If we compare this formulation with standard ways of modeling ratings such as in HFT, we can see that the major difference is the following. In standard models, the latent vectors of both users and items are unconstrained, i.e. both positive and negative values can be taken. This may cause problem interpreting the learned vectors. For example, when user u has a negative value for the kth latent factor and item i also has a negative value for the kth latent factor, the product of these two negative values results in a positive contribution to the rating of item i given by user u. But how shall we interpret these two negative values and their combined positive impact to the rating? In our model, we separate the latent factors into two groups. For one group of latent factors (product properties), we force the items to have non-negative values, while for the other group of latent factors (product aspects), we force the users to have non-negative values. By doing this, we improve the interpretability of the learned latent vectors.

3.1.2 Generation of Review Texts

In our model, for each latent factor, which can be either a product property or an aspect, there is a word distribution associated with it, which we denote by $\boldsymbol{\phi}_p$ for property p and $\boldsymbol{\psi}_a$ for aspect a.

We assume that a review of a product given by a particular user mainly consists of two types of information: properties this product possesses and evaluation of this product in the various aspects that this user cares about. Content related to product properties is mainly controlled by the property distribution of the product. For example, reviews on a Mexican restaurant may contain much information about Mexican food. Content related to aspects are mainly controlled by the user's aspect preference distribution. A user who values service more may comment more about a restaurant's service. Based on these assumptions, in the generative process of reviews, each word in a review document is sampled either from a product property or an aspect.

3.1.3 The Generative Process

Our model is shown in Figure 1. and the description of the generative process is as follows:

- For each product property p, sample a word distribution $\boldsymbol{\phi}_p \sim \text{Dirichlet}(\boldsymbol{\beta})$.
- For each aspect a, sample a word distribution $\boldsymbol{\psi}_a \sim \text{Dirichlet}(\boldsymbol{\beta})$.
- For each item
  - Sample a product property distribution $\boldsymbol{\theta}_i \sim \text{Dirichlet}(\boldsymbol{\alpha})$.
  - Sample an A-dimensional vector $\boldsymbol{v}^I_i$ where $v^I_{i,a} \sim \text{Normal}(0, \sigma^2)$.
  - Sample an item rating bias $b_i \sim \mathcal{N}(0, \sigma^2)$.
- For each user
  - Sample an aspect distribution $\boldsymbol{\pi}_u \sim \text{Dirichlet}(\boldsymbol{\alpha})$.
  - Sample a P-dimensional vector $\boldsymbol{v}^U_u$ where $v^U_{u,p} \sim \text{Normal}(0, \sigma^2)$.
  - Sample a user rating bias $b_u \sim \mathcal{N}(0, \sigma^2)$.
- For a user-item pair where a review and a rating exist
  - Sample the rating $r_{u,i} \sim \text{Normal}(\boldsymbol{\theta}_i \cdot \boldsymbol{v}^U_u + \boldsymbol{\pi}_u \cdot \boldsymbol{v}^I_i + b_i + b_u + b, \sigma^2)$
  - Sample the parameter for a Bernoulli distribution $\boldsymbol{\rho}_{u,i} \sim \text{Beta}(\boldsymbol{\gamma})$
  - For each word in the review
    * Sample $y_{u,i,n} \sim \text{Bernoulli}(\boldsymbol{\rho}_{u,i})$.
    * Sample $z_{u,i,n} \sim \text{Discrete}(\boldsymbol{\theta}_i)$ if $y_{u,i,n} = 0$ and $z_{u,i,n} \sim \text{Discrete}(\boldsymbol{\pi}_u)$ if $y_{u,i,n} = 1$.
    * Sample $w_{u,i,n} \sim \text{Discrete}(\boldsymbol{\phi}_{z_{u,i,n}})$ if $y_{u,i,n} = 0$ and $w_{u,i,n} \sim \text{Discrete}(\boldsymbol{\psi}_{z_{u,i,n}})$ if $y_{u,i,n} = 1$.

Here, α, β and γ are hyper-parameters for Dirichlet distribution, σ is the standard deviation for Gaussian distribution, $\rho_{u,i}$ is the switching probability distribution for review of user u on item i, $y_{u,i,n}$ and $z_{u,i,n}$ are the switching variable and topic assignment for word at position n of review on itme i from user u. We refer to our model as the Property-Aspect-Rating (PAR) model.

3.2 Parameter Estimation

Our goal is to learn the parameters that can maximize the log-likelihood of both review texts and ratings simultaneously. Formally speaking, we are trying to estimate the parameters $\boldsymbol{V}^U$, $\boldsymbol{V}^I$, $\boldsymbol{B}_U$, $\boldsymbol{B}_I$, $\boldsymbol{\pi}_U$, $\boldsymbol{\theta}_I$, $\boldsymbol{\rho}$, $\boldsymbol{\phi}_P$ and $\boldsymbol{\psi}_A$ that can optimize the following posterior probability.

$$P(\boldsymbol{V}^U, \boldsymbol{V}^I, \boldsymbol{B}_U, \boldsymbol{B}_I, \boldsymbol{\pi}_U, \boldsymbol{\theta}_I, \boldsymbol{\rho}, \boldsymbol{\phi}_P, \boldsymbol{\psi}_A | \boldsymbol{W}, \boldsymbol{R}).$$

Here $\boldsymbol{V}^U$ and $\boldsymbol{V}^I$ refer to all latent vectors for items and users, $\boldsymbol{B}_U$ and $\boldsymbol{B}_I$ refer to all the bias terms, $\boldsymbol{W}$ refers to all the words in the reviews and $\boldsymbol{R}$ refers to all the ratings. The hyperparameters are omitted in the formula. Equivalently, we will use the loglikelihood as our objective function. As there is no closed form solution for it, we use Gibbs-EM algorithm (Wallach, 2006) for parameter estimation.

E-step: In the E-step, we fix the parameters $\boldsymbol{\pi}_U$ and $\boldsymbol{\theta}_I$ and collect samples of the hidden variables $\boldsymbol{Y}$ and $\boldsymbol{Z}$ to approximate the distribution $P(\boldsymbol{Y}, \boldsymbol{Z} | \boldsymbol{W}, \boldsymbol{R}, \boldsymbol{\pi}_U, \boldsymbol{\theta}_I)$.

M-step: In the M-step, with the collected samples of $\boldsymbol{Y}$ and $\boldsymbol{Z}$, we seek values of $\boldsymbol{\pi}_U$, $\boldsymbol{\theta}_I$, $\boldsymbol{V}^U$, $\boldsymbol{V}^I$, $\boldsymbol{B}_U$ and $\boldsymbol{B}_I$ that maximize the following objective function:

$$\mathcal{L} = \sum_{(\boldsymbol{Y},\boldsymbol{Z}) \in S} \log P(\boldsymbol{Y}, \boldsymbol{Z}, \boldsymbol{W}, \boldsymbol{R} | \boldsymbol{\pi}_U, \boldsymbol{\theta}_I, \boldsymbol{V}^U, \boldsymbol{V}^I, \boldsymbol{B}_U, \boldsymbol{B}_I)$$

where S is the set of samples collected in the E-step.

In our implementation, we perform 600 runs of Gibbs EM. Because Gibbs sampling is time consuming, in each run we only perform one iteration of Gibbs sampling and collect that one sample. We then have 60 iterations of gradient descent. The gradient descent algorithm we use is L-BFBS, which is efficient for large scale data set.

4 Experiments

In this section, we present the empirical evaluation of our model.

Data Set	#Reviews	#W/R	Voc	#Users	#Items
SOFT	54,330	84.6	16,653	43,177	8,760
MP3	20,689	103.9	8,227	18,609	742
REST	88,865	86.5	21,320	8,230	3,395

Table 1: Statistics of our data sets.*#W/R stands for #Word/Review.

4.1 Data

We use three different review data sets for our evaluation. The first one is a set of software reviews, which was used by McAuley and Leskovec (2013). We refer to this set as SOFT. The second one is a set of reviews of MP3 players, which was used by Wang et al. (2011b). We refer to this set as MP3. The last one is a set of restaurant reviews released by Yelp[1] in Recsys Challenge 2013[2], which was also used by McAuley and Leskovec (2013). We refer to it as REST. Based on common practice in previous studies (Titov and McDonald, 2008a; Titov and McDonald, 2008b; Wang and Blei, 2011), we processed these reviews by first removing all stop words and then removing words which appeared in fewer than 10 reviews. We then also removed reviews with fewer than 30 words. Some statistics of the processed data sets are shown in Table 1.

4.2 Experiment Setup

As we have discussed in Section 1, the focus of our study is to modify the HFT model to capture both product properties and aspects. Note that HFT model is designed for both predicting ratings and discovering meaningful latent factors. Therefore, the goal of our evaluation is to test whether our PAR model can perform similarly to HFT in terms of rating prediction and latent factor discovery, and on top of that, whether our PAR model can well separate product properties and aspects, which HFT cannot do. In the rest of this section, we present our evaluation as follows. We first compare PAR with HFT in terms of finding meaningful latent factors. We then evaluate how well PAR separates properties and aspects. Finally, we compare PAR with HFT for rating prediction. Note that when we compare PAR with HFT in the first and the third tasks, we do not expect PAR to outperform HFT but we want to make sure PAR performs comparably to HFT.

In all our experiments, we use the same number

[1]http://www.yelp.com

[2]https://www.kaggle.com/c/yelp-recsys-2013

	Product Properties		Aspects	
	Number	Avg. # Relevant Words	Count	Avg. # Relevant Words
SOFT	18	11.3	9	9.2
MP3	6	5.0	13	9.9
REST	13	10.4	5	7.8

Table 2: Summary of the Ground Truth Latent Factors.

of latent factors for PAR and HFT. For PAR, the number of latent factors is the number of properties plus the number of aspects, i.e. $P + A$. After some preliminary experiments, we set the total number of latent factors to 30 for both models. For PAR, based on observations with the preliminary experiments, we empirically set P to 10 and A to 20. Although these settings may not be optimal, by using the same number of latent factors for both models, no bias is introduced into the comparison.

For other hyperparameters, we empirically tune the parameters using a development set and use the optimal settings. For PAR, we set $\alpha = 2$, $\beta = 0.01$, $\sigma = 0.1$ and $\gamma = 1$. For HFT, we set $\mu = 10$ for MP3 and SOFT and $\mu = 0.1$ for REST. All results reported below are done under these settings.

4.3 Annotation of Ground Truth

The major goal of our evaluation is to see how well the PAR model can identify and separate product properties and aspects. However, in all three data sets we use, there is no ground truth and we are not aware of any data set with ground truth labels we can use for our task. Therefore, we have to annotate the data ourselves.

Instead of asking annotators to come up with product properties and aspects, which would require them to manually go through all reviews and summarize them, we opted to ask them to start from latent factors discovered by the two models. We randomly mixed the latent factors learned by PAR and HFT. The top 15 words of each latent factor were shown to two annotators, and each annotator independently performed the following three steps of annotations. In the first step, an annotator had to determine whether a latent factor was meaningful or not based on the 15 words. In the second step, for latent factors labeled as meaningful, an annotator had to decide whether it was a product property or an aspect. In the third step, an annotator had to pick relevant words from the given list of 15 words for each latent factor. After the three-step independent annotation, the two annotators compared and discussed their results to come to a consensus. During this discussion, duplicate latent factors were merged and word lists for each latent factor were finalized. The annotators were required to exclude general words such that no two latent factors share a common relevant word. In the end, the annotators produced a set of product properties and another set of aspects for each data set. For each latent factor, a list of highly relevant words was also produced. Table 2 shows the numbers of ground truth properties and aspects as labeled by the annotators and the average numbers of relevant words per latent factor of the three data sets.

4.4 Discovery of Meaningful Latent Factors

In the first set of experiments, we would like to compare PAR and HFT in terms of how well they can discover meaningful latent factors. Here latent factors include both product properties and aspects.

4.4.1 Results

We show three numbers for each data set and each method. The first is the number of "good" latent factors discovered by a method. Here a good latent factor is one that matches one of the ground truth latent factors. A learned latent factor matches a ground truth latent factor if the top-15 words of the learned latent factor cover at least 60% of the ground truth relevant words of the ground truth latent factor. We find the 60% threshold reasonable because most matching latent factors appear to be meaningful.

We use Precision and Recall as the evaluation metric. We would like to point out that the recall defined in this way is higher than the real recall value, because our ground truth latent factors all come from the discovered latent factors, but there may exist meaningful factors that are not discovered by either HFT or PAR at all. Nevertheless, we can still use this recall to compare PAR with HFT. The results are shown in Table 3. As we

	SOFT			MP3			REST		
	# Good LF	Prec	Rec	# Good LF	Prec	Rec	# Good LF	Prec	Rec
PAR	20	0.67	0.74	14	0.47	0.74	10	0.33	0.56
HFT	20	0.67	0.74	12	0.40	0.63	10	0.33	0.56

Table 3: Results for Identification of Meaningful Latent Factors

can see from the table, PAR and HFT performed similarly in terms of discovering meaningful latent factors. PAR performed slightly better than HFT on the MP3 data set. Overall, between one-third to two-thirds of the discovered latent factors are meaningful for both methods, and both methods can discover more than half of the ground truth latent factors.

4.5 Separation of Product Properties and Aspects

In this second set of experiments, we would like to evaluate how well PAR can separate product properties and aspects. In order to focus on this goal, we first disregard the discovered latent topics that are not considered good latent topics according to the criterion used in the previous experiment.

We then show the 2×2 confusion matrix between the labeled two types of latent factors and the predicted two types of latent factors by PAR for each data set. The results are in Table 4. As we can see, our model does a very good job in separating the two types of latent factors for MP3 and REST. For SOFT, our model mistakenly labeled 4 product properties as aspects. Although this result is not perfect, it still shows that our model can separate properties from aspects well in different domains.

We find that properties in the software domain are mostly functions and types of software such as games, antivirus software and so on. Aspects of software include software version, user interface, online service and others. In the MP3 data set, properties are mainly about MP3 brands such as Sony and iPod while aspects are about batteries, connections with computers and some others. Properties of the restaurant data set are all types of cuisines and aspects include ambiance and service.

4.6 Rating Prediction

Finally we compare our model with HFT for rating prediction in terms of root mean squared error. The results are shown in Table 5. We can see that PAR outperforms HFT in two real data sets

Prediction	Ground Truth					
	SOFT		MP3		REST	
	P	A	P	A	P	A
P	8	2	3	0	8	0
A	4	6	1	10	0	2

Table 4: Confusion Matrices of PAR for all Data Sets. *P stands for property and A stands for aspect.

(SOFT, MP3) and gets the same performance for the data set REST. This means separating properties and aspects in the model did not compromise rating prediction performance, which is important because otherwise the learned latent factors might not be the best ones explaining the ratings.

	SOFT	REST	MP3
PAR	1.394	1.032	1.401
HFT	1.399	1.032	1.404

Table 5: Performance in Rating Prediction.

5 Conclusion and Future Work

We presented a joint model of product properties, aspects and numerical ratings for online product reviews. The major advantage of the proposed model is its ability to separate product properties, which are intrinsic to products, from aspects that are meant for comparing products in the same category. To achieve this goal, we combined probabilistic topic models with matrix factorization. We explicitly separated the latent factors into two groups and used both groups to generate both review texts and ratings. Our evaluation showed that compared with HFT our model could achieve similar or slightly better performance in terms of identifying meaningful latent factors and predicting ratings. More importantly, our model is able to separate product properties from aspects, which HFT and other existing models are not capable of.

References

Yang Bao, Hui Zhang, and Jie Zhang. 2014. TopicMF: Simultaneously exploiting ratings and reviews for recommendation. In *Proceedings of the Twenty-Eighth AAAI Conference on Artificial Intelligence*, pages 2–8.

Qiming Diao, Minghui Qiu, Chao-Yuan Wu, Alexander J. Smola, Jing Jiang, and Chong Wang. 2014. Jointly modeling aspects, ratings and sentiments for movie recommendation (JMARS). In *Proceedings of the 20th ACM SIGKDD International Conference on Knowledge Discovery and Data Mining*, pages 193–202.

Minqing Hu and Bing Liu. 2004. Mining and summarizing customer reviews. In *Proceedings of the Tenth ACM SIGKDD International Conference on Knowledge Discovery and Data Mining*, pages 168–177.

Julian J. McAuley and Jure Leskovec. 2013. Hidden factors and hidden topics: understanding rating dimensions with review text. In *Proceedings of the 7th ACM Conference on Recommender Systems*, pages 165–172.

Arjun Mukherjee and Bing Liu. 2012. Aspect extraction through semi-supervised modeling. In *Proceedings of the 50th Annual Meeting of the Association for Computational Linguistics*, pages 339–348.

Guang Qiu, Bing Liu, Jiajun Bu, and Chun Chen. 2011. Opinion word expansion and target extraction through double propagation. *Computational Linguistics*, 37:9–27.

Ruslan Salakhutdinov and Andriy Mnih. 2007. Probabilistic matrix factorization. In *Proceedings of the Twenty-First Annual Conference on Neural Information Processing Systems*, pages 1257–1264, Vancouver, British Columbia, Canada. Curran Associates, Inc.

Christina Sauper, Aria Haghighi, and Regina Barzilay. 2011. Content models with attitude. In *Proceedings of the 49th Annual Meeting of the Association for Computational Linguistics*, pages 350–358.

Ivan Titov and Ryan T. McDonald. 2008a. A joint model of text and aspect ratings for sentiment summarization. In *Proceedings of the 46th Annual Meeting of the Association for Computational Linguistics*, pages 308–316.

Ivan Titov and Ryan T. McDonald. 2008b. Modeling online reviews with multi-grain topic models. In *Proceedings of the 17th International Conference on World Wide Web*, pages 111–120.

Hanna M. Wallach. 2006. Topic modeling: Beyond bag-of-words. In *Proceedings of the 23rd International Conference on Machine Learning*, pages 977–984.

Chong Wang and David M. Blei. 2011. Collaborative topic modeling for recommending scientific articles. In *Proceedings of the 17th ACM SIGKDD International Conference on Knowledge Discovery and Data Mining*, pages 448–456.

Hongning Wang, Yue Lu, and ChengXiang Zhai. 2011a. Latent aspect rating analysis without aspect keyword supervision. In *Proceedings of the 17th ACM SIGKDD International Conference on Knowledge Discovery and Data Mining*, pages 618–626.

Hongning Wang, Yue Lu, and ChengXiang Zhai. 2011b. Latent aspect rating analysis without aspect keyword supervision. In *Proceedings of the 17th ACM SIGKDD International Conference on Knowledge Discovery and Data Mining*, pages 618–626.

Towards Opinion Summarization from Online Forums

Ying Ding
School of Information Systems
Singapore Management University
ying.ding.2011@smu.edu.sg

Jing Jiang
School of Information Systems
Singapore Management University
jingjiang@smu.edu.sg

Abstract

Summarizing opinions expressed in online forums can potentially benefit many people. However, special characteristics of this problem may require changes to standard text summarization techniques. In this work, we present our initial attempt at extractive summarization of opinionated online forum threads. Given the nature of user generated content in online discussion forums, we hypothesize that besides relevance, text quality and subjectivity also play important roles in deciding which sentences are good summary sentences. We therefore construct an annotated corpus to facilitate our study of extractive summarization of online discussion forums. We define a set of features to capture relevance, text quality and subjectivity, and empirically test their usefulness in choosing summary sentences. Using unpaired Student's t-test, we find that sentence length and number of sentiment words have high correlations with good summary sentences. Finally we propose some simple modifications to a standard Integer Linear Programming based summarization framework to incorporate these features.

1 Introduction

With the growing popularity of social media, people often share their experience and opinions openly on the Internet. Especially when a controversial event happens, there are many different opinions expressed in online forum threads, including judgement of the people and organizations involved in the event and suggestions for future changes. Since it is too time consuming to go through all the posts of a thread to understand every individual's opinion, summarizing online discussion forums becomes an important task that may benefit people including government policy makers and social scientists. While text summarization has been extensively studied, summarizing noisy and subjective user-generated content is still an under-explored area. A vast body of work has been done on summarizing online product reviews, but because of the special properties of product reviews, opinion summarization of product reviews tends to focus on product aspect identification and sentiment polarity classification. When it comes to summarizing general online discussions, particularly discussions on controversial topics such as a policy or a social issue, the challenges we face can be very different from summarizing product reviews.

Table 1 shows a set of summary sentences selected by a state-of-the-art summarization method (Gillick and Favre, 2009) from a forum thread on criticizing parliament ministers sleeping in a meeting. We can see that the summary contains low-quality sentences and some sentences do not express opinions. This result shows that traditional text summarization techniques, which only consider text representativeness, may not be able to summarize opinions from online forums very well.

In particular, we hypothesize that two important factors should be considered for summarizing online discussions. First, because forum posts are often noisy, with misspelling, broken sentences and online jargon, text quality should be considered for selecting good candidate summary sentences. Second, because the goal of summarizing discussion forums is mainly to capture online users' opinions, there should be a preference to choose subjective sentences for summaries.

To test the hypotheses above, we need ground truth summaries. Unfortunately, to the best of our knowledge we are not aware of existing bench-

Proceedings of Recent Advances in Natural Language Processing, pages 138–146,
Hissar, Bulgaria, Sep 7–9 2015.

1	Just For Laughs ....
2	P @ P shld change to NAP
3	otherwise , they are all fully awake .
4	If true..i suggest they better dnt attend the parliament .
5	Bottom people close eye means sleeping .
6	Top people close eye and snoozing means thinking very hard .
7	ministers / MPs must take parliament session very seriously .
8	becos in parliament , very important topics are being discussed and debated .
9	must pay attention and stay awake ! !
10	sleeping on the job ?
11	His face look like wks..
12	this is becoming the PAP 's official logo
13	Sleep and Dream

Table 1: Summary sentences selected by the ILP-based method (Gillick and Favre, 2009) from a thread on criticizing parliament ministers sleeping in a meeting.

mark data sets for online forum summarization. We thus construct a data set of extractive summaries of 10 online discussion threads. Using this data set we empirically test the importance of a set of features capturing the relevance, text quality and subjectivity of candidate sentences. We find that besides relevance, two other features that are significantly important are sentence length and the number of sentiment words. We further propose some simple modifications to an ILP (Integer Linear Programming)-based summarization framework to incorporate these features and show that the modified method achieves better summarization results.

Our main contributions are the following: (1) We provide a new data set for studying extractive summarization of online discussion forums. (2) We conduct an empirical study to test the importance of several sentence features capturing text quality and subjectivity for summary sentence selection. (3) We propose modifications to a standard ILP-based extractive summarization method to incorporate good sentence features, which are shown to achieve better results.

2 Related Work

Extractive multi-document summarization: Our work is related to extractive methods for multi-document summarization, which select sentences from the original documents to form summaries. While much work has been done for this general problem, existing methods do not focus on opinion summarization. Methods for extractive multi-document summarization generally considers two factors: to increase the representativeness of the selected summary sentences with respect to the original document set, and to reduce the redundancy in the selected sentences. Existing approaches include centroid-based methods (Radev et al., 2004), learning-based methods (Kupiec et al., 1995; Wong et al., 2008) and graph-based methods (Erkan and Radev, 2004; Mihalcea and Tarau, 2004; Mei et al., 2010). More recently, Lin and Bilmes have done a series of work modeling text summarization with submodular functions (Lin and Bilmes, 2011; Lin and Bilmes, 2010). To globally infer an optimal set of sentences as a summary, ILP-based document summarization has been used. It was first proposed by McDonald (2007) and Gillick and Favre (2009) proposed a scalable version.

Opinion summarization: Much work on opinion summarization is for product reviews (Hu and Liu, 2004; Popescu et al., 2005; Ganesan et al., 2012). As we have pointed out, summarizing opinions from online forums, where the topics can be social issues, is quite different from summarizing product reviews. For general opinion summarization, in 2008 the Text Analysis Conference (TAC) organized an opinion summarization task. But their task is different from the one we study here. Their task is a query-oriented summarization problem where a target topic is given together with some specific questions. The corpus they use is a large set of blogs. Our task is not query-oriented, and we aim to summarize the opinions found in a single thread discussing a focused topic.

Text summarization in social media: Recently with the explosion of social media, there has been much work on summarizing social media content. In particular, much attention has been paid to Twitter summarization (Chua and Asur, 2013; Meng et al., 2012). As Twitter posts are short and not naturally organized by topics, Twitter summarization is a very different problem than ours. There has also been some studies on forum summarization (Krishnamani et al., 2013; Ren et al., 2011; Tigelaar, 2008), but the focus of these studies is not on opinion summarization.

3 Data

Since we are not aware of any existing data set that satisfies our need, we opted to create our own data. First, we picked 10 threads discussing social issues in English from the online forum Asiaone[1], which is very popular in southeast Asia. We use the first 100 posts for each thread to study our summarization problem. On average, there are 256 sentences and 3652 tokens in each thread. The vocabulary size of our data set is 5661. For each thread, we asked 3 human annotators, who are all graduate students, to carefully read the 100 posts and write a summary with a length limit of 100 words. We specifically asked the human annotators to summarize the opinions rather than facts in these threads. We also encouraged the annotators to pick sentences directly from the data but they could also compose their own sentences if necessary. In the final human summaries, there are 172 unique sentences and 156 (91%) out of them are directly picked from the original data set. We used all sentences (from all annotators) directly picked from the data set as summary sentences and all other sentences as non-summary sentences. Based on this data set, we identified discriminative features and subsequently improved our summarization method.

4 Sentence Features

In this section, we identify a number of sentence features which we hypothesize to have correlations with whether a sentence is a good summary sentence for forum opinion summarization. While a large number of features have been examined in previous studies on standard summarization (Kupiec et al., 1995; Wong et al., 2008), in this work we hypothesize that for our problem the following characteristics of a sentence are the most important: (1) representativeness with respect to the entire thread, (2) text quality, and (3) subjectivity. The first one is important for any summarization, while the last two are special for forum opinion summarization.

[1]`http://www.asiaone.com/`

4.1 Representativeness

There are many different ways to measure the representativeness of a sentence with respect to the entire thread. Our objective here is not to find the best measure for representativeness but to compare the relative importance of the representativeness features with text quality features and subjectivity features for our problem. We consider two features for representativeness.

Cosine similarity. Cosine similarity has been widely used in previous summarization work (Kågebäck et al., 2014; Hu and Liu, 2004). For each sentence we calculate its cosine similarity to the entire thread, where the term vector for a sentence or for a thread is based on raw term frequency.

Concept coverage. Inspired by the concept-based ILP framework for summarization by (Gillick and Favre, 2009), we take all the bigrams (which are treated as concepts) in the original thread and use their frequencies as their weights. We then compute the weighted sum of the bigrams covered in a sentence. As the ILP-based summarization framework tries to maximize the overall concept coverage of all the selected summary sentences from one thread, a sentence with a higher concept coverage presumably is a better summary sentence candidate.

4.2 Text Quality

We hypothesize that text quality is especially important for summarizing forum posts because user-generated content tends to be of lower quality compared with traditional corpora. Typical characteristics of user-generated content that affect its text quality include use of Internet slang words, misspelling, grammatical errors, excess use of punctuation marks, etc. We hypothesize that low quality sentences are less likely to be chosen as summary sentences. While many features have been proposed to measure text quality (Pitler and Nenkova, 2008), based on our observation with our data, here we consider the following features:

4.2.1 Shallow Features

Sentence length. We use the length of a sentence in terms of the number of words as a feature. We observe that there are many short sentences in online forums and most of them do not carry much useful information. However, long sentences appear to be more informative and more useful. Thus we hypothesize that good summary sentences tend to be longer.

Percent of OOV (out of vocabulary) word. There exist a lot of Internet slang and abbreviations in user-generated content, such as "lol" and "hahaha." Sentences containing these words tend to be more informal and less informative. So we hypothesize that the more OOV words there are in a sentence, the less likely a sentence is a good summary sentence. Using a common English dictionary *British English Word Lists for Spell Checkers*[2], we count the number and ratio of OOV words in a sentence.

Percent of punctuation marks/emoticons. While this feature may not be important for traditional text, in user-generated content we observe that sometimes online users like to use many punctuation marks and emoticons to emphasize their emotions. We hypothesize that such sentences are not good summary sentences.

Percent of capitalized words. We also observe that in the threads we have collected, some sentences contain many capitalized words such as "HaHa" and "LOL." We hypothesize that the more capitalized words a sentence contains, the less likely it is a good summary sentence.

Average word length. This is the average length of a word in a sentence in terms of characters. With this feature, we would like to check whether good summary sentences tend to contain longer words.

4.2.2 Language Model based Feature

Log likelihood with respect to a reference corpus. Another way to measure how formal a sentence is is to use a high quality reference corpus such as a set of news articles to learn a unigram language model, and then to compute the log likelihood of generating a sentence from this language model (Pitler and Nenkova, 2008). Here we use a set of 20000 articles from Reuters as our reference corpus. Supposedly the higher the log likelihood of a sentence is, the more similar it is to the reference corpus, and we hypothesize that the more likely it is a good summary sentence. However, log likelihood is biased towards shorter sentences. We therefore take the average log likelihood per word of a sentence as our feature.

[2] `http://www.curlewcommunications.co.uk/wordlist.html`

4.2.3 POS based Features

Part-of-speech based grammatical features have been widely used in text quality prediction (Feng et al., 2010; Dell'Orletta et al., 2014). They can capture the linguistic and syntactic structure of sentence, which may affect its readability. In this work, we calculate the percentage of nouns, verbs, adjectives and adverbs in each sentence.

4.2.4 Parse Tree Height

The height of the parse tree of a sentence has been used in previous work to assess text quality (Dell'Orletta et al., 2014; Pitler and Nenkova, 2008; Schwarm and Ostendorf, 2005). Here we use Stanford PCFG Parser to extract this feature. We hypothesize that as summary sentences tend to be more informative and more well-written, they may be more complicated in terms of syntactic structure and their parse tree height are probably larger than non-summary sentences.

4.3 Subjectivity

Although online forums mostly contain opinions, people sometimes also share facts or perceived facts in forums. Since our problem is opinion summarization, the summary sentences presumably should be subjective. We therefore use the following feature to test our hypothesis.

Number of sentiment words. To measure subjectivity, we take a simple approach and count the number of sentiment words in a sentence using a sentiment lexicon. We use the MPQA subjectivity lexicon (Wilson et al., 2005).

5 Feature Analysis

5.1 Approach

In Section 3 we pointed out that the sentences directly picked from the original threads by the annotators are treated as summary sentences and all other sentences are treated as non-summary sentences for the purpose of identifying useful sentence features. With the features identified in Section 4, we would like to assess the discrimination power of these features in terms of picking up summary sentences. Knowing what features are useful can help us design better summarization methods for forum opinion summarization problem. Specifically, since all our feature values are numerical, we perform unpaired Student's t-test on each feature. Student's t-test is a statistical hypothesis test, which is used to determine if two sets of data are significantly different from each other. For each feature, we get two sets of values with one set extracted from summary sentences and the other set extracted from non-summary sentences. Then we apply Student's t-test to them. If these two sets of values are significant different, the corresponding feature is useful in picking up summary sentences .

5.2 Results

Table 2 shows the results of the Student's t-test for all the features we consider. Features that show statistical significance at a 95% confidence level are marked with an asterisk.

5.2.1 Representativeness

Both features capturing representativeness of a sentence, which are cosine similarity and concept coverage, are good features. This indicates that sentences representing the salient content of a forum thread are more likely to be summary sentences. This observation follows intuition well and reflects the nature of text summarization: extracting the main content.

5.2.2 Text Quality

Shallow Features: There is much variation among the text quality features. Although we hypothesize that the features we have identified are useful, it turns out that not all of them have a statistically significant impact on whether the sentence is a good summary sentence. In particular, we find that sentence length has a positive impact. This satisfies our hypothesis that longer sentence tend to be more informative and more likely to be selected as summary sentences. The percentage of capitalized words and percentage of punctuation/emotions have negative impact. This tells us that summary sentences tend to have less capitalized words and less punctuations and emoticons. In social media, capitalized words are often used for abbreviation or emphasis and they can make a sentence less readable and less informative. Punctuations and emoticons are used more often to purely express sentiment. Sentences with higher percentage of punctuations and emoticons are less likely to contain useful information.

However, features like percent of out-of-vocabulary words and average word length can not separate summary sentences from non-summary sentences. As these two features capture the formality of words, we can see that summary sentences are similar to non-summary sentences in term of word formality. We guess that word formality is not a significant factor influencing annotators' selection of summary sentences.

Language Model based feature: The likelihood of using a language model based on Reuters corpus does not have a significant impact on selecting summary sentences. It indicates summary sentences are not more formal compared with non-summary sentences. This is consistent with the result based on shallow features.

POS based Features: In this set of features, the percent of adjectives is the only discriminative one and it has a positive impact. As our task is opinion summarization, it is intuitive that summary sentences tend to have more adjectives as many opinions are expressed by using adjectives.

Parse Tree Height: Based on the statistic test result, parse tree height is a useful feature and summary sentences tend to have larger value on this feature. This result is consistent with our hypothesis that summary sentences carry more salient content and their tree structure may appear to be more complicated.

5.2.3 Subjectivity

The simple feature of number of sentiment words in a sentence turns out to be an important feature of selecting summary sentences. This satisfies our hypothesis that summary sentences of opinions from forum should carry more opinions.

6 Forum Opinions Summarization using ILP

In the last two sections we identified and analyzed a set of sentence features to understand what characteristics good summary sentences have for our problem. While we can extend this analysis and use a supervised learning approach to classify sentences from forum posts into summary and non-summary sentences, it may not be ideal as supervised approaches suffer from their dependence on labeled training data. Moreover, even if we classify sentences into summary and non-summary sentences, we still need to consider the redundancy problem when we select sentences to form a summary. We therefore choose an unsupervised approach with a global optimization framework.

ID	feature description	p-value	test statistic
1*	cosine similarity	<0.001	6.333
2*	concept coverage	<0.001	4.695
3*	percent of punctuation/emoticons	<0.001	-4.735
4*	percent of capitalized words	<0.001	-4.190
5*	sentence length	0.001	3.438
6	average word length	0.099	1.652
7	percent of OOV	0.126	-1.530
8	average log likelihood (Reuters)	0.952	0.061
9*	percent of adjectives	0.031	2.157
10	percent of adverbs	0.176	1.353
11	percent of verbs	0.277	1.087
12	percent of nouns	0.512	-0.656
13*	parse tree height	<0.001	3.931
14*	number of sentiment words	<0.001	5.370

Table 2: Results of statistical significance tests of the features. * indicates that the result is statistically significant at a 95% confidence level. Values less than 0.001 are denoted as < 0.001.

6.1 Integer Linear Programming for Document Summarization

McDonald (2007) proposed a global optimization model to solve document summarization by integer linear programming. The idea is to maximize the overall score of selected sentences while also minimizing the redundancy among selected sentences. However, his method can have an exponentially growing number of parameters and it cannot globally measure redundancy. To handle document summarization by globally considering both content coverage and redundancy, Gillick and Favre (2009) proposed a different framework. Their objective is to cover the "concepts" in the original documents. The quality of a summary is measured by the weighted sum of concepts it covers, and a concept is counted only once regardless of how many times it occurs in the selected summary sentences. The framework therefore intrinsically handles both content coverage and redundancy reduction. The formulation is as follows:

$$
\begin{aligned}
\text{Maximize:} \quad & \sum_i w_i c_i \\
\text{Subject to:} \quad & \sum_j l_j s_j \leq L \\
& s_j Occ_{ij} \leq c_i, \forall i, j \\
& \sum_j s_j Occ_{ij} \geq c_i, \forall i \\
& c_i \in \{0, 1\} \quad \forall i \\
& s_j \in \{0, 1\} \quad \forall j
\end{aligned}
$$

where w_i is the weight of concept i, c_i is a binary indicator for concept i which will be set to 1 when i is covered by the summary. s_j is the binary indicator for sentence j which is 1 when the sentence is selected as a summary sentence. Occ_{ij} is a binary variable indicating the occurrence of concept i in sentence j, which would be 1 if i occurs in j. l_j is the length of sentence j. We need to solve optimization problem and get the optimal values of c_i and s_j for all i and j.

6.2 Our Modifications

We can see that the above framework does not consider sentence quality or subjectivity. Based on the findings from Section 5, we propose the following modifications to the concept-based ILP framework.

LengthMod-1: Since we find that summary sentences from forums tend to be longer, we propose to minimize the total number of sentences in the summary as follows:

$$\text{Maximize:} \sum_i w_i c_i - \lambda \sum_j s_j.$$

where λ is a free parameter in all three modifications. The second term is essentially the total number of sentences selected. The other constraints for the optimization problem remain the same.

LengthMod-2: Alternatively, we propose the following objective function to favor longer sentences:

$$\text{Maximize:} \sum_i w_i c_i + \lambda \sum_j l_j^2 s_j.$$

With the total length of all selected sentences capped at L, the second term above favor the selection of fewer, longer sentences.

SubjectMod-1: To favor sentences with subjective words, we can formulate the following objective function:

$$\text{Maximize: } \sum_i w_i c_i + \lambda \sum_j o_j s_j,$$

where o_j is the sentiment score for sentence j, which is computed by counting the number sentiment words in j.

SubjectMod-2: Alternatively, to model the influence of sentiment words, we can change the way w_i is calculated. In the study by Gillick and Favre (2009), w_i is the frequency of concept i in the input documents. Here, we change it to be the frequency of i appearing in opinionated sentences. For simplicity, we treat sentences containing sentiment words as opinionated sentences. The intuition of the original method is try to cover as many frequent concepts as possible. The intuition of ours is to cover as many *opinion related* concepts as possible.

6.3 Results

	ROUGE-1	ROUGE-2
Baseline	0.3418	0.1062
LengthMod-1	0.3483	0.1187
LengthMod-2	0.3469	0.1182
SubjectMod-1	0.3399	0.0991
SubjectMod-2	**0.3576**	**0.1191**

Table 3: Summarization Performance

To test the effectiveness of our modifications, we applied both them and the baseline method on the forum data introduced in Section 3. The human editted summaries are used as the gold standard references. For our modifications, when summarizing one thread, we use all other 9 threads and the corresponding human summaries as training data to find the optimal λ. We use ROUGE-1 and ROUGE-2 as the evaluation metric.

In Table 3 we show the performance of the baseline method and our modifications. We can see that modifications that incorporate length into the objective function both give better performance over the baseline. This shows that our modified versions of the objective function can effectively bring in longer sentences for summaries. However, the two modified methods based on sentence subjectivity have very different performance. While SubjectMod-2 outperforms the baseline (and all other modifications), SubjectMod-1 does not outperform the baseline.

A deeper analysis of SubjectMod-1 and SubjectMod-2 can reveal their difference. SubjectMod-2 changes the way concept weights are calculated. In this method, concepts co-occurring more with sentiment words in the same sentence will be more important. The algorithm tries to cover as many sentiment related frequent concepts as possible. Coverage and subjectivity are incorporated and considered at the same time. However, SubjectMod-1 considers coverage and subjectivity separately. If a sentence contains some frequent but not opinion related concepts and a few sentiment words, it may be selected as a summary sentence by SubjectMod-1.

7 Conclusions

In this paper, we studied the problem of summarizing opinions from online forum threads. We first constructed a data set with human generated model summaries and then identified a number of sentence features which we hypothesized to be useful in characterizing good summary sentences. These features cover representativeness, text quality and subjectivity of a sentence. Based on the model summaries we have obtained, we evaluated the effectiveness of these features based on Student's t-test. We found that a number of these features are significantly discriminative in identifying summary sentences. We then proposed to modify an ILP-based summarization framework to take sentence length and subjectivity into consideration.

Our study provides insight into the general problem of summarizing online opinions from forum discussions, which has not been well studied. Our findings suggest that a number of factors other than content coverage are important to consider when it comes to summarizing opinions from social media. Our proposed modifications to a principled summarization framework show promising results. Our study is still preliminary. In the future, we plan to study how to further improve the ILP-based summarization framework to incorporate more considerations. We also expect that 1) it is useful to use fine-grained opinion extraction to extract and normalize opinions before they can be summarized, 2) social media properties like users' attributes and social effect can be helpful in summarizing text content.

References

Freddy Chong Tat Chua and Sitaram Asur. 2013. Automatic summarization of events from social media. In *Proceedings of the Seventh International Conference on Weblogs and Social Media*, pages 81 – 90.

Felice Dell'Orletta, Martijn Wieling, Andrea Cimino, Giulia Venturi, and Simonetta Montemagni. 2014. Assessing the readability of sentences: Which corpora and features? In *Proceedings of the Ninth Workshop on Innovative Use of NLP for Building Educational Applications*, page 163C173.

Günes Erkan and Dragomir R. Radev. 2004. Lexpagerank: Prestige in multi-document text summarization. In *Proceedings of the 2004 Conference on Empirical Methods in Natural Language Processing*, pages 365–371.

Lijun Feng, Martin Jansche, Matt Huenerfauth, and Noémie Elhadad. 2010. A comparison of features for automatic readability assessment. In *Proceedings of the 23rd International Conference on Computational Linguistics: Posters*, pages 276–284.

Kavita Ganesan, ChengXiang Zhai, and Evelyne Viegas. 2012. Micropinion generation: An unsupervised approach to generating ultra-concise summaries of opinions. In *Proceedings of the 21st International Conference on World Wide Web*, pages 869–878.

Dan Gillick and Benoit Favre. 2009. A scalable global model for summarization. In *Proceedings of the Workshop on Integer Linear Programming for Natural Langauge Processing*, pages 10–18.

Minqing Hu and Bing Liu. 2004. Mining and summarizing customer reviews. In *Proceedings of the Tenth ACM SIGKDD International Conference on Knowledge Discovery and Data Mining*, pages 168–177.

Mikael Kågebäck, Olof Mogren, Nina Tahmasebi, and Devdatt Dubhashi. 2014. Extractive summarization using continuous vector space models. In *Proceedings of the 2nd Workshop on Continuous Vector Space Models and their Compositionality*, pages 31–39.

Janani Krishnamani, Yanjun Zhao, and Rajshekar Sunderraman. 2013. Forum summarization using topic models and content-metadata sensitive clustering. In *Web Intelligence/IAT Workshops*, pages 195–198.

Julian Kupiec, Jan Pedersen, and Francine Chen. 1995. A trainable document summarizer. In *Proceedings of the 18th Annual International ACM SIGIR Conference on Research and Development in Information Retrieval*, pages 68–73.

Hui Lin and Jeff Bilmes. 2010. Multi-document summarization via budgeted maximization of submodular functions. In *Human Language Technologies: The 2010 Annual Conference of the North American Chapter of the Association for Computational Linguistics*, pages 912–920.

Hui Lin and Jeff Bilmes. 2011. A class of submodular functions for document summarization. In *Proceedings of the 49th Annual Meeting of the Association for Computational Linguistics*, pages 510–520.

Ryan McDonald. 2007. A study of global inference algorithms in multi-document summarization. In *Proceedings of the 29th European Conference on Information Retrieval Research*, pages 557–564.

Q. Mei, J. Guo, and D. Radev. 2010. Divrank: the interplay of prestige and diversity in information networks. In *Proceedings of the 16th ACM SIGKDD international conference on Knowledge discovery and data mining*, pages 1009–1018.

Xinfan Meng, Furu Wei, Xiaohua Liu, Ming Zhou, Sujian Li, and Houfeng Wang. 2012. Entity-centric topic-oriented opinion summarization in twitter. In *Proceedings of the 18th ACM SIGKDD International Conference on Knowledge Discovery and Data Mining*, pages 379–387.

Rada Mihalcea and Paul Tarau. 2004. Textrank: Bringing order into texts. In *Proceedings of the 2004 Conference on Empirical Methods in Natural Language Processing*, pages 404–411.

Emily Pitler and Ani Nenkova. 2008. Revisiting readability: A unified framework for predicting text quality. In *Proceedings of the Conference on Empirical Methods in Natural Language Processing*, pages 186–195.

Ana-Maria Popescu, Bao Nguyen, and Oren Etzioni. 2005. Opine: Extracting product features and opinions from reviews. In *Proceedings of the Human Language Technology Conference and Conference on Empirical Methods in Natural Language Processing*, pages 339–346.

D.R. Radev, H. Jing, M. Styś, and D. Tam. 2004. Centroid-based summarization of multiple documents. *Information Processing & Management*, 40(6):919–938.

Zhaochun Ren, Jun Ma, Shuaiqiang Wang, and Yang Liu. 2011. Summarizing web forum threads based on a latent topic propagation process. In *Proceedings of the 20th ACM International Conference on Information and Knowledge Management*, pages 879–884.

Sarah E. Schwarm and Mari Ostendorf. 2005. Reading level assessment using support vector machines and statistical language models. In *Proceedings of the 43rd Annual Meeting on Association for Computational Linguistics*, pages 523–530.

Almer S. Tigelaar. 2008. *Automatic discussion summarization : a study of Internet forums*. Ph.D. thesis, University of Twente.

Theresa Wilson, Janyce Wiebe, and Paul Hoffmann. 2005. Recognizing contextual polarity in phrase-level sentiment analysis. In *Proceedings of the Conference on Human Language Technology and Empirical Methods in Natural Language Processing*, pages 347–354.

Kam-Fai Wong, Mingli Wu, and Wenjie Li. 2008. Extractive summarization using supervised and semi-supervised learning. In *Proceedings of the 22Nd International Conference on Computational Linguistics*, pages 985–992.

Cross-lingual Synonymy Overlap

Anca Dinu[1], Liviu P. Dinu[2], Ana Sabina Uban[2]
[1]Faculty of Foreign Languages and Literatures, University of Bucharest
[2]Faculty of Mathematics and Computer Science, University of Bucharest
anca_d_dinu@yahoo.com, liviu.p.dinu@gmail.com, ana.uban@gmail.com

Abstract

We investigate in this paper the degree of overlap between synonym sets of translated word pairs across three languages: French, English and Romanian. We use for this purpose a French Synonym Dictionary, a Romanian Synonym Dictionary, Princeton's WordNet and Google Translate API. We build a database containing pairs of (translated) words from the three languages, along with their corresponding synonym sets. We use it in order to gain insight into the synonym overlap for each language pair, and thus, into their degree of common concept lexicalization, by various queries. While the overall percentage of common synonyms is (expectedly) quite small (averaging ~6% across all language pairs), the percentage of hard synonyms pairs (pairs that have at least one common synonym), reaching ~62%, is significant. This is encouraging for further use of this special kind of word translated pairs in tasks such as automatic enhancement of lexical databases (such as WordNet) for less resourced languages such as Romanian, based on corresponding English versions of these lexical databases. Another interesting query topic was obtaining distributions of hard synonym pairs, function of their part of speech: hard synonyms were most frequent among verbs for English, and among adjectives for Romanian and French.

Keywords: cross-lingual synonyms, French, Romanian, database

1 Introduction

We investigate in this paper the degree of overlap between synonym sets of translated word pairs in three different languages, namely French, English and Romanian. The main idea is to test whether the synonym sets of pairs of translated words are still semantically related, that is to measure the degree of synonym overlap.

Synonymy is a lexical semantic relation, that is, a relation between meanings of words. By definition, synonyms are 'words or expressions of the same language that have the same or nearly the same meaning in some or all senses' (Inc., 2004). Cross-linguistically, the question that we try to answer in this paper is how much of this common meaning is shared by pairs of translated words. Since synonymy closely associates different lexicalizations of the same concept (which is language-specific), the overlap between synonym sets across a pair of languages expresses a kind of concept lexicalization overlap.

Cross-lingual synonym sets prove to be useful in tasks such as, for instance, automatic translation of web pages. Since search engines are using more of the Latent Semantic Indexing, which associates keywords of an article or a page with its synonyms within the domain covered by the keywords, one needs to take into consideration the synonym set of the translated keywords and the overlap of two languages synonym sets.

2 Related Works

There are various NLP applications using synonyms, one of the most notable being automatic synonym detection or extraction (Wang and Hirst, 2011; Wang et al., 2010; Mohammad and Hirst, 2006; Bikel and Castelli, 2008), a. o., which in turn can help in tasks including machine translation, information retrieval, speech recognition, spelling correction, or text categorization (Budanitsky and Hirst, 2006).

A multilingual approach based on word alignment of parallel corpora proved to have (Van der Plas et al., 2011) higher precision and recall scores

Proceedings of Recent Advances in Natural Language Processing, pages 147–152,
Hissar, Bulgaria, Sep 7–9 2015.

for the task of synonym extraction than the monolingual approach. Other work on semantic distance between words and concepts (Mohammad et al., 2007) emphasise on the advantages of multilingual over the monolingual treatment.

3 Data and Tools

For Romanian language, we used a synonym dictionary (Dicționarul de sinonime al limbii Române, by Luiza Seche and Mircea Seche), which contains about 45.000 words and 230.000 synonym pairs. For English language we employed Princeton's WordNet, version 3.0, which contains about 150.000 words and 250.000 synonym pairs. For French language we used the synonyms dictionary developed by the CRISCO research centre, which contains almost 50.000 words and 400.000 synonyms relations. As a translation tool we used Google Translate API. We stored the data in a MySQL database.

4 Methodology

In the pre-processing step, we extracted and cleaned the data in the Romanian and French dictionary, and removed multiword expressions, obtaining 42.277 Romanian words with a total of 230.445 synonym pairs, 44.884 English words with a total of 145.898 synonyms, and 39.564 French words with a total of 344.600 synonyms. Of these, we analyzed the words for which translations were available using the Google Translate API; the number of such words for each language is illustrated in Table 1 below.

	Total words	Translation pairs		
		EN	FR	RO
EN	44.884	-	25.048	19.454
FR	39.564	19.302	-	20.209
RO	42.277	19.654	23.207	-

Table 1: Number of words and translation pairs

As a pre-processing step, Romanian words were stripped of accents (though in normal usage of the language Romanian characters don't usually have accents, in the dictionary some words are marked with accents to indicate their pronunciation), but the diacritics were left as they were found. The translations obtained with Google Translate API needed to be cleaned by removing non-alphanumeric characters and by matching the case to the translated word's case (lowercase if original word was lowercase, capitalized if original word was capitalized). Articles were also removed from the nouns among synonyms and translations for all languages, as well as infinitive markers from the verbs (*a* for Romanian, *to* for English), and sometimes pronouns for the Romanian verbs, such as *i* (*a i se năzări*) or *o* (*o șterge*), so as to ensure the canonical dictionary form of the verb. Reflexive pronouns (*se*) were kept, because they mark reflexive verbs (which may have a different meaning than their non-reflexive variant). To make sure the translations returned by the Google Translate API are valid dictionary words (since the API does not guarantee this), we only accepted for each language translations which we could find as words or synonyms in our dictionaries for that language, and discarded the rest.

Synonymy was considered a symmetric property - that is, for each *(w, s)* word-synonym pair found in the dictionaries, *(s, w)* was added as a synonym pair as well. Translation was treated as symmetric as well: for any word-translation pair *(w, t)* from *language A* to *language B* as found using the Google Translate API, *w* was considered to be the translation of *t* from *language B* to *language A*. This assumption was used to fill in missing data where translations for some words in certain languages were not found by the API.

For each of the Romanian, French and English words in the dictionaries, we obtained their synonym sets. For the English words, the synonyms were extracted from WordNet, where words are organized in synonym sets (or "synsets"), the synonyms of an English word were considered to be all the words in the union of all the synonym sets that include that word.

In the case of homonyms or polysemantic words, we merged all the synonyms for each sense of the word together, thus obtaining unique word forms across the entire word set (for either of the three languages), each associated with one synonym set.

We extracted information on each word's part of speech. In the Romanian synonym dictionary, possible parts of speech are {noun, verb, adjective, adverb, pronoun, article, interjection, numeral, preposition, conjunction}. In WordNet, words can have one of 4 parts of speech: {noun, verb, adjective, adverb}. In the French dictionary, possible parts of speech are {noun, verb, adverb, adjective, interjection, onomatopoeia, function word}. Considering we treated homonyms as the same word, for words where different senses of the word have different parts of speech, the word was considered to have multiple parts of speech.

For each pair of languages among the three languages analyzed, we generated word-translation pairs, we then computed statistics on their respective synonym sets, measuring overlaps between sets of synonyms from two perspectives: first translating the original word's synonyms in order to find their overlap with the translation's synonyms, and then translating the translation's synonyms in order to find their overlap with the original word's synonyms, resulting in two basic methods for measuring the synonyms' overlap.

Here are the steps we followed to obtain the statistics for word pairs and synonym sets, for a given pair of languages *language A* and *language B*, where *language A* and *language B* are both one of the three languages analyzed (English, French, Romanian): for each word in *language A*'s synonym dictionary:

1. We found its set of synonyms in *language A* (using *language A*'s synonym dictionary);
2. We obtained the word's translation into *language B* (given by Google Translate API);
3. We also obtained the set of synonyms for the *language B* translation (using *language B*'s synonym dictionary);
4. Finally, we found the translations in *language B* of the words in the *language A* set of synonyms (given by Google Translate API);

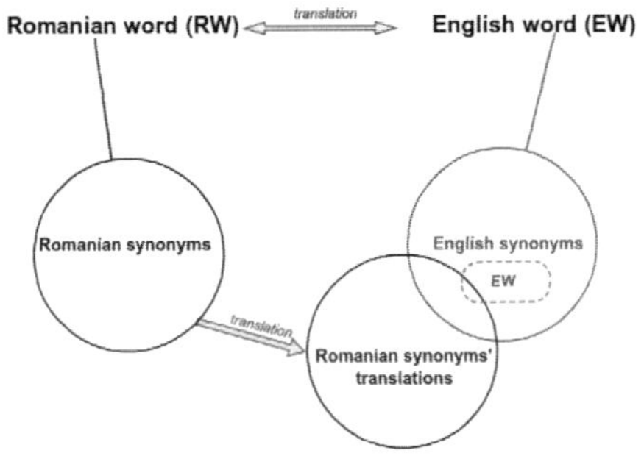

Figure 1: The method (for Romanian-English)

In order to test the overlap of *language A - language B* synonym sets, we counted the number of common words present in the synonym sets (consisting of words in *language B*) as computed above, for each word-translation pair. This process, exemplified for Romanian-English, is depicted in figure 1.

We applied the same algorithm the other way around. For each *language B* word the translation of which is found as an entry in the *language A* synonyms dictionary, one obtains its synonym set, its translation in *language A*, the synonym set for this translation and the translation into *language A* of the synonym set of the original *language B* word, then counts the common words present in these two resulted synonym sets (consisting of words in *language A*).

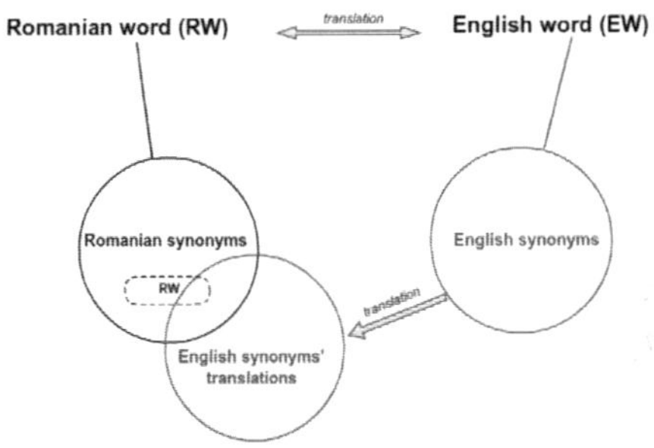

Figure 2: The method (for English-Romanian)

For measuring the intersections we used two methods: the first including only the synonyms of the two words (original *language A* word and its *language B* translation) and their translations, and the other including, along with the synonyms, the original target words as well (marked in the figures with the dotted border). We computed the overall percentage of common synonyms across synonym sets for all word pairs: for each word-translation pair, we measured the size of their joint synonym sets, as well as the size of these sets' overlap, as described above. We added these measures for all word pairs, and obtained the ratio of the number of common synonyms to the total size of all synonym sets.

We also counted the number of word-translation pairs for which at least one common synonym was found, or the synonym overlap contained at least one synonym (using any of the measures described above). These word pairs (along with their respective synonyms) will be called *hard synonyms*.

We organized the data in a MySQL database, in order to gain ease of access and to be able to instantiate various queries. The database consists of two tables: the first is the Word table - containing all words (words in either language, that have an entry in the dictionary or were just found as synonyms), as well as information on their translation, language and part of speech. There is a uniqueness constraint on the pair of columns (word, language), reflecting the uniqueness of word forms described above. The second table is WordsSynonyms - containing synonymy relations as references to pairs of words in the Word table.

This database structure straightforwardly allows for queries such as, for instance, queries on synonym set overlap, function of the word pair's part of speech tag.

Other queries may also be formulated in order to compute various statistics on words and their synonyms, such as average number of synonyms for words, function of their language or part of speech.

An example of such a query, that extracts the common synonyms for the Romanian-English word pair *nebunie - madness*, is depicted in figure 3 below.

```
mysql> SELECT rw.word AS "RO word", tw.word AS "EN translation",
    ->         rsw.word AS "RO synonym",
    ->         tsw.word AS "Common EN synonym" FROM (
    ->                 SELECT * FROM Word
    ->                  WHERE is_headWord AND language="RO"
    ->             ) AS rw
    ->             JOIN WordsSynonyms AS rs
    ->                  ON rw.id=rs.word_id
    ->             JOIN Word AS rsw
    ->                  ON rs.synonym_id=rsw.id
    ->             JOIN WordsSynonyms AS ts
    ->                  ON (ts.word_id=rw.translation_EN_id AND
    ->                     ts.synonym_id=rsw.translation_EN_id)
    ->             JOIN Word AS tw
    ->                  ON rw.translation_EN_id=tw.id
    ->             JOIN Word as tsw ON rsw.translation_EN_id=tsw.id
    ->             WHERE rw.word="nebunie";
+---------+----------------+-------------+-------------------+
| RO word | EN translation | RO synonym  | Common EN synonym |
+---------+----------------+-------------+-------------------+
| nebunie | madness        | ţicneală    | folly             |
| nebunie | madness        | mişelie     | folly             |
| nebunie | madness        | scrânteală  | craziness         |
| nebunie | madness        | zărgheală   | folly             |
+---------+----------------+-------------+-------------------+
```

Figure 3: An example of a database query

5 Results

The overall percentage of synonym overlap ranges from 4% to around 9% and is highest for the English-French and the French-Romanian language pairs: 9,29% for English-French (from a total of 319.624 words in both synonym sets, a total of 29.703 words are common), and 6,95% for French-Romanian (26.303 words are common from a total of 378.604 synonyms). These results were obtained using the second method described in the previous section, (e. g. including the target words in the synonym sets).

The average percent of hard synonym pairs is approximately 46,6% - with high scores for French-Romanian and Romanian-French, as well as English-French. The total number of hard synonyms for French-Romanian is 10.870 covering 53,79% of all 20.209 word pairs, while for Romanian-French the proportion of word pairs that are hard synonyms is 44,01%, and 62,02% for English-French. This is encouraging, since hard synonyms may have potential use tasks such as automatic enhancement of lexical databases (such as WordNet) for less resourced languages such as Romanian, based on corresponding English versions of these lexical databases. The percentages for Romanian and English are slightly lower (around 30%), as are those for the French-English language pair. Table 2 and 3 show the proportions of synonyms overlaps and hard synonym pairs respectively, for each of the language pairs considered and each of the two methods.

lang A	lang B	HS % (1)	HS % (2)
RO	FR	31,04%	44,01%
FR	RO	34,22%	53,79%
RO	EN	20,12%	33,36%
EN	RO	24,92%	46,85%
FR	EN	30,53%	39,86%
EN	FR	38,75%	62,02%

Table 2: Hard synonyms

lang A	lang B	Overlap%(1)	Overlap%(2)
RO	FR	3,79%	5,15%
FR	RO	4,51%	6,95%
RO	EN	3,05%	4,89%
EN	RO	3,67%	6,86%
FR	EN	3,31%	4,20%
EN	FR	5,96%	9,29%

Table 3: Total synonyms overlap

The distribution of hard synonym pairs, according to their part of speech, was also computed. The highest percentages of hard synonyms among words with a certain part of speech were obtained, in the case of language pairs including English (French-English, Romanian-English and their reversed analogues) for verbs, with as many as 74,03% of English verbs analyzed being part of an English-French hard synonyms pair (9.100 of 12.293 verb pairs). For French-English and English-French adverbs had the lowest proportion of hard synonyms - 51,45% and 62,52% respectively, whereas for English-Romanian and Romanian-English, nouns (50,14%) and adjectives respectively (37,24%) had the lowest percentages of hard synonyms. This hierarchy may look surprising at a first glance. One possible explanation is that particular object lexicalization varies more across languages than more abstract concepts (such as properties or events) lexicalization. It can be argued that these numbers support the hypothesis that language acquisition proceeds from general (abstract) concepts towards particularizations, and not the other way around (from particular cases towards generalizations).

	RO - FR	FR - RO
HS%	57,50% adj	78,88% adj
	53,57% noun	74,78% verb
	52,77% verb	70,76% noun
	52,14% adv	70,56% adv

Table 4: Distribution of hard synonyms across parts of speech for Romanian - French pairs

	RO - EN	EN - RO
HS%	49,60% verb	55,63% verb
	49,58% adv	55,48% adj
	42,17% noun	51,81% adv
	37,24% adj	50,14% noun

Table 5: Distribution of hard synonyms across parts of speech for Romanian - English pairs

	FR - EN	EN - FR
HS%	62,20% verb	74,03% verb
	54,04% adj	68,20% noun
	52,52% noun	67,51% adj
	51,45% adv	62,52% adv

Table 6: Distribution of hard synonyms across parts of speech for French - English pairs

For French-Romanian, on the other hand, (as well as for its reverse), the highest proportion of hard synonyms was found among adjectives: 78,88% of French adjectives are hard synonyms. Since some of the words in our database can have multiple parts of speech, the distribution of most common tuples of parts of speech that occur toghether for the same word among hard synonym pairs was also computed. The (adjective, noun) tuple was found to be especially rich in hard synonyms for the French-Romanian and Romanian-French word pairs (with 74,91% of French words that are both adjective and noun being part of a French-Romanian hard synonym pair). Table 7, 8 and 9 show the most common such part of speech tuples found among hard synonyms for each language pair.

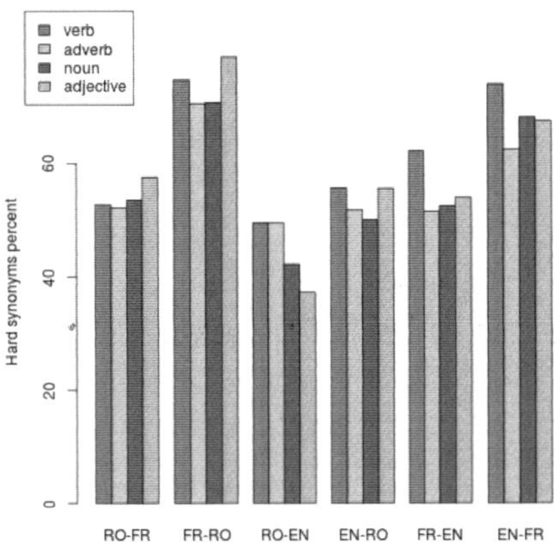

Figure 4: Hard synonyms proportion across parts of speech and language pairs

	RO - FR	FR - RO
HS%	53,63% adj,noun	74,91% adj,noun
	51,05% adj,adv	68,41% adj
	48,66% adj	65,04% verb
	44,75% noun	63,72% adv
	43,77% verb	59,71% noun

Table 7: Distribution of hard synonyms across words with multiple parts of speech, for most frequent combinations for French - Romanian pairs

6 Future Works

We leave for further research applying the same algorithm at deeper levels like synonym of syn-

	RO - EN	EN - RO
HS%	43,85% adv	63,49% adj,adv
	43,08% adj,adv	59,38% adj,verb
	40,06% verb	57,94% adj,noun,verb
	36,00% noun	50,77% adj,noun
	34,92% adj,noun	49,48% verb

Table 8: Distribution of hard synonyms across words with multiple parts of speech, for most frequent combinations for Romanian - English pairs

	FR - EN	EN - FR
HS%	58,28% verb	78,90% adj,noun,verb
	50,00% adj,noun	77,61% adj,adv
	45,58% noun	68,14% noun,verb
	45,47% adj	66,02% adj,noun
	44,20% adv	65,17% verb

Table 9: Distribution of hard synonyms across words with multiple parts of speech, for most frequent combinations for French - English pairs

onyms. Also, it would be interesting to test the distributional properties of the hard synonyms (as opposed to non-hard synonyms) on a parallel corpus. What one might hope to observe is a higher rate of co-occurrence of hard synonyms, since they express a common cross-lingual lexicalization of the same concept. Hard synonyms are also susceptible to be more reliable than non-hard synonyms with regard to the correlation between automatic word similarity judgements and human word similarity judgements.

7 Conclusions

We have presented a cross-lingual synonym overlap analysis for pairs of languages among three languages: French, English and Romanian, which can be quite straightforwardly extended for any other pair of languages. We have built a database containing pairs of (translated) words from the two languages along with their corresponding synonym sets and their synonym overlap set. Furthermore, we used it in order to gain insight into the synonym overlap of the three languages, and thus, into their degree of common concept lexicalization, by various queries. While the overall percentage of common synonyms is (expectedly) quite small (with an average of about 6% across all language pairs), the percentage of hard synonyms pairs (pairs that have at least one common synonym), as high as ~60%, is significant. This is encouraging for further use of this special kind of word translated pairs in tasks such as automatic enhancement of lexical databases (such as WordNet) for less resourced languages such as Romanian, based on corresponding English versions of these lexical databases. Another interesting query topic was obtaining distributions of hard synonym pairs, function of their part of speech: results varied with languages used in analysis: verbs had the biggest synonym overlap percentage for English hard synonyms (paired with any other of the two remaining languages), whereas adjectives and words that can be both adjectives and nouns were the most common for Romanian and French.

Acknowledgements

We thank the anonymous reviewers for their helpful and constructive comments. Research by UEFISCDI, PNII-IDPCE- 2011-3-0959.

References

Daniel M Bikel and Vittorio Castelli. 2008. Event matching using the transitive closure of dependency relations. In *Proceedings of the 46th Annual Meeting of the Association for Computational Linguistics on Human Language Technologies: Short Papers*, pages 145–148. Association for Computational Linguistics.

Alexander Budanitsky and Graeme Hirst. 2006. Evaluating wordnet-based measures of lexical semantic relatedness. *Computational Linguistics*, 32(1):13–47.

Merriam-Webster Inc. 2004. *Merriam-Webster's collegiate dictionary*. Merriam-Webster.

Saif Mohammad and Graeme Hirst. 2006. Distributional measures of concept-distance: A task-oriented evaluation. In *Proceedings of the 2006 Conference on Empirical Methods in Natural Language Processing*, pages 35–43. Association for Computational Linguistics.

Saif Mohammad, Iryna Gurevych, Graeme Hirst, and Torsten Zesch. 2007. Cross-lingual distributional profiles of concepts for measuring semantic distance. In *EMNLP-CoNLL*, pages 571–580.

Lonneke Van der Plas, Paola Merlo, and James Henderson. 2011. Scaling up automatic cross-lingual semantic role annotation. In *Proceedings of the 49th Annual Meeting of the Association for Computational Linguistics: Human Language Technologies: short papers-Volume 2*, pages 299–304. Association for Computational Linguistics.

Tong Wang and Graeme Hirst. 2011. Refining the notions of depth and density in wordnet-based semantic similarity measures. In *Proceedings of the Conference on Empirical Methods in Natural Language Processing*, pages 1003–1011. Association for Computational Linguistics.

Wenbo Wang, Christopher Thomas, Amit Sheth, and Victor Chan. 2010. Pattern-based synonym and antonym extraction. In *Proceedings of the 48th Annual Southeast Regional Conference*, page 64. ACM.

Barbecued Opakapaka: Using Semantic Preferences for Ontology Population

Ismail El Maarouf **Georgiana Marsic** **Constantin Orăsan**
University of Wolverhampton
{i.el-maarouf, georgie, c.orasan}@wlv.ac.uk

Abstract

This paper investigates the use of semantic preferences for ontology population. It draws on a new resource, the Pattern Dictionary of English Verbs, which lists semantic categories expected in each syntactic slot of a verb pattern. Knowledge of semantic preferences is used to drive and control bootstrapped pattern extraction techniques on the EnClueWeb09 corpus with the aim of identifying common nouns belonging to twelve semantic types. Evaluation reveals that syntactic patterns perform better than lexical and surface patterns, at the same time raising issues about assessing ontology population candidates out of context.

1 Introduction

This paper investigates the use of weakly supervised techniques driven by semantic preferences from the Pattern Dictionary of English Verbs (PDEV)[1] on the task of ontology population.

PDEV is the output of Corpus Pattern Analysis (CPA; Hanks, 2004), a technique in corpus lexicography for mapping meaning onto words in text. PDEV (Hanks and Pustejovsky, 2005; Hanks, 2013; El Maarouf et al., 2014) is a new resource which organizes the description of a verb entry according to its main patterns of use. Its major features are (1) that it only accounts for uses found in a corpus in a bottom-up data-driven approach, and (2) that the analysis focuses on the accurate description of word patterns, rather than on the analysis of word meanings in isolation.

Ontology population is defined as the automatic identification of the nouns classed under a semantic category in the CPA ontology[2].

[1] http://pdev.org.uk/

[2] http://pdev.org.uk/#onto

This paper describes ontology population techniques driven by PDEV semantic preferences applied to a web-scale corpus. The next section describes the resources used in this paper, section 3, the ontology population techniques, and section 4, the evaluation, before concluding in section 5.

2 Resources

2.1 The CPA Ontology

PDEV aims to provide a well-founded corpus-driven account of verb meaning, using semantic types (STs) to stand as prototypes for collocational clusters occurring in each clause role. Current CPA practice has shown that the scientific concepts from WordNet (Fellbaum, 1998), the most widely used semantic repository in NLP, do not map well onto words as they are actually used. This is partly because folk concepts, and not scientific concepts, form the foundation of meaning in natural language (Wierzbicka, 1984). For this reason, the CPA Ontology has been developed for PDEV, and it contrasts with WordNet in the following key aspects: (1) WordNet considers each synset (sense) as a node in the ontology while the CPA Ontology connects STs which cover multiple senses; thus WordNet synsets are either STs or word senses. (2) WordNet is intuition-based whereas the CPA Ontology is 'corpus-driven'.

The CPA ontology is inspired from the Brandeis Semantic Ontology (Pustejovsky et al., 2006), but has been gradually populated with STs based on the need to capture a verb's set of collocates. Each of the 220 STs currently included in the CPA Ontology is connected to at least one verb pattern, as can be observed on the public PDEV website.

2.2 Unambiguous PDEV Verb Patterns

PDEV uses STs to characterize the set of collocates found in the slots of a verb pattern. For example, the verb *barbecue* has only one pattern, as

Proceedings of Recent Advances in Natural Language Processing, pages 153–159,
Hissar, Bulgaria, Sep 7–9 2015.

Pattern	[[Human]] barbecues [[Food]]
Implicature	Human cooks Food on a rack over an open fire in the open air
Example	The South African environment department has refused permission to fishermen in Struisbaai to catch and barbecue a whale belonging to a species recognised as endangered.

Table 1: PDEV entry for *barbecue*

illustrated in Table 1. This suggests that *barbecue* is only used in this meaning, and that the subject can only be a Human, while the object can only be of type Food. In other words, one can unambiguously collect Food instances by looking at the nouns that occur as objects of the verb *barbecue*.

Out of the 9,200 subject and object slots included in the current version of PDEV that totals over 4,600 patterns, we identified 741 unambiguous slots. An unambiguous slot can either be the subject or the object slot of a verb that is characterized by no semantic alternation (i.e., only one ST) in that particular slot across all patterns of the verb which take the slot. We found that these 741 instances of unambiguous slots account for 66 different STs. We selected 12 of the most productive STs for our experiments. The experiments described in this paper focus on identifying common nouns that can populate the following target STs: Activity, Body_Part, Document, Eventuality, Food, Human_Group, Inanimate, Institution, Liquid, Location, Proposition, and State_of_Affairs. In total there are 70 verbs that take the STs above unambiguously as subject or object.

2.3 Web Corpus Data

For our experiments, we use the EnClueWeb09 corpus (Pomikalek et al., 2012; Kilgarriff et al., 2014), a large web-scale corpus (70 billion words) from which we extract for a given ST up to 50,000 concordances for each of the verbs that unambiguously take that particular ST in a subject or object slot. The resulting corpus, named Web-12, includes 3.6m sentences and 97m words, and has been parsed using the Stanford Parser (Klein and Manning, 2003).

2.4 Gold Standard for Automatic Evaluation

This paper proposes two different evaluations, an automatic one to evaluate system recall, and a manual one to evaluate system precision. The automatic evaluation is based on a gold standard ST lexicon, named WN, based on a mapping between WordNet synsets and the 12 STs, manually prepared by a CPA lexicographer[3]. Proper nouns and multi-word expressions were filtered out, as the techniques presented in this paper target single-word common nouns.

Two other gold standards were produced out of WN: WN-web containing nouns from WN that are also present in the Web-12 corpus, and WN-web-dep which contains nouns from WN which also occur in a dependency relation to one of the ST-indicative verbs according to the Stanford parser.

3 Ontology Population Techniques

This section describes the ontology population techniques implemented to automatically extract new instances belonging to each target ST.

3.1 Lexical Patterns

Hearst's patterns (Hearst, 1992) consist of regular expressions made up of lexical clues to collect hypernymy relations. Each pattern contains two slots: one for the hypernym (in our case the ST, e.g., Food), and one for the hyponym (in our case the ST instance, e.g., *fish*).

These patterns generally yield nouns with a satisfying precision. For this reason they are used as a starting point of more complex ontology population systems (Snow et al., 2005; Kozareva et al., 2008; Kozareva et al., 2009). In this paper, we use the patterns listed in (Etzioni et al., 2005). We evaluate two setups for our set of 12 STs: the first is applied to our Web-12 corpus (System S1), and the other is applied to the whole EnClueWeb09 repository (System S1+). Table 2 lists the most productive patterns used by System S1 together with the number of extractions and unique nouns identified across all 12 STs.

3.2 Surface Patterns

Another popular ontology population method is to automatically extract patterns that can reliably identify ST members. A pattern extraction technique particularly used for relation extraction relies on identifying sequences of words between

[3]The lexicographer identified links based on the gloss of a WordNet synset, and on the overlap between its hyponyms and the ST in the CPA ontology

<table>
<tr><th>Pattern</th><th>Extr.</th><th>Nouns</th></tr>
<tr><td colspan="3">System S1 (12 STs)</td></tr>
<tr><td>ST,? (such as|especially|including) N</td><td>353525</td><td>26062</td></tr>
<tr><td>ST,? (and|or) other N</td><td>225455</td><td>14226</td></tr>
<tr><td>such ST as N</td><td>3302</td><td>1873</td></tr>
<tr><td>N is a ST</td><td>1117367</td><td>58023</td></tr>
<tr><td colspan="3">System S2 (Food)</td></tr>
<tr><td>V ing N</td><td>82918</td><td>9675</td></tr>
<tr><td>V ed N</td><td>77005</td><td>7106</td></tr>
<tr><td>V d N</td><td>49553</td><td>9045</td></tr>
<tr><td colspan="3">System S2+ (Food)</td></tr>
<tr><td>, V ing N and</td><td>3056</td><td>157</td></tr>
<tr><td>, V ing N or</td><td>1187</td><td>30</td></tr>
<tr><td>, V d N ,</td><td>814</td><td>183</td></tr>
<tr><td colspan="3">System S3+ (Food)</td></tr>
<tr><td>||VBN| ||NN|nsubjpass |be||auxpass</td><td>7068</td><td>3484</td></tr>
<tr><td>||VBN| ||NN|dobj_enum ||NN|dobj_enum</td><td>6568</td><td>1247</td></tr>
<tr><td>||VBN| ||NNS|nsubjpass |be||auxpass</td><td>4090</td><td>2180</td></tr>
</table>

Table 2: Examples of patterns for each system

two entities of interest (Ravichandran and Hovy, 2002; Pantel and Pennacchiotti, 2006).

System 2 adapts this method by considering as relation boundaries the verb and the ST instance. Given a category and a set of seed words, it first extracts any string occurring between the verb and each seed. Patterns are built using the extracted strings and the verbs that unambiguously combine with an ST, and then applied to Web-12 to extract new instances of a given ST. The words extracted by these patterns are ordered by frequency.

This approach is evaluated in two setups, one deriving the pattern from only the string linking the verb to the noun (System S2), and another one that also includes a context word to the left and to the right of the verb and noun pair (System S2+). Table 2 provides examples of the most productive patterns for both setups applied to the Food ST. One may notice a dramatic drop in the number of extractions when including the outward context (System S2+), but also the fact that the most frequent patterns mostly capture suffix variation, determiners, prepositions, or punctuation. Clearly those patterns are applicable to many verbs, but specifically capture Food items due to the semantic preferences of the verbs they combine with.

3.3 Syntax-driven Techniques

Syntactic dependencies offer an attractive representation of the context of a verb which allows to abstract away from undesirable variation, such as word order, or insertion of modifiers or appositions. For example, the same direct object relation between *opakapaka* and *barbecue* holds in the following two sentences: *"he barbecued opakapakas"* and *"he barbecued several times opakapakas"*. Thus syntactic relations such as direct object can be used to retrieve instances of a ST in the predicted slot extracted from PDEV. System S3 relies on this assumption and populates a ST with all the nouns that occur in the unambiguous slots of the verbs that are indicative of that ST (e.g., for the Food ST, S3 will extract all the nouns that are direct objects of the verbs *barbecue*, *brown*, *fry*, *masticate*, *overcook*, *scoff*, *vomit*, and *wolf*).

Apart from this setting, we have experimented with learning syntactic patterns from the Web-12 corpus parsed with the Stanford parser. For each ST and each verb unambiguously taking the ST as subject/object, all verb occurrences were extracted together with their direct syntactic dependents, as well as dependents indirectly connected to the verb via coordination with a direct dependent. Each verb context is a combination of tokens represented as WORD|LEMMA|POS|DEPREL, where WORD, LEMMA, POS and DEPREL correspond, respectively, to the word, lemma, part of speech and dependency relation associated to the word. Patterns are then learned by System S3+, and examples of the most frequent patterns learned by S3+ are shown in Table 2.

3.4 Bootstrapped Learning and Ranking

Pattern-based approaches for ontology population are commonly used as part of a bootstrapping algorithm (Hearst, 1992; Ravichandran and Hovy, 2002; Etzioni et al., 2005; Pantel and Pennacchiotti, 2006). For comparison purposes, we apply an iterative ranking method inspired from the work of Thelen and Riloff (2002) to the output of the pattern-driven techniques presented above. At each iteration, the learned patterns are ranked according to their tendency to extract ST members and only the best patterns drive the extraction of new ST candidates which also undergo a ranking process to enable the selection of a fixed number of top nouns to be added to the ST lexicon. This method uses at each iteration the latest ST lexicon to rank and select a pattern pool. The bootstrapping process starts with the same set of 10 seeds which was used by the pattern extraction techniques, and the process is repeated until a certain number of extractions (in our case 500) is reached.

A pool of patterns is extracted from the whole set of patterns following a pattern ranking process that relies on scores calculated using Formula 1.

$$Score(pat_i) = \frac{F_i}{N_i} \times \log_2(F_i) \quad (1)$$

where F_i is the number of ST members extracted by pat_i, and N_i is the total number of nouns extracted by pat_i. This formula captures the insight that good patterns are those that capture a large portion of known category members at time t. The top $nP + i$ patterns are placed in the pattern pool, where nP is a fixed value, and i starts from 0 and is incremented at each iteration, to ensure constant addition of new patterns and renewal of the pattern pool. All the nouns extracted by patterns from the pattern pool are scored according to Formula 2.

$$S1(noun_i) = \frac{\sum_{j_i}^{P_i} \log_2(F_j + 1)}{P_i} \quad (2)$$

where P_i is the number of patterns that extract $word_i$, and F_j is the number of distinct category members extracted by pattern j. This formula captures the intuition that a good candidate is extracted by patterns that extract a large number of category members. The top nN candidates, where nN is a fixed number, are added to the ST lexicon which will be used in the next iteration.

4 Evaluation

4.1 Automatic Evaluation

The bootstrapping process described in Section 3.4 is applied in turn to each technique described in Sections 3.1, 3.2, and 3.3, with the exception of S1 which extracts very few nouns, and S3 which does not use patterns. A grid search is performed to obtain the best parameters for the number of patterns (nP) to be included in the pattern pool, and for the number of top nouns (nN) to be added to the lexicon at each iteration, using values from the set $5, 10, 20, 50$. The best systems were those which had the best macro-average precision at 500 extractions, specifically nN=5 and nP=50 for the lexical system S1+, nN=50 and nP=50 for both surface systems S2 and S2+, and nP=5 and nN=20 for the syntactic system S3+. Table 3 shows the results as averages over the 12 ST against WN-web-dep and can be compared to Table 4, which provides the results of each technique being applied only once on the Web-12 corpus and having its extractions ranked according to frequency of extraction. The results are somewhat surprising as the bootstrapped learning and ranking method has a particular negative effect on lexical and surface systems. This suggests that this bootstrapping method is better suited to syntactic patterns than to other systems. If we consider S1+ and S2, one reason might be that these systems extract patterns which have a large number of extractions (see table 2), and are therefore not sufficiently constrained. S2+, on the contrary, extracts more precise patterns in comparison with S2, but the trade-off is a lower number of extractions. Finally, syntactic patterns produce patterns which, on average, have a number of extractions only twice as much as noun types (see table 2), whereas lexical systems have a much larger discrepancy between the number of extractions and distinct noun types. We will explore this issue in future work, and investigate ranking methods which are more generic.

4.2 Manual Evaluation

In order to get a clear idea of systems' precision, a manual evaluation process focused on four STs (Document, Food, Liquid, and Location) and an annotation of the top 500 nouns extracted by bootstrapped learning and ranking with syntactic patterns[4] (S3+) was performed for each of the four STs. Each ST noun set was manually annotated by a different pair of 4 annotators. As the system extracts the nouns from the web, the extractions often yield knowledge unfamiliar to the annotator, and therefore, to be fair with the system, it is important to allow annotators access to encyclopaedia and dictionaries to learn what a word means (e.g. "opakapaka is a fish"), and if an established word use exists (e.g., *report* is not only a Speech Act: *His report of the conference was bleak.*, but also a Document: *He printed the report.*)

Human annotators had to assess whether a noun can or cannot be interpreted as a member of a given ST (i.e., provide a "yes"/"no" annotation for every noun in the top 500 extracted by the system), but at the same time the annotators had the option to provide a less categorical decision for nouns that they were unable to decide on (i.e., assign "maybe" to nouns they were unsure about). The annotation process consisted of two rounds. As the first round produced low agreement due to unforeseen difficulties, the guidelines were revised and clarified, and a second round was performed. The issues causing disagreement mainly concerned:

[4]This was the best performing ontology population technique, and was thus chosen as target for manual evaluation.

	Precision				Recall			
topN	S1	S2	S2+	S3+	S1	S2	S2+	S3+
100	0.037	0.070	0.047	0.312	0.002	0.020	0.011	0.058
200	0.036	0.068	0.047	0.285	0.005	0.035	0.017	0.107
300	0.036	0.057	0.043	0.254	0.010	0.044	0.021	0.141
400	0.033	0.050	0.044	0.236	0.012	0.053	0.023	0.167
500	0.036	0.045	0.044	0.218	0.017	0.059	0.023	0.188

Table 3: Bootstrapped ranking: precision and recall against WN-web-dep at 500 extractions

	Precision				Recall			
topN	S1+	S2	S2+	S3+	S1	S2	S2+	S3+
100	0.106	0.164	0.247	0.337	0.020	0.038	0.062	0.066
200	0.090	0.156	0.193	0.273	0.032	0.070	0.088	0.099
300	0.080	0.146	0.170	0.245	0.043	0.092	0.113	0.136
400	0.077	0.141	0.155	0.223	0.056	0.118	0.134	0.156
500	0.072	0.137	0.146	0.207	0.063	0.146	0.156	0.175

Table 4: Frequency ranking: precision and recall against WN-web-dep at 500 extractions

1. the difficulty in evaluating a noun out of context ('slice', 'course' for Food): the revised guidelines specified clearly that these cases should be marked as "maybe";
2. general nouns that are not prototypically ST instances, but can be used in a context to refer to an ST member without making the sentence semantically anomalous (e.g., *thing* standing for a Food item): these nouns should be marked as "maybe";
3. regular category shifts, e.g. the Food category includes Dishes (*pudding*), but also Animals, Vegetables, Insects, Fruits, etc.: these nouns should be assigned "yes".

Tables 5 and 6 report inter-annotator agreement for each annotation round. The output of the second annotation round shows a good/very good agreement and was used to build two gold standard sets for each ST. The instances considered by both annotators as true ST members ("yes") are included in the gold standard HUM-STRICT. To this set we add all potential ST members ("maybe") agreed on by both annotators to obtain the second gold standard HUM-RELAXED.

4.3 Manual Evaluation Results

The evaluations results of S3+ are presented in Tables 7 and 8: one strict evaluation against HUM-STRICT, and another relaxed evaluation against HUM-RELAXED, respectively. The difference between the results obtained on the two gold standards is less than 0.1 in precision, therefore the potential ST members have limited impact. Precision drops as more candidates are extracted, in agreement with the so-called 'semantic drift' tendency also observed by other authors (Komachi et al., 2008). We can also observe that precision drops more significantly for some categories such as Liquid and Document.

Category	Pairwise	Cohen K	Fleiss K
Document	66.7%	0.433	0.407
Food	89%	0.758	0.758
Liquid	87.2%	0.717	0.716
Location	73.3%	0.486	0.473

Table 5: Inter-annotator agreement, round 1

Category	Pairwise	Cohen K	Fleiss K
Document	85%	0.739	0.738
Food	92.6%	0.84	0.84
Liquid	96.8%	0.932	0.932
Location	88.2%	0.674	0.674

Table 6: Inter-annotator agreement, round 2

topN	Document	Liquid	Location	Food	Average
100	0.84	0.65	0.96	0.89	0.835
200	0.675	0.475	0.88	0.79	0.705
300	0.543	0.393	0.83	0.763	0.632
400	0.445	0.372	0.785	0.72	0.581
500	0.414	0.332	0.73	0.652	0.532

Table 7: Precision for S3+ on HUM-STRICT

topN	Document	Liquid	Location	Food	Average
100	0.92	0.67	0.96	0.9	0.863
200	0.745	0.49	0.925	0.8	0.74
300	0.627	0.41	0.89	0.78	0.677
400	0.525	0.39	0.85	0.748	0.628
500	0.498	0.352	0.798	0.678	0.582

Table 8: Precision for S3+ on HUM-RELAXED

However, when compared to results presented in Section 4.1, we can see a clear improvement, possibly due to a non-optimal mapping between the CPA Ontology and WordNet, but also explainable by ST members correctly extracted from the web, but absent from WordNet. The next subsection looks into this in more detail.

4.4 Comparison Between Gold Standards

Results on the manual reference have shown that a large portion of true candidates (HUM-STRICT) are not in WN, the resource built by mapping CPA STs to WordNet synsets and extracting all their hyponyms. An analysis of the nouns marked by annotators as true members of an ST (HUM-STRICT), but not included in WN, has revealed the following across the four target STs (Document, Food, Liquid, and Location). Out of the total number of 2,000 manually annotated nouns corresponding to the four STs, there are 623 nouns present in HUM-STRICT, but absent from WN. A percentage of 12% of these nouns are not in WordNet. They include foreign words used in English texts (e.g., Document: fiche <French for *index card* or *form*>, Food: pancetta <Italian for *bacon*> and *kielbasa* <Polish for *sausage*>), trademarks used as common nouns (e.g., Liquid: *frappuccino*, Food: *mcmuffin*), English common nouns absent from WordNet (e.g., Location: *forestland*), collapsed multiword expressions appearing as two-word expressions in WordNet (e.g., Food: *fastfood*, Liquid: *potlikker*), and obvious misspellings (e.g., Food: *vegtable*, *buritto*).

The remaining 88% of the nouns are present in WordNet, but are not included in WN due to two main reasons. Firstly, the mapping between the CPA Ontology and WordNet is not optimal and other WordNet subtrees can be added to each ST. The Food ST for example was populated with nouns found in the subtree corresponding to the synset *food#2*. An analysis of the nouns marked as food items by the annotators, but missing from the WN Food ST has revealed that the WordNet subtrees headed by *dish#2* and *course#7* can also be added to this ST. Secondly, there are cases when one would have to add many WordNet leaf synsets that are not grouped into a higher-level subhierarchy mappable to a CPA ST. In the case of the Liquid ST for example, there are many instances of liquid sauces (e.g., *vinegar*, *salsa*, *ketchup*) that are subsumed by *condiment#1*, but since many condiments come as powders, one cannot add the subtree headed by *condiment#1* to the Liquid ST, but should instead add individual synsets scattered across WordNet. Future work will address these issues in order to better align these resources.

5 Conclusions and Perspectives

Three types of ontology population techniques have been experimented in this paper: a lexical approach that draws on Hearst's patterns, a surface approach that looks at surface strings joining an ST-preferring verb with a candidate noun, and a syntactic approach that relies on patterns drawn from dependency relations connecting an ST-indicative verb with a candidate noun. A bootstrapped learning and ranking approach is then applied to each pattern-driven technique. These techniques are applied to a web corpus built by extracting a high number of concordance lines for 70 verbs unambiguously associated with 12 target STs via their semantic preferences extracted from PDEV, and then evaluated by ranking their outputs both frequency-wise and using the bootstrapped learning and ranking approach. The best 500 extractions yielded by each technique are assessed against a resource derived as a result of mapping each CPA ST to WordNet sub-hierarchies.

A manual annotation of the top 500 nouns extracted by the best system for four STs, namely Document, Food, Liquid and Location is then performed. All experiments indicate that the syntactic approach is superior to employing lexical patterns and surface patterns for ontology population.

The results of this article point to the difficulty in evaluating pattern-driven ontology population methods. The main reasons are that existing resources have limited coverage of nouns in a given usage, which is contextual. Intrinsic categorization of nouns offers a limited appreciation of system performance.

This work is the first to use semantic preferences from PDEV for ontology population from the web, therefore it is still work in progress. Particularly important is to investigate the best use of the ontology structure as part of pattern extraction algorithms. Bootstrapped learning and ranking has had limited impact on system precision, and we believe this is one place where future efforts should be concentrated. Since the present paper only investigates semantic preferences of PDEV verbs for 12 STs, it is important to extend this work to other categories. Another specific area of interest is the use of extractions from unambiguous semantic preferences data to disambiguate ambiguous contexts and verbs.

Acknowledgements

We are very grateful to anonymous reviewers for suggestions to improve this work. We would like to thank Emma Franklin for taking part in the annotation. This work was partly supported by a AHRC grant, [DVC, AH/J005940/1, 2012-2015], and the EXPERT project (People Programme (Marie Curie Actions) of the EU FP7 (REA grant agreement 317471)).

References

Guy Aston and Lou Burnard. 1998. *The BNC handbook*. Edinburgh University Press, Edinburgh.

Ismaïl El Maarouf, Jane Bradbury, Vít Baisa and Patrick Hanks. 2014. *Disambiguating Verbs by Collocation: Corpus Lexicography meets Natural Language Processing*. *Proceedings of LREC*, 1001–1006.

Oren Etzioni, Michael Cafarella, Doug Downey, Ana-Maria Popescu, Tal Shaked, Stephen Soderland, Daniel S. Weld, Alexander Yates. 2005. *Unsupervised named-entity extraction from the web: An experimental study*. *Artificial Intelligence*,165(1):91134.

Christiane Fellbaum. 1998. *WordNet: An Electronic Lexical Database*. MIT Press, Cambridge, MA.

Patrick Hanks and James Pustejovsky. 2005. *A Pattern Dictionary for Natural Language Processing*. *Revue Française de linguistique applique*, 10:2.

Patrick Hanks. 2004. *Corpus Pattern Analysis*. G. Williams and S. Vessier (eds.), *Euralex Proceedings*, Vol. 1.

Patrick Hanks. 2013. *Lexical Analysis: Norms and Exploitations*. MIT Press, Cambridge, MA.

Marti Hearst. 1992. *Automatic acquisition of hyponyms from large text corpora*. *Proceedings of COLING-92*, 539–545.

Adam Kilgarriff, Vít Baisa, Jan Bušta, Miloš Jakubíček, Vojtěch Kovář, Jan Michelfeit, Pavel Rychlý and Vít Suchomel. 2014. *The Sketch Engine: ten years on*. *Lexicography*, 1(1):7–36.

Dan Klein and Christopher D. Manning. 2003. *Accurate Unlexicalized Parsing*. *Proceedings of the 41st Meeting of the Association for Computational Linguistics*, 423–430.

Komachi, Mamoru and Kudo, Taku and Shimbo, Masashi and Matsumoto, Yuji. 2008. *Graph-based Analysis of Semantic Drift in Espresso-like Bootstrapping Algorithms*. *Proceedings of EMNLP*, 1011–1020.

Zornitsa Kozareva, Ellen Riloff and Eduard H. Hovy. 2008. *Semantic Class Learning from the Web with Hyponym Pattern Linkage Graphs*. *Proceedings of the 46th Annual Meeting of the Association for Computational Linguistics*, 1048–1056.

Zornitsa Kozareva and Eduard H. Hovy and Ellen Riloff. 2009. *Learning and Evaluating the Content and Structure of a Term Taxonomy*. *Learning by Reading and Learning to Read, Papers from the 2009 AAAI Spring Symposium, Technical Report SS-09-07*, 50–57.

Patrick Pantel and Marco Pennacchiotti. 2006. *Espresso: Leveraging Generic Patterns for Automatically Harvesting Semantic Relations*. *Proceedings of the 21st International Conference on Computational Linguistics and the 44th Annual Meeting of the Association for Computational Linguistics*, 113–120.

Jan Pomikalek, Miloš Jakubíček and Pavel Rychlý. 2012. *Building a 70 billion word corpus of English from ClueWeb*. *Proceedings of the Eighth International Conference on Language Resources and Evaluation (LREC12)*.

James Pustejovsky, Catherine Havasi, Jessica Littman, Anna Rumshisky and Marc Verhagen. 2006. *Towards a Generative Lexical Resource: The Brandeis Semantic Ontology*. *Proceedings of LREC 2006*.

Deepak Ravichandran and Eduard Hovy. 2002. *Learning surface text patterns for a question answering system*. *Proceedings of ACL-2002*, 41–47.

Philip Resnik. 1997. *Selectional Preferences and Sense Disambiguation*. *Proceedings of the ANLP Workshop "Tagging Text with Lexical Semantics: Why What and How?"*.

Rion Snow, Daniel Jurafsky and Andrew Y. Ng. 2005. *Learning syntactic patterns for automatic hypernym discovery*. *Advances in Neural Information Processing Systems 18 (NIPS 2005)*.

Michael Thelen and Ellen Riloff. 2002. *A Bootstrapping Method for Learning Semantic Lexicons Using Extraction Pattern Contexts*. *Proceedings of the ACL-02 Conference on Empirical Methods in Natural Language Processing*, Volume 10, 214–221.

Anna Wierzbicka. 1984. *Apples are not a kind of fruit: the semantics of human categorization*. *American Ethnologist*, Vol. 11, No. 2, 313–328.

Towards a Lexicon-grammar based Framework for NLP an Opinion Mining Application

Annibale Elia, Serena Pelosi,
Alessandro Maisto and Raffaele Guarasci
Department of Political, Social and Communication Science
University of Salerno
{elia,spelosi,amaisto,rguarasci}@unisa.it

Abstract

The present research exploits the large amount of linguistic resources developed into the Lexicon-grammar paradigm in the domain of the Opinion Mining. Grounded on the Semantic Predicates theory, the proposed system is able to automatically match the syntactic structures selected by special classes of verbs, indicating positive or negative Sentiment, Opinion or Physical acts, with the semantic frames evoked by the same lexical items. This methods has been tested on a large dataset composed of short texts, such as tweets and news headings.

1 Introduction

In our research we propose a computational use of the Lexicon-grammar (LG) theories in the domain of the Opinion Mining.

We take advantage of both the huge amount of linguistic facts, accurately formalized and described in the LG paradigm, and from the possibility to apply and test them on big data. The purpose is to build a fine grained Information Extraction tool able to locate meaningful information in raw texts and to characterize them with thorough semantic descriptions.

According with the Semantic Predicates theory (Gross, 1981), it has been possible to perform a matching between the definitional syntactic structures, attributed to each class of verbs, and the semantic information we attached in the database to every lexical entry.

This way we could create a strict connection between the arguments, selected by a given Predicate listed in our tables, and the actants involved into the same verb's Semantic Frame (Fillmore, 1976; Fillmore and Baker, 2001; Fillmore, 2006).

Thanks to our LG-based linguistic rules, anchored on the Semantic Predicates, we started with this research the development of an NLP framework that, on the base of sophisticated syntactic and semantic analyses, extracts real text occurrences and labels them with the semantic roles involved in every matched sentence.

This ambitious work, that in this preliminary stage focused just on the predicates indicating sentiments, opinions and physical acts, intends, in future works, to become a larger development of an LG-based Italian cross-platform open library for various kind of linguistic analyses.

We excluded from this work the Transfer, the Spatial and the also the Psychological Predicates, because they have been already tested on different kinds of raw data with satisfactory results (Vietri, 2014; Elia et al., 2010; Elia and Vietri, 2010; Elia et al., 2013; Maisto and Pelosi, 2014b).

2 Theoretical Background

The Lexicon-grammar (LG), the method and the practice of formal description of the natural language, introduced important changes in the way in which the relationship between lexicon and syntax was conceived. (Gross, 1971; Gross, 1975).

In the LG theoretical framework the minimum discourse units endowed with meaning are the whole nuclear sentences, generally anchored on the verbs, which hold together the relationships between the selected arguments.

That means that the sentence structure is already contained in the operator (Harris, 1971; Harris, 1976).

We chose this paradigm because of its compatibility with the purposes of the computational linguistics, that, in order to reach high performances in results, requires a large amount of linguistic data, as much as possible, exhaustive, reproducible and well organized.

The collection of the linguistic information is constantly registered into LG tables, binary matrices

Proceedings of Recent Advances in Natural Language Processing, pages 160–167,
Hissar, Bulgaria, Sep 7–9 2015.

that cross-check the lexical entries with transformational, distributional and structural properties (see Table 1).
The LG classification and description of the Italian verbs[1] (Elia et al., 1981; Elia, 1984; D'Agostino, 1992) is grounded on the differentiation of three different macro-classes: transitive verbs; intransitive verbs and verbs that select completive clauses as complement. Every LG class has its own definitional structure, that corresponds with the syntactic structure of the nuclear sentence selected by a given number of verbs[2]. All the lexical entries are, then, differentiated from one another in each class, by taking into account all the transformational, distributional and structural properties accepted or rejected by every item.
The formal notation used in the LG framework can be summarized in the following way: *N*, that always indicates a nominal group, is followed by a number, which specifies its nature. (*N0* stands for the sentence formal subject, N1 for the first complement and N2 for the second complement); *V* stands for the verbs; *Prep* for the prepositions and *Che F* suggests the presence of completive or subjective clauses.

2.1 Semantic Predicates

The whole set of syntactical structure of a given language (*Sy*) is linkable to the entire collection of the semantic items of the same language (*Se*) by means of specific interpretation rules. This is the basic assumption on which has been build the Semantic Predicates theory into the LG framework, that postulates a parallelism between the *Sy* actants and the *Se* aurguments (Gross, 1981). As an example, in [1]

[1] Quello slogan$^{[N0/h]}$ *offende*$^{[V/O]}$ le donne$^{[N1/t]}$
"That slogan offends the women"

the verb *offendere* "to offend", belonging to the LG class *20UM* (*N0 V N1hum*), will be associated to a Predicate with two variables, described by the function *O (h,t)*, through the following rules of interpretations (see Section 3 for the other semantic functions for the annotation of Semantic Predicates of different nature):

1. the Opinion Holder (*h* in the *Se*) corresponds to the formal subject (*N0* in *Sy*);
2. the opinion Target (*t* in the *Se*) is the human complement (*N1* in *Sy*).

As shown in [2], the syntactic transformations in which the same Predicate is involved do not modify the role played by its arguments, that, in order to be semantically labeled in a correct way, must be always led back to their original form [3].

[2] Il fuoriclasse *è stato offeso* da un politico messicano
"The champion has been offended by a Mexican politician"

[3] Un politico messicano$^{[N0/h]}$ *ha offeso*$^{[V/O]}$ Il fuoriclasse$^{[N1/t]}$
"a Mexican politician offended the champion"

Special kinds of Semantic Predicates have been already used in NLP applications into a lexicon-grammar context; we mention (Vietri, 2014; Elia et al., 2010; Elia and Vietri, 2010) that formalized and tested the Transfer Predicates on the Italian Civil Code; (Elia et al., 2013) that focused on the Spatial Predicates and (Maisto and Pelosi, 2014b) that exploited the Psychological Semantic Predicates for Sentiment Analysis purposes.

2.2 Frame Semantics

"Some words exist in order to provide access to knowledge of such frames to the participants in the communication process, and simultaneously serve to perform a categorization which takes such framing for granted" (Fillmore, 2006). With these words it has been depicted the Frame Semantics, which describes the sentences on the base of *predicators* able to bring to mind the *semantic frames* (inference structures, linked through linguistic convention to the lexical items meaning) and the *frame elements* (participants and props in the frame) involved in these frames (Fillmore, 1976; Fillmore and Baker, 2001; Fillmore, 2006).
A frame semantic description starts from the identification of the lexical items that carry out a given meaning and, then, explores the ways in which the frame elements and their constellations are realized around the structures that have such items as

[1]freely available at the address `http://dsc.unisa.it/composti/tavole/combo/tavole.asp`

[2]e.g. *V* for *piovere* "to rain" and all the verbs of the class 1; *N0 V* for *bruciare* "to burn" and the other verbs of the class 3; *N0 V da N1* for *provenire*"to come from" and the verbs belonging to the class 6; etc...

head (Fillmore et al., 2002).

Based on these principles, the FrameNet research project produced a lexicon of English for both human use and NLP applications (Baker et al., 1998; Fillmore et al., 2002; Ruppenhofer et al., 2006). Its purpose is to provide a large amount of semantically and syntactically annotated sentences endowed with information about the valences (combinatorial possibilities) of the items derived from annotated contemporary English corpus. Among the semantic domains covered there are also *emotion* and *cognition* (Baker et al., 1998).

For the Italian language, it has been developed LexIt, a tool that, following the FrameNet approach, automatically explores syntactic and semantic properties of Italian predicates in terms of distributional profiles. It performs frame semantic analyses using both *La Repubblica* corpus and the *Wikipedia* taxonomy (Lenci et al., 2012).

2.3 Case Study: Opinion Mining and Sentiment Analysis

Sentiment Analysis, also called opinion mining, subjectivity analysis, or appraisal extraction, consists in the computational treatment of opinions, and emotions freely expressed in texts. It represents a really active NLP field that includes as specific research challenges the Sentiment and Subjectivity Classification, the Feature-based Sentiment Analysis, Sentiment analysis of comparative sentences, the Opinion search and retrieval, or the Opinion spam detecting and, in the end, the Opinion Holder and Target extraction. This research fields have a large impact on many commercial, Government and Business Intelligence application.

The most used approaches in the Sentiment Analysis include, among others, the lexicon-based methods, that always start from the following assumption: the text sentiment orientation comes from the semantic orientations of words and phrases contained in it.

The most commonly used SO indicators are adjectives or adjective phrases (Hatzivassiloglou and McKeown, 1997; Hu and Liu, 2004; Taboada et al., 2006), but recently became really common the use of adverbs (Benamara et al., 2007)), nouns (Vermeij, 2005; Riloff et al., 2003)) and verbs as well (Neviarouskaya et al., 2009).

Among the most popular lexicons for the Sentiment Analysis we account: the General Inquirer (Stone et al., 1966), the Hatzivassiloglou Lexicon (Hatzivassiloglou and McKeown, 1997), WordNet-Affect (Strapparava et al., 2004), the Wilson Lexicon (Wiebe et al., 2004), SentiWordNet (Esuli and Sebastiani, 2006), the Appraisal Lexicon (Argamon et al., 2009), the Maryland dictionary (Mohammad et al., 2009) SentiFul (Neviarouskaya et al., 2011), the SO-CAL dictionary (Taboada et al., 2011), Q-WordNet (Agerri and García-Serrano, 2010), Velikovich Web-generated lexicon (Velikovich et al., 2010). and the SentiSense (de Albornoz et al., 2012).

N0=Nhum	N0= il fatto Ch F	**Verb**	N1= che F	N1= che Fcong	di N1hum	diN1-hum	di N1 contro N2	prep V-inf comp
+	-	profittare	+	+	+	+	+	-
+	-	ridersene	+	+	+	+	-	-
+	-	risentirsi	+	+	+	+	-	+
+	-	strafottersene	+	+	+	+	-	-
+	-	vergognarsi	+	+	+	+	-	+

Table 1: Extract of the Lexicon-grammar table of the verb Class 45.

3 Methodology

The starting point of our research are 66 Lexicon-grammar tables of the Italian verbs, developed at the Department of Communication Science of the University of Salerno. Among the 3000 lexical entries listed in such matrices, we manually extracted about 1000 verbs endowed with a defined semantic orientation. Furthermore, on this base, we manually built a set of electronic dictionaries enriched with both the properties listed in the LG tables (Table 1) and the Semantic details associated with each lexical item (Table 2). In detail, 28 LG classes contained at least one opinionated item.

The examples in Tables 1 and 2 concern a small group of verbs belonging to the Lexicon-grammar class 45. This class includes all the verbs that can entry into a syntactic structure such as *N0 V di N1*, in which the "subject" (*N0*) selected by the verb (*V*) is generally a human noun (*Nhum*) and the complement (*N1*) is a completive (*Ch F*) or infinitive (*V-inf comp*) clause, usually introduced by the preposition "di" (see Table1).

As shown in Table 2, our databases contain also semantic information concerning the nature, the semantic orientation and the strength of the Predi-

cates under consideration.
Differently from the most used Italian tagsets (Bosco et al., 2009), in order to avoid high computational costs, our lexical databases are provided with basic semantic description. In detail, the tagset used in this work is the following:

1. Type
   - (a) SENT, sentiment
   - (b) OP, opinion
   - (c) PHY physical act
2. Orientation
   - (a) POS, positive
   - (b) NEG, negative
3. Intensity
   - (a) STRONG, intense
   - (b) WEAK, feeble

Speaking in terms of Frame Semantics, we identified in the Opinion Mining and in the Emotion Detection field three Frames of interest, recalled by specific Predicates: *Sentiment*, *Opinion* and *Physical act*. The frame elements evoked by such frames are described below.

Sentiment. It refers to the expression of any given frame of mind or affective state. The "sentiment" words can be put in connection with some WordNet Affect categories (Strapparava et al., 2004), such as *emotion*, *mood*, *hedonic signal*. Examples are *sdegnarsi* "to be indignant" (class 10); *odiare* "to hate" (class 20); *affezionarsi* "to grow fond" (class 44B); *flirtare* "to flirt" (class 9); *disprezzare* "to despise" (class 20); *gioire* "to rejoice" (class 45).
Predicates of that kind evoke as frame elements an *experiencer* (e), that feels the emotion or other internal states, and a *causer* (c), an event or a person that instigates such states (Gildea and Jurafsky, 2002; Swier and Stevenson, 2004; Palmer et al., 2005). This semantic frame summarizes the FrameNet ones connected to emotions, such as *Cause_to_experience*, *Sensation Emotions*, *Cause_emotion*, *Emotions_of_mental_activity*, *Emotion_active*, etc...
In this work, they are described by a function of that sort: $S(e,c)$

Opinion. The type "Opinion", instead, is the expression of positive or negative viewpoints, beliefs or judgments, that can be personal or shared by most people. It comprises, among the WN-affect categories, *trait*, *cognitive state*, *behavior*, *attitude*. OP examples are *ignorare* "to neglect" (class 20); *premiare* "to reward" (class 20); *difendere* "to defend" (class 27); *esaltare* "to exalt" (class 22); *dubitare* "to doubt" (class 45); *condannare* "to condemn" (class 49); *deridere* "to make fun of" (class 50).
The frame elements they evoke are an *opinion holder* (h), that states an opinion about an object or an event, and an *opinion target* (t), that represents the event or the object on which the opinion is expressed about (Kim and Hovy, 2006; Liu, 2012).
Into the FrameNet frame *Opinion* and *Judgment*, the *opinion holder* is called *Cognizer*, but we preferred to use a word which is more common in the Sentiment Analysis and in the Opinion Mining literature.
$O(h,t)$ is the function by which they are semantically described.

Physical act. The type "Physical act" comprises verbs like *baciare* "to kiss" (class 18); *suicidarsi* "to commit suicide" (class 2); *vomitare* "to vomit" (class 2A); *sparare* "to shoot" (class 4); *schiaffeggiare* "to slap" (class 20); *palpeggiare* "to grope" (class 18).
For this group of predicates the selected frame elements ara a *patient* (z) that is the victim (for the negative actions) or the beneficiary (for the positive ones) of the physical act carried out by an *agent* (a) (Carreras and Màrquez, 2005; Màrquez et al., 2008).
It includes a large number of FrameNet frames, such as *Cause_bodily_experience*, *Cause_harm Killing*, *Rape*, *Sex*, *Shoot_projectiles*, *Violence*, etc...
The meaning of the sentences in which occur predicates of that kind is summarized in the function $P(z,a)$.

Semantic Orientation and Intensity. To perform the Orientation and the Intensity attribution, we manually explored the Italian LG tables of verbs and weighted the Prior Polarity (Osgood, 1952) of the words endowed with a positive or negative SO.
We created two separate scales for the evaluation of the strength (intense/weak) and of the polar-

Verb	LG Class	Type	Orientation	Intensity	Influence
profittare	45	op	neg	-	N0
ridersene	45	op	neg	weak	N1
risentirsi	45	sent	neg	-	N0
strafottersene	45	op	neg	strong	N1
vergognarsi	45	sent	neg	strong	N0

Table 2: Extract of the semantic description of the opinionated verbs belonging to the LG class 45.

ity (positive/negative) through the combination of four tags: POS, NEG, STRONG and WEAK, creating, this way, an evaluation scale that goes from -3 to +3 and a strength scale that ranges from -1 to +1.

Semantic Role Labeling. Thanks to lexical resources of this kind, it is possible to automatically extract and semantically describe real occurrences of sentences, like [4]

[4] Renzi$^{[N0/e]}$ *si vergogna*$^{[V/S]}$ di parlare di energia in Europa$^{[N1/c]}$
"Renzi feels ashamed of talking about energy in Europe"

in which the syntactic structure of the verb, *vergognarsi* "to feel ashamed", *N0 V (*di) Ch F*, is matched, by means of interpretation rules to the semantic function *S(e,c)*, that put in relation an *experiencer* (e) and a *causer* (c) thanks to a *Sentiment Semantic Predicate* (S).
Moreover, we provided our LG databases with the specification of the arguments (N0, N1, N2, etc...) that are semantically influenced by the semantic orientation of the verbs. The purpose is to correctly identify them as *features* of the opinionated sentences and to work on their base also into feature-based sentiment analysis tasks.

4 Experiment

4.1 Datasets

The reliability of the LG method on the Semantic Role Labeling in the Opinion Mining and the Emotion Detection tasks has been tested on three different datasets, two of which have been extracted from social network or web resources.
In detail, the first two datasets came from Twitter, the third was a free web news headings dataset provided by DataMediaHub (`www.datamediahub.it`) and Human Highway (`www.humanhighway.it`).
The tweets have been downloaded using the two hashtags #Mattarellapresidente, that groups together the user comments on the election of the Italian President Mattarella and #Masterchefit, that collects the comments on the homonymous Italian TV show.

1. Tweets (46.393 tweets)
   (a) #Mattarellapresidente (10.000 tweets)
   (b) #Masterchefit (36.393 tweets)
2. News Headings (80.651 titles)

4.2 System and Tools

The LG based approach includes the following basic steps:

1. a preprocessing pipeline, that includes two phases:
   (a) a cleaning up phase, carried out with Python routines, that aims to distinguish in the datasets linguistic elements from structural elements (e.g. markup informations, web specific elements);
   (b) an automatic linguistic analysis phase, with the goal to linguistically standardize relevant elements obtained from the cleaned datasets; in this phase texts are tokenized, lemmatized and POS tagged using TreeTagger (Schmid, 1994; Schmid et al., 2007) and, then, parsed using DeSR, a dependency-based parser (Attardi et al., 2009);
2. a Lexicon-grammar based automatic analysis, in which the raw data are semantically labeled according with the syntactic/semantic rules of interpretation connected with each LG verb class;

Figure 1 presents three headlines examples processed both with the dependency syntactic parser and the semantic LG-based semantic analyzer.
Notice that the elements of the traditional grammar automatically identified by DeSR, such as subjects and complements, have been renamed according with the lexico-grammar tradition.

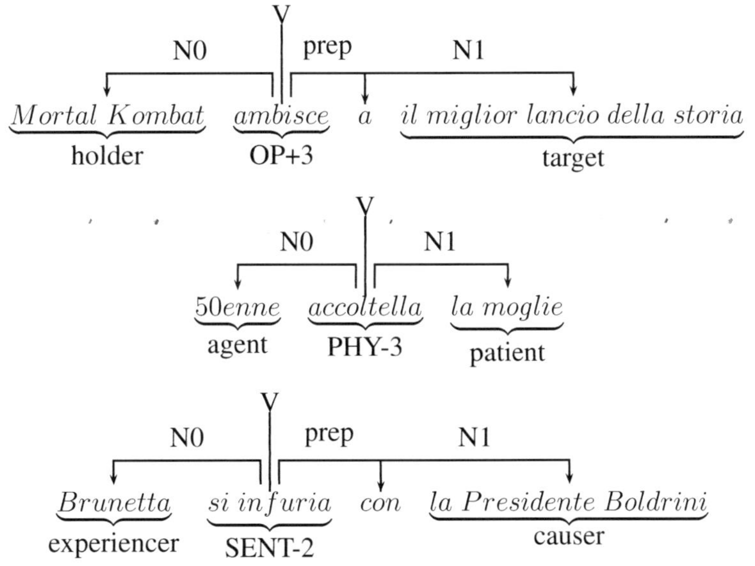

Figure 1: Examples of syntactically and semantically annotated sentences

4.3 Results and Open Issues

The corpus described in section 4.1, that counts 127,044 short texts, has been analyzed and semantically and syntactically annotated.
The representative sample on which the human evaluation has been performed, instead, has 42,348 texts.
The evaluation of the performances of our tool proved the effectiveness of the Lexicon-grammar approach. The average F-scores achieved in the different datasets are 0.71 in the Twitter and 0.76 in the Heading corpus.
Although such results, in this preliminary stage of the research, can be considered satisfactory, they shown that applying a lexicon-grammar method through a dependency parser is not the greatest solution for our purposes. The main goal of this work was, in fact, to demonstrate the validity and the reliability a LG based framework for NLP, but, in order to improve our performances, in future works we aim to build from scratch a syntactic parser completely inspired on the Lexicon-grammar theories, able to take into account not only the definitional syntactic structures of the LG verb classes, but also capable to handle every lemma's idiosyncrasies and any one of the properties systematically recorded into the LG tables.
In the end, it must be pointed out that this research represents just an aspect of a broader Sentiment Analysis framework, which involves not only the verbs in its lexicon, but also other, simple and compound, parts of speech, including special kinds of opinionated idioms (Maisto and Pelosi, 2014b; Maisto and Pelosi, 2014a). The novel aspect introduced in this work concerns, above all, the lexicon-grammar idea that in the lexicon are already contained syntactic clues.

5 Conclusion

This paper has introduced the possibility to apply and test the Lexicon-grammar theories and lexical resources on large corpora for different kinds of information extraction and content analysis purposes.
In detail, this research focused on the automatic extraction from raw data of sentences regarding Sentiments, Opinions and Physical Acts and on the semantic annotation of the roles involved in each one of the mentioned frames. Both the extraction and the analysis are anchored on a lexicon of Semantic Predicates, able to evoke, at the same time, the syntactic structures of their arguments in real text occurrences and the nature of the roles that those arguments play into specific semantic frames.
Furthermore, thanks to the tags which the Predicates are provided with, it has been possible to annotate the same sentences with information regarding their semantic orientation and intensity.
The aim of the research was to demonstrate the re-

liability of a Lexicon-grammar based framework for many kinds of NLP purposes. We started the experimentation on a corpus of tweets and news headlines, with satisfactory results.

References

Rodrigo Agerri and Ana García-Serrano. 2010. Q-wordnet: Extracting polarity from wordnet senses. In *LREC*.

Shlomo Argamon, Kenneth Bloom, Andrea Esuli, and Fabrizio Sebastiani. 2009. Automatically determining attitude type and force for sentiment analysis. pages 218–231.

Giuseppe Attardi, Felice DellOrletta, Maria Simi, and Joseph Turian. 2009. Accurate dependency parsing with a stacked multilayer perceptron. *Proceedings of EVALITA*, 9.

Collin F Baker, Charles J Fillmore, and John B Lowe. 1998. The berkeley framenet project. In *Proceedings of the 17th international conference on Computational linguistics-Volume 1*, pages 86–90. Association for Computational Linguistics.

Farah Benamara, Carmine Cesarano, Antonio Picariello, Diego Reforgiato Recupero, and Venkatramana S Subrahmanian. 2007. Sentiment analysis: Adjectives and adverbs are better than adjectives alone. In *ICWSM*.

Cristina Bosco, Simonetta Montemagni, Alessandro Mazzei, Vincenzo Lombardo, Felice DellOrletta, and Alessandro Lenci. 2009. Evalita09 parsing task: comparing dependency parsers and treebanks. *Proceedings of EVALITA*, 9.

Xavier Carreras and Lluís Màrquez. 2005. Introduction to the conll-2005 shared task: Semantic role labeling. In *Proceedings of the Ninth Conference on Computational Natural Language Learning*, pages 152–164. Association for Computational Linguistics.

Emilio D'Agostino. 1992. *Analisi del discorso: metodi descrittivi dell'italiano d'uso*. Loffredo.

Jorge Carrillo de Albornoz, Laura Plaza, and Pablo Gervás. 2012. Sentisense: An easily scalable concept-based affective lexicon for sentiment analysis. In *LREC*, pages 3562–3567.

Annibale Elia and Simonetta Vietri. 2010. Lexis-grammar & semantic web. *INFOtheca*, 11:15a–38a.

Annibale Elia, Maurizio Martinelli, and Emilio D'Agostino. 1981. *Lessico e Strutture sintattiche. Introduzione alla sintassi del verbo italiano*. Napoli: Liguori.

Annibale Elia, Simonetta Vietri, Alberto Postiglione, Mario Monteleone, and Federica Marano. 2010. Data mining modular software system. In *SWWS*, pages 127–133.

Annibale Elia, Daniela Guglielmo, Alessandro Maisto, and Serena Pelosi. 2013. A linguistic-based method for automatically extracting spatial relations from large non-structured data. In *Algorithms and Architectures for Parallel Processing*, pages 193–200. Springer.

Annibale Elia. 1984. Le verbe italien. *Les complétives dans les phrases à un complément*.

Andrea Esuli and Fabrizio Sebastiani. 2006. Determining term subjectivity and term orientation for opinion mining. 6:2006.

Charles J Fillmore and Collin F Baker. 2001. Frame semantics for text understanding. In *Proceedings of WordNet and Other Lexical Resources Workshop, NAACL*.

Charles J Fillmore, Collin F Baker, and Hiroaki Sato. 2002. The framenet database and software tools. In *LREC*.

Charles J Fillmore. 1976. Frame semantics and the nature of language*. *Annals of the New York Academy of Sciences*, 280(1):20–32.

Charles J Fillmore. 2006. Frame semantics. *Cognitive linguistics: Basic readings*, 34:373–400.

Daniel Gildea and Daniel Jurafsky. 2002. Automatic labeling of semantic roles. *Computational linguistics*, 28(3):245–288.

Maurice Gross. 1971. *Transformational Analysis of French Verbal Constructions*. University of Pennsylvania.

Maurice Gross. 1975. *Méthodes en syntaxe*. Hermann.

Maurice Gross. 1981. Les bases empiriques de la notion de prédicat sémantique. *Langages*, pages 7–52.

Zellig Sabbettai Harris. 1971. *Structures mathématiques du langage*, volume 3. Dunod.

Zellig Sabbetaï Harris. 1976. Notes du cours de syntaxe, traduction française par maurice gross. *Paris: Le Seuil*.

Vasileios Hatzivassiloglou and Kathleen R McKeown. 1997. Predicting the semantic orientation of adjectives. In *Proceedings of the 35th annual meeting of the association for computational linguistics and eighth conference of the european chapter of the association for computational linguistics*, pages 174–181. Association for Computational Linguistics.

Minqing Hu and Bing Liu. 2004. Mining opinion features in customer reviews. In *AAAI*, volume 4, pages 755–760.

Soo-Min Kim and Eduard Hovy. 2006. Extracting opinions, opinion holders, and topics expressed in online news media text. In *Proceedings of the Workshop on Sentiment and Subjectivity in Text*, pages 1–8. Association for Computational Linguistics.

Alessandro Lenci, Gabriella Lapesa, and Giulia Bonansinga. 2012. Lexit: A computational resource on italian argument structure. In *LREC*, pages 3712–3718.

Bing Liu. 2012. Sentiment analysis and opinion mining. *Synthesis Lectures on Human Language Technologies*, 5(1):1–167.

Alessandro Maisto and Serena Pelosi. 2014a. Feature-based customer review summarization. In *On the Move to Meaningful Internet Systems: OTM 2014 Workshops*, pages 299–308. Springer.

Alessandro Maisto and Serena Pelosi. 2014b. A lexicon-based approach to sentiment analysis. the italian module for nooj. In *Proceedings of the International Nooj 2014 Conference, University of Sassari, Italy*. Cambridge Scholar Publishing.

Lluís Màrquez, Xavier Carreras, Kenneth C Litkowski, and Suzanne Stevenson. 2008. Semantic role labeling: an introduction to the special issue. *Computational linguistics*, 34(2):145–159.

Saif Mohammad, Cody Dunne, and Bonnie Dorr. 2009. Generating high-coverage semantic orientation lexicons from overtly marked words and a thesaurus. In *Proceedings of the 2009 Conference on Empirical Methods in Natural Language Processing: Volume 2-Volume 2*, pages 599–608. Association for Computational Linguistics.

Alena Neviarouskaya, Helmut Prendinger, and Mitsuru Ishizuka. 2009. Compositionality principle in recognition of fine-grained emotions from text. In *ICWSM*.

Alena Neviarouskaya, Helmut Prendinger, and Mitsuru Ishizuka. 2011. Sentiful: A lexicon for sentiment analysis. *Affective Computing, IEEE Transactions on*, 2(1):22–36.

Charles E Osgood. 1952. The nature and measurement of meaning. *Psychological bulletin*, 49(3):197.

Martha Palmer, Daniel Gildea, and Paul Kingsbury. 2005. The proposition bank: An annotated corpus of semantic roles. *Computational linguistics*, 31(1):71–106.

Bo Pang and Lillian Lee. 2008. Opinion mining and sentiment analysis. *Foundations and trends in information retrieval*, 2(1-2):1–135.

Ellen Riloff, Janyce Wiebe, and Theresa Wilson. 2003. Learning subjective nouns using extraction pattern bootstrapping. In *Proceedings of the seventh conference on Natural language learning at HLT-NAACL 2003-Volume 4*, pages 25–32. Association for Computational Linguistics.

Josef Ruppenhofer, Michael Ellsworth, Miriam RL Petruck, Christopher R Johnson, and Jan Scheffczyk. 2006. Framenet ii: Extended theory and practice.

H Schmid, M Baroni, E Zanchetta, and A Stein. 2007. The enriched treetagger system. In *proceedings of the EVALITA 2007 workshop*.

Helmut Schmid. 1994. Probabilistic part-of-speech tagging using decision trees. In *Proceedings of the international conference on new methods in language processing*, volume 12, pages 44–49. Citeseer.

Philip J Stone, Dexter C Dunphy, and Marshall S Smith. 1966. The general inquirer: A computer approach to content analysis.

Carlo Strapparava, Alessandro Valitutti, et al. 2004. Wordnet affect: an affective extension of wordnet. In *LREC*, volume 4, pages 1083–1086.

Robert S Swier and Suzanne Stevenson. 2004. Unsupervised semantic role labelling. In *Proceedings of EMNLP*, volume 95, page 102.

Maite Taboada, Caroline Anthony, and Kimberly Voll. 2006. Methods for creating semantic orientation dictionaries. In *Proceedings of the 5th International Conference on Language Resources and Evaluation (LREC), Genova, Italy*, pages 427–432.

Maite Taboada, Julian Brooke, Milan Tofiloski, Kimberly Voll, and Manfred Stede. 2011. Lexicon-based methods for sentiment analysis. *Computational linguistics*, 37(2):267–307.

Leonid Velikovich, Sasha Blair-Goldensohn, Kerry Hannan, and Ryan McDonald. 2010. The viability of web-derived polarity lexicons. In *Human Language Technologies: The 2010 Annual Conference of the North American Chapter of the Association for Computational Linguistics*, pages 777–785. Association for Computational Linguistics.

MJM Vermeij. 2005. The orientation of user opinions through adverbs, verbs and nouns. In *3rd Twente Student Conference on IT, Enschede June*. Citeseer.

Simona Vietri. 2014. The italian module for nooj. In *In Proceedings of the First Italian Conference on Computational Linguistics, CLiC-it 2014*. Pisa University Press.

Janyce Wiebe, Theresa Wilson, Rebecca Bruce, Matthew Bell, and Melanie Martin. 2004. Learning subjective language. *Computational linguistics*, 30(3):277–308.

Using the Textual Content of the LMF-Normalized Dictionaries for Identifying and Linking the Syntactic Behaviours to the Meanings

Elleuch Imen
MIRACL Laboratory
B.P. 1088
3018 Sfax, Tunisia
imen.elleuch@fsegs.rnu.tn

Gargouri Bilel
MIRACL Laboratory
B.P. 1088
3018 Sfax, Tunisia
bilel.gargouri@fsegs.rnu.tn

Ben Hamadou Abdelmajid
MIRACL Laboratory
B.P. 242
3021 Sakiet-Ezzit Sfax, Tunisia
abdelmajid.benhamadou@isimsf.rnu.tn

Abstract

In this paper we propose an approach for identifying syntactic behaviours related to lexical items and linking them to the meanings. This approach is based on the analysis of the textual content presented in LMF normalized dictionaries by means of Definition and Context classes. The main particularity of these contents is their large availability and their semantically control due to their attachment to the meanings, which promotes the effective links between the syntactic behaviours and the meaning. In order to test the performance of the proposed approach, we tested it on an available Arabic LMF normalized dictionary. The experiment treats 9,800 verbs and allows us to evaluate the identified syntactic behaviours as well as their links to the meanings.

1 Introduction

A syntactic lexicon is essentially a linguistic resource describing the sub-categorization structure of lexical entries that specify the number and the type of arguments composing the syntactic behaviour. The creation of such a lexicon has been a very large and daunting task. Often, it is approved that the frontier of performance on NLP tasks is shaped entirely by the quality of the syntactic lexicon used. (Carroll and Fang, 2004) showed that the performance of syntactic parsers is improved by using an exhaustive and detailed large lexicon that contains the syntactic knowledge. In the same vein, (Jikoun and Rike, 2004; Surdeanu et al., 2011) argued that a syntactic lexicon represents the core component resource for information extraction, machine translation systems and word sense disambiguation. Due to their importance, several syntactic lexicons appeared for various languages. Regarding English, we can mention FrameNet (Baker et al., 2010), which is a lexical resource for English based on semantic frames and confirmed by attestations in corpus. It aims to document the syntactic and semantic combinatorial (or valence) for each lexical entry through manual annotation of representative lexicographical examples selected from corpus. VerbNet (Kipper et al., 2008) is another lexicon for the English language. It groups verbs sharing the same syntactic and semantic behaviours into classes based on the semantic classification of Levin (1993).

Concerning the French language, we can mention TLFi (Trésor de la Langue Française Informatisé) (Evelyne and Anne-Cécile, 2005), which is a large-scale public resource where sub-categorization is extracted from the dictionary "Trésor de la Langue Française Informatisé". This dictionary, although very structured, was conceived for human use. The lexicon-grammar (Gross, 1975) is another syntactic lexicon for French. It contains information on the syntax of verbs, nouns, adjectives and adverbs into tables.

As regards the Arabic language, we can cite the Arabic VerbNet (Mousser, 2010), which is a syntactic lexicon classifying Arabic verbs into classes based on Levin's verbs classification (Levin, 1993). Another resource for Arabic is ElixirFM (Bielický and Smrž, 2009), which is a functional morphological lexicon enriched with the Arabic verbal frame valence.

All cited lexicons suffer from a problem concerning their models and contents. Thus, such lexicons need to have a large coverage, to guarantee a high level of quality and to be directly usable in NLP tools.

To resolve these problems, the Lexical Markup Framework (LMF) (Francopoulo and George, 2008) ISO 24613 standard has been published providing a convenient solution for the modeling problem. But the enrichment problem still remains. In particular, these lexicons describe the

Proceedings of Recent Advances in Natural Language Processing, pages 168–175,
Hissar, Bulgaria, Sep 7–9 2015.

syntactic behaviours knowledge linked to lexical entries but not to their meanings.

The main goal of this paper is to propose an approach to recognize the syntactic behaviours of lexical entries in LMF dictionaries and to link them to their corresponding meanings. The basic concept of this approach is the analysis of textual contents such as definitions and contexts associated to each meaning of the lexical entries in LMF dictionaries. The main particularity of these contents is their large availability and their semantic control due to their association to the meanings, which promotes the effective links between the syntactic behaviours and the meaning.

The paper is organized as follows: Section 2 presents the proposed approach of self-enrichment of LMF normalized dictionaries with syntactic behaviour linked to the meanings of lexical entries; Section 3 describes our experimentation carried out on an available normalized Arabic dictionary with a discussion of the obtained results; Section 4 exposes related works and their comparison with our study; and finally, Section 5 concludes the paper with the announcement of some future works.

2 Proposed approach

2.1 Fundamentals

The LMF (Francopoulo and George, 2008) provides a standardized framework for the construction of computational lexicons as well as dictionaries for human use. This standard is represented as an object model for structured lexical knowledge by means of a series of extensions (i.e., morphological, syntactic, semantic and syntactico-semantic extensions). In this paper we are interested in the LMF syntactic extension that aims to describe the properties of a lexeme when combined with other lexemes in a sentence. Six classes are reserved to categorize the syntactic descriptions of a lexical entry. The first class is the Sub-categorization Frame that represents one syntactic construction that can be shared by all lexical entry instances. The second class is named the Sub-categorization Frame Set. It represents a set of syntactic constructions and possibly the relationship between them. The Lexeme Property is another class that characterizes one Sub-categorization Frame. Each Sub-categorization Frame is composed of different arguments, represented by the Syntactic Argument class, which allow its connection with the SynSemArgMap instance class. On the other hand, Syntactic Behaviour is the class that describes one of the possible behaviours of a lexeme and it can be attached to the Lexical Entry instance and optionally to the Sense instance.

In an LMF normalized dictionary, a class named Sense is reserved to represent the meaning of a lexical entry. This Sense can be attached to the Definition and Context classes. The Definition class is a narrative description of a Sense. It is reserved for the human user to facilitate his understanding of the meaning. As for the Context class, it represents a text string that describes an example of use of the lexical entry. So, this Context content is displayed for both human use and machine processing.

Benefiting from the particularities of the Context LMF class to be displayed for the computer programs on the one hand, and to describe the uses of the meanings related to the lexical entries on other hand, we propose to analyse this textual content in order to identify the syntactic behaviours of lexical entries then to associate them to the corresponding meanings in LMF normalized dictionaries.

Therefore, the analysis of the Context LMF class related to lexical entries in an LMF normalized dictionaries represents the fundamentals of the proposed approach to identify syntactic behaviours and to associate them to their corresponding meanings.

2.2 Steps of the approach

The proposed approach using the Context of the LMF normalized dictionaries for identifying and linking the syntactic behaviours to the meanings of lexical entries is composed of five steps as shown in Figure 1.

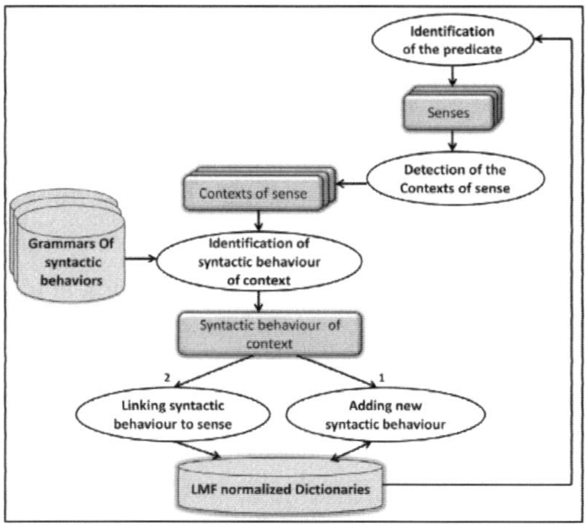

Figure 1: Proposed approach

In the following, we use the verb "to lease", which is extracted from the Oxford Advanced Learner's Dictionary[1] and represented as an LMF lexical entry to detail each step of the proposed approach. As shown in Figure 2 below, this verb has one sense described by four Contexts and one Definition and two syntactic behaviours.

```
▼<Lexicon>
  ▼<LexicalEntry id="53">
     <feat att="partOfSpeech" val="verb"/>
    ▼<Lemma>
       <feat att="writtenForm" val="to lease"/>
     </Lemma>
    ▼<Sense id="53P1">
      ▼<Context>
         <feat att="text" val="We lease all our computer equipment"/>
       </Context>
      ▼<Context>
         <feat att="text" val="They lease the land from a local farmer"/>
       </Context>
      ▼<Context>
         <feat att="text" val="A local farmer leased them the land"/>
       </Context>
      ▼<Context>
         <feat att="text" val="Parts of the building are leased out to tenants"/>
       </Context>
      ▼<Definition>
         <feat att="text" val="to use or let somebody use something, especially
          property or equipment, in exchange for rent "/>
         <feat att="source" val="Oxford Learner's Dictionary"/>
       </Definition>
     </Sense>
     <SyntacticBehaviour id="53C1" senses="53P1" subcategorizationFrames="SVC1C2"/>
     <SyntacticBehaviour id="53C2" senses="53P1" subcategorizationFrames="SVC1toC2"/>
   </LexicalEntry>
```

Figure 2: the verb "to lease" in the LMF dictionary

Identification of the predicate. The role of this step is twofold. Firstly, it searches the predicate to be processed, which can be a verb, an adjective, an adverb or a noun. After that, it aims to find out the meanings represented by the Sense LMF class attached to the processed predicate.

The application of the first step on the example presented in Figure2 identifies the predicate having 53 as identifier and "to lease" as lemma. One sense marks this predicate identified by the identifier "53P1", which corresponds to the first principal meaning of the "53" lexical entry in the LMF dictionary.

Detection of the Contexts of sense. A Context LMF class is used to describe the use of the lexical entry by means of a simple sentence. These Contexts are marked by their broad availability in the dictionary and by their semantic endorsement due to their association with the meanings. In order to find out syntactic behaviours and to link them to Senses, we propose to analyse these Contexts. Thus, the purpose of this step is to search for the processed sense related to lexical entry all linked Contexts.

[1]http://www.oxfordlearnersdictionaries.com/definition/english/lease_2

For the Sense "53P1" related to the verb "to lease", the second step of the proposed approach identifies four Contexts: (1) "We lease all our computer equipment", (2) "They lease the land from a local farmer", and (3) "A local farmer leased them the land" and (4) "Parts of the building are leased out to tenants".

Identification of the syntactic behaviour in Context. This step aims to identify the syntactic behaviour for each Context recognized in the previous step. To accomplish this objective, this step uses Grammars of syntactic behaviours. These Grammars must be constructed by means of linguistic tools and must be able to put a sentence in input in order to recognize its corresponding syntactic behaviour. At the end of this step, for each processed Context the syntactic behaviour is identified.

When we applied the third step to the Contexts obtained previously, we obtained the results described below. For the first context, "We lease all our computer equipment", Grammars of syntactic behaviour parses this sentence and recognizes the following: "We": the Subject, "lease": the processed predicate and "all our computer equipment": the Object. So, the corresponding syntactic behaviour is SVC (Subject Verb Complement). For the second Context, the SVC1fromC2 (Subject Verb First Complement "from" preposition Second Complement) syntactic behaviour is identified. Concerning the third Context, its related syntactic behaviour is SVC1C2 (Subject Verb First Complement, second Complement). As regards the fourth Context, the Grammars of syntactic behaviours identify the SVC1toC2 (Subject Verb First Complement "to" preposition Second Complement) syntactic behaviour.

Adding new syntactic behaviour. In the LMF normalized dictionaries, an existing list of syntactic behaviours can be linked to lexical entries, whereas the application of Grammars of syntactic behaviours to Contexts can identify new syntactic behaviours that do not appear in this list. At this stage, these new syntactic behaviours must be added to the list of syntactic behaviours related to the processed predicate.

Two syntactic behaviours, namely SVC1C2 and SVC1toC2, are linked to the predicate of the verb "to lease" in the example of Figure2. The application of Grammars of syntactic behaviours to Contexts identifies two new syntactic behaviours: SVC and SVC1fromC2. These later will take two new identifiers “53C2” and “53C3” having the sub-categorization Frames respectively: SVC and SVC1fromC2.

Linking syntactic behaviour to sense: At this stage, we have a final list of syntactic behaviours related to the processed lexical entry. Then, the objective is now to associate each syntactic behaviour to its corresponding Sense meaning.

For the verb “to lease”, all syntactic behaviours whatsoever, already existing or identified by the application of Grammars of syntactic behaviours, are related to the “53P1” sense. Thus, for each Syntactic Behaviour class an attribute named sense will be added having the value “53P1”.

3 Experiment and results

To consolidate our proposed approach, we tested it on an available Arabic LMF normalized dictionary. So, in this section we will present the available Arabic dictionary with its component knowledge. Then, we will detail the experimentation carried out and comment on the obtained results.

3.1 The LMF normalized Arabic dictionary

An Arabic LMF normalized dictionary named El-Madar[2] has been developed by (Khemakhem et al., 2013). The model of this dictionary takes into account the specificities of the Arabic language and covers the morphological, syntactic, semantic and syntactico-semantic levels. The current version of this dictionary contains about 37,000 lexical entries: 10,800 verbs, 22,400 nouns and 3,800 roots. Each lexical entry can include a morphological content like the part-of-speech, the lemma, some derived and inflected forms, etc. Also, it contains semantic knowledge such as the synonymy that can join senses of entries. Concerning the syntactic content, the El-Madar dictionary contains 155 general syntactic behaviours related to Arabic verbs where 5,000 verbs are connected to those behaviours.

3.2 The experiment

Our experimentation uses the El-Madar Arabic LMF dictionary. We are limited in this paper to processing verbal predicates. Apart from that, each step of the proposed approach will be experimented on the verbal predicate “وَهَبَ/ wahaba / to give” derived from El-Madar dictionary.

[2] http://elmadar.miracl-apps.com/

Experimentation of the “identification of the predicate” step. Figure3 presents the experimentation of the identification of the predicate step applied to the verb “وَهَبَ/ wahaba / to give”.

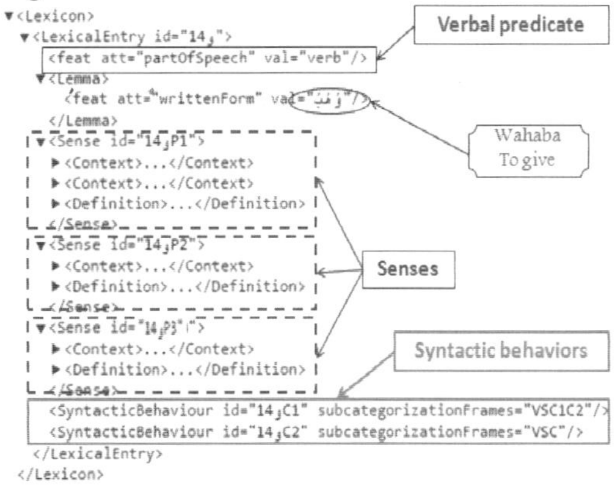

Figure 3: Experimentation of the identification of the predicate step

The lexical entry in Figure3 corresponds to the verbal predicate having the lemma “[3]وَهَبَ/wahaba/to give” and the identifier id=”14و”. This verb has three senses identified respectively “14وP1”, “14وP2” and “14وP3” and two syntactic behaviours “14وC1” and “14وC2”. This first step aims to recognize this verbal predicate.

Experimentation of the “detection of the contexts of sense” step. The same verbal predicate “وَهَبَ/wahaba/to give” is used at this stage to experiment the detection of the contexts of sense step. Figure 4 details this experimentation.

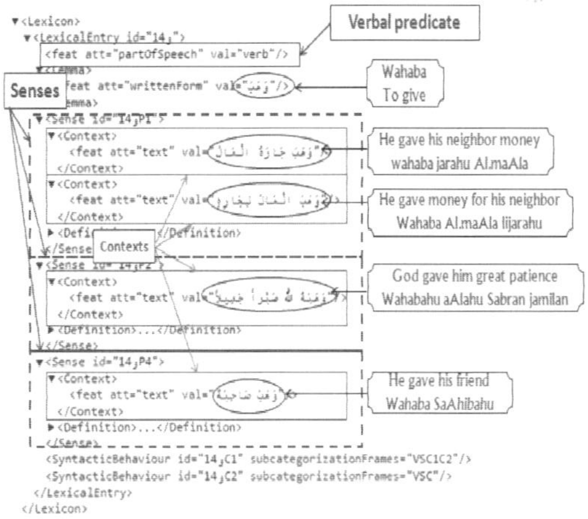

Figure 4: Detection of contexts of sense of the verb “وَهَبَ/wahaba/to give”

[3] the Arabic transliteration which has been used is Habash, Soudi and Buckwalter (Habash et al, 2007)

The experimentation of the second step on the verbal predicate "وَهَبَ/wahaba/to give" can recognize two contexts related to the sense1 id=" 14وP1": "وَهَبَ جَارَهُ الْمَالَ/wahaba jarahu Al.maAla/ He gave his neighbor money" and " وَهَبَ الْمَالَ لِجَارِهِ/ wahaba Al.maAla lijarihi/He gave money to his neighbor". For the second sense id=" 14وP2" one context is identified " وَهَبَهُ اللهُ صَبْراً جَمِيلاً/wahabahu Aalahu Sabran jamilan/ God gave him great patience". Regarding the third sense id="14 و P3" the only context found is " وَهَبَ صَاحِبَهُ /wahaba SaAhibahu/He gave his friend".

Experimentation of the "identification of syntactic behaviour of context" step. After searching contexts for each sense of the lexical entry "وَهَبَ/wahaba/ = to give", the identification of corresponding syntactic behaviours takes place.

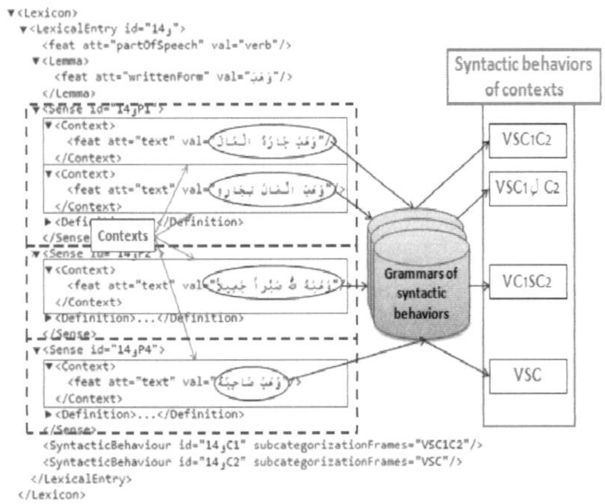

Figure 5: Experimentation of the "identification of syntactic behaviour of context" step

Figure5 demonstrates the recognition of syntactic behaviours of contexts of the verbal predicate "وَهَبَ/wahaba/to give". This identification is realized by the Grammars of syntactic behaviours. Those grammars (Elleuch et al., 2013) have been constructed using the NooJ[4] linguistic platform according to all existing Arabic syntactic patterns. They are able to identify for a simple sentence in input its corresponding syntactic behaviour. For example, when we applied Grammars of syntactic behaviours to the context " وَهَبَهُ اللهُ صَبْراً جَمِيلاً/wahabahu Aalahu Sabran jamilan/God gave him great patience" of the sense id="14وP2", the result of this application is VC1SC2. Indeed, the grammar parses the context in tokens: "وَهَبَهُ", "اللهُ", "صَبْراً" and "جَمِيلاً". The grammar can recognize "وَهَبَهُ/wahabahu/ gave him" as an agglutinate token composed of "وَهَبَ/wahaba/give", which is the verb (V), and "هُ/hu/him", which is a pronoun agglutinate to the verb representing the first complement (C1). "اللهُ/Aalahu/God" is a noun that fulfils the function subject (S). "صَبْراً/Sabran/patience" is a noun and "جَمِيلاً" is an adjective that describes "صَبْراً/Sabran/patience"; thus, " صَبْراً جَمِيلاً/Sabran jamilan/great patience" satisfies the function of second complement (C2).

The application of Grammars of syntactic behaviours to contexts finds the syntactic behaviours VSC1C2 and VSC1لـC2 for Sense1. The syntactic behaviour VC1SC2 is identified for the context of the second sense. Also, the syntactic behaviour VSC is recognized for Sense3 of the treated lexical entry "وَهَبَ".

Experimentation of the "addition of a new syntactic behaviour" step: Figure 6 below illustrates the experimentation of the enrichment of the "addition of a new syntactic behaviour" step.

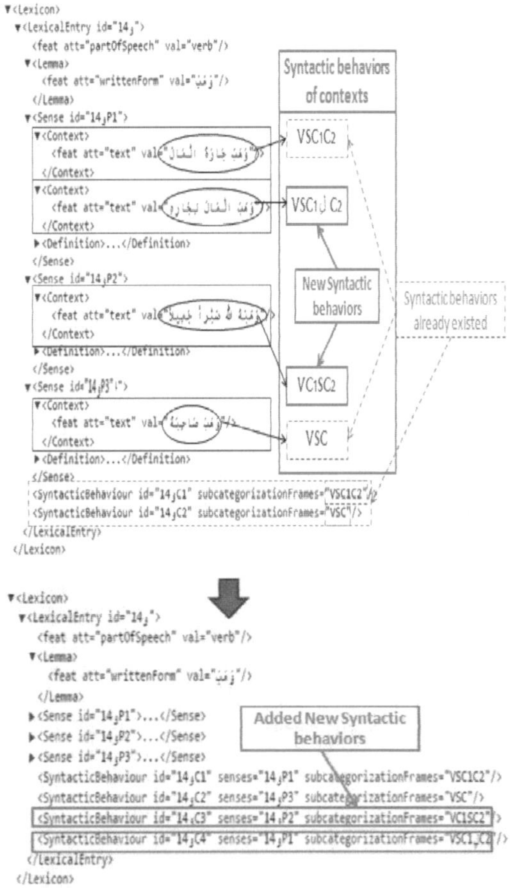

Figure 6: Adding new syntactic behaviour experiment

[4] www.nooj4nlp.net

As illustrated in Figure 6, this step makes a comparison between the already existing syntactic behaviours with the syntactic behaviours identified in the previous step. Indeed, when we compare the syntactic behaviours related to the predicate "وَهَبَ" with the syntactic behaviours identified for the contexts, we note that VSC1لC2 and VC1SC2 are newly detected syntactic behaviours. Then, the "addition of new syntactic behaviour" step appends those new syntactic behaviours to the predicate id="14و" "وَهَبَ". In this stage, the predicate "وَهَبَ" has four syntactic behaviours: VSC1C2, VSC, VSC1لC2 and VSC1C2.

Experimentation of the "linking syntactic behaviour to sense" step. The experimentation of the "linking syntactic behaviour to sense" step is presented in Figure7.

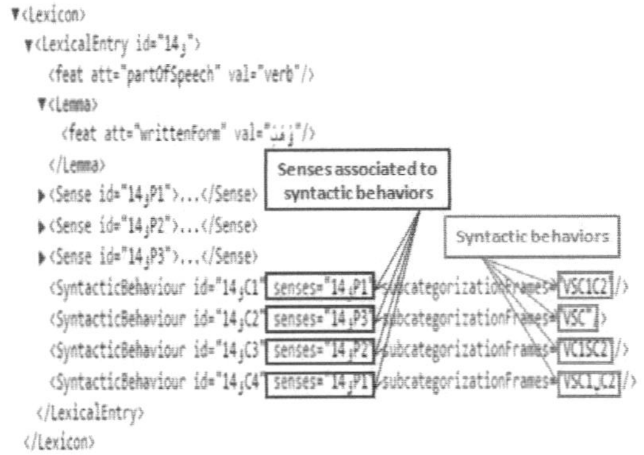

Figure 7: "Association of syntactic behaviour to sense" experiment

Figure7 represents the addition of the identifier of sense to each syntactic behaviour.

As VSC1C2 and VSC1لC2 are identified in the first sense, the identifier id="14وP1" of this sense is added to the syntactic behaviours VSC1C2 and VSC1لC2. Since the syntactic behaviour VC1SC2 is recognized in the context of the second sense, the id="14وP2" of the second sense is added to the syntactic behaviour VC1SC2. And finally, the id="14 و P3" of the third sense will be associated to the syntactic behaviour VSC where this behaviour is identified in the context of this sense.

3.3 Results

El-Madar dictionary (Khemakhem et al., 2013) contains up to now 10,800 verbs. Among them 1,000 verbs don't have the Sense classes. So, only 9,800 verbs have been treated by the experimentation we performed. 31,500 assignments between syntactic behaviours and meanings are the result of the experimentation of the proposed approach applied to El-Madar dictionary. A sample containing 2,000 resulting affectations representing the 155 kinds of Arabic syntactic behaviours have been assessed by a human expert. For these 2,000 affectations, the expert approves that 232 incorrect affectations and 140 missed ones are detected. Thus, for these 2,000 affectations the Precision is estimated to 0.88 and the Recall is equal to 0.92.

For error analysis, we can acknowledge that the sentence of the processed Context is represented as a complex structure and the Grammars of syntactic behaviours cannot analyse it and give wrong results. Also, we can accept that the Context written by the lexicographer is not appropriate to the exact syntactic behaviour of verbs.

4 Related works

In this section, we will present an overview of some Arabic syntactic lexicons. We can mention the ElixirFM lexicon (Bielický and Smrž, 2009), the Arabic syntactic lexicon (Loukil et al., 2010), and the Arabic VerbNet (Mousser, 2010) syntactic lexicons for the Arabic language since we have experimented the proposed approach on this language. At the end of this section, we will make a comparison between the three mentioned lexicons with our lexicon.

4.1 The ElixirFM Lexicon

ElixirFM (Bielický and Smrž, 2009) is a morphological lexicon enriched by the valency frame of Arabic verbs. This lexicon is based on the theoretical Functional Generative Description (FGD) approach. The valence of a verb is represented as a tree of dependencies. The lexicon contains about 3,500 frames of verb valence: 2,000 frames representing the intransitive verbs automatically created from the Buckwalter Arabic Morphological Analyzer and 1,500 frames manually formed. These frames take into account the thematic role of each argument which is composed of the syntactic behaviours of Arabic verbs and which also includes both obligatory and optional actants and only obligatory free modifications. In fact, this lexicon does not take into consideration the valency of modal, impersonal and defective verbs.

4.2 The Arabic Syntactic Lexicon

The Arabic syntactic lexicon (Loukil et al., 2010) is a lexical resource compliant to the LMF standard representing the syntactic features of Arabic verbs. The enrichment process used to populate this resource with syntactic behaviours is made semi-automatically by means of, the editor Lexus. Three steps compose the enrichment process. The first step is the manual identification of syntactic behaviours for Arabic verbs. The second one represents the use of the Lexus editor in order to enrich the lexicon with sub-categorizations of verbs. The last step details how to edit and affect sub-categorization frames to each processed verb. This lexicon includes 2,500 verb lemmas.

We can mention that the Arabic syntactic lexicon doesn't cover all syntactic behaviours of Arabic verbs because it considers only 17 sub-categorization frames. Also, the affectation of the sub-categorization frames is attached to the lexical entry but not to its meanings.

4.3 The Arabic VerbNet

The Arabic VerbNet (Mousser, 2010) is the Arabic version of the English VerbNet. It is a lexicon that classifies Arabic verbs based on Levin's classification (Levin, 1993). Thus, the same procedure, process and treatment used to build the English VerbNet were re-used to construct the Arabic VerbNet, with some adaptation for the Arabic language. This lexicon classifies verbs into classes. Each class groups verbs sharing syntactic and semantic properties represented into frames. Morphological, syntactic and semantic knowledge are presented into each frame. Indeed, the root, the derived forms, the present participle of the Arabic verb, the thematic roles of semantic arguments and the sub-categorization of each verb are included into each frame. 291 is the number of verb classes of the Arabic VerbNet including 7,937 verbs represented with 1,202 frames.

4.4 Synthesis

Even though all the approaches presented in the above studies on the Arabic language suggest some interesting ideas, each one of them includes some shortcomings. Indeed, ElixirFM does not present the explicit syntactic structure of verbs and neglects the syntactic functions of complements. The syntactic lexicon of (Loukil et al., 2010) is a very small lexicon representing only the syntactic aspects of very few Arabic verbs while the Arabic VerbNet does not represent the native features of Arabic verbs because it's a simple translation of the classes used in the English VerbNet with some adaptations.

A comparison between those three works and our lexicon according to different criteria is presented in Table 1, which is given below.

	ElixirFM Lexicon	Arabic Syntactic Lexicon	Arabic Verbnet	Our Lexicon
Normalized format	-	LMF standard	-	LMF standard
Linguistics levels covered				
Morphology	+	+	+	+
Semantic	+/-	-	+	+
Syntactic	+	+	+	+
Number of verbs	3500	2500	7937	9800
Classification	FGD	Verbal type hierarchy	Levin's class	Transitivity Intransitivity
Syntactic enrichment				
Process	Semi-automatic	Semi-automatic	Semi-automatic	Automatic
Formal representation	Frames	32 Rules	English Verbenet Frames	155 Grammars
Semantic features	+	-	+	-
Dictionaries	Printed	-	Printed	Electronic
	3		2	Arabic normalized LMF dictionary
Corpus	PADT	205 transliterated sentences	-	-
	CLARA			
	Arabic Gigaword			
Syntactic behavior				
Number	3500	17	1202	155
Related to	Meanings	Verbs	Meanings	Verbs Meanings

Table 1: Comparison with the existing Arabic syntactic lexicons

5 Conclusion and perspectives

We have presented an approach allowing us to find out the syntactic behaviours of lexical entries and linking them to their corresponding meanings in LMF normalized dictionaries. This approach uses the Context textual content to identify the syntactic behaviour. The main particularity of this content is its large availability and its semantic control due to this connection to the meanings, which promotes the effective links between the syntactic behaviour and the meaning. This approach is characterized by it genericity; thus it can be applied to any language. We have tested the proposed approach by its application to the Arabic language. For that purpose, an available Arabic LMF normalized dictionary named El-Madar was used to evaluate our approach. 9,800 verbs were treated in the experimentation giving 0.88 of Precision and 0.92 of Recall.

Future directions include extracting syntactic behaviours from other resources like corpora, and improving Grammars of syntactic behaviours in order to make them more sophisticated to support more complex linguistic rules.

References

Baker K., Bloodgood M. , Chris D., Bonnie W., Filardo N., Levin L., Miller S. and Piatko, C. 2010. *Semantically-Informed Machine Translation: A Tree-Grafting Approach.* Biennial Conference of the Association for Machine Translation in the Americas. Denver, Colorado, pp.411-438.

Bielický V. and Smrž O. 2009. *Enhancing the ElixirFM Lexicon with Verbal Valency Frames*, volume 2. International Conference on Arabic Language Resources and Tools (MEDAR 2009), Cairo, Egypt.

Carroll J., Fang A.C. 2004. *The Automatic Acquisition of Verb Subcategorisations and their Impact on the Performance of an HPSG Parser*, volume1. International Conference on Natural Language Processing, Sanya City, China.

Elleuch I., Gargouri B. and Ben-Hamadou, A. 2013. *Syntactic enrichment of Arabic dictionaries normalized LMF using corpora.* Language & Technology Conference (LTC). Poznan, Poland. pp.314-318.

Evelyne J. and Anne-Cécile N. 2005. *Vers un Lexique Syntaxique du Français : Extraction d'Informations de Sous-Catégorisation à Partir du TLFi.* Journée ATALA du 12 mars sur les lexiques syntaxiques, Paris.

Francopoulo G. and George M. 2008. *ISO/TC 37/SC 4 Rev.16. Language Resource Management – Lexical Markup Framework (LMF).*

Gross M. 1975. *Méthodes en Syntaxe: Régimes des Constructions Complétives.* Paris, Hermann.

Habash N., Soudi A. and Buckwalter T. 2007. *In Arabic Computational Morphology: Knowledge-based and Empirical Methods.* ISBN: 978-1-4020-6045-8.

Jikoun J.M. and Rike M. 2004. *Information Extraction for Question Answering: Improving recall Through Syntactic Patterns*, volume20. International Conference on Computational Linguistics

Khemakhem A., Gargouri B. and Ben Hamadou A. 2013. *LMF for Arabic, chapter in the book "LMF : Lexical Markup Framework".* TWiley Edictions, ISBN: 9781848214309, pp. 83-96.

Kipper K., Korhonen A., Ryant N. and Palmer, M. 2008. *A Large-Scale Classification of English Verbs*, volume 42. Journal of Language Resources and Evaluation, n° 1, pp. 21-40

Levin B. 1993. *English Verb Classes and Alternations.* Preliminary investigation, University of Chicago Press, Chicago and London.

Loukil N., Haddar K. and Ben Hamadou A. 2010. *A Syntactic Lexicon for Arabic Verbs.* International Conference on Language Resources and Evaluation, LREC, pp. 17-23, May, Valletta, Malta.

Mousser J. 2010. *A large Coverage Verb Taxonomy For Arabic.* International Conference on Language Resources and Evaluation, LREC, May, Valletta, Malta.

Surdeanu M., McClosky D., Smith M-R., Gusev, A. and Manning C-D. 2011. *Customizing an Information Extraction System to a New Domain.* In Proceedings of the ACL 2011 Workshop on Relational Models of Semantics (RELMS 2011), Portland, Oregon, USA, June 23, 2011. pp. 2–10.

Weakly Supervised Definition Extraction*

Luis Espinosa-Anke, Francesco Ronzano and **Horacio Saggion**
TALN - DTIC
Universitat Pompeu Fabra
Carrer Tànger, 122-134
08018 Barcelona
{luis.espinosa,francesco.ronzano,horacio.saggion}@upf.edu

Abstract

Definition Extraction (DE) is the task to extract textual definitions from naturally occurring text. It is gaining popularity as a prior step for constructing taxonomies, ontologies, automatic glossaries or dictionary entries. These fields of application motivate greater interest in well-formed encyclopedic text from which to extract definitions, and therefore DE for academic or lay discourse has received less attention. In this paper we propose a weakly supervised bootstrapping approach for identifying textual definitions with higher linguistic variability than the classic encyclopedic *genus-et-differentia* definition, and take the domain of Natural Language Processing as a use case. We also introduce a novel set of features for DE and explore their relevance. Evaluation is carried out on two datasets that reflect opposed ways of expressing definitional knowledge.

1 Introduction

Definition Extraction (DE) is the task to automatically extract textual definitions from text (Navigli and Velardi, 2010). It has received notorious attention for its potential application to glossary generation (Muresan and Klavans, 2002; Park et al., 2002), terminological databases (Nakamura and Nagao, 1988), question answering systems (Saggion and Gaizauskas, 2004; Cui et al., 2005), for supporting terminological applications (Meyer, 2001; Sierra et al., 2006), e-learning (Westerhout and Monachesi, 2007), and more recently for multilingual paraphrase extraction (Yan et al., 2013), ontology learning (Velardi et al., 2013) or hypernym discovery (Flati et al., 2014).

The corpora that have been used for evaluating DE systems are varied, although in general efforts have been greatly focused on academic and encyclopedic genres. Some prominent examples include German technical texts (Storrer and Wellinghoff, 2006), the IULA Technical Corpus (in Spanish) (Alarcón et al., 2009), the ACL Anthology (Jin et al., 2013; Reiplinger et al., 2012), the BNC corpus (Rodríguez, 2004), Wikipedia (Navigli and Velardi, 2010), ensembles of domain glossaries and Web documents (Velardi et al., 2008), or technical texts in various languages (Westerhout and Monachesi, 2007; Przepiórkowski et al., 2007; Borg et al., 2009; Degórski et al., 2008; Del Gaudio et al., 2013).

We propose a DE approach which, from a starting set of encyclopedic definition seeds, self-trains iteratively and gradually fits its classification capability to a target domain-specific test set. Evaluation is carried out on two corpora: First, a set of 50 abstracts of papers in the field of NLP[1]. Here, the target term is defined in the first sentence, and additional information may appear in the form of "syntactically plausible false definitions", i.e. sentences where the target term is also present, relevant information is provided, but do not constitute a definition

* This work is partially funded by the SKATER project, TIN2012-38584-C06-03, Ministerio de Economía y Competitividad, Secretaría de Estado de Investigación, Desarrollo e Innovación, España; and Dr. Inventor (FP7-ICT-2013.8.1 611383).

[1]Henceforth, we refer to this corpus as the *MSR-NLP* dataset.

Proceedings of Recent Advances in Natural Language Processing, pages 176–185,
Hissar, Bulgaria, Sep 7–9 2015.

(Navigli and Velardi, 2010). Second, the *W00* corpus (Jin et al., 2013), a subset of the ACL Anthology manually annotated with definitions, and which includes highly variable definitions both in terms of content and syntax. We achieve competitive results in both corpora.

The main contributions of our paper are: (1) A set of experiments demonstrating the soundness of our approach for DE in two different linguistic registers; (2) A novel set of features and an exploration of their influence in the learning process; and (3) A small, focused benchmarking dataset for DE evaluation in the NLP domain.

The remainder of this paper is structured as follows: Section 2 reviews prominent work in DE; Section 3 provides a detailed description of the datasets used; Section 4 presents the features used in our classification procedure and describes the bootstrapping algorithm; Section 5 shows the performance of our approach; Section 6 lists the best features at important iterations and discusses these findings; and finally Section 7 summarizes the main ideas contained in this paper and outlines potential directions for future work.

2 Background

Definitions are a well-studied topic, which traces back to the Aristotelian genus et differentia model of a definition, where the defined term (*definiendum*) is described by mentioning its immediate superordinate, usually a hypernym (*genus*), and the cluster of words that differentiate such definiendum from others of its class (*definiens*). Furthermore, additional research has elaborated on different criteria to take into consideration when deciding *what is a definition*: either by looking at their degree of formality (Trimble, 1985), the extent to which they are specific to an instance of an object or to the object itself (Seppälä, 2009), the semantic relations holding between definiendum and concepts included in the definiens (Alarcón et al., 2009; Schumann, 2011), the fitness of a definition for target users (Bergenholtz and Tarp, 2003; Fuertes-Olivera, 2010) or their stylistic and domain features (Velardi et al., 2008). In this work we elaborate on some ideas from the latter, especially on their *domain* and *stylistic* filters, which motivated the design of statistically-motivated features to describe a word's salience in terms of definitional knowledge (cf. Section 4).

Regarding DE, the earliest attempts focused on lexico-syntactic pattern-matching, either by looking at cue verbs (Rebeyrolle and Tanguy, 2000; Saggion and Gaizauskas, 2004; Sarmento et al., 2006; Storrer and Wellinghoff, 2006), or other features like punctuation or layout (Muresan and Klavans, 2002; Malaisé et al., 2004; Sánchez and Márquez, 2005; Przepiórkowski et al., 2007; Monachesi and Westerhout, 2008). As for supervised settings, let us refer to (Navigli and Velardi, 2010), who propose a generalization of word lattices for identifying definitional components and ultimately identifying definitional text fragments. Finally, more complex morphosyntactic patterns were used by (Boella et al., 2014), who model single tokens as relations over the sentence syntactic dependencies.

We refer now to unsupervised approaches to DE. (Reiplinger et al., 2012) benefit from hand crafted definitional patterns. Starting from a set of seed terms and patterns, term/definition pairs are iteratively acquired, together with bootstrapped new patterns. These are obtained via a generalization approach over part-of-speech and term wildcards. Additionally, two interconnected works are (De Benedictis et al., 2013) and (Faralli and Navigli, 2013), in that both bootstrap the web for acquiring large multilingual domain glossaries starting with a few seeds for term and gloss. While both systems behave similarly in extracting glosses and learning new patterns by exploiting *html* tags, they are substantially different in how acquired glosses are ranked. Specifically, the former exploits the bag-of-words representation of each extracted gloss and its intersection with the domain terminology, while the latter leverages Probabilistic Topic Models (PTM) by estimating the probability of words and term/gloss pairs to be pertinent to the domain.

3 Corpora

Our weakly supervised DE approach requires: (1) A general-domain (encyclopedic) set of seeds of textual definitions (TS) and (2) A domain-specific development set, e.g. a collection of papers (DS).

For our experiments, we use as TS the WCL Corpus (Navigli et al., 2010), a subset of Wikipedia manually annotated with definitions and hypernyms. This dataset is constructed under the intuition that the first sentence of a Wikipedia article constitutes its textual definition. It is important to highlight that, while this dataset includes semantic information manually annotated such as definiendum or hypernym, we do not exploit any of it, which makes the seed-construction step highly flexible as it only requires the sentence definition/non-definition class. We use as DS a subset of the ACL ARC corpus (Bird et al., 2008), processed with ParsCit (Councill et al., 2008). In this dataset, a well-formedness confidence score is given to each sentence (as these come from pdf parsing and noise is introduced in the process). We exploit this information and keep 500k sentences with a score of over .95.

For evaluation, we use two datasets: The MSR-NLP [2] and the W00 corpus. The MSR-NLP is a manually constructed small list of 50 abstracts in the NLP field, amounting to 304 sentences: 49 definitions and 255 non-definitions. They are extracted from the Microsoft Academic Research website[3], where abstracts including a definition provide a "Definition Context" section. This small dataset complies with the stylistic requirements of academic abstract writing, i.e. the use of well-developed, unified, coherent and concise language, and understandability to a wide audience[4]. A different register can be found in the W00 dataset, which includes many definitional sentences that are highly domain-specific, sometimes including the definition of a very specific concept, and showing higher linguistic variability (e.g. the definiendum might not appear at the beginning of the sentence, and unlike most abstracts, citations might be present). We illustrate this difference with two sentences containing a definition from the MSR-NLP (1) and the W00 (2) corpora:

(1) The Hidden Markov Model (HMM) is a probabilistic model used widely in the fields of Bioinformatics and Speech Recognition .

(2) This corpus is collected and annotated for the GNOME project (Poesio, 2000), which aims at developing general algorithms for generating nominal expressions

Note that in the case of (2), only the sequence "GNOME project aims at developing general algorithms for generating nominal expressions" is labelled as definition in the original dataset. In this work a definitional sentence is generalized as *being* or *containing* a definition, which enables casting the task as a sentence-classification problem, which is common practice in DE (Navigli and Velardi, 2010; Boella et al., 2014; Espinosa-Anke and Saggion, 2014).

Intuitively, we would expect a general-purpose DE system to be more likely to label sentence (1), as it includes the required elements for a canonical genus-et-differentia definition. This motivates our experiments, where we attempt to fit a model iteratively to be able to perform better in sentences like (2).

4 Modelling the Data

As mentioned in Section 3, we approach the DE task as a sentence classification problem, where a sentence can be either a definition (*def*) or not (*nodef*). However, instead of modelling sentence-level features like sentence length or depth of the parse tree, we rather encode word-level features in order to exploit individual items' characteristics in terms of position within the sentence, frequency or relevance in a definition corpus. These word-level features are used for classifying each word in a sentence (*def*|*nodef*).

We adopt two extraction strategies depending on whether we operate over DS or any of the two evaluation corpora (MSR-NLP and W00). In the case DS, the goal is to extract complete high-quality definitional and non-definitional sentences. Therefore, we only consider as potential candidates for bootstrapping those sentences where all the words have the same label (i.e. discarding, for example, a 10-word sentence where nine are tagged as *def* and one as *nodef*). This is in fact the most frequent case by a large margin, so we are confident that there are very few potentially relevant sentences being left out. Since evaluation is carried out at word level, this constraint does not apply.

[2] Available at http://www.taln.upf.edu/MSR-NLP_RANLP2015

[3] http://academic.research.microsoft.com/

[4] http://www.cameron.edu/~carolynk/Abstracts.html

We exploit the potential of the Conditional Random Fields[5] algorithm (Lafferty et al., 2001) to encode prior and posterior contextual information of a given element in a sequence (in our case, a word in a sentence). Specifically, we consider a context window of [-2,2]. For each word, we generate a feature vector consisting on the following features:

1. **sur**: Surface form of the current token without stemming.
2. **lem**: Lemma of the current token.
3. **pos**: Part-of-speech of the current token.
4. **bio-np**: Whether the current word is at the beginning (B), inside (I) or outside (O) a noun phrase. Noun phrases are obtained with the following regular expression over part-of-speech tags: [JN]*N.
5. **dep**: Dependency relation between the current token and its head.
6. **head-id**: The index of the head-word (or governor) in the syntactic dependency tree.
7. **bio-def**: An extension of the *bio-np* feature that also takes into account the definition-wise position. We perform this naïvely by finding the first verb of the sentence, and tagging all words before it as definiendum and the rest as definiens. We illustrate this feature below, where each word's NP-chunking comes from the bio-np feature, *D* refers to definiendum and *d* refers to definiens.

   The⟨o-D⟩ Abwehr⟨b-D⟩ was⟨o-d⟩ a⟨o-d⟩ German⟨b-d⟩ intelligence⟨i-d⟩ organization⟨i-d⟩ from⟨o-d⟩ 1921⟨o-d⟩ to⟨o-d⟩ 1944⟨o-d⟩ .

8. **termhood**: This metric determines the importance of a candidate token to be a terminological unit by looking at its frequency in general and domain-specific corpora (Kit and Liu, 2008). It is obtained as follows:

$$\text{Termhood(w)} = \frac{\text{r}_\text{D}(\text{w})}{|\text{V}_\text{D}|} - \frac{\text{r}_\text{B}(\text{w})}{|\text{V}_\text{B}|}$$

   Where r_D is the frequency-wise ranking of word w in a domain corpus (in our case, TS), and r_B is the frequency-wise ranking of such word in a general corpus, namely the Brown corpus (Francis and Kucera, 1979). Denominators refer to the token-level size of each corpus. If word w only appears in the general corpus, we set the value of Termhood(w) to $-\infty$, and to ∞ in the opposite case.

9. **tf-gen**: Frequency of the current word in the general-domain corpus r_B (Brown Corpus).
10. **tf-dom**: Frequency of the current word in the domain-specific corpus r_D (TS).
11. **tfidf**: Tf-idf of the current word over the training set, where each sentence is considered a separate document.
12. **def_prom**: We introduce the notion of Definitional Prominence aiming at establishing the probability of a word w to appear in a definitional sentence ($s = def$). For this, we consider its frequency in definitions and non-definitions in the TS as follows:

$$\text{DefProm(w)} = \frac{\text{DF}}{|\text{Defs}|} - \frac{\text{NF}}{|\text{Nodefs}|}$$

   where DF $= \sum_{i=0}^{i=n}(s_i = def \wedge w \in s_i)$ and NF $= \sum_{i=0}^{i=n}(s_i = nodef \wedge w \in s_i)$. Similarly as with the *termhood* feature, in cases where a word w is only found in definitional sentences, we set the DefProm(w) value to ∞, and to $-\infty$ if it was only seen in non-definitional sentences.

13. **D_prom**: We also introduce Definiendum Prominence in order to model our intuition that a word appearing more often in position of potential *definiendum* might reveal its role as a definitional keyword. This feature is computed as follows:

$$\text{DP(w)} = \frac{\sum_{i=0}^{i=n} w_i \in \text{term}_D}{|DT|}$$

   where term_D is a noun phrase (i.e. a term candidate) appearing in potential definiendum po-

[5] We use the CRF++ toolkit: http://crfpp.googlecode.com/svn/trunk/doc/index.html

sition and |DT| refers to the size of the candidate term corpus in candidate definienda position.

14. **d_prom**: Similarly computed as D_prom, but considering position of potential definiens.

4.1 Bootstrapping

As noted in Section 3, the initial TS consists of the WCL dataset, which makes our model suitable for DE in well-formed encyclopedic texts. However, our hypothesis that it would perform poorly in a linguistically more complex setting (e.g. in a corpus like the W00 dataset) is confirmed by the results at iteration 1 (see Table 1). Our bootstrapping approach is aimed at gradually obtaining a better fit model for W00, starting from our generic baseline trained exclusively on the WCL corpus. The following description of our approach is summarized in Algorithm 1.

As mentioned above, TS is a manually labelled dataset where each sentence $s \in S$ is given a label $d \in D = \{def, nodef\}$. Likewise, DS is an unlabelled subset of the ACL-ARC corpus, which amounts to 500k sentences. The first step is to initialize (1) The training set vocabulary V, which simply contains all the words in TS; and (2) The feature set F associated to each word $w \in V$. Then, for each iteration until we reach 200, the algorithm extracts the best-scoring sentences as predicted by our CRF-based classififer (recall that only sentences where all words are assigned the same label are considered) for both labels *def* and *nodef* (s' and s'' respectively), and uses them to increase the initial feature set and vocabulary. Next, it removes s' and s'' from DS, trains and evaluates a model on both the MSR-NLP and the W00 datasets, and repeats until it reaches our manually set end point: iteration 200th.

One important aspect to consider is that increasing the size of the training data does not have an effect of the features associated to a word. Incorporating definitions having concepts related to the target domain (NLP in our case) is a step forward, but their definitional salience (expressed by def_prom, D_prom and d_prom) remains the same, as they were calculated before firing the bootstrapping algorithm. For this reason, we include a feature update step at iteration 100, our sole motivation being that, for evaluation purposes, we will have the same number of iterations before and after such step. It consists in resetting F to $\emptyset$ and recalculating it. We hypothesize that the new feature values can reflect better the linguistic idiosyncrasies of a domain-specific definitional corpus. After 200 iterations, our bootstrapped dataset TS_{boot} includes the original training data and 400 new sentences: 200 definitions and 200 non-definitions.

As the bootstrapping process advances, s' and s'' show greater linguistic variability because the training data includes more non-canonical definitions (Table 1).

Algorithm 1 Bootstrapping for DE

Require:
$TS = \{(S, d \in D)\}$ Initial labelled train seeds.
$DS = \{S\}$ Subset of the ACL-ARC corpus.
MSR-NLP: Test set 1.
W00: Test set 2.

$V := \{w : \exists (s, d) \in TS \wedge w \in s\}$
$F := \{f_{TS}(w) : w \in V\}$
for $i = 0, i < 200, i++$ **do**
  $s' = argmax_{s \in DS}\ P(s = def)$
  $s'' = argmax_{s \in DS}\ P(s = nodef)$
  for $w \in s' \cup s''$ **do**
    if $w \notin V$ **then**
      $F = F \cup \{f_{TS}(w)\}$
      $V = V \cup \{w\}$
    end if
  end for
  $TS = TS \cup \{(s', def), (s'', nodef)\}$
  $DS = DS \setminus \{(s', def), (s'', nodef)\}$
  if $i = 100$ **then**
    $F = \emptyset$
    for $w \in V$ **do**
      $F = F \cup \{f_{TS}(w)\}$
    end for
  end if
  $model_i = trainModel(TS_i, F_i)$
  $evaluateModel(model_i, \{\text{MSR-NLP, W00}\})$
end for

4.2 Post Classification Heuristics

Our last step consists in applying a post-classification heuristic inspired by (Cai et al.,

Iter	Best definition in DS	MSR-NLP			W00		
		P	R	F	P	R	F
1	A term is a word or a word sequence	100	9.09	16.68	65.38	1.25	2.47
10	An abbreviation is defined as a shortened form of a written word or phrase used in place of the full form	83.13	44.4	57.88	69.84	11.35	19.53
120	A bunsetsu is one of the linguistic units in Japanese and roughly corresponds to a basic phrase in English	25.5	90.71	39.81	60.71	69.68	64.89
182	That is to say a site is a candidate site when it is found to have either an English page linking to its Chinese version or a Chinese page linking to its English version	22.92	92.53	36.74	62.55	76.63	68.88
200	Figure 1 and Figure 2 present the overall system configuration and data flow of the integrated system	23.34	96.72	37.6	62.27	78.45	69.43

Table 1: Definitions extracted throughout the bootstrapping process from the ACL ARC corpus and P/R/F results at that iteration on the two evaluation corpora (without post-classification heuristics). Note the gradual increase in syntactic and terminological variability in the extracted definitions.

2009). It consists in a set of rules for label-switching aimed at increasing the recall and ideally without hurting precision significantly. Let w_i be a word classified as not being part of a definition (*nodef*) at iteration i, we can rectify its class (w_i^{new}) to being part of a definition (*def*) as follows:

$$w_i^{new} = \begin{cases} def & \text{if } P(w_i) = def > \theta \\ def & \text{if } P(w_i) = nodef < \lambda, w_i^{\text{syn}} = P \end{cases}$$

Where w_i^{syn} refers to the dependency relation of the word examined at iteration i, and *P* is the *predicative* syntactic function of the word.

Our goal is to increase the number of *def* words in a sentence in cases where they were discarded by a small margin. We hypothesize that this could be particularly useful in "borderline" cases (some words classified in a sentence as *def*, some as *nodef*), where this heuristics helps our algorithm to make a decision always favouring definition labelling over non-definition. As for the constants, θ and λ are empirically set to .35 and .8 respectively after experimenting with several thresholds and inspecting manually the resulting classification.

5 Evaluation

We evaluate the performance of our approach at each iteration on both datasets (MSR-NLP and W00) using the classic Precision, Recall and F-Measure scores. All the scores reported in this article are at word-level.

The learning curves shown in Figure 1 demonstrate that our approach is suitable for fitting a model to a domain-specific dataset starting from general-purpose encyclopedic seeds. Unsurprisingly, performance on the MSR-NLP corpus drops soon after reaching its peak due to the fact that the training set gradually becomes less standard. Interestingly, the feature-update step has a dramatic influence in performance in both corpora: On one hand, the performance peak in a dataset with less linguistic variability (MSR-NLP) is reached early, and after iteration 100, where the feature update step occurs, Precision decreases, while Recall remains the same. On the other hand, the numbers in the W00 dataset are fairly stable until iteration 100, where a significant improvement in both Precision and Recall is achieved.

Let us look first at the results without applying recall-boosting post-classification heuristics: The performance of our models decreases in the MSR-NLP corpus after a few iterations (our best model is reached at iteration 23, where F=76.23), and this situation is unsurprisingly aggravated by the feature update step. However, our results improve significantly in the W00 dataset[6] after feature updating. Our best-performing model reaches F=70.72 at iteration 198.

Moreover, we observed a minor improvement after incorporating the label-switching heuristics in both corpora. Specifically, for the MSR-NLP corpus the improvement was from the aforementioned F=76.34 to F=77.46, while in the W00 dataset, it improved from F=70.72 to F=71.85. Tables 2 and 3 show Precision, Recall and F-Score for our best models in both datasets.

These numbers confirm that we are able to generate a domain and genre-sensitive model provided we have a development set available of similar characteristics. The discrepancy in terms of performance as the bootstrapping algorithm advances is an indicator that the models we obtain become more tailored towards the specific corpus, and therefore less apt for performing well in the encyclopedic genre. Our approach seems suitable for partially alleviating the lack of manually labelled domain-specific data in the DE field.

Let us also refer to the importance of having a development set as close as possible to the target corpus in terms of register and domain, and with a reasonable level of quality. In relation to this, we also performed experiments with a development set automatically constructed from the Web, but due to lack of preprocessing for noise filtering, results were unsatisfactory and therefore unreported in this paper.

As for comparative evaluation, we cannot contrast our results directly with the ones reported in (Jin et al., 2013), since while in both cases word-level evaluation is carried out, in our case we generalized all the words inside a sentence containing a definition to the label *def*. In addition, as it is pointed out in (Jin et al., 2013), only in (Reiplinger et al., 2012) there is an attempt to extract definitions from the ACL ARC corpus, but their evaluation relies on human judgement, and their reported coverage refers to a pre-defined list of terms.

[6]Note that since the W00 corpus is also a subset of the ACL ARC dataset, we first confirmed that it did not overlap with our dev-set.

	Iteration	P	R	F
Pre-PCH	198	62.69	81.11	70.72
Post-PCH	198	62.47	82.01	71.85

Table 2: Best results for the W00 dataset before (Pre-PCH) and after (Post-PCH) applying the post-classification heuristics.

	Iteration	P	R	F
Pre-PCH	23	80.69	72.24	76.23
Post-PCH	20	78.2	76.7	77.44

Table 3: Best results for both the MSR-NLP dataset before (Pre-PCH) and after (Post-PCH) applying the post-classification heuristics.

In general, the results reported in this article are consistent with the ones obtained in previous work for similar tasks. For instance, prior experiments on the WCL dataset showed results ranging from F=54.42 to F=75.16 (Navigli and Velardi, 2010; Boella et al., 2014). In the case of the W00 dataset, (Jin et al., 2013) reported numbers between F=40 and F=56 for different configurations. Since the availability of manually labelled gold standard is scarce, other authors evaluated Glossary/Definition Extraction systems in terms of manually assessed precision (Reiplinger et al., 2012; De Benedictis et al., 2013).

6 Feature Analysis

In order to understand the discriminative power of the features designed for our experiments, we computed Information Gain, which measures the decrease in entropy when the feature is present vs. ab-

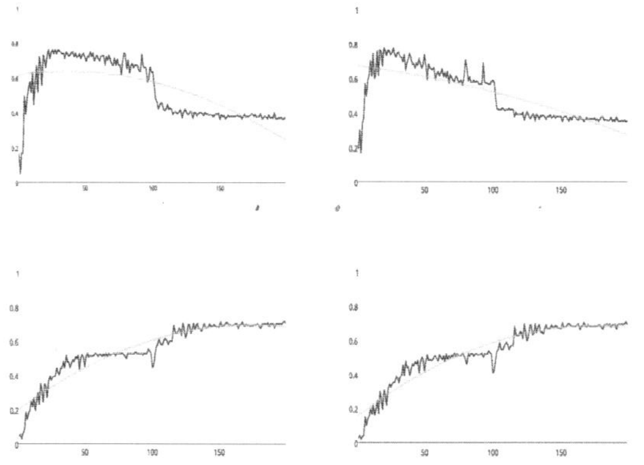

Figure 1: F-Score against iteration on the MSR-NLP (top row) and W00 datasets (bottom row), with bootstrapping + post-classification heuristics (left column) and only bootstrapping (right column).

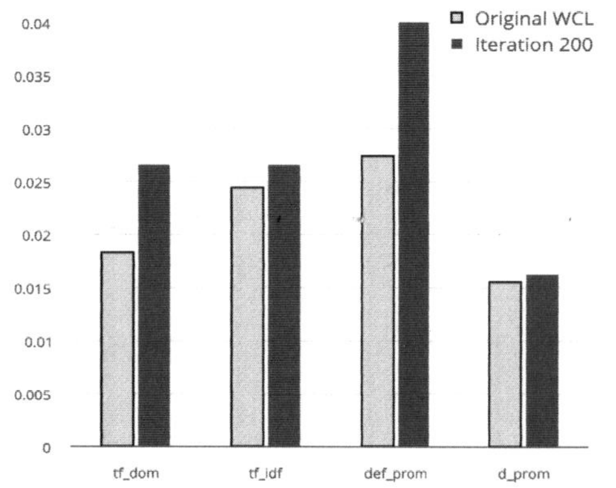

Figure 2: Information Gain for the best features at the end of the bootstrapping process. Note the substantial improvement in def_prom (definitional prominence).

sent (Forman, 2003), using the Weka toolkit (Witten and Frank, 2005). We did this for the original training set TS and the training set resulting at iteration 200 TS_{boot}. Then, we captured the top 30 features in TS_{boot}, and averaged their Information Gain score over all the available contexts. Finally, we compare these features in both datasets TS and TS_{boot} (see Figure 2).

We observe an improvement of definitionally-motivated features after iteration 100, which combined with the gradual improvement in performance in the W00 dataset, suggests that def_prom and d_prom contribute decisively to domain-specific DE, while D_prom proved less relevant. Note that in our setting, we do not focus in term/definition pairs, but rather a full-sentence definition. Therefore, we do not know a priori which term is the definiendum, and thus we do not perform a generalization step to convert it to a wildcard, which is common practice in the DE literature (Navigli and Velardi, 2010; Reiplinger et al., 2012; Jin et al., 2013; Boella et al., 2014). This provokes high sparsity in D_prom and we hypothesize that this may be the reason for this feature to not gain predictive power after many iterations or the feature update step.

7 Conclusions and Future Work

We have presented a weakly supervised DE approach that gradually increments the size of the training set with high quality definitions and clear examples of non-definitions. Two main conclusions can be drawn: (1) The definition-aware features we introduce show, in general, high informativeness for the task of DE; and (2) Our approach is valid for generating genre and domain specific training data capable of fitting corpora, even though this differs greatly in terms of content and register from the encyclopedic genre.

In addition, a small and focused benchmarking dataset of real-world definitions in the NLP domain has been released, which can be used both for linguistic and stylistic purposes and for evaluating DE systems.

These results motivate us to extend our experiments to several domains and textual genres, and to perform a longer iterative cycle where feature update is carried out more frequently. We believe that another interesting avenue for future work is multilingual definition extraction, which could benefit significantly from existing multilingual semantic networks and knowledge bases.

References

Rodrigo Alarcón, Gerardo Sierra, and Carme Bach. 2009. Description and evaluation of a definition extraction system for spanish language. In *Proceedings of the 1st Workshop on Definition Extraction*, WDE '09, pages 7–13, Stroudsburg, PA, USA. Association for Computational Linguistics.

Henning Bergenholtz and Sven Tarp. 2003. Two opposing theories: On h.e. wiegand's recent discovery of lexicographic functions. *Hermes, Journal of Linguistics*, 3-1:171–196.

Steven Bird, Robert Dale, Bonnie Dorr, Bryan Gibson, Mark Joseph, Min-Yen Kan, Dongwon Lee, Brett Powley, Dragomir Radev, and Yee Fan Tan. 2008. The acl anthology reference corpus: A reference dataset for bibliographic research in computational linguistics. In *Proceedings of the Sixth International Conference on Language Resources and Evaluation (LREC-08)*, Marrakech, Morocco, May. European Language Resources Association (ELRA). ACL Anthology Identifier: L08-1005.

Guido Boella, Luigi Di Caro, Alice Ruggeri, and Livio Robaldo. 2014. Learning from syntax generalizations for automatic semantic annotation. *Journal of Intelligent Information Systems*, pages 1–16.

Claudia Borg, Michael Rosner, and Gordon Pace. 2009. Evolutionary algorithms for definition extraction. In *Proceedings of the 1st Workshop in Definition Extraction*.

Peng Cai, HangZai Luo, and AoYing Zhou. 2009. Named entity recognition in italian using crf. In *EVALITA*.

Isaac G Councill, C Lee Giles, and Min-Yen Kan. 2008. Parscit: an open-source crf reference string parsing package. In *LREC*.

Hang Cui, Min-Yen Kan, and Tat-Seng Chua. 2005. Generic soft pattern models for definitional question answering. In *Proceedings of the 28th annual international ACM SIGIR conference on Research and development in information retrieval*, pages 384–391. ACM.

Flavio De Benedictis, Stefano Faralli, Roberto Navigli, et al. 2013. Glossboot: Bootstrapping multilingual domain glossaries from the web. In *ACL (1)*, pages 528–538.

Lukasz Degórski, Micha Marcińczuk, and Adam Przepiórkowski. 2008. Definition extraction using a sequential combination of baseline grammars and machine learning classifiers. In *Proceedings of the 6th International Conference on Language Resources and Evaluation (LREC)*, Marrakech, Morocco, may.

Rosa Del Gaudio, Gustavo Batista, and António Branco. 2013. Coping with highly imbalanced datasets: A case study with definition extraction in a multilingual setting. *Natural Language Engineering*, pages 1–33.

Luis Espinosa-Anke and Horacio Saggion. 2014. Applying dependency relations to definition extraction. In *Natural Language Processing and Information Systems*, pages 63–74. Springer.

Stefano Faralli and Roberto Navigli. 2013. Growing multi-domain glossaries from a few seeds using probabilistic topic models. In *EMNLP*, pages 170–181.

Tiziano Flati, Daniele Vannella, Tommaso Pasini, and Roberto Navigli. 2014. Two is bigger (and better) than one: the wikipedia bitaxonomy project. In *Proc. of the 52nd Annual Meeting of the Association for Computational Linguistics*.

George Forman. 2003. An extensive empirical study of feature selection metrics for text classification. *The Journal of machine learning research*, 3:1289–1305.

W Nelson Francis and Henry Kucera. 1979. Brown corpus manual. *Brown University*.

Pedro Fuertes-Olivera. 2010. *Specialised Dictionaries for Learners*. Berlin/New York: De Gruyter. Lexicographica Series Maior, 136.

Yiping Jin, Min-Yen Kan, Jun-Ping Ng, and Xiangnan He. 2013. Mining scientific terms and their definitions: A study of the ACL anthology. In *Proceedings of the 2013 Conference on Empirical Methods in Natural Language Processing*, pages 780–790, Seattle, Washington, USA, October. Association for Computational Linguistics.

Chunyu Kit and Xiaoyue Liu. 2008. Measuring monoword termhood by rank difference via corpus comparison. *Terminology*, 14(2):204–229.

John D. Lafferty, Andrew McCallum, and Fernando C. N. Pereira. 2001. Conditional Random Fields: Probabilistic Models for Segmenting and Labeling Sequence Data. In *Proceedings of the Eighteenth International Conference on Machine Learning*, ICML '01, pages 282–289, San Francisco, CA, USA. Morgan Kaufmann Publishers Inc.

Véronique Malaisé, Pierre Zweigenbaum, and Bruno Bachimont. 2004. Detecting semantic relations between terms in definitions. In Sophia Ananadiou and Pierre Zweigenbaum, editors, *International Conference on Computational Linguistics (COLING 2004) - CompuTerm 2004: 3rd International Workshop on Computational Terminology*, pages 55–62, Geneva, Switzerland, August 29.

Ingrid Meyer. 2001. Extracting knowledge-rich contexts for terminography. *Recent advances in computational terminology*, 2:279.

Paola. Monachesi and Eline. Westerhout. 2008. What can NLP techniques do for eLearning? In *International Conference on Informatics and Systems (INFOS08)*, pages 150–156.

A Muresan and Judith Klavans. 2002. A method for automatically building and evaluating dictionary resources. In *Proceedings of the Language Resources and Evaluation Conference (LREC*.

Jun-ichi Nakamura and Makoto Nagao. 1988. Extraction of semantic information from an ordinary english dictionary and its evaluation. In *Proceedings of the 12th Conference on Computational Linguistics - Volume 2*, COLING '88, pages 459–464, Stroudsburg, PA, USA. Association for Computational Linguistics.

Roberto Navigli and Paola Velardi. 2010. Learning word-class lattices for definition and hypernym extraction. In *Proceedings of the 48th Annual Meeting of the Association for Computational Linguistics*, ACL '10, pages 1318–1327, Stroudsburg, PA, USA. Association for Computational Linguistics.

Roberto Navigli, Paola Velardi, and Juana María Ruiz-Martínez. 2010. An annotated dataset for extracting definitions and hypernyms from the web. In Nicoletta Calzolari (Conference Chair), Khalid Choukri, Bente Maegaard, Joseph Mariani, Jan Odijk, Stelios Piperidis, Mike Rosner, and Daniel Tapias, editors, *Proceedings of the Seventh International Conference on Language Resources and Evaluation (LREC'10)*, Valletta, Malta, may. European Language Resources Association (ELRA).

Youngja Park, Roy J. Byrd, and Branimir K. Boguraev. 2002. Automatic Glossary Extraction: Beyond Terminology Identification. In *Proceedings of the 19th International Conference on Computational Linguistics*, pages 1–7, Morristown, NJ, USA. Association for Computational Linguistics.

Adam Przepiórkowski, Miroslav Spousta, Kiril Simov, Petya Osenova, Lothar Lemnitzer, Vladislav Kubo, and Beata Wójtowicz. 2007. Towards the automatic extraction of definitions in Slavic. In *Proceedings ofo the BSNLP workshop at ACL 2007*.

Josette Rebeyrolle and Ludovic Tanguy. 2000. Repérage automatique de structures linguistiques en corpus : le cas des énoncés définitoires. *Cahiers de Grammaire*, 25:153–174.

Melanie Reiplinger, Ulrich Schäfer, and Magdalena Wolska. 2012. Extracting glossary sentences from scholarly articles: A comparative evaluation of pattern bootstrapping and deep analysis. In *Proceedings of the ACL-2012 Special Workshop on Rediscovering 50 Years of Discoveries*, pages 55–65, Jeju Island, Korea, July. Association for Computational Linguistics.

Carlos Rodríguez. 2004. *Metalinguistic Information Extraction from Specialized Texts to Enrich Computational Lexicons*. Ph.D. thesis, Universitat Pompeu Fabra.

Horacio Saggion and Robert Gaizauskas. 2004. Mining on-line sources for definition knowledge. In *17th FLAIRS*, Miami Bearch, Florida.

A. Sánchez and J. Márquez. 2005. Hacia un sistema de extracción de definiciones en textos jurídicos. In *Actas de la 1er Jornada Venezolana de Investigación en Lingüística e Informática*, pages 1–10.

Luís Sarmento, Belinda Maia, Diana Santos, Ana Pinto, and Luís Cabral. 2006. Corpógrafo V3 From Terminological Aid to Semi-automatic Knowledge Engineering. In *5th International Conference on Language Resources and Evaluation (LREC'06)*, Geneva.

Anne-Kathrin Schumann. 2011. A bilingual study of knowledge - rich context extraction in russian and german. In *Proceedings of the Fifth Language and Technology Conference*, pages 516–520.

Selja Seppälä. 2009. A proposal for a framework to evaluate feature relevance for terminographic definitions. In *Proceedings of the 1st Workshop on Definition Extraction*, WDE '09, pages 47–53, Stroudsburg, PA, USA. Association for Computational Linguistics.

Gerardo Sierra, Rodrigo Alarcón, César Aguilar, and Alberto Barrón. 2006. Towards the building of a corpus of definitional contexts. In *Proceeding of the 12th EURALEX International Congress, Torino, Italy*, pages 229–40.

Angelika Storrer and Sandra Wellinghoff. 2006. Automated detection and annotation of term definitions in German text corpora. In *Conference on Language Resources and Evaluation (LREC)*.

L. Trimble. 1985. *English for Science and Technology: A Discourse Approach*. Cambridge Language Teaching Library.

Paola Velardi, Roberto Navigli, and Pierluigi D'Amadio. 2008. Mining the web to create specialized glossaries. *IEEE Intelligent Systems*, 23(5):18–25, September.

Paola Velardi, Stefano Faralli, and Roberto Navigli. 2013. Ontolearn reloaded: A graph-based algorithm for taxonomy induction. *Computational Linguistics*, 39(3):665–707.

Eline Westerhout and Paola Monachesi. 2007. Extraction of Dutch definitory contexts for elearning purposes. *Proceedings of the Computational Linguistics in the Netherlands (CLIN 2007), Nijmegen, Netherlands*, pages 219–34.

Ian H Witten and Eibe Frank. 2005. *Data Mining: Practical machine learning tools and techniques*. Morgan Kaufmann.

Yulan Yan, Chikara Hashimoto, Kentaro Torisawa, Takao Kawai, Jun'ichi Kazama, and Stijn De Saeger. 2013. Minimally supervised method for multilingual paraphrase extraction from definition sentences on the web. In *HLT-NAACL*, pages 63–73.

Jointly Embedding Relations and Mentions for Knowledge Population

Miao Fan[†,‡], **Kai Cao**[‡], **Yifan He**[‡] **and Ralph Grishman**[‡]
[†] CSLT, Division of Technical Innovation and Development,
Tsinghua National Laboratory for Information Science and Technology,
Tsinghua University, Beijing, 100084, China.
[‡]Proteus Group, New York University, NY, 10003, U.S.A.
fanmiao.cslt.thu@gmail.com, carson529@gmail.com;
me@yifanhe.org, grishman@cs.nyu.edu

Abstract

This paper contributes a joint embedding model for predicting relations between a pair of entities in the scenario of relation inference. It differs from most standalone approaches which separately operate on either knowledge bases or free texts. The proposed model simultaneously learns low-dimensional vector representations for both triplets in knowledge repositories and the mentions of relations in free texts, so that we can leverage the evidence both resources to make more accurate predictions. We use NELL to evaluate the performance of our approach, compared with cutting-edge methods. Results of extensive experiments show that our model achieves significant improvement on relation extraction.

1 Introduction

Relation extraction (Bach and Badaskar, 2007; Grishman, 1997; Sarawagi, 2008), which aims at discovering the relationships between a pair of entities, is a significant research direction for discovering more beliefs for knowledge bases. Most stand-alone approaches, however, either use local graph patterns in knowledge repositories, or extract features from text mentions, to individually help predict relations between two entities. The heterogeneity brings about a gap between structured repositories and unstructured free texts, which spoils the dream of sharing the evidence from both knowledge and natural language.

For studies in decades, scientists either compete the performance of their methods on the public text datasets such as ACE[1] (GuoDong et al., 2005) and MUC[2] (Zelenko et al., 2003), or look for effective approaches (Gardner et al., 2013; Lao et al., 2011) on improving the accuracy of link prediction within knowledge bases such as NELL[3] (Carlson et al., 2010) and Freebase[4] (Bollacker et al., 2007). Thanks to the research of distantly supervised relation extraction (Fan et al., 2014a; Mintz et al., 2009) which facilitates the manual annotation via automatically aligning with the relation mentions in free texts, NELL can not only extract triplets, i.e. $\langle head\_entity, relation, tail\_entity \rangle$, but also collect the texts between two entities as the evidence of relation mention. We take an example from NELL which originally records a belief: $\langle concept : city : caroline, concept : citylocatedinstate, concept : stateorprovince : maryland, County\ and\ State\ of \rangle$, where "$County\ and\ State\ of$" is the mention between the head entity $concept : city : caroline$, and the tail entity $concept : stateorprovince : maryland$, to indicate the relation $concept : citylocatedinstate$.

Fortunately, the embedding techniques (Fan et al., 2014b; Mikolov et al., 2013) enlighten us to break through the limitation of heterogeneous resources, and to establish a connection between a relation and its corresponding mention via learning a specific vector representation for each of the elements, including the entities and relations in triplets, and the words in mentions. More specifically, we propose a joint relation mention embedding (JRME) model in this paper, which simulta-

[1]http://www.itl.nist.gov/iad/mig/tests/ace/
[2]http://www.itl.nist.gov/iaui/894.02/related projects/muc/
[3]http://rtw.ml.cmu.edu/rtw/
[4]http://www.freebase.com/

Proceedings of Recent Advances in Natural Language Processing, pages 186–191,
Hissar, Bulgaria, Sep 7–9 2015.

neously learns low-dimensional vector representations for entities and relations in knowledge repositories, and in the meanwhile, each word in the relation mentions is also trained a dedicated embedding. This model helps us take advantage of the benefits from the two resources to make more accurate predictions. We use two different datasets extracted from NELL to evaluate the performance of JRME, compared with cutting-edge methods. It turns out that our model achieves significant improvement on relation extraction.

2 Related Work

We group some recent work on relation extraction into two categories, i.e. text-based approaches and knowledge-based methods. Generally speaking, both of the parties seek better evidences to make more accurate predictions. The text-based community focuses on linguistic features such as the words combined with POS tags that indicate the relations, but the other side conducts relation inference depending on the local connecting patterns between entity pairs learnt from the knowledge graph which is established by beliefs.

2.1 Text-based Approaches

It is believed that the text between two recognized entities in a sentence indicate their relationships to some extent. To implement a relation extraction system guided by supervised learning, a key step is to annotate the training data. Therefore, two branches emerge as follows,

- *Relation extraction with manual annotated corpora*: Traditional approaches compete the performance on the public text datasets which are annotated by experts, such as ACE and MUC. They choose different features extracted from the texts, like kernel features (Zelenko et al., 2003) or semantic parser features (GuoDong et al., 2005), and there is a comprehensive survey (Sarawagi, 2008) which shows more details about this branch.

- *Relation extraction with distant supervision*: Due to the limited scale and tedious labor caused by manual annotation, scientists explore an alternative way to automatically generate large-scale annotated corpora, named by distant supervision (Mintz et al., 2009). Even though this cutting-edge technique solves the issue of lacking annotated corpora, we still suffer from the problem of noisy and sparse features (Fan et al., 2014a).

2.2 Knowledge-based Methods

Knowledge bases contain millions of entries which are usually represented as triplets, i.e. $\langle head\_entity, relation, tail\_entity \rangle$, which intuitively inspire us to regard the whole repository as a graph, where entities are nodes and relations are edges. Therefore, one research community looks forward to predicting unknown relations which may exist between two entities via learning the linking patterns, and another promising research group tries to learn structured embeddings of knowledge bases.

- *Relation prediction with graph patterns*: Some canonical studies (Gardner et al., 2013; Lao et al., 2011) adopt a data-driven random walk model, which follows the paths from the head entity to the tail entity on the local graph structure to generate non-linear feature combinations to represent relations, and then uses logistic regression to select the significant features that contribute to classifying other entity pairs which also have the given relation.

- *Relation prediction with embedding representations*: Bordes et al. (Bordes et al., 2013; **?**) propose an alternative way that embedding the whole knowledge graph via learning a specific low-dimensional vector for each entity and relation, so that we just need simple vector calculation instead to predict relations.

Our model (JRME) benefits more from the latest and state-of-the art embedding approaches, TransE (Bordes et al., 2013) and IIKE (Fan et al., 2015a). Therefore, we re-implement them as the rival methods, and conduct extensive comparisons in the subsequent experiments.

3 Model

The heterogeneity between free texts and knowledge bases brings about a challenge that we can hardly take advantage of the features uniformly, since they are located in different spaces and have varies dimensions. Thankfully, the embedding techniques (Fan et al., 2014b; Mikolov et al., 2013; Fan et al., 2015b; Fan et al.,) leave an idea

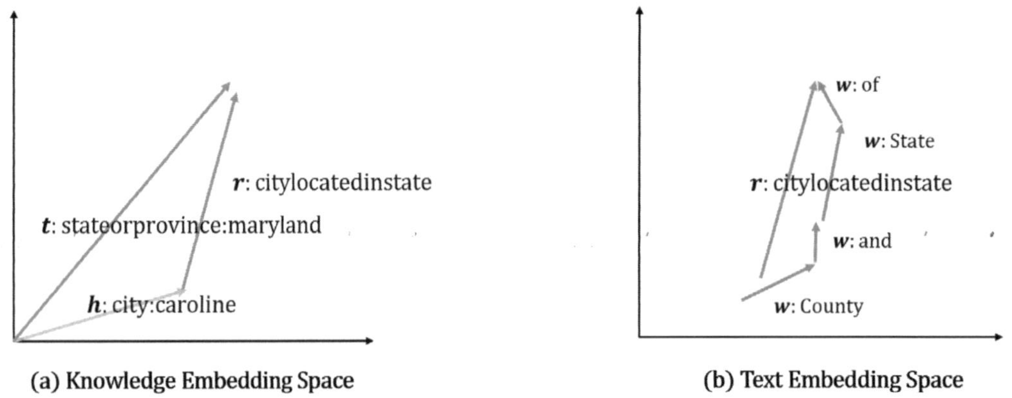

Figure 1: Given a belief, $\mathbf{h} : city : caroline, \mathbf{r} : citylocatedinstate, \mathbf{t} : stateorprovince : maryland$ and $\mathbf{m} : County\ and\ State\ of$ in NELL, (a) shows the distributed representations of a triplet in the knowledge space, and (b) illustrates word embeddings in the text space.

that almost all the elements, including words, entities, relations, can be learnt and assigned distributed representations, and the mission remaind for us is to jointly learn embeddings for entities, relations, and the words in the same feature space.

We arrange the subsequent content as follows: Section 3.1 and 3.2 describe how to model the knowledge and texts individually, and we finally talk about the proposed jointly embedding model in Section 3.3.

3.1 Knowledge Relation Embedding

Inspired by TransE (Bordes et al., 2013), we regard the relation r between a pair of entities, i.e. h and t, as a transition, due to the hierarchical structure of knowledge graphs. Therefore, we use $D_r(h, r, t)$ as follows to denote the plausibility of a triplet (h, r, t) illustrated by Figure 1(a):

$$D_r(h, r, t) = |\mathbf{h} + \mathbf{r} - \mathbf{t}|^2, \quad (1)$$

where the closer $\mathbf{h} + \mathbf{r}$ is to $\mathbf{t}$, the more likely the triplet (h, r, t) exists. The bold fonts indicate the vector representations, e.g. the embedding of the head entity h is $\mathbf{h} \in \mathbb{R}^d$ where d is short for dimension.

Assume that R is the set of relations. Given a correct triplet (h, r, t), we aim at pushing all the possible corrupt triplets with wrong relations $\{r'|r' \in R \,\&\, r' \neq r\}$ away. Therefore, we adopt a margin-based ranking loss function with a block α to separate all the negative triplets in the corrupted base K' from all the positives in the correct knowledge base K:

$$\arg\min_{r,r'} \mathcal{L}_r = \sum_{(h,r,t)\in K} \sum_{(h,r',t)\in K'} [\alpha + D_r(h, r, t) - D_r(h, r', t)]_+, \quad (2)$$

in which $[\,]_+$ is a hinge loss function, i.e. $[x]_+ = max(0, x)$.

3.2 Text Mention Embedding

Similar to the Knowledge Relation Embedding (KBE), we can also find an approach to measure the distance between the mention m and its corresponding relation r in Text Mention Embedding (TME). To denote the embedding of mention $\mathbf{m}$, we sum all the embeddings of words included by m as shown by Equation (3). Thanks to representing all the words and relations in vectors with the same dimension which is demonstrated by Figure 1(b), we can adopt inner product function shown by Equation (4) to calculate their similarity.

$$\mathbf{m} = \sum_{w\in m} \mathbf{w}, \quad (3)$$

$$D_m(r, m) = -\mathbf{r}^T\mathbf{m}. \quad (4)$$

Before using the margin-based ranking loss function to learn, we need to construct the negative set T' for each pair of relation mention (r, m) which appears in the correct training set T. To generate the negative pairs (r', m), we keep the mention m but iteratively change other relations from the set of relations R. The subsequent Formula (5) helps to discriminate between the two opponent sets with a margin β,

$$\arg\min_{r,m,r'} \mathcal{L}_m = \sum_{(r,m)\in T} \sum_{(r',m)\in T'} [\beta + D_m(r,m) - D_m(r',m)]_+. \tag{5}$$

3.3 Joint Relation Mention Embedding

Due to the uniform modeling standard of KBE and TME, we can jointly embed the relations and corresponding mentions (JRME) with Equation (6),

$$\begin{aligned}\arg\min_{r,m,r'} \mathcal{L} = \sum_{(h,r,t,m)\in KT} \sum_{(h,r',t,m)\in KT'} [\gamma \\ + D_r(h,r,t) - D_r(h,r',t) \\ + D_m(r,m) - D_m(r',m)]_+,\end{aligned} \tag{6}$$

in which each belief (h, r, t, m) belonging to the training set KT contains two entities, the relation and its corresponding mention.

If we achieve the learnt embeddings for all the entities, relations and words in mentions, we can simply use Equation (7) to measure the rationality of a relation r appearing between a pair of entities h, t with the evidence of m:

$$Score(h,r,t,m) = D_r(h,r,t) + D_m(r,m) \tag{7}$$

4 Experiments

We set up three objectives for evaluating the effectiveness of JRME, which are:

- testing the effectiveness of JRME in terms of different evaluation protocols/metrics;
- comparing the performances of JRME with other cutting-edge approaches;
- judging the robustness of the proposed model by using a larger but noisy dataset.

Section 4.1 and 4.2 display the different datasets and the various protocols we use to measure the performance compared with several state-of-the-art approaches, i.e TransE (Bordes et al., 2013) and IIKE (Fan et al., 2015a). Section 4.3 will show the results of the extensive experiments.

DATASET	NELL-50K	NELL-5M
#(ENTITIES)	29,904	177,635
#(RELATIONS)	233	236
#(TRAINING EX.)	57,356	5,000,000
#(VALIDATING EX.)	10,710	47,335
#(TESTING EX.)	10,711	47,335

Table 1: Statistics of the datasets used for relation prediction task.

4.1 Datasets

We prepare two datasets with different statistical characteristics. As illustrated by Table 1, both of them are generated by NELL (Carlson et al., 2010), a Never-Ending Language Learner which works on automatically extracting beliefs from the Web. NELL-50K is a medium size dataset, and each belief, which contains the head entity h, the tail entity t, the relation r between them, and the mention m indicate the relation, is validated by experts. However, NELL-5M is a much larger one with five million uncertain training examples automatically learnt from the Web by NELL.

4.2 Protocols

The scenario of experiments is that: given a pair of entities, a short text/mention to indicate the correct relations and a set of candidate relations, we compare the performance between our models and other state-of-the-art approaches, with the metrics as follows,

- *Average Rank*: Each candidate relation will gain a score calculated by Equation (7). We sort them in ascending order and compare with the corresponding ground-truth belief. For each belief in the testing set, we get the rank of the correct relation. The average rank is an aggregative indicator, to some extent, to judge the overall performance on relation extraction of an approach.
- *Hit@10*: Besides the average rank, scientists from the industrials concern more about the accuracy of extraction when selecting Top10 relations. This metric shows the proportion of beliefs that we predict the correct relation ranked in Top10.
- *Hit@1*: It is a more strict metric that can be referred by automatic system, since it demonstrates the accuracy when just picking the first predicted relation in the sorted list.

APPROACH	AVG. R.	HIT@10	HIT@1
TransE	131.8	16.3%	3.0%
KRE	29.1	44.3%	14.4%
TME	11.5	80.0%	56.0%
IIKE	*7.5*	*81.8%*	*56.8%*
JRME	**6.2**	**87.8%**	**60.2%**

Table 2: Performance of TransE, KRE, IIKE, TME and JRME on the metrics of Average Rank, Hit@10 and Hit@1 in NELL-50K dataset.

APPROACH	AVG. R.	HIT@10	HIT@1
TransE	77.1	5.4%	0.7%
KRE	57.5	17.9%	2.5%
TME	*3.6*	*96.3%*	*63.6%*
IIKE	4.5	82.6%	53.2%
JRME	**3.0**	**96.7%**	**68.0%**

Table 3: Performance of TransE, KRE, IIKE, TME and JRME on the metrics of Average Rank, Hit@10 and Hit@1 in NELL-5M dataset.

4.3 Hyperparameters

Before displaying the evaluation results, we need to elaborate the hyperparameters that have been tried, and show the best combination of hyperparameters we choose. Another advantage of embedding-based model is that it is unnecessary to tune many hyperparameters. For our model, we just need to set four, which are the uniform dimension d of entities, relations and the words in mentions, the margin α of KBE, the margin β of TME and the margin γ of JRME. To decide the ideal set of hyperparameters, we use the validation set to pick the best combination from $d \in \{10, 20, 50, 100, 200\}$, $\alpha \in \{0.1, 1.0, 2.0, 5.0, 10.0\}$, $\beta \in \{0.1, 1.0, 2.0, 5.0, 10.0\}$ and $\gamma \in \{0.1, 1.0, 2.0, 5.0, 10.0\}$. Finally, we choose $d = 100, \alpha = 1.0, \beta = 1.0$ and $\gamma = 2.0$ to train the embeddings, as this combination of hyperparameters helps perform best on the validation set.

4.4 Performance

Table 2 and 3 illustrate the results of experiments on NELL-50K and NELL-5M, respectively. Both of them show that JRME performs best among all the approaches we implemented. We can also figure out that text mentions contribute a lot to predicting the correct relations. Moreover, Table 3 also demonstrates that not only IIKE is robust to the noise in NELL-5M dataset, which consists with its characteristics emphasized by Fan et al. (Fan et al., 2015a), but also TME and JRME share this special "gene". Overall, JRME improves the average rank of relation prediction about 20% compared with state-of-the-art IIKE.

5 Conclusion

We engage in bridging the gap between unstructured free texts and structured knowledge bases to predict more accurate relations via proposing a joint embedding model between any given entity pair for knowledge population. The results of extensive experiments with various evaluation protocols on both medium and large NELL datasets effectively demonstrate that our model (JRME) outperforms other state-of-the-art approaches. Because of the uniform low-dimensional vector representations for entities, relations and even the words, evidence for prediction is compressed into embeddings to facilitate the information exchange and computing, which finally leads a huge leap forward in relation extraction.

There still remain, however, several open questions on this promising research direction in the future, such as exploring better ways to embed the whole beliefs or mentions without losing too much regularities of knowledge and linguistics.

Acknowledgments

The first author conducted this research while he was a joint-supervision Ph.D. student in New York University, and is also supported by China Scholarship Council. This paper is dedicated to all the members of the Proteus Project.

References

Nguyen Bach and Sameer Badaskar. 2007. A review of relation extraction. *Literature review for Language and Statistics II*.

Kurt Bollacker, Robert Cook, and Patrick Tufts. 2007. Freebase: A shared database of structured general human knowledge. In *AAAI*, volume 7, pages 1962–1963.

Antoine Bordes, Nicolas Usunier, Alberto Garcia-Duran, Jason Weston, and Oksana Yakhnenko. 2013. Translating embeddings for modeling multi-relational data. In *Advances in Neural Information Processing Systems*, pages 2787–2795.

Andrew Carlson, Justin Betteridge, Bryan Kisiel, Burr Settles, Estevam R. Hruschka Jr., and Tom M. Mitchell. 2010. Toward an architecture for never-ending language learning. In *Proceedings of the Twenty-Fourth Conference on Artificial Intelligence (AAAI 2010)*.

Miao Fan, Qiang Zhou, Andrew Abel, and Thomas Fang Zheng. Probabilistic belief embedding for large-scale knowledge population.

Miao Fan, Deli Zhao, Qiang Zhou, Zhiyuan Liu, Thomas Fang Zheng, and Edward Y. Chang. 2014a. Distant supervision for relation extraction with matrix completion. In *Proceedings of the 52nd Annual Meeting of the Association for Computational Linguistics (Volume 1: Long Papers)*, pages 839–849, Baltimore, Maryland, June. Association for Computational Linguistics.

Miao Fan, Qiang Zhou, Emily Chang, and Thomas Fang Zheng. 2014b. Transition-based knowledge graph embedding with relational mapping properties. In *Proceedings of the 28th Pacific Asia Conference on Language, Information, and Computation*, pages 328–337, Phuket,Thailand, December. Department of Linguistics, Chulalongkorn University.

Miao Fan, Qiang Zhou, and Thomas Fang Zheng. 2015a. Learning embedding representations for knowledge inference on imperfect and incomplete repositories. *arXiv preprint arXiv:1503.08155*.

Miao Fan, Qiang Zhou, Thomas Fang Zheng, and Ralph Grishman. 2015b. Probabilistic belief embedding for knowledge base completion. *arXiv preprint arXiv:1505.02433*.

Matt Gardner, Partha Pratim Talukdar, Bryan Kisiel, and Tom M. Mitchell. 2013. Improving learning and inference in a large knowledge-base using latent syntactic cues. In *EMNLP*, pages 833–838. ACL.

Ralph Grishman. 1997. Information extraction: Techniques and challenges. In *International Summer School on Information Extraction: A Multidisciplinary Approach to an Emerging Information Technology*, SCIE '97, pages 10–27, London, UK, UK. Springer-Verlag.

Zhou GuoDong, Su Jian, Zhang Jie, and Zhang Min. 2005. Exploring various knowledge in relation extraction. In *Proceedings of the 43rd Annual Meeting on Association for Computational Linguistics*, ACL '05, pages 427–434, Stroudsburg, PA, USA. Association for Computational Linguistics.

Ni Lao, Tom Mitchell, and William W. Cohen. 2011. Random walk inference and learning in a large scale knowledge base. In *Proceedings of the 2011 Conference on Empirical Methods in Natural Language Processing*, pages 529–539, Edinburgh, Scotland, UK., July. Association for Computational Linguistics.

Tomas Mikolov, Kai Chen, Greg Corrado, and Jeffrey Dean. 2013. Efficient estimation of word representations in vector space. *arXiv preprint arXiv:1301.3781*.

Mike Mintz, Steven Bills, Rion Snow, and Dan Jurafsky. 2009. Distant supervision for relation extraction without labeled data. In *Proceedings of the Joint Conference of the 47th Annual Meeting of the ACL and the 4th International Joint Conference on Natural Language Processing of the AFNLP: Volume 2-Volume 2*, pages 1003–1011. Association for Computational Linguistics.

Sunita Sarawagi. 2008. Information extraction. *Foundations and trends in databases*, 1(3):261–377.

Dmitry Zelenko, Chinatsu Aone, and Anthony Richardella. 2003. Kernel methods for relation extraction. *The Journal of Machine Learning Research*, 3:1083–1106.

Distributional Semantics for Resolving Bridging Mentions

Tim Feuerbach and **Martin Riedl** and **Chris Biemann**
Language Technology Group, CS Department, TU Darmstadt, Germany
uni@spell.work, {riedl, biem}@cs.tu-darmstadt.de

Abstract

We explore the impact of adding distributional knowledge to a state-of-the-art coreference resolution system. By integrating features based on word and context expansions from a distributional thesaurus (DT), automatically mined IS-A relationships and shallow syntactical clues into the Berkeley system (Durrett and Klein, 2013), we are able to increase its F1 score on bridging mentions, i.e. coreferent mentions with non-identical heads, by 8.29 points. Our semantic features improve over the Web-based features of Bansal and Klein (2012). Since bridging mentions are a hard but infrequent class of coreference, this leads to merely small improvements in the overall system.

1 Introduction

Automatically recognizing coreference – relating lexical items that refer to the same entity or context in a text – is an important semantic processing step for text understanding tasks such as fact extraction, information retrieval, and entity linking.

A common problem of coreference systems is their inability to resolve bridging mentions, i.e. coreferent mentions with non-identical heads (Vieira and Poesio, 2000). For example, a system requires semantic knowledge to detect the hypernymic relationship that holds between mentions like *a preliminary agreement* and *the pact*. Similarly, modeling selectional preference relies on information beyond the pronoun context itself.

There are two different kinds of approaches employed in the past to make this knowledge available as features to a coreference resolution system. The first class uses manually crafted resources like WordNet or Wikipedia (Poesio et al., 2004; Ponzetto and Strube, 2006). Despite their quality, they may decrease the performance when added to the system (Lee et al., 2011; Zhou et al., 2011). Further disadvantages are their limited size, slow growth and general-purpose nature. In contrast, using unsupervised/semi-supervised methods for generating knowledge is only limited by the size of input data and adapts to the target domain.

We present features exploiting automatically obtained distributional knowledge, following the distributional hypothesis formulated by Harris (1954) that words in similar contexts bear similar meanings. For that we resort to a distributional thesaurus (DT; Lin, 1998) listing semantically similar terms, as well as hyponym-hypernym relations (IS-As) acquired with Hearst patterns (Hearst, 1992), both made available by the JoBimText Project (Biemann and Riedl, 2013). When added to the state-of-the-art Berkeley Coreference Resolution System (Durrett and Klein, 2013), these features show a significant positive impact on bridging mentions.

2 Related Work

Our work is very similar to Bansal and Klein (2012), who created, among others, features based on IS-As, distributional clusters, and pronoun contexts. However, we chose to use a DT's list of similar words instead of clustering, and dependency relations as context features instead of N-gram neighborhood. We will compare our approach to Bansal and Klein's features below.

Distributional methods for coreference resolution are mostly pattern-based (Haghighi and Klein, 2009; Kobdani et al., 2011). Recent work by Recasens et al. (2013) used news events as context and exploited rewordings of the same story in different sources.

Semantic similarity for the resolution of bridging mentions has been employed by Poesio et al. (1998), Gasperin et al. (2004), and Versley (2007), yet all three works are applied to oracle anaphoric

Proceedings of Recent Advances in Natural Language Processing, pages 192–199,
Hissar, Bulgaria, Sep 7–9 2015.

mentions, thus not facing spurious mentions, i.e. phrases that are non-referring in the gold standard. Ng (2007) and Lee et al. (2012) made use of Lin's theasurus in a fully-featured system, but with a smaller expansion size (5 and 10 words, respectively).

3 Method

We added our features to the state-of-the-art Berkeley Coreference Resolution System (Durrett and Klein, 2013), which also acts as our baseline. It employs a mention-pair model by assigning each predicted mention a latent antecedent. The probability of a mention m having antecedent a is estimated using a log-linear model and competes with the likelihood of m being non-anaphoric. Features are binary and distinguished between features on mention pairs and features on anaphoricity resp. the candidate antecedent.

For our experiments, we used the system's FINAL feature set. Regarding anaphoricity and the candidate antecedent, it uses the mention's size in words, syntactic uni- and bigrams of the head, as well as lexicalizations of the head, first, last, preceding, and following word as features. Pairwise features are the distance between the two mentions, once as the number of sentences and once as the number of mentions; whether one mention is within the boundaries of the other; whether they belong to the same speaker; the candidate antecedent's number and gender using data by Bergsma and Lin (2006); the syntactic uni- and bigrams of both mentions; mention string match or containment; head string match or containment. See Durrett and Klein (2013) for a detailed description of the feature set.

The Berkeley System expands the feature space by feature conjunctions: If a pairwise feature f fires for current mention m_c and antecedent mention m_a, features $f \wedge \textit{type}(c)$ and $f \wedge \textit{type}(c) \wedge \textit{type}(a)$ are also activated, where type$(\cdot)$ returns a mention type literal based on the head's POS. For pronouns, this is the citation form; for proper and common nouns, PROPER and NOMINAL are returned, respectively.

Our distributional knowledge comes from a DT. Biemann and Riedl (2013) generalized Lin's thesaurus (Lin, 1998) by distinguishing between *terms* (e.g. words) and *context features* (e.g. dependency relations). The *holing operation* @ extracts terms and features from surface text and is used both for training and querying the DT. The DT lists for each term the n semantically most similar terms, where n is the expansion size parameter, and semantic similarity is defined as the number of shared significant contexts.

4 Experimental Setting

We adapted the training and evaluation data and splits from the CoNLL-2011 shared task on coreference resolution (Pradhan et al., 2011), which contains 2,999 documents from the OntoNotes v4.0 corpus (Hovy et al., 2006), and took the number and gender data from the task. Training and testing was performed with predicted mentions on the AUTO set of automatically preprocessed documents. We used the Berkeley System in version 1.0 and a DT created from 120M sentences of news texts ($n = 200$) using a dependency parse holing system (Biemann and Riedl, 2013, 72 f.) and including IS-As clustered into senses (Gliozzo et al., 2013).[1] Its terms are composed of a single word's lemma and its POS tag (e.g. *pact#NN*), while context features are neighbor terms in a dependency parse, complemented by the dependency label and governing direction (e.g. *governing#amod#preliminary#JJ*).

For evaluation, we used the standard coreference metrics MUC (Vilain et al., 1995), B^3 (Bagga and Baldwin, 1998), and $CEAF_e$ (entity/ϕ_4-CEAF; Luo, 2005), as well as their average, computed with the reference scorer v7 (Pradhan et al., 2014).

Additionally, we evaluate precision and recall on *system-bridging mentions*,[2] i.e. mentions that appear as bridging to the system, but not necessarily to a human. Let $\textit{head}(m_i)$ return the predicted head of the i-th mention in a document, $C(m_i)$ be the (gold or system) coreference chain of m_i, and $C^*(m_i) = \langle m_j : m_j \in C(m_i) \wedge j < i \wedge \textit{head}(m_j) \textit{ is a noun}\rangle$ be the sequence of noun antecedents of m_i. A mention m_i is *system-bridging* if head(m_i) is a noun, $C^*(m_i) \neq \emptyset$, and for all $m \in C^*(m_i)$ it holds that $\textit{head}(m) \neq \textit{head}(m_i)$. A bridging mention m_i from the gold chain C_G is a true positive (tp) if m_i and its immediate predecessor from $C^*_G(m_i)$ are members of the same system entity, and a false negative (fn) otherwise.

[1] model downloaded from `http://sourceforge.net/projects/jobimtext/files/data/models/en_news120M_stanford_lemma/`

[2] Our definition is based on *quasi-bridges* from the Berkeley System's source code (Durrett and Klein, 2013).

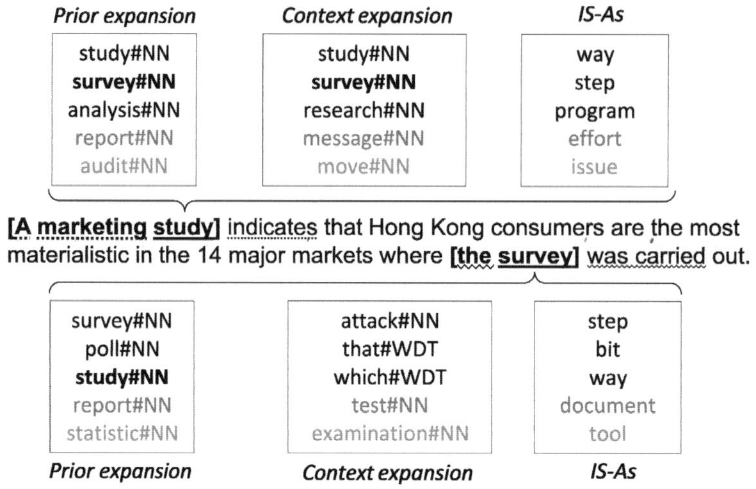

Feature values: PRIOR(t_1,t_2) = 2, PRIOR(t_2,t_1) = 3, SHARED_PRIOR = 0.4, IS-IS-A(t_1,t_2) = false, IS-IS-A(t_2, t_1) = false, SHARED_IS-As = 0.7, IN_C-EXPANSION(t_1, t_2) = 2, IN_C-EXPANSION(t_2, t_1) = 13.

Figure 1: Expansions and feature values for an example pair of bridging mentions from the development set. Dotted and wavy lines indicate dependency relations used in the context expansion.

A mention m_i' is considered a false positive (fp) if it is bridging in the system chain C_S, but is not coreferent with its immediate predecessor from $C_S^*(m_i')$ in the gold standard.

5 Additional Features

We added pairwise features from four different categories to the system, of which the last one (attribute features) is only loosely tied to a DT. Rank-based features have been discretized using equal-width binning (bin size: 20), though values from the interval $[-2, 20]$ were spelt out explicitly. Real values from the interval $[0, 1]$ were discretized by simply rounding to the first decimal digit. In the following feature description, t_1 and t_2 denote the heads of the current and antecedent candidate mention in term form. Each asymmetrical feature has an additional instance with t_1 and t_2 reversed. Furthermore, the function $\text{expansion}(\cdot)$ takes a term as its argument and returns the 200 most similar terms according to the DT. The position of a term t in an expansion is reported by $\text{rank}(t, \cdot)$.

1. **Prior** features target a head word's list of semantically similar terms as returned by the DT's expansion.

- PRIOR: Its value is 0 if $t_1 = t_2$, -2 if $\text{expansion}(t_2) = \emptyset$, -1 if $t_1 \notin \text{expansion}(t_2)$, and $\text{rank}(t_1, \text{expansion}(t_2))$ otherwise.
- SHARED_PRIOR: The overlap of two expansions: $(|\text{expansion}(t_1) \cap \text{expansion}(t_2)|)$ / $\min(|\text{expansion}(t_1)|, |\text{expansion}(t_2)|)$.

2. **IS-A** features operate on open class head words' hypernyms. To keep things simple, we treated all clusters equal.

- IS-IS-A: *True* if t_1 is among any of the IS-As of any cluster of t_2, *false* otherwise.
- SHARED_IS-As: Calculates the Dice index (Dice, 1945) between each IS-A cluster of t_1 and each of t_2 and returns the maximum value.

Since the data contains some noisy IS-As like *bit* (originating from *is a bit*), we added an additional lexicalized feature for SHARED_IS-A = *true* with the shared IS-A that has the highest frequency in the model.

3. A feature targeting the **context** of a mention's head to model selectional preference. For this, we define a context-based expansion (C-expansion). Similar to verb argument expectations (Lenci, 2011), we compose a list of the most likely words appearing in a given context, but do not restrict ourselves to verbs. We exploit the fact that term-context pairs are provided in the JoBimText model (Biemann and Riedl, 2013). Let C be the set of context features of a mention head in the text

		MUC			B^3			$CEAF_e$			
		P	*R*	F_1	*P*	*R*	F_1	*P*	*R*	F_1	*Average*
Development	BASELINE	69.88	63.25	66.40	61.86	52.98	57.08	57.69	54.31	55.95	59.81
	DUMMY	69.81	63.92†	66.74†	61.86	53.74†	57.52†	58.03	55.23†	56.60†	60.28†
	P	69.62	63.98†	66.68†	61.85	53.91†	57.60†	58.11	55.35†	56.69†	60.33†
	PI	69.73	64.12†	66.81†	62.00	54.13†	57.80†	58.24†	55.42†	56.79†	60.47†
	PIC	69.60	64.13†	66.76†	62.00	54.14†	57.81†	57.99	55.56†	56.75†	60.44†
	PICA	69.59	**64.54†**	**66.97†**	61.90	**54.73†**	**58.09†**	**58.31**	**56.04†**	**57.15†**	**60.74†**
	B&K (2012) CO	**70.09**	63.48	66.62	**62.77†**	53.35	57.68†	58.22†	54.69	56.40†	60.23†
	—"— +DUMMY	69.78	64.19†	66.87†	62.23	54.08†	57.87†	58.02	55.21†	56.58†	60.44†
Test	BASELINE	69.69	65.98	67.79	58.68	53.59	56.02	54.31	53.88	54.09	59.30
	PICA	69.17	**66.87†**	**68.00**	57.77	**54.49†**	56.08	**54.45**	**54.44†**	**54.44**	**59.51**
	B&K (2012) CO	69.30	66.11	67.67	58.10	53.62	55.77	54.31	53.63	53.97	59.14
	—"— +DUMMY	68.57	66.56†	67.55	57.12	54.12†	55.58	53.70	53.80	53.75	58.96

Table 1: Metric results achieved by the baseline, dummy setting, and incrementally adding features to the baseline (P = prior expansion, I = IS-A, C = C-expansion and A = attribute features). Also comparing to the Bansal and Klein (2012) co-occurrence feature. Scores with a dagger (†) are significantly better than the BASELINE (paired bootstrap resampling test with $N = 10000$ and $p = 0.05$ (Koehn, 2004)).

and $T = \{t_1, \ldots, t_n\}$ the set of terms for which there exists a $c_j \in C$ such that the pair (t_i, c_j) is a member of the model. We sort the members of T in the descending order of their probability $P(t_i|C)$ and take the first 200 elements as the target term's C-expansion. Defining $P(t_i|C)$, we assume conditional independence and calculate the plus-one-smoothed MLE as $\prod_{c_j \in C}(sig(t_i, c_j) + 1)/(V + \sum sig(*, c_j))$, with $sig(\cdot, \cdot)$ returning the significance value of a term-feature pair stored in the model, and V as the vocabulary size. The coreference feature IN_C-EXPANSION then returns the rank of t_1 in t_2's C-expansion with PRIOR's result semantics. If t_1 is from a closed word class, it is first mapped to the first open word class term from its own C-expansion. Unlike typical takes on selectional preference, we expand all mention heads, not only pronouns, to take their *contextual role* (Bean and Riloff, 2004) into account and to have at least some semantic knowledge for out-of-vocabulary terms.

4. **Attribute** features inspired by Vieira and Poesio (2000, 556 f.;560) guessing properties of mentions from dependency relations in the text. We consider as attributes all words in a copula, appositive, relative clause, or compound relation to a mention's head and added the following features:

- ATTR_PRIOR = $\{$*no attributes*, $-2, \ldots, 200\}$: Expands t_2, looks up each attribute of t_1 in t_2, and reports the best rank as in PRIOR.
- ATTR_IS-IS-A = $\{$*true*,*false*$\}$: Its value is *true* if t_1 is among any IS-A set of any attribute of t_2, *false* otherwise. If *true*, adds an additional version with the lexicalized IS-A.

Figure 1 illustrates the first three feature groups by means of a sentence from the development set. While the baseline treats those mentions as separate entities, our distributional features lead to their correct resolution.

6 Results

We present the results[3] of the modifications in Table 1. We also compare to a dummy system with the full feature set whose prior expansions return the identity, while the C-expansion and IS-A clusters are empty. This system profits from lemmatization as well as the syntactic clues provided by the attribute features.

While the BASELINE was unable to solve the introductory example, the distributional features provide the system enough confidence in assigning the mentions with the non-identical heads *pact* and *agreement* to the same entity. C-expansions had only low impact on performance. In a manual analysis, we observed many cases in which the sematically less preferable antecedent was selected, or in which non-coreferent pronouns were assigned to an entity, for example linking *you* in

[3]differences to reported scores in (Durrett and Klein, 2013) due to corrections of errors in the scoring script, see (Pradhan et al., 2014)

Thank you for your visit to a previous occurrence of *God* because of the common phrase *Thank God*. In comparison to PI, the recall on singleton pronouns decreased by 1 point, while the pairwise recall on anaphoric pronouns increased only by 0.4 points.

The final results on the test set in Table 1 were obtained by training on the conjunction of training and development data. We sacrifice some precision for better recall. Unfortunately, the increase in average F1 is not significant.

For comparison, we also integrated the feature set by Bansal and Klein (2012), computed on the Google Web N-gram corpus (Brants and Franz, 2006), into the Berkeley system. It includes the following features: *General co-occurrence* targets the general frequency of two head words appearing near to each other. *Hearst* works like our IS-IS-A feature. *Entity-based context* collects lists of seeds y in the pattern `h (is|are|was|were) (a|an|the)? y` in decreasing order of frequency, and reports whether there is a match in the top k seeds of the two head words. It also returns the dominant POS of the matched words. *Pronoun context* substitutes pronouns with their antecedent and estimates the likelihood of the new sequence. Finally, the *cluster* feature returns the sum of the earliest match positions of the two headwords' cluster ID lists, using phrasal clusters obtained by Lin et al. (2010).

We experimented with different permutations of these features, including the sets proposed in Bansal and Klein (2012), but found a set containing only the co-occurrence feature to perform best with regards to the average metrics score.[4] The results can be found in Table 1 noted as *B&K*. Remarkably, the feature rather increases precision than recall. The cluster feature led to a performance decrease already on the development set. This may stem from the many semantically unrelated word pairs, like *swords – elephants* or *definition – horror*, which share the same top cluster.

The models' results on bridging mentions are displayed in Table 2. We outperformed the baseline on both sets (F1 increased on test by 8.29 points). The positive impact on the metric scores is minor though, since only 7.6% of all mentions in the development set are bridging.

Again, we compare to the Bansal and Klein (2012) features, this time choosing the set performing best with regards to bridging mentions, which contains all features except *pronoun context*, which achieved an increase of 3.69 absolute F1 points on the test set. To assess whether these features are subsumed by our set or provide additional value, we also show the results of combining both in Table 2. The decrease in precision on the test set suggests that the Web features introduce too much noise to the system.

Bridging	P	R	F_1
BASELINE-Dev	36.21	15.51	21.72
DUMMY-Dev	41.36	17.45	24.55
PICA-Dev	**44.87**	23.82	31.12
B&K (2012)*-Dev	39.15	19.67	26.18
B&K (2012)*+Dummy-Dev	42.81	21.98	29.04
B&K (2012)*+PICA-Dev	44.19	**24.56**	**31.57**
BASELINE-Test	38.06	17.32	23.81
PICA-Test	39.47	27.05	**32.10**
B&K (2012)*-Test	37.97	21.56	27.50
B&K (2012)*+PICA-Test	36.84	**27.33**	31.38

Table 2: Precision, recall and F_1 scores on bridging mentions. Bolded improvements are significant over the baseline ($p = 0.05, N = 10000$).

7 Error Analysis

Error	BASELINE	PICA	Δ
Span	**399**	404	+5
Conflated entities	**1303**	1319	+16
Divided entities	1626	**1593**	-33
Extra entities	**521**	559	+38
Missing entities	881	**820**	-61
Extra mention	**577**	618	+41
Missing mention	862	**842**	-20

Table 3: Development set error counts comparison

As shown by an automatic classification of errors by the Berkeley Coreference Analyser (Kummerfeld and Klein, 2013) in Table 3, our system is prone to create spurious entities and mentions. The problem arises from semantic relations in the DT that are actually indicators of non-coreference (e.g. antonymy, co-hyponymy), but nevertheless ranked high. The similarity measure does not differentiate between these relations. This produced links like *Taipei – South Korea* and *the men – the women*. Since the hypothesis that a mention is non-referring has low probability if it begins with a determiner, the system desperately "searches" for an antecedent. Because of our semantic features, the system achieves higher confidence in

[4]For binning, we tried bin sizes 1, 0.5, and 0.25. For the entity features, we tried $k \in \{10, 20, 50, 100, 200\}$.

	ACR	ATT	CAN	DAT	DISC	HEAD	HYP	TATT	LEM	MET	SYN	INV	$\sum$
BASELINE	2	77	0	2	1	26	46	0	0	6	5	3	
PICA	3	99	1	3	4	31	97	1	1	6	9	3	
Total	23	235	50	32	171	58	409	13	10	38	32	12	1083

Table 4: Comparison of the numbers of resolved bridging mentions in the development set, broken down per type.

linking mentions with diverse heads if they bear at least some semantic similarity, creating spurious chains, which is punished by MUC and B^3 precision.

This intuition is backed by a manual analysis we conducted on 100 random errors not made by the baseline. When examining each of the system's antecedent decisions and their weights, we found that 23% of the wrong links were chosen because of distributional semantics features. The majority of these semantic errors were triggered by the PRIOR feature, whereas only one of them could be ascribed to the IS-A feature. Here, the recall-oriented clustering of IS-As in the DT (Gliozzo et al., 2013) produced an incorrect hypernymic relation between *Chaidamun Basin* and *the country*.

We classified the 1083 bridging mentions from the development set according to the knowledge required for resolution or their semantic relationship with a previous mention into the following categories:

ACR One head is an acronym of the other.

ATT One head is an attribute of the other as defined in Section 5.

CAN One head is in a CAN-BE relationship with the other, e.g. *pilot* and *man*.

DAT Temporal deixis like *today – the 30th*. We attribute the low recall of this class to the fact that the Berkeley system's FINAL feature set does not make use of named entity labels.

DISC Bridging mentions requiring textual entailment techniques, e.g. *my mother* and *Thelma Wahl*, sophisticated world knowledge as in the case of *Martha Stewart – the comeback queen*, or a discourse model to identify speakers or deixis.

HEAD Both heads are identical, but the system's head detection made a mistake. A large portion of these cases were Asian names, where the family name precedes the first name, and thus a strategy selecting the last word falls flat.

HYP The head of one mention is a hyponym of the other.

TATT Transitive attributes, i.e. one head is a hypernym, hyponym, acronym or synonym of one of the other mention's attributes, e.g. *Doctor Hunter* and *the physician*.

LEM Both heads have the same lemma.

MET The heads are in a metonymous relationship, e.g. *the Japanese government* and *Japan*.

SYN The heads are synonyms or near-synonyms, e.g. *dad* and *father*. This class also contains spelling variants and typos of proper names.

INV Invalid: At least one mention's head is a pronoun, but does not have the appropriate POS tag.

The results of both systems are shown in Table 4. Except for INV and MET, we increased the number of recalled mentions across all types. Hypernymic relationships form the largest class, making up more than a third of all system bridges in the development set. This was also the category with the strongest improvement: the number of recalled mentions doubled from 46 to 97 (23.7% of class size). We found that IS-A features are not solely responsible for this increase. For example, IS_IS-A did not fire for the links *a marketing study – the survey*, *the balloting – the elections* and *the insurrection – the Oct. 3 failed coup in Panama*, which were resolved thanks to the prior expansion. On the other hand, bridging mentions with attributes in transitive relationships, which inspired our attribute features, form only a small class with 13 members, from which we resolved 1 (baseline: 0).

8 Conclusion and Outlook

We have shown that our DT-based approach adds more than double the amount of absolute F1 points on bridging mentions in the test set than the semantic features described by Bansal and Klein (2012). However, undesired semantic relations present in the DT lead to a decrease in general resolution precision. A possible solution are asymmetrical *directional similarity measures* (Lenci, 2014) which bring preferred semantical relations to the top of the expansion, thus allowing the system to assign higher weights to these ranks. Also, classifiers using entity-mention or ranking models may profit from directly comparing ranks instead of learning separate weights like in the case of the Berkeley system's mention-pair model. While our results confirm that introducing semantic features in a coreference system is an "uphill battle" (Durrett and Klein, 2013), we have shown positive impact on a hard class of coreference using automatically acquired semantic information instead of manually constructed lexical resources. This will enable more domain-adaptive coreference resolution systems in the future, as well as open up avenues for adding semantic features for low-resourced languages.

Acknowledgment

This work has been supported by the German Federal Ministry of Education and Research (BMBF) within the context of the Software Campus project LiCoRes under grant No. 01IS12054.

References

Amit Bagga and Breck Baldwin. 1998. Algorithms for scoring coreference chains. In *Proc. Linguistic Coreference Workshop at LREC*, pages 563–566, Granada, Spain.

Mohit Bansal and Dan Klein. 2012. Coreference semantics from web features. In *Proc. ACL*, pages 389–398, Jeju Island, Korea.

David Bean and Ellen Riloff. 2004. Unsupervised learning of contextual role knowledge for coreference resolution. In *Proc. NAACL*, pages 297–304.

Shane Bergsma and Dekang Lin. 2006. Bootstrapping path-based pronoun resolution. In *Proc. ACL*, pages 33–40, Sydney, Australia.

Chris Biemann and Martin Riedl. 2013. Text: Now in 2D! A framework for lexical expansion with contextual similarity. *Journal of Language Modelling*, 1(1):55–95.

Thorsten Brants and Alex Franz. 2006. The Google Web 1T 5-gram corpus version 1.1. *LDC2006T13*.

Lee R. Dice. 1945. Measures of the amount of ecologic association between species. *Ecology*, 26(3):297–302.

Greg Durrett and Dan Klein. 2013. Easy victories and uphill battles in coreference resolution. In *Proc. EMNLP*, pages 1971–1982, Seattle, WA, USA.

Caroline Gasperin, Susanne Salmon-Alt, and Renata Vieira. 2004. How useful are similarity word lists for indirect anaphora resolution? In *Proc. DAARC*, S. Miguel, Azores, Portugal.

Alfio Gliozzo, Chris Biemann, Martin Riedl, Bonaventura Coppola, Michael R. Glass, and Matthew Hatem. 2013. JoBimText Visualizer: A graph-based approach to contextualizing distributional similarity. In *Proc. 8th TextGraphs at EMNLP*, Seattle, WA, USA.

Aria Haghighi and Dan Klein. 2009. Simple coreference resolution with rich syntactic and semantic features. In *Proc. EMNLP*, pages 1152–1161, Singapore.

Zellig S. Harris. 1954. Distributional structure. *Word*, 10(2-3):146–162.

Marti A. Hearst. 1992. Automatic acquisition of hyponyms from large text corpora. In *Proc. COLING*, volume 2, pages 539–545, Nantes, France.

Eduard Hovy, Mitchell Marcus, Martha Palmer, Lance Ramshaw, and Ralph Weischedel. 2006. OntoNotes: The 90% solution. In *Proc. NAACL-HLT*, pages 57–60, New York, NY, USA.

Hamidreza Kobdani, Hinrich Schütze, Michael Schiehlen, and Hans Kamp. 2011. Bootstrapping coreference resolution using word associations. In *Proc. ACL*, volume 1, pages 783–792, Portland, OR, USA.

Philipp Koehn. 2004. Statistical significance tests for machine translation evaluation. In *Proc. EMNLP*, pages 388–395, Barcelona, Spain.

Jonathan K. Kummerfeld and Dan Klein. 2013. Error-driven analysis of challenges in coreference resolution. In *Proc. EMNLP*, Seattle, WA, USA.

Heeyoung Lee, Yves Peirsman, Angel Chang, Nathanael Chambers, Mihai Surdeanu, and Dan Jurafsky. 2011. Stanford's multi-pass sieve coreference resolution system at the CoNLL-2011 shared task. In *Proc. CoNLL: Shared Task*, pages 28–34, Portland, OR, USA.

Heeyoung Lee, Marta Recasens, Angel Chang, Mihai Surdeanu, and Dan Jurafsky. 2012. Joint entity and event coreference resolution across documents. In *Proc. EMNLP-CoNLL*, pages 489–500, Jeju, Korea.

Alessandro Lenci. 2011. Composing and updating verb argument expectations: A distributional semantic model. In *Proc. CMCL*, pages 58–66, Portland, OR, USA.

Alessandro Lenci. 2014. Will distributional semantics ever become semantic? Talk at the 7th International Global WordNet Conference, Tartu, Estonia. `http://gwc2014.ut.ee/lenci_distributional_semantics_gwc2014.pdf`.

Dekang Lin, Kenneth Ward Church, Heng Ji, Satoshi Sekine, David Yarowsky, Shane Bergsma, Kailash Patil, Emily Pitler, Rachel Lathbury, Vikram Rao, et al. 2010. New tools for web-scale n-grams. In *Proc. LREC*, Valletta, Malta.

Dekang Lin. 1998. Automatic retrieval and clustering of similar words. In *Proc. COLING*, volume 2, pages 768–774, Montreal, QC, Canada.

Xiaoqiang Luo. 2005. On coreference resolution performance metrics. In *Proc. HLT-EMNLP*, pages 25–32, Vancouver, BC, Canada.

Vincent Ng. 2007. Shallow semantics for coreference resolution. In *Proc. IJCAI*, pages 1689–1694, Hyderabad, India.

Massimo Poesio, Sabine Schulte im Walde, and Chris Brew. 1998. Lexical clustering and definite description interpretation. In *Proc. AAAI Spring Symposium on Learning for Discourse*, pages 82–89, Stanford, CA, USA.

Massimo Poesio, Rahul Mehta, Axel Maroudas, and Janet Hitzeman. 2004. Learning to resolve bridging references. In *Proc. ACL*, Barcelona, Spain.

Simone Paolo Ponzetto and Michael Strube. 2006. Exploiting semantic role labeling, WordNet and Wikipedia for coreference resolution. In *Proc. NAACL-HLT*, pages 192–199, New York, NY, USA.

Sameer Pradhan, Lance Ramshaw, Mitchell Marcus, Martha Palmer, Ralph Weischedel, and Nianwen Xue. 2011. CoNLL-2011 shared task: Modeling unrestricted coreference in OntoNotes. In *Proc. CoNLL*, pages 1–27, Portland, OR, USA.

Sameer Pradhan, Xiaoqiang Luo, Marta Recasens, Eduard Hovy, Vincent Ng, and Michael Strube. 2014. Scoring coreference partitions of predicted mentions: A reference implementation. In *Proc. ACL*, pages 22–27, Baltimore, MD, USA.

Marta Recasens, Matthew Can, and Daniel Jurafsky. 2013. Same referent, different words: Unsupervised mining of opaque coreferent mentions. In *Proc. HLT-NAACL*, pages 897–906, Atlanta, GA, USA.

Yannick Versley. 2007. Antecedent selection techniques for high-recall coreference resolution. In *Proc. EMNLP-CoNLL*, pages 496–505, Prague, Czech Republic.

Renata Vieira and Massimo Poesio. 2000. An empirically based system for processing definite descriptions. *Computational Linguistics*, 26(4):539–593.

Marc Vilain, John Burger, John Aberdeen, Dennis Connolly, and Lynette Hirschman. 1995. A model-theoretic coreference scoring scheme. In *Proc. MUC-6*, pages 45–52, Columbia, MD, USA.

Huiwei Zhou, Yao Li, Degen Huang, Yan Zhang, Chunlong Wu, and Yuansheng Yang. 2011. Combining syntactic and semantic features by SVM for unrestricted coreference resolution. In *Proc. CoNLL: Shared Task*, pages 66–70, Portland, OR, USA.

Text Classification into Abstract Classes Based on Discourse Structure

Boris Galitsky
Knowledge Trail Inc.
San-Francisco, USA
bgalitsky@hotmail.com

Dmitry Ilvovsky
National Research University Higher School of Economics, Moscow, Russia
dilvovsky@hse.ru

Sergey O. Kuznetsov
National Research University Higher School of Economics, Moscow, Russia
skuznetsov@hse.ru

Abstract

The problem of classifying text with respect to belonging to a document or a meta-document is formulated and its application areas are proposed. An algorithm is proposed for document classification tasks where counts of words is insufficient do differentiate between such abstract classes of text as metalanguage and object-level. We extend the parse tree kernel method from the level of individual sentences towards the level of paragraphs, based on anaphora, rhetoric structure relations and communicative actions linking phrases in different sentences. Tree kernel learning technique is applied to these extended trees to leverage of additional discourse-related information. We evaluate our approach in the domain of action-plan documents.

1 Introduction

Solving text classification problems, keywords and their topicality usually suffice. These features provide abundant information to determine a topic of a text or document, such as apple vs banana, or adventures vs relaxing travel. At the same time, there is a number of document classification domains where distinct classes have similar words. In this case, style, phrasings and other kinds of text structure information need to be leveraged. To perform text classification in such domains, one needs to employ discourse information such as anaphora, rhetoric structure, entity synonymy and ontology, if available (Wu et al., 2011).

In this study, an issue of classifying a text with respect to being metalanguage or language object is addressed. We are concerned with differentiating between object-level documents, which inform us on how to do things, or how something has been done, and meta-documents, specifying how to write a document which explains how to do things, or how things have been done. Metalanguage is a symbolic system intended to express information, or analyze another language or symbolic system. In a natural language document, metalanguage is used as a special expressive means to ascend to the desired level of abstraction. To automatically recognize metalanguage patterns in text, one needs some implicit signals at the syntactic level. Naturally, just using keyword statistics is insufficient to differentiate between texts in metalanguage and language-object.

A presence of verbs for speech acts and mental states (such as knowing) may help to identify metalanguage patterns, but is an unreliable criterion: *I know the location of the highest mountain* vs *I know what he thinks about the highest mountain in the world*. The latter sentence contains a meta-predicate *think (who, about-what)* with the second variable ranging over a set of (object-level) expressions for thoughts about the *highest mountain*. Relying on syntactic parse trees would provide us with specific expressions and phrasings connected with a metalanguage. However, it will still be insufficient for a thorough description of linguistic features inherent to a metalanguage. It is hard to identify such features without employing a discourse structure of a document. This discourse structure needs to include anaphora, rhetoric relations, and interaction scenarios by means of communicative language (Galitsky and Kuznetsov, 2008). Furthermore, to systematically learn these discourse features associated with metalanguage, and differentiate them from the ones for language-object, one needs a unified approach to classify graph structures at the level of paragraphs (Galitsky et al., 2013).

The design of such features for automated learning of syntactic and discourse structures for classification is still done manually today. To overcome this problem, tree kernel approach has been proposed (Cumby and Roth, 2003). Tree kernels constructed over syntactic parse trees, as well as discourse trees (Galitsky et al., 2015) is one of the solutions to conduct feature engineer-

Proceedings of Recent Advances in Natural Language Processing, pages 200–207,
Hissar, Bulgaria, Sep 7–9 2015.

ing. Convolution tree kernel (Collins and Duffy, 2002; Haussler, 1999) defines a feature space consisting of all subtree types of parse trees and counts the number of common subtrees to express the respective distance in the feature space. They have found a broad range of applications in NLP tasks such as syntactic parsing re-ranking, relation extraction (Zhang et al., 2008), named entity recognition (Cumby and Roth, 2003), pronoun resolution (Kong and Zhou, 2011), question classification, and machine translation.

The kernel ability to generate large feature sets is useful to assure we have enough linguistic features to differentiate between the classes, to quickly model new and not well understood linguistic phenomena in learning machines. However, it is often possible to manually design features for linear kernels that produce high accuracy and fast computation time whereas the complexity of tree kernels may prevent their application in real scenarios. SVM (Vapnik, 1995) can work directly with kernels by replacing the dot product with a particular kernel function. This useful property of kernel methods, that implicitly calculates the dot product in a high-dimensional space over the original representations of objects such as sentences, has made kernel methods an effective solution to modeling structured linguistic objects (Moschitti, 2006).

An approach to build a kernel based on more than a single parse tree for search has been proposed (Galitsky et al., 2015). To perform classification based on additional discourse features, we form a single tree from a tree forest for a sequence of sentences in a paragraph of text.

A number of NLP tasks such as classification require computing of semantic features over paragraphs of text containing multiple sentences. Doing it at the level of individual sentences and then summing up the score for sentences will not always work. In the complex classification tasks where classes are defined in an abstract way, the difference between them may lay at the paragraph level and not at the level of individual sentences. In the case where classes are defined not via topics but instead via writing style, discourse structure signals become essential. Moreover, some information about entities can be distributed across sentences, and classification approach needs to be independent of this distribution. We will demonstrate the contribution of paragraph-level approach vs the sentence level in our evaluation.

2 Text Classification Based on Discourse Text Structure

2.1 The domain of documents and meta-documents

Our first example of the use of meta-language is the following text shared by an upset customer, doing his best to have a bank to correct an error: *The customer representative acknowledged that the only thing he is authorized to do is to inform me that he is not authorized to do anything.*
This is a good example for how people describe *thinking about thinking*. In this example, bank operations can be described in language-object, and bank employee's authorizations to perform these operations are actually described in meta-language. Here a document on banking operations is an object-level document, and authorization rules document is a meta-document relative to the operations document. The claim of this work is that this classification can be performed based on text analysis only without any knowledge of banking industry.

We define an ***action-plan*** (object-level) document as a document which contains a thorough and well-structured description of how to build a particular system or work of art, from engineering to natural sciences to creative art. According to our definition, action-plan document follows the reproducibility criteria of a patent or research publication; however format might deviate significantly. One can read such document and being proficient in the knowledge domain, can build such a system or work of art.

Conversely, a meta-document is a document explaining how to write object-level, action-plan documents. They include manuals, standard action-plan documents should adhere to, tutorials on how to improve them, and others.

We need to differentiate action-plan documents from the classes of documents which can be viewed as ones containing meta-language, whereas the genuine action-plan documents consists of the language-object patterns and should not include metalanguage ones. As to the examples of meta-documents, they include design requirements, project requirement document, operational requirements, design guidelines, design guides, tutorials, design templates (template for technical design document, research papers on system design, educational materials on system design, resume of a design professional, and others.

Naturally, action-plan documents are different from similar kinds of documents on the same topic in terms of style and phrasing. To extract these features, rhetoric relations are essential. Notice that meta-documents can contain object-level text, such as design examples. Object level documents (genuine action-plan docs) can contain some author reflections on the system design process (which are written in metalanguage). Hence the boundary between classes does not strictly separates metalanguage and language object. We use statistical language learning to optimize such boundary, having supplied it with a rich set of linguistic features up to the discourse structures. In the design document domain, we will differentiate between texts expressed mostly via meta-language and the ones mostly in language-object.

2.2 Discourse Structure of a Document

It turns out that sentence-level tree kernels are insufficient for classification in our domains. Since important phrases can be distributed through different sentences, one needs a sentence boundary – independent way of extracting both syntactic and discourse features. Therefore we intend to combine/merge parse trees to make sure we cover all the phrase of interest. Let us analyze the following text with respect of belonging to a document or meta-document.

This document describes the design of back end processor. Its requirements are enumerated below.

From the first sentence, it looks like an action-plan document. To process the second sentence, we need to disambiguate the preposition 'its'. As a result, we conclude from the second sentence that it is a requirements document, not an object-level action-plan one.

The structure of a document which can be potentially valuable for classification can be characterized by rhetoric relations that hold between the parts of a text. These relations, such as explanations or contrast, are important for text understanding in general since they contain information on how these parts of text are related to each other to form a coherent discourse. Naturally, we expect the structure of discourse for meta-language text patterns to be different to that of language-object text patterns.

Rhetorical Structure Theory, or RST (Mann, and Thompson, 1988; Mann et al., 1992; Marcu, 1997) is one of the most popular approaches to model extra-sentence as well as intra-sentence discourse. RST represents texts by labeled hierarchical structures, called Discourse Trees (DTs). The leaves of a DT correspond to contiguous Elementary Discourse Units (EDUs). Adjacent EDUs are connected by rhetorical relations (e.g., Elaboration, Contrast), forming larger discourse units (represented by internal nodes), which in turn are also subject to this relation linking. Discourse units linked by a rhetorical relation are further distinguished based on their relative importance in the text: nucleus being the central part, whereas satellite being the peripheral one. Discourse analysis in RST involves two subtasks: discourse segmentation is the task of identifying the EDUs, and discourse parsing is the task of linking the discourse units into a labeled tree. Discourse analysis explores how meanings can be built up in a communicative process, which varies between a text metalanguage and a text language-object. Each part of a text has a specific role in conveying the overall message of a given text.

For our classification tasks, just an analysis of a text structure can suffice for proper classification. Given a positive sequence

A hardware system contains classes such as GUI for user interface, IO for importing and exporting data between the emulator and environment, and Emulator for the actual process control. Furthermore, a class Modules is required which contains all instances of modules in use by emulation process.

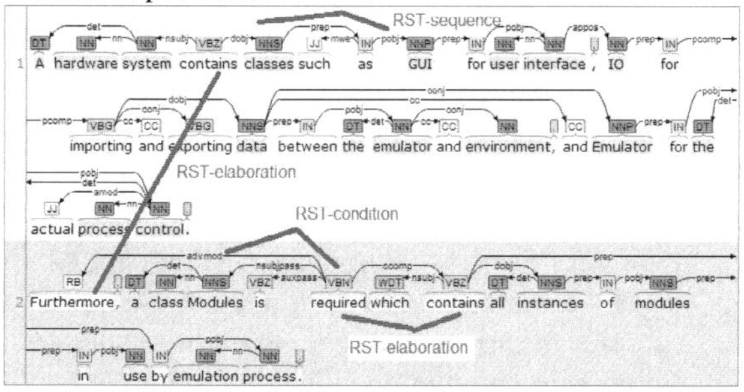

and a negative sequence

A socio-technical system is a social system sitting upon a technical base. Email is a simple example of such system. The term socio-technical was introduced in the 1950s by the Tavistok Institute.

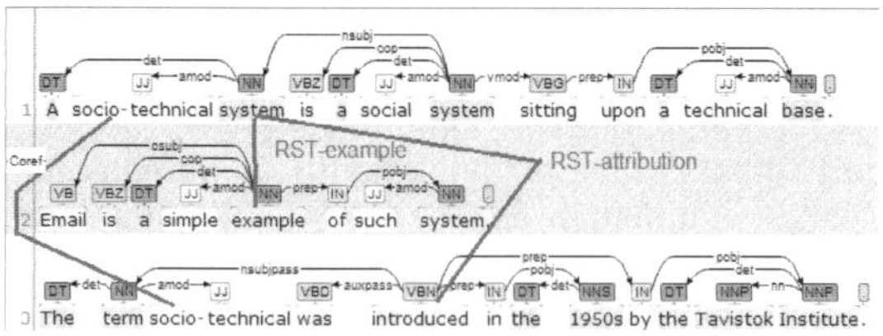

We want to classify the paragraph

A social network-based software ticket reservation system includes the following components.

They are the Database for storing transactions, Web Forms for user data input, and Business rule processor for handling the web forms. Additionally, the backend email processing includes the components for nightly transaction execution.

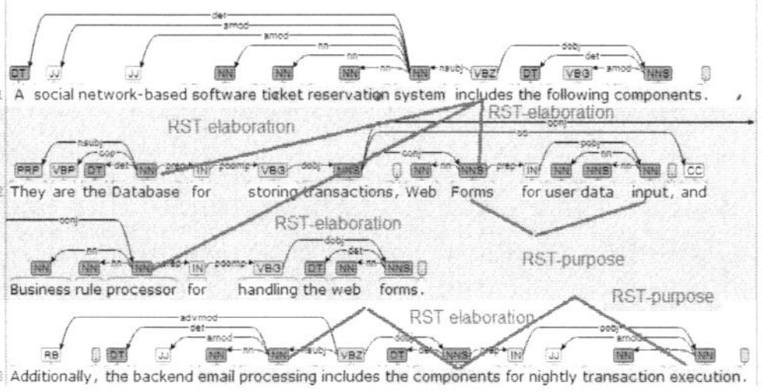

One can see that it follows the rhetoric structure of the top (positive) training set element, although it shares more common keywords with the bottom (negative) element. Hence we classify it as an action-plan document, being an object-level text, since it describes the system rather than introduces a terms (as the negative element does).

2.3 Anaphora and Rhetoric Relations for Classification Task

We introduce a classification problem where keyword and even phrase-based features are insufficient. This is due to the variability of ways information can be communicated in multiple sentences, and variations in possible discourse structures of text which needs to be taken into account.

We consider an example of text classification problem, where short portions of text belong to two classes:

- Tax liability of a landlord renting office to a business.
- Tax liability of a business owner renting an office from landlord.

I rent an office space. This office is for my business. I can deduct office rental expense from my business profit to calculate net income.

To run my business, I have to rent an office. The net business profit is calculated as follows. Rental expense needs to be subtracted from revenue.

To store goods for my retail business I rent some space. When I calculate the net income, I take revenue and subtract business expenses such as office rent.

I rent out a first floor unit of my house to a travel business. I need to add the rental income to my profit. However, when I repair my house, I can deduct the repair expense from my rental income.

I receive rental income from my office. I have to claim it as a profit in my tax forms. I need to add my rental income to my profits, but subtract rental expenses such as repair from it.

I advertised my property as a business rental. Advertisement and repair expenses can be subtracted from the rental income. Remaining rental income needs to be added to my profit and be reported as taxable profit.

Note that keyword-based analysis does not help to separate the first three paragraph and the second three paragraphs. They all share the same keywords *rental/office/income/profit/add/subtract.* Phrase-based analysis does not help, since both sets of paragraphs share similar phrases.

Secondly, pair-wise sentence comparison does not solve the problem either. Anaphora resolution is helpful but insufficient. All these sentences include '*I*' and its mention, but other links between words or phrases in different sentences need to be used.

Rhetoric structures need to come into play to provide additional links between sentences. The structure to distinguish between

renting for yourself and deducting from total income and

renting to someone and adding to income embraces multiple sentences. The second clause about *adding/subtracting incomes* is linked by means of the rhetoric relation of *elaboration* with the first clause for *landlord/tenant*. This rhetoric relation may link discourse units within a sentence, between consecutive sentences and even between first and third sentence in a paragraph. Other rhetoric relations can play similar role for forming essential links for text classification.

Which representations for these paragraphs of text would produce such common sub-structure between the structures of these paragraphs? We believe that extended trees, which include the first, second, and third sentence for each paragraph together can serve as a structure to differentiate the two above classes. The dependency parse trees for the first text in our set and its coreferences are shown below.

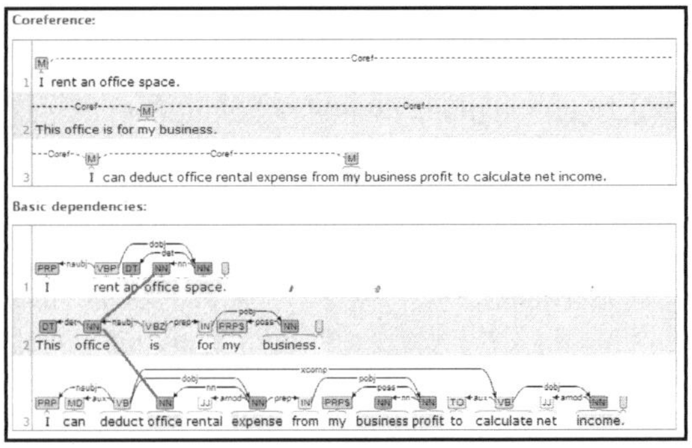

There are multiple ways the nodes from parse trees of different sentences can be connected: we choose the rhetoric relation of elaboration which links the same entity office and helps us to form the structure *rent-office-space – for-my-business – deduct-rental-expense* which is the base for our classification.

We show the resultant extended tree with the root *'I'* from the first sentence.

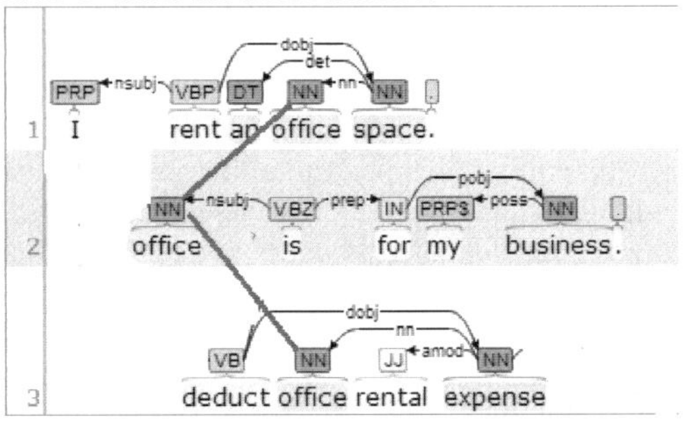

It includes the whole first sentence, a verb phrase from the second sentence and a verb phrase from the third sentence according to rhetoric relation of elaboration. Notice that this extended tree can be intuitively viewed as representing the 'main idea' of this text compared to other texts in our set. All extended trees need to be formed for a text and then compared with that of the other texts, since we don't know in advance which extended tree is essential. From the standpoint of tree kernel learning, extended trees are learned the same way as regular parse trees.

2.4 Learning on Extended Trees

For every inter-sentence arc which connects two parse trees, we derive the extension of these trees, extending branches according to the arc (Fig. 1).

In this approach, for a given parse tree, we will obtain a set of its extension, so the elements of kernel will be computed for many extensions, instead of just a single tree. The problem here is that we need to find common sub-trees for a much higher number of trees than the number of sentences in text, however by subsumption (sub-tree relation) the number of common sub-trees will be substantially reduced.

If we have two parse trees P_1 and P_2 for two sentences in a paragraph, and a relation R_{12}: $P_{1i} \rightarrow P_{2j}$ between the nodes P_{1i} and P_{2j}, we form the pair of extended trees $P_1 * P_2$:

$\ldots, P_{1i-2}, P_{1i-1}, P_{1i}, P_{2j}, P_{2j+1}, P_{2j+2}, \ldots$

$\ldots, P_{2j-2}, P_{2j-1}, P_{2j}, P_{1i}, P_{1i+1}, P_{2i+2}, \ldots,$

which would form the feature set for tree kernel learning in addition to the original trees P_1 and P_2.

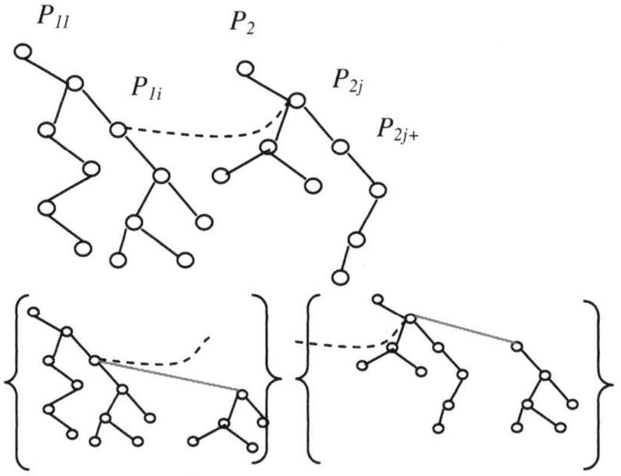

Fig. 1: An arc which connects two parse trees for two sentences in a text (on the top) and the derived set of extended trees (on the bottom).

The algorithm for building an extended tree for a set of parse trees T is presented below:

Input:
1) Set of parse trees T.
2) Set of relations R, which includes relations R_{ijk} between the nodes of T_i and T_j: $T_i \in T$, $T_j \in T$, $R_{ijk} \in R$. We use index k to range over multiple relations between the nodes of a parse tree for a pair of sentences.

Output: the exhaustive set of extended trees E.

Set $E = \varnothing$;
For each tree i=1:$|T|$
  For each relation R_{ijk}, k= 1: |R|
    Obtain T_j
    Form the pair of extended trees $T_i * T_j$;
    Verify that each of the extended trees do not have a super-tree in E
      If verified, add to E;
Return E.

Notice that the resultant trees are not the proper parse trees for a sentence, but nevertheless form an adequate feature space for tree kernel learning.

There are the following processing steps used in our classifier. Each paragraph of a document is subject to sentence splitting, part-of-speech tagging, dependency parsing and chunking. We also rely on additional tags to extend SVM feature space, finding similarities between trees. These additional tags include noun entities from Stanford NLP such as organization and title, and verb types from VerbNet. We then produce a graph-based representation for a document, applying anaphora and RST parser (Joty et al., 2012, 2013, 2014) for inter-sentence relations. To obtain the anaphora links, we employ coreferences from Stanford NLP (Lee et al., 2013; Recasens et al., 2013).

3 Evaluation

For the action-plan document domain, we formed a set of 940 action-plan documents from the web. We also compiled the set of meta- documents on similar engineering topics, mostly containing the same keywords. The list of documents obtained from the web is available at https://code.google.com/p/relevance-based-on-parse-trees/source/browse/src/test/resources/tree_kernel/action-plan-doc-list.csv. We split the data into 3 subsets for training/evaluation portions and cross-validation (Kohavi, 1995).

Table 1. Evaluation results.

Method	Precision	Recall	F-measure
*Nearest neighbor classifier (TF*IDF based)*	53.9	62	57.67+-0.62
Naive Bayesian classifier	55.3	59.7	57.42+-0.84
Tree kernel – regular parse trees	71.4	76.9	74.05+-0.55
Tree kernel SVM – extended trees for anaphora	77.8	81.4	79.56+-0.70
Tree kernel SVM – extended trees for RST	80.1	80.5	80+-1.03
Tree kernel SVM – extended trees for both anaphora and RST	**83.3**	**83.6**	**83.45+-0.78**

Table 1 shows evaluation results. Each row shows the results of the baseline classification methods, such as keyword statistics (Croft et al., 2008; Sulton and Buckley, 1998), Nearest-Neighbor classification and Naïve Bayes approach (Moore and Boyer, 1991; John and Langley, 1995).

Baseline approaches show rather low performance. The one of the tree kernel based methods improves as the sources of linguistic properties are expanded. For both domains, there is an improvement by a few percent due to the rhetoric relations compared with the baseline tree kernel SVM which employs parse trees only. For the literature documents, the role of anaphora is lower than for technical ones.

4 Discussion and Conclusions

In this study we addressed the issue of how semantic discourse features assist with solving such abstract classification problem as differentiating between natural language-object and natural meta-language. We demonstrated that the problem of such level of abstraction can nevertheless be dealt with statistical learning allowing automated feature engineering. Evaluation domain is selected so that the only differences between classes are in phrasing and discourse structures (not in keywords). We also demonstrated that both of these structures are learnable.

We draw the comparison with two following sets of linguistic features: (1) *The baseline set, parse trees for individual sentences*, and (2) *Parse trees and discourse information* and showed that the enhanced set indeed improves the classification performance for the same learning framework. One can see that the baseline text classification approaches does not perform well in the classification domain as abstract and complicated as recognizing metalanguage.

We considered the following sources of relations between words in sentences: coreferences, taxonomic relations such as sub-entity, partial case, predicates for subject etc., rhetoric structure relations, and dialogue structure. A number of NLP tasks including search relevance can be improved if search results are subject to confirmation by discourse structure plus syntactic structure generalization, when answers occur in multiple sentences. In this study we employed coreferences and rhetoric relation only to identify correlation with the occurrence of metalanguage in text. Although phrase-level analysis allows extraction of weak correlation with metalanguage in text, ascend to discourse structures makes detection of metalanguage more reliable. In our evaluation setting, using discourse improved the classification F-measure by 5.5 – 8.6% depending on a classification sub-domain.

There is a strong disattachment between modern text learning approaches and text discourse theories. Usually, learning of linguistic structures in NLP tasks is limited to keyword forms and frequencies. On the other hand, most theories of semantic discourse are not computational in nature. In this work we attempted to achieve the best of both worlds: learn complete parse tree information augmented with an adjustment of discourse theory allowing computational treatment.

In this paper, we used extended parse trees instead of regular ones, leveraging available discourse information, for text classification. This work describes one of the first applications of tree kernel to industrial scale NLP tasks. The advantage of this approach is that the manual thorough analysis of text can be avoided for complex text classification tasks where the classes are as high-level as documents vs meta-documents. The reason of the satisfactory performance of the proposed classification method is a robustness of statistical learning algorithms to noisy and inconsistent features extracted from documents.

The experimental environment, extended tree learning functionality and the evaluation framework are available at http://code.google.com/p/relevance-based-on-parse-trees.

Acknowledgements

This work was carried out by the authors within the project "Data mining based on applied ontologies and lattices of closed descriptions" supported by the Basic Research Program of the National Research University Higher School of Economics. This work has been also supported by the RFBR grant №13-07-00504/15.

References

Cumby, C. and Roth D. (2003) On Kernel Methods for Relational Learning. ICML, pp. 107-14.

Russell, S., Wefald, E, .Karnaugh, M., Karp, R., McAllester, D., Subramanian, D., Wellman, M. (1991) Principles of Metareasoning, Artificial Intelligence, pp 400--411, Morgan Kaufmann.

Collins, M., and Duffy, N. (2002) Convolution kernels for natural language. In Proceedings of NIPS, 625–32.

Mann, W. and Thompson, S. 1988. Rhetorical Structure Theory: Toward a functional theory of text organization, Text 8 (3), 243-281.

Galitsky, B. 2003. Natural Language Question Answering System: Technique of Semantic Headers. Advanced Knowledge International, Adelaide, Australia.

Galitsky, B., Usikov, D., and Kuznetsov S.O. 2013. Parse Thicket Representations for Answering Multi-sentence questions. 20th International Conference on Conceptual Structures.

Galitsky B., Ilvovsky, D., Kuznetsov, S.O. (2015) Text Integrity Assessment: Sentiment Profile vs Rhetoric Structure. CICLing-2015, Cairo, Egypt.

Wu, J., Xuan Z. and Pan, D. 2011. Enhancing text representation for classification tasks with semantic graph structures, International Journal of Innovative Computing, Information and Control (ICIC), Volume 7, Number 5(B).

Haussler, D. 1999. Convolution kernels on discrete structures. UCSB Technical report.

Kong, F. and Zhou G. 2011. Improve Tree Kernel-Based Event Pronoun Resolution with Competitive Information. Proceedings of the Twenty-Second International Joint Conference on Artificial Intelligence, 3 1814-19.

Moschitti, A. 2006. Efficient Convolution Kernels for Dependency and Constituent Syntactic Trees. 2006. In Proceedings of the 17th European Conference on Machine Learning, Berlin, Germany.

A. Severyn, A. Moschitti. 2012. Structural relationships for large-scale learning of answer re-ranking. SIGIR 2012: 741-750.

A. Severyn, A. Moschitti. 2012. Fast Support Vector Machines for Convolution Tree Kernels. Data Mining Knowledge Discovery 25: 325-357.

Mann, W., Matthiessen C. and Thompson S. 1992. Rhetorical Structure Theory and Text Analysis. Discourse Description: Diverse linguistic analyses of a fund-raising text. ed. by Mann W and Thompson S.; Amsterdam, John Benjamins. pp. 39-78.

Zhang, M.; Che, W.; Zhou, G.; Aw, A.; Tan, C.; Liu, T.; and Li, S. 2008. Semantic role labeling using a grammar-driven convolution tree kernel. IEEE transactions on audio, speech, and language processing. 16(7): 1315–29.

Lee, H., Chang, A., Peirsman, Y., Chambers, N., Surdeanu, M. and Jurafsky, D. 2013. Deterministic coreference resolution based on entity-centric, precision-ranked rules. Computational Linguistics 39(4), 885-916.

Marcu, D. 1997. From Discourse Structures to Text Summaries, in I. Mani and M.Maybury (eds) Proceedings of ACL Workshop on Intelligent Scalable Text Summarization, pp. 82–8, Madrid, Spain.

Kohavi, R. 1995. A Study of Cross-Validation and Bootstrap for Accuracy Estimation and Model Selection. International Joint Conference on Artificial Intelligence. 1137-43.

Recasens, M., de Marneffe M-C, and Potts, C.,2013. The Life and Death of Discourse Entities: Identifying Singleton Mentions. In Proceedings of NAACL.

Croft, B., Metzler, D., Strohman, T. 2009. Search Engines - Information Retrieval in Practice. Pearson Education. North America.

Salton, G. and Buckley, C. 1988. Term-weighting approaches in automatic text retrieval. Information Processing & Management 24(5): 513—23.

Moore, JS and Boyer RS. 1991. MJRTY - A Fast Majority Vote Algorithm, In R.S. Boyer (ed.), Automated Reasoning: Essays in Honor of Woody Bledsoe, Automated Reasoning Series, Kluwer Academic Publishers, Dordrecht, The Netherlands, pp. 105-17.

John G.H. and Langley, P. 1995. Estimating Continuous Distributions in Bayesian Classifiers. In Eleventh Conference on Uncertainty in Artificial Intelligence, San Mateo, 338-45.

Vapnik, V. (1995) The Nature of Statistical Learning Theory, Springer-Verlag.

Michael T. Cox and Anita Raja. (2007) Metareasoning: A manifesto.

S. Joty, G. Carenini, and R. T. Ng. 2012. A Novel Discriminative Framework for Sentence-Level Discourse Analysis. In Proceedings of the 2012 Joint Conference on Empirical Methods in Natural Language Processing and Computational Natural Language Learning, EMNLP-CoNLL'12, pages 904–915, Jeju Island, Korea. Association for Computational Linguistics.

S. Joty, G. Carenini, R. Ng, Y. Mehdad. 2013. Combining Intra- and Multi-sentential Rhetorical Parsing for Document-level Discourse Analysis. In Proceedings of the 51st Annual Meeting of the Association for Computational Linguistics, Sofia, Bulgaria.

Joty S. and Moschitti A. 2014. Discriminative Reranking of Discourse Parses Using Tree Kernels. In proceedings of EMNLP 2014.

Galitsky, B., Kuznetsov S. 2008. Learning communicative actions of conflicting human agents. J. Exp. Theor. Artif. Intell. 20(4): 277-317 .

Galitsky, B. 2012. Machine Learning of Syntactic Parse Trees for Search and Classification of Text. Engineering Applications of Artificial Intelligence. 26 (3), 1072-91

Enriching Word Sense Embeddings with Translational Context

Mehdi Ghanimifard
Department of Philosophy, Linguistics and Theory of Science
University of Gothenburg
mmehdi.g@gmail.com

Richard Johansson
Språkbanken, Department of Swedish
University of Gothenburg
richard.johansson@gu.se

Abstract

Vector-space models derived from corpora are an effective way to learn a representation of word meaning directly from data, and these models have many uses in practical applications. A number of unsupervised approaches have been proposed to automatically learn representations of word *senses* directly from corpora, but since these methods use no information but the words themselves, they sometimes miss distinctions that could be possible to make if more information were available.

In this paper, we present a general framework that we call *context enrichment* that incorporates external information during the training of multi-sense vector-space models. Our approach is agnostic as to which external signal is used to enrich the context, but in this work we consider the use of *translations* as the source of enrichment. We evaluated the models trained using the translation-enriched context using several similarity benchmarks and a word analogy test set. In all our evaluations, the enriched model outperformed the purely word-based baseline soundly.

1 Introduction

Word meaning representations derived from corpora have recently seen much attention in natural language processing (NLP), most importantly because they can be used very effectively to abstract over the word level in lexicalized NLP systems (Miller et al., 2004; Koo et al., 2008; Turian et al., 2010; Bansal et al., 2014; Guo et al., 2014; Sienčnik, 2015). These representations are derived from corpus statistics, building on the *distributional hypothesis* that the meaning of a word is reflected in statistical distributions of the contexts in which it appears (Harris, 1954). This intuition can be implemented in a number of ways in practice; in this work, we focus on models that represent word meaning as a point in a metric space (Widdows, 2005; Sahlgren, 2006; Turney and Pantel, 2010; Clark, 2015). In particular, one member of this family that has been particularly influential recently is the *skip-gram* learning algorithm (Mikolov et al., 2013a), which is derived from the log-bilinear language model by Mnih and Hinton (2007). The main reasons for its popularity are its computational efficiency (Mikolov et al., 2013b), its high performance in several evaluations, and the availability of an implementation in the form of the easily usable `word2vec` package.

In most cases distributional word representations disregard the fact that many words have more than one possible interpretation, or *word sense*, and in lexicographical descriptions of a language we will typically list the senses of a word in different sub-entries (Cruse, 1986). For instance, the English word *bass* can refer to a fish, a musical instrument, the low part of a musical range, etc. It is imaginable that we could use standard techniques to learn a vector-space semantic representation from a sense-annotated corpus, but this is infeasible in practice since fairly large corpora are needed to induce data-driven representations of a high quality, while corpora with hand-annotated sense identifiers are small and scarce. Instead, there have been several attempts to use *unsupervised* methods that create vectors representing the senses of ambiguous words, most of them based on some variant of the idea that was first proposed by Schütze (1998): that the different senses of a word can be discovered by applying a clustering algorithm to the set of contexts where it has appeared. Variations on this idea have turned up in a number of recent papers (Huang et al., 2012; Moen et al., 2013; Neelakantan et al., 2014; Kågebäck et al., 2015). However, unsupervised

Proceedings of Recent Advances in Natural Language Processing, pages 208–215,
Hissar, Bulgaria, Sep 7–9 2015.

models for discovering word senses are solipsistic in the sense that they are not *grounded* in the external world in the way that a language user is. This leads to the problem that they sometimes tend to discover different *discourses* or domains, rather than true word senses (Tahmasebi, 2013). Because of this lack of external signals, it seems natural to try to introduce additional sources of information into the learning process.

In this paper, we enrich the multi-sense skip-gram model (Neelakantan et al., 2014) by introducing external signals, which are implemented as additional context features during training. In particular, we use a *parallel corpus*, where the foreign-language words work as a source of external information that helps the algorithm form more distinct clusters. For instance, the fish sense of *bass* can be clearly distinguished from the musical senses if we have access to a Swedish translation: the fish is called *havsabborre*, while most of the musical senses would be translated as *bas*. Our approach can be seen as a form of *distant supervision* (Mintz et al., 2009), in contrast to the fully unsupervised approaches mentioned above.

We evaluated the context-enriched model on a collection of word similarity benchmarks and analogy tests, including the *contextual word similarity set* used in previous work on learning representations of different senses (Huang et al., 2012), and we saw large improvements when comparing to a baseline without access to the enriched context.

2 Background: the Skip-gram Model and its Multi-sense Extension

In the *skip-gram* model (Mikolov et al., 2013a), a target word w and a context feature c are represented using vectors from two different vector spaces, denoted $v_t(w)$ and $v_c(c)$ respectively. Intuitively, we would like the training algorithm to fit the vectors so that $v_c(c) \cdot v_t(w)$ is a high number if we are likely to see c near w, and a low number otherwise.

In the original formulation of the model, these two vectors are combined into probability of the occurrence of a context feature c near a target word w using the following equation:

$$\log P(c|w) = v_c(c) \cdot v_t(w) - \log Z(c)$$

where $Z(c)$ is a normalization factor so that the probabilities sum to 1. In principle, the model could be fit to a training corpus by maximizing the likelihood of all the contexts in the corpus, but due to the normalization factors $Z(c)$ – which are computed by summing over the whole vocabulary – this is computationally inefficient, leading to a number of approximations. Mikolov et al. (2013a) used a hierarchical decomposition, but after a simplification of the the idea of *noise-contrastive estimation* (Mnih and Kavukcuoglu, 2013), the most recent `word2vec` implementation estimates the word vectors using an approach called *skip-gram with negative sampling* (SGNS) (Mikolov et al., 2013b). This model treats word–context pairs actually occurring in a corpus as positive training examples, and synthetic pairs that were generated randomly as negative examples, and then fits a logistic model that discriminates between positive and negative examples:

$$P(\text{true pair}|c, w) = \frac{1}{1 + e^{-v_c(c) \cdot v_t(w)}}$$

During training of the SGNS model, when we consider a true pair (w, c), we generate N synthetic pairs (w, c') with the same word but with the c' randomly selected from the context vocabulary. While SGNS is not guaranteed to converge to the same solution as the original skip-gram model, it is more efficient and has achieved comparable results in evaluations.

The *multi-sense skip-gram* model (MSSG) by Neelakantan et al. (2014) generalizes SGNS by taking multiple senses into account. This algorithm uses context vectors as in the original skip-gram model, but it replaces the target word vector $v_t(w)$ for a word w with K different *sense vectors* $v_s(w, k)$.[1] In addition, it uses K vectors $\mu(w, k)$ that represent the centers of the clusters of contexts. The learning algorithm works in a fashion similar to SGNS, but extends it by introducing an additional sense discrimination step. When the algorithm encounters a word w, it first represents the full context window by building a sum $\bar{v}_c$ of the context vectors of the words appearing in the window. It then selects sense k whose context cluster $\mu(w, k)$ maximizes the dot product with $\bar{v}_c$. Finally, it carries out a gradient update (similar to that in SGNS) of the sense vector $v_s(w, k)$ and the context vectors $v_c(c)$, and adds $\bar{v}_c$ to the context cluster $\mu(w, k)$.

[1] Neelakantan et al. (2014) also described a *nonparametric* variant where the number of senses was determined automatically. We did not use that model since the distributed code did not include that part.

3 Context Enrichment

One of the fundamental criticisms against distributional word learning claims that the disembodiment from physical world will cause problems due to the fact that many concepts are actually grounded in perception and a sample text from a language alone does not carry all information about the concept behind the word (Andrews et al., 2009).[2] The perceptual information which has been claimed to improve these models are usually multi-modal data, for instance images as visual context of word usage in a language. In this work, we will instead enrich the training context with another type of supplementary text – the translation of the English text into Swedish – in order to improve the final word sense discrimination model.

In our method, we use a parallel corpus such as Europarl (Koehn, 2005), which provides sentence-by-sentence translations. Then by aligning words in each sentence we will add corresponding list of words in enhancing language into the list of words in skip-gram context window. Figure 1 illustrates why we expect this to be useful for forming better word sense clusters. In the figure, the first occurrence of the word *plant*, meaning an industrial or power plant, is translated by the Swedish word *anläggning*; the second example means a botanical plant and is translated as *planta*. This shows clearly that the external context in the form of a translation can be useful for discriminating between senses: an industrial plant would never occur in Swedish as *planta*, or vice versa.

Figure 1: Examples of two occurrences in Europarl of the English word *plant* and their respective translations into Swedish.

[2]One can also relate this problem to the "symbol grounding problem", by saying that the result of a distributional learning algorithm will be just meaningless symbolic relations between words. But the symbol grounding problem is a problem for specific application of these models in cognitive modeling, which is also mentioned by Harnad (1990).

3.1 Preprocessed Corpus

In order to facilitate and simplify the training process, we isolated the word alignment process from the rest of the training. In this isolated process in addition to the word alignment process which takes two parallel corpora and suggests one-to-many word alignments per sentence [3], we produce an enriched corpus by annotating the source corpus with words from the target corpus.

In order to get better results from word alignments, we applied a part-of-speech tagger on the Swedish and English words before running the aligner. Then we by taking the union of two word alignments with *fast_align* (Dyer et al., 2013) in both forward and reverse setups, we produced one-to-many mappings. We then read sentences from both corpora in parallel with their word mappings and generated the annotated corpus, which we refer to as the *enriched* or augmented corpus. The enriched corpus simply is the annotated source corpus which each word has its list of aligned words from target corpus.

During the training process, the Enriched Multi-Sense Skip-Gram Model will parse the annotated tokens, and add the enriched context to the skip-gram contexts as we describe in next section.

3.2 Enriched Multi-Sense Skip-Gram Model

The Enriched Multi-Sense Skip-Gram Model (EMSSG) extends the previous work by Neelakantan et al. (2014) by adding an extra step that incorporates external information into the context representation. In this procedure, sense vectors will be trained only for words in the source language; however, for any token occurring as context – including the translations – we produce a context vector. The enriched corpus is made of words and their enriched context (w, C). From each word from the source corpus $w_t \in W$ the corresponding enrichment is a subset of tokens from a parallel corpus $C_t \subset W'$:

$$W = \{w_t\}_{t \in 1,\ldots,T}, W' = \{w'_t\}_{t \in 1,\ldots,T'}$$

Basically, each token (w_t, C_t) is a result of word alignment which we produce in the preprocessing phase:

$$C_t = \{w'_{a_t(1)} \ldots w'_{a_t(m_t)}\}$$

[3]In more complicated translation alignments, such as phrase-to-phrase mappings, we still can take the one-to-many implementation of these alignments in our one directional process.

In the training process, the enrichment context C_t will be added to the skip-gram context words $C_{sg} = \{w_{t-R_t}, \ldots, w_{t-1}, w_{t+1}, \ldots, w_{t+R_t}\}$ to create a combined context: $C = C_t \cup C_{sg}$. As in the original MSSG, the vector representation of the combined context will then be used to predict the right sense for the observed context. We first build a representation of the full context by summing all the individual context vectors:

$$\bar{v}_c = \sum_{w \in C} v_c(w)$$

This vector is then compared to all the context cluster centroids in order to predict the sense:

$$s_t = \underset{k=1,2,\ldots,K}{\operatorname{argmax}} \; sim(\mu(w_t, k), \bar{v}_c)$$

Algorithm 1 shows the pseudocode of how we use the enriched context representation to improve the sense prediction and their corresponding clusters. The enriched context is only used during training as a form of distant supervision: at test time, only the skip-gram contexts are used when predicting the sense.

Algorithm 1 Training Algorithm of EMSSG model

input $(w_t, C_t)_{t \in \{1,2,\ldots,T\}}$, d, K, N.
for $t = 1, 2, \ldots, T$
for $k \in \{1, \ldots, K\}$
  initialize $\mu(w_t, k) = 0$
  randomly initialize $v_s(w_t, k)$, $v_c(w_t)$
for $t = 1, 2, \ldots, T'$
  randomly initialize $v_c(w'_t)$
for $t = 1, 2, \ldots, T$
    $R_t \sim \{1, \ldots, N\}$
    $C_{sg} \leftarrow \{w_{t-R_t}, \ldots, w_{t-1}, w_{t+1}, \ldots, w_{t+R_t}\}$
    $C \leftarrow C_t \cup C_{sg}$
    $\bar{v}_c \leftarrow \sum_{w \in C} v_c(w)$
    $s_t \leftarrow \operatorname{argmax}_{k=1,2,\ldots,K} sim(\mu(w_t, k), \bar{v}_c)$
    update cluster center:
     $\mu(w_t, s_t)$ with new context C
    for c words in C
      gradient update: $v_s(w_t, s_t)$ with $v_c(c)$
      gradient update: $v_c(c)$ with $v_s(w_t, s_t)$
    $C' \leftarrow Noisy\_Samples(C)$
    for c words in C'.
      negative gradient update:
       $v_s(w_t, s_t)$ with $v_c(c)$
return $v_s(w, k)$, $v_c(w)$, $v_c(w')$,$\mu(w, k)$
    for $w \in W, w' \in W', k \in 1, \ldots, K$

4 Experiments

To evaluate the enrichment model, we trained a baseline MSSG model without enrichment from English Europarl. Then by enriching the English Europarl with Swedish parallel corpus, as described in previous section, we trained the enriched model with the same setup.

In these models the dimension size is $d = 300$ and window size is $N = 5$, and number of senses is $k = 2$. To enable faster training we chose to train sense vectors only for top 1000 most frequent words, excluding stop words.

4.1 Word similarity tests

We evaluate our models with 3 different word similarity tests:

- the SimLex999 similarity test (Hill et al., 2014)
- the WordSim353 tests in both similarity and relatedness (Ponzetto and Strube, 2011)
- the Stanford Contextual Word Similarity test (Huang et al., 2012)

The evaluation procedures for word sense models in all of these test sets are identical:

- Disambiguate word senses for each pair of words.
- Quantify the similarity of pairs with the cosine similarity measure between two sense vectors.
- Calculate the correlation between gold standard and the estimated similarity.

In order to disambiguate the sense for a word, we need its context to find the most likely sense vector for that word. The sense disambiguation separate these tests in two groups: those with word contexts and those without word contexts.

4.1.1 Non-contextual tests

Both SimLex999 and WordSim353 are designed for evaluating word vector representations. Although the lack of context to describe the actual usage of word makes them unsuitable for word sense evaluation, they have been used to evaluate sense-aware vector-space models (Reisinger and Mooney, 2010; Neelakantan et al., 2014), so we include a comparison for completeness. However, despite the absence of context, human judges estimate their similarity based on their own understanding of senses of those words. Similar to *passive sense selection* in humans[4], we consider each word as context for the other word to select the best sense. With a twist, instead of using context vectors to predict the sense of the other one, we basically choose the most similar vectors pairs as desired vectors. This is equivalent to what Reisinger and Mooney (2010) term the *MaxSim* score.

To understand why we use this procedure, consider two very different words: in this case, we expect that all of their senses should be very different. Considering two words that the evaluators considered to be similar, it is likely that this does not apply to *all* of the senses, but only a specific pair. This motivates why we take the highest similarity of senses, and we think that this procedure is more meaningful than the *AvgSim* score used by (Reisinger and Mooney, 2010).

The English-Swedish Europarl's vocabulary covers 758 of word pairs in SimLex999 and 163 pairs in WordSim353 similarity test and 218 pairs WordSim353 relatedness test.

Table 1 shows the results of the evaluations on the three non-contextual benchmarks. As is customary in this type of evaluation, the similarity scores output by the model are compared to the gold standard using the Spearman correlation coefficient. In all three tests, the model with access to an enriched context representation clearly outperforms the baseline MSSG model.

Model	SL999	WS353-sim	WS353-rel
MSSG	0.29	0.44	0.35
EMSSG	0.36	0.52	0.39

Table 1: Spearman correlation values of the two systems when evaluated on the three non-contextual similarity test sets.

4.1.2 Contextual test

The Stanford Contextual Word Similarity test (Huang et al., 2012) consists of pairs of words and a sentence as an example for their usage. The sense disambiguation with the provided sample will be done by making a context vector as we have in MSSG models: the evaluation using this procedure is equivalent to the *localSim* procedure used by Neelakantan et al. (2014).

The English-Swedish Europarl's vocabulary covers 1498 samples of this dataset. In Table 2, we present the results (again, Spearman correlations) of the evaluation with this set. Again, the enriched model outperforms the baseline.

Model	Correlation
MSSG	0.45
EMSSG	0.53

Table 2: Evaluation on the Stanford contextual word similarity test set.

4.2 Word analogy test

The word analogy data set provided by Google (Mikolov et al., 2013c) is also another test for vector representations of words. The judgement on the word relation are based on their semantic or syntactic identity. For instance, an example of a semantic analogy is *Paris*:*France* = *Stockholm*:*Sweden*, while *sleeping*:*sleep* = *breaking*:*break* is an example of a syntactic analogy.

The test is about guessing the correct word vector by only having the three other word vectors. For instance, if the missing vector is $v_{gold} = v(\text{“}queen'')$, the nearest neighbour word vector to the vector $v_{analogy} = v(\text{“}king'') - v(\text{“}man'') + v(\text{“}woman'')$ should be v_{gold}. Similar to non-contextual word similarity tests, this test also needs a novel sense disambiguation method.

To find those word-senses that intended to be in each analogy test, we can suppose that correct senses in these tests should lead to only one correct answer. It means that the nearest neighbour to analogy vector $v_{analogy}$ should have a significant similarity comparing to other close neighbours of this vector. We can define a score to find the best analogy vector based on maximized margin from other neighbours. With k number of senses per word in the model, there are k^3 possible $v_{analogy}$.

For each possible $v_{analogy}$ and its top 10 closest sense vectors $V = \{v_1, ..., v_{10}\}$, we define the score of $v_{analogy}$ based on similarity of the nearest neighbour and its margin with other neighbours:

- δ_i is the *similarity margin* between $v_i \in V$

[4] Cruse (1986) used this term "*passive selection*" in contrast with "*productive selection*" as psycholinguistic matter, to describe sense selection among pre-established senses. Whenever we use this type of corpus driven word sense models, we only have passive selection because we only have pre-established senses. By using this term here, we want to emphasize that even in absence of context we can take most related senses as most obvious choice of sense

and the nearest neighbour v_1:

$$\delta_i = sim(v_1, v_{analogy}) - sim(v_i, v_{analogy})$$

- The score of $v_{analogy}$:

$$score = \frac{\sum_{i=1}^{10} \delta_i^2}{\delta_{10}^2}, \times sim(v_1, v_{analogy})$$

Higher score in this formula indicates that v_1, the most similar vector to $v_{analogy}$, has a significant similarity to $v_{analogy}$ compering to other possible neighbour vectors. By taking the best $v_{analogy}$ from all possible $v_{analogy}$, we automatically pick 3 sense vectors for analogy test.

Table 3 shows the results of the evaluation on the Google analogy test set (Mikolov et al., 2013c). For the third time, the translation-enriched model outperforms the MSSG baseline in all tests.

Model	Total	Syntactic	Semantic
MSSG	0.13	0.04	0.17
EMSSG	0.25	0.09	0.32

Table 3: Evaluation on the Google analogy test set.

5 Related Work

The idea of integrating different modalities into corpus-based vector representations has generated much interest recently (Lazaridou et al., 2014; Socher et al., 2014). The work in this area that is most similar to ours is that by Hill and Korhonen (2014) and : they extend the context representation of the skip-gram model with features representing the external information like we do, although they do not take word senses into account.

Parallel corpora have been used in a number of research projects in order to derive *crosslingual* word representations; this is different from our goal, which is to use them to help the monolingual model form better sense clusters. Klementiev et al. (2012) presented a neural multi-task learning model that used bilingual cooccurrence data as a way to connect the models in two languages, and Utt and Padó (2014) described a syntactically informed context-counting method. Faruqui and Dyer (2014) presented a method that combine two monolingual vector spaces into a multilingual one by Canonical Correlation Analysis. In addition to vector-space models, bilingual and multilingual corpora have been used to derive a number of non-geometric corpus-based representations, such as Brown clusters (Täckström et al., 2012) and topic models (Vulić et al., 2015).

Finally, the use of word translations as a way to distantly supervise word sense disambiguation and discrimination systems is an idea that goes far back (Dagan et al., 1991; Dyvik, 2004) and has reappeared many times. This intuition was behind a number of SemEval cross-lingual word sense disambiguation and lexical substitution tasks (Lefever and Hoste, 2010; Mihalcea et al., 2010).

6 Conclusions

We have presented a general technique called *context enrichment* that allows us to use external information to multi-prototype vector-space models of word meaning. The intention of this approach is that the external signal helps the model form more coherent and well-separated clusters during the training process, and it is not necessary during testing. The approach that we have evaluated is a straightforward extension of the multi-sense skip-gram model by Neelakantan et al. (2014), but we imagine that other models (for instance Huang el al., 2012) could be extended in a similar fashion. The model can integrate any kind of language-external signal as long as it can be represented as a contextual feature taken from a finite vocabulary. In this work, we enriched the context using word translations taken from the Europarl corpus (Koehn, 2005).

We evaluated the multi-sense vector models trained with translation-enriched contexts using a number of different benchmarks: word similarity tests, a contextual similarity test, and a word analogy test. In every experiment we tried, the enriched model outperformed the non-enriched baseline.

It seems straightforward to extend our work to a setting where other types of features are used, and we would like to explore this area further. In particular, we would like to integrate multimodal input (Hill and Korhonen, 2014), for instance with information extracted from images. This could lead to several interesting experiments where the effect of different modalities on word sense discovery could be investigated.

Acknowledgements

We would like to thanks the reviewers for their constructive comments. The second author was funded by the Swedish Research Council under grant 2013–4944, *Distributional methods to represent the meaning of frames and constructions.*

References

Mark Andrews, Gabriella Vigliocco, and David Vinson. 2009. Integrating experiential and distributional data to learn semantic representations. *Psychological review*, 116(3):463–498.

Mohit Bansal, Kevin Gimpel, and Karen Livescu. 2014. Tailoring continuous word representations for dependency parsing. In *Proceedings of the 52nd Annual Meeting of the Association for Computational Linguistics (Volume 2: Short Papers)*, pages 809–815, Baltimore, United States.

Stephen Clark. 2015. Vector space models of lexical meaning. In Shalom Lappin and Chris Fox, editors, *Handbook of Contemporary Semantics, second edition*. Wiley-Blackwell.

D. A. Cruse. 1986. *Lexical semantics*. Cambridge University Press.

Ido Dagan, Alon Itai, and Ulrike Schwall. 1991. Two languages are more informative than one. In *Proceedings of the 29th Annual Meeting of the Association for Computational Linguistics*, pages 130–137, Berkeley, United States.

Chris Dyer, Victor Chahuneau, and Noah A Smith. 2013. A simple, fast, and effective reparameterization of ibm model 2. In *HLT-NAACL*, pages 644–648. Citeseer.

Helge Dyvik. 2004. Translations as semantic mirrors: from parallel corpus to wordnet. *Language and computers*, 49(1):311–326.

Manaal Faruqui and Chris Dyer. 2014. Improving vector space word representations using multilingual correlation. In *Proceedings of the 14th Conference of the European Chapter of the Association for Computational Linguistics*, pages 462–471, Gothenburg, Sweden.

Jiang Guo, Wanxiang Che, Haifeng Wang, and Ting Liu. 2014. Revisiting embedding features for simple semi-supervised learning. In *Proceedings of the 2014 Conference on Empirical Methods in Natural Language Processing (EMNLP)*, pages 110–120, Doha, Qatar.

Stevan Harnad. 1990. Symbol Grounding Problem: Turing-Scale Solution Needed. 42:335–346.

Zellig Harris. 1954. Distributional structure. *Word*, 10(23).

Felix Hill and Anna Korhonen. 2014. Learning abstract concept embeddings from multi-modal data: Since you probably can't see what I mean. In *Proceedings of the 2014 Conference on Empirical Methods in Natural Language Processing (EMNLP)*, pages 255–265, Doha, Qatar.

Felix Hill, Roi Reichart, and Anna Korhonen. 2014. Simlex-999: Evaluating semantic models with (genuine) similarity estimation. *CoRR*, abs/1408.3456.

Eric H. Huang, Richard Socher, Christopher D. Manning, and Andrew Y. Ng. 2012. Improving word representations via global context and multiple word prototypes. In *Association for Computational Linguistics 2012 Conference (ACL 2012)*, Jeju Island, Korea.

Mikael Kågebäck, Fredrik Johansson, Richard Johansson, and Devdatt Dubhashi. 2015. Neural context embeddings for automatic discovery of word senses. In *Proceedings of the Workshop on Vector Space Modeling for NLP*, Denver, United States. To appear.

Alexandre Klementiev, Ivan Titov, and Binod Bhattarai. 2012. Inducing crosslingual distributed representations of words. In *Proceedings of COLING 2012*, pages 1459–1474, Mumbai, India.

Philipp Koehn. 2005. Europarl: A parallel corpus for statistical machine translation. In *MT Summit*, volume 5, pages 79–86.

Terry Koo, Xavier Carreras, and Michael Collins. 2008. Simple semi-supervised dependency parsing. In *Proceedings of ACL-08: HLT*, pages 595–603, Columbus, USA.

Angeliki Lazaridou, Elia Bruni, and Marco Baroni. 2014. Is this a wampimuk? cross-modal mapping between distributional semantics and the visual world. In *Proceedings of the 52nd Annual Meeting of the Association for Computational Linguistics (Volume 1: Long Papers)*, pages 1403–1414, Baltimore, United States.

Els Lefever and Véronique Hoste. 2010. Semeval-2010 task 3: Cross-lingual word sense disambiguation. In *Proceedings of the 5th International Workshop on Semantic Evaluation*, pages 15–20, Uppsala, Sweden.

Rada Mihalcea, Ravi Sinha, and Diana McCarthy. 2010. Semeval-2010 task 2: Cross-lingual lexical substitution. In *Proceedings of the 5th International Workshop on Semantic Evaluation*, pages 9–14, Uppsala, Sweden.

Tomáš Mikolov, Kai Chen, Greg Corrado, and Jeffrey Dean. 2013a. Efficient estimation of word representations in vector space. In *International Conference on Learning Representations, Workshop Track*, Scottsdale, USA.

Tomáš Mikolov, Ilya Sutskever, Kai Chen, Greg Corrado, and Jeff Dean. 2013b. Distributed representations of words and phrases and their compositionality. In *Advances in Neural Information Processing Systems 26*.

Tomáš Mikolov, Wen-tau Yih, and Geoffrey Zweig. 2013c. Linguistic regularities in continuous space word representations. In *Proceedings of the 2013 Conference of the North American Chapter of the Association for Computational Linguistics: Human Language Technologies*, pages 746–751, Atlanta, USA.

Scott Miller, Jethran Guinness, and Alex Zamanian. 2004. Name tagging with word clusters and discriminative training. In *HLT-NAACL 2004: Main Proceedings*, pages 337–342, Boston, SA.

Mike Mintz, Steven Bills, Rion Snow, and Daniel Jurafsky. 2009. Distant supervision for relation extraction without labeled data. In *Proceedings of the Joint Conference of the 47th Annual Meeting of the ACL and the 4th International Joint Conference on Natural Language Processing of the AFNLP*, pages 1003–1011, Suntec, Singapore.

Andriy Mnih and Geoffrey Hinton. 2007. Three new graphical models for statistical language modelling. In *Proceedings of the 24th International Conference on Machine Learning*, pages 641–648.

Andriy Mnih and Koray Kavukcuoglu. 2013. Learning word embeddings efficiently with noise-contrastive estimation. In *Advances in Neural Information Processing Systems 26*, pages 2265–2273.

Hans Moen, Erwin Marsi, and Björn Gambäck. 2013. Towards dynamic word sense discrimination with random indexing. In *Proceedings of the Workshop on Continuous Vector Space Models and their Compositionality*, pages 83–90, Sofia, Bulgaria.

Arvind Neelakantan, Jeevan Shankar, Alexandre Passos, and Andrew McCallum. 2014. Efficient non-parametric estimation of multiple embeddings per word in vector space. In *Proceedings of the 2014 Conference on Empirical Methods in Natural Language Processing (EMNLP)*, pages 1059–1069, Doha, Qatar.

Simone Paolo Ponzetto and Michael Strube. 2011. Taxonomy induction based on a collaboratively built knowledge repository. *Artificial Intelligence*, 175(9-10):1737–1756.

Joseph Reisinger and Raymond J Mooney. 2010. Multi-prototype vector-space models of word meaning. In *Human Language Technologies: The 2010 Annual Conference of the North American Chapter of the Association for Computational Linguistics*, pages 109–117. Association for Computational Linguistics.

Magnus Sahlgren. 2006. *The Word-Space Model*. Ph.D. thesis, Stockholm University.

Hinrich Schütze. 1998. Automatic word sense discrimination. *Computational Linguistics*, 24(1):97–123.

Scharolta Katharina Sienčnik. 2015. Adapting *word2vec* to named entity recognition. In *Proceedings of the 20th Nordic Conference of Computational Linguistics (NODALIDA 2015)*, pages 239–243, Vilnius, Lithuania.

Richard Socher, Andrej Karpathy, Quoc V. Le, Christopher D. Manning, and Andrew Y. Ng. 2014. Grounded compositional semantics for finding and describing images with sentences. *Transactions of the Association for Computational Linguistics*, 2:207–218.

Oscar Täckström, Ryan McDonald, and Jakob Uszkoreit. 2012. Cross-lingual word clusters for direct transfer of linguistic structure. In *Proceedings of the 2012 Conference of the North American Chapter of the Association for Computational Linguistics: Human Language Technologies*, pages 477–487, Montréal, Canada.

Nina N. Tahmasebi. 2013. *Models and Algorithms for Automatic Detection of Language Evolution*. Ph.D. thesis, Gottfried Wilhelm Leibniz Universität Hannover.

Joseph Turian, Lev-Arie Ratinov, and Yoshua Bengio. 2010. Word representations: A simple and general method for semi-supervised learning. In *Proceedings of the 48th Annual Meeting of the Association for Computational Linguistics*, pages 384–394, Uppsala, Sweden.

Peter D. Turney and Patrick Pantel. 2010. From frequency to meaning: Vector space models of semantics. *Journal of Artificial Intelligence Research*, 37:141–188.

Jason Utt and Sebastian Padó. 2014. Crosslingual and multilingual construction of syntax-based vector space models. *Transactions of the Association for Computational Linguistics*, 2:245–258.

Ivan Vulić, Wim De Smet, Jie Tang, and Marie-Francine Moens. 2015. Probabilistic topic modeling in multilingual settings: an overview of its methodology and applications. *Information Processing & Management*, 51(1):111–147.

Dominic Widdows. 2005. *Geometry and Meaning*. CSLI Publications.

Automatic Acquisition of Artifact Nouns in French

Xiaoqin Hu
Laboratory LDI
University of Paris 13
franhuxqin@hotmail.fr

Pierre-André Buvet
Laboratory LDI
University of Paris 13
pierreandre.buvet@gmail.com

Abstract

This article describes a method which allows acquiring artifact nouns in French automatically by extracting predicate-argument structures. Two strategies are presented: the supervised strategy and the semi-supervised strategy. In the supervised method, the semantic classes of artifact nouns are recognized by identifying the predicate-argument structures with the syntactic patterns of the given predicates. In the semi-supervised method, the extraction of predicate-argument structures is carried out from a semantic class of artifact nouns given in advance. The predicate candidates obtained from extracted predicate-argument structures are then intersected. Next, the syntactic patterns of predicates are automatically learned by probabilistic calculation. With the acquired predicates and the learned syntactic patterns, more artifact nouns are identified.

1 Introduction

The difficulties for automatic acquisition of terms might come from the linguistic techniques, the computational techniques or the limits of the natural language processing theory. Nowadays, many studies have been conducted for term extraction. This article presents a method for automatic acquisition of artifact nouns on the basis of syntactic-semantic analysis of predicates. Artifact nouns are the nouns of the artificial entities produced intentionally by human beings, with a view to a specific function. The automatic acquisition of artifact nouns is for completing the dictionary of semantic classes of laboratory LDI. There are two strategies for realizing this method: a supervised strategy in which the predicate-argument structures are extracted by the syntactic patterns of the given predicates and a semi-supervised strategy developed on the basis of the supervised strategy. The semi-supervised strategy consists of two steps. In the first step, it predicts which predicates are relevant by a probabilistic calculation. In the second step, it appeals to the supervised strategy. This article is organized as follows. Section 2 states the related work on term extraction in recent years. Section 3 presents the data model used in the proposed method. Section 4 explains in detail the proposed method including the semantic-syntactic analysis of appropriate predicates of artifact nouns. Section 5 presents the experiment results and the analysis of the results.

2 Related Work

In the as-built systems of term extraction, the part of linguistic model is often limited to morpho-syntactic descriptions and the part of statistical model, to a large extent, depends on the statistical knowledge. TERMINO (Lauriston, 1994) and LEXTER (Bourigault, 1996), two well-known semi-automatic systems of term extraction, are based on syntactic descriptions. The method of Hearst (1992) and the method of Snow et al. (2004) take advantage of morpho-syntactic patterns for automatically recognizing hyponyms and hypernyms. The statistical methods for term extraction can be based on Markov model (Jiang, 2012), co-occurrence, or vector support, etc. ANA (Enguehard, 1993) is a statistical method which is based on co-occurrence. Morlane-Hondère (2012) has presented a series of distributional methods realized with data mining techniques, such as mutual information, measures of association, log-likelihood or naive bays (Ibekwe-sanjuan, 2007). The method of Meilland and Bellot (2003) which extracts terms from annotated corpora, ACABIT (Daille, 1994) and the strategy of cooperation of many term extractors of Alecu et al. (2012) are

Proceedings of Recent Advances in Natural Language Processing, pages 216–223,
Hissar, Bulgaria, Sep 7–9 2015.

all the hybrid methods which combine linguistic model and statistical model. Furthermore, Seeker and Kuhn (2013) has proposed a method which identifies the morpho-syntactic patterns by statistical dependency Parsing, and Quiniou et al. (2012) has brought forward an approach aiming to identify the linguistic patterns via data mining techniques.

3 Data Model

3.1 Predicates, Arguments and Actualizers

The predicate is a linguistic unit defined as a language form of semantic relation between two entities. The entities linked by this relation are arguments. The actualizers are the linguistic elements which enable to register the predicates and arguments in grammatically correct statements. They can be grammatical units (such as prepositions, determiners...) or lexical units, such as modifying adjectives, adverbs, auxiliary verbs, support verbs, etc. The predicates semantically dominate the arguments.

3.2 Uses of Predicate

The predicates can be divided into verbal predicates, nominal predicates, adjective predicates, prepositional predicates and adverbial predicates in the conception of "uses of predicates" of Buvet (2009). The variations between the uses of predicate are morphosyntactic or interpretative. The interpretations of the uses result from a set of properties: type of state, type of action, processive aspect and stative aspect. A predicate can have one or more uses, for example, for the predicate *négocier* (*negotiate*), *négocier* (*negotiate*) is its verbal use, *négociation* (*negotiation*) is its nominal use and *négociable* (*negotiable*) is its adjective use.

3.3 Appropriate Predicates and Appropriate Relation

The appropriate predicates have a number of relatively limited semantic classes of arguments. This character of appropriate predicates allows predicting the semantic class to which their arguments belong. An appropriate predicate in a specific sense can define a semantic class of arguments. Nevertheless, the polysemy of most of the appropriate predicates necessitates delimiting the semantic class of arguments by gathering many appropriate predicates of one semantic class. For example, for the predicate *conduire* (*dive/take/lead*), it can be used in the following senses: *conduire mon enfant à l'école* (*drive my child to school*), *conduire une voiture* (*drive a car*) or *conduire une entreprise* (*lead a company*). The polysemy of *conduire* (*drive/take/lead*) prevents from isolating the semantic class of transport. However, with another appropriate predicate *réparer* (*repair*), we can predict that the arguments which can appear after both *conduire* (*drive/lead*) and *réparer* (*repair*) belong to the semantic class of transport. A set of appropriate predicates that allows delimiting a semantic class of arguments is defined as the definitional appropriate predicates of this semantic class of arguments (Buvet, 2009; Mejri, 2009). The definitional appropriate predicates characterize the semantics of their class of arguments.

4 Presentation of Method

4.1 Corpora

The corpora used for the method are composed of texts coming from about ten French websites (e.g., http://www.forum-auto.com/marques/index.htm, http://geekandfood.fr/blog/, etc.). The websites are selected around various themes: automobile, household appliances and decoration, cooking, beauty, fashion, health, etc. The chosen texts include the comments, the discussions on forum and the articles on the blog. The volume of the corpora reaches 22,858 Ko. They comprise 3,754,334 words. The texts of different themes occupy about the same proportion in the corpora. The texts of the different genres (the comments, the discussions on the forum and the articles on the blog) also occupy about the same proportion respectively.

4.2 Work Tool: Unitex

In the proposed method, both the preprocessing and the extraction of predicate-argument structures are carried out with local grammars through Unitex. With the integrated linguistic resources (such as Dela, Delac, etc.), Unitex makes it possible to represent a local grammar in the form of finite state automaton.

4.3 Supervised Method

In the supervised method, the predicate-argument structures are recognized automatically from a set of predicates given in advance. A series of syntactic patterns are established on the basis of the syntactic-semantic analysis of the appropriate predicates. The obtained arguments are then intersected for choosing the appropriate arguments of the given predicates.

4.3.1 Preprocessing

The constituents of multi-word expressions are often misrecognized by computer as the constituents of other syntactic structures, for example, in the sentence *Une fois acheté mon nouveau manteau, je suis rentré à la maison* (*once my new coat bought, I returned to home*), *fois acheté* (*time bought*) is often misrecognized as a noun phrase by computer with the syntactic pattern N+Adj. Nevertheless, *fois* (*time*) is the constituent of the multi-word expression *une fois* (*once*). To solve this problem, the following strategy is adopted: we appeal to the dictionary Delac in Unitex for labelling adjective multiword expressions, adverbial multi-word expressions, verbal multi-word expression and prepositional multi-word expressions ; these expressions are then replaced by the corresponding morphosyntactic label (like <ADV>, <ADJ>, <V> and <PREP>). Thus, the multiword expression *une fois acheté* becomes *<ADV> acheté* after the preprocessing.

The given predicates are labelled by the tool Unitex considering the different uses of each predicate. The morphosyntactic disambiguation of predicates depending on context is conducted at the same time. Thus, the given predicates are labeled by identifying the corresponding verbal phrases with the syntactic patterns such as, avoir+été+ADV+Vpp, se+faire+V, aller+être+ADV+Vpp, se+être+ADV+Vpp, avoir+Vpp, Vpp+Det+N, Vpr+DET+N,. For some lexical units of which the parts of speech are often used as reference for the morphosyntactic disambiguation of other lexical units, if they have multiple parts of speech, their entries of the lesser-used parts of speech in Dela are eliminated. For example, to decide a lexical unit is a noun or not depends on whether the lexical unit follows an article or not while some articles in French have more than one morphosyntactic interpretations (e.g., *un* (*a*) can be an article or a noun). Thus, the entry of *un* (*a*) as noun considered less used is eliminated in the preprocessing.

4.3.2 Automatic Extraction of Predicate-argument Structures

In French, the nominal distribution of an appropriate predicate can be situated in the position of subject, object complement (direct or indirect: the indirect object is introduced by the preposition in French), circumstantial complement of location or circumstantial complement of means. The syntactic position of nominal distribution often changes with the structural transformation of sentences (e.g., from an active sentence to a passive sentence). The analysis of syntactic-semantic distribution of appropriate predicates of artifact nouns is based on the elementary sentences of active form. The elementary sentences are the sentences containing only one conjugated verb. The complex sentences containing more than one conjugated verb can be obtained from a set of elementary sentences by the linguistic technique, i.e. transformation (Harris, 1976; Gross, 1986).

According to the syntactic position of nominal distribution of appropriate predicates, the appropriate predicates can be divided into four classes: the first class contains the appropriate predicates whose object complements (the object complement corresponds to the verb complement in English) are always artifact nouns; the second class contains the appropriate predicates whose object complements can be artifact nouns but whose circumstantial complements of means (it corresponds to the prepositional complement in English) are always artifact nouns; the third class includes the appropriate predicates whose object complements have less possibilities to be artifact nouns but whose circumstantial complements of location are always artifact nouns; the last class includes the appropriate predicates whose object complements are never artifact nouns but whose circumstantial complements (means or location) are always artifact nouns. Each class can be subdivided according to the syntactic features of the appropriate predicates. Table 1 lists all the classes that we made according to the syntactic-semantic distribution of appropriate predicates. For each class, some examples of predicates and corresponding syntactic patterns are given. In the formula expressions of syntactic-semantic distribution, V means verb, NAF indicates the artifact nouns and Nc refers to the nouns of other semantic classes.

Many other syntactic patterns are constructed considering language transformation from the basic syntactic patterns presented above. A series of graphs is established on the basis of the established syntactic patterns, and the predicate-argument structures are extracted through the tool

Classes	Appropriate Predicates	Syntactic-semantic Distribution
Class1		
Class_1	éteindre (turn off), inventer (invent), etc.	V+NAF
Class_1a	tirer (pull), retirer (remove), appuyer (support), etc.	V+dessus/dessous/sur...+NAF
Class_1b	jouer (play)	V+à/de+NAF
Class2		
Class_2	récurer (scrub), réparer (repaire), tracter (tow), etc.	V+de/avec/par+NAF
Class_2a	découper (cut out), fouiller (dig), décrasser (clean up), etc.	V+NAF/Nc+de/avec/par+NAF
Class_2b	équiper (equip), orner (decorate), etc.	V+NAF/Nc+de+NAF
Class3		
Class_3	ranger (arrange), installer (install), contenir (contain), etc.	V+NAF/Nc+sous/devant/sur/derrière...+NAF
Class_3a	transformer (transform)	V+NAF/Nc+en+NAF
Class_3b	connecter (connect)	V+NAF/Nc+à+NAF
Class4		
Class_4	verser(pour), enregistrer (record), etc.	V+Nc+dans+NAF
Class_4a	peigner (comb), maquiller(make up), farder (disguise), etc	V+Nc+avec/par/de+NAF
Class_4b	nourrir (nourish), alimenter (feed)	V+Nc+à+NAF
Class_4c	afficher (put up), placarder (placard), etc.	V+Nc+sur+NAF

Table 1: Analysis of syntactic-semantic distribution of appropriate predicates

Unitex. However, as the modifiers of a nominal phrase can be added without limits (especially when the modifiers are relative clauses), it is difficult to describe all types of constructions of sentence by the local grammar. In addition, an apposition often has a flexible position in one sentence. It can almost be inserted next to any noun phrase of a sentence. In the proposed method, the nominal phrases of more than five grams and the appositions are not taken into account.

4.3.3 Intersecting the Arguments

To intersect the arguments of different predicates is for finding the common arguments of the semantic class of predicates given in advance. As a semantic class of arguments is defined by a set of definitional appropriate predicates, the more an argument is shared by the given predicates, the more probably this argument belongs to the semantic class of the given predicates. The process of intersecting the arguments is shown in Figure 1. Pred$_i$ (i=1, 2, 3) refers to a predicate and Arg$_j$ (j=1, 2, 3) means an argument. The grey parts are the intersection of arguments. In fact, in our method, not only the common arguments of the given predicates are selected, but also the arguments shared by most of the given predicates. The number of different predicates that co-occur with an argument is noted as the intersecting frequency of this argument. For example, in Figure 1, the

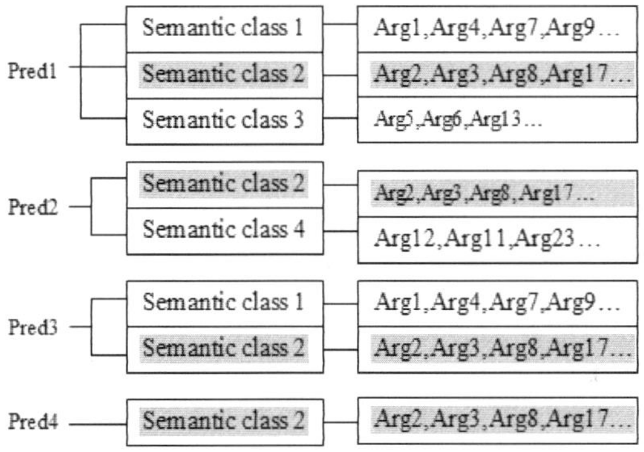

Figure 1: Intersecting the predicates

intersecting frequency of Arg2, Arg3, Arg8, and Arg17 is 4 because they are shared by all the four predicates and the intersecting frequency of Ar1, Arg4, Arg7, and Arg9 is 2 since they are shared by two predicates (Pred1 and Pred3).

4.4 Semi-supervised Method

In the semi-supervised method, the predicate-argument structures are identified with a semantic class of artifact nouns by local grammars. Then, all the predicates in the structures are extracted. Next, the predicates are intersected for determining which predicates belong to the semantic class of the given artifact nouns. The syntactic patterns associated with each predicate are also extracted. A probabilistic calculation is conducted in order to choose the most appropriate syntactic pattern for each predicate. With the selected predicates and their syntactic patterns, the nominal distribution of appropriate predicates can be located and the artifact nouns of the semantic class are finally acquired after intersecting the artifact nouns. With the obtained artifact nouns, the processes can be iterated for getting more artifact nouns.

4.4.1 Extraction of Predicate-argument Structures from a Semantic Class of Arguments

In the semi-supervised method, the predicate-argument relations are extracted from a set of arguments. However, with a set of appropriate predicates given in advance, the syntactic-semantic distribution can be predicted, but from the arguments, it is not certain to predict which syntactic-semantic relation is associated with the given argument. Thus, the following solution is adopted: all the possible syntactic relations between the artifact nouns and their appropriate predicates are firstly predicated; a probabilistic calculation is then carried out to the predicted syntactic relations in order to choose the appropriate syntactic pattern for each predicate. If the semantic distribution of artifact nouns can be situated in the position of noun complement without preposition introducing it (which concerns the direct complement of objet) and in the position of noun complement introduced by preposition (which concerns the indirect complement of objet, the circumstantial complement of location and the circumstantial complement of means), there should be three necessary constituents for forming a syntactic pattern allowing predicting a predicate-argument relation: verb, noun complement without preposition and noun complement introduced by preposition. With these three constituents, four combinations for forming the desired syntactic patterns can be obtained: V+NAF, V+NAF+prep+NAF, V+Nc+prep+NAF and V+prep+NAF (V means verb, prep refers to preposition and NAF indicates the artifact nouns). Other syntactic patterns (such as V+ADV+NAF, NAF+be+V+prep+NAF, NAF+V+prep+NAF+NAF or V+ADV+ADV+prep+NAF+NAF) are derived from these four basic syntactic patterns through the transformation of natural language.

With the established syntactic patterns, a series of graphs is constructed and the predicate-argument structures are labelled. In addition, the predicates, the arguments and the syntactic patterns associated with each predicate-argument structures are also labelled and extracted for the following processing.

4.4.2 Calculation of Syntactic Patterns

All the predicate-argument structures recognized by predicting the possible syntactic relations don't represent the real syntactic relation between a certain predicate and its arguments. For example, in *éteindre la lampe de poche* (*turn off the flashlight*), *éteindre* (*turn off*) can be identified by the syntactic pattern V+NAF+prep+NAF or V+NAF with the given artifact noun *lampe* (*lamp*) or *poche* (*pocket*); however, V+NAF+prep+NAF does not represent the syntactic-semantic distribution of the predicate *éteindre* (*turn off*). V+NAF+prep+NAF is misrecognized as the syntactic pattern of the predicate *éteindre* (*turn off*) because of the preposition *de* (*of*) which is a constituent of the compound noun *lampe de poche* (*flashlight*) rather than a preposition introducing a circumstantial complement. Thus, a probabilistic calculation of syntactic patterns is necessary for choosing the appropriate syntactic pattern for each predicate.

The syntactic pattern by which a predicate-argument structure is identified is recoded in the labels like *s=vactif_gnaf, s=vactif_gn_de_gnaf,...*, etc. The code *vactif* (*vpassif*) indicates the active (passive) form of the verb. The code *gn* means nominal phrase, and *gnaf* refers to a nominal phrase of artifact noun. The probability of having a direct object complement, $P(cod)$, is calculated by the formula:

$$P(cod) = \frac{c(gnaf) + c(gn)}{c(s)} \tag{1}$$

$c(gnaf)$ implies the frequency of occurrence of the syntactic patterns containing $gnaf$ in the position of direct object complement. For example, *s=vactif_gnaf, s=gnaf_va* and*gnaf_vpassif* are all the syntactic patterns including $gnaf$ in the position of direct object complement. $c(gn)$ indicates the frequency of occurrence of the syntactic patterns containing gn in the position of direct object complement. $c(s)$ indicates the frequency of occurrence of all the syntactic patterns associated with a predicate. The probability of having a direct object complement which is always artifact noun, $P(codnaf)$, is calculated according to the formula:

$$P(codnaf) = \frac{c(gnaf)}{c(s)} \quad (2)$$

and the probability of having an object complement introduced by a preposition, $P(codi)$, is calculated as follows:

$$P(codi) = \frac{c(prep)}{c(s)} \quad (3)$$

$c(prep)$ refers to the frequency of occurrence of the syntactic patterns containing a preposition. For each predicate, if its $P(codnaf)$ is greater than $P(cod)$-$P(codnaf)$, the direct object complement of this predicate is considered to be always artifact nouns;if $P(cod)$ equals to zero, this predicate is not considered to have the direct object complement; if $P(prep)$ is greater than 0.12, this predicate is considered as a predicate having an object complement introduced by preposition which is always artifact nouns. The threshold for $P(prep)$ is decided after several tests and it allows obtaining a more accurate syntactic information for each predicate. According to these probabilities about the syntactic positions, the most appropriate syntactic pattern is chosen for each predicate from the four basic syntactic pattern candidates. Finally, the extracted predicates are classified into four groups according to their syntactic-semantic patterns: the group of V+NAF, the group of V+NAF+prep+NAF, the group of V+Nc+prep+NAF, and the group of V+prep+NAF.

4.4.3 Intersecting the Predicates

The aim of intersecting the predicates is to find out common predicates of the given artifact nouns. The more a predicate is shared by the given arguments, the more probably it belongs to the semantic class of the given arguments. For a predicate, the number of different artifact nouns which cooccur with this predicate is noted as the intersecting frequency of this predicate. The threshold for intersecting the predicates is set at 2 after several tests. This threshold allows giving a better result.

4.4.4 Elimination of Basic Predicates

In the result obtained after intersecting, many basic predicates occupy the top place of the list. The basic predicates have a large semantic spectrum. They are not appropriate predicates of artifact nouns, but their nominal distribution cover the semantic class of artifact nouns. For the appropriate predicates which belong to the semantic class of given arguments, their frequencies of occurrence in the extracted predicate-argument structures (FC) and their frequencies of occurrence in the total corpus (FT) are more or less similar. On the contrary, for the basic predicates, there is a great disparity between their frequencies of occurrence in the extracted predicate-argument structures and their frequencies of occurrence in the total corpus, since the basic predicates have a larger and more general semantic spectrum. On the basis of this occurrence disparity, some of the basic predicates can be eliminated. The occurrence disparity (Ecart) is calculated as follows:

$$Ecart = \frac{FT - FC}{FT} \quad (4)$$

After several tests, we decided the threshold as 0.978 which gives a better result. If the $Ecart$ supasses the threshold, the corresponding predicate is considered as basic predicate.

4.4.5 Application of Supervised Method

With the filtered appropriate predicates and the learned syntactic-semantic patterns, a script is developed to automatically write the graphs for identifying the predicate-argument structures and labelling the arguments. Likewise, all the predicate-argument structures are extracted. The acquired arguments are then intersected. In this way, more artifact nouns are acquired from a small set of artifact nouns given in advance. The processes can be iterated for obtaining more artifact nouns.

5 Experiment and Evaluation

For the supervised method experiment, about one hundred appropriate predicates of artifact nouns are chosen, and a series of syntactic patterns are established on the basis of the syntactic-semantic distribution of the appropriate predicates. The semi-supervised method is tested with three semantic classes of arguments: container, cooker and road transport. For each semantic class, a list of arguments, including about twenty artifact nouns, is manually established. The evaluation is carried out by appealing to a dictionary of artifact nouns (including 13,400 entries) developed in the laboratory. The manual annotation is added because the dictrionary is not complet. Firstly, the

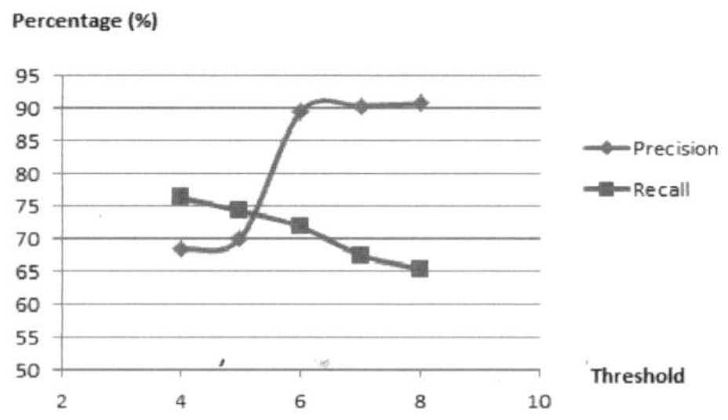

Figure 2: Experiment of threshold

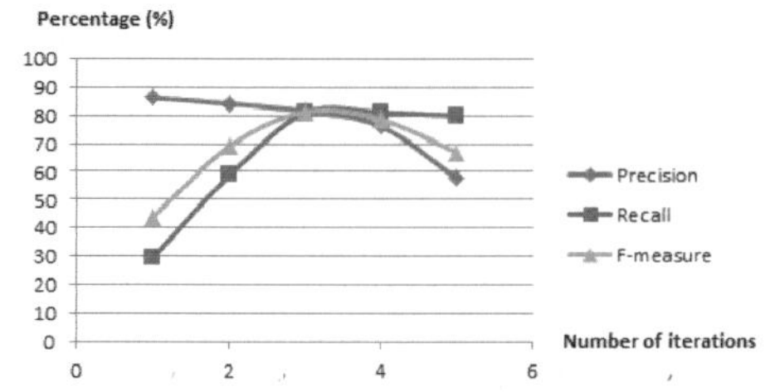

Figure 3: Experiment of iteration with semantic class "container"

artifact nouns in the corpus are labeled by the dictionary and the manual annotation. The result is considered as standard. Then, our method is applied for labelling the artifact nouns and another result is obtained. The result of our method is compared with the standard in order to calculate the precision, the recall and the F-measure.

For the supervised method, the threshold for intersecting the arguemnts is respectively set at 4, 5, 6, 7 and 8. Then, the precision, the recall and the F-measure are respectively calculated. The Evaluation results obtained with different thresholds are shown in Table 2. Figure 2 shows the comparision of the different evaluation results (F-measures) obtained with different thresholds. It is seen that the highest F-measure can be obtained when the threshold equals to 6.

Threshold	Precision	Recall	F-measure
4	68.31%	76.20%	72.03%
5	70.08%	74.16%	72.06%
6	89.40%	71.78%	79.63%
7	90.27%	67.45%	77.21%
8	90.59%	65.33%	75.91%

Table 2: Evaluation of supervised method

For the semi-supervised method, the experiment is firstly carried out with the artifact nouns of semantic calss "container". The processes of the semi-supervised method are iterated five times. The results obtained after each iteration are respectively evaluated. The threshold for intersecting the arguments is firstly set at 3. The result obtained by the semi-supervised method includes the grain terms. Table 3 shows the evaluation results obtained with different number of iterations, and Figure 3 shows the comparision of the evaluation resaults. It is found that the result obtained after three iterations has the highest F-measure. After four iterations, the precision falls down rapidly and the recall reaches a relatively stable value. The noise is brought by the nouns of other semantic classes obtained in each iteration. Then, the threshold is set at 2, 4, 5 and 6 respectively. The same experiment presented above is repeated for each threshold. Figure 4 shows a comparision of the highest F-measures that can be obtained with different thresholds. For the other two semantic classes, the same experiment and evaluation are conducted. Finally, we choose 3, 2 and 3 as the threshold for intersecting the arguments of the semantic class "container", "cooker" and "road transport" respectively and select 3, 3 and 4 as the number of iterations for the semantic class "container", "cooker" and "road transport" respectively. Table 4 shows the evaluation results of each semantic class with the defined threshold and number of iterations. The different quantity of apppropriate predicates of different semantic class in the copus makes the performance of our method different.

Number of iterations	Precision	Recall	F-measure
1	86.12%	29.41%	43.85%
2	84.07%	58.82%	69.21%
3	81.34%	81.02%	81.20%
4	76.10%	81.02%	78.48%
5	57.79%	79.87%	67.06 %

Table 3: Evaluation of iteration with semantic class "container"

Semantic classes	Precision	Recall	F-measure
Road transport	62.46%	58.53%	60.43%
Cooker	70.14%	76.87%	73.35%
Container	81.34%	81.02%	81.20%

Table 4: Evaluation of semi-supervised method

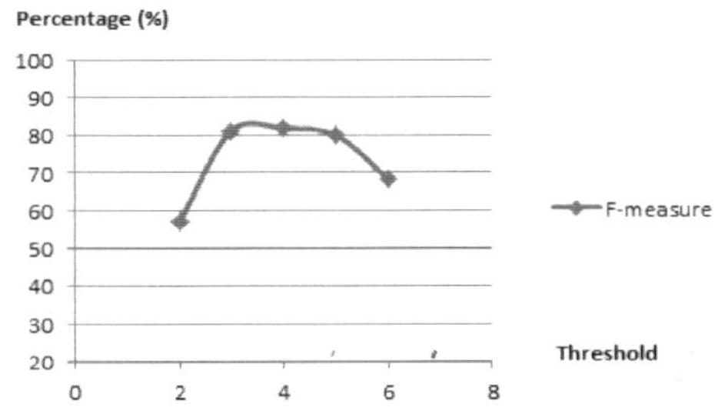

Figure 4: Experiment of threshold

6 Conclusion

The method in this article is based on the analysis of syntactic-semantic distribution of appropriate predicates of artifact nouns. The advantage of this method is that it allows locating not only the position of an artifact noun in each sentence but also the position of a nominal distribution which is composed of a semantic class of artifact nouns. A class of definitional appropriate predicate characterizes a semantic class of arguments and makes it possible to consider the polysemy. In addition, the identification of the nominal distributions of appropriate predicates also permits the identification of neologisms, misspelled artifact nouns or abbreviations. Although the performance of the proposed method is dependent on the accuracy and the completeness of the established local grammars, it allows obtaining lexicon resources with a relatively high precision and the obtained lexicon resources of semantic class can make a contribution to dialogue systems, natural language generation or other natural language processing applications.

References

B. P. Alecu, Izabella Thomas, and Julie Renahy. 2012. La "multi-extraction" comme stratégie d'acquisition optimisée de ressources terminologiques et non terminologiques. In *Actes de la 19e conférence sur le Traitement Automatique des Langues Naturelles*, pages 511–518. Grenoble.

D. Bourigault. 1996. Lexter: a natural language tool for terminology extraction. In *Proceedings of the 7th EURALEX International Congress*, pages 771–779. Göteborg.

P.-A. Buvet. 2009. Des mots aux emplois : la représentation lexicographique des prédicats. *Le Français Moderne*, 77(1):83–96.

B. Daille. 1994. Study and implementation of combined techniques for automatic extraction of terminology. In *The Balancing Act: Combining Symbolic and Statistical Approaches to Language, Proceedings of the Workshop of the 32nd Annual Meeting of the ACL*, pages 29–36. Las Cruces, New Mexico, USA.

Chantal Enguehard. 1993. Acquisition de terminologie à partir de gros corpuss. In *Actes Informatique & Langue Naturelle*, pages 373–384. Nantes.

M. Gross. 1986. *Grammaire transformationnelle du français : Syntaxe du verbe ; Syntaxe du nom*. Cantilène.

Z. S. Harris. 1976. *Notes du cours de syntaxe*. Le seuil.

M. A. Hearst. 1992. Automatic acquisition of hyponyms from large text corpora. In *Proceedings of the 14th conference on Computational linguistics*, volume 2, pages 539–545. Stroudsburg, PA, USA.

Fidelia Ibekwe-sanjuan. 2007. *Fouille de textes*. Lavoisier.

Jing Jiang. 2012. Information extraction from texte. In Charu C. Aggarwal and ChengXiang Zhai, editors, *Mining Text Data*, pages 18–22. Springer. US.

A. Lauriston. 1994. Automatic recognition of complex terms: problems and the termino solution. *Terminology*, 1(1):147–170.

Jean-Claude Meilland and Patrice Bellot. 2003. Extraction automatique de terminologie à partir de libellés textuels courts. In Geoffrey Williams, editor, *Linguistique de corpus*. Presses Universitaires de Rennes. France.

S. Mejri. 2009. Le mot, problématique théorique. *Le Français Moderne*, 77(1):68–82.

François Morlane-Hondère. 2012. *Une approche linguistique de l'évaluation des ressources extraites par analyse distributionnelle automatique*. Ph.D. thesis, Université Toulouse le Mirail. France.

Solen Quiniou, Peggy Cellier, Thierry Charnois, and Dominique Legallois. 2012. What about sequential data mining techniques to identify linguistic patterns for stylistics? In *Computational Linguistics and Intelligent Text Processing*, pages 166–177. Heidelberg.

Wolfgang Seeker and Jonas Kuhn. 2013. Morphological and syntactic case in statistical dependency parsing. *Computational Linguistics*, 39(1):23–55.

Rion Snow, Daniel Jurafsky, and Y. Ng Andrew. 2004. Learning syntactic patterns for automatic hypernym discovery. In *Advances in Neural Information Processing Systems*, pages 1297–1305. British Columbia.

Feature-Rich Part-Of-Speech Tagging Using Deep Syntactic and Semantic Analysis

Luchezar Jackov
Institute for Bulgarian Language
Bulgarian Academy of Sciences
lucho@skycode.com

Abstract

This paper describes the implementation, improvement and evaluation of the machine translation (MT) system proposed by Jackov (2014) when used as a feature-rich part-of-speech (POS) tagger for Bulgarian. The system does not rely on POS tagging for morphological disambiguation. Instead, all ambiguities are considered in parsing hypotheses that are scored and the best one is used for tagging. The system does not use automatic training on annotated corpora. Manually and automatically compiled linguistic resources are used for hypothesis derivation and scoring. BulTreeBank manually annotated corpus (Simov and Osenova, 2004) was used for evaluation, error detection and improvement.

1 Introduction

Part-of-speech (POS) tagging is the activity of labeling the words of a text with contextual tags describing the various grammatical features of the specific word usage. This is not trivial since many word forms are homonymous to other word forms. For instance, "*water*" is a noun in "*I drink water*" and a verb in "*They water the garden*". Linguists normally classify the words into at least eight basic POS classes: noun, pronoun, adjective, verb, adverb, preposition, conjunction, and interjection. Sometimes the list is extended with numerals, determiners, particles, etc. but the number of classes rarely exceeds 15.

Computational linguistics works with a larger inventory of POS tags, e.g., the Penn Treebank (Marcus et al., 1993) uses 48 tags: 36 for part-of-speech, and 12 for punctuation and currency symbols. The increase in the number of tags is partially due to finer granularity, e.g., there are special tags for determiners, particles, modal verbs, cardinal numerals, foreign words, existential *there*, etc., but also to the desire to encode morphological information as part of the tags.

POS tagging poses major challenges for morphologically complex languages whose tagsets encode a lot of additional morpho-syntactic features (for most of the basic POS categories), e.g., gender, number, person, etc. For example, BulTreeBank (Simov and Osenova, 2004) for Bulgarian uses 680 tags, while the Prague Dependency Treebank (Hajič, 1998) for Czech has over 1,400 tags (Georgiev et al., 2012).

POS tagging is a form of disambiguation and in many cases a deep syntactic and semantic analysis is needed for correct tagging.

An interesting approach for deep syntactic and semantic disambiguation was presented by Jackov (2014). However, the paper indicated that no evaluation of the system has been made. The goal of this paper is to present an evaluation of this system by using it as a feature-rich morphological tagger for Bulgarian and comparing the system output to the BulTreeBank manually annotated corpus for Bulgarian (Simov and Osenova, 2004).

The proposed approach considers the input text as a sequence of tokens. Then for each token all possible lemmas are derived. Lemma sequences of 1 or more tokens are looked up by the concept binder module in a synset lexicalization table for WordNet (Fellbaum, 1998) synsets. Each successful look-up is an assumption for a concept and constitutes an initial parsing hypothesis. The hypotheses contain assumptions about the concepts lying behind the input tokens, their syntactic roles and their dependency relations. Adjacent hypotheses are combined into new hypotheses for larger spans of the input sequence by using manually written hypothesis derivation rules. Each rule identifies, inherits and extends the syntactic and semantic assumptions of the constituting hypotheses. The rules are applied using a modified version of the Cocke–Younger–Kasami (CYK) algorithm (Cocke et al., 1970; Younger, 1967; Kasami, 1965) until all spans of

Proceedings of Recent Advances in Natural Language Processing, pages 224–231,
Hissar, Bulgaria, Sep 7–9 2015.

the input sequence are covered. To prevent hypothesis space explosion each hypothesis is scored against a knowledge database of dependency relations and only the n-best hypotheses are kept for each span of tokens.

Every hypothesis identifies one lemma per token and the best hypothesis is used for the tagging task. The data for the lemma consists of a set of values of morphological categories such as part of speech, gender, number, article, case, etc. These attribute values are used to compile the morphological tag assigned to each token.

The system was improved by correcting the handling of family names, by adding a category for explicit marking of verb transitiveness and importing verb transitiveness data from a dictionary, and by extending its lexical database using BulNet (Koeva, 2010).

The rest of the paper is organized as follows: Section 2 provides an overview of related work, Section 3 describes Bulgarian morphology in brief, Section 4 provides detailed description of the system, Section 5 describes modification of the system for the POS tagging task, Section 6 presents the work on the evaluation of the system and its improvement by using additional resources, Section 7 discusses in detail the process of error analysis and the resulting improvement, and Section 8 concludes and describes some promising directions for future work.

2 Related Work

A comprehensive review of the recent research on POS tagging is given by Georgiev et al. (2012). The rest of the paragraph is provided from the above-mentioned paper for informative purposes. Most previous work on Bulgarian POS tagging has started with large tagsets, which were then reduced. For example, Dojchinova and Mihov (2004) mapped their initial tagset of 946 tags to just 40, which allowed them to achieve 95.5% accuracy using the transformation-based learning of Brill (1995), and 98.4% accuracy using manually crafted linguistic rules. Similarly, Georgiev et al. (2009) who used maximum entropy and the BulTreeBank (Simov and Osenova, 2004) grouped its 680 fine-grained POS tags into 95 coarse-grained ones, and thus improved their accuracy from 90.34% to 94.4%. Simov and Osenova (2001) used a recurrent neural network to predict (a) 160 morpho-syntactic tags (92.9% accuracy) and (b) 15 POS tags (95.2% accuracy). Some researchers did not reduce the tagset: Savkov et al. (2011) used 680 tags (94.7% accuracy), and Tanev and Mitkov (2002) used 303 tags and the BULMORPH morphological analyzer (Krushkov, 1997), achieving P=R=95%. (Georgiev et al., 2012)

Chanev and Krushkov (2006) have also done a preliminary research on using HMM for POS tagging for Bulgarian, achieving precision of 92.16%.

A combined method for POS tagging, dependency parsing and co-reference resolution for Bulgarian has been proposed in Zhikov et al. (2013). The approach of Jackov is similar to the above-mentioned method in obviating the POS tagging step and the simultaneous resolution of all the morphological ambiguities together with the syntactic and semantic ambiguities. However, all of the linguistic data it uses is defined explicitly and only the dependency relations knowledge database may be automatically populated, while most of the other approaches rely on machine learning taking arbitrary features from training datasets. The predefined linguistic data is used to generate and score the hypotheses for the input sequence, eventually using the best hypothesis for output.

3 Bulgarian Morphology

Bulgarian language is highly inflective and with very rich morphology. Some of the pronouns have more than ten grammatical features, including case, gender, person, number, definiteness, etc.

There is a number of lexical and grammatical ambiguities in Bulgarian. For instance, many Bulgarian verbs have the same form for 2-nd and 3-rd singular aorist or imperfect, e.g. *Яде(ше) ли?* (meaning 'Did you/he eat'). There are also cross-POS ambiguities such as *става*, which means (a) 'joint' (a noun) or (b) 'become' (a verb, 3-rd person singular present). There is a systematic ambiguity between adverbs and neuter singular adjectives which all have the same surface form, e.g. *бърזо* is an adverb in *Той кара бързо* (meaning 'He drives fast') and an adjective in *бързо хранене* (meaning 'fast food'). Note that the example given in English has the same ambiguity. There is another notable ambiguity for the possessive clitic pronouns and the dative clitic personal pronouns. The situation is even worse for the conjunction *и* (meaning 'and') and *ѝ*, which is the clitic form of the possessive pronoun (meaning 'her') and the dative clitic form of the personal pronoun *тя* (meaning 'she'). Note that in the real world *ѝ* is often written without the stress mark, which makes it identical to the conjunction *u*.

An analysis of BulTreeBank shows that it consists of 59,924 different morphological entities (a word form and its morphological tag). 52,017 of them are unambiguous in terms of tagging, i.e. they are tagged the same within the corpus. However, the ambiguous word forms prevail in terms of usage statistics.

4 Detailed Description of the System

4.1 Overview

The system has been implemented in C++ and has a very compact binary data representation, approx. 60MB for 7 languages and 42 language translation directions. It has been used in offline translation applications for mobile devices, outperforming Google Offline Translator in both quality and size (the latter needs about 1.05GB of data for the above-mentioned 7 languages). It has also participated successfully in the iTranslate4 project, and can be tested online at http://itranslate4.eu (the SkyCode vendor). The system consists of a lemmatizer, a concept binder, a hypothesis generator, a dependency relations scorer and a synthesis unit. (Jackov, 2014)

The system implements an extensive inventory of categories and category values. A special category, the hypothesis type identifier (HTI), serves as the set of non-terminal values for the parsing rules, which are extended context-free grammar (CFG) rules used for production of hypotheses.

An elaborate description with many more examples is given by Jackov (2014).

4.2 Lemmatizer

The first step of the system operation is to apply the lemmatizer module on each input token, which produces a list of all lemmas for each token along with their category values. For instance, for the input token *ми,* the module will produce an entry for the dative clitic of the personal pronoun *аз* (meaning 'I'), an entry for the possesive pronoun clitic and two more entries for the second and third person singular aorist forms of the verb *мия* (meaning 'to wash'). The lemma of each lemmatization is kept as a lemma identifier, which is used later in the concept binder. The lemmatizer is built as a simple, yet very efficient stemmer allowing definition of arbitrary paradigms, one per HTI. The original system has 102,393 lemmas for Bulgarian.

4.3 Hypothesis Generator

The second step is to apply the hypothesis generator for every span of the input sequence of tokens. The module first runs the concept binder for spans of length less than 7 tokens, and then applies parsing rules over the adjacent sub-spans of each span.

4.4 Concept Binder

The concept binder finds the concepts (WordNet synset identifiers) matching a span of input tokens.

It uses a database of the possible lexicalizations for each WordNet synset. Each lexicalization entry in the database consists of a list of lemma identifiers, WordNet synset identifier, attribute restriction rules, attribute unification rules, and a list of additional attribute values. The list of additional values is used to define lexicalization level features such as sub-categorization frames, transitiveness and aspect for verbs, etc. The original system has 166,948 synset lexicalizations for Bulgarian.

4.5 Parsing Rules and Hypothesis Generation

The core of each parsing rule is an extended CFG rule defined for the HTI feature values of the constituting hypotheses. The parsing rule extends the CFG by defining additional attribute value restrictions, agreement restrictions, attribute unification rules and parsing rule score. It also defines syntactic and semantic roles, dependency relations and propagation rules so that the higher level hypothesis resulting from the rule application unifies those of the constituting hypotheses.

4.6 Dependency Relations Knowledge Database

The database contains entries that consist of a relation identifier, two WordNet synset identifiers and a weight value, which is normally 1 or -1.

The database is manually populated and currently has 1,803,446 entries.

Here are sample entries with words instead of WordNet synset identifiers for clarity:

(poss, study, woman, 1)

(nsubj, mushroom, study, 1)

The above entries are enough for disambiguating the sentence *Women's studies mushroom.*

4.7 Hypothesis Scoring

As a result each hypothesis contains a number of assumed concepts and their dependency relations and each concept is identified by its WordNet synset identifier. The set of the relations between the concepts is scored by looking up the dependency relations knowledge base. If the look-up is successful the dependency relation score is the weight of the matching entry, otherwise the score is zero. The hypothesis score is calculated by summing the dependency relation scores and the parsing rule score.

5 POS Tagging by the System

5.1 Overview

When the hypothesis generator finishes its work it yields a parsing hypothesis for the input sequence of tokens having the best score. While the lemmatizer assigns all possible lemmatizations for each token, each hypothesis contains exactly one lemmatization per token. The lemmatization data kept by the system contains the feature values associated with the input token, which in turn are used to compile the POS tag that is ultimately assigned to the token.

5.2 Translating Feature Values to Tags

The main issue when translating the feature values used within the system into the BulTreeBank tag set was the mapping of the large inventory of feature values (more than 1,000) into the large inventory of BulTreeBank tags (680).

Some of the work was easy due to the fact that the most common features and their values such as person, gender, number, etc. correspond in BulTreeBank and within the system of Jackov. For these features only a simple mapping of the feature values into the respective BulTreeBank mnemonic encodings and concatenating the resulting symbols was needed to correctly produce the BulTreeBank tags.

However, some of the word paradigms posed a problem. There are word forms in the lemmatizer that are handled by using derivation. The most notable examples are the verbal nouns, which are correctly annotated as nouns in BulTreeBank while being handled as derivational verb forms in the system. There are also others, e.g. various adjectives that are systematically derived from nouns and are handled as derivational noun forms within the system. Jackov motivated these deviations from the accepted linguistic models with much easier handling of such words within the system, their analysis, and translation. For instance, some of the derivational forms do not have WordNet synsets (at least in PWN3.0) as the verbal nouns have the verb semantics and the above-mentioned derivational adjectives in Bulgarian are semantically equivalent to English nouns used attributively.

6 Evaluation and Improvement by Using Additional Resources

6.1 Overview

A preliminary run of the system as a POS tagger for the BulTreeBank tagset produced result with accuracy of 88%. The error analysis showed the following deficiencies: (a) incomplete correspondence of category values to tags; (b) improper handling of family names; (c) lack of lemmas for some words; (d) lack of explicit transitiveness data in the lexicalization database; (e) lack of explicit adverb type description; (f) errors in the lemmatization data, the rules and the lexicalization data in the system. Handling these deficiencies is described in the below sub-sections.

6.2 Improving the Handling of Family Names

The BulTreeBank tagset annotates family names using a special hybrid tag because family names in Bulgarian are inflected by gender and number. In the system family names are entered as proper nouns. This has been improved by defining a new HTI feature value and a respective paradigm for the word forms. A simple algorithm based on the word endings was applied to derive the paradigms of the family names that had been defined as proper nouns. It was based on the heuristic that most Bulgarian family names have unchanging suffixes from which the lemma (the singular masculine form) can be derived and the inflection group identifier can be assigned, after which the transformation is complete.

6.3 Using BulNet

BulNet (Koeva, 2010) is the Bulgarian equivalent of Princeton WordNet (PWN) (Fellbaum, 1998). It is being developed by the Institute for Bulgarian Language (IBL) at the Bulgarian Academy of Sciences. The dataset was kindly provided by prof. Svetla Koeva from IBL.

A comparison between the dataset and the system lexicalization data showed that BulNet contained many lexicalizations that were not in the system and using BulNet will mitigate the deficiency of lacking some lexicalizations.

The use of the BulNet dataset was significantly eased by the fact that it uses the PWN 3.0 synset identifiers which are also used by the system.

6.4 Adding Explicit Transitiveness Feature Values

In the initial experiments the verb transitiveness was derived from the sub-categorization values that the system already had. However, this proved inconsistent with BulTreeBank. Apparently, the dictionary data for the transitiveness was used by the corpus annotators. To overcome this, an explicit transitiveness category has been added and the database has been populated with values by consulting the multi-volume Dictionary of Bulgarian Language by IBL.

6.5 Adding Explicit Adverb Type Feature Values

There is no adverb type categorization in the system, while most of the adverbs in BulTreeBank are tagged along with a type value. Since there was no other source for deriving this information, the most commonly used adverb tags have been used to populate the system database with explicit adverb type category values.

6.6 Using Unambiguous Word Forms as a Constraint

Additional improvement was achieved by analyzing the BulTreeBank corpus and extracting the unambiguous word forms (word forms that have unambiguous annotation), and using them as a constraint. For instance, this obviated the need of translating the category values for many pronouns which are elaborately annotated within BulTreeBank. However, using this technique also hides some of the corpus errors that become evident when comparing the POS tagging output of the system to the corpus.

6.7 Manual Improvement

After the above-mentioned improvements the precision of the POS tagging by the system reached 93%. The error analysis showed the following causes for errors: (a) improper correspondence of category values to tags; (b) improper rule application due to improperly defined constraints; (c) missing rules for certain linguistic phenomena; (d) improper or missing lexicalizations; (e) improper verb transitiveness and aspect data; (f) improper paradigm definitions; (g) tagging errors in the corpus.

Trying to address (a), (b), (c), (d), (e), and (f) for just one of the corpus files improved the overall precision to 95%, and the precision of the POS tagging for that file reached 96.54%.

Further analysis of the errors showed that some of them were indeed annotation errors in the corpus, while others come from different strategies for handling specific language phenomena. For instance, *много* (meaning 'many/much/very') is always annotated as adverbial numeral in BulTreeBank which does not reflect the ambiguity of the word – it is a numeral when meaning *many*, a quantifier adjective for one of the meanings of *much*, and an adverb for another of the meanings of *much* and also an intensifier adverb meaning *very*. After contacting Kiril Simov and Petya Osenova, it became clear that this type of annotation is correct in terms of the annotation model they had accepted.

The system makes the above distinctions which results in POS tagging differences which however are not errors. After manually correcting the discrepancies in the corpus file and correcting other annotation errors, the tagging precision for that file reached 97.998%. The percentage of errors and discrepancies for the corrected version of the file when compared to the original corpus file was 1.722%.

7 Error Analysis and Improvement

The careful error analysis has lead to:

- improving the system where the cause was incorrect description of the linguistic phenomena;
- improving the corpus by correcting incorrect annotations where the cause was an annotation errors.

It is worth mentioning that the error analysis lead to discovering errors in all resources used by the system. However, the goal of this paper is to evaluate the system using BulTreeBank, that is why the errors found in other resources are not discussed.

7.1. Error Analysis Leading to Improvement of the System

Some of the most useful cases of error detection and correction that lead to the most significant improvements of the system were those of a missing rule or improper constraint definitions for a certain rule. The lack of constraints in the rule definitions results in generation of parsing hypotheses that are not grammatical, which in turn leads to incorrect tagging.

Examples of linguistic phenomena that were not handled and were addressed by adding rules:

- repetitive coordinating conjunctions (e.g. *както ..., така и ...*, meaning '... as well as ...');
- handling personal pronoun dative clitics in front of a passive construction, i.e. *Писмата **му** бяха дадени* (meaning 'the letters were given **to him**').

Examples of linguistic phenomena whose handling was corrected by refining the rule constraints are:

- the personal and possessive pronoun clitics may appear before the verb. For instance, *ти **му** кажи това*, meaning 'you tell this **to him**'. However, it is unacceptable to start a sentence in Bulgarian with such pronoun. That constraint was added to the respective rules after inspecting tagging errors of *и* that should have been tagged as a conjunction (meaning 'and') but was erroneously tagged either as a dative clitic or a possessive clitic (meaning 'her');
- An adverbial phrase can appear between the verb and the direct object. For instance, *той прави **често** това*, meaning 'he **often** does this'. However, this is unacceptable when the direct object is a personal pronoun clitic.
- Possessive pronoun clitics may appear outside the noun phrase before the verb. For instance, *не **ми** забравяй рождения ден*, meaning 'Do not forget **my** birthday'. However, no other word (such as an adverb or adverbial phrase) is allowed between them.

The error analysis has also lead to a number of lexicalizations such as *играя театър* (meaning 'to pretend') being added to the concept database.

7.2 Error Analysis Leading to Improvement of the Corpus

Some of the differences between the corpus files and the POS tagging result of the system turned out to be annotation errors. Some of these errors were sporadic, while others appeared to be systematic. Below is a list of the most frequent systematic errors that were discovered:

- Errors in transitivity annotation. The transitivity of many Bulgarian verbs varies depending on the specific usage and often changes when the verb is used reflexively. 88 out of 148 tagging differences between the original and the edited corpus file are transitivity annotation errors. The above statistics are only for the 8,590-token file that was exhaustively inspected.
- Inconsistent annotation of the tokens *2/две/два* (meaning 'two'). These forms were annotated in a number of different ways. In 265 cases throughout the corpus *2* was annotated just as a numeral (M) without any other feature values. In 61 cases it was annotated as Mc-pi (plural cardinal numeral, no gender, indefinite article). In 90 cases it was annotated as Mcxpi (x stands for the various gender values and there were annotations for masculine, feminine and neuter). In all 291 cases *две* (meaning 'two' for feminine and neuter gender) was annotated as Mc-pi. In all 202 cases *два* (meaning 'two' for masculine gender) was annotated as Mcmpi. The same goes with other numerals ending in '2' where the linguistic expansion of the numeral would require the gender feature value.
- Inconsistent annotation of numerals representing years. Numerals like *19xx* most probably represent years. Most such numerals are either correctly annotated as Mofsi (ordinal numeral, feminine, singular, indefinite article) or incorrectly annotated just as a numeral (M) without any feature values. The distribution varies for the different numerals from 66% to 33% to more than 50% for the improper annotation (just M) for some of the year values (e.g. 1996).
- Inconsistent annotation of numerals representing days of the month. Days of month are normally annotated as ordinal numerals and a singular noun for the month. However, many numerals representing a day of month were annotated just as M.
- Inconsistent annotation of *часа* (meaning 'o'clock'). The correct annotation for this word form should be Ncmsh (single masculine noun with hybrid article). In many cases it was incorrectly annotated as Ncmpt (plural masculine noun count form). This may be caused by the constraint mentioned by Georgiev et al. (2012) in section 4. Apparently this rule is not appropriate for the above linguistic phenomenon.
- Inconsistent annotation of the article when annotating abbreviations. For in-

stance, *СДС* (meaning 'Union of democratic forces') in 248 cases is annotated as Npmsi (proper noun with indefinite article) and in 79 cases as a proper noun with definite article. The same goes for other abbreviations such as *БСП* (meaning 'Bulgarian socialist party'), and *МВР* (meaning 'Interior ministry'). While for some of the abbreviations it may be arguable whether to use definite article or not, in the case of *СДС* it is more often than not, in contrast with the above numbers.

- Inconsistent tagging of the auxiliary particle *да* as an affirmative particle in one of the corpus files. This error alone accounts for 2% error rate in the annotation of that file.

8 Conclusion and Future Work

8.1 Conclusion

The experiments of evaluating the system of Jackov as a feature-rich POS tagger for Bulgarian proved to be useful in several ways. After inexhaustive manual improvement the precision for one training file reached the state-of-the-art value of 97.98% for the full BulTreeBank tagset (Georgiev et al., 2012) and exceeded the value of 97.13% for the partially similar approach of Zhikov et al. (2013). The precision for a reduced set of 13 tags reached 99.94%. The overall precision of over 95% (98.43% for 13-strong tagset) can also be considered very good, having in mind the high rate of over 1.7% of annotation disagreements and errors.

It is worth noting that the above precision rate is measured for the corrected version of the corpus, which makes the result not directly comparable to other results. However, the corrections made to the corpus are linguistically motivated and linguistically motivated corrections are needed for further progress (Manning, 2011).

The rule-based nature of the system makes it a valuable tool for discovery of annotation errors – nearly a third of the differences between the output of the system and the corpus turned out to be annotation errors.

8.2 Future Work

The improvements made to the system in the process of using and refining it as a feature-rich POS tagger proved valuable as they improve the parsing accuracy and in turn the translation accuracy. A thorough review and corrective actions for POS tagging differences for all corpus files would (a) improve its parsing precision and translation quality and (b) improve the annotation precision of the corpus. It is also a good idea to evaluate the system using another POS-annotated corpus, e.g. BulPosCor[1] that was used by Dojchinova and Mihov (2004).

The good results and the improvement of the system in the process of evaluating it as a POS tagger imply that it is quite probable to achieve even better improvement and good results when evaluating it as a dependency parser by comparing its output to dependency-annotated corpora.

Another good direction of work is the use and evaluation of the system for semantic disambiguation, for instance using BulSemCor[2];

Some of the tagging errors imply that improving the co-referential resolution of the system may yield even better results when used as a POS tagger.

9 Acknowledgments

I wish to express my gratitude to my scientific advisor prof. Svetla Koeva for her help and encouragement to do the research described in the paper. I wish to thank assoc. prof. Petya Osenova and assoc. prof. Kiril Simov for the readily provided corpus data and their valuable comments on the research and when writing the paper. I also wish to thank the reviewers and my colleagues who have read the various versions of the paper and provided me with valuable comments.

References

Eric Brill. 1995. Transformation-based error-driven learning and natural language processing: a case study in part-of-speech tagging. *Comput. Linguist.*, 21:543-565.

A. Chanev, Hr. Krushkov. 2006. A Simple Part-of-Speech Tagger for Bulgarian, *In proceedings of the Conference on Mathematics, Informatics and Computer Science, Veliko Tarnovo, 2006,* pp. 195-198: https://www.researchgate.net/publication/278021899_A_SIMPLE_PART-OF-SPEECH-TAGGER_FOR_BULGARIAN

J. Cocke, and J. T. Schwartz. 1970. Programming Languages and Their Compilers: Preliminary Notes. Technical report. Courant Institute of Mathematical Sciences, New York University.

[1] http://bg.wikipedia.org/wiki/БулПосКор

[2] http://bg.wikipedia.org/wiki/БулСемКор

Veselka Dojchinova and Stoyan Mihov. 2004. High performance part-of-speech tagging of Bulgarian. In Christoph Bussler and Dieter Fensel, editors, AIMSA, volume 3192 of *Lecture Notes in Computer Science*, pages 246-255. Springer.

C. Fellbaum. 1998. WordNet: An Electronic Lexical Database. MIT Press.

Georgi Georgiev, Preslav Nakov, Petya Osenova, and Kiril Simov. 2009. Cross-lingual adaptation as a baseline: adapting maximum entropy models to Bulgarian. In *Proceedings of the RANLP'09 Workshop on Adaptation of Language Resources and Technology to New Domains*, AdaptLRTtoND '09, pages 35-38, Borovets, Bulgaria.

Georgi Georgiev, Valentin Zhikov, Kiril Ivanov Simov, Petya Osenova, and Preslav Nakov. 2012. Feature rich part-of-speech tagging for morphologically complex languages: Application to Bulgarian. In *EACL'12*, pages 492-502.

Jan Hajič. 1998. Building a Syntactically Annotated Corpus: The Prague Dependency Treebank. In Eva Hajičova, editor, *Issues of Valency and Meaning. Studies in Honor of Jarmila Panevova*, pages 12-19. Prague Karolinum, Charles University Press.

Luchezar Jackov. 2014. Machine translation based on WordNet and dependency relations, In *Proceedings of Computational Linguistics in Bulgaria 2014*, pages 64-72.

T. Kasami. 1965. An Efficient Recognition and Syntax-analysis Algorithm for Context-free Languages. *Scientific report AFCRL-65-758*. Bedford, MA: Air Force Cambridge Research Lab.

Svetla Koeva. 2010. Bulgarian Wordnet – current state, applications and prospects. In *Bulgarian-American Dialogues*, pages 120-132, Sofia: Prof. M. Drinov Academic Publishing House.

Hristo Krushkov. 1997. *Modelling and building machine dictionaries and morphological processors (in Bulgarian)*. Ph.D. thesis, University of Plovdiv, Faculty of Mathematics and Informatics, Plovdiv, Bulgaria.

Christopher D. Manning. 2011. Part-of-Speech Tagging from 97% to 100%: Is It Time for Some Linguistics? In Alexander Gelbukh (ed.), *Computational Linguistics and Intelligent Text Processing, 12th International Conference, CICLing 2011, Proceedings, Part I*. Lecture Notes in Computer Science 6608, pp. 171-189. Springer.

Mitchell P. Marcus, Mary Ann Marcinkiewicz, and Beatrice Santorini. 1993. Building a large annotated corpus of English: the Penn Treebank. *Comput. Linguist.*, 19:313-330.

Aleksandar Savkov, Laska Laskova, Petya Osenova, Kiril Simov, and Stanislava Kancheva. 2011. A web-based morphological tagger for Bulgarian. In Daniela Majchrakova and Radovan Garabik, editors, *Slovko 2011. Sixth International Conference. Natural Language Processing, Multilinguality*, pages 126-137, Modra/Bratislava, Slovakia. Helmut Schmid. 1994. Probabilistic part-of-speech

Kiril Simov and Petya Osenova. 2004. BTB-TR04: BulTreeBank morphosyntactic annotation of Bulgarian texts. Technical Report BTB-TR04, Bulgarian Academy of Sciences.

Hristo Tanev and Ruslan Mitkov. 2002. Shallow language processing architecture for Bulgarian. In *Proceedings of the 19th International Conference on Computational Linguistics,* COLING '02, pages 1-7, Taipei, Taiwan.

D. H. Younger. 1967. Recognition and parsing of context-free languages in time n3. *Information and Control 10 (2)*: 189-208.

Valentin Zhikov, Georgi Georgiev, Kiril Simov, Petya Osenova, 2013. Combining POS Tagging, Dependency Parsing and Coreferential Resolution for Bulgarian. *RANLP 2013*: 755-762.

The Application of Constraint Rules to Data-driven Parsing

Sardar Jaf
The University of Manchester
jafs@cs.man.ac.uk

Allan Ramsay
The University of Manchester
ramsaya@cs.man.ac.uk

Abstract

In this paper, we show an approach to extracting different types of constraint rules from a dependency treebank. Also, we show an approach to integrating these constraint rules into a dependency data-driven parser, where these constraint rules inform parsing decisions in specific situations where a set of parsing rule (which is induced from a classifier) may recommend several recommendations to the parser. Our experiments have shown that parsing accuracy could be improved by using different sets of constraint rules in combination with a set of parsing rules. Our parser is based on the arc-standard algorithm of MaltParser but with a number of extensions, which we will discuss in some detail.

1 Introduction

In this paper we present a new implementation of the arc-standard algorithm of MaltParser (Joakim, 2003; Nivre, 2006; Nivre, 2008). The key features of this implementation are that (i) it includes a new approach to handling non-projective trees (Section 3); (ii) it allows the inclusion of information about local subtrees as an extra guide to parsing (Section 8); (iii) the assignment of labels to arcs is carried out as a separate phase of analysis rather than during the determination of dependency relations between words (Section 5). We compare the performance of the arc-standard version of MaltParser with four different versions of our parser in Section 9.

2 Deterministic Shift-reduce Parsing

The arc-standard algorithm deterministically generates dependency trees using two data-structures: a queue of input words, and a stack of items that have been looked at by the parser. Three parse actions are applied to the queue and the stack: SHIFT, LEFT-ARC and RIGHT-ARC. SHIFT moves the head of the queue onto the top of the stack, LEFT-ARC makes the head of the queue a parent of the topmost item on the stack and pops this item from the stack, and RIGHT-ARC makes the topmost item on the stack a parent of the head of the queue, removing the head of the queue and moving the topmost item on the stack back to the queue. At each parse transition the parser uses a classifier trained on a dependency treebank for predicting the next parse action given the current state of the parser.

3 Non-projective Parsing

The arc-standard version of the MaltParser fails to deal with non-projective trees.

Figure 1 shows a well-known example of a Czech sentence with a non-projective dependency tree. Figure 2 shows the problem with the basic algorithm. In step *8* from Figure 2 the parser may perform either LEFT-ARC, RIGHT-ARC, or SHIFT, but none of these operations lead to producing a tree matching the original non-projective tree. According to the dependency relations that are extracted from the tree (as shown at the top of Figure 2), LEFT-ARC is not allowed. On the one hand, if the parser performs LEFT-ARC then this will lead to the production of a tree that will not match the original tree because that will make *5* the parent of *3*, which does not match any relations in the original tree. On the other hand, performing RIGHT-ARC, which is allowed , will make *3* the parent of *5*. However, performing RIGHT-ARC at this stage is not an ideal operation because *5* will not be available in subsequent stages when it is required to become the parent of *1*, which remains on the queue[1]. This means that *1* will subse-

[1]LEFT-ARC and RIGHT-ARC remove the dependent

Proceedings of Recent Advances in Natural Language Processing, pages 232–238,
Hissar, Bulgaria, Sep 7–9 2015.

quently receive the wrong parent, which will produce a tree that does not match the original tree. SHIFT will move *5* to the top of the stack, which means that both *5* and *3* will be on the stack and hence they will never be in a state where *3* can become the parent of *5*, therefore the parser will not produce a tree that matches the original tree.

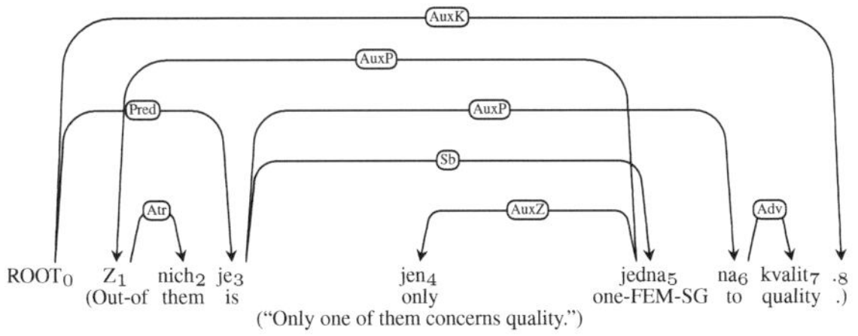

Figure 1: Non-projective dependency graph for a Czech sentence from the Prague Dependency Treebank (Nivre, 2008).

```
Dependency relations: (0,Pred,3)(0,AuxK,8)(1,Attr,2)(3,sb,5)
(3,AuxP,6)(5,AuxP,1)(5,AuxZ,4)(6,Adv,7)
```

Step	Action	Queue	Stack	Arcs
1	θ	[0,1,...]	[]	θ
2	SHIFT	[1,2,...]	[0]	θ
3	SHIFT	[2,3,...]	[1,0]	θ
4	RIGHT-ARC	[1,3,...]	[0]	A1=(1,Atr,2)
5	SHIFT	[3,4,...]	[1,0]	A1
6	SHIFT	[4,5,...]	[3,1,0]	A1
7	LEFT-ARC	[5,6,...]	[4,3,1,0]	A2=A1∪(5,AuxZ,4)
8	_	[5,6,...]	[3,1,0]	A2

Figure 2: Parsing the sentence in Figure 1 using the original arc-standard algorithm.

In order to overcome the limitation of the arc-standard algorithm of MaltParser, we allow for combining the head of the queue with an item on the stack that may or may not be the topmost item. Here, we introduce LEFT-ARC(N) and RIGHT-ARC(N) where N is any non-zero integer: LEFT-ARC(N) says 'Make the head of the queue the parent of the Nth item on the stack and pop the item from the stack', RIGHT-ARC(N) says 'Make the head of the queue a daughter of the Nth item on the stack, and roll the stack back onto the queue until you reach the Nth item'. LEFT-ARC(1) and RIGHT-ARC(1) are the arc-standard LEFT-ARC and RIGHT-ARC operations.

As part of this implementation we can reproduce the non-projective graph shown in Figure 1 given the dependency relations extracted from the graph. The parse transitions of the extended algorithm, as shown in Figure 3, reproduce the non-projective graph shown in Figure 1. The line in bold in steps `9` from Figure 3 shows the parse transition that the original algorithm would not have performed. In step `9`, the extended algorithm performs the LEFT-ARC(2) operation. It makes the head of the queue (`5`) the parent of the second item on the stack (`1`)[2].

```
Dependency relations: (0,Pred,3)(0,AuxK,8)(1,Attr,2)(3,sb,5)
(3,AuxP,6)(5,AuxP,1)(5,AuxZ,4)(6,Adv,7)
```

Step	Action	Queue	Stack	Arcs
1	θ	[0,1,...]	[]	θ
2	SHIFT	[1,2,...]	[0]	θ
3	SHIFT	[2,3,...]	[1,0]	θ
4	RIGHT-ARC(1)	[1,3,...]	[0]	A1=(1,Atr,2)
5	SHIFT	[3,4,...]	[1,0]	A1
6	SHIFT	[4,5,...]	[3,1,0]	A1
7	SHIFT	[5,6,...]	[4,3,1,0]	A1
8	LEFT-ARC(1)	[5,6,...]	[3,1,0]	A2=A1∪(5,AuxZ,4)
9	**LEFT-ARC(2)**	**[5,6,...]**	**[3,0]**	**A3=A2∪(5,AuxP,1)**
10	RIGHT-ARC(1)	[3,6,...]	[0]	A4=A3∪(3,Sb,5)
11	SHIFT	[6,7,8]	[3,0]	A4
12	SHIFT	[7,8]	[6,3,0]	A4
13	RIGHT-ARC(1)	[6,8]	[3,0]	A5=A4∪(6,Adv,7)
14	RIGHT-ARC(1)	[3,8]	[0]	A6=A5∪(3,AuxP,6)
15	RIGHT-ARC(1)	[0,8]	[]	A7=A6∪(0,Pred,3)
16	SHIFT	[8]	[0]	A7
17	RIGHT-ARC(1)	[0]	[]	A8=A7∪(0,AuxK,8)
18	SHIFT	[]	[0]	A8
19	θ	[]	[0]	A8

Figure 3: Parsing the sentence in Figure 1 using the extended version of the arc-standard algorithm.

A similar technique for processing non-projective sentences is proposed by Kuhlmann and Nivre (2010), which is the non-adjacent arc transitions. This technique allows for creating arcs between non-neighbouring arcs. This is achieved by extending the arc-standard to do the followings:

LEFT-ARC-2$_l$: This operation creates an arc by making the topmost item on the stack the parent of the third topmost item on the stack, and removes the topmost item.

RIGHT-ARC(2)$_l$: This operation creates an arc by making the third topmost item on the stack the parent of the topmost item on the stack, and removes the topmost item.

Although Attardi (2006) claims that LEFT-ARC(2)$_l$ and RIGHT-ARC-2$_l$ are sufficient for producing every non-projective tree Kuhlmann and Nivre (2010, p. 6) argues to the contrary.

Our re-implementation of the arc-standard algorithm, which is a generalisation of propos-

item from the queue or the stack so they will not be available in subsequent steps.

[2]The head of the queue was not combined with the topmost item on the stack in step `9` because that would have removed `5` from the queue, which will be needed later to be used as the parent of `1`.

als by Kuhlmann and Nivre (2010) and Attardi (2006), will handle all possible cases of non-projectivity because we allow N in LEFT-ARC(N) and RIGHT-ARC(N) to be a positive number larger than 2 if necessary. However, it contrasts the approach used by Kuhlmann and Nivre (2010) in that we combine the head of the queue with any item on the stack rather than combining the top items on the stack. Unfortunately, our approach broadens the range of possibilities available to the parser at each stage of the parsing process, and hence learning parse rules for enabling the parser to make the right choice at each stage becomes more difficult.

4 Assigning Scores to Parse States

Our parser generates one or more parse states from a given state. If the queue consists of one or more items and the stack is empty then the parser produces one state by performing SHIFT. For example, if the queue is `[1, 2, 3, 4]` and the stack is `[]` then the parser cannot recommend LEFT-ARC(N) or RIGHT-ARC(N) because these two operations require an item on the stack to be made the parent or the daughter of the head of the queue respectively.

If the queue consists of one or more items and the stack consists of one item only, then there are three possible moves: SHIFT, LEFT-ARC(1), and RIGHT-ARC(1). However, the parse model, which is based on a classification algorithm, will recommend only one operation (SHIFT, LEFT-ARC(1), or RIGHT-ARC(1)). Although in this kind of state our parser generates three states only one state will be given a positive score, which is based on recommendation of the parsing rules.

If the queue consists of one or more items and the stack consists of more than one item, then our parser may generate more than three states because it checks for relations between the head of the queue and any items on the stack; i.e., states that are generated by LEFT-ARC(N+1) and RIGHT-ARC(N+1), where N is a positive number.

In order to use a state from the newly generated states we assign a score to each new state, which is computed by using two different scores: (i) a score that is based on the recommendation made by the parsing rules. For example, we give a score of 1 for a SHIFT operation if it is recommended by a parsing rule, otherwise we give it a score of 0 (and the same applies to LEFT-ARC(N) and RIGHT-ARC(N)). Also (ii) we add the score from (i) to the score of the current state (which is the state that the new parse state is generated from). The sum of these two scores is assigned to the newly generated parse state(s).

There are two advantages of assigning a score to each parse state: (i) we can manipulate the assignment of various other scores to newly generated parse state(s), such as scores for the application of constraint rules to parse states, and (ii) we can rank a collection of parse states by using their scores and then process the state with the highest score, which we consider the most plausible state.

We store the states with various scores in an agenda ranked based on their scores, and the state with the highest score is explored by the parser.

5 Labelled Attachment Score

In this section we show the way we obtain labelled attachment scores, which is largely different from the way this is implemented in the original algorithm. As in the arc-standard algorithm, for each dependency relation between two words, a syntactic label is attached to indicate the syntactic role of the daughter item with its parent. However, the way we assign labels to dependency relations during parsing is that we extract patterns from the training data during training phase. This contrasts with the approach used in MaltParser whereby labels are predicted with the LEFT-ARC and RIGHT-ARC actions of the parser which are learned during training phase.

Each pattern or rule consists of a dependency parent, a list of n part-of-speech (POS) tagged items, a dependency daughter, a label, and the frequency of the pattern in the training data. A schema of a pattern is shown in Figure 4. The first element of the pattern is a parent item, the second element is a list of up to n POS tagged items between a parent item and its daughter in the original text, the third element is the daughter of a parent item, the fourth element is the label for the dependency relation and the last element is the frequency of the pattern recorded during the training phase. Figure 4 shows the rule format where `PARENT` is assigned as the parent of `DAUGHTER` and that there are up to n POS tagged items between them and the dependency label between the parent item and daughter item is `LABEL` where the last element indicates that the pattern occurred `j` times during the training phase.

```
PARENT,[POS1,...,POSn],DAUGHTER,LABEL,j
```

Figure 4: A schema of a pattern for a label.

6 Dataset

The kind of data that is suitable for developing a data-driven parser is an annotated treebank. There are a number of treebanks available for inducing a dependency parser for a number of natural languages. Some of the most popular treebanks for Arabic are: Penn Arabic Treebank (PATB) (Maamouri and Bies, 2004), Prague Arabic dependency treebank (PADT) (Smrž and Hajič, 2006), and Columbia Arabic treebank (CATiB) (Habash and Roth, 2009).

The linguistic information in PATB is sufficient for inducing a parser. However, the limitation for using this treebank directly for generating a parse model is that its annotation schemata is based on a phrase structure format, which cannot be used for dependency parsing. However, we have converted the phrase structure trees of the PATB to dependency structure trees using the standard conversion algorithm for transforming phrase structure trees to dependency trees, as described is detail by Xia and Palmer (2001).

Because we do not have access to the PATD and CATiB treebanks, we have used the PATB[3] part 1 version 3 for training and testing the arc-standard version of MaltParser and various versions of our parser.

In order to perform a 5-fold validation, we have systematically generated five sets of testing data and five sets of training data from the treebank, where the testing data is not part of the training data. The training data for each fold contains approximately 112,800 words while the testing data for each fold contains approximately 28,000 words. The average length of sentences is 29 words and the total number of testing sentences in each fold is about 970 sentences while the total number of sentences in the training data in each fold is about 3880 sentence. We use the training data for generating a set of parsing rules and for extracting a set of constraint rules; this way we are retrieving two different kinds of information from the training data.

[3]Catalogue number LDC2005T02 from the Linguistic Data Consortium (LDC). Available at: http://www.ldc.upenn.edu/Catalog/catalogEntry.jsp?catalogId =LDC2005T02

7 The Role of Constraint Rules in Parsing

Each intermediate state that is produced by following recommended parse operations by the parse model is checked to see whether it is plausible. We consider a state to be plausible if it obeys the constraint rules.

A parse state is assigned a score based on the recommendation of the parse model (see Section 4 for more details). We attempt to use constraint rules to assign an additional score to a state if the recommended parse operation by the parsing rules does not violate the constraint rules. This means that recommendations made by the parsing rules are validated by using a set of constraint rules to check whether they produce acceptable analyses. This way the parser benefits from the information provided by the parsing rules and from the information provided by the constraint rules.

The role of the constraint rules is particularly evident when the parser produces more than three states from one state. In situations where the parser is presented with a state whereby the queue contains one or more items and the stack contains more than one item, then the parser generates more than three states because it checks for relations between the head of the queue and any items on the stack. In this kind of situation, two or more parse operations may be recommended by the parsing rules; i.e., two or more states may be given a positive score. To determine which of the equally scored states should be explored next, the score given by the constraint rules to a parse state will influence the parser's decision. For example the lines in bold from Figure 5 where we assumed that the parsing rules recommended LEFT-ARC(1) (making 3 the parent of 2) and also LEFT-ARC(2) (making 3 the parent of 1) they are both given a score of 1, as shown in bold in Figure 5. Also, we assumed that the constraint rules encouraged the recommendation of the parse model and that they gave their scores to the two recommended operations, where LEFT-ARC(1) is given 0.25 and LEFT-ARC(2) is given 0.5. In this situation, LEFT-ARC(2), with a total score of 1.5, plus the score for the currently explored state (In this example the current score is set to 1), will be placed on the top of the agenda because it will have the highest score (2.5). In a situation like this, the constraint rules influence the decision of the parser whereby LEFT-ARC(2) is performed instead of LEFT-ARC(1).

States	Action	Queue	Stack	arcs	Curr. Sc	Sc	C. Sc	T. Sc
Current	θ	[3,4]	[2,1]	θ	1	θ	θ	1
New	SHIFT	[4]	[3,2,1]	θ	1	0	0	1
	RA(1)	[2,4]	[1]	2>3	1	0	0	1
	RA(2)	[1,2,4]	[]	1>3	1	0	0	1
	LA(1)	**[3,4]**	**[1]**	**3>2**	**1**	**1**	**0.25**	**2.25**
	LA(2)	**[2,3,4]**	**[]**	**3>1**	**1**	**1**	**0.5**	**2.5**

Figure 5: The generation of more than three states, LA = LEFT-ARC, RA = RIGHT-ARC, Curr = current, Sc = Score, C = Constraint, T = Total.

In Figure 5 we have shown the way the constraint rules may influence parse decisions. In the following sections, we describe different types of constraint rules that can be extracted automatically from a dependency treebank where we integrate them into our parser.

8 Extracting Constraint Rules from PATB

The main type of relations that are accounted for in dependency parsing are the parent-daughter relations between different words in a sentence. We devote the following sections to describing two different types constraint rules extracted from a set of dependency trees.

8.1 Parent-daughter Relations Extraction with Local Contextual Information

In the training phase, we use the dependency tree of each sentence as a grammar for parsing the sentence. During each LEFT-ARC(N) or RIGHT-ARC(N), the dependency relation between a parent and its daughter is recorded. The recorded relations contain different information: (i) the parent item (ii) the daughter item, (iii) a set of up to n POS tagged items from the queue and up to n POS tagged items from the stack[4], and (iv) the frequency of each rule. The frequency of each rule is used for computing the probability of the rule during parsing. The probability computation of a rule is calculated in three steps (i) obtaining the frequency of a rule, (ii) obtaining the sum of the frequency of all the rules with the same parent and daughter relation (regardless of the n POS tagged items that appear between them), (iii) dividing the number obtained in step (i) by the number obtained in step (ii). The probability of each rule is then used as a score for encouraging a parse operation suggested by the parse model.

[4]The number of items collected from the queue and the stack may vary between `1 ... n`.

The conditional probability for the constraint rule in Figure 6 is shown in equation (1), where r_i is a distinct rule with the same parent and daughter but a different set of intermediate items.

$$P(r_j) = \frac{|r_j|}{\sum_{i=1}^{n} |r_i|} \qquad (1)$$

In Figure 6 we show an example of a constraint rule with a window size of up to two items on the queue and up to two items on the stack. The rule in Figure 6 shows that a `VERB` is the parent of a `NOUN` if the first item in the queue is a `VERB`, the second item in the queue is a `PREP`, and there is only one item on the stack which is a `NOUN`. Since there is no second item on the stack the symbol '`-`' is used for representing unavailable items. The final element (`j`) of the rule represents the frequency of the rule during training.

```
r = (VERB,NOUN,[VERB,PREP,NOUN,-],j)
```

Figure 6: Dependency relations with local information.

We have evaluated our parser using this type of constraint rules where the best parsing performance is achieved when we recorded four items from the queue and three items from the stack for each dependency relation. The parsing performance is shown in Table 1.

8.2 Subtrees

Since LEFT-ARC(N) and RIGHT-ARC(N) result in the removal of a daughter item from the stack or queue, which may be required in subsequent parsing stages, it is vital to ensure that the daughter has collected all and only its daughters. Thus, subtrees can be used to encourage the parser to remove a daughter item only if there is evidence that it has collected all and only its daughters, this corresponds to completeness and cohesion in Lexical Functional Grammar (LFG) (Bresnan and Kaplan, 1982). This check is performed in two steps by using the subtrees: (i) collecting all the daughters of the dependent item from the tree that have been built by the parser, and (ii) finding a subtree (from a set of subtrees collected during training phase) that is headed by the dependent item with the same set of daughters that are collected in (i).

If a matching subtree is found then the parse operation can be encouraged by giving it a score. As shown in Figure 7, each daughter in a subtree is associated with a score, which represents the frequency of the subtree during training. The score is used for computing the probability of the subtree with a specific set of daughters, which is computed by dividing the frequency of the subtree by the total associated frequencies of all other daughters headed by the same item, this process resembles the approach used by Charniak (1996). The computed probability is then used for encouraging the parse operation.

Figure 7 shows two subtrees headed by a `VERB` where the first one has a `NOUN` as its daughter and it occurred `5` times during training while in the second rule the `VERB` has two `NOUN`s as its daughter and it occurred `10` times during training.

```
r = VERB,(5,[NOUN])
r = VERB,(10,[NOUN,NOUN])
```

Figure 7: Examples of unlexicalised subtree

The conditional probability for the subtrees in Figure 7 is shown in equation (2) where each r_k^f is a distinct rule.

$$P(r_k) = \frac{r_k^f}{\sum_{i=1}^{n} r_i^f} \tag{2}$$

9 Evaluation

In this section we compare the result we have obtained for testing the arc-standard algorithm of MaltParser[5] with different versions of our re-implementation of this algorithm: (i) DDParser, which is our re-implementation of the arc-standard of MaltParser; (ii) CDDParser, which is DDParser supplemented by parent-daughter constraint rules, i.e., the parsing rules and a set of parent-daughter constrain rules are used during parsing, (iii) SDDParser, which is DDParser supplemented by local subtrees, i.e., the parsing rules and a set of subtrees are used during parsing, and (iv) S-CD-DDParser, which is DDParser supplemented by a combination of subtrees and parent-daughter constrain rules. The performance of each parser is shown in Table 1.

We can note from Table 1 that DDParser is 43.8% more efficient than MaltParser. Although the unlabelled attachment score (UAS) of DDParser is slightly lower than that of MaltParser (0.7%) the labelled attachment score (LAS) and the labelled accuracy (LA) are more accurate than MaltParser by 1% and 1.4% respectively. We believe that this improved accuracy of LAS and LA occurred because we have used a different approach from MaltParser for assigning labels to dependency relations (see Section 5 for more details on our approach to label assignment).

Parsers	UAS (%)	LAS (%)	LA (%)	second/relation
MaltParser	75.2	70.0	92.2	0.144
DDParser	74.5	71.0	93.6	0.081
CDDParser	76.2	72.7	94.85	0.145
SDDParser	75.9	72.4	94.84	0.133
S-CD-DDParser	75.3	71.8	94.82	0.127

Table 1: Performance of MaltParser and our parsers.

The use of constraint rules has improved the parsing accuracy of DDParser but it has noticeably degraded its speed. This clearly indicates that the use of constraint rules improves parsing accuracy at the expense of speed. Having said that, the use of parent-daughter constraint rules improved the accuracy of our parser over the accuracy of MaltParser by 1% for UAS, 2.7% for LAS and 2.65% for LA while the parser remained as efficient as MaltParser.

The use of local subtrees as constraint rules also improved the accuracy of our parser over the accuracy of MaltParser by 0.7% for UAS, 2.4% for LAS and 2.64% for LA while its speed is quicker than MaltParser by 7.6%. These results show that the application of different types of constraint rules to a data-driven parser affects parsing performance differently. We have shown here that we can trade off parsing speed for parsing accuracy by using different constraint rules.

Additionally, we have combined the constraint rules and subtrees and applied them to DDParser. Applying both extensions to the parser did not lead to better results than using them individually. However, applying both extensions lead to better parsing accuracy than using none of them but the parsing speed degraded by about 36%.

It is worth noting that the training time of our parser, including the automatic extraction of constraint rules from the training data, was much shorter than the training time of the original algorithm. The training time for the original algorithm took approximately four hours. While the training time for our parser took approximately thirty

[5]Available at: http://www.maltparser.org/download.html

minutes. We assume that our training time was shorter because we have used the J48 classification algorithm (which is the Weka's[6] implementation of C4.5 (Quinlan, 1996)) instead of LiBSVM (Chang and Lin, 2011), which is used by the original algorithm[7].

In conclusion, from the experiments that we have conducted in this paper, we can note that applying constraint rules to a data-driven parser may improve the parsing accuracy but the parsing speed may degrade.

10 Future Work

Since there are a number of treebanks for different natural languages and that our method is language independent, we would like to evaluate our parser on different languages and examine its extendibility to other languages.

For this study, we have extracted a set of constraint rules from the same training data that we have used for generating a parse model. In the future, we would like to obtain a set of linguistic grammatical rules and apply them to our parser for validating operations recommended by the parse model.

11 Summary

In this paper we have shown an extension to the arc-standard algorithm of MaltParser. We have also shown a method to automatically extracting different kinds of constraint rules from a dependency treebank.

Our re-implementation of the arc-standard algorithm of MaltParser allows us to integrate different kinds of constraint rules to it. We have shown that the application of these constraint rules have improved the parsing accuracy at the expense of parsing speed. Although the application of constraint rules to parsing degraded the parsing speed the parser remained as efficient as the original algorithm.

Acknowledgements

This work was funded by the Qatar National Research Fund (grant NPRP 09-046-6-001).

[6] Available publicly at: http://www.cs.waikato.ac.nz/ml/weka/index.html

[7] We have experimented with a large number of classification algorithms with various features and settings for training our parser, but we cannot present them in this paper due to space limitation. See (Sardar, 2015) for more details on experiments on using different classifiers for parsing.

References

Giuseppe Attardi. 2006. Experiments with a multi-language non-projective dependency parser. In *Proceedings of the Tenth Conference on Computational Natural Language Learning*, CoNLL-X '06, pages 166–170, Stroudsburg, PA, USA. Association for Computational Linguistics.

Joan Bresnan and Ronald Kaplan. 1982. Lexical function grammar. In J.W. Bresnan, editor, *The Mental Representation of Grammatical Relations*, pages 173–281, Cambridge, MA. MIT Press.

Chih-Chung Chang and Chih-Jen Lin. 2011. LIBSVM: A library for support vector machines. *ACM Trans. Intell. Syst. Technol.*, 2(3):27:1–27:27, May.

Eugene Charniak. 1996. Tree-bank Grammars. In *Proceedings of the Thirteenth National Conference on Artificial Intelligence*, pages 1031–1036.

Nizar Habash and Ryan M. Roth. 2009. Catib: The columbia arabic treebank. In *Proceedings of the ACL-IJCNLP 2009 Conference Short Papers*, pages 221–224.

Nivre Joakim. 2003. An efficient algorithm for projective dependency parsing. In *Proceedings of the 8th International Workshop on Parsing Technologies (IWPT*, pages 149–160. Citeseer.

Marco Kuhlmann and Joakim Niver. 2010. Transition-based techniques for non-projective dependency parsing. *Northern European Journal of Language Technology*, 2:1–19.

Mohamed Maamouri and Ann Bies. 2004. Developing an Arabic treebank: methods, guidelines, procedures, and tools. In *Proceedings of the Workshop on Computational Approaches to Arabic Script-based Languages*, pages 2–9, Geneva.

Joakim Nivre. 2006. *Inductive dependency parsing*, volume 34 of *Text, Speech and Language Technology*. Springer.

Joakim Nivre. 2008. Algorithms for deterministic incremental dependency parsing. *Computational Linguistics*, 34:513–553.

John R. Quinlan. 1996. Improved use of continuous attributes in c4.5. *Journal of Artificial Intelligence Research*, 4:77–90.

Jaf Sardar. 2015. *The Application of Constraint Rules to Data-driven Parsing*. PhD Thesis, School of Computer Science, The University of Manchester.

Otakar Smrž and Jan Hajič. 2006. The other arabic treebank: Prague dependencies and functions. *Arabic Computational Linguistics: Current Implementations. CSLI Publications*, 104.

Fei Xia and Martha Palmer. 2001. Converting dependency structures to phrase structures. In *1st Human Language Technology Conference (HLT-2001)*, pages 1–5, San Diego.

Part-of-Speech Tagging for Code-Mixed English-Hindi Twitter and Facebook Chat Messages

Anupam Jamatia
National Institute of Technology
Agartala, Tripura, India
anupamjamatia@gmail.com

Björn Gambäck
Norwegian University of Science and Technology
Trondheim, Norway
gamback@idi.ntnu.no

Amitava Das
Indian Institute of Information Technology
Sri City, Andhra Pradesh, India
amitava.das@iiits.in

Abstract

The paper reports work on collecting and annotating code-mixed English-Hindi social media text (Twitter and Facebook messages), and experiments on automatic tagging of these corpora, using both a coarse-grained and a fine-grained part-of-speech tag set. We compare the performance of a combination of language specific taggers to that of applying four machine learning algorithms to the task (Conditional Random Fields, Sequential Minimal Optimization, Naïve Bayes and Random Forests), using a range of different features based on word context and word-internal information.

1 Introduction

Code-mixing occurs when a person changes language (alternates or switches code) below clause level, so internally inside a sentence or an utterance. This phenomenon is more abundant in more informal settings — such as in conversational spoken language and in social media text — and of course also more common in areas of the world where people are naturally bi- or multilingual, that is, in regions where languages change over short geospatial distances and people generally have at least a basic knowledge of the neighbouring languages. In particular, India is home to several hundred languages, with language diversity and dialectal changes instigating frequent code-mixing.

We will here look at the tasks of collecting and annotating code-mixed English-Hindi social media text, and on automatic part-of-speech (POS) tagging of these code-mixed texts. In contrast, most research on part-of-speech tagging has so far concentrated on more formal language forms, and in particular either on completely monolingual text or on text where code alternation occurs above the clause level. Most research on social media text has, on the other hand, concentrated on English tweets, whereas the majority of these texts now are written in other media and in other languages — or in mixes of languages.

Today, code-switching is generally recognised as a natural part of bi- and multilingual language use, even though it historically often was considered a sub-standard use of language. Conversational spoken language code-switching has been a common research theme in psycho- and sociolinguists for half a century, and the first work on applying language processing methods to code-switched text was carried out in the early 1980s (Joshi, 1982), while code-switching in social media text started to be studied in the late 1990s (Paolillo, 1996). Still, code alternation in conventional texts is not so prevalent as to spur much interest by the computational linguistic research community, and it was only recently that it became a research topic in its own right, with a code-switching workshop at EMNLP 2014 (Solorio et al., 2014), and a shared tasks at EMNLP and at Forum for Information Retrieval Evaluation, FIRE 2014.

Both these shared tasks were on automatic word-level language detection in code-mixed text, but here we will assume that the word-level languages are known and concentrate on the task of automatic part-of-speech tagging for these types of texts. We have collected a corpus consisting of Facebook messages and tweets (which includes all

Proceedings of Recent Advances in Natural Language Processing, pages 239–248,
Hissar, Bulgaria, Sep 7–9 2015.

possible types of code-mixing diversity: varying number of code alternation points, different syntactic mixing and language change orders, etc.), and carried out several experiments on this corpus to investigate the problem of assigning POS tags to code-mixed text.

The rest of the paper is organized as follows: In Section 2, we discuss the background and related work on part-of-speech tagging, social media text processing, and code-switching. The collection and annotation of a code-mixed corpus are described in Section 3, which also compares the complexity of the corpus to several other code-mixed corpora based on a code-mixing index. The actual part-of-speech tagging experiments are discussed in Section 4, starting by describing the features used, and then presenting the performance of four different machine learning methods. The results are elaborated on in Section 5, in particular how system performance is affected by the level of code-mixing, while Section 6 sums up the discussion and points to directions for future research.

2 Background and Related Work

In essence, this paper is concerned with the intersection of three topics: part-of-speech tagging, processing of social media text, and code-switching. In the present section, we will mainly discuss work related to the latter two topics, and tagging in relation to those.

First though, it should be noted that present-day POS taggers more or less receive 96+% performance on English news text with just about any method, with state-of-the-art systems going beyond the 97% point on the English Wall Street Journal corpus: Spoustová et al. (2009) report achieving an accuracy of 97.43% by combining rule-based and statistically induced taggers. However, most work on POS tagging has so far concentrated on a few European and East Asian languages, and on fairly formal texts, that is, texts of a quite different nature than the ones that are the topic of the present work.

2.1 Social Media and Code-Switching

The term 'social media text' will be used throughout this paper as referring to the way these texts are communicated, although it is important to keep in mind that social media in itself does not constitute a particular textual domain. Rather, there is a wide spectrum of different types of texts transmitted in this way, as discussed in detail by, e.g., Eisenstein (2013) and Androutsopoulos (2011). They both argue that the common denominator of social media text is not that it is 'noisy' and informal *per se*, but that it describes language in (rapid) change, which in turn has major implications for natural language processing: if we build a system that can handle a specific type of social media text today, it will be outdated tomorrow. Something which makes it very attractive to apply machine learning and adaptive techniques to the problem.

In all types of social media, the level of formality of the language depends more on the style of the writer than on the media as such; however, tweets (Twitter messages) tend to be more formal than chat messages in that they more often follow grammatical norms and use standard lexical items (Hu et al., 2013), while chats are more conversational (Paolillo, 1999), and hence less formal. Although social media often convey more ungrammatical text than more formal writings, Baldwin et al. (2013) show that the relative occurrence of non-standard syntax is fairly constant among many types of media, such as mails, tweets, forums, comments, and blogs, and argue that it should be tractable to develop NLP tools to process those, if focusing on English.

That is a large "if", though: first, the texts that we will discuss in this paper are not all in English, and — most importantly — not in one single language at all, but rather in a mix of languages, which clearly vastly complicates the issue of developing tools for these texts. Second, most previous research on social media text has focused on tweets, because of the ease of availability of Twitter; however, the conversational nature of chats tend to increase the level of code-mixing (Cárdenas-Claros and Isharyanti, 2009; Paolillo, 2011), so we will base our findings on data both from Twitter *and* from Facebook chats.

2.2 Code-Mixing and Tagging

There have been several efforts on social media text POS tagging in recent years, but almost exclusively on Twitter and mostly for English (Darling et al., 2012; Owoputi et al., 2013; Derczynski et al., 2013) and German (Rehbein, 2013; Neunerdt et al., 2014). Foster et al. (2011) introduce results for both POS tagging and parsing, but do not present a tool, and focus more on the parsing aspect. The two papers most similar to our work introduce the ARK tagger (Gimpel et al., 2011) and T-Pos (Ritter et al., 2011). The ARK tagger reaches 92.8% accuracy at token level, but uses a coarse, custom tagset. T-Pos is based on the Penn Treebank set and achieves an 88.4% token tagging accuracy. Neither paper reports sentence/whole tweet accuracy rates.

The first attempts at applying machine learning approaches to code-mixed language were by Solorio and Liu (2008a) who aimed to predict potential code alternation points, as a first step in the development of more accurate methods for processing code-mixed English-Spanish data. Only a few researchers have tried to tag code-mixed social media text: Solorio and Liu (2008b) addressed English-Spanish, while the English-Hindi mix was previously discussed by Vyas et al. (2014). Both used strategies based on combining the output of language-specific taggers, and we will utilize a similar solution in one of our experiments.

Turning to the specific problem of processing code-mixed Indian language data, Bhattacharja (2010) took a linguistic point of view on a particular type of complex predicates in Bengali that consist of an English word and a Bengali verb, in the light of different recent morphology models. Ahmed et al. (2011) noted that code-mixing and abbreviations add another dimension of transliteration errors of Hindi, Bengali and Telugu data when trying to understand the challenge of designing back-transliteration based input method editors. Mukund and Srihari (2012) proposed a tagging method that helps select words based on POS categories that strongly reflect Urdu-English code-mixing behavior. Das and Gambäck (2013) reported the first social media Indian code-mixing data (Bengali-Hindi-English), while Barman et al. (2014a) noted that character n-grams, part-of-speech, and lemmas were useful features for automatic language identification. Barman et al. (2014b) also carried out word-level classification experiments using a simple dictionary-based method. Bali et al. (2014) pointed out that structural and discourse linguistic analysis is required in order to fully analyse this type of code-mixing.

3 Data Collection and Annotation

For this work we have collected text both from Facebook and Twitter, initially 4,435 raw tweets and 1,236 Facebook posts. The tweets were on various 'hot' topics (i.e., topics that are currently being discussed in news, social media, etc.) and collected with the Java-based Twitter API,[1] while the Facebook posts were collected from campus-related university billboard postings (IIT Bombay Facebook Confession page).[2] The Facebook messages typically consist of a longer post (a "confession") followed by shorter, chat-like comments. The confessions are about "naughty" things that students have done on campus, and mainly concern cheating on exams or sex-related events.

Tokens	Facebook	Twitter	Total
Hindi	4.17	48.48	21.93
English	75.61	22.24	54.22
Universal	16.53	21.54	18.54
Named entity	2.19	6.70	3.99
Acronym	1.46	0.88	1.12
Mixed	0.02	0.08	0.05
Undefined	0.01	0.07	0.03

Table 1: Token Level Language Distribution (%)
('Universal' stands for punctuation marks, etc.)

3.1 Corpus

1,106 of the collected messages were randomly selected for manual annotation: 552 Facebook posts and 554 tweets. 20.8% of those messages are monolingual. Token level distribution of the corpus is reported in Table 1. Note that the Facebook messages are predominantly written in English, while the tweets mainly are in Hindi.

Utterance boundaries were manually inserted into the messages by two annotators, who initially agreed on 71% of the utterance breaks. After discussions and corrections, the agreement between the annotators was 94% and the resulting corpus has in total 2,583 utterances (1,181 from Twitter and 1,402 from Facebook), with 1,762 (68.2%) being monolingual. The sharp decrease in code-mixing when measured at the utterance level rather than message level shows the importance of the utterance boundary insertion, an issue we will get back to in Section 5.

Tokenization is an important preprocessing step which is difficult for social media text due to its

[1] http://twitter4j.org/

[2] www.facebook.com/Confessions.IITB

noisy nature. We used the CMU tokenizer,[3] which is a sub-module of the CMU Twitter POS tagger (Gimpel et al., 2011). Although the CMU tokenizer was originally developed for English, empirical testing showed that it works reasonably well also for the Indian languages.

3.2 Part-of-Speech Tagsets

We experimented with both coarse-grained and fine-grained tagsets, utilizing the fine-grained set during annotation. As can be seen in Table 2, this tagset includes both the Twitter specific tags introduced by Gimpel et al. (2011) and a set of POS tags for Indian languages that combines the IL-POST tags (Baskaran et al., 2008), the tags developed by the Central Institute of Indian Languages (LDCIL), and those suggested by the Indian Government's Department of Information Technology (TDIL),[4] that is, an approach similar to that taken for Gujarati by Dholakia and Yoonus (2014). The coarse-grained tagset instead combines Gimpel et al.'s Twitter specific tags with Google's Universal Tagset (Petrov et al., 2011).[5] The mapping between our fine-grained tagset and the Google Universal Tagset is also shown in Table 2.

3.3 Comparing Corpora Complexity

The error rates for various language processing applications would be expected to be higher for more complex code-mixed text. When comparing different code-mixed corpora to each other, it is thus desirable to have a measurement of the level of mixing between languages. Kilgarriff (2001) discusses various statistical measures that can be used to compare corpora more objectively, but all those measures presume the corpora to be monolingual.

In Das and Gambäck (2014) we instead suggested a *Code-Mixing Index*, CMI, to document the frequency of languages in a corpus, which we will use here as well. In short, the measure is defined as: if an utterance only contains language independent tokens, its CMI is zero; for other utterances, the CMI is calculated by counting the number of words belonging to the most frequent language in the utterance ($max\{w_i\}$) and dividing this by the total number of tokens (n) minus the number of language independent tokens (u):

$$\text{CMI} = \begin{cases} 100 \times [1 - \frac{max\{w_i\}}{n-u}] & : n > u \\ 0 & : n = u \end{cases}$$

which means that for mono-lingual utterances, CMI = 0 (since then $max\{w_i\} = n - u$).

In Gambäck and Das (2014), we describe the index further and suggest that a factor that could be included in the index is the number of code alternation points (P) in an utterance, since a higher

Category	Type	Description
Noun (G_N)	N_NN	Common Noun
	N_NNV	Verbal Noun
	N_NST	Spatio-temporal
	N_NNP	Proper Noun
Pronoun (G_PRP)	PR_PRP	Personal
	PR_PRL	Relative
	PR_PRF	Reflexive
	PR_PRC	Reciprocal
	PR_PRQ	Wh-Word
Verb (G_V)	V_VM	Main
	V_VAUX	Auxiliary
Adjective (G_J)	JJ	Adjective
Adverb (G_R)	RB_ALC	Locative Adverb
	RB_AMN	Adverb of Manner
Demonstrative (G_PRP)	DM_DMD	Absolute
	DM_DMI	Indefinite
	DM_DMQ	Wh-word
	DM_DMR	Relative
Quantifier (G_SYM)	QT_QTF	General
	QT_QTC	Cardinal
	QT_QTO	Ordinal
Particles (G_PRT)	RP_RPD	Default
	RP_NEG	Negation
	RP_INTF	Intensifier
	RP_INJ	Interjection
Residual (G_X)	RD_RDF	Foreign Word
	RD_SYM	Symbol
	RD_PUNC	Punctuation
	RD_UNK	Unknown
	RD_ECH	Echo Word
Conjunction, Pre- & Postposition	CC	Conjunction
	PSP	Pre-/Postposition
Numeral	&	Numeral
Determiner	DT	Determiner
Twitter-Specific (Gimpel *et al.* 2011) (G_X)	@	At-mention
	~	Re-Tweet/discourse
	E	Emoticon
	U	URL or email
	#	Hashtag

Table 2: POS Tagset

[3] www.ark.cs.cmu.edu/TweetNLP/

[4] www.ldcil.org/Download/Tagset/LDCIL/6Hindi.pdf resp. www.tdil-dc.in/tdildcMain/articles/780732DraftPOSTagstandard.pdf

[5] The Google Universal Tagset defines the following twelve POS tags: G_N (nouns), G_V (verbs), G_J (adjectives), G_R (adverbs), G_PRP (pronouns), G_DT (determiners and articles), G_PRE (prepositions and post-positions), G_NUM (numerals), G_CONJ (conjunctions), G_PRT (particles), G_SYM (punctuation marks) and G_X (a catch-all for other categories such as abbreviations or foreign words).

CMI Range	Facebook (%)	Twitter (%)	P (avg.)
$[0]$	84.80	48.19	0.00
$(0, 10]$	4.49	3.11	1.75
$(10, 20]$	4.42	15.39	1.91
$(20, 30]$	3.49	14.38	2.37
$(30, 40]$	1.71	11.10	2.65
$(40, 100)$	1.06	7.14	2.70

Table 3: Code Mixing and Code Alternation

number of switches in an utterance arguably increases its complexity. However, that paper does not extend the CMI with code alternation points, and in the following we just separately report the average number of code alternation points. Details for our corpus are given in Table 3, based on CMI rages and code alternation point distributions.

Testing the idea that the Code-Mixing Index can describe the complexity of code-switched corpora, we used it to compare the level of language mixing in our English–Hindi corpus (in total, and each of the Facebook and Twitter parts in isolation) to that of the English-Hindi corpus of Vyas et al. (2014), the Dutch-Turkish corpus introduced by Nguyen and Doğruöz (2013), and the corpora used in the 2014 shared tasks at FIRE and EMNLP.[6] Table 4 shows the average CMI values for these corpora, both over all utterances and over only the utterances having a non-zero CMI (i.e., the utterances that contain some code-mixing). The last column of the table gives the fraction of mixed utterances in the respective corpora.

Languages		CMI avg.	CMI mixed	P (avg.)	Mixed (%)
EN-HI	FB+TW	13.38	21.86	2.33	61.21
	FB	3.67	13.24	2.50	27.71
	TW	23.06	24.38	2.28	94.58
	Vyas	2.54	14.82	2.15	20.68
DU-TR		21.48	26.46	4.43	26.55
FIRE	EN-GU	5.47	25.47	1.56	21.47
	EN-KN	14.29	21.43	5.50	66.66
	EN-ML	18.74	25.33	2.47	74.00
	EN-TA	25.00	37.50	3.00	66.66
	EN-BN	29.37	32.27	0.91	91.00
	EN-HI	19.32	24.41	4.89	79.14
EMNLP	EN-ES	6.93	24.13	0.31	28.70
	EN-ZH	10.15	19.43	0.97	52.75
	EN-NE	18.28	25.11	1.42	72.79
	AR-AR	4.41	25.60	0.17	17.21

Table 4: Code-Mixing in Various Corpora

4 Part-of-Speech Tagging Experiments

This section discusses the actual tagging experiments, starting by describing the features used for training the taggers, and then reporting the results of using four different machine learning methods Finally, we contrast this with a strategy based on using a combination of language specific taggers.

4.1 Features

Feature selection plays a key role in supervised POS tagging. The important features for the POS tagging task have been identified based on the different possible combinations of available word and tag contexts. The features include the *focus word* (the current word), and its prefixes and suffixes from one-to-four letters (so four features each). Other features account for the previous word, the following word, whether the focus word starts with a digit or not, the previous word's POS tag, and the focus word's language tag.

Most of the features are self explanatory and quite obvious in POS tagging experiments, so we will only elaborate on prefix/suffix feature extraction: There are two different ways in which the focus word's suffix/prefix information can be used. The first and naïve one is to take a fixed length (say, n) suffix/prefix of the current and/or the surrounding word(s). If the length of the corresponding word is less than or equal to $n - 1$ then the feature value is not defined. The feature value is also not defined if the token itself is a punctuation symbol or contains any special symbol or digit.

The second and more helpful approach is to modify the feature to be binary or multiple valued. Variable length suffixes of a word can be matched with predefined lists of useful suffixes for different classes. Heuristic character extraction is generally not easy to motivate in theoretical linguistic terms, but the use of prefix/suffix information serves the practical purpose well for POS tagging of highly inflected languages, such as the Indian ones.

4.2 Machine Learning-based Taggers

We experimented with applying four machine learning-based classification algorithms to the

[6]The EMNLP corpora mix English with Spanish, Mandarin Chinese and Nepalese. The last EMNLP corpus is dialectal: Standard Arabic mixed with Egyptian (ARB-ARZ). The FIRE corpora mix English with Hindi, Gujarati, Bengali, Kannada, Malayalam and Tamil,. Note that the EN-KN and EN-TA corpora are very small (55 resp. 29 words), while EN-TA and EN-ML are only partially and inconsistently annotated, so those are not reliable as basis for comparison.

CMI Range	CRF FG	CRF CG	NB FG	NB CG	SMO FG	SMO CG	RF FG	RF CG
[0]	73.2	79.4	33.9	36.8	37.9	45.6	73.9	79.0
(0, 10]	64.0	71.5	36.0	40.1	39.0	45.9	68.7	75.3
(10, 20]	61.5	70.0	35.2	31.8	35.6	38.2	61.5	68.4
(20, 30]	60.4	68.0	33.3	42.0	36.3	46.6	58.2	67.3
(30, 40]	62.6	69.8	37.7	43.4	37.9	49.2	60.0	66.5
(40, 100)	64.5	71.1	39.2	44.3	39.0	49.3	62.4	67.6
avg.	64.3	71.6	35.8	39.7	37.6	45.8	64.1	70.6

Table 5: F_1 scores by CMI range distribution

Features	FG (F_1)	CG (F_1)
current word	62.0	67.7
+ next word	60.3	65.2
+ previous word	56.8	62.1
+ prefix	69.4	76.0
+suffix	72.2	78.9
+ start_with_digit	72.1	79.1
+ current_word_lang	73.3	79.8
+ prev_word_pos	73.3	79.8

Table 6: Feature Ablation for the RF-based Tagger

task: Conditional Random Fields (CRF), Sequential Minimal Optimization (SMO), Naïve Bayes (NB), and Random Forests (RF). For the CRF we used the MIRALIUM[7] implementation, while the other three were the implementations in WEKA.[8]

Table 5 reports performance after 5-fold cross validation of all the ML methods on the complete dataset (2,583 utterances), using both fine-grained (FG) and coarse-grained (CG) tagsets. As can be seen, Random Forests and CRF invariably gave the highest F scores (weighted average over all tags) on both tagsets, while SMO and Naïve Bayes consistently performed much worse. The difference between RF and CRF is not significant at the 99%-level in a paired two-tailed Student t-test.

To better understand the code-mixed POS tagging problem, we investigated which features are most important by performing feature ablation for RF-based tagger on the part of the corpus with CMI > 0. The feature ablation is reported in Table 6, with performance given by weighted average F-measure. As we see, including the previous or following word actually makes the performance decrease, while the other features contribute roughly the same to increase performance.

We then tested system performance on various

[7] code.google.com/p/miralium/

[8] www.cs.waikato.ac.nz/ml/weka/

From / To	CRF FG	CRF CG	NB FG	NB CG	SMO FG	SMO CG	RF FG	RF CG
EN-HI	12.4	9.0	21.2	18.9	21.2	17.8	12.1	8.5
HI-EN	5.4	5.6	19.2	18.1	18.2	16.6	4.8	4.6

Table 7: Error Rates (%) by Alternation Direction

number of code alternation points. Error rates at the alternation points are reported in Table 7, with the first column showing from which language the code alteration is taking place. The results indicate that all the ML methods have more problems with HI-EN alternation. A plausible reason is that most of the corpus is English mixed in Hindi, so the induced systems are biased towards Hindi syntactic patterns. More experiments are needed to better recognize which language is mixing into which, and to make the systems account for this; currently we are working on language modelling of code-mixed text for this purpose.

4.3 Combining Language Specific Taggers

Solorio and Liu (2008b) proposed a simple but elegant solution of tagging code-mixed English-Spanish text twice — once each with a tagger for each language — and then combining the output of the language specific taggers to find the optimal word-level labels.

The reported accuracy of the combined tagger of Solorio and Liu (2008b) was 89.72%, when word-level languages were known. They used the Penn Treebank tagset, which is comparable to our fine-grained tagset, but since the CMI value for their English-Spanish corpus is not known, it is hard to compare the performance figures.

However, Vyas et al. (2014) followed the same strategy as Solorio and Liu (2008b), reporting an accuracy of 74.87%, also given that the word-level languages were known. They used the Google Universal Tagset and therefore in this way is comparable to our coarse-grained tagset, although (as can be seen in Table 4) the English-Hindi corpus used by Vyas et al. (2014) is far less mixed (has an average CMI of 2.54) than our English-Hindi corpus (with an average CMI of 13.38), plausibly justifying a higher POS tagging accuracy.

Word sequence plays a major role for syntactic formation as well as semantic meaning of the language, and could as such strongly influence POS tagging. The combination tagging strategy could potentially break the word sequences, so using language specific taggers is not necessarily the optimal approach; still, we have also carried out

CMI Range	FG (%)	CG (%)
[0]	77.4	83.5
(0, 10]	69.5	75.9
(10, 20]	56.2	64.3
(20, 30]	59.9	68.2
(30, 40]	60.0	67.1
(40, 100)	66.4	72.8
avg.	64.9	72.0

Table 8: Accuracy of the Combination Tagger

experiments based on a similar language specific tagger combination, both for reasons of comparison and since the combination strategy is appealing in its straight-forward applicability.

The word-level language identifier of Barman et al. (2014b) (with a reported accuracy of 95.76%) was used to mark up our English-Hindi bilingual corpus with language tags for Hindi and English. To tag the Hindi tokens we then used the SNLTR[9] POS tagger, while CMU's ARK tagger was used to tag English and language independent tokens (i.e., universals, named entities, and acronyms).

As can be seen in Table 8, this gave an average accuracy of 71.97% on the coarse-grained tagset, marginally lower than the tagger's performance reported by Vyas et al. (2014), but compatible with the performance of the Random Forests and Conditional Random Field taggers described above. On the fine-grained tagset the tagger combination gave an average accuracy of 64.91%, also compatible with using the individual taggers.

5 Discussion

The ML-based taggers failed to out-perform the language specific combination tagger. One reason for this can be that the corpora used for training the machine learners is too small. Another reason might be that the Unknown Word Ratio (UWR) in these types of social media is very high. Unknown words typically cause problems for POS tagging systems (Giménez and Màrquez, 2004; Nakagawa et al., 2001). Our hypothesis was that the unknown word ratio increases with CMI. To test this, we calculated UWR on our English-Hindi corpus using both 10 folds and 5 folds, as shown in Table 9, getting numbers around 20% overall, with about 17% for the Facebook subpart and 29% for the Twitter

[9]http://nltr.org/snltr-software/

Folds	Facebook	Twitter	Total
5	17.03	29.95	20.49
10	16.68	29.27	19.79

Table 9: Average Unknown Word Ratios

part, supporting the hypothesis that the unknown word ratio indeed is high in these types of texts.

Working with social media text has several other fundamental challenges. One of these is sentence and paragraph boundary detection (Reynar and Ratnaparkhi, 1997; Sporleder and Lapata, 2006), which definitely is a problem in its own right — and obviously extra difficult in the social media context. The importance of obtaining the correct utterance splitting is shown by the level of code-mixing dropping in our corpus when measuring it at utterance level rather than message level. For example, the following tweet could be considered to consist of two utterances U1 and U2:

(1) listening to Ishq Wala Love (From " Student of the Year ") The DJ Suketu Lounge Mix

U1 listening to Ishq Wala Love (From " Student of the Year ")

U2 The DJ Suketu Lounge Mix

But one can also argue that this is one utterance only: even though the "The" is capitalized, it just starts a subordinate clause. In more formal language, it probably would have been written as:

(2) Listening to Ishq Wala Love (from "Student of the Year"), the DJ Suketu Lounge Mix.

Utterance boundary detection for social media text is thus a challenging problem in itself, which was not discussed in detail by Gimpel et al. (2011) or Owoputi et al. (2013). The main reason might be that those works were on tweets, that are limited to 140 characters, so even if the whole tweet is treated as one utterance, POS tagging results will not be strongly affected. However, when working with Facebook messages, we found several long posts, with a high number of code alternation points (6–8 alternation points are very common).

Automatic utterance boundary detection for social media text clearly demands separate solution mechanisms. In this work we have manually marked the utterance boundaries, but see Read et al. (2012) and López and Pardo (2015) for suggestions for how to address the problem.

6 Conclusion and Future Work

The paper has aimed to put the spotlight on the issues that make code-mixed text challenging for language processing. We report work on collecting, annotating, and measuring the complexity of code-mixed English-Hindi social media text (Twitter and Facebook posts), as well as experiments on automatic part-of-speech tagging of these corpora, using both a coarse-grained and a fine-grained tagset. Four machine learning algorithms were applied to the task (Conditional Random Fields, Sequential Minimal Optimization, Naïve Bayes, and Random Forests), and compared to a language specific combination tagger. The RF-based tagger performed best, but only marginally better than the combination tagger and the one based on CRFs.

There are several possible avenues that could be further explored on NLP for code-mixed texts, for example, transliteration, utterance boundary detection, language identification, and parsing. We are currently working on language modelling of code-mixed text to recognize which language is mixing into which. Language modelling has not before been applied to code-mixed POS tagging, but code-switched language models have previously been integrated into speech recognisers, although mostly by naïvely interpolating between monolingual models. Li and Funng (2014) instead obtained a code-switched language model by combining the matrix language model with a translation model from the matrix language to the mixed language. In the future, we also wish to explore language modelling on code-mixed text in order to address the problems caused by unknown words.

Acknowledgements

Thanks to all the researchers who have made their datasets and tools available: the organisers of the shared tasks on code-switching at EMNLP 2014 and in transliteration at FIRE 2014, Dong Nguyen (University of Twente The Netherlands), Seza Doğruöz (Tilburg University, The Netherlands), Monojit Choudhury and Kalika Bali (both at Microsoft Research India), and Utsab Barman (Dublin City University, Ireland).

References

Umair Z Ahmed, Kalika Bali, Monojit Choudhury, and Sowmya VB. 2011. Challenges in designing input method editors for Indian languages: The role of word-origin and context. In *Proceedings of the 5th International Joint Conference on Natural Language Processing*, pages 1–9, Chiang Mai, Thailand, November. AFNLP. Workshop on Advances in Text Input Method.

Jannis Androutsopoulos. 2011. Language change and digital media: a review of conceptions and evidence. In Tore Kristiansen and Nikolas Coupland, editors, *Standard Languages and Language Standards in a Changing Europe*, pages 145–159. Novus, Oslo, Norway,

Timothy Baldwin, Paul Cook, Marco Lui, Andrew MacKinlay, and Li Wang. 2013. How noisy social media text, how diffrnt social media sources? In *Proceedings of the 6th International Joint Conference on Natural Language Processing*, pages 356–364, Nagoya, Japan, October. AFNLP.

Kalika Bali, Jatin Sharma, Monojit Choudhury, and Yogarshi Vyas. 2014. "i am borrowing *ya* mixing?": An analysis of English-Hindi code mixing in Facebook. In *Proceedings of the 2014 Conference on Empirical Methods in Natural Language Processing*, pages 116–126, Doha, Qatar, October. ACL. 1st Workshop on Computational Approaches to Code Switching.

Utsab Barman, Amitava Das, Joachim Wagner, and Jennifer Foster. 2014a. Code mixing: A challenge for language identification in the language of social media. In *Proceedings of the 2014 Conference on Empirical Methods in Natural Language Processing*, pages 13–23, Doha, Qatar, October. ACL. 1st Workshop on Computational Approaches to Code Switching.

Utsab Barman, Joachim Wagner, Grzegorz Chrupała, and Jennifer Foster. 2014b. DCU-UVT: Word-level language classification with code-mixed data. In *Proceedings of the 2014 Conference on Empirical Methods in Natural Language Processing*, pages 127–132, Doha, Qatar, October. ACL. 1st Workshop on Computational Approaches to Code Switching.

Sankaran Baskaran, Kalika Bali, Tanmoy Bhattacharya, Pushpak Bhattacharyya, Monojit Choudhury, Girish Nath Jha, S. Rajendran, K. Saravanan, L. Sobha, and KVS Subbarao. 2008. A common parts-of-speech tagset framework for Indian languages. In *Proceedings of the 6th International Conference on Language Resources and Evaluation*, pages 1331–1337, Marrakech, Marocco, May. ELRA.

Shishir Bhattacharja. 2010. Bengali verbs: a case of code-mixing in Bengali. In *Proceedings of the 24th Pacific Asia Conference on Language, Information and Computation*, pages 75–84, Sendai, Japan, November.

Mónica Stella Cárdenas-Claros and Neny Isharyanti. 2009. Code switching and code mixing in internet chatting: between 'yes', 'ya', and 'si' a case study. *Journal of Computer-Mediated Communication*, 5(3):67–78.

William M. Darling, Michael J. Paul, and Fei Song. 2012. Unsupervised part-of-speech tagging in noisy and esoteric domains with a syntactic-semantic Bayesian HMM. In *Proceedings of the 13th Conference of the European Chapter of the Association for Computational Linguistics*, pages 1–9, Avignon, France, April. ACL. Workshop on Semantic Analysis in Social Media.

Amitava Das and Björn Gambäck. 2013. Code-mixing in social media text: The last language identification frontier? *Traitement Automatique des Langues*, 54(3):41–64.

Amitava Das and Björn Gambäck. 2014. Identifying languages at the word level in code-mixed Indian social media text. In *Proceedings of the 11th International Conference on Natural Language Processing*, pages 169–178, Goa, India, December.

Leon Derczynski, Alan Ritter, Sam Clark, and Kalina Bontcheva. 2013. Twitter part-of-speech tagging for all: Overcoming sparse and noisy data. In *Proceedings of the 9th International Conference on Recent Advances in Natural Language Processing*, pages 198–206, Hissar, Bulgaria, September.

Purva S. Dholakia and M. Mohamed Yoonus. 2014. Rule based approach for the transition of tagsets to build the POS annotated corpus. *International Journal of Advanced Research in Computer and Communication Engineering*, 3(7):7417–7422, July.

Jacob Eisenstein. 2013. What to do about bad language on the internet. In *Proceedings of the 2013 Conference of the North American Chapter of the Association for Computational Linguistics: Human Language Technologies*, pages 359–369, Atlanta, Georgia, June. ACL.

Jennifer Foster, Özlem Çetinoglu, Joachim Wagner, Joseph Le Roux, Stephen Hogan, Joakim Nivre, Deirdre Hogan, and Josef Van Genabith. 2011. #hardtoparse: POS tagging and parsing the twitterverse. In *Proceedings of the 25th National Conference on Artifical Intelligence*, pages 20–25, San Fransisco, California, August. AAAI. Workshop On Analyzing Microtext.

Björn Gambäck and Amitava Das. 2014. On measuring the complexity of code-mixing. In *Proceedings of the 11th International Conference on Natural Language Processing*, pages 1–7, Goa, India, December. 1st Workshop on Language Technologies for Indian Social Media.

Jesús Giménez and Lluís Màrquez. 2004. SVMTool: A general POS tagger generator based on support vector machines. In *Proceedings of the 4th International Conference on Language Resources and Evaluation*, pages 168–176, Lisbon, Portugal, May. ELRA.

Kevin Gimpel, Nathan Schneider, Brendan O'Connor, Dipanjan Das, Daniel Mills, Jacob Eisenstein, Michael Heilman, Dani Yogatama, Jeffrey Flanigan, and Noah A. Smith. 2011. Part-of-speech tagging for Twitter: Annotation, features, and experiments. In *Proceedings of the 49th Annual Meeting of the Association for Computational Linguistics: Human Language Technologies*, volume 2: short papers, pages 42–47, Portland, Oregon, June. ACL.

Yuhen Hu, Kartik Talamadupula, and Subbarao Kambhampati. 2013. *Dude, srsly?*: The surprisingly formal nature of Twitter's language. In *Proceedings of the 7th International Conference on Weblogs and Social Media*, Boston, Massachusetts, July. AAAI.

Aravind K. Joshi. 1982. Processing of sentences with intra-sentential code-switching. In *Proceedings of the 9th International Conference on Computational Linguistics*, pages 145–150, Prague, Czechoslovakia, July. ACL.

Adam Kilgarriff. 2001. Comparing corpora. *International Journal of Corpus Linguistics*, 6(1):97–133.

Ying Li and Pascale Funng. 2014. Code switch language modeling with functional head constraint. In *Proceedings of the 2014 International Conference on Acoustics, Speech and Signal Processing*, pages 4946–4950, Florence, Italy, May. IEEE.

Roque López and Thiago A.S. Pardo. 2015. Experiments on sentence boundary detection in user-generated web content. In Alexander Gelbukh, editor, *Computational Linguistics and Intelligent Text Processing: Proceedings of the 16th International Conference*, pages 357–368, Cairo, Egypt, March. Springer.

Smruthi Mukund and Rohini K. Srihari. 2012. Analyzing Urdu social media for sentiments using transfer learning with controlled translations. In *Proceedings of the 2012 Conference of the North American Chapter of the Association for Computational Linguistics: Human Language Technologies*, pages 1–8, Atlanta, Georgia, June. ACL. 2nd Workshop on Language in Social Media.

Tetsuji Nakagawa, Taku Kudoh, and Yuji Matsumoto. 2001. Unknown word guessing and part-of-speech tagging using support vector machines. In *Proceedings of the 6th Natural Language Processing Pacific Rim Symposium*, pages 325–331, Tokyo, Japan.

Melanie Neunerdt, Michael Reyer, and Rudolf Mathar. 2014. Efficient training data enrichment and unknown token handling for POS tagging of non-standardized texts. In Josef Ruppenhofer and Gertrud Faaß, editors, *Proceedings of the 12th Edition of the KONVENS Conference*, pages 186–192, Hildesheim, Germany, October. Universitätsverlag Hildesheim.

Dong Nguyen and A. Seza Doğruöz. 2013. Word level language identification in online multilingual communication. In *Proceedings of the 2013 Conference on Empirical Methods in Natural Language Processing*, pages 857–862, Seattle, Washington, October. ACL.

Olutobi Owoputi, Brendan O'Connor, Chris Dyer, Kevin Gimpel, Nathan Schneider, and Noah A. Smith. 2013. Improved part-of-speech tagging for online conversational text with word clusters. In *Proceedings of the 2013 Conference of the North American Chapter of the Association for Computational Linguistics: Human Language Technologies*, pages 380–390, Atlanta, Georgia, June. ACL.

John Paolillo. 1996. Language choice on soc.culture.punjab. *Electronic Journal of Communication*, 6(3), June.

John Paolillo. 1999. The virtual speech community: Social network and language variation on IRC. *Journal of Computer-Mediated Communication*, 4(4), June.

John Paolillo. 2011. "conversational" codeswitching on usenet and internet relay chat. *Language@Internet*, 8(article 3), June.

Slav Petrov, Dipanjan Das, and Ryan T. McDonald. 2011. A universal part-of-speech tagset. *CoRR*, abs/1104.2086.

Jonathon Read, Rebecca Dridan, Stephan Oepen, and Lars Jørgen Solberg. 2012. Sentence boundary detection: A long solved problem? In *Proceedings of the 24th International Conference on Computational Linguistics*, pages 985–994, Mumbai, India, December. ACL. Poster.

Ines Rehbein. 2013. Fine-grained POS tagging of German tweets. In *Proceedings of the 25th International Conference on Language Processing and Knowledge in the Web*, pages 162–175, Darmstadt, Germany, September. Springer.

Jeffrey C. Reynar and Adwait Ratnaparkhi. 1997. A maximum entropy approach to identifying sentence boundaries. In *Proceedings of the 5th Conference on Applied Natural Language Processing*, pages 803–806, Washington, DC, April. ACL.

Alan Ritter, Sam Clark, Mausam, and Oren Etzioni. 2011. Named entity recognition in tweets: An experimental study. In *Proceedings of the 2011 Conference on Empirical Methods in Natural Language Processing*, pages 1524–1534, Edinburgh, Scotland, August. ACL.

Thamar Solorio and Yang Liu. 2008a. Learning to predict code-switching points. In *Proceedings of the 2008 Conference on Empirical Methods in Natural Language Processing*, pages 973–981, Honolulu, Hawaii, October. ACL.

Thamar Solorio and Yang Liu. 2008b. Part-of-speech tagging for English-Spanish code-switched text. In *Proceedings of the 2008 Conference on Empirical Methods in Natural Language Processing*, pages 1051–1060, Honolulu, Hawaii, October. ACL.

Thamar Solorio, Elizabeth Blair, Suraj Maharjan, Steven Bethard, Mona Diab, Mahmoud Gohneim, Abdelati Hawwari, Fahad AlGhamdi, Julia Hirschberg, Alison Chang, and Pascale Fung. 2014. Overview for the first shared task on language identification in code-switched data. In *Proceedings of the 2014 Conference on Empirical Methods in Natural Language Processing*, pages 62–72, Doha, Qatar, October. ACL. 1st Workshop on Computational Approaches to Code Switching.

Caroline Sporleder and Mirella Lapata. 2006. Broad coverage paragraph segmentation across languages and domains. *ACM Transactions on Speech and Language Processing*, 3(2):1–35, July.

Drahomíra Spoustová, Jan Hajič, Jan Raab, and Miroslav Spousta. 2009. Semi-supervised training for the averaged perceptron POS tagger. In *Proceedings of the 12th Conference of the European Chapter of the Association for Computational Linguistics*, pages 763–771, Athens, Greece, March. ACL.

Yogarshi Vyas, Spandana Gella, Jatin Sharma, Kalika Bali, and Monojit Choudhury. 2014. POS tagging of English-Hindi code-mixed social media content. In *Proceedings of the 2014 Conference on Empirical Methods in Natural Language Processing*, pages 974–979, Doha, Qatar, October. ACL.

Sentiment Analysis in Twitter for Macedonian

Dame Jovanoski, Veno Pachovski
University American College Skopje
UACS, Macedonia
{jovanoski,pachovski}@uacs.edu.mk

Preslav Nakov
Qatar Computing Research Institute
HBKU, Qatar
pnakov@qf.org.qa

Abstract

We present work on sentiment analysis in Twitter for Macedonian. As this is pioneering work for this combination of language and genre, we created suitable resources for training and evaluating a system for sentiment analysis of Macedonian tweets. In particular, we developed a corpus of tweets annotated with tweet-level sentiment polarity (positive, negative, and neutral), as well as with phrase-level sentiment, which we made freely available for research purposes. We further bootstrapped several large-scale sentiment lexicons for Macedonian, motivated by previous work for English. The impact of several different pre-processing steps as well as of various features is shown in experiments that represent the first attempt to build a system for sentiment analysis in Twitter for the morphologically rich Macedonian language. Overall, our experimental results show an F_1-score of 92.16, which is very strong and is on par with the best results for English, which were achieved in recent SemEval competitions.

1 Introduction

The increasing popularity of social media services such as Facebook, Twitter and Google+, and the advance of Web 2.0 have enabled users to share information and, as a result, to have influence on the content distributed via these services. The ease of sharing, e.g., directly from a laptop, a tablet or a smart phone, have contributed to the tremendous growth of the content that users share on a daily basis, to the extent that nowadays social networks have no choice but to filter part of the information stream even when it comes from our closest friends.

Naturally, soon this unprecedented abundance of data has attracted business and research interest from various fields including marketing, political science, and social studies, among many others, which are interested in questions like these: *Do people like the new Apple Watch? What do they hate about iPhone6? Do Americans support ObamaCare? What do Europeans think of Pope's visit to Palestine? How do we recognize the emergence of health problems such as depression?*

Such questions can be answered by studying the sentiment of the opinions people express in social media. As a result, the interest for sentiment analysis, especially in social media, has grown, further boosted by the needs of various applications such as mining opinions from product reviews, detecting inappropriate content, and many others.

Below we describe the creation of data and the development of a system for sentiment polarity classification in Twitter for Macedonian: positive, negative, neutral. We are inspired by a similar task at SemEval, which is an ongoing series of evaluations of computational semantic analysis systems, composed by multiple challenges such as text similarity, word sense disambiguation, etc. One of the challenges there was on Sentiment Analysis in Twitter, at SemEval 2013-2015 (Nakov et al., 2013; Rosenthal et al., 2014; Rosenthal et al., 2015; Nakov et al., 2015), where over 40 teams participated three years in a row.[1] Here we follow a similar setup, focusing on message-level sentiment analysis of tweets, but for Macedonian instead of English. Moreover, while at SemEval the task organizers used Mechanical Turk to do the annotations, where the control for quality is hard (everybody can pretend to know English), our annotations are done by native speakers of Macedonian.

[1]Other related tasks were the Aspect-Based Sentiment Analysis task (Pontiki et al., 2014; Pontiki et al., 2015), and the task on Sentiment Analysis of Figurative Language in Twitter (Ghosh et al., 2015).

Proceedings of Recent Advances in Natural Language Processing, pages 249–257,
Hissar, Bulgaria, Sep 7–9 2015.

The remainder of the paper is organized as follows: Section 2 presents some related work. Sections 3 and 4 describe the datasets and the various lexicons we created for Macedonian. Section 5 gives detail about our system, including the preprocessing steps and the features used. Section 6 describes our experiments and discusses the results. Section 7 concludes with possible directions for future work.

2 Related Work

Research in sentiment analysis started in the early 2000s. Initially, the problem was regarded as standard document classification into topics, e.g., Pang et al. (2002) experimented with various classifiers such as maximum entropy, Naïve Bayes and SVM, using standard features such as unigram/bigrams, word counts/present, word position and part-of-speech tagging. Around the same time, other researchers realized the importance of external sentiment lexicons, e.g., Turney (2002) proposed an unsupervised approach to learn the sentiment orientation of words/phrases: positive vs. negative. Later work studied the linguistic aspects of expressing opinions, evaluations, and speculations (Wiebe et al., 2004), the role of context in determining the sentiment orientation (Wilson et al., 2005), of deeper linguistic processing such as negation handling (Pang and Lee, 2008), of finer-grained sentiment distinctions (Pang and Lee, 2005), of positional information (Raychev and Nakov, 2009), etc. Moreover, it was recognized that in many cases, it is crucial to know not just the polariy of the sentiment, but also the topic towards which this sentiment is expressed (Stoyanov and Cardie, 2008).

Early sentiment analysis research focused on customer reviews of movies, and later of hotels, phones, laptops, etc. Later, with the emergence of social media, sentiment analysis in Twitter became a hot research topic. The earliest Twitter sentiment datasets were both small and proprietary, such as the i-sieve corpus (Kouloumpis et al., 2011), or relied on noisy labels obtained from emoticons or hashtags. This situation changed with the emergence of the SemEval task on Sentiment Analysis in Twitter, which ran in 2013-2015 (Nakov et al., 2013; Rosenthal et al., 2014; Rosenthal et al., 2015). The task created standard datasets of several thousand tweets annotated for sentiment polarity. Our work here is inspired by that task.

In our experiments below, we focus on Macedonian, for which we only know two publications on sentiment analysis, none of which is about Twitter.

Gajduk and Kocarev (2014) experimented with 800 posts from the Kajgana forum (260 positive, 260 negative, and 280 objective), using SVM and Naïve Bayes classifiers, and features such as bag of words, rules for negation, and stemming.

Uzunova and Kulakov (2015) experimented with 400 movie reviews[2] (200 positive, and 200 negative; no objective/neutral), and a Naïve Bayes classifier, using a small manually annotated sentiment lexicon of unknown size, and various preprocessing techniques such as negation handling and spelling/character translation. Unfortunately, the datasets and the generated lexicons used in the above work are not publicly available, and/or are also from a different domain. As we are interested in sentiment analysis of Macedonian tweets, we had to build our own datasets.

In addition to preparing a dataset of annotated tweets, we further focus on creating sentiment polarity lexicons for Macedonian. This is because lexicons are crucial for sentiment analysis. As we mentioned above, since the very beginning, researchers have realized that sentiment analysis was quite different from standard document classification (Sebastiani, 2002), and that it crucially needed external knowledge in the form of suitable sentiment polarity lexicons. For further detail, see the surveys by Pang and Lee (2008) and Liu and Zhang (2012).

Until recently, such sentiment polarity lexicons have been manually crafted, and were of small to moderate size, e.g., LIWC (Pennebaker et al., 2001), General Inquirer (Stone et al., 1966), Bing Liu's lexicon (Hu and Liu, 2004), and MPQA (Wilson et al., 2005), all have 2000-8000 words. Early efforts in building them automatically also yielded lexicons of moderate sizes (Esuli and Sebastiani, 2006; Baccianella et al., 2010).

However, recent results have shown that automatically extracted large-scale lexicons (e.g., up to a million words and phrases) offer important performance advantages, as confirmed at shared tasks on Sentiment Analysis in Twitter at SemEval 2013-2015 (Nakov et al., 2013; Rosenthal et al., 2014; Rosenthal et al., 2015).

[2]There have been also experiments on movie reviews for the closely related Bulgarian language (Kapukaranov and Nakov, 2015), but there the objective was to predict user rating, which was addressed as an ordinal regression problem.

Similar observations were made in the Aspect-Based Sentiment Analysis task, which ran at SemEval 2014-2015 (Pontiki et al., 2014; Pontiki et al., 2015). In both tasks, the winning systems benefited from building and using massive sentiment polarity lexicons (Mohammad et al., 2013; Zhu et al., 2014). These large-scale automatic lexicons were typically built using bootstrapping, starting with a small seed of, e.g., 50-60 words (Mohammad et al., 2013), and sometimes even using just two emoticons.

3 Data

During a period of six months from November 2014 to April 2015, we collected about half a million tweet messages. In the process, we had to train and use a high-precision Naïve Bayes classifier for detecting the language, because the Twitter API often confused Macedonian tweets with Bulgarian or Russian. From the resulting set of tweets, we created training and testing datasets, which we manually annotated at the tweet level (using *positive*, *negative*, and *neutral/objective* as labels[3]).

The training dataset was annotated by the first author, who is a native speaker of Macedonian. In addition to tweet-level sentiment, we also annotated the sentiment-bearing words and phrases inside the *training* tweets, in order to obtain a sentiment lexicon.

The testing dataset was only annotated at the tweet level, and for it there was one additional annotator, again a native speaker of Macedonian. The value of the Cohen's Kappa statistics (Cohen, 1960) for the inter-annotator agreement between the two annotators was 0.41, which corresponds to *moderate* agreement (Landis and Koch, 1977); this relatively low agreement shows the difficulty of the task. For the final testing dataset, we discarded all tweets on which the annotators disagreed (a total of 474 tweets).

Table 1 shows the statistics about the training and the testing datasets. We can see that the data is somewhat balanced between positive and negative tweets, but has a relatively smaller proportion of neutral tweets.[4]

[3]Following (Nakov et al., 2013), we merged *neutral* and *objective* as they are commonly confused by annotators.

[4]It was previously reported that most tweets are neutral, but this was for English, and for tweets about selected topics (Rosenthal et al., 2014). We have no topic restriction; more importantly, there is a severe ongoing political crisis in Macedonia, and thus Macedonian tweets were full of emotions.

Dataset	Positive	Neutral	Negative	Total
Train	2,610 (30%)	1,280 (15%)	4,693 (55%)	8,583
Test	431 (38%)	200 (18%)	508 (44%)	1,139

Table 1: Statistics about the datasets.

We faced many problems when processing the tweets. For example, it was hard to distinguish advertisements vs. news vs. ordinary user messages, which is important for sentiment annotations. Here is an example tweet by a news agency, which should be annotated as neutral/objective:

Лицето АБВ е убиецот и виновен за убиството на БЦД. [5]

The above message has good grammatical structure, but in our datasets there are many messages with missing characters, missing words, misspellings and with poor grammatical structure; this is in part what makes the task difficult. Here is a sample message with missing words and misspellings:

брао бе, ги утепаа с....!!! [6]

Non-standard language is another problem. This includes not only slang and words written in a funny way on purpose, but also many dialectal words from different regions of Macedonia that are not used in Standard Macedonian. For example, in the Eastern part of the Republic of Macedonia, there are words with Bulgarian influence, while in the Western part, there are words influenced by Albanian; and there is Serbian influence in the North.

Finally, many problems arise due to our using a small dataset for sentiment analysis. This mainly affects the construction of the sentiment lexicons and the reason for this is the distribution of emoticons, hashtags and sentiment words. In particular, if we want to use hashstags or emoticons as seeds to construct sentiment lexicons, we find that very few tweet messages have emoticons or hashtags. Table 2 shows the statistics about the distribution of the emoticons and hashtags in the dataset (half a million tweet messages). That is why, in our experiments below, we do not rely much on hashtags for lexicon construction.

[5]Translation: *The person ABC is the killer, and he is responsible for the murder of BCD.*

[6]Translation: *That's great, they have smashed them with....!!!*

Token type	No. of messages
Without emoticons and hashtags	473,420
With emoticons	3,635
With hashtags	521
Total	477,576

Table 2: Number of tweets in our datasets that contain emoticons and hashtags.

4 Sentiment Lexicons

Sentiment polarity lexicons are key resources for the task of sentiment analysis, and thus we have put special efforts to generate some for Macedonian using various techniques.[7] Typically, a sentiment lexicon is a set of words annotated with positive and negative sentiment. Sometimes there is also a polarity score of that sentiment, e.g., *spectacular* could have positive strength of 0.91, while for *okay* that might be 0.3.

4.1 Manually-Annotated Lexicon

As we mentioned above, in the process of annotation of the training dataset, the annotator also marked the sentiment-bearing words and phrases in each tweet, together with their sentiment polarity in that context: positive or negative.

The phrases for the lexicon were annotated by two annotators, both native speakers of Macedonian. We calculated the Cohen's Kappa statistics (Cohen, 1960) for the inter-annotator agreement, and obtained the score of 0.63, which corresponds to *substantial* agreement (Landis and Koch, 1977).

We discarded all words with disagreement, a total of 122, and we collected the remaining words and phrases in a lexicon. The lexicon contained 1,088 words (459 positive and 629 negative).

4.2 Translated Lexicons

Another way to obtain a sentiment polarity lexicon is by translating a preexisting one from another language. We translated some English manually-crafted lexicons such as Bing Liu's lexicon (2,006 positive and 4,783 negative), and MPQA (2,718 positive and 4,912 negative), and an automatically extracted Bulgarian lexicon (5,016 positive and 2,415 negative), extracted from a movie reviews website (Kapukaranov and Nakov, 2015). For the translation of the lexicons we used Google Translate, and we further manually corrected the results, removing bad or missing translations.

[7] All lexicons presented here are publicly available at `https://github.com/badc0re/sent-lex`

4.3 Automatically-Constructed Lexicons

Sentiment lexicons can also be constructed automatically by using Pointwise Mutual Information as a way to calculate the semantic orientation of a word (Turney, 2002) or a phrase in a message (text). In sentiment analysis, using the orientation of a word, the positive and the negative score of a word/phrase can be calculated. The semantic orientation can be calculated as follows:

$$SO(w) = PMI(w, pos) - PMI(w, neg)$$

where PMI is the pointwise mutual information, and pos and neg are placeholders standing for any of the seed positive and negative terms.

A positive/negative value for $SO(w)$ indicates positive/negative polarity for w, and its magnitude shows the corresponding sentiment strength. In turn, $PMI(w, pos) = \frac{P(w,pos)}{P(w)P(pos)}$, where $P(w, pos)$ is the probability to see w with any of the seed positive words in the same tweet,[8] $P(w)$ is the probability to see w in any tweet, and $P(pos)$ is the probability to see any of the seed positive words in a tweet; $PMI(w, neg)$ is defined similarly.

Turney's PMI-based approach further serves as the basis for two popular large-scale automatic lexicons for English sentiment analysis in Twitter, initially developed by NRC for their participation in SemEval-2013 (Mohammad et al., 2013). The *Hashtag Sentiment Lexicon* uses as seeds hashtags containing 32 positive and 36 negative words, e.g., `#happy` and `#sad`; it then uses PMI and extracts 775,000 sentiment words from 135 million tweets. Similarly, the *Sentiment140* lexicon contains 1.6 million sentiment words and phrases, extracted from the same 135 million tweets, but this time using smileys as seed indicators for positive and negative sentiment, e.g., `:)`, `:-)` and `:))` serve as positive seeds, and `:(` and `:-(` as negative ones.

In our experiments, we used all words from our manually-crafted Macedonian sentiment polarity lexicon above as seeds, and then we mined additional sentiment-bearing words from a set of half a million Macedonian tweets. The number of tweets we used was much smaller in scale compared to that used in the *Hashtag Sentiment Lexicon* and in the *Sentiment140* lexicon, since there are much less Macedonian tweets (compared to English).

[8] Here we explain the method using number of tweets, as this is how we are using it, but Turney (2002) actually used page hits in the AltaVista search engine.

However, we used a much larger seed; as we will see below, this turns out to be a very good idea. We further tried to construct lexicons using words from the translated lexicons as seeds.

5 System Overview

The language of our tweet messages is Macedonian, and thus the text processing is a bit different than for English. As many basic tools that are freely available for English do not exist for Macedonian, we had to implement them in order to improve our model's performance. Our system uses logistic regression for classification, where words are weighted using TF.IDF.

5.1 Preprocessing

For pre-processing, we applied various algorithms, which we combined in order to achieve better performance. We used Christopher Potts' tokenizer,[9] and we had to be careful since we had to extract not only the words but also other tokens such as hashtags, emoticons, user names, etc. The pre-processing of the tweets goes as follows:

1. **URL and username removal**: tokens such as URLs and usernames (i.e., tokens starting with `@`) were removed.
2. **Stopword removal**: stopwords were filtered out based on a word list (146 words).
3. **Repeating characters removal**: consecutive character repetitions in a word were removed; also were removed repetitions of a word in the same token, e.g., 'какоооо' or 'дадада' (translated in English as 'what' and 'yes', respectively).
4. **Negation handling**: negation was addressed using a predefined list of negation tokens, then the prefix `NEG_CONTEXT_` was attached to the following tokens until a clause-level punctuation mark, in order to annotate it as appearing in a negated context, as suggested in (Pang et al., 2002). A list of 45 negative phrases and words was used to signal negation.
5. **Non-standard to standard word mapping**: non-standard words (slang) were mapped to an appropriate form, according to a manualy crafted predefined list of mappings.
6. **PoS tagging**: rule-based, using a dictionary.
7. **Tagging positive/negative words**: positive and negative words were tagged as `POS` and `NEG`, using sentiment lexicons.
8. **Stemming**: rule-based stemming was performed, which removes/replaces some prefixes/suffixes.

In sum, we started the transformation of an input tweet by converting it to lowercase, followed by removal of URLs and user names. We then normalized some words to Standard Macedonian using a dictionary of 173 known word transformations and we further removed stopwords (a list of 146 words). As part of the transformation, we marked the words in a negated context.

We further created a rule-based stemming algorithm with a list of 65 rules for removing/replacing prefixes and suffixes (Porter, 1980). We used two groups of rules: 45 rules for affix removal, and 20 rules for affix replacement. Developing a stemmer for Macedonian was challenging as this is a highly inflective language, rich in both inflectional and derivational forms. For example, here are some of the forms for the word навреда (English noun '*insult, offense*', verb '*offend, insult*'):

навредам	навредел
навредат	навредела
навредата	навределе
навредеа	навредело
навредев	навреден
навредевме	навредена
навредевте	...

In total, this word can generate over 90 inflected forms; in some cases, this involves a change in the last letter of the stem.

We further performed PoS (part-of-speech) tagging with our own tool based on averaged perceptron trained on MULTEXT-East resources (Erjavec, 2012). Here is an annotated tweet:

го/PN даваат/VB Глуп/NN и/CC Поглуп/NN на/CC Телма/NN[10]

Here are the POS tags used in the above example: (*i*) NN-noun; (*ii*) AV-adverb; (*iii*) VB-verb; (*iv*) AE-adjective; (*v*) PN-pronoun; (*vi*) PN-pronoun; (*vii*) CN-cardinal number; (*viii*) CC-conjunction.

[9] http://sentiment.christopherpotts.net/tokenizing.html

[10] The translation for this message is: *Dump and Dumper is on Telma.*

We also developed a lemmatizer based on *approximate fuzzy string matching*. First, we used the *candidate word* (the one we want to lemmatize) to retrieve word lemmata that are similar to it; we then used *Jaro–Winkler* distance and *Levenshtein* distance to calculate a score that will determine whether the word matches closely enough some of the retrieved words. Such techniques have been used by other authors for *record linkage* (Cohen et al., 2003). Finally, as a last step in the transformation, we weighed the words using TF.IDF.

5.2 Features

In order to evaluate the impact of the sentiment lexicon, we defined features that are fully or partially dependent on the lexicons. When using multiple lexicons at the same time, there are separate instances of these features for each lexicon. Here are the features we used:

(*i*) Unigrams/bigrams: each one is a feature and its value is its TF.IDF score; (*ii*) Number of positive words in the tweet; (*iii*) Number of negative words in the tweet; (*iv*) Ratio of the number of positive words to the total number of sentiment words in the tweet; (*v*) Ratio of negative words to the total number of sentiment words in the tweet; (*vi*) Sum of the sentiment scores for all dictionary entries found in the tweet; (*vii*) Sum of the positive sentiment scores for all dictionary entries found in the tweet; (*viii*) Sum of the negative sentiment scores for all dictionary entries found in the tweet; (*ix-x*) Number of positive and negative emoticons in the tweet.

For classification, we used logistic regression. Our basic features were TF.IDF-weighted unigram and bigrams, and also emoticons. We further included additional features that focus on the positive and negative terms that occur in the tweet together with their scores in the lexicon. In case of two or more lexicons being used together, we had a copy of each feature for each lexicon.

6 Experiments

Our evaluation setup follows that of the SemEval 2013-2015 task on Sentiment Analysis in Twitter (Nakov et al., 2013; Rosenthal et al., 2014; Rosenthal et al., 2015), where the systems were evaluated in terms of an F-score that is the average of the F_1-score for the positive, and the F_1-score for the negative class. Note that, even though implicit, the neutral class still matters in this score.

Features	**F-score**	**Diff.**
All	92.16	
All - stop words	86.24	-5.92
All - negation	87.51	-4.65
All - norm. words to STD. Macedonian	90.22	-1.94
All - repeated characters	91.10	-1.06
All - stemming	93.14	0.98
All - PoS	92.01	-0.15

Table 3: The impact of excluding the preprocessing steps one at a time.

Features	**F-score**	**Diff.**
All	92.16	
All - automatically-constructed lexicons	72.77	-19.39
All - our manually-crafted lexicon	79.32	-12.84
All - all translated lexicons	91.89	-0.27

Table 4: The impact of excluding the features derived from the sentiment polarity lexicons.

Table 3 shows the impact of each pre-processing step. The first row shows the results when using all pre-processing steps and all sentiment lexicons. The following rows show the impact of excluding each of the preprocessing steps, one at a time. We can see that stopword removal and negation handling are most important: excluding each of them yields a five point absolute from in F-score. Normalization to Standard Macedonian turns out to be very important too as excluding it yields a drop of two points absolute. Handling repeating characters and stemming are also important, each yielding one point drop in F-score. However, the impact of using POS tagging is negligible.

Table 4 shows the impact of excluding some of the lexicons. We can see that our manually-crafted lexicon is quite helpful, contributing 13 points absolute in the overall F-score. Yet, the bootstrapped lexicons are even more important as excluding them yields a drop of 19 points absolute.

7 Conclusion and Future Work

We have presented work on sentiment analysis in Twitter for Macedonian. As this is pioneering work for this combination of language and genre, we created suitable resources for training and evaluating a system for sentiment analysis of Macedonian tweets. In particular, we developed a corpus of tweets annotated with tweet-level sentiment polarity (positive, negative, and neutral), as well as with phrase-level sentiment, which we made freely available for research purposes.

We further bootstrapped several large-scale sentiment lexicons for Macedonian, motivated by previous work for English. The impact of several different pre-processing steps as well as of various features is shown in experiments that represent the first attempt to build a system for sentiment analysis in Twitter for the morphologically rich Macedonian language. Overall, our experimental results show an F_1-score of 92.16, which is very strong and is on par with the best results for English, which were achieved in recent SemEval competitions.

In future work, we are interested in studying the impact of the raw corpus size, e.g., we could only collect half a million tweets for creating lexicons and analyzing/evaluating the system, while Kiritchenko et al. (2014) built their lexicon on million tweets and evaluated their system on 135 million English tweets. Moreover, we are interested not only in quantity but also in quality, i.e., in studying the quality of the individual words and phrases used as seeds. An interesting work in that direction, even though in a different domain and context, is that of Kozareva and Hovy (2010). We are further interested in finding alternative ways for defining the sentiment polarity, including degree of positive or negative sentiment, and in evaluating them by constructing polarity lexicons in new ways (Severyn and Moschitti, 2015).

More ambitiously, we would like to extend our system to detecting sentiment over a period of time for the purpose of finding trends towards a topic (Nakov et al., 2013; Rosenthal et al., 2014; Rosenthal et al., 2015), e.g., predicting whether the sentiment is strongly negative, weakly negative, strongly positive, etc. We further plan application to other social media services, with the idea of analyzing the sentiment of an online conversation. We would like to see the impact of earlier messages on the sentiment of newer messages, e.g., as in (Vanzo et al., 2014; Barrón-Cedeño et al., 2015; Joty et al., 2015). Finally, we are interested in applying our system to help other tasks, e.g., by using sentiment analysis to finding opinion manipulation trolls in Web forums (Mihaylov et al., 2015a; Mihaylov et al., 2015b).

Acknowledgments

We would like to thank the anonymous reviewers for their constructive comments, which have helped us improve the final version of the paper.

References

Stefano Baccianella, Andrea Esuli, and Fabrizio Sebastiani. 2010. SentiWordNet 3.0: An enhanced lexical resource for sentiment analysis and opinion mining. In *Proceedings of the International Conference on Language Resources and Evaluation*, LREC '10, Valletta, Malta.

Alberto Barrón-Cedeño, Simone Filice, Gióvanni Da San Martino, Shafiq Joty, Lluís Màrquez, Preslav Nakov, and Alessandro Moschitti. 2015. Thread-level information for comment classification in community question answering. In *Proceedings of the 53rd Annual Meeting of the Association for Computational Linguistics and the 7th International Joint Conference on Natural Language Processing*, ACL-IJCNLP '15, pages 687–693, Beijing, China.

William Cohen, Pradeep Ravikumar, and Stephen Fienberg. 2003. A comparison of string metrics for matching names and records. In *Proceedings of the KDD workshop on data cleaning and object consolidation*, volume 3, pages 73–78, Washington, D.C., USA.

Jacob Cohen. 1960. A Coefficient of Agreement for Nominal Scales. *Educational and Psychological Measurement*, 20(1):37.

Tomaž Erjavec. 2012. MULTEXT-East: Morphosyntactic resources for Central and Eastern European languages. *Lang. Resour. Eval.*, 46(1):131–142.

Andrea Esuli and Fabrizio Sebastiani. 2006. SENTIWORDNET: A publicly available lexical resource for opinion mining. In *Proceedings of the International Conference on Language Resources and Evaluation*, LREC '06, pages 417–422, Genoa, Italy.

Andrej Gajduk and Ljupco Kocarev. 2014. Opinion mining of text documents written in Macedonian language. *arXiv preprint arXiv:1411.4472.*

Aniruddha Ghosh, Guofu Li, Tony Veale, Paolo Rosso, Ekaterina Shutova, John Barnden, and Antonio Reyes. 2015. SemEval-2015 task 11: Sentiment analysis of figurative language in Twitter. In *Proceedings of the 9th International Workshop on Semantic Evaluation*, SemEval '15, pages 470–478, Denver, CO, USA.

Minqing Hu and Bing Liu. 2004. Mining and summarizing customer reviews. In *Proceedings of the 10th ACM SIGKDD International Conference on Knowledge Discovery and Data Mining*, KDD '04, pages 168–177, Seattle, WA, USA.

Shafiq Joty, Alberto Barrón-Cedeño, Giovanni Da San Martino, Simone Filice, Lluís Màrquez, Alessandro Moschitti, and Preslav Nakov. 2015. Global thread-level inference for comment classification in community question answering. In *Proceedings of the Conference on Empirical Methods in Natural Language Processing*, EMNLP '15, Lisbon, Portugal.

Borislav Kapukaranov and Preslav Nakov. 2015. Fine-grained sentiment analysis for movie reviews in Bulgarian. In *Proceedings of the International Conference on Recent Advances in Natural Language Processing*, RANLP '15, Hissar, Bulgaria.

Svetlana Kiritchenko, Xiaodan Zhu, and Saif M Mohammad. 2014. Sentiment analysis of short informal texts. *Journal of Artificial Intelligence Research*, pages 723–762.

Efthymios Kouloumpis, Theresa Wilson, and Johanna Moore. 2011. Twitter sentiment analysis: The good the bad and the OMG! In *Proceedings of the International Conference on Weblogs and Social Media*, ICWSM '11, Barcelona, Spain.

Zornitsa Kozareva and Eduard Hovy. 2010. Not all seeds are equal: Measuring the quality of text mining seeds. In *Proceedings of the Annual Conference of the North American Chapter of the Association for Computational Linguistics*, NAACL-HLT '10, pages 618–626, Los Angeles, CA, USA.

J. Richard Landis and Gary G. Koch. 1977. The measurement of observer agreement for categorical data. *Biometrics*, 33(1):159–74, 3.

Bing Liu and Lei Zhang. 2012. A survey of opinion mining and sentiment analysis. In Charu C. Aggarwal and ChengXiang Zhai, editors, *Mining Text Data*, pages 415–463. Springer.

Todor Mihaylov, Georgi Georgiev, and Preslav Nakov. 2015a. Finding opinion manipulation trolls in news community forums. In *Proceedings of the Conference on Computational Natural Language Learning*, pages 310–314, Beijing, China.

Todor Mihaylov, Ivan Koychev, Georgi Georgiev, and Preslav Nakov. 2015b. Exposing paid opinion manipulation trolls. In *Proceedings of the Conference on Computational Natural Language Learning*, Hissar, Bulgaria.

Saif Mohammad, Svetlana Kiritchenko, and Xiaodan Zhu. 2013. NRC-Canada: Building the state-of-the-art in sentiment analysis of tweets. In *Proceedings of the Seventh international workshop on Semantic Evaluation Exercises*, SemEval '13, pages 321–327, Atlanta, GA, USA.

Preslav Nakov, Sara Rosenthal, Zornitsa Kozareva, Veselin Stoyanov, Alan Ritter, and Theresa Wilson. 2013. SemEval-2013 task 2: Sentiment analysis in Twitter. In *Proceedings of the Seventh International Workshop on Semantic Evaluation*, SemEval '13, pages 312–320, Atlanta, GA, USA.

Preslav Nakov, Sara Rosenthal, Svetlana Kiritchenko, Saif Mohammad, Zornitsa Kozareva, Alan Ritter, Veselin Stoyanov, and Xiaodan Zhu. 2015. Developing a successful SemEval task in sentiment analysis of Twitter and other social media texts. *Language Resources and Evaluation*.

Bo Pang and Lillian Lee. 2005. Seeing stars: Exploiting class relationships for sentiment categorization with respect to rating scales. In *Proceedings of the Annual Meeting of the Association for Computational Linguistics*, ACL '05, pages 115–124, Ann Arbor, MI, USA.

Bo Pang and Lillian Lee. 2008. Opinion mining and sentiment analysis. *Foundations and trends in information retrieval*, 2(1-2):1–135.

Bo Pang, Lillian Lee, and Shivakumar Vaithyanathan. 2002. Thumbs up?: Sentiment classification using machine learning techniques. In *Proceedings of the Conference on Empirical Methods in Natural Language Processing*, EMNLP '02, pages 79–86, Philadelphia, PA, USA.

James W. Pennebaker, Martha E. Francis, and Roger J. Booth. 2001. *Linguistic Inquiry and Word Count*. Lawerence Erlbaum Associates, Mahwah, NJ.

Maria Pontiki, Harris Papageorgiou, Dimitrios Galanis, Ion Androutsopoulos, John Pavlopoulos, and Suresh Manandhar. 2014. SemEval-2014 task 4: Aspect based sentiment analysis. In *Proceedings of the 8th International Workshop on Semantic Evaluation*, SemEval '14, pages 27–35, Dublin, Ireland.

Maria Pontiki, Dimitris Galanis, Haris Papageorgiou, Suresh Manandhar, and Ion Androutsopoulos. 2015. SemEval-2015 task 12: Aspect based sentiment analysis. In *Proceedings of the 9th International Workshop on Semantic Evaluation*, SemEval '2015, pages 486–495, Denver, CO, USA.

Martin F Porter. 1980. An algorithm for suffix stripping. *Program*, 14(3):130–137.

Veselin Raychev and Preslav Nakov. 2009. Language-independent sentiment analysis using subjectivity and positional information. In *Proceedings of the International Conference on Recent Advances in Natural Language Processing*, RANLP '09, pages 360–364, Borovets, Bulgaria.

Sara Rosenthal, Alan Ritter, Preslav Nakov, and Veselin Stoyanov. 2014. SemEval-2014 Task 9: Sentiment analysis in Twitter. In *Proceedings of the 8th International Workshop on Semantic Evaluation*, SemEval '14, pages 73–80, Dublin, Ireland.

Sara Rosenthal, Preslav Nakov, Svetlana Kiritchenko, Saif Mohammad, Alan Ritter, and Veselin Stoyanov. 2015. SemEval-2015 task 10: Sentiment analysis in Twitter. In *Proceedings of the 9th International Workshop on Semantic Evaluation*, SemEval '15, pages 450–462, Denver, CO, USA.

Fabrizio Sebastiani. 2002. Machine learning in automated text categorization. *ACM Comput. Surv.*, 34(1):1–47, March.

Aliaksei Severyn and Alessandro Moschitti. 2015. On the automatic learning of sentiment lexicons. In *Proceedings of the 2015 Conference of the North*

American Chapter of the Association for Computational Linguistics: Human Language Technologies, pages 1397–1402, Denver, CO, USA.

Philip J. Stone, Dexter C. Dunphy, Marshall S. Smith, and Daniel M. Ogilvie. 1966. *The General Inquirer: A Computer Approach to Content Analysis*. MIT Press.

Veselin Stoyanov and Claire Cardie. 2008. Topic identification for fine-grained opinion analysis. In *Proceedings of the 22nd International Conference on Computational Linguistics*, COLING '08, pages 817–824, Manchester, United Kingdom.

Peter D. Turney. 2002. Thumbs up or thumbs down?: Semantic orientation applied to unsupervised classification of reviews. In *Proceedings of the Annual Meeting of the Association for Computational Linguistics*, ACL '02, pages 417–424, Philadelphia, PA, USA.

Vasilija Uzunova and Andrea Kulakov. 2015. Sentiment analysis of movie reviews written in Macedonian language. In *ICT Innovations 2014*, pages 279–288. Springer.

Andrea Vanzo, Danilo Croce, and Roberto Basili. 2014. A context-based model for sentiment analysis in twitter. In *Proceedings of the 25th International Conference on Computational Linguistics*, COLING '14, pages 2345–2354, Dublin, Ireland.

Janyce Wiebe, Theresa Wilson, Rebecca Bruce, Matthew Bell, and Melanie Martin. 2004. Learning subjective language. *Comput. Linguist.*, 30(3):277–308, September.

Theresa Wilson, Janyce Wiebe, and Paul Hoffmann. 2005. Recognizing contextual polarity in phrase-level sentiment analysis. In *Proceedings of the Conference on Human Language Technology and Empirical Methods in Natural Language Processing*, HLT-EMNLP '05, pages 347–354, Vancouver, BC, Canada.

Xiaodan Zhu, Svetlana Kiritchenko, and Saif M. Mohammad. 2014. NRC-Canada-2014: Detecting aspects and sentiment in customer reviews. In *Proceedings of the International Workshop on Semantic Evaluation*, SemEval '14, pages 437–442, Dublin, Ireland.

About Emotion Identification in Visual Sentiment Analysis

Olga Kanishcheva
Institute of Information and Communication Technologies,
Bulgarian Academy of Sciences
kanichshevaolga@gmail.com

Galia Angelova
Institute of Information and Communication Technologies,
Bulgarian Academy of Sciences
galia@lml.bas.bg

Abstract

In this paper we present an approach for analysis of sentiments and emotions in image tagging using SentiWordNet as an external linguistic resource of emotional words. Our aim is to design and implement algorithms that assess the emotions and polarity given a set of image tags. The approach is not limited to object analysis only (considering informational keywords) but deals with the involvement tags and employs some techniques used for sentiment analysis in social networks. We consider the issue of tag sense disambiguation when image keywords are mapped to SentiWordNet. The Lesk algorithm helps to identify correctly the meaning of about 50% of the ambiguous single keywords of 200 images. The total number of tags we process is about 10,000. Calculating a "sentiment score" for each image, the system classifies images into three classes (positive, negative, neutral). These classes are compared to emotional assessments done *(i)* by humans and *(ii)* by training of a SVM classifier that provides the baseline of 69.7% precision, 29.9% recall and 41.8% F-measure. Our approach works with 63.53% precision, 58.7% recall and 61.02% F-measure. The experiments are performed using the annotations of the industrial auto-tagging platform Imagga that identifies automatically image objects with high precision.

1 Introduction

Folksonomies are recognized as a recent type of internet classification system where non-professional users add their own keywords (tags) to information objects. These tags could then be used by anyone to sort and share items. "*Folksonomy*" became the word most commonly used to refer to this annotation approach that is also known as ethnoclassification, social classification/tagging, collaborative tagging, social indexing and distributed classification.

Peters and Weller (2008) wrote that annotation development via crowdsourcing and the resulting folksonomies provide many advantages such as diverse opinions, independent decision-making, decentralization of power, and a way of aggregating opinions. Most current systems that facilitate tagging do not require any sort of text verification or controlled vocabulary. In this way the diversity of opinions allowed in tagging is limitless and the annotators independently select the tags they want to use. Finally, folksonomies provide the aggregation of opinions in the form of systems such as Flickr (https://www.flickr.com), Instagram (https://instagram.com/), Picasaweb (picasaweb.com/), Photobucket (http://photobucket.com/) and others.

Images in these large collections are retrieved using keywords specified by users. For example, searching with tag "*London*" returns the list of links to all photos annotated with this keyword. Thus the semantic information, which is saved up in the metadata, enables the development of various searching strategies that rely significantly on automatic text processing, lexical hierarchies and information search techniques.

Emotional words take special place among folksonomy tags. For instance Beaudoin (2007) suggests that the emotional elements and other parts of speech that express sentiments, such as adjectives, are classified in various categories. To define "tag sentiment", it is necessary to use tags from various categories. It is well known that user-defined tags in folksonomies contain a lot of emotional markers. Sentiments are most often expressed by adjectives (*attractive, cool, funny, pretty, beautiful, happy* etc.), verbs (*hate, admire*) and especially interjections – words that

Proceedings of Recent Advances in Natural Language Processing, pages 258–265,
Hissar, Bulgaria, Sep 7–9 2015.

bear no meaning by themselves but are well loaded with emotionality, such as *ah, wow, oops, hey,* etc. Besides users can enter emoticons and expressive lengthening of words for identification or strengthening the emotional relation to the image (*:D,* ☺, *coooool* etc.). All these emotional markers are considered as one category – the so-called "*subjective tags*" because they express users' opinion and emotion, e.g., *funny* or *cool.* They can help evaluating qualities and recommendations. Subjective tags are assigned to digital objects primarily with a motivation of self-expression.

In this paper we propose an integrated approach to sentiment analysis of image tags – coming from user-defined folksonomies and auto-tagging systems. The paper is organized as follows: Section 2 summarizes some related work; Section 3 overviews the sentiment analysis achievements and linguistic resources that provide information about emotional words. In Section 4 we present the Imagga Auto-Tagging Program (ATP) – the source of our test corpus of automatically annotated images. Section 5 describes the suggested approach in more detail; Section 6 presents current results. Section 7 contains the conclusion and plans for future work.

2 Related Work

A large number of research works appeared recently that address sentiment analysis and its relation to image annotation, including: visual aspects of sentiment analysis (Borth et al., 2013; Jia et al., 2012; Machajdik and Hunbury, 2010; Hailin et al., 2015) and hybrid approaches which analyze emotions using additional resources (Yang et al., 2013; Yang et al., 2014). The basic idea is to build a sophisticated feature space that can effectively represent the sentiment status of texts and/or images.

Jia et al. (2012) present a prediction of sentiment reflected in visual content. The authors propose a systematic, data-driven methodology to construct a large-scale sentiment ontology built upon psychology and web crawled folksonomies using SentiBank. The authors also used the psychological theory Plutchik's Wheel of Emotions as the guiding principle to construct a large-scale visual sentiment ontology that consists of more than 3,000 semantic concepts.

Chen et al. (2014) created a hierarchical system to model object-based visual sentiment concepts. The system handles sentiment concept classification in object-specific manner. It tackles the challenges of concept localization and resolving sentiment attribute ambiguity.

The systems presented in (Borth et al., 2013; Chen et al., 2014) are based only on analysis of Adjective Noun Pairs (ANP) such as "*beautiful flower*" or "*disgusting food*". The advantage of using ANPs, compared to nouns or adjectives only, is the potential to turn a neutral noun like "*dog*" into an ANP with strong sentiment like "*cute dog*" by adding an adjective with a strong sentiment. Authors claim that such phrases also make the concepts more detectable than single adjectives (e.g. "*beautiful*") which are typically abstract and difficult to detect.

Yang et al. (2014) applied a lexicon-based sentiment method from (Esuli and Sebastiani, 2006) to analyze the corresponding textual sentiment that is further used to cluster and rank the related images. Then, to link images in social networks that have similar emotions but different visual contents, the authors combine the social links with visual similarity between images, constructing a "*visual-social similarity matrix*" that quantifies image similarities from both visual and social perspectives. They propose the ViSoRank algorithm to identify representative images on the inferred visual-social similarity graph and the VSTRank algorithm to combine them together to discover the emotionally representative images for social events. Only two sentiment categories are used (positive and negative).

Ignacio Fernández-Tobías et al. (2013) present a model which is built upon an automatically generated lexicon that describes emotions by means of synonym and antonym terms, and that is linked to multiple domain-specific emotional folksonomies extracted from entertainment social tagging systems. Using these cross-domain folksonomies, the authors develop a number of techniques that automatically transform tag-based item profiles into emotion-oriented item profiles. This approach is applied for folksonomies in the movie and music domains.

Siersdorfer et al. (2010) consider the "bag-of-visual words" representation as well as the color distribution of images, and make use of the SentiWordNet thesaurus to extract numerical values for image sentiment from associated textual metadata. Then they perform a discriminative feature analysis based on information theoretic methods and apply machine learning techniques to predict the sentiment of images.

3 Modelling Sentiment

Sentiment analysis aims to determine the attitude of speaker or writer with respect to some topic or the overall contextual polarity of a document. The attitude may be his or her judgment or evaluation, affective state, or the intended emotional communication. The overall scheme of attitudes is often called "*tonality*".

In general approaches to tonality classification are based: *(i)* on dictionary matching, *(ii)* on (supervised or unsupervised) Machine Learning, and *(iii)* on hybrid methods. Some methods require dictionaries; others need annotated corpora. More sophisticated methods try to identify the mood and the object to which feelings are expressed. Tonality is measured by a predefined rank of emotional intensity of the feelings expressed by words or phrases. Often no text context is available in image tagging to help evaluating the emotional content as we deal mostly with isolated keywords.

In our work we use a dictionary-based approach for determining the tone of tags. Affective lexicons contain lists of words with tonality value for each word. One of the most popular linguistic resources for sentiment analysis is SentiWordNet, see Esuli and Sebastiani (2006).

SentiWordNet (http://sentiwordnet.isti.cnr.it/) is a lexical resource for opinion mining that consists of more 117,000 words. It appeared after automatic annotation of each WordNet synset with scores according to its degree of positivity, negativity, and objectivity. In this way three numerical values are assigned to each WordNet synset to define explicitly the objective, positive or negative component of the synset. Each value ranges in the interval [0,1] and their sum is 1. Words have various senses and therefore, can be assigned various respective values for objective, positive or negative components. SentiWordNet in used in our experiments because it is large enough to cover many tags we consider.

4 Auto-Tagging of Images

The company IMAGGA (http://imagga.com) has developed an original technology for image auto-tagging by English keywords. The technology is based on machine learning and assigns to each image a set of keywords depending on shapes that are recognized in the image. For each learned item the system "sees" in an image, appropriate tags are suggested. In addition the system proposes more tags based on multiple models that it has learned. They relate the visual characteristics of each image with associated tags of "similar" images in ImageNet or big external manually created data sets (e.g. Flickr). The intuition and motivation is that more tags serve better in searching because users may express their requests by different wordforms. The platform developers believe they have found the right practical way to offer best possible image annotation solution for a lot of use-cases.

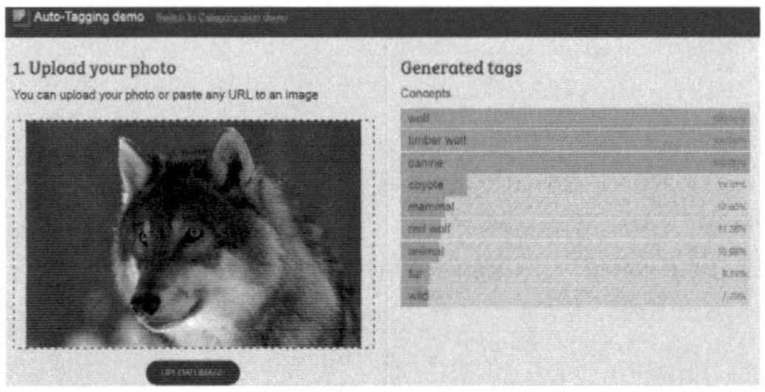

Figure1: Imagga's auto-tagging platform with automatically generated tags and their relevance scores: *wolf* 100%, *timber wolf* 100%, *canine* 100%, *coyote* 19%, *mammal* 12,6%, *red wolf* 11,36%, *animal* 10,98%, *fur* 8,15%, *wild* 7,79%

Quite often, when the image contains a close up object, Imagga's platform assigns correctly the most relevant tags to the central object (Fig. 1). In the right part of Fig. 1 keywords are ordered according to their relevance score. Associating external tags imports emotional keywords in the annotation of Imagga's images. We note that complex tags are not limited only to ANPs like in (Borth et al., 2013; Chen et al., 2014) – see e.g. "*timber wolf*" in Fig. 1.

5 Emotional Classification of Images

Our approach is sketched in Fig. 2: an image with folksonomy (i.e. manual) tags arrives to the system, then it is analyzed by the auto-tagging program and the central object is defined together with the corresponding tags. We designate the user-defined tags as t_{f_i}, $i=\overline{1,n}$, where n is the number of tags from the folksonomy. The tags assigned by the auto-tagging program are denoted by t_{p_j}, $j=\overline{1,m}$. Thus we receive a set of $n+m$ tags which characterize the image.

Keywords assigned by users have higher priority than tags calculated by the program. To distinguish the contribution of these tags' emotional content to the unified tagset sentiment, we define two addition coefficients α and β: the coefficient α shows the degree of priority of folksonomy (authos') tags and coefficient β denotes

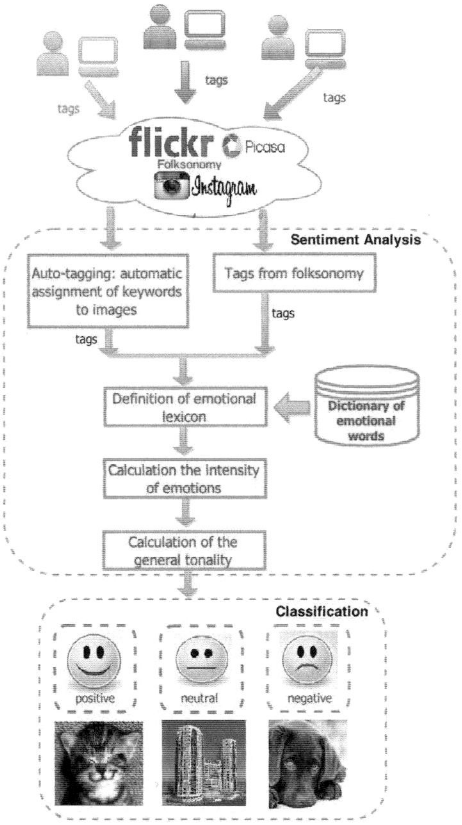

Figure 2: General scheme of our approach

the degree of priority of the ATP-keywords. SentiWordNet contains the predefined emotional polarity *p(w)* of a sense of the word *w* with values for its positive and negative components – *PosScore(w)*, *NegScore(w)* as shown in Table 1.

For each image annotated with tagset S_{tags} we define the value of the positive tag component *P* for this image: $P = \sum_{w \in S_{tags}} PosScore(w)$.

Pos-Score	Neg-Score	Synset Terms	Gloss
0.875	0	attractive#1	pleasing to the eye or mind especially through beauty or charm; "a remarkably attractive young man"; "an attractive personality"; "attractive clothes"; "a book with attractive illustrations"
0.125	0.375	long#9	having or being more than normal or necessary: "long on brains"; "in long supply"

Table 1: Structure of the SentiWordNet dictionary

The value of the negative tag component *N* is calculated similarly, by summing up all *NegScore*-s of the keywords. Note that *P* and *N* can be zero. Calculating positive and negative scores of certain image helps to measure the emotional intensity of the keywords as a whole, no matter whether it is positive or negative.

We introduce the notion of image sentiment *T*:

$$T = \begin{cases} \dfrac{\sum_{w \in t_f} \alpha \, PosScore(w) + \sum_{w \in t_p} \beta \, PosScore(w)}{\sum_{w \in t_f} \alpha \, NegScore(w) + \sum_{w \in t_p} \beta \, NegScore(w)} + \gamma N_{EE}, & N \neq 0 \\ 1 & N = 0, \; P = 0, \\ \sum_{w \in t_f} \alpha \, PosScore(w) + \sum_{w \in t_p} \beta \, PosScore(w) + \gamma N_{EE}, & N = 0, \; P \neq 0, \end{cases} \quad (1)$$

where γ is a coefficient defining the intensity of emotional elements and N_{EE} is the number of emotional elements in the tagset. The formula (1) takes into account the number of emotional elements such as emoticons (*:D*, ☺), lengthenings (*coool*), interjections (*bravo, oh*) etc. In our experiments, all emotional elements have equal weight given by the coefficient γ that ranges in the interval [0,1]. Note that image sentiment can be calculated for authors' tag and the auto-tags separately, for instance formula (1') defines image sentiment using folksonomy tags only:

$$T' = \begin{cases} \dfrac{\sum_{w \in t_f} \alpha \, PosScore(w)}{\sum_{w \in t_f} \alpha \, NegScore(w)} + \gamma N_{EE}, & N \neq 0 \\ 1 & N = 0, \; P = 0, \\ \sum_{w \in t_f} \alpha \, PosScore(w) + \gamma N_{EE}, & N = 0, \; P \neq 0, \end{cases} \quad (1')$$

After calculating the tonalities T_1, T_2, T_3, … of all images, we classify the latter into three categories *positive, negative,* and *neutral* and rank them within each group. Images with value $1 \leq T \leq 1.5$ are considered *neutral*; with $T > 1.5$ – *positive*; and with $T < 1$ – *negative*.

6 Experiments and Discussion

We deal with 200 images from 7 Flickr categories (people, animals, cars, houses, flowers, nature and miscellaneous) that have original author's annotation, in average 19 tags per image. To ensure independent opinion about their sentiment, all images were classified manually by two independent humans into three categories: *ExPos* (92 positive images), *ExNeg* (89 negative images) and *ExNeur* (19 neutral ones). No tags were shown to these annotators so they gave individual assessment looking at the image only. Images with controversial judgment are rejected. The resulting 200 pictures are the dataset we use.

In addition these 200 images were annotated by the Imagga ATP. Tables 2 and 3 present numbers of tags and their intersection with the SentiWordNet items. Note that "tags" come from the dataset but when mapping them to SentiWordNet we split them to tokens, e.g. "*Tokina 11-16mm f/2.8*" will be split into 3 sub-strings.

		Numbers
	Total tagsets	200
Tags assigned by authors	Total	3761
	of them unique	1715
Tags assigned by the ATP	Total	6103
	of them unique	597
Avg #tags per image, given	by authors	19
	by the ATP	30

Table 2: Assignment of 9864 tags in the test dataset

	Human tags	ATP tags	Total
Only pos-score	260	86	346
Only neg-score	233	75	308
Neutr(no score)	1505	746	2251
Pos.& neg. scores	107	38	145
Single sense	358	157	515
Many senses	1747	788	2535
Interjections	6		6
Lengthening	17		17

Table 3: Mapping test dataset' tags to SentiWordNet

Among the 9,864 tags in the test dataset, some 3,050 were found in SentiWordNet: 2,105 are assigned by authors and 945 by the ATP. Table 3 shows that 2,535 of these tags are polysemous so we used the Lesk WSD algorithm (Lesk, 1986) to distinguish which tag sense is mentioned in a particular image annotation. For each polysemous tag, we mapped the whole tagset of the respective image to a SentiWordNet gloss. The sense that overlaps maximally with the "annotation context" was considered to be the correct one. Some examples follow below:

***Example 1 for "homeless"*: Author's Tags** – Nikon D80 homeless man lisbon portugal obdachlos street life *poor* man; **SentiWordNet** homeless#2 – *poor* people who unfortunately do not have a home to live in ..... Here "*poor*" is a tag that appears in the gloss so "homeless#2" is chosen;

***Example 2 for "ancient"*: Program Tags** – architecture *old* ancient; **SentiWordNet** ancient#2 – very *old*; "an ancient mariner".... Here the sense ancient#2 is selected as the correct one due to the fact that the tag "*old*" appears in the SentiWordNet gloss.

The evaluation shows that the WSD precision in this case is about 50%. For empty overlaps the first sense in the SentiWordNet list is chosen.

Our experiment aims to study whether formula (1) provides a reasonable sentiment score for images. The tests support the rationality of including the keywords, assigned by the ATP, in the calculation of image sentiment. It happens often that the manually-annotated images have small amount of tags. But the ATP delivers further tags and then numerous keywords are associated from external collections with similar images, so the accumulated polarity increases.

We made a number of experiments to assess the behavior of coefficients in formula (1). To give an idea about these tests we present at Fig. 3 the changes of precision for positive and negative classes when α=1 and $\beta\in$ [0.1, 1]. The best results *Precision(positive)*=63.53% and *Precision(negative)*=58.93% were received for values α=1 and β=0.4. Similar test were performed for β=1 and $\alpha\in$ [0.1, 1].The optimal coefficient values are α=1 and β=0.4. We assumed that γ = 0.1.

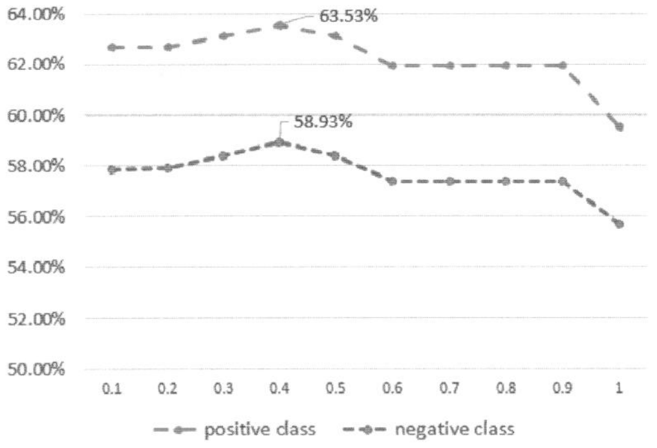

Figure 3: Tests with changes of coefficient β: the dash blue line corresponds to the positive class, the dot red line corresponds to the negative class.

For all pictures in the test collection, we compared the human-defined classes *ExPos*, *ExNeg* and *ExNeut* to image sentiments calculated using the ATP tags in formula (1). Regarding the 89 images in *ExNeg*, the histogram at Fig. 4 shows that the ATP assigned (correctly) keywords with negative tonality only to 57. However the ATP assigns also relevance scores to the keywords so we checked the tonality of auto-tags with relevance score higher than 20%. The success rate improves – 73% (65 out of 89 images) are annotated with negative sentiment by the ATP.

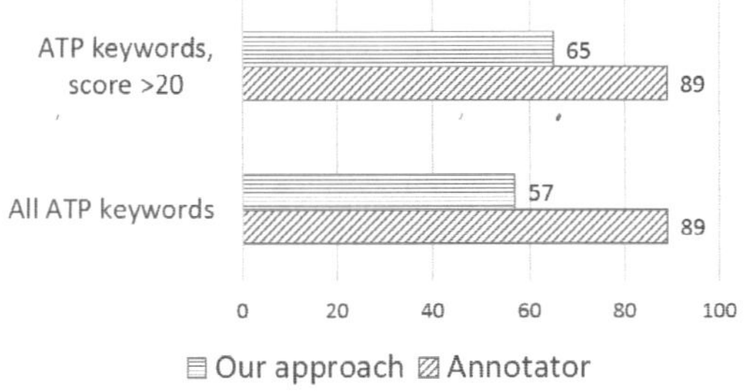

Fig. 4: Computing ATP tags' sentiment for ***ExNeg***

Fig. 5 shows that from all 92 images in *ExPos*, 67 (72.83%) are defined correctly when all ATP tags are considered. Filtering only the keywords with relevance score above 20% reduces also the images with positive sentiment to 54 (58.70%). Actually many ATP keywords with relevance scores lower than 20% are positive; therefore their removal influences significantly the calculations and the results are less successful for *ExPos* (but more successful for *ExNeg*).

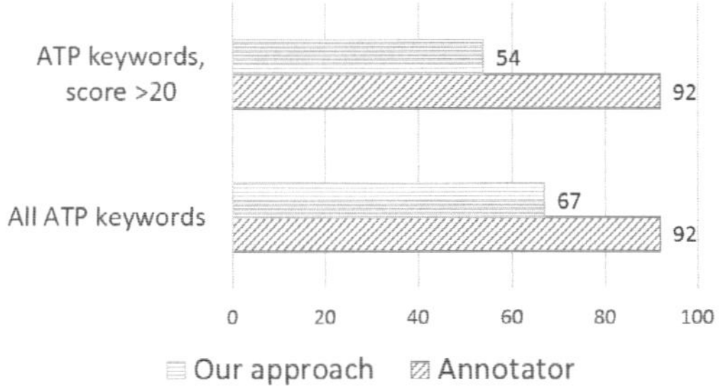

Fig. 5: Computing ATP tags' sentiment for ***ExPos***

The neutral class of 19 images turned to be the trickiest one. The default is – following the intuition behind formula (1) – that an image is "neutral" when it has no emotional tags at all, or when the sentiment of all the positive tags is equal or close to the sentiment of all negative tags. One of 19 images was classified incorrectly by the ATP. Another image with multiple correct tags was annotated with keywords that have strongly negative components in SentiWordNet:

NegScore(monkey) = 0.125,

NegScore(tropical) = 0.5

which lead to $T<1$ and assignment of negative sentiment. Apparently our approach significantly depends on the linguistic resources and the WSD success. In addition, SentiWordNet scores range in relatively small interval so one tag can change the image sentiment to either positive or negative. Due to this reason images are assigned different values (Fig. 6). To partially decrease these effects, *ExNeut* is defined for $T \in [1, 1.5]$.

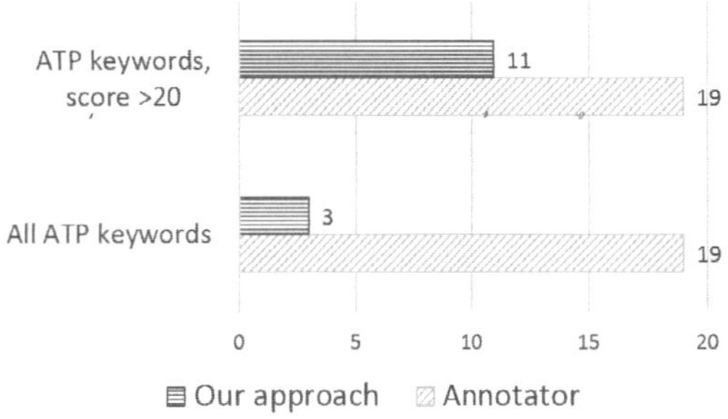

Fig. 6: Computing ATP tags' sentiment for ***ExNeut***

The test dataset contains ATP tags with relevance scores 7-100%. Fig. 7 shows how precision varies depending on the tags' relevance scores. The best precision is achieved for the class *ExPos* using only tags with relevance score>20%. This is related to the ATP features: all high relevance tags are not emotional.

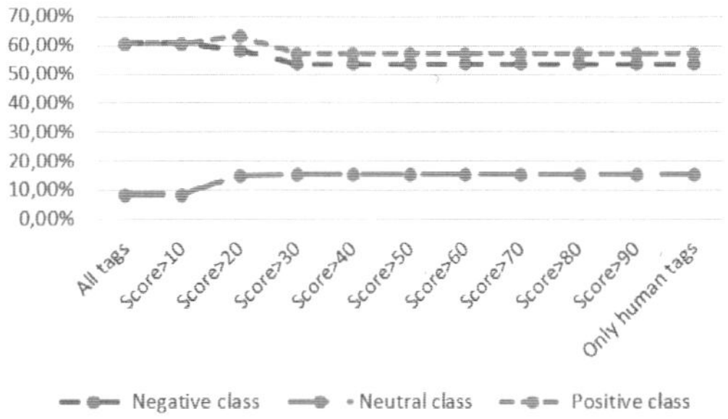

Figure 7: Precision in all classes (shown in Fig. 4, 5, and 6) depending on the tags' relevance scores

The emotional keywords in the test dataset have relevance scores from 20% to nearly 70%. But in general the majority of the positive tags, which are imported from external collection by Imagga's ATP, have relevance scores less than 20%. We remind that about 30% of all 9,864 tags are included in SentiWordNet. Table 3 shows that only 799 have a non-zero sentiment value.

Tables 4 and 5 summarize the comparison between the human-defined classes *ExPos*, *ExNeg* and *ExNeut* and the emotional image scores calculated using SentiWordNet. Table 4 shows calculations using only the author-defined tags and respectively, formula (1').

Low results for *ExNeut* are due to several reasons. First they illustrate the discrepancies of opinions of human-experts who defined *ExPos*, *ExNeg* and *ExNeut* (without seeing image tags)

Class	Recall	Precision	F_1-measure
ExPos	47%	57%	52%
ExNeut	74%	16%	26%
ExNeg	70%	53%	61%

Table 4: Mapping ***ExPos, ExNeg*** and ***ExNeut*** to calculations using formula (1'), for author-assigned tags

Class	Recall	Precision	F_1-measure
Positive	59%	63%	61%
Neutral	58%	15%	24%
Negative	73%	59%	65%

Table 5: Mapping ***ExPos, ExNeg*** and ***ExNeut*** to calculations using formula (1), for all ATP tags

and the picture authors. Table 6 shows further examples of various opinions and perspectives: authors's tags and the ATP keywords differ substantially. Second, emotional tags are relatively scarce in principle. Finally the lack of adequate linguistics resources prohibits the development of standardized datasets and gold standards.

Author's tags: *Derwentwater, Lake District, Weather, Wet, Very wet, Rain, Downpour, Torrential Rain, Cloud, Lake District Weather, Stair-rods, Heavy rain* ***Imagga's tags:*** *landscape 41.91%, water 38.13%, lake 34.06%, river 29.05%, trees 27.65%, tree 26.29%, forest 26.22%, ...* ***Calculated sentiment using SentiWordNet and formula (1):*** *neutral*	***Author's tags***: *garbage, dump* ***Imagga's tags***: *food 21.17%, honeycomb 15.97%, spice 15.32%, apiary 14.29%, healthy 12.93%, ...* ***Calculated sentiment using SentiWordNet and formula (1):*** *neutral*

Table 6: Sample images belonging to ***ExNeg***

Given the human-defined classes *ExPos*, *ExNeg* and *ExNeut*, we trained a SVM classifier on a subset of 80 images (i.e. 40% of the original dataset). More precisely we used SVM classifiers, which are binary by nature, and combined them into *n*-ary classifiers using the Sequential Minimization Optimization (SMO, Platt 1988) implemented in Weka (Witten, 2011). The remaining 60% of the experimental dataset are used as a test corpus for classifying images as *positive*, *negative* and *neutral*. Thus we have a "SMO-baseline" how tags are related to the human judgment of image sentiment. Fig. 8 shows precision, recall and F_1-measure for the positive class *ExPos*, where our approach is compared to the SMO results. The highest F_1-measure 61.02% is achieved for the suggested formula (1) despite the fact that less than 10% of all tags (799 of 9,864) have non-zero emotional values in SentiWordNet. The proposed idea looks feasible assuming that the activities on development of linguistic resources with affective words will grow.

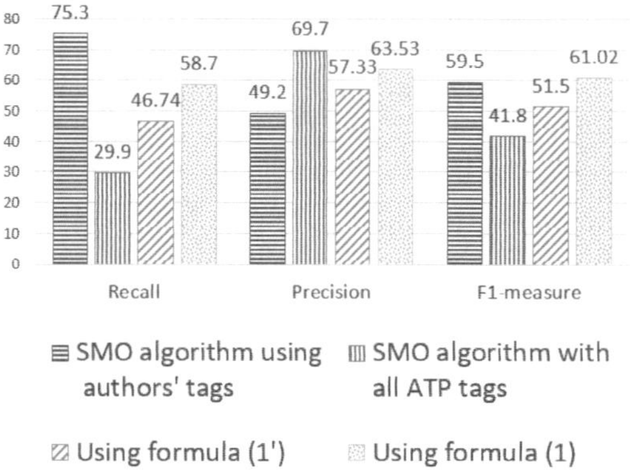

Figure 8: Precision, Recall and F_1-measure for ***ExPos*** using a SMO classification and our approach

Conclusion

The emotional classification of images depends on the individual opinion of each person, but we propose and investigate an idea how to compute image sentiment scores using external resources. Most keywords we use are meant for indexing the image content but the small percentage of positive/negative tags enables automatic calculations. The reported results are similar to those achieved in sentiment analysis and opinion mining where F-measures for evaluation of emotions in social networks are usually below 70%. As future work we plan at first to include colors in the emotional assessment of images.

Acknowledgements

This research is partially supported by the FP7 grant 316087 AComIn "Advanced Computing for Innovation", funded by the European Commission in 2012–2016. It is also related to the COST Action IC1307 iV&L Net. The authors are thankful to Imagga company for their comments, recommendations and experimental datasets.

References

Esuli A. and Sebastiani F. 2006. *Sentiwordnet: A publicly available lexical resource for opinion mining*. In Proc. of LREC, Vol. 6, pp. 417-422, 2006.

Beaudoin J. 2007. *Flickr Image Tagging: Patterns Made Visible*. In Bulletin of the American Society for Information Science and Technology (October/November, 2007), 26-29.

Borth D., R. Ji, Tao Chen, T. Breuel and Shih-Fu Chang. 2013. *Large-scale Visual Sentiment Ontology and Detectors Using Adjective Noun Pairs*. In Proc. of the 21st ACM Int. conference on Multimedia (Barcelona, Spain, October 21-25, 2013). MM'13 . ACM, New York, NY, 223-232. DOI= http://doi.acm.org/10.1145/2502081.2502282

Chen T., Felix X. Yu, Jiawei Chen, Yin Cui, Yan-Ying Chen and Shih-Fu Chang. 2014. *Object-Based Visual Sentiment Concept Analysis and Application*. In Proc. MM'14, 22st ACM Int. Conf. on Multimedia, ACM, NY, 367-376, 2014. DOI= http://doi.acm.org/ 10.1145/2647868.2654935

Hailin J., Jianchao Y., Quanzeng Y. and Jiebo L. 2015. *Robust Image Sentiment Analysis Using Progressively Trained and Domain Transferred Deep Networks*. In Proc. of the 29 AAAI Conference on AI (Austin Texas, USA), 381-388, 2015.

Peters I. andWeller K. 2008. *Tag Gardening for Folksonomy Enrichment and Maintenance*. Webology, Vol.5 (3).

Fernández-Tobías I., Cantador I. and Plaza L. 2013. *An Emotion Dimensional Model based on Social Tags: Crossing Folksonomies and Enhancing Recommendations E-Commerce and Web Technologies.*Lecture Notes in Business Information Processing, Vol. 152, 88-100, 2013.

Jia J., S. Wu, X. Wang, P. Hu, L. Cai, and J. Tang. 2012. *Can we understand van gogh's mood?: learning to infer affects from images in social networks*. In Proc. of the 20th ACM Int. conference on Multimedia (Nara, Japan). MM'12 . ACM, New York, NY, 857-860. DOI= http://doi.acm.org/10.1145/2393347.2396330

Lesk M. *Automatic sense disambiguation using machine readable dictionaries: how to tell a pine cone from an ice cream cone*. In SIGDOC '86: Proc. 5th Annual International Conference on Systems documentation, pp. 24-26, 1986 ACM, USA. DOI=10.1145/318723.318728

Machajdik J. and Hanbury A. 2010.*Affective image classification using features inspired by psychology and art theory*. In Proc. Int. Conf. on Multimedia (Firenze, Italy, October 25-29, 2010). MM'10 . ACM, New York, NY, 83-92. DOI= http://doi.acm.org/10.1145/1873951.1873965

Platt J. 1998. *Fast training of support vector machines using sequential minimal optimization*. In B. Schoelkopf, C. Burges, and A. Smola (eds.), Advances in Kernel Methods, Support Vector Learning. MIT Press, Cambridge, MA, USA.

Siersdorfer S., Minack E., Fan Deng and J. Hare. 2010. *Analyzing and Predicting Sentiment of Images on the Social Web*. In Proc. Int. Conf. on Multimedia (Firenze, Italy) ACM, NY, 715-718. DOI=http://doi.acm.org/10.1145/1873951.1874060

Witten I. H. 2011. *Data mining: practical machine learning tools and techniques*. – 3rd ed. / Ian H. Witten, Frank Eibe, Mark A. Hall. San Francisco: Morgan Kaufmann.

Yang, Y.,P. Cui, W. Zhu, and S. Yang. 2013. *User interest and social influence based emotion prediction for individuals*. In Proc. of the 21st ACM Int. Conf. on Multimedia (Barcelona, Spain), MM'13. ACM, NY, 785-788, 2013. DOI=http://doi.acm.org/10.1145/2647868.2654935

Yang Y., P. Cui, H. Vicky Zhao, Wenwu Zhu, Yuanyuan Shi and Shiqiang Yang. 2014. *Emotionally Representative Image Discovery for Social Events*. In Proc. Int. Conf. on Multimedia Retrieval (Glasgow, UK), ICMR'14. ACM, NY, 177-184. DOI=http://doi.acm.org/10.1145/2578726.2578749

Fine-Grained Sentiment Analysis for Movie Reviews in Bulgarian

Borislav Kapukaranov
Faculty of Mathematics and Informatics
Sofia University
Bulgaria
b.kapukaranov@gmail.com

Preslav Nakov
Qatar Computing Research Institute
HBKU
Qatar
pnakov@qf.org.qa

Abstract

We present a system for fine-grained sentiment analysis in Bulgarian movie reviews. As this is pioneering work for this combination of language and sentiment granularity, we create suitable, freely available resources: a dataset of movie reviews with fine-grained scores, and a sentiment polarity lexicon. We further compare experimentally the performance of classification, regression and ordinal regression in a 3-way, 5-way and 11-way classification setups, using as features not only the text from the reviews, but also contextual information in the form of metadata, e.g., movie length, director, actors, genre, country, and various scores: IMDB, Cinexio, and user-average. The results show that adding contextual information yields strong performance gains.

1 Introduction

With the recent explosion in the popularity of Web forums and social media, sentiment analysis has emerged as a hot research topic. As sentiment-annotated data became readily available, researchers tapped into it and started developing various models for sentiment polarity prediction. Nowadays, there are many applications for sentiment analysis, e.g., businesses getting automatically classified feedback from customers, automated review scoring in retail Web sites, exploration of positive and negative trends, etc.

Movie reviews are a popular and widely available source of sentiment-annotated data. Unlike reviews produced by critics, those contributed by users are typically short and serve primarily to provide brief justification of a user's rating. An important characteristic of movie reviews compared to other sentiment sources is that they are commonly scored on a 5-star scale.

This is very different from sentiment analysis on Twitter, where three-way sentiment classification schemes (*positive, negative, neutral*) have been preferred, e.g., at SemEval 2013-2015 (Nakov et al., 2013; Rosenthal et al., 2014; Rosenthal et al., 2015; Nakov et al., 2015). In contrast, the star system makes the task more fine-grained, thus allowing to capture user opinion better.

Here, we present experiments in predicting fine-grained stars, including halves, for Bulgarian movie reviews. This is a challenging task, that can be seen as (a) *multi-way classification*, i.e., choosing one out of eleven classes, (b) *regression*, i.e., predicting a real number, or (c) something in between, namely *ordinal regression*, i.e., predicting eleven values, but taking ordering into account, e.g., predicting 4 when the actual value is 3.5 would be better than predicting 1.

While sentiment classification in movie reviews has been extensively studied for English (movie reviews datasets were among the earliest to use for this task), it has not been tried for Bulgarian so far. Moreover, most research has focused on positive/negative/neutral classification and finer-grained schemes have been less popular (as they are harder). Even when used, the focus has typically been on having just five categories, not allowing halves. Thus, our contributions in this paper can be summarised as follows:

- We create a new dataset for movies in Bulgarian,[1] where each review is associated with an 11-scale star rating: 0, 0.5, 1, ..., 4.5, 5.
- We prepare a new sentiment lexicon for Bulgarian, which is also freely available.
- Most importantly, we present the first work for Bulgarian on predicting fine-grained sentiment.

[1]The dataset is freely available for research purposes at http://bkapukaranov.github.io/

Proceedings of Recent Advances in Natural Language Processing, pages 266–274,
Hissar, Bulgaria, Sep 7–9 2015.

The remainder of this paper is organized as follows: Section 2 introduces related work, Section 3 describes the dataset and teh lexicon we prepared, Section 4 presents the features we experiment with, Section 5 describes our experiments, and Section 6 discusses the results. Finally, Section 7 concludes and points to some possible directions for future work.

2 Related Work

Pang et al. (2002) were the first to look into text classification not in terms of topics, but focusing on how sentiment polarity is distributed in a document. They tried several machine learning algorithms on an English movie reviews dataset, and evaluated the performance of basic features such as n-grams and part of speech (POS) tags.

Movie reviews were one of the first research domains for sentiment analysis as they (*i*) have the properties of a short message, and (*ii*) are already manually annotated by the author, as the score generally reflects sentiment polarity. Popular features for score/sentiment prediction include POS tags, word n-grams, word lemmata, and various context features based on the distance from a topic word. The challenge with movie reviews is that only some of the words are relevant for sentiment analysis. In fact, often the review is just a short narrative of the movie plot. One way to approach the problem is to use a subjectivity classifier (Pang and Lee, 2004), which can be used to filter out objective sentences from the reviews, thus allowing the classifier then to focus on the subjective sentences only.

Early researchers realized the importance of external sentiment lexicons, e.g., Turney (2002) proposed an unsupervised approach to learn the sentiment orientation of words/phrases: positive vs. negative. Later work looked into the linguistic aspects of how opinions, evaluations, and speculations are expressed in text (Wiebe et al., 2004), into the role of context for determining the sentiment orientation (Wilson et al., 2005), of deeper linguistic processing such as negation handling (Pang and Lee, 2008), of finer-grained sentiment distinctions (Pang and Lee, 2005), of positional information (Raychev and Nakov, 2009), etc. Moreover, it was recognized that in many cases, it was crucial to know not just the sentiment, but also the topic towards which this sentiment was expressed (Stoyanov and Cardie, 2008).

Fine-grained sentiment analysis tries to predict sentiment in a text using a finer scale, e.g., 5-stars; Pang and Lee (2005) pioneered this sub-field. In their work, they looked at the problem from two perspectives: as one vs. all classification, and as a regression by putting the 5-star ratings on a metric scale. An interesting observation in their research is that humans are not very good at doing such kinds of highly granular judgments and are often off the target mark by a full star.

Naturally, most research in sentiment analysis was done for English, and very little efforts were devoted to other languages. We are not aware of other work on fine-grained sentiment analysis for Bulgarian. There is work on sentiment analysis by Bulgarian scolars (Raychev, 2009; Raychev and Nakov, 2009; Kraychev and Koychev, 2012; Kraychev, 2014).

We are aware of three publications for the closely-related Macedonian language,[2] which is mutually intelligible with Bulgarian.

Gajduk and Kocarev (2014) experimented with 800 posts from the Kajgana forum (260 positive, 260 negative, and 280 objective), using Support Vector Machines (SVM) and Naïve Bayes classifiers, and features such as bag of words, rules for negation, and stemming.

More closely related to our work, Uzunova and Kulakov (2015) experimented with 400 movie reviews (200 positive + 200 negative), and a Naïve Bayes classifier, using a small manually annotated sentiment lexicon of unknown size, and various preprocessing techniques such as negation handling and spelling/character translation.

Finally, Jovanoski et al. (2015) presented work on sentiment analysis of Macedonian tweets (8,583 for training + 1,139 for testing) using a 3-way tweet-level sentiment polarity classification scheme: positive, negative, and neutral/objective. They used standard features but variety of preprocessing steps, including morphological processing and POS tagging for Macedonian, negation handling, text standardization, tweet-specific processing, etc. More imporantly, they made use of several lexicons, some translated from other languages,[3] which they augmented with bootstrapping, ultimately achieving results that are on par with the state of the art for English.

[2]Some linguists consider Macedonian a dialect of Bulgarian; this is also the position of the Bulgarian government.

[3]In fact, they used, without translation, the Bulgarian lexicon that we present in this work.

Given the lack of previously developed datasets or sentiment polarity lexicons for Bulgarian, we had to create them ourselves. In addition to preparing a dataset of annotated movies, we further focused on building a sentiment polarity lexicon for Bulgarian. This is because lexicons are crucial for sentiment analysis. Since the very beginning, researchers have realized that sentiment analysis was quite different from standard document classification (Sebastiani, 2002), e.g., into categories such as *business*, *sport*, and *politics*, and that sentiment analysis crucially needed external knowledge in the form of suitable sentiment polarity lexicons. For further detail, see the surveys by Pang and Lee (2008) and Liu and Zhang (2012).

Until recently, such sentiment polarity lexicons were manually crafted, and were thus of small to moderate size, e.g., LIWC (Pennebaker et al., 2001), General Inquirer (Stone et al., 1966), Bing Liu's lexicon (Hu and Liu, 2004), and MPQA (Wilson et al., 2005), all have 2000-8000 words. Early efforts in building them automatically also yielded lexicons of moderate sizes (Esuli and Sebastiani, 2006; Baccianella et al., 2010).

However, recent results have shown that automatically extracted large-scale lexicons (e.g., up to a million words and phrases) offer important performance advantages, as confirmed at shared tasks on Sentiment Analysis on Twitter at SemEval 2013-2015 (Nakov et al., 2013; Rosenthal et al., 2014; Rosenthal et al., 2015). These lexicons were crucial for the top-performing teams in the competition in all three years.

Similar observations were made in the Aspect-Based Sentiment Analysis task at SemEval 2014-2015 (Pontiki et al., 2014). In both tasks, the winning systems benefited from building and using massive sentiment polarity lexicons (Mohammad et al., 2013; Zhu et al., 2014).

3 Data

Our dataset consist of 347 movies with a total of 10,198 Bulgarian reviews, which we crawled from the ticket-booking website Cinexio.[4] We chose only movies for which scored reviews in Bulgarian were present on the website. For each movie, we include a set of user reviews, each annotated with a score on an 11-point scale: 0, 0.5, 1, ..., 4.5, 5 stars. More detailed statistics about our movie reviews dataset can be found in Table 1.

[4]http://www.cinexio.com

Characteristic	**Count**
unique words	8,406
unique users	3,395
unique movie genres	23
unique movie countries	49
unique movie actors	1,668
unique movie directors	317

Table 1: Statistics about our dataset.

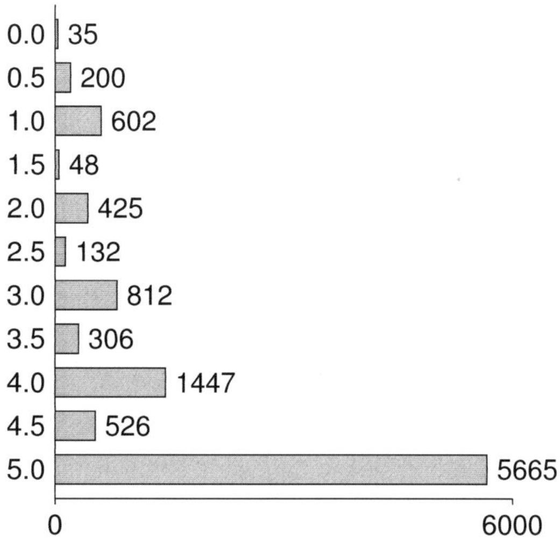

Figure 1: User rating distribution in our dataset.

Figure 1 shows a distribution of the user ratings in our movie reviews dataset. We can see that the distribution is generally skewed towards full scores, while scores with halves are much less frequent: people seem to prefer a 5-point scale, and would not take full advantage of an 11-point one. Moreover, the distribution is also skewed towards high scores, and quite heavily towards a 5-star rating in particular.

In addition to the movie reviews dataset, we further automatically generated a sentiment polarity lexicon for Bulgarian, using that dataset and pointwise mutual information (PMI) with respect to the positive and to the negative class, following the idea presented in (Turney, 2002):

$$pmi(w, class) = \log \left[\frac{p(w \,\&\, class)}{p(w)\, p(class)} \right] \quad (1)$$

Then, we calculated a sentiment polarity score:

$$polarity = pmi(w,\, pos) - pmi(w,\, neg) \quad (2)$$

Words with high positive/negative polarity were included in our sentiment polarity lexicon; this included 5,016 positive and 2,415 negative words.

Here, we list some examples of movie reviews (with English translations in footnotes):

- "добре, че го бастисаха накрая, че да се спре с тая пропаганда.. ;)"[5] with score 3.5

  This example is very interesting as it expresses cheerful and light mood, as indicated by the winking emoticon. Yet, it also mentions *propaganda*, which hints slight irritation about the way the movie plot developed.

- "Много добър филм"[6] with score 5.0

  Nothing really surprising here: typical positive comment, without going into specifics.

- "Много добър филм. Просто ни е далечен Американския патриотизъм."[7] with score 4.0

  Here, despite having the same text as the max-scored previous example, the review author has given a slightly lower score. From the text alone, we can conclude that the author likes the movie very much, but still makes a general remark on how the movie will be accepted culturally by Bulgarian viewers.

- "Не ме впечатли."[8] with score 3.0

  A typical mid-score comment: direct, clear.

- "Доста тъжно :("[9] with score 5.0

  This is a perfect example of why this problem is hard. The text alone shows clearly negative emotions both indicated by text and by the crying emoticon, but it seems that the author actually liked the movie very much and gave it a maximum score.

Negative reviews from other movies:

- "доста дълъг и поне да се случваше нещо..."[10] with 1.5 score

  On the low end of the scale, the scores become highly subjective, and often the same wording can be annotated with a full star difference in the score.

- "Филма е само част от трилогия, помнете че историята свършва най-интересното"[11] with score 2.0

  This is another confusing example. Did the author actually like the movie? Or was s/he affected by somebody else's opinion?

- "Доста повече екшън от първата част"[12] with score 3.0

  This is a great example showing that the perception of movies in a multipart series is influenced by earlier parts. It is not clear what people are scoring: the entire series or just the current (latest) part of the movie? People naturally try to compare with earlier series, which influences their scores.

In general, scores could be heavily biased, and also relative: if one has recently watched a bad movie, the following movie, even if just slightly better, could get an inflated score.

4 Features

In this section, we describe the features we experimented with: textual and contextual.

4.1 Textual Features

We used the following textual features:

- **words:** binary feature for each word;
- **emoticons:** binary feature for each positive/negative emoticon;
- ***n*-grams:** binary feature for each n-gram (we only used bigrams).
- **lexicon:** We further included two features based on our automatically generated movie reviews lexicon. They represent the positive and the negative overall score of the movie review, obtained by aggregating the lexicon scores of each word in the review text.

Note that our dataset lacks enough relevant instances to use features such as all-caps and punctuation, and thus we did not use them here.

Moreover, we found that using bigram features did not make much difference for this particular dataset, therefore the final feature set for the baseline system only used *bag of words*, *emoticons*, and the *lexicon* features.

[5]"it is good that they got him in the end, so the propaganda could finally be over.. ;)"

[6]"Very good movie"

[7]"Very good movie, we are just a little bit off on the American partriotic message"

[8]"Not impressed"

[9]"Quite sad :("

[10]"quite long, on top of that nothing actually happens..."

[11]"The movie is just the first part of a series, keep in mind the story ends in the most interesting part"

[12]"Definitely more action compared to the first part"

4.2 Contextual Features

In addition to the above textual features, we further added some contextual (metadata) features:

- **movie length**: numeric feature indicating the run-length of the movie;
- **country**: binary feature indicating the country the movie comes from;
- **genres**: indicator feature for each genre;
- **actors**: indicator feature for each actor;
- **director**: indicator feature for each director;
- **average user rating**: numeric feature with the user's average movie review score;
- **IMDB score**: numeric feature, current average score for this movie in IMDB;
- **Cinexio score**: numeric feature, current average score for this movie in Cinexio.

5 Experiments and Evaluation

Below we describe the class granularities we experimented with, the learning algorithms we used, and the evaluation results.

5.1 Class Granularity

In the original formulation, we have eleven classes: 0, 0.5, 1, ..., 4.5, 5. For model comparison purposes, we further experimented with aggregated classes. Thus, we ended up with three class inventories of various sizes:

- **11-way**: includes all labels, both integer and half-star;
- **5-way**: includes only the full stars;
- **3-way**: divides the scores into three classes, $positive \geq 3.5 > neutral \geq 2 > negative$.

5.2 Learning Algorithms

We performed experiments with three machine learning approaches: (*i*) classification, (*ii*) regression, and (*iii*) ordinal regression. We evaluated using a 5-fold cross validation. For scoring, we used the same metric for all class inventories and for all learning approaches, namely Mean Squared Error (MSE), which is standard for a task asking to predict ordinal values as in our case.

Classification. For classification, we used SVM with a linear kernel and L2-regularized L2-loss, as implemented in LibSVM (Chang and Lin, 2011). We used a one vs. all model, which we applied for each class inventory size: 3, 5, 11.

Regression. For regression, we used the same SVM tool and the same features and parameters as for classification, but we predicted a numerical value; this is known as *support vector regression* (Smola and Schölkopf, 2004)

Ordinal Regression. For this scenario, we used *ordinal logistic regression*. This model is also known as *proportional odds* and was introduced by McCullagh (1980).[13] The use of ordinal regression for sentiment analysis, is not very common, mostly because the ordinal formulation of the task is not very common, even though it was used by some researchers (Pang and Lee, 2005; Goldberg and Zhu, 2006; Baccianella et al., 2009). Yet, it makes a lot of sense to use it as it tries to fit the data into thresholded regions as a classification task would do, and at the same time tries to predict values with an established order and position in the label space. This makes it interesting especially in the 5-class setup, where we have a small number of labels and there is ordering between them.

5.3 Results

Our preliminary cross-validation experiments have shown that not all features that we have introduced above were really relevant; thus, we created a selected set of highly-relevant features: *words*, *emoticons*, *lexicons*, *Cinexio score*, and *average user rating*. We used this feature set when comparing the three machine learning algorithms (classification, regression, and ordinal regression), for the three class sizes (3, 5, and 11). The results are shown in Table 2.

Model	11-way	5-way	3-way
Classification	1.041	0.666	0.141
Regression	0.484	0.472	0.135
Ordinal regression	1.438	1.276	0.464

Table 2: **Evaluation using the selected features.** Shown is MSE for the three machine learning algorithms and for the three class sizes. (Lower scores are better.)

[13]There are several alternative machine learning approaches to ordinal regression, e.g., *support vector ordinal regression* (Chu and Keerthi, 2007).

Feature	MSE	ΔMSE
baseline (all textual features)	*0.745*	–
bl + IMDB score	0.689	-0.056
bl + Cinexio score	0.669	-0.076
bl + Cinexio + IMDB	0.658	-0.087
bl + user avg. score	0.520	-0.225
bl + user avg. score + Cinexio	0.484	-0.261
bl + movie length	0.484	-0.261
bl + director	0.732	-0.013
bl + country	0.723	-0.022
bl + actors	0.484	-0.261
bl + genres	0.723	-0.022

Table 3: **Impact of individual contextual features when added to the baseline.** Shown is MSE for the regression model with 11 classes.

Feature	MSE	ΔMSE
all (all textual + contextual features)	*0.515*	–
all – words	0.523	+0.008
all – lexicons	0.745	+0.230
all – emoticons	0.515	0.000
all – IMDB score	0.494	-0.021
all – Cinexio score	0.544	+0.029
all – user avg. score	0.736	+0.221
all – movie length	0.515	0.000
all – directors	0.515	0.000
all – country	0.514	-0.001
all – actors	0.515	0.000
all – genres	0.514	-0.001

Table 4: **Impact of individual features when excluded from the full feature set.** Shown is MSE for the regression model with 11 classes.

We can see in Table 2 that the best results are achieved for *regression*, where the mean squared error is within half a point away for the 11-way and the 5-way class inventories, and it is about four times lower for the 3-way one. The second-best performing machine learning approach is *classification*; its performance is very close to that of regression on the 3-way class inventory, but the gap widens with 5 classes (about 50% difference), and becomes huge with 11 classes (100% difference), where the predictions are on average a full point off from the target. Finally comes the worst-performing approach, *ordinal regression*, which consistently performs about four times worse than the standard regression.

Interestingly, while *classification* performs badly compared to *regression* on the 11-way class inventory, it quickly catches up for smaller numbers of classes, and the two learning approaches get quite close on the 3-way class inventory. This is expected, as classification usually struggles with too many class labels, especially in the case of uneven class distribution, and this is indeed our case, as we have seen in Figure 1.

However, the low performance of ordinal regression is quite surprising; the expectation was that it would perform the best. In future work, we plan to have a closer look at the reasons for these results. At this point, we can only note that we used SVM as the basic underlying classifier in our *classification* and *regression* experiments, but we used *logistic regression* as the basis for our *ordinal regression*. It is unclear whether this alone could explain the difference in performance, though.

Table 3, shows the impact of the individual context features (and some feature combinations) when added to the baseline textual features. We report results for 11-way classification with the *regression* model; and the last column shows the difference in MSE compared to the baseline. We can see that each of the features yields improvements, which means that they all are indeed relevant. The most important features turn out to be *movie length*, *actors*, and *user average score*.

Yet, some features might be redundant, i.e., having one feature might mean that we do not need to have some other ones. In order to study this, we performed experiments excluding features one at a time from the full set of features, both textual and contextual. The results are shown in Table 4. As before, we study 11-way classification with the *regression* model. The relative change in MSE compared to the full model is shown in the last column of the table. We can see that *lexicons* have the biggest impact, which is to be expected, as we know from previous work that they are among the most important resources for sentiment analysis. Another strong feature turns out to be the *user average score*, which also makes sense: a user who has been giving high scores in the past is likely to give high scores in the future. We can further see that many contextual features, e.g., *movie length, actors, director, genres* and *country*, made almost no difference. This is surprising as the first two yielded the largest improvements over the *baseline* features in Table 3; we believe this reflects feature interaction, but we plan closer investigation.

6 Discussion

We have seen in our experiments above that the best-performing model used *regression* and *contextual* features, in addition to *textual* ones. We believe that the kind of context we model, primarily metadata, is indeed important as, while it is not present in the text of the review, it has been taken into account when the author rated the movie.

Interestingly, we have found that factual information was not very useful. This is a good sign as it suggests that Cinexio users seem not to have prejudice about the expected quality of a movie based on its country of origin, director(s), or genre; however, actors playing do have impact.

One of the most useful contextual features was the *user average score*. Some users tend to give consistently high/low scores regardless of the movie, and thus knowing their average scores allows us to take this into account.

A related useful feature was the *Cinexio score* of the target movie. The idea is that if a movie has a high/low overall score, we should expect a new user also to give it a high/low score. While *IMDB scores* are quite similar, we had mixed results for them: they were quite helpful compared to the baseline, but were harmful with respect to the full set of features.

Given the difference between Cinexio and IMDB scores, we decided to have a closer look at how they relate to each other. This is shown in Figure 2. The blue line connects the corresponding Cinexio–IMDB scores, while the red line shows how perfect correlation would look like. Note that IMDB scores are in the 0–10 range.

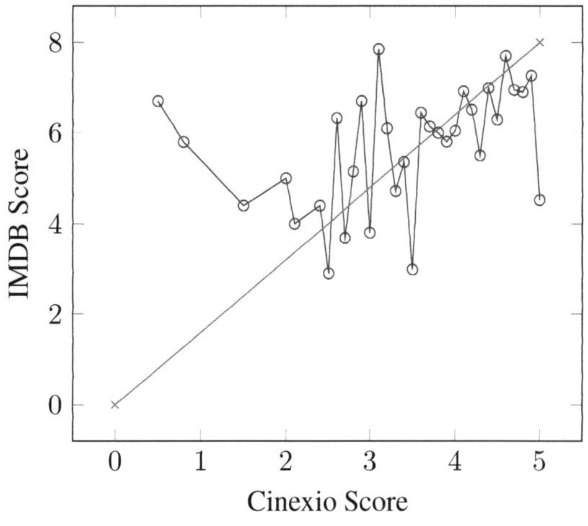

Figure 2: Cinexio vs. IMDB scores.

This is an interesting plot as it reflects how viewers (a) in Bulgaria and (b) worldwide feel about the same movie. We can see that the general correlation is there, especially for the mid-high scores. However, there is a lot of discrepancy with the extreme scores, i.e., what Bulgarian viewers see as extremely good is regarded as average at IMDB, and what they consider extremely bad, actually has an above-average score at IMDB.

This discrepancy in IMDB vs. Cinexio scores explains the mixed results we got when using the IMDB score as a feature. One way to fix this could be to split the IMDB feature into several features, each responsible for just a sub-interval of the possible values of the original feature. This might be useful for some other features with numerical values, which could show non-linearity, e.g., *Cinexio score*, *average user score*, or *movie length*.

7 Conclusion and Future Work

We presented the first research on fine-grained sentiment analysis for Bulgarian. As this is pioneering work for this language, we created a suitable dataset and a sentiment polarity lexicon, which we made freely available for research purposes; this should enable further research.

We further compared experimentally the performance of classification, regression and ordinal regression in a 3-way, 5-way and 11-way classification setups, using as features not only the text from the reviews, but also contextual information in the form of metadata, e.g., movie length, director, actors, genre, country, and various scores: IMDB, Cinexio, and user-average. The experimental results have shown that adding contextual information yields strong performance gains.

In future work, we plan to investigate the low performance of ordinal regression. We further want to experiment with more features, e.g., summary of the plot, subtitles, information from other websites such as IMDB, as well as with more linguistic processing of the text, e.g., stemming (Nakov, 2003b; Nakov, 2003a), POS tagging (Georgiev et al., 2012), and named entity recognition (Georgiev et al., 2009). We also want to see the impact of earlier comments on the sentiment of newer comments (Vanzo et al., 2014; Barrón-Cedeño et al., 2015; Joty et al., 2015). Finally, we would like to apply our system to help other tasks, e.g., finding trolls in Web forums (Mihaylov et al., 2015a; Mihaylov et al., 2015b).

References

Stefano Baccianella, Andrea Esuli, and Fabrizio Sebastiani. 2009. Multi-facet rating of product reviews. In *Proceedings of the 31th European Conference on IR Research on Advances in Information Retrieval*, ECIR '09, pages 461–472, Toulouse, France.

Stefano Baccianella, Andrea Esuli, and Fabrizio Sebastiani. 2010. SentiWordNet 3.0: An enhanced lexical resource for sentiment analysis and opinion mining. In *Proceedings of the International Conference on Language Resources and Evaluation*, LREC '10, Valletta, Malta.

Alberto Barrón-Cedeño, Simone Filice, Giovanni Da San Martino, Shafiq Joty, Lluís Màrquez, Preslav Nakov, and Alessandro Moschitti. 2015. Thread-level information for comment classification in community question answering. In *Proceedings of the 53rd Annual Meeting of the Association for Computational Linguistics and the 7th International Joint Conference on Natural Language Processing*, ACL-IJCNLP '15, pages 687–693, Beijing, China.

Chih-Chung Chang and Chih-Jen Lin. 2011. LIBSVM: A library for support vector machines. *ACM Transactions on Intelligent Systems and Technology*, 2:27:1–27:27.

Wei Chu and S. Sathiya Keerthi. 2007. Support vector ordinal regression. *Neural Comput.*, 19(3):792–815, March.

Andrea Esuli and Fabrizio Sebastiani. 2006. SENTIWORDNET: A publicly available lexical resource for opinion mining. In *Proceedings of the International Conference on Language Resources and Evaluation*, LREC '06, pages 417–422, Genoa, Italy.

Andrej Gajduk and Ljupco Kocarev. 2014. Opinion mining of text documents written in Macedonian language. *arXiv preprint arXiv:1411.4472*.

Georgi Georgiev, Preslav Nakov, Kuzman Ganchev, Petya Osenova, and Kiril Simov. 2009. Feature-rich named entity recognition for Bulgarian using conditional random fields. In *Proceedings of the International Conference Recent Advances in Natural Language Processing*, RANLP '09, pages 113–117, Borovets, Bulgaria.

Georgi Georgiev, Valentin Zhikov, Petya Osenova, Kiril Simov, and Preslav Nakov. 2012. Feature-rich part-of-speech tagging for morphologically complex languages: Application to Bulgarian. In *Proceedings of the 13th Conference of the European Chapter of the Association for Computational Linguistics*, EACL '12, pages 492–502, Avignon, France.

Andrew B. Goldberg and Xiaojin Zhu. 2006. Seeing stars when there aren't many stars: Graph-based semi-supervised learning for sentiment categorization. In *Proceedings of the First Workshop on Graph Based Methods for Natural Language Processing*, TextGraphs '06, pages 45–52, Sydney, Australia.

Minqing Hu and Bing Liu. 2004. Mining and summarizing customer reviews. In *Proceedings of the 10th ACM SIGKDD International Conference on Knowledge Discovery and Data Mining*, KDD '04, pages 168–177, Seattle, WA, USA.

Shafiq Joty, Alberto Barrón-Cedeño, Giovanni Da San Martino, Simone Filice, Lluís Màrquez, Alessandro Moschitti, and Preslav Nakov. 2015. Global thread-level inference for comment classification in community question answering. In *Proceedings of the Conference on Empirical Methods in Natural Language Processing*, EMNLP '15, Lisbon, Portugal.

Dame Jovanoski, Veno Pachovski, and Preslav Nakov. 2015. Sentiment analysis in Twitter for Macedonian. In *Proceedings of the International Conference on Recent Advances in Natural Language Processing*, RANLP '15, Hissar, Bulgaria.

Boris Kraychev and Ivan Koychev. 2012. Computationally effective algorithm for information extraction and online review mining. In *Proceedings of the 2nd International Conference on Web Intelligence, Mining and Semantics*, WIMS '12, pages 64:1–64:4, Craiova, Romania.

Boris Kraychev. 2014. *Extraction and Analysis of Opinions and Sentiments from Online Text*. Ph.D. thesis, Sofia University, January. (in Bulgarian).

Bing Liu and Lei Zhang. 2012. A survey of opinion mining and sentiment analysis. In Charu C. Aggarwal and ChengXiang Zhai, editors, *Mining Text Data*, pages 415–463. Springer.

Peter McCullagh. 1980. Regression models for ordinal data. *J. Roy. Statist. Soc. B*, 42:109–142.

Todor Mihaylov, Georgi Georgiev, and Preslav Nakov. 2015a. Finding opinion manipulation trolls in news community forums. In *Proceedings of the Conference on Computational Natural Language Learning*, pages 310–314, Beijing, China.

Todor Mihaylov, Ivan Koychev, Georgi Georgiev, and Preslav Nakov. 2015b. Exposing paid opinion manipulation trolls. In *Proceedings of the Conference on Computational Natural Language Learning*, Hissar, Bulgaria.

Saif Mohammad, Svetlana Kiritchenko, and Xiaodan Zhu. 2013. NRC-Canada: Building the state-of-the-art in sentiment analysis of tweets. In *Proceedings of the Seventh international workshop on Semantic Evaluation Exercises*, SemEval '13, pages 321–327, Atlanta, GA, USA.

Preslav Nakov, Sara Rosenthal, Zornitsa Kozareva, Veselin Stoyanov, Alan Ritter, and Theresa Wilson. 2013. SemEval-2013 task 2: Sentiment analysis in Twitter. In *Proceedings of the Seventh International Workshop on Semantic Evaluation*, SemEval '13, pages 312–320, Atlanta, GA, USA.

Preslav Nakov, Sara Rosenthal, Svetlana Kiritchenko, Saif Mohammad, Zornitsa Kozareva, Alan Ritter, Veselin Stoyanov, and Xiaodan Zhu. 2015. Developing a successful SemEval task in sentiment analysis of Twitter and other social media texts. *Language Resources and Evaluation*.

Preslav Nakov. 2003a. Building an inflectional stemmer for Bulgarian. In *Proceedings of the 4th International Conference on Computer Systems and Technologies*, CompSysTech '03, pages 419–424, Sofia, Bulgaria.

Preslav Nakov. 2003b. BulStem: Design and evaluation of an inflectional stemmer for Bulgarian. In *Proceedings of the Workshop on Balkan Language Resources and Tools*, Thessaloniki, Greece.

Bo Pang and Lillian Lee. 2004. A sentimental education: Sentiment analysis using subjectivity summarization based on minimum cuts. In *Proceedings of the 42nd Annual Meeting on Association for Computational Linguistics*, ACL '04, pages 271–278, Barcelona, Spain.

Bo Pang and Lillian Lee. 2005. Seeing stars: Exploiting class relationships for sentiment categorization with respect to rating scales. In *Proceedings of the Annual Meeting of the Association for Computational Linguistics*, ACL '05, pages 115–124, Ann Arbor, MI, USA.

Bo Pang and Lillian Lee. 2008. Opinion mining and sentiment analysis. *Foundations and trends in information retrieval*, 2(1-2):1–135.

Bo Pang, Lillian Lee, and Shivakumar Vaithyanathan. 2002. Thumbs up?: Sentiment classification using machine learning techniques. In *Proceedings of the Conference on Empirical Methods in Natural Language Processing*, EMNLP '02, pages 79–86, Philadelphia, PA, USA.

James W. Pennebaker, Martha E. Francis, and Roger J. Booth. 2001. *Linguistic Inquiry and Word Count*. Lawerence Erlbaum Associates, Mahwah, NJ.

Maria Pontiki, Harris Papageorgiou, Dimitrios Galanis, Ion Androutsopoulos, John Pavlopoulos, and Suresh Manandhar. 2014. SemEval-2014 task 4: Aspect based sentiment analysis. In *Proceedings of the 8th International Workshop on Semantic Evaluation*, SemEval '14, pages 27–35, Dublin, Ireland.

Veselin Raychev and Preslav Nakov. 2009. Language-independent sentiment analysis using subjectivity and positional information. In *Proceedings of the International Conference on Recent Advances in Natural Language Processing*, RANLP '09, pages 360–364, Borovets, Bulgaria.

Veselin Raychev. 2009. *Automatic Recognition of Positive/Negative Subjectivity in Text*. Ph.D. thesis, Sofia University, March. (in Bulgarian).

Sara Rosenthal, Alan Ritter, Preslav Nakov, and Veselin Stoyanov. 2014. SemEval-2014 Task 9: Sentiment analysis in Twitter. In *Proceedings of the 8th International Workshop on Semantic Evaluation*, SemEval '14, pages 73–80, Dublin, Ireland.

Sara Rosenthal, Preslav Nakov, Svetlana Kiritchenko, Saif Mohammad, Alan Ritter, and Veselin Stoyanov. 2015. SemEval-2015 task 10: Sentiment analysis in Twitter. In *Proceedings of the 9th International Workshop on Semantic Evaluation*, SemEval '15, pages 450–462, Denver, CO, USA.

Fabrizio Sebastiani. 2002. Machine learning in automated text categorization. *ACM Comput. Surv.*, 34(1):1–47, March.

Alex J. Smola and Bernhard Schölkopf. 2004. A tutorial on support vector regression. *Statistics and Computing*, 14(3):199–222, August.

Philip J. Stone, Dexter C. Dunphy, Marshall S. Smith, and Daniel M. Ogilvie. 1966. *The General Inquirer: A Computer Approach to Content Analysis*. MIT Press.

Veselin Stoyanov and Claire Cardie. 2008. Topic identification for fine-grained opinion analysis. In *Proceedings of the 22nd International Conference on Computational Linguistics*, COLING '08, pages 817–824, Manchester, United Kingdom.

Peter D. Turney. 2002. Thumbs up or thumbs down?: Semantic orientation applied to unsupervised classification of reviews. In *Proceedings of the Annual Meeting of the Association for Computational Linguistics*, ACL '02, pages 417–424, Philadelphia, PA.

Vasilija Uzunova and Andrea Kulakov. 2015. Sentiment analysis of movie reviews written in Macedonian language. In *ICT Innovations 2014*, pages 279–288. Springer.

Andrea Vanzo, Danilo Croce, and Roberto Basili. 2014. A context-based model for sentiment analysis in Twitter. In *Proceedings of the 25th International Conference on Computational Linguistics*, COLING '14, pages 2345–2354, Dublin, Ireland.

Janyce Wiebe, Theresa Wilson, Rebecca Bruce, Matthew Bell, and Melanie Martin. 2004. Learning subjective language. *Comput. Linguist.*, 30(3):277–308, September.

Theresa Wilson, Janyce Wiebe, and Paul Hoffmann. 2005. Recognizing contextual polarity in phrase-level sentiment analysis. In *Proceedings of the Conference on Human Language Technology and Empirical Methods in Natural Language Processing*, HLT-EMNLP '05, pages 347–354, Vancouver, BC, Canada.

Xiaodan Zhu, Svetlana Kiritchenko, and Saif M. Mohammad. 2014. NRC-Canada-2014: Detecting aspects and sentiment in customer reviews. In *Proceedings of the Workshop on Semantic Evaluation*, SemEval '14, pages 437–442, Dublin, Ireland.

Structural Alignment for Comparison Detection

Wiltrud Kessler and **Jonas Kuhn**
Institute for Natural Language Processing
University of Stuttgart
wiltrud.kessler@ims.uni-stuttgart.de

Abstract

There tends to be a substantial proportion of reviews that include explicit textual comparisons between the reviewed item and another product. To the extent that such comparisons can be captured reliably by automatic means, they can provide an extremely helpful input to support a process of choice. As the small amount of available training data limits the development of robust systems to automatically detect comparisons, this paper investigates how to use semi-supervised strategies to expand a small set of labeled sentences. Specifically, we use structural alignment, a method that starts out from a seed set of manually annotated data and finds similar unlabeled sentences to which the labels can be projected. We present several adaptations of the method to our task of comparison detection and show that adding the found expansion sentences slightly improves over a non-expanded baseline in low-resource settings, i.e., when a very small amount of training data is available.

1 Introduction

Sentiment analysis is an NLP task that has received considerable attention in recent years. If we consider the actual situations in which people are interested in aggregated subjective assessments of some product (or location, service etc.) by other users, a typical scenario is that they are in the process of making some choice – such as a purchase decision among a set of candidate products. It is clear that for this decision a plain polarity scoring for entire review texts is of limited use and we need a more detailed analysis. In this work, we focus on what is presumably the most useful kind of expression when it comes to supporting a process of choice: there tends to be a substantial proportion of reviews (about 10% of sentences) that include explicit textual comparisons, e.g., *"X is better than Y"*. To the extent that such subjective comparisons can be captured reliably by automatic means, they can provide an extremely helpful basis for coming up with a decision.

The analysis of comparisons has the disadvantage that data for supervised training can no longer be derived from star ratings. Existing manually annotated sentiment analysis data sets include some proportion of comparisons, however, for a reliable supervised training, a larger data set is required. Moreover, vocabulary differences across product categories make it advisable to use domain-specific training data.

If enough (human and/or financial) resources are available, the most effective approach is of course to invest in quality-controlled manual annotation of a relatively large amount of training data. However, since the higher-level semantic structure of comparisons as they appear in reviews is clear-cut, the problem setting could respond favorably to weakly supervised training strategies that start out from a seed set of manually annotated data. The experiments we present in this paper are exploring this very question.

Comparisons can be mapped to a predicate-argument structure, so we cast the task of detecting them as a semantic role-labeling (SRL) problem (Hou and Li, 2008; Kessler and Kuhn, 2013). Starting with a small set of labeled seed sentences, we use structural alignment (Fürstenau and Lapata, 2009), which has been successfully applied to SRL, to automatically find and annotate sentences that are similar to these seed sentences as a way to get more training data.

There are several challenges that make our task different from a typical SRL setting: Our data is not news, but user-generated data (product reviews), which is much more noisy. We have a

Proceedings of Recent Advances in Natural Language Processing, pages 275–281,
Hissar, Bulgaria, Sep 7–9 2015.

smaller, more fixed set of roles for the arguments (two entities that are compared in some aspect), but these arguments are further away from the predicates. And, like all sentiment-related task, we have to deal with subjectivity.

In this work we want to investigate whether structural alignment can successfully be used for getting additional training data for the task of comparison detection. We present some adaptations of the method to our task of comparison detection and experiment with varying numbers of seed sentences and gathered expansion sentences.

2 Related work

Sentiment analysis has in recent years moved from the document-level prediction of polarity or star rating to a more fine-grained analysis. Jindal and Liu (2006a) are the first to specifically distinguish comparison sentences from other sentences in product reviews. In follow-up work, Jindal and Liu (2006b) detect comparison arguments with label sequential rules and Ganapathibhotla and Liu (2008) identify the preferred entity in a ranked comparison. Xu et al. (2011) use Conditional Random Fields in relation extraction approach. We follow previous work (Hou and Li, 2008; Kessler and Kuhn, 2013) and tackle comparisons with a SRL approach, but move from a completely supervised setting to a semi-supervised one.

Several unsupervised or weakly supervised approaches have been presented for SRL. Gildea and Jurafsky (2002) – the first work that tackles SRL as an independent task – use bootstrapping, where an initial system is trained on the available data, applied to a large unlabeled corpus, and the resulting annotations are then used to re-train the model. Abend et al. (2009) do unsupervised argument identification by using pointwise mutual information to determine which constituents are the most probable arguments. Other approaches use the extensive resources that exist for SRL as a basis, e.g., Swier and Stevenson (2005) leverage VerbNet which lists possible argument structures allowable for each predicate. For comparison detection we do not have extensive resources to tap into. We do however think that a small seed set of comparison sentences can be annotated in reasonable time for any new domain or language. This set may not be sufficiently large for bootstrapping, but it can be used as an initial seed set. In this work, we use structural alignment (Fürstenau and Lapata, 2009) to expand this seed set with similar sentences in a semi-supervised way.

3 Approach

The goal of our work is to get more training data for comparison detection in a semi-supervised way. We implement structural alignment proposed by Fürstenau and Lapata (2009) and Fürstenau and Lapata (2012), a method for finding unlabeled sentences that are similar to existing labeled seed sentences (originally proposed for SRL). The basic hypothesis is that predicates that appear in a similar syntactic and semantic context will behave similarly with respect to their arguments so that the labels from the seed sentences can be projected to the unlabeled sentences. These newly labeled sentences can then be used as additional training data.

3.1 Outline of structural alignment

Given a small set of labeled sentences (seed corpus) and a large set of unlabeled sentences (expansion corpus). We collect expansion sentences for a predicate p of a seed sentence s with the follwing steps for every unlabeled sentence u.

1. *Sentence selection:* Consider u iff it contains a predicate compatible with p.
2. *Argument candidate creation:* Get all argument candidates from s and from u.
3. *Alignment scoring:* Score every possible alignment between the two argument candidate sets.
4. Store best-scoring alignment and its score iff at least one role-bearing node is covered.

When all unlabeled sentences have been processed, we choose the k sentences with the highest alignment similarity scores as expansion sentences for the seed predicate p. We project the labels of the arguments in the seed sentence onto their aligned words in these unlabeled sentences and add the newly labeled sentences to our data.

In the following we will discuss the main steps of the expansion algorithm and give some details. Figure 1 illustrates each step for a pair of example sentences from our data.

3.2 Sentence selection

We consider all sentences with the exact same lemma for the predicate as possible expansion sentences. In contrast to the original approach, we use the part of speech (POS) tag instead of the lemma

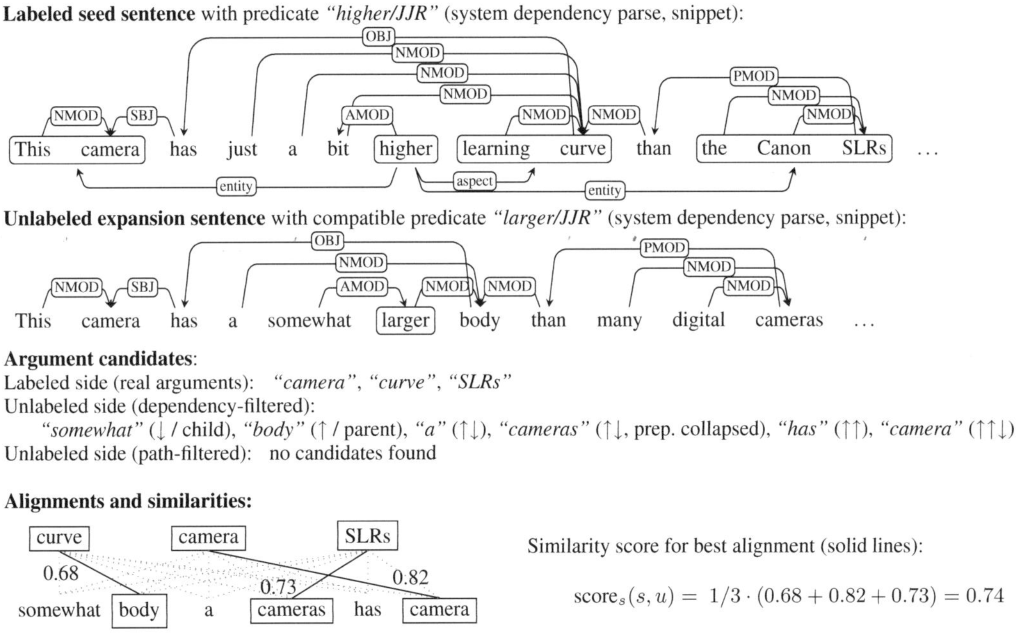

Figure 1: Steps of structural alignment for an example seed and an example unlabeled sentence.

for all adjectives and adverbs in comparative or superlative form (see Figure 1 where both predicates are *"JJR"*), as exchanging them is without any influence on the syntactic structure or the arguments of the comparison. Like the original approach, we only consider single-word predicates.

3.3 Argument candidate creation

Fürstenau and Lapata (2009) use the direct descendants and siblings of the predicate as argument candidates (both SRL arguments and non-arguments). In our labeled data, this find only 17% of the actual labeled comparison arguments.

The challenge is to enlarge the set of argument candidates, while keeping the number of candidates manageable so that alignments can be calculated in reasonable time. Similar to what has been proposed for SRL arguments (Xue and Palmer, 2004), we use all ancestors of the predicate until the root and their direct descendants, plus all descendants of the predicate itself. We remove prepositions (Fürstenau and Lapata, 2009) and conjunctions (Fürstenau and Lapata, 2012) which can never be arguments, and add their direct children to the candidate set. We also impose a distance limit and exclude numbers and punctuation. Applied to our labeled data, this *dependency-filtered* method finds 87% of all real arguments.

As a second method (*path-filtered*), we get the paths from the predicate to each argument in the labeled sentence and search for the exact same paths (compared by dependency relations) in the unlabeled sentence. All nodes on the path are extracted as candidates (Fürstenau and Lapata, 2012). The method is very precise, but also often fails to find any candidates.

On labeled side, we only take the actual labeled arguments of the comparison, as our candidate sets are relatively big and noisy and our interest is solely in finding good alignments for the projection of the real arguments. You can see the resulting candidates for the example in Figure 1.

3.4 Alignment scoring

The similarity of an alignment between two sentences s and u is the averaged sum of all word alignment similarities, themselves the averaged sum of different word similarity measures:

$$\text{score}_s(s,u) = \frac{1}{|M|}\sum_{i=1}^{|M|}\frac{1}{|S|}\sum_{j\in S}\text{sim}_j(w_i,\sigma(w_i))$$

where M is the set of candidates on labeled side, $w_i \in M$ one of these candidates, $\sigma(w_i)$ the candidate on unlabeled side aligned with w_i, and S is the set of similarities to calculate. Unaligned w_i receive a word similarity of zero.

name	value w_i	value $\sigma(w_i)$	$\text{sim}_j(\cdot)$	explanation
sim_{vs}	$\vec{v}$(slrs)	$\vec{v}$(cameras)	0.91	Cosine similarity of co-occurrence vectors $\vec{v}()$
$\text{sim}_{\text{neigh}}$	$\vec{v}$(canon), $\vec{v}$(i)	$\vec{v}$(digital), $\vec{v}$(but)	0.78	(sim_{vs} of left neighbors + sim_{vs} of right neighbors) / 2
sim_{dep}	PMOD, NNP	PMOD, NNS	0.75	Dependency relation similarity (0.5 same, 0 else) + POS sim. (0.5 same, 0.25 same universal POS, 0 else)
sim_{tok}	6	5	0.50	Similarity of distance (# tokens) of candidate from predicate $1/(\lvert d_{\text{tok}}(w_i, p) - d_{\text{tok}}(\sigma(w_i), \sigma(p))\rvert + 1)$.
sim_{lev}	$\uparrow 2 \downarrow 2$	$\uparrow 1 \downarrow 2$	0.75	Similarity in number of "up"s ($\uparrow$) and "down"s ($\downarrow$) on the dependency path from argument to predicate. The $\uparrow$ and $\downarrow$ parts are calculated separately and averaged.
sim_{path}	$\uparrow$ bit $\downarrow$ curve, than	$\downarrow$ body, than	0.70	Average sim_{dep} of all words on the the dependency path from argument to the predicate. The $\uparrow$ and $\downarrow$ parts are calculated separately, similarity for unpaired words is 0.

Table 1: Similarity measures for word alignment similarity. Columns 2–4 give the compared values and similarities for the example from Figure 1 with *"SLRs"* as w_i and *"cameras"* as $\sigma(w_i)$.

We compare the syntactic and semantic similarity of the two candidates with a variety of similarity measures that are listed in Table 1 along with values they take for the example from Figure 1.

We use two combinations of similarity measures: *flat* similarities only ($S = \{\text{vs}, \text{dep}\}$) which corresponds to the similarity measures used in the original work, and similarities that include *context* (all, $S = \{\text{vs}, \text{neigh}, \text{dep}, \text{tok}, \text{lev}, \text{path}\}$).

4 Experiments

4.1 Data

As our core labeled data set we use comparison sentences from English camera reviews[1] (Kessler and Kuhn, 2014). We divide the data into five folds and use one fold as seed data and the rest as test data. The full **seed data** contains 342 sentences with 415 predicates. The **test data** contains 1365 sentences with 1693 predicates.

As the unlabeled **expansion data**, we use a set of 280.000 camera review sentences from `epinions.com`. Note that expansion sentences are never used in testing, we always only test on human-annotated data.

To calculate vector space similarities we use co-occurrence vectors (symmetric window of 2 words, retain 2000 most frequent dimensions) extracted from a large set of reviews with a total of 40 million tokens. This set includes the above expansion corpus, the electronics part of the HUGE corpus (Jindal and Liu, 2008) and camera reviews from `amazon.com`.

[1] `http://www.ims.uni-stuttgart.de/forschung/ressourcen/korpora/reviewcomparisons/`

4.2 System for comparison detection

We retrain the MATE Semantic Role Labeling system (Björkelund et al., 2009)[2] on our data and use a typical pipeline setting with three classification steps: predicate identification, argument identification and argument classification. We distinguish three argument types: two entities and one aspect. We use standard SRL features (Johansson and Nugues, 2007) based on the output of the MATE dependency parser. This setup is equivalent to (Kessler and Kuhn, 2013).

4.3 Experimental setup

To evaluate whether the found expansion sentences are useful, we add the k best expansion sentences per seed predicate to the seed data and train on this expanded corpus. We use the test data for evaluation and compare classification performance of training on the expanded seed data with the **baseline** trained on the seed data only.

We test four versions of the expansion:

PATH-FLAT *path-filtered* candidate creation and *flat* similarities (closest to the original work).

DEP-FLAT *dependency-filtered* candidate creation and *flat* similarities.

PATH-CONTEXT *path-filtered* candidate creation and *context* similarities.

DEP-CONTEXT *dependency-filtered* candidate creation and *context* similarities.

There are two main questions we investigate:

1. How many seed sentences should be used (varying d)?
2. How many expansion sentences should be used per seed (varying k)?

[2] `http://code.google.com/p/mate-tools/`

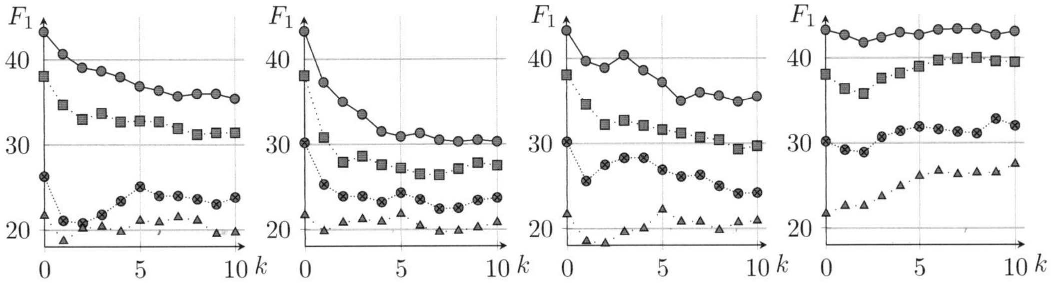

(a) PATH-FLAT (b) DEP-FLAT (c) PATH-CONTEXT (d) DEP-CONTEXT

Figure 2: F_1 score for argument identification when using different percentages d of the corpus as seed data (top to bottom: 100%, 50%, 25%, 10%) and expanding with different k numbers of candidates.

We expect that the training data expansion is helpful in low-resource and high-precision settings (i.e., d and k are small). This corresponds to a scenario where only a limited amount of sentences has been annotated for a new domain or language. We consider this to be a more realistic scenario for our task than the one used in (Fürstenau and Lapata, 2012), where a fixed number of training examples per frame is used, as in contrast to SRL we do not expect to know predicates or frames for comparisons in advance.

4.4 Results

Figure 2 shows some results for comparison argument identification in terms of F_1 score. The different curves represent expanding and training on different percentages d of the seed set, from 10% to 100% (full seed set). Note that the lowest setting uses only 34 seed sentences.

The x-axis shows k, the number of expansion sentences added per seed sentence. The value 0 corresponds to the baseline, i.e., training on the seed sentences only. In line with the results reported for SRL, for most cases as k gets larger, the amount of introduced noise outweighs the benefits of additional training data, so performance drops.

For PATH-FLAT, DEP-FLAT and PATH-CONTEXT, almost no setting manages to improve over the non-expanded baseline, every added expansion sentence only decreases performance. For DEP-CONTEXT, in some cases, especially for low values for d there is a small improvement. To illustrate the different sentences selected by the systems, consider this example:

(1) a. *"I felt **more** [comfortable]$_{\text{aspect}}$ with [XTi]$_{\text{entity}}$"*

b. *"I bought this because my wife didn't feel [comfortable]$_{\text{aspect}}$ with all the features/functions of the **more** complex [C5050Z]$_{\text{entity}}$."*

c. *"I was much **more** [comfortable]$_{\text{aspect}}$ with the [DSC-S75]$_{\text{entity}}$"*

Sentence 1a is the seed sentence, sentence 1b is the sentence selected by DEP-FLAT, sentence 1c is selected by DEP-CONTEXT. While choosing *"comfortable"* in sentence 1b to be aligned with the labeled aspect seems like a perfect match in isolation, 1c is a much better choice in context.

Figure 3 shows learning curves for argument identification for each system with the best setting for k (usually 1, 10 for DEP-CONTEXT). All systems except DEP-CONTEXT are nearly always below the baseline. The best value of k for DEP-CONTEXT in our experiments is 10, which is shown in the graph. The results are very similar for all $k \geq 5$, for lower values of k, the results drop below the baseline. The best setting manages to improve over the non-expanded baseline in low resource settings, but the curves get closer to each other when more seed data is added and the effect disappears at the end.

Due to space restrictions we are only able to show argument identification results, but the trends are very similar for predicate identification and argument classification.

4.5 Discussion

If we look at the sentences found by the expansion systems, we can identify two main problems with the extracted sentences.

One problem that affects all sentiment-related tasks is subjectivity. Often sentiment words (or in our case comparison words) appear in non-sentiment (non-comparative) contexts, but these contexts are very hard to distinguish from each other. Consider this example:

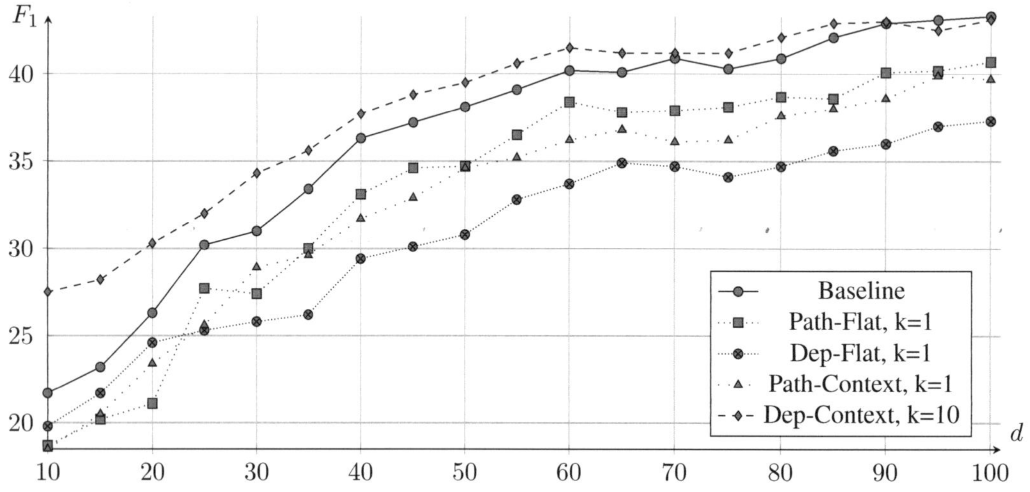

Figure 3: Learning curves (F_1 score for argument identification) with varying amounts of seed data d.

(2) a. *"This is largely a function of the much* ***smaller*** *[SD media]*$_{\text{entity}}$*."*

b. *"Plan for 8* ***higher*** *quality [pics]*$_{\text{entity}}$ *or about 24 medium quality pics with internal memory ."*

Sentence 2a is the seed sentence, sentence 2b is the best sentence selected by the context-aware system. Though the two phrases *"smaller SD media"* and *"higher quality pics"* are a very good match, the word *"higher"* in sentence 2b does not express a product comparison. Instead, it describes a type of picture. Such uses are relatively frequent and often mistakenly chosen as expansion sentences. Such "false positives" mainly affect predicate identification, but errors in this first step are propagated through the pipeline.

Another type of error is caused by the non-aligned part of sentences. Sentences are sometimes rather long and contain other predicates besides the expanded predicate. Consider this example (3a seed, 3b context-aware system):

(3) a. *"That said, the* ***larger*** *LCD [screen]*$_{\text{aspect}}$ *is really an improvement."*

b. *"The* ***smaller*** *2-inch [screen]*$_{\text{aspect}}$ *has higher resolution of 118,000 pixels!"*

The additional predicate *"higher"* in the expansion sentence is not detected, thereby creating a "false negative" example for the predicate identification classifier and the subsequent steps.

5 Conclusion

In this paper we investigate whether structural alignment, a semi-supervised method that has been successfully used for projecting SRL annotations to unlabeled sentences, can be adapted to the task of detecting comparisons. We find that some adjustments are necessary in order for the method to be applicable. First, we need to adapt the method of candidate selection to reflect that our arguments are further away from the predicate, while at the same time keeping the number of candidates manageable. Second, we need to adapt the similarity measure for scoring argument alignments to include context-aware measures. When we add the found expansion sentences to our training data, we can slightly improve over a non-expanded baseline in low-resource settings, i.e., when only a very small amount of training data in the desired domain or language is available.

There are many directions for future work. We have presented one possible context-aware similarity measure, but there are many other possibilities that can be explored. Two main issues are false positive and false negative predicates found by the expansion, the former being introduced by not detecting non-subjective usage of comparative words, the latter through other predicates besides the identified one being present in an expansion sentence. Doing subjectivity analysis to filter out non-comparative usages, and simplifying sentences or pre-selecting only short and simple sentences for expansion could improve results.

Acknowledgments

The work reported in this paper was supported by a Nuance Foundation grant.

References

Omri Abend, Roi Reichart, and Ari Rappoport. 2009. Unsupervised argument identification for semantic role labeling. In *Proceedings of ACL '09*, pages 28–36.

Anders Björkelund, Love Hafdell, and Pierre Nugues. 2009. Multilingual Semantic Role Labeling. In *Proceedings of CoNLL '09 Shared Task*, pages 43–48.

Hagen Fürstenau and Mirella Lapata. 2009. Semi-supervised semantic role labeling. In *Proceedings of EACL '09*, pages 220–228.

Hagen Fürstenau and Mirella Lapata. 2012. Semi-supervised semantic role labeling via structural alignment. *Computational Linguistics*, 38(1):135–171.

Murthy Ganapathibhotla and Bing Liu. 2008. Mining opinions in comparative sentences. In *Proceedings of COLING '08*, pages 241–248.

Daniel Gildea and Daniel Jurafsky. 2002. Automatic labeling of semantic roles. *Computational Linguistics*, 238(3):245–288.

Feng Hou and Guo-hui Li. 2008. Mining Chinese comparative sentences by semantic role labeling. In *Proceedings of ICMLC '08*, pages 2563–2568.

Nitin Jindal and Bing Liu. 2006a. Identifying comparative sentences in text documents. In *Proceedings of SIGIR '06*, pages 244–251.

Nitin Jindal and Bing Liu. 2006b. Mining comparative sentences and relations. In *Proceedings of AAAI '06*, pages 1331–1336.

Nitin Jindal and Bing Liu. 2008. Opinion spam and analysis. In *Proceedings of WSDM '08*, pages 219–230, New York, NY, USA. ACM.

Richard Johansson and Pierre Nugues. 2007. Syntactic representations considered for frame-semantic analysis. In *Proceedings of TLT Workshop '07*, page 12.

Wiltrud Kessler and Jonas Kuhn. 2013. Detection of product comparisons - How far does an out-of-the-box semantic role labeling system take you? In *Proceedings of EMNLP '13*, pages 1892–1897.

Wiltrud Kessler and Jonas Kuhn. 2014. A corpus of comparisons in product reviews. In *Proceedings of LREC '14*.

Robert Swier and Suzanne Stevenson. 2005. Exploiting a verb lexicon in automatic semantic role labelling. In *Proceedings of HLT/EMNLP '05*, pages 883–890.

Kaiquan Xu, Stephen Shaoyi Liao, Jiexun Li, and Yuxia Song. 2011. Mining comparative opinions from customer reviews for competitive intelligence. *Decis. Support Syst.*, 50(4):743–754, March.

Nianwen Xue and Martha Palmer. 2004. Calibrating features for semantic role labeling. In *Proceedings of EMNLP '04*, pages 88–94.

Recognition of Polish Temporal Expressions

Jan Kocoń†
G4.19 Research Group
Wrocław University of Technology
jan.kocon@pwr.edu.pl

Michał Marcińczuk
G4.19 Research Group
Wrocław University of Technology
michal.marcinczuk@pwr.edu.pl

Abstract

In this article we present the result of the recent research in the recognition of Polish temporal expressions. The temporal information extracted from the text plays major role in many information extraction systems, like question answering, event recognition or discourse analysis. We prepared a broad description of Polish temporal expressions, called PLIMEX. It is based on the state-of-the-art solutions for English, mostly TimeML specification. This solution can be used for the extraction of events and their attributes, in order to anchor events in time and to reason about the persistence of events. We prepared the annotation guidelines and we annotated all documents in Polish Corpus of Wrocław University of Technology (KPWr) using our specification. Here we describe results achieved by Liner2 machine learning system, adapted to recognise Polish temporal expressions.

1 Introduction

Recognition of temporal expressions and events became an active area of the research and plays a significant role in many natural language engineering systems. It is one of the major tasks in information extraction, which aim is to extract specific elements from unstructured data. In this research we focus on tracking changes over time in text written in natural language. Further reasoning about changes requires the information about temporally grounded events.

Textual references to time tell us how long something lasts, when something happens or how often occurs. People are usually conscious of their location in time — in most cases we know what is the current year, month and date and we use this information to capture the meaning of expressions like "yesterday", "tomorrow", "five days ago", "16th of November". Even in texts written in formal language (like newspaper articles), the global meaning of the given temporal expressions can be deduced by the analysis of the whole context of the document (often with metadata, such as document creation time). We can treat the global meaning of a temporal expression as a point in a timeline (e.g. "5th of December 2005"), a range (not always anchored to a specific point in a timeline, e.g. "two weeks") or even as a set of points in a timeline (e.g. "each Tuesday"). To determine the exact date, human (or machine learning system) often must know the full temporal context. These examples do not cover the complexity of the temporal expressions understanding. Sometimes a temporal expression is not the reference to the real world, but describes a fictional event. Sometimes a part of the text describes past or future, but it is not explicitly stated, but in other part of the document there are some clues to find out what tense is given. Also determining the temporal function of an expression can be a serious problem, even for a human, e.g. "four weeks" can be used to describe duration (how long something lasts) or point in time (e.g. "in four weeks"). An automatic system should distinguish between different categories of temporal expressions to capture its local and global semantic meaning properly. The extraction of temporal expressions identifies when something occurred by the recognition and normalization of expressions which refer to time. Often it is part of other reasoning systems, like in automatic question answering (Pustejovsky et al., 2005b) or event recognition (Andersen et al., 1992; Llorens et al., 2010b).

Mazur (2012) compared many state-of-the-art approaches to describe temporal expressions and divided these expressions into two main categories: instants and intervals. These are atoms

Proceedings of Recent Advances in Natural Language Processing, pages 282–290,
Hissar, Bulgaria, Sep 7–9 2015.

of time, which can be used to represent and reason about time. In the literature we can find many terms to describe instants, e.g. *a time point, a point, a point in time, a moment*. Also interval sometimes is called *period* (Benthem, 1983). Benthem (1983) uses interval as something that is between boundaries. On the other hand Allen (1995) finds interval temporal expressions in Benthem's meaning denoted by the term *duration*. The main difference between instants and intervals is that instants have no duration (treated as a feature of a period).

One of the most widely used specification for English to describe temporal information in natural language corpora is TimeML (Saurí et al., 2006). It was developed in the context of a workshop TERQAS[1], as a part of the ARDA-funded program AQUAINT[2] in a multi-project effort to improve the performance of question answering systems over documents written in natural language (Pustejovsky et al., 2005a). The aim of this research was to improve the access to information in the text through content rather than keywords. The main problem was the recognition of events and their temporal anchoring.

PLIMEX is a temporal annotation language suitable to describe temporal expressions in Polish text documents. It is based on TIDES Instruction Manual for the Annotation of Temporal Expressions (Ferro, 2001), which describes TIMEX2 annotation format. The TIDES manual is also the core of the TIMEX3 annotation format, used in the TimeML specification (Saurí et al., 2006). Both documents present how to use the special Standard Generalized Markup Language tags to annotate temporal expressions, by inserting them directly into the text. We adapted types of temporal expressions from TIMEX3: DATE, TIME, DURATION and SET.

TimeML was successfully adapted to many languages and one of the most widely used rule-based system *HeidelTime*[3] (Strötgen and Gertz, 2013; Strötgen et al., 2013) which uses the TIMEX3 annotation standard, currently supports 11 languages: English, German, Dutch, Vietnamese, Arabic, Spanish, Italian, French, Chinese, Russian, and Croatian. Our research gives the opportunity to create a cross-domain temporal tagger which supports Polish.

2 Types of Temporal Expression in PLIMEX

In this section we define the TimeML types of temporal expressions adapted to Polish. All English translations of Polish examples are given in parentheses. The extent of the annotation in text (if needed) is marked with square brackets.

2.1 DATE

DATE is a type of temporal expressions which denotes a point on a timeline, i.e. a unit of time greater than or equal to a day. The key question is *when*.

Examples of DATE:

(1) *[poniedziałek, 16 marca 1985 roku]*
([Monday, 16th March 1985])

(2) *to wydarzyło się [drugiego listopada]*
(it happened on [the second of November])

(3) *w [październiku 1963 roku]*
(in [October 1963])

(4) *to będzie we [wtorek osiemnastego]*
(it will be on [Tuesday, the eighteenth])

(5) *byłem nad jeziorem [latem tamtego roku]*
(I was at the lake in [the summer of that year])

2.2 TIME

It is a type of a point expression that describes temporal expressions which refer to the time of a day, even if it is not clearly defined. The key question is also *when*. For example *Smith wrócił (Smith returned)*:

(6) *[za dziesięć trzecia]*
(at [ten to three])

(7) *[dwadzieścia po dwunastej]*
(at [twenty past twelve])

(8) *o [ósmej rano]*
(at [eight in the morning])

(9) *o [9.00 w piątek 1 października 1999 roku]*
(at [9 am on Friday, October 1st, 1999])

(10) *[wczoraj późno w nocy]*
([yesterday late at night])

[1]Time and Event Recognition for Question Answering Systems. An Advanced Research and Development Activity Workshop on Advanced Question Answering Technology

[2]http://www.informedia.cs.cmu.edu/aquaint/index.html

[3]https://code.google.com/p/heideltime/

(11) *[wczoraj w nocy]*
([last night])

2.3 DURATION

DURATION, in contrast to DATE, has two points on a timeline associated with it — a start and an end point. An another name for it used in the literature is period (Saquete et al., 2003). The key question is *how long*.

Sometimes the range expressions are also included to this group (Mizobuchi et al., 1998), but these expressions can be treated as separate points in time (Mani and Wilson, 2000). For example *Smith był tutaj (Smith stayed there)*:

(12) *[dwa miesiące] (for [two months])*

(13) *[48 godzin] (for [48 hours])*

(14) *[trzy tygodnie] (for [three weeks])*

(15) *[całą ostatnią noc] ([all last night])*

(16) *[20 dni] w lipcu ([20 days] in July)*

(17) *przez [trzy godziny] w zeszły poniedziałek*
(for [three hours] last Monday)

If a specific piece of information, which relates to the calendar, occurs in the temporal expression, then DATE is the right type of annotation. This is true even if the context suggests that this type of temporal expression indicates the duration of an event, e.g. *[Cały 1985] przebywał na emigracji ([The entire 1985] he lived in exile)*.

2.4 SET

The SET expression is a type of temporal expressions which is related to more than one instance of a time unit — either a point or a period. The key question is *how often*. Examples – *Jan wraca pijany (John comes back drunk)*:

(18) *[dwa razy w tygodniu] ([twice a week])*

(19) *[co dwa dni] ([every two days])*

(20) *[każdej niedzieli] ([every Sunday])*

3 Inter-annotator Agreement

The inter-annotator agreement was measured on randomly selected 100 documents from the Corpus of Wrocław University of Technology called KPWr. We used the positive specific agreement (Hripcsak and Rothschild, 2005) as it was measured for T3Platinum corpus (UzZaman et al., 2012) and two domain experts to annotate the subset of 100 documents from KPWr. We calculate the value of positive specific agreement (PSA) for each category. The results are presented in Table 1.

Type	1 and 2	only 1	only 2	PSA [%]
date	182	12	22	91.46
time	28	13	8	72.73
duration	13	3	4	78.79
set	6	2	9	52.17
$\sum$	229	30	43	86.25

Table 1: The value of positive specific agreement (PSA) calculated on the subset of 100 documents from KPWr, annotated independently by two domain experts using PLIMEX 1.0 guidelines. *1 and 2* means all annotations in which annotators 1 and 2 agreed. *Only 1* is the number of annotations made only by annotator 1 and *only 2* – the number of annotations made only by annotator 2.

According to (UzZaman et al., 2012) the best quality of data was achieved for TempEval-3 platinum corpus (T3Platinum) and it was annotated and reviewed by the organizers. Every file was annotated independently by at least two expert annotators. The result of overall T3Platinum inter-annotator positive specific agreement (PSA) at the level of annotating of temporal expressions with types was 0.88. In our case for 100 randomly selected documents the PSA value achieved was 86.25 (annotating using PLIMEX 1.0 specification).

4 Recognition

Many state of the art systems which recognize time expressions use supervised sequence labelling methods, mostly Conditional Random Fields (CRFs) (Lafferty et al., 2001). Recent studies in comparison of temporal expressions recognition systems for English like TempEval-2 and TempEval-3 (UzZaman et al., 2013) show a shift in the state-of-the-art. While normalisation is done best by rule-engineered systems, recognition is done well by a variety of methods. The conclusion is that rule-engineering and machine learning are equally good at timex recognition (UzZaman et al., 2013). Two best machine learning systems (comparing results of recognition, not normalization) reported by UzZaman et al. (2013) — ClearTK (Steven, 2013) and TIPSem (Llorens et al., 2010a) — utilize CRFs in recognition of temporal expressions.

Our approach is based on *Liner2* tool[4] (Marcińczuk et al., 2013), which uses CRF++ toolkit[5]. This tool was successfully used in other natural language engineering tasks, mainly in named entities recognition (NER) (Marcińczuk and Kocoń, 2013; Marcińczuk et al., 2013).

5 Features

In recognition, the values of features are obtained at the token level. As a baseline we used a default set of features available in the Liner2 tool which was used to train models for named entity recognition (Marcińczuk and Kocoń, 2013; Marcińczuk et al., 2013). The set includes the following types of features:

Morphosyntactic — lemma, grammatical class, case, number, gender, complete morphological tag;

Orthographic — word, word shape (pattern), prefix, suffix, starts with upper case, starts with lower case, starts with symbol, starts with digit, has upper case, has symbol, has digit;

Semantic — word synonym, hypernym;

Dictionary — person first name, person last name, country name, city name, road name, person prefix, country prefix, person noun, person suffix, road prefix, specific triggers (country, district, geographic name, organization name, person name, region, settlement).

We decided to implement special features, which better characterize timexes' constituents:

Orthographic

is_number — is word a number;

structure — each character composing a word is converted to: **x** (if character is a letter), **d** (if character is a digit), **-** (in other case);

structure_packed — each sequence of the same characters in *structure* is converted to a single character, e.g. **ddd** $\rightarrow$ **d**;

other features describing word shape: is number, all upper, all letters, all digits, all alphanumeric, no letters, no alphanumeric, regex, word length

Semantic — *tophyper*: this feature uses plWordNet (Piasecki et al., 2014; Maziarz et al., 2013) to find the possible root of the given word in a graph built from the hyponymy relations joining lexical units in plWordNet. This process is currently not preceded by word sense disambiguation (Kedzia et al., 2014).

Dictionary — *timex*: a lexicon prepared by a domain expert, which contains words referring to time, e.g. **godzina** (Eng. *hour*), **minuta** (Eng. *minute*), etc.

6 Evaluation

We performed evaluation of temporal expressions recognition as it was proposed by UzZaman et al. (2013). The evaluation process is based on Task A of TempEval 2013, described in UzZaman et al. (2013), which aim is to determine the extent of temporal expressions in text as defined by the TimeML TIMEX3 tag and determine the class of expression (date, time, duration or set). To evaluate if the extents of entities and the classes are correctly identified (*exact match* evaluation) we used *precision, recall* and F_1*-score*. We also performed a relaxed match if there is an overlap between the *system entity* and *gold entity*, e.g. "sunday" vs "sunday morning". A detailed instruction for the relaxed match test score can be found in (Chinchor, 1998). Metrics used for *relaxed match*: **COR** – number correct, **ACT** – number actual, **POS** – number possible. Metrics used for *strict match*: **TP** – true positive, **FP** – false positive, **FN** – false negative. Measures used for both *strict* and *relaxed match*: **P** – precision, **R** – recall, $\mathbf{F_1}$ – F_1-score.

KPWr corpus consists of 1635 documents. A *train* set is 50% of all documents (819) and both *test* and *tune* evaluation data sets are 25% of all documents (408 on each set).

[4] http://nlp.pwr.wroc.pl/en/tools-and-resources/liner2

[5] http://crfpp.sourceforge.net/

6.1 Baseline

The baseline models utilize a set of features used for named entity recognition for Polish (Marcińczuk and Kocoń, 2013; Marcińczuk et al., 2013).

Annotation	TP	FP	FN	P [%]	R [%]	F_1 [%]
timex	2272	338	677	87.05	77.04	81.74
date	1760	201	353	89.75	83.29	86.40
time	111	56	177	66.47	38.54	48.79
duration	280	75	200	78.87	58.33	67.07
set	17	2	51	89.47	25.00	39.08
TOTAL	2168	334	781	86.65	73.52	79.55

Table 2: *Exact match* evaluation of TIMEX3 recognition (10-fold cross-validation on train set) — baseline features.

Annotation	COR	ACT	POS	P [%]	R [%]	F_1 [%]
timex	4694	526	1199	89.92	79.65	84.48
date	3594	328	628	91.64	85.13	88.26
time	243	91	330	72.75	42.41	53.58
duration	583	127	376	82.11	60.79	69.86
set	34	4	102	89.47	25.00	39.08
TOTAL	4454	550	1436	89.01	75.62	81.77

Table 3: *Relaxed match* evaluation of TIMEX recognition (10-fold cross-validation on train set) — baseline features.

Table 2 shows the results of the *exact match* evaluation of Polish temporal expressions recognition, performed as 10-fold cross-validation on the train set (see Table **??**). Table 3 shows the same result using *relaxed match* evaluation. Each table contains the result of two models: *4-class* (boundaries recognition and classification of temporal expressions; available classes: DATE, TIME, DURATION and SET) and *1-class* (boundaries recognition only, all classes casted to a single class named *timex*). Each model utilizes the baseline set of features.

6.2 Baseline with New Features

We added new features (described in Section 5) to the baseline set. The evaluation procedure is the same as described in Section 6.1.

Table 4 shows the results of the *exact match* evaluation of models which utilize both baseline and new features. Table 5 shows the same result using *relaxed match* evaluation. Each table contains the result of two models: *4-class* (boundaries recognition and classification of temporal expressions; available classes: DATE, TIME, DURATION and SET) and *1-class* (boundaries recognition only, all classes cast to a single class called *timex*).

Annotation	TP	FP	FN	P [%]	R [%]	F_1 [%]
timex	2389	367	560	86.68	81.01	83.75
date	1830	231	283	88.79	86.61	87.69
time	114	62	174	64.77	39.58	49.14
duration	299	104	181	74.19	62.29	67.72
set	18	3	50	85.71	26.47	40.45
TOTAL	2261	400	688	84.97	76.67	80.61

Table 4: *Exact match* evaluation of TIMEX recognition (10-fold cross-validation on train set) – baseline + new features.

Annotation	COR	ACT	POS	P [%]	R [%]	F_1 [%]
timex	4944	568	949	89.70	83.90	86.70
date	3733	389	491	90.56	88.38	89.46
time	259	93	316	73.58	45.04	55.88
duration	625	181	334	77.54	65.17	70.82
set	36	6	100	85.71	26.47	40.45
TOTAL	4653	669	1241	87.43	78.94	82.97

Table 5: *Relaxed match* evaluation of TIMEX recognition (10-fold cross-validation on train set) – baseline + new features.

We can see that adding new features improved F_1 for each model and for each match evaluation. Detailed analysis of these results is presented in Section 7.

6.3 Feature Selection

Feature selection methods can be divided into three categories: wrapper, filter and embedded methods (Blum and Langley, 1997; Hou and Jiao, 2010; Kohavi and John, 1997). We managed to find most suitable method, which can be applied to the CRFs probabilistic framework in order to avoid overfitting and reduce the storage and computational problem without the significant loss of F_1-score.

In this work we used the wrapper approach, where the feature subset selection is performed using the induction algorithm as a black box. The same algorithm is used to estimate the accuracy of the classifier trained on a selected subset of features. Each selection step depends on the result of the classifier evaluation. We utilized the method described by Zhu (2010), which contains the following steps:

1. Let $M = \varnothing$ be the initial set of features.
2. Let C be the candidate feature set as atomic features. These are usually predicates on simple combination of words and tags, e.g.(x = John, z = PERSON), (x = John, z = LOCATION), (x = John, z = ORGANIZATION), etc. We used a context window size of 5.
3. Build an individual CRF model with features $M \cup \{f\}$ for each candidate feature $f \in C$. Select the candidate feature f^* which improve the CRF model the most (e.g., by the result of model evaluation). Let $M = M \cup \{f^*\}$, and $C = C - \{f^*\}$.
4. Go to step 3 until enough features have been added to the CRF model or there is no F_1-score gain after the current iteration.

Table 6 shows the result of the feature selection for TIMEX recognition. The procedure was performed for both *1-class* and *4-class* model. The initial set of features was the baseline with new features. We used average *exact match* F_1-score of 10-fold cross-validation on train set to evaluate the result after each step of the selection.

Model	Iter.	Selected feature	F_1 [%]	Gain [pps]
1-class	1	prefix-3	71.33	71.333
	2	hypernym1	77.59	6.260
	3	pattern	80.35	2.756
	4	dict_timex_base	81.46	1.114
	5	top4hyper1	81.46	0.947
	6	case	82.77	0.363
	7	structP	83.00	0.226
	8	dict_trigger_int_district	83.09	0.094
	9	starts_with_upper_case	83.15	0.055
	10	prefix-1	83.17	0.018
	11	hypernym2	83.40	0.231
4-class	1	prefix-3	70.03	70.031
	2	hypernym1	75.39	5.361
	3	struct	78.40	3.014
	4	dict_timex_base	79.10	0.695
	5	top4hyper4	79.89	0.789

Table 6: Result of the feature selection for TIMEX recognition (2 models: boundaries recognition and 4-class model). Used measure: average *exact match* F_1-score of 10-fold cross-validation on train set. Initial set of features: baseline + new features.

We can see that most of the proposed new features were selected (*dict_timex_base, top4hyper1, structP, starts_with_upper_case* for *1-class* model and *struct, dict_timex_base, top4hyper4* for *4-class* model). None of the proposed features were selected in the first or the second iteration. The most discriminative feature for both models is orthographic *prefix-3* and the second is semantic *hypernym1*.

Table 7 and Table 8 show the results of match evaluation of models which utilize features after the selection (*B+new*).

Annotation	TP	FP	FN	P [%]	R [%]	F_1 [%]
timex	225	42	47	84.27	82.72	83.49
date	1801	240	312	88.24	85.23	86.71
time	108	60	180	64.29	37.50	47.37
duration	296	106	184	73.63	61.67	67.12
set	17	2	51	89.47	25.00	39.08
TOTAL	2222	408	727	84.49	75.35	79.66

Table 7: *Exact match* evaluation of TIMEX recognition (10-fold cross-validation on train set) – after feature selection (see Table 6).

Annotation	COR	ACT	POS	P [%]	R [%]	F_1 [%]
timex	465	69	78	87.08	85.64	86.35
date	3673	409	547	89.98	87.04	88.48
time	247	89	316	73.51	43.87	54.95
duration	622	182	337	77.36	64.86	70.56
set	34	4	102	89.47	25.00	39.08
TOTAL	4576	684	1302	87.00	77.85	82.17

Table 8: *Relaxed match* evaluation of TIMEX recognition (10-fold cross-validation on train set) – after the features selection (see Table 6).

Detailed analysis of these results is presented in Section 7.

6.4 Processing Time

Table 6.4 shows the processing time of TIMEX recognition for the given feature sets: baseline, baseline with added new features (B+new) and features selected after the feature selection process (the initial set was B+new).

We see that *1-class* model after selection is about 3.6 times faster in recognition processing time than *baseline* and about 5 times faster than *B+new*. *4-class* model after selection is about 4.2 times faster than *baseline* and about 5.2 times faster than *B+new*. The selection process signifi-

Model	Fold	Baseline [s]	B+new [s]	Selection [s]
1-class	1	127.41	168.81	39.19
	2	114.98	148.92	29.13
	3	115.53	163.08	31.44
	4	112.65	158.13	31.15
	5	111.61	168.60	31.24
	6	113.70	151.39	30.93
	7	106.88	162.24	30.05
	8	111.81	158.49	30.94
	9	114.17	152.16	30.39
	10	111.95	159.34	31.14
	$\sum$	1140.68	1591.15	315.59
4-class	1	296.99	376.95	67.13
	2	263.21	335.42	69.44
	3	291.32	330.95	62.04
	4	276.87	334.62	73.17
	5	291.37	358.58	66.23
	6	273.14	354.18	69.02
	7	296.39	359.58	67.36
	8	282.13	340.85	66.72
	9	297.54	352.18	66.87
	10	276.97	369.55	70.42
	$\sum$	2845.93	3512.86	678.39

Table 9: Comparison of TIMEX recognition processing time (in seconds) for different feature sets on train set (10-fold cross-validation).

Set	Model	Match	Baseline [%]	B+new [%]	Selection [%]
train	1-class	exact	81.74	**83.75**	**83.29**
		relaxed	84.48	**86.70**	**86.30**
	4-class	exact	79.55	**80.61**	79.66
		relaxed	81.77	**82.97**	82.17
tune	1-class	exact	79.37	80.91	80.06
		relaxed	82.81	**84.87**	**84.16**
	4-class	exact	77.75	**79.49**	77.96
		relaxed	80.30	**82.19**	80.89

Table 10: Comparison of results (F_1-score) achieved on different sets (*train* – 10-fold cross-validation on *train* set; tune – model is trained on *train* set and evaluated on *tune* set). Variants with *1 class* are boundaries recognition only. The difference between baseline and results in bold are statistically significant.

cantly improved the overall speed of the recognition.

7 Conclusions

Table 10 shows the comparison of results (F_1-score) achieved on different sets. We performed 10-fold cross-validation on the train set. Then each model was trained using the train set and evaluated on the tune set, divided into 10 parts. All the given results are averaged. We analyzed the statistical significance of differences between the baseline and the other models. To check the statistical significance of F_1-score difference we used paired-differences Student's t-test based on 10-fold cross-validation with a significance level $\alpha = 0.05$ (Dietterich, 1998). The statistically significant improvement with respect to the baseline is marked in bold.

We made the following observations:

- Adding special features (see Section 5) to the baseline (*B+new* column) significantly improved the result for each evaluation variant except *exact match* for boundaries recognition (1 class) performed on tune set (the improvement is not statistically significant in that case).
- Performing the feature selection (see Section 6.3) statistically improved the results for 3 evaluation variants, only in boundaries detection. In each case we can see small improvement according to the baseline, but most of them (all 4-class recognition variants) are not statistically significant.
- Selection of features reduced the quality of the recognition (comparing to B+new) but the difference is not statistically significant.
- Each proposed model evaluation result is not worse comparing to the baseline result, most of them (10 of 16) are significantly better.
- The selection process significantly improved the overall speed of the recognition.

Acknowledgements

Work financed by the Polish Ministry of Science and Higher Education, a program in support of scientific units involved in the development of a European research infrastructure for the humanities and social sciences in the scope of the consortia CLARIN ERIC and ESS-ERIC, 2015-2016.

References

James Allen. 1995. *Natural Language Understanding (2Nd Ed.)*. Benjamin-Cummings Publishing Co., Inc., Redwood City, CA, USA.

Peggy M. Andersen, Philip J. Hayes, Alison K. Huettner, Linda M. Schmandt, Irene B. Nirenburg, and Steven P. Weinstein. 1992. Automatic extraction of facts from press releases to generate news stories. In *In: Processing of the Third Conference on Applied Natural Language Processing*, pages 170–177.

Johan van Benthem. 1983. *The logic of time : a model-theoretic investigation into the varieties of temporal ontology and temporal discourse*. Synthese library. D. Reidel, Dordrecht, London, Boston.

Avrim L. Blum and Pat Langley. 1997. Selection of relevant features and examples in machine learning. *Artificial Intelligence*, 97(1–2):245 – 271. Relevance.

Nancy Chinchor. 1998. MUC-7 test scores introduction (appendix b). In *Proceedings of the 7th Message Understanding Conference*.

Thomas G. Dietterich. 1998. Approximate statistical tests for comparing supervised classification learning algorithms. *Neural Computation*, 10:1895–1923.

Lisa Ferro. 2001. Instruction manual for the annotation of temporal expressions.

Cuiqin Hou and Licheng Jiao. 2010. Selecting features of linear-chain conditional random fields via greedy stage-wise algorithms. *Pattern Recognition Letters*, 31(2):151 – 162.

George Hripcsak and Adam S Rothschild. 2005. Agreement, the f-measure, and reliability in information retrieval. *Journal of the American Medical Informatics Association*, 12(3):296–298.

Paweł Kedzia, Maciej Piasecki, Jan Kocoń, and Agnieszka Indyka-Piasecka. 2014. Distributionally extended network-based word sense disambiguation in semantic clustering of polish texts. *IERI Procedia*, 10(0):38 – 44. International Conference on Future Information Engineering (FIE 2014).

Ron Kohavi and George H. John. 1997. Wrappers for feature subset selection. *Artificial Intelligence*, 97(1–2):273 – 324. Relevance.

John D. Lafferty, Andrew McCallum, and Fernando C. N. Pereira. 2001. Conditional random fields: Probabilistic models for segmenting and labeling sequence data. In *Proceedings of the Eighteenth International Conference on Machine Learning*, ICML '01, pages 282–289, San Francisco, CA, USA. Morgan Kaufmann Publishers Inc.

Hector Llorens, Estela Saquete, and Borja Navarro. 2010a. Tipsem (english and spanish): Evaluating crfs and semantic roles in tempeval-2. In *Association for Computational Linguistics*, pages 284–291.

Hector Llorens, Estela Saquete, and Borja Navarro-Colorado. 2010b. TimeML events recognition and classification: Learning CRF models with semantic roles. In *Proceedings of the 23rd International Conference on Computational Linguistics*, COLING '10, pages 725–733, Stroudsburg, PA, USA. Association for Computational Linguistics.

Inderjeet Mani and George Wilson. 2000. Robust temporal processing of news. In *Proceedings of the 38th Annual Meeting on Association for Computational Linguistics*, ACL '00, pages 69–76, Stroudsburg, PA, USA. Association for Computational Linguistics.

Michał Marcińczuk and Jan Kocoń. 2013. Recognition of Named Entities Boundaries in Polish Texts. In *ACL Workshop Proceedings (BSNLP 2013)*.

Michał Marcińczuk, Jan Kocoń, and Maciej Janicki. 2013. Liner2 – a customizable framework for proper names recognition for Poli. In Robert Bembenik, Lukasz Skonieczny, Henryk Rybinski, Marzena Kryszkiewicz, and Marek Niezgodka, editors, *Intelligent Tools for Building a Scientific Information Platform*, pages 231–253.

Marek Maziarz, Maciej Piasecki, Ewa Rudnicka, and Stanisław Szpakowicz. 2013. Beyond the transfer-and-merge wordnet construction: plwordnet and a comparison with wordnet. In *Proc. RANLP*, pages 443–452.

Paweł Mazur. 2012. *Broad-Coverage Rule-Based Processing of Temporal Expressions*. Ph.D. thesis, Politechnika Wrocławska.

Shoji Mizobuchi, Toru Sumitomo, Masao Fuketa, and Jun-ichi Aoe. 1998. A method for understanding time expressions. In *Systems, Man, and Cybernetics, 1998. 1998 IEEE International Conference on*, volume 2, pages 1151–1155 vol.2, Oct.

Maciej Piasecki, Marek Maziarz, Stanisław Szpakowicz, and Ewa Rudnicka. 2014. Plwordnet as the cornerstone of a toolkit of lexico-semantic resources. In *Proc. 7th International Global Wordnet Conference*, pages 304–312.

James Pustejovsky, Bob Ingria, Roser Sauri, Jose Castano, Jessica Littman, Rob Gaizauskas, Andrea Setzer, Graham Katz, and Inderjeet Mani. 2005a. The specification language timeml. *The language of time: A reader*, pages 545–557.

James Pustejovsky, Robert Knippen, Jessica Littman, and Roser Saurí. 2005b. Temporal and event information in natural language text. *Language Resources and Evaluation*, 39(2-3):123–164.

Estela Saquete, Rafael Muñoz, and Patricio Martínez-Barco. 2003. Terseo: Temporal expression resolution system applied to event ordering. In Václav Matoušek and Pavel Mautner, editors, *Text, Speech and Dialogue*, volume 2807 of *Lecture Notes in Computer Science*, pages 220–228. Springer Berlin Heidelberg.

Roser Saurí, Jessica Littman, Robert Gaizauskas, Andrea Setzer, and James Pustejovsky. 2006. TimeML annotation guidelines, version 1.2.1.

Bethard Steven. 2013. Cleartk-timeml: A minimalist approach to tempeval 2013. pages 10–14.

Jannik Strötgen, Julian Zell, and Michael Gertz. 2013. Heideltime: Tuning english and developing spanish resources for tempeval-3. In *Second Joint Conference on Lexical and Computational Semantics (*SEM), Volume 2: Proceedings of the Seventh International Workshop on Semantic Evaluation (SemEval 2013)*, pages 15–19, Atlanta, Georgia, USA, June. Association for Computational Linguistics.

Jannik Strötgen and Michael Gertz. 2013. Multilingual and cross-domain temporal tagging. *Language Resources and Evaluation*, 47(2):269–298.

Naushad UzZaman, Hector Llorens, James F. Allen, Leon Derczynski, Marc Verhagen, and James Pustejovsky. 2012. Tempeval-3: Evaluating events, time expressions, and temporal relations. *CoRR*, abs/1206.5333.

Naushad UzZaman, Hector Llorens, Leon Derczynski, Marc Verhagen, James Allen, and James Pustejovsky. 2013. Semeval-2013 task 1: Tempeval-3: Evaluating time expressions, events, and temporal relations. *Atlanta, Georgia, USA*, page 1.

Xiaojin Zhu. 2010. Conditional random fields. CS769 Advanced Natural Language Processing.

Domain Adaptation with Filtering for Named Entity Extraction of Japanese Anime-Related Words

Kanako KOMIYA [1] Daichi EDAMURA [2] Ryuta TAMURA [2]
Minoru SASAKI [1] Hiroyuki SHINNOU [1] Yoshiyuki KOTANI [2]
Ibaraki University [1] Tokyo University of Agriculture and Technology [2]
{kkomiya, msasaki, shinnou}@mx.ibaraki.ac.jp
edaedaichi@gmail.com, {50015646125@st, kotani@cc}.tuat.ac.jp

Abstract

We developed a system to extract Japanese anime-related words, i.e., Japanese NEs (named entities) in the anime-related domain. Since the NEs in the area, such as the titles of anime or the names of characters, were domain-specific, we started by building a tagged corpus and then used it for the experiments. We examined to see if the existing corpora were useful to improve the results. The experiments conducted using Conditional Random Fields showed that the effect of domain adaptation varied according to the genres of the corpora, but the filtering of the source data not only reduced the time for training but also assisted in the domain adaptation work.

1 Introduction

Japanese pop culture such as that exemplified by manga, anime, and gaming has recently gained popularity with the younger generations. They are commercially important; if the NEs (named entities) in the area, such as the titles of the anime and the names of the character could be automatically obtained, they would be useful for the product search, identification, or recommendation. Therefore, we developed a system to extract Japanese NEs in these areas using Conditional Random Fields (CRF). Since the NEs in the area (see Section 3), such as the titles of the anime or the names of the characters, are domain-specific, we build a tagged corpus in the anime domain (see Section 5). We examined to see if the existing corpora were useful with the anime corpus using domain adaptation, since tagging of corpora is time-consuming. The experiments (see Sections 4 and 6) showed that the effect of domain adaptation varied according to the genres of the corpora, but filtering the source data not only reduced the time for training but also asisted in the domain adaptation work. The F-measure was the best when the newspaper and anime corpora were used simultaneously with the domain adaptation after the filtering of the newspaper data (see Section 7).

2 Related Work

Named entity recognition (NER), which involves seeking to locate and classify elements in text into predefined categories, such as the names of people, organizations, and locations, has recently been intensively studied. There are two types of NER methods, i.e., NER using pattern matching and NER using supervised machine learning. NER using pattern matching finds elements in text that match the manually predefined patterns, i.e., the character strings that tend to co-occur with the NEs, e.g., "Mr." or "University" (Takemoto et al., 2001). There are some works on analyzing or creating these patterns; (Lertcheva and Aroonmanakun, 2011) have analyzed the patterns of the product names used in Thai economic news. NER using pattern matching can extract the NEs that precisely match the patterns, but cannot extract the NEs that do not match the patterns. Therefore, it is difficult to use these types of methods in our system because the anime-related NEs such as the titles of an anime often do not match the patterns.

On the other hand, NER using supervised machine learning trains the patterns to extract the NEs using a tagged corpus. (Yamada et al., 2002) have carried out NER using a support vector machine (SVM). (Nakano and Hirai, 2004) have proposed conducting NER using a bunsetsu feature. Considerable achievements have been made using these methods. In addition, the Hidden Markov Model (HMM) and CRF are often used for NER (Ponomareva et al., 2007), (Ekbal and Bandyopadhyay, 2007). (Asahara and Matsumoto, 2004) have also proposed a character-based chunking method to address the unit problem where NER using su-

Proceedings of Recent Advances in Natural Language Processing, pages 291–297,
Hissar, Bulgaria, Sep 7–9 2015.

pervised machine learning in Japanese originally cannot extract NEs that are smaller than morphemes because cascading morphological analysis and chunking is usually used for any NE extraction in Japanese. (An et al., 2003) have automatically collected NE tagged corpora from World Wide Web to alleviate the problem: building corpus is time-consuming.

There are some works on the adaptation of NER. (Shen et al., 2003) have investigated the effective features of a Hidden Markov model-based NE recognizer for the biomedical domain. (Chiticariu et al., 2010) have improved NER rule language (NERL) for the pattern-based domain adaptation of NER. (Guo et al., 2009) have proposed a domain adaptation method using latent semantic association.

We developed a system to extract Japanese anime-related words using machine learning method, i.e., CRF, for this paper. Since our purpose is to use the anime-related words for the product search, identification, or recommendation, we only extracted them and did not automatically classify them into sub-classes. We examined to see if the existing corpora were useful with the corpus that we built using domain adaptation and showed that the filtering of the source data assisted in the domain adaptation work.

3 Definition of Anime-related Words

We defined the anime-related NEs based on Sekine's extended NE hierarchy (Sekine, 2008). The time and numerical representations were removed because they usually do not appear only in anime but also in real life. Place names were also removed because it is difficult to distinguish place names that appear only in anime from those that appear in real life.

We had two kinds of anime-related words: interior and exterior. The former contains the titles of anime and the anime-related NEs that appear in the anime, and the latter is those that do not, such as the animators. Our system covered both of these. The interior anime-related words include the titles of anime, the names of characters, animals, imaginary creatures, gods, organizations, facilities, products, events, natural objects such as stones, and states such as diseases that appear in the anime. The exterior anime-related words include the names of people such as the authors of the original story, animators, and game creators, the names of organizations such as the production companies and broadcasting companies, the names of related products, and the names of relevant sites, related events, and so on. Table 1 lists some examples of the anime-related words.

4 System to Extract Anime-related Words

The CRF was used as a sequential labeling method to extract anime-related words. There are four steps in the extraction of anime-related words:

1. The parameters are learned through the training corpus.
2. When the text is input into the system, the morphological analysis is carried out and the features are automatically generated.
3. Sequential labeling is carried out using CRF based on the generated features.
4. The NEs are extracted with tags.

We used the BIESO tags (B-beginning, I-intermediate, E-end, S-single token concept, O-outside), for the CRF. Five types of feature, i.e., morpheme, Part-of-speech (POS), finer subcategory of POS, character type, and No. of characters were introduced to train the model of the CRF. They were extracted from the surrounding words of the target morpheme. We used the character type as a feature because the Japanese language has many types of characters and it seemed to be related to the ability of the morphemes to be NEs, especially for anime-related words. The values of the types are hiragana, katakana, alphabetical letters, Chinese characters, and others including punctuation marks. We used the type of the initial character of the morpheme for this feature.

5 Data

We used an anime corpus that we built for the experiments. The texts consisted of 50 anime articles from Wikipedia. The morphological analysis was automatically carried out but the errors in the word segmentations and the POS tags of personal names were manually corrected. After that, all the NEs that we defined above were manually annotated. We used the extended NE tagged corpora (Hashimoto et al., 2008), which were based on the Balanced Corpus of Contemporary Japanese (BCCWJ) (Maekawa, 2008), for a reference when we built the corpus.

Detailed conception	Example	Translation or Explanation
Name of animal character	ポチ	Pochi(Dog's name)
Name of special weapon	かめはめ波	Kame Hame Ha
Name of character	宿海仁太	Yadomi Zhinta
Nickname of character	じんたん	Zintan

Table 1: Examples of anime-related words

The anime-related NE tagged BCCWJ were created based on the extended NE tagged corpora on BCCWJ and they were also used for the training data. We investigated to see if they could be used for the training data on their own and could be used with the corpus that we built with and without domain adaptation. Table 2 summarizes the number of characters, morphemes, NEs, and O tags in the anime corpus and the BCCWJ. The number of O tags after filtering, where all the tokens with an O tag outside of the window of the NEs were filtered out, is also itemized in the table. The genres we used in the BCCWJ are Q&A sites, blogs, novels, magazines, and newspapers. Although the POS were manually annotated on the corpora, the morphological analysis was automatically carried out on them when we used them for the training data; the POS tags should be the same as the anime corpus to train the CRF. After that, the morphemes that have NE tags similar to those of the anime corpus were listed. Then, the BIESO tags were automatically annotated on all the morphemes in the BCCWJ, based on their orthography or spelling using the list of NEs. The NE tags that we used were Product_Other, Character, Doctrine_Method_Other, Company, Broadcast_Program, Occasion_Other, Person, Show_Organization, Movie, Company_group, School, Organization_Other, Country, Music, Offense, Book, National_Language, Event_Other, Class, Food_Other, Corporation_Other, Ethnic_Group_Other, Animal_Disease, Period_Other, Award, Clothing, Magazine, Military, and Name_Other.

Although the NEs that are irrelevant to anime are not tagged on the anime corpus, because they are outside the scope of our research, the BCCWJ contains many of them. Therefore, the anime corpus has many NEs whose POS subcategories are proper name whereas the BCCWJ have many general noun ones.

6 Experiment

CRF++ [1] and MeCab [2] were used as the CRF tool and as a morphological analyzer, respectively. The morphemes were used as tokens in CRF++ and each of the alphabetical words was processed as one token. The parameters *f* and *c* in CRF++ were set to two and one, respectively, according to the results from preliminary experiments.

We used three types of features, i.e., the morphemes, the POS, and the finer subcategory of POS inside a window size of 5, the character type inside a window size of 3, and the number of the characters inside a window size of 1. These window sizes were determined according to the results from preliminary experiments.

Table 3 specifies an example of the tagged anime corpus. The meanings of the morphemes are also shown in the table for reference. If "戦い" (Fight) was the target morpheme, the features within "帝国" (Empire), "と" (Against), "戦い" (Fight), "、" (,). and "未知" (Unknown) are used for the three types of features, the features within "と" (Against), "戦い" (Fight) and, "、" (,) are used for the character type, and the features within "戦い" (Fight) are used for the number of the characters.

We used input-level unigrams, bigrams, trigrams, and 4grams for the POS and the finer subcategories of POS within the window size of 5. However, only the unigrams in the window size of 5 and the bigrams in the window size of 3 were used for the morphemes, because their combination number would be extremely large. The combination of the POS and the finer subcategory of POS of the target morpheme, and the combinations of the previous output and target morpheme were also used in all the experiments. When the character type and the number of characters were used, POS and morpheme combination, and that of the finer subcategory of POS and the morpheme

[1] http://crfpp.googlecode.com/svn/trunk/doc/index.html
[2] http://mecab.googlecode.com/svn/trunk/mecab/doc/index.html

Type	Anime	Q&A site	Blog	Novel	Magazine	Newspaper
Total No. of characters	44,829	177,636	189,474	369,345	388,941	56,2206
Total No. of morphemes	26,948	108,182	116,885	228,721	236,369	353,882
Total No. of NEs	1,570	2,202	4,173	5,042	7,758	13,629
NEs of S tag	742	1,282	2,772	3,163	4,409	6,928
NEs of BIE tags	828	920	1,401	1,879	3,349	6,701
O tags	23,824	104,377	109,922	220,753	222,259	327,939
O tags after filtering	No filtering	7,792	14,013	18,228	27,080	47,324

Table 2: No. of characters, morphemes, NEs, and O tags in BCCWJ and anime corpus

of the target morpheme were also used. Five-fold cross validation [3] was used in the experiments.

We examined to see if the existing corpora, the BCCWJ, were useful for extracting anime-related words, and if they were useful for the training data on their own and together with the anime corpus, using domain adaptation. The experiments were carried out without domain adaptation, as a reference. (Daumé III, 2007) was used as the domain adaptation method, where an input space was augmented and general, source-specific, and target-specific triple length features were made. The mappings were $\Phi_s(x) =< x, x, 0 >$, $\Phi_t(x) =< x, 0, x >$, where $\Phi_s(x)$ and $\Phi_t(x)$ denoted the mappings to map the source and target data, respectively, $< x >\in \mathbb{R}^F$ was the original input, and $0 =< 0, 0, ..., 0 >\in \mathbb{R}^F$ was the zero vector.

We also investigated to see if the filtering of the source data, where all the tokens with an O tag outside of the window of the NEs were filtered out, assisted in the domain adaptation work. We assumed the recall would be improved when many tokens with O tags were filtered out.

7 Results

The experimental results, i.e., the tag accuracy, the recall, the precision, and the F-measure, according to the corpora and the filtering on a single corpus are listed in Table 4. The experimental results according to the corpora and the filtering when the anime corpus and BCCWJ were used together with a simple augmentation and using Daumé's method of domain adaptation, respectively, are summarized in Tables 5 and 6. The results in bold denote the results that were superior to those of the system trained using only the anime corpus and the underline means the value is the best result overall.

The recall, precision, and F-measure were evaluated based on chunks. In other words, the NEs with a BIE tag are correct only if all the tags from the initial B to the last E in the chunk are correct. The tag accuracy is the number of correct tags in the total number of tags.

8 Discussion

First, let us focus on the results with no filtering. The results listed in Table 4 show that the recalls are very low and the precisions are not very good when the BCCWJ are used for the training on their own. According to Table 5, when the BCCWJ and anime corpus are used together using simple augmentation, the recalls are not very good but the precisions are comparable to (The average is slightly better than) the results when using only the anime corpus. Finally, the results in Table 6 show that the recalls are slightly better than and the precisions are slightly worse than the results when only the anime corpus is used. However, the averaged F-measure is slightly worse than that of the anime corpus. These results show that the domain adaptation slightly improved the recalls and reduced the level of precision and that the F-measures did not change very much.

Next, let us consider the experimental results when using the filtering. The results in Table 4 show that the recalls greatly improved but the precisions considerably decreased when the filtering was used. We think this is because many tokens with O tags were deleted; it makes the system extract more NEs. We can see from Table 5 that the situation is almost the same, when the corpora are used together with the simple augmentation: the recalls improved but the precision decreased when the filtering was used, which has no effect on the F-measures. According to Table 6, the improvement of the recalls is not very large

[3] The full source corpus and the four fifth anime corpus were used for the training and the rest one fifth anime corpus was used for the test.

Meaning	Morpheme	POS	Finer subcategory of POS	Char. type	N of Chars	Tag
Yamato	ヤマト	Noun	Proper name-organization	Katakana	3	S
Topic-marking	は	Particle	Linking particle	Hiragana	1	o
Gamirasu	ガミラス	Noun	General	Katakana	4	B
Empire	帝国	Noun	General	Chinese	2	E
Against	と	Particle	Case-marking-general	Hiragana	1	o
Fight	戦い	Verb	Independent word	Chinese	2	o
,	、	Mark	Punctuation	Punctuation	1	o
Unknown	未知	Noun	General	Chinese	2	o
Of	の	Particle	Adnominalize	Hiragana	1	o
Universe	宇宙	Noun	General	Chinese	2	o
Space	空間	Noun	General	Chinese	2	o
In	における	Particle	Case-marking-collocation	Hiragana	4	o
Obstacle	障害	Noun	General	Chinese	2	o
Object-marking	を	Particle	Case-marking-general	Hiragana	1	o
Overcome	乗り越え	Verb	Independent word	Chinese	4	o

Table 3: Example of tagged anime corpus

Filtering	Corpora	Tag accuracy	Recall	Precision	F-measure
No	Anime	94.92%	68.47%	84.65%	75.70%
No	Q&A site	91.59%	33.95%	70.88%	45.91%
No	Blog	92.19%	42.80%	77.42%	55.13%
No	Novel	93.16%	48.28%	82.93%	61.03%
No	Magazine	93.50%	48.47%	**86.18%**	62.05%
No	Newspaper	92.64%	46.31%	76.69%	57.74%
No	Avg.	92.62%	43.96%	78.82%	56.37%
Yes	Q&A site	78.76%	**72.04%**	26.57%	38.82%
Yes	Blog	81.36%	**77.13%**	30.95%	44.17%
Yes	Novel	93.07%	**80.45%**	30.20%	60.45%
Yes	Magazine	83.19%	<u>**80.83%**</u>	32.29%	46.15%
Yes	Newspaper	81.76%	**76.11%**	30.23%	43.27%
Yes	Avg.	81.36%	**77.31%**	30.05%	43.27%

Table 4: Experimental results according to corpora and filtering on single corpus

Filtering	Corpora	Tag accuracy	Recall	Precision	F-measure
No	Q&A	94.55%	62.80%	83.56%	71.71%
No	Blog	94.40%	61.85%	84.14%	71.29%
No	Novel	94.36%	61.15%	**85.18%**	71.19%
No	Magazine	94.62%	60.06%	<u>**88.13%**</u>	71.44%
No	Newspaper	94.24%	58.79%	83.08%	68.85%
No	Avg.	94.43%	60.93%	**84.82%**	70.90%
Yes	Q&A	94.21%	**75.10%**	70.85%	72.91%
Yes	Blog	94.70%	**76.43%**	73.22%	74.79%
Yes	Novel	94.33%	**77.96%**	68.88%	73.14%
Yes	Magazine	94.38%	**79.68%**	69.38%	74.18%
Yes	Newspaper	93.75%	**78.09%**	66.20%	71.65%
Yes	Avg.	94.28%	**77.45%**	69.71%	73.33%

Table 5: Experimental results according to corpora and filtering using simple augmentation

Filtering	Corpora	Tag accuracy	Recall	Precision	F-measure
No	Q&A	**94.99%**	**69.17%**	83.73%	**75.76%**
No	Blog	**94.95%**	**69.36%**	83.26%	75.68%
No	Novel	**94.95%**	**68.98%**	83.63%	75.60%
No	Magazine	94.80%	68.09%	83.19%	74.89%
No	Newspaper	94.89%	**69.11%**	83.59%	75.66%
No	Avg.	94.92%	**68.94%**	83.48%	75.52%
Yes	Q&A	**94.95%**	**69.30%**	83.95%	**75.92%**
Yes	Blog	**95.01%**	**68.92%**	83.42%	75.48%
Yes	Novel	**95.00%**	**69.55%**	83.94%	**76.07%**
Yes	Magazine	**95.11%**	**69.62%**	84.53%	**76.35%**
Yes	Newspaper	**95.08%**	**70.13%**	83.92%	**76.41%**
Yes	Avg.	**95.03%**	**69.50%**	83.95%	**76.05%**

Table 6: Experimental results according to corpora and filtering using domain adaptation

but the decrease in the level of precision is also not very large, because the degree of improvement increased and the degree of decrease lessened when using the filtering. However, the F-measures improved. These results show that the filtering with domain adaptation could improve the recalls while not affecting the level of precision too much.

Method	Filtering	S	BIE
Original	No	436.8	436.2
Original	Yes	2,279.0	1,768.0
Simple aug.	No	589.6	538.8
Simple aug.	Yes	883.4	863.6
DA	No	658.0	638.6
DA	Yes	663.6	636.2

Table 7: Averaged number of NEs that system output

As described above, the filtering made the system extract more NEs. Table 7 lists the averaged number of the NEs that the system extracted. The filtering did not affect the number of NEs that the system output when domain adaptation was used, but the numbers of correct answers increased by the filtering.

The results in Tables 4, 5, and 6 show that only the systems using domain adaptation can outperform the system trained using only the anime corpus. In addition, the results in Table 6 show that the effect of the domain adaptation varies according to the genre of the corpora; only the Q&A site data could improve the F-measure of the system without filtering. However, the other results in this table show that four-fifths of the system improved the F-measures. The F-measure was the best when the newspaper and anime corpora were used together using the domain adaptation after the newspaper data was filtered.

Finally, the filtering has another advantage: the time for training, which was reduced to only 15% of that of the system trained with full corpora.

9 Conclusion

We developed a system to extract Japanese anime-related words using CRF and examined to see if the corpora whose genre were not anime were useful for improving the results. We investigated to see if they could be used for the training data on their own and could be used with the anime corpus that we built with and without domain adaptation. We also examined to see if the filtering of the source data, where all the tokens with an O tag outside of the window of the NEs were filtered out, assisted the domain adaptation work. The experiments showed that (1) the non-anime corpora could improve the F-measure when they were used with the anime corpus using only domain adaptation, (2) the effect of the domain adaptation varies according to the genre of the corpora, and (3) the domain adaptation with the filtering improved the recalls without effecting the level of precision too much, which improved the F-measure. Moreover, the training time was reduced to only 15% of that of the system trained with full corpora.

Acknowledgment

We thank Mr. Masaki TAKASE, who built the annime corpus and developed a baseline system. This work was partially supported by JSPS KAKENHI Grant Number 24700138.

References

Joohui An, Seungwoo Lee, and Gary Geunbae Lee. 2003. Automatic acquisition of named entity tagged corpus from world wide web. In *Proc. of ACL'03*, pages 165–168.

Masayuki Asahara and Yuji Matsumoto. 2004. A word unit problem in japanese named entity extraction. *IPSJ Journal (In Japanese)*, Vol. 45(No. 5):1442–1450.

Laura Chiticariu, Rajasekar Krishnamurthy, Yunyao Li, Frederick Reiss, and Shivakumar Vaithyanathan. 2010. Domain adaptation of rule-based annotators for named-entity recognition tasks. In *Proceedings of the 2010 Conference on EMNLP*, pages 1002–1012.

Hal Daumé III. 2007. Frustratingly easy domain adaptation. In *Proceedings of the 45th Annual Meeting of the Association of Computational Linguistics*, pages 256–263.

Asif Ekbal and Sivaji Bandyopadhyay. 2007. A hidden markov model based named entity recognition system: Bengali and hindi as case studies. In *Proceedings of the 2nd international conference on Pattern recognition and machine intelligence*, pages 545–552.

Honglei Guo, Huijia Zhu, Zhili Guo, Xiaoxun Zhang, Xian Wu, and Zhong Su. 2009. Domain adaptation with latent semantic association for named entity recognition. In *Proceedings of the 2009 Annual Conference of the NAACL*, pages 281–289.

Taiichi Hashimoto, Takashi Inui, and Koji Murakami. 2008. Constructing extended named entity annotated corpora. In *IPSJ SIG Notes 2008 (In Japanese)*, pages 113–120.

Nattadaporn Lertcheva and Wirote Aroonmanakun. 2011. Product name identification and classification in thai economic news. In *Proc. of IJCNLP 2011 Named Entities Workshop*, pages 58–61.

Kikuo Maekawa. 2008. Balanced corpus of contemporary written japanese. In *Proceedings of the 6th Workshop on Asian Language Resources (ALR)*, pages 101–102.

Keigo Nakano and Yuzo Hirai. 2004. Japanese named entity extraction with bunsetsu features. *IPSJ Journal (In Japanese)*, Vol. 45(No. 3):934–941.

Natalia Ponomareva, Paolo Rosso, Ferran Pla, and Antonio Molina. 2007. Conditional random fields vs. hidden markov models in a biomedical named entity recognition task. In *Proceedings of the Recent Advances in Natural Language Processing 2007*, pages 1–7.

Satoshi Sekine. 2008. Extended named entity ontology with attribute information. In *Proceedings of the 5th International Conference on Language Resources and Evaluation*, pages 52–57.

Dan Shen, Jie Zhang, Guodong Zhou, Jian Su, and Chew-Lim Tan. 2003. Effective adaptation of a hidden markov model-based named entity recognizer for biomedical domain. In *Proceedings of the Whorkshop on NLP Bionmedicine, ACL*, pages 49–56.

Yoshikazu Takemoto, Toshikazu Fukushima, and Hiroshi Yamada. 2001. A japanese named entity extraction system based on building a large-scale and high-quality dictionary and pattern-matching rules. *IPSJ Journal (In Japanese)*, Vol. 42(No. 6):1580–1591.

Hiroyasu Yamada, Taku Kudo, and Yuji Matsumoto. 2002. Japanese named entity extraction using support vector machine. *IPSJ Journal (In Japanese)*, Vol. 43(No. 1):44–53.

Feature Extraction for Native Language Identification Using Language Modeling

Vincent Kríž, Martin Holub, Pavel Pecina
Charles University in Prague
Faculty of Mathematics and Physics
Institute of Formal and Applied Linguistics
{kriz, holub, pecina}@ufal.mff.cuni.cz

Abstract

This paper reports on the task of Native Language Identification (NLI). We developed a machine learning system to identify the native language of authors of English texts written by non-native English speakers. Our system is based on the language modeling approach and employs cross-entropy scores as features for supervised learning, which leads to a significantly reduced feature space. Our method uses the SVM learner and achieves the accuracy of 82.4 % with only 55 features. We compare our results with the previous similar work by Tetreault et al. (2012) and analyze more details about the use of language modeling for NLI. We experiment with the TOEFL11 corpus (Blanchard et al., 2013) and provide an exact comparison with results achieved in the *First Shared Task in NLI* (Tetreault et al., 2013).

1 Introduction

We present a system for identifying the native language (L1) of a writer based solely on a sample of their writing in a second language (L2). In this work we focus on English as the second language.

According to the weak Contrastive Analysis Hypothesis (Lado, 1957), speakers and writers of the same L1 can sometimes be identified by similar L2 errors. These errors may be a result of linguistic interference. Common tendencies of a speaker's L1 are superimposed onto their L2. Native Language Identification (NLI) is an attempt to exploit these errors in order to identify the L1 of the speaker from texts written in L2. In the present study we approach NLI exclusively as a classification task where the set of the L1 languages is known a priori.

1.1 Motivation and Possible Applications

The NLI task is a quickly growing subfield in NLP. The task is motivated by two types of questions:

1. questions about the native language influence in non-native speakers' speech or writing, and
2. questions about the accuracy of the NLI classification that is achievable, which also includes the technical details of the classification systems.

Native Language Identification can be used in educational settings. It can provide useful feedback to language learners about their errors. Smith and Swan (2001) showed that speakers of different languages make different kinds of errors when learning a foreign language. A system which can detect the L1 of the learner will be able to provide more targetted feedback about the error and contrast it with common properties of the learner's L1.

The knowledge of the native language can be used as a feature for authorship analysis (Stamatatos, 2009). The plethora of available electronic texts (e.g., e-mail messages, online forum messages, blogs, source code, etc.) presents the potential of authorship analysis in various applications including criminal law (e.g., identifying writers of harassing messages, verifying the authenticity of suicide notes), civil law (e.g., copyright disputes), and forensic linguistics. In the end, it includes the traditional applications to literary research (e.g., attributing anonymous or disputed literary works to known authors). Bergsma et al. (2012) consider the NLI task as a sub-task of the authorship analysis task.

Relatively similar to NLI is the task of Language Variety Identification. It has been recently addressed by the research community (Zampieri and Gebre, 2012; Sadat et al., 2014; Maier and Gómez-Rodríguez, 2014).

Proceedings of Recent Advances in Natural Language Processing, pages 298–306,
Hissar, Bulgaria, Sep 7–9 2015.

2 Related Work

2.1 Known Approaches to the Task

Most researchers use a system involving the Support Vector Machines (SVM) trained on n-gram based features. The most common features include character n-grams, function words, parts of speech, spelling errors, and features of writing quality, such as grammatical errors, style markers, and so forth.

In contrast, Swanson and Charniak (2012) introduced the Tree Substitution (TSG) structures, learned by Bayesian inference. Bykh et al. (2013) used recurring n-grams, inspired by the variation n-gram approach to corpus error annotation detection (Dickinson and Meurers, 2003). Ionescu et al. (2014) propose a combination of several string kernels and use multiple kernel learning. Malmasi and Cahill (2015) provide a systematic study of feature interaction and propose a function to measure feature independence effectiveness.

The most important related work is the recent paper by Tetreault et al. (2012), which was, to our best knowledge, the first extensive study involving the use of language modeling and entropy-based features for the sake of NLI. The comparison with our work is summarized in Sections 5.4 and 6.

2.2 Results Achieved on the ICLE Corpus

Studies before 2012 experimented with the texts included in the International Corpus of Learner English (ICLE) (Granger et al., 2002). Since the ICLE corpus was not designed with the task of NLI in mind, the usability of the corpus for this task is further compromised by idiosyncrasies in the data such as topic bias.

The highest NLI accuracy was 90.1%, which was reported by Tetreault et al. (2012). The authors used a system involving SVM with the L1-regularized logistic regression solver and default parameters. The system reported in the study by Tetreault et al. (2012) classified between seven L1s. The reported accuracy is higher than any of the previous NLI studies that examined the same number (Bykh et al., 2013) or even a smaller number of L1s in the ICLE.

The ensemble method used by Tetreault et al. (2012) involved the creation of separate classifier models for each category of features; the L1 affiliations of individual texts were later predicted by the combined probabilities produced by the different classifier models. The authors pointed out that combining all features into a single classifier gave them an NLI accuracy of only 82.6%, which falls far short of the 90.1 % they achieved through the ensemble method.

The study by Jarvis and Paquot (2012) presents a system that examines 12 L1s in the ICLE. Their system uses a combination of features that includes only lexical n-grams (1-grams, 2-grams, 3-grams, and 4-grams). The system provides the highest classification accuracy of only 53.6 %.

2.3 The First NLI Shared Task (2013)

The First Native Language Identification Shared Task (Tetreault et al., 2013), henceforth the Shared Task, was intended to unify the community and help the field progress. Tetreault et al. (2013) report the methods most participants used, the data they evaluated their systems on, the results achieved by the different teams, and some suggestions and ideas about what we can do for the next iteration of the NLI shared task.

The Shared Task used the new corpus TOEFL11 (Blanchard et al., 2013) designed specifically for the NLI task and provided a common set of L1s as well as evaluation standards for this competition. This allows a direct comparison of approaches. The corpus was published by the Linguistic Data Consortium[1] in 2014.

The Shared Task consisted of three sub-tasks. We consider our system to be a part of the *Closed* sub-task, which is the 11-way classification task using only the TOEFL11 data for training. Although we use English texts from the Wikipedia to build the language model of general English, this common data are not connected with the task.

In total, 29 teams competed in the Shared Task competition. The majority of teams used Support Vector Machines. The teams used ensemble methods for combining their classifiers. There were a few other teams that tried different methods, such as Maximum Entropy, Discriminant Function Analysis, and K-Nearest Neighbors. The most successful approaches are reported and compared with our system in Table 5.

In this work we experiment with exactly the same data, using the same cross-validation splits as the participants of the Shared Task, so we can provide the exact comparison with the published results.

[1] `https://catalog.ldc.upenn.edu/LDC2014T06`

3 Development Data

3.1 Basic Characteristics of the TOEFL11

The TOEFL11 corpus (Blanchard et al., 2013) contains 12,100 essays uniformly balanced between 11 target L1 languages. In addition, it is sampled as evenly as possible from 8 topics (*prompts*) along with 3 *proficiency levels* (low, medium, high) for each essay. The proficiency level has been determined by assessment experts using a consistent rating procedure for the entire corpus. The 11 target L1 languages covered by the corpus are: Arabic (ARA), Chinese (CHI), French (FRE), German (GER), Hindi (HIN), Italian (ITA), Japanese (JAP), Korean (KOR), Spanish (SPA), Telugu (TEL), and Turkish (TUR).

The number of essays per target L1 language is perfectly balanced. It is also almost perfectly balanced in relation to the prompts written about. All eight prompts are reflected in all target L1 languages. For 4 target languages (ARA, CHI, JAP, KOR), all prompts are almost equally represented with a proportion of approximately 12.5% per prompt. In other L1s, there is more variability. The distribution of the proficiency levels is even more variable. In conclusion, the TOEFL11 is not a perfectly balanced corpus, but it is much larger than the ICLE and involves fewer prompts, which are more evenly distributed across the L1 groups.

3.2 Experiment Settings

For the purposes of the Shared Task, the corpus was split into three sets: training (TOEFL11-TRAIN), development (TOEFL11-DEV), and test (TOEFL11-TEST). The training corpus consisted of 900 essays per L1, the development set consisted of 100 essays per L1, and the test set consisted of another 100 essays per L1. The Shared Task organizers asked the participants to perform 10-fold cross-validation on a data set consisting of the union of TOEFL11-TRAIN and TOEFL11-DEV. For a direct comparison with the Shared Task participants, we experiment with the same folds as in the competition.

4 Feature Engineering

We define a small set of cross-entropy based features computed over different language models, which leads to significant reduction of the usual feature space based on n-grams. The features are then used by a SVM classifier.

4.1 Use of Language Modeling

Our system is inspired by Moore and Lewis (2010). They show how to select a good subset of the available data as a training portion for a language model that improves the match between the language model from that data source and the desired application output. In their work they score text segments by the difference of the cross-entropy of a text segment according to the in-domain language model compared to the cross-entropy of the text segment according to a language model trained on a random sample of the data source from which the text segment is drawn. The introduced cross-entropy difference selection method produces language models that are both a better match to texts in a restricted domain and require less data for training than any of the other data selection methods tested.

Moreover, Axelrod et al. (2011) reported an improvement of their end-to-end machine translation system using domain adaptation based on extracting sentences from a large general-domain parallel corpus that are most relevant to the target domain selected with simple cross-entropy based methods.

4.2 Cross-entropy Scoring

We apply the idea of scoring texts by the difference in cross-entropy and developed the system for classifying target L1 languages. We built 11 special language models of English, each based on the texts with the same L1 language available in the training data. To compare these special language models with general English, we have built a general language model of English, using Wikipedia. Then we use cross-entropy to measure the similarity between a given test instance and target L1 languages. These cross-entropy scores then serve as features for the SVM classifier.

Formally, the cross-entropy of text t with empirical n-gram distribution p given a language model M with distribution q is

$$\mathsf{H}(t, M) = -\sum_{x} p(x) \log q(x).$$

For each L1 to be classified ($\mathcal{L}_1, \ldots, \mathcal{L}_{11}$) we built a language model M_i. We also built a model of general English M_G. Then we define the *normalized cross-entropy score*:

$$D_G(t, M_i) = \mathsf{H}(t, M_i) - \mathsf{H}(t, M_G).$$

In the subsequent machine learning process, the scores $D_G(t, M_i)$, for $i = 1, \ldots, 11$, are used as elements of the feature vector describing text t. The usage of the language model of general English is motivated by the idea that we are interested only in text features which distinguish author's L2 language (i.e. his or her specific English) from other authors with different L1 languages. Correct language constructions typically occurring in general English are removed from the comparison.

4.3 Computing the L1 Language Models

To build the L1 language models M_i with as many training data as possible, we used the *leave-one-out* method.

Let t_i be the i-th training instance and $gs(t_i)$ is the true L1 of text t_i. To calculate the cross-entropy for the instance t_i, using the language model for language $\mathcal{L}_j \neq gs(t_i)$, we built the model M_j using all available training instances t_k such that $gs(t_k) = \mathcal{L}_j$.

To calculate the cross-entropy for the instance t_i, using the language model for language $\mathcal{L}_j = gs(t_i)$, we built M_j using all available training instances t_k except the instance t_i itself: $t_k, \mathcal{L}_j = gs(t_i), k \neq i$.

Because of this approach, the cross-entropy scores proposed in Section 4.2, are only approximate. Each cross-entropy was computed with respect to a slightly different vocabulary, resulting in a different out-of-vocabulary (OOV) rate. OOV tokens in the scoring text were excluded from the computation, so the measurements are not strictly comparable.

We believe that this drawback is reasonable: (1) it allows us to compute scores for all training instances, and (2) we do not have to split the training data into two parts – one for building the language model and the other for the cross-entropy calculation.

4.4 Language Model of General English

We built a language model of general English M_G using Wikipedia. The official Wikipedia dumps contain a lot of technical pages and it is not straightforward to extract meaningful sentences and portions useful for language modeling. In order to avoid the duplication of the laborious efforts, we gratefully used the project TC Wikipedia[2] provided by Artiles and Sekine (2009).

[2] `http://nlp.cs.nyu.edu/wikipedia-data/`

4.5 Cross-entropy Based Features

We adopted and experimented with all successful feature families used in the previous works reported in Section 2.

For each feature family, we defined 11 cross-entropy scores derived from the 11 language models coresponding to the 11 target L1 languages.

- **Tokens (T)**. Token based language model.
- **Characters (C)**. Character based language model.
- **Suffixes (S_n)**. Language models built on token suffixes of the length $n \in \{2, ..., 6\}$.
- **POS tags (P)**. Language model built on POS tags. We tagged the TOEFL11 corpus as well as the whole Wikipedia by the Stanford tagger (Toutanova et al., 2003).

For each feature family we built and compared the performance of two language models: one from the original text, and the other using the same, but lower-cased text. Moreover, we experimented with and compared different smoothing methods, as described in details in Section 5.2.

4.6 Other features

To complete the list of feature families, we added 9 statistical **(ST)** and two categorical **(PR)** features:

Text length characteristics include the number of sentences, number of tokens and number of characters for the given instance. It also includes the average sentence length (# of tokens / # of sentences) and average token length (# of characters / # of tokens).

Lexical variety family includes the number of unique tokens (in the original as well as the lower-cased text) and the so called *lexical variety*. It is defined as the ratio between a unique number of tokens and the overall number of tokens in the classified instance. We provide two features for both the original and the lower-cased text.

Prompt and proficiency (PR) are two categorical features available for each TOEFL11 instance, which encode the topic of the essay and the proficiency level of the writer, respectively.

5 Results and Discussion

The experiments presented in this paper represent the results of exploring a range of various features and machine learning approaches. We describe

Smoothing method	Maximum n-gram order 3	4	5	6	7	8
Witten and Bell (1991)	61.3	61.8	61.8	61.9	62.0	62.0
Witten and Bell (1991)*	65.8	66.4	66.4	66.3	66.3	66.2
Ristad (1995)	69.6	69.7	69.6	69.7	69.6	69.8
Chen and Goodman (1996)	56.8	58.5	58.8	68.8	59.0	59.0
Kneser and Ney (1995)	59.0	60.6	61.0	61.2	61.2	61.3
Kneser and Ney (1995)*	77.5	77.8	77.8	77.9	77.9	77.9

Table 1: The influence of different smoothing methods and n-gram ranges (from [1,3] to [1,8]) on the system accuracy. Each system uses 11 cross-entropy based features over token based language models.

ID	Feature family	Maximum n-gram order 3	4	5	6	7	8
C	Characters	61.4	70.5	73.0	74.1	74.6	74.9
S_2	Suffixes (2)	68.8	68.4	68.3	68.3	68.3	68.2
S_3	Suffixes (3)	73.6	73.2	73.2	73.2	73.1	73.0
S_4	Suffixes (4)	75.5	75.3	75.4	75.5	75.4	75.4
S_5	Suffixes (5)	77.1	76.9	77.2	77.1	77.1	77.1
S_6	Suffixes (6)	77.7	77.8	77.8	77.8	77.7	77.8
T	Tokens	78.0	78.0	77.9	78.0	77.9	78.0
P	POS tags	53.1	53.2	52.0	50.4	49.1	48.2

Table 2: Accuracy of the system using background language models built on different feature families and n-gram ranges (from [1,3] to [1,8]). Each system uses 11 cross-entropy based features over specified language model.

a number of models and compare: (1) different smoothing methods; (2) performance of different feature families; (3) different n-gram range used by language model; (4) different combinations of feature families.

5.1 SVM Settings

Our most successful system uses a linear SVM multiclass classifier. In our experiments, we did not observe any gain from using either polynomial or RBF kernels. This observation is exactly in line with previous research (see Section 2). The parameter *Cost* was optimized through cross validation.

In this work, the SVM implementation of the R package *e1071*[3] is applied, which is based on the LIBSVM library (Chang and Lin, 2011). To provide a multiclass classifier, we experimented with two common strategies: (i) *one-vs-one* and (ii) *one-vs-all*. The first strategy yields consistently better results.

5.2 Best Smoothing Method

We used the SRILM software[4] (Stolcke, 2002) to build langauge models (LM) as well as to calculate cross-entropy based features. This software offers several smoothing algorithms. Experiments showed that selecting an appropriate smoothing method is essential for model quality. Table 1 presents averaged accuracies from the cross validation over TOEFL11-TRAIN. The token-based LMs are built with different smoothing strategies.

Witten-Bell (Witten and Bell, 1991) and Kneser-Ney smoothing (Kneser and Ney, 1995) currently support *interpolation.* This option causes the discounted n-gram probability estimates at the specified order n to be interpolated with lower-order estimates. This sometimes yields better models with some smoothing methods. In Table 1, interpolated smoothing methods are marked with *.

According to the results from Table 1, we selected the Kneser and Ney (1995) discounting with interpolation as the most successful smoothing al-

[3]http://cran.r-project.org/web/packages/e1071/

[4]http://www.speech.sri.com/projects/srilm/

ID	Feature family	Original	Lower-case
C	Characters	44.4	61.4
S_2	Suffixes (2)	55.9	68.8
S_3	Suffixes (3)	67.4	73.6
S_4	Suffixes (4)	70.3	75.5
S_5	Suffixes (5)	71.7	77.1
S_6	Suffixes (6)	73.2	77.7
T	Tokens	74.6	78.0

Table 3: Accuracy of the system using background language models built on original texts compared with language models built on lower-cased texts.

gorithm and we used it in all next experiments.

5.3 Individual Feature Families

The results presented in this section are averaged accuracies over the 10-fold cross-validation on the combined TOEFL11-TRAIN and TOEFL11-DEV sets. The cross-validation folds were exactly defined by the organizers of the Shared Task. Statistical significance was computed using the corrected resampled (two tailed) t-Test (Nadeau and Bengio, 2003), which is suitable for cross-validation based experiments. The test significance was 0.05.

We experimented with almost all types of n-gram features used by the participants of the Shared Task. For each feature family we built 6 different LMs based on a different n-gram range (from [1,3] to [1,8]).

Table 2 shows the classifier performance using different feature families individually. For each family we selected the most successful n-gram range. We noticed that a higher n-gram order improves only character based features. For other feature families the differences in performance were not statistically significant. In such cases we selected the lowest n-gram order to keep the model as simple as possible.

The accuracies presented in Table 2 were obtained using language models built from the lower-cased texts. Table 3 shows the accuracy improvement based on the lower-case transformation. We consider language models built on original training data to be too sparse. Transformation to lower-case makes the data less sparse and language models more expressive. Each model in Table 3 uses 11 cross-entropy based features. Language models contains n-grams from the range [1, 3].

C	T	S_4	P	PR	ST	Accuracy
x	x	x	x	x	x	82.43 ± 0.5
x	x	x	x	x		82.18 ± 0.8
x	x	x		x		82.16 ± 0.6
	x	x	x	x		81.97 ± 0.5
x	x	x		x	x	81.91 ± 0.6
x	x	x				81.31 ± 0.4
	x	x				81.07 ± 0.5
x	x					80.94 ± 0.7
x		x	x	x	x	78.29 ± 0.7
	x					77.99 ± 0.7

Table 4: Accuracy with confidence intervals of the system using combinations of different feature families, as defined in Section 4.5: C – characters, T – tokens, S_4 – suffixes of length 4, P – POS tags, PR – proficiency, and prompt, ST – statistical features.

5.4 Feature Families Combinations

To obtain the best performance we tried to find out the most successful combination of the proposed feature families. Table 4 shows several interesting combinations.

The individual suffix model achieved best performance with the length of 6 (see Table 2). However, in combination with other families, it finally appeared that the best performance was achieved with the suffixes with the length of 4, which was found using the cross-validation on the training data set. Our hypothesis is that the suffix models with the length greater than 4 are rather similar to the token models, since many tokens have less than 5 characters, which implies that the gain from their combination is quite poor. Therefore the choice of S_4 does not seem to be dependent on the training data set.

The full combination of the feature families consists of 55 features. We wanted to examine whether we could reduce this amount even more. According to Table 4, the most important family is the token feature family. Its removal from the model causes a large decrease in accuracy. On the other hand, the removal of the statistical feature family (ST) and POS tags feature family (P) leads to almost the same system performance.

Our models based only on token- or character-n-grams language models significatly outperform the system reported by Tetreault et al. (2012). Their model based on 5-gram language models reaches 73.9 % accuracy (see Table 3 in the cited

System	# of feat.	Acc.	Approach
Gebre et al. (2013)	-	84.6	n-grams (tokens, characters, POS, spelling errors)
Jarvis et al. (2013)	400,000	84.5	n-grams (tokens, lemmas, POS)
Lynum (2013)	867,479	83.9	n-grams (tokens, characters, suffixes)
Malmasi et al. (2013)	-	82.5	n-grams (tokens, function words, POS, syntactic features)
Our system	**55**	**82.4**	**language models (tokens, characters, POS, suffixes)**
Bykh et al. (2013)	-	82.4	n-grams (tokens, POS, syntactic dependences, suffixes)

Table 5: Final comparison of different NLI systems submitted to the *closed* sub-task. Number of features is not provided for the Shared Task participants who did not specified it in their reports.

paper), while our models with the accuracy between 78 % and 81.3 % are significantly better. Since we do not know all details of their implementation, we can only hypothesize that the big difference in accuracy is mainly due to different smoothing methods used, or perharps due to different computation of the entropic scores.

5.5 Best Shared Task Systems – Comparison

Our experiment settings are perfectly in line with the Shared Task guidelines, so we can directly compare the performance of our system with the best participants of the Shared Task, see Table 5. All the best systems used n-grams of tokens, characters, and POS tags. Two systems (Malmasi et al., 2013; Bykh et al., 2013) used also syntactically based n-grams and function words. The systems differ in the value type provided for n-gram feature vectors. The most successful systems (Gebre et al., 2013; Lynum, 2013) used TF-IDF. Other systems used binary values as well as absolute and relative frequencies.

In fact, all compared systems work with hundreds of thousands of n-gram features. Training models with such a huge number of features requires specific hardware and could be time consuming. Of course, our model also deals with a huge number of n-grams, but are hidden in the language models consisting of smoothed linear combinations of n-grams. All the statistical information extracted and collected when the 11 language models are learned from the training data is finally comprised in a small number of features. The resulting benefit is that the SVM learner then works only with a few already trained and smoothed linear n-gram combinations and in contrast to the other compared models it does not need to learn a huge number of parameters/weights for all n-gram features.

6 Conclusion

We described our system for identifying the native language (L1) of a non-native English writer. Our research was focused on the use of a significantly reduced feature space. The language modeling approach and using cross-entropy scores led to an enormous decrease in the feature space dimension: from hundreds of thousands to 55 features.

In comparison with the recent work by Tetreault et al. (2012), who also examined the use of language models in a similar way, we obtained a better result when using only the features based on language modeling, which is probably due to the fact that (1) we used a different (and for our purpose significantly better) smoothing method, and (2) we succesfully combined several approches to language modeling using different types of n-grams. Another difference is in using our "normalized cross-entropy scores" as features in contrast to their "perplexity scores", the exact effect of which, however, is not known.

We experimented with and combined several feature families and a number of different language models. Cross-validation testing on the TOEFL11 corpus revealed that our best model accuracy is 82.4 % in categorizing essays into 11 L1 languages, which is a result comparable to the state-of-the-art.

Acknowledgements

This research work has been supported by the Czech Science Foundation, grant project no. P103/12/G084, and partially also by SVV project number 260 224. We gratefully thank to our colleagues Barbora Hladká for her useful feedback, and Silvie Cinková for her English corrections. Last but not least, we thank to all anonymous reviewers for their valuable comments.

References

Javier Artiles and Satoshi Sekine. 2009. Tagged and cleaned wikipedia (TC wikipedia). http://nlp.cs.nyu.edu/wikipedia-data/.

Amittai Axelrod, Xiaodong He, and Jianfeng Gao. 2011. Domain adaptation via pseudo in-domain data selection. In *Proceedings of the 2011 Conference on Empirical Methods in Natural Language Processing*, pages 355–362, Edinburgh, United Kingdom. Association for Computational Linguistics.

Shane Bergsma, Matt Post, and David Yarowsky. 2012. Stylometric analysis of scientific articles. In *Proceedings of the 2012 Conference of the North American Chapter of the Association for Computational Linguistics: Human Language Technologies*, NAACL HLT '12, pages 327–337, Stroudsburg, PA, USA. Association for Computational Linguistics.

Daniel Blanchard, Joel Tetreault, Derrick Higgins, Aoife Cahill, and Martin Chodorow. 2013. TOEFL11: A corpus of non-native english. *ETS Research Report Series*, 2013(2):i–15.

Serhiy Bykh, Sowmya Vajjala, Julia Krivanek, and Detmar Meurers. 2013. Combining shallow and linguistically motivated features in native language identification. In *Proceedings of the Eighth Workshop on Innovative Use of NLP for Building Educational Applications*, pages 197–206, Atlanta, Georgia, June. Association for Computational Linguistics.

Chih-Chung Chang and Chih-Jen Lin. 2011. Libsvm: A library for support vector machines. *ACM Trans. Intell. Syst. Technol.*, 2(3):27:1–27:27, May.

Stanley F. Chen and Joshua Goodman. 1996. An empirical study of smoothing techniques for language modeling. In *ACL-96*, pages 310–318, Santa Cruz, CA. ACL.

Markus Dickinson and Walt Detmar Meurers. 2003. Detecting inconsistencies in treebanks. In *Proceedings of TLT*, volume 3, pages 45–56.

Binyam Gebrekidan Gebre, Marcos Zampieri, Peter Wittenburg, and Tom Heskes. 2013. Improving native language identification with TF-IDF weighting. In *Proceedings of the Eighth Workshop on Innovative Use of NLP for Building Educational Applications*, pages 216–223, Atlanta, Georgia, June. Association for Computational Linguistics.

Sylvaine Granger, Estelle Dagneaux, and Fanny Meunier. 2002. *International Corpus of Learner English: Version 1.1; Handbook and CD-ROM*. Pr. Univ. de Louvain, Louvain-la-Neuve.

Radu-Tudor Ionescu, Marius Popescu, and Aoife Cahill. 2014. Can characters reveal your native language? A language-independent approach to native language identification. In Alessandro Moschitti, Bo Pang, and Walter Daelemans, editors, *Proceedings of the 2014 Conference on Empirical Methods in Natural Language Processing, EMNLP 2014, October 25-29, 2014, Doha, Qatar, A meeting of SIGDAT, a Special Interest Group of the ACL*, pages 1363–1373. ACL.

Scott Jarvis and Magali Paquot. 2012. Exploring the role of n-grams in L1 identification. In Scott Jarvis and Scott A. Crossley, editors, *Approaching Language Transfer Through Text Classification: Explorations in the Detectionbased Approach*, Second language acquisition, pages 71–105. Multilingual Matters, Bristol, United Kingdom.

Scott Jarvis, Yves Bestgen, and Steve Pepper. 2013. Maximizing classification accuracy in native language identification. In *Proceedings of the Eighth Workshop on Innovative Use of NLP for Building Educational Applications*, pages 111–118, Atlanta, Georgia, June. Association for Computational Linguistics.

Reinhard Kneser and Hermann Ney. 1995. Improved backing-off for m-gram language modeling. In *In Proceedings of the IEEE International Conference on Acoustics, Speech and Signal Processing*, volume I, pages 181–184, Detroit, Michigan, May.

Robert Lado. 1957. *Linguistics Across Cultures: Applied Linguistics for Language Teachers*. University of Michigan Press.

André Lynum. 2013. Native language identification using large scale lexical features. In *Proceedings of the Eighth Workshop on Innovative Use of NLP for Building Educational Applications*, pages 266–269, Atlanta, Georgia, June. Association for Computational Linguistics.

Wolfgang Maier and Carlos Gómez-Rodríguez. 2014. Language variety identification in spanish tweets. In *Proceedings of the EMNLP'2014 Workshop on Language Technology for Closely Related Languages and Language Variants*, pages 25–35, Doha, Qatar, October. Association for Computational Linguistics.

Shervin Malmasi and Aoife Cahill. 2015. Measuring feature diversity in native language identification. In *Proceedings of the Tenth Workshop on Innovative Use of NLP for Building Educational Applications*, pages 49–55, Denver, Colorado, June. Association for Computational Linguistics.

Shervin Malmasi, Sze-Meng Jojo Wong, and Mark Dras. 2013. Nli shared task 2013: Mq submission. In *Proceedings of the Eighth Workshop on Innovative Use of NLP for Building Educational Applications*, pages 124–133, Atlanta, Georgia, June. Association for Computational Linguistics.

Robert C. Moore and William Lewis. 2010. Intelligent selection of language model training data. In *Proceedings of the ACL 2010 Conference Short Papers*, pages 220–224, Uppsala, Sweden. Association for Computational Linguistics.

Claude Nadeau and Yoshua Bengio. 2003. Inference for the generalization error. *Machine Learning*, 52(3):239–281.

Eric Sven Ristad. 1995. A natural law of succession. *CoRR*, abs/cmp-lg/9508012.

Fatiha Sadat, Farzaneh Kazemi, and Atefeh Farzindar. 2014. Automatic identification of arabic language varieties and dialects in social media. In *Proceedings of the Second Workshop on Natural Language Processing for Social Media (SocialNLP)*, pages 22–27. Association for Computational Linguistics and Dublin City University, 08/2014.

Bernard Smith and Michael Swan. 2001. *Learner English: A teacher's guide to interference and other problems*. Ernst Klett Sprachen.

Efstathios Stamatatos. 2009. A survey of modern authorship attribution methods. *Journal of the American Society for Information Science and Technology*, 60(3):538–556.

Andreas Stolcke. 2002. Srilm-an extensible language modeling toolkit. In *Proceedings International Conference on Spoken Language Processing*, pages 257–286, November.

Benjamin Swanson and Eugene Charniak. 2012. Native language detection with tree substitution grammars. In *Proceedings of the 50th Annual Meeting of the Association for Computational Linguistics (Volume 2: Short Papers)*, pages 193–197. Association for Computational Linguistics.

Joel Tetreault, Daniel Blanchard, Aoife Cahill, and Martin Chodorow. 2012. Native tongues, lost and found: Resources and empirical evaluations in native language identification. In *Proceedings of COLING 2012*, pages 2585–2602. The COLING 2012 Organizing Committee.

Joel Tetreault, Daniel Blanchard, and Aoife Cahill. 2013. A report on the first native language identification shared task. In *Proceedings of the Eighth Workshop on Innovative Use of NLP for Building Educational Applications*, pages 48–57, Atlanta, Georgia, June. Association for Computational Linguistics.

Kristina Toutanova, Dan Klein, Christopher D. Manning, and Yoram Singer. 2003. Feature-rich part-of-speech tagging with a cyclic dependency network. In *Proceedings of the 2003 Conference of the North American Chapter of the Association for Computational Linguistics on Human Language Technology - Volume 1*, NAACL '03, pages 173–180, Stroudsburg, PA, USA. Association for Computational Linguistics.

Ian H. Witten and Thomas C. Bell. 1991. The zero-frequency problem: Estimating the probabilities of novel events in adaptive text compression. *IEEE Transactions on Information Theory*, 37(4):1085–1094.

Marcos Zampieri and Binyam Gebre. 2012. Automatic identification of language varieties: The case of Portuguese. In Jeremy Jancsary, editor, *Proceedings of KONVENS 2012*, pages 233–237. ÖGAI, September. Main track: poster presentations.

Learning Agglutinative Morphology of Indian Languages with Linguistically Motivated Adaptor Grammars

Arun Kumar
Universitat Oberta de Catalunya
akallararajappan@uoc.edu

Lluís Padró
Universitat Politècnica de Catalunya
padro@cs.upc.edu

Antoni Oliver
Universitat Oberta de Catalunya
aoliverg@uoc.edu

Abstract

In this paper an automatic morphology learning system for complex and agglutinative languages is presented. We process complex agglutinative morphology of Indian languages using Adaptor Grammars and linguistic rules of morphology. Adaptor Grammars are a compositional Bayesian framework for grammatical inference, where we define a morphological grammar for agglutinative languages and morphological boundaries are inferred from a corpora of plain text. Once it produces morphological segmentation, regular expressions for orthography rules are applied to achieve final segmentation. We test our algorithm in the case of three complex languages from the Dravidian family and evaluate the results comparing to other state of the art unsupervised morphology learning systems and show significant improvements in the results.

1 Introduction

Morphological processing is an important step for natural language processing systems, specially for morphology-rich or agglutinative languages. In morphological processing a word is segmented in corresponding morphemes that are required for later stages of language processing. Most of the morphological systems are hand-built, which is a time consuming and costly process –e.g. finite state methods based morphology learning (Beesley, 1998). For this reason, least resourced languages lack this important component which act as major hurdle for building NLP systems. Unsupervised learning of morphology is a solution for dealing with this problem. In the case of unsupervised morphology learning systems –refer to (Hammarström and Borin, 2011) for details–, morphology of languages is learned using a corpus of plain text using statistical measures. Unsupervised morphology learning systems produce state-of-the-art results for many languages, such as English and Finnish (Creutz and Lagus, 2005; Goldsmith, 2001). In the case of Dravidian languages, poor results are obtained because of lack of knowledge of orthographical and morphological complexities, such as *Sandhi*, a morpho-phonemic change that happens in boundaries of word or morpheme concatenation.

Our method is a combination of statistical and rule based methods. The orthography related issues are solved by using a set of orthographic rules in the form of finite state transducer, which is rule based and morphological segmentation is achieved using statistical model of morphology based on Adaptor Grammar.

Adaptor Grammars are Bayesian non parametric models that can be used to learn linguistic structures. They are non parametric version of Probabilistic Context Free Grammar (PCFG). It is designed for unsupervised structure learning and successfully used in various natural language processing applications, such as word segmentation. We use Adaptor Grammars to learn model of morphology and once the model produce output we use regular expressions created from morphological rules and orthography to refine the results. The major idea behind the model is as these languages are agglutinated, suffixes are stacked to together to create a large word sequence. It indicates as the length of the word increase more number of morphemes are present in the word. With this intuition we define a model of morphology. We test our system on three major languages from Dravidian family. We choose three highly agglutinative and inflected languages from the family for experimentation such as Tamil, Malayalam and Kannada.

The structure of the paper as follows: In Section 2.1, we briefly discuss morphological prop-

Proceedings of Recent Advances in Natural Language Processing, pages 307–312,
Hissar, Bulgaria, Sep 7–9 2015.

erties and orthography of main languages in Dravidian family that make unsupervised learning difficult. In Section 2.2, we give an informal definition of Adaptor Grammars and inference procedure. In the following Section 4, we give the details of Adaptor Grammar model on Dravidian languages. The details of experiments and data used for experiments are explained in section 5. This section also includes a comparison of results with state of the art systems. Last section concludes the paper with future research directions.

2 Background

2.1 Challenges Related to Dravidian Languages

Dravidian languages are highly agglutinative like Turkish and inflected like Finnish. The major ones of the family are Tamil, Telugu, Kannada and Malayalam. They are major languages of southern part of India having millions of native speakers. In this study we focus on Tamil, Kannada and Malayalam.

These languages use alpha syllabic writing systems in which vowels are represented in the form of dependent symbols to consonant symbols i.e. consonant symbols are ligatures. The vowel symbols also can occur in the atomic form if they are not connected to consonants. For example, in the case of Malayalam (Taylor and Olson, 1995), (ക ka) represents a consonant ligature consisting of (ക് k) and a short vowel (അ a). As these languages use alpha syllabic writing system, symbols are syllables instead of individual characters like in English, and phonological changes occur during the concatenation of morphemes and words, resulting in a change in orthography. This process refereed as *Sandhi changes*. For example (Steever, 1998), in the Tamil word (நரி, nari, *fox*) + (ஆ ā) → (நரிய nariyā, *Is it a fox?*). The syllable (ஆ ā, *(interrogative)*) suffers a change in script and is changed to (யா, Yā).

They also contain large number of diacritics and digraphs. As a result, morpheme boundaries are marked at syllabic level. Dravidian languages are agglutinative and generate long word sequences with orthographic changes. All these languages are highly inflected: nouns inflected with cases, gender, number and post positions. Verbs are inflected with tenses, mood , aspect and gender.

- (எழுத்துப்பூர்வமாக, El̲uttuppūrvamāka, *writing*)
- (പൂർത്തിയാക്കിക്കഴിഞ്ഞു , pūrttiyākkikkal̲iññu, *finished*)

Compounding is another challenge in unsupervised morphology learning of these languages. Dravidian languages can generate a large number of compounds, which can in turn become components of larger compounds (Mohanan, 1986). For example; a compound word from Malayalam (ammāyiamma, *mother-in-law*) is a combination of two stems (ammāyi, *aunt*) and (amma, *mother*).

These languages contain co-compounds and sub-compounds with phonological changes (Inkelas, 2014), Some examples from Malayalam:

- kāṭṭilemaraṁ *forest-tree* (tree forest)
- tīvaṇṭi *fire-vehicle* (train)

Here the word kāṭṭilemaraṁ is a sub-compound since it is a combination of stems (kāṭṭile - *forest*, and maraṁ - *tree*). The word tīvaṇṭi is a co-compound because it contains just a head (vaṇṭi - *vehicle*) and a modifier (tī - *fire*). Named entities and proper names are also inflected and agglutinative with cases and number markers. It becomes more difficult when the named entity is a loaned foreign word. E.g., in Malayalam kampyūṭṭaṟinṟe is the combination of an English word *computer* and Malayalam genitive case marker.

2.2 Adaptor Grammar

An Adaptor Grammar is a 7-tuple $\langle N, W, R, S, \theta, A, C\rangle$, where $\langle N, W, R, S, \theta\rangle$ is a PCFG with a set of non terminals N, a set of terminals W, starting symbol $S \in N$, and a set of rewriting rules R where each $r \in R$ has probability $\theta_r \in \theta$. $A \subseteq N$ is a set of *adapted non terminals*, and C is a vector of adaptors indexed by elements of A, such that C_X is an adaptor for adapted non terminal $X \in A$, that is, C_X is a mapping from the set T_X of sub trees with root X to a base probability distribution H_X, determined by the probabilities of PCFG rules expanding X. Inference on the model is done using Markov Chain Monte Carlo techniques. For technical details see (Johnson et al., 2007)

Various non parametric probabilistic processes can be used as adaptors, like Dirichlet Process. Johnson uses Dirichlet Process as adaptor for word segmentation of Sesotho (Johnson, 2008).

3 Related Work

Recent research in morphology learning has shifted to semi-supervised learning, obtaining better results than fully unsupervised learning, such as (Kohonen et al., 2010a) and (Kohonen et al., 2010b). But In the case of Indian languages unsupervised morphology is rarely applied. As state of the art morphology learning systems give good results in the case of European languages, there are some efforts to test Dravidian languages on these systems. But obtained results are rather poor (Bhat, 2012). These studies give an idea of a rule and statistics based model that can work well on Indian languages. In the case of Adaptor Grammars, they are applied to various NLP tasks such as: Word segmentation (Johnson, 2008), named entity recognition (Elsner et al., 2009), and machine transliteration (Wong et al., 2012).

4 Adaptor Grammars on Dravidian Languages and Inference Procedure

We use a Pitman-Yor process based adaptor (Pitman, 2002) for learning the complex morphology of Dravidian languages. Pitman-Yor process is a stochastic model that can be represented in the form of a Chinese Restaurant Process metaphor. This representation helps to do inference on the model. The Pitman-Yor process is used as an adaptor that means our non terminals are placed with prior distribution, which is Pitman-Yor process.

We define a model similar to (Goldwater et al., 2005), but our model is more complex because they consider that one word is composed of one stem and one suffix, which is not a valid assumption in the case of agglutinative languages. In the case of agglutinative languages, many suffixes can be stacked together to form a word consisting of many morphemes. Considering this factor we define a complex model where a stem can be followed by many suffixes. For instance, an agglutinative word phrase from Malayalam `sansthānaṅṅaḷileānnāṉ` can be represented in a PCFG trees. A PCFG tree can represent any segmentation of a particular word phrase like `san + sthāna + ṅṅaḷil + eānnāṉ`, but we need only the right morpheme segmentation, in this case it is `sansth + ānaṅṅaḷileā + nnāṉ`. Adaptor Grammar enable us to learn these tree fragments and allows to define a general model of morphology. From this we define a general model of the morpheme structure of the languages. We model agglutinative morphology using the following grammar:

$$
\begin{aligned}
&Word \rightarrow Stem \mid Stem\, Suffixes\\
&Stem \rightarrow chars\\
&Suffixes \rightarrow Aspect\\
&Suffixes \rightarrow Tenses\\
&Suffixes \rightarrow Mood\\
&Suffixes \rightarrow Case\\
&Suffixes \rightarrow Gender\\
&Suffixes \rightarrow Gender\, Number\\
&Suffixes \rightarrow Gender\, Case\\
&Suffixes \rightarrow Number\, Case\\
&Gender \rightarrow chars\\
&Number \rightarrow chars\\
&Case \rightarrow chars\\
&Aspect \rightarrow chars\\
&Tenses \rightarrow chars
\end{aligned}
$$

where $chars$ is any sequence of characters, and $Suffixes$ is an adapted non terminal. We place a Pitman-Yor process prior on $Suffixes$ non terminals. So it can be expanded according to rewrite rules and a rule probability defined by the Pitman-Yor Process. $Case$, $Gender$, $Number$, $Tense$ and $Mood$ are adapted non terminals, which represent the morphological variations. Each $Case$, $Gender$, $Number$, $Tense\ Aspect$ and $Mood$ act as a *submorph* as in (Sirts and Goldwater, 2013) and this grammar is similar to compounding grammar described by them. The tree based model can represent all possible segmentation. But we place a Pitman-Yor process on the adapted non terminal $Suffixes$. It enables the expansion of PCFG tree in two ways: one based on the PCFG rule probability, and another based on rule probability sampled from the Pitman-Yor adaptor. Because of the caching property of the Pitman-Yor process, frequent morphemes are clustered together in tables of the Chinese Restaurant process. It also important to note that word morphemes are not completely independent entities, since there are various interdependencies between them. We consider bi-gram dependencies so the grammar we defined above is similar to *Collocation Adaptor Grammar* described in (Johnson, 2008), where terminals are syllables. We use the Metropolis Hasting inference algorithm described in (Johnson and Goldwater, 2009) for the inference procedure.

4.1 Rule Based Transliteration

We use a simple program that handles orthography and *Sandhi* rules. The main idea of the program

	Tamil	Kannada	Malayalam
Token frequency	500K	500 K	500 K
No. Segmented tokens	10K	10K	10K
No. R E expressions	34	62	34
No orthographic rules	89	67	96

Table 1: Corpus information

is to transliterate between native syllabic script in original texts, and phonetic romanized transcript. The program works in both directions, and is used to interface the Adaptor Grammar model with the input/output texts.

For example: an agglutinated Malayalam word phrase അടയാളപ്പെടുത്തുകയായിരുന്നു is converted to corresponding ISO romanized form which is (`aṭayāḷappeṭuttukayāyirunnu`, *have been marked*) to get unique phonological representation. And the unique form is converted to its syllabic structure. It is possible to track the Sandhi changes by converting the script into syllabic form. The changes can be insertion, deletion or substitution of syllables (e.g. മഴ + ആണ് → മഴയാണ്, `maḻayāṇ`, *raining*). When we convert the ISO form of the corresponding word all the syllables that are inserted (യ *y*) and the vowel in atomic form (ആ *ā*). This distinction is important for handling Sandhi.

We created rules for these orthographic conversions. If a syllable indicating vowel is inside the segmentation we transliterate the corresponding syllable to a dependent vowel. Otherwise the vowel symbol in atomic form is produced. Rules handle also consonant digraphs: if two consonants are together with a marker of diacritic syllable we produce a digraph character instead of individual consonants. For example: when a word such as `gujaṟātt` is encountered, we convert the syllable `tt` as ത്ത instead of individual `t` symbols (ത ത).

We apply this conversion rules for two purposes: at first for conversion of orthographic script to syllabic form to fed it to the adaptor sampler and after sampling converting the syllables back to corresponding orthographic scripts.

5 Data and Experiments

For testing our method, we have extracted from Wikipedia and news websites a corpus of five million words of each language, and normalized the fonts to Unicode 6.1 version. The overall corpora was converted to 8-bit extended ASCII transcription using rule based transliteration. The conversion script works as follows: A Malayalam word (e.g. തുരുത്തുകൾ) is converted to `tutarcl`, where Unicode character `ṭ` is converted to ASCII character `t`, which represents a syllable in our internal representation. We keep a single space between syllables. These syllables act as terminals of our PCFG trees. We convert 500K unsegmented tokens of each language as described above. Named entities and proper names are not removed, as they can also be inflected. Then we ran Adaptor Grammar model and inference algorithms for 100 iterations, and the sampled syllables are fed to the transliteration module, which produces the corresponding orthographic form.

For the evaluation of presented algorithms, we have morphologically segmented 10K words of each language[1], which is manually created. The details of corpus used in table presented in the Table 1, The evaluation is based on how well the methods predict the morpheme boundaries and calculated as precision, recall and F-score. Information of data used for experiments is provided in Table 1. We used python suite provided in the morpho-challenge website for evaluation purposes. We also trained as baselines Morfessor[2], Morfessor-CAP[3], and Morepheme++[4] with the same amount of tokens. As these software perform very well for inflected and agglutinative languages, such as Finnish and Turkish. All the software except Morepheme++ trained with 500 K tokens and models are created. The trained models applied to our 10K words in unsegmented form and evaluated the results with their morphological segmentation in orthographic form. In the case of Morpheme++, we ran the software on the 10K test tokens and compared the results with its corresponding morphological segmentation in ortho-

[1] Available in http://anonymized-URL

[2] https://pypi.python.org/pypi/Morfessor

[3] http://www.cis.hut.fi/project/morpho/morfessorcatmap-downloadform.shtml

[4] http://www.hlt.utdallas.edu/~sajib/Morphology-Software-Distribution.html

graphical form as the system is not model based.

The result of the experiment is presented in Table 2. It includes precision (P), recall (R) and F-score (F) based on the morphological segmentation produced in orthographic levels. We have performed a manual analysis of results to understand the improvement in precision and the errors.

- Since our method uses a rule based transliteration module, it handles better the orthography, which is very important. Other systems do not considering the digraphs as single entities, and thus, they wrongly segment the digraphs, resulting in lower performance.
- Also, our system is the only that handles *Sandhi* changes.
- In the case of Kannada all systems show good performance because the language has a smaller amount of digraphs.
- When the word stem is a loaned word, all systems failed to segment it.

6 Conclusion and Future Research

We have presented a semi supervised morphology learning technique that uses Adapter Grammars and linguistic rules. And the result show that a method that is a combination of statistical and rule based method can give better performance than a fully unsupervised method in complex languages. We also show that handling orthography of Indian languages using rules is useful for handling morpho-phonemic complexities. In the future research, we will extend the system to other languages in the Dravidian family such as Tulu and Telugu.

References

Kenneth R Beesley. 1998. Arabic morphology using only finite-state operations. In *Proceedings of the Workshop on Computational Approaches to Semitic languages*, pages 50–57. Association for Computational Linguistics.

Suma Bhat. 2012. Morpheme segmentation for kannada standing on the shoulder of giants. In *24th International Conference on Computational Linguistics*, page 79.

Mathias Creutz and Krista Lagus. 2005. *Unsupervised morpheme segmentation and morphology induction from text corpora using Morfessor 1.0*. Helsinki University of Technology.

Micha Elsner, Eugene Charniak, and Mark Johnson. 2009. Structured generative models for unsupervised named-entity clustering. In *Proceedings of Human Language Technologies: The 2009 Annual Conference of the North American Chapter of the Association for Computational Linguistics*, pages 164–172. Association for Computational Linguistics.

John Goldsmith. 2001. Unsupervised learning of the morphology of a natural language. *Computational linguistics*, 27(2):153–198.

Sharon Goldwater, Mark Johnson, and Thomas L Griffiths. 2005. Interpolating between types and tokens by estimating power-law generators. In *Advances in neural information processing systems*, pages 459–466.

Harald Hammarström and Lars Borin. 2011. Unsupervised learning of morphology. *Computational Linguistics*, 37(2):309–350.

Sharon Inkelas. 2014. *The interplay of morphology and phonology*. Oxford University Press.

Mark Johnson and Sharon Goldwater. 2009. Improving nonparametric Bayesian inference: Experiments on unsupervised word segmentation with Adaptor Grammars. In *naacl09*, pages 317–325.

Mark Johnson, Thomas L. Griffiths, and Sharon Goldwater. 2007. Bayesian inference for PCFGs via Markov chain Monte Carlo. In *naacl07*.

Mark Johnson. 2008. Unsupervised word segmentation for sesotho using adaptor grammars. In *Proceedings of the Tenth Meeting of ACL Special Interest Group on Computational Morphology and Phonology*, pages 20–27. Association for Computational Linguistics.

Oskar Kohonen, Sami Virpioja, and Krista Lagus. 2010a. Semi-supervised learning of concatenative morphology. In *Proceedings of the 11th Meeting of the ACL Special Interest Group on Computational Morphology and Phonology*, pages 78–86. Association for Computational Linguistics.

Oskar Kohonen, Sami Virpioja, Laura Leppänen, and Krista Lagus. 2010b. Semi-supervised extensions to morfessor baseline. In *Proceedings of the Morpho Challenge 2010 Workshop*, pages 30–34.

Karuvannur P Mohanan. 1986. The theory of lexical phonology: Studies in natural language and linguistic theory. *Dordrecht: D. Reidel.*

Jim Pitman. 2002. Combinatorial stochastic processes. Technical report, Technical Report 621, Dept. Statistics, UC Berkeley, 2002. Lecture notes for St. Flour course.

Kairit Sirts and Sharon Goldwater. 2013. Minimally-supervised morphological segmentation using adaptor grammars. *Transactions of the Association for Computational Linguistics*, 1:255–266.

Method	Kannada			Malayalam			Tamil		
	P	R	F	P	R	F	P	R	F
Morfessor-base	67.92	59.02	45.63	38.21	41.59	48.54	41.75	41.59	41.78
Morfessor-CAP	70.32	53.77	62.1	62.64	47.11	53.77	59.48	41.07	44.09
Adaptor Grammar & rule	**73.63**	**59.82**	**66.01**	**65.66**	**54.32**	**59.66**	**53. 10**	**53. 17**	**53.13**
Morepheme ++	40.98	47.17	43.86	64.08	27.12	38.22	30.34	29.88	30.11

Table 2: Results; Compared to state of art systems

Sanford B Steever. 1998. *The Dravidian Languages*. Routledge London.

Insup Taylor and David R Olson. 1995. *Scripts and literacy: Reading and learning to read alphabets, syllabaries, and characters*, volume 7. Springer Science & Business Media.

Sze-Meng Jojo Wong, Mark Dras, and Mark Johnson. 2012. Exploring adaptor grammars for native language identification. In *Proceedings of the 2012 Joint Conference on Empirical Methods in Natural Language Processing and Computational Natural Language Learning*, pages 699–709. Association for Computational Linguistics.

Statistical Sandhi Splitter and its Effect on NLP Applications

Prathyusha Kuncham
Prathyusha.kuncham@gmail.com
IIIT-Hyderabad

Kovida Nelakuditi
nelakuditi.kovida@research.iiit.ac.in
IIIT-Hyderabad

Radhika Mamidi
radhika.mamidi@iiit.ac.in
IIIT-Hyderabad

Abstract

This paper revisits the work of (Kuncham et al., 2015) which developed a statistical sandhi splitter (SSS) for agglutinative languages that was tested for Telugu and Malayalam languages. Handling compound words is a major challenge for Natural Language Processing (NLP) applications for agglutinative languages. Hence, in this paper we concentrate on testing the effect of SSS on the NLP applications like Machine Translation, Dialogue System and Anaphora Resolution and show that the accuracy of these applications is consistently improved by using SSS. We shall also discuss in detail the performance of SSS on these applications.

1 Introduction

Sandhi which has its origin from Sanskrit '*samdhi*' meaning "combination", it refers to a set of morphophonological changes i.e. fusion of final and initial sounds/characters at either morpheme or word boundaries. Sandhi is of two types; (i) Internal sandhi and (ii) External sandhi. "Macdonell, 1926"

Internal Sandhi: It refers to morphophonological changes that occur within a word i.e. across morpheme boundaries. For example, consider an English word "impatient" where /n/ in the negative morpheme "in-" has changed to /m/. This is seen for all the words starting with bilabial sounds that are prefixed with the "in-" morpheme.

External Sandhi: It refers to morphophonological changes that occur across word boundaries. When different words combine to form a compound word, we call it external sandhi. This type of sandhi occurs predominantly in Italian "Absalom et al., 2006" and Dravidian languages.

Ex[1]: 'pUjayyAkA' -> 'pUja'+'ayyAkA'
after having finished the prayer *prayer* *finished*

Here, we can observe the morphophonological change (a -> a + a) at the word boundaries.

"Kuncham et al., (2015) handled one type of external sandhi that is prominent in many agglutinative languages and poses many challenges to NLP applications as seen below."

Machine Translation

akkaDikeLLu -> akkaDiki + veLLu
go there *there* *go*

When 'akkaDikeLLu' is given as input to Google "Telugu to English" Translate, it could not analyze the input and the English translation was 'Akkadikellu' which is wrong. But if the compound word is split and then given as input, Google Translate gave correct translation as 'Go there'.

Anaphora Resolution

nEnoccAnu -> nEnu + vaccAnu
I came *I* *came*

For the proper functioning of the Anaphora Resolution system, it is important to identify the pronoun 'nEnu' *(I)* in the input which is only possible by splitting the input.

Dialogue System

raMgEmiTi -> raMgu + EmiTi
what is the color *color* *what*

If the compound word is given as input to a Dialogue system, it is very important to identify the question word 'EmiTi' *(what)* to give the correct answer.

From the above examples, we can see the importance of sandhi splitter in NLP applications. In this paper we show the performance and the effect of SSS on three NLP systems namely, (i) Telugu-English Machine Translation system, (ii) Dialogue System for 'Tourism' domain in Telugu and (iii) Anaphora Resolution system for Telugu.

[1] All the examples are from Telugu language.

Proceedings of Recent Advances in Natural Language Processing, pages 313–319,
Hissar, Bulgaria, Sep 7–9 2015.

2 Related Work

Previous efforts on sandhi splitting primarily concentrated on building rule based systems to identify different words in the compound word. "Nair and Peter (2011) developed rules to identify all possible splits in any compound word i.e. both external and internal sandhi in Malayalam, an agglutinative language." "Joshi Shripad, (2012) implemented a rule based algorithm to split compound words into meaningful subwords in Marathi."

Apart from the traditional rule based systems, there are statistical systems for sandhi splitting as well. "Vempaty and Nagalla (2011) proposed a method using simple finite state automata for finding possible words in a given compound word." Finite state transducer (FST) is built from the syllables of base words and is used to identify possible candidates for a compound word. This approach fails for out-of-vocabulary (OOV) words i.e. if base word of any compound word doesn't exist in the FST. "Kuncham et al., (2015) built a statistical sandhi splitter (SSS) which identifies and generates meaningful words in a compound word using conditional random fields (CRFs)." "Natarajan and Charniak (2011) used statistical methods like Dirichlet Process and Gibbs Sampling for Sanskrit sandhi splitting."

In the recent years, the use of hybrid systems is increasing. Hybrid systems combine both statistical and rule based techniques. "Devadath, (2014) identifies split point statistically and uses character level rules specific to language to split the compound word accordingly."

"Popović et al., (2006) and Macherey et al., (2011) have discussed the challenges faced in machine translation due to compound words and handled compound words within the machine translation task." To the best of our knowledge, no one has shown the effect of sandhi splitting on various NLP applications.

In this paper, we discuss the effect of SSS (which gives better performance than the existing systems in Telugu language) on three different NLP applications i.e. Machine Translation, Anaphora Resolution and Dialogue System in Telugu. The results show that the performance of these systems is better after adopting SSS.

3 Statistical Sandhi Splitter (SSS)

In agglutinative languages, it is a common phenomenon to combine different words to form a compound word. So, sandhi splitting is an important step for any NLP application for these languages. SSS uses a statistical approach using CRF for the task of sandhi splitting. The approach consists of two stages namely, Segmentation and Word Generation.

3.1 Segmentation

In this stage, the boundaries between different words i.e. positions where morphophonological changes occur in a compound word are identified using CRF. The input for this task is a word and the output is the segments that show the boundary/split points in the input. The resulting segments may or may not be meaningful words which can be seen in the below example.

Example:

Input: 'rAmuDoccADu' *(Ramudu came)*

Output: 'rAmuD'-'occADu'

Here, 'rAmuDoccADu'->'rAmuDu'+'vaccADu'

Ramudu came *Ramudu* *came*

In this example we can see that the segments 'rAmuD', 'occADu' are not meaningful words in Telugu language.

3.2 Word Generation

In this stage, meaningful words are generated from the segments obtained from the Segmentation stage. The input for this stage is the segments of a compound word and output is a meaningful word for each segment in the input. This stage consists of two components, (i) Class Label Assignment and (ii) Word Formation.

3.2.1 Class Label Assignment

The number of morphophonological changes occurring in any word is finite. The change can be either addition or deletion of characters at the end or at the starting of the segment. Each such change is taken as a separate class. Classes are extracted from the training data automatically. In this stage a class label is assigned to each segment using CRF.

Example:

In continuation to the example discussed in Segmentation stage, we have,

Class Label Assignment: 'rAmuD' _u

'occADu' -o+va

In this example, we already know that the segments 'rAmuD' and 'occADu' are not meaningful. The first segment will be meaningful if "u" is added at its end and for the second segment to be meaningful, 'o' is removed and 'va' is added in its place. So these two segments fall into '_u' and '-o+va' classes respectively.

3.2.2 Word Formation

This component generates meaningful words from the segments using class label information from Class Label Assignment stage.

The output of the Word Formation step for the example 'rAmuDoccADu' discussed in section 3.1 and 3.2.1 is as follows.

'rAmuDoccADu' -> 'rAmuDu' + 'vaccADu'

Ramudu came *Ramudu* *came*

4 Effect on NLP applications

"Kuncham et al., (2015) claim that compound words pose a problem for various NLP applications and that SSS is an attempt to reduce this effect." Here, we examine that claim by using SSS as a plugin before NLP applications like Machine Translation, Anaphora Resolution and Dialogue system. In this section we report our observations with respect to each of these applications.

4.1 Machine Translation

We use Google Translate[2] for Telugu-English Translation because it is one of the state-of-the-art commercial machine translation systems used today. Google Translate applies statistical learning techniques to build a translation model based on both monolingual text in the target language and aligned text consisting of examples of human translations between the languages.

We tested on 514 Telugu sentences which had 1890 words.

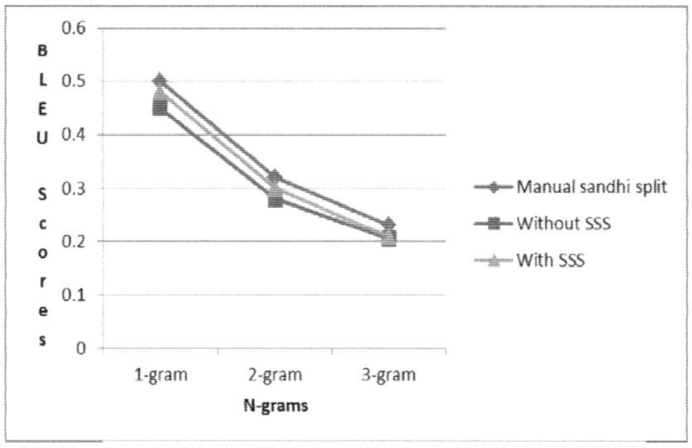

Fig 1: Cumulative N-gram BLEU scores on Telugu sentences in different experiment scenarios

BLEU score reported on manually sandhi divided data is 0.5003. This BLEU score would be the benchmark. BLEU score on sandhi combined data is 0.4506. We can observe the difference in the BLEU scores which tells us the importance of sandhi splitting in machine translation. As Telugu is a relatively morphologically rich language than English, it is very important that we split the compound words in Telugu when translating from Telugu to English. The BLEU score obtained by using SSS is 0.4810, which shows an improvement of **0.0304** over the sandhi combined data.

From the above reported BLEU scores, we can see that Google Translate fails to perform well in certain scenarios owing to the differences in the languages and mainly due to the high existence of compound words in Telugu. We will discuss through various examples how the differences in languages and compound words pose a challenge to machine translation. We further discuss the effect of SSS on Google Translate.

Different languages view the world with microscopes of different sensitivities. We may not find two languages with one to one mapping in their vocabulary and rules of the language. This is the very reason, Machine Translation is a challenging area of research. Following are some special constructions in Telugu that pose a problem for Machine Translation.

Examples

1. panIpATa cEsukuMTuMdi. -> At panipata
   She is doing her work.

If we observe the above sentence from the source language (Telugu), the word 'panIpATa' is a compound word which has two words namely, 'panI', 'pATa', where the first word means work and the second word means 'things done after/during work' when used along with the former. This kind of word formation is unique in Indian languages and not found in English. Translating such kinds of words is problematic and not dealt by Google Translate which can be seen from its output 'At panipata'.

2. eMduku mAneSAvu. -> Why quit
   why did you stop

Indian languages are pro drop languages whereas English is not. If we observe this example, the Telugu sentence has no word mapping to "you". The verbs in Telugu are inflected with gender, number and person information which helps to understand the meaning even if the subject is dropped. 'vu' in the verb 'mAneSA**vu**' *(stop)* gives 2nd person information, but the exact pronoun is dropped. This dropping is not possible in English language. In Telugu to English translation, accounting for the pro drop is a challenging

[2] http://translate.google.com/translate_t

task and we see that it is not properly handled by Google Translate.

3. rAmulu pAlu tAne pitukutADu .
Ramulu himself milks.
-> Ramulu he milked milk.

Ellipsis poses a problem for translation in any language. In this example, the English translation for the Telugu sentence is "Ramulu himself milks". Here, we can observe that the object of verb "milk" is missing and it is only from the context we understand the sentence as "Ramulu milks the cows himself." Handling such cases require contextual knowledge. Recognizing ellipsis and bringing out the missing information in the target languages is a big challenge.

	Positive	Negative
True	119	1655
False	61	55

Table 1: Confusion matrix of SSS on Telugu sentences

Now we discuss the problems of compound words and the performance of SSS on machine translation. Table 1 gives the confusion matrix of SSS on 514 sentences which are discussed below in detail.

True positives
This category includes all the compound words that should be split and are correctly split by SSS.

1. ***Correct split, correct translation***
WS:[3] tana iMTiki vacci koMceM annaM tecciMdi. *(She came to her house and brought some rice.)*
GT: To come to his house and brought some rice.

WoS: tana iMTikocci koMceM annaM tecciMdi.
GT: Intikocci brought her a little rice.

'iMTikocci' *(came home)* is the compound word which is not recognized by Google Translate. But once it is correctly split into these two words 'iMTiki' *(home)*, 'vacci' *(came)* the translator not only recognizes the words but also gives an answer close to the correct translation.

[3] WS –With SSS
WoS – Without SSS
GT – Google Translate Output
AS – Actual Split

WS: tulasi lEdu ani aDDaMgA tala UpiMdi. *(Tulasi shaked her head.)*
GT: Shakes head across the basil.

WoS: tulasi **lEdani** aDDaMgA talUpiMdi .
GT: The basil is **not** repeated horizontally.

In this example, we can observe that the compound word 'lEdani' *(not)* is recognized by Google Translate but is not translated correctly into English. When the compound word is split, the output of Google Translate is close to the correct translation.

2. ***Correct split, wrong translation***

WS: ippuDu tulasiki nayamu ayiMdi. *(Now Tulasi is healed.)*
GT: Now tulasiki was serious.
WoS: ippuDu tulasiki nayamayiMdi .
GT: Tulasiki healing now.

In this example, even though the compound word 'nayamayiMdi' *(healed)* is correctly split, the translation is incorrect to the extent that it gives an opposite sense.

True negatives
This category includes all the compound words that should not be split and are not split by SSS.

WS: I gOlIlu vEsuko. *(Take these tablets)*
GT: This can be marble.
This sentence does not contain any compound word, so no split is required.

False positives
This category includes words that should not be split but are split by SSS.

WS: sAyaM kAlaM rAmulu vaccADu. *(Ramulu came in the evening.)*
GT: Ramulu came to the aid of the season.

WoS: sAyaMkAlaM rAmulu vaccADu
GT: Ramulu returned in the evening.
Here, 'sAyaMkAlaM' *(evening)* is the word that ideally should not be split, but SSS splits it.

False negatives
This category includes (a) compound words that should be split but not split by SSS and (b) compound words that are wrongly split.

(a) **WS:** raktaMtO idaMdutuMdi. *(This is supplied with blood.)*
GT: Idandutundi blood.

'idaMdutuMdi' *(this is supplied)* should be split into 'idi' *(this)* and 'aMdutuMdi' *(supplied)*, but SSS doesn't split it resulting in non-identification of the word and thus incorrect translation by Google Translate.

(b) **WS:** vALLa mIda ottiDu ekkuva. *(More pressure on them)*
GT: More pressure on them.
AS: vALLa mIda ottiDi ekkuva
GT: Another pressure

Here, there are two compound words 'vALLamIda' *(on them)* and 'ottiDekkuva' *(more pressure)*. The first word is correctly split into 'vALLa' *(them)* and 'mIda' *(on)* whereas the latter is wrongly split. The correct split for the second one is 'ottiDi' *(pressure)*, ekkuva' *(more)* which can be seen in **AS** (Actual Split). But strangely, Google Translate gives correct translation for the wrong split instead of the correct split.

Some Special Cases:

1(a). **WS:** kAni mUTa **kanipiMca lEdu**. *(But the package is not seen.)*
GT: But the package is not visible.
WoS: kAni mUTa **kanipiMcalEdu** .
GT: But the package did not.

1(b). **WS:** idi aMtA jariginA raMgaDu **lEva lEdu**. *(Rangadu did not get up even after all this)*
GT: Lev rangadu not it at all.
WoS: idaMwA jariginA raMgaDu **lEvalEdu**
GT: Rangadu risen at all this.

In the above sentences, SSS splits 'lEdu' *(not)* from words - 'kanipiMcalEdu' *(not visible)*, 'levalEdu' *(did not get up)*. Google Translate gives correct translation in sentence 1 (a) but not in sentence 1(b). The decision to split in this case is dependent on context, which SSS doesn't take into consideration.

2(a). **WS:** I mUTalanu mA tAta**ki** aMdiMcAli. *(Give these packages to my grandfather.)*
GT: These kits provide our tataki.
Manual split: I mUTalanu mA tAta**ku** aMdiMcAli .
GT: These kits provide our grandfather.

In WS, 'tAtaki' *(to grandfather)* is not identified by the Translator as we can see, it is just transliterated in the English translation. But a variant of 'tAtaki', 'tAtaku' *(to grandfather)* (in manual split) is identified by the Google Translate. In general both these words are used alternatively in Telugu.

2(b). **WS:** civara**ki** oka cOTa pani dorikiMdi. *(Finally found a work at one place.)*
GT: Finally found a place to work.
Manual split: civara**ku** oka cOTa pani doVrikiMdi
GT: Finally found a place to work.

In 2(a), the variants 'tAtaki' and 'tAtaku' are translated differently whereas in 2(b), the similar variants 'civaraki' *(finally)* and 'civaraku' are translated to same meaning in English.

4.2 Anaphora resolution

Anaphora resolution is the problem of resolving references to earlier or later items in the discourse. These items are usually noun phrases representing objects in the real world called referents but can also be verb phrases, whole sentences or paragraphs.

An effort was made for building an Anaphora Resolution system for Telugu dialogues at IIIT-H. This system is a rule based system that handles nominal pronominal anaphora for human to human conversations. We examine the effect of SSS on this system and present our results in this section.

The corpus we used consists of 95 human conversations, each conversation may contain around 2-8 dialogues. Total pronouns in the corpus are 413. Most of the conversations in the corpus have been taken from the web.

	#pronouns correctly resolved	**#pronouns wrongly resolved**	**Accuracy**
Without SSS	179	224	43.30
With SSS	254	159	**61.50**

Table 2: Accuracy of Anaphora Resolution system with and without using SSS

Here, we can see an improvement of 18.2% accuracy if SSS is used as a plugin before the Anaphora Resolution system. This improvement is because SSS could identify 53 more pronouns that were initially not identified by the Anaphora Resolution system as seen in Table 3.

Total pronouns	#pronouns identified without SSS	#pronouns identified with SSS
413	359	412

Table 3: Pronouns identified with and without SSS by Anaphora Resolution system

Even though the number of pronouns identified by SSS is close to total pronouns in the corpus, there is a 5% error in splitting the compound words by SSS. The errors are of two types; (i) Wrong split and (ii) No split.

Wrong split:

ninnanE -> **ninnu** + anE
only yesterday ***you*** *particle*

In Telugu, 'ninnanE' has two senses, (a) 'only you' and (b) 'only yesterday'. If the word occurs with sense (a), it should be split and not in the case of (b) and the sense is decided only from the context. Here, 'ninnanE' should not be split but the split resulted into a pronoun 'ninnu' *(you)* which is wrong. From our analysis, this type of error was more than others i.e. 2.5% of total errors.

AvidelA -> Avida + elA
how she *she* *how*

This is the correct split for the compound word 'AvidelA' but the output from SSS is 'Avidu' and 'elA'. 'Avidu' is an unknown word in Telugu. This type of error constitutes of 1.6% of total errors.

No split:

In this type of error, SSS could not split some compound words like the following example. This error constitutes of about 0.9% of total errors.

EMTadi -> EMTi + adi
what is that *what* *that*

Here, 'EMtadi' is not split by SSS.

4.3 Dialogue System:

A Dialogue System is a computer program that is designed to communicate with humans in a natural way in natural language. As mentioned in "Sravanthi et al., 2015", Sandhi is a challenge to Dialogue Systems and the effect of SSS on this system is discussed in this section.

We prepared 281 questions on 'Tourist places in Hyderabad' domain in Telugu. Accuracy of the Dialogue System with and without using SSS is shown in Table 4.

	#Correctly Answered questions	Accuracy
Without SSS	156	55.51
With SSS	175	**62.27**

Table 4: Accuracy of Dialogue system with and without SSS

From this table we can see that there is an improvement in the overall accuracy of Dialogue system after using SSS but the increase in the accuracy is only 6.8%. This is because of the following reasons.

1. Borrowing of English words is common in Telugu language. If the compound words contain English words, it makes the split difficult for SSS. Moreover, occurrence of English words in 'Tourism' domain is high resulting in the increase in the percentage of errors.

gOlkoMDekkaDuMdi -> gOlkoMDa +
where is Golconda *Golconda*
ekkaDa + uMdi
where *present*

This is the actual split for the compound word 'gOlkoMDekkaDuMdi' but SSS gives wrong split as 'gOlkoMD**u**', 'ekkaDa', 'uMdi'. Since 'gOlkoMDa' (Golconda) is not identified in the question, the Dialogue system gives wrong answer.

TaimiMgsEMTi -> TaimiMgs + EMTi
what are the timings *timings* *what*

The above is the correct split for 'TaimiMgsEMTi' but SSS couldn't split it. It fails to split if English words like 'timings', 'address', 'monuments' etc., occur in the compound words.

2. Presence of context dependent particles.

gOlkoMDan**E** Taimulo cUDaccu?
What time can Golconda be visited?

The clitique 'E' is ambiguous and the split depends on the context as discussed in "Kuncham et al., 2015". Here, 'E' acts as a question marker which should be split to get the correct answer. But this type of context dependent cases is not handled by SSS.

3. Wrong splits by SSS.

cirunAmA *(address)* which should not be split but split by SSS as 'ciruni' and 'Ama' which have no sense in Telugu.

5 Conclusion

In conclusion, we can say that the presence of compound words degrade the performance of any NLP application for agglutinative languages which can be improved significantly by using SSS. We have presented our efforts in discussing the detail analysis of the performance and the effect of SSS on different NLP applications. As discussed in sections 4.2 and 4.3, splitting of some words depend on contextual information. SSS can be extended to handle these context dependent particles by considering whole sentences for training and learning features.

Acknowledgement:

This work is partially supported by Information Technology Research Academy (ITRA), Government of India under ITRA-Mobile grant ITRA/15(62)/Mobile/VAMD/01

References

Kuncham, P., Nelakuditi, K., Nallani, S., and Mamidi, R. (2015). Statistical sandhi splitter for agglutinative languages. In Computational Linguistics and Intelligent Text Processing, pages 164–172. Springer.

A. A. Macdonell, *A Sanskrit Grammar for students.* New Delhi, India: D.K. Printworld (P) Ltd., 1926.

M. Absalom and J. Hajek, "Prosodic phonology and raddoppiamento sintattico: a re-evaluation," in *Selected Papers from the 2005 Conference of the Australian Linguistic Society, Melbourne: Monash University. http://www. arts. monash. edu. au/ling/als, 2006.*

Nair, L. R. and Peter, S. D. (2011). Development of a rule based learning system for splitting compound words in malayalam language. In Recent Advances in Intelligent Computational Systems (RAICS), 2011 IEEE, pages 751–755. IEEE.

Joshi Shripad, S. (2012). Sandhi splitting of Marathi compound words. Int. J. on Adv. Computer Theory and Engg, 2(2).

Vempaty, P. C. and Nagalla, S. C. P. (2011). Automatic sandhi spliting method for telugu, an indian lan-guage. Procedia-Social and Behavioral Sciences, 27:218–225.

Natarajan, A. and Charniak, E. (2011). S3-statistical sam. dhi splitting.

Devadath V V, Litton J Kurisinkel, D. M. S. V. V. (2014). A sandhi splitter for malayalam.(accepted but yet to be published in proceedings of ICON 2014.)

Popović, M., Stein, D., and Ney, H. (2006). Statistical machine translation of german compound words. In Advances in Natural Language Processing, pages 616–624. Springer.

Macherey, K., Dai, A. M., Talbot, D., Popat, A. C., and Och, F. (2011). Language-independent compound splitting with morphological operations. In Proceedings of the 49th Annual Meeting of the Association for Computational Linguistics: Human Language Technologies-Volume 1, pages 1395–1404. Association for Computational Linguistics.

Sravanthi, M. C., Prathyusha, K., and Mamidi, R. (2015). A Dialogue System for Telugu, a resource-poor language. In Computational Linguistics and Intelligent Text Processing, pages 364–374. Springer.

Automatically Identifying Periodic Social Events from Twitter

Florian Kunneman
Centre for Language Studies
Radboud University
f.kunneman@let.ru.nl

Antal van den Bosch
Centre for Language Studies
Radboud University
a.vandenbosch@let.ru.nl

Abstract

Many events referred to on Twitter are of a periodic nature, characterized by roughly constant time intervals in between occurrences. Examples are annual music festivals, weekly television programs, and the full moon cycle. We propose a system that can automatically identify periodic events from Twitter in an unsupervised and open-domain fashion. We first extract events from the Twitter stream by associating terms that have a high probability of denoting an event to the exact date of the event. We compare a timeline-based and a calendar-based approach to detecting periodic patterns from the event dates that are connected to these terms. After applying event extraction on over four years of Dutch tweets and scanning the resulting events for periodic patterns, the calendar-based approach yields a precision of 0.76 on the 500 top-ranked periodic events, while the timeline-based approach scores 0.63.

1 Introduction

As a popular communication channel for both sharing news, experiences, and intentions, Twitter has been found to provide an accurate reflection of many aspects of the real world (Bollen et al., 2011; Zhao et al., 2011). For example, the periodicity of daily life can be exposed by visualizing the frequency of hashtags such as '#breakfast' and '#goodmorning' (Preoţiuc-Pietro and Cohn, 2013). In addition, real-world events can be automatically detected by signaling a sudden rise and fall of word occurrences in tweets (Petrović et al., 2010; McMinn et al., 2013). We propose a system that can identify *periodic* events from Twitter: provided with a continuous stream of raw tweets, it returns an overview of periodic social events.

Surprisingly, this topic of periodicity has not yet been studied in the context of events mentioned on Twitter, while the identification of periodicity in recurring events has obvious gains for a system that detects events in the Twitter stream. Detected periodicity patters can be used to predict future events before they are referred to on Twitter. For instance, if World Food Day is detected on the 16th of October for a number of consecutive years, it can be expected and put on the calendar for the next year.

The rich set of references to the real world made on Twitter make it a suitable platform to mine for periodic patterns in relation to events of any type. At the same time, the non-standard language and large amount of streaming messages make it a challenging task. We facilitate this task by applying an event extraction approach that identifies terms that might represent a social event, and that relates them to a frequently and explicitly mentioned date of the event. After this first event extraction stage, periodicity detection can be applied to the clean date sequences linked to event terms.

2 Related Work

Finding periodic patterns is a valuable task in many contexts of sequential data, such as DNA or protein sequences (Zhang et al., 2007), market basket data (Mahanta et al., 2008), and complex signals such as sound (Sethares and Staley, 1999). Elfeky et al. (2005) distinguish between 'segment periodicity' and 'symbol periodicity'. The first refers to the repetition of a specific sequence, while the second refers to single symbols in a sequence that recur at roughly constant time intervals. The latter is what we aim to detect.

Several patterns of periodicity have been analyzed in social media. Chu et al. (2012a) aim to distinguish bots from human user accounts on Twitter, and find that the periodicity of tweet postings is a strong indicator to recognize bots. They

Proceedings of Recent Advances in Natural Language Processing, pages 320–328,
Hissar, Bulgaria, Sep 7–9 2015.

estimate periodicity by the entropy rate of post intervals, where a low entropy points to a non-random, periodic pattern. Chu et al. (2012b) adopt this entropy-based periodicity feature to help distinguish spam campaigns from proper campaigns on Twitter. Fan et al. (2014) analyze temporal patterns in topics discussed on Weibo, and find that the topic 'business' displays a highly periodic pattern. Yang et al. (2013) aim to classify Twitter users in predefined categories. They find that the periodicity pattern of words linked to a category is a strong indication, as users tend to mention their topic of interest at similar times of the day and week. At the word level, Preoţiuc-Pietro et al. (2013) apply Gaussian processes to model the periodicity of hashtag mentions. They use this information to predict hashtag frequencies at any hour.

The automatic identification of periodic patterns related to events has not been applied in the context of Twitter. The detection of single events, on the other hand, is a popular strand of research. Many studies have leveraged the notion of burstiness, the sudden rise and fall of word frequency, to find events from Twitter. Either by looking at the rapid growth of tweet clusters (Petrović et al., 2010; McMinn et al., 2013; Diao et al., 2012) or words with peaky behavior (Weng and Lee, 2011; Li et al., 2012). The explicit reference to events in tweets has also been shown to help find scheduled events; social events in particular (Ritter et al., 2012). A possible reason the aforementioned approaches have not been employed to search for periodically recurring events, is that it requires a longitudinal effort to increase the chances of observing periodic behavior. To this end, we make use of TwiNL (Tjong Kim Sang and van den Bosch, 2013), a database of IDs of Dutch tweets gathered from December 2010 onwards.

3 Approach

3.1 Open-domain Event Extraction

Our approach to event extraction is similar to Ritter et al. (2012). The approach relies on explicit references to a future point in time combined with terms, and favors date–term pairs with a strong connection. We apply this approach to Dutch tweets, though most of its components are language-independent.

3.1.1 Tweet Processing

Each incoming tweet from a stream is initially scanned for future referring time expressions. We manually specified a set of rules that focus on a future date in time as expressed in the Dutch language. Examples of the English equivalents of these rules are displayed in Table 1.[1]

Category	Examples (English)
Date	Sept. 13th 2014
Exact	in a month
Weekday	this Wednesday

Table 1: Examples of the three types of rules for the extraction of time expressions

The set of rules can be divided in three categories that each relate to different types of conversion of the time expression into a date. The 'Date' category of rules consists of the different variations of date mentions, and link directly to a future date. The 'Exact' rules comprise a variety of phrase combinations that specify an exact number of days remaining to the event. The 'Weekday' rules match a mention of a weekday, preceded by a future referring phrase like 'deze' ('this') or 'volgende week' ('next week').

Tweets found to have a future referring time expression are subsequently scanned for meaningful words and word n-grams that might denote an event. We refer to such n-grams as 'event terms' henceforth. As off-the-shelf named entity taggers display a poor performance when applied on the non-standard language in social media (Ritter et al., 2011), as alternative we applied the commonness metric (Meij et al., 2012) and extracted any hashtag as event term.

Commonness is formulated as the prior probability of a concept c (the n-gram) to be used as an anchor text q in Wikipedia (Meij et al., 2012):

$$Commonness(c, q) = \frac{|L_{q,c}|}{\sum_{c'} |L_{q,c'}|} \quad (1)$$

Where $L_{q,c}$ denotes the set of all links with anchor text q pointing to the Wikipedia page titled c, and $\sum_{c'} |L_{q,c'}|$ is the sum of occurrences of q as an anchor text linking to other concepts.

[1] Although commonly available time taggers such as Heideltime (Strötgen and Gertz, 2010) could be applied to this end, Heideltime does not specialize in future time expressions.

We downloaded the Dutch Wikipedia dump of 2015/02/05[2], and parsed it with the Annotated-WikiExtractor[3]. Then, we used Colibri Core[4] to calculate the commonness of any concept that has its own Wikipedia article, and is used as an anchor text on other Wikipedia pages at least once. These statistics are used to extract event terms from a tweet. Tweets that match a future time reference in the first stage are stripped of this time reference, and n-grams with $n \leq 5$ (covering the length of most event names) are extracted. Any n-gram found to have a commonness score above 0.05 is extracted as an event term. We set the threshold based on analyzing a sample n-grams with their score.

Aside from concepts with an above-threshold commonness score, we directly selected any hashtag in tweets with future time references as event terms. Hashtags can be seen as user-designated keywords, and are often employed as event markers.

3.1.2 Event Ranking

Not all pairs of dates and event terms that result from the tweet processing stage represent a significant event. Some candidate terms might not refer to an event, and some terms might denote a personal rather than a social event. A first step to identify significant events is to employ a minimum threshold of five tweets in which an event term should co-occur with the same date. Following Ritter et al. (2012), event terms more frequently mentioned with a specific date are seen as the more significant events. We therefore calculate the fit between any frequent event term and the date with which it is mentioned, by means of the G_2 log likelihood ratio statistic:

$$G_2 = \sum_{z \in \{e, \neg e\}, y \in \{d, \neg d\}} O_{z,y} \times \ln\left(\frac{O_{z,y}}{E_{z,y}}\right) \quad (2)$$

The fit between any event term e and date d is calculated by the observed (O) and expected (E) frequency of the four pairs $\{e, d\}$,$\{e, \neg d\}$,$\{\neg e, d\}$ and $\{\neg e, \neg d\}$. The expected frequency is calculated by multiplying the observed frequencies of z (denoting either e or $\neg e$) and y (denoting either d or $\neg d$) and dividing them by the total number of tweets in the set.

We prioritize events that are tweeted about by many different users, by multiplying the G_2 log likelihood ratio statistic with the fraction of different users that mention the event. The events are ranked by the resulting G_2u score:

$$G_2u = \left(\frac{u}{t}\right) * G_2 \quad (3)$$

Here, u is the number of unique users that mention the date and entity in the same tweet, while t is the number of tweets in which the date and entity are both mentioned.

The calculation of G_2u for each pair results in a ranked list of date–term pairs. To reduce subsequent computational costs, all pairs with a rank number below 2,500 are discarded.

As an event might be described by multiple event terms, it is likely that the ranked list of date–term pairs contains several event terms that describe the same event. To de-duplicate these, we cluster event terms based on the content of the tweets in which they are mentioned. Each set of tweets in which the same date–term pair occurs is aggregated into one big document. The documents are converted into a feature vector with $tf * idf$ weighting, where the idf value is based on all aggregated documents in the set of 2,500 date–term pairs. A similarity matrix is generated for each set of date–term pairs labeled with the same date. These documents are then clustered by means of Agglomerative Hierarchical Clustering (Day and Edelsbrunner, 1984). The advantage of this algorithm is that it does not require a fixed number of clusters as parameters. Pairs of tweet sets are clustered together if their similarity is above an empirically set threshold of 0.7.

3.1.3 Performance

We tested the approach to event extraction on a large sample of Dutch tweets posted in August 2014, which we collected from TwiNL (Tjong Kim Sang and van den Bosch, 2013). We evaluated the top-250 extracted events, and compared the outcomes with an n-gram baseline, in which the commonness approach to entity extraction is replaced by extracting all n-grams. The results are displayed in Table 2.

The output of the system was rated by a set of four annotators; the results are presented by the

[2] http://dumps.wikimedia.org/nlwiki/nlwiki-20150205-pages-articles.xml.bz2

[3] https://github.com/jodaiber/Annotated-WikiExtractor

[4] http://proycon.github.io/colibri-core/doc/

	50%	75%	100%	Mutual F-score
Ngram	0.52	-	0.42	0.89
Commonness	0.87	0.80	0.63	0.90

Table 2: Precision@250 of output identified as event by human annotators

minimal percentage of annotators that agreed on the event status. A majority of 75% of the annotators agrees that 80% of the output represents an event. In comparison, only 52% of the top-250 output of the n-gram baseline system was rated as event by at least one of two annotators. We also scored the inter-annotator agreement by Mutual F-score, which provides an insight into the agreement for the positive (event) class. On average, annotators yield an F-score of 0.9 on classifying the event class if the decisions of another annotator are seen as the gold standard.

3.2 Online Extraction of Events

The approach described above extracts events from a *fixed* set of tweets. To apply the event extraction in a *streaming* fashion, the procedure should be repeated for any new batch of tweets. We chose to work with a window size of one month. We set the step size to one day, to ensure that events are extracted from any monthly periodic sequence. For each daily event extraction step, the top-2500 events are selected.

This overlapping sliding window setting leads to a large amount of duplicate events in the output. To build a calendar of unique events, a merging procedure is performed after each event extraction. The events in the output are each compared with the existing set of events with the same date. If over 10% of the tweets in the new event overlap with an existing event, the events are merged by adding any new tweets and event terms to the existing event. New events that do not overlap with an existing event are added as a new event.

3.3 Periodicity Detection

The event extraction procedure results in a set of events represented as one or more event terms linked to a date. Next, periodic events can be found by scanning for events that are linked to at least three dates, between which two periods of time occur that are roughly equal.

We compare two approaches to finding periodic patterns from the date sequence related to an event term: a timeline-based approach and a calendar-based approach. We refer to them as 'PerTime' and 'PerCal'.

3.3.1 PerTime

PerTime leverages the intervals between sequences of at least three dates. Any date sequence that has roughly similar intervals is seen as periodic. The intervals are measured at the level of days. We estimate the similarity by computing the relative standard deviation over the intervals, RSD:

$$RSD = \frac{s}{\bar{x}} * 100\% \tag{4}$$

The RSD relates the average $\bar{x}$ to the standard deviation s, returning the standard deviation as the percentage of the average values in a set. The RSD is a sensible approach to scoring the periodicity of date intervals, as any deviation in big intervals, such as 365 days, is less penalized than the deviation in smaller intervals, such as 7 days. We set the minimum interval length to 6 days, ensuring weekly events as the minimal periodicity.

3.3.2 PerCal

Rather than looking for regular intervals between dates, PerCal searches for similarities between the dates in a sequence. An event term like 'Christmas Day' would be mostly linked to '25 December'. Likewise, an event term might recur with 'the third Saturday of May'. The calendar-based approach scans a date sequence for such repetitions.

The detection of calendar periodicity has mainly been the focus in studies that aim to find periodic transactional patterns (Li et al., 2001; Li et al., 2003; Mahanta et al., 2008). Li et al. (2001) propose an intuitive calendar scheme to describe a periodic pattern. The pattern has the form of ⟨year,month,day⟩. Any of these fields can be filled with a specific value, while the '*'-character is used to denote 'every'. For example, the pattern ⟨*,2,1⟩ represents 'every year on the 1st of February', while ⟨2011,*,12⟩ denotes 'every twelfth day of the month in 2011'. We adopt this pattern scheme, and extend it with the additional fields week, weekday, and #weekday (the index of a given weekday within a month). We add the '-' character as a possible value, to account for fields that are irrelevant to a pattern. As an additional extension, we allow the model to describe patterns

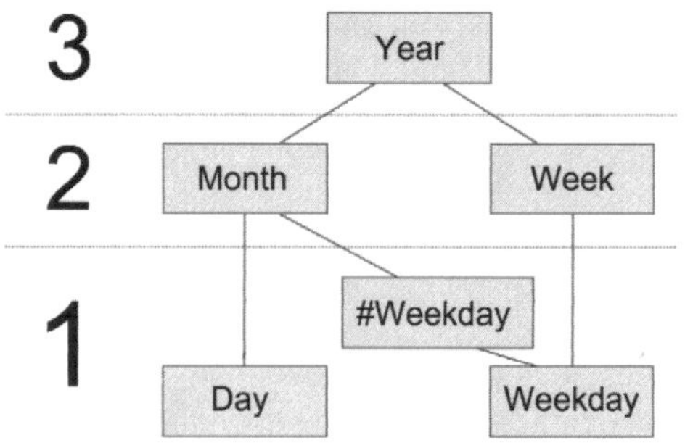

Figure 1: Diagram of included calendar fields and their relation on three levels.

like 'every six months' or 'every two years', by specifying a step size that relates to the field that is described by 'every'. For example, ⟨*2,1,-,-,Sunday,2⟩ denotes 'every two years on the second Sunday of January', and ⟨2011,*,-,1,-,-⟩ denotes 'every first day of the month in 2011'.

The relationship between the included calendar fields is illustrated in Figure 1. The scheme has three levels of granularity. On the first level are 'day' (1–31), 'weekday' (Monday–Sunday) and '#weekday' (1–5). The 'day' field relates to 'month' (1–12) at the second level; any combination between the two values can be made. '#weekday' has a connection to both 'weekday' and 'month', and represents the index of a weekday in a month (for example: the *third* Wednesday of October). Finally, 'weekday' connects directly to 'week' (1–53), which enables relations like 'every Wednesday' or 'Monday on week 40'. At the top level is the 'year' field, so as to describe yearly patterns or patterns during a specific year.

A periodic calendar pattern can be detected by ascending the hierarchy of calendar fields and looking for regularities. Like PerTime, weekly periodicity is the smallest pattern that is searched for. Starting from the lower-level fields (day, weekday and the weekday-#weekday combination), the algorithm scans whether any of the values of these fields occurs three times or more (the minimum requirement for a periodic pattern). If this requirement is met, the dates that contain this value are selected and passed on to the higher level: month (if the day or the weekday-#weekday combination is periodic) or week (if the weekday is periodic). Because the patterns we look for can describe either a sequence on this second level (like 'every two months' or 'every week') or a sequence of years on the third level, we scan both for a sequence and a repetition of the month or the week values on this second level. If a sequence is found, the pattern is finalized. If a repetition is found, the algorithm proceeds to find a yearly pattern.

A sequence of weeks, months or years might have steps of unequal size. In such a case we describe the pattern with the smallest step size found. Any date between larger steps is denoted as a missing date. In the sequence '2014/03/04 – 2014/04/04 – 2014/06/04' there is a monthly sequence of step size '1', with a missing date '2014/05/04'.

Some patterns show stronger periodicity than others. As mentioned above, a sequence might contain missing dates, decreasing the evidence for periodicity. In addition, not all dates linked to an event term may combine into a pattern. Following Li et al. (2001), we quantify these two inconsistencies as *confidence* and *support* estimates. Confidence is estimated by dividing the dates that could fill in a pattern (from the first date to the last) by the number of dates that are actually seen. Support is the percentage of all dates that are linked to an event term that satisfy the pattern. To obtain an overall score of the quality of a pattern, we calculate the average of these two metrics.

PerCal searches for periodic patterns at different levels. As a result, it may find multiple patterns in the same date sequence. If two patterns overlap, the one with the highest overall score is selected.

3.3.3 Clustering of Periodic Terms

To de-duplicate output from both the PerTime and PerCal approaches, we cluster event terms with a periodic sequence together. For both approaches, we aggregate all tweets linked to the periodic pattern of an event term, to form big documents. Any pair of terms with 90% overlapping dates for PerTime and any pair with a similar pattern for PerCal were tested as clusters. Clustering was applied in the same fashion as described at the end of Section 3.1.2. The threshold for clustering was set to a cosine similarity above 0.5.

4 Experimental Set-up

4.1 Data

We tested our system on all Dutch tweets that were collected from the Tweet IDs in TwiNL, from the start of the database, December 16th 2010, up to February 16th 2015, amounting to 2.73 billion tweets in total. After processing these tweets, 24,162,633 were found to have a matching time expression.

4.2 Procedure

We applied the event extraction module on the span of tweets as specified in Section 3.2, with a sliding window of a month and a daily sliding frequency. Events were merged if they were extracted from (partly) the same tweet IDs. After all tweets were processed, a calendar was filled with 94,526 events.

Periodicity detection is applied to single event terms; we kept a log of the dates linked to each term. We searched for periodic patterns in this log by starting with events that took place in 2014. For both PerTime and Percal, whenever a date in 2014 or later was appended to an event term log, the approach was applied to the updated date sequence. If a periodic pattern was already found for an event term, it was overwritten with the pattern that was extracted from the updated sequence. We clustered terms with a similar periodic pattern after all events were processed.

4.3 Evaluation

We ranked the periodic event patterns returned by the two approaches by their respective metrics to score periodicity: RSD for PerTime and the average value of support and coverage for PerCal. One of the authors manually assessed the top-500 patterns from both rankings, deciding for each output whether it represents a regularly recurring sequence of events, rather than events or event terms that share a coincidental temporal regularity. The terms, dates, and tweets linked to each output, and if needed the Google search engine, were consulted to guide this decision.

In order to acquire a sense of agreement for the annotations, a second author annotated the top-200 events of the two systems. The mutual F-score of positive annotations was 0.92 for the PerTime output and 0.93 for the PerCal output.

5 Results

PerTime assigned a periodicity score to 5,301 events out of the total of 94,526 events. PerCal found 7,018 periodic patterns [5]. The precision and recall of their top-500 output are presented in Table 3. 315 correct periodic events were confirmed from the output of PerTime, and 379 from the output of PerCal, resulting in precision-at-500 scores of 0.63 and 0.76, respectively. We approximated a recall score by comparing the periodic event terms that were found by both approaches (637 in total), and calculating which percentage of these was returned by either of them. The recall scores are lower than the precision scores, due to an overlap of only 116 events (18%) between PerTime and PerCal.

	Precision	Recall
PerTime	0.63	0.52
PerCal	0.76	0.69

Table 3: Periodicity detection quality after manual evaluation of the top-500 deteced periodic events by the two approaches.

Precision-at-curves of the top-500 rankings are given in Figure 2. For PerTime, the RSD at rank 500 is 10.2 days. A perfect RSD score of 0.0 was maintained up to rank 81. The ranks of events with equal scores were randomly shuffled. The curve shows a progressing decay towards the end. The temporally increasing precision at rank 200 is due to the detection of a number of periodic events that are characterized by changing intervals, such as Easter and Pentecost, and share the same non-perfect RSD score.

For PerCal, the pattern score at rank 500 is 0.65. In contrast to PerTime, precision is decreasing at a slower rate with lower-ranked events.

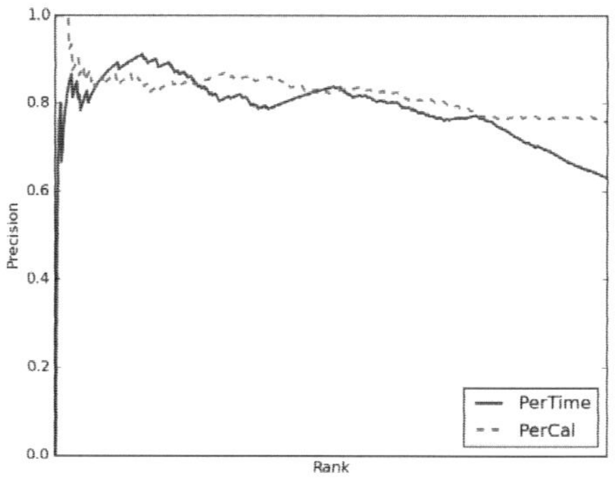

Figure 2: Precision-at-curves for PerTime and PerCal

[5]A dataset with the tweet ID's that relate to all 94,526 events, as well as the periodic event patterns that were found by both systems, will be made publicly available from `http://cls.ru.nl/~fkunneman/data_periodicity.zip`

	Event term(S)	Dates	Timeline pattern	Calendar pattern
Periodic events found by both approaches	#trendrede	2011/09/13,2012/09/11, 2013/09/10, 2014/09/09	364 -364 - 364	⟨*,9,-,-,Tuesday,2⟩
	#valentinesday	2013/02/14, 2014/02/14, 2015/02/14	365 - 365	⟨*,2,-,14,-,-⟩
Periodic events only found by timeline approach	romantische muziek	2011/08/14, 2012/08/12, 2013/08/25, 2014/08/24	364 - 378 - 364	-
	paaszondag	2011/04/24, 2012/04/08, 2013/03/31, 2014/04/20, 2015/04/05	350 - 357 - 385 - 350	-
Periodic events only found by calendar approach	#7hloop	2011/11/20, 2012/11/18, 2014/11/16	364 - 728	⟨*,11,-,-,Sunday,3⟩
	fortarock	2011/07/02, 2012/06/02, 2012/11/09, 2013/06/01, 2014/05/31, 2015-06-06	336 - 160 - 204 - 364 - 371	⟨*,-,22,-,Saturday,-⟩

Table 4: Examples of periodic events in the top 500 output of the timeline and calendar approach

6 Analysis

Examples of detected periodic events are given in Table 4. To give an idea of the strength of both approaches, a distinction is made between events that are only found by one of them, or by both. An example of a periodic event found by both approaches is '#valentinesday'. Events like this, linked to a fixed date, are characterized by equal yearly intervals (only allowing for a minor deviation of 366 instead of 365 days in leap years).

The event 'romantische muziek' (referring to the 'Day of Romantic Music') is not found by PerCal, which is due to an inconsistent pattern of dates. PerTime can typically deal with such small inconsistencies. The event described by 'paaszondag' ('Easter Sunday') follows the lunisolar calendar, while the calendar approach follows a Gregorian calendar scheme[6]. Again, PerTime only penalizes the inconsistencies in day intervals, without discarding the event altogether.

While PerTime can deal with inconsistencies in the intervals between dates, PerCal displays a higher tolerance towards missing dates. An example is '#7hloop' (a running event in The Netherlands), which was not found by the event extraction module in 2013. The resulting interval of 728 days (two years) at this point results in a poor periodicity score for PerTime. PerCal, having detected the overall pattern, gives a smaller penalty for the missing entry in 2013. The support for these days is 1.0, while the confidence is 0.75, leading to an overall score of 0.88. Similarly, noisy date sequences in which only part of the dates form a periodic pattern can only be dealt with by PerCal. PerTime assigns a low overall periodicity score to the date sequence associated with 'Fortarock' (a music festival in The Netherlands), due the irregular intervals.

[6]To find events like Easter, the framework of PerCal could be extended by including a lunisolar scheme or other existing schemes.

7 Conclusion

We have presented a framework that extracts a calendar of events from the Twitter stream and detects periodic event sequences in this calendar. Applying the procedure to over 4 years of Dutch tweets, a timeline-based and calendar-based approach to periodicity detection yield a precision-at-500 of 0.63 and 0.76, respectively.

As far as we know this is the first work that deals with the task of periodic event detection on Twitter data, which serves to extract long-range patterns from Twitter, detect periodic events among those patterns, and predict events before they are mentioned on Twitter. Although we obtained encouraging results, there is room for improvement. To clarify whether the event extraction approach that we applied is most suitable as a first step before periodicity detection, other approaches to event detection or extraction, such as burstiness, may be applied as well during this stage for comparison.

The calendar-based approach may be extended in a knowledge-driven way with schemes that describe the lunisolar calendar, the lunar calendar, as well as other historical and religious calendars, so as to enable the detection of periodic patterns that relate to Easter, the Ramadan, and Hindu festivals for example.

Acknowledgements

This research was funded by the Dutch national program COMMIT. We thank Erik Tjong Kim Sang for the development and support of the http://twiqs.nl service.

References

Johan Bollen, Huina Mao, and Alberto Pepe. 2011. Modeling public mood and emotion: Twitter sentiment and socio-economic phenomena. In *ICWSM*.

Zi Chu, Steven Gianvecchio, Haining Wang, and Sushil Jajodia. 2012a. Detecting automation of twitter accounts: Are you a human, bot, or cyborg? *IEEE Transactions on Dependable and Secure Computing*, 9(6):811–824.

Zi Chu, Indra Widjaja, and Haining Wang. 2012b. Detecting social spam campaigns on twitter. In *Applied Cryptography and Network Security*, pages 455–472. Springer.

William H. E. Day and Herbert Edelsbrunner. 1984. Efficient algorithms for agglomerative hierarchical clustering methods. *Journal of classification*, 1(1):7–24.

Qiming Diao, Jing Jiang, Feida Zhu, and Ee-Peng Lim. 2012. Finding bursty topics from microblogs. In *Proceedings of the 50th Annual Meeting of the Association for Computational Linguistics: Long Papers-Volume 1*, pages 536–544. Association for Computational Linguistics.

Mohamed G. Elfeky, Walid G. Aref, and Achmed K. Elmagarmid. 2005. Periodicity detection in time series databases. *Knowledge and Data Engineering, IEEE Transactions on*, 17(7):875–887.

Rui Fan, Jichang Zhao, Xu Feng, and Ke Xu. 2014. Topic dynamics in weibo: Happy entertainment dominates but angry finance is more periodic. In *2014 IEEE/ACM International Conference on Advances in Social Networks Analysis and Mining (ASONAM)*, pages 230–233. IEEE.

Yingjiu Li, X. Sean Wang, and Sushil Jajodia. 2001. Discovering temporal patterns in multiple granularities. In *Temporal, Spatial, and Spatio-Temporal Data Mining*, pages 5–19. Springer.

Yingjiu Li, Peng Ning, X. Sean Wang, and Sushil Jajodia. 2003. Discovering calendar-based temporal association rules. *Data & Knowledge Engineering*, 44(2):193–218.

Chenliang Li, Aixin Sun, and Anwitaman Datta. 2012. Twevent: segment-based event detection from tweets. In *Proceedings of the 21st ACM international conference on Information and knowledge management*, pages 155–164. ACM.

Anjana K. Mahanta, Fokrul A. Mazarbhuiya, and Hemanta K. Baruah. 2008. Finding calendar-based periodic patterns. *Pattern Recognition Letters*, 29(9):1274–1284.

Andrew J. McMinn, Yashar Moshfeghi, and Joemon M. Jose. 2013. Building a large-scale corpus for evaluating event detection on twitter. In *Proceedings of the 22nd ACM international conference on Conference on information & knowledge management*, pages 409–418. ACM.

Edgar Meij, Wouter Weerkamp, and Maarten de Rijke. 2012. Adding semantics to microblog posts. In *Proceedings of the fifth ACM international conference on Web search and data mining*, pages 563–572. ACM.

Saša Petrović, Miles Osborne, and Victor Lavrenko. 2010. Streaming first story detection with application to twitter. In *Human Language Technologies: The 2010 Annual Conference of the North American Chapter of the Association for Computational Linguistics*, pages 181–189. Association for Computational Linguistics.

Daniel Preoţiuc-Pietro and Trevor Cohn. 2013. A temporal model of text periodicities using gaussian processes. In *Proceedings of the 2013 Conference on Empirical Methods in Natural Language Processing*, pages 977–988.

Alan Ritter, Sam Clark, and Oren Etzioni. 2011. Named entity recognition in tweets: an experimental study. In *Proceedings of the Conference on Empirical Methods in Natural Language Processing*, pages 1524–1534. Association for Computational Linguistics.

Alan Ritter, Mausam, Oren Etzioni, and Sam Clark. 2012. Open domain event extraction from twitter. In *Proceedings of the 18th ACM SIGKDD international conference on Knowledge discovery and data mining*, KDD '12, pages 1104–1112, New York, NY, USA. ACM.

William A. Sethares and Thomas W. Staley. 1999. Periodicity transforms. *IEEE Transactions on Signal Processing*, 47(11):2953–2964.

Jannik Strötgen and Michael Gertz. 2010. Heideltime: High quality rule-based extraction and normalization of temporal expressions. In *Proceedings of the 5th International Workshop on Semantic Evaluation*, pages 321–324. Association for Computational Linguistics.

Erik Tjong Kim Sang and Antal van den Bosch. 2013. Dealing with big data: The case of twitter. *Computational Linguistics in the Netherlands Journal*, 3:121–134, 12/2013.

Jianshu Weng and Bu-Sung Lee. 2011. Event detection in twitter. In *Proceedings of the AAAI conference on weblogs and social media (ICWSM-11)*, pages 401–408.

Tao Yang, Dongwon Lee, and Su Yan. 2013. Steeler nation, 12th man, and boo birds: classifying twitter user interests using time series. In *2013 IEEE/ACM International Conference on Advances in Social*

Networks Analysis and Mining (ASONAM), pages 684–691. IEEE.

Minghua Zhang, Ben Kao, David W. Cheung, and Kevin Y. Yip. 2007. Mining periodic patterns with gap requirement from sequences. *ACM Transactions on Knowledge Discovery from Data (TKDD)*, 1(2):7.

Siqi Zhao, Lin Zhong, Jehan Wickramasuriya, and Venu Vasudevan. 2011. Human as Real-Time sensors of social and physical events: A case study of Twitter and sports games. Technical Report TR0620-2011, Houston, TX: Rice University and Motorola Labs.

Collecting and Evaluating Lexical Polarity with a Game With A Purpose

Mathieu Lafourcade
LIRMM
Univ. Montpellier, France
lafourca@lirmm.fr

Nathalie Le Brun
Imagin@t
34400 Lunel, France
imaginat@imaginat.name

Alain Joubert
LIRMM
Univ. Montpellier, France
aj@lirmm.fr

Abstract

Sentiment analysis from a text requires amongst others having a polarity lexical resource. We designed LikeIt, a GWAP (Game With A Purpose) that allows to attribute a positive, negative or neutral value to a term, and thus obtain a resulting polarity for most of the terms of the freely available lexical network of the JeuxDeMots project. We present a quantitative analysis of data obtained through our approach, together with the comparison method we developed to validate them qualitatively.

1 Introduction

Being able to evaluate feelings is essential in natural language processing, whether to analyze political speeches or opinion of the general public on the provision of services, tourist, cultural, or about consumer goods. Whatever type of approach, statistics supervised or more linguistic one (Brun, 2011), such ability requires referring to a polarity lexical resource, in wich terms are endowed with positive, negative and neutral values. The polarity can be expressed using a single numerical value (Taboada *et al.*, 2011), or more: two values (positive/negative) are used in Emolex (Saif and Turney, 2013), a lexical polarity / feelings resource in English, produced by crowdsourcing (using Amazon Mechanical Turk, which can be problematic, see Fort *et al.* (2014)). SentiWordNet (Esuli and Sebastiani, 2006), as well as WordNet Affect (Strapparava and Valitutti, 2004) are extensions of WorldNet in which terms are polarized along three values (positive, negative, objective) of which the last one is opposed to the first two. Approaches through propagation by starting from a manual core (see Gala and Brun (2012) and Lafourcade and Fort (2014)) have also been performed, but such approaches may not exactly reflect the views of speakers. Learning algorithms and compositional approaches can use such polarity data (Kim and Hovy, 2004) and (Turney, 2002). The GWAP (Game With A Purpose) JeuxDeMots (JDM) (Lafourcade, 2007) resulted in a lexical network in constant expansion, in which terms are linked by lexical-semantic relations. Contributive approaches with non-experts have been analysed in (Snow *et al.*, 2013) and proven quite efficient. Within the JDM project, some alternative type of games allow to validate and verify lexical relations produced through the main game (Lafourcade *et al.*, 2015). The JDM project thus provides suitable context to test various methods of polarity information acquisition.

It may be relevant to assign to words some information in the form of finite sets of values. Thus, the polarity can be defined by three values: positive, negative and neutral. It may be noticed that many semantic features can be characterized in this way, i.e. associated with such variable-sized sets of values: feelings/emotions (anger, fear, joy, love, sadness ...), or colors (red, blue, yellow, green, orange, violet, black, white ...). Since this type of association cannot be obtained through the main game of the JDM project, we designed several other games for characterizing the words according to various criteria (I like/I don't like, associated feeling, associated color...). Applications of these data are numerous, either in discourse analysis or disambiguation. But such an annotation is complex because it is subjective and heavily influenced by the context: for example, the same remark can be considered a trait of humor, an advice, a criticism or a reprimand ... according to the enunciator, the interlocutor and context.

In this article, we firstly introduce LikeIt, a GWAP designed to collect polarization data, and how the polarization of the terms spreads within the lexical network. Then, we present the results obtained through a quantitative and qualitative analysis. Our method of qualitative assess-

Proceedings of Recent Advances in Natural Language Processing, pages 329–337,
Hissar, Bulgaria, Sep 7–9 2015.

ment, based on a comparison between the polarity data and the feelings data (i.e. feelings that people spontaneously associate with a given term) is described in detail. Finally, we discuss the prospects that this work allows to consider.

2 LikeIt, a Polarity Game

Similarly to social networks, the game is to assign the assessment *I like*, *I do not like* or *I don't care* to a displayed term. Of course, this assessment is not only very subjective, but closely linked to the context. However, we hypothetise that many words have intrinsic polarity that it is possible to gather, by asking enough people. A majority polarity may emerge from answers, and if so, we can verify which one.

2.1 How Does it Work?

The player has to answer *yes*, *no* or *I do not care* to the question *do you like the idea of* followed by a term. This framework seems to be the most flexible and most comprehensive way to enrich the lexical network with polarity information. This allows in particular to distinguish between the terms for which people are mostly indifferent (majority of *I do not care, neutral* polarity) and those that raise sharply divided opinions (roughly equal amounts of *yes* and *no*, polarity equally divided between *positive* and *negative*). Within the context of word sense disambiguation, preliminary results show that polarity is sufficient for selecting the correct meaning of a term in about 50% of cases. Polarity data may also be used in opinions analysis, by combining the polarities of highly polarized terms (i.e. those whose highest polarity is greater than 50% of the cumulative values of the three possible polarities). Figure 1 shows screenshots of LikeIt game. Among the qualities that make this vote game by consensus an effective GWAP (Lafourcade *et al.*, 2015), it can be emphasized:

- **simplicity**: although the response procedure (*yes, no, I don't care*) is identical to that of surveys, diversity of vocabulary and topics is such that people do not feel they complete a survey. In addition, the response by a simple click makes possible to play from a smartphone or tablet, to pass the time during relatively short waiting situations (waiting room, queue, transport, ...). Quantitatively, very short games and immediate rerun make likeIt a very effective game to collect data.
- **diversity of vocabulary and topics and variability of response**: a number of words elicit mixed feelings, even opposing (e.g., the term *operating room*, theoretically seen as positive, but negative if we are personally concerned), and the feelings of a player can evolve over time and according to circumstances. Thus the word *bachelor* or *school exam* creates a negative feeling among high school students, but significantly positive for graduates. The choice to provide some very general vocabulary makes it interesting and varied game.
- **reactivity**: as soon he answered, the player can see the percentage of people who share his opinion, which may induce some emotions about the fact of being or not like everyone. Direct feedback is thus given, while the game is immediately rerun with a new question.

2.2 The Collected Data

For each word, the responses of players generate a triplet of values representing the number of votes for each of the three possible polarities. Their percentage distribution represents what we call the polarization of the term, similar to a three-component vector, whose norm can be calculated. The higher are the intensity (i.e. the number of votes for the word) and the vector norm, the more reliable the polarization is. The minimum intensity from which the polarization can be considered as reliable is difficult to define because various factors are involved, but we can estimate the minimum number of votes as 20 times the number of poles (i.e. at least 20 votes for a monopolarity, 40 votes for bipolarity, and 60 votes for a tripolarity). A word is highly polarized when one of the three values is greater than 50%. Table 1 shows some examples of different polarizations, with corresponding intensities and norms.

Although this is out of the scope of this article, we should note that considering polarization as a vector of the three polarities (with possibly null polarities) lead us to very interesting manipulation, comparison and combination possibilities pertaining to vectors and to norms. Basically, the Manhattan norm is the count of votes, and the p-norm with $p = 2$ is the Euclidian norm (the one mentioned here). Roughly speaking, in the context of sentiment analysis of a given text, combining polarizations of contained words means adding such normed vectors.

Figure 1: Two consecutive screenshots of LikeIt. Further to the answer given in the left screen (*barrier*), the player immediately can see at the top of the next screen (right image and bottom zoom), the percentage of players who share his view: the game thus provides a feedback to the player while being immediately rerun with a new question.

Term	Distribution of polarities (%)	Intensity
gift	**POS: 82** NEUT: 14 NEG: 4	Nb votes : 280 norm : 232.73
retirement	POS: 48 NEUT: 18 NEG: 34	Nb votes : 303 norm : 190.60
policemen	POS: 29 NEUT: 15 **NEG: 56**	Nb votes : 274 norm : 177.45
autumn	POS: 37 NEUT: 44 NEG: 18	Nb votes : 277 norm : 168.34

Table 1: Examples of polarizations obtained with LikeIt: the term *gift* is strongly positively monopolarized, while others show a more heterogeneous distribution. The norm value is the norm of the vector composed of the values of positive, neutral and negative polarities. The higher the norm, the more confident we can be in the the representativeness of the polarity distribution.

2.3 The Term Selection Algorithm

A very large proportion of words having a neutral overall polarity, if we randomly select the terms within the network, the game may be monotonous and boring for the player. In addition, the network includes highly specialized terms, which is interesting if you know the term, but discouraging otherwise. For these reasons, the terms are selected within the network via a propagation algorithm whose principle is:

- A term T whose neutral polarity represents less than 50% in the distribution of the three polarities is selected randomly;
- The proposed word is either T, with a probability p of 0.5, either a neighbor N that is randomly selected among neighbors of T, with probability *1-p*;
- In order to accelerate the propagation, the probability p is changed under various conditions (empirically determined). If the total number of votes is under 30 (resp. over 300, over 1000) for N, then $p = 0.25$ (resp. 0.75, 0. 9);
- The propagation algorithm was initiated by manually assigning a positive polarity to the term *good* (1 *positive* vote) and a negative polarity to the word *bad* (1 *negative* vote).

This simple algorithm performs within the network a propagation between the words for which polarity information is relevant, i.e. those that are not strongly neutral, and this while partially avoiding the terms that have already a lot of polarity votes. Thus, a neutral term will be mostly selected through its neighbors. A highly linked term (to other terms in the network) will be polarized more quickly than others as it will be more often reached through neighboring (at least as long as the number of votes remains below the set threshold).

2.4 Observed Experimental Biases

A first bias observed is due to polysemy: for a polysemous term, it is possible that the player's response is influenced by an anecdotal sense, but strongly negative or positive. Thus, polarization of *vache* (cow), whose the dominant sense, the animal, is broadly neutral (or even slightly positive) can be influenced by the meaning *vache (méchant)* (nasty), which is strongly negative. Indeed, the players, who are *de facto* in a polarity context, think at first to the most polarized sense and thus they assign it a negative polarity. It is the same for *fumier* (dominant sense: manure, substituted sense: insult), *cellule* (cell) (dominant sense: biology, substituted sense: jail cell), etc. However, the refinements of these terms show a polarization consistent with that expected. Some terms are bipolarized because the polarity can vary depending on the diegetic perspective (the player identifies with the character and is involved in the context) or extradiegetic (he adopts an external perspective). Thus *dragon, orc, vampire, witch,* etc. are both negative (diegetic perspective) and positive (extradiegetic perspective). It is a second bias. A third bias, which tends to favour the positive polarization, is explained in the next section.

3 Evaluation of Polarity Data

3.1 Quantitative Evaluation

During the first three months, more than 25,000 terms were polarized (i.e. characterized with information on the polarity) with a total of over 150,000 votes. Within 3 years, more than 385,000 words were polarized with more than 100 million votes. The network containing about 490,000 words, we see that about 75% were reached by the propagation algorithm [1] .

283 votes per term on average
178 votes per positive polarity on average
88 votes per neutral polarity on average
83 votes per negative polarity on average
120 votes per polarity on average

Table 2: Quantitative data of polarity obtained with LikeIt: the average number of votes for terms and polarities.

We can clearly see on table 2 that the average number of positive votes is higher than neutral and negative votes altogether. Hence players seem more reluctant to vote neutral or negative than positive. This could be interpreted as an analogy to what happens on social networks, where people are invited to click *like* to show their approval, but where there is no way to indicate that one do not like, disapprove, or even just is indifferent. Thus, it is possible that many people unconsciously behave in a "socially correct" way, i.e. giving only positive opinions and passing over terms that would generate a negative one. We should note however than the mean number might not always be a good indicator of the distribution of the votes, especially when the distribution roughly follows a power law. The median value is certainly more meaningful.

As regards the global distribution of polarities (table 3), there is a slight predominance of neutral polarity, which is not surprising. Although the algorithm is designed not to offer too many neutral terms, current vocabulary still remains predominantly neutral. On the other hand, the positive polarities are almost twice as high as the negative ones, which may be explained in different ways, in addition to the above assumption.

Data in tables 3 and 5 thus appear to be biased towards the positive polarity that represents 55% of votes. Indeed, interviewing the players, it turns out that many terms rather perceived as neutral (e.g. *Odonata*) are often labeled positively. The bias seems to be the result of the adage that "I love what I do not hate". It is difficult to assess the impact of such a bias because the terms that would be positive or neutral are not known *a priori*, but this effect would be in addition to the one mentioned above (reluctance to express a negative opinion) to explain the strong predominance of positive votes.

The positive bias can also be explained as an effect of the term selection algorithm : the proposed terms are mostly named entities or words in fields which usually arouse approval : thus the vast majority of famous people are perceived rather positively, especially actors and actresses; in the same way, named entities of works (films, paintings, novels. . .) mainly generate positive feelings, as well as most of the culinary vocabulary , especially names of culinary specialty, of drinks . . .

The distribution of polarities according to number of votes in table 4 has a median value around 80 (it means that there are so many polarities with a number of votes lower than 80, as of polarities with a number of votes higher than 80). It is quite enough votes for being statistically meaningful. We could consider that at least 20 votes are

[1]all data are freely available at the following url in realtime: url anonymized

336,461	positive polarities	(37.1 %)
373,403	neutral polarities	(41.1 %)
198,103	negative polarities	(21.8 %)
907,967	polarities	(100 %)

59,943,107	positive votes	(54.9 %)
32,879,876	neutral votes	(30.1 %)
16,332,188	negative votes	(15 %)
109,155,171	votes	(100 %)

Table 3: Quantitative data obtained with LikeIt: distribution of polarities (left) and votes (right). We can see the distribution of polarities does not stick exactly to the distribution of votes. There is a majority of neutral polarities but a majority of positive votes.

needed to define a representative polarity; 811,666 polarities are above this threshold (89% of all polarities).

The average (120 see table 2) is shifted to the right due to a number of relations with a very high number of votes. These are the "hub" terms of the network, *i.e.* the very general terms, which are connected to several tens of thousands of words. For instance, the term *animal* has more than 26,052 outcoming relations. Such terms are more often proposed than less connected words, and thus rapidly collect a large number of votes.

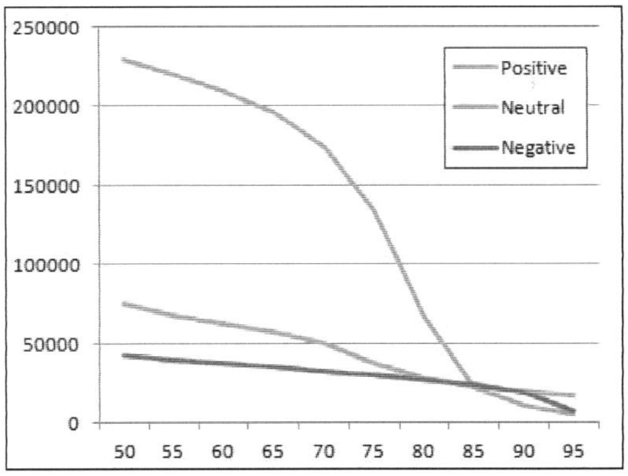

Figure 2: This figure shows the distribution of the majority polarities (> 50%). Such polarities are largely positive and are twice the number of neutral and negative polarities altogether. However for higher distributions (from 60% to 80%) number of positive drops sharply.

In table 5 we see that the dominating polarities combinations are: positive/neutral bipolarity (43%, not necessarily with the same weight) and "positive/neutral/negative" tripolarity (42%, not necessarily evenly distributed). For the first, it confirms that people tend to vote either neutral or positive, or more precisely to vote positively even if they are rather indifferent. Conversely, a negative vote would truly reflect a marked opinion. For the second, it indicates that many words arouse an opinion shared, although in these polarities distributions there may be a strong dominance of one among the three. This distribution also shows that unanimity is rare: only 6.4% shows a single polarity. Figure 3 is cumulative and shows that there are many (in proportion) negative and neutral polarities with a low number of votes, and significantly more positive polarities over 200 votes. This is consistent with the hypothesis mentioned above : people seem more likely to vote positively than negatively or neutrally. In figure 4, the distribution of polarities according to their weight (linear and log) shows that over approximately 400 votes, negative polarities are more numerous than others. This is due to the presence in the network of very negative "hubs" : hightly connected words for which the vote is almost always negative, as *death, illness, accident, cancer* ...Ups and downs are a consequence of the structure of the network, the algorithm and the fact that players can pass over, all combined.

6,835	terms with positive polarity only	(1.8 %)
13,006	terms with neutral polarity only	(3.4 %)
4,388	terms with negative polarity only	(1.1 %)
167,396	terms with positive/neutral polarity only	(43.4 %)
627	terms with positive/negative polarity only	(0.2 %)
31,563	terms with neutral/negative polarity only	(8.2 %)
161,752	terms with positive/neutral/negative polarity	(42 %)
385567	terms with at least one polarity	(100 %)

Table 5: Quantitative data of polarity obtained with LikeIt: the distribution of terms according to mono, bi or tripolarization.

3.2 Qualitative Evaluation Method

The problem of the qualitative evaluation of our data is complex insofar as there is no lexical resource of polarity to which the polarity data from LikeIt could be compared. A manual assessment which would be to check the relevance of the polarity assigned to a number of terms is unthink-

53,881 polarities < 10 votes	854,086 polarities ≥ 10 votes
96,301 polarities < 20 votes	811,666 polarities ≥ 20 votes
222,988 polarities < 40 votes	684,979 polarities ≥ 40 votes
➤ 468,072 polarities < 80 votes	439,895 polarities ≥ 80 votes ◀
639,269 polarities < 160 votes	268,698 polarities ≥ 160 votes
863,043 polarities < 320 votes	44,924 polarities ≥ 320 votes
907,261 polarities < 640 votes	706 polarities ≥ 640 votes
907,926 polarities < 1280 votes	41 polarities ≥ 1280 votes

Table 4: Distributions of polarities depending upon the number of votes which median value is around 80, the median for each polarity being given in table 3.

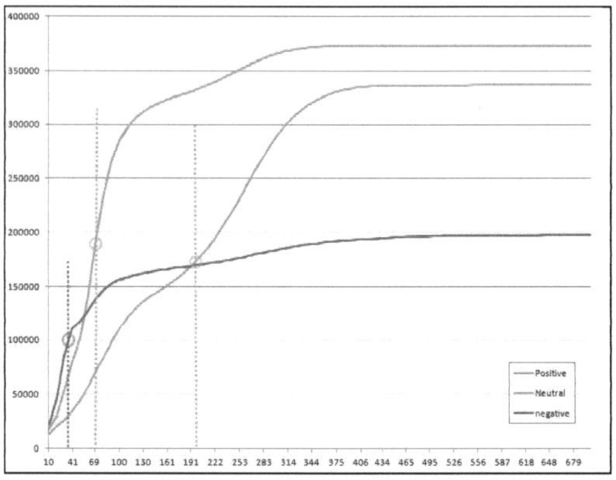

Figure 3: Cumulative number of polarities according to the number of votes (weight). The median values concerning the negative and neutral polarities (resp. 36 and 70) are significantly lower than the median value for positive polarities (about 200).

able due to the data size. In addition, how would we select the terms to be checked? Within the project JDM, two games allow associations between terms and the feelings they evoke: terms relative to feelings can be proposed openly via a text field in the main game, and in a semi-open way (chosen by clic or given through free answer in advanced mode) in Emot game (Lafourcade *et al.*, 2015) (url anonymized) .

So, for each term, we get a list of weighted associated feelings as follows:

- **gift**: joy (1712)(+); surprise (1142)(+); happiness (980)(+); love (780)(+); pleasure (741)(+); friendship (660)(+); gratitude (310)(+); disappointment (260)(-); amazement (222)(+); gratefulness (210)(+); generosity (200)(+); satisfaction (160)(+); contentment (140)(+); enjoyment (120)(+); desire (100)(+); embar-rassment (90)(-); emotion (81)(+); delight (80)(+); impatience (70)(-); jealousy (70)(-); happy (60)(+); party (50)(+); liking (50)(+); frustration (50)(-); awkwardness (50)(-);
- **policeman**: security (1027)(+); fear (1007)(-); violence (817)(-); hatred (357)(-); apprehension (297)(-); anger (186)(-); strength (137)(*); protection (127)(+); repression (127)(-); insecurity (127)(-); anxiety (117)(-); revolt (117)(-); insecurity (127)(-); injustice (97)(-); brutality (97)(-); panic (97)(-); respect (97)(+); terror (87)(-); aggressiveness (117)(-); fury (87)(-); distrust (87)(-); worry (77)(-); pain (77)(-); reject (77)(-); blue funk (67)(-); blindness (66)(-); mistrust (65)(-); shame (63)(-); incomprehension (57)(-); distress (57)(-); relief (57)(+); fright (32)(-); disquietude (32)(-);
- **arm**: strength (110)(*); protection (100)(+); support (80)(+); union (5)(-); indifference (4)().

The terms concerning feelings were the first to be reached by the propagation algorithm, so they are polarized. In the list above, for each feeling term, following the weight of the relation, a symbol in brackets indicates the majority polarity (which accounts for over 50% of votes) or the absence of a dominant polarity. The (+) corresponds to a positive dominant polarity, (-) indicates a negative dominant polarity, () a predominantly neutral polarity, and (*) indicates the absence of a majority polarity. We so notice that the term *strength*, associated with *arm* and with *policeman* does not present any majority polarity.

A polarization can thus be calculated for a term, by making the sum of polarity vectors of every feeling term associated, and it can be compared to that stemming from the LikeIt game. We compare then a polarity inferred to a polarity directly

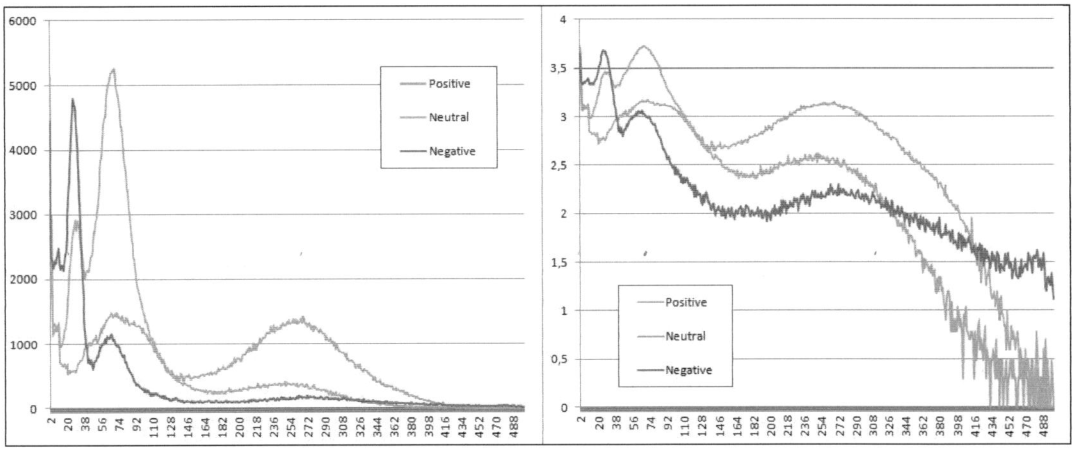

Figure 4: Distribution of polarities (on the left) and of the log of polarities (on the right) according to their number of votes (weight). The number of polarities above 500 votes is low (see table 4) - they are not shown on these figures.

established by the players. This is done via a *cosine* measure and a measure of the *max* (*max*=1 if both dominant polarities coincide). The advantage of such an approach is that it can be automated, so we can reserve the effort of manual inspection for divergent cases. We calculated the *cos* and *max* values, and ordered the first 5,000 terms by decreasing weights for the feelings relation (thus the most often played for this relation at the first).

The average of the maximal polarities from the game (*mpa*) can be seen as the maximum rate of agreement reached on average by the general opinion, for the *n* most played words. Between 1,000 and 5,000 first most played words, the difference between *mpa* and unanimity (100-*mpa*) varies between 15 and 12 %: it seems logic that the number of divergent opinions increases with the number of votes. The manual review of cases of divergence (*max* = 0) shows that they mainly concern the terms that can be perceived from a diegetic or extradiegetic perspective, such as:

thesis, earwig, analysis, moray, micropenis, woman [agent-of] express something, dragon, custard pie attack...

To associate feelings with a given term, the player seems to get a diegetic perspective, while he adopts an external one (extradiegetic perception) to assign one polarity to a given word with LikeIt. Indeed, all the cases of difference concern words polarized negatively via the associated feelings, and positively via LikeIt. Note that the highly polarized words are not concerned by the perspective diegetic / extradiegetic. Moreover, we emphasize that the terms that elicit the most subjectivity of opinion display a heterogeneous polarity, but its distribution into *positive/negative/neutral* is consistent in both modes of assessment.

4 Conclusion and Future Work

Our results and the method we developed to characterize the polarity through various GWAP allow to consider a number of perspectives. First, it is to continue the double approach (polarity inferred from associated feelings, and polarity directly assigned through the game LikeIt) to further expand the already abundant lexical resource of polarity (385,000 words with a polarity information as a freely available resource).

Then, our approach can be extrapolated: indeed, all types of characteristics (size, temperature, weight / balance, temporality, location ...) may be characterized and quantified using crowdsourcing through GWAP. But a preliminary study to identify the most useful and informative has necessarily to be undertaken, to avoid boring and thus demotivating the players by multiplying this type of games. Note that the data generated through these games, that require only knowledge and a good command of language, are of good quality, which justifies this approach.

It is also necessary to keep in mind that the polarities data are not static but potentially fluctuating, especially in time, and depending on the circumstances. For example, the term *volcano* rather arouses curiosity or indifference, but when an im-

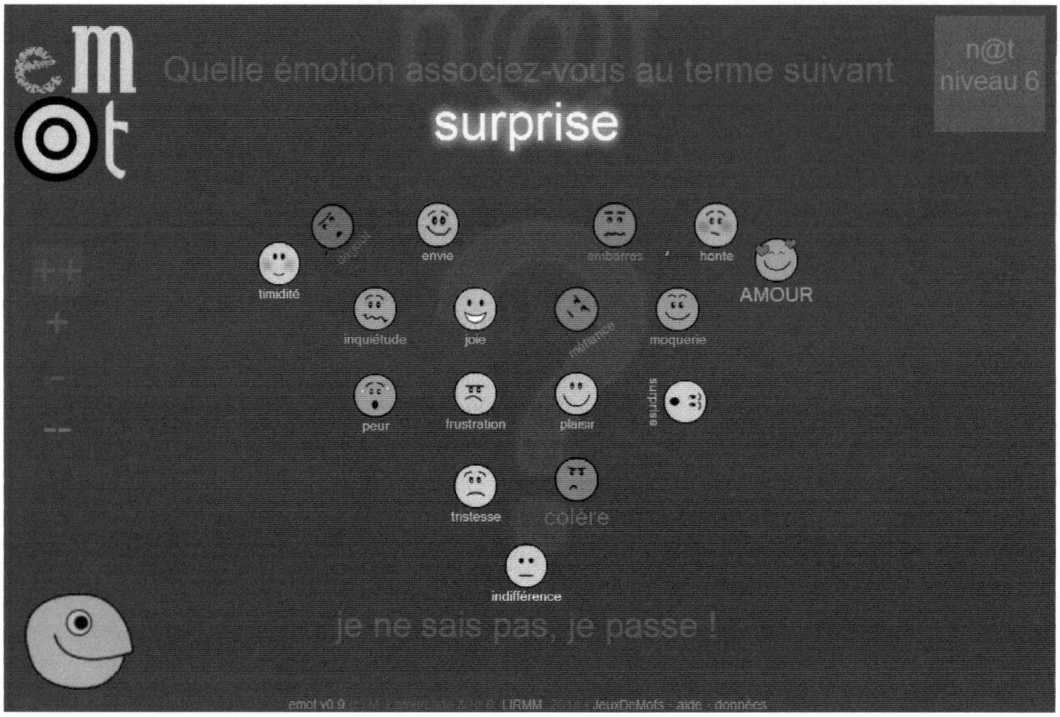

Figure 5: A screenshot of the Emot game. The player is invited to choose one associated feeling aroused by the word *surprise*. The data obtained with Emot allow us to cross-evaluate those obtained with LikeIt.

n first terms	**Cos average**	**Max average**	**Maximal polarities average**
1 000	0.80	0.76	85.65 %
2 000	0.83	0.79	86.55 %
3 000	0.80	0.75	87.40 %
4 000	0.82	0.77	87.49 %
5 000	0.83	0.79	87.63 %

Table 6: Qualitative assessment of polarization data from LikeIt compared with those calculated from the associated feelings. There is a significant correlation between the polarization defined by LikeIt and that induced by the associated feelings.

minent eruption threatens populations or air traffic, anxiety and fear become the majority among the feelings expressed. Similarly, feelings about a celebrity, or a work (named entities) can be very fluctuating over time, and if contradictory feelings appear for the same word in the network, introduce a notion of context may be interesting, for example *DSK [context] IMF*, and *DSK[context] Sofitel.*

We could polarize the words automatically, based on their relations within the network: for example, the relation *characteristic* is very polarizing; *widow [characteristic] sad* allows to assign a negative polarity to *widow*. However, the crowdsourcing approach is generally more reliable and faster, both for highly monopolarized words and those whose polarity is more heterogeneous.

The approach and tools presented in this article are relatively new, and the number of polarized terms represents a significant proportion (70%) of the entire network. It can be assumed that the most interesting common words are those which are the most played in JeuxDeMots, hence the most appropriately linked to other words, as claimed in (Chamberlain *et al.*, 2006). As our propagation algorithm selects the vast majority of such terms, we may conclude that our approach allows to effectively polarize them. Given the results, we reckon we have demonstrated the feasibility, the interest and the perspective of our project, and broadly undertook to build the corresponding resource.

References

Agarwa C. and Bhattachary P. 2006. Augmenting Wordnet with Polarity Information on Adjectives. *3rd International Wordnet Conference*, Jeju Island, Korea, South Jeju (Seogwipo), 2006, 7 p.

Brun C. 2011. Detecting opinions using Deep Syntactic Analysis. *Proceedings of Recent Advances in Natural Language Processing*, (RANLP 2011), Hissar, Bulgaria, pp. 392-398.

Chamberlain J., Fort K., Kruschwitz U., Lafourcade M. and Poesio M. 2013. Using Games to Create Language Resources: Successes and Limitations of the Approach. *Theory and Applications of Natural Language Processing.* Gurevych, Iryna; Kim, Jungi (Eds.), Springer, ISBN 978-3-642-35084-9, 2013, 42 p.

Esuli A. and Sebastiani F. 2006. SentiWordNet: a publicly available lexical resource for opinion mining. *Proceedings of LREC-06*, Gêne, Italie, 6 p.

Fort K., Adda G., Sagot B., Mariani J. and Couillaut A. 2014. Crowdsourcing for Language Resource Development: Criticisms about Amazon Mechanical Turk Overpowering Use. *Lecture Notes in Artificial Intelligence*,Springer, pp. 303-314, 2014, 978-3-319-08957-7.

Gala N. and Brun C. 2012. Propagation de polarités dans des familles de mots : impact de la morphologie dans la construction d'un lexique pour l'analyse d'opinions. *Actes de Traitement Automatique des Langues Naturelles*, (TALN 12), Grenoble, juin 2012, pp. 495-502.

Kim S. and Hovy E. 2004. Determining the sentiment of opinions. *Proceedings of COLING- 04*, (TALN 12), Barcelone, Espagne, pp. 1367-1373.

Lafourcade M. 2007. Making people play for Lexical Acquisition. *Proceedings of 7th Symposium on Natural Language Processing*, Thailand, 13-15 December 2007, 8p.

Lafourcade M., Le Brun N. and Joubert A. 2015. Jeux et intelligence collective – résolution de problèmes et acquisition de données sur le Web. *Collection Science cognitive et management des connaissances (sous la direction de Joseph Mariani et Patrick Paroubek)*, ISTE éditions, 2015, 156 p.

Lafourcade M. and Fort K. 2014. Propa-L: a semantic filtering service from a lexical network created using Games With A Purpose. *Proceedings of the Ninth International Conference on Language Resources and Evaluation*, Reykjavik, Islande, 26-31 May 2014, pp. 1676-1681.

Saif M. and Turney P. 2013. Crowdsourcing a Word-Emotion Association Lexicon. *Computational Intelligence*, 29 (3), pp. 436-465.

Snow R., OConnor B., Jurafsky D., and Y. Ng A. 2008 Cheap and Fast But is it Good? Evaluating Non-Expert Annotations for Natural Language Tasks. *Proceedings of the 2008 Conference on Empirical Methods in Natural Language Processing*, Honolulu, Association for Computational Linguistics, pp. 254263.

Strapparava C. and Valitutti A. 2004. WordNet Affect: an affective extension of WordNet. *Proceedings 4th International conference on Language Resources and Evaluation*, (LREC-04), Lisbon, Portugal, pp. 1083-1086.

Taboada M., Brooke J., Tofiloski M., Voll K. and Stede M. 2011. Lexicon-based methods for sentiment analysis. *Computational Linguistics,* Volume 37 (2), pp. 267-307.

Turney P. 2002. Thumbs up or thumbs down? Semantic orientation applied to unsupervised classification of reviews. *Proceedings of ACL-02*, Philadelphia, USA, pp. 417-424.

Vegnaduzzo V. 2004. Acquisition of subjective adjectives with limited resources. *AAAI spring symposium on exploring attitude and affect in text: Theories and Applications*, Stanford, USA.

Medical Imaging Report Indexing: Enrichment of Index through an Algorithm of Spreading over a Lexico-semantic Network

Mathieu Lafourcade
LIRMM
University of Montpellier
France
mathieu.lafourcade@lirmm.fr

Lionel Ramadier
IMAIOS
34090 Montpellier
France
lionel.ramadier@lirmm.fr

Abstract

In medical imaging domain, digitized data is rapidly expanding Therefore it is of major interest for radiologists to be able to do an efficient and accurate extraction of imaging and clinical data (radiology reports) which are essential for a rigorous diagnosis and for a better management of patients. In daily practice, radiology reports are written using a non-standardized language which is often ambiguous and noisy. The queries of radiological images can be greatly facilitated through textual indexing of associated reports. In order to improve the quality of the analysis of such reports, it is desirable to specify an index enlargement algorithm based on spreading activations over a general lexical-semantic network. In this paper, we present such an algorithm along with its qualitative evaluation.

1 Introduction

Widespread digitalization in the health care sector and the implementation of customized electronic medical record result in a rapid increase in the volume of digital medical data. The medical computer systems allow to archive many and varied information (for example medical record, results of medical analyses, X-rays and radiological reports…). Thus, these data are accessible, either to be completed and compared with new results or to adapt the management of patients, or to provide decision support to improve the quality of care. The ability to have easily and efficiently access to these medical data has become a primary objective for health professionals. Thus, a proper indexing of medical reports (surgical, radiological...) optimizes the search for information, not only in a clinical purpose, but also educational. Dinh *and al.*, (2010) then realized a semantic indexing of patients' medical records in order to make it support for some information search procedures. Their indexing method uses MeSH (Medical Subject Headings), involves disambiguation, the extraction of clinical values, and weighting of concepts. Pouliquen, (2002) also performed an automatic indexation through recognition and extraction of medical concepts. He took into account the compound words and word associations to convert a sentence in reference words with the help of a medical thesaurus.

In the field of the medical imaging, the quantity of images and reports increases so much that being able to find quickly and easily the information becomes a major stake. But take full advantage of such a collection of radiological images means being able to quickly identify relevant information and requires that they are properly indexed from their reports. To be effective and useful for practitioners, indexing must consider their requests. Several authors, including Hersh et al., (2001) and Huang et al., (2003) automatically indexed radiological reports using the UMLS metathesaurus. To improve the accuracy of their results, they used a subsection of UMLS terminology, and Hersh *et al.,* (2001) deliberately choose not to include some parts of reports, especially the *indications* section. They thus obtained an index limited to strictly medical terms. However, in practice, in order to efficiently search, practitioners must have the possibility to specify in their requests not only medical specific terms (*digestive perforing, glioblastoma*), but also expressions, compound words, and circumlocutions of general sense (*skiing accident, breast disease in young women, hangman fracture, trauma of the lower limbs*).

Proceedings of Recent Advances in Natural Language Processing, pages 338–345,
Hissar, Bulgaria, Sep 7–9 2015.

Automatic extraction of relevant information from medical corpus is complex for several reasons: firstly, most texts are not structured and contain abbreviations, ellipsis and inaccuracies, on the other hand the amount of information to be analyzed is large and relevance is difficult to determine. The obstacles that hinder relevant indexing are of all kinds: difficulty of automatic semantic analysis (especially the precise analysis of negations, as shown by Huang *et al.*, (2007)), of identifying apocopes *(flu for influenza)* or unfamiliar terms (i.e. absent from the knowledge base), of recognition of medical entities often present in a distorted writing style, of extraction of semantic relations present in the text (Bundschus *et al.*, 2008), etc. To carry out a good indexing, it is crucial to have a knowledge base not only broad-spectrum (i.e. not limited to standardized forms) but also dynamic (i.e. able to evolve and enrich itself by permanent learning).

As far as we know, until now, the automatic indexing of radiological reports has concerned mainly medical terms without considering the general information. However, Xu *et al.*, (2014) were able to identify named entities of anatomical terms using some general resources like Wikipedia and Wordnet besides the usual medical resources i.e. UMLS, RadLex, MeSH et BodyPart3D (http://lifesciencedb.jp/bp3d/). Another type of resource, which had never been used in the medical or biomedical framework allows to consider not only the words and concepts of specialty, but also the common language used in reports (including the *indications* section). This is the lexical-semantic JeuxDeMots network (http://www.jeuxdemots.org) we use as a basis of knowledge and support for automatic indexing of radiological reports.

One objective of IMAIOS project (that we are conducting in collaboration with radiologists from Montpellier) is to achieve efficient indexing of radiological reports. To this end, we do not use only a description of the terms and concepts of specialty, but we are also working to determine the meaning and usage of terms and abbreviations very common in medicine. McInnes and Stevenson (2014) stressed the difficulty of indexing in the biomedical field, and Ramadier *et al.*, (2014) tries to make the task easier by using annotations and inferences from semantic relations. In this article we show how one can, from the semantic information of reports (in French), set an enlargement of raw built index to improve the recall of information retrieval. Indeed, radiologists may express their queries using generic terms (e.g. *benign brain tumor, brain tumor, benign tumor, tumor*) or consequences, or circumstances, etc. without these terms or expressions are explicitly present in reports. This semantic indexation may be also combined with the content-based image retrieval (CBIR) (Kurtz *et al.* (2014)).

In this article we first present the knowledge base used to achieve this indexing in French langage, i.e. the lexical network JeuxDeMots, then we describe precisely what an enlarged index relative to raw index is, and the index enlargement algorithm based on a spread over the lexical network. Finally we discuss experiments and analyze the results.

2 Index Enlargement and Spreading

The knowledge base on which our radiological reports indexing strategy relies is the lexical network JeuxDeMots (Lafourcade 2007). Although this network is general, it contains many specialty data, including medicine/radiology, which we have added within the framework of IMAIOS project. The network is the basis for a propagation algorithm that aims to increase the raw index obtained through conventional methods of information retrieval.

2.1 The JeuxDeMots Lexical Network

JDM network is a lexical-semantic graph for the French language whose lexical relations are generated both through GWAP (Games With A Purpose, see Lafourcade *et al.*, (2015)) and via a contributory tool called Diko (manual insertion and automatic inferences with validations). At the time of this writing, the JDM network contains over 20 million relations between around 500,000 terms. The properties of this network that are important in the context of our work are the following:

- among about 80 lexico-semantic relations of the network, those which are relevant for our indexation project are the relations essentially semantic like hyperonymy, typical features, typical places, typical parts, target, etc.;
- polysemous terms are connected by the relation "refinement" with their various senses. About 9,000 polysemous terms are linked to approximately 25,000 meanings.

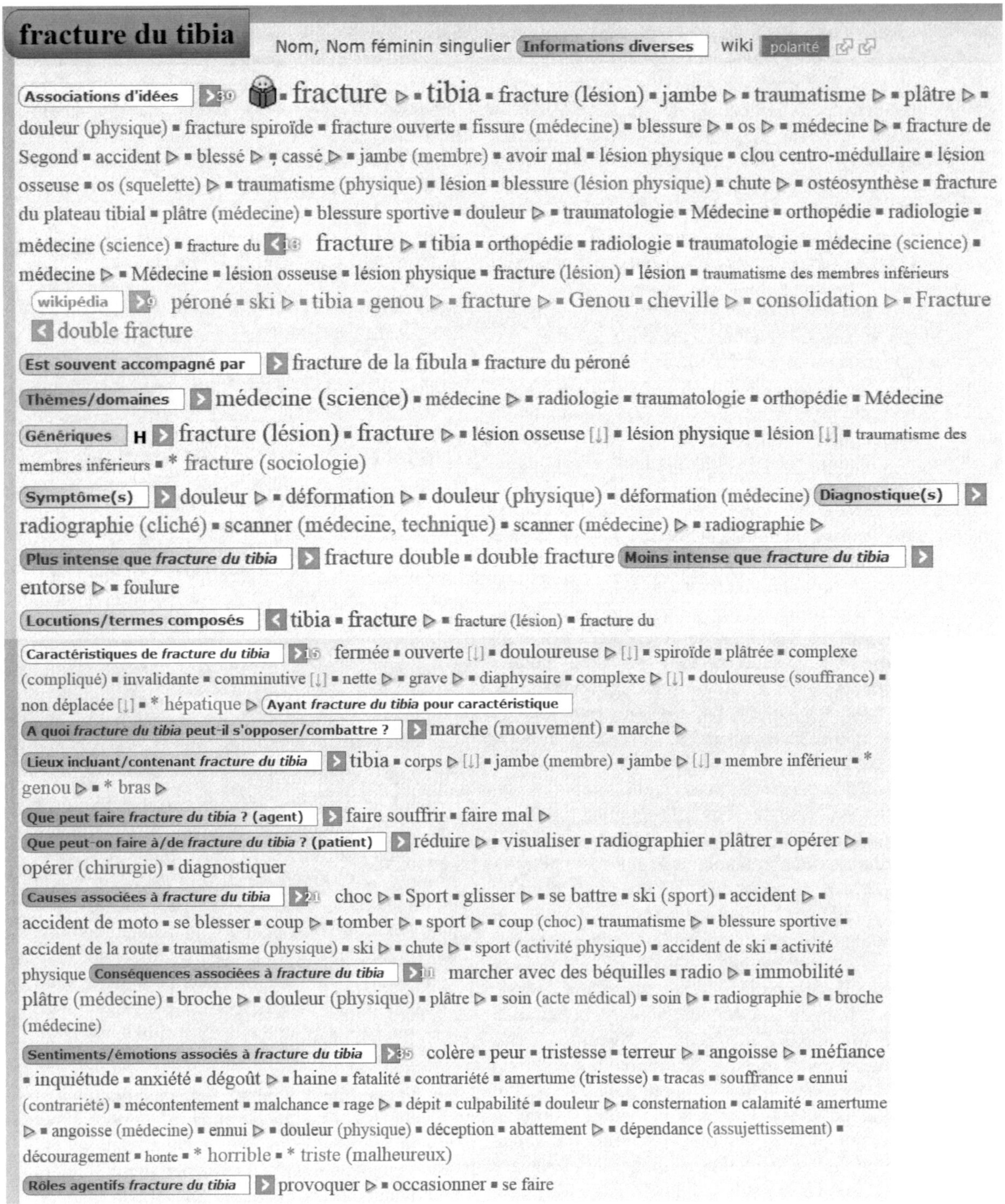

Figure 1. Screenshot of the contributory tool Diko showing the entry "tibia fracture". Diko is the online tool of visualization and of contribution of the JeuxDeMots lexical network. Note that the entry *tibia fracture* includes both specific medical relations (such as symptoms, diagnostic ...) and more general associations (such as causes, consequences, etc.).

For example, fracture → fracture (injury), fracture (break), fracture (sociology). The term in brackets is a *gloss* that allows to know or guess the meaning (refinement) of the polysemous word;

- relations are weighted, the weight reflects the strength of association between terms. Approximately 70,000 relations have negative weights, indicating a wrong relation (wrong relations are kept as they may be interesting within the framework of lexical disambiguation). An example is : *fracture du tibia *hypernym (< 0)* fracture (sociology: social dislocation) ;
- when a term *t* is associated with one of the meanings of a polysemous term, there is a relation of inhibition between the other meanings and the term *t*. For example: fracture *inhibition* talus (inclination), talus (printing), talus (embankment), astragale (architecture), astragale (botany), There is at least another meaning of talus or of astragale which are related to the term fracture: talus (os) and astragale (os).

The indexing of keywords in the medical field is often limited to certain aspects of a disease (Andrade, 2000) or to a part of the anatomy. But as the purpose of this indexation is to retrieve documents using also everyday language, we index not only anatomical terms (*knee, anterior wall of the colon, the genu of the corpus callosum, ...*), clinical signs (*plantar reflex*) and the names of diseases (*carcinoma*), but also everyday words (*fall in the bathtub*) likely to be used by the radiologist in his query.

The following table provides an order of size of the amount of information we have at our disposal about the specialty areas that are particularly relevant in the IMAIOS project:

Term	Outgoing links	Incoming links
medicine	21408	22666
anatomy	10477	11453
radiology	382	502
accident	741	956
medical imaging	541	556

Table 1: Number of relations of some key terms within the JDM lexical network.

2.2 Standard Indexing Report

Our corpus includes approximately 40,000 radiology reports (Example 1) concerning the different medical imaging techniques (MRI, scanner, ultrasonography, X-ray radiology, vascular radiology, scintigraphy ...). These reports are written in semi-structured way: they are generally divided into four parts (*indications, technique, results*, and an optional *conclusion*). Each part is written by the radiologist in a very free style, often with a profusion of acronyms (ATCD for of antecedent, ACR for American College of Radiology, tt for treatment, etc.), of elisions (*the anterior communicating* instead of *the anterior communicating artery*), and all sorts of various improprieties (*influenza* instead of *influenza virus*). Reports contain a lot of implicit information which need to be explicit to realize an indexation meeting the needs of practitioners. For instance it may be very interesting to explicit the expression *middle cerebral artery territory.*

The creation of the index starting from the reports is made by the traditional methods of information retrieval, i.e. term frequency (TF) and document frequency (DF) to calculate the IDF (Inverse Document Frequency). The identification of the compound terms is made upstream compared to the content of JeuxDeMots network. We use the underscore to separate the two parts of a compound word so that it is considered as an entity at the time of the extraction (*tibia_fracture*).

indications : fracture du tibia droit, chute de ski **technique** : une série de coupes axiales transverses sur l'ensemble de la cheville droite sans injection de produit de contraste **étude** : en fenêtres parties molles et osseuses. **résultats** : fractures diaphysaires spiroïdes à trois fragments principaux du 1/3 distal du tibia et de la fibula avec discret déplacement vers l'avant, sans retrait de refend articulaire. Fractures de la base de M2 et de M3 non articulaire et non déplacée. Fracture articulaire de la partie interne de la base de M1 non déplacée. Atrophie avec dégénérescence marquée des corps musculaires de l'ensemble des loges.	atrophie • cheville • chute • corps musculaire • coupe axiale transverse • dégénérescence • déplacement • fibula • fracture • fracture du tibia • loge • non articulaire • non déplacée • ski • spiroïde • tibia

Example 1: typical radiological report (left) and raw index (right). The raw index is the list of extracted terms, ordered alphabetically (the weights are not mentioned and the list is simplified). Compound words are extracted if they are present in the same form in the JDM network.

Despite the frequency filtering, we keep the words in the vicinity of medicine, even for low TF-IDF values. If a word of the report is connected to *medicine* (neighbor at a distance of 1) in the JDM network, then it is added to the index. In the same way, non-medical words (*motorcycle accident*, *influence of drugs*) are captured and added to the index if they are linked to a term itself linked to *medicine* (neighbor at a distance of 2): thus *motorcycle accident* is added because it is linked to *polytrauma* through the consequence relation and *polytraumat* is itself related to *medicine* through the field relation

Moreover, if a term of raw index is polysemous, it is interesting to try to determine the proper refinement: for example, in the above report the words *fracture (fracture), cheville (ankle), chute (fall)* and *loge (compartment)* are polysemous. We will see later that the identification of proper refinement is important. Moreover, the algorithm does not handle negation but in the phrase "*no articular fracture*", the term "*no articular*" will be detected because it belongs to the network JDM.

Thus, the *enlargement is a process intended for adding to the index some terms which are relevant, although they are not in the text.*

accident de ski • **accident de sports d'hiver** • atrophie • cheville • **cheville>anatomie** • chute • **chute>tomber** • corps musculaire • coupe axiale transverse • dégénérescence • **dégénérescence musculaire** • déplacement • fibula • fracture • **fracture articulaire** • **fracture des membres inférieurs** • **fracture multiple** • **fracture diaphysaire** • **fracture du tibia** • **fracture non articulaire** • **fracture non déplacée** • **fracture spiroïde** • **fracture avec déplacement** • **fracture>lésion** • **imagerie médicale** • **jambe** • **lésion** • **lésion osseuse** • loge • **loge>anatomie** • **médecine** • non articulaire • non déplacée • **péroné** • **radiologie** • ski • **spiroïde** • **sports d'hiver** • tibia • **traumatisme des membres inférieurs** • ...

Example 2: Enlarged index corresponding to raw index above (the terms are listed alphabetically with the added words in bold). We can see that the general themes of the text are properly identified (*medicine, medical imaging, radiology*), and the polysemous terms were refined with the correct meaning depending on the context.

2.3 Enlargement through Spreading Algorithm

The enlargement strategy is to propagate signals originating from the terms of the raw index over the JDM network. The signal consists in "lighting up" the terms of the raw index within the network and retrieve related terms that light up in their turn.

At each iteration, the terms discharge their current activation to their neighbors. Thus, the total activation is none other than the sum of discharges received by a term during the entire process. For negatively weighted relations (i.e. inhibitory relations), the activation is removed instead of added. A term with negative CA cannot discharge. Iterated sequence is performed synchronously for all terms. Note that the distribution of the signal is proportional to the logarithm of the weight (and not proportional to the weight itself).

Specifically, we can describe the algorithm informally as follows:

Init: terms T of network are associated with a pair of values (CA, TA), *current activation* and *total activation*.

1 for the terms **T** belonging to raw index, we set CA = TA = 1. the terms **T** are sources of activation

2 for all other terms, AC= AT = 0.

3 we set a number of iterations NBI

4 we repeat NBI times the following operation :

5 for each term T of network having neighbors $\{t_1, \ldots, t_n\}$ via a relation *r* from T to t_i with a positive weight w_i, we modify CA and TA of t_i :

$$CA(t_i) = CA(t_i) + CA(T) \times \frac{\log(w_i)}{\sum_{k=0}^{n} \log(w_k)}$$

$$TA(t_i) = TA(t_i) + CA(t_i)$$

// activation received by t_i is stored in $TA(t_i)$

6 $AT(\mathbf{T}) = 1$

// all T discharged their activation, we recharge the **T**

7 activated terms are filtered using a percentage of surface S; the remaining activated terms are returned.

Algorithm 1: calculation of an enlarged index starting from a raw index, using a propagation over the JDM lexical network. The two main parameters are NBI (number of iterations) and S (% of retained surface for the filter).

NBI \ S	10 %	20 %	30 %	40 %	50 %
1	22 / 82 %	45 / 80 %	67 / 78 %	93 / 53 %	127 / 38 %
2	31 / 95 %	55 / 92 %	83 / 89 %	211 / 57 %	439 / 41 %
3	48 / 99 %	90 / 97 %	139 / 95 %	356 / 53 %	755 / 34 %
4	111 / 97 %	223 / 92 %	335 / 87 %	747 / 45 %	1259 / 23 %
5	387 / 96 %	774 / 87 %	1161 / 76 %	1671 / 26 %	2089 / 15 %

Table 3 : The *nouv/pert* values depending on NBI and S parameters. NBI is the number of iterations performed in the lexical network. S is the retained part of the area under the curve of the cumulative weights of terms reached by the propagation algorithm.

After the iterations (lines 5-7), we obtain a weighted list of terms that are then ranked in order of decreasing weights. We retain by filtering N terms of the highest weight, such that the sum of their weights is S% of the total weight of the terms of the list.

We chose not to use all relations available in the lexical network JDM; indeed, some of them are too lexical: in the context of our work, they could degrade accuracy. We use the following relations (Table 2) (their relative importance, if different from 1 (default weighting) is indicated in brackets): associated ideas (weight of 1/2), hypernyms (weight of 2), synonyms, typical features, symptoms, diagnostics, parts/whole, typical place, causes, consequences, field, and frequently associated with. In the above algorithm, for simplicity, all relations are equally important (default weighting of 1, otherwise, their relative importance should be placed on both sides of the fraction).

r_associated	free associated terms
r_synonym	synonyms or quasi-synonyms
r_syn_strict	strict synonyms
r_isa	generic term
r_carac	typical characteristics
r_target	target of disease (people, organ etc).of diseases
r_symptoms	symptoms of diseases
r_location	typical location
r_cause	typical causes
r_consequence	typical consequences
r_accomp	what comes often with

Table 2: the relations through which the algorithm spreads to enlarge the index

3 Evaluation of Enlarged Index

We conducted a statistical evaluation of our propagation algorithm by randomly selecting 200 enlarged indexes (from a total of 30,000 calculated). We manually reviewed every term of the enlarged index to determine whether it was relevant or not. A *relevant term* is a term that is considered as appropriate for the description of the report. The presence of irrelevant terms increases the amount of noise when requesting documents. The absence of relevant terms decreases recall.

The pairs of values in Table 3 are *nouv/pert*, where *nouv* is the average number of terms of enlarged index that are not in the raw index and *pert* the average percentage of the relevant terms in enlarged index.

In practice, the *pert* value is assessed manually just once, regardless of the NBI and S parameters. Indeed we examine for each report all terms obtained in order of decreasing weights, for all parameter values, and then we assess the adequacy of each term. If we find a succession of 5 irrelevant terms, it is considered that the following are also irrelevant. The *nouv* value can be calculated automatically. For the same number of iterations, the greater the retained part is, the larger the number of terms is (low filtering). This means that if the recall is more important, in consideration accuracy tends to decrease (or even to collapse beyond 30%), because the terms added to the raw index are less and less relevant. Conversely, the more the number of iterations increases, the more the relevant terms are likely to be often reached and through multiple paths starting from the terms of the raw index, thus to be reinforced. The lexical network contains loops (direct and indirect) that act as self-reinforcement structures. The computation time dramatically increases with each new iteration, as the number of terms discharging their activation increases very strongly. For NBI = 5, almost the entire network is reached (if we exclude filtering S), its diameter being of about 6 (JDM is small-world network). Overall the conditions that seem most interesting for a reasonable computation time (a few seconds) are 3-4 iterations and an area of less than 30%.

All ambiguous terms have correctly been disambiguated. This means that the enlarged index systematically included proper refinement when refinement was proposed (this is not necessarily the case for low values of NBI and S). If we recalculate the enlarged index while preventing access to refined terms, the *pert* value decline globally by 10%, regardless of the values of NBI and S. Try to select the correct meaning of ambiguous words can be carried out jointly with the selection of relevant terms and would even tend to favor it. Finally, all the specialty areas identified by the algorithm turned out relevant. Add the relevant specialties in the raw index before the enlargement process does not significantly improve the results (nor degrade them). Note that if we recalculate the raw and enlarged index while giving access, during propagation, only to immediate neighbors of the word *medicine*, whatever the relation, then the *pert* value decline in average by 12%. The use of a wide knowledge base, no limited to the only specialty field would thus improve largely the relevance of the produced index. Thus, the choice not to separate specialized and common vocabulary proves judicious and effective regarding the analysis of radiological reports. Moreover the algorithm is fast and well suited to handle the amount of data generated daily in radiology centers.

One can also notice that the overall process presented above works thematically on the text and semantically on the lexical network. A sharp semantic analysis of the reports would in all likelihood involve a chunk and dependencies analysis. The errors we found (23 terms for 200 indexes, which represent 23 errors for about 10,000 terms) may have different causes:

- lack of information in the knowledge base (20% of error cases);
- lack of semantic role, implying the need for a detailed analysis (55%);
- chimerism - two parts of the report have brought about an irrelevant term (25%).

As mentioned above, the network is characterized by a *never ending learning* approach (adding relations and refinement occurs permanently) in the spirit of Carlson *et al.* (2010). We can therefore reasonably hope that the knowledge base being constantly enriching, errors due to lack of knowledge will rapidly decrease over time. Similarly, the ability to identify the semantic relations and especially semantic roles within the reports would minimize the 2nd and 3rd source of errors.

4 Conclusion and prospects

Our objective is to automatically index radiological reports, using not only the medical terms but also words of common language that may be included in users' queries, especially hospital practitioners. To increase recall without significantly degrading the accuracy, we add in the raw index some implied words or expressions, using the JeuxDeMots lexical-semantic network as a support of knowledge. As far as we know, very few studies take into account the non-medical items in the radiological reports or carry out implicit inference for identify relevant terms. Conventional approaches to improve recall consist primarily of adding some terms more general (hyperonyms) starting from a medical ontology. But it is tangible that when information of general sense is present, the results are improved: the assumption that it would be better not to separate general knowledge and specialized one seems to be confirmed, at least in the context of our indexing works.

The results presented here are preliminary and require a substantive assessment of indexes on the whole corpus. These first results look promising, but we need to be able to automate the evaluation in order to do it on a larger scale. We could then further analyze the reports by seeking to extract relations between words using analogy/comparison with the relations of the JeuxDeMots lexical-semantic network. Another improvement would be to develop automated means for recognizing negation. So, the indexation would concern not only the terms, but also the semantic relations between them. One objective of the IMAIOS project is also to extract from medical reports some new knowledge to enrich the lexical network. Finally, we also plan to deduct from the corpus some rules of inference and thus make an authentic reasoning, i.e. to propose by deduction and by induction new medical information or even diagnosis.

References

Andrade M. A. and Bork, P. 2000. *Automated extraction of information in molecular biology.* FEBS letters, Elsevier, 476/1, pp. 12–17.

Bundschus M., Dejori M., Stetter M., Tresp V. and Kriegel H.-P. 2008. *Extraction of semantic biomedical relations from text using conditional random fields.* BMC bioinformatics, **9**:207, 14 p.

Carlson A., Betteridge J., Kisiel B., Settles B., Hruschka E. R., and Mitchell T. M. 2010. *Toward an architecture for never-ending language learning.* In AAAI, 2010, 8 p.

Dinh D., Tamine L. *et al.* 2010. *Vers un modèle d'indexation sémantique adapté aux dossiers médicaux de patients.* In Conférence francophone en Recherche d'Information et Applications, CORIA 2010, pp. 325–336.

Hersh W., Mailhot M., Arnott-Smith C. and Lowe H. 2001. *Selective automated indexing of findings and diagnoses in radiology reports.* Journal of biomedical informatics, 34(4), pp. 262–273.

Huang Y. and Lowe H. J. 2007. A *novel hybrid approach to automated negation detection in clinical radiology reports.* Journal of the American Medical Informatics Association, 14(3), pp. 304–311.

Huang Y., Lowe H. J. and Hersh W. R. (2003. A pilot study of contextual UMLS indexing to improve the precision of concept-based representation in xml-structured clinical radiology reports. Journal of the American Medical Informatics Association, 10(6), pp. 580–587.

Kurtz, C., Beaulieu, C. F., Napel, S., & Rubin, D. L. (2014). A hierarchical knowledge-based approach for retrieving similar medical images described with semantic annotations. *Journal of biomedical informatics*, *49*, pp. 227-244.

Lafourcade M. (2007). *Making people play for lexical acquisition with the JeuxDeMots prototype.* In SNLP'07 : 7th international symposium on natural language processing.

Lafourcade M., Le Brun N., Joubert A. (2015) *Games with a Purpose (GWAPS),* John Wiley & Sons, ISBN: 978-1-84821-803-1, 158 p.

Langlotz C. P. 2006. Radlex : A new method for indexing online educational material. Radiographics, 26(6), pp. 1595–1597.

Mcinnes B. T. and Stevenson M. 2014. *Determining the difficulty of word sense disambiguation.* Journal of biomedical informatics, 47, pp. 83–90.

Pouliquen B. 2002. *Indexation de textes médicaux par extraction de concepts, et ses utilisations.* Thèse de doctorat, Faculté de Médecine, Université Rennes 1, juin 2002, 163 p.

Ramadier L., Zarrouk M., Lafourcade M. and Micheau A. 2014. *Annotations et inférences de relations dans un réseau lexico-sémantique : application à la radiologie.* TALN 2014, Marseille, juillet 2014, pp. 103-112.

Ramos J. 2003. *Using TF-IDF to Determine Word Relevance in Document Queries.* In Proceedings of the first instructional conference on machine learning., 4 p.

Robertson S. E. and Jones K. S. 1976. *Relevance weighting of search terms.* Journal of the American Society for Information science, 27(3), pp. 129–146.

Robertson, S. 2004. "Understanding inverse document frequency: On theoretical arguments for IDF". *Journal of Documentation* **60** (5): pp. 503–520.

Xu Y., Hua J., Ni Z., Chen Q., Fan Y., Ananiadou S., Eric I., Chang C. and Tsujii J. 2014. *Anatomical entity recognition with a hierarchical framework augmented by external resources.* PloS one, 9(10), e108396.

Zarrouk M., Lafourcade M. and Joubert A. 2013. *Inference and reconciliation in a crowdsourced lexical semantic network.* Computación y Sistemas, 17(2), pp. 147–159.

Taxonomy Beats Corpus in Similarity Identification, but Does It Matter?

Minh Ngoc Le
VU University Amsterdam
m.n.le@vu.nl

Antske Fokkens
VU University Amsterdam
antske.fokkens@vu.nl

Abstract

We present extensive evaluations comparing the performance of taxonomy-based and corpus-based approaches on SimLex-999. The results confirm our hypothesis that taxonomy-based approaches are more suitable to identify similarity. We introduce two new measures of evaluation that show that all measures perform well on a coarse-grained evaluation and that it is not always clear which approach is most suitable when a similarity score is used as a threshold. This leads us to conclude that the inferior performance of corpus-based approaches may not (always) matter.

1 Introduction

Similarity measures are used in a wide variety of Natural Language Processing (NLP) tasks (see Pilehvar et al. (2013), among others for examples). They may be used, e.g. to increase coverage of an approach by using information from similar words for unseen data, or to establish average similarity between a question and a potential answer.

Due to its importance, similarity measures have received steady attention in computational linguistics. There are two widely followed, but different, schools: taxonomy-based approaches and distributional, or corpus-based, approaches. Apart from a few exceptions, these approaches have mostly been studied separately.

Our main goal is to examine how the approaches perform when identifying true similarity, in contrast to the more general relatedness, which also includes association, between word-pairs. We evaluate the approaches on the new gold-standard SimLex-999 (Hill et al., 2014b). We compare taxonomy-based approaches that use WordNet (Fellbaum, 1998) to the corpus-based approaches that performed best on SimLex-999 in Hill et al. (2014a). We hypothesize that taxonomy-based approaches outperform corpus-based approaches on a true similarity set, because corpus-based approaches tend to mix-up similarity and association.

We carry out several evaluations which investigate (i) the difference in performance on pure similarity sets and sets that combine similarity and association, (ii) the influence of associative pairs while identifying true similarity, and (iii) various evaluation metrics that compare similarity measures to the gold standard of SimLex-999.

We perform more than one evaluation metric for two reasons. First, different ranking coefficients can lead to a completely different outcome when evaluating similarity scores (Fokkens et al., 2013). Second, we want to gain more insight into the differences between individual measures. To do so, we introduced two new, more flexible, evaluation methods which reveal high results for all similarity measures. We argue that these new evaluations provide a better insight into how suitable similarity measures are to be used in NLP tasks than the commonly used Spearman's correlation (henceforth Spearman ρ).

Our results show that most of the evaluations confirm our hypothesis. The few cases where corpus-based methods outperformed taxonomy-based approaches reveal much smaller differences than the many cases where taxonomy-based approaches have higher results. However, all similarity measures perform very well when they are evaluated on the relative ranking of word-pairs that are further apart in the gold-standard. We therefore conclude that, even though taxonomy-based are better at identifying similarity than corpus-based approaches, this may not (always) matter.

The rest of this paper is structured as follows. In Section 2, we motivate our approach and address related work. Section 3 describes the similarity measures we investigate. In Section 4, we

Proceedings of Recent Advances in Natural Language Processing, pages 346–354,
Hissar, Bulgaria, Sep 7–9 2015.

outline our experimental methodology, including used datasets and evaluation methods. The results are presented in Section 5, and our conclusions and future work in Section 6.

2 Background and Motivation

Several gold-standards have been created that rank word-pairs based on their similarity. Agirre et al. (2009) point out that association and similarity are mixed up in these sets, where associated pairs such as *coffee* and *cup* rank higher than truly similar pairs such as *car* and *train*. The confusion directly influences the performance of corpus-based approaches, which also tend to have difficulties distinguishing association from similarity (Hill et al., 2014a).

Hill et al. (2014b) introduce a new gold standard dataset that is annotated with pure semantic similarity and larger than previously created similarity sets, such as Rubenstein and Goodenough (1965) and Agirre et al. (2009)'s sets. Hill et al. (2014a) evaluate corpus-based approaches and show that they indeed have trouble identifying similarity, performing well-below the upperbound of agreement between human annotators.

It is not surprising that corpus-based approaches confuse similarity and association: semantically related words tend to occur close to each other and hence in similar contexts. Approaches that make use of a relatively narrow context window perform slightly better, because they can capture more subtle differences in context to some extend.

Taxonomies represent word meanings in hypernym and hyponym hierarchies, directly capturing their similarity. The closer two terms are in the hierarchy, the more similar they are. Similarity measures that make use of this structure are less likely to confuse whether two terms are similar or related in some other way.

These well-known properties of corpus-based and taxonomy-based approaches led to the following hypothesis:

> Taxonomy-based approaches are better suited to identify similarity than corpus-based approaches

Agirre et al. (2009) seem to contradict this hypothesis showing that corpus-based approaches can be as good at identifying similarity (when the right model is based on enough data). However, Hill et al. (2014b) point out that Agirre et al.'s evaluation set does not form a representative set for measuring similarity, even after they made an alternative set that separates association and similarity. We therefore expected that the hypothesis would nevertheless hold on SimLex-999.

The outcome of our experiments confirmed our hypothesis, thus contradicting Agirre et al. (2009)'s results and being, to our knowledge, the first to show this on such a large and reliable benchmark. Banjade et al. (2015) also applies WordNet-based and corpus-based similarity measures to SimLex-999, but do not examine or discuss the difference between taxonomy-based approaches and corpus-based approaches in detail. Instead, they focus on the strength of combining several approaches to yield better results.[1] We investigate the difference between the approaches in various evaluations showing that taxonomy-based approaches outperform corpus-based approaches, a conclusion that cannot be drawn (clearly) from Banjade et al. (2015)'s results. It should be noted that our conclusions only apply to the task of identifying pure similarity. Markert and Nissim (2005) show, for instance, that a corpus-based approach with sufficiently large corpus works better than WordNet for anaphora resolution.

The next step in our investigation was to determine the strengths and weaknesses of each approach. The original idea was to investigate pairs that are ranked more or less correctly by one approach, but are far off in the other to identify patterns of errors in each approach. We did not find such patterns, partially because the examples that have large differences in ranking compared to the gold are relatively rare.

We therefore developed two alternative evaluation methods that are less sensitive to minor differences in ranking. The first evaluation directly tests the comparison of pairs and, more importantly, allows us to study the contribution of partitions of the dataset. The second evaluation revolves around thresholds for similarity. In this evaluation, we set thresholds to establish a binary distinction between highly similar pairs and other pairs. The pairs above the similarity threshold are compared to those falling above the threshold in the gold (see Section 4.2).

Many studies compare similarity measures (see Baroni et al. (2014) and Pedersen (2010), among

[1] We independently confirmed this result in our own experiments, but decided to leave it out of this paper because our results did not add much to Banjade et al. (2015).

others) but, to our knowledge, Agirre et al. (2009) and Banjade et al. (2015) are the only ones that look at both taxonomy-based approaches and distributional approaches. As mentioned above, they do not dive into the details of the differences between the two. Furthermore, apart from Fokkens et al. (2013), who do not propose new rankings, we are not aware of studies applying multiple evaluation metrics for similarity-based rankings.

3 Similarity Measures

This section describes the similarity measures compared in this paper.

3.1 Taxonomy-based Similarity Measures

WordNet (Fellbaum, 1998) organizes nouns and verbs in hierarchies of hypernym-hyponym relations. We selected WordNet for our taxonomy-based experiments, because it is widely used and probably the most popular taxonomy when it comes to determining word similarity. Many measures of similarity based on WordNet have been proposed over the years. Early work (Rada et al., 1989) advocates the use of *is-a* hierarchy and later approaches continue to use it heavily. In order to make a clean comparison between WordNet and distributional models, we do not include in our study measures that make use of a corpus such as Resnik (1995) and Jiang and Conrath (1997).

Path length similarity takes the inverse of the path length (i.e. the distance in number of nodes) from s_1 to s_2 plus one.

$$\text{PL} = \frac{1}{\text{d}(s_1, s_2) + 1}$$

Wu and Palmer's similarity (Wu and Palmer, 1994) takes the fact into account that senses deeper in the hierarchy tend to be more specific than those high up. It therefore incorporates the depth of the hierarchy in their similarity calculation:

$$\text{WUP} = \frac{2\text{depth}(lcs)}{\text{d}(s_1, lcs) + \text{d}(s_2, lcs) + 2\text{depth}(lcs)}$$

Leacock and Chodorows similarity (Leacock and Chodorow, 1998) normalizes path-based scores by the maximum depth D of the hierarchy. This corrects for the difference in the depth of verb and noun hierarchy:

$$\text{LCH} = -\log \frac{\text{d}(s_1, s_2) + 1}{2D}$$

3.2 Distributional Semantic Models

We selected two representative models from the large and growing literature on corpus-based models of lexical semantics: Word2vec (Mikolov et al., 2013, W2V) and dependency-based word embeddings (Levy and Goldberg, 2014a, DEPS).

Word2vec is the first model to use a Skip-Gram with Negative Sampling (SGNN) algorithm for constructing semantic models and performed best on SimLex-999 in Hill et al. (2014a). Levy and Goldberg (2014b) argue that SGNN implicitly factorizes a shifted positive mutual information word-context matrix, not unlike traditional distributional semantic models. The use of a small window size and the weighting scheme that favors nearby contexts are supported by a systematic study of Kiela and Clark (2014) that shows the superiority of small windows. Moreover, Sahlgren (2006) presents empirical evidence that smaller windows lead to a cleaner distinction between syntagmatic and paradigmatic relations (which can be considered the linguistic version of similarity and association).

Levy and Goldberg (2014a) extend SGNN to work with arbitrary contexts and experiment with dependency structures. It is generally believed that dependency structures are better at capturing similarity (Padó and Lapata, 2007) although Kiela and Clark (2014) found mixed results.

The Skip-gram model captures the distribution $p(c|t)$ of a context word c within a certain window around a target word t. For a vocabulary of millions, computing normalized probabilities (i.e. summing to one) for each example can be prohibitively expensive. Negative sampling was used to avoid the cost.

For each context-target pair (c, t) taken from training data, we replace the context by random words drawn from the vocabulary to obtain new pairs $\{(c', t)\}$. We call $D \ni (c, t)$ *positive distribution* and $N \ni (c', t)$ *negative distribution*. The task of the model is to identify which pairs come from D and which from N. Formally. that is to maximize the negative log likelihood:

$$\ell = -\left(\sum \log p(D|c, t) + \sum \log p(N|c', t)\right)$$

The probability is calculated using *target embeddings* $e_t \in \mathbb{R}^d$ and *context embeddings* $\hat{e}_c \in \mathbb{R}^d$ such that:

$$p(D|c, t) = \sigma(e_t \cdot \hat{e}_c),$$

where $\sigma(x) = 1/(1 + e^{-x})$ is a monotonic function that maps any value in $(-\infty, +\infty)$ to a valid probability.

The training objective encourages to increase $p(D|c, t)$ which can be achieved by aligning e_t and $\hat{e}_c$ in similar directions. On the other hand, the objective also encourages a small $p(N|c, t)$, creating an uniform "repelling force" between all pairs of words. After a lot of updating iterations, similar words come close together while dissimilar words are pulled apart.

We used the trained embeddings from Mikolov et al. (2013) and Levy and Goldberg (2014a).[2] Word2vec embeddings are 300-dimensional vectors obtained by training on 100 billion words of Google News dataset. Dependency-based embeddings were harvested from English Wikipedia automatically annotated with dependency structures. Although the dependency-based model was trained on a significantly smaller corpus, it achieves comparable results as we will show in Section 5.

4 Experimental Setup

In this section, we describe the experimental setup used in our evaluations. We first describe the datasets and then the evaluation metrics we use.

4.1 Gold-standard Datasets

We evaluate the approaches on three datasets. WordSim-353 and MEN allow us to compare performance on sets that mix association and similarity. SimLex-999's ranking is based on similarity only.

WordSim-353 (Finkelstein et al., 2001) includes 353 word pairs scored for *relatedness* on a scale from 0 to 10 by 13 or 16 subjects. The inter-annotator agreement is 0.611 defined as the average pairwise Spearman's correlation. Researchers have reported correlation as high as 0.81 (Yih and Qazvinian, 2012). Agirre et al. (2009) later divided WordSim-353 into a "similarity" and "relatedness" set. However, Hill et al. (2014b) rightly point out that both remain relatedness datasets, because this is what the annotators rated.

MEN (Bruni et al., 2012) is composed of 3,000 word pairs, sampled to include a balanced range of relatedness. Annotators were asked to choose which of two pairs of words is more related, an arguably more intuitive task than assigning a score.

SimLex-999 (Hill et al., 2014b) carefully distinguishes between similarity and association and provides a balanced range of similarity, concreteness and parts-of-speech. The authors sampled 900 associated pairs from the University of South Florida Free Association Database (Nelson et al., 2004) and randomly coupled them to create 999 unassociated pairs. Subjects were asked to judge the similarity of word pairs on a 0-6 scale. Their answers were averaged to produce the final score.

All three datasets are lemma-based. The way two words can be compared, however, is more likely via their *senses* (e.g. *queen* is not similar to *princess* when referring to a chess piece). We follow Resnik (1995) in using maximally similar senses in our taxonomy-based approaches.

4.2 Evaluation Metrics

The first evaluation measure we use compares between the gold ranking and a measurement's ranking using **Spearman's ρ**, the most widely used evaluation metric for similarity score.

Hill et al. (2014b) report performance on a subset of highly associated word pairs, but its contribution to the overall performance is unclear. We wish to gain deeper insight into how different subsets in the data contribute to the overall score. This is not possible with Spearman's ρ due to its holistic nature. We overcome this by using **ordering accuracy** following Agirre et al. (2009). The scale is defined as:

$$a = a_{G,G} = \frac{1}{|G|^2} \sum_{(u,v)\in G} \sum_{(x,y)\in G} m_{s,G}(u,v,x,y)$$

where G stands for the gold standard and $m_{s,G}(\cdot)$ is a matching function that returns 1 for those two word-pairs whose relative ranking is the same in the gold standard and in the ranking of the similarity measure and 0 otherwise. We also experiment with a variation of m where ties get half score. As shown in Figure 1, ordering accuracy highly correlates with Spearman's ρ.

If G can be partitioned into n subsets g_i (i.e. $\bigcap g_i = \emptyset$ and $\bigcup g_i = G$) then a can be decomposed as the weighted sum of the accuracy on different subsets. The weights are proportional to their size:

$$a = \frac{1}{|G|^2} \sum_i \sum_j |g_i||g_j| a_{g_i,g_j}$$

[2]The models are available at: https://code.google.com/p/word2vec/ and https://levyomer.wordpress.com/2014/04/25/dependency-based-word-embeddings

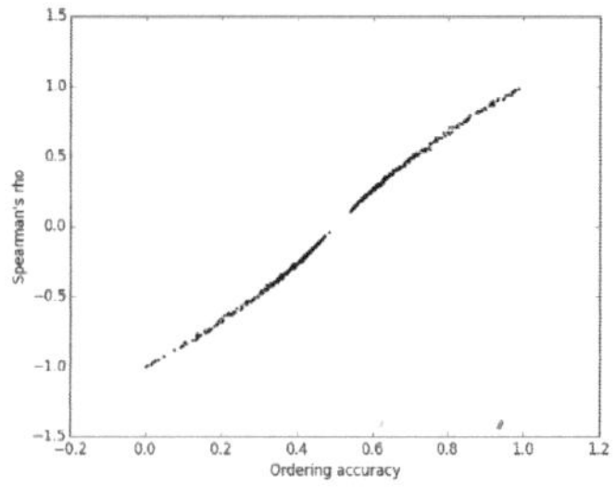

Figure 1: Ordering accuracy and Spearman's ρ on a synthesized dataset of 100 word pairs.

Model	SL-999$_{nv}$	MEN$_{nv}$	WS-353
WUP	0.47	0.39	0.35
PL	0.52	0.39	0.30
LCH	0.55	0.39	0.31
W2V	0.42	0.77	0.70
DEPS	0.45	0.61	0.63

Table 1: Spearman's correlation of models to similarity benchmarks.

The final evaluation measure is based on the observation that many approaches use a threshold to determine which words are similar enough to be used for contributing features or approximations, or to be candidates for lexical substitution (McCarthy and Navigli, 2009; Biran et al., 2011, e.g.). **Threshold accuracy** sets a similarity threshold and determines how many of the n-highest ranking word pairs in a given measurement are also in the top-n pairs of the gold standard. In other words, this evaluation determines whether the right word-pairs would end up above the threshold of being similar.

5 Results

We calculated the similarity scores of all noun and verb pairs in SimLex-999 (a set of 888 pairs), MEN (2,034 pairs), and all pairs in WordSim-353 using the measures outlined in Section 3 and ranked the word pairs according to the outcome.

5.1 Spearman's Rank Correlation

Table 1 shows the performance of models on all three benchmarks. Taxonomy based approaches perform higher on SimLex-999, whereas corpus-based approaches reveal high performance on MEN and WordSim-353 and score significantly lower on SimLex-999. This result confirms that taxonomy-based approaches capture similarity rather than association, whereas corpus-based approaches do not clearly distinguish the two.

Model	SL-999 *nv*	SL-999 *nv*	SL-999 *nv,assoc*	Diff. *assoc*
		Using tie corrections		
WUP	64.9	66.6	67.3	+0.7
PL	61.1	68.0	68.2	+0.2
LCH	65.1	69.2	69.1	-0.1
W2V	64.4	64.6	57.5	-7.1
DEPS	65.5	65.6	60.9	-4.7

Table 2: Ordering accuracy (percentage) of similarity measures on SimLex-999$_{nv}$.

5.2 Ordering Accuracy

Table 2 presents the evaluation of our metrics using ordering accuracy. The first column indicates the standard score. The scores in the second and third column are calculated while giving partial credits to ties. Note that this only affects the performance of taxonomy-based approaches, where it is common for word pairs to have identical scores.

Without correction for ties, scores for taxonomy-based and corpus-based measures are highly similar, with the corpus-based DEPS leading to the highest results. Taxonomy-based approaches uniformly beat corpus-based approaches again when we do correct for ties, confirming the outcome of our Spearman ρ evaluation.

We also evaluate on a subset of highly-associated words. The results are presented in column 3 of Table 2. Sizeable decrease is observed in corpus-based measures for highly associated terms while taxonomy-based measures remain largely unaffected. This result confirms our hypothesis once more that taxonomy-based measures are more suited to capture similarity and that corpus-based methods tend to have difficulties separating similarity from association.

5.3 Decomposition of Ordering Accuracy

Palmer et al. (2007) showed that making subtle sense distinction is hard for human subjects leading to evaluations where both coarse-grained and fine-grained word senses are considered (Palmer et al., 2007; Navigli et al., 2007). Similarly, establishing which word-pair is more similar than another is challenging when pairs are close in sim-

$\Delta = 0$	
pollution-president	forget-learn
take-leave	succeed-try
army-squad	girl-child
emotion-passion	collect-save
sheep-lamb	attention-awareness
$\Delta = 1$	
spoon-cup	argue-differ
remind-sell	apple-candy
book-topic	argument-agreement
corporation-business	kidney-organ
alcohol-wine	beach-island

Table 3: Is the pair in the left or in the right more similar? (All pairs are extracted from SimLex-999)

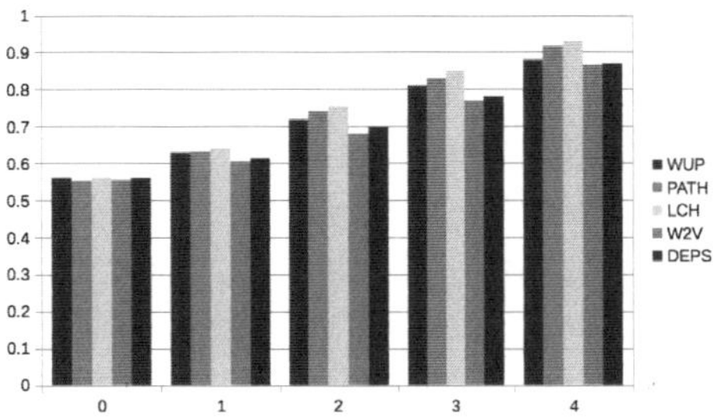

Figure 2: Ordering accuracy varies with degrees of granularity on SimLex-999_{nv}. $\Delta = 0$ means two pairs fall in the same range of similarity (e.g. 0-2); $\Delta = 1$ means they fall in neighboring ranges of similarity (e.g. 0-2 and 2-4), etc.

ilarity. This is illustrated by the sample pairs in Table 3. The fact that ranking such pairs is highly challenging for humans leads to the question how meaningful differences in performance of similarities measures on these pairs actually are.

To overcome this issue and gain deeper insight into how often low performance is the result of many small errors piling up and how often it is the result of a set of pairs being ranked completely wrongly, we apply our ordering accuracy to a decomposed dataset. We divide SimLex-999_{nv} into five equal similarity ranges $\{g_i\}$ based on SimLex-999's original ranges. The first range g_1 contains highly dissimilar pairs of words with a similarity between 0 and 2. Final set g_5 contains very similar or synonymous pairs with a similarity from 8 to 10.

We use different granularity levels Δ ($\Delta = 0, ..., 4$). Component accuracy is calculated by comparing each pair in g_i to every pair in g_j such that $|i - j| = \Delta$.

The results reported in Figure 2 show that all models perform consistently well on coarse-grained similarity while only marginally beating chance-level at the most fine-grained level. Furthermore, taxonomy-based approaches only outperform corpus-based approaches when comparing pairs that are further apart in the gold ranking.

Because the two most fine-grained components ($\Delta = 0$ and $\Delta = 1$) together have a weight of 58%, the ordering accuracy as reported in Table 2 is dominated by fine-grained similarity comparison. Spearman's ρ highly correlates with ordering accuracy, indicating that fine-grained differences also had a major impact on previous work. It is questionable whether it is really necessary for these measures to capture the small differences in similarity that are even difficult for humans to find. This outcome shows that similarity measures perform better than they seem to do according to recent evaluations in the literature.

5.4 Threshold Evaluation

The final evaluation we carry out is the so-called *threshold* evaluation. It evaluates how well a threshold performs that separates highly similar terms from less similar terms based on a specific score. We use the 10% and 20% most similar terms as a starting point. In a total set of 888 examples, this means we compare the top 89 and top 178 pairs of each measurement's output with the top pairs of the gold data. We report on the accuracy (i.e. percentage of pairs correctly classified as highly similar) of each scores. As mentioned above, taxonomy-based approaches often assign the same score to multiple pairs. If this was the case for the pairs around the threshold, we extended the range of comparison as to include all pairs with an identical score. Table 4 provides an overview of the results.

The top-n sets increase significantly for taxonomy-based approaches. Because approaches tend to fare better when the size of the group changes, we calculated the scores for W2V and DEPS with the top-n ranks found in the taxonomy-based scores. Table 5 shows the results of this analysis. The scores of the relevant taxonomy-based approach are repeated in the third row.

The threshold based evaluation shows more

Model	10%-based		20%-based	
	n	%	n	%
WUP	94	42.6	191	50.3
PATH	172	43.5	645	80.8
LCH	172	53.5	305	61.0
W2V	89	32.6	178	38.2
DEPS	89	33.7	178	43.8

Table 4: Threshold based evaluation, comparing the set of top-n similar pairs

model	n-value				
	94	172	191	305	645
W2V	33.0	38.4	39.8	48.5	**82.0**
DEPS	31.9	43.6	42.9	52.8	81.4
taxo.	**42.6**	43.5/**53.5**	**50.3**	**61.0**	80.8

Table 5: Scores of corpus-based methods on the n-values used for taxonomy-based scores.

variation than our other metric. In three out of twelve cases,[3] the corpus-based approach leads to more accurate results than the taxonomy-based score. In combination with the outcome of the accuracy ordering result, this outcome underlines the importance of using a variety of evaluation metrics.

Overall, the outcome seems to confirm that taxonomy-based approaches are better at identifying similarity. First, taxonomy-based approaches outperformed corpus-based approaches on identifying the most accurate pairs. Second, corpus-based approaches only beat taxonomy-based ones in few measures and with comparatively small margins (the largest difference being 1.2%, compared to differences up to 15.1%).

6 Discussion and Conclusions

This paper investigated the difference in performance of taxonomy-based approaches and corpus-based approaches on identifying similarity. The outcome of our experiments confirmed our hypothesis that taxonomy-based approaches are better at identifying similarity. This is mainly due to the fact that corpus-based approaches have difficulties distinguishing association from similarity, as also noted by Hill et al. (2014a).

We presented several results that confirm our hypothesis by (i) comparing performance of taxonomy-based and corpus-based methods on a dataset designed to capture similarity, (ii) relating this to the results of the same measures on evaluation sets that measure both association and relatedness, and (iii) looking what the influence is of testing against a set that consists of associated terms.

The results show that taxonomy-based approaches excel at identifying similarity whereas corpus-based approaches yield high results when similarity and association are not distinguished. Furthermore, taxonomy-based approaches are not influenced by association between words whereas performance of corpus-based measures drop when their task is to identify similarity.

We applied more than one evaluation to compare the models' performance on SimLex-999. This was done for two reasons. First, different evaluation measures can sometimes lead to different conclusions even if they are meant to address the same question on the same dataset. This also happened in our evaluation, where ordering accuracy without tie-correction and some thresholds led to different results. Second, the evaluation metrics revealed different aspects of the performance. Most notably, the results of our decomposed ordering accuracy showed that all similarity measures are quite good in a coarse-grained setting.

Together with the mixed outcome of the threshold-evaluation, this shows that corpus-based approaches have good potential to be used when similarity needs to be detected. In particular, when taxonomy-based approaches run into coverage issues, they may be the preferred choice. We therefore believe that it will ultimately depend on the application which approach works best. Future work will need to show whether and how these approaches differ when used in actual applications.[4]

Acknowledgments

The research for this paper was supported by the Netherlands Organisation for Scientific Research (NWO) via the Spinoza-prize Vossen projects (SPI 30-673, 2014-2019) and the BiographyNet project (Nr. 660.011.308), funded by the Netherlands eScience Center (`http://esciencecenter.nl/`). We would like to thank the anonymous reviewers for their feedback.

[3]We compare eight corpus-based outcomes with one taxonomy score and two with two scores for n=172, leading to twelve comparisons in total.

[4]All our code is published on `https://bitbucket.org/ulm4/kcsim`.

References

Eneko Agirre, Enrique Alfonseca, Keith Hall, Jana Kravalova, Marius Paşca, and Aitor Soroa. 2009. A study on similarity and relatedness using distributional and wordnet-based approaches. In *Proceedings of Human Language Technologies: The 2009 Annual Conference of the North American Chapter of the Association for Computational Linguistics*, NAACL '09, pages 19–27, Stroudsburg, PA, USA. Association for Computational Linguistics.

Rajendra Banjade, Nabin Maharjan, Nobal B. Niraula, Vasile Rus, and Dipesh Gautam. 2015. Lemon and tea are not similar: Measuring word-to-word similarity by combining different methods. In *Computational Linguistics and Intelligent Text Processing*, pages 335–346. Springer.

Marco Baroni, Georgiana Dinu, and Germán Kruszewski. 2014. Dont count, predict! A systematic comparison of context-counting vs. context-predicting semantic vectors. In *Proceedings of the 52nd Annual Meeting of the Association for Computational Linguistics*, pages 238–247.

Or Biran, Samuel Brody, and Noémie Elhadad. 2011. Putting it simply: a context-aware approach to lexical simplification. In *Proceedings of the 49th Annual Meeting of the Association for Computational Linguistics: Human Language Technologies: short papers-Volume 2*, pages 496–501. Association for Computational Linguistics.

Elia Bruni, Gemma Boleda, Marco Baroni, and Nam-Khanh Tran. 2012. Distributional semantics in technicolor. In *Proceedings of the 50th Annual Meeting of the Association for Computational Linguistics: Long Papers-Volume 1*, pages 136–145. Association for Computational Linguistics.

Christiane Fellbaum, editor. 1998. *WordNet: An Electronic Lexical Database*. MIT Press, Cambridge, MA.

Lev Finkelstein, Evgeniy Gabrilovich, Yossi Matias, Ehud Rivlin, Zach Solan, Gadi Wolfman, and Eytan Ruppin. 2001. Placing search in context: The concept revisited. In *Proceedings of the 10th international conference on World Wide Web*, pages 406–414. ACM.

Antske Fokkens, Marieke Erp, Marten Postma, Ted Pedersen, Piek Vossen, and Nuno Freire. 2013. Offspring from reproduction problems: What replication failure teaches us. In *Proceedings of the 51st Annual Meeting of the Association for Computational Linguistics (Volume 1: Long Papers)*, pages 1691–1701. Association for Computational Linguistics.

Felix Hill, KyungHyun Cho, Sébastien Jean, Coline Devin, and Yoshua Bengio. 2014a. Not all neural embeddings are born equal. *NIPS 2014 Workshop on Learning Semantics*.

Felix Hill, Roi Reichart, and Anna Korhonen. 2014b. SimLex-999: Evaluating Semantic Models with (Genuine) Similarity Estimation. *ArXiv e-prints*, August.

Jay J Jiang and David W Conrath. 1997. Semantic similarity based on corpus statistics and lexical taxonomy. In *Proceedings of the 10th Research on Computational Linguistics International Conference*, pages 19–33. The Association for Computational Linguistics and Chinese Language Processing (ACLCLP).

Douwe Kiela and Stephen Clark. 2014. A Systematic Study of Semantic Vector Space Model Parameters. In *Proceedings of EACL 2014, Workshop on Continuous Vector Space Models and their Compositionality (CVSC)*, pages 21–30. Association for Computational Linguistics.

Claudia Leacock and Martin Chodorow. 1998. Combining local context and WordNet similarity for word sense identification. *WordNet: An electronic lexical database*, 49(2):265–283.

Omer Levy and Yoav Goldberg. 2014a. Dependency-based word embeddings. In *Proceedings of the 52nd Annual Meeting of the Association for Computational Linguistics (Volume 2: Short Papers)*, pages 302–308, Baltimore, Maryland, June. Association for Computational Linguistics.

Omer Levy and Yoav Goldberg. 2014b. Neural word embedding as implicit matrix factorization. In Z. Ghahramani, M. Welling, C. Cortes, N.D. Lawrence, and K.Q. Weinberger, editors, *Advances in Neural Information Processing Systems 27*, pages 2177–2185. Curran Associates, Inc.

Katja Markert and Malvina Nissim. 2005. Comparing Knowledge Sources for Nominal Anaphora Resolution. *Computational Linguistics*, 31(3):367–402, September.

Diana McCarthy and Roberto Navigli. 2009. The english lexical substitution task. *Language Resources and Evaluation*, 43(2):139–159.

Tomas Mikolov, Greg Corrado, Kai Chen, and Jeffrey Dean. 2013. Efficient Estimation of Word Representations in Vector Space. *ICLR Workshop*.

Roberto Navigli, Kenneth C. Litkowski, and Orin Hargraves. 2007. Semeval-2007 task 07: Coarse-grained english all-words task. In *Proceedings of the Fourth International Workshop on Semantic Evaluations (SemEval-2007)*, pages 30–35, Prague, Czech Republic, June. Association for Computational Linguistics.

Douglas L. Nelson, Cathy L. McEvoy, and Thomas A. Schreiber. 2004. The university of south florida free association, rhyme, and word fragment norms. *Behavior Research Methods, Instruments, & Computers*, 36(3):402–407.

Sebastian Padó and Mirella Lapata. 2007. Dependency-based construction of semantic space models. *Computational Linguistics*, 33(2):161–199.

Martha Palmer, Hoa Trang Dang, and Christiane Fellbaum. 2007. Making fine-grained and coarse-grained sense distinctions, both manually and automatically. *Natural Language Engineering*, 13(02):137–163.

Ted Pedersen. 2010. Information content measures of semantic similarity perform better without sense-tagged text. In *Human Language Technologies: The 2010 Annual Conference of the North American Chapter of the Association for Computational Linguistics*, pages 329–332. Association for Computational Linguistics.

Taher Mohammad Pilehvar, David Jurgens, and Roberto Navigli. 2013. Align, disambiguate and walk: A unified approach for measuring semantic similarity. In *Proceedings of the 51st Annual Meeting of the Association for Computational Linguistics (Volume 1: Long Papers)*, pages 1341–1351. Association for Computational Linguistics.

Roy Rada, Hafedh Mili, Ellen Bicknell, and Maria Blettner. 1989. Development and application of a metric on semantic nets. *Systems, Man and Cybernetics, IEEE Transactions on*, 19(1):17–30, Jan.

Philip Resnik. 1995. Using information content to evaluate semantic similarity in a taxonomy. In *Proceedings of the 14th international joint conference on Artificial intelligence-Volume 1*, pages 448–453. Morgan Kaufmann Publishers Inc.

Herbert Rubenstein and John B Goodenough. 1965. Contextual correlates of synonymy. *Communications of the ACM*, 8(10):627–633.

Magnus Sahlgren. 2006. The word-space model: Using distributional analysis to represent syntagmatic and paradigmatic relations between words in high-dimensional vector spaces.

Zhibiao Wu and Martha Palmer. 1994. Verbs semantics and lexical selection. In *Proceedings of the 32nd annual meeting on Association for Computational Linguistics*, pages 133–138. Association for Computational Linguistics.

Wen-tau Yih and Vahed Qazvinian. 2012. Measuring word relatedness using heterogeneous vector space models. In *Proceedings of the 2012 Conference of the North American Chapter of the Association for Computational Linguistics: Human Language Technologies*, pages 616–620. Association for Computational Linguistics.

Semantic Parsing via ℓ_0-norm-based Alignment

Zhihua Liao
Foreign Studies College
Hunan Normal University
Changsha, China
liao.zhihua61@gmail.com

Qixian Zeng
Foreign Studies College
Hunan Normal University
Changsha, China
wanyouto@qq.com

Qiyun Wang
Foreign Studies College
Hunan Normal University
Changsha, China
qywang@qq.com

Abstract

In this paper, we explore the IBM Model with a ℓ_0-norm prior to the semantic parsing which parses a sentence to its corresponding meaning representation, and compare two supervised probabilistic Combinatory Categorial Grammar (PCCG) online learning approaches that are Unification-Based Learning (UBL) method and Factored Unification-Based Learning (FUBL) one. Specially, we extend manually GeoQuery and ATIS datasets from English to Chinese *pinyin*-format string. The experiment on such benchmark datasets in both English and Chinese with two different meaning representations (i.e., lambda-calculus and variable-free expressions) demonstrates that both methods adopted this IBM Model with ℓ_0-norm outperform trivially those that used the IBM Model without ℓ_0-norm, and also shows small improvements of around $0.1\% \sim 0.7\%$ of *F1* for the two algorithms on nearly all conditions.

1 Introduction

Learning the mapping from natural language sentences to formal meaning representations has become one of the main targets in natural language processing. Recent research has focused on learning the semantic parsers directly from corpora that consist of sentences paired with their meaning representations (Artzi and Zettlemoyer, 2011; Artzi and Zettlemoyer, 2013; Kwiatkowski et al., 2010; Kwiatkowski et al., 2011; Lu et al., 2008; Zettlemoyer and Collins, 2005; Zettlemoyer and Collins, 2007; Zettlemoyer and Collins, 2009; Zettlemoyer and Collins, 2012). They usually employ corpus-based probabilistic methods. Furthermore, some research work has been explored to learn to map any natural language to a wide variety of logical expressions of linguistic meaning (Kwiatkowski et al., 2011; Liao and Zhang, 2013). For example, the training data can consist of Turkish, Spanish, Japanese and English sentences paired with lambda-calculus expressions or variable-free logical ones.

Our approach is inspired by the principle of minimum description length (Barron et al., 1998; Ashish et al., 2012). The main motivation is that through adding a ℓ_0-norm prior this extension of the IBM model can enable it to encourage the sparsity in word-to-word alignment model. It uses an efficient training algorithm based on projected gradient descent. In this paper, we will apply this method to the semantic parsing. Our work focus on the *Initialization* procedure that the weights for lexeme features are initialized according to coocurrance statistics between words and logical constants. They are implemented with the modification of GIZA++ toolkit which is viewed as the drop-in replacement for GIZA++ (Ashish et al., 2012).

We evaluate our approach on two benchmark corpora (i.e., GeoQuery and ATIS) annotated with Chinese *pinyin*-format string. The GeoQuery corpus has complex sentence and meaning representation pairs whereas the ATIS corpus contains spontaneous and unedited text so that it is difficult to analyze within formal grammar expression. We compare the performances of both PCCG online learning methods using the IBM Alignment Model with and without ℓ_0-norm. The experimental results demonstrate the effect of this extended IBM Model with ℓ_0-norm.

2 Background

We start with a brief review of the IBM word alignment model, then present a detailed description about how to add the ℓ_0-norm into the baseline IBM Model. Besides, we also review the CCG

Proceedings of Recent Advances in Natural Language Processing, pages 355–361,
Hissar, Bulgaria, Sep 7–9 2015.

grammar (CCG) formalism, the probabilistic CCG (PCCG), and the factored CCG lexicon, as well as the lambda-calculus and higher-order unification.

2.1 IBM Model

Assume that a natural language sentence x is parsed using the CCG lexicon to form a logical expression z. Let a natural language sentence x consist of word-based string $x_1 \dots x_j \dots x_k$, and let the output meaning representation z consist of logical forms $z_1 \dots z_j \dots z_k$. Then this model describes the process by which the meaning representation is generated by the sentence via the alignment $\hat{a} = a_1, \dots, a_j, \dots, a_k$. Each a_j is a hidden variable that indicates which x_{a_j} word the logical form z_j is aligned to.

In IBM model, the joint probability of the sentence and alignment can be defined as follows:

$$P(z, \hat{a}|x) = \Pi_{j=1}^{m} d(a_j|a_{j-1}, j) t(z_j|x_{a_j})$$

Here, the two parameters of this equation are the distortion probability $d(a_j|a_{j-1}, j)$ and the translation probability $t(z_j|x_{a_j})$, respectively.

Let θ stand for all the parameters of this model. The standard training process is to find the parameter values to maximize the likelihood. That is, it is to minimize the negative log-likelihood of the observed data as defined by

$$\hat{\theta} = \arg\min_{\theta}(-\log P(z|x, \theta))$$

$$= \arg\min_{\theta}(-\log \sum_{\hat{a}} P(z, \hat{a}|x, \theta))$$

This can be completed by using the expectation-maximization (EM) algorithm.

2.2 MAP-EM Algorithm with ℓ_0-norm

In the statistical machine translation field the dominant approach has been the IBM model together with the HMM model. Because it is unsupervised, this can enable it apply to any language pair on an available parallel text. Barron et al. (1998) proposed the principle of minimum description length in the word-to-word translation model, which can reduce the overfitting and result in the garbage collection effect. Then the IBM/HMM model by addition with the ℓ_0-norm prior to encourage the sparsity has been extended (Ashish et al., 2012). This extension makes use of an efficient training method based on projected gradient descent and line search to constrained optimization problem. It can scale up to the large dataset in word-to-word alignment. Therefore, this provides significant improvement in the alignment quality.

In word alignment by incorporating a smoothed ℓ_0 prior, the maximum of a posteriori (MAP) objective function is defined as

$$\hat{\theta} = \arg\min_{\theta}(-\log P(z|x, \theta) P(\theta))$$

where

$$P(\theta) \propto \exp(-\alpha \|\theta\|_0^\beta)$$

and

$$\|\theta\|_0^\beta = \Sigma_{x,z}(1 - \exp \frac{-t(z \mid x)}{\beta})$$

Here, $P(\theta)$ is a smoothed approximation of the ℓ_0-norm and the hyperparameter β controls the tightness of approximation.

Next, for an EM procedure the M-step is defined as:

$$\hat{\theta} = \arg\min_{\theta}(-\Sigma_{x,z} E[C(x, z)] \log t(z|x))$$

Here, the count $C(x, z)$ is the number of times that z occurs aligned to x.

Eventually, MAP-EM is given by:

$$\hat{\theta} = \arg\min_{\theta}(-\Sigma_{x,z} E[C(x, z)] \log t(z|x)$$

$$-\alpha \Sigma_{x,z} \exp \frac{-t(z|x)}{\beta})$$

This optimization problem is non-convex and can be intractable in a closed-form solution. In order to solve this optimization problem, a projected gradient descent has been employed. Therefore, this extension to IBM model can be implemented as a modification to the open-source toolkit GIZA++[1]. Due to its simplicity and generality, this modified model can be utilized to compute cooccurrence statistics in **IBM Model 1** between words and logical constants during the *Initialization* procedure.

[1] http://www.isi.edu/ avaswani/giza-pp-10.html

2.3 Combinatory Categorial Grammars (CCGs)

CCGs are a linguistically-motivated formalism for modeling a wide range of language phenomena (Steedman, 1996; Steedman, 2000). A CCG is defined by a lexicon and a set of combinators. The lexicon contains entries that pair words or phrases with categories like the following (Liao and Zhang, 2013):

alasijia:-NP : alaska:s

alasijiazhou:-NP : alaska:s

alasijia:-NP : alaska:n

alasijiazhou:-NP : alaska:n

zhijiage:-NP : chicago:c

zhijiageshi:-NP : chicago:c

zhijiage:-NP : chicago:n

zhijiageshi:-NP : chicago:n

Lexical entries share much information while their decompositions can lead to more compact lexicons. When beginning from lexical entries, each intermediate parse node is constructed with one of a small set of CCG combinators. These nodes can capture jointly syntax and semantic information. The combinators contain the functional application, coordination, composition, type-raising and type-shifting.

2.4 Probabilistic CCGs (PCCGs)

It is much obvious for extending CCGs to PCCGs. The primary motivation is to deal with the ambiguity by ranking alternative parses for a sentence in order of probability (Kwiatkowski et al., 2010). Given a CCG lexicon Λ, each sentence may contains many possible parses. The parse with the most likelihood can be selected by using a log-linear model. This model usually consists of a feature vector ϕ and a parameter vector θ. Therefore the joint probability of a logical form z constructed with a parse y, given a sentence x is defined as:

$$P(y, z|x; \theta, \Lambda) = \frac{e^{\theta \cdot \phi(x,y,z)}}{\Sigma_{(y',z')} e^{\theta \cdot \phi(x,y',z')}}$$

2.5 Factored CCG Lexicon

In general, traditional CCG lexicon lists lexical items that pair words and phrases with syntactic and semantic content. This lexicon might be inefficient when some words appear repeatedly with closely related lexical content. Recently, Kwiatkowshi et al. introduced a factored CCG lexicon representation (Kwiatkowski et al., 2011). Each lexical item is composed of a lexeme and a template such as:

hangban:-N:$\lambda x.flight(x)$

hangban:-N$/(S|NP)$:$\lambda f \lambda x.flight(x) \wedge f(x)$

boshidun:-NP:bos

boshidun:-N $\backslash$ N:$\lambda f \lambda x.from(x, bos) \wedge f(x)$

piaojia:-N:$\lambda x.cost(x)$

piaojia:-N$/(S|NP)$:$\lambda f \lambda x.cost(x) \wedge f(x)$

piaojia:-N $\backslash$ N:$\lambda f \lambda x.cost(x) \wedge f(x)$

jiage:-N:$\lambda x.cost(x)$

jiaqian:-N:$\lambda x.cost(x)$

This factored lexicon includes both of lexeme to model word meaning and template to model systematic variation in word usage. It also allows the reuse of common syntactic structures through a small set of templates. In order to induce a factored lexicon, two procedures are adopted for those factor lexical items into lexemes and templates. Next, these factoring operations are integrated into the complete learning algorithm.

2.6 Lambda Calculus and Higher-Order Unification

Suppose that sentence meaning is represented by use of logical expression. This logical form is defined as the typed lambda-calculus expression (Kwiatkowski et al., 2010). The basic type e stands for an entity, t stands for a truth value, and i for a number. Function types of the form $\langle e, t \rangle$ are assigned to lambda expressions. For example, $\lambda x.state(x)$ take an entity x and return a truth value. The meaning of words and phrases are represented by lambda-calculus forms. They contain constants, quantifiers, logical connectors, and lambda abstractions. Due to its generality, the meaning of each words and phrases can be arbitrary lambda-calculus expressions.

The higher-order unification problem involves finding a substitution for the free variables in a pair of lambda-calculus form which makes the expression equal each other when applied. This problem is remarkable complex and intractable. In the unrestricted case, there can be infinitely many solution pairs (f, g) for a given logical expression h. Instead, the restricted higher-order unification is tractable. For example, given an expression h, let find an expression for f and g such that either $h = f(g)$ or $h = \lambda x.f(g(x))$. The limited form of the unification problem can define the ways to split h into subparts so that these subparts can be recombined with CCG parsing operations to reconstruct h.

3 Methodology

This section describes two different PCCG online learning methods, namely, Unification-Based Learning (UBL) method and Factored Unification-Based Learning (FUBL) one.

3.1 UBL Algorithm

This subsection describes the UBL algorithm (Kwiatkowski et al., 2010). This algorithm steps through the data incrementally and performs two-step procedure for each training example. First, new lexical items are induced for the training instance by splitting and merging nodes in the best correct parse given the current parameters. Next, the parameters of the PCCG are updated by computing a stochastic gradient update on the marginal likelihood given the updated lexicon.

3.2 FUBL Algorithm

Although the UBL algorithm can effectively use a higher-order-unification-based lexical induction method to define the space of possible grammars in a language-string and a meaning-representation-independent manner, it can not scale well to some challenging spontaneous and unedited natural language input. At the same time, the FUBL algorithm for inducing factored lexicons is also language independent, but can scale well to these challenging sentences (Kwiatkowski et al., 2011). Assuming training data where each example is a sentence paired with a logical form, the algorithm induces a factored PCCG which includes the lexemes, templates and parameters. This online algorithm repeatedly performs both lexical expansion and a parameter update for each training example. First, the learning algorithm adds lexemes and templates to the factored model by performing manipulations on the highest score pairs of the current training example. Next, a stochastic gradient descent update on the parameter of the parsing model is used to update parameter.

4 Experiments

This section describes our experimental setup and comparisons of the result. We follow the setup of Zettlemoyer and Collins (2005; 2007; 2009; 2012) and Kwiatkowski et al. (2010; 2011) except with manually extending two datasets from English to Chinese *pinyin*-format string, including datasets and initialization as well as system, as reviewed below. Finally, we report the experimental results.

Datasets We evaluate on two benchmark datasets. GeoQuery[2] is made up of natural language queries to a database of geographical information, while ATIS contains natural language queries to a flight booking system (Deborah et al., 1994). Specially, we have made both of original English corpora (i.e., GeoQuery and ATIS) manually translate into the corresponding Chinese *pinyin*-format string ones by five native quite fluent Chinese speaker, who major in English-Chinese translation during their graduate studying stages. Therefore, Chinese GeoQuery and ATIS corpora are new. Furthermore, GeoQuery contains both lambda-calculus and variable-free meaning representations whereas ATIS only includes lambda-calculus expression. The Geo880 dataset has 880(English sentence or Chinese one, logical form) pairs split into a training set of 600 pairs and a test set of 280 ones. The Geo250 is a subset of the Geo880 and is used 10-fold cross validation experiments with the same splits of the data. Figures 1 and 2 show the examples with both lambda-calculus and variable-free meaning representations in Chinese Geo880 dataset, respectively. The ATIS dataset contains 5410 (English sentence or Chinese one, logical form) pairs split into a 5000 example development set and a 450 example test set. Here, Figure 3 shows some examples with lambda-calculus expression in the Chinese ATIS dataset. Next, we report exact match *Recall*, *Precision* and *F1*. For ATIS we also report partial match *Recall*, *Precision* and *F1*.

neige zhou yv mixiegen jierang

(lambda $0 e (and (state:t $0) (next_to:t $0 michigan:s)))

ehaiezhou jingnei de zhuyao chengshi you neixie

(lambda $0 e (and (major:t $0) (city:t $0) (loc:t $0 ohio:s)))

akensezhou zuididian shi nali

(argmin $0 (and (place:t $0) (loc:t $0 arkansas:s)) (elevation:i $0))

[2]http://www.cs.utexas.edu/users/ml/geo.html

neixie zhou yv qiaozhiyaya rjierang

(lambda $0 e (and (state:t $0) (next_to:t $0 georgia:s)))

niuyue you duoshao tiao heliu

(count $0 (and (river:t $0) (loc:t $0 new_york:s)))

Figure 1:Examples with lambda-calculus expression in Chinese Geo880.

neige zhou yv mixiegen jierang

(answer (state (next_to_2 (stateid michigan:e))))

ehaiezhou jingnei de zhuyao chengshi you neixie

(answer (major (city (loc_2 (stateid ohio:e)))))

akensezhou zuididian shi nali

(answer (lowest (place (loc_2 (stateid arkansas:e)))))

neixie zhou yv qiaozhiyaya rjierang

(answer (state (next_to_2 (stateid georgia:e))))

niuyue you duoshao tiao heliu

(answer (count (river (loc_2 (stateid new_york:e)))))

Figure 2: Examples with variable-free expression in Chinese Geo880.

neixie hangban cong dalasi feiwang feinikesi

(lambda $0 e (and (flight $0) (from $0 dallas:ci) (to $0 phoenix:ci))

neixie hangban cong feinikesi feiwang yanhucheng

(lambda $0 e (and (flight $0) (from $0 phoenix:ci) (to $0 salt_lake_city:ci))

wo xvyao yitang zaodian de hangban cong mierwoji feiwang danfo

(lambda $0 e (and (flight $0) (during_day $0 early:pd) (from $0 milwaukee:ci) (to $0 denver:ci))

zai danfo you neixie dimian jiaotong leixing kede

(lambda $v0 e (and (ground_transport $v0) (to_city $v0 denver:ci)))

Figure 3:Examples with lambda-calculus expression in Chinese ATIS.

Initialization For the fair comparison, we first use the baseline IBM Model without ℓ_0-norm to the *Initialization* procedure. The weights for lexeme features are initialized according to coocurrance statistics between words and logical constants. These are estimated with the GIZA++ implementation of IBM Model 1 (Och and Ney, 2003; Och and Ney, 2004). For UBL algorithm, we set the initial weight for each ϕ_L to ten times the average score the (word, constant) pairs in L except for the weights of seed lexical entries in Λ_{NP} which are set to 10. The learning rate α_0 is set to 1.0 and cooling rate C in all training scenarios set to 10^{-5} and the algorithm is ran for $T = 20$ iterations. For FUBL algorithm, the initial weights for templates are set by adding -0.1 for each slash in the syntactic category and -2 if the template contains logical constants. Features on (lexeme, template) pairs and all parse features are initialized to zero.

Next, we use the modification of IBM model with ℓ_0-norm to initialize the weights of lexeme features according to coocurrance statistics between word and logical constants. We have implemented this model as an open-source extension to GIZA++. Usage of the extension is identical to the standard GIZA++. The only differences are that the user needs to switch the ℓ_0 prior on or off, and to adjust both hyperparameters α and β. We first set $\alpha = 10$ and $\beta = 0.05$, then ran five iterations of this Model with the smoothed ℓ_0-norm. Besides them, the other parameters remain the same as the those of IBM Model without ℓ_0-norm.

System We employ both supervised PCCG online learning approaches. They include UBL system (Kwiatkowski et al., 2010) and FUBL one (Kwiatkowski et al., 2011). They are implemented after the *Initialization* procedure in which GIZA++ with and without the ℓ_0-norm is used.

Results Tables 1-7 present the results for all of the experiments. In aggregate, they demonstrate that both UBL and FUBL systems achieve some small improvements for adding the ℓ_0-norm across languages with lambda-calculus and variable-free expressions. The results that both algorithms are used to test Chinese GeoQuery and ATIS corpora are new. In all cases, FUBL with ℓ_0-norm performs at or near state-of-the-art recall and precision when compared to those comparable systems.

For the Geo250 domain, Tables 1 and 2 show exact match performances of UBL and FUBL systems with and without ℓ_0-norm between English and Chinese for both different meaning representations. And the systems with ℓ_0-norm achieve the best scores. For the Geo880 domain, the results from Tables 3 and 4 indicate that the performances of both systems with ℓ_0-norm exceed slightly those ones without ℓ_0-norm.

For the ATIS development set, Table 5 shows the exact match performances of both systems with and without ℓ_0-norm between English and Chinese with lambda-calculus expression. It can

IBM Model without ℓ_0-norm	English Rec.	Pre.	F1	Chinese Rec.	Pre.	F1
UBL	81.8	83.5	82.6	81.9	86.6	84.1
FUBL	83.7	83.7	83.7	83.9	86.8	85.2
IBM Model with ℓ_0-norm	**English Rec.**	**Pre.**	**F1**	**Chinese Rec.**	**Pre.**	**F1**
UBL	82.0	83.6	82.8	82.4	86.8	84.6
FUBL	83.9	83.8	83.9	84.2	87.0	85.6

Table 1: Exact match performance across languages on Geo250 dataset with lambda-calculus expressions.

IBM Model without ℓ_0-norm	English Rec.	Pre.	F1	Chinese Rec.	Pre.	F1
UBL	80.4	80.8	80.6	78.6	79.3	78.9
FUBL	82.7	83.2	82.9	80.0	81.6	80.8
IBM Model with ℓ_0-norm	**English Rec.**	**Pre.**	**F1**	**Chinese Rec.**	**Pre.**	**F1**
UBL	80.8	81.0	80.9	79.0	79.6	79.3
FUBL	82.8	83.5	83.1	80.4	81.8	81.2

Table 2: Exact match performance across languages on Geo250 dataset with variable-free expressions.

be seen that both algorithms with ℓ_0-norm also outperforms trivially those without ℓ_0-norm over $0.2\% \sim 0.5\%$. For the ATIS test set, Tables 6 and 7 present the exact and partial match performances of both systems with and without ℓ_0-norm. The results demonstrate that the systems with ℓ_0-norm are superior to the ones without ℓ_0-norm once again.

5 Conclusion

In this paper, we develop a novel method to the semantic parsing which applies a modified IBM Alignment Model to initialize the weights of all lexical features. During *Initialization* procedure for two PCCG online learning algorithms, because of the addition to ℓ_0-norm this can enable it to better alignment performances between words and logical expressions. On benchmark datasets in both English and Chinese with two different meaning representations, the experimental results demonstrate that the small improvements have been achieved by the addition of ℓ_0-norm.

Acknowledgments

We are grateful to the anonymous reviewers for their valuable feedback on an earlier version of this paper. This research was supported in part by Undergraduate Innovative Research Training project of Hunan Normal University (grant no.201401021) and the Social Science Foundation (grant no.14YBA260) in Hunan Province, China.

IBM Model without ℓ_0-norm	English Rec.	Pre.	F1	Chinese Rec.	Pre.	F1
UBL	87.9	88.5	88.2	88.1	90.8	89.4
FUBL	88.6	88.6	88.6	88.8	92.0	91.2
IBM Model with ℓ_0-norm	**English Rec.**	**Pre.**	**F1**	**Chinese Rec.**	**Pre.**	**F1**
UBL	88.2	88.6	88.4	88.5	91.0	89.8
FUBL	88.9	88.9	88.9	89.0	92.1	91.3

Table 3: Exact match performance across languages on Geo880 test set with lambda-calculus expressions.

IBM Model without ℓ_0-norm	English Rec.	Pre.	F1	Chinese Rec.	Pre.	F1
UBL	84.3	85.2	84.7	82.0	84.0	83.0
FUBL	85.7	86.4	86.2	83.8	84.6	84.2
IBM Model with ℓ_0-norm	**English Rec.**	**Pre.**	**F1**	**Chinese Rec.**	**Pre.**	**F1**
UBL	84.5	85.6	85.1	82.3	84.1	83.2
FUBL	86.0	86.5	86.3	84.2	84.6	84.4

Table 4: Exact match performance across languages on Geo880 test set with variable-free expressions.

IBM Model without ℓ_0-norm	English Rec.	Pre.	F1	Chinese Rec.	Pre.	F1
UBL	65.6	67.1	66.3	66.8	69.0	68.4
FUBL	81.9	82.1	82.0	83.3	83.8	83.5
IBM Model with ℓ_0-norm	**English Rec.**	**Pre.**	**F1**	**Chinese Rec.**	**Pre.**	**F1**
UBL	65.8	67.5	66.6	67.0	69.4	68.7
FUBL	82.2	82.6	82.4	83.8	84.0	83.9

Table 5: Exact match performance across languages on ATIS development set with lambda-calculus expressions.

IBM Model without ℓ_0-norm	English Rec.	Pre.	F1	Chinese Rec.	Pre.	F1
UBL	71.4	72.1	71.7	72.6	73.0	72.8
FUBL	82.8	82.8	82.8	83.6	83.5	83.6
IBM Model with ℓ_0-norm	**English Rec.**	**Pre.**	**F1**	**Chinese Rec.**	**Pre.**	**F1**
UBL	72.0	72.6	72.3	72.8	73.4	73.1
FUBL	83.2	83.4	83.3	84.0	84.0	84.0

Table 6: Exact match performance across languages on ATIS test set with lambda-calculus expressions.

IBM Model without ℓ_0-norm	English Rec.	Pre.	F1	Chinese Rec.	Pre.	F1
UBL	78.2	98.2	87.1	79.2	98.6	88.0
FUBL	95.2	93.6	94.6	95.3	93.8	94.6
IBM Model with ℓ_0-norm	**English Rec.**	**Pre.**	**F1**	**Chinese Rec.**	**Pre.**	**F1**
UBL	78.6	98.5	87.8	80.0	98.6	88.5
FUBL	95.6	94.0	94.8	95.9	94.4	95.2

Table 7: Partial match performance across languages on ATIS test set with lambda-calculus expressions.

References

Andrew Barron, Jorma Rissanen, and Bin Yu. 1998. *The Minimum Description Length Principle in Coding and Modeling. IEEE Transaction on Information Theory*, 44(6):2743-2760.

Ashish Vaswani, Liang Huang, and David Chiang. 2012. *Smaller Alignment Models for Better Translations: Unsupervised Word Alignment with the L0-norm. In Proceedings of the 50th Annual Meeting of the Association for Computational Linguistics (ACL)*, pages 311–319.

Deborah A. Dahl, Madeleine Bates, Michael Brown, William Fisher, Kate Hunicke-Smith, David Pallett, Christine Pao, Alexander Rudnicky, and Elizabeth Shriberg. 1994. *Expanding the scope of the ATIS task: the ATIS-3 corpus. ARPA Human Language Technology Workshop*, pages 43–48.

Franz Joseph Och and Hermann Ney. 2003. *A Systematic comparison of Various Statistical Alignment Models. Computational Linguistics*, 29(1):19–51.

Franz Joseph Och and Hermann Ney. 2004. *The Alignment Template Approach to Statistical Machine Translation. Computational Linguistics*, 30:417–449.

Luke S. Zettlemoyer and Michael Collins. 2005. *Learning to Map Sentences to Logical Form: Structured Classification with Probabilistic Categorial Grammars. In Proceedings of UAI*, pages 658–666.

Luke S. Zettlemoyer and Michael Collins. 2007. *Online Learning of Relaxed CCG Grammars for Parsing to Logical Form. In Proceedings of EMNLP-CoNLL*, pages 678–687.

Luke S. Zettlemoyer and Michael Collins. 2009. *Learning Context-Dependent Mappings from Sentences to Logical Form. In Proceedings of ACL-IJCNLP*, pages 976–984.

Luke S. Zettlemoyer and Michael Collins. 2012. *Learning to Map Sentences to Logical Form: Structured Classification with Probabilistic Categorial Grammars. CoRR abs.*

Philipp Koehn, Franz Joseph Och, and Daniel Marcu. 2003. *Statistical Phrase-based Translation. In Proceedings of NAACL.*

Steedman Mark. 1996. *Surface Structure and Interpretation. The MIT Press.*

Steedman Mark. 2000. *The Syntactic Process. The MIT Press.*

Tom Kwiatkowski, Luke Zettlemoyer, Sharon Goldwater, and Mark Steedman. 2010. *Inducing Probabilistic CCG Grammars from Logical Form with Higher-order Unification. In Proceedings of the Conference on Empirical Methods in Natural Language Processing (EMNLP)*, Cambridge, MA.

Tom Kwiatkowski, Luke Zettlemoyer, Sharon Goldwater, and Mark Steedman. 2011. *Lexical Generalization in CCG Grammar Induction for Semantic Parsing. In Proceedings of the Conference on Empirical Methods in Natural Language Processing (EMNLP)*, Edinburgh, UK.

Tom Kwiatkowski, Luke Zettlemoyer, Sharon Goldwater, and Mark Steedman. 2012. *A Probabilistic Model of Syntactic and Semantic Acquisition from Child-Directed Utterances and their Meanings. In Proceedings of the European Chapter of the Association for Computational Linguistics (EACL)*, Avignon, France.

Wei Lu, Hwee Tou Ng, Wee Sun Lee, and Luke S. Zettlemoyer. 2008. *A Generative Model for Parsing Natural Language to Meaning Representations. In Proceedings of The Conference on Empirical Methods in Natural Language Processing (EMNLP)*, pages 783–792.

Yoav Artzi and Luke Zettlemoyer. 2011. *Bootstrapping Semantic Parsers from Conversations. In Proceedings of the Conference on Empirical Methods in Natural Language Processing (EMNLP).*

Yoav Artzi and Luke Zettlemoyer. 2013. *Weakly Supervised Learning of Semantic Parsers for Mapping Instructions to Actions. Transactions of the Association for Computational Linguistics (TACL).*

Zhihua Liao and Zili Zhang. 2013. *Learning to Map Chinese Sentences to Logical Forms. In Proceedings of the 7th International Conference on Knowledge Science, Engineering and Management (KSEM)*, pages 463–472.

A Supervised Semantic Parsing with Lexical Extension and Syntactic Constraint

Zhihua Liao
Foreign Studies College
Hunan Normal University
Changsha, China
liao.zhihua61@gmail.com

Qixian Zeng
Foreign Studies College
Hunan Normal University
Changsha, China
wanyouto@qq.com

Qiyun Wang
Foreign Studies College
Hunan Normal University
Changsha, China
qywang@qq.com

Abstract

Existing semantic parsing research has steadily improved accuracy on a few domains and their corresponding meaning representations. In this paper, we present a novel supervised semantic parsing algorithm, which includes the lexicon extension and the syntactic supervision. This algorithm adopts a large-scale knowledge base from the open-domain Freebase to construct efficient, rich Combinatory Categorial Grammar (CCG) lexicon in order to supplement the inadequacy of its manually-annotated training dataset in the small closed-domain while allows for the syntactic supervision from the dependency-parsed sentences to penalize the ungrammatical semantic parses. Evaluations on both benchmark closed-domain datasets demonstrate that this approach learns highly accurate parser, whose parsing performance benefits greatly from the open-domain CCG lexicon and syntactic constraint.

1 Introduction

Semantic parsers convert natural language sentences to logical forms through a meaning representation language. Recent research has focused on learning such parsers directly from corpora made up of sentences paired with logical meaning representations (Artzi and Zettlemoyer, 2011; Lu et al., 2008; Lu and Tou, 2011; Liao and Zhang, 2013; Kwiatkowski et al., 2010; Kwiatkowski et al., 2011; Kwiatkowski et al., 2012; Zettlemoyer and Collins, 2005; Zettlemoyer and Collins, 2007; Zettlemoyer and Collins, 2009; Zettlemoyer and Collins, 2012). And its goal is to learn a grammar that can map new, unseen sentences onto their corresponding meanings, or logical expressions.

For decades there have been many algorithms that learn probabilistic CCG grammars. These grammars are well suited to the semantic parsing because of the close linking with syntactic and semantic information. Thus, they are used to model a wide range of complex linguistic phenomena and are strongly lexicalized, which store all language-specific grammatical information directly with the words and the CCG lexicon. This CCG lexicon is useful for learning parser. However, it often suffers from the sparsity and the diversity in the training and testing datasets. Consequently, we hold that a large-scale knowledge base should play a key role in the semantic parsing. That is, it might be quite favorable in training such parser and resolving these syntactic ambiguities. Using the knowledge base which contains rich semantic information from the open-domain such as Freebase, can improve efficiently the parser's ability to solve complex syntactic parsing problem and benefit the accuracy. Besides, many previous approaches do not involve the syntactic constraint to penalize the ungrammatical parses when semantic parsing.

This paper presents a supervised approach to learn semantic parsing task using a large-scale open-domain knowledge base and syntactic constraint. The semantic parser is trained to learn parsing via a large-scale open-domain CCG lexicon while simultaneously producing parses that syntactically agree with their dependency parses. Combining these two elements allows us to train a more accurate semantic parser. In particular, it also contains a factored CCG lexicon from the closed-domain GeoQuery and ATIS. Therefore, our approach not only includes two traditional CCG lexicons from the closed-domain GeoQuery and ATIS, and from the open-domain Freebase, but also includes the factored lexicon from the closed-domain GeoQuery and ATIS. This joint of such different lexicons does well in dealing with

Proceedings of Recent Advances in Natural Language Processing, pages 362–370,
Hissar, Bulgaria, Sep 7–9 2015.

the sparsity and the diversity of the dataset where some words or phrases have been never appeared during the training and testing procedures.

This paper is structured as follows. We first provide some background information about Freebase dataset, Combinatory Categorial Grammar, probabilistic CCG (PCCG) and syntactic constraint function in Section 2. Section 3 describes how we use FUBL algorithm to construct a semantic parser FUBLLESC, and Section 4 presents our experiments and reports the results. Section 5 describes the related work. Finally, we make the conclusion and give the future work in Section 6.

2 Background

2.1 Freebase Dataset

Freebase is a free, online, user-contributed, relational database covering many different domains of knowledge (Cai and Yates, 2013; Cai and Yates, 2014; Reddy et al., 2014). The full schema and contents are available for download[1]. One main motivation we adopt Freebase is that it provides a much rich knowledge base to build a large-scale CCG lexicon for semantic parsing than traditional benchmark database like GeoQuery. The GeoQuery database contains only a single geography domain, 7 relations, and 698 total instances. However, the "Freebase Commons" subset of Freebase consists of 86 domains, an average of 25 relations per domain (total of 2134 relations), and 615000 known instances per domain (53 million instances total). The total dataset can be divided into 11 different subsets in terms of the domain types.

2.2 Combinatory Categorial Grammar

CCG is a linguistic formalism that tightly couples syntax and semantic (Steedman, 1996; Steedman, 2000). It can be used to model a wide range of language phenomena. A traditional CCG grammar includes a lexicon Λ with entries like the following:

$$flights \vdash N : \lambda x.flight(x)$$

$$to \vdash (N\backslash N)/NP : \lambda y.\lambda f.\lambda x.f(x) \wedge to(x,y)$$

$$Boston \vdash NP : bos$$

where each lexical item $w \vdash X : h$ has words w, a syntactic category X, and a logical form h. For the first example, these are flights, N, and $\lambda x.flight(x)$. Furthermore, we also introduce the factored lexicon as *(lexeme,template)* pairs, as described in Subsection 3.3.

[1]http://www.freebase.com

CCG syntactic categories may be atomic (such as S or NP) or complex (such as $(N\backslash N)/NP$) where the slash combinators encode word order information. CCG uses a small set of combinatory rules to build syntactic parses and semantic representations concurrently. It includes forward (>) and backward (<) application rules, and forward (>**B**) and backward (<**B**) composition rules as well as coordination rule. Except for the standard forward and backward slashes of CCG we also include a vertical slash for which the direction of application is underspecified.

2.3 Probabilistic CCG

Due to the ambiguity in both the CCG lexicon and the order in which combinators are applied, there will be many parses for each sentence. We discriminate between competing parses using a log-linear model which has a syntactic constraint function Φ that will be described in the next Subsection 2.4, a feature vector ϕ, and a parameter vector θ. The probability of a parse y that returns logical form $z_i, i = 1 \ldots n$, given a sentence $x_i, i = 1 \ldots n$ and a weak supervision variable μ is defined as:

$$P(y, z_i, \mu | x_i; \theta, \Lambda) = \frac{\Phi(x_i, y, \mu) e^{\theta \cdot \phi(x_i, y, z_i, \mu)}}{\Sigma_{y', z', \mu'} \Phi(x_i, y', \mu') e^{\theta \cdot \phi(x_i, y', z', \mu')}} \quad (1)$$

Subsection 4.3 fully defines the set of features used in the system presented. The most important of these control the generation of lexical items from (lexeme,template)pairs. Each (lexeme, template) pair used in a parse fires three lexical features as we will see in more details in Subsection 4.3.

The parsing or inference problem done at the testing step requires us to find the most likely logical form z given a sentence x_i and a weak supervision variable μ to encourage the agreement between the semantic parses and syntactic-based dependency ones, assuming that the parameters θ and lexicon Λ are known:

$$f(x_i) = \arg\max_z p(z | x_i; \theta, \Lambda) \quad (2)$$

where the probability of the logical form is found by summing over all parses that produce it:

$$p(z | x_i; \theta, \Lambda) = \Sigma_{y \in Y st.\mu=1} p(y, z, \mu | x_i; \theta, \Lambda) \quad (3)$$

In this approach the distribution over parse trees y is modeled as a hidden variable. Thereby, the parse tree y must agree with a dependency parse of the same sentence x_i. That is, it must guarantee the weak supervision variable μ value to be **1**. For each sentence x_i, we perform a beam search to produce all possible semantic parse y, then check the value of the syntactic constraint function Φ for each generated parse and eliminate parses which are not consistent with their dependency parses. The sum over parses can be calculated efficiently using the inside-outside algorithm with a CKY-style parsing algorithm.

To estimate the parameters themselves, we use stochastic gradient updates. Given a set of n sentence-meaning pairs $(x_i, z_i) : i = 1 \ldots n$, we update the parameters θ iteratively, for each example i, by following the local gradient of the conditional log-likelihood objective $O_i = \log P(z_i|x_i; \theta, \Lambda)$. The local gradient of the individual parameter θ_j associated with feature ϕ_j and training instance (x_i, z_i) is given by:

$$\frac{\partial O_i}{\partial \theta_j} = E_{p(y,\mu|x_i,z_i;\theta,\Lambda)}[\phi_j(x_i, y, z_i, \mu)] - E_{p(y,z,\mu|x_i;\theta,\Lambda)}[\phi_j(x_i, y, z, \mu)] \tag{4}$$

All of the expectations in above equation are calculated through the use of the inside-outside algorithm on a pruned parse chart. For a sentence of length m, each parse chart span is pruned using a beam width proportional to $m^{\frac{2}{3}}$, to allow larger beams for shorter sentences.

2.4 Syntactic Constraint Function Φ

A main problem within the above semantic parsing is that it admits a large number of ungrammatical parses. This may result in the waste of time for searching the parse space. Our motivation using the syntactic constraint is that it can shrink the space of searching parse tree and reduce the time of finding the correct parse. Thus, it will enhance the efficiency of semantic parsing. The syntactic constraint function penalizes ungrammatical parses by encouraging the semantic parser to produce parse trees that agree with a dependency parse of the same sentence (Krishnamurthy and Mitchell, 2012; Krishnamurthy and Mitchell, 2013; Krishnamurthy and Mitchell, 2015). Specifically, the syntactic constraint requires the predicate-argument structure of the CCG parse to agree with the predicate-argument structure of the dependency parse.

Therefore, the agreement can be defined as a function of each CCG rule application in y. In the parse tree y, each rule application combines two subtrees, y_h and y_c, into a single tree spanning a larger portion of the sentence x_i. A rule application AGREE(y,t) is consistent with a dependency parse t if the head words of y_h and y_c have a dependency edge between them in t. Here, the weak supervision variable μ is defined as AGREE(y,t). Therefore, the syntactic Constraint function $\Phi(\mu, y, x_i)$ is true if and only if every rule application AGREE(y,t) in y is consistent with t.

$$\Phi(\mu, y, x_i) = \begin{cases} 1 & \text{if } \mu = \textsc{Agree}(y, \textsc{DepParse}(x_i)) \\ 0 & \text{otherwise} \end{cases} \tag{5}$$

3 Learning Factored PCCGs with Lexicon Extension and Syntactic Constraint

Our factored unification based learning method with lexicon extension and syntactic constraint (FUBLLESC) extends the factored unification based learning (FUBL) algorithm (Kwiatkowski et al., 2011) to induce an open-domain lexicon, while also simultaneously adding dependency-based syntactic constraint to permit semantic parsing. In this section, we first define knowledge base K - Freebase and construct the open-domain CCG lexicon Λ_O, then provide the factored lexicon Λ_F from the closed-domain GeoGuery and ATIS, and finally present our FUBLLESC algorithm.

3.1 Knowledge Base K - Freebase

The main input in our system is a propositional knowledge base $K = (E, \Re, C, \Delta)$ (Hoffmann et al., 2011). It contains entities E, categories C, relations $\Re$, and relation instances Δ. The categories and relations are predicates which operate on the entities and return truth values; the categories $c \in C$ are one-place predicates and the relations $r \in \Re$ are two-place predicates. The entity $e \in E$ represents a real-world entity and has a set of known text names. Examples of such knowledge base come from the open-domain Freebase.

This knowledge base influences the semantic parser by two ways. Firstly, CCG logical forms are constructed by combining the categories, relations and entities from the knowledge base with logical connectives; hence, the predicates in the knowledge base determine the expressivity of the parser's semantic representation. Secondly, the known relation instances $r(e_1, e_2) \in \Delta$ are used to train the semantic parser.

3.2 Construct the Open-domain CCG Lexicon Λ_O

The first step in constructing the semantic parser is to define a open-domain CCG lexicon Λ_O. We construct Λ_O by applying simple dependency-parse-based heuristics to sentences in the training corpus (i.e., NYT-Freebase[2]). Here we adopt MALTPARSER (Nivre et al., 2006) as the dependency-parser. The resulting lexicon Λ_0 captures a variety of linguistic phenomena, including verbs, common nouns, noun compounds and prepositional modifiers. Next, we use the mention identification procedure to identify all mentions of entities in the sentence set $x_i, i = 1 \dots n$. Here we adopt sentential relation extractor MULTIR (Hoffmann et al., 2011), which is a state-of-the-art weakly supervised relation extractor for multi-instance learning with overlapping relation that combines a sentence-level extraction model with a simple, corpus-level component for aggregating the individual facts. This process results in (e_1, e_2, x_i) triple, consisting of sentences with two entity mentions. The dependency path between e_1 and e_2 in x_i is then matched against the dependency parse patterns in Table 1. Each matched pattern adds one or more lexical entries to Λ_O.

Each pattern in Table 1 has a corresponding lexical category template, which is a CCG lexical category containing parameters e, c and r that are chosen at initialization time. Given the triple (e_1, e_2, x_i), the relations r are chosen such that $r(e_1, e_2) \in \Delta$, and the categories c are chosen such that $c(e_1) \in \Delta$ or $c(e_2) \in \Delta$. The template is then instantiated with every combination of these e, c and r values.

3.3 Factored Lexicon Λ_F

A factored lexicon includes a set L of lexemes and a set T of lexical templates (Kwiatkowski et al., 2011). A lexeme $(w, \vec{c})$ pairs a word sequence with an ordered list of logical constants $\vec{c} = [c_1 \dots c_m]$. For example, lexemes can contain a single lexeme (flight, [flight]). It also can contain multiple constants, for example (cheapest, [arg max,cost]). A lexical template takes a lexeme and produces a lexical items. Templates have the general form $\lambda(\omega, \vec{v}).[\omega \vdash X : h_{\vec{v}}]$, where $h_{\vec{v}}$ is a logical expression that contains variables from the list $\vec{v}$. Applying this template to input lexeme $(w, \vec{c})$ gives the full lexical item $w \vdash X : h$ where the variable ω has been replaced with the wordspan w and the logical form h has been created by replacing each of the variables in $\vec{v}$ with the counterpart constants from $\vec{c}$. Then the lexical items are constructed from the specific lexemes and templates.

3.4 The FUBLLESC Algorithm

Figure 1 shows the FUBLLESC learning algorithm. We assume training data $\{(x_i, z_i) : i = 1 \dots n\}$ where each example is a sentence x_i paired with a logical form z_i. The algorithm induces a factored PCCG with lexicon extension and syntactic constraint, including traditional CCG lexicon Λ_T from the closed-domain GeoQuery and ATIS, the CCG lexicon Λ_O from the open-domain Freebase, the lexeme L, templates T, the factored lexicon Λ_F from the closed-domain GeoQuery and ATIS, and parameter θ.

This algorithm is online, repeatedly performing both lexical expansion (**Step 1**) and parameter update (**Step 2**) procedures for each training example. The overall approach is closely related to the FUBL algorithm (Kwiatkowski et al., 2011), but includes a large-scale CCG lexicon from the open-domain Freebase knowledge base and the syntactic constraint function from the dependency parser.

Inputs: Training set$\{(x_i, z_i) : i = 1 \cdots n\}$ where each example is a sentence x_i paired with a logical form z_i. Set of entity name lexemes L_e. Number of iteration J. Learning rate parameter α_0 and cooling rate parameter c. Set of entity name lexemes L_e. Empty lexeme set L. Empty template set T. Set of NP lexical items l_F from the factored lexicon Λ_F. Set of NP lexical items l_T from the closed-domain CCG lexicon Λ_T. Set of NP lexical items l_O from the open-domain CCG lexicon Λ_O.

Definitions: NEW-LEX(y) returns a set of new lexical items from a parse y. MAX-FAC(l) generates a (lexeme, template) pair from a lexical item $l \in l_F \cup l_T \cup l_O$. PART-FAC($y$) generates a set of templates from parse y. The distributions $p(y, \mu | x, z; \theta, \Lambda_F)$ and $p(y, z, \mu | x; \theta, \Lambda_F)$ are defined by the log-linear model.

Initialization: Let

- For $i = 1 \cdots n$.
  - $(\Psi, \pi) =$ MAX-FAC $(x_i \vdash S : z_i)$
  - $L = L \cup \Psi, T = T \cup \pi$
- set $L = L \cup L_e$.

[2]http://iesl.cs.umass.edu/riedel/data-univSchema/

Part of Speech	Dependency Parse Pattern	Lexical Category Template
Proper Noun	(name of entity e) Sacramento	$w := N : \lambda x.x = e$ $Sacramento := N : \lambda x.x = Sacramento$
Common Noun	$e_1 \stackrel{SBJ}{\Longrightarrow} [is, are, was, \ldots] \stackrel{OBJ}{\Longleftarrow} w$ Sacramento is the capital	$w := N : \lambda x.c(x)$ $capital := N : \lambda x.City(x)$
Noun Modifier	$e_1 \stackrel{NMOD}{\Longleftarrow} e_2$ Sacramento, California	Type change $N : \lambda x.c(x)$ to $N\|N : \lambda f.\lambda x.\exists y.c(x) \wedge f(y) \wedge r(x,y)$ $N : \lambda x.City(x)$ to $N\|N : \lambda f.\lambda x.\exists y.City(x) \wedge f(y) \wedge LocatedIn(x,y)$
Preposition	$e_1 \stackrel{NMOD}{\Longleftarrow} w \stackrel{PMOD}{\Longleftarrow} e_2$ Sacremento in California $e_1 \stackrel{SBJ}{\Longrightarrow} VB^* \stackrel{ADV}{\Longleftarrow} w \stackrel{PMOD}{\Longleftarrow} e_2$ Sacramento is located in California	$w := (N\backslash N)/N : \lambda f.\lambda g.\lambda x.\exists y.f(y) \wedge g(x) \wedge r(x,y)$ $in := (N\backslash N)/N : \lambda f.\lambda g.\lambda x.\exists y.f(y) \wedge g(x) \wedge LocatedIn(x,y)$ $w := PP/N : \lambda f.\lambda x.f(x)$ $in := PP/N : \lambda f.\lambda x.f(x)$
Verb	$e_1 \stackrel{SBJ}{\Longrightarrow} w^* \stackrel{OBJ}{\Longleftarrow} e_2$ Sacramento governs California $e_1 \stackrel{SBJ}{\Longrightarrow} w^* \stackrel{ADV}{\Longleftarrow} [IN, TO] \stackrel{OBJ}{\Longleftarrow} e_2$ Sacramento is located in California $e_1 \stackrel{NMOD}{\Longrightarrow} w^* \stackrel{ADV}{\Longleftarrow} [IN, TO] \stackrel{OBJ}{\Longleftarrow} e_2$ Sacramento located in California	$w^* := (S\backslash N)/N : \lambda f.\lambda g.\exists x,y.f(y) \wedge g(x) \wedge r(x,y)$ $governs := (S\backslash N)/N : \lambda f.\lambda g.\exists x,y.f(y) \wedge g(x) \wedge LocatedIn(x,y)$ $w^* := (S\backslash N)/PP : \lambda f.\lambda g.\exists x,y.f(y) \wedge g(x) \wedge r(x,y)$ $islocated := (S\backslash N)/PP : \lambda f.\lambda g.\exists x,y.f(y) \wedge g(x) \wedge LocatedIn(x,y)$ $w^* := (S\backslash N)/PP : \lambda f.\lambda g.\lambda y.f(y) \wedge g(x) \wedge r(x,y)$ $located := (S\backslash N)/PP : \lambda f.\lambda g.\lambda y.f(y) \wedge g(x) \wedge LocatedIn(x,y)$
Forms of "to be"	(none)	$w^* := (S\backslash N)/N : \lambda f.\lambda g.\exists x.g(x) \wedge f(x)$

Table 1: Dependency parse pattern used to instantiate lexical categories for the semantic parser lexicon Λ_O. Each pattern is followed by an example phrase that instantiates it. An $*$ indicates a position that may be filled by multiple consecutive words in the sentence. e_1 and e_2 are the entities identified in the sentence, r represents a relation where $r(e_1, e_2)$, and c represents a category where $c(e_1)$. Each template may be instantiated with multiple values for the variables e, c, r.

- set $\Lambda_F = (L, T)$.
- set $\Lambda_F = \Lambda_F \cup \Lambda_T \cup \Lambda_O$.
- Initialize θ using coocurrence statistics.

Algorithm: For $t = 1 \cdots J, i = 1 \cdots n$:

Step 1: Add Lexemes and Templates

- Let $y^* = \arg\max_{y,\mu_i} p(y, \mu_i | x_i, z_i; \theta, \Lambda_F)$
- For $l \in$ NEW-LEX(y^*)
  - * $(\Psi, \pi) =$ MAX-FAC(l)
  - * $L = L \cup \Psi, T = T \cup \pi, \Lambda_F = \Lambda_F \cup (\Psi, \pi)$
- $\Pi =$ PART-FAC (y^*), $T = T \cup \Pi$

Step 2: Update Parameters with Syntactic Constraint

- Let $\gamma = \frac{\alpha_0}{1 + c \times k}$ where $k = i + t \times n$.
- Let $\mu_i = \text{AGREE}(y, \text{DEPPARSE}(x_i))$.
- Let

$$\begin{aligned} \Delta &= E_{p(y,\mu_i|x_i,z_i;\theta,\Lambda_F)}[\phi(x_i, y, z_i, \mu_i)] \\ &- E_{p(y,z,\mu_i|x_i;\theta,\Lambda_F)}[\phi(x_i, y, z, \mu_i)] \end{aligned}$$

- Set $\theta = \theta + \gamma\Delta$

Output: Lexeme L, template T, factored lexicon Λ_F, and parameters θ.

Figure 1: The FUBLLESC algorithm.

Initialization This model is initialized with two traditional CCG lexicons and a factored lexicon as follow. Firstly, a traditional CCG lexicon Λ_T is built from the closed-domain GeoQuery and ATIS whereas another CCG lexicon Λ_O is constructed from the open-domain Freebase. Secondly, we start to build the factored lexicon Λ_F from the closed-domain GeoQuery and ATIS. MAX-FAC is a function that takes a lexical item l and returns the maximal factoring of it, that is the unique, maximal (lexeme,template) pair that can be combined to construct l. We apply MAX-FAC to each of the training examples (x_i, z_i), creating a single way of producing the desired meaning z from a lexeme containing all of the words in x_i. The lexemes and templates created in this way provide the initial factored lexicon Λ_F. Finally, we combine the initial factored lexicon Λ_F with these two traditional CCG lexicons Λ_T and Λ_O to create a new larger factored lexicon Λ_F.

Step 1: The first step of the learning algorithm adds lexemes and templates to the factored model given by performing manipulations on the highest scoring correct parse y^* of the current training example (x_i, z_i). NEW-LEX function generates lexical items by splitting and merging nodes in the best parse tree of each training example. The splitting procedure is a three-step process that first splits the logical form h, then splits the CCG syntactic category X and finally splits the string w. The merging procedure is to recreate the original parse tree $X : h$ spanning w by recombining two new lexical items with CCG combinators (application or composition). First, the NEW-LEX procedure is run on y^* to generate new lexical items. We then use the function MAX-FAC to create the maximal factoring of each of these new lexical items and these are added to the factored representation of the lexicon Λ_F. New templates can also be introduced through partial factoring of internal parse nodes. These templates are generated by using the function PART-FAC to abstract over the wordspan and a subset of the constants contained in the internal parse nodes of y^*. This step allows for templates that introduce new semantic content to model elliptical language.

Step 2: The second step does a stochastic gradient descent update on the parameter θ used in the parsing model. In particular, this update first computes the weak supervision variable μ_i value for each parse tree y through the syntactic constraint function Φ and then judges whether the punishment need to be done. More details about this update are described in Subsection 2.3.

4 Experimental Setup

This section describes our experimental setup and comparisons of the result. We follow the setup of Zettlemoyer and Collins (2007; 2009) and Kwiatkowski et al. (2010; 2011), including datasets, features, evaluation metrics, and initialization as well as systems, as reviewed below. Finally, we report the experimental results.

4.1 Datasets

We evaluate on two benchmark closed-domain datasets. GeoQuery is made up of natural language queries to a database of geographical information, while ATIS contains natural language queries to a flight booking system (Zettlemoyer and Collins, 2007; Zettlemoyer and Collins, 2009; Zettlemoyer and Collins, 2012; Kwiatkowski et al., 2010; Kwiatkowski et al., 2011). The Geo880 dataset has 880(English sentence, logical form) pairs split into a training set of 600 pairs and a test set of 280 ones. The Geo250 dataset is a subset of the Geo880, and is used 10-fold cross validation experiments with the same splits of this subset. The ATIS dataset contains 5410 (English sentence, logical form) pairs split into a 5000 example development set and a 450 example test set.

4.2 Evaluation Metrics

We report exact math *Recall*, *Precision* and *F1*. *Recall* is the percentage of sentences for which the correct logical form was returned, *Precision* is the percentage of returned logical forms that are correct, and *F1* is the harmonic mean of *Precision* and *Recall*. For ATIS we also report partial match *Recall*, *Precision* and *F1*. Partial match *Recall* is the percentage of correct literals returned. Partial match *Precision* is the percentage of returned literals that are correct.

4.3 Features

We introduce two types of features to discriminate among parses: lexical features and logical-form features. First, for each lexical item $L \in \Lambda_T \cup \Lambda_O$ from the closed-domain CCG lexicon Λ_T and the open-domain CCG lexicon Λ_O, we include a feature ϕ_L that fires when L was used. Second, For each (lexeme, template) pair used to create another lexical item $(l, t) \in \Lambda_F$ about the factored lexicon Λ_F we have indicator features ϕ_l for the lexeme used, ϕ_t for the template used, and $\phi_{l,t}$ for the pair that was used. Thereby, the lexical feature includes ϕ_L and $\phi_{l,t}$. We assign the features on the lexical templates a weight of 0.1 to prevent them from swamping the far less frequent but equally informative lexeme features. For each logical-form feature, it is computed on the lambda-calculus expression z returned at the root of the parse. Each time a predicate p in the output logical expression z takes a argument a with type $T(a)$ in position i, it triggers two binary indicator features: $\phi_{(p,a,i)}$ for the predicate-argument relation and $\phi_{(p,T(a),i)}$ for the predicate argument-type relation.

4.4 Initialization

The weights for lexeme features are initialized according to coocurrance statistics between words and logical constants. They are estimated with the GIZA++ implementation of IBM Model 1 (Och and Ney, 2003; Och and Ney, 2004). The weights of the seed lexical entries from the closed-domain CCG lexicon Λ_T and the open-domain CCG lexicon Λ_O are set to 10 that can be equivalent to the highest possible coocurrence score. The initial weights for templates are set by adding -0.1 for each slash in the syntactic category and -2 if the template contains logical constants. Features on (lexeme, template) pairs and all parse features are initialized to zero. We use the learning rate $\alpha_0 = 1.0$ and cooling rate $c = 10^{-5}$ in all training, and run the algorithm for $J = 20$ iterations.

4.5 Systems

We compare this performance to those recently-published and directly-comparable results. For GeoQuery, they include the ZC07 (Zettlemoyer and Collins, 2007), λ-WASP (Wong and Mooney, 2007), UBL (Kwiatkowski et al., 2010) and

system	Rec.	Pre.	F1
ZC07	74.4	87.3	80.4
UBL	65.6	67.1	66.3
FUBL	81.9	82.1	82.0
FUBLLESC	85.2	**92.8**	88.8

Table 3: Performance of Exact Match on the ATIS development set.

FUBL (Kwiatkowski et al., 2011). For ATIS, we report results from ZC07 (Zettlemoyer and Collins, 2007), UBL (Kwiatkowski et al., 2010) and FUBL (Kwiatkowski et al., 2011).

4.6 Results

Tables 2-4 present all the results on the GeoGuery and ATIS domains. In all cases, FUBLLESC achieves at state-of-the-art recall and precision when compared to directly comparable systems and it significantly outperforms FUBL and ZC07. Most importantly, it is obvious that on precision our FUBLLESC remarkably exceeds other systems because of the joint effect about the addition of an open-domain CCG lexicon and the usage of syntactic constraint. As shown in Table 2, on Geo250 FUBLLESC achieves the highest recall 86.2% and precision 92.0%, whereas on Geo880 the only higher recall and precision (90.8% and 95.6%) are also achieved by FUBLLESC. On the ATIS development set, FUBLLESC outperforms FUBL by 3.3% of recall and by 10.7% of precision, which is shown in Table 3. Table 4 indicates that on the ATIS test set FUBLLESC significantly outperforms FBUL by 10% of precision on Exact Match and 5% of precision on Partial Match, respectively.

5 Related Work

Semantic parsers have been thought of mapping sentences to logical representations of their underlying meanings. There has been significant work on supervised learning for inducing semantic parsers. Various techniques were applied to this problem including machine translation (Wong and Mooney, 2006; Wong and Mooney, 2007), using CCG to building meaning representations (Zettlemoyer and Collins, 2005; Zettlemoyer and Collins, 2007; Zettlemoyer and Collins, 2009; Zettlemoyer and Collins, 2012), higher-order unification (Kwiatkowski et al., 2010; Kwiatkowski et al., 2011), modeling child language acquisition (Kwiatkowski et al., 2012),generative model (Ruifang and Mooney, 2006; Lu et al., 2008), inductive logic programming (Zelle and Mooney, 1996; Thompson and Mooney, 2003; Tang and Mooney, 2000), probabilistic forest to string model for language generation (Lu and Tou, 2011), and the extension from English to Chinese (Liao and Zhang, 2013). The algorithm we develop in this paper builds on some previous work on the supervised learning CCG parsers (Kwiatkowski et al., 2010; Kwiatkowski et al., 2011), as described in Section 3.4.

Recent research in this field has focused on learning for various forms of relatively weak but easily gathered supervision. This includes unannotated text (Poon and Domingos, 2009; Poon and Domingos, 2010), learning from question-answer pairs (Liang et al., 2011; Berant et al., 2013), via paraphrase model (Berant and Liang, 2014), from conversational logs (Artzi and Zettlemoyer, 2011), with distant supervision (Krishnamurthy and Mitchell, 2012; Krishnamurthy and Mitchell, 2013; Krishnamurthy and Mitchell, 2015; Cai and Yates, 2013; Cai and Yates, 2014), and from sentences paired with system behaviors (Artzi and Zettlemoyer, 2013) as well as via semantic graphs (Reddy et al., 2014).

Our approach builds on a number of existing algorithm ideas which include adopting PCCG to building the meaning representation (Kwiatkowski et al., 2010; Kwiatkowski et al., 2011), using the weakly supervised parameter leaning with the syntactic constraint (Krishnamurthy and Mitchell, 2012; Krishnamurthy and Mitchell, 2013), and employing the open-domain Freebase to semantic parsing (Cai and Yates, 2013).

6 Conclusion and Future Work

This paper presents a novel supervised method for semantic parsing which induces PCCG from sentences paired with logical forms. This approach contains an open-domain Freebase lexicon and syntactic constraint which employs dependency parser to penalize uncorrect CCG parsing tree. The experiments on both benchmark datasets (i.e., GeoQuery and ATIS) show that our method achieves higher performances.

In the future work, we are interested in exploring morphological model and containing more open-domain lexicons as well as more syntactic

(a) The Geo250 test set

system	Rec.	Pre.	F1
λ-WASP	75.6	91.8	82.9
UBL	81.8	83.5	82.6
FUBL	83.7	83.7	83.7
FUBLLESC	86.2	**92.0**	89.0

(b) The Geo880 test set

system	Rec.	Pre.	F1
ZC07	86.1	91.6	88.8
UBL	87.9	88.5	88.2
FUBL	88.6	88.6	88.6
FUBLLESC	90.8	**95.6**	93.1

Table 2: Performance of Exact Match between the different GeoQuery test sets.

(a) Exact Match

system	Rec.	Pre.	F1
ZC07	84.6	85.8	85.2
UBL	71.4	72.1	71.7
FUBL	82.8	82.8	82.8
FUBLLESC	86.4	**92.8**	89.5

(b) Partial Match

system	Rec.	Pre.	F1
ZC07	96.7	95.1	95.9
UBL	78.2	98.2	87.1
FUBL	95.2	93.6	94.6
FUBLLESC	97.2	**98.6**	97.9

Table 4: Performance of Exact and Partial Matches on the ATIS test set.

information. Besides, it will also be important to better model some variations within the existing lexemes.

Acknowledgments

We are grateful to the anonymous reviewers for their valuable feedback on an earlier version of this paper. This research was supported in part by Undergraduate Innovative Research Training project of Hunan Normal University (grant no.201401021) and the Social Science Foundation (grant no.14YBA260) in Hunan Province, China.

References

Cynthia A. Thompson and Raymond J. Mooney. 2003. *Acquiring Word-Meaning Mappings for Natural Language Interfaces. Journal of Artificial Intelligence Research*, 18:1–44.

Franz Joseph Och and Hermann Ney. 2003. *A Systematic Comparison of Various Statistical Alignment Models. Computational Linguistics*, 29(1):19–51.

Franz Joseph Och and Hermann Ney. 2004. *The Alignment Template Approach to Statistical Machine Translation. Computational Linguistics*, 30:417–449.

Ruifang Ge and Raymond J. Mooney. 2006. *Discriminative Reranking for Semantic Parsing. In Proceedings of the Conference of the Association for Computational Linguistics (ACL).*

Jayant Krishnamurthy and Tom M. Mitchell. 2012. *Weakly Supervised Training of Semantic Parsers. In Proceedings of the 2012 Joint Conference on Empirical Methods in Natural Language Processing and Computatioanl Natural Language Learning (EMNLP-CoNLL).*

Jayant Krishnamurthy and Tom M. Mitchell. 2013. *Joint Syntactic and Semantic Parsing with Combinatory Categorial Grammar. In Proceedings of the 52th Annual Meeting of the Association for Computational Linguistics (ACL).*

Jayant Krishnamurthy and Tom M. Mitchell. 2015. *Learning a Compositional Semantics for Freebase with an Open Predicate Vocabulary. Transactions of the Association for Computational Linguistics (TACL).*

Joakim Nivre, Johan Hall, and Jens Nilsson. 2006. *Maltparser: A Data-driven Parser-denerator for Dependency Parsing. In Proceedings of the 21st International Conference on Computatonal Lianguistics and 44th Annual Meeting of the Association for Computational Linguistics (ACL).*

Jonathan Berant, Andrew Chou, Roy Frostig, and Percy Liang. 2013. *Semantic Parsing on Freebase from Question-Answer Pairs. In Proceedings of EMNLP.*

Jonathan Berant and Percy Liang. 2014. *Semantic Parsing via Paraphrasing. In Proceedings of ACL.*

John M. Zelle and Raymond J. Mooney. 1996. *Learning to Parse Database Queries using Inductive Logic Programming. In Proceedings of the National Conference on Artificial Intelligence (AAAI).*

Lappoon R. Tang and Raymond J. Mooney. 2000. *Automated Construction of Database Interfaces: Integrating Statistical and Relational Learning for Semantic Parsing. In Proceedings of the Joint Conference of Empirical Methods in Natural Language Procesing and Very Large Corpora (EMNLP).*

Luke S. Zettlemoyer and Michael Collins. 2005. *Learning to Map Sentences to Logical Form: Structured Classification with Probabilistic Categorial Grammars. In Proceedings of UAI*, pages 658–666.

Luke S. Zettlemoyer and Michael Collins. 2007. *Online Learning of Relaxed CCG Grammars for Parsing to Logical Form. In Proceedings of EMNLP-CoNLL*, pages 678–687.

Luke S. Zettlemoyer and Michael Collins. 2009. *Learning Context-Dependent Mappings from Sentences to Logical Form. In Proceedings of ACL-IJCNLP*, pages 976–984.

Luke S. Zettlemoyer and Michael Collins. 2012. *Learning to Map Sentences to Logical Form: Structured Classification with Probabilistic Categorial Grammars. CoRR abs.*

Percy Liang, Michael I. Jordan, and Dan Klein. 2011. *Learning Dependency-based Compositional Semantics. In Proceedings of the Conference of the Association for Computational Linguistics (ACL).*

Poon Hoifung and Pedro Domingos. 2009. *Unsupervised Semantic Parsing. In Proceedings of the Conference on Empiricial Methods in Natural Language Processing (EMNLP).*

Poon Hoifung and Pedro Domingos. 2010. *Unsupervised Ontology Induction from Text. In Proceedings of the Conference of the Association for Computational Linguistics (ACL).*

Qingqing Cai and Alexander Yates. 2013. *Semantic Parsing Freebase: Towards Open-domain Semantic Parsing. In Proceedings of the Second Joint Conference on Lexical and Computational Semantics (SEM).*

Qingqing Cai and Alexander Yates. 2014. *Large-scale Semantic Parsing via Schema Matching and Lexicon Extension. In Proceedings of the Annual Meeting of the Association for Computational Linguistics (ACL).*

Raphael Hoffmann, Congle Zhang, Xiao Ling, Luke S. Zettlemoyer, and Daniel S. Weld. 2011. *Knowledge-based Weak Supervision for Information Extraction of Overlapping Relations. In Proceedings of the 49th Annual Meeting of the Association for Computational Linguistics: Human Language Technologies (ACL).*

Siva Reddy, Mirella Lapata, Mark Steedman. 2014. *Large-scale Semantic Parsing without Question-Answer Pairs. Transactions of the Association for Computational Linguistics (TACL).*

Steedman Mark. 1996. *Surface Structure and Interpretation. The MIT Press.*

Steedman Mark. 2000. *The Syntactic Process. The MIT Press.*

Tom Kwiatkowski, Luke Zettlemoyer, Sharon Goldwater, and Mark Steedman. 2010. *Inducing Probabilistic CCG Grammars from Logical Form with Higher-order Unification. In Proceedings of the Conference on Empirical Methods in Natural Language Processing (EMNLP)*, Cambridge, MA.

Tom Kwiatkowski, Luke Zettlemoyer, Sharon Goldwater, and Mark Steedman. 2011. *Lexical Generalization in CCG Grammar Induction for Semantic Parsing. In Proceedings of the Conference on Empirical Methods in Natural Language Processing (EMNLP)*, Edinburgh, UK.

Tom Kwiatkowski, Luke Zettlemoyer, Sharon Goldwater, and Mark Steedman. 2012. *A Probabilistic Model of Syntactic and Semantic Acquisition from Child-Directed Utterances and their Meanings. In Proceedings of the European Chapter of the Association for Computational Linguistics (EACL)*, Avignon, France.

Wei Lu, Hwee Tou Ng, Wee Sun Lee, and Luke S. Zettlemoyer. 2008. *A Generative Model for Parsing Natural Language to Meaning Representations. In Proceedings of The Conference on Empirical Methods in Natural Language Processing (EMNLP)*, pages 783–792.

Wei Lu and Hwee Tou Ng. 2011. *A Probabilistic Forest-to-String Model for Language Generation from Typed Lambda Calculus Expressions. In Proceedings of The Conference on Empirical Methods in Natural Language Processing (EMNLP)*, pages 1611–1622.

Yoav Artzi and Luke Zettlemoyer. 2011. *Bootstrapping Semantic Parsers from Conversations. In Proceedings of the Conference on Empirical Methods in Natural Language Processing (EMNLP).*

Yoav Artzi and Luke Zettlemoyer. 2013. *Weakly Supervised Learning of Semantic Parsers for Mapping Instructions to Actions. Transactions of the Association for Computational Linguistics (TACL).*

Yuk Wah Wong and Raymond J. Mooney. 2006. *Learning for Semantic Parsing with Statistical Machine Translation. In Proceedings of the Human Language Technology Conference of the North American Association for Computational Linguistics (NAACL).*

Yuk Wah Wong and Raymond J. Mooney. 2007. *Learning Synchronous Grammars for Semantic Parsing with Lambda Calculus. In Proceedings of the Conference of the Association for Computational Linguistics (ACL).*

Zhihua Liao and Zili Zhang. 2013. *Learning to Map Chinese Sentences to Logical Forms. In Proceedings of the 7th International Conference on Knowledge Science, Engineering and Management (KSEM)*, pages 463–472.

Predicting the Level of Text Standardness in User-generated Content

Nikola Ljubešić[*‡] Darja Fišer[†] Tomaž Erjavec[*] Jaka Čibej[†]
Dafne Marko[†] Senja Pollak[*] Iza Škrjanec[†]

[*] Dept. of Knowledge Technologies, Jožef Stefan Institute
`name.surname@ijs.si`
[†] Dept. of Translation studies, Faculty of Arts, University of Ljubljana
`name.surname@ff.uni-lj.si`
[‡] Dept. of Inf. Sciences, Faculty of Humanities and Social Sciences, University of Zagreb

Abstract

Non-standard language as it appears in user-generated content has recently attracted much attention. This paper proposes that non-standardness comes in two basic varieties, technical and linguistic, and develops a machine-learning method to discriminate between standard and non-standard texts in these two dimensions. We describe the manual annotation of a dataset of Slovene user-generated content and the features used to build our regression models. We evaluate and discuss the results, where the mean absolute error of the best performing method on a three-point scale is 0.38 for technical and 0.42 for linguistic standardness prediction. Even when using no language-dependent information sources, our predictor still outperforms an OOV-ratio baseline by a wide margin. In addition, we show that very little manually annotated training data is required to perform good prediction. Predicting standardness can help decide when to attempt to normalise the data to achieve better annotation results with standard tools, and provide linguists who are interested in non-standard language with a simple way of selecting only such texts for their research.

1 Introduction

User-generated content (UGC) is becoming an increasingly frequent and important source of human knowledge and people's opinions (Crystal, 2011). Language use in social media is characterised by special technical and social circumstances, and as such deviates from the norm of traditional text production. Researching the language of social media is not only of great value to (socio)linguists, but also beneficial for improving automatic processing of UGC, which has proven to be quite difficult (Sproat, 2001). Consistent decreases in performance on noisy texts have been recorded in the entire text processing chain, from PoS-tagging, where the state-of-the-art Stanford tagger achieves 97% accuracy on Wall Street Journal texts, but only 85% accuracy on Twitter data (Gimpel et al., 2011), to parsing, where double-digit decreases in accuracy have been recorded for 4 state-of-the-art parsers on social media texts (Petrov and McDonald, 2012).

Non-standard linguistic features have been analysed both qualitatively and quantitatively (Eisenstein, 2013; Hu et al., 2013; Baldwin et al., 2013) and they have been taken into account in automatic text processing applications, which either strive to normalise non-standard features before submitting them to standard text processing tools (Han et al., 2012), adapt standard processing tools to work on non-standard data (Gimpel et al., 2011) or, in task-oriented applications, use a series of simple pre-processing steps to tackle the most frequent UGC-specific phenomena (Foster et al., 2011).

However, to the best of our knowledge, the level of (non-)standardness of UGC has not yet been measured to improve the corpus pre-processing pipeline or added to the corpus as an annotation

Proceedings of Recent Advances in Natural Language Processing, pages 371–378,
Hissar, Bulgaria, Sep 7–9 2015.

layer in comprehensive corpus-linguistic analyses. In this paper, we present an experiment in which we manually annotated and analysed the (non-)standardness level of Slovene tweets, forum messages and news comments. The findings were then used to train a regression model that automatically predicts the level of text standardness in the entire corpus. We believe this information will be highly useful in linguistic analyses as well as in all stages of text processing, from more accurate sampling to build representative corpora to choosing the best tools for processing the collected documents, either with tools trained on standard language or with tools specially adapted for non-standard language varieties.

The paper is organised as follows. Section 2 presents the dataset. Section 3 introduces the features used in subsequent experiments, while Section 4 describes the actual experiments and their results, with an emphasis on feature evaluation, the gain when using external resources, and an analysis of the performance on specific subcorpora. The paper concludes with a discussion of the results and plans for future work.

2 The Dataset

This section presents the dataset used in subsequent experiments, starting with our corpus of user-generated Slovene and the sampling used to extract the dataset for manual annotation. We then explain the motivation behind having two dimensions of standardness, and describe the process of manual dataset annotation.

2.1 The Corpus of User-generated Slovene

The dataset for the reported experiments is taken from our corpus of user-generated Slovene, which currently contains three types of text: tweets, forum posts, and news site comments. The complete corpus contains just over 120 million tokens.

Tweets were collected with the TweetCaT tool (Ljubešić et al., 2014b), which was constructed specifically for compiling Twitter corpora of smaller languages. The tool uses the Twitter API and a small lexicon of language specific Slovene words to first identify the users that predominantly tweet in Slovene, as well as their friends and followers. TweetCaT continuously collected the users' tweets for a period of almost two years, also updating the list of users. This resulted in the Slovene tweet subcorpus, which contains 61 million tokens. Currently, most of the collected tweets were written between 2013 and 2014. It should be noted that the majority of these tweets did not turn out to be user-generated content, but rather news feeds, advertisements, and similar material produced by professional authors.

For forum posts and news site comments, six popular Slovene sources were chosen as they were the most widely used and contained the most texts. The selected forums focus on the topics of motoring, health, and science, respectively. The selected news sites pertain to the national Slovene broadcaster RTV Slovenija, and the most popular left-wing and right-wing weekly magazines. Because the crawled pages differ in terms of structure, separate text extractors were developed using the Beautiful Soup[1] module, which enables writing targeted structure extractors from HTML documents. This allowed us to avoid compromising corpus content with large amounts of noise typically present in these types of sources, e.g. adverts and irrelevant links. It also enabled us to structure the texts and extract relevant metadata from them.

The forum posts contribute 47 million tokens to the corpus, while the news site comments amount to 15 million tokens. As with tweets, the majority of the collected comments were posted between 2013 and 2014. The forum posts cover a wider time span, with similar portions of text coming from each of the years between 2006 and 2014.

The corpus is also automatically annotated. The texts were first tokenised and the word tokens normalised (standardised) using the method of Ljubešić et al. (2014a), which employs character-based statistical machine translation. The CSMT translation model was trained on 1000 keywords taken from the Slovene tweet corpus (compared to a corpus of standard Slovene) and their manually determined standard equivalents. Then, using the models for standard Slovene the standardised word tokens were PoS-tagged and lemmatised.

2.2 Samples for Manual Annotation

For the experiments reported in this paper, we constructed a dataset containing individual texts that were semi-randomly sampled from the corpus of tweets, forum posts and comments. The dataset was then manually annotated.

To guarantee a balanced dataset, we selected

[1] `http://www.crummy.com/software/BeautifulSoup/`

equal proportions (one third) of texts for each text type. For forum posts and comments, we included equal proportions of each of their six sources. In order to obtain a balanced dataset in terms of language (non-)standardness from a corpus heavily skewed towards standard language, we used a heuristic to roughly estimate the degree of text (non-)standardness, which makes use of the corpus normalisation procedure. For each text, we computed the ratio between the number of word tokens that have been changed by the automatic normalisation, and its overall length in words. If this ratio was 0.1 or less, the text was considered as standard, otherwise it was considered as non-standard. The dataset was then constructed so that it contained an equal number of "standard" and "non-standard" texts. It should be noted that this is only an estimate, and that the presented method does not depend on an exact balance. Different rough measures of standardness could also be taken, e.g. a simple ratio of out-of-vocabulary words to all words, given a lexicon of standard word forms.

2.3 Dimensions of Standardness

It is far from easy to tell how "standard" a certain text is. While it could be regarded as a single dimension of a text (as is usually the case with e.g. sentiment annotation), standardness turns out to comprise a very disparate set of features. For example, some authors use standard spelling, but no capital letters. Others make many typos, while some will typeset their text in a standard fashion, but use colloquial or dialectal lexis and morphology.

To strike a balance between the adequacy and the complexity of the annotation, we decided to use two dimensions of standardness: technical and linguistic. The score for technical text standardness focuses on word capitalisation, the use of punctuation, and the presence of typos or repeated characters in the words. The score for linguistic standardness, on the other hand, takes into account the knowledge of the language by the authors and their more or less conscious decisions to use non-standard language, involving spelling, lexis, morphology, and word order.

These two dimensions are meant to be straightforward enough to be applied by the annotators, informative enough for NLP tools to appropriately apply possibly different normalisation methods, and relevant enough to linguists for filtering relevant texts when researching non-standard language.

2.4 Manual Annotation and Resulting Dataset

The annotators, who were postgraduate students of linguistics, were presented with annotation guidelines and criteria for annotating the two dimensions of non-standardness. Each given text was to be annotated in terms of both dimensions using a score between 1 (standard) and 3 (very non-standard), with 2 marking slightly non-standard texts. We used a three-score system as the task is not (and can hardly be) very precisely defined. Using this scale would also allow us to better observe inter-annotator agreement. In addition, for learning standardness models, we used a regression model, which returns a degree of standardness, rather than a classification one. In this particular case, a slightly more fine-grained scoring is beneficial.

To give an idea of the types of features taken into account for each dimension, two examples of short texts are presented below:

- T=1 / L=3
  Original: *Ma men se zdi tole s poimenovanji oz s poslovenjenjem imen mest čist mem.*
  Standardised: *Meni se zdi to s poimenovanji oz. s poslovenjenjem imen mest čisto mimo.*
  English: *To-me Refl. it-seems this with naming i.e. with making-into-Slovene names of-cities completely wrong.*
  Differences: Colloquial particle ("ma"), colloquial form of pronoun ("tole" vs. "to"), phonetic transcription of dialectal word forms ("men" vs. "meni", "čist" vs. "čisto", "mem" vs. "mimo")

- T=3 / L=1
  Original: *se pravi,da predvidevaš razveljavitev*
  Standardised: *Se pravi, da predvidevaš razveljavitev?*
  English: *Refl. this-means, that you-foresee annuling?*
  Differences: No capital letter at the start of sentence, no space after the comma, no sentence-final punctuation.

The annotators were told to mark with 0 those texts that were out of scope for the experiment, e.g. if they were written in a foreign language, automatically generated (such as news or advert lead-ins in tweets) or if they contained no linguistic material (e.g. only URLs, hashtags, and emoticons). These texts were then not included in the manually annotated dataset.

After a training session in which a small set of texts was annotated and discussed by all annotators, the experimental data was annotated in two campaigns. A first batch of 904 text instances was annotated, each by a single annotator, and was subsequently used as the development data in our experiments. For the second batch, each of 402 text instances was annotated by two annotators. In 8 of these instances, the difference between the annotations made by separate annotators in at least one dimension was two. This means that the first annotator marked a text as standard in at least one dimension, while the other marked it as very non-standard. This is why these data points were removed from the dataset, leaving 394 instances that constituted the testing set for the experiments. The response variables for the experiments were computed as the average of the values given by two annotators.

3 The Feature Space

We defined 29 features to describe the technical and linguistic text properties. The features can be grouped in two main categories. Character-based features (listed in Table 1 and described in 3.1) concern the incorrect use of punctuation and spaces, character repetition, the ratio of alphabetic vs. non-alphabetic characters, vowels vs. consonants, etc. Token-based features (listed in Table 2 and described in 3.2) describe word properties. Some are very general, e.g. proportions of very short words, capitalised words, etc., while others depend on the use of language-specific lexicons and mostly compute the proportion of words not included in these lexicons.

3.1 Character-based Features

This category contains features dealing either with the use of punctuation and brackets or the use of alphanumeric characters.

In terms of punctuation and brackets, we calculate the ratio of punctuation compared to all characters, ratio of paragraphs ending with an end-of-sentence punctuation sign, and the ratio of spaces preceding or not following a punctuation sign.

Name	Description
punc_space _ratio	ratio of punctuations followed by a space
space_punc _ratio	ratio of punctuations following a space
ucase_char _ratio	ratio of upper-case characters
punc_ratio	ratio of punctuation characters
sentpunc _ucase_ratio	ratio of sentence endings followed by an upper-case character
parstart _ucase_ratio	ratio of paragraph beginnings with an upper-case character
parend_sent punc_ratio	ratio of paragraphs ending with a punctuation
alpha_ratio	ratio of letter characters
weirdbracket _ratio	ratio of brackets with unexpected spaces
weirdquote _ratio	ratio of quotes with unexpected spaces
char_repeat _ratio	ratio of character repetitions of n={2,3}
alpha_repeat _ratio	ratio of letter repetitions of n={2,3}
char_length	text length in characters
cons_alpha _ratio	ratio of consonants among letters
vow_cons _ratio	ratio of vowels and consonants
alphabet _ratio	ratio of Slovene alphabet characters

Table 1: Overview of character-based features

Similarly, we calculate the ratio of opening or closing brackets that are preceded and followed by spaces.

For the alphanumeric characters, we calculate the ratios of alphabetic and alphanumeric characters in the text, the ratio of uppercase letters, and the ratios of sentences and paragraphs starting with an uppercase letter. One feature is based on the ratio between vowels and consonants in the text, while another encodes the ratio of characters from the Slovene alphabet. Two other features are based on repeating characters, one covering any character, the other focusing on alphabetic characters only.

Name	Description
alphanum _token_ratio	ratio of tokens consisting of alphanumeric characters
token_rep _ratio	ratio of token repetitions
ucase_token _ratio	ratio of upper-case tokens
tcase_token _ratio	ratio of title-case tokens
short_token _ratio	ratio of short tokens (up to 3 characters)
oov_ratio	ratio of OOVs given a lexical resource
short_oov _ratio	ratio of OOVs among short tokens (up to 4 characters)
lowercased _names_ratio	ratio of names written in lowercase

Table 2: Overview of token-based features

3.2 Token-based Features

In this category, we discriminate between string-based and lexicon-based features, the latter being dependent on external data sources.

In terms of string-based features, we compute the ratio of title-case and upper-case words, as well as word repetitions. Another feature is the ratio of words composed only of consonants. We also consider the ratio of very short words.

A large part of lexicon-based features uses the Sloleks lexicon[2] (Krek and Erjavec, 2009), consisting of Slovene words with all their word forms. The lexicon consists of 961,040 forms since Slovene is a morphologically rich language and each lexeme has many possible word forms.

The features based on this resource are the ratio of out-of-vocabulary (OOV) words (sloleks), the ratio of words that are OOVs, but are missing a vowel character (sloleks_vowel), the ratio of short words that are OOVs (sloleks_short), and the number of lower-case forms covered by a title- or upper-case entry in the lexicon only (sloleks_names).

We experimented with another source of lexical information – the KRES balanced corpus of standard Slovene (Logar Berginc et al., 2012). We produced two lexicons from the corpus, one consisting of all letter-only tokens occurring at least ten times (70,249 entries, kresleks_10), and the other with the frequency threshold of 100 (4,339 entries, kresleks_100). We used both resources to calculate OOV ratios.

Finally, we used a very small lexical resource of 195 most frequent non-standard forms of Slovene (nonstdlex). We produced this resource by calculating the log-likelihood statistic of each token from our corpus with respect to its frequency in the KRES corpus. We manually inspected the 250 highest-ranked tokens, cleaning out 55 irrelevant entries.

4 Experiments and Results

In this section, we describe our regressor optimisation and evaluation, the analysis of feature coefficients, the dependence on external information sources, the learning curve of the problem, and the independence from the text genre.

4.1 Regressor Optimisation

In the first set of experiments, we used the development set to perform grid search hyperparameter optimisation via 10-fold cross-validation on the SVR regressor using an RBF kernel. As our scoring function throughout the paper, we use the mean absolute error as it is more resistant to outliers than the mean squared error, and is also easier to interpret.

The results obtained from the optimised regressor, presented in Table 3, showed that the task of predicting technical standardness is simpler than that of predicting linguistic standardness, which was expected.

Dimension	Mean absolute error
technical	0.451 ± 0.033
linguistic	0.544 ± 0.033

Table 3: Results obtained from the dev set

4.2 Test Set Evaluation

Once we had optimised our hyperparameters on the development set, we performed an evaluation of the system on our test set. Given that the test set was double-annotated, with opposite-label instances removed and neighbouring labels averaged, we expected a lower level of error compared to the development data.

In Table 4 we compare our system with multiple baselines. The first two baselines (baseline_linear

[2]Sloleks is available under the CC BY-NC-SA license at http://www.slovenscina.eu/.

and baseline_SVR) are supervised equivalents to what researchers mostly use in practice – the OOV ratio heuristic. Those baselines use only one feature – the OOV ratio on the Sloleks lexicon (sloleks). The first baseline (baseline_linear) is algorithmically simpler as it uses linear regression, thereby linearly mapping the [0-1] range of the OOV ratio heuristic to the expected [1, 3] range of our response variables. The second baseline (baseline_SVR) uses SVR with an RBF kernel.

The last two baselines are random baselines that produce random numbers in the [1,3] range. The baseline_test was evaluated on our test set and the baseline_theoretical was evaluated on another randomly generated sequence of values in the [1,3] range. Both baselines were evaluated on drastically longer test sets (either by repeating our test set or by generating longer sequences of random numbers) to produce accurate estimates.

We can observe that the mean absolute error of our final system did, as expected, go down in comparison to the 10-folding result obtained on the development data from Table 3. There are two reasons for this: 1) most incorrect annotations in the testing data were removed, and 2) the 3-level scale was transformed to a 5-level scale. The error level on the technical dimension is still lower compared to the linguistic dimension, although the distance between those two dimensions has shrunk from 0.09 points to 0.05 points.

Comparing our system to baseline_linear on the linguistic dimension shows that using more variables than just the OOV ratio and training a non-linear regressor does produce a much better system, with an error reduction of more than 0.17 points. When using a non-linear regressor as a baseline (baseline_SVR), the error difference falls to 0.12 points, which argues for using non-linear regressors on this problem.

For the technical dimension, as expected, the OOV ratio heuristic is not optimal, producing, differently than when using all the features, similar or worse results compared to the linguistic dimension.

The two random baselines show that both our system and the OOV baselines are a safe distance away from these weak baselines.

Beside the fact that using multiple features enhances our results, we want to stress that using a supervised system should not be questioned at all, since the output of heuristics such as the OOV ratio is very hard to interpret by the final corpus user, in contrast to the [1, 3] range defined in this paper.

	Technical	Linguistic
final system	**0.377**	**0.424**
baseline_linear	0.594	0.597
baseline_SVR	0.584	0.548
baseline_test	0.713	0.749
baseline_theoretical	0.889	0.889

Table 4: Final evaluation and comparison with the baselines via mean absolute error.

4.3 Feature Coefficients

Our next experiment focused on the usefulness of specific features by training a linear kernel SVR on standardised data and analysing its coefficients. We thereby inspected which variables demonstrate the highest prediction strength for each of our two dimensions.

For the technical dimension, the most prominent features are the ratio of alphabetic characters, the number of character repetitions, the ratio of upper-case characters and the ratio of spaces after punctuation.

On the other hand, for the linguistic dimension, the most prominent features are the OOV rate given a standard lexicon (sloleks), the OOV rate given a lexicon of non-standard forms (nonstdlex), and the ratio of short tokens.

As expected, for the technical dimension, character-based features are of greater importance. As for the linguistic dimension, token-based features, especially the lexicon-based ones, carry more weight.

4.4 External Information Sources

Our next experiment looked into how much information is obtained from external information sources used in lexicon-based features. With this experiment, we wanted to measure our dependence on these resources and the level of prediction quality one can expect if some of those resources are not available.

The results obtained with information sources that influence prediction quality the most are given in Table 5. While the technical prediction in general does not suffer a lot when removing external information sources, the linguistic one does suffer an 0.11-point increase in error when all the resource-dependent features are removed (none). The most informative resource is the lexicon of standard language (sloleks), yielding a 0.07-out-of-0.11-points error reduction. Producing a lexicon from a corpus of standard language (kresleks_100) does not come close to that, producing just a 0.02-point error reduction. While the small lexicon of non-standard forms (nonstdlex) does reduce the error by 0.06 points, using all standard-lexicon-related features (sloleks_all) comes 0.03 points closer to the final result obtained with all features (all).

Information source	Technical	Linguistic
all	0.377	0.424
none	0.384	0.537
kresleks_100	0.385	0.514
sloleks	0.379	0.461
sloleks_vowel	0.378	0.488
sloleks_all	0.380	0.445
nonstdlex	0.379	0.476

Table 5: Dependence of prediction quality on external information sources

4.5 Learning Curve

This set of experiments focused on the impact of the amount of data available for training on our prediction quality. We compared three predictors: the technical one, the linguistic one and the linguistic one without using any external information sources. The three learning curves are depicted in Figure 1. They show that useful results can be obtained with just a few hundred annotated instances. The learning of the technical and linguistic dimensions seem to be equally hard when there are up to 100 instances available for learning, the technical dimension taking off after that. The linguistic dimension is obviously harder to learn when external information sources are not used. Both learning curves seem to be parallel, showing that a larger amount of training data, at least for the features defined, cannot compensate for the lack of external knowledge.

4.6 Genre Dependence

Our final experiment focused on the dependence of the results on the genre of the training and testing data. We took into consideration the three genres present in the corpus: tweets, news comments and forum posts. On each side, training and testing, we experimented with using either data from just one genre or from all genres together. On the training side, we made sure to use the same number of instances in each experiment. The results of the genre dependence experiment are presented in Table 6.

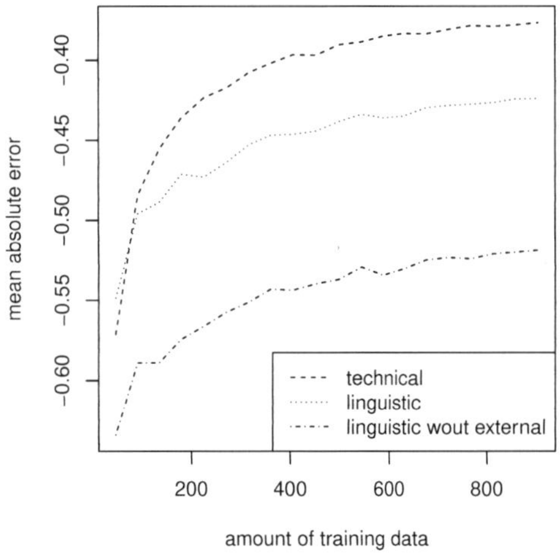

Figure 1: Mean absolute error as a function of training data size

Technical				
	Tweet	Comment	Forum	All
Tweet	0.384	0.451	0.485	0.440
Comment	0.519	0.389	0.400	0.437
Forum	0.514	0.408	0.370	0.431
All	0.426	0.382	0.417	0.409
Linguistic				
	Tweet	Comment	Forum	All
Tweet	0.410	0.452	0.503	0.455
Comment	0.453	0.429	0.510	0.465
Forum	0.444	0.458	0.500	0.467
All	0.395	0.439	0.507	0.448

Table 6: Impact of the genre of training (rows) and testing data (columns)

In the technical dimension, we observe best results when training and testing data comes from the same genre. There are no significant differences between the genres.

In the linguistic dimension, Twitter data proves to be easiest to perform prediction on, and forum data the most complicated. Interestingly, the best predictions are not made if training data comes from the same genre, but if all genres are combined.

5 Conclusion

In this paper, we presented a supervised-learning approach to predicting the text standardness level. While we differentiated between two dimensions of standardness, the technical and the linguistic one, we explained both with the same 29 features, most of which were independent from external information sources.

We showed that we outperform the supervised baselines that rely on the traditionally used OOV ratio only. We outperformed those baselines even when not using any external information sources, which makes our predictor highly language-independent.

Both predictors outperformed the supervised baselines when only a few tens of instances are available for training. Most of the learning is performed on the first 500 instances. This makes building the training set for a language an easy task that can be completed in day or two.

While the single most informative external information source was the lexicon of standard language, adding information from very small lexicons of frequent non-standard forms or from automatically transformed lexicons of standard language significantly improved the results.

Finally, we showed that the predictors are, in general, genre-independent. The technical dimension is slightly more genre-dependent than the linguistic one. While predicting linguistic standardness on tweets is the simplest task, predicting the same on forums proves to be much more difficult.

Future work includes applying more transformations to the lexicon of standard language than just vowel dropping, inspecting the language independence of features without relying on manually annotated data in the target language, and using lexical information from the training data to improve prediction.

Acknowledgments

The work described in this paper was funded by the Slovenian Research Agency, project J6-6842 and by the European Fund for Regional Development 2007-2013, grant RC.2.2.08-0050 (Project RAPUT).

References

Timothy Baldwin, Paul Cook, Marco Lui, Andrew MacKinlay, and Li Wang. 2013. How Noisy Social Media Text, How Diffrnt Social Media Sources. In *Sixth Intl. Joint Conference on NLP*, pages 356–364.

David Crystal. 2011. *Internet Linguistics: A Student Guide*. Routledge, New York, NY, 10001, 1st edition.

Jacob Eisenstein. 2013. What to Do About Bad Language on the Internet. In *NAACL-HLT*, pages 359–369. ACL, June.

Jennifer Foster, Ozlem Cetinoglu, Joachim Wagner, Joseph Le Roux, Joakim Nivre, Deirdre Hogan, and Josef van Genabith. 2011. From News to Comment: Resources and Benchmarks for Parsing the Language of Web 2.0. In *IJCNLP*, pages 893–901, Chiang Mai, Thailand. Asian Federation of NLP.

Kevin Gimpel, Nathan Schneider, Brendan O'Connor, Dipanjan Das, Daniel Mills, Jacob Eisenstein, Michael Heilman, Dani Yogatama, Jeffrey Flanigan, and Noah A. Smith. 2011. Part-of-Speech Tagging for Twitter: Annotation, Features, and Experiments. In *ACL (Short Papers)*, pages 42–47. ACL.

Bo Han, Paul Cook, and Timothy Baldwin. 2012. Automatically Constructing a Normalisation Dictionary for Microblogs. In *EMNLP-CoNLL*, pages 421–432, Jeju Island, Korea.

Yuheng Hu, Kartik Talamadupula, and Subbarao Kambhampati. 2013. Dude, srsly?: The surprisingly formal nature of twitter's language. In *ICWSM*.

Simon Krek and Tomaž Erjavec. 2009. Standardised Encoding of Morphological lexica for Slavic languages. In *MONDILEX Second Open Workshop*, pages 24–9, Kyiv, Ukraine. National Academy of Sciences of Ukraine.

Nikola Ljubešić, Tomaž Erjavec, and Darja Fišer. 2014a. Standardizing Tweets with Character-Level Machine Translation. In *CICLing*, Lecture notes in computer science, pages 164–75. Springer.

Nikola Ljubešić, Darja Fišer, and Tomaž Erjavec. 2014b. TweetCaT: a Tool for Building Twitter Corpora of Smaller Languages. In *Ninth LREC*, Reykjavik. ELRA.

Nataša Logar Berginc, Miha Grčar, Marko Brakus, Tomaž Erjavec, Špela Arhar Holdt, and Simon Krek. 2012. *Korpusi slovenskega jezika Gigafida, KRES, ccGigafida in ccKRES: gradnja, vsebina, uporaba*. Zbirka Sporazumevanje. Trojina, zavod za uporabno slovenistiko: Fakulteta za družbene vede, Ljubljana.

Slav Petrov and Ryan McDonald. 2012. Overview of the 2012 Shared Task on Parsing the Web. *First Workshop on Syntactic Analysis of Non-Canonical Language (SANCL)*, 59.

Richard Sproat. 2001. Normalization of Non-Standard Words. *Computer Speech & Language*, 15(3):287–333, July.

Predicting Inflectional Paradigms and Lemmata of Unknown Words for Semi-automatic Expansion of Morphological Lexicons

Nikola Ljubešić
University of Zagreb
nljubesi@ffzg.hr

Miquel Esplà-Gomis
Universitat d'Alacant
mespla@dlsi.ua.es

Filip Klubička
University of Zagreb
fklubick@ffzg.hr

Nives Mikelić Preradović
University of Zagreb
nmikelic@ffzg.hr

Abstract

In this paper we describe a semi-automated approach to extend morphological lexicons by defining the prediction of the correct inflectional paradigm and the lemma for an unknown word as a supervised ranking task trained on an already existing lexicon. While most ranking approaches rely only on heuristics based on a single information source, our predictor uses hundreds of features calculated on the candidate stem, corpus evidence and statistics calculated from the existing lexicon. On the example of the Croatian language we show that our approach significantly outperforms a heuristic-based baseline, yielding correct candidates in 77% of cases on the first position and in 95% of cases on the first five positions.

1 Introduction

Morphological lexicons are a vital resource in automatic processing of morphologically rich languages and their construction is a tedious and costly process.

The most reasonable approach to organizing inflectional morphological lexicons of morphologically rich languages is to define inflectional paradigms and assign them to corresponding lexemes. In this way, every entry in the morphological lexicon becomes a pair (l, p) of a lemma l and a paradigm p which allow to derive all the possible surface forms of a given word.

In this paper we frame the problem of assisting a process of extending an existing morphological lexicon as a supervised ranking problem. Namely, for each unknown word of a language we generate all possible pairs (l, p) and rank them with the goal of positioning existing pairs as high as possible. The result of the raking process is presented to a linguist through a graphical interface for labelling the correct pairs (l, p).drastically lower than would be the case if the lexicon was built manually.

2 Related Work

A significant amount of research has focused on the problem of enhancing the process of producing morphological resources. The most widely used approach is ranking pairs (l, p) of lemmas and paradigms by various scoring functions which rely on corpus evidence, the most popular being the coverage of all inflected forms derived from a pair (l, p) in a given monolingual corpus (Clément et al., 2004; Tadić and Oliver, 2004; Sagot, 2005; Šnajder et al., 2008; Esplà-Gomis et al., 2011). While our approach follows the same ranking paradigm, we argue that a significant amount of additional information can be gained from corpora and other information sources, supervised machine learning being the obvious solution for combining those.

The approach by Lindén (2009) does not rely on corpus evidence only, but uses the existing lexicon as well, showing that by combining corpus and lexicon evidence significant gains can be achieved.

The first approach to exploit machine learning over multiple sources of information for extending morphological lexicons is the work of Kaufmann and Pfister (2010) who use the information from a morphological lexicon, a morphological grammar and a corpus, and combine it via a machine-learning approach to guess the stem and morphosyntactic information for unknown words. Using a different approach, Ahlberg et al. (2014) learns paradigms from an initial collection of inflection tables, and new words are assigned to these paradigms by using a confidence score. This approach is later extended by Ahlberg et al. (2015) to use multi-class classification (using support vector machines) for choosing the best paradigm. In this work, all the possible suffixes and prefixes from a given surface form are used as binary features,

Proceedings of Recent Advances in Natural Language Processing, pages 379–387,
Hissar, Bulgaria, Sep 7–9 2015.

after applying feature selection in order to optimise the performance.

Regarding supervised approaches, it is worth noting the work by Durrett and DeNero (2013), in which patterns are built from morphologically analysed corpora to infer paradigms. For a given new surface form, they are applied in order to obtain all the inflections, and a hidden Markov model is used to choose the likeliest paradigm.

The work most similar to ours, on which we build upon, is the one by Šnajder (2012) who defines a set of string and corpus features and exploits them in a supervised learning setting, framing the problem as a binary classification task, i.e. predicting whether a candidate pair (l, p) is correct or not. This approach enables both a fully automatic lexicon construction process and the fact that a surface form can be a realisation of more than one (l, p) pair. However, results show that, although quite a high accuracy of 92% is reported (on an artificially balanced dataset), the approach is not sufficient for the positively labeled instances to be included in a morphological lexicon without human inspection, while exposing linguists to a collection of pairs (l, p) that are classified as correct is far from optimal as, in case of a false positive, alternatives are not given.

Our approach tries to facilitate the best of the two worlds – producing a ranked output for every unknown word as this is the optimal representation for the necessary human inspection, and combining all available information sources and the supervised learning paradigm to produce an output with the highest quality possible.

The remainder of the paper is structured as follows: in the following section we describe the components of our method. Section 4 describes the experimental setting while Section 5 gives the discussion of the results of the experiments. The paper ends with the conclusions in Section 6.

3 The Method

Our approach for producing a ranked list of candidate pairs (l, p) for each unknown word consists of three steps: 1) generating candidates; 2) extracting features from each candidate; and 3) ranking the candidates by supervised learning. We describe those in detail in the remainder of this section.

3.1 Candidate Generation

When we want to add an unknown surface form to a morphological lexicon we first need to know which pairs (l, p) are compatible with it. In this work, we focus on languages using suffixing for morphological inflection. This strategy is the most frequent for languages all around the world (Dryer, 2013), and it is the one specifically used by Croatian, which is our case of study. For suffixing languages, a paradigm in a morphological lexicon adds suffixes to a given stem in order to produce surface forms. Therefore, a good hint to find out the candidate paradigms from an unknown word is the inflection suffix. Unfortunately, finding out which is the suffix of a surface form without knowing its paradigm is not straightforward. Our strategy consists in checking which suffixes in the whole collection of suffixes generated by all the paradigms in a morphological lexicon match the unknown word, so we can obtain a collection of $(\mathrm{stem}, \mathrm{suffix})$ candidate pairs (l, p). Having these candidates it is possible to identify which paradigms produce the suffixes and consequently to obtain a collection of candidate pairs (l, p).

To simplify the search of candidate suffixes for a given unknown word, we use a *generalised suffix tree* (McCreight, 1976) containing all the possible suffixes from the paradigms in our lexicon.[1] Each of these suffixes is labeled with the index of the corresponding paradigms that can produce it. The generalised suffix tree data structure allows to retrieve the paradigms compatible with an unknown word by efficiently searching for all the compatible suffixes; when a suffix is found, the collection of paradigms generating it is retrieved and the list of candidates is enlarged with the new pairs (l, p).

3.2 Ranking the Candidates

Our approach is aimed at producing a ranked list of candidate pairs (l, p) for a given unknown surface form to be added to the lexicon. To do so, we use a binary classification approach which classifies each candidate pair (l, p) as either correct or incorrect, as well as a certainty measure for the candidate pair to belong to the positive class. We finally use that certainty measure to rank our candidates from the most suitable to the least suitable one.

To train our prediction models we define several features by which each candidate in our dataset is

[1] Note that this method could be easily adapted to prefixing languages by using a prefix tree instead a suffix tree.

represented. A significant part of the features we use are those proven to be informative by Šnajder (2012). We extended that list of features with those using probabilities of paradigm-conditioned suffixes of different length, probabilities of paradigm-conditioned prefixes, coverage of morphosyntactic classes, and coverage of surface forms tagged in the corpus with the corresponding morphosyntactic description (MSD).

The rest of this section describes the specific groups of features.

3.2.1 Stem Features

Stem features capture information about the stem obtained from the surface form after removing the suffix according to the pair (l, p) to be evaluated. These features are the following:

EndsIn – categorical feature containing the last character of the stem
EndsInCons – binary feature whether the stem ends with a consonant
EndsInPals – binary feature whether the stem ends with a palatal voice
EndsInVelars – binary feature whether the stem ends with a velar voice
NumSyllables – number of the syllables of the stem
OneSyllable – binary feature whether the stem contains one syllable only
StemLength – length of the stem

3.2.2 Lexicon Features

The lexicon features represent the information from the existing lexicon about the relation between a paradigm and suffixes and prefixes of stems and lemmata that belong to that paradigm. This information is encoded as paradigm-conditioned probabilities of affixes of length n, i.e. $P(\text{affix}_n|\text{paradigm})$. The features are the following:

LemmaSuffixProb_n – probability of a lemma suffix of length n given the paradigm
StemSuffixProb_n – probability of a stem suffix of length n given the paradigm
StemPrefixProb_n – probability of a stem prefix of length n given the paradigm

For each of these features $n \in \{1, 2, 3\}$, meaning that there are all together 9 different lexicon features.

3.2.3 Corpus Features

The corpus features are extracted from an external monolingual corpus. If such a corpus is available, it can be used to confirm the existence of the word forms derived from the pair (l, p) and to measure whether the observed frequency distribution of different forms is close to the expected one as calculated on existing lexicon entries. Additionally, we propose here to use a morphosyntactically annotated corpus which allows us to indirectly introduce the contextual information used by the tagger in its decision process. The corpus features are the following:

Freq – corpus frequency of the unknown word
LemmaAttested – binary feature whether the candidate lemma was attested in the corpus
NumAttForms – number of attested word forms from the expanded candidate paradigm
NumAttTags – number of morphosyntactic tags with at least one attested word form
PropAttForms – proportion of attested word forms
PropAttTags – proportion of morphosyntactic tags with at least one attested word form
PropAttFormsPoS – proportion of attested words forms tagged with the corresponding PoS
PropAttFormsMSD – proportion of attested words forms tagged with the corresponding morphosyntactic description
SumAttForms – sumation of corpus frequencies of word forms generated
SimTagDistrJS – Jensen-Shannon divergence between the expected paradigm-conditioned probability distribution of morphosyntactic categories (measured on the training portion of the existing lexicon and the corpus) and the observed probability distribution of morphosyntactic categories of the candidate (measured on the candidate and the corpus)
SimTagDistrCos – cosine distance of distributions used to obtain SimTagDistrJS

3.2.4 Other Features

Two categorical features are included in this category: the paradigm and the part-of-speech (PoS) of a given candidate. These features enable the model to capture the a-priori probability of each paradigm and PoS and possible dependences of other features on the paradigm or PoS. To clarify the latter with an example, the number of syllables of a stem is hardly a good predictor of the correctness of a candidate if it is not joined with the information on the paradigm of the candidate. Namely, there are paradigms that prefer stems with a specific number of syllables.

4 Experimental Setting

4.1 The Datasets

The two main sources of information we use in building our system are an existing morphological lexicon of Croatian and a corpus of Croatian. While we use both for extracting features (see Sections 3.2.2 and 3.2.3), we use the lexicon for producing the annotated dataset we train our predictor on.

4.1.1 The Lexicon

The morphological lexicon of Croatian we use in our experiments is part of the Apertium rule-based machine translation system (Forcada et al., 2011). It is the only freely available morphological lexicon of Croatian which contains both definitions of paradigms and lexemes attached to these paradigms.[2]

At the time we ran our experiments, the lexicon consisted of 413 paradigms from open-word classes, out of which 204 were noun paradigms, 167 were verbal and 42 adjectival. There were 10,183 lexemes in the lexicon annotated with one of the 413 paradigms. The whole lexicon was, up to that point, produced manually by the members of the Apertium community.

These lexemes produce almost 70 thousand different surface forms. Once those surface forms are used to generate all candidate pairs (l, c), which are the instances we perform classification and ranking on, we end up with around 7 million instances, with a ratio of positive and negative examples of 1:100.

Given that the amount of the available training data is huge, we randomly split the existing lexicon in two parts: 80% of the lexical entries were used for development, while the remaining 20% of the entries were put aside for testing.

The final development set contains 55,458 surface forms, while the test set consists of 12,089 surface forms. Each of these surface form has at least one pair (l, p) from which it could be derived. While 90% surface forms can be only derived from one pair (l, p), 9% can be derived from two of them and the remaining 1% can be derived from up to 7 pairs (l, p).[3] Generating candidate pairs (l, p) for the surface forms produced 6.1 million development and 1.3 million testing instances.

4.1.2 The Corpus

For gathering corpus evidence we used the largest available corpus of Croatian: the second version of the Croatian web corpus *hrWaC* (Ljubešić and Klubička, 2014), consisting of 2 billion words. The corpus is morphosyntactically tagged and lemmatised (Agić et al., 2013) with tools trained on a 90k-token training corpus (Agić and Ljubešić, 2014).

4.2 The Classifiers

We consider two classifiers for our task: support vector machines (SVM) and Random Forests (RF). While SVM has proven to be the best performing classifier on many different problems, the strengths of RF are comparable prediction strength and much higher speed. We use the Scikit-learn implementations of the two classifiers (Pedregosa et al., 2011).

Given that the RF classifier is a stochastic process, each experiment on that classifier is run 10 times and we report the mean and standard deviation of the scoring function.

For optimising our binary classifiers, we use randomised search for RF as the number of hyperparameters is quite high, while we perform grid search on SVM with the RBF kernel.

During classifier optimisation we use the F1 of the positive class as our scoring function since the dataset is highly unbalanced, having for each positive instance 100 negative ones.

4.3 Ranking

For producing ranked results we opt for the simple pointwise ranking approach in which we use certainty of the positive class on the binary classification problem as our ranking function.

We do not take pairwise ranking under consideration as we expect 1.1 correct answers among 100 candidates, making the computational cost of a drastically higher number of necessary classifications for pairwise ranking hard to argue for.

We perform ranking with both of our classifiers. In case of RF we rank the candidates by the descending probability of the positive class, while

[2] `http://sourceforge.net/p/apertium/svn/HEAD/tree/languages/apertium-hbs/`

[3] The high amount of surface forms which can be derived from two paradigms can be explained by the fact that different verbal paradigms exist regarding verb's aspect, transitivity and reflexivity. Consequently, if a verb is biaspectual, it is given two paradigms.

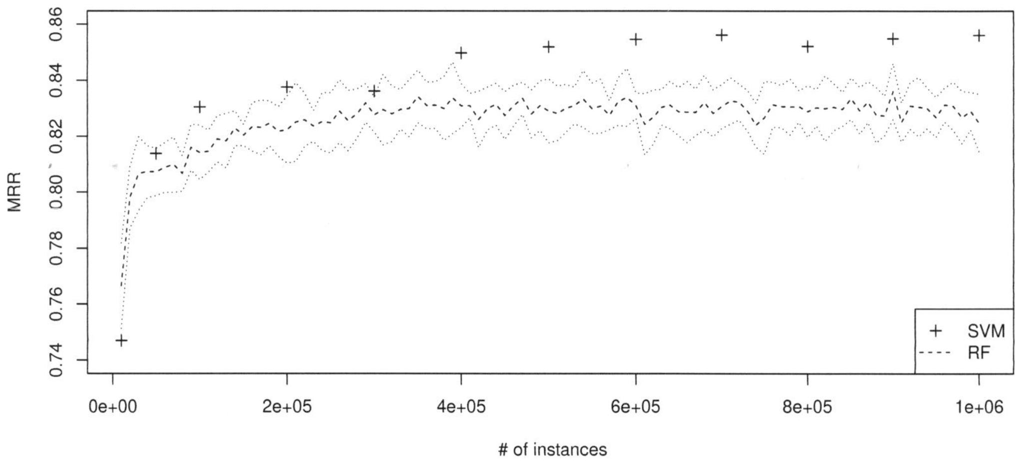

Figure 1: Ranking performance of both classifiers as a function of training data size

with SVMs we use the descending distance of each instance to the separating hyperplane.

We evaluate the ranking results via mean reciprocal rank (MRR) (Craswell, 2009) as for most of the surface forms there exists only one correct candidate pair. While reciprocal rank of a ranked result is the multiplicative inverse of the position of the (first) correct pair (l, p) in the ranking, the MRR is the average of reciprocal ranks of all the ranked results.

As our heuristic-based baseline, we take the scoring function from Esplà-Gomis et al. (2011). Given a pair (l, p), this approach produces the collection of surface forms that can be derived from it and calculates a confidence score based on the number of these surface forms attested in the corpus.

5 Results

We perform two sets of experiments. In the first set, we optimise both classifiers on the binary classification task, using F1 score on the positive class as our scoring function. In the second set of experiments we use the optimised classifiers for pointwise ranking, using MRR as our scoring function.

5.1 Classification

Given that optimising classifiers on multiple millions of instances would be extremely time-consuming, we limit our development data on 500 thousand instances, as it showed to produce stable results during our early experiments. On both classifiers we perform optimisation via 10-fold cross-validation on the development data. We perform a final evaluation of the optimised classifiers on our test data.

The result on the binary classification task obtained on the test data for SVM is 70.4% and for RF 59.8$\pm$2.4%. Regarding the time necessary for training and annotating the test set, SVM takes 215.86 and 99.04 seconds, while RF takes 3.28 and 0.46 seconds.

These results show quite clearly that, while the RF classifier is magnitudes faster on both training and testing, SVM outperforms RF with a wide margin.

5.2 Ranking

In the first ranking experiment we compare the two optimised classifiers while taking into account the amount of data used for training. We plot the results in form of learning curves in Figure 1. For RF we vary the training data size from 10 thousand instances to 1 million instances in 10k-size steps. Given that the training time for SVM is much higher than for RF, we evaluate SVMs by increasing the amount of training data by 100k instances.

The results show that on the pointwise ranking task SVM still outperforms RF, but not as drastically as on the classification task.

Regarding the impact of the amount of training data on the ranking output, we observe a steep learning curve up to 100k learning instances (climb-

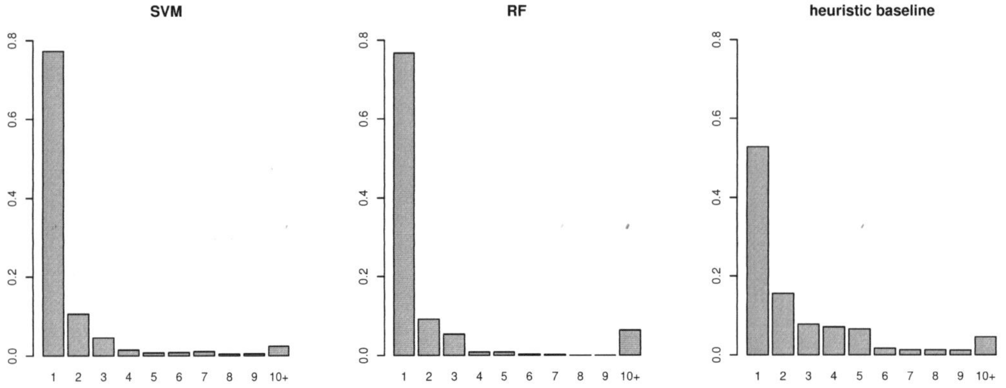

Figure 2: Distribution of positions of first correct candidates with both classifiers and the heuristic baseline

ing up to 0.831 MRR with SVM), with a moderate increase in MRR up to 500k (0.852 with SVM). The improvement obtained when doubling the amount of training data to one million instances is just 0.004 MRR (0.856 with SVM). Therefore we will perform the remainder of our experiments by using 500k training instances.

The heuristic-based baseline (Esplà-Gomis et al., 2011) does not depend on the amount of training data and produces an MRR of 0.674. Therefore we can conclude that our machine learning approaches significantly outperform our heuristic baseline.

5.3 Analysis of the Results

In this section we perform a deeper analysis of the ranking results obtained by using 500k training instances.

In Figure 2 we plot the distribution of the position of the first correct candidate for both our classifiers and compare it to our heuristic-based baseline. With both classifiers we position the correct candidate on the first position in 77% of cases. A slight difference in the classifier performance can be seen when we compare the percentage of surface forms for which a correct candidate can be found on the first three positions, where SVM reports 92.4% and RF 91.4%. If we assume that a human annotator can easily inspect the first 5 positions, correct candidates can be found with SVM in 94.7% and with RF in 93.1% of cases.

The heuristic-based approach shows significantly worse results, actually quite worse than reported in (Esplà-Gomis et al., 2011), which is due to the much higher morphological complexity of the language used in these experiments.While for only 52.8% of surface forms correct candidates are found on the first position, the first three and five positions contain correct candidates for 77.1% and 90.9% of surface forms respectively.

part of speech	RF	SVM
all	0.833 ± 0.004	0.852
noun	0.816 ± 0.010	0.827
verb	0.778 ± 0.009	0.838
adjective	0.935 ± 0.007	0.903

Table 1: Ranking performance by part of speech

In Table 1 we show the MRR score obtained on each part-of-speech of the surface form. The noticeably best results are obtained on adjectives, which is to be expected as their inflection is quite regular in Croatian. Worst results are obtained on verbs although nouns have the highest number of candidate paradigms. This can be explained by a much more complex inflectional system of verbs, part of which is used very infrequently.

Interestingly, the more successful SVM classifier performs slightly better on "hard" parts-of-speech, especially verbs, while RF outperforms SVM on the "easy" adjectival class.

5.4 Feature Analysis

In this section we inspect the impact of the defined features on our task by measuring the loss in MRR as they are either removed or used exclusively. Given the large number of features and the consequently large number of necessary experiments, we perform these with the faster RF classifier only.

	except	only
stem	0.708 ± 0.012	0.452 ± 0.001
corpus	**0.651 ± 0.009**	**0.737 ± 0.006**
lexicon	0.865 ± 0.007	0.398 ± 0.003
other	0.818 ± 0.010	0.569 ± 0.000

Table 2: Ranking performance of RF as features of a specific group are either removed (except) or used exclusively (only)

In the first experiment we either remove a feature group, as defined in section 3.2, or remove all but that feature group. The results of this experiment are shown in Table 2.

While removing feature groups, a significant loss in performance can be observed when removing corpus features. When removing lexicon features, a slight increase in MRR can be observed pointing to the conclusion that performing feature reduction on this feature group should be performed. First insights point to the conclusion that the features deteriorating our predictions are StemPrefix_2 and StemPrefix_3 while all the remaining features of this group improve our predictions. We leave this task for future work.

On the other hand, when using feature groups exclusively, i.e. using each of them separately, the best performance is obtained with corpus features. Lexicon features show to be of least help when used alone.

A reasonable performance is obtained when using the "other" feature group only. This group models the a priori probability of a paradigm given its part-of-speech and can be considered the most-frequent-paradigm baseline.

In the final experiment we focus on the most informative group of features – the corpus group. Again, we run experiments when removing a specific feature, or when training our predictor on that feature only.

The first thing we observe is that proportions of attested entities alone, as one would expect, are more informative than the numbers of the same. The most informative type of corpus information when used alone is the proportion of attested forms, outperforming the proportion of attested tags. Using annotated corpora, i.e. constraining attested forms only to those annotated with the expected morphosyntactic description (MRR 0.646) or part of speech (MRR 0.619), does outperform using raw text only (MRR 0.593). Distribution distances alone are not very informative (MRR 0.185), but generate the biggest loss in MRR once they are removed, proving the uniqueness of the information they provide.

5.5 Linguist Speed Improvements

A final inquiry was made in the speed improvements obtained by using the presented tool. A linguist very well acquainted with the paradigms at his disposal required on average 66 seconds for an entry when not using the tool, 76 seconds when using the candidate generator without the ranker, and 42 seconds when using both. From this we conclude that the tool brings a productivity increase by a factor of 1.6 while presenting unranked candidates does not bring any productivity gains.

6 Conclusion

In this paper we have presented a supervised ranking approach to assisting the expansion of an existing morphological lexicon. We have shown that such approach outperforms the traditional heuristic-based scoring approach by a wide margin.

We have used two classifiers during our experiments, one more accurate, the other much faster. While SVM does perform better than RF, in a production scenario the difference is not crucial and if computational capacity is limited, one should opt for RF.

An inspection of specific types of features showed the corpus type to be the most informative. Inside that feature type the proportion of attested word forms that are tagged in the corpus with the expected morphosyntactic description is proven to be the overall most informative feature.

An initial inquiry in speed gains when using the predictor showed to increase the linguists productivity by a factor of 1.6. A potential increase in accuracy has to be verified with future experiments.

Future work should also include a feature selection process. Namely, we have noticed that, regardless of using classifiers that perform implicit feature selection, there are some features among the lexicon-based ones that do deteriorate our results.

Finally, as the features using annotations from the corpora have shown to be more informative than those using raw text only, additional features using that information source should be added to the feature space.

Acknowledgments

The research leading to these results has received funding from the European Fund for Regional Development 2007-2013 under grant agreement no. RC.2.2.08-0050 (project RAPUT) and from the European Union Seventh Framework Programme FP7/2007-2013 under grant agreement no. PIAP-GA-2012-324414 (project Abu-MaTran).

References

Željko Agić and Nikola Ljubešić. 2014. The SETimes.HR linguistically annotated corpus of Croatian. In *Proceedings of the Ninth International Conference on Language Resources and Evaluation*, LREC'14, Reykjavik, Iceland.

Željko Agić, Nikola Ljubešić, and Danijela Merkler. 2013. Lemmatization and morphosyntactic tagging of croatian and serbian. In *Proceedings of the Fourth Biennial International Workshop on Balto-Slavic Natural Language Processing*, pages 48–57, Sofia, Bulgaria, August.

Malin Ahlberg, Markus Forsberg, and Mans Hulden. 2014. Semi-supervised learning of morphological paradigms and lexicons. In *Proceedings of the 14th Conference of the European Chapter of the Association for Computational Linguistics*, pages 569–578, Gothenburg, Sweden.

Malin Ahlberg, Markus Forsberg, and Mans Hulden. 2015. Paradigm classification in supervised learning of morphology. In *Proceedings of the 2015 Conference of the North American Chapter of the Association for Computational Linguistics: Human Language Technologies*, pages 1024–1029, Denver, USA.

Lionel Clément, Bernard Lang, and Benoît Sagot. 2004. Morphology based automatic acquisition of large-coverage lexica. In *Proceedings of the Fourth International Conference on Language Resources and Evaluation*, LREC'04, pages 1841–1844, Lisbon, Portugal, May.

Nick Craswell. 2009. Mean reciprocal rank. In Ling Liu and M.Tamer Özsu, editors, *Encyclopedia of Database Systems*, pages 1703–1703. Springer US.

Matthew S. Dryer, 2013. *The World Atlas of Language Structures Online*, chapter "Prefixing vs. Suffixing in Inflectional Morphology". Max Planck Institute for Evolutionary Anthropology, Leipzig, Germany.

Greg Durrett and John DeNero. 2013. Supervised learning of complete morphological paradigms. In *Proceedings of the Human Language Technologies: Conference of the North American Chapter of the Association of Computational Linguistics*, pages 1185–1195, Atlanta, USA.

Miquel Esplà-Gomis, Víctor M. Sánchez-Cartagena, and Juan Antonio Pérez-Ortiz. 2011. Enlarging monolingual dictionaries for machine translation with active learning and non-expert users. In *Proceedings of Recent Advances in Natural Language Processing*, RANLP'11, pages 339–346, Hissar, Bulgaria, September.

Mikel L. Forcada, Mireia Ginest-Rosell, Jacob Nordfalk, Jim ORégan, Sergio Ortiz-Rojas, Juan Antonio Prez-Ortiz, Felipe Snchez-Martnez, Gema Ramrez-Snchez, and Francis M. Tyers. 2011. Apertium: a free/open-source platform for rule-based machine translation. *Machine Translation*, 25(2):127–144.

Tobias Kaufmann and Beat Pfister. 2010. Semi-automatic extension of morphological lexica. In *Proceedings of the 2010 International Multiconference on Computer Science and Information Technology*, IMCSIT'10, pages 403–409, Wisla, Poland, October.

Krister Lindén. 2009. Entry generation by analogy – encoding new words for morphological lexicons. *Northern European Journal of Language Technology*, 1(1):1–25.

Nikola Ljubešić and Filip Klubička. 2014. {bs,hr,sr}WaC – web corpora of Bosnian, Croatian and Serbian. In *Proceedings of the 9th Web as Corpus Workshop*, WaC-9, pages 29–35, Gothenburg, Sweden.

Edward M. McCreight. 1976. A space-economical suffix tree construction algorithm. *Journal of the Association for Computing Machinery*, 23(2):262–272, April.

Fabian Pedregosa, Gaël Varoquaux, Alexandre Gramfort, Vincent Michel, Bertrand Thirion, Olivier Grisel, Mathieu Blondel, Peter Prettenhofer, Ron Weiss, Vincent Dubourg, Jake Vanderplas, Alexandre Passos, David Cournapeau, Matthieu Brucher, Matthieu Perrot, and Édouard Duchesnay. 2011. Scikit-learn: Machine learning in Python. *Journal of Machine Learning Research*, 12:2825–2830, November.

Benoît Sagot. 2005. Automatic acquisition of a slovak lexicon from a raw corpus. In Václav Matoušek, Pavel Mautner, and Tomáš Pavelka, editors, *Text, Speech and Dialogue*, volume 3658 of *Lecture Notes in Computer Science*, pages 156–163. Springer Berlin Heidelberg.

Jan Šnajder. 2012. Guessing the correct inflectional paradigm of unknown Croatian words. In *Proceedings of the Eighth Language Technologies Conference*, pages 173–178, Ljubljana, Slovenia, October.

Marko Tadić and Antoni Oliver. 2004. Enlarging the Croatian morphological lexicon by automatic lexical acquisition from raw corpora. In *Proceedings of the Fourth International Conference on Language Resources and Evaluation*, LREC'04, pages 1259–1262, Lisbon, Portugal, May.

J. Šnajder, B. Dalbelo Bašić, and M. Tadić. 2008. Automatic acquisition of inflectional lexica for morphological normalisation. *Information Processing & Management*, 44(5):1720–1731.

Predicting Correlations Between Lexical Alignments and Semantic Inferences

Simone Magnolini
University of Brescia
FBK, Trento, Italy
magnolini@fbk.eu

Bernardo Magnini
FBK, Trento, Italy
magnini@fbk.eu

Abstract

While there is a strong intuition that word alignments (e.g. synonymy, hyperonymy) play a relevant role in recognizing text-to-text semantic inferences (e.g. textual entailment, semantic similarity), this intuition is often not reflected in the system performances and there is a general need of a deeper comprehension of the role of lexical resources. This paper provides an empirical analysis of the dependencies between data-sets, lexical resources and algorithms that are commonly used in text-to-text inference tasks. We define a *resource impact index*, based on lexical alignments between pairs of texts, and show that such index is significantly correlated with the performance of different textual entailment algorithms. The result is an operational, algorithm-independent, procedure for predicting the performance of a class of available RTE algorithms.

1 Introduction

In the last decade text-to-text semantic inference has been a relevant topic in Computational Linguistics. Driven by the assumption that language understanding crucially depends on the ability to recognize semantic relations among portions of text, several text-to-text inference tasks have been proposed, including recognizing paraphrasing (Dolan and Brockett., 2005), recognizing textual entailment (RTE) (Dagan et al., 2005), and semantic similarity (Agirre et al., 2012). A common characteristic of such tasks is that the input are two portions of text, let's call them $Text1$ and $Text2$, and the output is a semantic relation between the two texts, possibly with a degree of confidence of the system. For instance, given the following text fragments:

Text1: *George Clooneys longest relationship ever might have been with a pig. The actor owned Max, a 300-pound pig.*
Text2: *Max is an animal.*

a system should be able to recognize that there is an "entailment" relation among $Text1$ and $Text2$.

While the task is very complex, requiring in principle to consider syntax, semantics and also pragmatics, current systems adopt rather simplified techniques, based on available linguistic resources. For instance, many RTE systems (Dagan et al., 2012) would attempt to take advantage of the fact that, according to WordNet, the word *animal* in $Text2$ is a hypernym of the word *pig* in $Text1$. A relevant aspect in text-to-text tasks is that data-sets are usually composed of textual pairs for positive cases, where a certain relation (e.g. entailment) holds, and negative pairs, where the semantic relation does not hold. For instance, the following pair:

Text1: *John has a cat, named Felix, in his farm, it's a Maine Coon, it's the largest domesticated breed of cat.*
Text2: *Felix is the largest domesticated animal in John's farm.*

shows a case of "non-entailment". It is worth to notice that in both the examples, although the entailment judgment is different, still there is an high degree of lexical alignments between words in $Text1$ and $Text2$ (e.g. $Max \longrightarrow Max, pig \longrightarrow animal, cat \longrightarrow animal$).

In the paper we systematically investigate the relations between the distribution of lexical associations in textual entailment data-sets and the system performance. As a result we define a "resource impact index" for a certain lexical resource with respect to a certain data-set, which indicates the capacity of the resource to discrimi-

Proceedings of Recent Advances in Natural Language Processing, pages 388–397,
Hissar, Bulgaria, Sep 7–9 2015.

nate between positive and negative pairs. We show that the "resource impact index" is homogeneous across several data-sets and tasks, and that it correlates with the performance of available entailment systems.

The paper is structured as follows. Section 2 provides the relevant background about the ongoing discussion on the use of lexical resources in textual entailment. Section 3 defines the Resource Impact Index that will be used in the experimental section. Section 4 reports on the experimental setting, including data-sets, resources and algorithms that we have been using. Section 5 discusses the results in term of the correlation between the Resource Index on a certain data-set and the accuracy obtained by two different algorithms using a single lexical relation at time. Section 6 shows how we can combine the Resource Index in case of multiple resources, while still maintaining the correlation with the algorithm performance. Finally, Section 7 highlights the potential impact of the paper within the current research on text-to-text semantic inferences.

2 Background on Lexical Resources and Text-to-Text Inferences

The role of lexical resources for recognizing text-to-text semantic relations (e.g. paraphrasing, textual entailment, textual similarity) has been under discussion for several years. This discussion is well reflected in the data reported by the RTE-5 "ablation tests" initiative (Bentivogli et al., 2009), where the performance of an algorithm was measured removing one resource at a time.

Challenge	**T1/T2 Overlap (%)**		
	YES	**NO ENTAILMENT**	
		Unknown	**Contradiction**
RTE - 1	68.64	64.12	
RTE - 2	70.63	63.32	
RTE - 3	69.62	55.54	
RTE - 4	68.95	57.36	67.97
RTE - 5	77.14	62.28	78.93

Table 1: Comparison among the structure of different RTE data-sets (Bentivogli et al., 2009).

As an example, participants at the RTE evaluation reported that WordNet was useful (i.e. improved performance) 9 of the times, while 7 out of 16 it was not. In addition, Table 1, again extracted from (Bentivogli et al., 2009), suggests that the degree of word overlap among positive and negative pairs might be a key to understand the complexity of a text-to-text inference task, and, as a consequence, a key to interpret the system's performance. Particularly, we can notice that the word overlap for the "Yes" cases and the "Contradiction" cases in the RTE-4 data-set is very similar, and even higher for the RTE-5 data-set. While this fact confirms the intuition that contradiction is generated when there is high overlap in meaning (de Marneffe, 2012), it also means that word overlap is not a discriminatory feature.

In this paper we claim that the two issues raised at RTE-5 (i.e. mixed evidence for the use of WordNet, and the fact that word overlap was not discriminative) are very much related, and, actually, are part of the same phenomenon. To support our claim, we build on top of previous work (Magnolini and Magnini, 2014), which we generalize considering: (i) lexical associations with different polarity (e.g. synonyms and antonyms); (ii) data-sets with different characteristics, (e.g. task, length of the pairs, languages); (iii) different algorithms for calculating textual entailment. We are interested to capture correlations between the use of lexical resources (both single resources and in combination) and the performance of inference algorithms. Particularly, the goal is to predict the behavior of an entailment algorithm given the characteristics of both the resource and the data-set.

There are several factors which, in principle, can affect our experiments, and that we have carefully considered.

Lexical Resources. First, the impact of a resource depends on the quality of the resource itself. Lexical resources, particularly those that are automatically acquired, might include noisy data, which can negatively affect performance. On the other hand, manually developed resources such as WordNet (Fellbaum, 1998) are particularly complex (i.e. a dozen of different relations, deep taxonomic structure, fine grained sense distinctions) and their use needs tuning. In order to face with these issues, we have selected manually constructed lexical resources, with a high degree of precision. In our experiments we have used lexical relations separately, in order to keep as much as possible under control their effect. Under this use, when we refer to a lexical resource we actually mean a resource that provides a specific lexical relation: for instance, a resource for lexical derivation, a resource for the hyperonymy relation, and so on. In addition, in the paper we consider both lexical resources that are supposed to provide similarity/compatibility alignments (e.g. synonyms) and resources/relations that are supposed to provide lexical oppositions (e.g. antonyms).

Inference Algorithms. Second, different algorithms may use different strategies to take advantage of resources. For instance, algorithms that calculate a distance or a similarity between $Text1$ and $Text2$ may assign different weights to a certain word association, on the basis on human intuitions (e.g. synonyms preserve entailment more than hypernyms). In our experiments we avoided as much as possible the use of settings not supported by empirical evidences and we use algorithms that are publicly available in order to maximize the replicability of the experiments.

Data-sets. Finally, data-sets representing different inference phenomena, may manifest different behaviors with respect to the impact of a certain resource, which can be specific for each inference type (e.g. entailment and semantic similarity). Although reaching a high level of generalization is limited by the existence of a limited number of data-sets, we have conducted experiments both on several textual entailment data-sets, also for different languages, and on a semantic similarity data-set.

3 Resource Impact Index

In this Section we define the general model through which we estimate the impact of a lexical resource. The idea behind the model is quite simple: the impact of a resource on a data-set should be correlated to the capacity of the resource to discriminate positive pairs from negative pairs in the data-set. We measure such capacity as the number of *lexical alignments* that the resource can establish on positive and negative pairs, and then we calculate the difference among them. We call this measure the *resource impact differential* - RID. The smaller the RID, the smaller the impact of the resource on that data-set. In the following we provide a more precise definition both of lexical alignments (Section 3.1) and of the model for calculating the resource impact differential (Section 3.2).

3.1 Defining Lexical Alignments

The idea that the entailment relation is related to the degree of lexical alignments between the words in a $(T1, T2)$ pair was introduced in (Dagan et al., 2012) as a useful generalization over the use of lexical resources in Recognizing Textual Entailment. In our work we adopt their definition of alignment, and we apply it to the RID calculation. More precisely, we say that two tokens in a $(T1, T2)$ pair are aligned when there is at least one semantic association relation, including equality, between the two tokens. For instance, synonyms and morphological derivations are different types of lexical alignments.

In addition, we extend the (Dagan et al., 2012) definition, allowing both positive and negative alignments. In fact, alignments inherit the polarity of the resource from which they are generated. We have a *Positive Alignment* when the semantic relation of the alignment is derived from a resource bringing positive associations (see Section 2), and we have a *Negative Alignment* when the source is negative (e.g. antonyms).

Finally, in the experiments reported in this paper we consider both word-to-word alignments and phrase alignments, where n-gram sequences are involved.

3.2 Defining the Impact Index

The Resource Impact Index is defined over a certain data-set D and a certain lexical resource LR.

Data-set (D). A data-set is a set of text pairs $D = \{(T1, T2)\}$, including both positive $(T1, T2)^p$ and negative $(T1, T2)^n$ pairs for a certain semantic relation (e.g. entailment, similarity). As reported in Section 2, this is a quite standard composition of benchmarks for text-to-text inferences.

Lexical Resource (LR). We define a Lexical Resource as any potential source of alignments among words. In most of the cases, rather than generic lexical resources (e.g. WordNet) we are interested in specific semantic relations provided by a resource. For instance, WordNet is a source for alignments based on synonyms. As discussed in Section 2, we consider both resources that are supposed to provide similarity-based alignments, which we call *positive lexical resources*, denoted with LR^+, and resources that are supposed to provide opposition-based alignments, which we call *negative lexical resources*, denoted with LR^-.

Resource Impact (RI). The impact of a resource LR on a data-set D is calculated as the number of lexical alignments returned by LR on all pairs, both positive and negative, normalized on the number of potential alignments for the data-set D. We use $|T1| * |T2|$ ($|T|$ is the number of tokens in text T) as potential number of potential alignments (Dagan et al., 2012, page 52), although there might be other options, such as $|T1| + |T2|$, and $max(|T1|, |T2|)$.

RI ranges from 0, when no alignment is found, to 1, when all potential alignments are returned by LR.

$$RI_{(LR,D)} = \frac{\sum_{i \in D} LexAl(T1_i, T2_i)}{\sum_{i \in D} |T1_i| * |T2_i|} \quad (1)$$

Resource Impact Differential (RID). The impact of a resource LR on a certain data-set D is given by the difference between the RI on positive pairs $(T1, T2) \in D^p$ and on negative pairs $(T1, T2) \in D^n$.

A RID for a positive lexical resource ranges from -1, when the RI is 0 for the positive pairs (i.e. when entailment holds) and 1 for negative entailed pairs, to 1, when the RI is 1 for entailed and 0 for not-entailed pairs.

$$RID_{(LR^+,D)} = RI_{(LR,D^p)} - RI_{(LR,D^n)} \quad (2)$$

For a resource with negative polarity (e.g. antonyms) the RID is expected to be the difference between the Resource Impact on negative and on positive pairs (equation 3).

$$RID_{(LR^-,D)} = RI_{(LR,D^n)} - RI_{(LR,D^p)} \quad (3)$$

The RID measure is not affected by the length of the pairs in the data-set, because it is normalized on the potential number of alignments for each pair. As far as the relation between RID and the impact of the lexical resource (i.e. the number of lexical alignments produced by the resource), being the RID a difference, we can consider the impact as an upper bound of the RID (see equation 4).

$$\left|RID_{(LR,D)}\right| \leq \frac{\sum_{i \in D} LexAl(T1_i, T2_i)}{\sum_{i \in D} |T1_i| * |T2_i|} \quad (4)$$

4 Experiments

In this section we apply the model described in Section 3 to different data-sets and resources, taking advantage of different sources of lexical and phrase alignments.

4.1 Data-sets

We use four different data-sets in order to experiment different characteristics of the corpora used for benchmarking text-to-text inferences.

RTE-3 eng. The RTE-3 data-set (Giampiccolo et al., 2007) for English has been used in the context of the Recognizing Textual Entailment shared tasks. It has been constructed mainly using application derived text fragments, and it is balanced between positive and negative pairs (about 1600 in total).

RTE-3 ita. The Italian RTE-3 data-set[1] is the translation of the English one. The goal is to monitor the behaviour of the RID while changing the language.

RTE-5 eng. The RTE-5 data-set (Bentivogli et al., 2009) is similar to RTE-3, although $T1$ pairs are usually much longer, which, in our terms, means that a higher number of alignments can be potentially generated by the same number of pairs.

SICK eng. Finally the SICK data-set (Sentences Involving Compositional Knowledge) (Marelli et al., 2014) has been recently used to highlight distributional properties. SICK is not balanced (1299 positive and 3201 negative pairs), and $T1$ and $T2$, differently from RTE pairs, have similar length.

4.2 Sources for Lexical Alignments

We carried out experiments using six different sources of lexical alignments, whose use is quite diffused in the practice of text-to-text inference systems, and with different expected behavior, as far as the polarity of the lexical resource is concerned.

Lemmas. The first source consists of a simple match among the lemmas in $T1$ and $T2$: if two lemmas are equal (case insensitive), then we count it as an alignment between $T1$ and $T2$. The expected polarity of alignments based on lemmas is positive, as we assume that they increase the similarity between $T1$ and $T2$.

[1] http://www.excitement-project.eu/index.php/results/178-public-resources

Synonyms. The second source considers alignments due to the synonymy relation (e.g. *home* and *habitation*). The sources are WordNet (Fellbaum, 1998), version 3.0 for English, and MultiWordNet (Pianta et al., 2002) for Italian. If two lemmas are found in the same synset, then we count it as an alignment.The expected polarity of alignments based on synonyms is positive.

Hypernyms. The third source considers the hyperonymy relation (e.g. *dog* and *mammal*): as for synonymy we use WordNet and MultiWordNet, counting as an alignment all the cases where two lemmas are in the hypernym hierarchy, at any distance. The expected polarity of alignments based on hypernyms is positive.

Morphological Derivations. The fourth source of alignment are morphological derivations (e.g. *invention* and *invent*). As for English, derivations are covered again by WordNet, while for Italian we used MorphoDerivIT, a resource developed within the EXCITEMENT project[2], which has the same structure of CATVAR (Habash and Dorr, 2003) for English. The expected polarity of alignments based on morphological derivations is positive.

Antonyms. The fifth source of alignment are antonyms (e.g. *man* and *woman*). Antonyms are provided by WordNet for English and by MultiWordNet for Italian. The expected polarity of alignments based on antonyms is negative, as we assume that they increase the opposition between $T1$ and $T2$.

Paraphrase Tables. The sixth source of alignment are paraphrase tables (e.g. *can be modified* and *may be revised*). We built paraphrase tables from the Meteor translation tables (Denkowski and Lavie, 2014). The idea is that if an n-gram n_s in the source language s is translated into n-gram n_t in the target language t, and if n_t has multiple translations back into s, then all these translations are potential paraphrases of each other. The probability of translation from one language to another can be used to compute the probability that two n-grams in language s are paraphrases of each other. To compute this probability we use all shared translations into the target language t of the two n-grams (both in source language s). There are two main reasons to consider paraphrase tables: (i) they cover alignments that are only partially covered by the other sources that we considered; (ii) most of the phrases are n-grams, which allows us to test the RID behavior on sequences longer than single tokens. The expected polarity of alignments based on paraphrase tables is positive.

0-Knowledge. Finally, in order to investigate the behavior of the RID in absence of any lexical alignment, we include a 0-Knowledge experimental baseline, where the system does not have access to any source of lexical alignment. As no alignment is produced (including token match), the RID of the 0-Knowledge baseline is always 0.

4.3 Algorithms

In order to verify our hypothesis that the RID index is correlated with the capacity of a system to correctly recognize textual entailment, we run experiments using two different RTE algorithms, i.e. EDITS and P1EDA, which take advantage of lexical resources in different ways. The two algorithms are both supervised, in the sense that they use training data to build a model. As the goal of our experiments is to monitor the behavior of the RID index in different settings, rather than to assess the performance of the two algorithms, we decided to simplify as much as possible the experimental setting, and we calculated accuracy and F1 for the two algorithms using the training section of the data-sets[3].

EDITS (Negri et al., 2009), is a distance-based RTE algorithm based on calculating the Edit Distance between $T1$ and $T2$, defined as the minimum-weight sequence of edit operations (i.e. deletion, insertion and substitution) that transforms $T1$ into $T2$. The intuition is that the less the cost of transforming $T1$ into $T2$, the more likely the entailment relation between the two texts. The final decision is taken on the basis of a threshold, empirically estimated over training data. For all the experiments, the cost of edit operations is set as follows: 0 for substitution if two words are aligned; 1 for substitution if two words are not aligned; 1 for insertion; 0 for deletion. The algorithm is normalized on the number of words of $T1$ and $T2$, after stop

[2]http://www.excitement-project.eu/index.php/results/178-public-resources

[3]We will investigate the behavior of the RID between test and training data-sets in future work.

words are removed. As for linguistic processing, the Edit Distance algorithm needs tokenization, lemmatization and Part-of-Speech tagging (in order to access resources). We used TreeTagger (Schmid, 1995) for English and TextPro (Pianta et al., 2008) for Italian. In addition we removed stop words, including some very common verbs.

P1EDA (Noh et al., 2015) is an alignment-based RTE algorithm, developed and fully documented in the software website[4], based on alignments between $T1$ and $T2$. The intuition is that the more the portions of $T2$ are aligned with portions of $T1$, the higher the probability of the entailment relation. First the algorithm extracts all possible alignments between portions in $T1$ and $T2$, then it extracts a number of features from the alignments, which are finally given as input to a multinomial logistic regression classifier trained on annotated data. The features implemented in the P1EDA version used for our experiments are the following: (i) the ratio of words in $T2$ aligned with $T1$; (ii) the ratio of content words in $T2$ aligned with $T1$ and, (iii) the ratio of verbs in $T2$ aligned with $T1$. As for linguistic processing, P1EDA needs tokenization, lemmatization and Part-of-Speech tagging. As in the case of EDITS we used TreeTagger (Schmid, 1995) for English and TextPro (Pianta et al., 2008) for Italian.

All the experiments reported in the paper have been conducted using the Excitement Open Platform (EOP), (Padó et al., 2014) (Magnini et al., 2014), a generic architecture and a comprehensive implementation for textual inference in multiple languages. The platform includes state-of-art algorithms, a large number of knowledge resources and facilities for experimenting and testing innovative approaches. The architecture is based on the concept of modularization with pluggable and replaceable components to enable extensions and customizations, this way helping to control that experiments are conducted in the proper way, with easily observable intermediate steps. The EOP platform includes both the algorithms and the lexical resources used in our experiments, and it is distributed as an open source software.[5]

[4]https://github.com/hltfbk/EOP-1.2.3/wiki/AlignmentEDAP1

[5]http://hltfbk.github.io/Excitement-Open-Platform/

5 Results

Table 2 and Table 3 report the results of the experiments on the four data-sets and the seven sources of alignment (including the 0-Knowledge baseline) described in Section 4[6]. For each resource we show the RID of the resource (given the very low values, RIDs are shown multiplied by a 10^4 factor), and the accuracy achieved both by the EDITS and the P1EDA algorithms. The last row of the tables shows the Pearson correlation between the RID and the accuracy of the algorithms for each data-set, calculated as the mean of the correlations obtained for each resource on that data-set.

A first observation is that all RID values are very close to 0, indicating a low expected impact of the resources. Even the highest RID (i.e. 523.342 for lemmas on SICK), corresponds to a 5% of the potential impact of the resource. Negative RID values for positive resources, mean that the resource, somehow contrary to the expectation, produces more alignments for negative pairs than for positive (this is the case, for instance, of synonyms on the English RTE-3). On the same line, negative RID values for negative resources mean that a resource with negative polarity produces more alignments for positive pairs than for negative (this case does not appear in the results).

Alignment on lemmas is by far the resource with the best impact, while alignments produced by paraphrases produce very negative RID.

Finally, results fully confirm the initial hypothesis that the RID is correlated with the system performance; i.e. the accuracy for balanced data-sets and the F1 for the unbalanced one. The Pearson correlation shows that R is close to 1 for all the RTE data-sets (the slightly lower value on SICK reveals the different characteristics of the data-set), indicating that the RID is a very good predictor of the system performance, at least for the class of inference algorithms represented by EDITS and P1EDA. The low values for RID are also reflected in absolute low performance, showing again that when the system uses a low impact resource the accuracy is close to the baseline (i.e. the 0-Knowledge configuration).

Although improving the performance of RTE systems is not the direct goal of our experiments, it is worth noting that P1EDA outperformed EDITS,

[6]The EDITS implementation available in the EOP platform does not allow n-gram alignments, so we could not run paraphrases with EDITS.

EDITS	RTE-3 eng		RTE-3 ita		RTE-5 eng		SICK eng	
	RID	Accuracy	RID	Accuracy	RID	Accuracy	RID	F1
0-Knowledge	0	0.542	0	0.543	0	0.536	0	0.004
Lemmas	97.215	0.635	84.594	0.641	43.221	0.62	523.342	0.347
Synonyms	-4.876	0.536	5.343	0.537	10.138	0.561	12.386	0.093
Hypernyms	-5.333	0.532	-1.791	0.543	12.921	0.555	48.665	0.221
Derivations	-1.747	0.571	-0.024	0.536	5.722	0.553	-6.436	0
Antonyms (*)	1.076	0.542	0	0.543	1.013	0.54	28.479	0
R Correlation	0.943		0.990		0.988		0.862	

Table 2: Experimental results on different data-sets with different resources using EDITS. (*) Antonyms have negative polarity.

P1EDA	RTE-3 eng		RTE-3 ita		RTE-5 eng		SICK eng	
	RID	Accuracy	RID	Accuracy	RID	Accuracy	RID	F1
0-Knowledge	0	0.527	0	0.517	0	0.506	0	0
Lemmas	97.215	0.682	84.594	0.706	43.221	0.601	523.342	0.485
Synonyms	-4.876	0.533	5.343	0.516	10.138	0.521	12.386	0
Hypernyms	-5.333	0.527	-1.791	0.512	12.921	0.543	48.665	0.038
Derivations	-1.747	0.553	-0.024	0.512	5.722	0.528	-6.436	0.018
Antonyms (*)	1.076	0.532	0	0.517	1.013	0.52	28.479	0
Paraphrases	-11.668	0.52	18.049	0.5075	33.803	0.563	-67.148	0.015
R Correlation	0.987		0.967		0.959		0.983	

Table 3: Experimental results on different data-sets with different resources using P1EDA. (*) Antonyms have negative polarity.

	RID_C	Accuracy (P1EDA)	R Correlation
0-knowledge	0	0.527	
Lemmas+Synonyms	92.338	0.683	
Synonyms+Hypernyms	-10.209	0.526	
Hypernyms+Antonyms	-6.409	0.528	
			0.996
ALL resources	84.181	0.687	
			0.995
Paraphrases+Synonyms	-16.296	0.523	
			0.993

Table 4: Results on combining multiple resources using P1EDA.

and it achieved results (i.e. 0.68 on English RTE-3, 0.70 on Italian RTE-3, 0.60 on RTE-5) which can be considered at the state-of-art for publicly available systems.

6 Combining RIDs of Multiple Sources

While the previous sections have confirmed our hypothesis that the RID index is correlated with the performance of RTE algorithms using single resources, the aim of this Section is to show that the RID obtained from a combination of resources is still correlated with the algorithm performance.

We define the RID of multiple resources, called Combined Resource Index Differential (RID_C) as the sum of the RIDs of the single resources. For instance, in Table 4, the combined RID_C of Lemmas+Synonyms (i.e. 92.338) is obtained summing the RID for Lemmas (97.215, see Table 3) with the RID for Synonyms (i.e. -4.876). Intuitively, the sum of two RIDs for the resources $LR1$ and $LR2$ corresponds to the RID

of a single resource composed by $LR1$ and $LR2$, under the assumption that they are disjoint, i.e. that the set of alignments that $LR1$ and $LR2$ produce is disjoint. In order to take into consideration the combination of non-disjoint resources, the RID of the intersection has to be subtracted, as shown in equation 5 (combining positive resources) and equation 6 (combining a positive and a negative resource).

$$RID_{C(LR_1^+,LR_2^+,D)} = RID_{(LR_1^+,D)} + RID_{(LR_2^+,D)} - RID_{(LR_1^+ \cap LR_2^+,D)} \tag{5}$$

$$RID_{C(LR_1^+,LR_2^-,D)} = RID_{(LR_1^+,D)} - RID_{(LR_2^-,D)} - RID_{(LR_1^+ \cap LR_2^-,D)} \tag{6}$$

We conducted a number of RID combination experiments, reported in Table 4. First, we used four disjoint resources, whose RIDs show different characteristics on the RTE-3 dataset. As reported in Table 3, lemmas have a high and positive RID; synomyms and hypernyms are both resources with positive polarity, and both have a slightly negative RID; antonyms is a resource with negative polarity and slightly positive RID. For each pairwise combination, we run P1EDA for calculating entailment judgments, and then we computed the correlation between the accuracy of the algorithm and the RID of the combination, calculated summing the RIDs.

Then, we experimented a combination of the five resources (including the 0-Knowledge baseline). The result ("All resources" line in Table 4), again shows very high correlation with the accuracy of the system. We think that the minor decrease in the correlation (i.e. from 0.996 to 0.995) is due to few cases of overlap among the resources, particularly some synonyms are also hypernyms, which we did not filter out.

Finally, we run a combination experiment using paraphrases and synonyms, two resources that show a relatively high level of overlap in RTE-3. Here the goal is to test that subtracting the RID of the intersection of the two resources results in a better correlation. Accordingly, we have calculated both the simple RID (i.e. without subtracting the RID of the intersection) and the combined RID_C. We note that the alignments in the intersection are almost equally distributed between positive and negative pairs, resulting in very close RIDs, namely -16.544 for the simple RID, and -16.296 for the combined one.

7 Final Discussion and Conclusion

According to the initial working hypothesis, we have shown that the RID index is highly correlated with the accuracy of RTE systems, a result that allows to use the RID as a reliable indicator of the impact both of a single resource and of a combination of them. We now have both an empirical explanation of the impact of a lexical resource over a certain inference task, and an operational, algorithm-independent procedure for predicting the performance of a class of available RTE algorithms.

We now discuss what we can learn from the achievements reported in the paper, and how we can take advantage of our findings in order to design more effective text-to-text inference systems.

A first finding is that RIDs of popular lexical relations among words are quite close to 0, which indicates that their distribution is not useful to discriminate positive and negative pairs in current text-to-text data-sets. As a second finding, the Resource Impact RI (equation 1), which tells us how much a resource is used for a certain data-set, is very dis-homogeneous. To give an idea, the following are the RIs of our resources on the English RTE-3 data-set: lemmas 682.266, synonyms 72.709, hypernyms 157.055, morphological derivations 62.757, antonyms 3.885, paraphrases 316.717. Finally, although we do not have quantitative data supporting our intuition, we are convinced that the coverage of our resources (i.e. the alignments produced by a resources with respect to the alignments it should produce) is pretty good, indicating that there is no much room for improving the resources themselves.

Given the above three elements, i.e. low RID of resources (even in combination), not homogeneous impact of different semantic relations, and good coverage over the data-sets, we think that future improvements in text-to-text inference should consider more discriminative features, i.e. resources with higher absolute value of RID (e.g. a wider range of lexical opposition phenomena). In addition, our findings support the intuition that lexical phenomena do not exhaust the complexity of textual entailment and that local compositional aspects of meaning (e.g. verb argument structure, scope of negation), need to be exploited.

Acknowledgments

This work was partially supported by the EC-funded project EXCITEMENT (FP7ICT-287923).

References

Eneko Agirre, Daniel Cer, Mona Diab, and Aitor Gonzalez-Agirre. 2012. SemEval-2012 task 6: A pilot on semantic textual similarity. In *Proceedings of the International Workshop on Semantic Evaluation*, pages 385–393, Montréal, Canada.

Luisa Bentivogli, Bernardo Magnini, Ido Dagan, Hoa Trang Dang, and Danilo Giampiccolo. 2009. The fifth PASCAL recognising textual entailment challenge. In *Proceedings of the TAC Workshop on Textual Entailment*, Gaithersburg, MD.

Ido Dagan, Oren Glickman, and Bernardo Magnini. 2005. The PASCAL Recognising Textual Entailment Challenge. In *Proceedings of the PASCAL Challenges Workshop on Recognising Textual Entailment*, pages 177–190, Southampton, UK.

Ido Dagan, Dan Roth, and Fabio Massimo Zanzotto. 2012. *Recognizing Textual Entailment: Models and Applications*. Number 17 in Synthesis Lectures on Human Language Technologies. Morgan & Claypool.

Marie-Catherine de Marneffe. 2012. *What's that supposed to mean?* Ph.D. thesis, Stanford Univeristy.

Michael Denkowski and Alon Lavie. 2014. Meteor universal: Language specific translation evaluation for any target language. In *Proceedings of the EACL 2014 Workshop on Statistical Machine Translation*.

William B. Dolan and Chris Brockett. 2005. Automatically constructing a corpus of sentential paraphrases. In *Proceedings of the Third International Workshop on Paraphrasing (IWP2005), Asia Federation of Natural Language Processing*.

Christiane Fellbaum, editor. 1998. *WordNet: An Electronic Lexical Database*. The MIT Press, Cambridge, MA; London.

Danilo Giampiccolo, Bernardo Magnini, Ido Dagan, and Bill Dolan. 2007. The Third PASCAL Recognising Textual Entailment Challenge. In *Proceedings of the ACL-PASCAL Workshop on Textual Entailment and Paraphrasing*, Prague, Czech Republic.

Nizar Habash and Bonnie Dorr. 2003. A categorial variation database for english. In *Proceedings of the 2003 Conference of the North American Chapter of the Association for Computational Linguistics on Human Language Technology-Volume 1*, pages 17–23. Association for Computational Linguistics.

Bernardo Magnini, Roberto Zanoli, Ido Dagan, Kathrin Eichler, Günter Neumann, Tae-Gil Noh, Sebastian Padó, Asher Stern, and Omer Levy. 2014. The excitement open platform for textual inferences. In *Proceedings of the 52nd Meeting of the Association for Computational Linguistics, Demo papers*.

Simone Magnolini and Bernardo Magnini. 2014. Estimating lexical resources impact in text-to-text inference tasks. In *Proceedings of the First Italian Conference on Computational Linguistics CLiC-it 2014*, Pisa, Italy.

Marco Marelli, Stefano Menini, Marco Baroni, Luisa Bentivogli, Raffaella Bernardi, and Roberto Zamparelli. 2014. A sick cure for the evaluation of compositional distributional semantic models. In Nicoletta Calzolari (Conference Chair), Khalid Choukri, Thierry Declerck, Hrafn Loftsson, Bente Maegaard, Joseph Mariani, Asuncion Moreno, Jan Odijk, and Stelios Piperidis, editors, *Proceedings of the Ninth International Conference on Language Resources and Evaluation (LREC'14)*, Reykjavik, Iceland, may. European Language Resources Association (ELRA).

Matteo Negri, Milen Kouylekov, Bernardo Magnini, Yashar Mehdad, and Elena Cabrio. 2009. Towards extensible textual entailment engines: the EDITS package. In *Proceeding of the Conference of the Italian Association for Artificial Intelligence*, pages 314–323, Reggio Emilia, Italy.

Tae-Gil Noh, Sebastian Padó, Vered Shwartz, Ido Dagan, Vivi Nastase, Kathrin Eichler, Lili Kotlerman, and Meni Adler. 2015. Multi-level alignments as an extensible representation basis for textual entailment algorithms. In *Proceedings of the Fourth Joint Conference on Lexical and Computational Semantics (*SEM 2015)*.

Sebastian Padó, Tae-Gil Noh, Asher Stern, Rui Wang, and Roberto Zanoli. 2014. Design and realization of a modular architecture for textual entailment. *Journal of Natural Language Engineering*. `doi:10.1017/S1351324913000351`.

Emanuele Pianta, Luisa Bentivogli, and Christian Girardi. 2002. Developing an aligned multilingual database. In *Proc. 1st Intl Conference on Global WordNet*.

Emanuele Pianta, Christian Girardi, and Roberto Zanoli. 2008. The textpro tool suite. In Bente Maegaard Joseph Mariani Jan Odijk Stelios Piperidis Daniel Tapias Nicoletta Calzolari (Conference Chair), Khalid Choukri, editor, *Proceedings of the Sixth International Conference on Language Resources and Evaluation (LREC'08)*, Marrakech, Morocco, may. European Language Resources Association (ELRA). http://www.lrec-conf.org/proceedings/lrec2008/.

Helmut Schmid. 1995. Treetagger - a language independent part-of-speech tagger. *Insti-*

tut für Maschinelle Sprachverarbeitung, Universität Stuttgart, 43:28.

Learning the Impact of Machine Translation Evaluation Metrics for Semantic Textual Similarity

Simone Magnolini
University of Brescia,
Fondazione Bruno Kessler
Trento, Italy
magnolini@fbk.eu

Ngoc Phuoc An Vo
University of Trento,
Fondazione Bruno Kessler
Trento, Italy
ngoc@fbk.eu

Octavian Popescu
IBM Research, T.J. Watson
Yorktown, US
o.popescu@us.ibm.com

Abstract

We present a work to evaluate the hypothesis that automatic evaluation metrics developed for Machine Translation (MT) systems have significant impact on predicting semantic similarity scores in Semantic Textual Similarity (STS) task for English, in light of their usage for paraphrase identification. We show that different metrics may have different behaviors and significance along the semantic scale [0-5] of the STS task. In addition, we compare several classification algorithms using a combination of different MT metrics to build an STS system; consequently, we show that although this approach obtains state of the art result in paraphrase identification task, it is insufficient to achieve the same result in STS.

1 Introduction

Semantic related tasks have become a noticed trend in Natural Language Processing (NLP) community. Particularly, the Semantic Textual Similarity (STS) task has captured a huge attention in the NLP community despite being recently introduced since SemEval 2012 and continuing in SemEval 2013, 2014 and 2015 (Agirre et al., 2012; Agirre et al., 2013; Agirre et al., 2014; Agirre et al., 2015). Basically, the task requires to build systems which can compute the similarity degree between two given sentences. The similarity degree is scaled as a real score from 0 (no relevance) to 5 (semantic equivalence). The evaluation is done by computing the correlation between human judgment scores and systems' predictions by the mean of Pearson correlation method.

In contrast, Machine Translation evaluation metrics are designed to assess if the output of a MT system is semantically equivalent to a set of reference translations. In SemEval 2012, the system made by (de Souza et al., 2012) and then the system (Barrón Cedeño et al., 2013) in SemEval 2013 introduced the approach of using a set of MT evaluation metrics together with other lexical and syntactic features to predict the semantic similarity scores in STS. Although this approach shows promising results, there was no in-depth analysis on the impact of the evaluation metrics to the overall performance and how each metric behaves on STS data. Moreover, as being inspired by the literature (Madnani et al., 2012) for paraphrase recognition, which obtains the state of art result on the Microsoft Research paraphrase corpus (MSRP) (Dolan et al., 2004), we decide to analyze the impact of MT evaluation metrics in STS.

Our aim consists of two folds, (1) to obtain a clear idea of how each individual metric behaves and correlates with the human-judgement semantic similarity, and (2) to examine the approach of combining a set of chosen metrics to build regression models for predicting the semantic similarity scores and analyze the incorporation of these metrics in regarding to the overall performance of the system. To achieve our goal, we divide our research in two main aspects: first, we evaluate the correlation between each single MT metric and the human-annotation scores; and second, we evaluate how different classification algorithms perform using these metrics as features.

The remainder of this paper is organized as follows: Section 2 presents the description of different MT evaluation metrics, Section 3 reports the experimental settings, Section 4 is the evaluation and discussion, and finally, Section 5 is conclusions and future work.

Proceedings of Recent Advances in Natural Language Processing, pages 398–403,
Hissar, Bulgaria, Sep 7–9 2015.

2 Machine Translation Evaluation Metrics

Technically, the MT evaluation metric assesses the semantic equivalence between the translation hypothesis produced by a MT system and the reference translation. In STS task, the idea of using MT evaluation metrics is adopted to improve the word alignment job between two given sentences which consequently leads to better prediction of semantic similarity scores. In this study, we employ four commonly used metrics from two different groups of MT evaluation metrics, (1) the n-gram based metrics (METEOR and BLEU), and (2) the edit-distance based metrics (TER and TERp).

METEOR (Metric for Evaluation of Translation with Explicit ORdering). We use the latest version (1.5) of METEOR (Denkowski and Lavie, 2014) that finds alignments between sentences based on exact, stem, synonym and paraphrase matches between words and phrases. Segment and system level metric scores are calculated based on the alignments between sentence pairs.

BLEU (BiLingual Evaluation Understudy). We use BLEU (Papineni et al., 2002) because it is one of the most commonly used metrics and it has a high reliability. The BLEU metric computes as the amount of n-gram overlap, for different values of n=1,2,3 and 4, between the system output and the reference translation, in our case between sentence pairs. The score is tempered by a penalty for translations that might be too short. BLEU relies on exact matching and has no concept of synonymy or paraphrasing.

TER (Translation Error Rate). We use the 0.7.25 version of TER (Snover et al., 2006). TER computes the number of edits needed to "fix" the translation output so that it matches the reference. TER differs from word error rate (WER) in which it includes a heuristic algorithm to deal with shifts in addition to insertions, deletions and substitutions.

TERp (TER-Plus). The last metrics that we use is TERp (Snover et al., 2009) building upon the core TER algorithm and providing additional edit operations based on stemming, synonymy and paraphrase.

year	dataset	pairs	source
2012	MSRpar	1500	newswire
2012	MSRvid	1500	video descriptions
2012	OnWN	750	OntoNotes, WordNet glosses
2012	SMTnews	750	Machine Translation evaluation
2012	SMTeuroparl	750	Machine Translation evaluation
2013	headlines	750	newswire headlines
2013	FNWN	189	FrameNet, WordNet glosses
2013	OnWN	561	OntoNotes, WordNet glosses
2013	SMT	750	Machine Translation evaluation
2014	headlines	750	newswire headlines
2014	OnWN	750	OntoNotes, WordNet glosses
2014	Deft-forum	450	forum posts
2014	Deft-news	300	news summary
2014	Images	750	image descriptions
2014	Tweet-news	750	tweet-news pairs
2015	image	750	image description
2015	headlines	750	news headlines
2015	answers-students	750	student answers,reference answers
2015	answers-forum	375	answers in stack exchange forums
2015	belief	375	forum data exhibiting committed belief

Table 1: Summary of STS datasets in 2012, 2013, 2014, 2015.

3 Experiments

3.1 Datasets

The STS (for English) dataset consists of several datasets: STS 2012, STS 2013, STS 2014 and STS 2015 (Agirre et al., 2012; Agirre et al., 2013; Agirre et al., 2014; Agirre et al., 2015). Each sentence pair is annotated with the semantic similarity score in the scale [0-5]. Table 1 shows the summary of STS datasets and sources over the years. For training, we use all data in STS 2012, 2013 and 2014; and for testing, we use STS 2015 datasets.

3.2 Evaluation Methods

We use two different evaluation methods to evaluate the impact of the metrics on our training dataset, (1) the Pearson correlation between the metric outputs and the gold standards which is the official evaluation method used in STS task; and (2) the RELIEF (Robnik-Sikonja and Kononenko, 1997) analysis implemented in WEKA (Hall et al., 2009) to estimate the quality of MT evaluation metric output in regression.

3.3 Settings

Firstly, we employ the four metrics to compute the semantic similarity between given sentences on the training dataset. We use the default configuration for all metrics, except the "-norm" option for METEOR that tokenizes and normalizes punctuation and lowercase, as suggested in its documentation; and the "-c" option for TER and TERp that roofs the score to 100. Then we normalize all the output results to the scale [0-1].

Next, we combine the outputs of these four metrics to build eight different regression models using different classification algorithms in WEKA (e.g. IsotonicRegression, LeastMedSq, MultilayerPerceptron, SimpleLinearRegression, LinearRegression, M5Rules, M5 Model Trees, and DecisionTable). We only use the default settings of each algorithm without tuning any parameter because our goal is to compare the results of different approaches, not to obtain high performance. We evaluate each model twice, (i) by a 10-fold cross validation on training data, and (ii) we evaluate the model on the test data (STS 2015 dataset). For the comparison, we use the official baseline of STS task which uses the bag-of-words approach to represent each sentence as a vector in the multi-dimensional token space (each dimension has 1 if the token is present in the sentence, 0 otherwise) and computes the cosine similarity between vectors.

4 Evaluations and Discussions

4.1 Evaluation of Individual Metric

The Pearson correlation and RELIEF analysis of each single metric compared to the human-annotation scores are presented in Table 2. According to both methods, the METEOR tends to be the superior metric, while in contrast TERp has low values in both. We split the BLEU metric into four values for 1-gram, 2-gram, 3-gram and 4-gram. The Pearson correlation shows that the smaller size of n-gram overlap, the more correlation with the human judgment obtained. In overall, except TER that has inverse correlation which is the more negative result, the better correlation with human annotation scores, other metrics have reasonable correlation. Nevertheless, another error metric, TERp does not perform well and returns a positive correlation, opposite to the TER metric.

We also investigate the behaviour of each metric deeper inside each score bracket in the STS semantic scale. We plot the output of each metric in corresponding to each score bracket [0-1], [1-2], [2-3], [3-4] and [4-5] to see how each MT metric behaves on each score bracket. The results of RELIEF analysis and Pearson correlation in Figure 1 and 2 show that most of the metrics perform well in two particular score brackets [0-1] and [4-5]. This means that by deploying MT evaluation metrics for STS task, the system will be able to obtain a high precision of predicting the semantic similarity for two cases "not/almost not relevant" and "equivalent/almost equivalent". This investigation can help to significantly improve the overall performance of a STS system by increasing the accuracy of predicting the scores in brackets [0-1] and [4-5]. In contrast, both figures have a central region where the correlation scores decrease significantly, and even worst for TERp where Pearson correlation changes signs, that means that in some regions this metric switches from direct to inverse correlation.

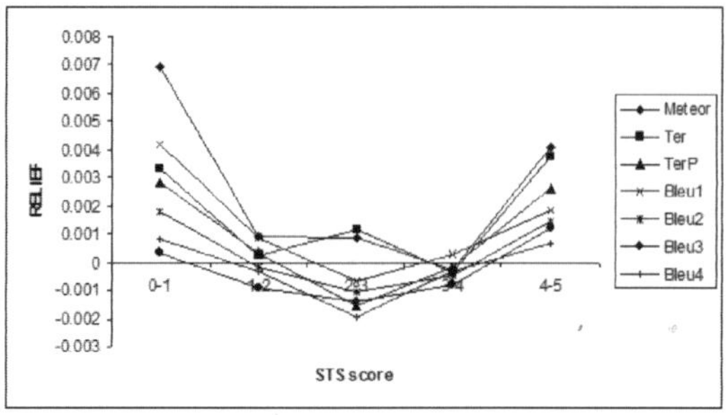

Figure 1: RELIEF analysis.

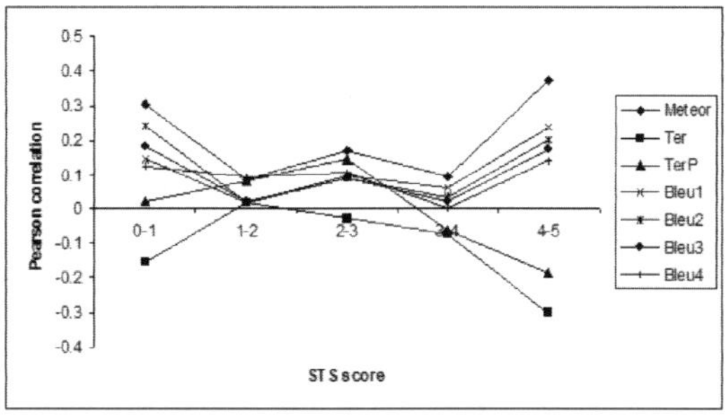

Figure 2: Pearson correlation.

	RELIEF	Pearson
METEOR	0.00503	0.56065
TER	-0.00157	-0.25673
TERp	-0.00098	0.21047
BLEU-1	-0.00145	0.36800
BLEU-2	-0.00201	0.31801
BLEU-3	-0.00203	0.27074
BLEU-4	-0.00249	0.27233

Table 2: Evaluation of the different features on the training dataset.

	IR	LMS	MLP	SLR	LR	M5R	M5P	DT	Baseline	BestSys
Cross-validation	0.610	0.629	0.606	0.560	0.653	0.737	0.739	0.698	0.382	-
Test set	0.702	0.643	0.694	0.688	0.612	0.609	0.611	0.588	0.587	**0.801**
Standard deviation	0.429	0.458	0.475	0.444	0.404	0.363	0.363	0.386	0.579	-

Table 3: Evaluation of the different algorithms: Pearson coefficient (IR: IsotonicRegression, LMS: LeastMedSq, MLP: MultilayerPerceptron, SLR: SimpleLinearRegression, LR: LinearRegression, M5R: M5Rules, M5P: M5 Model Trees, DT: DecisionTable, Baseline: STS Baseline, BestSys: 1st ranked system in STS 2015).

This enlightens an important difference between the impact of these metrics on STS task and on the paraphrase recognition task: while MT metrics show acceptable performance distinguishing the border regions, i.e. the most similar (almost paraphrase) and the most dissimilar, they have worse performance in the middle regions.

4.2 Evaluation of Metric Combination

We examine the impact of the combination of all metrics to the overall performance in STS by building several regression models using all the metric outputs as features. Since every metric and also the STS score is a numeric value we use normal regression algorithms. The results of these analysis are reported in Table 3 which shows, (i) the average of the 10-Folds cross-validation on the training data, (ii) the overall performance on the test data, and (iii) to better describe the different algorithms, we also report the standard deviation (SD) of the ten standard deviations from ten folds; we use this measure as an index to evaluate if the performances of the classifier during cross-validation are uniform or present some instability due to specific fold.

We group the models into two groups by a threshold of the standard deviation (SD $= 0.41$) in which the lower SD, the more reliable model is and vice versa. It is interesting to notice that more stable models (on the right hand side) perform well the cross-validation on the training dataset, but obtain low performance on the test dataset, in a margin of 10% (except the LR having margin of 1%). Nevertheless, the less stable models (on the left hand side) obtain better results on the test dataset and low performance on the cross-validation, in a margin of 2-10%. From our observation, another important aspect is that not all the algorithms use all given features in the same way, but during the training phase Isotonic Regression (IR) and Simple Linear Regression (SLR) discard other features and use only METEOR metric.

Another interesting observation is the different learning approaches of different algorithms taking advantage from MT metrics. Some algorithms can learn more information from the combination of these metrics and perform well the cross validation on training data, but when being evaluated on the test data, the model is strongly penalized by the domain-independence datasets in STS. In our case the STS 2012, 2013 and 2014 datasets are different from the STS 2015, which leads to an overfitting of the systems that builds the model using all these features. On the other hand, algorithms which are not so optimized can use MT metrics in a more flexible way to obtain good result on the test dataset.

In overall, all the regression models using combination of MT metrics outperform the task baseline in both cross validation on training dataset (by a large margin of 22-36%) and performance on test dataset (by a margin of 0.1-12%). However, none of these models can compare to the best system on the test dataset, the difference between the best model and the best system is a large margin of 10%. This proves that using only MT metric is not sufficient and efficient enough to solve the STS task. But combining MT metrics with other linguistic features may return promising result.

5 Conclusions and Future Work

In this study, we show the notable characteristic of the MT metrics as features for the STS task. The distribution of correlation between MT metrics and STS human judgment indicates that this feature is reliable only in the border regions of the [0-5] scale, in particular in [0-1] and [4-5]. This result means that, MT metrics have interesting degrees of correlation with STS, so they are useful features for the task, but from the other side it means that they can not be used alone, because their performance are very low in the [1-4] range. Among the different metrics, METEOR has superior property compared to others and it proves to be an useful feature, even alone, to build acceptable STS systems.

In future we want to investigate more on the impact of other MT metrics on STS task. In this paper we have focused on the distribution of correlation on the [0-5] scale, but a study of the distribution on the different domain would give other important information on these features. Our aim is to find the most useful MT metric or the best combination of metrics among others, and the most reliable and effective algorithm to obtain better performance on the STS task. We also want to extend the study to multilingual STS, for instance, STS for Spanish, to learn if the impact and behavior of MT evaluation metrics remain the same in other languages.

References

Eneko Agirre, Mona Diab, Daniel Cer, and Aitor Gonzalez-Agirre. 2012. Semeval-2012 task 6: A pilot on semantic textual similarity. In *Proceedings of the First Joint Conference on Lexical and Computational Semantics-Volume 1: Proceedings of the main conference and the shared task, and Volume 2: Proceedings of the Sixth International Workshop on Semantic Evaluation*, pages 385–393. Association for Computational Linguistics.

Eneko Agirre, Daniel Cer, Mona Diab, Aitor Gonzalez-agirre, and Weiwei Guo. 2013. *SEM 2013 shared task: Semantic textual similarity. In *Second Joint Conference on Lexical and Computational Semantics (*SEM), Proceedings of the Main Conference and the Shared Task.*

Eneko Agirre, Carmen Banea, Claire Cardie, Daniel Cer, Mona Diab, Aitor Gonzalez-Agirre, Weiwei Guo, Rada Mihalcea, German Rigau, and Janyce Wiebe. 2014. Semeval-2014 task 10: Multilingual semantic textual similarity. In *Proceedings of the 8th International Workshop on Semantic Evaluation (SemEval 2014)*, pages 81–91.

Eneko Agirre, Carmen Banea, Claire Cardie, Daniel Cer, Mona Diab, Aitor Gonzalez-Agirre, Weiwei Guo, Inigo Lopez-Gazpio, Montse Maritxalar, Rada Mihalcea, German Rigau, Larraitz Uria, and Janyce Wiebe. 2015. SemEval-2015 Task 2: Semantic Textual Similarity, English, Spanish and Pilot on Interpretability. In *Proceedings of the 9th International Workshop on Semantic Evaluation (SemEval 2015)*, Denver, CO, June. Association for Computational Linguistics.

Luis Alberto Barrón Cedeño, Lluís Màrquez Villodre, Maria Fuentes Fort, Horacio Rodríguez Hontoria, Jorge Turmo Borras, et al. 2013. UPC-CORE: What can machine translation evaluation metrics and wikipedia do for estimating semantic textual similarity? In *Proceedings of the Joint Conference on Lexical and Computational Semantics. "*SEM 2013: The Second Joint Conference on Lexical and Computational Semantics".*

José Guilherme C de Souza, Matteo Negri, and Yashar Mehdad. 2012. Fbk: machine translation evaluation and word similarity metrics for semantic textual similarity. In *Proceedings of the First Joint Conference on Lexical and Computational Semantics-Volume 1: Proceedings of the main conference and the shared task, and Volume 2: Proceedings of the Sixth International Workshop on Semantic Evaluation*, pages 624–630. Association for Computational Linguistics.

Michael Denkowski and Alon Lavie. 2014. Meteor universal: Language specific translation evaluation for any target language. In *Proceedings of the EACL 2014 Workshop on Statistical Machine Translation.*

Bill Dolan, Chris Quirk, and Chris Brockett. 2004. Unsupervised construction of large paraphrase corpora: Exploiting massively parallel news sources. In *Proceedings of the 20th international conference on Computational Linguistics*, page 350. Association for Computational Linguistics.

Mark Hall, Eibe Frank, Geoffrey Holmes, Bernhard Pfahringer, Peter Reutemann, and Ian H Witten. 2009. The weka data mining software: an update. *ACM SIGKDD explorations newsletter*, 11(1):10–18.

Nitin Madnani, Joel Tetreault, and Martin Chodorow. 2012. Re-examining machine translation metrics for paraphrase identification. In *Proceedings of the 2012 Conference of the North American Chapter of the Association for Computational Linguistics: Human Language Technologies*, pages 182–190. Association for Computational Linguistics.

Kishore Papineni, Salim Roukos, Todd Ward, and Wei-Jing Zhu. 2002. Bleu: a method for automatic evaluation of machine translation. In *Proceedings of the 40th annual meeting on association for computational linguistics*, pages 311–318. Association for Computational Linguistics.

Marko Robnik-Sikonja and Igor Kononenko. 1997. An adaptation of relief for attribute estimation in regression. In Douglas H. Fisher, editor, *Fourteenth International Conference on Machine Learning*, pages 296–304. Morgan Kaufmann.

Matthew Snover, Bonnie Dorr, Richard Schwartz, Linnea Micciulla, and John Makhoul. 2006. A study of translation edit rate with targeted human annotation. In *Proceedings of association for machine translation in the Americas*, pages 223–231.

Matthew G Snover, Nitin Madnani, Bonnie Dorr, and Richard Schwartz. 2009. Ter-plus: paraphrase, semantic, and alignment enhancements to translation edit rate. *Machine Translation*, 23(2-3):117–127.

Norwegian Native Language Identification

Shervin Malmasi[◇] **Mark Dras**[◇] **Irina Temnikova**[♡]

[◇]Macquarie University, Sydney, NSW, Australia
[♡]Qatar Computing Research Institute, HBKU, Qatar

shervin.malmasi@mq.edu.au, mark.dras@mq.edu.au
itemnikova@qf.org.qa

Abstract

We present a study of Native Language Identification (NLI) using data from learners of Norwegian, a language not yet used for this task. NLI is the task of predicting a writer's first language using only their writings in a learned language. We find that three feature types, function words, part-of-speech n-grams and a hybrid part-of-speech/function word mixture n-gram model are useful here. Our system achieves an accuracy of 79% against a baseline of 13% for predicting an author's L1. The same features can distinguish non-native writing with 99% accuracy. We also find that part-of-speech n-gram performance on this data deviates from previous NLI results, possibly due to the use of manually post-corrected tags.

1 Introduction

Native Language Identification (NLI) is the task of identifying a writer's native language (L1) based only on their writings in a second language (the L2). NLI works by identifying language use patterns that are common to groups of speakers of the same native language. This process is underpinned by the presupposition that an author's L1 disposes them towards certain language production patterns in their L2, as influenced by their mother tongue. This relates to cross-linguistic influence (CLI), a key topic in the field of Second Language Acquisition (SLA) that analyzes transfer effects from the L1 on later learned languages (Ortega, 2009).

It has been noted in the linguistics literature since the 1950s that speakers of particular languages have characteristic production patterns when writing in a second language. This language transfer phenomenon has been investigated independently in various fields from different perspectives, including qualitative research in SLA and more recently though predictive computational models in NLP (Jarvis and Crossley, 2012).

Recently this has motivated studies in Native Language Identification (NLI), a subtype of text classification where the goal is to determine the native language (L1) of an author using texts they have written in a second language or L2 (Tetreault et al., 2013).

The motivations for NLI are manifold. The use of such techniques can help SLA researchers identify important L1-specific learning and teaching issues. In turn, the identification of such issues can enable researchers to develop pedagogical material that takes into consideration a learner's L1 and addresses them. It can also be applied in a forensic context, for example, to glean information about the discriminant L1 cues in an anonymous text. In fact, recent NLI research such as that related to the work presented by Perkins (2014) has already attracted interest and funding from intelligence agencies (Perkins, 2014, p. 17).

While most NLI research to date has focused on English L2 data, there is a growing trend to apply the techniques to other languages in order to assess their cross-language applicability (Malmasi and Dras, 2014c).

The current work presents the first NLI experiments on Norwegian data using a corpus of examination essays collected from learners of Norwegian, as described in section 3. Given the differences between English and Norwegian (which we outline in section 2.1), the main objective of the present study is to determine if NLI techniques previously applied to L2 English can be effective for detecting L1 transfer effects in L2 Norwegian.

Another unique aspect of this data is the availability of manually corrected part-of-speech (POS) tag annotations. This is something that has not been generally considered in previous NLI research and we aim to analyze how these results compare to previous studies in this regard.

Proceedings of Recent Advances in Natural Language Processing, pages 404–412,
Hissar, Bulgaria, Sep 7–9 2015.

2 Background and Related Work

NLI work has been growing in recent years, using a wide range of syntactic and more recently, lexical features to distinguish the L1. A detailed review of NLI methods is omitted here for reasons of space, but a thorough exposition is presented in the report from the very first NLI Shared Task that was held in 2013 (Tetreault et al., 2013).

Most English NLI work has been done using two corpora. The *International Corpus of Learner English* (Granger et al., 2009) was widely used until recently, despite its shortcomings[1] being widely noted (Brooke and Hirst, 2012). More recently, TOEFL11, the first corpus designed for NLI was released (Blanchard et al., 2013). While it is the largest NLI dataset available, it only contains argumentative essays, limiting analyses to this genre.

Research has also expanded to use non-English learner corpora (Malmasi and Dras, 2014a; Malmasi and Dras, 2014c). Recently, Malmasi and Dras (2014b) introduced the Jinan Chinese Learner Corpus (Wang et al., 2015) for NLI and their results indicate that feature performance may be similar across corpora and even L1-L2 pairs. In this work we attempt to follow this exploratory pattern by extending NLI research to Norwegian, which has not yet been studied for this task.

NLI is now also moving towards using linguistic features to generate SLA hypotheses. Swanson and Charniak (2014) approach this by using both L1 and L2 data to identify features exhibiting non-uniform usage in both datasets, creating lists of candidate transfer features. Malmasi and Dras (2014d) propose a different method, using linear SVM weights to extract lists of overused and underused linguistic features for each L1 group.

Many of these studies have investigated using syntactic information such as parse trees or part-of-speech (POS) tags as classification features (Kochmar, 2011). This is generally achieved by using taggers and parsers based on statistical models to automatically annotate the documents. For example, Tetreault et al. (2012) use the Stanford Tagger (Toutanova et al., 2003) to extract POS tags from the TOEFL11 data.

One issue to consider here is that the models used by these statistical taggers are trained on well-formed text from a standard variety of the language written by native speakers (*e.g.* news articles). When tested on such data, the models generally achieve high accuracies of 95% or higher. However, it cannot be assumed that these tools will achieve similar levels of accuracy on learner data, a distinct genre which they were not trained on.

This is a consideration that has not gone unnoticed and several researchers have investigated this question. Van Rooy and Schäfer (2002) investigated this issue and report that "learner spelling errors contributed substantially to tagging errors", causing up to 38% of the tagging errors. Díaz-Negrillo et al. (2010) argue that the properties of learner language are systematically different from those assumed for the standard variety of the language and that this interlanguage cannot be considered a noisy variant of the native language. Instead of viewing this as a robustness issue, they suggest that a new POS model for learner language may be more suitable. Based on the results of their empirical analysis they highlight several issues with standard POS models and they propose a new tripartite POS annotated model that encodes properties based on the lexical stem, distribution and morphology.

This evidence points to a performance degradation on learner data and suggests that the POS annotations used in many previous studies are vulnerable to tagging errors. Such errors could reduce their efficacy in distinguishing the different syntactic patterns used by different L1 groups. The availability of post-corrected POS tags in our data, as described in §3, can provide some insight into how much this issue affects NLI by comparing its performance with previously reported results.

2.1 Norwegian

Norwegian can be considered as one of the mainland Scandinavian languages. Along with Danish and Swedish, these languages share their heritage and have descended from a common Nordic language. Even today, a degree of mutual intelligibility continues to exist among these languages.

Norwegian itself is written in two distinguishable forms: Bokmål and Nynorsk with the former being more commonly used for writing, including in our data. The language has a number of properties that make it interesting to examine for NLI.

Norwegian grammar shares many similarities with English since both are Germanic languages. However, a number of differences also exist.

Norwegian has three genders: male, female and neuter. Definite and indefinite articles also ex-

[1]The issues exist as the corpus was not designed for NLI.

ist for all three genders, but the definite article is added to nouns as a suffix. Nouns are categorized by gender and in addition to definiteness, they are also inflected for plurality. Pronouns are classified by gender, person and number; they are also declined in nominative or accusative case. Adjectives must agree with gender of their head nouns and are also marked for plurality and definiteness. Norwegian verbs, although not marked for person or plurality, can have several different tenses and moods, leading to a rich morphology.

An important point to consider here is that this additional complexity also increases the possibility and number of potential learner errors. A more in-depth exposition of Norwegian syntax and morphology can be found in Haugen (2009).

3 Data

In this study we use data from the ASK Corpus (*Andrespråkskorpus*, Second Language Corpus). The ASK Corpus (Tenfjord et al., 2013; Tenfjord et al., 2006b; Tenfjord et al., 2006a) is a learner corpus composed of the writings of learners of Norwegian. These texts are essays written as part of a test of Norwegian as a second language. Each text also includes additional metadata about the author such as age or native language. An advantage of this corpus is that all the texts have been collected under the same conditions and time limits. The corpus also contains a control subcorpus of texts written by native Norwegians under the same test conditions. The corpus also includes error codes and corrections, although we do not make use of this information here.

There are a total of 1,700 essays written by learners of Norwegian as a second language with ten different first languages: German, Dutch, English, Spanish, Russian, Polish, Bosnian-Croatian-Serbian, Albanian, Vietnamese and Somali. The essays are written on a number of different topics, but these topics are not balanced across the L1s.

Detailed word level annotations (lemma, POS tag and grammatical function) have been first obtained automatically using the Oslo-Bergen tagger. These annotations have then been manually post-edited by human annotators since the tagger's performance can be substantially degraded due to orthographic, syntactic and morphological learner errors. These manual corrections can deal with issues such as unknown vocabulary or wrongly disambiguated words.

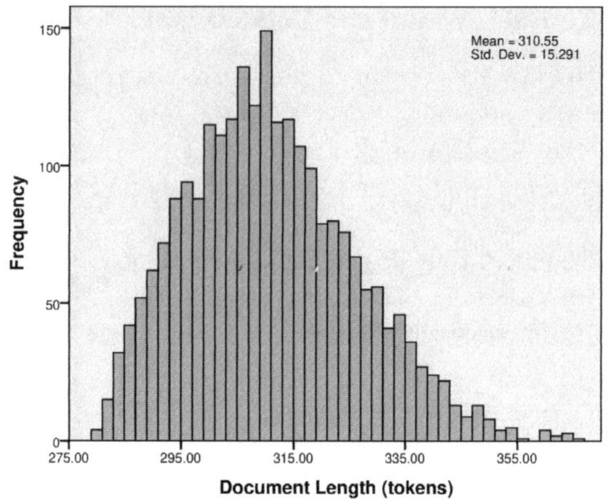

Figure 1: A histogram of the number of tokens per document in the dataset that we generated.

In this work we extracted 750k tokens of text from the ASK corpus in the form of individual sentences. Following the methodology of Brooke and Hirst (2011) and Malmasi and Dras (2014b), we randomly select and combine the sentences from the same L1 to generate texts of approximately 300 tokens on average, creating a set of documents suitable for NLI. This methodology ensures that the texts for each L1 are a mix of different authorship styles, topics and proficiencies. It also means that all documents are similar and comparable in length.

The 10 native languages and the number of texts generated per class are listed in Table 1. In addition to these we also generate 250 control texts written by natives. A histogram of the number of tokens per document is shown in Figure 1. The documents have an average length of 311 tokens with a standard deviation of 15 tokens.

3.1 Part-of-Speech Tagset

The ASK corpus uses the Oslo-Bergen tagset[2] which has been developed based on the Norwegian Reference Grammar (Faarlund et al., 1997).

Here each POS tag is composed of a set of constituent morphosyntactic tags. For example, the tag `subst-appell-mask-ub-fl` signifies that the token has the categories "noun common masculine indefinite plural". Similarly, the tags `verb-imp` and `verb-pres` refer to imperative and present tense verbs, respectively.

[2]http://tekstlab.uio.no/obt-ny/english/tagset.html

Native Language	Documents
Albanian	121
Dutch	254
English	273
German	280
Polish	281
Russian	257
Serbian	259
Somali	90
Spanish	243
Vietnamese	100
Total	2,158

Table 1: The 10 L1 classes included in this experiment and the number of texts we generated for each class.

Given its many morphosyntactic markers and detailed categories, the ASK dataset has a rich tagset with over 300 unique tags.

4 Experimental Methodology

In this study we employ a supervised multi-class classification approach. The learner texts are organized into classes according to the author's L1 and these documents are used for training and testing in our experiments. A diagram conceptualizing our NLI system is shown in Figure 2.

4.1 Classifier

We use a linear Support Vector Machine to perform multi-class classification in our experiments. In particular, we use the LIBLINEAR[3] package (Fan et al., 2008) which has been shown to be efficient for text classification problems such as this. More specifically, it has been demonstrated to be the most effective classifier for this task in the 2013 NLI Shared Task (Tetreault et al., 2013).

4.2 Evaluation

In the same manner as many previous NLI studies and also the NLI 2013 shared task, we report our results as classification accuracy under k-fold cross-validation, with $k = 10$. In recent years this has become a *de facto* standard for reporting NLI results.

[3]http://www.csie.ntu.edu.tw/%7Ecjlin/liblinear/

5 L1 Identification Experiment

We experiment using three syntactic feature types described in this section. As the ASK corpus is not balanced for topic, we do not consider the use of lexical features such as word n-grams in this study. Topic bias can occur as a result of the subject matters or topics of the texts to be classified not evenly distributed across the classes (Koppel et al., 2009). For example, if in our training data all the texts written by English L1 speakers are on topic A, while all the French L1 authors write about topic B, then we have implicitly trained our classifier on the topics as well. In this case the classifier learns to distinguish our target variable through another confounding variable.

Norwegian Function Words As opposed to content words, function words are topic-independent grammatical words that indicate the relations between other words. They include determiners, conjunctions and auxiliary verbs. Distributions of English function words have been found to be useful in studies of authorship attribution and NLI. Unlike POS tags, this model analyzes the author's specific word choices.

In this work we used a list of 176 function words obtained from the distribution of the Apache Lucene search engine software.[4] This list includes stop words for the Bokmål variant of the language and contains entries such as *hvis* (whose), *ikke* (not), *jeg* (I), *så* (so) and *hjå* (at). We also make this list available on our website.[5]

In addition to single function words, we also extract function word bigrams, as described by Malmasi et al. (2013). Function word bigrams are a type of word n-gram where content words are skipped: they are thus a specific subtype of skip-gram discussed by Guthrie et al. (2006). For example, the sentence *We should all start taking the bus* would be reduced to *we should all the*, from which we would extract the n-grams.

Part-of-Speech n-grams In this model POS n-grams of order 1–3 were extracted. These n-grams capture small and very local syntactic patterns of language production and were used as classification features. Previous work and our experiments showed that sequences of size 4 or greater achieve

[4]https://github.com/apache/lucene-solr

[5]http://web.science.mq.edu.au/%7Esmalmasi/data/norwegian-funcwords.txt

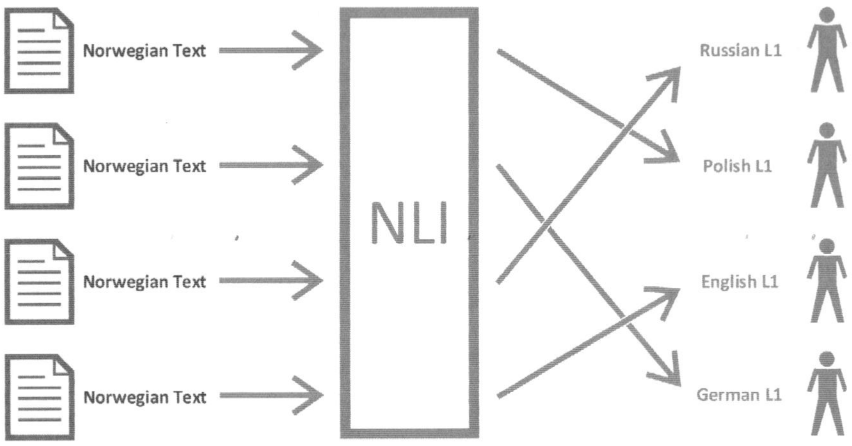

Figure 2: Illustration of our NLI system that identifies the L1 of Norwegian learners from their writing.

lower accuracy, possibly due to data sparsity, so we do not include them.

We observe 328 different tags in the data resulting in 9k unique bigrams and 61k trigram features.

Mixed POS-Function Word n-grams Previously Wong et al. (2012) proposed the use of POS n-grams which retained the surface form of function words instead of using their POS tag. Example mixed trigrams include "`the NN that`" or "`NN that VBZ`". They demonstrated that such features can outperform their pure POS counterparts. Here we also use our above-described function word list to generate such mixed n-grams.

5.1 Results

The results for all of our features are shown in Table 2. We compare against a majority class baseline of 13% which is calculated by using the largest class, in this case Polish, as the default classification label chosen for all texts.

The distribution of function word unigrams and bigrams is highly discriminative, yielding accuracies of 51.1% and 50.0%, respectively. These are well-above the baseline and suggest the presence of L1-specific grammatical and lexical choice patterns that can help distinguish the L1, potentially due to cross-linguistic transfer. Such lexical transfer effects have been previously noted by researchers and linguists (Odlin, 1989). These effects are mediated not only by cognates and similarities in word forms, but also word semantics.

Feature	**Accuracy (%)**
Majority Baseline	13.0
Function Words	51.1
Function Word bigrams	50.0
Part-of-Speech unigrams	61.2
Part-of-Speech bigrams	66.5
Part-of-Speech trigrams	62.7
POS/Function Word trigrams	78.1
All features combined	**78.6**

Table 2: Norwegian Native Language Identification accuracy for the features used in this study.

The purely syntactic POS n-gram models are also very useful for this task, with the best accuracy of 66.5% for POS bigrams. This is the highest NLI accuracy achieved using POS n-grams. Using the 11-class TOEFL11 data, none of the shared task entries or subsequent studies have achieved accuracies of 60% or higher, with results usually falling in the 40–55% range. We also note that our POS n-gram performance plateaus with bigrams. This deviates from previous NLI results where trigrams usually yield the highest accuracy. This, alongside the higher accuracy, could potentially be a result of the tags being manually corrected by annotators, leading to more accurate tags and thus classification accuracy. However, this does not entirely explain why performance degrades when using trigrams. This could be due to tagset size and the number of features because with 328 tags, this is the largest tagset used for NLI to date.

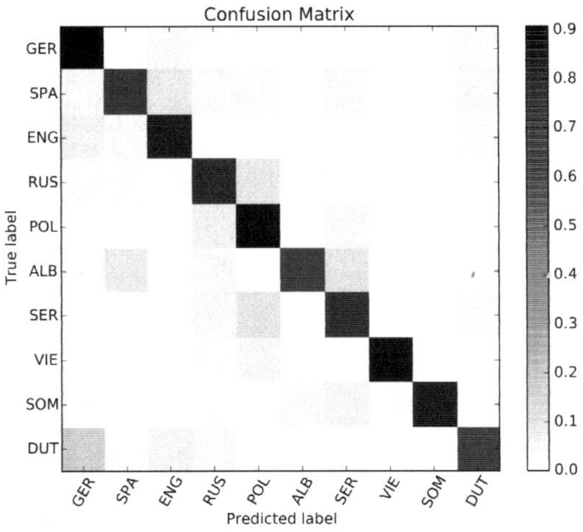

Figure 3: Confusion matrix for our 10 classes.

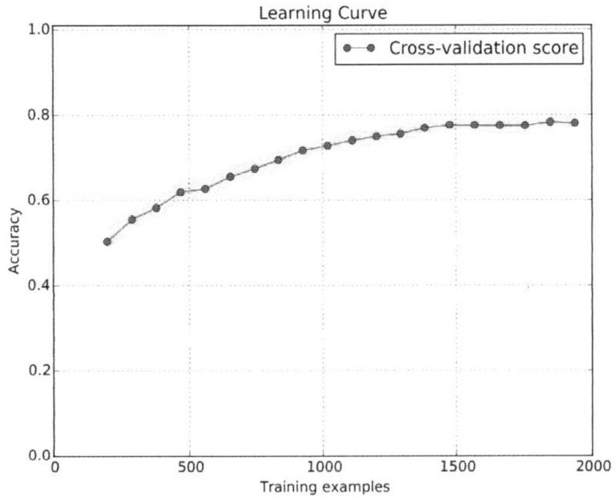

Figure 4: A learning curve for our Norwegian NLI system trained on all features.

The mixture of POS and function word n-grams provides the best result for a single feature with 78.1% accuracy. This is consistent with previous findings about this feature type.

Finally, combining all of the models into a single feature vector provides the highest accuracy of 78.6%, which is only slightly better than the best single feature type.

Figure 3 shows the normalized confusion matrix for our results. German and Polish are the most correctly classified L1s, while the highest confusion is between Dutch–German followed by Serbian–Polish and Russian-Polish. This is not surprising given that these pairs are from the same families: Germanic and Slavic. We were however surprised by the substantial confusion between Albanian and Spanish, even though the languages are not typologically related.

We also analyze the rate of learning for our classifier. A learning curve for a classifier trained on all features is shown in Figure 4. We observe that while there is a rapid initial increase in accuracy, performance begins to level off after around 1,500 training documents.

6 Identifying Non-Native Writing

Our second experiment involves using the above-described features to classify Norwegian texts as either Native or Non-Native. To achieve this we use 250 control texts we generated from the ASK Corpus that were written by native Norwegian speakers; these texts represent the Native class. This is contrasted against the Non-Native class which includes 250 texts sampled from each language[6] listed in Table 1.

Feature	**Accuracy (%)**
Random Baseline	50.0
Function Words	90.0
Function Word bigrams	94.2
Part-of-Speech unigrams	95.0
Part-of-Speech bigrams	98.4
Part-of-Speech trigrams	98.5
POS/Function Word trigrams	98.6
All features combined	**98.8**

Table 3: Accuracy for classifying Norwegian texts as either Native or Non-Native.

6.1 Results

The results of our final experiment for distinguishing non-native writing are listed in Table 3. They demonstrate that these feature types are highly useful for discriminating between Native and non-Native writings, achieving 98.8% accuracy by using all feature types. POS/Function Word mixture trigrams are the best single feature in this experiment.

These results show that the language productions of native speakers are very different to those of learners, enabling our models to distinguish them with almost perfect accuracy.

[6]We sample evenly with 25 texts per non-native L1 class.

7 Discussion and Conclusion

We presented the first Norwegian NLI experiments, achieving high levels of accuracy that are comparable with previous results for English and other languages. A key objective here was to investigate the efficacy of syntactic features for Norwegian, a language which is different to English in some aspects such as morphological complexity. The features employed here could also identify non-native documents with 99% accuracy.

Another contribution of this work is the identification of a new dataset for NLI. Tasks focused on detecting L1-based language transfer effects – such as NLI – require copious amounts of data. Contrary to this requirement, researchers have long noted the paucity of suitable corpora[7] for this task (Brooke and Hirst, 2011). This is one of the research issues addressed by this work. The introduction of this corpus can assist researchers test and verify their methodology on multiple datasets and languages.

This study is also novel in its use of post-corrected POS tags. As noted in §5.1, while the POS-based results here are different from those of previous studies that have used automated tagging methods, it is unclear if this is due to the use of post-edited tags or the large size of the tagset. This is an issue that merits further investigation. Additional results from a fully experimental setup using multiple sets of automatic and gold standard POS tags for the same texts can help provide better insight here. The ASK corpus does not include the original POS tags obtained automatically using the Oslo-Bergen tagger prior to human editing and the texts would need to be re-annotated for such a study. This is left for future work.

There are a number of directions for future research. There have been a number of interesting NLI that could also be tested on this data. These include oracles for determining the upper-bound on classification accuracy (Malmasi et al., 2015), analyses of feature diversity and interaction (Malmasi and Cahill, 2015), and large-scale cross-corpus experiments (Malmasi and Dras, 2015b).

The application of more linguistically sophisticated features also warrants further investigation, but this is limited by the availability of Norwegian NLP tools and resources. For example, the use of a Norwegian constituency parser could be used to study the overall structure of grammatical constructions as captured by context-free grammar production rules (Wong and Dras, 2011). Another possible improvement is the use of classifier ensembles to improve classification accuracy. This has previously been applied to other classification tasks (Malmasi and Dras, 2015a) and English NLI (Tetreault et al., 2012) with good results.

[7] An ideal NLI corpus should have multiple L1s, be balanced by topic, proficiency, texts per L1 and be large in size.

Acknowledgments

We would like to thank Kari Tenfjord and Paul Meurer for providing access to the ASK corpus and their assistance in using the data.

References

Daniel Blanchard, Joel Tetreault, Derrick Higgins, Aoife Cahill, and Martin Chodorow. 2013. TOEFL11: A Corpus of Non-Native English. Technical report, Educational Testing Service.

Julian Brooke and Graeme Hirst. 2011. Native language detection with 'cheap' learner corpora. Presented at the *Conference of Learner Corpus Research*, University of Louvain, Belgium.

Julian Brooke and Graeme Hirst. 2012. Measuring interlanguage: Native language identification with L1-influence metrics. In *Proceedings of the Eight International Conference on Language Resources and Evaluation (LREC'12)*, pages 779–784, Istanbul, Turkey, May.

Ana Dıaz-Negrillo, Detmar Meurers, Salvador Valera, and Holger Wunsch. 2010. Towards interlanguage POS annotation for effective learner corpora in SLA and FLT. In *Language Forum*, volume 36, pages 139–154.

Jan Terje Faarlund, Svein Lie, and Kjell Ivar Vannebo. 1997. *Norsk referansegrammatikk*. Columbia University Press.

Rong-En Fan, Kai-Wei Chang, Cho-Jui Hsieh, Xiang-Rui Wang, and Chih-Jen Lin. 2008. LIBLINEAR: A library for large linear classification. *Journal of Machine Learning Research*, 9:1871–1874.

Sylviane Granger, Estelle Dagneaux, Fanny Meunier, and Magali Paquot. 2009. *International Corpus of Learner English (Version 2)*. Presses Universitaires de Louvain, Louvian-la-Neuve.

David Guthrie, Ben Allison, Wei Liu, Louise Guthrie, and Yorick Wilks. 2006. A Close Look at Skip-gram Modelling. In *Proceedings of the Fifth International Conference on Language Resources and Evaluation (LREC 2006)*, pages 1222–1225, Genoa, Italy.

Einar Haugen. 2009. Danish, norwegian and swedish. In Bernard Comrie, editor, *The world's Major Languages*, pages 197–216. Routledge.

Scott Jarvis and Scott Crossley, editors. 2012. *Approaching Language Transfer Through Text Classification: Explorations in the Detection-based Approach*, volume 64. Multilingual Matters Limited, Bristol, UK.

Ekaterina Kochmar. 2011. Identification of a writer's native language by error analysis. Master's thesis, University of Cambridge.

Moshe Koppel, Jonathan Schler, and Shlomo Argamon. 2009. Computational methods in authorship attribution. *Journal of the American Society for Information Science and Technology*, 60(1):9–26.

Shervin Malmasi and Aoife Cahill. 2015. Measuring Feature Diversity in Native Language Identification. In *Proceedings of the Tenth Workshop on Innovative Use of NLP for Building Educational Applications*, pages 49–55, Denver, Colorado, June. Association for Computational Linguistics.

Shervin Malmasi and Mark Dras. 2014a. Arabic Native Language Identification. In *Proceedings of the Arabic Natural Language Processing Workshop (EMNLP 2014)*, pages 180–186, Doha, Qatar, October. Association for Computational Linguistics.

Shervin Malmasi and Mark Dras. 2014b. Chinese Native Language Identification. pages 95–99, Gothenburg, Sweden, April. Association for Computational Linguistics.

Shervin Malmasi and Mark Dras. 2014c. Finnish Native Language Identification. In *Proceedings of the Australasian Language Technology Workshop (ALTA)*, pages 139–144, Melbourne, Australia.

Shervin Malmasi and Mark Dras. 2014d. Language Transfer Hypotheses with Linear SVM Weights. In *Proceedings of the 2014 Conference on Empirical Methods in Natural Language Processing (EMNLP)*, pages 1385–1390, Doha, Qatar, October. Association for Computational Linguistics.

Shervin Malmasi and Mark Dras. 2015a. Language Identification using Classifier Ensembles. In *Proceedings of LT4VarDial - Joint Workshop on Language Technology for Closely Related Languages, Varieties and Dialects*, Hissar, Bulgaria, September.

Shervin Malmasi and Mark Dras. 2015b. Large-scale Native Language Identification with Cross-Corpus Evaluation. In *Proceedings of the 2015 Conference of the North American Chapter of the Association for Computational Linguistics (NAACL-HLT 2015)*, pages 1403–1409, Denver, CO, USA, June. Association for Computational Linguistics.

Shervin Malmasi, Sze-Meng Jojo Wong, and Mark Dras. 2013. NLI Shared Task 2013: MQ Submission. In *Proceedings of the Eighth Workshop on Innovative Use of NLP for Building Educational Applications*, pages 124–133, Atlanta, Georgia, June. Association for Computational Linguistics.

Shervin Malmasi, Joel Tetreault, and Mark Dras. 2015. Oracle and Human Baselines for Native Language Identification. In *Proceedings of the Tenth Workshop on Innovative Use of NLP for Building Educational Applications*, Denver, Colorado, June. Association for Computational Linguistics.

Terence Odlin. 1989. *Language Transfer: Cross-linguistic Influence in Language Learning*. Cambridge University Press, Cambridge, UK.

Lourdes Ortega. 2009. *Understanding Second Language Acquisition*. Hodder Education, Oxford, UK.

Ria Perkins. 2014. *Linguistic identifiers of L1 Persian speakers writing in English: NLID for authorship analysis*. Ph.D. thesis, Aston University.

Ben Swanson and Eugene Charniak. 2014. Data driven language transfer hypotheses. *EACL 2014*, page 169.

Kari Tenfjord, Hilde Johansen, and Jon Erik Hagen. 2006a. The "Hows" and the "Whys" of Coding Categories in a Learner Corpus (or "How and Why an Error-Tagged Learner Corpus is not ipso facto One Big Comparative Fallacy"). *Rivista di psicolinguistica applicata*, 6(3):1000–1016.

Kari Tenfjord, Paul Meurer, and Knut Hofland. 2006b. The ASK corpus: A language learner corpus of Norwegian as a second language. In *Proceedings of the 5th International Conference on Language Resources and Evaluation (LREC)*, pages 1821–1824.

Kari Tenfjord, Paul Meurer, and Silje Ragnhildstveit. 2013. Norsk andrespråkskorpus - A corpus of Norwegian as a second language. In *Learner Corpus Research Conference (LCR 2013)*.

Joel Tetreault, Daniel Blanchard, Aoife Cahill, and Martin Chodorow. 2012. Native Tongues, Lost and Found: Resources and Empirical Evaluations in Native Language Identification. In *Proceedings of COLING 2012*, pages 2585–2602, Mumbai, India, December. The COLING 2012 Organizing Committee.

Joel Tetreault, Daniel Blanchard, and Aoife Cahill. 2013. A Report on the First Native Language Identification Shared Task. In *Proceedings of the Eighth Workshop on Innovative Use of NLP for Building Educational Applications*, pages 48–57, Atlanta, Georgia, June. Association for Computational Linguistics.

Kristina Toutanova, Dan Klein, Christopher D. Manning, and Yoram Singer. 2003. Feature-rich part-of-speech tagging with a cyclic dependency network. In *IN PROCEEDINGS OF HLT-NAACL*, pages 252–259.

Bertus Van Rooy and Lande Schäfer. 2002. The effect of learner errors on POS tag errors during automatic POS tagging. *Southern African Linguistics and Applied Language Studies*, 20(4):325–335.

Maolin Wang, Shervin Malmasi, and Mingxuan Huang. 2015. The Jinan Chinese Learner Corpus. In *Proceedings of the Tenth Workshop on Innovative Use of NLP for Building Educational Applications*, pages 118–123, Denver, Colorado, June. Association for Computational Linguistics.

Sze-Meng Jojo Wong and Mark Dras. 2011. Exploiting Parse Structures for Native Language Identification. In *Proceedings of the 2011 Conference on Empirical Methods in Natural Language Processing*, pages 1600–1610, Edinburgh, Scotland, UK., July. Association for Computational Linguistics.

Sze-Meng Jojo Wong, Mark Dras, and Mark Johnson. 2012. Exploring Adaptor Grammars for Native Language Identification. In *Proc. Conf. Empirical Methods in Natural Language Processing (EMNLP)*, pages 699–709.

Automatic construction of complex features in Conditional Random Fields for Named Entities Recognition

Michał Marcińczuk
Institute of Informatics
Wrocław University of Technology
michal.marcinczuk@pwr.edu.pl

Abstract

Conditional Random Fields (CRFs) have been proven to be very useful in many sequence labelling tasks from the field of natural language processing, including named entity recognition (NER). The advantage of CRFs over other statistical models (like Hidden Markov Models) is that they can utilize a large set of features describing a sequence of observations. On the other hand, CRFs potential function is defined as a linear combination of features, what means, that it cannot model relationships between combinations of input features and output labels. This limitation can be overcome by defining the relationships between atomic features as complex features before training the CRFs. In the paper we present the experimental results of automatic generation of complex features for the named entity recognition task for Polish. A rule-induction algorithm called RIPPER is used to generate a set of rules which are latter transformed into a set of complex features. The extended set of features is used to train a CRFs model.

1 Background

Named entity recognition (NER) is an information extraction task and its goal is to identify and categorize text fragments which refer to some objects. Objects can be referred to by proper names, definite descriptions and noun phrases (LDC, 2008). From the perspective of information extraction tasks proper names are the most valuable as they identify the objects by their unique (to some extends) name. In this paper we will focus on identification of proper names for Polish.

There exist several tools for named entity recognition for Polish, including Liner2[1] (Marcińczuk et al., 2013) and Nerf[2] (Savary and Waszczuk, 2012). So far, the existing tools do not solve the problem of named entity once and for all. For a limited set of named entities (first names, last names, names of countries, cities and roads) the results are 70.53% recall with 91.44% precision (Marcińczuk and Janicki, 2012). Results for a wider range of entities are even lower, i.e. recall of 54% with 93% precision for 56 categories of named entities (Marcińczuk et al., 2013). Savary and Waszczuk (2012) presented a statistical model which obtained 76% recall with 83% precision for names of people, places, organizations, time expressions and name derivations tested on the National Corpus of Polish[3] (Przepiórkowski et al., 2012).

The recent works on named entity recognition focus mainly on improving the machine learning-based approaches. One direction is to decompose the task into two stages: named entity boundary detection and classification (Marcińczuk and Kocoń, 2013). The other is identification of new features which will provide better information to identify the named entities (Marcińczuk and Kocoń, 2013). Another direction is combination of different machine learning methods into a single classifier (Speck and Ngonga Ngomo, 2014). There is also another tendency which is based on increasing the size of training data by their automatic generation from Wikipedia (Al-Rfou et al., 2015). Last but not least direction is improvement of named entity recognition for noisy data, like "tweets" (Piskorski and Ehrmann, 2013; Küçük et al., 2014).

In our study we will follow another route whose goal is to generate a set of complex features based on an existing set of token features. In Section 2

[1] Web page: http://nlp.pwr.wroc.pl/liner2.
[2] Web page: http://zil.ipipan.waw.pl/Nerf.
[3] Home page: http://nkjp.pl

Proceedings of Recent Advances in Natural Language Processing, pages 413–419,
Hissar, Bulgaria, Sep 7–9 2015.

we present the motivation for complex features generation and explain, why the current state-of-the-art approach based on Conditional Random Fields cannot model complex dependences between features and classes on its own. In Section 3 we present a baseline set of features and propose three new auxiliary token features. Section 4 presents a procedure for generation complex features for a predefined set of basic features utilizing an existing algorithm for rule induction called RIPPER. In Section 5 we present the results of empirical evaluation and, finally, in Section 6 we discuss the obtained results.

2 Motivation for complex features

CRFs are type of discriminative models which are trained to maximize the conditional probability of observations (x) and classes (y) sequences $P(y|x)$. The conditional probability distribution is represented as a multiplication of feature functions exponents:

$$P(y|x) = \frac{1}{Z_0} exp\left(\sum_{i=1}^{n}\sum_{k=1}^{m}\lambda_k f_k(y_{i-1}, y_i, x) + \sum_{i=1}^{n}\sum_{k=1}^{m}\mu_k g_k(y_i, x)\right) \quad (1)$$

where Z_0 is a normalization factor, $f_k(y_{i-1}, y_i, x)$ and $g_k(y_i, x)$ are feature functions, and λ_k, μ_k are weights of feature functions which are set during learning process. This probability distribution does not model the relationships between combinations of feature functions and classes. In other words, if a combination of two or more feature functions is a good class indicator, the CRFs will not be able to discover the relationship. However, if the relationship between observation features is known then it can be presented to the CRFs as a set of feature functions. The feature functions which are a combination of two or more observation features will be called complex features. The complex feature functions can be represented as:

$$f'_k(y_{i-1}, y_i, x) = y_{i-1} \circ y_i \circ concat(h_1(x), ..., h_j(x)) \quad (2)$$

$$g'_k(y_i, x) = y_i \circ concat(h_1(x), ..., h_j(x)) \quad (3)$$

where $h_1(x)$, ..., $h_k(x)$ are some observation features. This leads to a conclusion, that the complex dependences between observation features and classes must be predefined in a form of separate feature functions.

To verify the above conclusion we performed the following experiment. Let assume we have a training instance with eight observations ($x_1, ..., x_8$), two observation features h_1 and h_2, and two possible classes A and B. The vectors with observation feature values are presented in Table 1. If we treat every observation as a separate one-element sequence the CRFs model trained with only simple feature functions ($g_k(y_i, x) = y_i \circ h_j(x)$) will not learn to distinguish between classes A and B[4]

x	$h_1(x)$	$h_2(x)$	y
x_1	0	0	A
x_2	0	1	B
x_3	1	0	B
x_4	1	1	A
x_5	0	0	A
x_6	0	1	B
x_7	1	0	B
x_8	1	1	A

Table 1: Feature vectors for observations $x_1, ..., x_8$ and features $h_1(x)$ and $h_2(x)$.

We can observe, that there is a relationship between h_1, h_2 and y, i.e. $y = B$ if $h_1(x) <> h_2(x)$. This relationship can be transformed into a complex function, i.e.:

$$h_3(x) = (h_1 \circ h_2)(x) = concat(h_1(x), h_2(x))$$

If we include the feature $h_3(x)$ (see Table 2) and repeat the training and testing procedure, then the CRFs model will correctly classify the observations. This confirms that the complex dependences between observation features and classes must be beforehand identified and included in the training procedure as a separate set of feature functions.

In the context of named entity recognition tasks the *observation* is a single token. The *class* is a label from a predefined set of labels, i.e. $\{B\text{-}nam, I\text{-}nam, O\text{-}nam\}$, where $B\text{-}nam$ is assigned to tokens starting a named entity, $I\text{-}nam$ is assigned to tokens which are part of a named entity and O is assigned to tokens which are not part

[4]Here we used the CRF++ tool to train and test the model.

x	$h_1(x)$	$h_2(x)$	$h_3(x)$	y
x_1	0	0	00	A
x_2	0	1	01	B
x_3	1	0	10	B
x_4	1	1	00	A
x_5	0	0	00	A
x_6	0	1	01	B
x_7	1	0	10	B
x_8	1	1	00	A

Table 2: Feature vectors for observations $x_1, ..., x_8$ and features $h_1(x)$, $h_2(x)$ and $h_3(x)$.

of any named entity. An *observation feature* is a token attribute, for example an orthographic form, a part of speech or a presence in a gazetteer. A *complex feature* will be a combination of *observation features*, for example *the current token is upper case and the preceding is lower case*.

3 Feature space

3.1 Baseline set of features

The baseline set of features contains features used by Marcińczuk and Kocoń (2013) in recognition of named entities boundaries for Polish. It contains orthographic, morphological, lexicon-based and wordnet-base features. The set contains only one complex feature, i.e. *agreement*. This feature checks the number, case and gender agreement between adjacent tokens.

3.2 New features

Before generating complex features we revised the baseline set of features. After error analysis we have identified three main types of errors which are related to incorrect boundaries detection. The errors are:

- names which are splitted into several tokens which are not separated by white spaces are partially recognized. For example "EX-8.5" (name of an engine model) is splitted into five tokens: *[EX][-][8][.][5]* and only the first token is marked as a named entity, i.e. "*EX*".
- names which are quoted are partially recognized. For example in "(...) lecture 'New media and social changes' (...)" only "*New media*" is annotated.
- names in brackets are also partially recognized.

To solve the above problems we introduced three new basic features: *quotation*, *bracket* and *nospace*. The features are described in the following subsections.

3.2.1 The *Nospace* feature

Nospace feature indicates if there is or not a space (or any white space character) between the current and the preceding token.

$$nospace(n) = \begin{cases} 1 & \text{if there is a whitespace character} \\ & \text{between } n-1\text{-th and } n\text{-th tokens} \\ 0 & \text{otherwise} \end{cases}$$

3.2.2 The *Quotation* feature

Quotation feature indicates if the token is between an opening and a closing quotation marks.

$$quotation(n) = \begin{cases} B & \text{if } n\text{-th token is an opening} \\ & \text{quotation mark} \\ I & \text{if } n\text{-th token is between an opening} \\ & \text{and a closing quotation mark} \\ E & \text{if } n\text{-th token is a closing} \\ & \text{quotation mark} \\ O & \text{otherwise} \end{cases}$$

3.2.3 The *Bracket* feature

Bracket feature indicates if the token is between an opening and a closing bracket.

$$bracket(n) = \begin{cases} B & \text{if } n\text{-th token is an opening bracket} \\ I & \text{if } n\text{-th token is between an opening} \\ & \text{and a closing brackets} \\ E & \text{if } n\text{-th token is a closing bracket} \\ O & \text{otherwise} \end{cases}$$

4 Complex feature generation

RIPPER (Repeated Incremental Pruning to Produce Error Reduction) is a rule learning algorithm that can efficiently handle large and noisy datasets. According to Cohen (1995) RIPPER scales nearly linearly with number of examples in a dataset.

We used Java implementation of RIPPER called JRip, which is a part of Weka software (Hall et al., 2009). The set of rules was induced on the tune part of the KPWr corpus (Broda et al., 2012) which contains 62k instances of O class, 3.7k instances of $B - nam$ class and 3k instances of $I - nam$ class. For each token feature we used five features for the adjacent tokens — two preceding tokens, the current token and two following tokens. A sample of token feature vectors for a single feature *orth* is presented in Table 3.

n	orth	orth-2	orth-1	orth-0	orth+1	orth+2
1	Tom	NULL	NULL	Tom	lives	in
2	lives	NULL	Tom	lives	in	Paris
3	in	Tom	lives	in	Paris	NULL
4	Paris	lives	in	Paris	NULL	NULL

Table 3: Token feature vectors for a sample sentence and a single feature *orth* (orthographic form of token)
.

The rule induction process took 2.5 hours on a single 2.4 GHz CPU. The final set of rules consists of 29 rules for $B\text{-}nam$ class and 24 rules for $I\text{-}nam$ class. The accuracy of the rules on the tune part was 96.6%. The detailed results are presented in the Table 4.

Class	P	R	F
$B\text{-}nam$	82.5%	79.2%	80.8%
$I\text{-}nam$	86.2%	63.8%	73.3%
O	97.7%	99.1%	98.4%
All	96.6%	96.6%	96.4%

Table 4: Evaluation of the rules on the tune part of the KPWr corpus.

A sample rule generated by JRip is presented on Figure 1. The rule says: *the current token starts a named entity* (B-nam) if *the current token has an upper case letter* (has_upper_case+0 = 1) and *the preceding token does not have only upper case letters* (all_upper-1 = 0) and *the preceding token have only lower case letters* (pattern-1 = ALL_LOWER) and *the following token has an upper case letter* (has_upper_case+1 = 1).

Table 5 contains a list of features which appeared in the rules generated by JRip accompanied with the number of rules containing the feature. The most common features where *has_upper_case* (29 rules), *starts_with_lower_case* (24 rules) and *starts_with_upper_case* (23 rules). These are orthographic features which refer to presence of upper and lower case letters — in Polish upper case letters indicate most of named entity. The new features described in Section 3.2 also appeared in the rules — *parenthesis* and *nospace* appeared in 8 rules and *quotation* in 1 rule. This means that the new features combined with other features are useful in named entity boundary detection.

The set of rules was finally transformed into a set of template features. The transformation consists of removing feature values and keeping only feature names. A feature template for the sample rule from Figure 1 is presented on Figure 2. We use CRF++ [5] implementation of CRFs which generates all possible combinations of feature values for given feature template during the training process. This way CRF++ can explore all combinations of feature values (including the one generated by JRip) and evaluate them in the context of sequence labelling task. The final evaluation of the generated complex features is presented in Section 5.

```
(has_upper_case+0 = 1)
  and (all_upper-1 = 0)
  and (pattern-1 = ALL_LOWER)
  and (has_upper_case+1 = 1)
=> iobtag=B-nam
```

Figure 1: A sample rule generated by JRip on the tune part of KPWr.

```
has_upper_case:0/all_upper:-1/
  pattern:-1/has_upper_case:1
```

Figure 2: A complex feature converted from the sample rule from Figure 1.

5 Evaluation

We have evaluated three set of features: *baseline* (described in Section 3.1), *baseline with new features* (described in Section 3.2) and *baseline with complex features* (baseline features with new features and automatically generated complex features according to the procedure presented in Section 4).

We decided not to evaluate the set of rules generated by JRip on their own as we did not expect to obtain good results. The performance of the rules on the tune set (set on which the rules were generated) was relatively low and on unseen data it might be even lower.

The evaluation was performed by training CRF-based statistical model using 10-fold cross validation on the train part of the KPWr (see Table 6).

[5]Web page: `http://crfpp.googlecode.com/svn/trunk/doc/index.html`

Feature	Count
has_upper_case	29
starts_with_lower_case	24
starts_with_upper_case	23
ctag	14
pattern	14
agr1	12
class	12
dict_person_first_nam	10
all_upper	9
orth	9
case	8
parenthesis	8
nospace	8
has_lower_case	7
gender	6
length	7
all_alphanumeric	4
all_digits	2
all_letters	3
has_digit	2
number	2
suffix-1	2
struct	2
no_letters	1
prefix-1	1
quotation	1
starts_with_digit	1
suffix-2	1

Table 5: A list of features used to construct the set of rules with a number of rules in which the feature appeared.

We also validate the generality of the feature sets by training the model on the train and tune part of KPWr and testing on the test part of KPWr (see Table 6).

We present results for *strict* and *partial* matching evaluation (Chinchor, 1992). In the *strict* matching the boundaries of recognized annotations must be exactly the same as in the reference corpus. In the *partial* matching the recognition of annotations presence and its boundaries are evaluated separately. This means that annotations which do not exactly match the expected boundaries are treated as partial success.

To check the statistical significance of difference between results we used Student's t-test with a significance level $\alpha = 0.05$ (Dietterich, 1998).

Application of the new three features (*nospace*, *quotation* and *bracket*) improved the F-measure for strict evaluation from 80.30% to 81.13%. The difference is statistically significant for $\alpha = 0.05$ what means that the additional features are useful for the recognition of named entities boundaries. Further improvement was achieved by extending the feature set with the complex features generated with RIPPER algorithm. The F-measure increased to 82.61% and the difference is also statistically significant.

Similar increase of F-measure was observed for the test part of KPWr. The initial value of F-measure increased from 82.40% for baseline set of features to 84.50% for the baseline set of features extended with complex features.

Evaluation	P	R	F
Baseline			
Strict	81.92%	78.74%	80.30%
Partial	88.11%	84.83%	86.44%
Baseline with new features			
Strict	82.79%	79.54%	81.13%
Partial	88.52%	85.22%	86.84%
Baseline with complex features			
Strict	84.10%	81.16%	82.61%
Partial	89.07%	86.25%	87.64%

Table 6: 10-fold cross validation on the train part of KPWr corpus.

Evaluation	P	R	F
Baseline			
Strict	84.25%	80.63%	82.40%
Partial	89.78%	85.80%	87.74%
Baseline with new features			
Strict	84.94%	81.72%	83.29%
Partial	90.22%	86.75%	88.45%
Baseline with complex features			
Strict	86.04%	83.02%	84.50%
Partial	90.73%	87.63%	89.15%

Table 7: Evaluation on the test part of the KPWr corpus.

6 Conclusions

A rule learning algorithms such as RIPPER can be successfully used to improve the performance of a CRF-based statistical model. RIPPER can find a dependences between token features and their classes. The dependences can be expressed as a set of rules which can be latter transformed into a set of feature templates for CRFs.

Despite the improvement we achieved, the final performance of named entity recognition is still far from perfect. There are same possible reasons for that. First of all, the complex features generated by RIPPER have form of conjunction of positive assertions. This means that RIPPER will not produce rules with negation (i.e. if $h_j(x) <>' b'$ then ...). This can be achieved by enumerating all possible values for feature h_j and constructing a set of negated features but this approach might be ineffective due to large space of possible values (especially orthographic and base forms).

The other limitation of this approach is lack of long distance dependences modelling. For example, if a sequence of tokens T in one sentence has labelling L, then there is high probability that the same sequence in an another sentence will have the same labelling. In the current approach there is no linking between the same sequences of tokens.

Also the discrepancy between strict and partial matching evaluation shows, that there is still a problem with proper boundary detection of named entities. This is a problem for long names, like titles which are not quoted. In such cases there is no orthographic indication, where the title ends and its ending is recognized incorrectly.

Acknowledgement Work financed by the Polish Ministry of Science and Higher Education, a program in support of scientific units involved in the development of a European research infrastructure for the humanities and social sciences in the scope of the consortia CLARIN ERIC and ESS-ERIC, 2015-2016

References

Rami Al-Rfou, Vivek Kulkarni, Bryan Perozzi, and Steven Skiena. 2015. Polyglot-NER: Massive multilingual named entity recognition. *Proceedings of the 2015 SIAM International Conference on Data Mining, Vancouver, British Columbia, Canada, April 30 - May 2, 2015*, April.

Bartosz Broda, Michał Marcińczuk, Marek Maziarz, Adam Radziszewski, and Adam Wardyński. 2012. KPWr: Towards a Free Corpus of Polish. In Nicoletta Calzolari, Khalid Choukri, Thierry Declerck, Mehmet Uğur Doğan, Bente Maegaard, Joseph Mariani, Jan Odijk, and Stelios Piperidis, editors, *Proceedings of LREC'12*. ELRA.

Nancy Chinchor. 1992. MUC-4 Evaluation Metrics. In *Proceedings of the Fourth Message Understanding Conference*, pages 22–29.

William W. Cohen. 1995. Fast effective rule induction. In *Twelfth International Conference on Machine Learning*, pages 115–123. Morgan Kaufmann.

Thomas G. Dietterich. 1998. Approximate statistical tests for comparing supervised classification learning algorithms. *Neural Computation*, 10(7):1895–1924.

Mark Hall, Eibe Frank, Geoffrey Holmes, Bernhard Pfahringer, Peter Reutemann, and Ian H. Witten. 2009. The weka data mining software: An update. *SIGKDD Explor. Newsl.*, 11(1):10–18, November.

Dilek Küçük, Guillaume Jacquet, and Ralf Steinberger. 2014. Named entity recognition on turkish tweets. In Nicoletta Calzolari, Khalid Choukri, Thierry Declerck, Hrafn Loftsson, Bente Maegaard, Joseph Mariani, Asunción Moreno, Jan Odijk, and Stelios Piperidis, editors, *Proceedings of the Ninth International Conference on Language Resources and Evaluation (LREC-2014), Reykjavik, Iceland, May 26-31, 2014.*, pages 450–454. European Language Resources Association (ELRA).

LDC. 2008. ACE (Automatic Content Extraction) English Annotation Guidelines for Relations (Version 6.2).

Michał Marcińczuk and Maciej Janicki. 2012. Optimizing CRF-Based Model for Proper Name Recognition in Polish Texts. In Alexander F. Gelbukh, editor, *CICLing (1)*, volume 7181 of *Lecture Notes in Computer Science*, pages 258–269. Springer.

Michał Marcińczuk, Jan Kocoń, and Maciej Janicki. 2013. Liner2 - A Customizable Framework for Proper Names Recognition for Polish. In Robert Bembenik, Łukasz Skonieczny, Henryk Rybiński, Marzena Kryszkiewicz, and Marek Niezgódka, editors, *Intelligent Tools for Building a Scientific Information Platform*, volume 467 of *Studies in Computational Intelligence*, pages 231–253. Springer.

Michał Marcińczuk and Jan Kocoń. 2013. Recognition of named entities boundaries in polish texts. In *Proceedings of the 4th Biennial International Workshop on Balto-Slavic Natural Language Processing*, pages 94–99, Sofia, Bulgaria, August. Association for Computational Linguistics.

Jakub Piskorski and Maud Ehrmann. 2013. On named entity recognition in targeted twitter streams in polish. In *Proceedings of the 4th Biennial International Workshop on Balto-Slavic Natural Language Processing*, pages 84–93, Sofia, Bulgaria, August. Association for Computational Linguistics.

Adam Przepiórkowski, Mirosław Bańko, Rafał L. Górski, and Barbara Lewandowska-Tomaszczyk, editors. 2012. *Narodowy Korpus Języka Polskiego [Eng.: National Corpus of Polish]*. Wydawnictwo Naukowe PWN, Warsaw.

Agata Savary and Jakub Waszczuk. 2012. Narzędzia do anotacji jednostek nazewniczych. In Adam Przepiórkowski, Mirosław Bańko, Rafał L. Górski, and Barbara Lewandowska-Tomaszczyk, editors, *Narodowy Korpus Języka Polskiego*. Wydawnictwo Naukowe PWN. Creative Commons Uznanie Autorstwa 3.0 Polska.

René Speck and Axel-Cyrille Ngonga Ngomo. 2014. Ensemble learning for named entity recognition. In Peter Mika, Tania Tudorache, Abraham Bernstein, Chris Welty, Craig Knoblock, Denny Vrandečić, Paul Groth, Natasha Noy, Krzysztof Janowicz, and Carole Goble, editors, *The Semantic Web – ISWC 2014*, volume 8796 of *Lecture Notes in Computer Science*, pages 519–534. Springer International Publishing.

Pattern Construction for Extracting Domain Terminology

Yusney Marrero García
Agrarian University of Havana, Cuba
yusneym@unah.edu.cu

Paloma Moreda Pozo
University of Alicante, Spain
moreda@dlsi.ua.es

Rafael Muñoz Guillena
University of Alicante, Spain
rafael@dlsi.ua.es

Abstract

The extraction of domain terminology is a task that is increasingly used for different application processes of natural language such as the information recovery, the creation of specialized corpus, question-answering systems, the creation of ontologies and the automatic classification of documents. This task of the extraction of domain terminology is generally performed by generating patterns. In literature we could find that the patterns which are used to extract such terminology often change from one domain to another, it means the intervention of human experts to the generation and validation of these patterns. This article deals with a methodology for automatic obtaining patterns (Basic Patterns and Definitory Verbal Patterns) for extracting domain terminology and minimizing the manual work of the experts. The obtained methodology was evaluated in the computer science domain obtaining a 97 percent in the case of the values of the basic patterns and a 98 percent of the definitory verbal patterns. Then the methodology was tested in three other domains with similar results, Agricultural Engineering (a 96 percent of the basic patterns and a 97 percent of the definitory verbal patterns), Veterinary Medicine (98% of the basic pattern and the definitory verbal patterns) and Agronomy (96% of the basic pattern and the definitory verbal patterns), showing that methodology can be applied in any specialty curriculum documents.

1 Introduction

The extraction of terms that characterizes a document is a task of vital importance in the development of recovery systems and information extraction.

It is very important to get the patterns that characterize these terms for the proper functioning of such systems.

In the present systems of natural language processes, there is a tendency which minimizes the human labor, leaving the processing of the whole information to the system but the final validation made by experts remains irreplaceable in many cases.

Sometimes the obtained patterns change from one domain to another, so there are some methods to minimize the human intervention. It would be a great step forward for the work of such systems.

The research paper is organized as follows: after presenting the state of the art (Section 2), we present in Section 3 Pattern Generation Process, Selection of the corpus (Section 3.1), Definitory context (Section 3.2), Definitory verbal patterns (Section 3.3) and Our proposal (Section 3.4). Then, the processes of Evaluation – Analysis for the Computer Science domain (Section 4) and then the evaluation of the obtained methodology in other domains will be presented (Section 4.1) and the ending with conclusions and future work (section 5).

2 State of the Art

Obtaining patterns for the extraction systems are a task whose success will depend on the correct operation of the system that uses it, the values of recall and precision have a direct correspondence with the obtained information in mapping with patterns.

Several proposals have been introduced to try to solve this problem such as (Riloff, 1993) and (Soderland et al., 1995). In these proposals as well as in the presented methodology extraction patterns are generated and are based on annotated corpus of training. The process of annotation of a corpus is clearly easier than the creation of a pattern dictionary manually, although it is true that it requires a domain expert that conducts and supervises the labeling of the

Proceedings of Recent Advances in Natural Language Processing, pages 420–426,
Hissar, Bulgaria, Sep 7–9 2015.

corpus.

Other proposals have avoided the annotation process like (Riloff and Shoen, 1995) in this case an annotated corpus is not required but preclassified, that is to say that the texts which are received as input must have been previously classified and (Huffman, 1995) in which a user is allowed to identify entities of interest that may represent events of interest.

3 Pattern Generation Process

It is very important to identify the recurrent syntactic structures of the terms that characterize these texts so as to extract domain terminology in specialized texts automatically. These structures represent patterns that follow the terminology that characterizes this domain. (Saneifar et al., 2009), (Sierra et al., 2006).

So as to develop an automatic terminology extraction domain which is based on patterns, the correct identification of these structures is a key factor for its proper operation.

In specialized texts it is very common to find many of the terms that characterize the texts.

In this section and these subsections our methodology is presented. It deals with the automatic generation of patterns to extract domain terminology in Spanish as well as other elements needed to understand it. The proposed methodology is based on two sets of patterns, the Basic Patterns and Definitory Verbal Patterns, the latter are incorporated in the methodology with the aim of improving the obtained precision of values which is based on the idea that most of the terms are defined in domain texts, belonging to them, which are framed in defining contexts as proposed by (Alarcon et al., 2007).

Next, a description of the corpus selection process is presented and the reasons for their selection.

3.1 Selection of the Corpus.

The selection of the corpus to use is a difficult but important task, because it is going to get the language patterns of the terms that are going to be used for tests and evaluation processes.

As proposed by (Dubuc and Lauriston, 1997), so as to elect the corpus we must take into account that:

- The text must be representative. The document scanning object has to reflect the use of experts in a specialty field.
- The nature of the publication largely determines the importance of contexts it contains. Textbooks, manuals, monographs, are excellent sources that provide explicit information of concepts and terms. The analysis of random samples of texts in a publication may determine its usefulness for terminology research.
- We must pursue a minimum of presentation and reliability. In general, poorly written texts with many grammatical mistakes provide a little solid base of terminological analysis.

Following the recommendations of Dubuc and Lauriston, some documents have been selected as corpus (120 documents in Spanish) these documents deal with the subjects belonging to the Curriculum Base and Own of the study Plan "D" of the Computer Science career of the Agrarian University of Havana paying special attention to the texts of each curriculum that are generally representative, reviewed and approved by experts in each domain, they are variegated in different areas where each domain is composed by a continuous updating. Texts provide a very important content having a correct presentation and reliability due to the staff and the destination where they will be used.

3.2 Definitory Contexts.

In (Sierra, 2009), a study with different approaches to the concept of Context Definitory (CD) is made in terminology (De Bessé, 1991), (Auger, 1997), (Pearson, 1998) and (Meyer, 2001).

In (Alarcon et al., 2007), the term CD deals with any textual fragment of a specialized document where a term is defined. CDs are formed by a term (T) and a definition (D), which are connected by a defining pattern (PD). They may optionally include a pragmatic pattern (PP), that is to say, structures that provide conditions using this term or qualifying its meaning. Figure 1

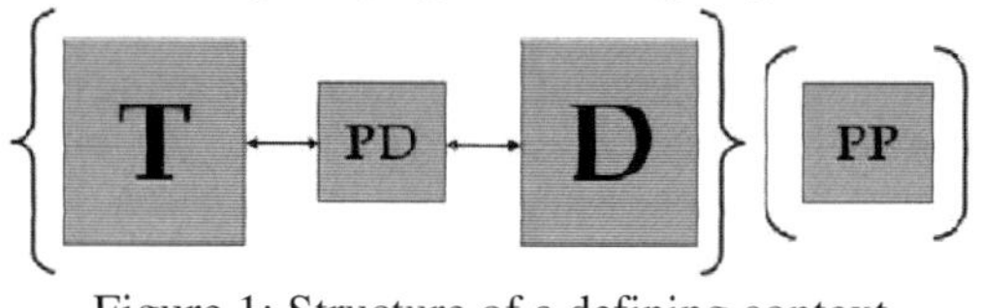

Figure 1: Structure of a defining context

3.3 Definitory Verbal Patterns.

(Alarcon, 2009) suggests that there are syntactic patterns that connect the term with its definition, if such connectors have a verb as the nucleus, then we have a Definitory Verbal Pattern (DVP).

In this sense we could find specialized texts with DVP.

Example 1:

Así, **se define** el *estándar XML* **como** el formato universal para documentos y datos estructurados en Internet y podemos explicar las características de su funcionamiento a través de 7 puntos importantes, tal y como la propia W3C recomienda.

Example 2:

cliente servidor: **Es una** tendencia de los actuales sistemas de operación que consiste en instrumentar la mayoría de las funciones en procesos usuarios, construyendo un "kernel" mínimo.

In the above examples we observe that the defining information is composed by the verbs *define* and *be*. Furthermore, the occurrence of the pronoun *se* to the verb *define*, and the adverb *como* to form the pattern *se define como*. In Example 2, we have the combination *es un*, a prototypical structure to define a term.

3.4 Our Proposal

In Figure 2 we present our methodology of automatic extraction of patterns where every step is described below.

1. Selection of the corpus belonging to the domain.

The first step of our methodology is to select the corpus we are going to use. This corpus should be divided into two parts; one part is used in the process of obtaining patterns and the remaining part in the evaluation process.

2. Semi-automatic annotation of terms belonging to the domain in question (Human expert validation)

For the labeling process we have constructed the **TermEt** tool which basically has two functions:

a) If you do not have a set of patterns already obtained, you have to show a view of the text and experts will be able to mark and write notes about the terms which belong to the domain.

b) If there is a set of patterns, the application allows their input showing the word or strings of words to be mapped with the previously introduced patterns, allowing the expert labelling or not the terms with the same tags.

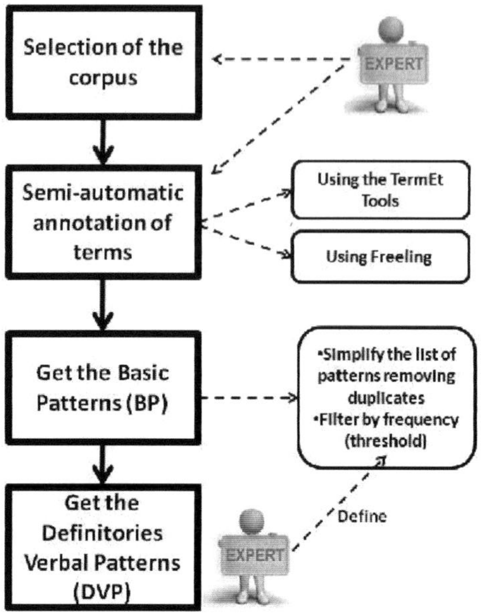

Figure 2: Our Methodology

In both cases, a morphological analysis is performed to the text using the Freeling[1] tool, and as an output an XML file is provided with the processed text and the terms which have been listed with their corresponding grammatical categories.

3. Get the basic patterns. This process involves the extraction of the label string obtained from a morphological analysis to the words that were annotated in the corpus as a term. Simplify the list of patterns removing duplicates and filter it through its frequency.

From the XML the obtained file as an output from the previous step and the list of strings for the terms which were included in the processed documents were extracted and a first set of possible patterns is obtained. Table 1 shows a fragment of the initial list of obtained patterns.

Patterns	
N	Noun
NJ	Noun+ Adjective
N	Noun
N	Noun
NPN	Noun+Preposition+Noun
NPNJ	Noun+Preposition+Noun+Adjective
N	Noun
NJCJ	Noun+Adjective+Conjuntion+Adjective

Table 1: Initial list of patterns

[1] http://nlp.lsi.upc.edu/freeling/

The number of obtained patterns may be very large, in order to simplify this pattern list we have to eliminate duplicated patterns and the frequency of each one is stored A filtering process is then performed, its frequency of appearance in the text is emphasized, experts can set a threshold and all patterns that its frequency in the text do not exceed this threshold will be deleted from the final list of patterns.

Table 2 shows the final list of resulting patterns after making the pro-filtering process considering the frequency of occurrence in each of the patterns.

This set of obtained patterns are called Basic Patterns (BP), and they represent the basic structures that follow the terms of a particular domain.

Patterns		Frequency
N	Noun	F1
NJ	Noun+ Adjective	F2
NPN	Noun+Preposition+Noun	F3

Table 2: Basic Patterns

As we can see if we use this set of obtained patterns we will surely obtain the terms that define that domain, but they are so basic that a lot of noise will be introduced affecting the precision values severely.

Next we show you some examples that constitute noise and they are structures that are extracted by the mapping of these patterns and there are not any terms that characterize that domain.

Pattern **Examples of Noise**

N estudiante (student), diccionario(dictionary)
NJ diccionario grande (big dictionary)
NPN etapa de trabajo (stage work).

4. Get the Definitory Verbal Patterns

So as to minimize the noise the obtained BP is introduced and a set of DVP to use has been defined.

In (Alarcon et al., 2007), it is shown that the verbs that can operate more as connectors between a term and a definition are conceive and define as well as the prototypical use of the verb to be better than a determiner which is known as ISA relationship.

In a previous study (Alarcon and Sierra 2003) the different definitory verbal patterns were found and they can constitute these verbs, although it is necessary to clarify that, depending on the defined pattern the terms and their definitions can occupy different positions in the constitutive elements.

Based on these two criteria (the verbs are used and the different positions that a term can occupy and its definition in the DVP context) for our methodology we have defined the following DVP:

- o BP? DVP + BP?+"como"+*definition*+ BP?
- o BP+":"+" DVP "+ *definition*

where:

BP: are obtained in step 3 of the proposed methodology.

DVP: they can be defined taking into consideration the verbs *conceive* and *define*, and the prototypical *is-a* according to the following structures:

SE = Impersonal pronoun *se*
Vaux = Auxiliary verb
VDef_Inf = Definitory verb, impersonal infinitive form.
VDef_Par = Definitory verb, impersonal participle form.
VDef_Con = Definitory verb, personal conjugate form
Pron = pronoun

Definitory verb, impersonal infinitive form.
SE (Pron) VAux VDef_Inf | VAux VDef_Inf (SE | Pron) | VDef_Inf (Pron)
Example: puede definir (se | lo)
Definitory verb, impersonal participle form.
(SE VAux | Vaux{1,2}) Vdef_Par
Example: se ha definido
Definitory verb, personal conjugate form
(SE) VDef_Con
Example: se define

Table 3: Defining Verbal Patterns

In the table above auxiliary verbs (Vaux) can be personal or impersonal forms of any of the above verbs and items in brackets are optional.

With this we are ensuring that the terms that are extracted using these DVP have a defined structure that follows the terms belonging to the domain.

4 Evaluation-Analysis

For the evaluation and analysis processes that follow the proposed methodology the remaining 50% of the selected corpus was used.

Once the corpus is obtained for the evaluation. Table 4 shows some examples of computer science domain terms which are associated to the obtained basic patterns with frequency (F1,F2,...Fn) higher or equal to 80%. (Step 3 of our methodology)

Generally in the BP the precision and recall of the obtained terms from mapping with those patterns were measured. Table 5

Pattern/ Domain	Computer Science
N	computadora (computer) teclado (keyboard)
NJ	programación paralela (parallel programming) sistema operativo (operating system)
NPN	lenguaje de programación (programming language) ingeniería de software(software engineering)

Table 4: List of examples of the basic patterns in the computer science domain

Patterns	Precision (%)	Recall (%)
BP	38,23	97,43

Table 5: Precision and recall values in the BP

We notice that the values of recall for those basic patterns are very good, since most terms have been detected with these structures, however as they are general patterns they introduce much noise, causing the precision values are very low.

In the case of DVP (step 4 for our methodology), we obtain satisfactory precision values, demonstrating that if we include the BP in the DVP we can solve the problem of low precision. However, the covering values are decreasing to a 18%.

Patterns	Precision (%)	Recall (%)
DVP	98,35	18,23

Table 6: Precision and recall values in the DVP

The recall results are low because the definitory verbal patterns only recognize the terms of the corpus that are defined and they do not consider other undefined terms that belong to the domain.

Example: A **computer** *is an* equipment which is made up of a CPU and peripherals.

The PVD only extract the term computer and not the terms CPU and peripherals.

4.1 Evaluation of the Obtained Methodology in Other Domains

In order to test the applicability of the proposal methodology in other domains Agricultural Engineering, Veterinary Medicine and Agronomy were selected.

After a validation process we have proved that the terms that characterize these domains correspond to the above basic patterns. Some examples of terminology are shown in Tables 7,8 and 9. Each domain associated respectively with the patterns is also shown.

Pattern/ Domain	Agricultural Engineering
N	agrícola (agricultural)
NJ	maquinaria agrícola (agricultural machinery) producción agropecuaria(agricultural production)
NPN	procesos de poscosecha (post-harvest processes) acidez del suelo (soil acidity) rotación de cultivos (crop rotation)

Table 7: Example list of the obtained basic patterns in Agricultural Engineering domain

Pattern/ Domain	Veterinary Medicine
N	zootecnia (animal husbandry) andrología (andrology)
NJ	medicina veterinaria (veterinary medicine) andrología veterinaria (veterinary andrology)
NPN	transferencia de embriones (embryo transfer)

Table 8: Example list of the obtained basic patterns in Veterinary Medicine domain

Pattern/ Domain	Agronomy
N	Fitotecnia (plant science), hortícola (horticulture)
NJ	producción agrícola (agricultural production) sanidad vegetal (plant health)
NPN	elementos de agroecología (elements of agroecology)

Table 9: List of examples of the obtained basic patterns in Agronomy domain

Similar behavior of the computer science domain corresponded to the results of accuracy and recall in both BP and DVP in each evaluated domain. Table 10 shows the results.

Domain	Patterns	Precision (%)	Recall (%)
Agricultural Engineering	BP	36,34	96,32
	DVP	97,47	20,18
Veterinary Medicine	BP	39,65	98,24
	DVP	98,06	19,56
Agronomy	BP	35,08	96,45
	DVP	96,43	17,18

Table 10: Precision and recall values which were obtained in the domains of Agricultural Engineering, Veterinary Medicine and Agronomy

5 Conclusions and Future Work

In this article we have proposed a methodology for automatic construction of patterns for extracting domain terminology in the Spanish language; it represents a contribution of some importance to this field. The methodology was initially applied to the domain of Computer Science and then was tested in Agricultural Engineering, Veterinary Medicine and Agronomy domains, getting excellent results, showing that it can be applied in any domain of specialty curriculum documents.

In the process of evaluation we have demonstrated that if we only use the BP, we could solve the problem of recall but you know they are very general patterns therefore the problem of accuracy will be affected as well as all nouns, nouns + adjectives, etc will be extracted too.

Incorporating these BP to DVP, we would solve the problem of accuracy, but it is true that the terms of specialty are generally defined in specialized texts, most of these terms are only found in those texts where they are precisely defined, so we could only obtain the terms that are defined in each document.

We propose to use both patterns BP and the DVP due to the fact that the patterns in an extracted system of terminology are an intermediate step in the process, then each extracted system that uses them must validate a set of characteristics either language statistics or semantics that allow them to refine a list of candidates from obtained terms through patterns that were presented here.

As future works we propose to analyze how to combine both sets of patterns (BP and VDP) to obtain the best values of precision and recall. Add new patterns to extract non defined terms in the corpus belonging to the domain and then to use the presented methodology for the creation of an extracted system of terminology that is independent from the domain with the aim of generating a semantic network that can be used in several applications of natural language processing as mentioned above with extracted terms and some linguistic resources EuroWordNet (Vossen, 2001), Babelnet (Navigli, Ponzetto, 2010), DBPedia (S.Auer, 2007) and others.

References

Alarcón, Rodrigo. 2009. Extracción automática de contextos definitorios en corpus especializados. Tesis de Doctorado, Universidad Pompeu Fabra, Barcelona.

Navigli, R. & Ponzetto, S. P. 2010. Babelnet: building a very large multilingual semantic network. In proceedings of the 48th annual meeting of the Association for Computational Linguistics, ACL '10. Stroudsburg, PA, USA, 216–225.

Vossen Piek, 2001. Building a multilingual database with wordnets for several European languages. Language Resources, Language Engineering. 2001.

Sören Auer, Christian Bizer, Georgi Kobilarov, Jens Lehmann, Richard Cyganiak, and Zachary Ives, 2007. DBpedia: A Nucleus for a Web of Open Data.

Ellen Riloff. 1993. Automatically constructing a dictionary for information extraction task. In *Procceding of the Eleventh National Conference on Artificial Intelligence.*

Stephend Soderland, David Fisher, Jonathan Aseltine, and Wendy Lehnert. 1995. Crystal: Inducing a conceptual dictionary. In *Proccedings of the Fourteenth International Joint Conference on Artificial Intelligence.*

Ellen Riloff & Jay Shoen. 1995. Automatically acquiring conceptual patterns whitout and annotated corpus. In *Procceding of the Third Workshop on Very Large Corpora,* pages 148-161.

Scott B Huffman. 1995. Learning information extraction patterns from examples. In *IJCAI-95 Workshop on New Approaches to Learning for NLP.*

Neus Catalá & Núria Castell. 1997. Construcción automática de diccionarios de patrones de extracción de información.

Dubuc, R. & Lauriston, A. 1997. "Terms and Contexts". In *Handbook of Terminology Management.* Volume 1. Wright, S.E. and Budin, G. (eds). Amsterdam/Philadelphia: John Benjamins Publishing Company, 80-87.

De Bessé, Bruno. 1991. Le Contexte Terminographique. *Meta* 26(1):111-120.

Auger, Alain. 1997. Repérage des énoncé d'intérêt définitoire dans les bases de données textuelles. Tesis de doctorado, Neuchâtel, Universidad de Neuchâtel.

Pearson, Jennifer. 1998. *Terms in Context*, Philadelphia, John Benjamins.

Meyer, Ingrid. 2001. Extracting a knowledgerich contexts for terminography: A conceptual and methodological framework. In *Recent Advances in Computational Terminology,* edited by Bourigault, D.; Jaquemin, C. & L'Homme, M.C. Philadelphia: John Benjamins.

Alarcón, R. & Sierra, G. 2003. El rol de las predicaciones verbales en la extracción automática de conceptos, Estudios de Lingüística Aplicada 38, México DF, Universidad Nacional Autónoma de México-Centro de Enseñanza en Lenguas Extranjeras, pp. 129-144.

Sierra, Gerardo. 2009. Extracción de contextos definitorios en textos de especialidad a partir del reconocimiento de patrones lingüísticos. Universidad Nacional Autónoma de México.

Hassan Saneifar, Stephane Bonniol, Anne Laurent, Pascal Poncelet and Mathieu Roche, 2009. Terminology Extraction from Log Files.

Gerardo Sierra, Alfonso Medina, Rodrigo Alarcón, César A. Aguilar, 2006. Towards the Extraction of Conceptual Information from Corpora.

A Procedural Definition of Multi-word Lexical Units

Marek Maziarz
Wrocław University of Technology, Wrocław, Poland
mawroc@gmail.com

Stan Szpakowicz
University of Ottawa, Ottawa, Ontario, Canada
szpak@eecs.uottawa.ca

Maciej Piasecki
Wrocław University of Technology, Wrocław, Poland
maciej.piasecki@pwr.wroc.pl

Abstract

Multi-word expressions evade a closed definition. Linguists and computational linguists rely on intuition or build lists of MWE types; while practical, that is scientifically and aesthetically unsatisfying. Without presuming to solve a daunting theoretical problem, we propose a decision procedure which steers a lexicographer toward acceptance or rejection of an N-gram as a lexical unit: a decision tree classifies N-grams as MWE or not MWE. It will succeed if it agrees with the native speakers' judgment. We need a small, linguistically credible set of features, to contend with the multiplicity of adequate trees. Decision tree induction works with a fixed set of annotated classification examples, but the lexical material for MWE recognition is too large to make annotation feasible. We rely on small-scale statistically significant sampling, and on intuition. Of a few decision trees produced by informed trial and error, we select one we consider best in our circumstances. That tree, deployed in a large-scale wordnet construction project, allowed us to gather dependable statistics on its usefulness in lexicographers' work. Our goal: systematic expansion of a wordnet by tens of thousands of MWEs in a manner as free of personal biases as possible.

1 Motivation

Multi-word expressions (MWEs) are present in almost every lexical resource. Their recognition can facilitate many natural language engineering tasks: information extraction, automated indexing, question answering and machine translation, to name a few. The unwavering interest in MWEs contends with the vagueness of the notion itself. There are too many, and too divergent, descriptions of just what an MWE is. Computational linguists have sought – with mixed success – a clear, "closed-formula" definition. It turns out that not only is the term "multi-word expression" not visible in linguistic literature, but that there also is no consensus on fixed phraseological expressions, non-compositional expressions, idiomatic expressions, lexicalised expressions, collocations *etc.* Most sources in traditional and computational linguistics alike seem to make do with a list of types of lexical connections in lieu of a definition. That may be practical, but it is neither scientifically nor aesthetically satisfying.

Piasecki et al. (2009) and Maziarz et al. (2013) present plWordNet, a very large wordnet and a comprehensive lexical resource for Polish. It describes most of Polish single-word lexical units and many multi-word expressions, but the coverage of the latter must increase significantly. Before that has happened, one needs to decide what *are* MWEs which merit inclusion in plWordNet, and how to make a group of lexicographers apply the definition consistently when they work on wordnet expansion.

We aim to develop a decision procedure which steers a lexicographer toward unequivocal acceptance or rejection of an N-gram as a unit in the lexical system of the language at hand. Just like a formal grammar sets precise boundaries to include things intuitively ungrammatical and exclude things intuitively grammatical, an MWE decision procedure cannot be perfect. It will be a success if it agrees to a high degree with the

Proceedings of Recent Advances in Natural Language Processing, pages 427–435,
Hissar, Bulgaria, Sep 7–9 2015.

native speakers' judgment. We do not presume to offer a solution to a theoretical problem of a clearly daunting magnitude, but we do propose a kind of practical solution which appears to work in the development of plWordNet, and which can be adapted to other languages and resources.[1]

2 An Intuitive Definition of Multi-word Lexical Unit

There is no commonly accepted definition of multi-word lexical units (MWLUs) (Granger and Paquot, 2008, p. 31). Many characteristics have been proposed as distinguishing MWLUs from regular, productive expressions in natural languages (Zgusta, 1971). Let us note two interwoven perspectives: lexicalisation and restrictedness. The former fits well the goal of building a dictionary (wordnets *are* dictionaries, among other things). An MWLU is a unit of the lexical system, stored in what is often called a *mental lexicon* (Nooteboom, 2011, p. 3).[2]

The restrictedness perspective emphasises restrictions on an MWLU's syntactic structure, meaning and use. A variety of restrictedness criteria have been proposed (Zgusta, 1971). The most frequently invoked one is semantic non-compositionality (Malmkjær, 1991, p. 291).[3] Idioms are par excellence non-compositional, and semantically the most restricted, but there are many other less pronounced cases. Restrictedness can be only considered on a continuous scale, where natural characteristic points – breaks between classes – are hard to come by.[4]

We aim to define MWLU in the spirit of lexicalisation by using means (linguistic tests) developed according to restrictedness. We will favour criteria more constrictive, and easier to work with, than complex notion of semantic non-compositionality (Svensson, 2008).

From our point of view, then, a multi-word lexical unit is fundamentally

> an expression built from more than one word, associated with a definite meaning somehow stored in one's mental lexicon and immediately retrieved from memory as a whole.

As a result, an MWLU is intuitively perceived by lexicographers as worth including in a dictionary.

Such an intuitive definition is hopelessly impractical, so, for the needs of the lexical resource building practice, we have also formulated an operational definition which takes the form of a combination of criteria implemented as linguistic tests. The criteria are meant to be applied to a MWLU candidate in appropriate, pre-defined sequences. The following sections will introduce both the criteria and the way of combining them.

3 Evaluating the Quality of the Intuitive Definition

We gave the intuitive definition (ID) from section 2, and a set of 129 monosemous word combinations, to 14 linguists who work on plWordNet. The composition of the set, collected by hand, was motivated by a few sources: Polish phraseology publications, *e.g.,* (Lewicki, 2003; Nowakowska, 2005; Müldner-Nieckowski, 2007), and a general dictionary (Dubisz, 2006). We balanced it so as to represent various stages of lexicality. The subjects answered *Yes*, *Don't know* or *No* when asked if a given *stimulus* – word combination – was a lexical unit. The 14 answers for each word combination were mapped into numbers (*Yes* $\rightarrow$ 1, *Don't know* $\rightarrow$ 0, *No* $\rightarrow$ -1) and then summed up.

Figure 1 shows that some word combinations achieved the maximum score of 14 (*e.g., szkoła podstawowa* 'primary school'), and some the minimum of -14 (*e.g., pies Marka* 'Mark's dog'). The intermediate possibilities include *mały ekran* 'the small screen = TV', *samolot transportowy* 'a freight plane' and *zjawisko językowe* 'linguistic phenomenon', all scoring at 0. The distribution is clearly not normal.

Consider a linguist's choices as they arise from probability distribution. The Central Limit Theorem says that if independent random variables X_i, $i = 1, 2, \ldots$ have the same distribution, finite mean and variance, then the sum $X_1 + X_2 +$

[1] We believe that it is unique to rely on machine learning algorithms and to use Cohen's κ to test the whole procedure on many subjects. That is why there is no related-work section in this paper. Müldner-Nieckowski (2003) arranged certain criteria into one procedure, but his proposal differed in several ways: (1) he based the procedure only on his knowledge and intuition, (2) he applied points to a candidate MWE, then a score was calculated and the final decision made according to an arbitrary threshold, (3) he proposed no tests of decision consistency between many people.

[2] «The basic prerequisite for according lemma status to a multi-word items is that it has undergone some kind of lexicalisation, *i.e.,* that it has been stored in our mental lexicon as a unit.'» (Svensén, 2009, pp. 102-3).

[3] The meaning of non-compositional MWLU cannot be reproduced from the meaning of its parts (Granger and Paquot, 2008, p. 31).

[4] «It is impossible to establish a sharp boundary between free combinations and set ones. It can be shown that there are different degrees of 'setness'.» (Zgusta, 1971, p. 154).

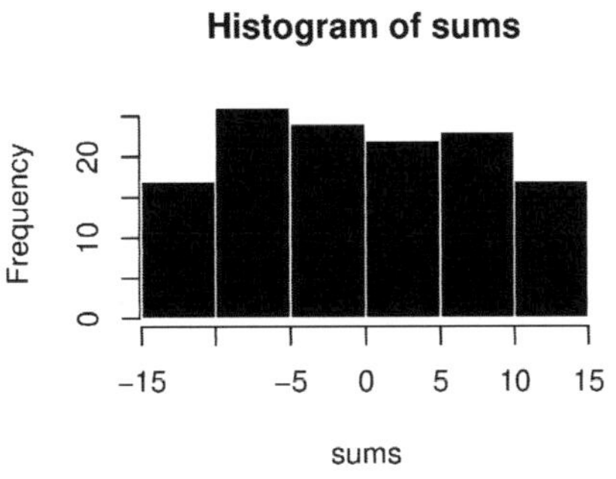

Figure 1: A histogram of summed decisions of 14 linguists for 129 word combinations, in groups of five. The Shapiro-Wilk test shows that the distribution differs from the normal distribution (W = 0.9605, p-value = 0.0008472).

... converges to normal distribution N (Meester, 2008, p. 179). The empirical distribution of $X_1 + \ldots + X_{14}$ shown in Figure 1 obviously is not normal, which leads us to the finding that, although independently, linguists reacted similarly to the same word combination stimuli.

It seems that linguists have an *intuition* on the lexicality of multi-word combinations. What many of the subjects share is perhaps the same, or quite similar, mental lexicon. But is this intuition consistent from one subject to another?

The histogram in Figure 1 suggests that many word combinations are judged inconsistently (about 1/3 of them score close to 0). There is rather low inter-annotator agreement between pairs of subjects on this set of 129 word combinations. We assume that both -1 and 0 signal non-lexical multi-word combinations, while +1 means a lexical unit. On the overall list of 129 items, the average Cohen's κ = 0.317, a "fair" value according to Landis and Koch (1971, p. 165). In computational linguistics such a result could be rejected, because a common assumption puts the κ value which guarantees reliable results at no less than 0.8, with κ above 0.67 deemed only tolerable.[5] For phraseologists, however, a value a little over 0.3 is not surprising at all, because everyone has their own mental lexicon or intuition on lexical items (Müldner-Nieckowski, 2003). The question

[5]Reidsma and Carletta (2008) show that this rule of thumb does not always work. Sometimes lower κ makes the results reliable, sometimes even $\kappa \geq 0.8$ does not suffice. The authors recommend checking whether differences between annotators are systematic or random.

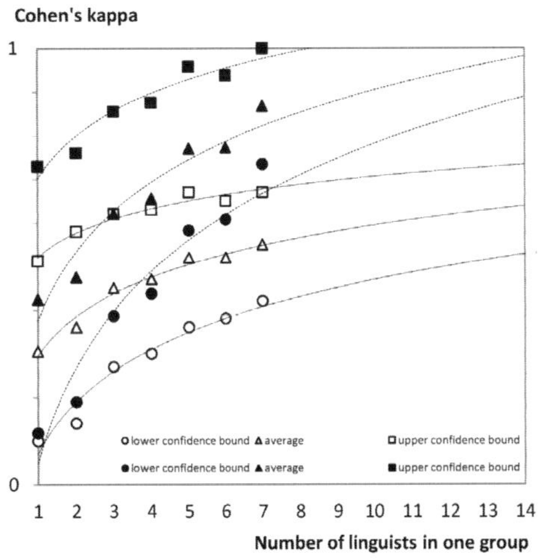

Figure 2: Cohen's κ between the summed decisions of two groups of $k = 1..7$ linguists. Confidence intervals at $\alpha = 0.05$. We start the diagram from $k = 1$, the ordinary two-subject inter-annotator agreement (one linguist per group). White figures stand for all word combinations, black figures – for word combinations with certain status: $\left|\sum_{i=1}^{14} X_i\right| > 3$.

now arises whether these lexicons are comparable, and how to achieve better κ values.

It is an open question whether averaging the independent judgments of two or more subjects increases κ. To seek an answer, we gathered the answers of 14 linguists and averaged their decisions within two independent groups. Given a matrix of judgments with 129 rows (word combinations) and 14 columns (linguists), we sampled $2k$ columns without repetition, k going into group A and k into group B, k = 1..7. Next, we sampled 129 rows with repetition for all $2k$ linguists, summed up group A and group B separately. A positive sum made the word combination an LU, a non-negative sum – not an LU. Cohen's κ was calculated for groups A and B as if they were individual annotators. This sampling was repeated 10,000 times. For a 95% simple percentile confidence interval, we took the values #250 and #9751 (DiCiccio and Efron, 1996; DiCiccio and Romano, 1988; Artstein and Poesio, 2008). The lower and upper confidence bounds appear in Figure 2 (white figures, dotted lines).

It is noticeable that increasing k increases κ. For 7-subject virtual teams, we have a confidence interval of 0.42 to 0.67, much better, but still below the level of agreement desirable in computational linguistics. The extrapolation of confidence bounds into higher values of k via logarithmic functions ($R^2 \geq 0.95$) gives even higher κ values, CI = (0.53, 0.74) for k = 14. If the logarithmic extrapolation works for k > 14, we can say that we finally reach acceptable κ.

If we remove the least stable word combinations,[6] Cohen's κ increases a good deal, as Figure 2 (black figures, dashed lines) shows. As we can see, we get very good κ values even for teams of 5-7 people.

It is worth remarking that such increasing curves for κ would never emerge by chance. This proves that our definition mirrors linguists' intuition quite well. If we gathered many linguists, gave them the definition and asked to agree on the status of each multi-word combination, we would end up with a fairly appropriate dictionary of multi-word lexical units.

We have studied the quality of decision procedures by comparing their results with averaged decisions of 14 ($L1$-varia) or 5 ($L2$-plWN, $L3$-NAcoll) linguists (after the removal of word combinations of the least certain status, *i.e.*, $\left|\sum_{i=1}^{14} X_i\right| \leq 3$ and $\left|\sum_{i=1}^{5} X_i\right| \leq 1$ respectively.

4 Using the Intuitive Definition

Grouping linguists into teams of 14 (or more) significantly reduces inconsistencies of their decisions. Despite this advantage, it must be said that such a procedure is unacceptably labour-intensive. If we want to build a large dictionary of multi-word items, we must seek another solution.

We have decided to use the intuitive definition only to calibrate a special procedure of applying the status of lexicality or non-lexicality to virtually every given word combination. We posited four requirements for such a procedure.

- It must reflect common intuition of a team of linguists adjusting their decisions on what is and what is not lexical. (This is measured by precision, recall and F_1-score.)
- It must guarantee that linguists who follow it will work consistently. (We check this point using Cohen's κ.)
- It must agree with linguistic and phraseological knowledge about lexicality. (This condition was met up-front: our procedures build on criteria taken from phraseology literature.)
- It must not be too complicated. (That is why we tended to prefer simpler models over more complex ones. This criterion relies on the procedure designer's intuition.)

The calibration was performed on three sets of word combinations:

1. $L1$-varia – the already discussed set of 129 monosemous word combinations taken from various sources, annotated by 14 people (section 3). This set is the most universal, because of the largest annotator group but also various multi-word combination types (idioms, terms, compounds, collocations and loose word combinations).
2. $L2$-plWN – the set of 200 multi-word items randomly taken from plWordNet, annotated by 5 people. This representative sample set contains mainly multi-word lexical units but also some non-lexical ones, inherited from the "pre-theoretic" early stages of the development of plWordNet.
3. $L3$-NAcoll – the set of 200 Noun+Adjective collocations, drawn randomly from a set of 10,000 best Noun+Adjective pairs according to a point-wise mutual information algorithm (Bouma, 2009). The set was also annotated by 5 linguists. This type is the most common in plWordNet (almost 50% of multi-word lexical unit instances – see Figure 3).

After having many subjects annotate the lists, we chose a few people from each group of annotators (3 from the $L1$ group, 2 from $L2$ and 4 from $L3$) and gave them several linguistic criteria out of which we wanted to construct the final procedure. Here are the criteria, operationalised in the form of substitution tests.

- The specialist character of a word combination – specialist register and its terminological character (Zgusta, 1971, p. 144).
- Non-compositionality of a word combination – its metaphoric character (Müldner-Nieckowski, 2007, 117), hyponymy between a word combination and its syntactic head, ability to be paraphrased (Zgusta, 1971, p. 144).
- Syntactic criteria of non-separability and fixed word order (Bright, 1992, pp. 286-8),

[6] Those with the sum of 14 votes oscillating around 0. We did throw out word combinations with $\left|\sum_{i=1}^{14} X_i\right| \leq 3$.

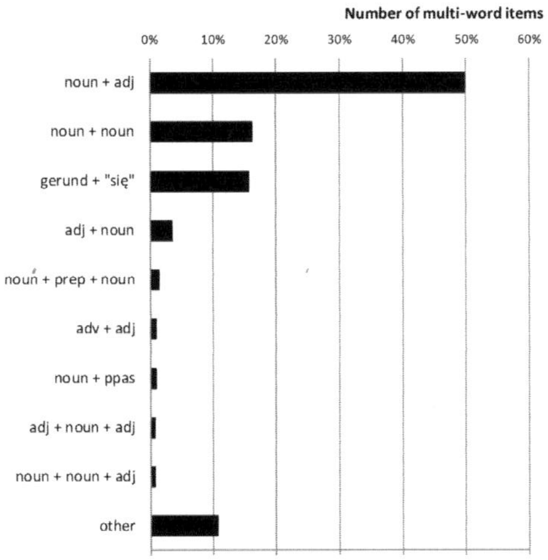

Figure 3: Multi-word items in plWordNet by syntactic pattern.

(Pike, 1967), (Müldner-Nieckowski, 2007, p. 100).

- A derivational criterion of the possibility of forming a one-word derivative from a multi-word lexical unit base (Svensén, 2009, pp. 102-103).
- An ontological criterion of a multi-word combination being a sign for a unique object type (Szober, 1967, p. 113), (Svensén, 2009, pp. 102-103).

We excluded from tests those criteria which seemed unproductive, *e.g.*, having one-word counterpart in another language.[7] Equipped with this criterion repertoire, the linguists described every multi-word combination.

The three matrices of linguists' choices now consist of independent variables (linguistic criteria) and a predicted variable (the level of lexicality measured by the sum of linguists' choices). These matrices were given to machine learning algorithms which tried to perform the best classification from linguistic criteria into the lexicality score. We worked in the Weka environment (Hall et al., 2009), and found that decision tree induction gave the best results.

5 Planting Trees

The decision trees, the embodiment of our procedure, were evaluated in accordance with the four requirements listed in section 4. We applied Cohen's κ measure for inter-annotator agreement and standard model efficiency measures. Figure 4 presents one of those trees, made by Weka's J48 decision tree induction for the set $L2$-plWN.

[7]What is lexical in one language need not be lexical in another. Otherwise, there would be no lexical gaps.

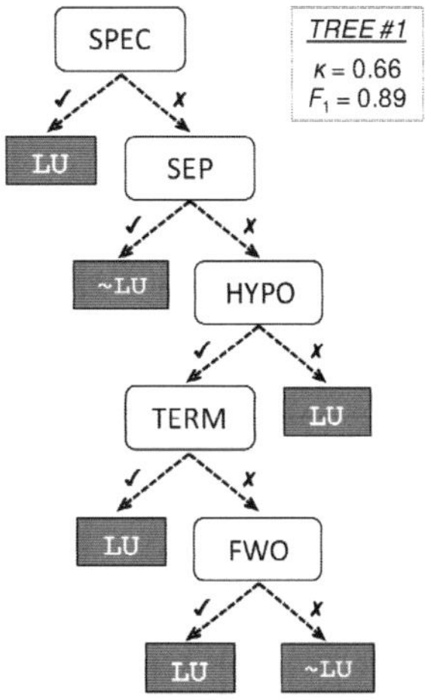

Figure 4: Tree #1 for the set $L2$-plWN. Legend: SPEC – specialist register, SEP – separability, HYPO – hyponymy between a word combination and its syntactic head, TERM – terminology, FWO – fixed word order, LU – MWLU, $\sim$LU – loose combination.

The results were initially promising: averaged $F_1 = 89\%$, $P_{LU} = 96\%$, $R_{LU} = 84\%$. It turned out fast, however, that trees adequate for LUs already in plWordNet were disappointing when applied to the more general set of $L1$-varia word combinations. Apart from acceptable Cohen's κ, we had inferior procedure performance, with F_1 = 52%. Table 1 shows more details.

Tree #2 behaved similarly: good κ and good model performance for LUs in plWordNet did not turn into a good F_1-score for the $L1$-varia set. Cohen's κ was reasonable. See Table 1 again.

We then started from a more general set $L1$, but good trees were hard to obtain. The best was tree #3, but the results were inconclusive (Table 2): very good behaviour, but κ still low. What is more important, the tree was very complicated, so it would be difficult to improve κ.

At the end of the day, we found ourselves with a couple of trees made for the $L2$ set which worked poorly on $L1$, and one tree for $L1$ which also worked on $L2$ but with moderate values of κ.

That is why we have decided to construct a de-

Procedure	tree #1			tree #2		
	$L2$-plWN, κ=0.66			$L2$-plWN, κ=0.67		
	P	R	F_1	P	R	F_1
LU	96%	84%	90%	90%	78%	83%
~LU	81%	96%	88%	80%	91%	85%
Averaged	88%	90%	**89%**	85%	84%	**84%**
	$L1$-varia, κ=0.58			$L1$-varia, κ=0.59		
	P	R	F_1	P	R	F_1
LU	65%	34%	45%	86%	21%	34%
~LU	47%	80%	59%	47%	96%	63%
Averaged	56%	57%	**52%**	66%	58%	**48%**

Table 1: Precision, recall and F_1-measure of trees #1 and #2 for the sets $L2$-plWN and $L1$-varia.

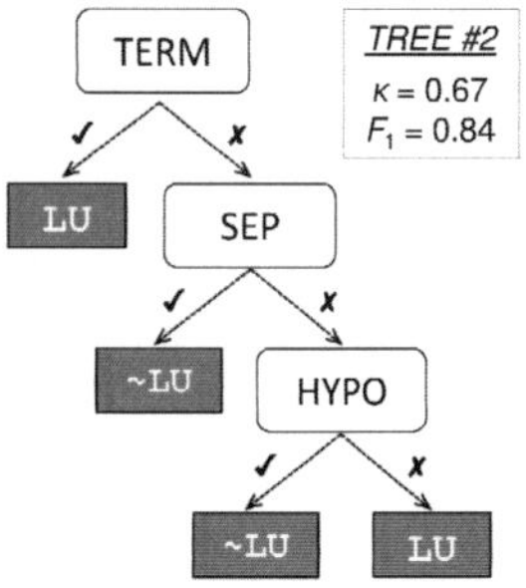

Figure 5: Tree #2 for the set $L2$-plWN. Legend: TERM - terminology, SEP – separability, HYPO – hyponymy between a word combination and its syntactic head, LU – MWLU, ~LU – loose combination.

cision tree for the most frequent structural type Noun+Adjective. Since the performance of the tree on the set $L3$-NAcoll was very good, we generalised it onto other structural types and checked it on the most general set $L1$-varia. We also inspected the κ values for the $L2$-plWN set. A brief description appears in section 6.

6 Collocations of the Noun+Adjective Type

The ability to have a paraphrase is a criterion aimed at detecting non-compositionality, similarly to criteria for a word combination being a hyponym of its own syntactic head (HYPO in Figures 4 and 5) and metaphoricity (MET in Figure 6). A word being specialist or being a term are also very close criteria. The combination of non-compositionality and terminology can be traced in all of the trees we present here.

Among many other trees, Weka gave us a lexicographically intriguing tree #4 (Figure 7). We have finally decided to use the criteria TERM and PAR in a very simple decision procedure called TP. Further experiments were run on the TP tree and noun+adjective word combinations from the $L3$-NAcoll set,[8] on all structural types from the most general set $L1$, and from plWordNet ($L2$-plWN set).

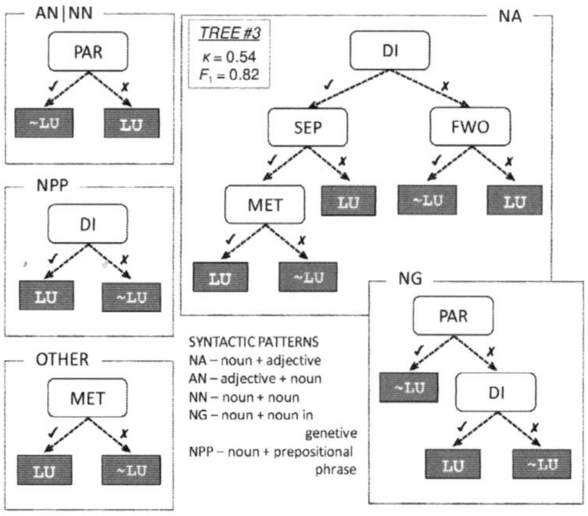

Figure 6: Tree #3 for the set $L1$-varia. Legend: DI – intuitive definition, SEP – separability, HYPO – hyponymy between a word combination and its syntactic head, MET – metaphoricity, PAR – paraphraseability, LU – MWLU, ~LU – loose combination.

tree #3			
$L1$-varia, κ=0.54	P	R	F_1
LU	93%	74%	82%
~LU	74%	93%	82%
Average	82%	82%	82%
$L2$-plWN, κ=0.49	P	R	F_1
LU	100%	92%	96%
~LU	67%	100%	81%
Average	84%	96%	88%

Table 2: Precision, recall and F_1-measure of tree #3 for the sets $L2$-plWN and $L1$-varia.

In order to improve the recall of LU recognition, we added the criteria of separability and fixedness based on the IPI PAN Corpus (IPIC) counts to the criteria for tree #5 (Figure 8); we call it TP_{IPIC}.[9] The tree is a hybrid, since it binds human-driven decision paths with the semi-automatic verification of syntactic irregularities.

[8] Recall that Noun+Adj combinations are the most frequent in plWordNet: 50%.

[9] `http://korpus.pl/`

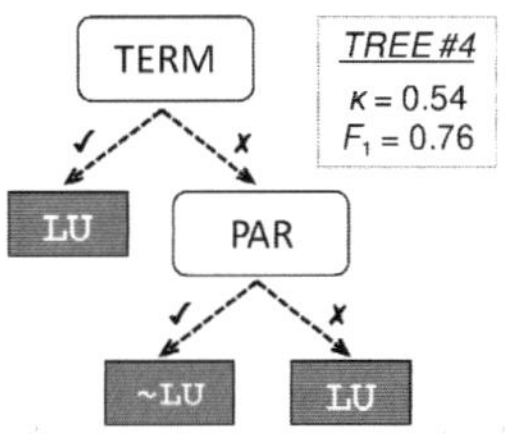

Figure 7: Tree #4 for the set $L3$-NAcoll. Legend: TERM – terminology, PAR – paraphraseability, LU – MWLU, ~LU – loose combination.

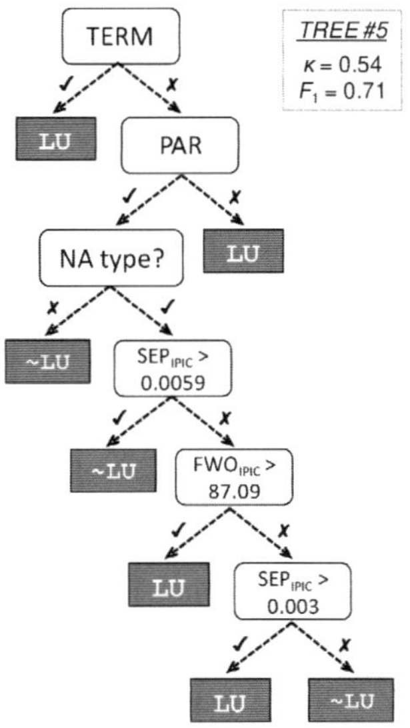

Figure 8: Tree #5 for the set $L3$-NAcoll. Legend: TERM – terminology, PAR – paraphraseability, NA type? – noun and a postposed adjective, SEP$_{IPIC}$ – separability according to corpus statistics, FWO$_{IPIC}$ – fixed word error according to corpus statistics, LU – MWLU, ~LU – loose combination.

We checked the performance of both trees on the $L3$-NAcoll set (thoroughly) and on the $L1$-varia set. For the plWordNet set ($L2$-plWN), we only have checked κ. We looked if the trees achieved high precision and recall in recognising LUs and F-score,[10] as well as sufficient Cohen's κ, and compared them to decision procedure based only on our intuitive decision (ID). In a series of experiments with 2 to 6 linguists, we found that precision and F-score of simple ID procedure was

[10]We aim to construct a wordnet, so we focus mainly on LUs, not on word combinations rejected by linguists.

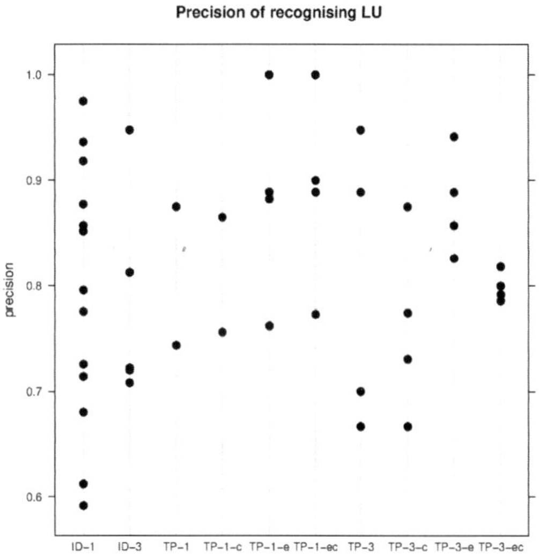

Figure 9: Precision of recognising a LU by procedures TP, TP$_{IPIC}$ and ID. Experiments for Noun+Adj word combinations on the $L3$-NAcoll set, and for all structural types on the $L1$-varia. Legend: ID – intuitive definition, TP – tree #4 procedure, 'c' – signals tree #5 procedure, digits 3 and 1 denote the $L3$ and $L1$ set, 'e' marks procedures run by experienced annotators. Precision values in experiments 'TP-1' & 'TP-3', 'TP-3-c' & 'TP-1-c', 'TP-3-e' & 'T-1-e', and 'TP-3-ec' & 'T-1-ec', are indistinguishable.

comparable to TP and TP$_{IPIC}$ (Figures 9 and 10), but the inter-annotator agreement of plWordNet editors pairs was the best for TP$_{IPIC}$ (Figure 11).

It is interesting that the κ values improved visibly when we compared experienced linguists, who have worked with the procedure for several months (scores marked with 'e') with inexperienced linguists. Please inspect in particular the similarly rising κ values in the sequence of tests 'TP1' < 'TP1c' < 'TP1e' < 'TP1ec' and 'TP3' < 'TP3c' < 'TP3e' < 'TP3ec' in Figure 11.

Good performance of our procedures on different word combination sets (NA in $L3$ set, all structural types in $L1$ and $L2$ sets), tested by many subjects (2-6, experienced and inexperienced), shows that these procedures are useful. Thus, from low-to-moderate κ, the procedures lift us to the area of acceptable κ.

7 Final Thoughts

Using procedures TP and TP$_{IPIC}$ boosts κ. Using them for a few months results in an even steeper

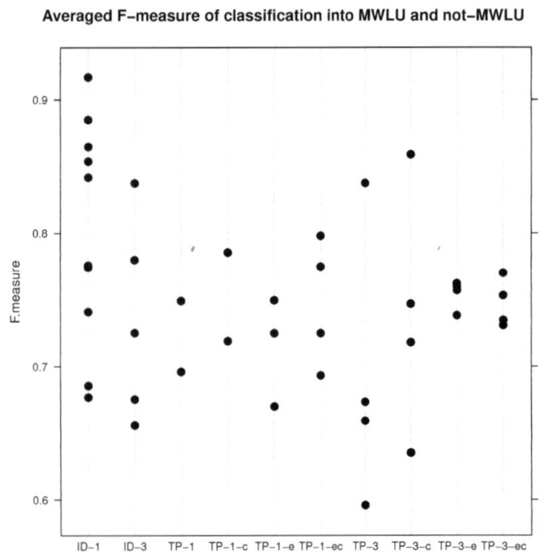

Figure 10: An averaged F-score for three procedures (TP, TP_{IPIC} and ID). Experiments performed for noun+adjective word combinations on the $L3$-NAcoll set and for all structural types on the $L1$-varia. Marks as in previous legend. Be aware of small variance in the case of experienced linguists ('e').

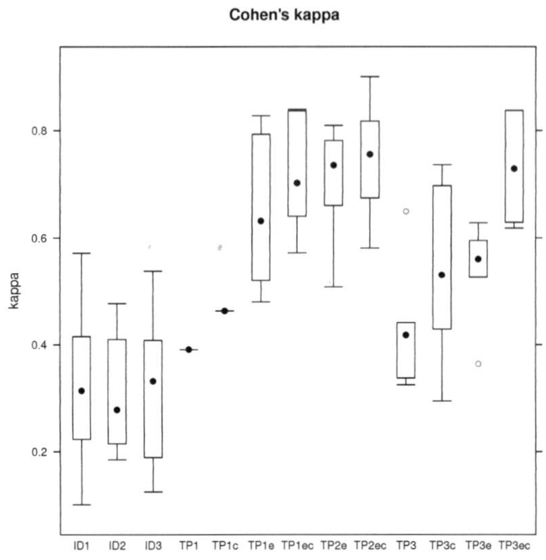

Figure 11: Boxplots of Cohen's κ for three procedures: (i) simple ID procedure performed on the sets $L3$-NAcoll ('ID3', 5 linguists), $L2$-plWN ('ID2', 4 linguists) and $L1$-varia ('ID1', 14 linguists), (ii) TP procedure ('TP1' on $L1$, 'TP3' on $L3$), (ii) TP_{IPIC} procedure, *i.e.,* TP with extensions for syntactic irregularities measured on the IPI PAN Corpus ('TP3c' ran on $L3$ and 'TP1c' checked on $L1$), e – signals TP and TP_{IPIC} performed by experienced plWordNet editors. The t-test performed for the $L3$ set found the means of ID procedure, the TP procedure used by experienced linguists ('TP3e') and TP_{IPIC} (used both by experienced and inexperienced linguists: 'TP3c', 'TP3ec') statistically different with the p-value $\approx$ 0.005. For sets $L1$-varia and $L2$-plWN we can prove statistical differences between 'ID1' and 'ID2' procedures and for experienced linguists applying procedures TP and TP_{IPIC} ('TP1e', 'TP2e', 'TP1ec' & 'TP2ec', respectively). Note a perfect fit of the boxplots of κ for the ID procedure ran on sets $L1$, $L2$, $L3$.

κ rise ('TPne' and 'TP$n$ec' in Figure 11). In the end, we get a workable procedural definition of a multi-word lexical unit.

Taking the perspective of a large wordnet as a comprehensive reference lexico-semantic resource, we divided MLUs into three classes:

- *terms* – multi-word terminological units,
- *idioms* – semantically non-compositional units,
- *compounds* – units which manifest syntactic irregularity.

The latter class is represented in plWordNet by noun+adjective pairs which show syntactic irregularity, *e.g.,* non-separability and fixed word order.

Using this procedure, nearly 30,000 word combinations were annotated in plWordNet.

Here is a simple conclusion from the work presented in this paper: one *can* leverage vague linguistics intuitions about multi-word lexical units into a constructive classification procedure. Another conclusion: while it is not the ultimate goal to use machine learning to build up a wordnet, machine learning can still be a lot of help.

Acknowledgments

Work supported by the Polish Ministry of Education and Science, Project CLARIN-PL, the European Innovative Economy Programme project POIG.01.01.02-14-013/09, and by the EU's 7FP under grant agreement No. 316097 [ENGINE].

References

Ron Artstein and Massimo Poesio. 2008. Inter-Coder Agreement for Computational Linguistics. *Computational Linguistics*, 34(4):555–596.

Gerlof Bouma. 2009. Normalized (Pointwise) Mutual Information in Collocation Extraction. In *Proceedings of the Biennial GSÇL Conference*.

William Bright, editor. 1992. *International Encyclopaedia of Linguistics*, volume II. Oxford University Press, Oxford.

Thomas J. DiCiccio and Bradley Efron. 1996. Bootstrap Confidence Intervals. *Statistical Science*, 11(3):189–212.

Thomas J. DiCiccio and Joseph P. Romano. 1988. A Review of Bootstrap Confidence Intervals. *Journal of the Royal Statistical Society. Series B (Methodological)*, 50(3):338–354.

Stanisław Dubisz. 2006. Wstęp [Introduction]. In Stanisław Dubisz, editor, *Uniwersalny słownik języka polskiego PWN. Wersja 3.0 (elektroniczna na CD) [A universal dictionary of Polish. Version 3.0 (electronic on CD)]*. Polish Scientific Publishers PWN.

Sylviane Granger and Magali Paquot. 2008. Disentangling the phraseological web. In Sylviane Granger and Fanny Meunier, editors, *Phraseology: An interdisciplinary perspective*. John Benjamins Publishing Company.

Mark Hall, Eibe Frank, Geoffrey Holmes, Bernhard Pfahringer, Peter Reutemann, and Ian H. Witten. 2009. The WEKA Data Mining Software: An Update. *SIGKDD Explorations*, 11(1):10–18.

J. Richard Landis and Gary G. Koch. 1971. The Measurement of Observer Agreement for Categorical Data. *Biometrics*, 33(1):159–174.

Andrzej Maria Lewicki. 2003. *Studia z teorii frazeologii [Research in the theory of phraseology]*. Leksem.

Kirsten Malmkjær, editor. 1991. *The Linguistics Encyclopedia*. Routledge, London & New York.

Marek Maziarz, Maciej Piasecki, and Stanisław Szpakowicz. 2013. The chicken-and-egg problem in wordnet design: synonymy, synsets and constitutive relations. *Language Resources and Evaluation*, 47(3):769–796.

Ronald Meester. 2008. *A Natural Introduction to Probability Theory*. Birkhäuser, 2nd edition.

Piotr Müldner-Nieckowski. 2003. *Wielki słownik frazeologiczny języka polskiego [Grand phraseological Polish dictionary]*. Świat Książki.

Piotr Müldner-Nieckowski. 2007. *Frazeologia poszerzona: Studium leksykograficzne [Extended phraseology: Lexicographic study]*. Oficyna Wydawnicza Volumen, Warszawa.

Sieb Nooteboom. 2011. Self-monitoring for speech errors in novel phrases and phrasal lexical items. In *Yearbook of Phraseology*. de Gruyter.

Alicja Nowakowska. 2005. *Świat roślin w polskiej frazeologii [The plant kingdom in Polish phraseology]*. Acta Universitatis Wratislaviensis 2755. Wydawnictwo Uniwersytetu Wrocławskiego.

Maciej Piasecki, Stanisław Szpakowicz, and Bartosz Broda. 2009. *A Wordnet from the Ground Up*. Wrocław University of Technology Press.

Kenneth Lee Pike. 1967. *Language in Relation to a Unified Theory of the Structure of Human Behaviour*. Mouton, The Hague.

Dennis Reidsma and Jean Carletta. 2008. Squibs: Reliability measurement without limits. *Computational Linguistics*, 34(3):319–326.

Maria Helena Svensson. 2008. A very complex criterion of fixedness: Non-compositionality. In *Phraseology: An interdisciplinary perspective*. John Benjamins Publishing Company.

Bo Svensén. 2009. *A handbook of lexicography: the theory and practice of dictionary-making*. Cambridge University Press.

Stanisław Szober. 1967. *Gramatyka języka polskiego [A grammar of Polish]*. Polish Scientific Publishers PWN.

Ladislav Zgusta. 1971. *Manual of Lexicography*. Janua Linguarum. Series Maior. de Gruyter.

Semi-Supervised Never-Ending Learning in Rhetorical Relation Identification

Erick G. Maziero[1,2], Graeme Hirst[1]
[1]Department of Computer Science
University of Toronto
Toronto, ON, M5S 3G4, Canada
erick,gh@cs.toronto.edu

Thiago A. S. Pardo[2]
[2]Department of Computer Science
University of São Paulo
São Carlos, SP, 13566-590, Brazil
taspardo@icmc.usp.br

Abstract

Some languages do not have enough labeled data to obtain good discourse parsing, specially in the relation identification step, and the additional use of unlabeled data is a plausible solution. A workflow is presented that uses a semi-supervised learning approach. Instead of only a predefined additional set of unlabeled data, texts obtained from the web are continuously added. This obtains near human perfomance (0.79) in intra sentential rhetorical relation identification. An experiment for English also shows improvement using a similar workflow.

1 Introduction

A text is composed of coherent propositions (phrases and sentences, for example) ordered and connected according to the intentions of the author of the text. This composition may be recognized and structured according to many theories and this type of information is valuable to many natural language processing applications. A process to recognize, automatically, the coherent or discursive (or also rhetorical) structure of a text is named discourse parsing (DP).

The most prominent theory in Computational Linguistics to structure the discourse of a text is the Rhetorical Structure Theory (RST) proposed by Mann and Thompson (1987). In this theory, the text is segmented into elementary discourse units (EDUs), which each contain a proposition (basic idea) of the text. The theory proposes a set of rhetorical relations that may hold between

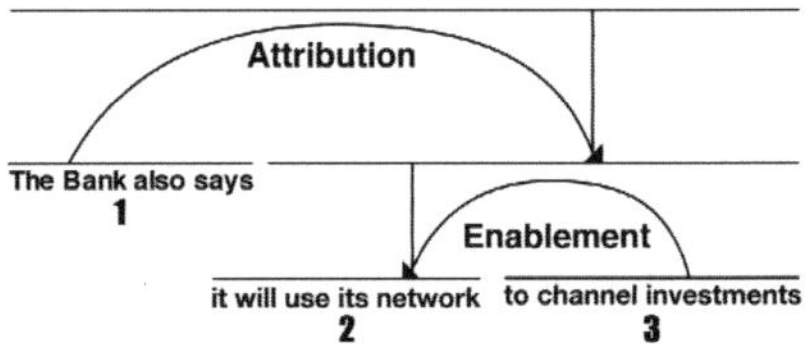

Figure 1: An example of sentence-level structure according to RST. From Soricut and Marcu (2003).

the EDUs, explicating the intentions of the author. For example, consider the sentence in Figure 1. It is segmented into three EDUs, numbered from 1 to 3. EDUs 2 and 3 are related by the relation *Enablement*, forming a new span of text, which is related to 1 by the relation *Attribution*. In each relation, EDUs can be *Nucleus* (more essential) or *Satellite* to the writer's purpose.

Many approaches have been used in DP, the majority of them using machine learning algorithms, such as probabilistic models (Soricut and Marcu, 2003), SVMs (Reitter, 2003; duVerle and Prendinger, 2009; Hernault et al., 2010; Feng and Hirst, 2012) and dynamic conditional random field (Joty et al., 2012). To obtain acceptable results, these approaches need plenty of labeled data. But even more than other levels of linguistic information, such as morphology or syntax, the annotation of discourse is an expensive task. Given this fact, what can we do when there is not enough data to perform effective learning of DP, as in languages with little annotated data?

This paper describes a methodology to overcome the problem of insufficient labeled data in the task of identifying rhetorical relations between

Proceedings of Recent Advances in Natural Language Processing, pages 436–442,
Hissar, Bulgaria, Sep 7–9 2015.

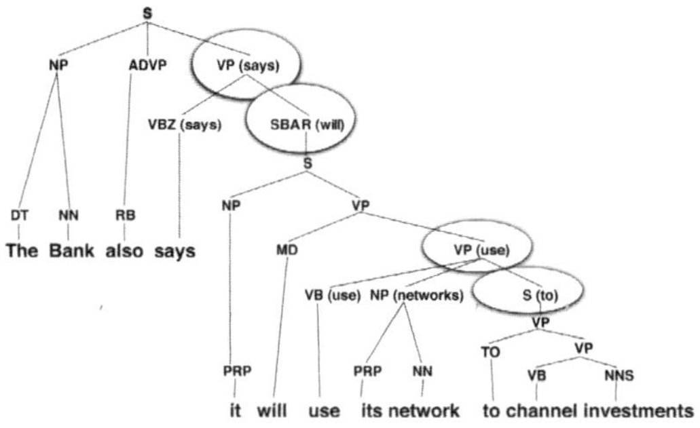

Figure 2: Lexicalized syntactic tree used by SPADE. The circles indicate the node used as the most indicative information to identify the rhetorical relation and structure.

EDUs, which is the most important step during DP. The language used in our work is Portuguese and two well-known systems of DP for English were adapted to this language. Portuguese is a language with insufficient annotated data to obtain a good discourse parser, but has all the tools to adapt some English discourse parsers. A framework of semi-supervised never-ending learning (SSNEL) (see Section 2.2 below) was created and evaluated with the adapted models. The results show that this approach improved the results to achieve near-human perfomance, even with the use of automatic tools (syntax parser and discourse segmenter).

2 Related Work

2.1 Supervised Discourse Parsing

Soricut and Marcu (2003) use two probabilistic models to perform a sentence-level analysis, one for segmentation and other to identify the relations and build the rhetorical structure. The parser is named SPADE (Sentence-level Parsing of DiscoursE) and the authors base their model on lexical and syntactic information, extracting features from a lexicalized syntactic tree. They assume that the features extracted at the jointing point of two discursive segments are the most indicative information to identify the rhetorical structure of the sentence. For example, in Figure 2, the circled nodes correspond to the most indicative cues to identify the structure and relation between each two adjacent segments.

The authors report a F-measure of 0.49 in a set of 18 RST relations. The human performance in this same task is 0.77 (measured by inter-annotation agreement). The authors, then, use the probabilistic model with manual segmentation and syntactic trees to see the impact of this information in the parsing and the model achieves 0.75.

Hernault et al. (2010) use support vector machine (SVM) classifiers to perform DP. This discourse parser is named HILDA (HIgh-Level Discourse Analyser). This work used a set of 41 rhetorical relations and achieves a F-measure of 0.48 in the step of relation identification, both intra-sentential and inter-sentential.

Feng and Hirst (2012) improve HILDA by incorporating new proposed features and some adapted from Lin et al. (2009). Another important decision was the specification of features for intra-sentential and inter-sentential relationships and the use of contextual features in the building of the rhetorical tree. Considering the approach to intra-sentential relation identification, with 18 RST relations this work achieves a macro average F-measure of 0.49 and weighted average F-measure of 0.77 in relation identification.

Joty et al. (2012) use a joint modelling approach to identify the structure and the relations at the sentence-level using DCRFs (dynamic conditional random fields) and a non-greedy bottom-up method in the construction of the rhetorical structure. The features used in this work were similar to those used by HILDA. They achieve a F-measure of 0.77, using manual segmentation, and 0.65 using automatic segmentation.

Some languages, such as Portuguese, do not have enough data to train a good DP and there is no work treating this limitation in this language. The first attempt to perform DP in Portuguese was made by Pardo and Nunes (2006), who used an approach based on lexical patterns extracted from an RST-annotated corpus of academic texts to create DiZer (Discourse analyZer). More than 740 lexical patterns were manually extracted from the corpus. A lexical pattern is composed of the discursive markers, its position in the EDU, and corresponding nuclearity. The use of lexical patterns is a unique approach for Portuguese, and achieves a F-measure of 0.625 in relation detection when evaluated in academic texts; in news texts, DiZer achieves an F-measure of 0.405.

2.2 Semi-supervised Discourse Parsing

All the above cited approaches to DP use annotated data to extract discursive knowledge and are limited to the availability of this resource, which is expensive to obtain. Specially, it is important to note that, to obtain good performance in the task more data is necessary. Semi-supervised learning (SSL) is employed in scenarios in which there is some labeled data and large availability of unlabeled data, and manual annotation is an expensive task (Zhu, 2008).

Related to the use of SSL in DP, Marcu and Echihabi (2002) used naive Bayes to train binary classifiers to distinguish between some types of relations, as *Elaboration* vs. *Cause-Explanation-Evidence*. For example, for this binary classifier, applying SSL, the accuracy increased from approximately 0.6 to 0.95 after the use of millions of new instances. Chiarcos (2012) used SSL to develop a probabilistic model mapping the occurrence of discourse markers and verbs to rhetorical relations. For Italian, Soria and Ferrari (1998) conducted work in the same direction. Sporleder and Lascarides (2005) performed similar work to Marcu and Echihabi, with similar results for a different set of relations and a more sophisticated classifier. Building on this, there is an interesting idea, known as never-ending learning (NEL) by Carlson et al. (2010), in which they apply SSL with infinite unlabeled data. The needed data is widely and freely available on the web. Their architecture runs 24 hours per day, forever, obtaining new information and performing a learning task.

With the aim of surpassing the limitation of labeled RST in Portuguese to develop a good DP, we employ SSNEL in the task by adapting the work of Soricut and Marcu (2003) and Hernault et al. (2010). This choice for SSLNEL was made considering the large and free availability of news texts on the web.

3 RST Corpora

RST-DT (RST Discourse TreeBank) (Carlson et al., 2001) is the most widely used corpus annotated with RST in English. Table 1 compares it with available Portuguese corpora labeled according to RST (these corpora will be referred to as RST-DT-PT hereafter). The corpora CSTNews (Cardoso et al., 2011), Summ-it (Collovini et al., 2007) and two-thirds of Rhetalho (Pardo and Seno, 2005) are composed of news texts, and the corpus CorpusTCC (Pardo and Nunes, 2004) and the reminder of Rhetalho are composed of scientific texts. The RST-DT contains more documents (45) and many more words (55,536) than RST-DT-PT.

Corpus	Language	Documents	Words
RST-DT-PT	PT	340	120,847
CSTNews		140	47,240
Rhetalho		50	2,903
Summ-it		50	16,704
CorpusTCC		100	53,000
RST-DT	EN	385	176,383

Table 1: Size of the RST-DT-PT and its components, and of the RST-DT.

This work focuses on the identification of rhetorical relations at the sentence level, and as is common since the work of Soricut and Marcu (2003), fine-grained relations were grouped: 29 sentence-level rhetorical relations were found and grouped into 16 groups. The imbalance of the relations is a natural characteristic in discourse and, to avoid overfitting of a learning model on the less-frequent relations, no balancing was made. The relation *Summary*, for example, occurs only 2 times, and *Elaboration* occurs 1491 times, making very difficult the identification of the *Summary* relation.

4 Adapted Models

Syntactic information is crucial in SPADE (Soricut and Marcu, 2003) and for Portuguese the parser most similar to that used by Soricut and Marcu is the LX-parser (Stanford parser trained to Portuguese (Silva et al., 2010)). After the parsing of the text by the syntactic parser, the same lexicalization procedure (Magerman, 1995) was applied and adapted according to the tagset used by LX-parser. In this adaptation, only pairs of adjacent segments at sentence-level were considered, and nuclearity was not considered, in order to avoid sparseness in the data. Training the adapted model (here called SPADE-PT) using the RST-DT-PT achieved F-measure of 0.30. The precision was 0.69, but the recall was only 0.19.

The same features used by HILDA (Hernault et al., 2010) were extracted from the pairs of adjacent segments at sentence-level and many machine learning algorithms were tested, besides the SVM, which was used in the original work. The algorithm which obtained the best F-measure was

J48, an implementation of decision trees (Quinlan, 1993). The RST-DT-PT corpora was used and the adaptation (here called of HILDA-PT) achieved an F-measure of 0.548, which is much better than that of SPADE-PT. A possible explanation is that the feature set in SPADE is composed only of syntactic tags and words. The resulting probabilistic model is sparse and many equal instances may indicate different relations (classes). However HILDA adds more features over which the classifier can work better, even when some values are absent.

Given the results of the adapted models, HILDA-PT was chosen to be incorporated into the SSNEL, explicated below.

5 Semi-supervised Never-ending Learning Workflow

Here, an adaptation of Carlson et al. (2010) self-training algorithm was used. Two different approaches to relation identification are used, that is to say, a lexical pattern set *LPS* (the relation identification module of DiZer), and a multi-class classifier *C* generated according to some machine learning algorithm. All the new instances obtained from the lexical module are used together with the more confident classifications of *C* to retrain this last. For each classification, J48 returns a confidence value used to choose the most confident classifications.

Also, there is interest in observing the behaviour of the classifier in each iteration of the semi-supervision, searching for the best F-measure it may achieve. In this way, a workflow of never-ending learning (NEL) was proposed and is presented in Figure 3. Workflow 1 is presented as an alternative visualization to the illustration in Figure 3. Continuously, a crawler gets pages from online news on the web and performs cleaning to obtain the main text (*Text*). In a first iteration, a *Segmenter* (Maziero et al., 2007) is applied to obtain the EDUs in each sentence and, for each pair of adjacent EDUs (*PairEDUs*), the C_1 classifier (C_1 initially trained with the $LabeledData_1$ from the RST-DT-PT) and the lexical pattern set *LPS* are used to identify the relations between the segments. To retrain C_1, all the new instances from the lexical pattern set *LabeledDataLPS* (as *LPS* does not provide a confidence value, all the labelled instances are

```
Data: LabeledData_1 and Text

train a classifier C_1 using LabeledData_1

while exist some Text do
    get one Text from NewsTexts
    apply Segmenter on Text to obtain PairEDUs
    Index <- 1

    forall the PairEDUs do
        apply LPS to obtain LabeledDataLPS
        apply C_Index to obtain LabeledDataC

        forall the LabeledDataC as newInstanceC do

            if confidence of newInstanceC >= 0.7 then
                LabeledDataCConfident <-
                            newInstance
            end
        end
        LabeledData_Index+1 <-
                LabeledDataLPS+
                LabeledDataCConfident
        train a new classifier C_Index+1
                using LabeledData_Index+1
        apply Monitor and obtain
                FmC_Index+1
        plot FmC_Index+1 in the graph G if

        FmC_index+1 < FmC_Index then
            discard C_Index+1
            C_Index+1 <- C_Index
        end
    end
end
```

Workflow 1: Workflow of the SSNEL using two models to identify rhetorical relations between each *PairEDUs*.

used in the semi-supervision) and the classifications *LabeledDataC* with confidence greater than 0.7 by C_1 are joined with $LabeledData_1$ to obtain $LabeledData_2$ ($LabeledData_2 = LabeledDataLPS + LabeledDataC$). After the retraining, a *Monitor* verifies the new F-measure of C_2 (FmC_2, obtained using 10-fold cross validation) and, if it decreased compared with the F-measure of C_1 (FmC_1), C_2 is discarded and, for the next iteration, C_1 will continue to be used. If FmC_1 did not decrease, C_2 will be used in the next iteration. *Monitor* also plots a graph *G* to present the behaviour of *FmC* during SSNEL. This process continues iteratively.

It is important to note that, given the small size of the training data, we opted to use 10-fold cross-validation during the training and testing of the

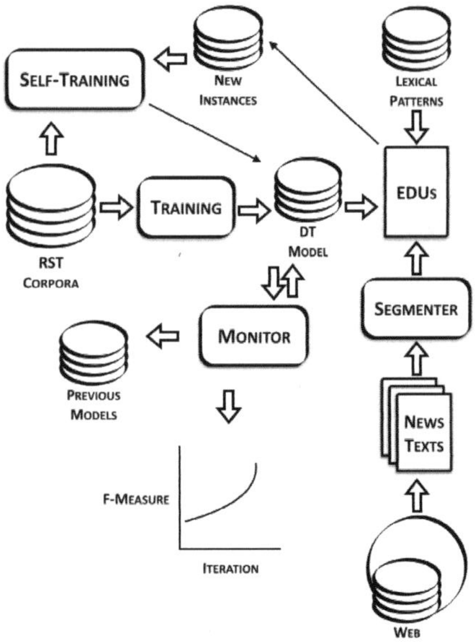

Figure 3: SSNEL workflow.

classifiers, instead of separating the data into three sets (training, development, and test). The total number of instances was 6163 and some relations, such as *Restatement* with 28 instances, would have few relations when split into three sets.

During the semi-supervision of SPADE-PT, the model of relation identification was incrementally obtained at each iteration, since the addition of a new instance only modifies the probabilities of the instances already present in the model. If the instance is new, it is added to the model and the probabilities are adjusted. However, in the semi-supervision of the HILDA-PT, the algorithm J48 does not allow incremental learning. There are some implementations of incremental decision trees, but the resulting models are not as accurate as J48 because they work with an incomplete set of training instances. As we want the best F-measure for relation identification, the algorithm J48 was employed, even though it is not an incremental learning.

Another important decision is to monitor the concept-drift (CD) (Klinkenberg, 2004) during the SSNEL, given that a concept may change over time. In this work, CD refers to different sources and topics to which the classifier is applied. To treat CD, the algorithm may detect the evolution of the concept and be able to modify the model to accommodate the concept, avoiding the decrease

Method	F-measure		Instances
	Initial	Final	
DiZer	0.22	-	-
Elaboration Relation	0.26	-	-
SPADE-PT	0.30	0.34	1,592
HILDA-PT	0.55	**0.79**	21,740

Table 2: Comparison of results considering the two adapted models (SPADE-PT and HILDA-PT) with two baselines (Elaboration Relation and DiZer).

in the performance of the model being generated. One technique to monitor the CD is *statistical process control* (SPC) (Gama et al., 2004). This technique constantly analyses the error during the learning: if the F-measure drops, it may indicate some changes in the concept and the model needs to be modified. In the SSNEL workflow, this is treated by the *Monitor*, which discards new instances used to retrain the model if its F-measure decreases, ensuring that the learned model always acquires correct new learning.

6 Experiments

Considering Workflow 1, the two adapted models were instantiated as *C*, and many iterations were executed. After 1,640 iterations and the addition of 1,592 new training instances, the F-measure of SPADE-PT increased only 0.05. HILDA-PT, after 180 iterations and with the addition of 21,740 new instances, increased 0.24, achieving 0.79 using automatic segmentation. Table 2 presents a summary of the results. As explained in Section 4, the features used by SPADE-PT lead to a sparse model (when there is not enough initial data), and this is the reason that, during 1,640 iterations, only 1,592 new instances were acquired, compared to the number of iterations and new instances during the experiment with HILDA-PT.

To evaluate the parsers, two baselines were considered. One of them (Elaboration Relation) is the labeling of all the instances with the most frequent relation in the corpus (*Elaboration*); the second is the use of *LPS* (DiZer) applied to all *PairEDUs* in RST-DT-PT. SPADE-PT, even after many iterations in SSNEL, performed lower than the two baselines. HILDA-PT, since even before the use of SSNEL, performed better than the baselines.

The class composed of relations *Interpretation*, *Evaluation* and *Conclusion* had 40 labeled examples, initially. After the iterations, its F-measure increased from 0.054 to 0.916. Except for *Comparison* and *Summary*, all the other relations increased their F-measures. This reinforces the results obtained by Marcu and Echihabi (2002), which increased (the result of a binary classifier to distinguish between two relations) from 0.6 to 0.95 after the use of millions of new instances. The relation *Summary*, however, with only 2 labeled instances, continued its zero F-measure.

SSNEL of HILDA-PT was executed for 23 days. Documents used had on average 28 sentences and 749 words. The choice of only 10 documents per batch is to have a fine-grained control over the new instances, given that if a new classifier decreases the F-measure, it is discarded. Out of 70 generated classifiers were discarded.

As the use of 10-fold cross-validation in the SSNEL may lead to some overfitting on the data which was already classified in the workflow, two other SSNEL experiments were performed, for English and Portuguese, with separated training and test sets. These experiments had less time to run, and, in order to determine whether the improvements during the SSNEL were statistically significant, paired T-tests were employed to compare initial classifier and the best classifier obtained during iterations in the workflow. The test shown improvements (at the level $p < .1$), even though they are low for both experiments. Probably, with many more iterations the results would be better. Table 3 shows the improvements in the accuracy during the SSNEL, the number of iterations, and the number of new instances incorporated in the training data. Although a direct comparison between the experiments is not fair, due to different corpora, the improvements show that this workflow is promising to increase the accuracy of classifiers with unlabeled data.

The experiment with SSNEL for English was realized in order to see the results that could be obtained when large annotated corpora are available. In the SSNEL for English, only decision-tree classifiers were used to classify new instances. For Portuguese, a symbolic model (lexical patterns) was also used together with the classifiers.

The improved results presented in Table 2 and 3 are very different due to differing evaluation strategies. Using separated test data, we tried to avoid possible overfitting on training data, but the size of test data may not lead to a fair evaluation

Experiment	Accuracy		Instances	Iterations
	Initial	Final		
Portuguese	0.531	**0.556**	1,247	200
English	0.635	**0.645**	565	25

Table 3: Results of SSNEL applied to Portuguese and English languages using training and test sets.

of some relations with very few examples.

We do not compare our results to those of Soricut and Marcu (2003) or Joty et al. (2012), since HILDA-PT used different corpora (RST-DT-PT instead of RST-DT), and some reported results are for the complete DP. However, our results show the potential of the SSNEL workflow when not enough labeled data is available for supervised learning, since the same approach for relation identification of Hernault et al. (2010) was used in HILDA-PT and 0.531 was initially obtained. These results constitute the state of art for rhetorical relation identification for Portuguese and it is believed that with more time (iterations in SSNEL), the results may increase.

7 Conclusion

Even though the results obtained in the SSNEL were satisfactory, new features will be added to the HILDA-PT, for example, types of discourse signals, beyond the discourse markers (Taboada and Das, 2013), and the use of semantic information, as synonymity. Also, given that the number of features will increase, feature selection may be applied to select the most informative features in each iteration of the SSNEL.

Since this work treats only rhetorical relations, without nuclearity, a classifier of nuclearity was trained (with the same features of HILDA-PT) and obtained a F-score of 0.86. As done by Feng and Hirst (2012), a better set of features will be selected to identify relations between inter-sentential spans. A procedure similar to tree building used by Feng and Hirst (2012) will be employed in the future DP.

Acknowledgments

This work was financially supported by grant♯2014/11632-0, São Paulo Research Foundation (FAPESP), the Natural Sciences and Engineering Research Council of Canada and by the University of Toronto.

References

Paula C.F. Cardoso, Erick G. Maziero, Maria L.C. Jorge, Eloize M.R. Seno, Ariani Di Felippo, Lucia H.M. Rino, Maria G.V. Nunes, and Thiago A.S. Pardo. 2011. CST-News: A discourse-annotated corpus for single and multi-document summarization of news texts in Brazilian Portuguese. In *Proceedings of the 3rd RST Brazilian Meeting*, pages 85–105. Cuiaba/Brazil.

Andrew Carlson, Justin Betteridge, Bryan Kisiel, Burr Settles, Estevam R. Hruschka, and Tom M. Mitchell. 2010. Toward an architecture for never-ending language learning. In *Proceedings of Association for the Advancement of Artificial Intelligence*, volume 5, pages 1306–1313.

Lynn Carlson, Daniel Marcu, and Mary E. Okurowski. 2001. Building a discourse-tagged corpus in the framework of Rhetorical Structure Theory. In *Proceedings of Second SIGdial Workshop on Discourse and Dialogue*, volume 16, pages 1–10.

Christian Chiarcos. 2012. Towards the unsupervised acquisition of discourse relations. In *Proceedings of 50th Annual Meeting of the Association for Computational Linguistics*, pages 213–217.

Sandra Collovini, Thiago I. Carbonel, Jorge C.B. Coelho, Juliana T. Fuchs, and Renata Vieira. 2007. Summ-it: um corpus anotado com informações discursivas visando à sumarização automática. *Congresso Nacional da SBC*, pages 1605–1614.

David A. duVerle and Helmut Prendinger. 2009. A novel discourse parser based on support vector machine classification. In *Proceedings of Joint Conference of the 47th Annual Meeting of the ACL and the 4th International Joint Conference on Natural Language Processing of the AFNLP*, volume 2, pages 665–673.

Vanessa W. Feng and Graeme Hirst. 2012. Text-level discourse parsing with rich linguistic features. In *Proceedings of 50th Annual Meeting of the Association for Computational Linguistics*, volume 1, pages 60–68.

João Gama, Pedro Medas, Gladys Castillo, and Pedro Rodrigues. 2004. Learning with drift detection. In *Proceedings of 17th Brazilian symp. on Artif. Intell. SBIA*, pages 286–295.

Hugo Hernault, Helmut Prendinger, David A. duVerle, and Mitsuru Ishizuka. 2010. HILDA: A discourse parser using support vector machine classification. *Dialogue and Discourse*, 1(3):1–33.

Shafiq Joty, Giuseppe Carenini, and Raymon T. Ng. 2012. A novel discriminative framework for sentence-level discourse analysis. In *Proceedings of the 2012 Joint Conference on Empirical Methods in Natural Language Processing and Computational Natural Language Learning*, EMNLP-CoNLL '12, pages 904–915. Association for Computational Linguistics, Stroudsburg, PA, USA.

Ralf Klinkenberg. 2004. Learning drifting concepts: Example selection vs. example weighting. *Intelligent Data Analysis*, 8(3):281–300.

Ziheng Lin, Min-Yen Kan, and Hwee Tou Ng. 2009. Recognizing implicit discourse relations in the Penn Discourse Treebank. In *Proceedings of 2009 Conference on Empirical Methods in Natural Language Processing*, volume 1, pages 343–351.

David M. Magerman. 1995. Statistical decision-tree models for parsing. In *Proceedings of Association for Computational Llinguistics 1995*, pages 276–283. Cambridge, Massachusetts.

William C. Mann and Sandra A. Thompson. 1987. Rhetorical Structure Theory: Toward a functional theory of text organization. *Text*, 8(3):243–281.

Daniel Marcu and Abdessamad Echihabi. 2002. An unsupervised approach to recognizing discourse relations. In *Proceedings of 40th Annual Meeting of the Association for Computational Linguistics*, pages 368–375.

Erick G. Maziero, Thiago A.S. Pardo, and Maria G.V. Nunes. 2007. Identificação automática de segmentos discursivos: o uso do parser Palavras. Technical Report 305, University of Sao Paulo.

Thiago A.S. Pardo and Maria G.V. Nunes. 2004. Relações retóricas e seus marcadores superficiais: Análise de um corpus de textos científicos em Português do Brasil. Technical Report 231, University of Sao Paulo.

Thiago A.S. Pardo and Maria G.V. Nunes. 2006. Review and evaluation of DiZer: An automatic discourse analyzer for Brazilian Portuguese. In *Proceedings of 7th Workshop on Computational Processing of Written and Spoken Portuguese - PROPOR (Lecture Notes in Computer Science 3960)*, pages 180–189.

Thiago A.S. Pardo and Eloize R.M. Seno. 2005. Rhetalho: um corpus de referência anotado retoricamente. In *Proceedings of V Encontro de Corpora*.

J. Ross Quinlan. 1993. *C4.5: Programs for Machine Learning*. Morgan Kaufmann Publishers Inc., San Francisco, CA, USA.

David Reitter. 2003. Simple signals for complex rhetorics: On rhetorical analysis with rich-feature support vector models.

Joao Silva, António Branco, Sérgio Castro, and Reis Reis. 2010. Out-of-the-box robust parsing of portuguese. In *Proceedings of 9th International Conference on the Computational Processing of Portuguese*, PROPOR'10, pages 75–85. Springer-Verlag, Berlin, Heidelberg.

Claudia Soria and Giacomo Ferrari. 1998. Lexical marking of discourse relations - some experimental findings. In *Proceedings of ACL-98 Workshop on Discourse Relations and Discourse Markers*, pages 36–42.

Radu Soricut and Daniel Marcu. 2003. Sentence level discourse parsing using syntactic and lexical information. In *Proceedings of the 2003 Conference of the North American Chapter of the Association for Computational Linguistics on Human Language Technology*, volume 1, pages 149–156.

Caroline Sporleder and Alex Lascarides. 2005. Exploiting linguistic cues to classify rhetorical relations. In *Proceedings of Recent Advances in Natural Language Processing (RANLP-05)*, pages 157–166. Bulgaria.

Maite Taboada and Debopam Das. 2013. Annotation upon annotation: Adding signalling information to a corpus of discourse relations. *Dialogue and Discourse*, 4(2):249–281.

Xiaojin Zhu. 2008. Semi-supervised learning literature survey. Technical Report 1530, University of Wisconsin-Madison.

Exposing Paid Opinion Manipulation Trolls

Todor Mihaylov, Ivan Koychev
FMI
Sofia University
tbmihailov@gmail.com
koychev@fmi.uni-sofia.bg

Georgi D. Georgiev
Ontotext AD
Sofia, Bulgaria
georgiev@ontotext.com

Preslav Nakov
Qatar Computing Research Institute
HBKU, Qatar
pnakov@qf.org.qa

Abstract

Recently, Web forums have been invaded by *opinion manipulation trolls*. Some trolls try to influence the other users driven by their own convictions, while in other cases they can be organized and paid, e.g., by a political party or a PR agency that gives them specific instructions what to write. Finding paid trolls automatically using machine learning is a hard task, as there is no enough training data to train a classifier; yet some test data is possible to obtain, as these trolls are sometimes caught and widely exposed. In this paper, we solve the training data problem by assuming that a user who is called a *troll* by several different people is likely to be such, and one who has never been called a troll is unlikely to be such. We compare the profiles of (*i*) paid trolls vs. (*ii*) "mentioned" trolls vs. (*iii*) non-trolls, and we further show that a classifier trained to distinguish (*ii*) from (*iii*) does quite well also at telling apart (*i*) from (*iii*).

1 Introduction

During the 2013-2014 Bulgarian protests against the Oresharski cabinet, social networks and news community forums became the main "battle grounds" between supporters and opponents of the government. In that period, there was notable censorship in the media, and many people who lived outside the capital did not really know what was actually happening. Moreover, there was a very notable presence of government supporters in Web forums. In series of leaked documents in the independent Bulgarian media Bivol,[1] it was alleged that the ruling Socialist party was paying Internet trolls with EU Parliament money.

[1] https://bivol.bg/en/category/b-files-en/b-files-trolls-en

The Bivol's leaked documents revealed for the first time such a practice by a political party despite the problem with opinion manipulation being generally notable across Eastern Europe. The reputation management documents described the following services: *"Monthly posting online of 250 comments by virtual users with varied, typical and evolving profiles from different (non-recurring) IP addresses to inform, promote, balance or counteract. The intensity of the provided online presence will be adequately distributed and will correspond to the political situation in the country."*

The practice of using Internet trolls for opinion manipulation has been reality since the rise of Internet and community forums. It has been shown that user opinions about products, companies and politics can be influenced by opinions posted by other online users (Dellarocas, 2006). This makes it easy for companies and political parties to gain popularity by paying for "reputation management" to people that write in discussion forums and social networks fake opinions from fake profiles. Yet, over time, forum users developed sensitivity about trolls, and started publicly exposing them.

2 Related Work

A popular way to manipulate public opinion in Internet is by making controversial posts on a specific topic that aim to win the argument at any cost, usually accompanied by untruthful and deceptive information. The problem of deceptive opinion spam is studied in (Ott et al., 2011), where the authors integrated work from both psychology and computational linguistics trying to detect fake opinions that were written to sound authentic. Malicious troll users posting misinformation posts have also been studied using graph-based approaches over signed social networks (Ortega et al., 2012; Kumar et al., 2014). A related problem is that of trustworthiness of statements on the Web (Rowe and Butters, 2009).

Proceedings of Recent Advances in Natural Language Processing, pages 443–450,
Hissar, Bulgaria, Sep 7–9 2015.

Troll detection and offensive language use are understudied problems (Xu and Zhu, 2010). They have been addressed using analysis of the semantics and the sentiment in posts (Cambria et al., 2010); there have been also studies of general troll behavior (Herring et al., 2002; Buckels et al., 2014). Another approach has been to use lexico-syntactic features about user's writing style, structure, and cyber-bullying content (Chen et al., 2012); cyber-bullying was detected using user profile and post metadata (Galn-Garca et al., 2014), and sentiment analysis (Xu et al., 2012).

A related problem is that of Web spam detection, usually addressed as text classification (Sebastiani, 2002), e.g., using spam keyword spotting (Dave et al., 2003), lexical affinity of arbitrary words to spam content (Hu and Liu, 2004), frequency of punctuation and word co-occurrence (Li et al., 2006). See (Castillo and Davison, 2011) for an overview on adversarial Web search.

3 Data

We crawled the largest media community forum in Bulgaria, that of Dnevnik.bg[2], a daily newspaper that requires users to be signed in to comment (all in Bulgarian), which makes it easy to track them. The platform allows users to comment on news, to reply to other users' comments and to vote on them with thumbs up/down. Each publication has a category, a subcategory, and a list of manually selected tags (keywords).

We crawled the *Bulgaria*, *Europe*, and *World* categories for the period 01-Jan-2013 to 01-Apr-2015, together with the comments and the corresponding user profiles: 34,514 publications on 232 topics and with 13,575 tags, 1,930,818 comments (897,806 of them replies), and 14,598 users.

We have three groups of users: known paid trolls (as exposed in Bivol), "mentioned" trolls (called trolls by a certain number of different users), and non-trolls (never called trolls, despite having a high number of posts). Looking at users with at least 150 comments, we have 314 "mentioned" trolls (mentioned by five or more users) vs. 964 non-trolls (vs. some in between); we further have 15 paid trolls from Bivol. Here is an example post with troll accusation (translated):

"To comment from "Rozalina": You, trolls, are so funny :) I saw the same signature under other comments:)"

[2] `http://dnevnik.bg`

4 Method

We train a classifier to distinguish "mentioned" trolls vs. non-trolls; we experiment both with balanced and (natural) imbalanced classes. Then, at test time, we evaluate how well the classifier performs at discriminating paid trolls vs. non-trolls. We use a support vector machine (SVM) classifier (Chang and Lin, 2011) with a radial basis function (RBF) kernel, and features motivated by several publications about troll behavior.

Note that we perform the classification at the user level, i.e., based on user activity history, from which we extract statistics summarizing the user activity. In particular, for each user, we count the number of comments posted, the number of days in the forum, the number of days with at least one comment, and the number of publications commented on. All other features are scaled with respect to these statistics, which makes it possible for us to handle users that registered only recently (which we need to do at test time). Our features can be divided in the following general groups:

Vote-based features. We calculate the number of comments with positive and negative votes for each user. This is useful as we assume that non-trolls are likely to disagree with trolls, and to give them negative votes. We use the sum from all comments as a feature. We also count separately the comments with high, low and medium positive to negative ratio. Here are some example features: (a) the number of comments where $(\text{positive}/\text{negative}) < 0.25$, and (b) the number of comments where $(\text{positive}/\text{negative}) < 0.50$.

Comment-to-publication similarity. These features measure the similarity between comments and publications. We use cosine and TF.IDF-weighted vectors for the comment and for the publication. The idea is that trolls might try to change or blurr the topic of the publication if it differs from his/her views or agenda.

Comment order-based features. We count how many user comments the user has among the first k. The idea is that trolls might try to be among the first to comment to achieve higher impact.

Top loved/hated comments. We calculate the number of times the user's comments were among the top 1, 3, 5, 10 most loved/hated comments in some thread. The idea is that in the comment thread below many publications there are some trolls that oppose all other users, and usually their comments are among the most hated.

Comment replies-based features. These are features that count how many comments by a given user are replies to other users' comments, how many are replies to other replies, and so on. The assumption here is that trolls post not only a large number of comments, but also a large number or replies, as they want to dominate the conversation, especially when defending a specific cause. We further generate complex features that combine user comment reply features and vote counts-based features, thus generating even more features that model the relationship between replies and user agreement/disagreement.

Time-based features. We generate features from the number of comments posted during different time periods on a daily or on a weekly basis. We assume that users who are paid or who could be activists of political parties probably have some usual times to post, e.g., maybe they do it as a full-time job. On the other hand, most non-trolls work from 9:00 to 18:00, and thus we could expect that they should probably post less comments during this part of the day. We have time-based features that count the number of comments from 9:00 to 9:59, from 12:00 to 12:59, during working hours 9:00-18:00, etc.

Note that all the above features are scaled, i.e., divided by the number of comments, by the number of days the user has spent in the forum, by the number of days in which the user posted more than one comment, etc. Overall, we have a total of 338 such scaled features. In addition, we define a new set of features, which are non-scaled.

Non-scaled features. The non-scaled features are features based on the same statistics as above, but they are not divided by the number of comments / number of days in the forum / number of days with more that one comment, etc. For example, one non-scaled feature is the number of times a comment by the target user was voted negatively, i.e., as thumbs down, by other users. As a non-scaled feature, we would use this number directly, while above we would scale it by dividing it by the total number of user's comments, by the total number of publications the user has commented on, etc. Obviously, there is a danger in using non-scaled features: older users are likely to have higher values for them compared to recently-registered users. Yet, we found unscaled features useful in previous experiments (Mihaylov et al., 2015), so we included them here as well.

5 Experiments and Evaluation

In previous work (Mihaylov et al., 2015), we have already experiments with distinguishing "mentioned" trolls vs. non-trolls, achieving accuracy of 88-94%. Here, we are interested in discriminating between *paid* trolls and non-trolls.

Unfortunately, we only know fifteen paid trolls (from the publication in Bivol), which is too little to use for training and testing. Thus, we trained on "mentioned" trolls vs. non-trolls, but we then tested on *paid* trolls vs. non-trolls. We focused on the top four known paid trolls with the highest number of posts, as they had more than 100 comments, which means that we had enough information about them.[3] Thus, for testing we used the four trolls with 100 posts or more, to which we added four non-trolls (i.e., users who have never been called *trolls*). For training, we used 314 "mentioned" troll with 150 posts or more, to which we added 314 non-trolls, also with 150+ posts.

For the experiments, we extracted the features described in the previous section, both scaled and non-scaled, and we normalized them in the -1 to 1 interval. We then trained a support vector machine (SVM) classifier (Chang and Lin, 2011) with a radial basis function (RBF) kernel with C=32 and g=0.0078125. We chose these values using cross-validation on the training dataset. The testing results are shown in Tables 1 and 2.

Table 1 shows that we can find paid trolls with 100% precision and 75% recall, which is quite good. However, we should be very cautious about any conclusions we draw, as we only had eight testing examples. Yet, let us try to do some analysis. First, note that the best F-score is achieved when using All Scaled features. Moreover, features based on reply status, similarity, up/down votes, number of triggered replies seem to have no impact on the classification performance, as excluding them from the All Scaled features does not affect the results either way. However, excluding time-related features and reply comments vote-based features results in bad score, which means that these features have the most impact on finding paid trolls. Finally, excluding all vote-related features results in zero precision and recall on paid trolls evaluation, which means that these features are key for finding paid trolls.

[3]There were six known paid trolls with more than 40 comments, and the remaining nine known paid trolls from Bivol had less than 40 comments.

Features	Accuracy	Precision	Recall	F-score
All Scaled (AS)	0.88	1.00	0.75	0.86
AS - comment order (Scaled - S)	0.88	1.00	0.75	0.86
AS - is reply (S)	0.88	1.00	0.75	0.86
AS - is reply to has reply (S)	0.88	1.00	0.75	0.86
AS - similarity (S)	0.88	1.00	0.75	0.86
AS - similarity top (S)	0.88	1.00	0.75	0.86
AS - topl oved hated (S)	0.88	1.00	0.75	0.86
AS - total comments (S)	0.88	1.00	0.75	0.86
AS - triggered replies range (S)	0.88	1.00	0.75	0.86
AS - triggered replies total (S)	0.88	1.00	0.75	0.86
AS - vote updown total (S)	0.88	1.00	0.75	0.86
AS - time (S)	0.75	1.00	0.50	0.67
AS - time hours (S)	0.75	1.00	0.50	0.67
AS - vote up/down reply status (S)	0.75	1.00	0.50	0.67
AS - time day of week (S)	0.63	1.00	0.25	0.40
AS + Non Scaled (NS)	0.63	1.00	0.25	0.40
AS - vote up/down all (S)	0.38	0.00	0.00	0.00

Table 1: Results for classifying 4 paid trolls vs. 4 non-trolls for All Scaled (AS) '−' (minus) some scaled feature group. We train on 314 "mentioned" trolls vs. 314 non-trolls. (The bottom features are better, as they yield the highest drop in accuracy and F1 when excluded from All Scaled.)

Features	Accuracy	Precision	Recall	F-score
only day of week (S)	0.88	0.80	1.00	0.89
only reply status (S)	0.75	0.75	0.75	0.75
only time hours (S)	0.75	0.75	0.75	0.75
only top loved hated (S)	0.75	1.00	0.50	0.67
only comment order (S)	0.63	0.67	0.50	0.57
only vote updown is reply (S)	0.63	0.67	0.50	0.57
only similarity top (S)	0.63	1.00	0.25	0.40
only triggered replies range (S)	0.63	1.00	0.25	0.40
only is reply to has reply (S)	0.50	0.50	0.25	0.33
only similarity (S)	0.50	0.50	0.25	0.33
only time (S)	0.50	0.50	0.25	0.33
only total comments (S)	0.50	0.50	0.25	0.33
only triggered replies total (S)	0.50	0.50	0.25	0.33
only vote up/down all (S)	0.50	0.50	0.25	0.33
only vote up/down total (S)	0.50	0.50	0.25	0.33
All Unscaled	0.50	0.00	0.00	0.00

Table 2: Results for classifying 4 paid trolls vs. 4 non-trolls for individual Scaled (S) feature groups. We train on 314 "mentioned" trolls vs. 314 non-trolls. (The top features are better, as they perform well when used alone.)

Table 2 shows the performance of selected feature groups when used in isolation. We can see that features such as time of posting and votes are among the most important ones; yet, in our previous research, we have found them to be virtually irrelevant for finding "mentioned" trolls vs. non-trolls (Mihaylov et al., 2015).

Table 2 also shows that the best score is achieved by the day of the week feature, which confirms our assumption that paid trolls tend to write on working days. Next come the time-related features, which includes hour-related features and number of comments posted during working hours vs. in the evenings.

6 Discussion

Recall that our objective in this work was to identify paid opinion manipulation trolls in Internet forums. Unfortunately, we could not train a classifier to do that directly, as we did not have enough known paid trolls. Thus, we resorted to a simple trick: we considered as trolls those users who were accused of being such by other users. The assumption was that some of these "mentioned" trolls could have actually been paid. However, this is much of a witch hunt and despite our good overall results, the training data is not 100% reliable. For example, some trolls, whether paid or not, could have accused some non-trolls of being trolls, by mistake or on purpose.

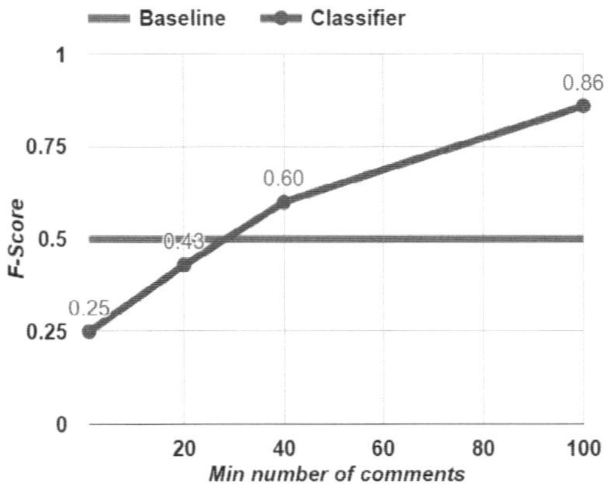

Figure 1: Finding paid trolls with different min number of comments. Training with AS features, and 314 "mentioned" trolls vs. 314 non-trolls.

Recall also that, in our experiments above, we used for testing only four of the fifteen known paid trolls: those with 100 or more comments. It is interesting to see how our classifier would perform if tested on trolls with different minimum number of comments (and the corresponding number of non-trolls). This is shown in Figure 1: we can see that most known paid users with less than 40 comments cannot be exposed as trolls using "mentioned" trolls as training examples.

Next, we vary the number of mentions (by different people) needed for us to consider a user a troll; we try 3, 4 and 6, in addition to 5 as above. Table 3 shows the results when testing on paid trolls with 100+ mentions (4 trolls + 4 non-trolls), where we trained with All Scaled features, and users with 150+ comments and varying minimum number of mentions as a troll.

min mentions	**3**	**4**	**5**	**6**
"mentioned" trolls	536	416	314	259
non-trolls	536	416	314	259
accuracy	0.75	0.88	0.88	0.75
F-score	0.67	0.86	0.86	0.67

Table 3: Finding paid trolls with 100+ mentions (4 trolls + 4 non-trolls). Training with AS features, and users with 150+ comments and varying minimum number of mentions as a troll.

min mentions	**3**	**4**	**5**	**6**
"mentioned" trolls	536	416	314	259
non-trolls	536	416	314	259
accuracy	0.83	0.87	0.91	0.92
F-score	0.83	0.87	0.91	0.92

Table 4: Finding "mentioned" trolls (cross-validation on the training dataset). Training with AS features, and users with 150+ comments and varying minimum number of mentions as a troll.

Table 4 shows results when training on the same datasets as in Table 3, but this time evaluating with cross-validation on the training data.

We can see that the best results when testing with paid trolls are achieved for "mentioned" trolls with a minimum of 4 or 5 mentions (Table 3), while when both training and evaluating with "mentioned" trolls (Table 4), the best results are with 6 mentions. This could mean that paid trolls behave more like moderately "mentioned" trolls rather than like highly "mentioned" trolls. More experiments, with a higher number of known paid trolls, are needed in order to confirm this.

Finally, we built and analyzed aggregated profiles for the three kinds of users we considered: (*i*) paid trolls vs. (*ii*) "mentioned" trolls vs. (*iii*) non-trolls.[4] For this purpose, we selected average values for the most notable features for the users with the highest number of comments from each group. We then normalized these values with value/max. The result is shown on Figure 2.

(1 - Active days to all time rate) shows that "mentioned" trolls write at least one comment in 52% of their days of all time being in the forum, while non-trolls do so 36% of the time, and paid trolls only do it 15% of the time. This suggests that paid trolls are less active, maybe because they only write comments when they are paid to do it.

[4]Note that we excluded from our analysis users with too few comments or with too few mentions as a troll.

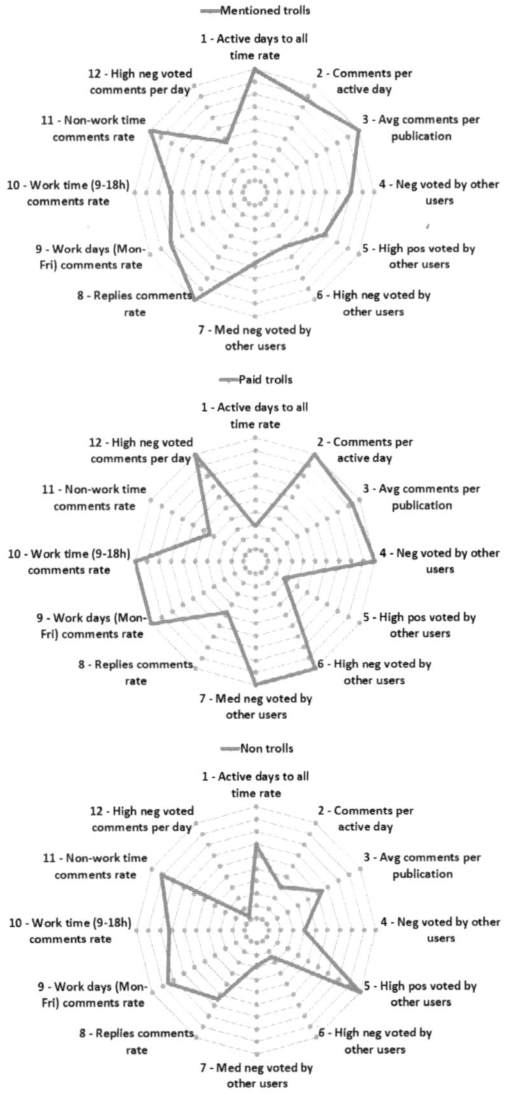

Figure 2: "Mentioned" trolls vs. paid trolls vs. non-trolls based on average feature values.

(2 - Comments per active day) shows that paid trolls and "mentioned" trolls write twice as many comments as non-trolls per day.

(3 - Avg comments per publication) shows that both paid and "mentioned" trolls post more comments per publication than non-trolls.

(4 - Neg voted by other users), (6 - High neg voted by other users), (7 - Med neg voted by other users) show that both paid and "mentioned" trolls have much more negatively voted comments than non-trolls. Yet, this is higher for paid trolls, which could mean that they have more influence compared to the self-driven "mentioned" trolls.

(5) - "mentioned" trolls have more positively voted comments compared to paid trolls.

(8 - Replies comments rate) - "mentioned" trolls are more likely to write comments that are replies to other user's comments compared to non-trolls, while paid trolls prefer to write specific comments and not to enter personal "battles". Moreover, paid trolls are more likely to write comments on working days (9 - Work days (Mon-Fri) comments rate) (Mon-Fri), and during working hours (9-18h) ((10 - Work time (9-18h) comments rate),(11 - Non-work time comments rate)) while "mentioned" trolls and non-trolls would write comments at anytime, though mostly during non-working hours.

These observations confirm our assumptions that paid trolls write comments primarily for the money, while "mentioned" trolls do so anytime, and are "self-driven". Yet, note that some of our "mentioned" trolls might be actually paid.

7 Conclusion and Future Work

We have presented experiments in trying to distinguish *paid* opinion manipulation trolls vs. non-trolls in Internet forums. As we did not have enough known paid trolls, for training we used "mentioned" trolls, assuming that a user who is called a *troll* by several different people is likely to be one, while one who has never been called a troll is unlikely to be such. We compared the profiles of (*i*) paid trolls vs. (*ii*) "mentioned" trolls vs. (*iii*) non-trolls, and we have shown that a classifier trained to distinguish (*ii*) from (*iii*) does quite well also at telling apart (*i*) from (*iii*).

Our further analysis has shown that the most important features were the number of comments, of positive and of negative votes, of posted replies, and the time of commenting. Overall, paid trolls looked roughly like the "mentioned" trolls, except that they were posting most of their comments on working days and during working hours.

Unfortunately, our features only worked well for trolls with high number of posts. Thus, in future work, we plan to add keywords, topics, named entities, sentiment analysis (Kapukaranov and Nakov, 2015; Jovanoski et al., 2015), etc, in order to be able to detect "fresh" trolls; this would require stemming (Nakov, 2003b; Nakov, 2003a), POS tagging (Georgiev et al., 2012), and named entity recognition (Georgiev et al., 2009). We also plan to analyze the comment threads as a whole (Barrón-Cedeño et al., 2015; Joty et al., 2015).

References

Alberto Barrón-Cedeño, Simone Filice, Giovanni Da San Martino, Shafiq Joty, Lluís Màrquez, Preslav Nakov, and Alessandro Moschitti. 2015. Thread-level information for comment classification in community question answering. In *Proceedings of the 53rd Annual Meeting of the Association for Computational Linguistics and the 7th International Joint Conference on Natural Language Processing*, ACL-IJCNLP '15, pages 687–693, Beijing, China.

Erin E Buckels, Paul D Trapnell, and Delroy L Paulhus. 2014. Trolls just want to have fun. *Personality and individual Differences*, 67:97–102.

Erik Cambria, Praphul Chandra, Avinash Sharma, and Amir Hussain. 2010. Do not feel the trolls. In *Proceedings of the 3rd International Workshop on Social Data on the Web*, SDoW '10, Shanghai, China.

Carlos Castillo and Brian D. Davison. 2011. Adversarial web search. *Found. Trends Inf. Retr.*, 4(5):377–486, May.

Chih-Chung Chang and Chih-Jen Lin. 2011. LIBSVM: A library for support vector machines. *ACM Transactions on Intelligent Systems and Technology*, 2:27:1–27:27.

Ying Chen, Yilu Zhou, Sencun Zhu, and Heng Xu. 2012. Detecting offensive language in social media to protect adolescent online safety. In *Proceedings of the 2012 International Conference on Privacy, Security, Risk and Trust and of the 2012 International Conference on Social Computing*, PASSAT/SocialCom '12, pages 71–80, Amsterdam, Netherlands.

Kushal Dave, Steve Lawrence, and David M Pennock. 2003. Mining the peanut gallery: Opinion extraction and semantic classification of product reviews. In *Proceedings of the 12th International World Wide Web conference*, WWW '03, pages 519–528, Budapest, Hungary.

Chrysanthos Dellarocas. 2006. Strategic manipulation of internet opinion forums: Implications for consumers and firms. *Management Science*, 52(10):1577–1593.

Patxi Galn-Garca, JosGaviria de la Puerta, CarlosLaorden Gmez, Igor Santos, and PabloGarca Bringas. 2014. Supervised machine learning for the detection of troll profiles in Twitter social network: Application to a real case of cyberbullying. In lvaro Herrero, Bruno Baruque, Fanny Klett, Ajith Abraham, Vclav Snel, Andr C.P.L.F. de Carvalho, Pablo Garca Bringas, Ivan Zelinka, Hctor Quintin, and Emilio Corchado, editors, *International Joint Conference SOCO13-CISIS13-ICEUTE13*, volume 239 of *Advances in Intelligent Systems and Computing*, pages 419–428. Springer International Publishing.

Georgi Georgiev, Preslav Nakov, Kuzman Ganchev, Petya Osenova, and Kiril Simov. 2009. Feature-rich named entity recognition for Bulgarian using conditional random fields. In *Proceedings of the International Conference Recent Advances in Natural Language Processing*, RANLP '09, pages 113–117, Borovets, Bulgaria.

Georgi Georgiev, Valentin Zhikov, Petya Osenova, Kiril Simov, and Preslav Nakov. 2012. Feature-rich part-of-speech tagging for morphologically complex languages: Application to Bulgarian. In *Proceedings of the 13th Conference of the European Chapter of the Association for Computational Linguistics*, EACL '12, pages 492–502, Avignon, France.

Susan Herring, Kirk Job-Sluder, Rebecca Scheckler, and Sasha Barab. 2002. Searching for safety online: Managing "trolling" in a feminist forum. *The Information Society*, 18(5):371–384.

Minqing Hu and Bing Liu. 2004. Mining and summarizing customer reviews. In *Proceedings of the 10th ACM SIGKDD International Conference on Knowledge Discovery and Data Mining*, KDD '04, pages 168–177, Seattle, WA, USA.

Shafiq Joty, Alberto Barrón-Cedeño, Giovanni Da San Martino, Simone Filice, Lluís Màrquez, Alessandro Moschitti, and Preslav Nakov. 2015. Global thread-level inference for comment classification in community question answering. In *Proceedings of the Conference on Empirical Methods in Natural Language Processing*, EMNLP '15, Lisbon, Portugal.

Dame Jovanoski, Veno Pachovski, and Preslav Nakov. 2015. Sentiment analysis in Twitter for Macedonian. In *Proceedings of the International Conference on Recent Advances in Natural Language Processing*, RANLP '15, Hissar, Bulgaria.

Borislav Kapukaranov and Preslav Nakov. 2015. Fine-grained sentiment analysis for movie reviews in Bulgarian. In *Proceedings of the International Conference on Recent Advances in Natural Language Processing*, RANLP '15, Hissar, Bulgaria.

Srijan Kumar, Francesca Spezzano, and VS Subrahmanian. 2014. Accurately detecting trolls in slashdot zoo via decluttering. In *Proceedings of the 2014 IEEE/ACM International Conference on Advances in Social Network Analysis and Mining*, ASONAM '14, pages 188–195, Beijing, China.

Wenbin Li, Ning Zhong, and Chunnian Liu. 2006. Combining multiple email filters based on multivariate statistical analysis. In *Foundations of Intelligent Systems*, pages 729–738. Springer.

Todor Mihaylov, Georgi Georgiev, and Preslav Nakov. 2015. Finding opinion manipulation trolls in news community forums. In *Proceedings of the Nineteenth Conference on Computational Natural Language Learning*, CoNLL '15, pages 310–314, Beijing, China.

Preslav Nakov. 2003a. Building an inflectional stemmer for Bulgarian. In *Proceedings of the 4th International Conference on Computer Systems and Technologies*, CompSysTech '03, pages 419–424, Sofia, Bulgaria.

Preslav Nakov. 2003b. BulStem: Design and evaluation of an inflectional stemmer for Bulgarian. In *Proceedings of the Workshop on Balkan Language Resources and Tools*, Thessaloniki, Greece.

F. Javier Ortega, José A. Troyano, Fermín L. Cruz, Carlos G. Vallejo, and Fernando Enríquez. 2012. Propagation of trust and distrust for the detection of trolls in a social network. *Computer Networks*, 56(12):2884 – 2895.

Myle Ott, Yejin Choi, Claire Cardie, and Jeffrey T. Hancock. 2011. Finding deceptive opinion spam by any stretch of the imagination. In *Proceedings of the 49th Annual Meeting of the Association for Computational Linguistics: Human Language Technologies - Volume 1*, HLT '11, pages 309–319, Portland, Oregon.

Matthew Rowe and Jonathan Butters. 2009. Assessing Trust: Contextual Accountability. In *Proceedings of the First Workshop on Trust and Privacy on the Social and Semantic Web*, SPOT '09, Heraklion, Greece.

Fabrizio Sebastiani. 2002. Machine learning in automated text categorization. *ACM computing surveys (CSUR)*, 34(1):1–47.

Zhi Xu and Sencun Zhu. 2010. Filtering offensive language in online communities using grammatical relations. In *Proceedings of the Seventh Annual Collaboration, Electronic Messaging, Anti-Abuse and Spam Conference*, CEAS '10, pages 20–29, Redmond, WA, USA.

Jun-Ming Xu, Xiaojin Zhu, and Amy Bellmore. 2012. Fast learning for sentiment analysis on bullying. In *Proceedings of the International Workshop on Issues of Sentiment Discovery and Opinion Mining*, WISDOM '12, pages 10:1–10:6, New York, NY, USA.

Extractive Summarization by Aggregating Multiple Similarities

Olof Mogren, Mikael Kågebäck, Devdatt Dubhashi
Department of Computer Science and Engineering
Chalmers University of Technology,
412 96 Göteborg, Sweden
mogren@chalmers.se

Abstract

News reports, social media streams, blogs, digitized archives and books are part of a plethora of reading sources that people face every day. This raises the question of how to best generate automatic summaries. Many existing methods for extracting summaries rely on comparing the similarity of two sentences in some way. We present new ways of measuring this similarity, based on sentiment analysis and continuous vector space representations, and show that combining these together with similarity measures from existing methods, helps to create better summaries. The finding is demonstrated with MULTSUM, a novel summarization method that uses ideas from kernel methods to combine sentence similarity measures. Submodular optimization is then used to produce summaries that take several different similarity measures into account. Our method improves over the state-of-the-art on standard benchmark datasets; it is also fast and scale to large document collections, and the results are statistically significant.

1 Introduction

Extractive summarization, the process of selecting a subset of sentences from a set of documents, is an important component of modern information retrieval systems (Baeza-Yates et al., 1999). A good summarization system needs to balance two complementary aspects: finding a summary that captures all the important topics of the documents (*coverage*), yet does not contain too many similar sentences (*non-redundancy*). It follows that it is essential to have a good way of measuring the similarity of sentences, in no way a trivial task. Consequently, several measures for sentence similarity have been explored for extractive summarization.

In this work, two sets of novel similarity measures capturing deeper semantic features are presented, and evaluated in combination with existing methods of measuring sentence similarity. The new methods are based on sentiment analysis, and continuous vector space representations of phrases, respectively.

We show that summary quality is improved by combining multiple similarities at the same time using kernel techniques. This is demonstrated using MULTSUM, an ensemble-approach to generic extractive multi-document summarization based on the existing, state-of-the-art method of Lin and Bilmes (2011). Our method obtains state-of-the-art results that are statistically significant on the de-facto standard benchmark dataset DUC 04. The experimental evaluation also confirm that the method generalizes well to other datasets.

2 MULTSUM

MULTSUM, our approach for extractive summarization, finds representative summaries taking multiple sentence similarity measures into account. As Lin and Bilmes (2011), we formulate the problem as the optimization of monotone nondecreasing submodular set functions. This results in a fast, greedy optimization step that provides a $(1 - \frac{1}{e})$ factor approximation. In the original version, the optimization objective is a function scoring a candidate summary by coverage and diversity, expressed using cosine similarity between sentences represented as bag-of-terms vectors. We extend this method by using several sentence similarity measures M^l (as described in Section 3) at the same time, combined by multiplying them together element-wise:

$$M_{\mathbf{s}_i,\mathbf{s}_j} = \prod M^l_{\mathbf{s}_i,\mathbf{s}_j}.$$

Proceedings of Recent Advances in Natural Language Processing, pages 451–457,
Hissar, Bulgaria, Sep 7–9 2015.

In the literature of kernel methods, this is the standard way of combining kernels as a conjunction (Duvenaud, 2014; Schölkopf et al., 2004, Ch 1).

3 Sentence Similarity Measures

Many existing systems rely on measuring the similarity of sentences to balance the coverage with the amount of redundancy of the summary. This is also true for MULTSUM which is based on the existing submodular optimization method. Similarity measures that capture general aspects lets the summarization system pick sentences that are representative and diverse in general. Similarity measures capturing more specific aspects allow the summarization system to take these aspects into account.

We list some existing measures in Table 3 (that mainly relies on counting word overlaps) and in Sections 3.1 and 3.2, we present sentence similarity measures that capture more specific aspects of the text. MULTSUM is designed to work with all measures mentioned below; this will be evaluated in Section 4. Interested readers are referred to a survey of existing similarity measures from the litterature in (Bengtsson and Skeppstedt, 2012). All these similarity measures require sentence splitting, tokenization, part-of-speech tagging and stemming of words. The Filtered Word, and TextRank comparers are set similarity measures where each sentence is represented by the set of all their terms. The KeyWord comparer and LinTFIDF represent each sentence as a word vector and uses the vectors for measuring similarity.

DepGraph first computes the dependency parse trees of the two sentences using Maltparser (Nivre, 2003). The length of their longest common path is then used to derive the similarity score.

The similarity measure used in TextRank (Mihalcea and Tarau, 2004) will be referred to as TRComparer. The measure used in submodular optimization (Lin and Bilmes, 2011) will be referred to as LinTFIDF. All measures used in this work are normalized, $M_{\mathbf{s}_i,\mathbf{s}_j} \in [0,1]$.

Name	Formula
Filtered	$M_{\mathbf{s}_i,\mathbf{s}_j} = \lvert(\mathbf{s}_i \cap \mathbf{s}_j)\rvert / \sqrt{\lvert(\mathbf{s}_i)\rvert + \lvert(\mathbf{s}_j)\rvert}$
TRCmp.	$M_{\mathbf{s}_i,\mathbf{s}_j} = \lvert\mathbf{s}_i \cap \mathbf{s}_j\rvert / (log\lvert\mathbf{s}_i\rvert + log\lvert\mathbf{s}_j\rvert)$
LinTFIDF	$M_{\mathbf{s}_i,\mathbf{s}_j} = \frac{\sum_{w \in \mathbf{s}_i} tf_{w,i} \cdot tf_{w,j} \cdot idf_w^2}{\sqrt{\sum_{w \in \mathbf{s}_i} tf_{w,\mathbf{s}_i} idf_w^2} \sqrt{\sum_{w \in \mathbf{s}_j} tf_{w,\mathbf{s}_j} idf_w^2}}$
KeyWord	$M_{\mathbf{s}_i,\mathbf{s}_j} = \frac{\sum_{w \in \{\{\mathbf{s}_i \cap \mathbf{s}_j\} \cap K\}} tf_w \cdot idf_w}{\lvert\mathbf{s}_i\rvert + \lvert\mathbf{s}_j\rvert}$
DepGraph	*See text description.*

Table 1: Similarity measures from previous works.

3.1 Sentiment Similarity

Sentiment analysis has previously been used for document summarization, with the aim of capturing an average sentiment of the input corpus (Lerman et al., 2009), or to score emotionally charged sentences (Nishikawa et al., 2010). Other research has shown that negative emotion words appear at a relative higher rate in summaries written by humans (Hong and Nenkova, 2014). We propose a different way of making summaries sentiment aware by comparing the level of sentiment in sentences. This allows for summaries that are both representative and diverse in sentiment.

Two lists, of positive and of negative sentiment words respectively, were manually created[1] and used. Firstly, each sentence $\mathbf{s}_i$ is given two sentiment scores, $positive(\mathbf{s}_i)$ and $negative(\mathbf{s}_i)$, defined as the fraction of words in $\mathbf{s}_i$ that is found in the positive and the negative list, respectively. The similarity score for positive sentiment are computed as follows:

$$M_{\mathbf{s}_i,\mathbf{s}_j} = 1 - \lvert positive(\mathbf{s}_i) - positive(\mathbf{s}_j)\rvert$$

The similarity score for negative sentiment are computed as follows:

$$M_{\mathbf{s}_i,\mathbf{s}_j} = 1 - \lvert negative(\mathbf{s}_i) - negative(\mathbf{s}_j)\rvert$$

3.2 Continuous Vector Space Representations

Continuous vector space representations of words has a long history. Recently, the use of deep learning methods has given rise to a new class of continuous vector space models. Bengio et al. (2006) presented vector space representations for words that capture semantic and syntactic properties. These vectors can be employed not only to find similar words, but also to relate words using multiple dimensions of similarity. This means that words sharing some sense can be related using

[1]To download the sentiment word lists used, please see `http://www.mogren.one/`

translations in vector space, e.g. $v_{king} - v_{man} + v_{woman} \approx v_{queen}$.

Early work on extractive summarization using vector space models was presented in (Kågebäck et al., 2014). In this work we use a similar approach, with two different methods of deriving word embeddings. The first model (CW) was introduced by Collobert and Weston (2008). The second ($W2V$) is the skip-gram model by Mikolov et al. (2013).

The Collobert and Weston vectors were trained on the RCV1 corpus, containing one year of Reuters news wire; the skip-gram vectors were trained on 300 billion words from Google News.

The word embeddings are subsequently used as building blocks for sentence level phrase embeddings by summing the word vectors of each sentence. Finally, the sentence similarity is defined as the cosine similarity between the sentence vectors.

With MULTSUM, these similarity measures can be combined with the traditional sentence similarity measures.

4 Experiments

Our version of the submodular optimization code follows the description by Lin and Bilmes (2011), with the exception that we use multiplicative combinations of the sentence similarity scores described in Section 3. The source code of our system can be downloaded from `http://www.mogren.one/`. Where nothing else is stated, MULTSUM was evaluated with a multiplicative combination of TRComparer and FilteredWordComparer.

4.1 Datasets

In the evaluation, three different datasets were used. DUC 02 and DUC 04 are from the Document Understanding Conferences, both with the settings of task 2 (short multi-document summarization), and each consisting of around 50 document sets. Each document set is comprised of around ten news articles (between 111 and 660 sentences) and accompanied with four gold-standard summaries created by manual summarizers. The summaries are at most 665 characters long. DUC 04 is the de-facto standard benchmark dataset for generic multi-document summarization.

Experiments were also carried out on Opinosis (Ganesan et al., 2010), a collection of short user reviews in 51 different topics. Each topic consists of between 50 and 575 one-sentence user reviews by different authors about a certain characteristic of a hotel, a car, or a product. The dataset includes 4 to 5 gold-standard summaries created by human authors for each topic. The the gold-standard summaries is around 2 sentences.

4.2 Baseline Methods

Our baseline methods are Submodular optimization (Lin and Bilmes, 2011), DPP (Kulesza and Taskar, 2012), and ICSI (Gillick et al., 2008). The baseline scores are calculated on precomputed summary outputs (Hong et al., 2014).

4.3 Evaluation Method

Following standard procedure, we use ROUGE (version 1.5.5) for evaluation (Lin, 2004). ROUGE counts n-gram overlaps between generated summaries and the gold standard. We have concentrated on recall as this is the measure with highest correlation to human judgement (Lin and Hovy, 2003), on ROUGE-1, ROUGE-2, and ROUGE-SU4, representing matches in unigrams, bigrams, and skip-bigrams, respectively.

The Opinosis experiments were aligned with those of Bonzanini et al. (2013) and Ganesan et al. (2010)[2]. Summary length was 2 sentences. In the DUC experiments, summary length is 100 words[3].

5 Results

Our experimental results show significant improvements by aggregating several sentence similarity measures, and our results for ROUGE-2 and ROUGE-SU4 recall beats state–of–the–art.

5.1 Integrating Different Similarity Measures

Table 2 shows ROUGE recall on DUC 04. MULTSUM[4] obtains ROUGE scores beating state-of-the-art systems, in particular on ROUGE-2 and ROUGE-SU4, suggesting that MULTSUM produce summaries with excellent fluency. We also note, that using combined similarities, we beat original submodular optimization.

Figure 5.1 shows, for each $n \in [1..9]$, the highest ROUGE-1 recall score obtained by MULTSUM, determined by exhaustive search

[2]ROUGE options on Opinosis: -a - m -s -x -n 2 -2 4 -u.

[3]ROUGE options on DUC: -a -n 2 -m -l 100 -x -c 95 -r 1000 -f A -p 0.5 -t 0 -2 4 -u.

[4]Here, MULTSUM is using TRComparer and FilteredWordComparer in multiplicative conjunction.

	ROUGE-1	ROUGE-2	ROUGE-SU4
$MULTSUM$	39.35	**9.94**	**14.01**
$ICSISumm$	38.41	9.77	13.62
DPP	**39.83**	9.62	13.86
$SUBMOD$	39.18	9.35	13.75

Table 2: ROUGE recall scores on DUC 04. Our system MULTSUM obtains the best result yet for ROUGE-2 and ROUGE-SU4. DPP has a higher ROUGE-1 score, but the difference is not statistically significant (Hong et al., 2014).

1	2	3	4
1.0	0.00038	0.00016	0.00016

Table 3: p-values from the Mann-Whitney U-test for combinations of similarity measures of size $n \in [1..4]$, compared to using just one similarity measure. Using 2, 3, or 4 similarity measures at the same time with MULTSUM, gives a statistically significant improvement of the ROUGE-1 scores. Dataset: DUC 04.

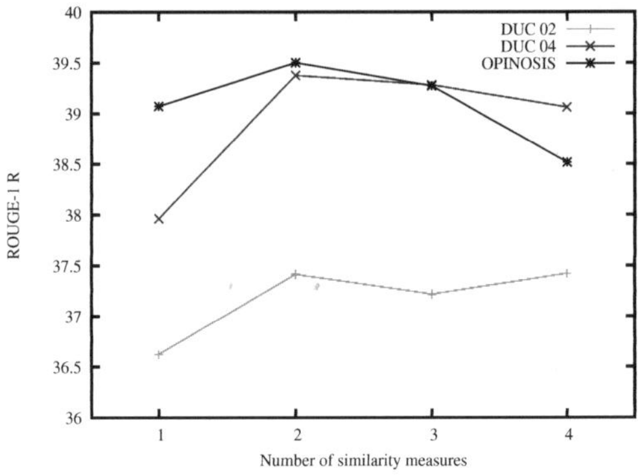

Figure 1: MULTSUM ROUGE-1 recall performance for each top-performing combination of up to four similarity measures. On all datasets, using combinations of two, three, and four similarity measures is better than using only one.

among all possible combinations of size n. The performance increases from using only one sentence similarity measure, reaching a high, stable level when $n \in [2..4]$. The behaviour is consistent over three datasets: DUC 02, DUC 04 and OPINOSIS. Based on ROUGE-1 recall, on DUC 02, a combination of four similarity measures provided the best results, while on DUC 04 and Opinosis, a combination of two similarity scores provided a slightly better score.

Table 3 shows p-values obtained using the Mann-Whitney U-test (Mann et al., 1947) on the ROUGE-1 scores when using a combination of n similarities with MULTSUM, compared to using only one measure. The Mann-Whitney U-test compares two ranked lists A and B, and decides whether they are from the same population. Here, A is the list of scores from using only one measure, and B is the top-10 ranked combinations of n combined similarity measures, $n \in [1..4]$). One can see that for each $n \in [1..4]$, using n sentence similarity measures at the same time, is significantly better than using only one.

On DUC 02, the best combination of similarity measures is using CW, LinTFIDF, NegativeSentiment, and TRComparer. Each point in Figure 5.1 represents a combination of some of these four similarity measures. Let n be the number of measures in such a combination. When $n = 1$, the "combinations" are just single similarity measures. When $n = 2$, there are 6 different ways to choose, and when $n = 3$, there are four. A line goes from each measure point through all combinations the measure is part of. One can clearly see the benefits of each of the combination steps, as n increases.

5.2 Evaluation with Single Similarity Measures

In order to understand the effect of different similarity measures, MULTSUM was first evaluated using only one similarity measure at a time. Table 4 shows the ROUGE recall scores of these experiments, using the similarity measures presented in Section 3, on DUC 04.

We note that MULTSUM provides summaries of high quality already with one similarity measure (e.g. with TRComparer), with a ROUGE-1 recall of 37.95 Using only sentiment analysis as the single similarity measure does not capture enough information to produce state-of-the-art summaries.

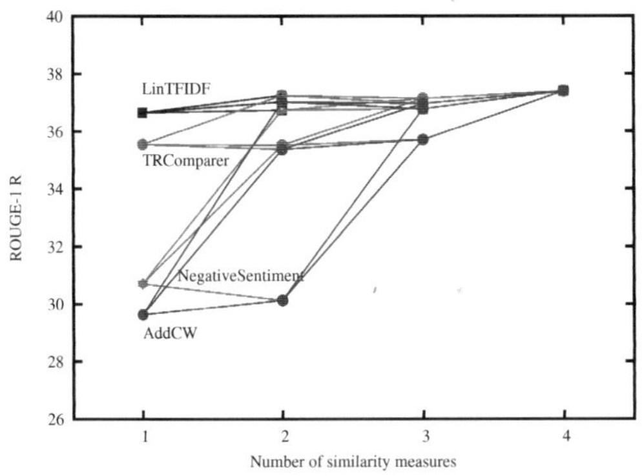

Figure 2: ROUGE-1 recall for the top-performing four-combination on DUC 2002 (CW, LinTFIDF, NegativeSentiment, and TRComparer), and all possible subsets of these four similarity measures. (When the number of similarity measures is one, only a single measure is used).

	ROUGE-1	ROUGE-2	ROUGE-SU4
$TRComparer$	**37.95**	**8.94**	**13.19**
$Filtered$	37.51	8.26	12.73
$LinTFIDF$	35.74	6.50	11.51
$KeyWord$	35.40	7.13	11.80
$DepGraph$	32.81	5.43	10.12
$NegativeSent.$	32.65	6.35	10.29
$PositiveSent.$	31.19	4.87	9.27
$W2V$	32.12	4.94	9.92
CW	31.59	4.74	9.51

Table 4: ROUGE recall of MULTSUM using different similarity measures, one at a time. Dataset: DUC 04. The traditional word-overlap measures are the best scoring when used on their own; the proposed measures with more semantical comparisons provide the best improvements when used in conjunctions.

6 Discussion

Empirical evaluation of the method proposed in this paper shows that using several sentence similarity measures at the same time produces significantly better summaries.

When using one single similarity at a time, using sentiment similarity and vector space models does not give the best summaries. However, we found that when combining several similarity measures, our proposed sentiment and continuous vector space measures often rank among the top ones, together with the TRComparer.

MULTSUM, our novel summarization method, based on submodular optimization, multiplies several sentence similarity measures, to be able to make summaries that are good with regards to several aspects at the same time. Our experimental results show significant improvements when using multiplicative combinations of several sentence similarity measures. In particular, the results of MULTSUM surpasses that of the original submodular optimization method.

In our experiments we found that using between two and four similarity measures lead to significant improvements compared to using a single measure. This verifies the validity of commonly used measures like TextRank and LinTFIDF as well as new directions like phrase embeddings and sentiment analysis.

There are several ideas worth pursuing that could further improve our methods. We will explore methods of incorporating more semantic information in our sentence similarity measures. This could come from systems for Information Extraction (Ji et al., 2013), or incorporating external sources such as WordNet, Freebase and DBpedia (Nenkova and McKeown, 2012).

7 Related Work

Ever since (Luhn, 1958), the field of automatic document summarization has attracted a lot of attention, and has been the focus of a steady flow of research. Luhn was concerned with the importance of words and their representativeness for the input text, an idea that's still central to many current approaches. The development of new techniques for document summarization has since taken many different paths. Some approaches concentrate on what words should appear in summaries, some focus on sentences in part or in whole, and some consider more abstract concepts.

In the 1990's we witnessed the dawn of the data explosion known as the world wide web, and research on multi document summarization took off. Some ten years later, the Document Understanding Conferences (DUC) started providing researchers with datasets and spurred interest with a venue for competition.

Luhn's idea of a frequency threshold measure for selecting topic words in a document has lived on. It was later superseded by $tf \times idf$, which measures the specificity of a word to a document,

The two bombers who carried out Friday's attack, which led the Israeli Cabinet to suspend deliberations on the land-for-security accord signed with the Palestinians last month, were identified as members of Islamic Holy War from West Bank villages under Israeli security control. The radical group Islamic Jihad claimed responsibility Saturday for the market bombing and vowed more attacks to try to block the new peace accord. Israel radio said the 18-member Cabinet debate on the Wye River accord would resume only after Yasser Arafat's Palestinian Authority fulfilled all of its commitments under the agreement, including arresting Islamic militants.

Table 5: Example output from MULTSUM. Input document: d30010t from DUC 04. Similarity Measures: W2V, TRComparer, and FilteredWordComparer.

something that has been used extensively in document summarization efforts. RegSum (Hong and Nenkova, 2014) trained a classifier on what kinds of words that human experts include in summaries. (Lin and Bilmes, 2011) represented sentences as a $tf \times idf$ weighted bag-of-words vector, defined a sentence graph with weights according to cosine similarity, and used submodular optimization to decide on sentences for a summary that is both representative and diverse.

Several other methods use similar sentence-based formulations but with different sentence similarities and summarization objectives (Radev et al., 2004; Mihalcea and Tarau, 2004).

(Bonzanini et al., 2013) introduced an iterative sentence removal procedure that proved good in summarizing short online user reviews. CLASSY04 (Conroy et al., 2004) was the best system in the official DUC 04 evaluation. After some linguistic preprocessing, it uses a Hidden Markov Model for sentence selection where the decision on inclusion of a sentence depends on its number of signature tokens. The following systems have also showed state–of–the–art results on the same data set. ICSI (Gillick et al., 2008) posed the summarization problem as a global integer linear program (ILP) maximizing the summary's coverage of key n-grams. OCCAMS_V (Davis et al., 2012) uses latent semantic analysis to determine the importance of words before the sentence selection. (Kulesza and Taskar, 2012) presents the use of Determinantal point processes (DPPs) for summarization, a probabilistic formulation that allows for a balance between diversity and coverage. An extensive description and comparison of these state–of–the–art systems can be found in (Hong et al., 2014), along with a repository of summary outputs on DUC 04.

Besides the aforementioned work, interested readers are referred to an extensive survey (Nenkova and McKeown, 2012). In particular, they discuss different approaches to sentence representation, scoring and summary selection and their effects on the performance of a summarization system.

8 Conclusions

We have demonstrated that extractive summarization benefits from using several sentence similarity measures at the same time. The proposed system, MULTSUM works by using standard kernel techniques to combine the similarities. Our experimental evaluation shows that the summaries produced by MULTSUM outperforms state-of-the-art systems on standard benchmark datasets. In particular, it beats the original submodublar optimization approach on all three variants of ROUGE scores. It attains state-of-the-art results on both ROUGE-2 and ROUGE-SU4, showing that the resulting summaries have high fluency. The results are statistically significant and consistent over all three tested datasets: DUC 02, DUC 04, and Opinosis.

We have also seen that sentence similarity measures based on sentiment analysis and continuous vector space representations can improve the results of multi-document summarization. In our experiments, these sentence similarity measures used separately are not enough to create a good summary, but when combining them with traditional sentence similarity measures, we improve on previous methods.

Acknowledgments

This work has been done within "Data-driven secure business intelligence", grant IIS11-0089 from the Swedish Foundation for Strategic Research (SSF). We would like to thank Gabriele Capannini for discussion and help and Jonatan Bengtsson for his work on sentence similarity measures.

References

Ricardo Baeza-Yates, Berthier Ribeiro-Neto, et al. 1999. *Modern information retrieval*, volume 463. ACM press New York.

Yoshua Bengio, Holger Schwenk, Jean-Sébastien Senécal, Fréderic Morin, and Jean-Luc Gauvain. 2006. Neural probabilistic language models. In *Innovations in Machine Learning*. Springer.

Jonatan Bengtsson and Christoffer Skeppstedt. 2012. Automatic extractive single document summarization. Master's thesis, Chalmers University of Technology and University of Gothenburg.

Marco Bonzanini, Miguel Martinez-Alvarez, and Thomas Roelleke. 2013. Extractive summarisation via sentence removal: condensing relevant sentences into a short summary. In *SIGIR*, pages 893–896.

Ronan Collobert and Jason Weston. 2008. A unified architecture for natural language processing: Deep neural networks with multitask learning. In *Proceedings of ICML*, pages 160–167.

John M Conroy, Judith D Schlesinger, Jade Goldstein, and Dianne P O'leary. 2004. Left-brain/right-brain multi-document summarization. In *DUC 2004*.

Sashka T Davis, John M Conroy, and Judith D Schlesinger. 2012. Occams–an optimal combinatorial covering algorithm for multi-document summarization. In *ICDMW*. IEEE.

David Duvenaud. 2014. *Automatic model construction with Gaussian processes*. Ph.D. thesis, University of Cambridge.

Kavita Ganesan, ChengXiang Zhai, and Jiawei Han. 2010. Opinosis: a graph-based approach to abstractive summarization of highly redundant opinions. In *Proceedings of COLING*, pages 340–348. ACL.

Dan Gillick, Benoit Favre, and Dilek Hakkani-Tur. 2008. The icsi summarization system at tac 2008. In *Proceedings of TAC*.

Kai Hong and Ani Nenkova. 2014. Improving the estimation of word importance for news multi-document summarization. In *Proceedings of EACL*.

Kai Hong, John M Conroy, Benoit Favre, Alex Kulesza, Hui Lin, and Ani Nenkova. 2014. A repository of state of the art and competitive baseline summaries for generic news summarization. *LREC*.

Heng Ji, Benoit Favre, Wen-Pin Lin, Dan Gillick, Dilek Hakkani-Tur, and Ralph Grishman. 2013. Open-domain multi-document summarization via information extraction: Challenges and prospects. In *Multi-source, Multilingual Information Extraction and Summarization*, pages 177–201. Springer.

Mikael Kågebäck, Olof Mogren, Nina Tahmasebi, and Devdatt Dubhashi. 2014. Extractive summarization using continuous vector space models. *Proceedings of (CVSC)@ EACL*, pages 31–39.

Alex Kulesza and Ben Taskar. 2012. Determinantal point processes for machine learning. *arXiv:1207.6083*.

Kevin Lerman, Sasha Blair-Goldensohn, and Ryan McDonald. 2009. Sentiment summarization: Evaluating and learning user preferences. In *Proceedings of EACL*, pages 514–522. ACL.

Hui Lin and Jeff Bilmes. 2011. A class of submodular functions for document summarization. In *ACL*.

Chin-Yew Lin and Eduard Hovy. 2003. Automatic evaluation of summaries using n-gram co-occurrence statistics. In *Proceedings of NAACL/HLT*, pages 71–78.

Chin-Yew Lin. 2004. Rouge: A package for automatic evaluation of summaries. In *Text Summarization Branches Out: Proc. of the ACL-04 Workshop*, pages 74–81.

Hans Peter Luhn. 1958. The automatic creation of literature abstracts. *IBM Journal*, 2(2):159–165.

Henry B Mann, Donald R Whitney, et al. 1947. On a test of whether one of two random variables is stochastically larger than the other. *The annals of mathematical statistics*, 18(1):50–60.

Rada Mihalcea and Paul Tarau. 2004. Textrank: Bringing order into texts. In *Proceedings of EMNLP*, volume 4.

Tomas Mikolov, Kai Chen, Greg Corrado, and Jeffrey Dean. 2013. Efficient estimation of word representations in vector space. *arXiv:1301.3781*.

Ani Nenkova and Kathleen McKeown. 2012. A survey of text summarization techniques. In Charu C. Aggarwal and ChengXiang Zhai, editors, *Mining Text Data*, pages 43–76. Springer.

Hitoshi Nishikawa, Takaaki Hasegawa, Yoshihiro Matsuo, and Genichiro Kikui. 2010. Optimizing informativeness and readability for sentiment summarization. In *Proceedings of ACL*, pages 325–330. ACL.

Joakim Nivre. 2003. An efficient algorithm for projective dependency parsing. In *Proceedings of IWPT*. Citeseer.

Dragomir R. Radev, Timothy Allison, Sasha Blair-Goldensohn, John Blitzer, Arda Çelebi, Stanko Dimitrov, Elliott Drábek, Ali Hakim, Wai Lam, Danyu Liu, Jahna Otterbacher, Hong Qi, Horacio Saggion, Simone Teufel, Michael Topper, Adam Winkel, and Zhu Zhang. 2004. Mead - a platform for multidocument multilingual text summarization. In *LREC*.

Bernhard. Schölkopf, Koji. Tsuda, and Jean-Philippe. Vert. 2004. *Kernel methods in computational biology*. MIT Press, Cambridge, Mass.

STATISTICAL MACHINE TRANSLATION IMPROVEMENT BASED ON PHRASE SELECTION

Cyrine Nasri
SMarT, LORIA
Campus Scientifique BP 139,
54500 Vandoeuvre Lès Nancy
Cedex, France
cyrine.nasri@loria.fr

Chiraz Latiri
LIPAH laboratory
Faculty of Sciences of Tunis
University of Tunis El Manar
Tunisia
chiraz.latiri@gnet.tn

Kamel Smaïli
SMarT, LORIA
Campus Scientifique BP 139,
54500 Vandoeuvre Lès Nancy
Cedex, France
smaili@loria.fr

Abstract

This paper describes the importance of introducing a phrase-based language model in the process of machine translation. In fact, nowadays SMT are based on phrases for translation but their language models are based on classical ngrams. In this paper we introduce a phrase-based language model (PBLM) in the decoding process to try to match the phrases of a translation table with those predicted by a language model. Furthermore, we propose a new way to retrieve phrases and their corresponding translation by using the principle of conditional mutual information.
The SMT developed will be compared to the baseline one in terms of BLEU, TER and METEOR. The experimental results show that the introduction of PBLM in the translation decoding improve the results.

1 INTRODUCTION

Language modeling is a crucial task in many areas of natural language processing (NLP) like Automatic Speech Recognition (ASR), Statistical Machine Translation (SMT), Optical Character Recognition (OCR), etc. Every improvement in the language model performance can impact the previously cited applications
Many researches on language modeling have been proposed in the literature over the past decades (Yoshua et al., 2003), (Schwenk, 2007) and (Wu et al., 2012). Nowadays, the new language models are based on deep learning techniques (Arsoy et al., 2012). Some studies were proposed to improve the language model quality by adding external informations (syntactic, morphological, etc). Significant improvements were noted (Charniak et al., 2003) (Kirchhoff and Yang, 2005) (Sarikaya and Deng, 2007) (L. Schwartz and et al., 2011), (Xiao et al., 2011).
In the following, we will be interested by variable-length models. In fact, words are commonly used as the basic lexical unit in standard language model, however in automatic speech recognition, some works were based on variable-length models where the basic unit is variable in terms of length. These variable-length ngrams correspond to phrases as defined in the speech recognition and machine translation communities. The models shown that they reduce the perplexity of the language model and sometimes they improve the performance of the ASR (Giachin, 1995) (Dietrich, 1998) (G. Riccardi and Riley, 1997) (K.F. Ries and Waibel, 1996) (Zitouni et al., 2003).
In SMT, (Baisa, 2011), first proposed the chunk-based language model (including phrase-based) in machine translation but did not give a solution. Recently, (Xu and Chen., 2015) designed a direct algorithm for phrase-based language model in statistical machine translation. In their method, phrase can be any word sequence. The phrase vocabulary is huge and the data sparsity problem is very serious. It leads to difficulty in probability estimation for phrase-based language model.
Language model is considered as the one of the most important component in SMT. Its role is to assign a probability to each translation hypothesis. In this paper, we propose to extend the standard language model to a variable-length one by considering phrases as atomic units in a language model.
This approach has the following major advantages: the first is that the phrase-based language model can easily capture a relationship between words over a long distance, within a sentence. The second advantage, is the compatibility of the translation hypotheses with that of the language model, ensuring more consistency in the decoding process. It means that we hope that the translation

Proceedings of Recent Advances in Natural Language Processing, pages 458–464,
Hissar, Bulgaria, Sep 7–9 2015.

hypotheses would correspond to the units of the language models.

We integrated this new language model in two statistical translation systems: baseline phrase-based SMT system (Koehn et al., 2003), and inter-lingual triggers based machine translation (Nasri et al., 2014).

This paper is structured as follows: first we give an overview of inter-lingual triggers. Second we present our method for training phrases for SMT. Then we describe our approach to derive a new phrase-based language model to be included as such a new statistical machine translation system. Finally, we present results of the proposed translation system using the new phrase-based language model. We end with a conclusion which points out the strength of our method and gives some tracks about the future work.

2 INTER-LINGUAL TRIGGERS

Inter-lingual triggers are inspired from triggers concept used in statistical language modeling (Tillmann and Ney, 1997). A trigger is a set composed of words and its best correlated triggered words in terms of mutual information (MI). In (Lavecchia et al., 2007), authors proposed to determine correlations between words belonging to two different languages. Each inter-lingual trigger is composed of a triggering source linguistic unit and its best correlated triggered target linguistic units. Based on this idea, they found among the set of triggered target units, potential translations of the triggering source words. Inter-lingual triggers are determined on a parallel corpus according to mutual information measure namely:

$$MI(a,b) = P(a,b)log\frac{P(a,b)}{P(a)P(b)} \quad (1)$$

Where a and b are respectively a source and a target words. *P(a, b)* is the joint probabilities and *P(a)* and *P(b)* are marginal probabilities. For each source unit a, the authors kept its k best target triggered units. This approach has been extended to take into account triggers of phrases (Lavecchia et al., 2008). The drawback of this method is that phrases are built in an iterative process starting from single words and joining others to them until the expected size of phrases is reached. In other words, at the end of the first iteration, sequences of two words are built, the following iteration produces phrase of three words and so on until the stop-criteria is reached. Then, once all the source phrases are built, their corresponding phrases in the target language are retrieved by using n-to-m inter-lingual trigger approach which means that a phrase of n words triggers a phrase of m words. In order to avoid the propagation of errors due to the cascade of steps in the previous method, we propose a new approach which is based on a conditional mutual information which allows retrieving target phrases given source ones.

3 A NEW METHOD FOR LEARNING PHRASE TRANSLATIONS

In this section, we present our new approach to learn a translation model based on conditional mutual information (CMI). Before presenting our approach, we introduce some necessary formalizations related to CMI.

3.1 A REVIEW OF CONDITIONAL MUTUAL INFORMATION (CMI)

In order to capture the relationship between several words at least 3, we decided to use conditional mutual information which is defined as follows for discrete random variables:

$$CMI(X,Y|Z) = \sum_{z\in Z}\sum_{y\in Y}\sum_{x\in X} P(x,y,z) \; log\frac{P(x,y,z)P(z)}{P(x,z)P(y,z)} \quad (2)$$

Where P is the joint or the marginal probability depending on the number of the parameters.

We suppose that random variables X and Z and Y and Z are both independent, the preceding formula could be written as follows:

$$CMI(X,Y|Z) = \sum_{z\in Z}\sum_{y\in Y}\sum_{x\in X} P(x,y,z) \; log\frac{P(x,y,z)}{P(x)P(y)P(z)} \quad (3)$$

When we would like to calculate the CMI for only 3 values which correspond to 3 words in our case, the preceding formula is rewritten as follows:

$$CMI(x,y,z) = P(x,y,z)log\frac{P(x,y,z)}{P(x)P(y)P(z)} \quad (4)$$

3.2 A NEW ALGORITHM FOR LEARNING TRANSLATION PAIRS

We describe our learning phrase translations algorithm. This algorithm does not require an initial word-to-word alignment, nor an initial segmentation of the monolingual text (Costa-Jussà et al., 2010). It uses the conditional mutual information between the source and target words to identify directly phrase pairs.

Once all phrase pairs are extracted, we segment source and target training corpus in terms of the best phrases. Then, we associate to each source phrase its best target translation.

Conditional mutual information calculates the correlation relationship between n variables. This principle is interesting since it allows to associate n words in the target language to a source phrase.

Such as in Lavecchia 2008, our objective is to use the principle of inter-lingual triggers except that we use multivariate mutual information. As illustrative example, guess that we are interested by phrases of length 2 which are translated by one word. For instance, *good morning* is translated by *bonjour* in French. We can then calculate directly the correlation degree between these two linguistic units as follows:

According to formula 4, for this example x = *good*, y = *morning* and z =*bonjour*.

This formula can capture this strength relationship between the words of the source phrase and the word of the target language. In fact, the equation takes into account the relationship between each component of the source phrase and the word of the target language. We believe that this will lead to more realistic phrases with more relevant translations.

Given a sentence pair (f, e), where f is a sentence in a source language and e a sentence in a target language. First, we calculate a Source-to-Target two-to-one (Trig 2-1) trigger model since CMI permits to find triggers like $x, y \longrightarrow z$ where x, y are contiguous words on a source language and z is a word in a target language. Only the k best triggers for each source phrase are kept to be incorporated into the dictionary. Then, the source phrases of the resulting triggers are sorted in a decreasing order of the CMI value. These phrases are useful to segment the source training corpus by merging two different words into one phrase.

Once the source training corpus is segmented into phrases, we determine for each source phrase its best translations in the target language. For this, we compute a Target-to-Source two-to-one triggers model like $\langle x, y \rangle \rightarrow z$, where x, y represent words in the target language and z is a token (single word or phrase) in the source language. This process is iterated to extend the length of phrases until we reach the maximum length of phrases.

The correponding process is given in Algorithm 1. At the end of this process, we get a list of triggers of source phrases with their best phrase translations, some of them are presented in Table1.

The phrases get are used to rewrite the training corpus, Table 2 gives an overview of the obtained corpus.

Algorithm 1 A phrase model based on CMI

1: S is a source corpus and T is a target corpus.
2: Train a trigger model $2 \longrightarrow 1$ where the left phrase come from S and the right one from T. For each source phrase, only the k best ones are kept.
3: Sort the phrases (the right member of the triggers) in a decreasing order of the CMI.
4: Segment the source corpus with the source phrases.
5: Execute 2, 3 and 4 but switch the source and the target corpora.
6: Calculate triggers $1 \longrightarrow 1$ where the left sequence come from S and the right one from T.
7: Go to step 2 which will increase the size of phrases until the expected length is achieved.

4 GETTING A NEW PHRASE-BASED LANGUAGE MODELS

The role of the language model in machine translation is to measure the fluency and the well-formness of a translation. Common applications of language models include estimating the distribution based on N-gram coverage of words, to predict word and word orders (Lafferty et al., 2001) (Stolcke, 2002). In this work, we propose to model the prediction of phrase and phrase orders. By considering all word sequences as phrases, the dependency inside a phrase, is preserved. In other words, word-based language model is a special case of phrase-based language model if only single word phrases are considered. Intuitively our approach has the following advantages:

Source phrases	Target phrases	CMI
parlement+européen	european+union	**0.65**
	the parlement+européen	0.52
	parlement	0.5
	européen	0.31
prendre+en+considération	bare+in+mind	**0.42**
	consider	0.32
	take+into+account	0.25
je+voudrais+remercier	I+want+to+thank	**0.62**
	I+thank	0.35
	thank+you	0.11

Table 1: Example of interlingual phrases

we must bare+in+mind the community as+a+whole. nous devons prendre+en+considération la communauté dans+son+ensemble.
mr+president I wish+to+congratulate mrs+poulen on her report. monsieur+le+président je tiens+à+féliciter madame+poulen sur+son+rapport.
madam+president the last+week the mep karla+peijs was attacked in brussels. madame+la+présidente la semaine+dernière le mep karla+peijs a été attaqué à bruxel.
you have requested a+debate+on+this+subject in the course of the+next+few+days during this part+session. tu as demandé un+débat+sur+ce+sujet au cours des+prochains+jours au cours de cette+partie +de+session.

Table 2: Example of sentences in the training corpus

Source	il faut prendre en considération le fait que les compagnies d'assurance ont besoin d'un certain temps.
Baseline	it must be taken into account the fact that insurance companies need some time.
Interlingual Triggers	Account must+be+taken of the+fact that insurance companies request a certain amount of time.
Interlingual Triggers + PBLM	we must bare+in+mind the+fact that insurance companies need some time.
Source	Dans ce contexte, il faut veiller, si une partie à l'accord opère au niveau régional.
Baseline	In this connection, we have to make sure that if the party to an agreement operates at regional level, .
Interlingual Triggers	In+this+context, it+must+be+ensured, if a party to the agreement operates at regional+level.
Interlingual Triggers + PBLM	In+this+context, we+have+to+make+sure, if a party to the agreement operates at regional+level.

Table 3: Few examples of translations based on the phrase-based language model

- To take into account long distance dependency: the phrase-based language model can easily capture the long distance relationship between the different components of the sentence.
- To ensure a consistency between phrases of the language model and those of the translation table: Considering the pertinent phrases as single units will reduce the entropy of the language model. More importantly, the current statistical machine translations are performed on phrases, which are considered as translation units. The objective is to ensure that the translated segment correspond to the phrase predicted by a language model.

To build the new phrase-based language model (PBLM), we use a segmented target training corpus in terms of phrases. It consists of 600.000 sentences extracted from the European parliament corpus Europarl. The segmentation has been achieved by using the phrases of translation, as described in the previous section. To train the model, we use SRILM (Stolcke, 2002) to build a 5-gram language model.

5 EXPERIMENTAL EVALUATION AND RESULTS

This section describes the performance of the proposed language model in a machine translation task. The system used in this test is based upon MOSES, briefly described in (Koehn et al., 2007). The parallel corpus used for training consists of French, English text from Europarl Parliament proceeding corpus (Europarl) version 6 described in Table 4. In the baseline phrase-based SMT system four models have been used, namely: four models namely: a translation table, a language model, a distortion model and a penality which reflects the difference in size between the proposed translation and the sentence to be translated. To estimate the optimal value of each weight, the Minimum Error Rate Training (MERT) algorithm is used on a development corpus. In this work, we assume that the maximum size of a phrase is 8 words. In (Nasri et al., 2014), the authors showed that the quality of translation does not increase with phrase size greater than 8 words. The development and test corpus must be rewritten in the same way as the training corpus with phrases. In case of conflict between two phrases, the algorithm will prefer the phrase with the highest CMI value.

Corpus		**French**	**English**
Training	**Sentences**	1M	
	Words	23362869	20498748
	Vocabulary	968081	967065
Dev	**Sentences**	1400	
	Words	38741	34839
Test	**Sentences**	500	
	Words	5.8k	5.3k

Table 4: Description of Europarl corpus

In this evaluation, we compare the performance of the following translation systems in terms of BLEU (Papineni et al., 2002), METEOR (Lavie and Agarwal, 2005) and TER (Snover et al., 2006): the baseline translation system (Koehn et al., 2007) using a standard ngram language model, and the inter-lingual trigger based translation system (Nasri et al., 2014) using both models (ngram and phrase-based language model). Table 3 shows some examples of translations based on the phrase-based language model. Table 4, 5 and 6 present respectively the results in terms of BLEU, METEOR and TER.

System	Dev	Test
Baseline	30.42	28.56
Baseline + PBLM	30.76	28.8
Triggers	28.58	26.66
Triggers + PBLM	29.60	27.54

Table 5: Evaluation of translation systems using different LM (ngram PBLM) in terms of BLEU

System	Dev	Test
Baseline	50.22	49.32
Baseline + PBLM	50.91	49.61
Triggers	48.31	47.03
Triggers + PBLM	48.42	47.21

Table 6: Evaluation of translation systems using different LM (ngram PBLM) in terms of METEOR

The Phrase-Based Language Model (PBLM) while outperforms slightly the translation quality of the baseline phrase-based SMT system what-

System	Dev	Test
Baseline	35.32	30.59
Baseline + PBLM	35.24	30.29
Triggers	38.68	32.33
Triggers + PBLM	38.51	32.21

Table 7: Evaluation of translation systems using different LM (ngram PBLM) in terms of TER

ever the measures. In fact, in terms of BLEU the improvement is equal to 0.34% on Dev2010, and 0.24% on test2010. In terms of METEOR, an increase of 0,69% and 0.29% have been achieved on DEV20110 and Test2010. While for the TER we observed a reduction of TER of 0,08 and 0,12 on respectively DEV2010 and Test2010. In trigger-based machine translation, the PBLM improves also the translation quality measured by BLEU, METEOR and TER. In term of BLEU, the improvement is equal to 1.02% on Dev2010, and 0.88% on test2010. METEOR also increased of 0.11% on Dev2010 and 0.18% on test2010. TER decreased of 0,17% and 0,12% on respectively DEV2010 and Test2010.

6 CONCLUSION

In this paper, we have presented a new phrase-based language model for statistical machine translation. We first, gave the definition of inter-lingual triggers. Then, we described a new algorithm for learning translation pairs without an initial word-to-word alignments, nor an initial segmentation of the monolingual text. Finally, we designed a new phrase based langue model.
The experiments on French-to-English translation demonstrated that the proposed phrase-based language model improve the quality of translation by proposing another kind of language model. In fact, a variable-length language model has the ability to use potentially the same phrases as those of the partial translations which reinforces the quality of translation.

References

E. Arsoy, T. N. Sainath, B. Kingsbury, and B. Ramabhadran. 2012. Deep neural network language models. In *In Proceedings of NAACL-HLT 2012 Workshop: Will We Ever Really Replace the N-gram Model? On the Future of Language Modeling for HLT*, pages 20–28.

V. Baisa. 2011. Chunk-based language model and machine translation. Master's thesis.

E. Charniak, K. Knight, and K. Yamada. 2003. Syntax-based language models for statistical machine translation. In *In MT Summit IX. Intl. Assoc. for Machine Translation*, pages 40–46.

M. R. Costa-Jussà, V. Daudaravicius, and R. E. Banchs. 2010. Using collocation segmentation to extract translation units in a phrase-based statistical machine translation system. *Procesamiento del Lenguaje Natural*, 45:215–220.

K. Dietrich. 1998. Language-model optimization by mapping of corpora. In *Proceedings of the International Conference on Acoustics, Speech, and Signal Processing*, pages 701–704, Seattle, USA. International Conference on Acoustics, Speech, and Signal Processing.

A. Ljolje G. Riccardi, A. L. Gorin and M. Riley. 1997. A spoken language system for automated call routing. In *Proceedings of the International Conference on Acoustics, Speech, and Signal Processing*, pages 1143–1146, Munich, Germany. International Conference on Acoustics, Speech, and Signal Processing.

E. Giachin. 1995. Phrase bigrams for continuous speech recognition. In *Proceedings of the International Conference on Acoustics, Speech, and Signal Processing*, pages 225–228, Detroit, Michigan, USA. International Conference on Acoustics, Speech, and Signal Processing.

D. Buo K.F. Ries and A. Waibel. 1996. Class phrase models for language modeling. In *Proceedings of the International Conference on Spoken Language Processing*, pages 398–401, Philadelphia, USA. The Fourth International Conference on Spoken Language Processing.

K. Kirchhoff and M. Yang. 2005. Improved language modeling for statistical machine translation. In *Proceedings of the ACL Workshop on Building and Using Parallel Texts*, pages 125–128, Ann Arbor, Michigan. Association for Computational Linguistics.

P. Koehn, F.J Och, and D. Marcu. 2003. Statistical phrase-based translation. In *Proceedings of the 2003 Conference of the North American Chapter of the Association for Computational Linguistics on Human Language Technology - Volume 1*, NAACL '03, pages 48–54, Edmonton, Canada. Association for Computational Linguistics.

P. Koehn, H. Hoang, A. Birch, C. Callison-Burch, M. Federico, N. Bertoldi, B. Cowan, W. Shen, C. Moran, R. Zens, C. Dyer, O. Bojar, A. Constantin, and E. Herbst. 2007. Moses: Open source toolkit for statistical machine translation. In *Proceedings of the 45th Annual Meeting of the ACL on Interactive Poster and Demonstration Sessions*, pages 177–180,

Prague, Czech Republic. Association for Computational Linguistics.

C. Callison-Burch L. Schwartz and, W. Schuler, and S. Wu. 2011. Incremental syntactic language models for phrase-based translation.

J.D. Lafferty, A. McCallum, and F.C.N. Pereira. 2001. Conditional random fields: Probabilistic models for segmenting and labeling sequence data. In *Proceedings of the Eighteenth International Conference on Machine Learning*, ICML '01, pages 282–289, San Francisco, CA, USA. Morgan Kaufmann Publishers Inc.

C. Lavecchia, K. Smaili, D. Langlois, and J.P Haton. 2007. Using inter-lingual triggers for machine translation. In *INTERSPEECH*, pages 2829–2832. ISCA.

C. Lavecchia, D. Langlois, and K. Smaili. 2008. Discovering phrases in machine translation by simulated annealing. In *INTERSPEECH*, pages 2354–2357. ISCA.

A. Lavie and A. Agarwal. 2005. Meteor: An automatic metric for mt evaluation with improved correlation with human judgments. pages 65–72.

C. Nasri, K. Smaili, and C. Latiri. 2014. Training phrase-based smt without explicit word alignment. In *Proceedings of the 15th International Conference on Intelligent Text Processing and Computational Linguistics*, pages 233–241, Nepal.

K. Papineni, S. Roukosand W. Todd, and Z. Wei-Jing. 2002. Bleu: A method for automatic evaluation of machine translation. In *Proceedings of the 40th Annual Meeting on Association for Computational Linguistics*, ACL '02, pages 311–318, Stroudsburg, PA, USA. Association for Computational Linguistics.

R. Sarikaya and Y. Deng. 2007. Joint morphological-lexical language modeling for machine translation. In *Proceedings of the 45th Annual Meeting of the ACL on Interactive Poster and Demonstration Sessions*, Prague, Czech Republic. Association for Computational Linguistics.

H. Schwenk. 2007. Continuous space language models. *Computer Speech and Language*, 21(3):492 – 518.

M. Snover, B. Dorr, R. Schwartz, L. Micciulla, and J. Makhoul. 2006. A study of translation edit rate with targeted human annotation. In *In Proceedings of Association for Machine Translation in the Americas*, pages 223–231.

A. Stolcke. 2002. Srilm - an extensible language modeling toolkit. In *SRILM - An Extensible Language Modeling Toolkit*, pages 901–904.

C. Tillmann and H. Ney. 1997. Word triggers and the em algorithm. In *IN PROCEEDINGS OF THE WORKSHOP COMPUTATIONAL NATURAL LANGUAGE LEARNING (CONLL 97*, pages 117–124.

Y. Wu, X. Lu, H. Yamamoto, S. Matsuda, C. Hori, and H. Kashioka. 2012. Factored language model based on recurrent neural network.

T. Xiao, J. Zhu, and M. Zhu. 2011. Language modeling for syntax-based machine translation using tree substitution grammars: A case study on chinese-english translation. pages 18:1–18:29.

J. Xu and G. Chen. 2015. Phrase based language model for statistical machine translation. arXiv preprint arXiv:1501.04324.

B. Yoshua, D. Réjean, V. Pascal, and J. Christian. 2003. A neural probabilistic language model. *J. Mach. Learn. Res.*, 3:1137–1155, March.

I. Zitouni, K. Smaili, and J.P. Haton. 2003. Statistical language modeling based on variable-length sequences. volume 17, pages 27–41.

A Simple and Efficient Method to Generate Word Sense Representations

Luis Nieto Piña and **Richard Johansson**
Språkbanken, Department of Swedish, University of Gothenburg
Box 200, SE-40530 Gothenburg, Sweden
{luis.nieto.pina, richard.johansson}@svenska.gu.se

Abstract

Distributed representations of words have boosted the performance of many Natural Language Processing tasks. However, usually only one representation per word is obtained, not acknowledging the fact that some words have multiple meanings. This has a negative effect on the individual word representations and the language model as a whole. In this paper we present a simple model that enables recent techniques for building word vectors to represent distinct senses of polysemic words. In our assessment of this model we show that it is able to effectively discriminate between words' senses and to do so in a computationally efficient manner.

1 Introduction

Distributed representations of words have helped obtain better language models (Bengio et al., 2003) and improve the performance of many natural language processing applications such as named entity recognition, chunking, paraphrasing, or sentiment classification (Turian et al., 2010; Socher et al., 2011; Glorot et al., 2011). Recently, the Skip-gram model (Mikolov et al., 2013a; Mikolov et al., 2013b) was proposed, which is able to produce high-quality representations from large collections of text in an efficient manner.

Despite the achievements of distributed representations, polysemy or homonymy are usually disregarded even when word semantics may have a large influence on the models. This results in several distinct senses of one same word sharing a representation, and possibly influencing the representations of words related to those distinct senses under the premise that similar words should have similar representations. Some recent attempts to address this issue are mentioned in the next section.

We present a simple method for obtaining sense representations directly during the Skip-gram training phase. It differs from most previous approaches in that it does not need to create or maintain clusters to discriminate between senses, leading to a significant reduction in the model's complexity. It also uses a heuristic approach to determining the number of senses to be learned per word that allows the model to use knowledge from lexical resources but also to keep its ability to work withouth them. In the following sections we look at previous work, describe our model, and inspect its results in qualitative and quantitative evaluations.

2 Related Work

One of the first steps towards obtaining word sense embeddings was that by Reisinger and Mooney (2010). The authors propose to cluster occurrences of any given word in a corpus into a fixed number K of clusters which represent different word usages (rather than word senses). Each word's is thus assigned multiple prototypes or embeddings.

Huang et al. (2012) introduced a neural language model that leverages sentence-level and document-level context to generate word embeddings. Using Reisinger and Mooney (2010)'s approach to generate multiple embeddings per word via clusters and training on a corpus whose words have been substituted by its associated cluster's centroid, the neural model is able to learn multiple embeddings per word.

Neelakantan et al. (2014) tried to expand the Skip-gram model (Mikolov et al., 2013a; Mikolov et al., 2013b) to produce word sense embeddings using the clustering approach of Reisinger and Mooney (2010) and Huang et al. (2012). Notably, Skip-gram's architecture allows the model to, given a word and its context, select and train a word sense embedding jointly. The authors

Proceedings of Recent Advances in Natural Language Processing, pages 465–472,
Hissar, Bulgaria, Sep 7–9 2015.

also introduced a *non-parametric* variation of their model which allows a variable number of clusters per word instead of a fixed K.

Also based on the Skip-gram model, Chen et al. (2014) proposed to maintain and train context word and word sense embeddings conjunctly, by training the model to predict both the context words and the senses of those context words given a target word. To avoid using cluster centroids to represent senses, the number of sense embeddings per word and their initial values are obtained from a knowledge network.

Our system for obtaining word sense embeddings also builds upon the Skip-gram model (which is described in more detail in the next section). Unlike most of the models described above, we do not make use of clustering algorithms. We also allow each word to have its own number of senses, which can be obtained from a dictionary or using any other heuristic suitable for this purpose. These characteristics translate into *a*) little overhead calculations added on top of the initial word-based model; and *b*) an efficient use of memory, as the majority of words are monosemic.

3 Model Description

3.1 From Word Forms to Senses

The distributed representations for word forms that stem from a Skip-gram (Mikolov et al., 2013a; Mikolov et al., 2013b) model are built on the premise that, given a certain target word, they should serve to predict its surrounding words in a text. I.e., the training of a Skip-gram model, given a target word w, is based on maximizing the log-probability of the context words of w, $c_1, \ldots, c_n$:

$$\sum_{i=1}^{n} \log p(c_i|w). \tag{1}$$

The training data usually consists of a large collection of sentences or documents, so that the role of target word w can be iterated over these sequences of words, while the context words c considered in each case are those that surround w within a window of a certain length. The objective then becomes maximizing the average sum of the log-probabilities from Eq. 1.

We propose to modify this model to include a sense s of the word w. Note that Eq. 1 equals

$$\log p(c_1, \ldots, c_n|w) \tag{2}$$

if we assume the context words c_i to be independent of each other given a target word w. The notation in Eq. 2 allows us to consider the Skip-gram as a Naïve Bayes model parameterized by word embeddings (Mnih and Kavukcuoglu, 2013). In this scenario, including a sense would amount then to adding a latent variable s, and our model's behaviour given a target word w is to select a sense s, which is in its turn used to predict n context words $c_1, \ldots, c_n$. Formally:

$$\begin{aligned} p(s, c_1, \ldots, c_n|w) &= \\ p(s|w) \cdot p(c_1, \ldots, c_n|s) &= \\ p(s|w) \cdot p(c_1|s) \ldots p(c_n|s)&. \end{aligned} \tag{3}$$

Thus, our training objective is to maximize the sum of the log-probabilities of context words c given a sense s of the target word w plus the log-probability of the sense s given the target word:

$$\log p(s|w) + \sum_{i=1}^{n} \log p(c_i|s). \tag{4}$$

We must now consider two distinct vocabularies: V containing all possible word forms (context and target words), and S containing all possible senses for the words in V, with sizes $|V|$ and $|S|$, resp. Given a pre-set $D \in \mathbb{N}$, our ultimate goal is to obtain $|S|$ dense, real-valued vectors of dimension D that represent the senses in our vocabulary S according to the objective function defined in Eq. 4.

The neural architecture of the Skip-gram model works with two separate representations for the same vocabulary of words. This double representation is not motivated in the original papers, but it stems from `word2vec`'s code[1] that the model builds separate representations for context and target words, of which the former constitute the actual output of the system. (A note by Goldberg and Levy (2014) offers some insight into this subject.) We take advantage of this architecture and use one of these two representations to contain senses, rather than word forms: as our model only uses target words w as an intermediate step to select a sense s, we only do not need to keep a representation for them. In this way, our model builds a representation of the vocabulary V, for the context words, and another for the vocabulary S of senses, which contains the actual output. Note that the

[1] `http://code.google.com/p/word2vec/`

representation of context words is only used internally for the purposes of this work, and that context words are word forms; i.e., we only consider senses for the target words.

3.2 Selecting a Sense

In the description of our model above we have considered that for each target word w we are able to select a sense s. We now explain the mechanism used for this purpose. The probability of a context word c_i given a sense s, as they appear in the model's objective function defined in Eq. 4, $p(c_i|s)$, $\forall i \in [1, n]$, can be calculated using the *softmax* function:

$$p(c_i|s) = \frac{e^{v_{c_i}^{\intercal} \cdot v_s}}{\sum_{j=1}^{|V|} e^{v_{c_j}^{\intercal} \cdot v_s}} = \frac{e^{v_{c_i}^{\intercal} \cdot v_s}}{Z(s)}, \quad (5)$$

where v_{c_i} (resp. v_s) denotes the vector representing context word c_i (resp. sense s), $v^{\intercal}$ denotes the transposed vector v, and in the last equality we have used $Z(s)$ to identify the normalizer over all context words. With respect to the probability of a sense s given a target word w, for simplicity we assume that all senses are equally probable; i.e., $p(s|w) = \frac{1}{K}$ for any of the K senses s of word w, senses(w).

Using Bayes formula on Eq. 3, we can now obtain the posterior probability of a sense s given the target word w and the context words $c_1, \ldots, c_n$:

$$\begin{aligned} p(s|c_1, \ldots, c_n, w) = \\ \frac{p(s|w) \cdot p(c_1, \ldots, c_n|s)}{\sum_{s_k \in \text{senses}(w)} p(s_k|w) \cdot p(c_1, \ldots, c_n|s_k)} = \quad (6) \\ \frac{e^{(v_{c_1} + \cdots + v_{c_n}) \cdot v_s} \cdot Z(s)^{-n}}{\sum_{s_k \in \text{senses}(w)} e^{(v_{c_1} + \cdots + v_{c_n}) \cdot v_{s_k}} \cdot Z(s_k)^{-n}}. \end{aligned}$$

During training, thus, given a target word w and context words $c_1, \ldots c_n$, the most probable sense $s \in$ senses(w) is the one that maximizes Eq. 6. Unfortunately, in most cases it is computationally impractical to explicitly calculate $Z(s)$. From a number of possible approximations, we have empirically found that considering $Z(s)$ to be constant yields the best results; this is not an unreasonable approximation if we expect the context word vectors to be densely and evenly spread out in the vector space. Under this assumption, the most probable sense s of w is the one that maximizes

$$\frac{e^{(v_{c_1} + \cdots + v_{c_n}) \cdot v_s}}{\sum_{s_k \in \text{senses}(w)} e^{(v_{c_1} + \cdots + v_{c_n}) \cdot v_{s_k}}} \quad (7)$$

For each word occurrence, we propose to select and train only its most probable sense. This approach of *hard sense assignments* is also taken in Neelakantan et al. (2014)'s work and we follow it here, although it would be interesting to compare it with a *soft* updates of all senses of a given word weighted by the probabilities obtained with Eq. 6.

The training algorithm, thus, iterates over a sequence of words, selecting each one in turn as a target word w and its context words as those in a window of a maximum pre-set size. For each target word, a number K of senses s is considered, and the most probable one selected according to Eq. 7. (Note that, as the number of senses needs to be informed –using, for example, a lexicon–, monosemic words need only have one representation.) The selected sense s substitutes the target word w in the original Skip-gram model, and any of the known techniques used to train it can be subsequently applied to obtain sense representations. The training process is drafted in Algorithm 1 using Skip-gram with Negative Sampling.

Negative Sampling (Mikolov et al., 2013b), based on Noise Contrastive Estimation (Mnih and Teh, 2012), is a computationally efficient approximation for the original Skip-gram objective function (Eq. 1). In our implementation it learns the sense representations by sampling N_{neg} words from a noise distribution and using logistic regression to distinguish them from a certain context word c of a target word w. This process is also illustrated in Algorithm 1.

4 Experiments

We trained the model described in Section 3 on Swedish text using a context window of 10 words and vectors of 200 dimensions. The model requires the number of senses to be specified for each word; as a heuristic, we used the number of senses listed in the SALDO lexicon (Borin et al., 2013). Note, however, that such a resource is not vital and could be substituted by any other heuristic. E.g., a fixed number of senses per word, as Neelakantan et al. (2014) do in their parametric approach.

As a training corpus, we created a corpus of 1 billion words downloaded from Språkbanken, the Swedish language bank.[2] The corpora are distributed in a format where the text has been tokenized, part-of-speech-tagged and lemmatized.

[2] `http://spraakbanken.gu.se`

Algorithm 1: Selection of senses and training using Skip-gram with Negative Sampling. (Note that v_x denotes the vector representation of word/sense x.)

Input: Sequence of words $w_1, \ldots, w_N$, window size n, learning rate α, number of negative words N_{neg}
Output: Updated vectors for each sense of words w_i, $i = 1, \ldots, N$

for $t = 1, \ldots, N$ **do**
  $w = w_i$
  $K \leftarrow$ number of senses of w
  context(w) = $\{c_1, \ldots, c_n \mid c_i = w_{t+i},\ i = -n, \ldots, n,\ i \neq 0\}$
  for $k = 1, \ldots, K$ **do**
    $p_k = \frac{e^{(v_{c_1} + \cdots + v_{c_n}) \cdot v_{s_k}}}{\sum_{j=1}^{K} e^{(v_{c_1} + \cdots + v_{c_n}) \cdot v_{s_j}}}$
  $s = \arg\max_{k=1,\ldots,K} p_k$
  for $i = 1, \ldots, n$ **do**
    $f = \frac{1}{1+e^{v_{c_i} \cdot v_s}}$
    $g = \alpha(1 - f)$
    $\Delta = g \cdot v_{c_i}$
    $v_{c_i} = v_{c_i} + g \cdot v_s$
    for $j = 1, \ldots, N_{neg}$ **do**
      $d_j \leftarrow$ word sampled from noise distribution, $d_j \neq c_i$
      $f = \frac{1}{1+e^{v_{d_j} \cdot v_s}}$
      $g = -\alpha \cdot f$
      $\Delta = \Delta + g \cdot v_{d_j}$
      $v_{d_j} = v_{d_j} + g \cdot v_s$
    $v_s = v_s + \Delta$

Compounds have been segmented automatically and when a lemma was not listed in SALDO, we used the parts of the compounds instead. The input to the software computing the embeddings consisted of lemma forms with concatenated part-of-speech tags, e.g. *dricka*-verb for the verb 'to drink' and *dricka*-noun for the noun 'drink'.

The training time of our model on this corpus was 22 hours. For the sake of time performance comparison, we run an off-the-shelf `word2vec` execution on our corpus using the same parameterization described above; the training of word vectors took 20 hours, which illustrates the little complexity that our model adds to the original Skip-gram.

4.1 Inspection of nearest neighbors

We evaluate the output of the algorithm qualitatively by inspecting the nearest neighbors of the senses of a number of example words, and comparing them to the senses listed in SALDO.

Table 1 shows the nearest neighbor lists of the senses of two words where the algorithm has been able to learn the distinctions used in the lexicon. The verb *flyga* 'to fly' has two senses listed in SALDO: to travel by airplane and to move through the air. The adjective *öm* 'tender' also has two senses, similar to the corresponding English word: one emotional and one physical. The lists are semantically coherent, although we note that they are topical rather than substitutional; this is expected since the algorithm was applied to lemmatized and compound-segmented text and we use a fairly wide context window.

flyg 'flight'	*flaxa* 'to flap wings'
flygning 'flight'	*studsa* 'to bounce'
flygplan 'airplane'	*sväva* 'to hover'
charterplan 'charter plane'	*skjuta* 'to shoot'
SAS-plan 'SAS plane'	*susa* 'to whiz'

(a) *flyga* 'to fly'

kärleksfull 'loving'	*svullen* 'swollen'
ömsint 'tender'	*ömma* 'to be sore'
smek 'caress'	*värka* 'to ache'
kärleksord 'word of love'	*mörbulta* 'to bruise'
ömtålig 'delicate'	*ont* 'pain'

(b) *öm* 'tender'

Table 1: Examples of nearest neighbors of the two senses of two example words.

In a related example, Figure 1 shows the projections onto a 2D space[3] of the representations for the two senses of *åsna*: 'donkey' or 'slow-witted person', and those of their corresponding nearest neighbors.

For some other words we have inspected, we fail to find one or more of the senses. This is typically when one sense is very dominant, drowning out the rare senses. For instance, the word *rock*

[3]The projection was computed using `scikit-learn` (Pedregosa et al., 2011) using multidimensional scaling of the distances in a 200-dimensional vector space.

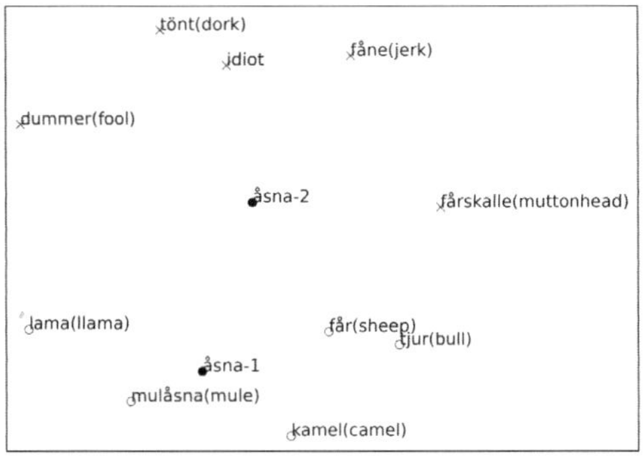

Figure 1: 2D projections of the two senses of *åsna* ('donkey' and 'slow-witted person') and their nearest neighbors.

has two senses, 'rock music' and 'coat', where the first one is much more frequent. While one of the induced senses is close to some pieces of clothing, most of its nearest neighbors are styles of music.

In other cases, the algorithm has come up with meaningful sense distinctions, but not exactly as in the lexicon. For instance, the lexicon lists two senses for the noun *böna*: 'bean' and 'girl'; the algorithm has instead created two bean senses: bean as a plant part or bean as food. In some other cases, the algorithm finds genre-related distinctions instead of sense distinctions. For instance, for the verb *älska*, with two senses 'to love' or 'to make love', the algorithm has found two stylistically different uses of the first sense: one standard, and one related to informal words frequently used in social media. Similarly, for the noun *svamp* 'sponge' or 'mushroom'/'fungus', the algorithm does not find the sponge sense but distinguishes taxonomic, cooking-related, and nature-related uses of the mushroom/fungus sense. It's also worth mentioning that when some frequent foreign word is homographic with a Swedish word, it tends to be assigned to a sense. For instance, for the adjective *sur* 'sour', the lexicon lists one taste and one chemical sense; the algorithm conflates those two senses but creates a sense for the French preposition.

4.2 Quantitative Evaluation

Most systems that automatically discover word senses have been evaluated either by clustering the instances in an annotated corpus (Manandhar et al., 2010; Jurgens and Klapaftis, 2013), or by measuring the effect of the senses representations in a downstream task such as contextual word similarity (Huang et al., 2012; Neelakantan et al., 2014). However, Swedish lacks sense-annotated corpora as well as word similarity test sets, so our evaluation is instead based on comparing the discovered word senses to those listed in the SALDO lexicon. We selected the 100 most frequent two-sense nouns, verbs, and adjectives and used them as the test set.

To evaluate the senses discovered for a lemma, we generated two sets of word lists: one derived from the lexicon, and one from the vector space. For each sense s_i listed in the lexicon, we created a list L_i by selecting the N senses (for other words) most similar to s_i according to the graph-based similarity metric by Wu and Palmer (1994). Conversely, for each sense vector v_j in our vector-based model, a list V_j was built by selecting the N vectors most similar to v_j, using the cosine similarity. We finally mapped the senses back to their corresponding lemmas, so that the two sets $L = \{L_i\}$ and $V = \{V_j\}$ of word lists could be compared.

These lists were then evaluated using standard clustering evaluation metrics. We used three different metrics:

- *Purity/Inverse-purity F-measure* (Zhao and Karypis, 2001), where each of the lexicon-based lists L_i is matched to the vector-based list V_j that maximizes the F-measure, the harmonic mean of the cluster-based precision and recall:

  $$P(V_j, L_i) = \frac{|V_j \cap L_i|}{|C_j|} \quad R(V_j, L_i) = \frac{|V_j \cap L_i|}{|L_i|}$$

  The overall F-measure is defined as the weighted average of individual F-measures:

  $$F = \sum_i \frac{|L_i|}{\sum_k |L_k|} \max_j F(V_j, L_i)$$

- *B-cubed F-measure* (Bagga and Baldwin, 1998), which computes individual precision and recall measures for every item occurring in one of the lists, and then averaging all precision and recall values. The F-measure is the harmonic mean of the averaged precision and recall.

- *V-measure* (Rosenberg and Hirschberg, 2007), the harmonic mean of the *homogeneity* and the *completeness*, two entropy-based metrics. The homogeneity is defined as the relative reduction of entropy in V when adding the information about L:

$$h(V, L) = 1 - \frac{H(V|L)}{H(V)}$$

Conversely, the completeness is defined

$$c(V, L) = 1 - \frac{H(L|V)}{H(L)}.$$

Both measures are set to 1 if the denominator is zero.

Table 2 shows the results of the evaluation for nouns, verbs, and adjectives, and for different values of the list size N. As a strong baseline, we also include an evaluation of the sense representations discovered by the system of Neelakantan et al. (2014), run with the same settings as our system. This system is available only in its parametric version. (I.e., the number of senses per word is a fixed parameter.) As the words used in the experiments always have two senses assigned, this parameter is set to 2. This accounts for fairness in the comparison with our approach, which is given the *right* number of senses by the lexicon (and thus in this case also 2). We used the three metrics mentioned above: Purity/Inverse-purity F-measure (*Pu-F*), B-cubed F-measure (*B^3-F*), and V-measure (*V*). As we can see, our system achieves higher scores than the baseline in almost all the evaluations, despite using a simpler algorithm that uses less memory. Only for the V-measure the result is inconclusive for verbs and adjectives; for nouns, and for the other two evaluation metrics, our system is consistently better.

	Pu-F		**B^3-F**		**V**	
N	N-14	ours	N-14	ours	N-14	ours
10	9.4	**10.7**	2.5	**2.8**	8.9	**10.6**
20	9.5	**10.8**	2.1	**2.4**	6.7	**8.9**
40	9.0	**9.9**	1.8	**2.0**	5.1	**7.2**
80	7.8	**8.9**	1.4	**1.7**	4.3	**5.6**
160	7.4	**8.2**	1.3	**1.5**	3.9	**4.7**

(a) Nouns.

	Pu-F		**B^3-F**		**V**	
N	N-14	ours	N-14	ours	N-14	ours
10	9.1	**10.8**	2.0	**2.5**	**11.3**	7.6
20	8.1	**9.3**	1.4	**1.7**	6.7	**7.5**
40	7.3	**8.2**	1.0	**1.3**	4.5	**4.5**
80	7.5	**8.7**	1.0	**1.3**	**3.7**	3.2
160	8.2	**10.3**	1.2	**1.7**	1.2	**1.5**

(b) Verbs.

	Pu-F		**B^3-F**		**V**	
N	N-14	ours	N-14	ours	N-14	ours
10	6.8	**7.6**	1.4	**1.7**	9.4	**10.7**
20	6.5	**7.6**	1.3	**1.5**	**8.5**	7.2
40	6.4	**7.3**	1.1	**1.3**	5.4	**5.8**
80	6.5	**7.0**	1.0	**1.1**	**5.2**	4.7
160	6.9	**7.5**	1.0	**1.1**	4.1	**4.4**

(c) Adjectives.

Table 2: Evaluation of the senses produced by our system and that of Neelakantan et al. (2014).

5 Conclusions and Future Work

In this paper, we present a model for automatically building sense vectors based on the Skip-gram method. In order to learn the sense vectors, we modify the Skip-gram model to take into account the number of senses of each target word. By including a mechanism to select the most probable sense given a target word and its context, only slight modifications to the original training algorithm are necessary for it to learn distinct representations of word senses from unstructured text.

To evaluate our model we train it on a 1-billion-word Swedish corpus and use the SALDO lexicon to inform the number of senses associated to each word. Over a series of examples in which we analyse the nearest neighbors of some of the represented senses, we show how the obtained sense representations are able to replicate the senses defined in SALDO, or to make novel sense distinctions in others. On instances in which a sense is dominant we observe that the obtained representations favour this sense in detriment of less common ones.

We also give a quantitative evaluation of the sense representations learned by our model using a variety of clustering evaluation metrics, and compare its performance with that of the model proposed by Neelakantan et al. (2014). In most instances of this evaluation our model obtains higher scores than this baseline, despite its relative lower complexity. Our model's low complexity is characterized by *a*) the simple word sense disambiguation algorithm introduced in Section 3.2, which allows us to fit word sense embeddings into Skip-gram's existing architecture with little added computations; and *b*) the flexible number of senses per word, which takes advantage of the monosemic condition of most words to make an efficient use of memory. This low complexity is demonstrated by our training algorithm's small increase in running time with respect to that of the original, word-based Skip-gram model.

In this work, our use of a lexicon is limited to setting the number of senses of a given word, While this information proves useful for obtaining coherent sense representations, an interesting line of research lies in further exploiting existing knowledge resources for learning better sense vectors. E.g., leveraging the network topology of a lexicon such as SALDO, that links together senses of semantically related words, could arguably help improve the representations for those rare senses with which our model currently struggles, by learning their representations taking into account those of neighbour senses in the network.

Acknowledgments

We would like to thank the reviewers for their constructive comments. This research was funded by the Swedish Research Council under grant 2013–4944, *Distributional methods to represent the meaning of frames and constructions*.

References

Amit Bagga and Breck Baldwin. 1998. Algorithms for scoring coreference chains. In *Proceedings of the 1st International Conference on Language Resources and Evaluation*, pages 563–566, Granada, Spain.

Yoshua Bengio, Réjean Ducharme, Pascal Vincent, and Christian Jauvin. 2003. A neural probabilistic language model. *Journal of Machine Learning Research*, 3:1137–1155.

Lars Borin, Markus Forsberg, and Lennart Lönngren. 2013. SALDO: a touch of yin to WordNet's yang. *Language Resources and Evaluation*, 47:1191–1211.

Xinxiong Chen, Zhiyuan Liu, and Maosong Sun. 2014. A unified model for word sense representation and disambiguation. In *Proceedings of the 2014 Conference on Empirical Methods in Natural Language Processing (EMNLP)*, pages 1025–1035.

Xavier Glorot, Antoine Bordes, and Yoshua Bengio. 2011. Domain adaptation for large-scale sentiment classification: A deep learning approach. In *Proceedings of the 28th International Conference on Machine Learning (ICML-11)*, pages 513–520.

Yoav Goldberg and Omer Levy. 2014. word2vec explained: deriving Mikolov et al.'s negative-sampling word-embedding method. *arXiv preprint arXiv:1402.3722*.

Eric H Huang, Richard Socher, Christopher D Manning, and Andrew Y Ng. 2012. Improving word representations via global context and multiple word prototypes. In *Proceedings of the 50th Annual Meeting of the Association for Computational Linguistics: Long Papers-Volume 1*, pages 873–882. Association for Computational Linguistics.

David Jurgens and Ioannis Klapaftis. 2013. SemEval-2013 task 13: Word sense induction for graded and non-graded senses. In *Second Joint Conference on Lexical and Computational Semantics (*SEM), Volume 2: Proceedings of the Seventh International Workshop on Semantic Evaluation (SemEval 2013)*, pages 290–299, Atlanta, United States.

Suresh Manandhar, Ioannis Klapaftis, Dmitriy Dligach, and Sameer Pradhan. 2010. Semeval-2010 task 14: Word sense induction & disambiguation. In *Proceedings of the 5th International Workshop on Semantic Evaluation*, pages 63–68, Uppsala, Sweden.

Tomas Mikolov, Kai Chen, Greg Corrado, and Jeffrey Dean. 2013a. Efficient estimation of word representations in vector space. *arXiv preprint arXiv:1301.3781*.

Tomas Mikolov, Ilya Sutskever, Kai Chen, Greg S Corrado, and Jeff Dean. 2013b. Distributed representations of words and phrases and their compositionality. In *Advances in Neural Information Processing Systems*, pages 3111–3119.

Andriy Mnih and Koray Kavukcuoglu. 2013. Learning word embeddings efficiently with noise-contrastive estimation. In *Advances in Neural Information Processing Systems*, pages 2265–2273.

Andriy Mnih and Yee Whye Teh. 2012. A fast and simple algorithm for training neural probabilistic language models. *arXiv preprint arXiv:1206.6426*.

Arvind Neelakantan, Jeevan Shankar, Alexandre Passos, and Andrew McCallum. 2014. Efficient non-parametric estimation of multiple embeddings per word in vector space. In *Proceedings of EMNLP*.

Fabian Pedregosa, Gaël Varoquaux, Alexandre Gramfort, Vincent Michel, Bertrand Thirion, Olivier Grisel, Mathieu Blondel, Peter Prettenhofer, Ron Weiss, Vincent Dubourg, Jake VanderPlas, Alexandre Passos, David Cournapeau, Matthieu Brucher, Matthieu Perrot, and Edouard Duchesnay. 2011. Scikit-learn: Machine learning in Python. *Journal of Machine Learning Research*, 12:2825–2830.

Joseph Reisinger and Raymond J Mooney. 2010. Multi-prototype vector-space models of word meaning. In *Human Language Technologies: The 2010 Annual Conference of the North American Chapter of the Association for Computational Linguistics*, pages 109–117. Association for Computational Linguistics.

Andrew Rosenberg and Julia Hirschberg. 2007. V-measure: A conditional entropy-based external cluster evaluation measure. In *Proceedings of the 2007 Joint Conference on Empirical Methods in Natural*

Language Processing and Computational Natural Language Learning (EMNLP-CoNLL), pages 410–420, Prague, Czech Republic.

Richard Socher, Eric H Huang, Jeffrey Pennin, Christopher D Manning, and Andrew Y Ng. 2011. Dynamic pooling and unfolding recursive autoencoders for paraphrase detection. In *Advances in Neural Information Processing Systems*, pages 801–809.

Joseph Turian, Lev Ratinov, and Yoshua Bengio. 2010. Word representations: a simple and general method for semi-supervised learning. In *Proceedings of the 48th Annual Meeting of the Association for Computational Linguistics*, pages 384–394. Association for Computational Linguistics.

Zhibiao Wu and Martha Palmer. 1994. Verb semantics and lexical selection. In *Proceedings of the 32nd Annual Meeting of the Association for Computational Linguistics*, pages 133–138, Las Cruces, United States.

Ying Zhao and George Karypis. 2001. Criterion functions for document clustering: Experiments and analysis. Technical Report TR 01-040, Department of Computer Science, University of Minnesota.

TBXTools: A Free, Fast and Flexible Tool for Automatic Terminology Extraction

Antoni Oliver
Universitat Oberta de Catalunya
aoliverg@uoc.edu

Mercè Vàzquez
Universitat Oberta de Catalunya
mvazquezga@uoc.edu

Abstract

The manual identification of terminology from specialized corpora is a complex task that needs to be addressed by flexible tools, in order to facilitate the construction of multilingual terminologies which are the main resources for computer-assisted translation tools, machine translation or ontologies. The automatic terminology extraction tools developed so far either use a proprietary code or an open source code, that is limited to certain software functionalities. To automatically extract terms from specialized corpora for different purposes such as constructing dictionaries, thesauruses or translation memories, we need open source tools to easily integrate new functionalities to improve term selection. This paper presents TBXTools, a free automatic terminology extraction tool that implements linguistic and statistical methods for multiword term extraction. The tool allows the users to easily identify multiword terms from specialized corpora and also, if needed, translation candidates from parallel corpora. In this paper we present the main features of TBXTools along with evaluation results for term extraction, both using statistical and linguistic methodology, for several corpora.

1 Introduction

Automatic terminology extraction (ATE) is a relevant natural language processing task involving terminology which has been used to identify domain-relevant terms applying computational methods (Oliver et al., 2007a; Foo, 2012).

Automatic term extraction is a relevant task that can be useful for a wide range of tasks, such as ontology learning, machine translation, computer-assisted translation, thesaurus construction, classification, indexing, information retrieval, and also text mining and text summarisation (Heid and McNaught, 1991; Frantzi and Ananiadou, 1996; Vu et al., 2008).

The automatic terminology extraction tools developed in recent years allow easier manual term extraction from a specialized corpus, which is a long, tedious and repetitive task that has the risk of being unsystematic and subjective, very costly in economic terms and limited by the current available information. However, existing tools should be improved in order to get more consistent terminology and greater productivity (Gornostay, 2010).

In the last few years, several term extraction tools have been developed, but most of them are language-dependent: French and English –Fastr (Jacquemin, 1999) and Acabit (Daille, 2003); Portuguese –Extracterm (Costa et al., 2004) and ExATOlp (Lopes et al., 2009); Spanish-Basque –Elexbi (Hernaiz et al., 2006); Spanish-German –Autoterm (Haller, 2008); Arabic (Boulaknadel et al., 2008); Slovene and English –Luiz (Vintar, 2010); English and Italian –KX (Pianta and Tonelli, 2010); or English and German (Gojun et al., 2012).

Some tools are adapted to a specialized domain: TermExtractor (Sclano and Velardi, 2007), TerMine (Ananiadou et al., 2009) or BioYaTeA (Golik et al., 2013), for example. Specific tools have been developed to extract corpus-specific lexical items comparing technical and non-technical corpus: TermoStat (Drouin, 2003). And other tools are based on under-resourced language –TWSC (Pinnis et al., 2012)–, or use semantic and contextual information –Yate (Vivaldi and Rodríguez, 2001).

Furthermore, there was TermSuite, which was developed during the European project TTC (*Terminology Extraction, Translation Tools and Com-*

Proceedings of Recent Advances in Natural Language Processing, pages 473–479,
Hissar, Bulgaria, Sep 7–9 2015.

parable Corpora). This project focused on the automatic or semi-automatic acquisition of aligned bilingual terminologies for computer-assisted translation and machine translation. To this end, automatic terminology extraction is part of the process of identifying terminologies from comparable corpora (Blancafort et al., 2010).

This paper presents TBXTools, a free automatic term extraction tool which allows multiword terms from specialized corpora to be identified easily, combining statistical and linguistic methods.

This paper is structured as follows: in the next section we present the TBXTools implementation and statistical and linguistic methods, as well as the automatic finding of translation equivalents. The experimental settings are described in detail in section 3. The paper concludes with some final remarks and ideas for future work.

2 TBXTools

2.1 Description

TBXTools is a Python class that implements a set of methods for ATE along with other utilities related to terminology management. This tool has a free software licence and can be downloaded from SourceForge[1]. TBXTools is an evolution of previous tools developed by the authors (Oliver and Vàzquez, 2007; Oliver et al., 2007b).The tool is still under development but it already implements a set of methods that permit the following functionalities:

- Statistical term extraction using n-grams and stop words and allowing some normalizations: capital letter normalization, morphological normalization and nested candidate detection.
- Linguistic term extraction using morpho-syntactic pattern and a tagged corpus. Any external tagger and a connection with a server running Freeling (Padró and Stanilovsky, 2012) are implemented. The tool uses an easy formalism for the expression of patterns, allowing the use of regular expressions and lemmatization of some of the components, if required.
- Detection of translation candidates in parallel corpora, using a statistical strategy.
- Automatic learning of morphological patterns from a list of reference terms.

[1]http://sourceforge.net/projects/tbxtools/

Nowadays TBXTools does not have a user interface, but it will be developed in the future. At present the extraction is done by means of simple Python scripts calling the TBXTools class. In this paper we will see the code of some of these scripts. Several examples of scripts can be found in the TBXTools distribution.

2.2 Statistical Terminology Extraction

The statistical strategy for terminology extraction is based on the calculation of n-grams, that is, the combination of n words appearing in the corpus. After this calculation, filtering with stop words is performed, eliminating all the candidates beginning or ending with a word from a list. Some normalizations, such as case normalization, nesting detection and morphological normalization, can be performed. Here we can see a complete code for terminology extraction:

```
from TBXTools import *
e=TBXTools()
e.load_sl_corpus("corpus.txt")
e.load_stop_l1("stop-eng.txt")
e.set_nmin(2)
e.set_nmax(3)
e.statistical_term_extraction()
e.case_normalization()
e.nesting_detection()
e.load_morphopatterns("morpho-eng.txt")
e.morpho_normalization()
e.save_term_candidates("candidates.txt")
```

The code, as can be seen, is very simple. First of all, we import TBXTools and create a TBXTools object, called e in the example. This code calculates the term candidates from the corpus in the $corpus.txt$ file using the stop words in the $stop.txt$ file. Afterwards, we fix the minimum n to 2 and the maximum to 3, in order to calculate bigrams and trigrams term candidates. The next step in the code performs the statistical term extraction. After that, the following normalizations are implemented:

- Case normalization: it tries to collapse the same term appearing with a different case: for example, "interest rate", "Interest Rate" and "INTEREST RATE" into "interest rate".
- Nesting detection: sometimes shorter term candidates are not terms in and of themselves, but are part of a longer term. For example, the bigram term candidate "national central" is a part of the trigram term candidate "national central bank".

- Morphological normalization: it tries to collapse several forms at the same time into a single form, for example, to collapse the plural term candidate "economic policies" into "economic policy". To perform this normalization, a simple set of morphological patterns is used. After all these normalizations, the term candidates are saved into the text file *candidates.txt*. The candidates are stored in descending frequency order and the value of frequency is also stored, as in the following example:

```
53 euro banknotes
51 central bank
47 payment institution
23 payment instrument
```

2.3 Linguistic Terminology Extraction

To perform linguistic terminology extraction we need a POS-tagged corpus. The tagging can be performed with any tagger offering lemma and POS tags. TBXTools can be easily used with Freeling. In the following example we will perform linguistic extraction from a tagged corpus (*ct.txt*) using a set of patterns (*p*) and storing the term candidates into the file *candidates.txt*. The Python script would look like this:

```
from TBXTools import *
e=TBXTools()
e.load_tagged_corpus("ct.txt")
e.load_ling_termextract_patterns("p.txt")
e.ling_term_extract()
e.save_term_candidates("candidates.txt")
```

If our tagged corpus uses the Penn Treebank POS tags, the patterns should be expressed with these same tags, for example NN NN or JJ NN. If we want to use the lemma instead of the word form in a pattern, we use square brackets, as in NN [NN.*]. Note that in this pattern we have also used regular expressions to make it more general. The formalism also allows for the inclusion of the lemmas and word forms in the patterns, as in [N.*] /of/ [N.*], where the lemma *of* is used.

TBXTools is able to calculate the translation equivalent for a given term using a parallel corpus. If the given term appears several times in the corpus, TBXTools can use simple statistical calculations to try to select the translation equivalent in the target language. In the following code we can observe how this task can be performed:

```
from TBXTools import *
import codecs
e=TBXTools()
e.load_tabtxt_corpus("corpus.txt")
e.load_stop_l2("stop.txt")
...
tr=e.get_statistical_translation_
candidate(t, candidates=5)
print(t,tr)
...
```

With this code we load a parallel corpus and a list of stop words for the target language. Then we calculate the translation equivalent (*tr*) from the term (*t*) and ask to return 5 candidates. The output would as follows:

```
payment institution entidad de pago:
servicios de pago:dinero electrónico:
entidad de crédito:Estado miembro:
```

In this example we want to find the translation of "payment institution" and we get 5 candidates in Spanish. In this case the first one is the correct one ("entidad de pago").

3 Experimental Settings

3.1 Resources

We performed some experiments on terminology extraction using controlled corpora, that is, we knew in advance which terms are in these corpora. We used a subset of 1,000 segments from the ECB (European Central Bank) corpus and EMEA (European Medicines Agency documents corpus) corpus (Tiedemann, 2012) in English.

A manual selection of terms in these corpus subsets was performed. Terms in the corpus were manually annotated and those in plural form were lemmatized. This annotation task was performed independently by two terminologists, and those cases with no agreement were discussed and a common solution adopted. Having these annotated corpora, we extracted a list of all terms and their frequencies. Two different lists were extracted for each corpus: a list containing the terms as they appeared in the corpus (in plural or lemma form), and another list containing only the lemmatized terms. These lists of extracted terms from the manually annotated corpora were used to evaluate the extraction results.

3.2 Methodology

In our experiments we performed and evaluated 3 different tasks for both corpus subsets:

- Statistical terminology extraction for English
- Linguistic terminology extraction for English
- Automatic extraction of translation equivalents into Spanish

In all these experiments we used TBXTools. The programs used have been described in section 2.

3.3 Evaluation and Results

Since we have a list of all terms appearing in both corpus subsets, evaluation of the automatic terminology extraction experiments could be done automatically. We have evaluated precision for different values of frequency. TBXTools has a method that, given a set of translation candidates, a list of terms and a value of frequency, calculates the precision and recall values. Here we can see a piece of code for the evaluation task:

```
...
e.load_evaluationterms("ref_terms.txt")
(p,r)=extractor.eval_prec_recall_byfreq(5)
...
```

This code returns the value of precision (p) and recall (r) for all candidates with a frequency of 5 or higher.

The task of automatic extraction of translation equivalents has been evaluated manually by a terminologist.

Statistical Approach

In tables 1 to 4 we can see the evaluation results for the statistical approach. We have presented figures of precision (*P.*) and reacall (*R.*) for bigrams and trigrams and for the ECB and EMEA subsets of 1,000 segments. As we can observe in all results, for high values of frequency we get very few term candidates and the values of precision are not significant, as recall is too low.

In Table 1 we can observe the results for the statistical approach using the subset of the ECB corpus. The total number of candidates for bigram word forms are 720, and for bigram lemmata 696. If we focus on figures for frequency equal to 2, we get 280 candidates with a precision of 43.21% for word forms and 274 candidates with a precision of 27.37% for lemmata. This significant difference between these two values (15.84 points) indicates that the simple approach to lemmatization based on morphological normalization using simple morphological patterns is not very accurate.

	Word forms		Lemmata	
Freq	**P.**	**R.**	**P.**	**R.**
50	100.00	0.34	50.00	0.41
20	100.00	2.06	71.43	2.03
10	61.54	5.50	57.14	6.50
5	59.09	13.40	41.27	10.57
2	43.21	41.58	27.37	30.49
1	29.58	73.20	17.10	48.37

Table 1: Results for statitistical approach using ECB corpus for bigrams

In Table 2 we can observe the results for trigrams. The total number of candidates for trigram word forms are 726, and for trigram lemmata 722. As we can see, the precision values for trigrams are worse than for bigrams (for frequency equal to 2, from 43.21% to 18.72% for word forms and from 27.37% to 5.47% for lemmata).

	Word forms		Lemmata	
Freq	**P.**	**R.**	**P.**	**R.**
50	0	0	X	X
20	100.00	1.87	50.00	2.38
10	75.00	2.80	33.33	4.76
5	50.00	9.35	25.00	11.90
2	18.72	35.51	5.47	26.19
1	10.06	68.22	2.08	35.71

Table 2: Results for statistical approach using ECB corpus for trigrams

In tables 3 and 4 the results for the EMEA subcorpus are presented. The total number of candidates for bigram word forms is 432, and for bigram lemmata, 422, whereas for trigrams the total is 367 both for word forms and lemmata. The behaviour here is very similar to that of the ECB corpus, but here the number of bigram and trigram candidates is lower than for the ECB corpus.

Linguistic Approach

In tables 5 to 8 the results for the linguistic approach are presented.

	Word forms		Lemmata	
Freq	**P.**	**R.**	**P.**	**R.**
50	0	0	0	0
20	100.00	1.90	100.00	2.84
10	77.78	8.86	66.67	8.51
5	52.24	22.15	42.42	19.86
2	30.41	70.25	22.50	57.45
1	27.78	75.95	20.38	60.99

Table 3: Results for statistical approach using EMEA corpus for bigrams

	Word forms		Lemmata	
Freq	**P.**	**R.**	**P.**	**R.**
50	0	0	0	0
20	100.00	2.33	100.00	2.38
10	28.57	4.65	14.29	2.38
5	13.89	11.63	8.33	7.14
2	9.70	67.44	6.69	47.62
1	8.45	72.09	5.99	52.38

Table 4: Results for statistical approach using EMEA corpus for trigrams

	Word forms		Lemmata	
Freq	**P.**	**R.**	**P.**	**R.**
20	100.00	0.69	66.67	0.81
10	66.67	2.75	75.00	4.88
5	58.14	8.59	57.50	9.35
2	41.10	33.33	36.48	34.55
1	25.82	67.70	23.26	69.11

Table 5: Results for linguistic approach using ECB corpus for bigrams

	Word forms		Lemmata	
Freq	**P.**	**R.**	**P.**	**R.**
20	100.00	0.93	0	0
10	33.33	0.93	0	0
5	30.77	3.74	15.38	4.76
2	13.95	16.82	6.98	21.43
1	9.36	49.53	3.55	47.62

Table 6: Results for linguistic approach using ECB corpus for trigrams

	Word forms		Lemmata	
Freq	**P.**	**R.**	**P.**	**R.**
20	100.00	2.53	100.00	3.55
10	87.50	8.86	83.33	10.64
5	66.67	21.52	66.00	23.40
2	29.77	81.01	29.12	86.52
1	28.69	84.81	27.97	90.07

Table 7: Results for linguistic approach using EMEA corpus for bigrams

For the extraction of bigrams candidates we have used a set of patterns that have been learnt

	Word forms		Lemmata	
Freq	**P.**	**R.**	**P.**	**R.**
20	0	0	0	0
10	16.67	2.33	16.67	2.38
5	12.00	6.98	11.11	7.14
2	9.27	67.44	9.74	71.43
1	8.71	72.09	9.43	78.57

Table 8: Results for linguistic approach using EMEA corpus for trigrams

with TBXTools. This feature uses the tagged corpus and a set of reference terms and returns a list of patterns. This list should be manually revised and modified in order to make the patterns more general.

In Table 7 the results for the linguistic approach using the ECB corpus for bigrams are presented. For frequency equal to 2, a precision of 41.10% for word forms and 36.48% for lemmata is achieved. If we now observe the difference between these values (a difference of 4.62 points instead of the 15.84 points for morphological normalization in the statistical approach), we can conclude that the linguistic approach performs much better in the task of normalizing the terms into their base form.

Automatic Extraction of Translation Equivalents in Parallel Corpora

In this section we present the results for the experiments with automatic extraction of translation equivalents in parallel corpora. The Spanish equivalents selection for the English terms (in lemma form) in ECB and EMEA subcorpora was done by two experts translators. As TBXTools is able to return several translation candidates for each corpora, we assessed if the first candidate was correct (P_1) and if any of the first five candidates were correct (P_5). As the algorithm did not produce Spanish translations for many English terms, we also presented a corrected precision ($P*_1$ and $P*_5$), taking only into account the English terms for which the algorithm returned some translation candidates. In some cases we failed to find the translation of a term because we searched using the lemma form and the term always appeared in plural in the corpus. Tables 9 and 10 shows the recall values.

Table 9 shows the evaluation results using a parallel corpus consisting of the first 1,000 seg-

	P_1	P_5	$P*_1$	$P*_5$	R_1	R_5
ECB 2g	12.60%	26.01%	27.93%	57.66%	12.60%	26.01%
ECB 3g	2.78%	12.96%	10%	46.67%	2.78%	12.96%
EMEA 2g	23.40%	43.97%	34.02%	63.92%	23.40%	43.97%
EMEA 3g	2.38%	35.70%	4.00%	60.00%	2.38%	35.71%

Table 9: Results for automatic extraction of translation equivalents for 1,000 segments subcorpora

	P_1	P_5	$P*_1$	$P*_5$	R_1	R_5
ECB 2g	30.89%	47.15%	46.63%	71.17%	30.89%	47.15%
ECB 3g	11.11%	36.11%	21.05%	68.42%	11.11%	31.48%
EMEA 2g	49.65%	68.79%	56.00%	77.60%	49.65%	62.25%
EMEA 3g	16.67%	52.38%	22.58%	70.97%	16.67%	52.35%

Table 10: Results for automatic extraction of translation equivalents for the full corpora

ments of the corpora (the same subset used for extracting the English term candidates). It is evident that precision for bigrams is much higher than precision for trigrams. This is mainly due to the fact that, in general, frequency for trigram terms is much lower than for bigram terms. This fact becomes less important when we correct the results excluding these terms with no translation candidates.

Table 10 shows the evaluation results using the full corpora for finding the translation candidates. As can be observed, precision and recall values are now much higher, as more English sentences can be found containing the desired term, and therefore there are more Spanish sentences with which to find the translation equivalent.

4 Conclusions and Future Work

This paper has presented a free automatic terminology extraction tool. This tool is written in Python and it can work under any popular operating system. The tool is designed to achieve the following:

- The tool is fast and efficient.
- The tool is flexible, allowing several techniques and normalizations to be used.
- It works in terminal and the user only needs to write simple Python scripts. No Python programming knowledge is required, as scripts are simple and readable. The user can make new scripts by copying and modifying example scripts.
- It is designed to work under Python 2.X and 3.X, without the need for external libraries, avoiding installation problems.

This tool is still under development but it can be used to build monolingual or bilingual terminology glossaries in a fast and efficient way.

In the near future we plan to add the following features:

- Statistical measures for term candidate reordering.
- Improved algorithm for automatic learning of patterns for linguistic terminology extraction.
- Implementation of an algorithm for learning morphological variants of term candidates.
- Development of a simple visual user interface, to make the use of TBXTools even more easy.

In this paper we have also presented the results of the experiments for statistical and linguistic monolingual terminology extraction and for the automatic detection of translation equivalents in parallel corpora.

References

Sophia Ananiadou, Brian Rea, Naoaki Okazaki, Rob Procter, and James Thomas. 2009. Supporting systematic reviews using text mining. *Social Science Computer Review*.

Helena Blancafort, Béatrice Daille, Tatiana Gornostay, Ulrich Heid, Claude Méchoulam, and Serge Sharoff. 2010. TTC: Terminology Extraction, Translation Tools and Comparable Corpora. In European association for lexicography, editor, *14th EURALEX International Congress*, pages 263–268, Leeuwarden/Ljouwert, Netherlands, July.

Siham Boulaknadel, Beatrice Daille, and Driss Aboutajdine. 2008. A multi-word term extraction program for arabic language. In *Proceedings of the 6th International Conference on Language Resources and Evaluation (LREC 2008)*, page 1485–1488, Marràqueix, Marroc. European Language Resources Association.

Rute Costa, Raquel Silva, and Maria Teresa Lino. 2004. Extracterm: an extractor for portuguese language. In *Proceedings of the 4th International Conference on Language Resources and Evaluation (LREC04)*, pages 1–5.

Béatrice Daille. 2003. Conceptual structuring through term variations. In *Proceedings of the ACL 2003 workshop on Multiword expressions: analysis, acquisition and treatment-Volume 18*, pages 9–16. Association for Computational Linguistics.

Patrick Drouin. 2003. Term extraction using non-technical corpora as a point of leverage. *Terminology*, 9(1):99–115.

Jody Foo. 2012. *Computational Terminology: Exploring Bilingual and Monolingual Term Extraction.* Ph.D. thesis, Linköping University, Linköping, Suècia.

Katerina Frantzi and Sophia Ananiadou. 1996. A hybrid approach to term recognition. In *Proceedings of the International Conference on Natural Language Processing and Industrial Applications (NLP-IA 1996)*, volume 1, page 93–98, Moncton, Canadà.

Anita Gojun, Ulrich Heid, Bernd Weissbach, Carola Loth, and Insa Mingers. 2012. Adapting and evaluating a generic term extraction tool. In *LREC*, pages 651–656.

Wiktoria Golik, Robert Bossy, Zorana Ratkovic, and Nédellec Claire. 2013. Improving term extraction with linguistic analysis in the biomedical domain. In *Proceedings of the 14th International Conference on Intelligent Text Processing and Computational Linguistics (CICLing13), Special Issue of the journal Research in Computing Science*, pages 24–30.

Tatiana Gornostay. 2010. Terminology management in real use. In *Proceedings of the 5th International Conference Applied Linguistics in Science and Education*, pages 25–26.

Johann Haller. 2008. Autoterm: Term candidate extraction for technical documentation (spanish/german). *Tradumàtica: traducció i tecnologies de la informació i la comunicació*, (6).

Ulrich Heid and John McNaught. 1991. EUROTRA-7 study: Feasibility and project definition study on the reusability of lexical and terminological resources in computerised applications. Final report. CEC-DG XIII.

Antton Gurrutxaga Hernaiz, Xavier Saralegi Urizar, Sahats Ugartetxea, and Iñaki Alegría Loinaz. 2006. Elexbi, a basic tool for bilingual term extraction from spanish-basque parallel corpora. In *Atti del XII Congresso Internazionale di Lessicografia: Torino, 6-9 settembre 2006*, pages 159–165.

Christian Jacquemin. 1999. Syntagmatic and paradigmatic representations of term variation. In *Proceedings of the 37th annual meeting of the Association for Computational Linguistics on Computational Linguistics*, pages 341–348. Association for Computational Linguistics.

Lucelene Lopes, Paulo Fernandes, Renata Vieira, and Guilherme Fedrizzi. 2009. Eχatolp–an automatic tool for term extraction from portuguese language corpora. In *Proceedings of the 4th Language & Technology Conference: Human Language Technologies as a Challenge for Computer Science and Linguistics (LTC), Faculty of Mathematics and Computer Science of Adam Mickiewicz University*, pages 427–431.

Antoni Oliver and Mercè Vàzquez. 2007. A free terminology extraction suite. Londres. Information Management.

Antoni Oliver, Joaquim Moré, and Salvador Climent. 2007a. *Traducció i tecnologies*, volume 116 of *Manuals*. Editorial UOC, Barcelona.

Antoni Oliver, Mercè Vázquez, and Joaquim Moré. 2007b. Linguoc lexterm: una herramienta de extracción automática de terminología gratuita. *Translation Journal*, 11(4).

Lluís Padró and Evgeny Stanilovsky. 2012. Freeling 3.0: Towards wider multilinguality. In *Proceedings of the Language Resources and Evaluation Conference (LREC 2012)*, Istanbul, Turkey, May. ELRA.

Emanuele Pianta and Sara Tonelli. 2010. Kx: A flexible system for keyphrase extraction. In *Proceedings of the 5th international workshop on semantic evaluation*, pages 170–173. Association for Computational Linguistics.

Marcis Pinnis, Nikola Ljubešić, Dan Ştefănescu, Inguna Skadiņa, Marko Tadić, and Tatiana Gornostay. 2012. Term extraction, tagging, and mapping tools for under-resourced languages. In *Proceedings of the 10th Conference on Terminology and Knowledge Engineering (TKE 2012), June*, pages 20–21.

Francesco Sclano and Paola Velardi. 2007. Termextractor: a web application to learn the shared terminology of emergent web communities. In *Enterprise Interoperability II*, pages 287–290. Springer.

Jörg Tiedemann. 2012. Parallel data, tools and interfaces in opus. In Nicoletta Calzolari, Khalid Choukri, Thierry Declerck, Mehmet Uğur Doğan, Bente Maegaard, Joseph Mariani, Jan Odijk, and Stelios Piperidis, editors, *Proceedings of the Eighth International Conference on Language Resources and Evaluation (LREC-2012)*, pages 2214–2218, Istanbul, Turkey, May. European Language Resources Association (ELRA). ACL Anthology Identifier: L12-1246.

Špela Vintar. 2010. Bilingual term recognition revisited the bag-of-equivalents term alignment approach and its evaluation. *Terminology*, 16(2):141–158.

Jorge Vivaldi and Horacio Rodríguez. 2001. Improving term extraction by combining different techniques. *Terminology*, 7(1):31–48.

Thuy Vu, Ai Ti Aw, and Min Zhang. 2008. Term extraction through unithood and termhood unification. In *Proceedings of the 3rd International Joint Conference on Natural Language Processing (IJCNLP 2008)*, volume 1, pages 631–636, Hyderabad, Índia.

Enlarging the Croatian Wordnet with WN-Toolkit and CroDeriV

Antoni Oliver
Universitat Oberta de Catalunya
aoliverg@uoc.edu

Krešimir Šojat
Sveučilište u Zagrebu
ksojat@ffzg.hr

Matea Srebačić
Sveučilište u Zagrebu
msrebaci@unizg.hr

Abstract

Wordnet is a standard semantic resource for several Natural Language Processing tasks and it is available for an increasing number of languages. The Croatian Wordnet (CroWN) was a relatively small resource with 10.026 synsets and 31.367 synset-variant pairs covering only 45.91% of the so-called Core WordNet. Comparing these figures with the size of the Princeton WordNet for English version 3.0, that has 117,659 synsets and 206,975 synset-variant pairs, it is clear that the CroWN should be expanded. First experiments for the expansion of the CroWN were performed using the WN-Toolkit, a set of Python programs for wordnet creation and expansion using dictionary, Babelnet and parallel-corpora based strategies. The WN-Toolkit was previously successfully applied to other languages as Spanish, Catalan and Galician. After this first expansion, CroWN reached 70.63% of the core wordnet. In the second step we used CroDeriv, a derivational database for Croatian and the manual creation of 1,457 synset-variant pairs until reaching 100% of the Core WordNet. After second step was completed, CroWN reached 23,137 synsets and 47,931 synset-lemma pairs.

1 Introduction

In this paper we explain the methodology and results of the experiments for the enlargement of the Croatian Wordnet using the WN-Toolkit and the derivational database CroDeriV. The paper is organised as follows: first, we will explain the development of the previous version of CroWN and we will present some figures about the size of this wordnet before and after the expansion. Then we will present the WN-Toolkit and its main features. After that, in section 4, we will present the CroDeriV, morphological database of Croatian verbs which was used in one of our experiments. Next, the experimental methodology is presented followed by the results of the experiments. After that the main sources of errors are presented and analyzed. Finally, the conclusions and future work are presented.

2 CroWN and wordnets for other languages

The Croatian Wordnet has been developed under the Central and South-East European Resources (CESAR) project, funded by the European Commission (50%) and the Ministry of Science, Education and Sports of the Republic of Croatia (50%). The first version of the Croatian Wordnet had 10.026 synsets and 31.252 synset-variant pairs. The synset ID's are those of the Princeton WordNet for English v 3.0.

The Princeton WordNet for English version 3.0 has 117,659 synsets and 206,975 synset-variant pairs. In table 1 we can observe the number of synset variant pairs both in old and new versions of CroWN. In table 2 the number of synsets in both versions is shown. The starting version of the Croatian Wordnet covered 45.91% of the so-called Core WordNet (Boyd-Graber et al., 2006), that is, approximately the 5,000 most frequently used word senses. After the automatic expansion described in this paper 100% of the core synsets were covered.

The Open Multilingual Wordnet[1] (OMW) (Bond and Paik, 2012) provides free access to several wordnets in a common format. The new CroWN is also distributed in the Open Multilingual Wordnet website. In table 3 we can observe all the wordnets in OML with the relative position

[1] http://compling.hss.ntu.edu.sg/omw/

Proceedings of Recent Advances in Natural Language Processing, pages 480–487,
Hissar, Bulgaria, Sep 7–9 2015.

POS	Old version	New version
Overall	31,252	47,901
Nouns	16,726	27,001
Verbs	13,669	17,904
Adjectives	857	2,594
Adverbs	0	402

Table 1: Number of synset-variant pairs in old and new versions of CroWN

POS	Old version	New version
Overall	10,026	23,120
Nouns	7,373	16,178
Verbs	2,351	4,736
Adjectives	302	1,814
Adverbs	0	392

Table 2: Number of synsets in old and new versions of CroWN

regarding the number of synsets (on the left) and the % of the Core WordNet (on the right), both for the old version (hrv-o) and the new version (hrv-n) of the CroWN. As we can observe in the table, regarding the number of synsets, the old CroWN occupied the 21st position, and the new version reached the 17th. With respect to the % of the Core WordNet, the old version occupied the 24th position and the new one, as it reached the 100%, occupies the 4th position.

These figures indicate that the CroWN, after the enlargement described in this paper, is a much more valuable resource, although there is still a lot of work to be done.

3 The WN-Toolkit

The WN-Toolkit[2] (Oliver, 2014) is a set of programs developed in Python for the automatic creation of wordnets following the expand model (Vossen, 1998), that is, by translation of the variants (words) associated with the Princeton WordNet synsets. The toolkit also provides some free language resources. These resources are preprocessed so they can be easily used with the toolkit.

The WN-Toolkit implements the following strategies for WordNet creation:

- Dictionary based methodology: This strategy uses bilingual dictionaries to translate the English variants associated with each synset. This direct translation using dictionaries can be performed only on those English variants being monosemic, that is, variants associated to a single synset. About 82% of the English variants in the Princeton WordNet 3.0 are monosemic. These figures show us that a large percentage of a target wordnet can be implemented using this strategy, but we would not be able to extract the most frequent variants, as common words are usually polysemic.

[2]The WN-Toolkit can be freely downloaded from `http://sourceforge.net/projects/wn-toolkit/`

P	lang	synsets	lang	% CORE
1	eng	117,659	eng	100
2	fin	116,763	fin	100
3	tha	73,350	cmn	100
4	fra	59,091	**hrv-n**	**100**
5	jpn	57,184	bul	100
6	ind	51,822	ind	99
7	cat	45,826	zsm	99
8	por	43,895	swe	99
9	zsm	42,679	jpn	95
10	slv	42,583	fra	92
11	cmn	42,312	slv	86
12	spa	38,512	por	84
13	ita	34,728	ita	83
14	eus	29,413	tha	81
15	pol	28,757	cat	81
16	**hrv-n**	**23,120**	dan	81
17	glg	19,312	nob	81
18	ell	18,049	spa	76
19	fas	17,759	eus	71
20	arb	10,165	nno	66
21	**hrv-o**	**10,026**	ell	57
22	swe	6,796	pol	49
23	heb	5,448	arb	48
24	bul	4,999	**hrv-o**	**45.91**
25	qcn	4,913	fas	41
26	als	4,676	glg	36
27	dan	4,476	als	31
28	nob	4,455	qcn	28
29	nno	3,671	heb	27

Table 3: Number of synsets in old (hrv-o) and new (hrv-n) versions of CroWN

- Babelnet based strategies: BabelNet (Navigli and Ponzetto, 2010) is a semantic network and a multilingual encyclopedic dictionary with lexicographic and encyclopedic coverage of terms. Entries are connected in a very large network of semantic relations. BabelNet covers 50 languages, Croatian among them. In this methodology we simply extract the data from the BabelNet file to get the target wordnet. This strategy can only be applied to old versions of Babelnet, as new versions have a use restriction not allowing the creation of wordnets from its data.

- Parallel corpus based methodologies: In order to extract wordnets from a parallel corpus we need this parallel corpus to be semantically tagged with Princeton WordNet synsets in the English part. As these corpora are not easily available, we use two strategies for the automatic construction of the required corpora:

- By machine translation of sense-tagged corpora.
- By automatic sense-tagging of English-Croatian parallel corpora.

The WN-Toolkit also provides some resources, as dictionaries and preprocessed bilingual corpora.

4 The CroDeriV database

CroDeriV (Šojat et al., 2014) is a database that contains information about the morphological structure and derivational relatedness of verbs in Croatian. Nowadays it contains 14,192 Croatian verbs that are morphologically analyzed, that is, segmented into lexical, derivational and inflectional morphemes. The structure of CroDeriV enables the detection of verbal derivational families in Croatian as well as the distribution and frequency of particular affixes and lexical morphemes. Derivational families consist of a verbal base form and all prefixed or suffixed derivatives detected in available Croatian dictionaries and corpora. Language data structured in this way was further used for the expansion of other language resources for Croatian, such as Croatian WordNet and the Croatian Morphological Lexicon (Šojat and Srebačić, 2014; Šojat et al., 2014). Matching the data from CroDeriV on one side, and Croatian WordNet and the Croatian Morphological Lexicon on the other, resulted in significant enrichment of Croatian WordNet and enlargement of the Croatian Morphological Lexicon.

In this paper we present the procedure for using CroDeriV to further expand the Croatian WordNet.

5 Experimental methodology

In order to automatically evaluate the results, we compare the obtained wordnet with the existing Croatian Wordnet. If we get some variant for a synset, we compare if in the Croatian WordNet there is a variant for this synset, and if this variant is the same as the extracted one. If we got one of the variants in the reference wordnet, the result is evaluated as correct. If there are some variants in the reference wordnet, but not the one we extracted, this is evaluated as incorrect. If we don't have any variant in the reference wordnet for the particular synset, the result remains unevaluated, that is, we don't take into account this obtained variant in the evaluation results. The automatic precision values obtained in this way tend to be lower than the real values. Sometimes we obtain a variant that is correct, but we have other correct variants for the same synset in the reference wordnet. In these cases we evaluate our result as incorrect. On the other hand, as the reference Croatian Wordnet is not very big, we leave a lot of obtained variants without evaluation.

As we stated in the previous section, automatically evaluated values of precision tend to be lower than the real values. For this reason, for each experiment we have manually evaluated a subset of the non-evaluated and incorrect results in order to calculate a corrected value of precision.

We offer two values of corrected precision values:

- strict: we have also considered small errors (as capitalization, plural forms, etc.) as errors
- non-strict: we have considered small errors as correct

6 Experimental results

6.1 Dictionary-based strategy

6.1.1 Resources

In the table 4 we can observe the dictionaries (English-Croatian) we have used for the experiments along with the number of entries. As can be seen in the table, only freely available resources have been used.

Dictionary	Website	Entries
OmegaWiki	http://www.omegawiki.org/	1,692
Wiktionary	http://www.wiktionary.org/	29,216
Wikipedia	http://www.wikipedia.org/	70,387
Geonames	http://www.geonames.org/	1,353
Wikispecies	http://species.wikimedia.org/	1,785

Table 4: Dictionaries used for the dictionary-based strategy

The Wiktionary dictionary contains words in Croatian, Bosnian and Serbian, some of them written in Cyrillic. We have filtered the dictionary with the Croatian Morphological Dictionary (Tadić and

	Omegawiki	Wiktionary	Wikipedia	Geonames	Wikispecies	Combination
Total	646	1,905	4,196	429	772	7,247
Evaluated	176	522	409	0	183	1,156
Precision	83.52	79.31	57.95	-	75.96	70.33
Precision N	57.14	80.65	57.95	-	75.96	70.49
Precision V	-	67.86	-	-	-	66.10
Precision A	-	83.33	-	-	-	83.33

Table 5: Results for the dictionary-based strategy using automatic evaluation

Fulgosi, 2003; Oliver and Tadić, 2004) in order to get a list of Croatian words, so words in the Wiktionary dictionary not being in the Croatian Morphological Dictionary are deleted from the dictionary. After the filtering 7.437 entries remained. Entries from the Wikipedia are all with the first letter in uppercase. Once we have extracted the wordnet from Wikipedia we had to normalize the capitalization of the results. We have done this in an automatic way by comparing capitalization of entries from the Wikipedia with the capitalization of the variants of the same synset in the Princeton English WordNet. Entries in the Wikispecies dictionary are with the first letter in uppercase. In this case we have simply changed all to lowercase.

6.1.2 Results and evaluation

In the table 5 we present the results of the automatic evaluation for all the dictionaries and for the combination of all of them:

The value in the row Total shows the number of synset-variants pairs extracted using the given dictionary or the combination of all dictionaries. The value in Evaluated indicates the number of synset-variant pairs that could be automatically evaluated, that is, the number of synset-variant pairs already present in the Croatian WordNet. In the case of Geonames no single synset-variant pair was present, so we couldn't calculate figures of precision. We show the overall precision along with the precision for nouns, verbs, adjectives and adverbs. Note that we couldn't evaluate the precision for any adverb, as no adverbs were present in the previous version of the Croatian WordNet.

As we can see, an overall automatic calculated precision of 70.33% is achieved. We have manually evaluated 10% of the non-evaluated synset-variant pairs and 10% of the evaluated as incorrect. For strict precision we have achieved 84.49% (more than 14 points higher than automatic evaluation) and for non-strict 90.72% (more than 20 points higher).

The dictionary-based strategy has allowed to extract 6,091 new synset-variant pairs.

6.2 BabelNet based strategy

6.2.1 Resources

For our experiments we have used BabelNet version 2. In this strategy we simply extract the information for Croatian from the BabelNet file.

6.2.2 Results and evaluation

In table the results of automatic evaluation are presented.

Total	12949
Evaluated	1,934
Precision	66.65
Precision N	66.65

Table 6: Results for the BabelNet-based strategy using automatic evaluation

Note that with this strategy we have only been able to extract synset-variant pairs for nouns. 10% of the non-evaluated synset-variant pairs, as well as 20% of the evaluated as incorrect have been manually evaluated. A strict value of 88.96% and a non-strict value of 96.8% have been calculated.

6.3 Machine translation of sense-disambiguated corpora

6.3.1 Resources

In order to extract wordnets from a parallel corpus we need this parallel corpus to be semantically tagged with wordnet synsets in the English part. As these corpora are not easily available, we use two strategies for the automatic construction of the required corpora:

- By machine translation of sense-tagged corpora. We use manually sense tagged English corpora (as Semcor, for example) and we automatically translate the English text into the target language. We are using Google Translate, as it is a statistical system capable to perform a quite good lexical selection task when translating, that is, in some cases is capable to

	Semcor	PWGC	Senseval 2	Senseval 3	Combination
Total	3,111	4,916	144	135	7,123
Evaluated	1,616	2,066	73	82	2,853
Precision	83.17	79.77	83.56	81.71	80.41
Precision N	84.8	80.77	77.08	78.23	81.29
Precision V	78.71	74.25	95	90.63	75.82
Precision A	80.11	85.26	100	50	89.12

Table 7: Results for the parallel corpus strategy using automatic evaluation and machine translation of sense-tagged corpora

select the correct translation of a polysemic word.

- By automatic sense-tagging of English-Croatian parallel corpora. To perform the sense-tagging we have used Freeling and UKB (Padró et al., 2010) (Agirre and Soroa, 2009). The tagging has been performed sentence by sentence.

In both cases, we need to POS tag the Croatian text, getting both the lemma and the POS information. We have used Hunpos with a model for Croatian, and we have developed a program to get the associated lemma from the Croatian Morphological Lexicon. Once we have these corpora, the task of extracting a wordnet is equal to word-alignment task. We have used GIZA++ to align the lemmatized parallel corpora and we have developed a script (that will be included in the WN-Toolkit) to extract the wordnets from the aligned files. In the table 8 we can see the information about the sense-tagged corpora for machine translation strategy.

Corpus	Sentences	Tokens eng	Tokens hrv
Semcor	37,176	794,748	721,282
PWGC	113,404	1.529,105	1,303,386
Senseval 2	238	5,493	5,129
Senseval 3	300	5,530	5,022

Table 8: English sense-tagged corpora used in the experiments

The algorithm for wordnet creation from parallel corpora allows to adjust two parameters:

- Minimum frequency: the minimum value of frequency of the synset in the corpus.
- Minimum percent: The relation between the frequency of the first candidate and the second candidate.

In our experiments for Croatian we have fixed these values to:

- minimum frequency: 5 (except for very small corpora, as for example Senseval 2 and Senseval 3)
- minimum percent: 50.

These values have been fixed after performing several extraction experiments using the Croatian-English parallel corpus.

6.3.2 Results and evaluation

In table 7 we can observe the values of precision, calculated in an automatic way, for the strategy of machine translation of sense-tagged corpora. No distinction between monosemic and polysemic variants is done here, offering an overall value. As expected, for bigger corpora we are obtaining more synset-variant pairs. We are again not obtaining precision values for adverbs, as no adverbs were found in the previous version of CroWN.

We have manually evaluated 10% of the non-evaluated synset-variant pairs, as well as 20% of the evaluated as incorrect. This allowed us to calculate a corrected strict precision of 87.76% (7 points higher than automatic precision) and a non-strict precision of 94.26% (more than 13 points higher than automatic precision).

6.4 Automatic sense tagging of parallel corpora

6.4.1 Resources

In table 9 we can observe the information for the corpus used in the automatic sense-tagging strategy.

Corpus	Sentences	Tokens eng	Tokens hrv
cro-eng p.c.	62,566	1,790,041	1,590,637
EUBookshop	6,104	131,217	126,607
hrenWaC	47,475	1,282,007	1,152,552
SETIMES 2	205,910	4,629,877	4,662,863

Table 9: English sense-tagged corpora used in the experiments

6.4.2 Results and evaluation

In table 10 the results for automatic sense-tagging of English-Croatian parallel corpora are shown. Here again, no distinction between monosemic and polysemic variants has been made.

6.5 Use of CroDeriV

6.5.1 Resources

In our experiments we have used CroDeriV to expand the verbal subset of the CroWN. Using this derivational database we have created a list of 13,781 verb lemmata. Once we have created the verb list we have tried to find their translation in a free Croatian-English on-line dictionary[3]. We have used a script to automatically query this on-line dictionary in case the verb is not already in the CroWN. In this way we have done queries and obtained a list of 10,463 Croatian verbs with translations into English. For each Croatian verb we have assigned the synsets of the English verb, which we obtained as a translation variant.

6.5.2 Results and evaluation

Candidates	10463
New verbal synset-variant pairs	2921
New verbal synsets	2271

Table 11: Number of candidates, synset-variant pairs and synsets for verbal expansion using CroDeriV

In table 11 we can observe the number of candidates, synset-variant pairs and synsets obtained by using CroDeriV for the expansion of the verbal part of the CroWN. The obtained precision is very low, only 27.91%, due to the fact that verbs are highly polysemous units and all of the synsets in which the translation of the Croatian verbal lemma occurs were listed among the candidates, which resulted in an average of 6,8 candidate synsets per verbal lemma. However, in the majority of cases at least one of the candidate synsets was correct. Moreover, numerous candidates were not completely incorrect, since only the reflexivity of the Croatian verb in question had to be corrected in order to correspond to the offered PWN synset. All of these cases were manually corrected. Finally, the results show that in some cases more than one synset-variant pair per synset was found, and in the final step the synset-variant pairs corresponding to the same PWN synset were grouped into same synset in CroWN as well.

Although the overall precision of this procedure is not as high as with monosemous units, it yielded a rather satisfactory number of both new synset-variant pairs and new synsets. However, this method significantly contributed to the improvement of the CroWN's coverage of lemmas from various Croatian corpora.

[3]http://www.rjecnik.net/

6.6 Manual creation until reaching 100% of Core WordNet

After applying WN-Toolkit strategies, CroWN encompassed 70.63% of the Core synsets. We decided to add the remaining part of this set, namely 1,456 synsets. The majority of these synsets comprise senses of polysemous units. The following procedure was applied to polysemous units:

1. the literals from these synsets were automatically translated into Croatian;

2. the obtained results were manually checked and corrected.

A manual evaluation and correction of the remaining 1,456 Core synsets was performed. The results of this procedure can be divided into following groups as far as:

1. only one of the translation candidates was correct,

2. two or more translation candidates were correct,

3. none of the translation candidates was correct.

For the first and the second group additional synset-variants in synsets with at least one automatically obtained correct translation was provided. For the last group at least one correct translation for all synsets was provided. The result of these procedure is 100% of Core WordNet synsets represented in CroWN 2.0.

7 Main source of errors

The manual revision of the results has allowed us to devise the main source of errors. We can highlight the following:

	cro-eng p.c.	EUBookshop	hrenWaC	SETIMES 2	Combination
Total	2,209	673	3,834	5,583	7,395
Evaluated	866	344	1,560	1,908	2,569
Precision	79.56	75.29	78.46	71.96	70.07
Precision N	78.81	74.73	78.64	71.83	69.73
Precision V	77.39	72.34	70.97	68.42	66.67
Precision A	91.94	87.5	90.63	85.05	86.47

Table 10: Results for the parallel corpus strategy using automatic evaluation and automatic sense-tagging of English-Croatian parallel corpora

- For dictionary-based and Babelnet-based strategies one important source of errors is the capitalization of the entries. In some of the used dictionaries (for example Wikipedia and Wikispecies), all the entries begin with a capital letter, regardless they are proper or common names.

- For dictionary-based and Babelnet-based strategies other important source of errors are some entries in forms other than nominative singular. Some of the dictionary entries are in nominative plural.

- For strategies based on parallel corpora (both machine translation of sense-tagged corpora and automatic sense-tagging of parallel corpora) numerous errors are produced by the Croatian tagger. As stated earlier, we have used a simple Hunpos tagger with a model for Croatian and a simple script for adding the lemmata. This tagger is not able to cope with multiword expressions and is not able to attach the reflexive particle *se* of reflexive verbs to the lemma.

- For the strategy based on parallel corpora using machine translation, another important source of errors is the quality of the machine translation system. We have used Google Translate, a state-of-the-art machine translation system, so we don't expect to make any improvement in this aspect.

- For strategy based on parallel corpora using automatic word sense-disambiguation of the English part, one important source of errors is the word sense disambiguation, as it is a very difficult task. We have used a state-of-the-art word sense algorithm (Freeling+UKB), so we don't expect to make any improvement in the tagger. In these experiments the corpora were sense tagged sentence by sentence, thus reducing the context information available for the UKB algorithm. In future experiments we plant to sense tag the corpora grouping several sentences of the same document.

8 Conclusions and future work

In this paper we have described the procedures applied for the automatic acquisition of new CroWN synsets based on various dictionaries and parallel corpora. The results were both automatically and manually evaluated, and approximately 5,000 new synsets were detected as candidates for CroWN. As it has been stated above, the procedures proved valuable for the detection of monosemous vocabulary. However, it became obvious that the detection of correct senses of polysemous words is a highly challenging task. This especially pertains to procedures relying on sense-tagged parallel corpora, previously lemmatized and POS tagged. The main problem is non-availability of sense-tagged corpora for Croatian that could be used for more comprehensive approach. Further problems arise from not completely satisfactory results of lemmatization and POS tagging. One of our future goals is thus to create a Freeling module (including lemmatizer and POS tagger) for Croatian. In order to make the CroWN a more representative resource for Croatian, we plan to compare the list of words from CroWN and frequency list of lemmas from Croatian corpora. This procedure should enable the detection of gaps in the coverage of Croatian vocabulary and should result in a more balanced and usable wordnet for Croatian. Moreover, since CroDeriV is currently being expanded with other POS, we will use it for further expansion of other lexical hierarchies in CroWN. All these steps should also result in a sense-tagged corpus of Croatian that could be used for various NLP tasks.

As a future work we also plan to improve the WN-Toolkit. One of the improvements will be the inclusion of a methodology allowing to deal with polysemous English variants. This methodology will make use of the definitions and the semantic relations in the dictionary and will try to match them with the definitions and relations in the Princeton English WordNet. This will allow us to match the correct target language translation to a given meaning. With the new version of the toolkit we plan to create wordnets for as much languages as possible and to contribute to the extension of the Extended Open Multilingual Wordnet[4] (Bond and Foster, 2013).

Acknowledgments

This research has been partially conducted thanks to a Networds Grants for Short visits, references 6500, 7008 and 7009, from the ESF Research Networking Programmes.

This research has been carried out thanks to the Project SKATER (TIN2012-38584-C06-01 and TIN2012-38584-C06-06) supported by the Ministry of Economy and Competitiveness of the Spanish Government.

The automatic translation of sense-tagged corpora have been performed thanks to an academic agreement with Google .

References

Eneko Agirre and Aitor Soroa. 2009. Personalizing pagerank for word sense disambiguation. In *Proceedings of the 12th Conference of the European Chapter of the Association for Computational Linguistics*, pages 33–41. Association for Computational Linguistics.

Francis Bond and Ryan Foster. 2013. Linking and extending an open multilingual wordnet. In *Proceedings of the 51st Annual Meeting of the Association for Computational Linguistics (ACL-2013)*, Sofia, Bulgaria. 1352–1362.

Francis Bond and Kyonghee Paik. 2012. A survey of wordnets and their licenses. In *Proceedings of the 6th Global WordNet Conference (GWC 2012)*, Matsue, Japan. 64–71.

Jordan Boyd-Graber, Christiane Fellbaum, Daniel Osherson, and Robert Schapire. 2006. Adding dense, weighted connections to wordnet. In Petr Sojka, Key-Sun Choi, Christine Fellbaum, and Piek Vossen, editors, *Proceedings of the 3rd International WordNet Conference*, pages 29–36. Global Wordnet Association.

Roberto Navigli and Simone Paolo Ponzetto. 2010. BabelNet: building a very large multilingual semantic network. In *Proceedings of the 48th Annual Meeting of the Association for Computational Linguistics*, ACL '10, Stroudsburg, PA, USA. Association for Computational Linguistics. ACM ID: 1858704.

Antoni Oliver and Marko Tadić. 2004. Enlarging the Croatian Morphological Lexicon by Automatic Lexical Acquisition from Raw Corpora. In Maria Teresa Lino Lino, Maria Francisca Xavier, Fátima Ferreira, Rute Costa, and Raquel Silva, editors, *Proceedings of the Language Resources and Evaluation - LREC'04*, pages 3366 – 3370, Lisbon, Portugal. European Language Resources Association, ELRA.

Antoni Oliver. 2014. WN-Toolkit: Automatic generation of WordNets following the expand model. In Heili Orav, Christianne Fellbaum, and Piek Vossen, editors, *Proceedings of the 7th Global WordNet Conference*, pages 7–15, Tartu, Estonia. Global Wordnet Association.

Lluís Padró, Samuel Reese, Eneko Agirre, and Aitor Soroa. 2010. Semantic services in freeling 2.1: Wordnet and ukb. In Pushpak Bhattacharyya, Christiane Fellbaum, and Piek Vossen, editors, *Principles, Construction, and Application of Multilingual Wordnets*, pages 99–105, Mumbai, India, February. Global Wordnet Conference 2010, Narosa Publishing House.

Marko Tadić and Sanja Fulgosi. 2003. Building the croatian morphological lexicon. In *Proceedings of the EACL2003 Workshop on Morphological Processing of Slavic Languages*, pages 41 – 46.

Piek Vossen. 1998. Introduction to eurowordnet. In Piek Vossen, editor, *EuroWordNet: A multilingual database with lexical semantic networks*, pages 1–17. Springer Netherlands.

Krešimir Šojat and Matea Srebačić. 2014. Morphosemantic relations between verbs in Croatian WordNet. In Heili Orav, Christianne Fellbaum, and Piek Vossen, editors, *Proceedings of the 7th Global WordNet Conference*, pages 262–267, Tartu, Estonia. Global Wordnet Association.

Krešimir Šojat, Matea Srebačić, Tin Pavelić, and Marko Tadić. 2014. CroDeriV: a New Resource for Processing Croatian Morphology. In N. Calzolari, K. Choukri, T. Declerck, H. Loftsson, Maegaard B., Mariani, J., A. Moreno, J. Odijk, and S. Piperidis, editors, *Proceedings of the Language Resources and Evaluation - LREC'14*, pages 3366 – 3370, Reykjavik, Iceland. European Language Resources Association, ELRA.

[4]http://compling.hss.ntu.edu.sg/omw/summx.html

A Comparative Study of Different Sentiment Lexica for Sentiment Analysis of Tweets

Canberk Özdemir and Sabine Bergler
CLaC Labs, Concordia University
1455 de Maisonneuve Blvd West
Montreal, Quebec, Canada, H3G 1M8
ozdemir.berkin@gmail.com, bergler@cse.concordia.ca

Abstract

We report on interoperability of different sentiment lexica with each other and with the linguistic notions *negation* and *modality* for sentiment analysis of tweets in a comprehensive ablation study and in competition results for SemEval 2015. Our approach performed well at the tweet level, but excelled in the presence of figurative language.

1 Introduction

Increasing interest in social media is reflected in SemEval competitions on sentiment analysis of tweets. Sentiment analysis categorizes text into positive or negative sentiment, possibly with an additional neutral category (Pang and Lee, 2008). Tweets use more informal and non-standard language than other text forms posing additional challenges. The winners of the past two years made heavy use of their specially designed NRC lexicon (Mohammad et al., 2013; Kiritchenko et al., 2014), a large lexical resource extracted from tweets with hashtags that are unmistakably positive or negative. This leads to the question we address here: is a bigger lexicon (proportionally) more useful? Is there something special about the NRC lexicon? Is a lexicon that is designed like the NRC lexicon but ten times its size more useful? And finally, can linguistic contexts *negation* and *modality* improve the lexicon and the final classification?

We compiled a NRC-inspired lexical resource, Gezi, of seven times the size of the NRC lexicon. We used several lexica in various combinations: Gezi, NRC, Bing Liu's lexicon (Hu and Liu, 2004), MPQA (Wilson et al., 2005), and aFinn (Nielsen, 2011), and add negation and modality sensitive features, performing comprehensive ablation experiments. The system competed in SemEval 2015 and ranked 9/40 in Task 10B, sentiment classification of tweets, and 1/35 in Task 11, tweets featuring figurative language.

2 Previous Work

Since Pang and Lees pioneering work on movie review classification into thumbs up—thumbs down (Pang et al., 2002), the major resource for sentiment determination was a sentiment lexicon, modelled after the independently and previously created Harvard General Inquirer (Stone et al., 1966), a list of words labelled as positive or negative sentiment carriers. Rule-based approaches yielded strong baselines that depended mainly on the coverage of the lexicon used, leading to various efforts to compile dedicated sentiment lexica (Esuli and Sebastiani, 2006; Wilson et al., 2005). The growing number of sentiment laden text on social media led to more efforts to annotate corpora, enabling machine learning approaches which monopolize the current exercises on sentiment annotation of tweets at SemEval (Rosenthal et al., 2015; Rosenthal et al., 2014; Nakov et al., 2013). The lexicon is still the major tool used, and for the non-standard use of language encountered in tweets, special resources have been compiled using the annotations displayed by the tweets themselves. Go et al. (2009), for instance, collected corpora using tweets containing positive or negative emoticons. In a similar way, Kiritchenko et al. (2014) use selected positive and negative hashtags to retrieve positive or negative tweets, computing association scores to the words occurring in tweets of each polarity. The resulting NRC lexicon was used by the winning team in SemEval 2013 and

Proceedings of Recent Advances in Natural Language Processing, pages 488–496,
Hissar, Bulgaria, Sep 7–9 2015.

2014, together with a simple negation feature.

The attention paid to sentiment in tweets led to the development of the CMU tagger Gimpel et al. (2011), a tokenizer and a POS tagger for tweets, as well as a named-entity recognizer for tweets (Ritter et al., 2011).

3 SemEval Datasets

The datasets for the SemEval exercises have been annotated using Amazon's Mechanical Turk[1] for Task 10 and CrowdFlower[2] for Task 11. The resulting annotations include, as expected, mislabelings and borderline judgements in the gold standard, such as:

labelled as negative *I haven't eaten chicken nuggets since I was like 6 or 7.. Who wants to get some McDonald's with me tomorrow?*

labelled as neutral *Class early in the mornjng =\it's bedtime! But do get to see my Sam tomorrow :)*

Polarity Classification Dataset Tweets with at least one term of SentiWordNet (Esuli and Sebastiani, 2006) association score greater than 0.3 or less than -0.3 form the corpus that is then manually labelled as positive, negative, or neutral.

The different test sets for 2013 (Nakov et al., 2013), 2014 (Rosenthal et al., 2014) and 2015 (Rosenthal et al., 2015) show a skewed distribution: with the exception of 2014, the majority of test cases are neutral and negative tweets form the smallest class, with the distribution changing slightly from year to year, see Table 1, where 'tw' stands for 'tweet', 'lj' for 'LiveJournal' entries, and 'sarc' for 'sarcastic tweets', different sources for test data for comparison.

Dataset	Positive	Negative	Neutral
tw-train	3,662	1,466	4,600
tw-dev	575	340	739
2013-tw-test	1,572	601	1,640
2013-sms-test	492	394	1,207
2014-tw-test	982	202	669
2014-sarc-test	33	40	13
2014-lj-test	427	304	411
2015-tw-test	1,038	365	987

Table 1: Dataset composition for Task10B.

Figurative Language Dataset The training set, consisting of 8000 tweets containing 5000 sarcastic, 1000 ironical and 2000 metaphorical tweets, was annotated on an 11 point scale (-5, . . . , +5) and released in two formats: tweets with integer or real-valued sentiment scores. The nature of figurative language tends to be negative Ghosh et al. (2015), Table 2 shows the distribution of instances for each integer sentiment score for training and test set.

Sentiment Value	Test Size	Training Size
-5	4	4
-4	99	434
-3	836	2,741
-2	1,540	2,546
-1	679	811
0	297	297
1	168	171
2	154	206
3	200	107
4	110	52
5	4	5

Table 2: Composition of datasets for Task 11.

4 Linguistic Notions

Following the successful use of a simple negation heuristic in (Kiritchenko et al., 2014), we further develop the use of the linguistic phenomena *negation* and *modality*. Negation and modality change the effect of the terms that occur in their scope, even though this change is not always one of total sentiment reversal for negation (a) or weakening for modality (b).

a. *Just watched the whole 2nd season of AHS in less then 24 hours. I'm not even ashamed.*

b. *Max might have to get put down tomorrow <3 absolutely heart breaking if I have to see my puppy go. Love you Maxy*

We use modality triggers *would like, would love, should, ought to, must, may, might, could, will, would, can, ca, cant, cannot, able, unable*; negation triggers from Rosenberg (2013); scope rules of Rosenberg et al. (2012).

Negation The simplest instances of negation parallel the logic operator: negation reverses the truth value of a proposition (*I'll do the dishes for you — NOT!*) but in natural language, usage is more varied, and negation is used to create contrast along other dimension, not only truth value, but also veridicity, and belief (*I don't believe that she did the dishes for you.*), to name but two. The degree to which a basic proposition is challenged is even more nuanced when modality (*I could do the dishes for you if you*

[1]https://www.mturk.com/mturk/
[2]http://www.crowdflower.com/

could take the garbage out.) and negation interact (*She might not have done the dishes for you.*). This impacts tasks of information extraction from on-line texts and while these phenomena have long been neglected as comparatively rare and benign in information retrieval contexts, precision-oriented information extraction has addressed negation and recently modality in a series of challenge tasks (BioNLP Shared Tasks 2008-2010 (Kim et al., 2009), CoNLL 2010 (Farkas et al., 2010), *Sem(Morante and Blanco, 2012), QA4MRE (Morante and Daelemans, 2012)).

Negation and modality affect sentiment (*I am not happy!* does not convey positive sentiment). Even simple negation heuristics are beneficial: consider the scope of the negation to span from a negation trigger to the next punctuation mark (Mohammad et al., 2013) or to occupy a fixed window around the negation trigger (Günther and Furrer, 2013). Our system uses a syntax-aware negation trigger and scope detection system developed by Rosenberg (2013).

The effect that negation is interpreted to have on the interpretation of a text varies. Kennedy and Inkpen (2005) encode negation as a simple reverser of polarity values (multiplying them by -1). However, negation does not always reverse the effects of the sentiment carriers, as the case of judgements illustrates: *This isn't awful.* does not mean *This is fantastic.* Since negated sentiment carriers do not default to one fixed resulting sentiment value but have to be assessed in their linguistic context, we do not resolve the negation numerically, but encode its occurrence in a separate feature (*negated-positive, negated-negative, negated-neutral*), a technique similar to Kennedy and Inkpen (2006).When computing the association scores for our Gezi lexical resource, a negation context results in multiplying sentiment association scores of sentiment carriers by -0.5, an empirically derived value.

Modality Modality indicates possibility, it dampens the asserted veridicity of a statement, often accompagnied by the reason for the hedging: second hand information, belief, hypothetical, ... In utility texts like newspaper articles or UNIX documentation, modality is a rare phenomenon. But in journal articles in the life sciences or in tweets, it is frequent and carries important meaning aspects. The BioNLP Shared Task series (Kim et al., 2009) paid special attention to speculative language, and QA4MRE (Morante and Daelemans, 2012) additionally addressed the interaction of negation and modality. Following Rosenberg et al. (2012), whose treatment at the QA4MRE pilot dominated the competition, we treat modality the same as we treat negation: a trigger list and scope annotation indicate the modalized material and we represent this and its interaction with negation by doubling our encoded features to include for example *mod-positive, negation-positive, mod-negation-positive* (see Table 5).

5 Lexical Resources

A number of sentiment lexica are available and have been used in various systems. To our knowledge, they have not been compared critically on the same task to assess their respective contribution alone or in combination. We perform such a comparative ablation exercise on some of the more widely used lexica in order to assess our own new lexical resource, Gezi.

5.1 Manually Compiled Lexica

We include MPQA lexicon and Bing Lius Opinion Lexicon, which includes MPQA entries and thus provides a first means to compare how size impacts performance. To complete the picture, we also use the much smaller aFinn lexicon.

MPQA (Wilson et al., 2005), manually compiled with prior polarities for over 8000 words, distinguishing *positive, negative*, and *neutral*. The terms also have pseudo-POS tag information for disambiguation purposes.

Opinion Lexicon of Bing Liu (Hu and Liu, 2004), manually selected lexicon of around 6800 terms, only *positive* and *negative*.

aFinn (Nielsen, 2011), lexicon of words manually rated for valence scores with an integer between -5 and 5 together with their prior polarities, around 2500 words.

5.2 Automatically Compiled Lexica

NRC Hashtag Sentiment Lexicon (Mohammad et al., 2013) This open source lexicon was key in the winning entry for the last two years. It is a large, automatically compiled resource that uses seed hashtags that carry unambiguous, strong sentiment as proxy for true tweet sentiment. The polarity of the seed hashtag is used to calculate PMI [3] based association scores (Church and Hanks, 1990), substituting seed hashtags for emoticons in the technique championed by (Go et al., 2009). The lexicon contains 54,129 unigrams, 316,531 bigrams and 480,010 skip bigrams extracted from their tweet collection.

Gezi (Özdemir and Bergler, 2015) further develops this technique: nearly 20 million tweets are processed to calculate PMI scores for 376,863 unigrams, 922,773 bigrams and 850,074 dependency triples. Seed hashtags stem from 35 positive and 34 negative synonyms of *good* and *bad* in the Oxford American Writers Thesaurus (Moody and Lindberg, 2012).

We remove duplicates, retweets, and modified tweets; tweets with mixed negative and positive seed hashtags; tweets who consist mostly of URLs, hashtags, and usernames. Then, we label the tweets with the unique sentiment of their seed hashtag(s) after deleting URLs. Finally, we preprocess the collection and extract features. The tweet collection is tokenized using the CMU and Annie tokenizers (Gimpel et al., 2011; Cunningham et al., 2002), and parsed using the Stanford parser (Socher et al., 2013; de Marneffe and Manning, 2008). Negation and modality triggers are identified and their scope is determined (Rosenberg et al., 2012) in order to extract the context-aware sentiment association values[4] with PMI for unigrams, bigrams, and dependency triples (type-governor-dependent).

6 Validating Gezi on Subtask 10E

SemEval 2015 included a pilot task, Subtask 10E, which asked to determine association scores of given target terms with sentiment in tweets.

We tested our Gezi unigrams and bigrams together with the smallest but very effective aFinn lexicon in a simple rule-based approach:

1. If a target term is covered by a Gezi bigram, only this bigram score is used, to avoid double counting the unigram sentiment carrier and negation annotation, if they exist.
2. If a carrier is in a negation scope, its prior sentiment score is multiplied with -0.5.
3. Sentiment scores from aFinn and Gezi are normalized to a common scale and averaged.
4. Each prior sentiment score is scaled to [0,1]
5. If the target term cannot be assigned a score with the preceding rules, the score assigned is 0.5 (neither positive nor negative).

This approach ranked 4th among 10 submitted systems in both Kendall and Spearman correlation coefficient (Nelson, 2001) evaluations: Our Kendall rank correlation coefficient is 0.584, where other results range between 0.625 and 0.254, and our Spearman rank correlation coefficient is 0.777, where others range between 0.817 and 0.373, validating Gezi unigrams and bigrams.

7 Association Ratios to Prior Polarities

Association ratios yield continuous values and require thresholds to assign discrete prior polarities to lexicon entries.

For Gezi, we partitioned the association ratios into five categories, *strong positive, positive, exclusion, negative,* and *strong negative*. The middle category (association score close to 0) denotes terms that occur nearly as often in tweets labelled negative as in positive ones and a clear classification is not possible. The reason may be that the term is sentiment neutral (*box*) or that it can take on different sentiment in different contexts (*positive* carries negative sentiment in infection-related contexts). Rather than calling these terms *neutral*, we eliminate them entirely from Gezi.

For a term to fall into the positive categories, it has to occur at least twice as often in positive tweets as in negative tweets, thus positive terms have association scores greater than 1. For a term to be categorized as strongly positive, its score has to be greater than the geometric mean of the positive space $gMean(1, 8) = \sqrt{8} = 2.83$. Analogously, a term is considered negative if its association score lies below -1 and as strongly negative if its association score lies below -2.83. We partition the NRC Hashtag Sentiment Lexicon accordingly.

Table 3 shows the resulting composition of Gezi and the NRC lexicon for each polarity class. We see that after removing the elimination category of association scores close to 0, Gezi is roughly ten times bigger than the NRC lexicon and that the size ratio is almost equal in all the categories.

[3] pointwise mutual information

[4] Note that words have separate entries for different part-of-speech.

polar class	NRC unigrams	Gezi unigrams
strong-positive	3,390	24,739
positive	10,276	108,685
negative	8,447	62,333
strong-negative	3,605	24,639
no neutral	25,721	220,339
all	54,126	376,863

Table 3: Prior polarity class distribution.

8 Term Overlap for Different Lexica

To assess the relationship of size to unique content, we paired the five corpora and determined the size of the *Intersection* of the terms covered, indicating separately in how many cases the assigned sentiment value is the same (*Agreement*). Here, $Ratio = \frac{Agreement}{Intersection}$.

Lex A	Lex B	Intersection	Agreement	Ratio
aFinn	NRC	989	822	0.831
aFinn	Gezi	1,911	1,624	0.85
Liu	NRC	1,840	1,488	0.809
Liu	Gezi	4,028	3,386	0.841
MPQA	NRC	1,819	1,340	0.737
MPQA	Gezi	4,105	2,993	0.729
NRC	Gezi	16,868	13,957	0.827
MPQA	Liu	5,414	5,369	0.992
aFinn	Liu	1,314	1,298	0.988
MPQA	aFinn	1,246	1,202	0.965

Table 4: Intersection and agreement of lexica.

Unsurprisingly, the greatest agreement is between the smaller, manually curated lexica, which are based in part on common material (like the Harvard General Inquirer and the MPQA corpus). As expected, MPQALiu displays the greatest degree of agreement among these lexica, since MPQA formed the seed for Liu. But the lowest agreement is between MPQA and Gezi, the biggest lexicon (explained in part by the lack of the neutral category in Gezi), while Gezi-Liu has fifth-highest agreement. These observations suggest that bigger is not proportionally better: while the smaller lexica encode more of a consensus set of clear sentiment carriers, the larger lexica encode increasing amounts of low-frequency terms from the sentiment fringe, which makes their out of domain performance more volatile.

9 Experimental Setup

For the SemEval 2015 challenges, we process tweets in GATE (Cunningham et al., 2013) to extract features and run supervised machine learning algorithms using Weka (Witten and Frank, 2011).

Tokenization and POS Tagging The GATE plugin Annie tokenizer (Cunningham et al., 2002) is mature and robustly trained outside Twitter. It deals well with complex tokens, but it is not adapted to tweet-specific tokens. The CMU tokenizer (Gimpel et al., 2011) is a new tool that has been trained on Twitter data and expressly targets non-standard tokens such as emoticons, urls, exclamations (*!!!!!*), hashtags, etc. We prioritize the CMU tagger and use its tokens and POS tags when they are Twitter-specific, otherwise we use the Annie tokens, unless Ritter et al. (2011) suggests fusing multi-word entity names.

Text Normalization excludes Twitter-specific tokens that occur at the beginning and end of a sentence to improves parser performance.

Sentiment Lookup All lexical resources were transformed into gazetteer lists for each sentiment category. We use POS tag information to disambiguate senses where necessary and exclude sentiment carriers from the body of named entities.

Parsing by the Stanford parser and dependency module Version 3.4.1 (Socher et al., 2013; de Marneffe and Manning, 2008) forms the basis for NEGATOR (Rosenberg, 2013) to identify negation and modality triggers and their scope.

Feature Creation To represent our features compactly, we use compound *primary features* that encode *polarity class in linguistic context* as described above paired with the *lexical resource* that supplied this score. Abstracting away from actual sentiment terms to their polarity class helps to manage the feature space dimensionality. It also smoothes over the different lexical gaps of each lexicon. Primary features from a lexical resource are bundled under the name of that lexicon.

Table 5 shows the primary features created from the aFinn for Example 1. The only sentiment carrier term from *aFinn* is *perfect*, with a *positive* score of *3*. There is also a negation trigger which scopes over *perfect*, the scope is underlined. The resulting feature is *positive-aFinn-negated* with a score of -0.5*3=-1.5 in Table 5.

(1) El Classico on a Sunday Night is*n't* *perfect* for the Monday Morning !!

Secondary features are a collection of ad hoc features, such as specific annotations (i.e. emoticons, implicit-explicit negation triggers, modality triggers, named-entities, contrastive discourse

feature	value
positive-aFinn	0
positive-aFinn-negated	1
positive-aFinn-mod	0
positive-aFinn-mod-negated	0
negative-aFinn	0
negative-aFinn-negated	0
negative-aFinn-mod	0
negative-aFinn-mod-negated	0
aFinn-score	-1.5

Table 5: aFinn subset features for Example 1.

connectors and markers), frequencies and sentiment association scores for tokens with specific POS tags, POS tags and sentiment association scores of the first and last two tokens of tweets, and the highest and lowest sentiment association scores within tweets, see Table 6.

ids		# feat's
	Primary Feature Subsets	
f_1	aFinn	9
f_2	MPQA	12
f_3	BingLiu	8
f_4	NRC unigrams	17
f_5	NRC bigrams	17
f_6	Gezi unigrams	17
f_7	Gezi bigrams	17
f_8	dependency scores	13
f_9	dependency counts	8
	Secondary Feature Subsets	
f_{10}	POS tag based scores and counts	9
f_{11}	frequencies of specific annotations	12
f_{12}	position and top-lowest scores	6

Table 6: Feature subset bundles with IDs.

Feature Combinations We combined the twelve feature bundles of Table 6 in all possible combinations for a comprehensive ablation study. Feature combinations are processed with libSVM (Chang and Lin, 2011) with RBF kernel and parameters of cost=5, gamma=0.001 and weights=[neutral=1; positive=2; negative=2.9] in Weka (Witten and Frank, 2011) for Subtask 10B and M5P (Wang and Witten, 1997), a decision tree regressor, to predict continuous values for Task 11. These were exhaustively combined with the technique of (Shareghi and Bergler, 2013).

10 SemEval Results and Ablation

For Task 10B, tweet polarity classification, we submitted the results of $f_{1,2,3,6,8,9,10,11,12}$ containing feature subsets of aFinn, MPQA, Liu, Gezi unigrams, dependencies and secondary feature set, 94 features in total. Our submission achieved an average F-measure of positive and negative classes of 62.00, 9th among 40 submissions. Table 7 details our performance on all datasets scored. The top-performing submission achieved 64.84 f-measure. The fact that the results were this close makes it difficult to attribute them to the techniques reported wholesale and more comparison experiments need to be conducted.

dataset	F1	Rank
Twitter2015	62.00	9/40
Twitter2015Sarcasm	58.55	9/40
LiveJournal2014	73.59	6/40
SMS2013	63.05	18/40
Twitter2013	70.42	7/40
Twitter2014	70.16	9/40
Twitter2014Sarcasm	51.43	10/40

Table 7: Official results for SemEval Task 10B.

For Task 11, sentiment degree association to tweets of figurative language, we submitted $f_{1,2,3,6,7,10,11,12}$ containing aFinn, MPQA, Liu, Gezi unigrams-bigrams, and secondary feature set, totally 90 features. The challenge uses two evaluation metrics: cosine similarity and mean-squared error. According to both metrics, our submission ranked first, see Table 8.

MSE				
Overall	Sarcasm	Irony	Metaphor	Other
2.117	1.023	0.779	3.155	3.411
Cosine				
Overall	Sarcasm	Irony	Metaphor	Other
0.758	0.892	0.904	0.655	0.584

Table 8: Official results for SemEval Task 11.

Ablation studies Table 9 compares results for different feature bundles from our ablation studies. The results in italics represent official challenge results, while results in bold represent the best performing bundle for given datasets.

Our choice of system for Task 10B was informed by good performance on both, 2013 and 2014 datasets. Our best performing feature bundle is only marginally better and leaves a 2% gap to the competition winner.

For Task 11 we chose the best performing combination in 10-fold-cross validation. Our competition submission did not include dependency features. If we include them instead of MPQA and Liu feature subsets, performance increases by a cosine difference of .01.

feature ids	Task 10B F1 measures 2015	2014	2013	Task 11 Cosine
$f_{1,3,5,6,7,8,9,10,11,12}$	**62.64**	69.57	70.61	0.763
$f_{1,2,3,6,7,8,9,10,11,12}$	62.38	69.9	**70.85**	0.767
$f_{1,2,3,4,5,6,7,8,9,10,11,12}$	62.18	69.98	70.81	0.765
$f_{1,2,3,6,8,9,10,11,12}$	*62.0*	**70.16**	70.42	0.761
$f_{1,3,6,7,8,9,10,11,12}$	61.88	68.97	70.03	0.765
$f_{1,6,7,8,9,10,11,12}$	61.31	68.63	70.06	**0.768**
$f_{1,3,4,5,7,8,9,10,11,12}$	61.25	67.96	70.36	0.757
$f_{3,6,7,8,9,10,11,12}$	60.77	67.8	68.37	0.763
$f_{1,2,3,6,7,10,11,12}$	60.17	65.8	66.91	*0.758*
$f_{1,6}$	58.28	65.48	65.4	0.576
$f_{1,4}$	57.33	63.01	64.15	0.617

Table 9: Performance of different feature bundles.

No single feature bundle performs best on all datasets, however, since the best performers for each dataset include almost all features with small variations, we conclude that the different features are compatible and at least to a small degree encode complementary information. However, the feature bundle that contains all features is never the top performer, indicating some interference between features. Note that among the four top performing bundles in Table 9, only NRC unigrams is not present at all! This surprising result is probably due to Gezi being very similar but bigger, which is supported by the comparison bundles that include only aFinn and NRC or aFinn and Gezi: Gezi outperforms NRC for Task 10B by a very small margin, considering its ten-fold size difference. For Task 11, however, NRC outperforms Gezi in this baseline combination.

Table 9 shows the secondary feature bundles $f_{10,11,12}$ in every combination. These are corrective measures that were frequent and obvious enough to catch our eye and are thus very effective. More surprising is the strong performance of simple dependency feature association scores, present in all top performing feature bundles.

Impact of Size Expectedly, performing worst are the single feature bundles, in particular each lexicon used as the sole feature for the classification task, see Table 10.The surprise: aFinn, the smallest (ca. 1% of Gezi), manually curated lexicon not only dominates the others, but enhanced with our linguistic context annotations performs only 12% worse than the best bundle on 2015 data. We speculate that the reason is the design criterion (Nielsen, 2011) for aFinn to eliminate entries that may have conflicting sentiment labels altogether. This sends a very simple and clear message: reliability ranks above quantity. This of course limits aFinn to the uncontroversial core of the fuzzy set of sentiment carriers, but below that glass ceiling, it is the one to beat. Gezi, with its 100-fold size advantage trails aFinn by a mere 0.3%, which gives hope that automatically extracted lexica that include the volatile fringe can, with enough training data, approximate aFinns performance (and likely surpass it in time, as it already does for the 2014 data). The NRC lexicon which is 10-fold aFinns size, trails its performance by 5%.

feature ids	Task 10B F1 measures 2015	2014	2013	Task 11 Cosine
f_1:aFinn	54.97	60.26	62.19	0.558
f_6:Gezi uni	54.65	60.81	57.86	0.554
f_3:Liu	53.88	53.9	57.2	0.555
f_2:MPQA	52.22	51.42	53.39	0.548
f_4:NRC uni	49.83	52.39	50.9	0.609

Table 10: Task 10B's lexical sets results.

Comparing Gezi to NRC, we see that adding negation scope while enlarging the size of the tweet collection for automatically creating a resource increases its efficiency, supported by the fact that Gezi intersects and agrees with manually created lexica to a higher degree than NRC, see Table 4. But NRC outperforms Gezi in the two-lexicon-only runs $f_{1,6}$ and $f_{1,4}$ of Table 9.

11 Conclusion

Gezi, a new, large Twitter-derived sentiment lexicon that encodes the linguistic context in which a sentiment carrier occurs, was run together with certain ad hoc features on recent SemEval tasks. For comparison purposes and to improve performance, four sentiment lexica from the literature were added. A comprehensive ablation study of all the subgroupings of the resulting features shows several surprises: the smallest lexicon, aFinn, is the best solo performer. Our automatically derived Gezi lexicon marginally improves on the smaller NRC lexicon of similar design and approaches aFinns performance. We demonstrated that features do not add improvements linearly but are largely compatible with each other and effective in different subsets on different datasets, thus a careful vetting of features for each corpus is essential. Our performance in different SemEval 2015 challenge tasks shows that our approach is robust.Ranking first on the figurative language pilot task without specially geared feature additions underscores this fact and makes it a strong contender for applications across domains and tasks.

Acknowledgments

This work has been funded by a grant from Canada's Natural Science and Engineering Research Council (NSERC).

References

Chih-Chung Chang and Chih-Jen Lin. 2011. LIBSVM: A library for support vector machines. *ACM Trans. Intell. Syst. Technol.*, 2(3):27:1–27:27.

Kenneth Ward Church and Patrick Hanks. 1990. Word association norms, mutual information, and lexicography. *Computational Linguistics*, 16(1).

Hamish Cunningham, Diana Maynard, Kalina Bontcheva, and Valentin Tablan. 2002. GATE: an architecture for development of robust HLT applications. In *Proceedings of 40th Annual Meeting of the Association for Computational Linguistics, July 2002 (ACL'02)*, pages 168–175, Philadelphia, Pennsylvania, USA.

Hamish Cunningham, Valentin Tablan, Angus Roberts, and Kalina Bontcheva. 2013. Getting more out of biomedical documents with GATE's full lifecycle open source text analytics. *PLoS Computational Biology*, 9(2).

Marie-Catherine de Marneffe and Christopher D. Manning. 2008. The Stanford typed dependencies representation. In *COLING 2008: Proceedings of the Workshop on Cross-Framework and Cross-Domain Parser Evaluation, 18-22 August 2008*, CrossParser '08, pages 1–8, Manchester, United Kingdom.

Andrea Esuli and Fabrizio Sebastiani. 2006. Sentiwordnet: A publicly available lexical resource for opinion mining. In *In Proceedings of the 5th Conference on Language Resources and Evaluation (LREC'06, 24-26 May 2006, Genoa, Italy*, pages 417–422.

Richárd Farkas, Veronika Vincze, György Móra, János Csirik, and György Szarvas. 2010. The CoNLL-2010 shared task: Learning to detect hedges and their scope in natural language text. In *Proceedings of the Fourteenth Conference on Computational Natural Language Learning — Shared Task, July 15-16, 2010*, CoNLL '10: Shared Task, pages 1–12, Uppsala, Sweden.

Aniruddha Ghosh, Guofu Li, Tony Veale, Paolo Rosso, Ekaterina Shutova, John Barnden, and Antonio Reyes. 2015. SemEval-2015 Task 11: Sentiment analysis of figurative language in Twitter. In *Proceedings of the 9th International Workshop on Semantic Evaluation (SemEval 2015), 1-5 June 2015*, pages 470–478, Denver, CO, USA.

Kevin Gimpel, Nathan Schneider, Brendan O'Connor, Dipanjan Das, Daniel Mills, Jacob Eisenstein, Michael Heilman, Dani Yogatama, Jeffrey Flanigan, and Noah A. Smith. 2011. Part-of-speech tagging for Twitter: Annotation, features, and experiments. In *Proceedings of the 49th Annual Meeting of the Association for Computational Linguistics: Human Language Technologies: Short Papers - Volume 2, 19-24 June 2011*, HLT '11, pages 42–47, Portland, Oregon, USA.

Alec Go, Richa Bhayani, and Lei Huang. 2009. Twitter sentiment classification using distant supervision. *CS224N Project Report, Stanford*, pages 1–12.

Tobias Günther and Lenz Furrer. 2013. GU-MLT-LT: Sentiment analysis of short messages using linguistic features and stochastic gradient descent. In *Second Joint Conference on Lexical and Computational Semantics (*SEM), Volume 2: Proceedings of the Seventh International Workshop on Semantic Evaluation (SemEval 2013), June 2013*, pages 328–332, Atlanta, Georgia, USA.

Minqing Hu and Bing Liu. 2004. Mining and summarizing customer reviews. In *Proceedings of the Tenth ACM SIGKDD International Conference on Knowledge Discovery and Data Mining, August 22-25, 2004*, KDD '04, pages 168–177, Seattle, WA, USA.

Alistair Kennedy and Diana Inkpen. 2005. Sentiment classification of movie and product reviews using contextual valence shifters. In *Workshop on the Analysis of Informal and Formal Information Exchange during Negotiations, FINEXIN 2005, May 26-27 2005*, Ottawa, Canada.

Alistair Kennedy and Diana Inkpen. 2006. Sentiment classification of movie reviews using contextual valence shifters. *Computational Intelligence*, 22(2):110–125.

Jin-Dong Kim, Tomoko Ohta, Sampo Pyysalo, Yoshinobu Kano, and Jun'ichi Tsujii. 2009. Overview of BioNLP'09 shared task on event extraction. In *Proceedings of the Workshop on Current Trends in Biomedical Natural Language Processing: Shared Task, June 4-5 2009*, BioNLP '09, pages 1–9, Boulder, CO, USA.

Svetlana Kiritchenko, Xiaodan Zhu, and Saif M. Mohammad. 2014. Sentiment analysis of short informal texts. *Journal of Artificial Intelligence Research (JAIR)*, 50:723–762.

Saif Mohammad, Svetlana Kiritchenko, and Xiaodan Zhu. 2013. NRC-Canada: Building the state-of-the-art in sentiment analysis of tweets. In *Second Joint Conference on Lexical and Computational Semantics (*SEM), Volume 2: Proceedings of the Seventh International Workshop on Semantic Evaluation (SemEval 2013), June 14-15, 2013*, pages 321–327, Atlanta, Georgia, USA.

Rick Moody and Christine A Lindberg. 2012. *Oxford American Writer's Thesaurus*. Oxford University Press.

Roser Morante and Eduardo Blanco. 2012. *SEM 2012 shared task: Resolving the scope and focus of negation. In *Proceedings of the First Joint Conference on Lexical and Computational Semantics - Volume 1: Proceedings of the Main Conference and the Shared Task, and Volume 2: Proceedings of the Sixth International Workshop on Semantic Evaluation, 7-8 June 2012*, SemEval '12, pages 265–274, Montréal, Canada.

Roser Morante and Walter Daelemans. 2012. Annotating modality and negation for a machine reading evaluation. In Pamela Forner, Jussi Karlgren, and Christa Womser-Hacker, editors, *CLEF (Online Working Notes/Labs/Workshop), 17-20 September 2012, Rome Italy*.

Preslav Nakov, Sara Rosenthal, Zornitsa Kozareva, Veselin Stoyanov, Alan Ritter, and Theresa Wilson. 2013. SemEval-2013 Task 2: Sentiment analysis in Twitter. In *Second Joint Conference on Lexical and Computational Semantics (*SEM), Volume 2: Proceedings of the Seventh International Workshop on Semantic Evaluation (SemEval 2013), June 14-15, 2013*, pages 312–320, Atlanta, Georgia, USA.

Roger B. Nelson. 2001. Kendall Tau metric. *Encyclopaedia of Mathematics*, 3.

Finn Årup Nielsen. 2011. A new ANEW: evaluation of a word list for sentiment analysis in microblogs. In *Proceedings of the ESWC2011 Workshop on 'Making Sense of Microposts': Big things come in small packages, Heraklion, Crete, Greece, May 30, 2011*, pages 93–98.

Canberk Özdemir and Sabine Bergler. 2015. CLaC-SentiPipe: SemEval2015 Subtasks 10 B, E, and Task 11. In *Proceedings of the 9th International Workshop on Semantic Evaluation (SemEval 2015), 1-5 June 2015*, pages 479–485, Denver, CO, USA.

Bo Pang and Lillian Lee. 2008. Opinion mining and sentiment analysis. *Found. Trends Inf. Retr.*, 2(1-2):1–135.

Bo Pang, Lillian Lee, and Shivakumar Vaithyanathan. 2002. Thumbs up?: Sentiment classification using machine learning techniques. In *Proceedings of the ACL-02 Conference on Empirical Methods in Natural Language Processing - Volume 10, July 6-7, 2002*, EMNLP '02, pages 79–86.

Alan Ritter, Sam Clark, Mausam, and Oren Etzioni. 2011. Named entity recognition in tweets: An experimental study. In *Proceedings of the Conference on Empirical Methods in Natural Language Processing, July 27-29, 2011*, EMNLP '11, pages 1524–1534, Edinburgh, United Kingdom.

Sabine Rosenberg, Halil Kilicoglu, and Sabine Bergler. 2012. CLaC Labs: Processing modality and negation. working notes for QA4MRE pilot task at CLEF 2012. In *CLEF 2012 Evaluation Labs and Workshop, Online Working Notes, Rome, Italy, September 17-20, 2012*.

Sabine Rosenberg. 2013. Negation triggers and their scope. Master's thesis, Department of Computer Science and Software Engineering, Concordia University.

Sara Rosenthal, Alan Ritter, Preslav Nakov, and Veselin Stoyanov. 2014. SemEval-2014 Task 9: Sentiment analysis in Twitter. In *Proceedings of the 8th International Workshop on Semantic Evaluation (SemEval 2014), August 23-24, 2014*, pages 73–80, Dublin, Ireland.

Sara Rosenthal, Preslav Nakov, Svetlana Kiritchenko, Saif M. Mohammad, Alan Ritter, and Veselin Stoyanov. 2015. SemEval-2015 Task 10: Sentiment analysis in Twitter. In *Proceedings of the 9th International Workshop on Semantic Evaluation (SemEval 2015), 1-5 June 2015*, pages 451–463, Denver, CO, USA.

Ehsan Shareghi and Sabine Bergler. 2013. Feature combination for sentence similarity. In Osmar Zaefane and Sandra Zilles, editors, *Advances in Artificial Intelligence: 26th Canadian Conference on Artificial Intelligence, Canadian AI 2013, Regina, Canada, May 28-31, 2013*, volume 7884 of *Lecture Notes in Computer Science*, pages 150–161. Springer Berlin Heidelberg.

Richard Socher, John Bauer, Christopher D. Manning, and Andrew Y. Ng. 2013. Parsing with compositional vector grammars. In *Proceedings of the 51st Annual Meeting of the Association for Computational Linguistics, ACL 2013, 4-9 August 2013, Sofia, Bulgaria, Volume 1: Long Papers*, pages 455–465.

Philip J. Stone, Dexter C. Dunphy, and Marshall S. Smith. 1966. *The General Inquirer: a Computer Approach to Content Analysis*. M.I.T. studies in comparative politics. M.I.T. Press, Cambridge, MA, USA.

Yong Wang and Ian H. Witten. 1997. Induction of model trees for predicting continuous classes. In *Poster in Proceedings of the 9th European Conference on Machine Learning, April 23-25 1997*, Prague, Czech Republic. Faculty of Informatics and Statistics.

Theresa Wilson, Janyce Wiebe, and Paul Hoffmann. 2005. Recognizing contextual polarity in phrase-level sentiment analysis. In *Proceedings of the Conference on Human Language Technology and Empirical Methods in Natural Language Processing, October 6-8, 2005*, HLT '05, pages 347–354, Vancouver, British Columbia, Canada.

Ian H. Witten and Eibe Frank. 2011. *Data Mining: Practical Machine Learning Tools and Techniques*. Morgan Kaufmann Publishers, 3rd edition.

Classification of Attributes in a Natural Language Query into Different SQL Clauses

Ashish Palakurthi[†], **Ruthu S. M.**[†], **Arjun R. Akula**[†,*] **and Radhika Mamidi**[†]
[†]Language Technologies Research Center, IIIT Hyderabad, India.
[*]IBM Research, Bangalore, India.
ashish.palakurthi@research.iiit.ac.in,
ruthus.m@students.iiit.ac.in, arakula@in.ibm.com,
radhika.mamidi@iiit.ac.in

Abstract

Attribute information in a natural language query is one of the key features for converting a natural language query into a Structured Query Language[1] (SQL) in Natural Language Interface to Database systems. In this paper, we explore the task of classifying the attributes present in a natural language query into different SQL clauses in a SQL query. In particular, we investigate the effectiveness of various features and Conditional Random Fields for this task. Our system uses a statistical classifier trained on manually prepared data. We report our results on three different domains and also show how our system can be used for generating a complete SQL query.

1 Introduction

Databases have become one of the most efficient ways to store and retrieve information. Database systems require a user to have the knowledge of structured languages in order to be able to retrieve information from them. As a result, it becomes difficult for people of non-technical background to use databases. Natural Language Interface to Database (NLIDB) (Androutsopoulos et al., 1995; Catalina Hallett and David Hardcastle, 2008; Pazos et al., 2002; Popescu et al., 2003; Giordani and Moschitti, 2009; Gupta et al., 2012) systems provide an interface through which a user can ask a query in natural language and get the required information from the database. NLIDB systems translate the user's natural language (NL) query into a SQL query, thereby allowing the user to retrieve the answer from the database. However, NLIDB systems are not widely used because of their inability to process ambiguity and complexity of natural language, which makes them more error prone. Thus, it becomes very important to capture even the smallest of the information from a NL query before converting it into a SQL query.

A relational database contains objects called tables in which information is stored. These tables contain columns and rows. The column names in the tables are known as attributes. A SQL query is composed of different SQL clauses like SELECT, FROM, WHERE, GROUP BY, HAVING and ORDER BY. Since clauses in a SQL query have attributes, attribute information becomes very important for an effective conversion of a NL query into a SQL query. Explicit attributes are the attributes mentioned by the user in the NL query text. When a NL query is converted into SQL query, explicit attributes may belong to different SQL clauses. In this paper, we use Conditional Random Fields (CRF) for classifying the explicit attributes in a NL query to different SQL clauses.

2 Related Work

There have been significant research efforts in the area of NLIDB systems. Different approaches have been proposed to deal with these systems.

In (Gupta et al., 2012), the authors propose a NLIDB system based on Computational Paninian Grammar (CPG) Framework (Bharati et al., 1996). They emphasize on syntactic elements as well as the semantics of the domain. They convert a NL query into a SQL query by processing the NL query in three stages, viz. the syntactic stage, the semantic stage and the graph processing stage. In the semantic stage, they identify attribute-value pairs for various entities using noun frames. The problem with this proposal is that it becomes costly in terms of space to use high number of frames in large domains. In (Khalid et al., 2007), machine learning was used in Question Answering systems.

[1]Structured Query Language is a specialized language used for relational database management and data manipulation.

Proceedings of Recent Advances in Natural Language Processing, pages 497–506,
Hissar, Bulgaria, Sep 7–9 2015.

The system proposed by them maps an input query to certain tables containing attributes which can provide the required answer. They specify that identifying the related tables and attributes from the knowledge base is very important for answering an incoming question. Amany Sarhan (2009) emphasized on the importance of identifying the table names of attributes in a NL query. He shows that attribute and table information help in minimizing the effort to build SQL queries. Thus, attribute information plays a very important role in both NLIDB systems and Question Answering systems. To our knowledge, this work is the first attempt to classify attributes directly from a NL query to different SQL clauses in their SQL queries. In (Srirampur et al., 2014), the authors address the problem of Concepts Identification of a NL query in NLIDB, which plays a crucial role for our system to generate a complete SQL query.

The remainder of this paper is structured as follows. Section 3 describes the problem. In section 4, we illustrate the concept of explicit attribute classification. Section 5 explains the methodology along with the features adopted for the classification. We also discuss on generating the complete SQL query. In section 6, we show experimentations and results along with error analysis. We conclude in section 7.

3 Problem

An attribute in a NL query can correspond to various SQL clauses. We define two types of attributes which can be found in a NL query.

Explicit attributes: Explicit attributes are the attributes which are directly mentioned by the user in the NL query.

Implicit attributes: Implicit attributes are not directly mentioned by the user in the NL query. These attributes are identified with the help of values mentioned by the user in the NL query. For identifying these attributes, domain dictionaries can be used. Table 1 shows a sample domain dictionary. The following examples illustrate explicit and implicit attributes in a user query.

Example 1: *List the grades of all the students in Mathematics.*

In this example, *grade* is an explicit attribute as it is directly mentioned by the user in the NL query. The user also mentions the value *Mathematics.* This value when checked in the domain dictionary gives the attribute course_name as *Mathematics* is the name of a course. Thus, course_name is an implicit attribute. The attribute *students* or student_name is another explicit attribute in the above example.

Example 2: *What course does Smith teach?*

In this example, *course* or course_name is an explicit attribute as it is directly mentioned by the user. The user mentions the value *Smith.* This value when checked in the domain dictionary gives the attribute professor_name if *Smith* is a name of a professor. Thus, the attribute professor_name is an implicit attribute.

Implicit attributes generally correspond to the WHERE clause in a SQL query as they are associated with a value. This paper focusses on classifying explicit attributes into different SQL clauses in a SQL query.

Value	Attribute
Smith	professor_name
ABCD	lab_name
John	student_name
Science	course_name

Table 1: Sample domain dictionary

4 Explicit Attribute Classification

In this section, we illustrate the classification of explicit attributes from a NL query into different clauses in a SQL query. In all the examples shown in Figure 1, course_name (courses) is explicitly mentioned by the user. In each example, the attribute course_name belongs to a different SQL clause. In Example 1 (Figure 1), course_name belongs to the SELECT clause as the user has asked to the list courses taught by Smith. In Example 2 (Figure 1), course_name belongs to the WHERE clause as it gives information about a course (Science). Note that Science can be identified as course_name from the domain dictionary as well. In Example 3, the user is asking to show a student from each course. So it is required to group the students according to their course (course_name) and then list them. Thus, the attribute course_name should belong to the GROUP BY clause. Note that, in the same example the user has also mentioned another attribute (students) explicitly. Since he has asked to list the students, the attribute student_name will belong to the SELECT clause. In Example 4, the two explicit attributes mentioned by the user are professors and courses. Here, the user is asking to list only those professors who teach more than two courses. Here, we group according to professors and then for each professor, we count the number of courses taught. Only if the count is greater than 2, we select the professor and list his name. Thus, professor_name belongs to the GROUP BY clause. The condition on professors is COUNT *(course_name)* > 2. Therefore, the attribute *courses* or course_name belongs to the HAVING clause. In this way, by identifying the clauses to which the attributes belong, we can improve the translation of NL queries to SQL queries. In the next section, we describe how we classify these explicit attributes to their SQL clauses.

1. *What are the courses taught by Smith?*
SELECT course_name
FROM COURSES, TEACH, PROFESSOR
WHERE professor_name= "Smith" AND
prof_id=prof_teach_id AND
course_teach_id=course_id.
2. *Who teaches Science course?*
SELECT professor_name
FROM COURSES, TEACH, PROFESSOR
WHERE course_name="Science" AND
course_id =course_teach_id AND
prof_teach_id=prof_id
3. *List a student from each course.*
SELECT student_name, course_name
FROM STUDENTS, REGISTER, COURSES
WHERE stud_id=stud_reg_id AND
reg_id=course_id
GROUP BY course_name
4. *Who are the professors teaching more than 2 courses?*
SELECT professor_name
FROM COURSES, TEACH, PROFESSOR
WHERE course_id=course_teach_id AND
prof_teach_id =prof_id
GROUP BY professor_name
HAVING COUNT(course_name) > 2

Figure 1: Examples of NL queries and their SQL queries

5 Methodology

We manually prepared a dataset of queries on the Academic domain of our university. The university database was used as the source of information. Examples of tables in the database schema are *courses, labs, students* consisting of attributes like course_name, course_id, student_name, lab_name etc. The database has relations like register (between student and course), teach (between professor and course) etc. Each token in the sentence is given a tag and a set of features. If a token is an attribute, it is assigned a tag which corresponds to a SQL clause to which the attribute belongs. If a token is not an attribute, it is given a NULL (O) tag. The tagging was done manually. Our tag set is simple and consists of only 4 tags, where each tag corresponds to a SQL clause. The tags are SELECT, WHERE, GROUP BY, HAVING. Formally, our task is framed as assigning label sequences to a set of observation sequences.

Token	Attribute	Tag
What	0	O
are	0	O
the	0	O
courses	1	GROUP BY
with	0	O
less	0	O
than	0	O
25	0	O
students	1	HAVING
?	0	O

Table 2: Example of tagging scheme

We followed two guidelines while tagging sentences. Sometimes it is possible that an attribute can belong to more than one SQL clause. If an attribute belongs to both SELECT and GROUP BY clause, we tag the attribute as a GROUP BY clause attribute. This is done with an aim to identify higher number of GROUP BY clause attributes as SELECT clause attributes are very common and are comparatively easier to identify. The second guideline that we followed was, if an attribute belongs to both the SELECT and the WHERE clause, we tag the attribute as a SELECT clause attribute. This is done because the WHERE clause attributes can often be identified through a domain dictionary. Table 2 shows an example of the tagging scheme. Each token in a sentence is given a set of features and a tag. In Table 2, we have shown only one feature due to space constraints. We trained our data and created models for testing. We used Conditional Random Fields (Lafferty et al., 2001) for the machine learning task. The next subsection describes the features employed for the classification of explicit attributes in a NL query.

5.1 Classification Features

The following features were used for the classification of explicit attributes in a NL query.

Token-based Features These features are based on learning of tokens in a sentence. The *isSymbol* feature checks whether a token is a symbol (>, <) or not. Symbols like > (greater than), < (less than) are quite commonly used as aggregations in NL queries. This feature captures such aggregates. We also took lower case form of a token as a feature for uniform learning. We considered a particular substring as a feature. If that substring is found in the token, we set the feature to 1 else 0 (for example, in batch wise or batchwise, the attribute *batch* is identified as GROUP BY clause attribute using substring *wise*).

Grammatical Features POS tags of tokens and grammatical relations (e.g. nsubj, dobj) of a token with other tokens in the sentence were considered. These features were obtained using the Stanford parser[2] (Marneffe et al., 2006).

Contextual Features Tokens preceding and following (*local context*) the current token were also considered as features. In addition, we took the POS tags of the tokens in the local context of the current token as features. Grammatical relations of the tokens in local context of the current token were also considered for learning.

Other Features:

isAttribute This is a basic and an important feature for our problem. If a token is an attribute, we set the feature to 1, else 0.

Presence of other attributes This feature aims to identify the GROUP BY clause attributes only. In SQL, the HAVING clause generally contains a condition on the GROUP BY clause. If a NL query is very likely (>95%) to have a HAVING clause attribute, then the SQL clause will certainly have a GROUP BY clause as well. This feature is marked as 1 for an attribute if it has a local context which may trigger a GROUP BY clause and at the same time if the NL query is very likely to have the HAVING clause attribute. The likeliness of the HAVING clause attribute is again decided based on the local context of the attribute. Thus, GROUP BY clause attribute is not just identified using its local context, but also depending on the presence of HAVING clause attribute. In simple terms, this feature increases the weight of an attribute to belong to the GROUP BY clause of the SQL query.

Trigger words An external list is used to determine whether a word in the local context of an attribute may trigger a certain SQL clause for the attribute. (eg., the word *each* may trigger GROUP BY clause).

5.2 Completing the SQL Query

Until now, we have only identified attributes and their corresponding SQL clauses. But this is not sufficient to get a complete SQL query. In this section, we describe how we can generate a complete SQL query after the classification of attributes. To build a complete SQL query we would require:

1. Complete attribute and entity information.
2. Concepts[3] of all the tokens in the given query.
3. Mapping of identified entities and relationships in the Entity Relationship schema to get the joint conditions in WHERE clause.

Our system can extract attribute information using explicit attribute classifier for explicit attributes and domain dictionaries for implicit attributes. Sometimes, we may not have complete attribute information to form a SQL query. That is, there can be attributes other than explicit attributes and implicit attributes in a SQL query. For example, consider:

Example 1: *Which professor teaches* NLP *?*

Example 2: *Who teaches* NLP *?*

The SQL query for both the examples is:

SELECT professor_name
FROM prof, teach, course
WHERE course_name= NLP AND
course_id=course_teach_id AND
prof_teach_id=prof_id .

In example 1, our system has complete attribute information to form the SQL query. Since professor is explicitly mentioned by the user in the query, here professor_name is identified as a SELECT clause attribute by our system. But in example 2, we do not have complete attribute information. Here identifying the SELECT clause attribute professor_name is a problem, as there is no clue (neither explicit attribute nor implicit attribute) in the query which points us to the attribute professor_name. To identify attributes which cannot be identified as implicit attributes or explicit at-

[2]http://nlp.stanford.edu/software/lex-parser.shtml

[3]Concept of a NL token maps the NL token to the database schema. The tables, attributes and relations in the database schema constitute concepts.

tributes, Concepts Identification (Srirampur et al., 2014) is used. In Concepts Identification, each token in the NL query is tagged with concepts. Using Concepts Identification, we can directly identify *Who* as professor_name. These attributes are known as the *Question class* attributes. Most of the times, since question words are related to the SELECT clause, the attribute professor_name can be mapped to the SELECT clause, thereby giving us complete information of attributes. We also use Concepts Identification to identify relations in the NL query. In both the examples, *teach* which is a relationship in the Entity Relationship schema can be identified through Concepts Identification (CI). Once the attributes are identified, entities can be extracted. For example, entities for the attributes course_name, professor_name are COURSES and PROFESSOR respectively. The identified entities and relationships are added to the FROM clause.

All the identified entities and relationships can now be mapped to the Entity Relationship (ER) schema to get the joint conditions (Arjun Reddy Akula, 2015) in the WHERE clause. We create an ER graph using the ER schema of the database with entities and relationships as vertices in the ER graph. We apply a Minimum spanning tree (MST) algorithm on the ER graph to get a non-cyclic path connecting all the identified vertices in the ER graph. With this, we get the required join conditions in the WHERE clause. Arjun Reddy Akula (2015) discusses the problem of handling joint conditions in detail. Note that new entities and relationships can also be identified while forming the MST. These extra entities and relationships are added to the FROM clause in the SQL query. We now have a complete SQL query.

6 Experiments and Discussions

6.1 Data

We manually prepared a rich dataset ensuring that NL queries when converted into SQL queries, a wide variety of SQL queries are covered for the classification. We tested our classifier on these queries. Apart from the Academic domain, we also experimented on Mooney's dataset[4]. We considered the Restaurant and the Geoquery domains (Wong and Mooney, 2006) in Mooney's dataset. The Geoquery dataset (GEO880) consisted of 880 queries. Since we are not addressing nested SQL queries, we removed queries which when converted to SQL queries, involve nested SQL queries. This task was done manually. There were 256 nested SQL queries in the Geoquery dataset. Regarding classification, we mainly focused on the Academic domain as it consists of queries with the SELECT, WHERE, GROUP BY and the HAVING clause attributes. The Restaurant and Geoquery domains had queries with only the SELECT and WHERE clause attributes. This is one of the reasons why we prepared the data ourselves. Table 3 shows the number of sentences considered for training and testing in each domain.

Domain	Train	Test
Academic	711	305
Restaurant	150	100
Geoquery	400	224

Table 3: Corpus statistics

6.2 Experimental Results

We used the metrics of Precision (P), Recall (R) and F-measure[5] (F) for evaluation.

6.2.1 Baseline Method

We first determine the majority class C of an explicit attribute A found in the training data. The baseline system then labels all occurrences of A found in the test data with class C, irrespective of the context of the attribute. In all the three domains, SELECT clause attribute was the majority class attribute. Table 4 summarizes the results of the baseline method in all the domains.

Domain	P(%)	R(%)	F(%)
Academic	46.29	46.37	46.33
Restaurant	47.75	43.80	45.69
Geoquery	63.08	63.08	63.08

Table 4: Baseline method results

6.2.2 Conditional Random Fields

We used Conditional Random Fields for the classification experiments since it represents the state of the art in sequence modeling and has also

[4]http://www.cs.utexas.edu/users/ml/nldata.html

[5]
$$F - measure = \frac{2 * P * R}{P + R}$$

been very effective at Named Entity Recognition (NER). As our problem is very similar to NER, we used CRF. CRF++[6] tool kit was used for this. CRFs are a probabilistic framework used for labeling sequence data. CRF models effectively solve the label bias problem, which make it better than HMMs which are generally more likely to be susceptible to the label bias problem. Our discussions mainly focus on Academic domain.

We conducted experiments in three phases. Phase one involved using features only for the current token. The system achieved a F-measure of 60.27%.

Domain	Clause	P(%)	R(%)	F(%)
Academic	SELECT	60.94	89.80	72.61
	WHERE	48.81	57.75	52.90
	GROUP BY	72.37	38.73	50.46
	HAVING	14.29	1.52	2.74
	Overall	**60.04**	**60.50**	**60.27**
Restaurant	SELECT	81.08	92.31	86.33
	WHERE	96.30	92.86	94.55
	Overall	**87.50**	**92.56**	**89.96**
Geoquery	SELECT	78.21	98.05	87.01
	WHERE	94.12	53.33	68.09
	Overall	**81.54**	**81.54**	**81.54**

Table 5: Results obtained without considering contextual features.

In phase two, we added contextual features as well. The contextual features include tokens surrounding the current token, POS tags of the tokens surrounding the current token and also the grammatical relations of the tokens surrounding the current token.

Domain	Clause	P(%)	R(%)	F(%)
Academic	SELECT	88.12	93.88	90.91
	WHERE	56.41	92.96	70.21
	GROUP BY	96.58	79.58	87.26
	HAVING	96.88	46.97	63.27
	Overall	**83.49**	**83.97**	**83.73**
Restaurant	SELECT	94.64	81.54	87.60
	WHERE	100.00	98.21	99.10
	Overall	**97.30**	**89.26**	**93.10**
Geoquery	SELECT	89.04	99.02	93.76
	WHERE	97.94	79.17	87.56
	Overall	**91.69**	**91.69**	**91.69**

Table 6: Results obtained on adding contextual features.

[6] https://code.google.com/p/crfpp

Incorporating contextual features showed a significant improvement in the classification. At the end of phase two, the F-measure of the system was 83.73%. This shows that the local context of an attribute is important in deciding its SQL clause. Table 5 and Table 6 show the classification results of phase one and phase two respectively. By local context, we mean the neighbouring tokens or features of neighbouring tokens of the attribute in the NL query. After a few pilot experiments, context window of size three was found to be optimal in Academic domain and context window of size one was enough for Restaurant and Geoquery domains. Window size of three was required specially for HAVING clause attributes. This is probably because HAVING clause attributes are generally associated with aggregations. Hence, local context of an attribute is very important for the HAVING class attributes. As can be seen from Table 5 and Table 6, adding contextual features increased the F-measure of HAVING clause attributes by 60.53 percentage points. The presence of attribute feature is very important for identifying the GROUP BY clause attributes. F-measure of GROUP BY clause attributes increased by 11.72 percentage points on adding this feature. The reason for higher F-measures in the Restaurant and the Geoquery domains is mainly because these domains had NL queries with only the SELECT and the WHERE clause attributes, thus making classification much easier. Moreover, the randomness found in queries was comparatively lesser than the Academic domain. In addition, the problem of contextual conflicts was not seen in these domains. Contextual conflicts are discussed in the error analysis section.

Train	Test	P(%)	R(%)	F(%)
Academic	Restaurant	69.63	77.69	73.44
Academic	Geoquery	70.99	70.77	70.88
Restaurant	Academic	52.55	51.15	51.84
Restaurant	Geoquery	80.66	60.31	69.01
Geoquery	Academic	50.57	50.95	50.76
Geoquery	Restaurant	87.50	92.56	89.96

Table 7: Cross domain results

In phase three, we performed cross domain experiments. Here, we train a model on a dataset of one domain and test the model on the dataset of a different domain. We do not consider current token as a feature since the attributes are different in each domain. But, features like POS and grammatical relations of the current token were taken. Contextual tokens and other features of contextual tokens were considered. Table 7 shows the results of phase three experiments. Using contextual features in a supervised machine learning framework captures a strong generalization for classifying the attributes.

Finally, we compare the final results we were able to achieve to the state-of-the-art. Many NLIDB systems have been proposed using different approaches. We discuss few of them. PRECISE (Popescu et al., 2003) is a system which converts semantic analysis to a graph matching problem using schema elements. A class of semantically tractable queries is proposed and the system can form SQL queries only if a query belongs to the proposed class. PRECISE achieves an overall F-measure of 87% on 700 tractable queries from the GEO880 (Geoquery domain) corpus and a recall of 95% in restaurant domain. In KRISP (Kate et al., 2006), a user query is mapped to its formal meaning representations using kernel based classifiers. These classifiers were trained on string subsequence kernels and were used to build complete meaning representation of the user query. They achieve a precision of 94% and recall of 78% on the GEO880 corpus.

Support Vector Machines with kernel methods (Giordani et al., 2009) were adopted to represent syntactic relationships between NL and SQL queries. The authors apply different combinations of kernels and derive an automatic translator of NL query to SQL query. Their system achieves an overall accuracy of 76% and 84.7% for forming SQL queries in the Geoquery and the Restaurant domains respectively.

A set of candidate SQL queries (Giordani et al., 2012) are produced using lexical dependencies and metadata of the database. These SQL queries are then re-ranked using SVM with tree kernels. Using few heuristics they generate final list of SQL queries. They achieved F-measure of 85% on the GEO880 corpus. Recent work (Clarke et al., 2010) tackles semantic parsing using supervision. Here, the system predicts complex structures based on feedback of external world. From the GEO880 corpus, they randomly select 250 queries for training and 250 queries for testing and achieved an overall F-measure of 73%.

However, there have not been any efforts in mapping NL queries to SQL queries exclusively from an attribute point of view. Attributes being the building blocks of a SQL query, we focus on attributes to build a SQL query. After attribute classification, Concept Identification and identification of the joint conditions in the WHERE clause, we evaluate the overall SQL query formation. Even if one attribute is wrongly tagged, we consider the SQL query wrong. After accounting to Concepts Identification errors and domain dictionary errors, the final accuracies achieved by our system were 75%, 71% and 64% in Restaurant, Geoquery[7] and Academic domains respectively.
We define accuracy as

$$Accuracy = \frac{\text{Number of correctly retrieved SQL queries}}{\text{Total Number of queries}}$$

These accuracies[8] are on the same test datasets used for attribute classification(Table 3). Apart from wrong tagging of attributes, one interesting error we found while forming SQL queries was domain dictionary error. For example, consider the query, *What length is the Mississippi?*. Here, the user is talking about Mississippi river, but the domain dictionary tags Mississippi as state_name. However, if the query had been asked as *What length is the Mississippi river ?*, the system uses the explicit attribute *river* and retrieves Mississippi as river_name. In summary, we achieve competitive results using a novel approach and move towards tackling domain independency.

6.3 Error Analysis in Attribute Classification

Most of the errors occurred due to contextual conflicts which are of two types. Contextual conflict between two attributes *A* and *B* is an instance wherein both the attributes *A* and *B* have same local context but are found to be classified under different SQL clauses $\hat{A}$ and $\hat{B}$. We say that there is a contextual conflict between $\hat{A}$ and $\hat{B}$ clause attributes. The observed contextual conflicts (> 90%) were:

SELECT clause vs GROUP BY clause attributes. For example, consider *List the courses in our college* and *List the batches in our college with more*

[7]The results on Geoquery domain may actually be worse as the data (Table 3) we considered is a subset of the GEO880.

[8]Various state-of-the-art approaches show results on different train-test data splits. We achieved an accuracy of 74% in restaurant domain using standard 10-fold cross validation method. We do not show 10-fold cross validation results for Geoquery domain as the corpus we considered in this domain is a subset of the GEO880 dataset. However, the difference in results is likely not statistically significant.

than 100 students. Here, context of *courses* and *batches* is same. In the first example, the attribute *courses* (course_name) is a SELECT clause attribute and in the second example, the attribute batches (batch_name) is a GROUP BY clause attribute. But *batches* was misclassified as SELECT clause attribute. It should belong to the GROUP BY clause according to our annotation guidelines.

WHERE clause vs HAVING clause attributes.
In the examples, *Who are the students with more than 8 marks in NLP?* and *What are the batches with more than 8 students?*, the prefix context of *marks* in the first example is same as the prefix context of *students* (more than 8) in the second example. The attribute *marks* in the first example belongs to the WHERE clause and *students* in the second example belongs to the HAVING clause. But *students* was misclassified as WHERE clause attribute. Another reason why one yields WHERE and the other HAVING is due to the way the database is organized internally. If the *batch* table has a *number of students* attribute, then the second example would also yield a WHERE clause. This is an inherent limitation of the NLIDB approach, not related to the features, classifier or the overall approach used.

Contextual conflicts were less in the Restaurant and the Geoquery domains when compared to the Academic domain, as they consisted of only SELECT and WHERE clause attributes. Errors in these domains were mainly token based errors.

7 Conclusion and Future Work

In this paper, we investigate a CRF model to classify attributes present in a NL query into different SQL clauses in a SQL query. We believe that this is the core part of SQL query formation. For explicit attribute classification, our system achieved overall F-measures of 83.73%, 93.10%, 91.69% in Academic, Restaurant and Geoquery domains respectively. We also achieved accuracies of 64%, 75% and 71% in forming SQL queries in Academic, Restaurant and Geoquery domains respectively. The main contributions of this paper are:

- We show that within a sentence, attributes can be used to build a SQL query. For this, the local context of an attribute can be helpful to identify its clause in the SQL query
- We primarily focus on attribute classification as they are the building blocks of the SQL query. We then use an existing system to complete the SQL formation. We achieved promising results in forming SQL queries using a novel approach.
- The work presents a significant study on SQL clauses like GROUP BY and HAVING by manually creating a new dataset. To the best of our knowledge, benchmark datasets do not cover these SQL clauses as good as they cover SQL clauses like SELECT and WHERE.
- Experiments in cross domain datasets suggest that the proposed feature set learns a strong generalization for classifying the attributes in the NL query. To an extent, this certainly addresses the disadvantage of domain independency in NLIDB systems. Another advantage of learning the context of an attribute is that, it can be useful in classifying an unseen attribute within the same domain.

Finally, we claim that attributes are an important part of a user query to a NLIDB system. Exploring patterns on how these attributes are used by a user in a NL query can be useful to form a SQL query. The proposed approach may break down with NL queries having less explicit attributes, where the NL query may require deeper semantic processing. It would be interesting if we can combine our approach with existing parsing based approaches. In our future work, we will further improve the explicit attribute classification, incorporate semantic features to improve SQL query formation and handle nested SQL queries.

Acknowledgements

We would like to thank the anonymous reviewers for the valuable feedback on this work. This research was supported in part by the Information Technology Research Academy (ITRA), Government of India under ITRA-Mobile grant ITRA/15(62)/Mobile/VAMD/01. Any opinions, findings, conclusions or recommendations expressed in this publication are those of the authors and do not necessarily reflect the views of the ITRA.

References

Rashid Ahmad, Mohammad Abid Khan, and Rahman Ali 2009. Efficient Transformation of a Natural Language Query to SQL for Urdu. In *Proceedings of the Conference on Language & Technology*, page p53.

Arjun R. Akula, Rajeev Sangal, Radhika Mamidi. 2013. A Novel Approach Towards Incorporating Context Processing Capabilities in NLIDB System. *In Proceedings of the International Joint Conference on Natural Language Processing (IJCNLP)*,pages 1216-1222, Nagoya, Japan.

Arjun R. Akula. 2015. A Novel Approach Towards Building a Generic, Portable and Contextual NLIDB System. International Institute of Information Technology Hyderabad.

Ioannis Androutsopoulos, Graeme D. Ritchie, and Peter Thanisch. 1995. Natural language interfaces to databasesan introduction. *Natural language engineering*,1(01), 29-81.

Raffaella Bernardi and Manuel Kirschner. 2008. Context modeling for iqa: the role of tasks and entities. In *Coling 2008: Proceedings of the workshop on Knowledge and Reasoning for Answering Questions,* pages 2532. Association for Computational Linguistics.

Nuria Bertomeu, Hans Uszkoreit, Anette Frank, Hansulrich Krieger and Brigitte Jorg. 2006. Contextual phenomena and thematic relations in database qa dialogues: results from a wizard-of-oz experiment. In *Proceedings of the Interactive Question Answering Workshop at HLT-NAACL* , pages 1-8 Association for Computational Linguistics.

Akshar Bharati, Medhavi Bhatia, Vineet Chaitanya, and Rajeev Sangal. 1996. Paninian grammar framework applied to English. In *Technical Report TRCS-96-238,CSE,IIT Kanpur, Tech.Rep.*

Joyce Y Chai and Rong Jin. 2004. Discourse structure for context question answering. In *Proceedings of the Workshop on Pragmatics of Question Answering at HLT-NAACL*, pages 23-30.

James Clarke, Dan Goldwasser, Ming-wei Chang and Dan Roth. 2010. Driving semantic parsing from the worlds response. In *ACL Conference on Natural Language Learning (CoNLL).*

Faraj A. El-Mouadib, Zakaria Suliman Zubi, Ahmed A.Almagrous, I. El-Feghi 2009. Generic interactive natural language interface to databases(GINLIDB). In *International Journal of Computers* 3(3).

Alessandra Giordani. 2008. Mapping Natural Language into SQL in a NLIDB. *In Natural Language and Information Systems* (pp. 367-371). Springer Berlin Heidelberg.

Alessandra Giordani and Alessandro Moschitti. 2009. Syntactic structural kernels for natural language interfaces to databases. *In Machine Learning and Knowledge Discovery in Databases,* pages 391406. Springer.

Alessandra Giordani and Alessandro Moschitti. 2009. Semantic Mapping between Natural Language Questions and SQL Queries via Syntactic Pairing. In *14th International Conference on Applications of Natural Language to Information Systems, Saarbrucken, Germany.*

Alessandra Giordani and Alessandro Moschitti. 2010. Corpora for Automatically Learning to Map Natural Language Questions into SQL Queries. In *Proceedings of the Seventh conference on International Language Resources and Evaluation(LREC), Malta.*

Alessandra Giordani and Alessandro Moschitti. 2012. Generating SQL Queries Using Natural Language Syntactic Dependencies and Metadata. *NLDB* 164-170.

Alessandra Giordani and Alessandro Moschitti. 2012. Automatic Generation and Reranking of SQL-Derived Answers to NL Questions. In *Proceedings of the Joint workshop on Intelligent Methods for Software System Engineering (JIMSE)held in ECAI 2012. Montpellier, France.*

Alessandra Giordani and Allesandro Moschitti 2012. Translating Questions to SQL Queries with Generative Parsers Discriminatively Reranked *COLING.*

Abhijeet Gupta, Arjun Akula, Deepak Malladi, Puneeth Kukkadapu, Vinay Ainavolu and Rajeev Sangal. 2012. A novel approach towards building a portable nlidb system using the computational paninian grammar framework. *In Asian Language Processing (IALP), 2012 International Conference on* (pp. 93-96). IEEE.

Catalina Hallett and David Hardcastle 2008. Towards a bootstrapping nlidb system In *Natural Language and Information Systems,* Springer, 2008, pp. 199-204.

Xiaofei Jia, and Mengchi Liu. 2003. Towards an Intelligent Information System *SBBD.*

Rohit J. Kate and Raymond J.Mooney. 2006. Using string-kernels for learning semantic parsers. In *Proceedings of the 21st International Conference on Computational Linguistics and the 44th annual meeting of the Association for Computational Linguistics. ACL.*

Mahboob Alam Khalid, Valentin Jijkoun and Maarten de Rijke 2007. Machine learning for question answering from tabular data. In *Proceedings of Database and Expert Systems Applications*:392-396. IEEE.

John Lafferty, Andrew McCallum, and Fernando CN Pereria. 2001. Conditional random fields: Probabilistic models for segmenting and labeling sequence data. In *Int.Conf. Machine Learning, San Francisco, CA*.

Yunyao Li, Huahai Yang, and HV Jagadish 2005. Nalix: an interactive natural language interface for querying xml. In Proceedings of the 2005 ACM SIGMOD international conference on Management of data, pages 900902. ACM.

Marie-Catherine de Marneffe, Bill MacCartney and Christopher D.Manning. 2006. Generating Typed Dependency Parses from Phrase Structure Parses. In *Proceedings of LREC*.

Xiaofeng Meng and Shan Wang. 2001 Nchiql: The chinese natural language interface to databases. In *Database and Expert Systems Applications* pages 145154. Springer.

M.Minock, Peter Olofsson and Alexander Nasslund. 2008. Towards building robust natural language interfaces to databases. In *Natural language and Information systems. Springler Berlin Heidelberg.* 187-198.

Ana-Maria Popescu, Oren Etzioni and Henry Kautz 2003. Towards a theory of natural language interfaces to databases. In *Proceedings of the 8th international conference on Intelligent user interfaces. ACM.*

Filipe P. Porfirio , and Nuno J. Mamede. 2000. Databases and Natural Language Interfaces *JISBD*.

Rodolfo A. Pazos Rangel , Alexander Gelbukh , J. Javier Gonzlez Barbosa , Erika Alarcn Ruiz , Alejandro Mendoza Meja , and A. Patricia Domnguez Snchez 2002. Spanish Natural Language Interface for a Relational Database Querying System. In *Sojka, P., Kopeek, I., Pala, K. (eds.) TSD 2002. LNCS (LNAI),* vol. 2448, pp. 123-130. Springer, Heidelberg (2002).

Amany Sarhan. 2009. A proposed architecture for dynamically built NLIDB systems. In *Knowledge-based and Intelligent Engineering Systems Journal* 13(2),IOS.

Saikrishna Srirampur, Ravi Chandibhamar, Ashish Palakurthi and Radhika Mamidi. 2014 Concepts identification of an NL query in NLIDB systems. In *Asian Language Processing (IALP), 2014 International Conference* on, pp. 230-233. IEEE.

Niculae Stratica, Leila Kosseim, and Bipin C Desai 2005 Using semantic templates for a natural language interface to the cindi virtual library. *Data and Knowledge Engineering*, 55(1):4-19.

Lappoon R. Tang and Raymond J. Mooney. 2001. Using Multiple Clause Constructors in Inductive Logic Programming for semantic Parsing In *Proceedings of the 12th European Conference on Machine Learning(ECML):*466-477.

Kristina Toutanova, Dan Klein, Christopher Manning and Yoram Singer. 2003. Feature-Rich Part-of-Speech Tagging with a Cyclic Dependency Network. In *Proceedings of HLT-NAACL* 252-259.

Y. W. Wong and R. J. Mooney. 2006. Learning for semantic parsing with statistical machine translation. In *In Proceedings of HLT-NAACL-06*, pages 439-446, New York City, NY.

Classifying Idiomatic and Literal Expressions Using Vector Space Representations

Jing Peng
Montclair State University
pengj@mail.montclair.edu

Anna Feldman
Montclair State University
feldmana@mail.montclair.edu

Hamza Jazmati
Montclair State University
jazmatih1@mail.montclair.edu

Abstract

We describe an algorithm for automatic classification of idiomatic and literal expressions. Our starting point is that idioms and literal expressions occur in different contexts. Idioms tend to violate cohesive ties in local contexts, while literals are expected to fit in. Our goal is to capture this intuition using a vector representation of words. We propose two approaches: (1) Compute inner product of context word vectors with the vector representing a target expression. Since literal vectors predict well local contexts, their inner product with contexts should be larger than idiomatic ones, thereby telling apart literals from idioms; and (2) Compute literal and idiomatic scatter (covariance) matrices from local contexts in word vector space. Since the scatter matrices represent context distributions, we can then measure the difference between the distributions using the Frobenius norm. We provide experimental results validating the proposed techniques.

1 Introduction

Despite the common belief that idioms are always idioms, potentially idiomatic expressions, such as *hit the sack* can appear in literal contexts. Fazly et al. (2009)'s analysis of 60 idioms from the British National Corpus (BNC) has shown that close to half of these also have a clear literal meaning; and of those with a literal meaning, on average around 40% of their usages are literal. Therefore, idioms present great challenges for many Natural Language Processing (NLP) applications. Most current translation systems rely on large repositories of idioms. In this paper we describe an algorithm for automatic classification of idiomatic and literal expressions. Similarly to Peng et al. (2014), we treat idioms as semantic outliers. Our assumption is that the context word distribution for a literal expression will be different from the distribution for an idiomatic one. We capture the distribution in terms of covariance matrix in vector space.

2 Previous Work

Previous approaches to idiom detection can be classified into two groups: 1) type-based extraction, i.e., detecting idioms at the type level; 2) token-based detection, i.e., detecting idioms in context. Type-based extraction is based on the idea that idiomatic expressions exhibit certain linguistic properties such as non-compositionality that can distinguish them from literal expressions (Sag et al., 2002; Fazly et al., 2009). While many idioms do have these properties, many idioms fall on the continuum from being compositional to being partly unanalyzable to completely non-compositional (Cook et al., 2007). Katz and Giesbrech (2006), Birke and Sarkar (2006), Fazly et al. (2009), Sporleder and Li (2009), Li and Sporleder (2010), among others, notice that type-based approaches do not work on expressions that can be interpreted idiomatically or literally depending on the context and thus, an approach that considers tokens in context is more appropriate for idiom recognition.To address these problems, Peng et al. (2014) investigate the bag of words *topic* representation and incorporate an additional hypothesis– contexts in which idioms occur are more affective. Still, they treat idioms as semantic outliers.

3 Proposed Techniques

We hypothesize that words in a given text segment that are representatives of a common topic of discussion are likely to associate strongly with a literal expression in the segment, in terms of projection (or inner product) of word vectors onto the

Proceedings of Recent Advances in Natural Language Processing, pages 507–511,
Hissar, Bulgaria, Sep 7–9 2015.

vector representing the literal expression. We also hypothesize that the context word distribution for a literal expression in word vector space will be different from the distribution for an idiomatic one.

3.1 Projection Based On Local Context Representation

The local context of a literal target verb-noun construction (VNC) must be different from that of an idiomatic one. We propose to exploit recent advances in vector space representation to capture the difference between local contexts (Mikolov et al., 2013a; Mikolov et al., 2013b).

A word can be represented by a vector of fixed dimensionality q that best predicts its surrounding words in a sentence or a document (Mikolov et al., 2013a; Mikolov et al., 2013b). Given such a vector representation, our first proposal is the following. Let v and n be the vectors corresponding to the verb and noun in a target verb-noun construction, as in *blow whistle*, where $v, n \in \Re^q$. Let $\sigma_{vn} = v + n \in \Re^q$. Thus, σ_{vn} is the word vector that represents the composition of verb v and noun n, and in our example, the composition of *blow* and *whistle*. As indicated in (Mikolov et al., 2013b), word vectors obtained from deep learning neural net models exhibit linguistic regularities, such as additive compositionality. Therefore, σ_{vn} is justified to predict surrounding words of the composition of, say, *blow* and *whistle*.

For a given vocabulary of m words, represented by matrix $V = [v_1, v_2, \cdots, v_m] \in \Re^{q \times m}$, we calculate the projection of each word v_i in the vocabulary onto σ_{vn}

$$P = V^t \sigma_{vn} \tag{1}$$

where $P \in \Re^m$, and t represents transpose. Here we assume that σ_{vn} is normalized to have unit length. Thus, $P_i = v_i^t \sigma_{vn}$ indicates how strongly word vector v_i is associated with σ_{vn}. This projection forms the basis for our proposed technique.

Let $D = \{d_1, d_2, \cdots, d_l\}$ be a set of l text segments, each containing a target VNC (i.e., σ_{vn}). Instead of generating a term by document matrix, where each term is *tf-idf* (product of term frequency and inverse document frequency), we compute a term by document matrix $M_D \in \Re^{m \times l}$, where each term in the matrix is

$$p \cdot idf, \tag{2}$$

the product of the projection of a word onto a target VNC and inverse document frequency. That is, the term frequency (tf) of a word is replaced by the projection (inner product) of the word onto σ_{vn} (1). Note that if segment d_j does not contain word v_i, $M_D(i,j) = 0$, which is similar to *tf-idf* estimation. The motivation is that topical words are more likely to be well predicted by a literal VNC than by an idiomatic one. The assumption is that a word vector is learned in such a way that it best predicts its surrounding words in a sentence or a document (Mikolov et al., 2013a; Mikolov et al., 2013b). As a result, the words associated with a literal target will have larger projection onto a target σ_{vn}. On the other hand, the projections of words associated with an idiomatic target VNC onto σ_{vn} should have a smaller value.

We also propose a variant of $p \cdot idf$ representation. In this representation, each term is a product of p and typical *tf-idf*. That is,

$$p \cdot tf \cdot idf. \tag{3}$$

3.2 Local Context Distributions

Our second hypothesis states that words in a local context of a literal expression will have a different distribution from those in the context of an idiomatic one. We propose to capture local context distributions in terms of scatter matrices in a space spanned by word vectors (Mikolov et al., 2013a; Mikolov et al., 2013b).

Let $d = (w_1, w_2 \cdots, w_k) \in \Re^{q \times k}$ be a segment (document) of k words, where $w_i \in \Re^q$ are represented by a vectors (Mikolov et al., 2013a; Mikolov et al., 2013b). Assuming w_is have been centered, we compute the scatter matrix

$$\Sigma = d^t d, \tag{4}$$

where Σ represents the local context distribution for a given target VNC.

Given two distributions represented by two scatter matrices Σ_1 and Σ_2, a number of measures can be used to compute the distance between Σ_1 and Σ_2, such as Choernoff and Bhattacharyya distances (Fukunaga, 1990). Both measures require the knowledge of matrix determinant. In our case, this can be problematic, because Σ (4) is most likely to be singular, which would result in a determinant to be zero.

We propose to measure the difference between Σ_1 and Σ_2 using matrix norms. We have experimented with the Frobenius norm and the spectral norm. The Frobenius norm evaluates the difference between Σ_1 and Σ_2 when they act on a standard basis. The spectral norm, on the other hand, evaluates the difference when they act on the direction of maximal variance over the whole space.

4 Experiments

4.1 Methods

We have carried out an empirical study evaluating the performance of the proposed techniques. For comparison, the following methods are evaluated: **1** *tf-idf*: compute term by document matrix from training data with *tf-idf* weighting; **2** *p-idf*: compute term by document matrix from training data with proposed *p-idf* weighting (2); **3** *p*tf-idf*: compute term by document matrix from training data with proposed p*tf-idf weighting (3); **4** $CoVAR_{Fro}$: compute literal and idiomatic scatter matrices from training data (4). For a test example, compute a scatter matrix according to (4). Calculate the distance between the test scatter matrix and training scatter matrices using Frobenius norm; and **5** $CoVAR_{Sp}$: compute literal and idiomatic scatter matrices from training data (4). For a test text segment, compute a scatter matrix according to (4). Calculate the distance between the test scatter matrix and training scatter matrices using the spectral norm.

For methods from **1** to **3**, we compute a latent space from a term by document matrix obtain from the training data that captures 80% variance. To classify a test example, we compute cosine similarity between the test example and the training data in the latent space to make a decision.

4.2 Data Preprocessing

We use BNC (Burnard, 2000) and a list of verb-noun constructions (VNCs) extracted from BNC by Fazly et al. (2009), Cook et al. (2008) and labeled as L (Literal), I (Idioms), or Q (Unknown). The list contains only those VNCs whose frequency was greater than 20 and that occurred at least in one of two idiom dictionaries (Cowie et al., 1983; Seaton and Macaulay, 2002). The dataset consists of 2,984 VNC tokens. For our experiments we only use VNCs that are annotated as I or L. We only experimented with idioms that can have both literal and idiomatic interpretations.

We use the original SGML annotation to extract paragraphs from BNC. Each document contains three paragraphs: a paragraph with a target VNC, the preceding paragraph and following one.

Since BNC did not contain enough examples, we extracted additional from COCA, COHA and GloWbE (http://corpus.byu.edu/). Two human annotators annotated this new dataset for idioms and literals. The inter-annotator agreement was relatively low (Cohen's kappa = .58); therefore, we merged the results keeping only those entries on which the two annotators agreed.

Table 1: Datasets: Is = idioms; Ls = literals

Expression	Train	Test
BlowWhistle	20 Is, 20 Ls	7 Is, 31 Ls
LoseHead	15 Is, 15 Ls	6 Is, 4 Ls
MakeScene	15 Is, 15 Ls	15 Is, 5 Ls
TakeHeart	15 Is, 15 Ls	46 Is, 5 Ls
BlowTop	20 Is, 20 Ls	8 Is, 13 Ls
BlowTrumpet	50 Is, 50 Ls	61 Is, 186 Ls
GiveSack	20 Is, 20 Ls	26 Is, 36 Ls
HaveWord	30 Is, 30 Ls	37 Is, 40 Ls
HitRoof	50 Is, 50 Ls	42 is, 68 Ls
HitWall	90 Is, 90 Ls	87 is, 154 Ls
HoldFire	20 Is, 20 Ls	98 Is, 6 Ls
HoldHorse	80 Is, 80 Ls	162 Is, 79 Ls

4.3 Word Vectors

For our experiments reported here, we obtained word vectors using the word2vec tool (Mikolov et al., 2013a; Mikolov et al., 2013b) and the text8 corpus. The text8 corpus has more than 17 million words, which can be obtained from `mattmahoney.net/dc/text8.zip`. The resulting vocabulary has 71,290 words, each of which is represented by a $q = 200$ dimension vector. Thus, this 200 dimensional vector space provides a basis for our experiments.

4.4 Datasets

Table 1 describes the datasets we used to evaluate the performance of the proposed technique. All these verb-noun constructions are ambiguous between literal and idiomatic interpretations. The examples below (from the corpora we used) show how these expressions can be used *literally*.

BlowWhistle: *we can immediately turn towards a high-pitched sound such as whistle being blown. The ability to accurately locate a noise* ··· **LoseHead**: *This looks as eye-like to the predator as the real eye and gives the prey a fifty-fifty chance of losing its head. That was a very nice bull I shot, but I lost his head.* **MakeScene**: ··· *in which the many episodes of life were originally isolated and there was no relationship between the parts, but at last we must make a unified scene of our whole life.* **TakeHeart**: ··· *cutting off one of the forelegs at the shoulder so the heart can be taken*

Table 2: Average accuracy of competing methods on 12 datasets

Method	BlowWhistle			LoseHead			MakeScene			TakeHeart		
	Pre	Rec	Acc	Pre	Rec	Acc	Pre	Rec	Acc	Pre	Rec	Acc
tf-idf	0.23	0.75	0.42	0.27	0.21	0.49	0.41	0.13	0.33	0.65	0.02	0.11
p-idf	0.29	0.82	0.60	0.49	0.27	0.48	0.82	0.48	0.53	0.90	0.43	0.44
p*tf-idf	0.23	0.99	0.37	0.31	0.30	0.49	0.40	0.11	0.33	0.78	0.11	0.18
$CoVAR_{Fro}$	**0.65**	**0.71**	**0.87**	**0.60**	**0.78**	**0.58**	**0.84**	**0.83**	**0.75**	**0.95**	**0.61**	**0.62**
$CoVAR_{sp}$	0.44	0.77	0.77	0.62	0.81	0.61	0.80	0.82	0.72	0.94	0.55	0.56
	BlowTop			**BlowTrumpet**			**GiveSack**			**HaveWord**		
	Pre	Rec	Acc	Pre	Rec	Acc	Pre	Rec	Acc	Pre	Rec	Acc
tf-idf	0.55	0.93	0.65	0.26	0.85	0.36	0.61	0.63	0.55	0.52	0.33	0.52
p-idf	0.59	0.58	0.68	0.44	0.85	0.69	0.55	0.47	0.62	0.52	0.53	0.54
p*tf-idf	0.54	0.53	0.65	0.33	0.93	0.51	0.54	0.64	0.55	0.53	0.53	0.53
$CoVAR_{Fro}$	**0.81**	**0.87**	**0.86**	**0.45**	**0.94**	**0.70**	**0.63**	**0.88**	**0.72**	0.58	0.49	0.58
$CoVAR_{sp}$	0.71	0.79	0.79	0.39	0.89	0.62	0.66	0.75	0.73	**0.56**	**0.53**	**0.58**
	HitRoof			**HitWall**			**HoldFire**			**HoldHorse**		
	Pre	Rec	Acc	Pre	Rec	Acc	Pre	Rec	Acc	Pre	Rec	Acc
tf-idf	0.42	0.70	0.52	0.37	0.99	0.39	0.91	0.57	0.57	0.79	0.98	0.80
p-idf	0.54	0.84	0.66	0.55	0.92	0.70	0.97	0.83	0.81	0.86	0.81	0.78
p*tf-idf	0.41	0.98	0.45	0.39	0.97	0.43	0.95	0.89	0.85	0.84	0.97	0.86
$CoVAR_{Fro}$	**0.61**	**0.88**	**0.74**	**0.59**	**0.94**	**0.74**	**0.97**	**0.86**	**0.84**	**0.86**	**0.97**	**0.87**
$CoVAR_{sp}$	0.54	0.85	0.66	0.50	0.95	0.64	**0.96**	**0.87**	**0.84**	0.77	0.85	0.73

out still pumping and offered to the god on a plate. **BlowTop**: *Yellowstone has no large sources of water to create the amount of steam to blow its top as in previous eruptions.*

5 Results

Table 2 shows the average precision, recall and accuracy of the competing methods on 12 datasets over 20 runs. The best performance is in bold face. The best model is identified by considering precision, recall, and accuracy together for each model. We calculate accuracy by adding true positives and true negatives and normalizing the sum by the number of examples.

As for the individual model performance, the $CoVAR$ model outperforms the rest of the models. Interestingly, the Frobenius norm outperforms the spectral norm. One possible explanation is that the spectral norm evaluates the difference when two matrices act on the maximal variance direction, while the Frobenius norm evaluates on a standard basis. That is, Frobenius measures the difference along all basis vectors. On the other hand, the spectral norm evaluates changes in a particular direction. When the difference is a result of all basis directions, the Frobenius norm potentially provides a better measurement. The projection methods (p-idf and p*tf-idf) outperform tf-idf overall but not as pronounced as $CoVAR$.

Finally, we have noticed that even the best model ($CoVAR_{Fro}$) does not perform as well on certain idiomatic expressions. We hypothesized that the model works the best on highly idiomatic expressions. Idiomaticity is a continuum. Some idioms seem to be more easily interpretable than others. We conducted a small experiment, in which we asked two human annotators to rank VNCs in our dataset as "highly idiomatic" to "easily interpretable/compositional" (in context) on a scale of 5 to 1 (5: highly idiomatic; 1: low idiomaticity). While we cannot make strong claims based on a such small-scale experiment, the results of our pilot study suggest that there is a correlation between the idiomaticity scores and the performance of our model – the highly idiomatic expressions seem to be detected better. We plan to conduct an experiment with more human annotators and on an larger dataset to verify our hypothesis.

6 Conclusions

In our experiments we used a subset of Fazly et al. (2009)'s dataset plus some additional examples extracted from other corpora. Similarly to us, Fazly et al. (2009)'s goal is to determine whether a given VNC is idiomatic or literal in context. Our model is comparable to and often outperforms Fazly et al. (2009)'s unsupervised CForm model. Our method can also be compared with Peng et al. (2014) who also experiment with LDA, use similar data, and frame the problem as classification.

Acknowledgements

This material is based in part upon work supported by the U.S. National Science Foundation under Grant Number 1319846. Any opinions, findings, and conclusions or recommendations expressed in this material are those of the authors and do not necessarily reflect the views of the National Science Foundation.

References

Julia Birke and Anoop Sarkar. 2006. A clustering approach to the nearly unsupervised recognition of nonliteral language. In *Proceedings of the 11th Conference of the European Chapter of the Association for Computational Linguistics (EACL'06)*, pages 329–226, Trento, Italy.

Lou Burnard, 2000. *The British National Corpus Users Reference Guide*. Oxford University Computing Services.

Paul Cook, Afsaneh Fazly, and Suzanne Stevenson. 2007. Pulling their weight: Exploiting syntactic forms for the automatic identification of idiomatic expressions in context. In *Proceedings of the ACL 07 Workshop on A Broader Perspective on Multiword Expressions*, pages 41–48.

Paul Cook, Afsaneh Fazly, and Suzanne Stevenson. 2008. The VNC-Tokens Dataset. In *Proceedings of the LREC Workshop: Towards a Shared Task for Multiword Expressions (MWE 2008)*, Marrakech, Morocco, June.

Anthony P. Cowie, Ronald Mackin, and Isabel R. McCaig. 1983. *Oxford Dictionary of Current Idiomatic English*, volume 2. Oxford University Press.

Afsaneh Fazly, Paul Cook, and Suzanne Stevenson. 2009. Unsupervised Type and Token Identification of Idiomatic Expressions. *Computational Linguistics*, 35(1):61–103.

K. Fukunaga. 1990. *Introduction to statistical pattern recognition*. Academic Press.

Graham Katz and Eugenie Giesbrech. 2006. Automatic Identification of Non-compositional Multiword Expressions using Latent Semantic Analysis. In *Proceedings of the ACL/COLING-06 Workshop on Multiword Expressions: Identifying and Exploiting Underlying Properties*, pages 12–19.

Linlin Li and Caroline Sporleder. 2010. Using gaussian mixture models to detect figurative language in context. In *Proceedings of NAACL/HLT 2010*.

Tomas Mikolov, Kai Chen, Greg Corrado, and Jeffrey Dean. 2013a. Efficient estimation of word representations in vector space. In *Proceedings of Workshop at ICLR*.

Tomas Mikolov, Ilya Sutskever, Kai Chen, Greg Corrado, and Jeffrey Dean. 2013b. Distributed representations of words and phrases and their compositionality. In *Proceedings of NIPS*.

Jing Peng, Anna Feldman, and Ekaterina Vylomova. 2014. Classifying idiomatic and literal expressions using topic models and intensity of emotions. In *Proceedings of the 2014 Conference on Empirical Methods in Natural Language Processing (EMNLP)*, pages 2019–2027, Doha, Qatar, October. Association for Computational Linguistics.

Ivan A. Sag, Timothy Baldwin, Francis Bond, Ann Copestake, and Dan Flickinger. 2002. Multiword expressions: A Pain in the Neck for NLP. In *Proceedings of the 3rd International Conference on Intelligence Text Processing and Computational Linguistics (CICLing 2002)*, pages 1–15, Mexico City, Mexico.

Maggie Seaton and Alison Macaulay, editors. 2002. *Collins COBUILD Idioms Dictionary*. HarperCollins Publishers, second edition.

Caroline Sporleder and Linlin Li. 2009. Unsupervised Recognition of Literal and Non-literal Use of Idiomatic Expressions. In *EACL '09: Proceedings of the 12th Conference of the European Chapter of the Association for Computational Linguistics*, pages 754–762, Morristown, NJ, USA. Association for Computational Linguistics.

Extraction of the Multiword Lexical Units in the Perspective of the Wordnet Expansion

Maciej Piasecki
Wrocław Univ. of Technology
maciej.piasecki@pwr.edu.pl

Michał Wendelberger
Wrocław Univ. of Technology
michal.wendel@gmail.com

Marek Maziarz
Wrocław Univ. of Technology
mawroc@gmail.com

Abstract

The paper focuses on selecting an optimal set of the Multiword Expressions Extraction methods used as a tool during wordnet expansion. Wordnet multiword lexical units are a broad class and it is difficult to find a single extraction method fulfilling the task. Many extraction association measures were tested on very large corpora and a very large wordnet, namely plWordNet. Several new measures are proposed and compared with selected methods in the literature. Two ways of combining measures into ensembles were analysed too. We showed that method selection and the tuning of their parameters can be transferred between two large corpora. The comparison of the extracted collocations with the huge set of plWordNet multiword lexical units revealed that the performance of the methods is much below the optimistic levels reported in the literature. However, the carefully selected set and combination of the methods can be a valuable tool for lexicographers.

1 Introduction

A large number of different methods for the extraction Multiword Expressions (henceforth, MWE) have been proposed in literature. Most of them are focused on particular properties of MWEs, e.g. non-compositionality. Before applying selected methods as the support for the construction of a large lexicon we have to answer several questions.

- What method should we select if we need to extract MWEs of different subtypes?
- How effective are different methods in helping lexicographers who use a complex but well specified definition of Multiword Lexical Units (MLUs)[1] (Maziarz et al., 2015a)?
- What is the performance of the known extraction methods when they are applied to big corpora (e.g. >1 billion words) and next evaluated against very large lexicons of MWEs?

We aim at the development of a method for the extraction of MLUs from large corpora for the needs of wordnet expansion. MLUs encompass a broad spectrum of MWEs: from non-compositional MWEs to specialist terminology. The starting point for this work were the seminal papers of Pečina, e.g. (Pečina, 2010), including tests of a very large number of MWE extraction methods. However, those tests were done on relatively limited data set. The corpus used by Pečina in his experiments consisted of about 1.5 million words. In our work we utilised different corpora including the testing *Merged Corpus* of 1.6 billion words covering rich variety of topics and genres[2]. So, it was more than 1 000 times bigger than that used in (Pečina, 2010).

We wanted to perform large scale evaluation done on big corpora, utilising a very large lexicon of MWEs and focused on Polish, a language which is significantly different from English. The first experiments (completed) inspired us also to the development of a couple of additional association measures focused on selected MWE subtypes and meant to enrich the variety of MWE types covered by the combined measure.

[1] MLUs are, shortly speaking, MWEs that are elements of a lexical system, see Sec. 2

[2] The Merged Corpus combines Polish Wikipedia (http://pl.wikipedia.org/) the version from 28th Apr. 2012 and the corpus of electronic edition of the Rzeczpospolita newspaper (Rze, 2008). It was completed with texts collected from the internet. All texts from the internet were filtered: only larger texts with a relatively small number of words not recognised by the morphological analyser Morfeusz (Woliński, 2006) have been included in the corpus.

Proceedings of Recent Advances in Natural Language Processing, pages 512–520,
Hissar, Bulgaria, Sep 7–9 2015.

2 Background

plWordNet is a wordnet of Polish. Every wordnet is a lexico-semantic network describing lexical meanings in terms of lexico-semantic relations (Fellbaum, 1998). There are about 40 types of relations with more than 90 subtypes in total in plWordnet (Maziarz et al., 2013). After the series of projects starting 2005, plWordNet has now become the largest wordnet worldwide. The version 2.3 published in the year 2015 includes more than 171 000 lemmas, 244 000 lexical units (LUs)[3] and 184 000 synsets[4]. It has achieved very comprehensive coverage of Polish LUs that is comparable to the largest Polish dictionaries.

Because plWordNet 2.1 contained mainly one-word lemmas[5] contrary to most dictionaries, we have decided to add also many MLUs to plWordNet 3.0. We have estimated that the future plWordNet 3.0 should be expanded with about 60 000 multi-word LUs in comparison to 2.1.

plWordNet has been developed on the basis of the corpus-based semi-automatic method with all editing decisions having been made by linguists. In order to follow this development model, word combinations that seem to be good candidates for MLUs should be extracted from the large corpora, verified by lexicographers and added to plWordNet in this semi-automated way. In this paper we concentrate on the first phase: extraction MLU candidates from large corpora in a way facilitating their manual verification.

The crucial point in the evaluation procedure of extraction algorithms (Sec. 6) was the utilization of plWordNet as a gold-standard. We sought for such algorithms which gave us good precision in recognising MLUs from plWordNet. It must be emphasised that in previous versions of plWordNet MLUs were added on the basis of linguists' intuition of what is and what is not lexical. This intuition was supported by lexicographic resources, mainly general, phraseological and specialist dictionaries, lexicons and encyclopaedias.

The newest version of plWordNet now contains more than 30k MLUs added with the usage of detailed guidelines. The procedure of assessing lexicality of a given MLU candidate is presented in (Maziarz et al., 2015b) and (Maziarz et al., 2015a) in this volume. Summarising, it is based on a decision tree guiding linguists. Every extracted collocation is analysed in a sequence of tests before it is rejected or accepted as a plWordNet MLU. The application of with the guidelines tree improved consistency of lexicographers' decisions.

In order to check trustworhtiness of plWordNet as a gold-standard lexical resource we asked 5 linguists to intuitively assess lexicality of 200 MLUs randomly taken from plWordNet 2.1. They were given a definition pointing to the notion of LU being the part of our mental lexicon[6] and non-reproducibility of a word combination (whether it is set or free). Having averaged their answers we found that the confidence interval for the proportion of genuine MLUs is 90-98% (α=0.05). For instance, linguists rejected such word combinations as *koszt zakupu* 'the cost of buying something' or *kolor włosów* 'hair coloring', while accepted *płaca minimalna* 'minimum wage' or *ośrodek zdrowia* 'health centre'. [7] Thus, finally, we obtained a good argument for basing the estimation procedure on plWordNet.

3 Starting Point: Association Measures for MWEs

MWE elements occur together in text more frequently than it would be caused by chance. This idea has been expressed in more than hundred association measures based on statistical association measures, information theory or just heuristics, e.g. cf a rich overview in (Pečina, 2010). It would be difficult to repeat such an overview in a short paper, so our starting point were the results reported in (Pečina, 2010) and the set of the best performing measures according to those tests, e.g. Unigram Subtuples, Frequency Biased Mutual Dependency, Mutual Expectation or Pearsonś Chi2̂, see the complete list in Sec. 5.2. Next, we extended this basic set with several more measures reported in the literature as having good performance: e.g. Contonni T1 (Paradowski, 2015) or Specific Exponential Correlation (Buczyński, 2004), see Sec. 5.2.

[3] A lexical unit is understood here technically as a triple: a lemma plus sense number plus a part of speech; MLUs have multi-word lemmas.

[4] Synsets are traditionally sets of near synonyms (Fellbaum, 1998), in plWordNet they group lexical units sharing the same lexico-semantic relations (Maziarz et al., 2013).

[5] In version 2.1 of plWordNet 1/5 of all LUs were MLUs.

[6] «The basic prerequisite for according lemma status to a multi-word items is that it has undergone some kind of lexicalisation, i.e., that it has been stored in our mental lexicon as a unit.» (Svensén, 2009, pp. 102-3).

[7] (Maziarz et al., 2015a) provide arguments for taking averaged decision of 5 linguists as a fair sign of lexicalicity.

On the basis of the first experiments and analysis of the measure similarity in (Paradowski, 2015), we formulated our own unique measures: W Specific Correlation, W Order, W Term Frequency Order and W Specific Exponential Correlation that are presented in Sec. 4. The last two measures have parameters and were tested for their different values.

We have also adopted from (Pečina, 2010) the method of combining by means of Machine Learning many association measures into one complex of better performance. Every MWE candidate is described by a vector of the measure values. Candidates that are know to be MWE define positive examples, the rest of candidates is used as negative examples. Several learning methods were used in (Pečina, 2010), namely: Linear Logistic Regression, Linear discriminant analysis, SVM (Support Vector Machines) and Multi-layer Perceptron (a neural network). A complex measure based on the Multi-layer Perceptron expressed the best performance, but the other complex measures were on the similar level.

Pečina tried to combine almost all single measures. However, (Paradowski, 2015) showed that many of them are correlated and even can be obtained from the same basic equation by changing its parameters. Such correlated measures are redundant attributes from the Machine Learning point of view and should not be used together.

Our approach differs significantly from the previous ones by the scale of the evaluation tests in terms of the size of: corpora used for the extraction and the MWE lexicon used for the comparison. Concerning the former we used the Merged Corpus of Polish described in Sec. 1, concerning the latter we used MLUs for plWordNet 2.2 as the gold set that includes almost 50 000 MWEs.

In (Pečina, 2010) the evaluation was performed on the basis of the *Prague Dependency Treebank* 2.0 that consists of 1 504 847 words from which 635 952 different word bi-grams were extracted. After Part of Speech based filtering 26 450 bi-grams were left. Next, all bi-grams occurring less than 6 times were removed and the bi-gram set was reduced to only 12 232. Those MWE candidates were evaluated manually by linguists according to the 5 MWE categories defined. The same definitions were used by all evaluators, but the inter-annotator agreement was moderate, cf. (Pečina, 2010). 2 557 bi-grams, i.e. 20.9% of the evaluated set, were found to be MWEs.

Summing up, hundreds of association measures were proposed in the literature, cf. (Pečina, 2010). On the basis of the evaluation results presented in the literature, especially for Polish data (Buczyński, 2004), and the possible generalisation of some measure to one equation with parameters (Paradowski, 2015), this set can be reduced to a much smaller number of the most promising ones. As a baseline we used the raw frequency of lemma bi-grams assuming that the more frequent bi-grams are more likely to be MWEs.

4 Extension: Additional Measures and the Complex Measure

4.1 W Specific Exponential Correlation

Pointwise Mutual Information, shortly mentioned in Eq. 1, is often used and expresses relatively good performance. In Eq. 1, x and y are words, $p(x)$, $p(y)$ and $p(x,y)$ are Maximum Likelihood Estimations of the probabilities, respectively, of single (marginal) and joint occurrences. However, PMI is known to overestimate the importance of infrequent events.

$$PMI(x,y) = log_2 \frac{p(x,y)}{p(x)p(y)} \quad (1)$$

PMI was modified in different ways to cope with this problem, e.g. one possibility is to refer to the 'full' Mutual Information in which the logarithm is multiplied by $p(x,y)$ probability. Applying this analogy to PMI, we obtain W Specific Correlation in Eq. 2 proposed in (Hoang et al., 2009a).

$$W\_SC(x,y) = p(x,y) log_2 \frac{p(x,y)}{p(x)p(y)} \quad (2)$$

Mutual Dependency in Eq. 3 is another modification of PMI in which the x and y joint frequency is emphasised inside the logarithm:

$$MD(x,y) = log_2 \frac{p(x,y)^2}{p(x)p(y)} \quad (3)$$

Buczyński (Buczyński, 2004) increased the power of the nominator to 3 and called this measure *Frequency Biased Mutual Dependency.* It produced good results in two evaluations on large Polish corpora (Buczyński, 2004) and (Broda et al., 2008). Later, Buczyński generalised his measure exchanging "3" to "$2 + \alpha$".

Finally, inspired by (Petrovica et al., 2010), we combined all the above modifications in a measure that is called *W Specific Exponential Correlation* and presented in Eq. 4.

$$W\_SEC(x, y) = p(x, y)log_2\frac{p(x, y)^e}{p(x)p(y)} \quad (4)$$

In *W_SEC* the frequency of the pair increases both components of the measure: one inside the logarithm and the one outside of it. The *W_SEC* behaviour is controlled by the parameter e and can be adapted to the task to some extent.

Following (Petrović et al., 2010) and (Van de Cruys, 2011, p. 2), *W_SEC* can be also easily modified for the extraction of candidates with n constituents, see Eq. 5.

4.2 W Order

Several criteria can be used in the MWE recognition. One of them is how the word order of the candidate is fixed. The more constrained possible linear word orders of the MWE candidate constituents are, the more likely it is an MWE. In order to test this, we need to calculate the number of possible word orders for the given candidate. This assumption is the basis for the *W Order* measure proposed in Eq. 6 where t is a sequence of the candidate constituents (words), S is a set of all possible orders of the same constituents, $S(t)_i$ – ith tuple from the set $S(t)$ and $f(\ldots)$ is the frequency.

$$W\_Ord(t) = \frac{1}{\prod_{i=1}^{n}(1 + \frac{f(S(t)_i))}{max(f(S(t)))+1})} \quad (6)$$

In *W Order* the components are multiplied and the result of this multiplication is the biggest if all of them are equal. The smallest result is 0 if one of them is 0 – in the extreme situation only one is non-zero and equals the whole sum. Thus, the larger the multiplication result is, the more distributed the word orders are. It means that we need to reverse the fraction in order to get the needed behaviour of the measure.

W Order abstracts from the interpretation of the word order, i.e. it does not give any preference to any word order. The measure tests the number of the orders and their relative frequencies. The value of the measure does not depend on the exact frequencies of the candidate tuples, but it tests their mutual ratio.

By adding 1 to every frequency value in the denominators in Eq. 6, we wanted to secure against possible zero values, e.g. caused by one zero-frequency tuple. Secondly, we avoid assigning the same value of the measure and the position in the ranking to those candidates that have at least one zero frequency tuple. As a result, candidates with the greater number of zero frequency tuples obtain higher values of the measure, which promotes more fixed word order candidates. Thirdly, adding 1 causes that the amount of statistical information collected about a given candidate is taken into account in the measure. If the product of the tuple frequencies for different order variants of a given candidate is equal, a candidate with more statistical information, i.e. such that occurred more times, will be promoted. Finally, adding 1 modifies the range of possible values of the measure, eliminates problems with dividing and practically increases the number of possible values produced by the measure.

W Order does not require generalisation, as it is defined already for n-element tuples.

4.3 W Term Frequency Order

The frequency of a candidate is a very simple feature that is not sufficient on its own. However, it is correlated with the acceptance of candidates as MWE. Thus, we proposed also a *W Order* version, Eq. 7, in which the raw candidate frequency increases the measure value. It is already defined for n-element candidates.

$$W\_TFO(t) = f(t)W\_Ord(t) \quad (7)$$

4.4 Combined Measure

Complex measures are built as follows:

1. for each measure a ranking of the candidates is created;
2. each ranking is multiplied by the weights assigned to the measures;
3. weighted rankings are combined into the resulting ranking of the complex measures.

Weights for the individual measures were optimised by the genetic algorithm using a system described in (Kłyk et al., 2012). Genotypes consisted of measure weights. The precision of the extracted candidates in comparison to plWordNet MWEs

$$W\_SEC(x_1,\dots,x_n) = p(x_1,x_2,...,x_n)log_2\frac{p(x_1,x_2,...,x_n)^e}{\prod_{i=1}^{n} p(x_i)} \quad (5)$$

was used as the fitness function value. By mapping all candidate extraction results on the rankings we remove different ranges of different measures. The linear combination of the rankings has clear interpretation. The applied genetic algorithm is very flexible and does not need any assumptions concerning the combined measures. The algorithm was run on the tuning corpus only. For the test corpus, we used weights optimised on the test corpus. Henceforth, the complex measure will be called *VAM* (*Vector Attribute Measure*).

5 Experimental Setting

5.1 Data Sets

We used two corpora: the first one for tuning the measure parameters and the second for testing. The tuning corpus was also utilised for training different versions of the complex VAM.

As a tuning corpus we used *The Corpus of IPI PAN of Polish* (IPIC) (Przepiórkowski, 2004) – the first large corpus of Polish, still the only bigger Polish corpus available and used in many different experiments. IPIC consists of 255 516 328 tokens (of the word level) from which we extracted 19 752 289 possible word bi-grams.

All tests were performed on the Merged Corpus, cf Sec. 1. It consists of 1 610 753 950 tokens. 77 770 719 word bi-grams of different types were extracted from it. There is no overlapping between the tuning corpus (i.e. IPIC) and the test corpus. We checked for duplicated texts and removed them from the test corpus.

MWEs from the plWordNet version 17th April2015 were used as a gold standard set. The set contains 48 735 multi-word lemmas that represent a larger number of MLUs but all corpora were processed on the level of words not word senses.

5.2 Association Measures

On the basis of the results reported in the literature, we selected a number of association measures for the tests plus our own measures: Contonni T1 (Paradowski, 2015), Contonni T2 (Paradowski, 2015), Sorgenfrei (Paradowski, 2015), Dice (Pečina, 2010), Jaccard (Pečina, 2010), Unigram Subtuples (Pečina, 2010), Frequency Biased Mutual Dependency (Pečina, 2010), Mutual Expectation (Pečina, 2010), W Specific Correlation (Hoang et al., 2009b), T-Score (Pečina, 2010), Z-Score (Pečina, 2010), Pearson's Chi$\hat{2}$ (Pečina, 2010), Loglikelihood (Pečina, 2010), Specific Exponential Correlation (Buczyński, 2004), W Specific Exponential Correlation, W Order, and W Term Frequency Order.

5.3 Candidate Extraction Process

In the case of inflectional languages like Polish, a direct application of the statistical measures to word forms would not be feasible for the extraction of MWE candidates. There are too many word forms and each candidate has several inflectional forms on average. Thus, both corpora were first preprocessed by the morphosyntactic tagger WCRFT2 (Radziszewski, 2013) that maps words on their lemmas[8]. Next, the extraction process was performed on the level of lemmas annotated with morphosyntactic information.

MLUs in plWordNet are described with complex information including: multi-word lemmas, partial description of the syntactic structure and syntactic heads, cf (Kurc et al., 2012). The partial description of a MLU is expressed in the WCCL language of morpho-syntactic constraints (Radziszewski et al., 2011). Each MLU is assigned a minimal set of constraints that refer to its lemma and enable recognition of its occurrences in text, e.g. the constraints define the order of constituents (if it is fixed) and morphosyntactic agreements between them. plWordNet editors tried to use the same single constraint set for the description of many MLUs. As a result a limited set of structural classes of MWEs was defined. About 100 MWE structural classes are used in plWordNet, but most of them represent Proper Names and specific idioms. Due to the large size of plWordNet we can assume that the set of MWE classes is representative for Polish.

Annotated lemma bi-grams extracted from the tagged corpus were filtered with morpho-syntactic patterns, cf (Seretan, 2011), written in WCCL language[9] (Radziszewski et al., 2011) and acquired

[8]A lemma is a basic morphological form representing a set of word forms that differ only in the values of the morphosyntactic categories.

[9]See also: `http://nlp.pwr.wroc.pl/redmine/`

from the MWE representation in plWordNet. Only 38 more frequent MWE classes were used, e.g. classes describing Proper Names were excluded.

The extracted statistical data concerning all extracted candidates were stored in a contingency table to be available for the computation of different association measures.

The total number of candidates extracted from the tuning corpus and filtered by 38 WCCL-based patterns was 13 384 814. Most candidates, i.e. 8 249 314, 61,63% of all, were covered by only two patterns that require a noun or a word not recognised by the morphological analyser used in the WCRFT tagger.

All extracted and pre-filtered candidates were used during the extraction process. However the final ranking was created by post-filtering based on a narrow subgroup of only 6 WCCL pattern related to nouns and adjectives. This subgroup was selected on the basis of the frequency of MWEs represented in plWordNet[10]. Only patterns covering the largest number of plWordNet MWEs that were found among the candidates extracted from the corpus were preserved. The selected patterns decreased the number of candidates to 878 096, but the precision was increased very much, as only infrequent classes were removed.

In the case of the test corpus, the initial non-filtered set of 77 770 719 was reduced by the selected 6 patterns to 3 867 835 candidates. However, we could observe that most of them are very infrequent, i.e. below 5 occurrences (for more than 1.6 billion tokens). As such infrequent MWEs would not be interesting for extending plWordNet, we decided to add post-filtering based on the candidate frequency. The threshold was set to at least 6 occurrences. This threshold reduced the number of candidates to 524 760 that is still large number beyond the possibility of the manual verification before adding to plWordNet.

6 Results

Results of experiments are presented in Table 1. First, we tried to optimise the parameter values for different measures on IPIC – the tuning corpus, cf Sec. 5. IPIC was also used for learning weights for the individual measures in the complex VAM measure. In Table 1 we present also the results obtained on the large test set – the Merged Corpus, cf Sec. 5. Parameter values established on the tuning corpus were used during the tests. As both corpora do not have any overlap, we can notice how stable the applied measures are when moved between corpora. It s was especially important for our intended application to the plWordNet expansion, since with the advancement of the work we are interested in new MWEs not yet covered and we use bigger and bigger corpora. The process of collecting texts for the merged corpora is ongoing.

The weights established for the single measures in VAM on the running corpus are as follows: Mutual Expectation: -0.21, T-Score: 0.97, Loglikelihood: 0.68, Jaccard: -0.57, Sorgenfrei: 0.39, Unigram Subtuples: 0.46, SEC($E = 2.8$): 0.77, WSEC($E = 1.1$): -0.65, W Order: 0.04, W Term Frequency Order: 0.52, Contonni T1: 0.63, Contonni T2: -0.58.

In order to evaluate the results we applied two different evaluation measures. The first measure, called *Average Precision* in Table 1 was taken from (Pečina, 2010) and it is based on calculating cut-off precisions for every ranking position on which a true MWE (from plWordNet) was found. Next, in a similar way to (Pečina, 2010), values lower than 0.1 and greater than 0.9 were filtered out. From the rest, the average was computed and used as an evaluation result for the given measure.

As the second evaluation measure we used a simple cut-off precision, called *Cut-off* in Table 1. In this case, the same cut-off ranking position was used for all measures. As the tuning and test corpus have very different size we set the cut-off ranking position on 7 685 for IPIC (tunning) and on 19 687 for the Merged Corpus (test). These values were defined as the minimal number of candidates after filtering across all measures tested, i.e. no measure produced less candidates after filtering, but many extracted more. With the help of the cut-off precision we analyse what is the percentage of extracted candidates on the ranking up to this position that are included in plWordNet. The cut-off precision is a simple measure and does not show the distribution of MWEs across different ranking positions. In the worst case they can be all grouped at the end of the ranking. However, the cut-off value signals what is the estimated percentage of good hints for new MLUs (the real value should be higher, as many MWEs are not included in the

`projects/joskipi/wiki/`

[10]MWEs have been added mostly to noun and adjective parts of plWordNet

Measure	Average Precision		Cut-off Precision	
	IPIC	Merged Corpus	IPIC	Merged Corpus
Frequency	0.2660	0.2116	0.2636	0.2292
Frequency Biased MD	**0.3585**	**0.2709**	**0.3256**	**0.2643**
Loglikelihood	0.3125	0.2202	0.2882	0.2286
Mutual Expectation	0.3150	0.2246	0.2990	0.2353
Pearsons Chi 2	0.3231	0.2523	0.2982	0.2598
Sorgenfrei	0.3239	0.2543	0.2986	0.2601
Specific Exp. Corr. E=2.8	**0.3592**	**0.2715**	**0.3266**	**0.2642**
Tscore	0.2895	0.2223	0.2766	0.2345
Unigram Subtuples	0.2375	0.1893	0.2373	0.2099
W Order	0.2476	0.1169	0.2393	0.1530
W Specific Correlation	0.3240	**0.2410**	0.2993	0.2434
W Specific Exp. Corr. E=1.1, E=0.9	**0.3339**	0.2394	**0.3049**	0.2442
W Term Frequency Order	0.2915	0.2027	0.2744	0.2263
Zscore	0.3234	0.2525	0.2982	**0.2597**
Jaccard	0.2799	0.2168	0.2743	0.2403
Dice	0.2799	0.2168	0.2743	0.2403
Consonni T1	0.1180	0.0962	0.1447	0.1331
Consonni T2	0.1180	0.0962	0.1447	0.1331
Vector Association Measure	**0.3929**	**0.3114**	**0.3521**	**0.2835**

Table 1: Average and cut off precision of MWEs extracted from tuning corpus (IPIC – the IPI PAN Corpus) and the test corpus (Merged Corpus) and plWordNet the version 17th Apr. 2015 as a source of MLUs to be used as a gold-standard.

applied version of plWordNet).

As we could expect, the results obtained on the test corpus are worse than those on tuning corpus. However, the test corpus is several times larger than the tuning corpus. This can negatively influence the average precision. For the cut-off precision we set much higher cut-off level for the test corpus. Surprisingly, not all measures performed better than the simple *Frequency* measure that can be treated as a baseline.

The complex measure VAM appeared to be the best in all tests. In the case of tuning corpus this was expected, as VAM was optimised on this corpus. However its improvement is even larger on the test corpus. It means that VAM improves moving the false candidates down to the more remote ranking positions. The next two best measures were well known Frequency Biased MD and SEC in the generalised version proposed by us. W Order produced results below the expected level. However, W Order is sensitive to the fixed word order of candidates while many MWEs in plWordNet have non-constrained word order. Other measures proposed by us were close to the top ones. It is worth to emphasise that VAM combines all single measures but with different weights.

Most measures showing good performance in tests in (Pečina, 2010) are also among higher results in our tests. The only difference is the poor performance o Unigram Subtuples – the best single measure in (Pečina, 2010) .

7 Conclusions

We have verified and confirmed the idea of Pečina of combining together many simple association measures. However, tests were done on much larger corpora and a lager set of manually described MWEs.

The obtained results show that a complex measure, even if it is so simple as a linear combination of individual association measures can produce results better than any single measure. What is more, the combined measure was trained on a different corpus and still it expresses better results on a different test corpus. During tests on two large corpora we revisited the evaluation performed by Pečina on much smaller scale and for a different language. In general, we conformed his findings, however, we added to the tests several additional measures including a couple of original measures proposed by us. Any single measure is not as good as their combination, but our results show that some measures, e.g. FBMD, SEC, are worth more attention than the others. Moreover, measures with better performance are interesting components for the complex combined measure. Following observations of (Paradowski, 2015), it is important to avoid combining together correlated measures that produce identical rankings.

Acknowledgments

Work financed by the Polish Ministry of Science and Higher Education, a program in support of scientific units involved in the development of a European research infrastructure for the humanities and social sciences in the scope of the consortia CLARIN ERIC (`www.clarin-pl.eu`) and ESS-ERIC, 2015-2016.

References

B. Broda, M. Derwojedowa, and M. Piasecki. 2008. Recognition of structured collocations in an inflective language. *Systems Science*, 34(4):27–36. The previous version was published in the Proceedings of AAIA'08, Wisła Poland.

A. Buczyński. 2004. Pozyskiwanie z internetu tekstów do badań lingwistycznych. Master's thesis, Wydział Matematyki Informatyki i Mechaniki Uniwersytetu Warszawskiego, Warsaw.

Ch. Fellbaum, editor. 1998. *WordNet — An Electronic Lexical Database*. The MIT Press.

H. H. Hoang, S. N. Kim, and M.-Y. Kan. 2009a. A re-examination of lexical association measures. In *Proceedings of the 2009 Workshop on Multiword Expressions, ACL-IJCNLP 2009*, pages 31–39. ACL.

H. H. Hoang, S. N. Kim, and M.-Y. Kan. 2009b. A re-examination of lexical association measures. In *Proceedings of the 2009 Workshop on Multiword Expressions, ACL-IJCNLP 2009*, pages 31–39, Singapore. Suntec.

Ł. Kłyk, P. B. Myszkowski, B. Broda, M. Piasecki, and D. Urbansky. 2012. Metaheuristics for tuning model parameters in two natural language processing applications. In Allan Ramsay and Gennady Agre, editors, *Proceedings of the 15th International Conference on Artificial Intelligence: Methodology, Systems, Applications*, volume 7557 of *Lecture Notes in Computer Science*, pages 32–37, Varna, Bulgaria. Springer.

R. Kurc, M. Piasecki, and B. Broda. 2012. Constraint based description of polish multiword expressions. In N. Calzolari, K. Choukri, T. Declerck, M. Uğur Doğan, B. Maegaard, J. Mariani, J. Odijk, and S. Piperidis, editors, *Proceedings of the Eight International Conference on Language Resources and Evaluation (LREC'12)*, pages 2408–2413, Istanbul, Turkey, may. European Language Resources Association (ELRA).

M. Maziarz, M. Piasecki, and S. Szpakowicz. 2013. The chicken-and-egg problem in wordnet design: Synonymy, synsets and constitutive relations. *Language Resources and Evaluation*, 47(3):769–796.

M. Maziarz, S. Szpakowicz, and M. Piasecki. 2015a. A procedural definition of multi-word lexical units. In *Proceedings of the International Conference Recent Advances in Natural Language Processing RANLP 2015*, page this volume, Hissar, Bulgaria, September. INCOMA Ltd. Shoumen, BULGARIA.

M. Maziarz, S. Szpakowicz, M. Piasecki, and A. Dziob. 2015b. Jednostki wielowyrazowe. Procedura sprawdzania leksykalności połączeń wyrazowych [Multi-word units. A procedure for testing the lexicality of collocations]. Technical Report PRE-11, Faculty of Computer Science and Management, Wrocław University of Technology. `http://clarin-pl.eu/wp-content/uploads/2015/05/Jednostki-wielowyrazowe_Procecura-sprawdzania-leksykalno%C5%9Bci-po%C5%82%C4%85cze%C5%84-wielowyrazowych.pdf`.

M. Paradowski. 2015. On order equivalence relation of binary association measures. *International Journal of Applied Mathematics and Computer Science*, 25(3):*to appear*.

S. Petrović, J. Šnajder, and B. D. Bašić. 2010. Extending lexical association measures for collocation extraction. *Computer Speech and Language*, 24(2):383–394.

S. Petrovica, J. Šnajder, and B. D. Bašic. 2010. Extending lexical association measures for collocation extraction. *Computer, Speech and Language*, 24:383–394.

P. Pečina. 2010. Lexical association measures and collocation extraction. *Language Resources and Evaluation*, 44:137–158.

A. Przepiórkowski. 2004. *The IPI PAN Corpus, Preliminary Version*. Institute of Computer Science PAS.

A. Radziszewski, A. Wardyński, and T. Śniatowski. 2011. WCCL: A morpho-syntactic feature toolkit. In I. Habernal and V. Matoušek, editors, *Text, Speech and Dialogue, Plzen 2011*, LNAI 6836, pages 434–441. Springer.

A. Radziszewski. 2013. A tiered CRF Tagger for polish. In *Intelligent Tools for Building a Scientific Information Platform. Studies in Computational Intelligence*, volume 467, pages 215–230. Springer Verlag.

2008. Korpus Rzeczpospolitej. [on-line] `www.cs.put.poznan.pl/dweiss/rzeczpospolita`. Corpus of text from the online edtion of Rzeczpospolita.

V. Seretan. 2011. *Syntax-Based Collocation Extraction*, volume 44 of *Text, Speech and Language Technology*. Springer Netherlands.

B. Svensén. 2009. *A Handbook of Lexicography: the Theory and Practice of Dictionary-making*. Cambridge University Press.

T. Van de Cruys. 2011. Two multivariate generalizations of pointwise mutual information. In *Proceedings of the Workshop on Distributional Semantics and Compositionality*, pages 16–20, Portland.

M. Woliński. 2006. Morfeusz – a practical tool for the morphological analysis of Polish. In Mieczysław A. Kłopotek, Sławomir T. Wierzchoń, and Krzysztof Trojanowski, editors, *Intelligent Information Processing and Web Mining – Proceedings of the International IIS: IIPWM '06 Conference held in Wisła, Poland, June, 2006*, Advances in Soft Computing, pages 511–520, Berlin. Springer.

A New Approach to Automated Text Readability Classification based on Concept Indexing with Integrated Part-of-Speech n-gram Features

Abigail R. Razon
University of Birmingham
ARR125@cs.bham.ac.uk

John A. Barnden
University of Birmingham
J.A.BARNDEN@cs.bham.ac.uk

Abstract

This study is about the development of a learner-focused text readability indexing tool for second language learners (L2) of English. Student essays are used to calibrate the system, making it capable of providing realistic approximation of L2s' actual reading ability spectrum. The system aims to promote self-directed (i.e. self-study) language learning and help even those L2s who can not afford formal education.

In this paper, we provide a comparative review of two vectorial semantics-based algorithms, namely, Latent Semantic Indexing (LSI) and Concept Indexing (CI) for text content analysis. Since these algorithms rely on the *bag-of-words* approach and inherently lack grammar-related analysis, we augment them by incorporating Part-of-Speech (POS) n-gram features to approximate syntactic complexity of the text documents.

Based on the results, CI-based features outperformed LSI-based features in most of the experiments. Without the integration of POS n-gram features, the difference between their mean exact agreement accuracies (MEAA) can reach as high as 23%, in favor of CI. It has also been proven that the performance of both algorithms can be further enhanced by combining POS bi-gram features, yielding as high as 95.1% and 91.9% MEAA values for CI and LSI, respectively.

1 Introduction

Text Readability is often defined as how easily documents can be read and understood. Moreover, **Text Readability Indexing** (TRI) is the process wherein texts are classified according to their difficulty level based on educational standards set by institutions.

We take it as one of our working hypotheses that language learning is something personal and that text interpretations are greatly influenced by the learner's personality, preferences, experiences, and beliefs which are not something that can be easily set to a particular standard. Thus, TRI systems should be modelled from the learners themselves and that these systems should have the ability to adapt to the learner's learning progression.

Past researches on this domain, such as (Si and Callan, 2001) and (Heilman et al., 2007), rely greatly on syntactic features as indicators of text readability. Such features include sentence length, syllable and character counts per word, part-of-speech (POS) tags, and word frequency. Although these features are important linguistic components, these have not been sufficient to model reading difficulty levels. As a result, recent studies are geared towards using content learning techniques from the Natural Language Processing (NLP) area. Such techniques include Latent Semantic Indexing (LSI) and Concept Indexing (CI) which have the ability to extract text content features that can be used to model learner profiles within each school grade level.

There have been several attempts to combine grammar- and content-based features in readability analysis. However, it still hasn't been fully investigated so far and, to the best of our knowledge, the combined analysis of CI, a vectorial semantics-based algorithm similar to LSI, and POS n-gram features hasn't been explored at all for text readability indexing.

In this paper, we present a comparative study on LSI and CI with the integration of POS n-gram features. Section 2 and 3 give the summaries of related work and existing LSI versus CI researches, respectively. Our study's working assumptions are

Proceedings of Recent Advances in Natural Language Processing, pages 521–528,
Hissar, Bulgaria, Sep 7–9 2015.

then presented in Section 4. Section 5 describes the datasets we used in the experiments and details of the sampling procedure done on these datasets are provided in Section 6. Section 7 contains the discussion on methodology, followed by the experimental details and results presented in Sections 8 and 9, respectively. Finally, the conclusion of the study is provided in Section 10.

2 Related Work

In this section, we will discuss three researches which focused on the combination of features for text readability indexing. Authors of these studies were able to conclude that combining several text feature sets could yield improved classification metrics.

The study in (Si and Callan, 2001) combined content-based and surface linguistic features into a single text readability level classifier. The *Expectation Maximization* (EM) algorithm was then utilized to automatically calculate the weight values for their proposed models, namely, the *unigram language model* (i.e. using words in text) and the *sentence length distribution model*. The authors hypothesized that 1.) readability measures should be sensitive to content as well as to surface linguistic features and 2.) statistical language models could capture the content information related to reading difficulty. Experiments showed that 1.) Sentence length is a useful feature for readability analysis on their dataset since its mean value increases as the readability level of texts increase, while 2.) Syllable count is not a useful feature as it did not exhibit the same behavior. Si and Callan also achieved higher accuracy value of 70.5% for the unigram language model than the sentence length distribution model which only yielded 42.6%. Moreover, by combining these two models together, they were able to achieve their highest accuracy of 75.4%.

In (Schwarm and Ostendorf, 2005), binary *Support Vector Machines* (SVM) were utilized to approximate the syntactic and semantic complexities of texts. Several text features including sentence length, syllable count, word instances- and uniqueness-based features, part-of-speech (POS) features (e.g. tags, parse tree height, average number of noun phrases, average number of verb phrases), and word uni-, bi-, and tri-gram features were used to train the classifiers. In the experiments, Schwarm and Ostendorf observed the contribution of individual features to the overall performance of the SVM classifiers and found out that 1.) no feature stood out as the most important one, and 2.) system performance was degraded when any particular feature was removed. They also realized that trigram models were noticeably more accurate than bigrams and unigrams. Results showed that their system could sometimes achieve *precision* value of 75%, *recall* of 87% and adjacent accuracy classification error (percentage of articles which are misclassified by more than one grade level) of 3.3%.

In (Heilman et al., 2007), the authors had concluded from their interactions with instructors of second language learners of English that combining grammatical and lexical features as predictors of text readability could outperform those measures based solely on one of the two. Heilman et al. combined vocabulary-based approach using *Multinomial Naive Bayes* classifier on unigrams, and grammar-based approach using *k-Nearest Neighbor* algorithm on parse trees, sentence length, verb forms, and part-of-speech tags features to evaluate text readability. Results of their study showed that vocabulary-based approach alone is better than grammar-based approach. However, the combined approach was proven to further enhance the performance of their system, reducing the mean squared error value by as much as 21% from 0.51 to 0.4.

3 LSI versus CI

LSI has been a well-known information retrieval algorithm. It was patented in 1988 by Scott Deerwester, Susan Dumais, George Furnas, Richard Harshman, Thomas Landauer, Karen Lochbaum and Lynn Streeter (Deerwester et al., 1989). CI, on the other hand, was proposed more recently by George Karypis and Eui-Hong (Sam) Han in 2000 (Karypis and Han, 2000) as a faster alternative for LSI. In this section, we present existing researches comparing the performances of LSI and CI on text content and readability analyses.

3.1 English Essay Content Analysis

The study presented in (Razon, 2010) focused on comparing LSI and CI as applied on English essay scoring. Both algorithms are based on vectorial semantics using dimensionality reduction.

Through several experiments, the study was able to prove that CI can outperform LSI in grading essays using content features alone. Below is the result of one of the experiments the authors conducted, where *accuracy* was calculated based on the exact agreement between the system's predicted scores and actual essay scores given by human checkers. As indicated on Table 1, CI outperformed LSI on all datasets reaching as high as 84.21% accuracy. It is also important to note that, as shown in the Grade8 dataset results, the difference between the accuracies of the two algorithms can reach as high as 18.75% in favor of CI.

Dataset	LSI Accuracy	CI Accuracy
Grade7	78.95	84.21
Grade8	62.50	81.25
Grade9 Set1	50.00	58.82
Grade9 Set2	64.10	69.23

Table 1: LSI vs. CI Accuracies (%) using Normalized Raw Term Frequency in (Razon, 2010)

3.2 Filipino Essay Content Analysis

The study in (Ong, 2011) was an attempt to implement a CI-based Filipino essay grader. Filipino language experts were consulted to validate the outputs. Experiments comparing CI and LSI showed that CI may perform better than LSI for some experts. The experimental results have proven that the system has a 95% probability of achieving accuracy from 75.5% to 79.9% in predicting the actual essay score given by human raters using the CI-based system. This range of accuracy values is comparable to those achieved among human raters which is between 70.6% and 70.9%.

As also stated in (Ong, 2011), CI, with small number of vectors representing each pre-defined class or group in the dataset, can run faster than LSI. The time complexity for CI is $O(iekn)$ while LSI is $O(en^2)$, where i is the number of iterations until convergence is achieved, k is the number of vectors representing each pre-defined class, e is the number of vocabulary entries, and n is the number of essays.

3.3 Tagalog Text Readability Indexing

A comparative study between LSI- and CI-based algorithms, as applied on readability analysis for **Tagalog** text documents, was conducted in (Razon et al., 2011). In the experiments, the authors applied *Spearman's rho* onto the training and test cosine similarity matrices, such that, each test document vector of cosine similarity scores with respect to the semantic space created using the training documents, is correlated against the training set's vectors of cosine similarity scores. Grade levels were then assigned to each test document based on the grade level of the training document with the highest correlation to it.

	RTF		TF-IDF	
Grade Level	LSI	CI	LSI	CI
2	61.67	80.00	76.67	66.67
3	40.00	52.00	62.00	52.00
4	16.67	36.67	23.33	33.33
6	65.00	47.50	32.50	20.00

Table 2: Exact Agreement Accuracy (%) using Raw Term Frequency (RTF) and Term Frequency-Inverse Document Frequency (TF-IDF) Weighting Schemes in (Razon et al., 2011)

As shown on Table 2, CI using raw term frequency (RTF) weighting scheme outperformed LSI on all the datasets except Grade 6. On the other hand, for the term frequency-inverse document frequency (TF-IDF) case, LSI performed better than CI except on Grade 4 dataset.

4 Our Assumptions

Our main assumption in this study is that ***written essays by students can be used to approximate their lowest possible reading level***. This assumes that whatever the students can write, they can also read. In (Metametrics, 2009), it was empirically proven that people's reading ability is consistently higher than their writing ability, hence providing a justification to this claim. Aside from this main assumption, we have also drawn out the following working assumptions from the researches discussed in Section 2 and other references cited in this paper:

1. *Statistical and n-gram analysis of POS tags can yield useful information to approximate text readability levels.* (Schwarm and Ostendorf, 2005; Heilman et al., 2007)

2. *Combined grammar-related and content-based analyses can yield better results for text readability analysis.* (Heilman et al., 2007; Landauer and Way, 2012)

5 Our Datasets

One of the challenges in this study is creating a suitable dataset to model and test readability levels of reading materials. There are two categories of data in this project. The first one is composed of English essays written by high school students. Under this category, we have the *2010 Gr 7-9* and *2014 Gr 7-9* datasets. These are used to model student reading abilities per school grade level. Each of these datasets is divided into two, $\frac{2}{3}$ for **training** and $\frac{1}{3}$ for **test**. The second data category is the teacher-prepared instructional materials which we call the *Reading Mats* dataset. These materials are selected by the schools' instructional materials experts and are classified from grade 7 to grade 9. In the experiments, these are used to create the **reference** set for both the training and testing processes which will be discussed in the later sections of this paper.

Dataset	Grade7	Grade8	Grade9	Total
2010 Gr 7-9	47	54	112	213
2014 Gr 7-9	67	62	64	193
Reading Mats	12	6	10	28

Table 3: Summary of Datasets Used

6 Our Sampling Procedure

Sampling is another very important factor to consider in the implementation of the system. For both the 2010 Grade7-9 and 2014 Grade7-9 datasets, a stratified 3-fold cross-validation is implemented, such that, essays in each grade level (i.e. Grade7, Grade8, Grade9) are roughly divided into three equal static partitions. One partition is always set aside for testing and the other two for training. Note that since there 3 grade levels with 3 partitions each, 27 Test-Training combinations are created to exhaust all possible partition combinations with 1:2 test-to-training partition ratio for each grade level.

7 Our Methodology

7.1 Content-based Analysis

7.1.1 Matrix Representation

After creating the vocabulary list from text samples, the three sets (i.e. training, test and reference) are converted to their term-by-document matrix representation. In this representation, each column is equivalent to one text sample vector, each row represents one word or term in the vocabulary, and each entry in the matrix is the number of occurrences of each term in each text sample.

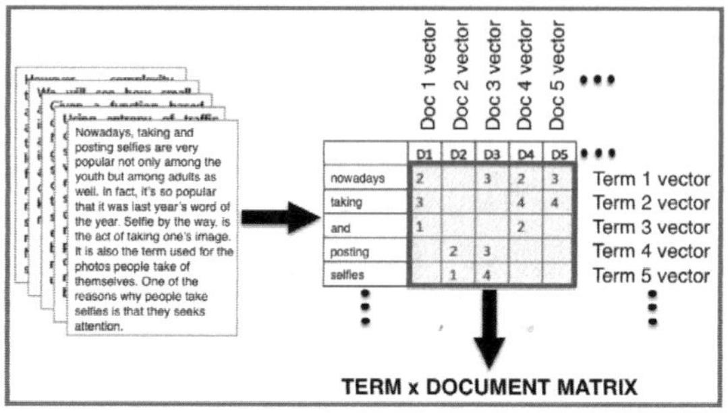

Figure 1: Term-by-Document Matrix

7.1.2 Dimensionality Reduction

As in the study of Razon in (Razon, 2010), both LSI and CI dimensionality reduction strategies are implemented separately on the training sets. These are *Singular Value Decomposition* (SVD) for LSI and *Concept Decomposition* (CD) for CI. SVD is defined as the decomposition of matrix X using $X = UDV^T$ where $U = XX^T$, $V = X^TX$ and D is a matrix whose diagonals are the singular values of matrix X. On the other hand, CD is defined as the decomposition of matrix X using $X_p = C_pZ^*$, where C_p is a matrix created using the normalized mean column vectors of each sub-cluster in the training set, and Z^* is the least-squares approximation with closed-form solution of $Z^* = (C_k^TC_k)^{-1}C_k^TX$ (Karypis and Han, 2000). A *sub-cluster* (sub) is derived from the stratified clustering of the vector representations of text documents by grade level. *K-means* clustering algorithm is utilized to accomplish this task.

7.1.3 Folding-In

Folding-in refers to the projection of the original training, test and reference document vectors onto the reduced semantic space derived in the previous step. For LSI, this process involves solving the equation $q_i = q_i^TU_kD_k^{-1}$ for all document vectors q_i of the training, reference and test sets. For CI, we solve the equation $q^* = (C_p^TC_p)^{-1}C_p^Tq$, where q^* is the reduced dimensionality matrix representation of the original training, reference or test matrix.

7.1.4 Similarity Measurement

After folding-in all column vectors of the training, test and reference sets onto the LSI- and CI-based reduced semantic spaces, cosine similarity values between the column vectors of both the training and test sets, against the column vectors of the reference set are calculated. Consequently, this step yields two sets of similarity vectors as shown in Figure 2. One set corresponds to the similarity values between all reference set vectors against a training document vector and the other corresponds to the similarity values between all reference set vectors against a test document vector. We will refer to these vectors as *training document-to-reference similarity vector* and *test document-to-reference similarity vector*, respectively. These vectors serve as training and test inputs of our SVM classifier.

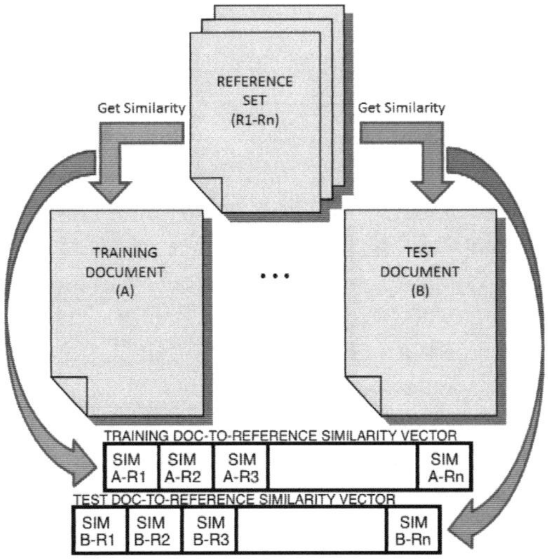

Figure 2: Similarity Vector Diagram

7.2 POS-based Grammar Analysis

Grammar features are necessary to model texts for each grade level. As part of our working assumptions discussed in Section 4, POS n-grams can be used to provide a rough approximation of the texts' syntactic information at the least. For example, POS unigrams can provide information regarding which of the POS tags are prevalent for each grade level and which are not. On the other hand, POS bi- and tri-grams can capture grammar-related information which can serve as basis for syntax complexity.

In this study, `Apache OpenNLP Maxent POS Tagger` is used to tag all documents. After getting uni-, bi- and tri-gram features from the text documents, we constructed the term-by-document matrices for the training, test and reference sets, where the POS n-grams are treated as the terms of the said matrices (i.e. POS-n-gram-by-document matrices). Next, we constructed the corresponding *training document-to-reference* and *test document-to-reference similarity vectors* for these matrices the same way as discussed in Section 7.1.4. Finally, *sparsification* of these matrices have been considered to further enhance the performance of the systems.

Sparsification is the removal of sparse term vectors (i.e. n-gram vectors) or the exclusion of those term vectors which have mostly zero values. This procedure aims to reduce the dimensionality of the POS n-gram-by-document matrix without sacrificing the loss of significant information inherent in the matrix. In this study, the term *sparsity* refers to the maximum sparse percentage, called the *sparse index* (SI), to consider in the experiment. For example, SI value of 0.7 means that all term vectors which are 70% sparse and below will be considered. Therefore, higher sparsity values allow more POS n-gram vectors to be included in the analysis.

8 Our Experiments

Five (5) feature sets are investigated in this study. These are: 1.) **POS**: POS n-gram features only, 2.) **LSI**: LSI-based features only, 3.) **CI**: CI-based features only, 4.) **LSI+POS**: Combined LSI-based and POS n-gram features, and 5.) **CI+POS**: Combined CI-based and POS n-gram features.

The following experimental phases are implemented using the training and test document-to-reference similarity vectors discussed in Sections 7.1.4 and 7.2

1. **Phase 1**: Baseline Experiments using Feature Sets 1, 2 and 3
2. **Phase 2**: Combined Grammar and Content Features Experiments using Feature Sets 4 and 5 with NO Sparsification
3. **Phase 3**: POS n-gram Sparsification Experiments using Feature Sets 1, 4 and 5 with SI from 0.1 to 0.9

Radial basis function (RBF) is used as the kernel function for all SVM classifiers in all the experiments. For each phase discussed above, the following SVM parameters are held constant: 1.) γ: kernel parameter which controls the shape of the RBF, 2.) C: misclassification cost or penalty constant, and 3.) k: number of folds in training cross-validation (i.e. k-fold cross-validation constant). Having constant values for these parameters allows us to focus our investigation on the

POS n-gram sparsification and the primary parameter of each baseline feature set, namely, the n in POS n-grams (i.e. uni-, bi-, tri-), LSI's dimensionality constant, dim, with values from 0.5 to 0.9, and CI's number of sub-cluster representations per grade level, sub, with values from 1 to 5.

Optimal values for dim and sub are derived in Phase 1. Then, LSI- and CI-based features corresponding to these values are combined with the full POS uni-, bi- and tri-gram feature sets in Phase 2, where we aim to find out 1.) if the combination of content- and grammar-based feature sets could yield higher mean exact agreement accuracy (MEAA), and 2.) which of the combined feature sets would perform best among the others. Finally, an investigation on the effect of POS n-grams' sparsity index is performed in Phase 3 to optimize the LSI+POS and CI+POS combination processes.

9 Our Experimental Results

9.1 Phase 1: Baseline Experiments

Baseline experiments are those experiments done using isolated feature sets (i.e. POS only, LSI only and CI only). For the 2010 Grade 7-9 dataset, the highest MEAA of 89.72% is achieved by CI using 2-sub-cluster vector representation per grade level. This is followed by POS bigrams with a value of 85.39%, making LSI the last with a value of 68.28% at reduced dimensionality of 50%. Furthermore, baseline CI-based features also outperformed LSI- and POS-based features yielding as high as 93.40% MEAA for the 2014 Grade 7-9 dataset. This is also followed by POS bigrams with a value of 87.38%, making LSI the last again with a value of 79.80% at reduced dimensionality of 70%.

9.2 Phase 2: Combined Features Experiments

In this phase, we directly combined the LSI- and CI-based features with POS n-gram features (i.e. LSI+POS and CI+POS) **without sparsification**. In general, LSI's performance has improved while the reverse is true for CI.

Referring to Tables 4 and 5, we can see that both, LSI+POS uni-grams and CI+POS uni-grams, have achieved higher MEAA values than POS uni-grams alone. It is also important to note that the MEAA for the combination of POS bi- and tri-grams with CI and LSI have resulted to values equal to or very close to that of isolated POS bi- and tri-grams, respectively. Therefore, it can be inferred that POS bi- and tri-gram features dominate the content-based features from CI and LSI, clipping the MEAA to the values achieved in the POS n-grams baseline experiments and this consequently affected CI's MEAA values negatively. Hence, we can say that simply adding the features together, which has been a common practice in other existing researches, does not guarantee a much better feature set. This anomalous behaviour led us to go forward and conduct Phase 3 to investigate the effects of POS n-gram sparsification.

Feature Set	**Primary Param.**	**2010 Gr7-9**		**2014 Gr7-9**	
		MEAA	SD	MEAA	SD
POS n-gram	n=1, uni	0.749	0.064	0.786	0.096
	n=2, bi	**0.854**	0.027	**0.874**	0.041
	n=3, tri	0.853	0.035	0.845	0.044
CI	sub=1	0.891	0.052	0.933	0.039
	sub=2	**0.897**	0.051	**0.934**	0.041
	sub=3	0.884	0.071	0.931	0.042
	sub=4	0.873	0.045	0.927	0.042
	sub=5	0.882	0.053	0.929	0.042
LSI	dim=0.5	**0.683**	0.054	0.781	0.056
	dim=0.6	0.660	0.055	0.783	0.050
	dim=0.7	0.666	0.040	**0.798**	0.048
	dim=0.8	0.659	0.044	0.789	0.053
	dim=0.9	0.655	0.039	0.785	0.060

Table 4: Phase 1: Baseline Experiment Summary

Base Feature	**Modified Feature Set**	**2010 Gr7-9**		**2014 Gr7-9**	
		MEAA	SD	MEAA	SD
CI (sub=2)	CI+POS uni	0.838	0.064	0.850	0.073
	CI+POS bi	0.854	0.027	0.874	0.041
	CI+POS tri	0.853	0.035	0.845	0.044
LSI (dim-0.7)	LSI+POS uni	0.768	0.060	0.816	0.058
	LSI+POS bi	0.854	0.027	0.874	0.041
	LSI+POS tri	0.855	0.033	0.852	0.041

Table 5: Phase 2: Combined Features Experiment Summary

9.3 Phase 3: POS n-gram Sparsification

As evident on Figures 3 and 4, the MEAA tends to increase as we increase the SI value, reaching its peak in the range of 0.6 to 0.9 for all n-grams (i.e. uni-grams, bi-grams, tri-grams). Results also show that CI with POS bi-grams has yielded the highest MEAA of 90.9% and 95.1%, with low standard deviations (SD) of 0.045 and 0.021, on both the 2010 and 2014 Grade 7-9 datasets, respectively.

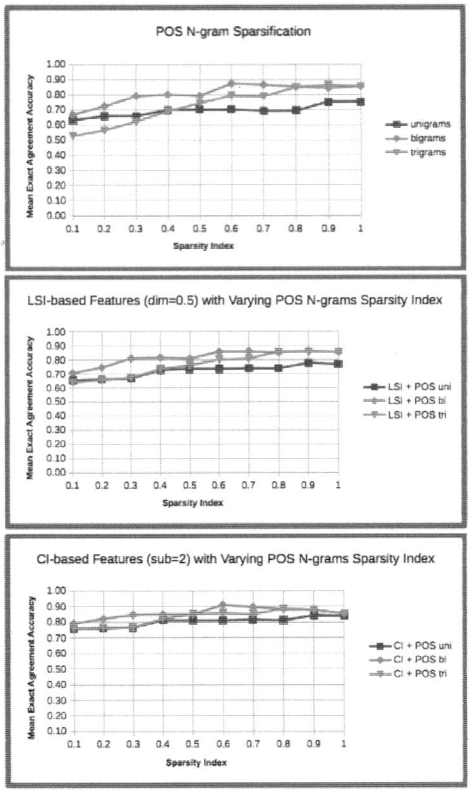

Figure 3: POS n-grams Sparsification Experimental Results on the 2010 Grade 7-9 Dataset using Feature Sets 1-POS only, 4-LSI+POS and 5-CI+POS

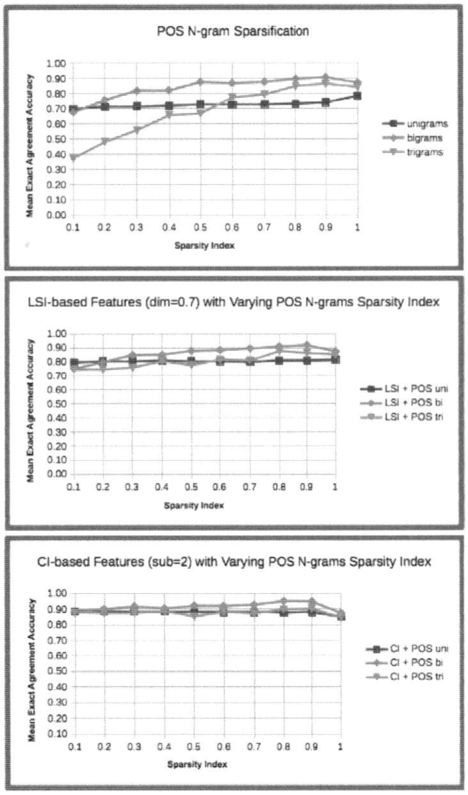

Figure 4: POS n-grams Sparsification Experimental Results on the 2014 Grade 7-9 Dataset using Feature Sets 1-POS only, 4-LSI+POS and 5-CI+POS

9.4 General Observations

The following statements summarize the overall results of the experiments:

1. For baseline experiments, CI-based similarity features alone can yield good results, outperforming the LSI- and POS-based similarity features.

2. LSI's performance can be greatly improved by combining it with the full set POS-based features (i.e. SI=1.0, no sparsification). However, the opposite is true for CI's.

3. The combined CI and POS Bi-grams feature sets (i.e. CI+POS bi-grams) consistently yield the highest MEAA in Phase 3, ranging from 80% to 95% for SI values between 0.2 to 0.8 as shown by the red lines on Figures 3 and 4.

4. POS N-gram features sparsification improves the MEAA of isolated POS-, combined LSI+POS-, and combined CI+POS-based feature sets (i.e. feature sets 1, 4 and 5 as discussed in Section 8). Optimal MEAA values can be achieved within 0.6 to 0.8 SI values, then slope downwards all the way to 1.0. Note that at SI=1.0, no term is removed from the feature sets' vocabulary (i.e. full combined vocabulary is being used without sparsification).

5. POS bi-gram feature set is superior among the other n-grams' (i.e. uni- and tri-grams). This is exhibited on Figures 3 and 4, where bi-grams almost always yield the highest MEAA all throughout the SI spectrum.

6. SI has greater influence on bi- and tri-grams than uni-grams in terms of MEAA. Unigrams tend to exhibit gradual changes in the MEAA graphs.

10 Conclusion

In this study, we have successfully implemented a learner-based text readability indexer using combined content and grammar features for the English language. Superiority of the combined CI and POS bi-grams feature set has been established in the experiments, yielding as high as 95.1% MEAA. Moreover, the results of the Phase2 and Phase3 experiments also prove that POS n-gram sparsification is important to optimize the feature combination process. This goes to show that careful analysis is necessary in combining feature sets and that merely adding the features together does not guarantee a better feature set.

For future work, it would be interesting to find out what happens if we use the combined POS n-gram features such that we have: 1.) uni-grams and bi-grams, 2.) bi-grams and tri-grams, 3.) uni-grams and tri-grams, and 4.) uni-grams, bi-grams, and tri-grams, together with CI- or LSI-based features. Then, we can also attempt to optimize the combination process through sparsification as we did in this study. Adding more grade levels and text documents into the system can also be done to further validate the results. Furthermore, the flexibility of the system can be tested by applying it on languages other than English.

Acknowledgments

We would like to acknowledge the support provided by the Department of Science and Technology (DOST) of the Philippines through its Engineering Research and Development for Technology (ERDT) program. We would also like to thank the University of the Philippines Integrated School (UPIS) for giving us permission to use their essay samples and reading materials as data.

References

Scott C. Deerwester et al. (Bell Communications Research, Inc.). *Computer Information Retrieval using Latent Semantic Structure.* US Patent 4,839,853. June 13, 1989.

George Karypis and Euihong Han. 2000. *Concept Indexing: A Fast Dimensionality Reduction Algorithm with Applications to Document Retrieval and Categorization.* In *Proc. of the 9th International Conference on Information and Knowledge Management* McLean, Virginia.

Luo Si and Jamie Callan. 2001. *A Statistical Model for Scientific Readability.* In *Proc. of the 2001 ACM CIKM. 10th International Conference on Information and Knowledge Management*, Atlanta, GA, USA.

Kevyn Collins-Thompson and Jamie Callan. 2004. *A Language Modeling Approach to Predicting Reading Difficulty.* In *Proc. of HLT/NAACL 2004*, Boston, USA.

Constantinos Boulis and Mari Ostendorf. 2005. *Text Classification by Augmenting the Bag-of-Words Representation with Redundancy-Compensated Bigrams.* In *Proc. of the SIAM International Conference on Data Mining at the Workshop on Feature Selection in Data Mining.*

Sarah E. Schwarm and Mari Ostendorf. 2005. *Reading Level Assessment using Support Vector Machines and Statistical Language Models.* In *Proc. of the 43rd Annual Meeting on Association for Computational Linguistics*, Michigan, USA.

Patric Larsson. 2006 *Classification into Readability Levels - MS Thesis.* Uppsala University, Uppsala, Sweden.

Michael J. Heilman et al. 2007. *Combining Lexical and Grammatical Geatures to Improve Readability Measures for First and Second Language Texts.* In *Proc. of NAACL HLT 2007*, Rochester, New York.

Sarah E. Petersen and Mari Ostendorf. 2009. *A Machine Learning Approach to Reading Level Assessment.* In *Journal of Computer Speech and Language, Volume 23 Issue 1*, London, United Kingdom.

Malbert Smith III. 2009. *The Reading-Writing Connection. MetaMetrics Position Paper*, Durham, North Carolina.

Abigail R. Razon. 2010. *A New Approach to Automated Essay Content Analysis using Concept Indexing - MS Thesis.* University of the Philippines-Diliman, Manila, Philippines.

Abigail R. Razon et al. 2011. *Readability Analysis of Grade School Reading Books using Concept Learning with K-Means Clustering.* In *Proc. of 2011 International Symposium on Multimedia and Communication Technology*, Hokkaido, Japan.

Darrel Alvin N. Ong. 2011. *Automated Content Scoring of Filipino Essays using Concept Indexing - MS Thesis.* University of the Philippines-Diliman, Manila, Philippines.

Thomas Landauer and Denny Way. 2012 *Improving Text Complexity Measurement through the Reading Maturity Metric.* In *Annual meeting of the National Council on Measurement in Education*, Vancouver, British Columbia, Canada.

Jessica Nelson et al. 2012. *Measures of Text Difficulty: Testing their predictive value for grade levels and student performance. Council of Chief State School Officers*, Washington, DC.

Classification of Lexical Collocation Errors in the Writings of Learners of Spanish

Sara Rodríguez-Fernández
Universitat Pompeu Fabra

Roberto Carlini
Universitat Pompeu Fabra

Leo Wanner
ICREA and
Universitat Pompeu Fabra

{sara.rodriguez.fernandez, roberto.carlini, leo.wanner}@upf.edu

Abstract

It is generally acknowledged that *collocations* in the sense of idiosyncratic word co-occurrences are a challenge in the context of second language learning. Advanced miscollocation correction is thus highly desirable. However, state-of-the-art "collocation checkers" are merely able to detect a possible miscollocation and then offer as correction suggestion a list of collocations of the given keyword retrieved automatically from a corpus. No more targeted correction is possible since state-of-the-art collocation checkers are not able to identify the type of the miscollocation. We suggest a classification of the main types of lexical miscollocations by US American learners of Spanish and demonstrate its performance.

1 Introduction

In the second language learning literature, it is generally acknowledged that it is in particular idiosyncratic word co-occurrences of the kind *take* [*a*] *walk*, *make* [*a*] *proposal*, *pass* [*an*] *exam*, *weak performance*, *hard blow*, etc. that make language learning a challenge (Granger, 1998; Lewis, 2000; Nesselhauf, 2004; Nesselhauf, 2005; Lesniewska, 2006; Alonso Ramos et al., 2010). Such co-occurrences (in lexicography known as "collocations") are language-specific. For instance, in Spanish, you 'give a walk' (*dar* [*un*] *paseo*), while in French and German you 'make' it (*faire* [*une*] *promenade* / [*einen*] *Spaziergang machen*). In English you *take a step*, while in German you 'make' it ([*einen*] *Schritt machen*) and in Spanish you 'give' it (*dar* [*un*] *paso*). In English, you can *hold* or *give* [*a*] *lecture*, in Spanish you 'give' (*dar* [*una*] *clase*), but you do not 'hold' it, and in German you 'hold' it ([*eine*] *Vorlesung halten*), but do not 'give' it. And so on.

Several proposals have been put forward for how to verify automatically whether a collocation as used by a language learner is correct or not and, in the case that it is not, display a list of potential collocations of the keyword (*walk*, *step*, and *lecture* above) of the assumingly incorrect collocation. For instance, a Spanish learner of English may use **approve* [*an*] *exam* instead of *pass* [*an*] *exam*. When this miscollocation is entered, e.g., into the MUST collocation checker[1] for verification, the program suggests (in this order) *pass exam*, *sit exam*, *take exam*, *fail exam*, and *do exam* as possible corrections. That is, the checker offers all possible <verb> + *exam* collocations found in a reference corpus or dictionary. However, the display of a mere list of correct collocations of a given keyword is unsatisfactory for learners since they are left alone with the problem of picking the right one among several (potentially rather similar) choices. On the other hand, no further restriction of the list of correction candidates or any meaningful reordering is possible because the collocation checker has no knowledge about the type of the error of the miscollocation.

In order to improve the state of affairs, and be able to propose a more targeted correction, we must be able to identify the type of error of the collocation proposed by the learner (and thus also the meaning the learner intended to express by the miscollocation). While this seems hardly feasible with isolated collocations submitted by a learner for verification (as above), error type recognition in the writings of learners is more promising. Such an error type recognition procedure is taken for granted in grammar checkers, but is still absolutely unexplored in collocation checkers. In what follows, we outline how some of the most prominent errors in collocations identified in the writings of US American students learning Spanish can be

[1] http://miscollocation-richtrf.rhcloud.com/

Proceedings of Recent Advances in Natural Language Processing, pages 529–536,
Hissar, Bulgaria, Sep 7–9 2015.

classified with respect to a given collocation error typology.

2 Background on Collocations and Collocation Errors

Given that the notion of collocation has been discussed and interpreted in lexicology from different angles, we first clarify our usage of the term. Then, we outline the miscollocation typology that underlies our classification.

2.1 On the Nature of Collocations

The term "collocation" as introduced by Firth (1957) and cast into a definition by Halliday (1961) encompasses the statistical distribution of lexical items in context: lexical items that form high probability associations are considered collocations. It is this interpretation that underlies most works on automatic identification of collocations in corpora; see, e.g., (Choueka, 1988; Church and Hanks, 1989; Pecina, 2008; Evert, 2007; Bouma, 2010). However, in contemporary lexicography and lexicology, an interpretation that stresses the idiosyncratic nature of collocations prevails. According to Hausmann (1984), Cowie (1994), Mel'čuk (1995) and others, a collocation is a binary idiosyncratic co-occurrence of lexical items between which a direct syntactic dependency holds and where the occurrence of one of the items (the *base*) is subject of the free choice of the speaker, while the occurrence of the other item (the *collocate*) is restricted by the base. Thus, in the case of *take* [*a*] *walk*, *walk* is the base and *take* the collocate, in the case of *high speed*, *speed* is the base and *high* the collocate, etc. It is this understanding of the term "collocation" that we find reflected in general public collocation dictionaries and that we follow in our work since it seems most useful in the context of second language acquisition. However, this is not to say that the two main interpretations of the term "collocation", the distributional and the idiosyncratic one, are disjoint, i.e., necessarily lead to a different judgement with respect to the collocation status of a word combination. On the contrary: two lexical items that form an idiosyncratic co-occurrence are likely to occur together in a corpus with a high value of *Pointwise Mutual Information* (PMI) (Church and Hanks, 1989):

$$PMI = \log\left(\frac{P(a \cap b)}{P(a)P(b)}\right) = \log\left(\frac{P(a|b)}{P(a)}\right) = \log\left(\frac{P(b|a)}{P(b)}\right) \quad (1)$$

The PMI indicates that if two variables *a* and *b* are independent, the probability of their intersection is the product of their probabilities. A PMI equal to 0 means that the variables are independent; a positive PMI implies a correlation beyond independence; and a negative PMI signals that the co-occurrence of the variables is lower than the average. Two lexemes are thus considered to form a collocation when they have a positive PMI, i.e., they are found together more often that this would happen if they would be independent variables.

PMI has been a standard collocation measure throughout the literature since Church and Hank's proposal in 1989. However, a mere use of PMI or any similar measure neglects that the lexical dependencies between the base and the collocate are not symmetric (recall that PMI is commutative, i.e., $PMI(a, b) = PMI(b, a)$). Only a few studies take into consideration the asymmetry of collocations; see, e.g., Gries (2013), who proposes an asymmetric association measure, ΔP, and Carlini et al. (2014), who propose an assymmetric normalization of PMI; see Eq. (2). In our work, we use Carlini et al. (2014)'s asymmetric $NPMI_C$.

$$NPMI_C = \frac{PMI(collocate, base)}{-log(p(collocate))} \quad (2)$$

2.2 Typology of Collocation Errors

Alonso Ramos et al. (2010) proposed a detailed three-dimensional typology of collocation errors. The first dimension defines which element of the collocation (the base or the collocate) is erroneous or whether it is the collocation as a whole. The second (descriptive) dimension details the type of error that was produced. Three different global types are distinguished: register, lexical, and grammatical. The third dimension, finally, details the possible interpretation of the origin of the error (e.g., calque from the native language of the learner, analogy to another common collocation, etc.). In the experiments presented in this paper, we focus on the lexical branch of the descriptive dimension.

Lexical errors are divided into five different types; the first two affect either the base or the collocate; the other three the collocation as a whole:[2]

[2]Given that we work on a Spanish learner corpus, the examples of miscollocations are in Spanish. The consensual-

1. *Substitution errors*: Errors resulting from an inappropriate choice of a lexical unit that exists in the language as either base or collocate. This is the case, e.g., with **realizar una meta* 'to reach a goal', lit. 'to make, to carry out a goal', where both the base and the collocate are existing lexical units in Spanish, but the correct collocate *alcanzar*, lit. 'to achieve' has been substituted by *realizar*.

2. *Creation errors*: Errors resulting from the use of a non-existing (i.e., "created" or invented) lexical unit as the base or as the collocate. An example of this type of error is **estallar confrontamientos*, instead of *estallar confrontaciones*, lit. '(make) explode a confrontation', where the learner has used the non-existing form *confrontamientos*.

3. *Synthesis errors*: Errors resulting from the use of a non-existing lexical unit instead of a collocation, as, for instance, **escaparatear*, instead of *ir de escaparates* 'to go window-shopping'.

4. *Analysis errors*: Errors that are inverse to synthesis errors, i.e., that result from the use of an invented collocation instead of a single lexical unit expression. An example of this type of error is **sitio de acampar* 'camping site', which in Spanish would be better expressed by the lexical unit *camping*.

5. *Different sense errors*: Errors resulting from the use of a correct collocation, but with meaning different from the intended one. An example of this type of error is **el próximo día*, instead of *el día siguiente* 'the next day'.

Our studies show that 'Substitution', 'Creation' and 'Different sense' errors are the most common types of miscollocations. In contrast, learners tend to make rather few 'Synthesis' and 'Analysis' errors. Therefore, given that 'Synthesis' errors are not comparable to any other error class, we decided not to consider them at this stage of our work. 'Analysis' errors show in their appearance a high similarity to 'Substitution' errors, such that they could be merged with them without any major distortion of the typology. Therefore, we deal below with miscollocation classification with respect to three lexical error classes: 1. 'Extended Substitution', 2. 'Creation', and 3. 'Different Sense'.

ized judgement whether a given collocation is a miscollocation or a correct collocation has in all cases been made by a team of lexicographers who are native speakers of Peninsular Spanish.

3 Towards Automatic Collocation Error Classification

In corpus-based linguistic phenomenon classification, it is common to choose a supervised machine learning method that is then used to assign any identified phenomenon to one of the available classes. In the light of the diversity of the linguistic nature of the collocation errors and the widely diverging frequency of the different error types, this procedure seems not optimal for miscollocation classification. A round of preliminary experiments confirmed this assessment. It is more promising to target the identification of each collocation error type separately, using for each of them the identification method that suits its characteristics best. Furthermore and as a matter of fact, it cannot be excluded that a miscollocation may contain more than one type of error. Thus, it may contain an error in the base and another error in the collocate, or it might have a lexical and a grammatical error or two lexical errors (one per element) at the same time. An example of a collocation containing two lexical errors is *afecto malo* 'bad effect', where both the base and the collocate are incorrect. *Afecto* 'affect' is chosen instead of *efecto* 'effect', and *malo* 'bad' instead of *nocivo* 'damaging'.

In what follows, we describe the methods that we use to identify miscollocations of the three types that we target. All of these methods perform a binary classification of all identified incorrect collocations as 'of type X' / 'not of type X'. The methods for the identification of 'Extended substitution' and 'Creation' errors receive as input the incorrect collocations (i.e., grammatical, lexical or register-oriented miscollocations) recognized in the writing of a language learner by a collocation error recognition program[3], together with their sentential contexts. The method for the recognition of 'Different sense' errors receives as input 'different sense' errors along with the correct

[3]Since in our experiments we focus on miscollocation classification, we use as "writings of language learners" a learner corpus in which both correct and incorrect collocations have been annotated manually and revised by different annotators. Only those instances for which complete agreement was found were used for the experiments.

collocations identified in the writing of the learner.

Extended Substitution Error Classification. For the classification of incorrect collocations as 'extended substitution error' / 'not an extended substitution error', we use supervised machine learning. This is because 'extended substitution' is, on the one side, the most common type of error (such that sufficient training material is available), and, on the other side, very variant (such that it is difficult to be captured by a rule-based procedure). After testing various ML-approaches, we have chosen the Support Vector Machine (SMO) implementation from the Weka toolkit (Hall et al., 2009).[4]

Two different types of features have been used: lexical features and co-occurrence (or PMI-based) features. The lexical features consist of the lemma of the collocate and the bigram made up of the lemmas of the base and collocate. The PMI-based features consist of: $NPMI_C$ of the base and the collocate, $NPMI_C$ of the hypernym of the base and the collocate, $NPMI$ of the base and its context, and $NPMI$ of the collocate and its context, considering as context the two immediate words to the left and to the right of each element. Hypernyms were taken from the Spanish WordNet; $NPMI$s and $NPMI_C$s were calculated on a 7 million sentences reference corpus of Spanish.

Creation Error Classification. For the detection of creation errors among all miscollocations, we have designed a rule-based algorithm that uses linguistic (lexical and morphological) information; see Algorithm 1.

If both elements of a collocation under examination are found in the reference corpus (RC) with a sufficient frequency ($\geq$50 for our experiments), they are considered valid tokens of Spanish, and therefore 'Not creation' errors. If one of the elements has a low frequency in the RC (<50), the algorithm continues to examine the miscollocation. First, it checks whether a learner used an English word in a Spanish sentence, considering it as a 'transfer Creation error'. If this is not the case, it checks whether the gender suffix is wrong, considering it as a 'gender Creation error', as in, e.g., **hacer regala* instead of *hacer regalo*, lit. 'make present'. This is done by alternating the gender suffix and checking the resulting token in the RC.

[4]Weka is University of Waikato's public machine learning platform that offers a great variety of different classification algorithms for data mining.

Algorithm 1: Creation Error Classification

Given a collocation '$b + c$' that is to be verified
do
if b_L,c_L $\in$ RC
// with 'b_L'/'c_L' as lemmatized base/collocate
  and freq('b_L') > 50
  and freq('c_L') > 50
 then echo "Not a creation error"
else if $b_L \vee c_L \in$ English dictionary
 then echo "Creation error (Transfer)"
else if check_gender(b_L) = false
 then echo "Creation error (Incorrect gender)"
else if check_affix(b_r) || check_affix(c_r)
// with 'b_r'/'c_r' as stems of base/collocate
 then echo: "Creation error (Incorrect derivation)"
else if check_ortography(b_L) || check_ortography(c_L)
 then echo "Not a creation error (Ortographic)"
else if freq('b_L') > 0 **or** freq('c_L') > 0
 then echo "Not a creation error"
else
echo "Creation error (Unidentified)"

If no gender-influenced error could be detected, the algorithm checks whether the error is due to an incorrect morphological derivation of either the base or the collocate — which would imply a 'derivation Creation error', as in, e.g. **ataque terrorístico* instead of *ataque terrorista* 'terrorist attack'. For this purpose, the stems of the collocation elements are obtained and expanded by the common nominal / verbal derivation affixes of Spanish to see whether any derivation leads to the form used by the learner. Should this not be the case, the final check is to see whether any of the elements is misspelled and therefore we face a 'Not creation error'. This is done by calculating the edit distance from the given forms to valid tokens in the RC.

In the case of an unsuccessful orthography check, we assume a 'Creation' error if the frequency of one of the elements of the miscollocation is '0', and a 'Not creation' error for element frequencies between '0' and '50'.

Different Sense Error Classification. Given that 'Different Sense Errors' capture the use of correct collocations in an inappropriate context, the main strategy for their detection is to compare the context of a learner collocation with its prototypical context. The prototypical context is represented by a centroid vector calculated using the lexical contexts of the correct uses of the collocation found in the RC.

The vector representing the original context is compared to the centroid vector in terms of cosine similarity; cf. Eq. (3).

$$sim(A, B) = \frac{A \cdot B}{\|A\| \, \|B\|} \quad (3)$$

A specific similarity threshold must be determined in order to discriminate correct and incorrect uses. In the experiments we carried out so far, 0.02543 was empirically determined as the best fitting threshold. However, further research is needed to design a more generic threshold determination procedure.

4 Experiments

In this section, we first describe the experiment set up and present then the results of the experiments.

4.1 Experiment Setup

For our experiments, we use a fragment of the Spanish Learner Corpus CEDEL2 (Lozano, 2009), which is composed of writings of learners of Spanish whose first language is American English. The writings have an average length of 500 words and cover different genres. Opinion essays, descriptive texts, accounts of some past experience, and letters are the most common of them. The levels of the students range from 'low-intermediate' to 'advanced'. In the fragment of CEDEL2 (in total, 517 writings) that we use (our working corpus), both the correct and incorrect collocation occurrences are tagged.[5] As stated above, collocations were annotated and revised, and only those for which a general agreement regarding their status was found, were used for the experiments.

Table 1 shows the frequency of the correct collocations and of the five types of lexical miscollocations in our working corpus. The numbers confirm our decision to discard synthesis miscollocations (there are only 9 of them – compared to, e.g., 565 substitution miscollocations) and to merge analysis miscollocations (19 in our corpus) with substitution miscollocations.[6]

To be able to take the syntactic structure of collocations into account, we processed

Class	# Instances
Correct collocations	3245
Analysis errors	19
Substitution errors	565
Creation errors	69
Synthesis errors	9
Different sense errors	48

Table 1: Number of instances of the different types of lexical errors and correct collocations in our working corpus.

CEDEL2 with Bohnet (2010)'s syntactic dependency parser[7].

As a reference corpus, we used a seven million sentence corpus, from Peninsular Spanish newspaper material. The reference corpus was also processed with Bohnet (2010)'s syntactic dependency parser.

4.2 Results of the Experiments

Table 2 shows the performance of the individual collocation error classification methods. In the '+' column of each error type, the accuracy is displayed with which our algorithms correctly detect that a miscollocation belongs to the error type in question; in the '−' column, the accuracy is displayed with which our algorithms correctly detect that a miscollocation does not belong to the corresponding error type.

	'Ext. subst'		'Creation'		'Diff. sense'	
	+	-	+	-	+	-
Baseline	0.395	0.902	0.391	0.986	0.5	0.453
Our model	0.832	0.719	0.681	0.942	0.583	0.587

Table 2: Error detection performance. The lower row displays the achieved accuracy.

To assess the performance of our classification, we use three baselines, one for each type of error. To the best of our knowledge, no other state-of-the-art figures are available with which we could compare its quality further. For the 'Extended substitution' miscollocation classification, we use as baseline a simplified version of the model, trained only with one of our lexical features, namely bigrams made up of the lemmas of the base and

[5]The tagging procedure has been carried out manually by several linguists. The first phase of it was already carried out by (Alonso Ramos et al., 2011). We carried on the tagging work by Alonso Ramos et al. to have for our experiments a corpus of a sufficient size.

[6]Recall that we argued that synthesis miscollocations are too different from the other types of errors to be merged with any other type.

[7]Processing tools' performance on non-native texts is lower than on texts written by natives. We evaluated the performance of the parser on our learner corpus and obtained the following results: LAS:88.50%, UAS:87.67%, LA:84.54%.

the collocate of the collocation. For 'Creation' miscollocation classification, the baseline is an algorithm that judges a miscollocation to be of the type 'Creation' if either one of the elements (the lemma of the base or of the collocate) or both elements of the miscollocation are not found in the reference corpus. Finally, for the 'Different sense' miscollocation classification, we take as baseline an algorithm that, given a bag of the lexical items that constitute the contexts of the correct uses of a collocation in the RC, judges a collocation to be a miscollocation of the 'Different sense' type, if less than half of the lexical items of the context of this collocation in the writing of the learner is not found in the reference bag.

5 Discussion

Before we discuss the outcome of the experiments, let us briefly make some generic remarks on the phenomenon of a collocation in the experiments.

5.1 The Phenomenon of a Collocation

The decision whether a collocation is correct or incorrect is not always straightforward, even for native expert annotators. Firstly, a certain number of collocations was affected by spelling and inflective errors. Consider, e.g., *tomamos cervesas* 'we drank beer', instead of *cervezas*; *sacque una mala nota* 'I got a bad mark', where *saqué* is the right form, or *el dolor disminúe* 'the pain decreases', instead of *disminuye*. In such cases, we assume that these are orthographical or morphological mistakes, rather than collocational ones. Therefore, we consider them to be correct. On the other hand, collocations may also differ in their degree of acceptability. Consider, e.g., *asistir a la escuela, tomar una fotografía* o *mirar la televisión*. Collocations that were doubtful to one or several annotators were looked up in th RC. If their frequency was higher than a certain threshold, they were annotated as correct. Otherwise, they were considered incorrect. From the above examples, *asistir a la escuela* was the only collocation considered as correct after the consultation of the RC.

5.2 The Outcome of the Experiments

The performance figures show that the correct identification of 'Different sense' miscollocations is still a challenge. With an accuracy somewhat below 60% for both the recognition of 'Different sense' miscollocations and recognition of 'Correctly used' collocations, there is room for improvement. Our cosine-measure quite often leads to the classification of correct collocations as 'Different sense' miscollocations (cf., e.g., *ir en coche* 'go by car' , *tener una relación* 'have a relationship', *tener impacto* 'have impact', *tener capacidad* 'have capacity') or classifies 'Different sense' errors as correctly used collocations, such as *gastar el tiempo* (intended *pasar el tiempo* 'spend time' or *tener opciones* instead of *ofrecer posibilidades* 'offer possibilities'. This shows the limitations of an exclusive use of lexical contexts for the judgement whether a collocation is appropriately used: on the one hand, lexical contexts can, in fact, be rather variant (such that the learner may use a collocation correctly in a novel context), and, on the other hand, lexical contexts do not capture the *situational* contexts, which determine even to a major extent the appropriateness of the use of a given expression. Unfortunately, to capture situational contexts remains a big challenge.

6 Conclusions and Future Work

We discussed a classification of collocation errors made by American English learners of Spanish with respect to the lexical branch of the miscollocation typology presented in Alonso Ramos et al. (2010). The results are very good for two of the three error types we considered, 'Substitution' and 'Creation'. The third type of miscollocation, 'Different sense', is recognized to a certain extent, but further research is needed to be able to recognize it as well as the other two error types. But already with the provided classification at hand, learners can be offered much more targeted correction aids than this is the case with the state-of-the-art collocation checkers. We are now about to implement such aids, which will also offer the classification and targeted correction of grammatical collocation errors (Rodríguez-Fernández et al., 2015), into the collocation learning workbench HARenES (Wanner et al., 2013; Alonso Ramos et al., 2015).

7 Acknowledgements

This work is funded by the Spanish Ministry of Economy and Competitiveness (MINECO), through a predoctoral grant (BES-2012-057036), in the framework of the project HARenES (FFI2011-30219-C02-02).

References

Margarita Alonso Ramos, Leo Wanner, Orsolya Vincze, Gerard Casamayor, Nancy Vázquez, Estela Mosqueira, and Sabela Prieto. 2010. Towards a Motivated Annotation Schema of Collocation Errors in Learner Corpora. In *Proceedings of the 7th International Conference on Language Resources and Evaluation (LREC)*, pages 3209–3214, La Valetta, Malta.

Margarita Alonso Ramos, Leo Wanner, Orsolya Vincze, Rogelio Nazar, Gabriela Ferraro, Estela Mosqueira, and Sabela Prieto. 2011. Annotation of collocations in a learner corpus for building a learning environment. In *Proceedings of the Learner Corpus Research 2011 Conference*, Louvain-la-Neuve, Belgium.

Margarita Alonso Ramos, Roberto Carlini, Joan Codina-Filba, Ana Orol, Orsolya Vincze, and Leo Wanner. 2015. Towards a Learner Need-Oriented Second Language Collocation Writing Assistant. In *Proceedings of the EURCALL Conference*, Padova, Italy.

Bernd Bohnet. 2010. Very high accuracy and fast dependency parsing is not a contradiction. In *Proceedings of the 23rd International Conference on Computational Linguistics (COLING)*, pages 89–97. Association for Computational Linguistics.

Gossa Bouma. 2010. Collocation extraction beyond the independence assumption. In *Proceedings of the ACL 2010, Short paper track*, Uppsala.

Roberto Carlini, Joan Codina-Filba, and Leo Wanner. 2014. Improving Collocation Correction by ranking suggestions using linguistic knowledge. In *Proceedings of the 3rd Workshop on NLP for Computer-Assisted Language Learning*, Uppsala, Sweden.

Yakov Choueka. 1988. Looking for needles in a haystack or locating interesting collocational expressions in large textual databases. In *Proceedings of the RIAO*, pages 34–38.

Keith Church and Patrick Hanks. 1989. Word Association Norms, Mutual Information, and Lexicography. In *Proceedings of the 27th Annual Meeting of the ACL*, pages 76–83.

Anthony Cowie. 1994. Phraseology. In R.E. Asher and J.M.Y. Simpson, editors, *The Encyclopedia of Language and Linguistics, Vol. 6*, pages 3168–3171. Pergamon, Oxford.

Stefan Evert. 2007. Corpora and collocations. In A. Lüdeling and M. Kytö, editors, *Corpus Linguistics. An International Handbook*. Mouton de Gruyter, Berlin.

John Firth. 1957. Modes of meaning. In J.R. Firth, editor, *Papers in Linguistics, 1934-1951*, pages 190–215. Oxford University Press, Oxford.

Sylviane Granger. 1998. Prefabricated patterns in advanced EFL writing: Collocations and Formulae. In A. Cowie, editor, *Phraseology: Theory, Analysis and Applications*, pages 145–160. Oxford University Press, Oxford.

Stefan Th Gries. 2013. 50-something years of work on collocations: what is or should be next. *International Journal of Corpus Linguistics*, 18(1):137–166.

Mark Hall, Eibe Frank, Geoffrey Holmes, Bernhard Pfahringer, Peter Reutemann, and Ian H. Witten. 2009. The WEKA Data Mining Software: An Update. *SIGKDD Explorations*, 11(1).

Michael Halliday. 1961. Categories of the theory of grammar. *Word*, 17:241–292.

Franz-Joseph Hausmann. 1984. Wortschatzlernen ist Kollokationslernen. Zum Lehren und Lernen französischer Wortwendungen. *Praxis des neusprachlichen Unterrichts*, 31(1):395–406.

Justyna Lesniewska. 2006. Collocations and second language use. *Studia Lingüística Universitatis Iagellonicae Cracoviensis*, 123:95–105.

Michael Lewis. 2000. *Teaching Collocation. Further Developments in the Lexical Approach*. LTP, London.

Cristóbal Lozano. 2009. CEDEL2: Corpus escrito del español L2. In C.M. Bretones Callejas, editor, *Applied Linguistics Now: Understanding Language and Mind*, pages 197–212. Universidad de Almería, Almería.

Igor Mel'čuk. 1995. Phrasemes in Language and Phraseology in Linguistics. In M. Everaert, E.-J. van der Linden, A. Schenk, and R. Schreuder, editors, *Idioms: Structural and Psychological Perspectives*, pages 167–232. Lawrence Erlbaum Associates, Hillsdale.

Nadja Nesselhauf. 2004. How learner corpus analysis can contribute to language teaching: A study of support verb constructions. In G. Aston, S. Bernardini, and D. Stewart, editors, *Corpora and language learners*, pages 109–124. Benjamins Academic Publishers, Amsterdam.

Nadja Nesselhauf. 2005. *Collocations in a Learner Corpus*. Benjamins Academic Publishers, Amsterdam.

Pavel Pecina. 2008. A machine learning approach to multiword expression extraction. In *Proceedings of the LREC 2008 Workshop Towards a Shared Task for Multiword Expressions (MWE 2008)*, pages 54–57, Marrakech.

Sara Rodríguez-Fernández, Roberto Carlini, and Leo Wanner. 2015. Classification of Grammatical Collocation Errors in the Writings of Learners of Spanish. In *Proceedings of the Annual Spanish Computational Linguistics Conference (SEPLN)*, Alicante, Spain.

Leo Wanner, Serge Verlinde, and Margarita Alonso Ramos. 2013. Writing Assistants and Automated Lexical Error Correction: Word Combinatorics. In *Proceedings of eLex 2013: Electronic Lexicography in the 21st Century*, Tallinn, Estonia.

Measuring Semantic Similarity for Bengali Tweets Using WordNet

Dwijen Rudrapal
CSE Department
NIT Agartala, India
dwijen.rudrapal@gmail.com

Amitava Das
CSE Department
IIIT, Sricity, India
amitava.santu@gmail.com

Baby Bhattacharya
CSE Department
NIT Agartala, India
babybhatt75@gmail.com

Abstract

Similarity between natural language texts, sentences in terms of meaning, known as textual entailment, is a generic problem in the area of computational linguistics. In the last few years researchers worked on various aspects of textual entailment problem, but mostly restricted to English language. Here in this paper we present a method for measuring the semantic similarity of Bengali tweets using WordNet. Moreover we defined partial textual entailment (PTE) as in real data partial entailment cases are equally prevalent with the complete/direct entailment. Although by definition entailment is a directional relationship, but here we consider entailment more as semantic similarity.

Keywords: Semantic similarity; WordNet; Synonym;

1 Introduction

Variations of natural language expression make it difficult to determine semantically equivalent sentences. The beauty of natural languages is similar meaning could be expressed in countless ways; therefore it is a very complex task to measure relatedness of natural language sentences. Morpho-Syntactic variations of similar meaning expressions are more prevalent in social media text due to its informal nature. Semantic similarity score plays important role in many Natural Language Applications (NLP) such as multi-document summarization (MDS), question answering(QA), information extraction(IE) (Bhagwani et al., 2012). Several researchers have explored numbers of semantic similarity methods mostly for English but very less for Indian languages and almost nothing for Bengali. Technically these methods can be categorized into two groups: dictionary/thesaurus-based (one such example is edge counting-based) methods and corpus-based (one such method is information theory-based) methods (Li et al., 2003). Edge counting based methods use only **semantic links** and corpus based methods combine corpus statistics with **taxonomic distances**.

The objective of this work is to design a system to measure semantic similarity score between two Bengali tweets. We adopted a lexical based method; the words are grouped into clusters in terms of their senses along with their synonyms. Our proposed method centered on analyzing shared words similarity among tweets.

Partial Textual Entailment (PTE) is defined as a bidirectional relationship among a sentence/tweet pair. It defines partial/complete meaning inference from one sentence/text from another text. We define these following 4 detailed PTE categories:

1. **Type 1**: If both the given texts are having same information and mean same, then it is a case of direct entailment and should be noted as (*X*=*X*).
2. **Type 2:** If the first/second given text has any extra information than the second/first text respectively then it is been categorized as PTE2. This type may have two variations like: (*X*=*X*+*Z* or *X*+*Z*=*X*).
3. **Type 3:** If the first given text has all the information of the second given text and has some extra information, then its 3rd variation of PTE, noted as (*X*+*Z*=*X*+*Y*).
4. **Type 4:** If both the given texts are not having common information then it is a *NOT-Entailed* case.

In all the above cases *X, Y, Z* represents a block of information in a given text.

The remainder of this paper is organized as follows. Section 2 describes corpus acquisition and annotation process, followed by section 3 introduced WordNet structure and the preprocessing step. Section 4 details experiment and evaluation setup. In the section 5 we reported performance of the baseline system. Section 6 is a discussions section on errors in results. Section 7 reviews related work and finally the section 8 concludes the paper.

Proceedings of Recent Advances in Natural Language Processing, pages 537–544,
Hissar, Bulgaria, Sep 7–9 2015.

2 Corpus Acquisition and Annotation

2.1 Corpus

To create Bengali tweet corpus for the proposed entailment problem we targeted tweets on specific contemporary popular topics. The rationale behind topic based tweets collection is to capture people's natural way of explaining an event using different synonymous words and varied syntactic formations while expressing the same meaning. A paid Twitter API[1] has been used for this purpose. Total 6500 Bengali tweets have been collected for the period of 2 months (August 2014-September 2014) on 25 different topics covering various domains like international and national politics, sports, natural disasters, political campaigns and elections. For example Jamayet Strike issue in Bangladesh, Cheat fund scam in Orissa and Bengal, Flood in Kashmir, Ukraine crisis, Knight Riders performance in IPL, Bi-election in West Bengal etc.

In few topics tweets were surprisingly higher, more than 2000, in some topics number of tweets were less or around 100.

2.2 Annotation and Corpus Statistics

For the manual annotation of semantic similarity among tweets, we involved two human annotators, who are native Bengali speakers but not linguist. An automatic cosine similarity method applied to same topic cluster to prune tweet pairs for the annotation from the corpus. An experimentally chosen threshold then set to create annotation pairs. Finally tweet pairs are being manually marked according to the PTE types. Annotation agreement has been measured on a small subset, randomly chosen on one topic: having 100 sentence pairs. We found the annotation consensus is of 0.86 *kappa* (Cohen J, 1960). One empirical question could be raised here that cosine similarity based pruning is a biased method, whereas empirically there are countless ways to express same meaning with different set of words (synonyms). To make sure we thoroughly analyzed our left out part of the corpora (left out after cosine pruning) and found only handful cases (3-4%) where people use different wordings altogether.

The annotation process produced a set of 804 tweet pairs, among them 350 tweet pairs were found as entailed and 454 tweets pair annotated as negative cases. The exact distribution of the different PTE classes in the annotated data is shown in following table 1.

TWT pairs	PTE types			
	type 01	type 02	type 03	type 04
804	350 (43.5%)	94 (11.69%)	74 (9.20%)	286 (35.57%)

Table 1: Distribution of tweet pairs in PTE classes

It could be noticed that there are significant presence of PTE 2 and 3 classes in the real corpus, whereas the majority class is till the direct entailment case. Now an argument could be raised that why these negative examples i.e. PTE-04 type is so essential to include. The rationale is, these negative examples are so important because this is the exclusion set made by annotators despite of high cosine similarity value with their peers. The average cosine similarities score of the negative examples are 0.25 and for PTE-03 is **0.35**. Ranges and average cosine similarity scores on the golden set is reports in the Table 2. For example:

বৃহস্পতি ও রোববার হরতাল ডেকেছে জামায়াত

ENG: *Thursday and Sunday Jamayet called strike.*

সিরাজগঞ্জে জামায়াতের নিরুত্তাপ হরতাল

ENG: *Jamayet called strike is peacefully in Shirajganj.*

Cosine similarity: 0.516

SN	Types	Cosine Similarity	
		Ranges	Avg.
1	Entailed	> 0.70	0.70
2	Not-Entailed	< 0.70	0.35
3	PTE-type 1	> 0.70	0.70
4	PTE- type 2	0.40 - 0.69	0.46
5	PTE- type 3	0.30 - 0.39	0.35
6	PTE- type 4	< 0.30	0.25

Table 2: Ranges of cosine similarity scores

3 Bengali WordNet

WordNet is a lexical semantic network to hold semantic relations like synonyms and word-senses as the nodes of the network and relations of the synonyms and word-senses are the edges of the network. In WordNet, meaning of each word is represented by a unique word-sense and a set of its synonyms called synset. We have collected the Bengali WordNet developed by Das and Bandyopadhyay as described in (Das and Bandyopadhyay 2010), consists total 12K numbers of synsets.

3.1 Pre-Processing

Text pre-processing is a vital pre-requisite while working with noisy social media text. Pre-

[1] http://www.tweetarchivist.com

processing involves splitting tweet into valid tokens: words and symbols, stemming, moving out stop words and part-of-speech tagging. The CMU tweet tokenizer (Gimpel et al., 2011) has been used here. Although it is primarily developed for English but also works well for other languages like Bengali. We used the Bengali stop word list, made available publicly by ISI Kolkata[2]. For the POS tagging the system developed by (Dandapat et al., 2007) has been used. Although the POS tagger is not trained on social media text and accuracy of the tagger on tweet has not been measured. This is something we would like to do next.

To trim all the surface word forms into corresponding root we developed one simple rule based Bengali Stemmer. Our stemmer concentrated on framing rules for stemming word categories like noun, verb adverb and adjectives. To frame the rules for stripping suffixes and prefixes we drew inspirations and knowledge from (Dash, 2014) and (Das and Bandyopadhyay, 2010).

3.2 Similarity Computation

We devised two kinds of similarity measurement methods for word level then accumulated those word-level similarities to sentence level.

3.2.1 Computation of Word Similarity

Study from different psychological experiments demonstrates that semantic similarity is obviously context-dependent (Medin et al., 1993), (Tversky, 1977). Meaning of a word in sentence is context-dependent, which effects semantic similarity. For example,

খাওয়ার আগে হাত ভালো করে ধুয়ে নেবে

ENG: Before the meal, wash hands properly

রিয়ানুজ এর হত্যাকান্ডে ওর ও হাত ছিল

ENG: He was also involved in the Riyanuj murder case.

Two above cited sentences have a common word "হাত/hand", but the word meaning is different in two sentences. In the first sentence "হাত" implies a part of human body and in 2nd sentence "হাত" implies association/involvement in one event.

For the semantic similarity calculation among two given words w_1 and w_2, we computed a scalar distance of these words in the meaning-spaces based on the synsets of these words extracted from the WordNet. If w_1 and w_2 both belong to same sysnset i.e. w_1 is a synonym of w_2 or vice versa, then the distance (d) between w_1 and w_2 is 0 and the semantic similarity score is 1, otherwise, the distance (d) between w_1 and w_2 is 1 and semantic similarity score is 0.

$$\text{Sim}(w_1, w_2) = \begin{cases} 1 & (\textit{if } d = 0) \\ 0 & (\text{if } d = 1) \end{cases} \quad (1)$$

For example:

w_1: অভিজ্ঞ (Experienced)

w_2: পারদর্শী (Expert)

Calculated semantic similarity score is 1.

3.2.2 Sentence Similarity Computation

For the sentence level similarity calculation we performed two sets of experiments. One with fine-grained entailment PTE classes i.e. the 4 classes and the other is a binary classification task: entailed or not entailed.

To determine the semantic similarity score of two given tweets A and B, we first pre-processed the tweets as described in the section 2.2 and calculated the length of tweets. Say, x is the length of tweet A and y is the length of tweet B. Then a semantic similarity matrix R[x,y] has been developed of each pair of words w_i and w_j where i and j are the indices of words. If a word at any position in A is not available in the WordNet, we computed the word similarity based on presence of same word in B. If such a word from A gets complete word match with any word in B, then similarity score is 1 between the words else 0. For example names and abbreviations like স. পা (Samajbadi Party), বিজেপি (BJP) which are the abbreviations of political party name, are not available in WordNet. Their similarity measured based on character matching of each word in the tweets.

Every token of tweet A represents a row and every token of tweet B represents a column in the semantic similarity relative matrix R[x,y].Figure 1 1illustrates an example similarity matrix representation of two example tweets as cited below. Each cell represents the word level similarity scores. For example:

সাঈদীর আমৃত্যু কারাদণ্ড প্রদান করায় হরতাল ডেকেছে জামায়াত

ENG: Jamayet called strike on the lifetime imprisonment issue of Sighdi.

জামায়াতের বনধ চলছে, সাঈদীর আজীবন কারাদণ্ড দেওয়ার প্রতিবাদে

ENG: Jamayet's strike is going on, in protest of Sighdi's lifetime imprisonment.

Computed semantic similarity score is 0.923

[2]http://www.isical.ac.in/~clia/resources.html

	সাঙ্গীদী Sighdi	আমৃত্যু Life-Time	কারাদণ্ড Impris-onment	প্রদান Anou-nced	হরতাল Strike	জামায়াত Jama-yet
জামায়াত Jama-yet	0	0	0	0	0	1
বনধ Strike	0	0	0	0	1	0
সাঙ্গীদী Sighdi	1	0	0	0	0	0
আজীবন Life-time	0	1	0	0	0	0
কারাদণ্ড Impris-onment	0	0	1	0	0	0
দেওয়া Anno-unce	0	0	0	1	0	0
প্রতিবাদ Prot-est	0	0	0	0	0	0

Figure1: Semantic similarity matrix between tweets.

Matching weight of tweet *A* computed by summing all the row wise cell weight and Matching weight of tweet *B* computed by summing all the column wise cell weight. In above cited example matching weight of both tweet *A* and *B* is 6. Following formula is used to determine the semantic similarity score between tweet *A* and tweet *B*.

$$\text{sim}(\text{A}, \text{B}) = \frac{\sum total\ matching\ weight(A,B)}{\sum length(A,B)} \quad (2)$$

An important point is that the proposed similarity value is based on each of the individual word similarity values, so that the overall similarity always reflects the influence of each word and its senses. According to the proposed semantic similarity score formulation, similarity values ranges from 0 to 1. If all the words of tweet *A* get semantically similar to all the words in tweet *B*, score will be 1, and will be 0 if there is no match.

4 Performance

System performance has been evaluated in two folds: with the binary (entailed or not) classes and with the fine-grained PTE classes. For performance evaluation we measured similarity score of all the tweet pairs in a class. Then experimentally, we set threshold to achieve optimum accuracy for each class. Decided threshold values are reported in the table 3.

SN	PTE	Threshold Range
1	**Entailed**	> 0.75
2	**Not-entailed**	< 0.75
3	**Type 1**	> 0.75
4	**Type 2**	0.2 - 0.29
5	**Type 3**	0.3 - 0.74
6	**Type 4**	< 0.2

Table 3: Threshold values of semantic similarity for Bengali tweets.

Accuracy results of our proposed system on binary class and fine-grained classes considering the pre-set threshold values are reported in Table 4 and 5.

Types	Precision	Recall	F1
Entailed	98.23	63.42	77.08
Not-Entailed	77.85	99.11	87.2
Avg.	88.04	81.265	82.14

Table 4: Performance on binary entailment classes

PTE classes	Precision	Recall	F1
PTE- 01	98.23	63.42	77.08
PTE- 02	26.15	36.17	30.35
PTE- 03	16.54	60.81	26.01
PTE-Type 04	86.36	53.14	65.8
Avg.	56.82	53.385	49.81

Table 5: Performance on the PTE classes

We setup another experiment on English tweets to evaluate the proposed approach and for the purpose of comparison. From SemEval 2015 task 1[3], we collected POS tagged corpus of tweet pairs. We involved two human annotators and tagged 639 tweets pair according to the PTE classes. To measure inter-annotator agreement, randomly 100 tagged pairs have been chosen. We found inter-annotator agreement is 0.709. Detail distribution of the tweet pair according to PTE classes is shown in table 6.

TWT pairs	PTE types			
	type 01	type 02	type 03	type 04
639	48 (7.5%)	61 (9.5%)	83 (12.9%)	447 (69.95%)

Table 6: English tweet pairs in PTE classes

Then we applied our proposed algorithm to determine the semantic similarity using English WordNet[4] (Boyd-Graber et al., 2006). All the POS tagged tweets are pre-processed by removing stop words[5] and lemmatization (Manning et al, 2014). System performance on these English tweet pairs measured in two folds: binary classes and fine-grained PTE classes. For each fold we achieved optimum accuracy with the pre-defined threshold values as mentioned in the table 7.

SN	PTE-Type	Threshold Range
1	**Entailed**	> 0.65
2	**Not-entailed**	< 0.65
3	**Type 1**	> 0.65
4	**Type 2**	0.5 to 0.64
5	**Type 3**	0.4 to 0.49
6	**Type 4**	< 0.4

Table 7: Threshold ranges for Eng. tweets.

[3] http://alt.qcri.org/semeval2015/task1/

[4] http://wordnetcode.princeton.edu/standoff-files/core-wordnet.txt

[5] http://www.lextek.com/manuals/onix/stopwords1.html

Performance of the proposed system on the SemEval English tweets is reported in the Table 8 and 9.

Types	Precision	Recall	F1
Entailed	22.75	79.16	35.34
Not-Entailed	97.88	78.17	86.92
Avg.	60.32	78.67	61.13

Table 8: Performance on the binary entailment classes for English tweets

PTE classes	Precision	Recall	F1
PTE- 01	31.40	79.16	44.97
PTE- 02	14.28	16.39	15.26
PTE- 03	13.63	14.45	14.03
PTE-Type 04	94.58	66.44	78.05
Avg.	38.47	44.11	38.07

Table 9: Performance on the PTE classes for English tweets

Results on English tweets are directly comparable with (Xu et al., 2014), named as MULTIP, make use of features like string comparison, POS and topic words. The reported final accuracy was 71.5 (F-Measure), whereas feature ablation shows string + POS features achieved 49.6 (F-measure), is directly comparable with our system's result: 61.13 on binary classes, while our system is only using WordNet based lexical features. Performance degradation on fine-grained classes is quite natural NLP phenomena. Integration of POS and topic words feature into our system could be straight-forward but extracting those features for Bengali tweets, demands research endeavors as those NLP tools are unavailable presently for the language.

5 Baseline System and Performance

SN	PTE	Threshold Range	F1
1	Entailed	> 0.75	72.89
2	Not-entailed	< 0.75	84.7
3	Type 1	> 0.75	73.48
4	Type 2	0.2 - 0.29	4.60
5	Type 3	0.3 - 0.74	11.9
6	Type 4	< 0.2	75.87

Table 10: Baseline system Performance on the PTE classes for Bengali tweets.

We have developed a very basic system to categorize Bengali tweets according to the defined PTE classes. Two tweets compared using only word matching and without WordNet information. This simple method returns a similarity score among two tweets. We calculated similarity score for all the PTE class tweets and experimentally set threshold for each class to achieve highest accuracy. Threshold values for each class and the accuracy of the system reported in table 10.

Performance of the proposed system over the baseline system shows better accuracy and also clarifying the fact that PTE recognition is more challenging than the classical unidirectional textual entailment recognition.

6 Discussion

System's poor performance on the fine-grained classes is a natural phenomenon for any NLP system. This is an ongoing work. Here in this section we are discussing on challenges related with the PTE classes.

Let us first explain why PTE classes identification is required. Common information boundary detection is essential for various applications for example multi-document summarization (MDS). A MDS needs to remove common information chunks before the aggregation.

Indeed automatic PTE detection for social media text is a challenging problem. Moreover additional NLP resources for a resource scarced language like Bengali are not well developed. Looking at the error types we decided to go for a system can take both the feature input: lexical and syntactic, but dependency parser development for Bengali tweets is a separate problem altogether.

Confusion matrix is drawn for Bengali tweets (Figure 2) and English tweets (Figure 3) to understand overlap between PTE classes and it has been observed PTE02-PTE03 are closely overlapped with each other on both the data set.

		System tagged				
		PTE 01	PTE 02	PTE 03	PTE 04	Total
Golden	PTE 01	222	03	125	0	350
	PTE 02	2	34	43	15	94
	PTE 03	2	18	45	9	74
	PTE 04	0	75	59	152	286
Total		226	130	272	176	804

Figure 2: Confusion matrix for Bengali tweets.

		System tagged				
		PTE 01	PTE 02	PTE 03	PTE 04	Total
Golden	PTE 01	38	8	1	1	48
	PTE 02	41	10	7	3	61
	PTE 03	42	16	12	13	83
	PTE 04	46	36	68	297	447
Total		167	70	88	314	639

Figure 3: Confusion matrix for English tweets.

7 Related Works

Automatic detection of textual entailment is a well-studied discipline, but most of the endeavors so far concentrated on English, almost no work on Indian languages especially on Bengali. There are many approaches to measure semantic similarity of words and sentences based on simple organizational schemes like Dictionary to complex organizational schemes like WordNet [Fellbaum, 2010] and ConceptNet [Liu et al., 2004]. The model proposed by [Tversky, 1977] is one of the early works in this area.

Technically these methods can be categorized into two groups: edge counting-based (or dictionary/thesaurus-based) methods and information theory-based (or corpus-based) methods (Li et al., 2003). Among two approaches, very less research work done on edge counting based method. Rada et al. (Rada, R et al., 1989), proposed a metric called distance, which determines the average minimum path length over all pair wise combinations of nodes between two subsets of nodes. Distance measure has been used to assess the conceptual distance between sets of concepts when used on a semantic net of hierarchical relations and represents the relatedness of two words

Due to the specific applications of edge counting based method like medical semantic nets (Li et al., 2003), most of the research on semantic similarity followed information theory based method (Resnik, 1993a) work is the first work on information theory based system which proposed modeled the selectional behavior of a predicate as its distributional effect on the conceptual classes of its arguments. This model experiment result suggests that many lexical relationships are better viewed in terms of underlying conceptual relationships. In a later work (Resnik, 1993b) focuses on two selectional preferences and semantic similarity as information-theoretic relationships involving conceptual classes and demonstrates the applicability of these relations to measure semantic similarity between two words. A model proposed by (Lee et al., 1993) also measured the distance of the nodes using edge weights between adjacent nodes in a graph as an estimator of semantic similarity. The work by (Richardson et al., 1994) has proposed a WordNet based scheme for Hierarchical Conceptual Graphs (HCG) to measure semantic similarity between words. System proposed by (Li et al., 2006), uses a semantic-vector approach to measure sentence similarity. Sentences are transformed into feature vectors having individual words from the sentence pair as a feature set. System proposed (Liu et al., 2008) an approach to determine sentence similarity, which takes into account both semantic information and word order. They define semantic similarity of sentence 1 relative to sentence 2 as the ratio of the sum of the word similarity weighted by information content of words in sentence 1 to the overall information content included in both sentences. The method proposed by (Liu et al., 2013) presents an information theory based approach of calculating the similarity between very short texts and sentences using WordNet, common-sense knowledge base and human intuition.

For Bengali text the work by (Sinha et al., 2012) design and develop a Bangla lexicon based on semantic similarity among Bangla words from Samsad Samarthasabdokosh. The lexicon is hierarchically organized into categories and subcategories. The words are grouped into clusters along with their synonyms. Weighted edges between different types of words related to same or different concepts or categories exist, denoting the semantic distance between them. (Sinha et al., 2014) proposed a hierarchically organized semantic lexicon in Bangla and also a graph based edge-weighting approach to measure semantic similarity between two Bangla words.

Our work is on information theory based method rather edge counting based method. Edge counting method is expedient for particular applications with constrained taxonomies (Li et al., 2003). In this paper, our work explains an approach to determine semantic relatedness between any two tweets.

8 Conclusion and Future Work

This paper presents an initial approach to measure semantic similarity between two Bengali tweets, based on the words meanings. Bengali tweets are less noisy in nature compared to English. In general people do use less abbreviated forms ('gr8' for great), word play ('goooood' for good) and etc., but Romanization / transliterated writing and code-mixing is very much prominent in Indian social media. Even romanization of Indian languages has no writing standard. People are literally whimsical about spelling over social media; for example pyari (beloved) could be written in various phonetically similar spellings: pyaari, payari, piari, and etc. We are currently working on PTE detection on code-mixed Bengali tweets.

References

A Das and S. Bandyopadhyay, "Morphological Stemming Cluster Identification for Bangla", In Knowledge Sharing Event-1: Task 3: Morphological Analyzers and Generators, Mysore, January, 2010.

Boyd-Graber, J., Fellbaum, C., Osherson, D., and Schapire, R. (2006). "Adding dense, weighted connections to WordNet." In: Proceedings of the Third Global WordNet Meeting, Jeju Island, Korea, January 2006.

Cohen J.,"A coefficient of agreement for nominal scales". Educational and Psychological Measurement.1960; 20 (1):37–46.

D.L. Medin, R.L. Goldstone, and D. Gentner, "Respects for Similarity," Psychological Rev., vol. 100, no. 2, pp. 254-278, 1993.

Dandapat S., Sarkar S. and Basu A "Auto-matic Part-of-Speech Tagging for Bengali: An approach for Morphologically Rich Languages in a Poor Resource Scenario". In Proceedings of the Association of Computational Linguistics (ACL 2007), Prague, Czech Republic.

Das, A. and Bandyopadhyay, S. "Semanticnet-perception of human pragmatics". In Proceedings of the 2nd Workshop on Cognitive Aspects of the Lexicon, pages 2–11, Beijing, China, 2010.

Fellbaum, C. (2010). "WordNet." *Theory and Application of Ontology: Computer Applications.* New York: Springer, 231-243.

Hongzhe Liu, Pengfei Wang, "Assessing Sentence Similarity Using WordNet based Word Similarity", JOURNAL OF SOFTWARE, VOL. 8, NO. 6, JUNE 2013.

Kevin Gimpel, Nathan Schneider, Brendan O'Connor, Dipanjan Das, Daniel Mills, Jacob Eisenstein, Michael Heilman, DaniYogatama, Jeffrey Flanigan, and Noah A. Smith, "Part-of-Speech Tagging for Twitter: Annotation, Features, and Experiments", In Proceedings of ACL 2011.

Lee, J., Kim, M., and Lee, Y. (1993). "Information retrieval based on conceptual distance in is-a hierarchy". Journal of documentation, 49(2):188–207.

Liu, H. and Singh, P. (2004). "Conceptnet—a practical commonsense reasoning tool-kit".BT technology journal, 22(4):211–226.

Manjira Sinha, Abhik Jana, Tirthankar Dasgupta, Anupam Basu, "A New Semantic Lexicon and Similarity Measure in Bangla", Proceedings of the 3rd Workshop on Cognitive Aspects of the Lexicon (CogALex-III), pages 171–182,COLING 2012, Mumbai, December 2012.

Manjira Sinha,Tirthankar Dasgupta, Abhik Jana, Anupam Basu, "Design and Development of a Bangla Semantic Lexicon and Semantic Similarity Measure", International Journal of Computer Applications (0975 – 8887), Volume 95– No.5, June 2014.

Manning, Christopher D., Surdeanu, Mihai, Bauer, John, Finkel, Jenny, Bethard, Steven J., and McClosky, David. 2014. The Stanford CoreNLP Natural Language Processing Toolkit. In Proceedings of 52nd Annual Meeting of the Association for Computational Linguistics: System Demonstrations, pp. 55-60

Niladri Sekhar Dash, "A Descriptive Study of Bengali Words" Cambridge University Press, December 2014.

Rada, R., Mili, H., Bicknell, E., and Blettner, M. (1989). "Development and application of a metric on semantic nets". Systems, Man and Cybernetics, IEEE Transactions on, 19(1):17–30.

Resnik, P. "Selection and information: a class-based approach to lexical relationships". IRCS Technical Reports Series, page 200, 1993.

Resnik, P. "Semantic classes and syntactic ambiguity". In Proc. of ARPA Workshop on Human Language Technology, pages 278–283, 1993.

Richardson, R., Smeaton, A., and Murphy, J. (1994). "Using wordnet as a knowledge base for measuring semantic similarity between words". Technical report, Technical Report Working Paper CA-1294, School of Computer Applications, Dublin City University.

Sumit Bhagwani, Shrutiranjan Satapathy, Harish Karnic, "sranjans: Semantic Textual Similarity using Maxi mal Weighted Bipartite Graph Matching", First Joint Conference on Lexical and Computational Semantics (*SEM), pages 579–585, Montr´eal, Canada, June 7-8, 2012.

Tversky, A. (1977). "Features of similarity". Psychological review, 84(4):327.

Xiao-Ying Liu, Yi-Ming Zhou, Ruo-Shi Zheng. "Measuring Semantic Similarity Within Sentences". Proceedings of the Seventh International Conference on Machine Learning and Cybernetics, Kunming, 2008.

Xu, W., Ritter, A., Callison-Burch, C., Dolan, W. B., and Ji, Y. (2014). Extracting lexically divergent paraphrases from Twitter. Transactions of the Association for Computational Linguistics (TACL), 2(1).

Yuhua Li, David McLean, Zuhair A. Bandar, James D. OShea, and Keeley Crockett. "Sentence Similarity Based on Semantic Nets and Corpus Statistics". IEEE Transections on Knowledge and Data Engineering, Vol. 18, No. 8, 2006.

Yuhua Li, Zuhair A. Bandar, and David McLean, "An Approach for Measuring Semantic Similarity between Words Using Multiple Information Sources", IEEE Transactions On Knowledge And Data Engineering, vol. 15, no. 4, july/august 2003

Ordering adverbs by their scaling effect on adjective intensity

Josef Ruppenhofer[*], Jasper Brandes[*], Petra Steiner[*], Michael Wiegand[†]
[*]Hildesheim University
Hildesheim, Germany
{ruppenho|brandesj|steinerp}@uni-hildesheim.de
[†]Saarland University
Saarbrücken, Germany
michael.wiegand@lsv.uni-saarland.de

Abstract

In recent years, theoretical and computational linguistics has paid much attention to linguistic items that form scales. In NLP, much research has focused on ordering adjectives by intensity (*tiny* < *small*). Here, we address the task of automatically ordering English adverbs by their intensifying or diminishing effect on adjectives (e.g. `extremely` *small* < `very` *small*).

We experiment with 4 different methods: 1) using the association strength between adverbs and adjectives; 2) exploiting scalar patterns (such as *not only X but Y*); 3) using the metadata of product reviews; 4) clustering. The method that performs best is based on the use of metadata and ranks adverbs by their scaling factor relative to unmodified adjectives.

1 Introduction

Being able to recognize the intensity associated with scalar expressions is a basic capability needed for tackling any NLP task that can be reduced to textual entailment. For instance, as illustrated by de Marneffe et al. (2010), when interpreting dialogue (A: *Was it good?* B: *It was ok / great / excellent.*), a yes/no question involving a gradable predicate may require understanding the entailment relations between that predicate and another contained in the answer. Another application is within sentiment analysis, where assessing the strength of subjective expressions (e.g. *good* < *great* < *excellent*) is one of the central tasks besides subjectivity detection and polarity classification (Rill et al., 2012b; Sheinman et al., 2013; de Melo and Bansal, 2013; Ruppenhofer et al., 2014, *inter alia*). It is also well known that subjective adjectives are frequently modified by adverbs that increase (`very` *expensive*) or decrease (`fairly` *expensive*) their intensity. As Benamara et al. (2007) have shown, it is useful to take such adverbial intensification into account when predicting document-level sentiment scores. However, Benamara et al. (2007) used human-assigned scores to model adverbs' effect on adjectives.

As far as we know, there is no well-established automatic method that can determine for degree adverbs what their effect will be on the intensity of various adjectives. In this paper, we explore several methods on English data that might be used towards that purpose, evaluating them against a new gold standard data set that we collected. All new resources that were created in the context of our investigation will be made publicly available.

The remainder of this paper is structured as follows. We present our data in §2. We describe the construction of our gold standard in §3 and the methods we use in §4. This is followed by the presentation of our experiments and results in §5. We discuss related work in §6 and conclude in §7.

2 Data

For our experiments we use two large corpora (Table 1). The first is a large set of Amazon reviews, which consist of numerical star ratings and textual assessments. Since both express the writers' evaluation, they are strongly correlated. Accordingly, we project the numerical star ratings onto the adjectives and adverbs in the texts as intensity scores (cf. §4.2). Second, we also use the ukWaC webcorpus, which is even larger than the review corpus, as general language data on which we compute association measures (cf. §4.1) and which we mine for linguistic patterns (cf. §4.3, §4.4).

Corpora	Tokens	Reference
Amazon reviews	~1.06 B	Jindal and Liu (2008)
ukWaC	~2.25 B	Baroni et al. (2009)

Table 1: Corpora used

Proceedings of Recent Advances in Natural Language Processing, pages 545–554,
Hissar, Bulgaria, Sep 7–9 2015.

3 Construction of human gold standard

To be able to assess adverb rankings produced by automatic methods, we collected human ratings for adverb and adjective combinations through an online survey. All combinations were rated individually, in randomized order, under conditions intended to minimize the effects of bias, habituation, fatigue etc. on the results. Participants were asked to use a horizontal slider, dragging it in the desired direction, representing polarity, and releasing the mouse at the desired intensity, ranging from -100 to $+100$. To indicate the intended word sense of each item, the scale was labeled accordingly. For instance, we specified that *cool* should be interpreted in terms of Temperature (*cool day*) rather than Desirability (*cool app*).

Through Amazon Mechanical Turk (AMT), we recruited subjects with the following qualifications: US residency, a HIT-approval rate of at least 97%, and 500 prior completed HITs. We collected 20 ratings per item but had to exclude some participants' answers as unusable, which reduced our sample for some items.

3.1 Adjectives

The adjectives we used – shown in Table 2 – cover four semantic areas, two of them (more or less) objective, namely Duration and Temperature, and two of them subjective, namely Quality and Intelligence. They are a subset of those used by Ruppenhofer et al. (2014) for ordering adjectives by intensity (cf. §4.1). Following Paradis (1997; 2001), we classify adjectives into three types. **Scalar adjectives** are ones that combine with scalar degree adverbs (fairly *long*, very *good*, terribly *nasty*). The mode of oppositeness that characterizes scalar adjectives is antonymy (e.g. *good - bad*). **Extreme adjectives** combine with reinforcing totality adverbs (absolutely *terrible*, totally *brilliant*, utterly *disastrous*). Like scalar adjectives, these adjectives are also antonymic (*hot - cold*) and they are conceptualized according to a scale. However, extreme adjectives do not represent a range on a scale but an (end-)point on the scale. The third type, **limit adjectives**, also combines with totality adverbs (completely *dead*, absolutely *true*, almost *identical*). This type differs from the others in that it is not associated with a scale but conceptualized in terms of either-or. It is not represented in our data elicitation but it is used by one of the automatic ranking methods (cf. §4.1, §5.1.)

Adjective	Scale	Polarity	Type
dumb	Intelligence	neg	scalar
smart	Intelligence	pos	scalar
brainless	Intelligence	neg	extreme
brainy	Intelligence	pos	extreme
bad	Quality	neg	scalar
good	Quality	pos	scalar
mediocre	Quality	neg	scalar
super	Quality	pos	extreme
cool	Temperature	neg	scalar
warm	Temperature	pos	scalar
frigid	Temperature	neg	extreme
hot	Temperature	pos	extreme
short	Duration	neg	scalar
long	Duration	pos	scalar
brief	Duration	neg	scalar
lengthy	Duration	pos	scalar

Table 2: Adjectives used and their classification

Maximizer	Booster
absolutely	awfully
completely	extremely
perfectly	very
quite	highly
Moderator	**Diminisher**
quite	slightly
fairly	a little
pretty	somewhat
Approximator	**Control**
almost	*none*

Table 3: Adverbs used and their classification

3.2 Adverbs

The adverbs in our surveys as well as their classification are inspired by Paradis (1997). The adverbs belong to five types plus a control condition as shown in Table 3. As Table 4 shows, maximizers and approximators are totality adverbs, they target adjectives that belong to the limit or extreme class. The other adverb classes are scalar adverbs that target scalar adjectives. In the control condition (*none*), subjects rate the unmodified adjective.

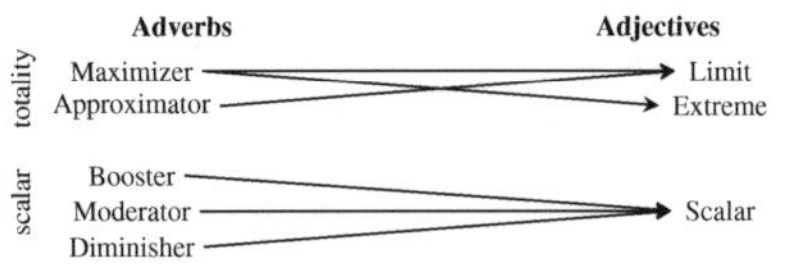

Table 4: Prototypical associations between adverb and adjective types according to Paradis (1997)

3.3 Design

We designed four parallel surveys, each eliciting data for degree modification of four adjectives, to be completed by non-overlapping sets of participants (enforced via AMT Worker IDs). In each survey, participants first were asked for metadata such as age, residency, native language etc. Subsequently, pairs of main and distractor block followed until at the end feedback on difficult survey items was solicited. Each main block used one adjective, which participants first had to rate unmodified before giving ratings for seven combinations of the adjective with half the available adverbs.

Each main block was followed by a distractor block in which participants had to match verbs to related adjectives. As the combinations of an adjective with all adverbs were spread out over two main blocks, each survey had a total of 8 main blocks. The adverbs used with the first main block for an adjective were sampled randomly from our list, the remaining adverbs were put into the second main block featuring the adjective.

Note that we elicited data for all possible combinations of adjective and degree adverb. As shown by Desagulier (2014) and Erman (2014) for moderators and maximizers, respectively, some adverb-adjective combinations are highly entrenched, while others are likely to be rare or unfamiliar and thus possibly more difficult to rate.

3.4 Final ranking

Table 5 shows the ranking of adverb-adjective combinations, generalized over all 16 adjectives. The score per combination is the sum of all absolute scores for the adverb with any adjective across all participants, renormalized into the range [0,100]. Note that rank 8 is occupied by the cases where the relevant adjectives are not modified by any adverb. The results closely match expectations based on linguistic theory. We have booster and maximizer adverbs occupying ranks higher than the unmodified adjective, while we find moderators and diminishers occupying lower ranks. The ranking for the ambiguous *quite* seems to reflect its moderator use more than its maximizer use. The ordering among the moderators (*quite* > *pretty* > *fairly*) matches that reported as expert linguistic analysis by Paradis (1997, 148-155).

We next apply the method for building a gold standard described above to the combinations of all adverbs with each single adjective. The correlations between the 14 different resulting adverb rankings are high throughout with Spearman values >0.900. This argues that the ranking that we get when summing over all adjectives (cf. Table 5) also applies to the adjectives individually.

Finally, we constructed a relative ranking based

#	score	adverb	#	score	adverb
1	91.1	extremely †	9	59.9	quite †,○
2	89.2	absolutely ⋆	10	52.5	pretty ○
3	84.2	completely ⋆	11	42.1	fairly ○
4	79.3	highly †	12	35.9	somewhat ▷
5	78.6	very †	13	30.5	slightly ▷
6	75.2	awfully †	14	27.4	almost ♣
7	74.8	perfectly ⋆	15	26.7	a little ▷
8	62.7	*none*			

Table 5: Gold standard ranking of adverb-adjective intensity, based on absolute scores (†=maximizer, ⋆=booster, ○=moderator, ▷=diminisher, ♣=approximator)

on the number of raters for whom the combination of adverb A with a given adjective had a higher score than the combination involving adverb B. That method produces essentially the same result: the Spearman rank correlation with the absolute ranking in Table 5 is ρ=0.993. Due to space limitations, we only report results relative to the absolute gold standard in the remainder of the paper.

In order to be able to experiment with more than the 14 prototypical and frequent adverbs that we could collect ratings for, we make use of the intensity ratings for 93 adverbs provided by Taboada et al.'s (2011) SoCaL resource. While various lexical resources provide polarity scores for nouns, verbs, and adjectives (Wilson et al., 2005; Thelwall et al., 2010; Taboada et al., 2011, *inter alia*), few resources cover and assign scores to degree adverbs. The adverb ranking obtained from the SoCaL resource for our 14 adverbs correlates strongly with our two gold standards, with coefficients of 0.969 against the absolute gold standard and 0.976 against the relative one. This gives us confidence that we can use the SoCaL ratings as an extended gold standard. Note that the set of 93 adverbs from SoCaL contains many adverbs that are less frequent and less grammaticized than the 14 adverbs from the smaller set.

4 Methods

Our methods to determine the intensifying effect of adverbs on adjectives are all corpus-based.

4.1 Collostructional analysis (Collex)

Our first method, **distinctive-collexeme analysis** (**Collex**) (Gries and Stefanowitsch, 2004) has previously been successfully applied to the intensity ordering of both subjective and objective adjectives (Ruppenhofer et al., 2014), with stable correlation results as evaluated against a human gold standard (Spearman's ρ of 0.732-0.837).

For the task of ordering adverbs according to their intensifying effect on an adjective, we assume that adverbs with different intensifying effects co-occur with different types of adjectives, as shown by Table 4 in §3.2. We identify two different constructions an adverb can occur in: modification of scalar adjectives such as *dumb* or modification of limit and extreme adjectives such as *brainless*. Booster, moderator, and diminisher adverbs co-occur with scalar adjectives (e.g. `very/rather` *dumb*), while limit and extreme adjectives are modified by maximizer and approximator adverbs (e.g. `absolutely/almost` *brainless*). Our hypothesis is that if adverb A has a higher preference for the limit and extreme adjective construction than adverb B, then A has a greater scaling effect than B. An adjective's preference for occurring in either construction is used to derive an ordering of the given adverbs by their effect on the intensity of adjectives. This preference is determined using the Fisher exact test (Fisher, 1922; Pedersen, 1996). It makes no distributional assumptions and does not require a minimum sample size. The direction in which observed frequencies differ from expected ones is taken to indicate the preference for one of the two constructions and is measured by the p-value.

We ran a distinctive-collexeme analysis for both the smaller and the larger set of degree adverbs on ukWaC with two different settings. First, we used the 16 adjectives from the survey differentiated into the two types *scalar* and *extreme* as presented in Table 2. We refer to the output as $\textbf{Collex}_{surveyAdj}$. Second, we used a larger set of 188 adjectives culled from the literature (Paradis, 1997; Erman, 2014; Desagulier, 2014). The adjectives are distributed across the three classes as follows: 26 extreme (**xtrm**), 123 limit (**lim**) and 39 **scalar**. We refer to the output as $\textbf{Collex}_{moreAdj}$.

4.2 Mean star ratings (MeanStar)

Another method we evaluate employs **Mean star ratings** (**MeanStar**) from product reviews as described by Rill et al. (2012b). Unlike Collex, this method uses no linguistic properties of words or phrases. Instead, it derives intensity values for words or phrases in review texts from the numeric star ratings that reviewers (manually) assign to products. The star ratings encode a polar score on the document level. Since the ratings are not binary but on a five-point scale, they can also be used as source for deriving intensity information. The basic idea is to count how many instances of a word or phrase occur in reviews with a given star rating (score) within a review corpus.

Following Rill et al. (2012b)'s model for simple adjectives, we generically define the intensity score for a word or phrase as the mean of the star ratings $SR_i = \frac{\sum_{j=1}^{n} S_j^i}{n}$, where i designates a distinct word or phrase, j is the j-th occurrence of the word or phrase, S_j^i is the star rating associated with i in j, and n is the number of observed instances of i. We experiment with three methods that are based on MeanStar. They differ a) in how the item *i* that is to be scored is defined (as a word or phrase) and b) in whether the resulting scores are used directly to generate a ranking or only after further processing.

Adverbs only In the simplest application of MeanStar, we calculate for each adverb the average star level of the reviews it occurs in, and then rank the adverbs by these scores.

Adjective-specific In a different mode of using the star-based scores, we do not build a general ordering of adverbs. Instead, we only order combinations of adverbs with specific adjectives. Accordingly, we perform a rank correlation of adverb-adjective combinations against the gold standard *per adjective* and report the average of the absolute Spearman rank correlation results.

Scaling factor The third method, **Scaling**, builds a global ranking of adverbs by comparing the MeanStar scores of adverb-adjective combinations to those of unmodified adjectives. The benefit of this is that we can make use of each adverb-adjective combination independently of any other and do not need to rely only on adjectives that are attested with all or many of the adverbs that we need to rank, which is rarely the case. The algorithm works as presented in Algorithm 1.

An important facet of the algorithm is the filtering in step 4. In order to get clearly polar cases, we retain only combinations with a score >=3.75 ('positive') or with a score <=2.5 ('negative'). It is known that the average review tends to have a slightly higher score than three. For that reason, the threshold for positive reviews is slightly more extreme than that for negative reviews. We discard combinations: 1) that are observed only once; 2) where the adjective contains characters other than letters or a hyphen; or 3) where the adjective never occurs unmodified in the corpus.

Algorithm 1 Rank by scaling factor (sf)

```
1: take a stratified random sample of n items from the set of adverbs
2: for each adverb adv in the sample do
3:     retrieve all combinations of adv with any adjective
4:     filter combinations
5:     sort combinations
6:     for combination in top k combinations do
7:         calculate scaling factor relative to unmodified adjective
8:         classify as intensifying or diminishing
9:     end for
10:     if length(intensifying_uses) > length(diminishing_uses) then
11:         if length(pos_intensifying_uses) / length(neg_intensifying_uses)
    > Threshold then
12:             average_sf=mean(pos_intensifying_uses)
13:         else:
14:             average_sf=mean(pos_intensifying_uses+neg_intensifying_uses)
15:         end if
16:     else if length(diminishing_uses) > length(intensifying_uses) then
17:         if length(neg_diminishing_uses) / length(pos_diminishing_uses)
    > Threshold then
18:             average_sf=mean(neg_diminishing_uses)
19:         else
20:             average_sf=mean(pos_diminishing_uses+neg_diminishing_uses)
21:         end if
22:     end if
23: end for
24: rank adverbs by their average scaling factor (average_sf)
```

In steps 7 and 8, we look at the *k* most frequent combinations per adverb. For each combination, we calculate a scaling factor in the interval [-1,+1] relative to the unmodified adjective. For intensifying adverbs we measure what fraction of the distance from the simple adjective to the highest score (5 for positive adjectives) or lowest score (1 for negative adjectives) the adjective has been 'pushed' by the adverb. For diminishing adverbs, we measure what fraction of the unmodified adjective's distance to the neutral score (3) the adjective has been 'pushed'. For each adverb, we keep track of the scaling factors for all *k* combinations. The classification as intensifying or diminishing is corpus-driven: an adverb in combination with a specific adjective is intensifying/diminishing, if the combination's value is more/less extreme than that of the unmodified adjective.

In lines 10-22, we perform two levels of checks before deciding how to assign the final scaling factor to the adverb. On the first level, we discard whichever type of uses is in the minority, intensifying or diminishing uses. On the second level, we identify whether the uses retained in the previous step have mostly been observed with positive adjectives or with negative ones. If the quotient exceeds a certain threshold, we again choose to ignore the evidence from the minority class. With both checks, the idea is to obtain a clearer signal of what the adverb's effect is.

Finally, we rank all adverbs by their aggregate scaling factor and perform a rank correlation test against a gold standard.

	Adjectives in X and Y	
Pattern	**Any**	**Identical**
X(,) and in fact Y	0	0
X(,) or even Y	15	3
X(,) if not Y	64	1
be X(,) but not Y	60	5
not only X(,) but Y	7	0
not X, let alone Y	0	0
not Y, not even X	0	0
$\sum$	146	9

Table 6: Phrasal patterns in the ukWaC

4.3 Horn patterns

Horn (1976) put forth a set of **pattern-based diagnostics** for acquiring information about the relative intensity of linguistic items that express different degrees of some shared property. The complete set is shown in the first column of Table 6. For all patterns, the item in the Y slot needs to be stronger than that in the X slot. The two slots can be filled by different types of expressions such as nouns, verbs, and adjectives. We are interested in the case, shown in sentences 1 and 2, where adverb-adjective combinations occupy both slots.

(1) This is [`very` *good*], if not [`extremely` *good*].

(2) It's not just [`mildly` *entertaining*] but [`very` *entertaining*].

As shown above, we can apply Horn patterns to our task by requiring X and Y to be adverb-adjective combinations where the adjective is identical and the adverbs are two distinct items from the 93 adverbs from SoCaL. Based on the frequencies with which different adverbs occur in the X and Y slots, we can induce a ranking of the adverbs. Table 6 shows the number of matches one gets when querying the ukWaC for instances of the 7 patterns with the above constraints. We get only 146 unique hits overall. Moreover, we get only 9 where the adjective in slot X is identical to the one in slot Y. The coverage problem we observe is familiar from earlier work on ordering adjectives, where it could be overcome through the use of web-scale n-grams and a sophisticated interpolation technique by de Melo and Bansal (2013). However, in the case of adverbs the problem is more severe. Furthermore, looking for the patterns in web-scale n-grams is not possible since the instances of these diagnostic patterns all exceed 5 tokens when X and Y are complex adjective phrases: at this time, no web-scale n-gram collection for n $>$ 5 is available.

4.4 Cluster analysis

Cluster analysis aims to group data objects into different groups based on object-specific features.

Gold	Configuration	Corr.
Ours	Collex$_{surveyAdj}$	0.055
	Collex$_{moreAdj-xtrm+scalar}$	-0.099
	Collex$_{moreAdj-lim+scalar}$	0.165
	Collex$_{moreAdj-xtrm+lim+scalar}$	0.191
SoCaL	Collex$_{surveyAdj}$	0.003
	Collex$_{moreAdj-xtrm+scalar}$	0.152
	Collex$_{moreAdj-lim+scalar}$	-0.188
	Collex$_{moreAdj-xtrm+lim+scalar}$	-0.154

Table 7: Spearman rank correlations for Collex

While it does not produce a ranking of adverbs according to their intensifying/diminishing effect, we can consider it a fallback method in case no robust ranking method can be found. The aim would be to obtain groups of adverbs that have a similar intensifying/diminishing effect on a modified adjective. Potentially, the clusters could subsequently be converted into a ranking (with tied ranks) by another method.

The features we use to cluster the adverbs are the co-occurrence frequencies with the top 35 adjectival collocates of each adverb, following Desagulier (2014). The adjectival collocates of each adverb are determined via Collexeme analysis (cf. Gries and Stefanowitsch, 2004). Furthermore, we use the *Canberra* distance measure (Lance and Williams, 1966) and *Ward.D* clustering algorithm (Ward, 1963), as this setting has produced clusters that are coherent with Paradis' (1997) classification of degree adverbs (Desagulier, 2014).

We performed hierarchical cluster analysis on both the 14 adverbs from our gold standard as well as on 93 single-term degree adverbs that are included in Taboada et al.'s (2011) SoCaL resource. We refer to the output as **Cluster**$_{surveyAdj}$ and **Cluster**$_{SoCaLAdj}$, respectively.

5 Experiments

For our evaluation, we compute the similarity between a gold standard ranking – either that based on our data elicitation (cf. Table 5), or that based on the degree adverbs in SoCaL (cf. §3.4) – and any other ranking that we are interested in, as Spearman's rank correlation coefficient (Spearman's ρ).

5.1 Collex

For the output of Collex, we constructed a ranking of the adverbs as follows: The adverb with the highest preference for extreme adjectives was placed at the top of the ranking. The remaining adverbs with preference for extreme adjectives were placed below that, ordered by descending p-values. Then, we continued with the adverb that had the lowest preference for scalar adjectives and added the remaining adverbs, placing the adverb with the highest preference for scalar adjectives at the bottom of the ranking. This approach of building a ranking has produced good results for the intensity ordering of adjectives (Ruppenhofer et al., 2014) and we adopt it with the idea of now exploiting the connection between adjectives and adverbs in the reverse direction.

The results of the pairwise Spearman rank correlations between the gold standard of either of the two adverb sets and the rankings derived from Collex are shown in Table 7. **Collex**$_{surveyAdj}$, the adverb ranking obtained from a distinctive-collexeme analysis performed on the 16 adjectives from our survey, produces no correlation with either gold standard. **Collex**$_{moreAdj}$, the adverb ranking derived from a distinctive-collexeme analysis ran on a larger set of adjectives, yields minimal positive and negative correlations against both gold standards. One way to interpret this result has to do with the associations between adjectives and adverbs as shown in Table (4). In the earlier work of Ruppenhofer et al. (2014) on ordering adjectives, maximizers and approximators were grouped as one pole of attraction for adjectives, and boosters, moderators, and diminishers as another. The gold ranking to be matched for adjectives has a relatively simple structure since extreme adjectives (e.g. *brilliant*) are simply more intensive than scalar adjectives (e.g. *smart*). When we go in the opposite direction, such a clear delimitation is not the case: as Table 5 shows, some boosters actually have a higher scaling effect than maximizers. Similarly, we have a problem in that approximators push intensity towards neutrality whereas maximizers push towards the extreme: Collex treats them as if they are pushing in the same direction. The structural properties of the adjective-adverb interaction may thus make Collex only suitable in one direction.

5.2 MeanStar

Table 8 shows the results for the three variants of MeanStar. Note that an asterisk in the last column marks experiments where results are averaged over 10 runs and each run is based on a stratified random sample of adverbs from SoCaL. The first four rows for **Adv** in Table 8 show the results for the adverb-only approach: while the cor-

Method	Configuration	Gold	Corr.	Adverbs
Adv	MeanStar$_{global-any}$	Ours	0.283	14
	MeanStar$_{global-title}$	Ours	0.446	14
	MeanStar$_{global-any}$	SoCaL	0.311	*30
	MeanStar$_{global-title}$	SoCaL	0.531	*30
Spec	MeanStar$_{specific-any}$	Ours	-0.091	14
	MeanStar$_{specific-title}$	Ours	0.203	14
Scaling	MeanStar$_{global-any}$	Ours	0.382	14
	MeanStar$_{global-title}$	Ours	0.787	14
	MeanStar$_{global-any}$	SoCaL	0.780	*30
	MeanStar$_{global-title}$	SoCaL	0.930	*30

Table 8: Spearman rank correlations for MeanStar
(* experiments involve adverbs randomly selected from SoCaL)

relation results are not very high, performance is better when using data from review titles alone (0.446 against our gold standard; 0.531 against SoCaL). This was to be expected since titles reflect the tenor of the star rating more directly than sentences in the body of a review.

The results for the adjective-specific variant of MeanStar are shown in the two rows marked **Spec**. We cannot evaluate against the larger set of adverbs in SoCaL because SoCaL contains no information on specific adverb-adjective combinations. For the results shown, we use only adverb-adjective combinations that occur at least twice. Regardless of whether we use only titles or full reviews, we face data sparsity problems as we do not see instances of all combinations between our adjectives and the adverbs. Coverage is better, if we use the reviews as a whole (11.5 vs. 4.4). By contrast, the correlation results, though low overall, are better if we use titles only (0.203 vs. -0.091). If we used the absolute values of the correlations, then the average correlation would be higher for full reviews (0.644 vs. 0.612).

As we can see, the Scaling method performs very well, even without having been optimized. For instance, the 2:1 margin for the second-level check is not based on any work with a development set but simply a rough guess. Omitting the second-level checks on steps 11 and 17 of the algorithm drops the score for **MeanStar**$_{global-title}$ with 30 random adverbs from 0.930 to 0.880 and for **MeanStar**$_{global-any}$ from 0.780 to 0.720, which are still good levels of performance.

5.3 Cluster analysis

To assess the quality of the clustering, we report on an external cluster validation performed against an expert classification of the adverbs. For the 14 gold standard adverbs we use the classification by Paradis (1997), while for the 93 adverbs from SoCaL (Taboada et al., 2011), we use

Degree adverbs	N Adverbs	N Clusters	ARI	Purity
Cluster$_{surveyAdj}$	14	5	0.572	0.857
Cluster$_{SoCaLAdj}$	93	5	-0.066	0.623

Table 9: External cluster evaluation for a cluster analysis based on Canberra distance measure and Ward.D clustering algorithm

a grouping of these adverbs into Paradis' (1997) five adverb classes that two of the authors worked out collaboratively. Results are shown in Table 9.

The quality of the clustering results is measured by the *adjusted Rand index* (ARI) and *Cluster purity* (Purity). ARI measures the accuracy of the clustering, that is the percentage of correctly clustered objects based on the given classes and corrects the basic Rand Index (RI) for chance (Hubert and Arabie, 1985). For Purity, in turn, we assign each cluster to the adverb class that is most frequent in the cluster. Then, the accuracy of this assignment, i.e. the percentage of the correctly assigned adverbs is measured (Manning et al., 2008, 356-360). Purity can take values between 0 and 1, where 0 represents a "bad clustering" and a value of 1 indicates a perfect fit with a given (manual) classification. For ARI, the interpretation of the [0,1] range is the same. However, ARI can sometimes produce negative values when the original RI is smaller than the expected index. These negative values also represent bad clusterings. It is easy for Purity to achieve a value of 1 - as is the case when each object has its own cluster (Manning et al., 2008, 357). We therefore report results for both evaluation metrics.

By using the top adjectival collocates of each adverb as clustering features, we get a good clustering for the 14 degree adverbs for which we elicited human ratings as compared to the classification of Paradis (1997). For the larger set of 93 adverbs from SoCaL, we obtain very poor results. Figure 1 illustrates the clustering result for the smaller set of adverbs, **Cluster**$_{surveyAdj}$.

5.4 Summary

We found the MeanStar method that computes a scaling factor to perform best. Unlike the adverb-only variant of MeanStar, it makes use of the fact that the score of an adverb-adjective combination also depends on the adjective. And unlike the adjective-specific version of MeanStar, it builds a global ranking and is able to combine evidence from adverb-adjective combinations independently of which other combinations have been

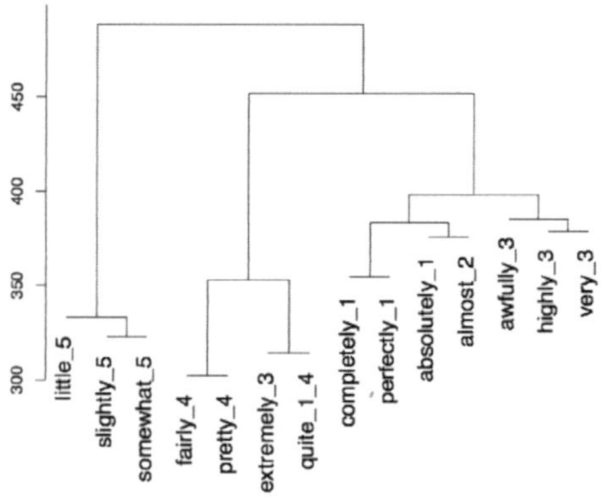

Figure 1: Dendrogram for the 14 adverbs from the survey. Indices show Paradis' (1997) classes.

observed. Somewhat surprisingly, the methods that are more directly grounded in linguistic theory performed worse (collostructional analysis) or proved unusable (Horn patterns). One possible reasons for the inferior Collex and clustering results may be that the relation between adverbs and adjectives is asymmetric to begin with, and easier to exploit in one direction than the other. Another is that the 5-way classification of adverbs and the assumptions about their common interaction with three types of adjectives cannot readily be extended beyond the set of well-known and highly grammaticized degree adverbs such as *very, quite, absolutely* to the much larger set of less grammaticized cases such as *mind-bogglingly* or *blisteringly*. The metadata approach, notably makes no assumptions about adverb or adjective classes.

6 Related work

Benamara et al. (2007) show the usefulness of taking adverbial intensification of adjectives into account when predicting document-level sentiment scores for news articles and blog posts. They divide adverbs into 5 classes based on the work of Quirk et al. (1985) and Bolinger (1972). The various scoring functions they explore for the adverb-adjective combinations are sensitive both to an adverb's class and to its score. The score of an adverb could lie between 0 and 1, with 0 meaning that the adverb has no impact on an adjective and 1 signifying that the adverb pushes the score of the combination to the minimum or maximum of the [-1,+1] scale. However, Benamara et al. (2007) lack an automatic way of scoring adverbs and rely on scores gathered from annotators.

Rill et al. (2012a) present a method for gathering opinion-bearing words and phrases, including adjective-phrases, from Amazon review data and assigning polarity scores on a continuous range between -1 and +1 to the entries based on the star ratings associated with the reviews. In subsequent work, Rill et al. (2012b) mention ways to infer the scores of unobserved adverb-adjective combinations based on observed combinations involving other, similar adjectives. However, the authors do not implement and evaluate these ideas.

Finally, a great deal of research on intensity has focused on acquiring prior polarity scores for individual words, and specifically adjectives. Various methods have been explored, including phrasal patterns (Sheinman et al., 2013; de Melo and Bansal, 2013); the use of star ratings (Rill et al., 2012b); extracting knowledge from lexical resources Gatti and Guerini (2012); and collostructional analysis (Ruppenhofer et al., 2014).

7 Conclusion

We examined various methods for ranking degree adverbs by their effect on the intensity of adjectives. We evaluated the methods against a new carefully-built gold standard that we collected experimentally as well as against a larger expert-constructed gold standard that we found to correlate well with ours for the overlapping members. While we found one method, Horn surface patterns, to currently not be workable at all due to the lack of suitable n-gram resources, we developed a MeanStar-based method that produces very good results using ratings metadata from product reviews to compute a scaling factor for adverb-adjective combinations relative to unmodified adjectives. Conspicuously, this scaling method makes no assumptions about any inherent properties of adverbs or adjectives, unlike the Collex and clustering approaches. In future work, we plan on looking more closely into the low results for the collostructional analysis approach, which had produced good results on the adjective ordering task, to ascertain if the asymmetries in the adverb-adjective associations (cf. §5.1) really are what prevents better results. Similarly, we plan on revisiting the typologies of adverbs and adjectives that we adopted from linguistic theory in order to see if they could be extended or revised in a way to give better clustering results.

Acknowledgments

The authors were partially supported by the German Research Foundation (DFG) under grants RU 1873/2-1 and WI 4204/2-1.

References

Marco Baroni, Silvia Bernardini, Adriano Ferraresi, and Eros Zanchetti. 2009. The WaCky Wide Web: A Collection of Very Large Linguistically Processed Web-Crawled Corpora. *Language Resources and Evaluation*, 43(3):209–226.

Farah Benamara, Carmine Cesarano, Antonio Picariello, Diego Reforgiato, and VS Subrahmanian. 2007. Sentiment Analysis: Adjectives and Adverbs are Better than Adjectives Alone. In *Proceedings of the International Conference on Weblogs and Social Media (ICWSM)*.

Dwight Bolinger. 1972. *Degree words*. Mouton, the Hague.

Marie-Catherine de Marneffe, Christopher D. Manning, and Christopher Potts. 2010. "Was It Good? It Was Provocative." Learning the Meaning of Scalar Adjectives. In *Proceedings of the 48th Annual Meeting of the Association for Computational Linguistics*, ACL '10, pages 167–176, Stroudsburg, PA, USA. Association for Computational Linguistics.

Gerard de Melo and Mohit Bansal. 2013. Good, Great, Excellent: Global Inference of Semantic Intensities. *Transactions of the Association for Computational Linguistics*, 1:279–290.

Guillaume Desagulier, 2014. *Corpus Methods for Semantics*, chapter Visualizing distances in a set of near-synonyms, pages 145–178. John Benjamins Publishing Company, Amsterdam, Philadelphia.

Britt Erman. 2014. There is no such thing as a free combination: a usage-based study of specific construals in adverb-adjective combinations. *English Language and Linguistics*, 18:109–132.

R. A. Fisher. 1922. On the Interpretation of 2 from Contingency Tables, and the Calculation of P. *Journal of the Royal Statistical Society*, 85(1):87–94, January.

Lorenzo Gatti and Marco Guerini. 2012. Assessing Sentiment Strength in Words Prior Polarities. In *Proceedings of the International Conference on Computational Linguistics (COLING)*, pages 361–370, Mumbai, India.

Stefan Th. Gries and Anatol Stefanowitsch. 2004. Extending collostructional analysis: a corpus-based perspective on 'alternations'. *International Journal of Corpus Linguistics*, 9(1):97–129.

Laurence Robert Horn. 1976. *On the Semantic Properties of Logical Operators in English*. Indiana University Linguistics Club.

Lawrence Hubert and Phipps Arabie. 1985. Comparing partitions. *Journal of classification*, 2(1):193–218.

Nitin Jindal and Bing Liu. 2008. Opinion Spam and Analysis. In *Proceedings of the International Conference on Web Search and Web Data Mining (WSDM)*, pages 219–230, Palo Alto, USA.

G. N. Lance and W. T. Williams. 1966. Computer programs for hierarchical polythetic classification ("similarity analyses"). *The Computer Journal*, 9(1):60–64.

Christopher D. Manning, Prabhakar Raghavan, and Hinrich Schütze. 2008. *Introduction to Information Retrieval*, volume 1. Cambridge University Press, Cambridge,UK.

Carita Paradis. 1997. *Degree modifiers of adjectives in spoken British English*, volume 92. Lund University Press.

Carita Paradis. 2001. Adjectives and boundedness. *Cognitive Linguistics*, (12):47–65.

Ted Pedersen. 1996. Fishing for exactness. In *Proceedings of the South-Central SAS Users Group Conference*, Austin, TX, USA.

Randolph Quirk, Sydney Greenbaum, Geoffrey Leech, and Jan Svartvik. 1985. *A Comprehensive Grammar of the English Language*. Longman.

Sven Rill, Sven Adolph, Johannes Drescher, Dirk Reinel, Jörg Scheidt, Oliver Schütz, Florian Wogenstein, Roberto V. Zicari, and Nikolaos Korfiatis. 2012a. A phrase-based opinion list for the German language. In Jeremy Jancsary, editor, *Proceedings of KONVENS 2012*, pages 305–313. ÖGAI.

Sven Rill, Johannes Drescher, Dirk Reinel, Jörg Scheidt, Oliver Schütz, Florian Wogenstein, and Daniel Simon. 2012b. A Generic Approach to Generate Opinion Lists of Phrases for Opinion Mining Applications. In *Proceedings of the KDD-Workshop on Issues of Sentiment Discovery and Opinion Mining (WISDOM)*, Beijing, China.

Josef Ruppenhofer, Michael Wiegand, and Jasper Brandes. 2014. Comparing methods for deriving intensity scores for adjectives. In *Proceedings of the 14th Conference of the European Chapter of the Association for Computational Linguistics, volume 2: Short Papers*, pages 117–122, Gothenburg, Sweden, April. Association for Computational Linguistics.

Vera Sheinman, Christiane Fellbaum, Isaac Julien, Peter Schulam, and Takenobu Tokunaga. 2013. Large, huge or gigantic? Identifying and encoding intensity relations among adjectives in WordNet. *Language Resources and Evaluation*, 47(3):797–816.

Maite Taboada, Julian Brooke, Milan Tofiloski, Kimberly Voll, and Manfred Stede. 2011. Lexicon-Based Methods for Sentiment Analysis. *Computational Linguistics*, 37(2):267–307.

Mike Thelwall, Kevan Buckley, Georgios Paltoglou, and Di Cai. 2010. Sentiment Strength Detection in Short Informal Text. *Journal of the American Society for Information Science and Technology*, 61(12):2544–2558.

Joe H Ward. 1963. Hierarchical grouping to optimize an objective function. *Journal of the American statistical association*, 58(301):236–244.

Theresa Wilson, Janyce Wiebe, and Paul Hoffmann. 2005. Recognizing Contextual Polarity in Phrase-level Sentiment Analysis. In *Proceedings of the Conference on Human Language Technology and Empirical Methods in Natural Language Processing (HLT/EMNLP)*, pages 347–354, Vancouver, BC, Canada.

bRol: The Parser of Syntactic and Semantic Dependencies for Basque

Haritz Salaberri, Olatz Arregi, Beñat Zapirain
IXA Group - Faculty of Computer Sciences
University of the Basque Country, Spain
{haritz.salaverri, olatz.arregi, benat.zapirain}@ehu.eus

Abstract

This paper presents *bRol*, the first fully automatic system to be developed for the parsing of syntactic and semantic dependencies in Basque. The parser has been built according to the settings established for the *CoNLL-2009* Shared Task (Hajič et al., 2009), therefore, *bRol* can be thought of as a standard parser with scores comparable to the ones reported in the shared task. A second-order graph-based MATE parser has been used as the syntactic dependency parser. The semantic model, on the other hand, uses the traditional four-stage SRL pipeline.

The system has a labeled attachment score of 80.51%, a labeled semantic F_1 of 75.10, and a labeled macro F_1 of 77.80.

1 Introduction

Since 1999 *The Conference on Natural Language Learning* (CoNLL) has been holding shared tasks focusing around different topics which concern human language processing. The CoNLL Shared Task aims to evaluate such applications in a standard setting, and to establish, as a result, the evaluation measures according to which these systems are evaluated and compared with one another.

In 2009 participants had to choose between two tasks: the joint parsing of syntactic and semantic dependencies or a SRL-only task. In both cases dependencies had to be parsed for propositions centered around verbal and, in some cases, nominal predicates in seven different languages (Catalan, Chinese, Czech, English, German, Japanese and Spanish). The representation used to perform and evaluate SRL was a dependency-based representation for both the syntactic and the semantic dependencies. Our focus is on the parsing of syntactic and semantic dependencies for Basque. In addition to describing our parser and presenting our results we also attempt to make a correct reading of these by taking into account the morphological and typological nature of Basque.

bRol is implemented as a sequence of five cascaded subtasks: Syntactic parsing (D), predicate identification (PI), predicate classification (PC), argument identification (AI) and argument classification (AC). Additionally, a post-process method is performed in order to relabel the duplicated role labels that may be assigned to predicate arguments in the AC subtask. Each of these subtasks is addressed by using a separate component with no backwards feedback between them.

Section 2 lists the resources used, section 3 and 4 describe the syntactic submodel and the semantic submodel, respectively. Results are shown in section 5 and section 6 presents our conclusions.

2 Resources

In order to develop *bRol*, the Basque corpus EPEC, also known as the *Basque PropBank*, is used (Aldezabal et al., 2010). EPEC is a corpus of text annotated with information about basic semantic propositions. Predicate-argument relations were added to the syntactic trees in the corpus using the *Basque Verb Index* (BVI) verb lexicon, also known as the *Basque VerbNet* (Aldezabal et al., 2013). Each entry in BVI is linked to the corresponding verb entry in well-known resources such as PropBank, VerbNet, WordNet and the Levin classes. A Basque NomBank, which has not been developed yet, is necessary in order to build a parser capable of labeling arguments for nominal predicates.

2.1 The EPEC Corpus

One half of the text contained in EPEC was extracted from the *Statistical Corpus of 20th Century Basque*. The other half was extracted from newspaper extracts from the *Euskaldunon*

Proceedings of Recent Advances in Natural Language Processing, pages 555–562,
Hissar, Bulgaria, Sep 7–9 2015.

Egunkaria, the only daily newspaper written entirely in Basque.

Syntax is annotated following the dependency-based formalism used in the *Prague Dependency Treebank* and the syntactic tag set consists of 30 different labels. Regarding semantic arguments we distinguish A0, A1, A2, A3, A4 and AM, which corresponds to adjuncts. There are 12 different types of adjuncts. Some other features of the corpus are: (1) the number of different verbs is 1,242; (2) there are 10,379 sentences and 161,812 tokens; (3) the language variety is the standard variety of Basque; and (4) all preprocessing steps (e.g. lemmatization) and the annotations of linguistic features (PoS, syntax, SRL, etc) in the corpus are manual.

Statistics on our data can be seen and compared to the ones in the CoNLL-2009 Shared Task in tables 1, 2 and 3. These statistics reflect several key features of the addressed languages, such as the degree of inflectionality, as well as features related to the annotation specification and conventions used.

2.2 The BVI Verb Lexicon

The Basque Verb Index (BVI) was created manually. Initially, it contained the verbs in the Database for Basque Verbs (EADB) proposed in (Aldezabal, 2004), an in-depth study of 100 verbs selected from the 622 that occur in the *Statistical Corpus of 20th Century Basque*. When EPEC was built BVI was extended from the initial 100 verbs to 243 verbs. These verbs are the ones with a minimum of 30 occurrences in the corpus.

3 Syntactic Dependency Parsing

The two main approaches to dependency parsing are transition-based dependency parsing (Nivre, 2003) and Maximum Spanning Tree-based dependency parsing (McDonald and Pereira, 2006). Our system uses MATE (Bohnet, 2010), a Maximum Spanning Tree-based dependency parser (also known as graph-based or MST-based). In MST-based dependency parsing the directed graph $G_x = (V_x, E_x)$ is defined for each sentence x where

$$V_x = \{x_0 = root, x_1, ..., x_n\}$$
$$E_x = \{(i,j) : x_i = x_j, x_i \in V_x, x_j \in V_x - root\}$$

That is, G_x is a graph where all the words and the root symbol are vertices and there is a directed edge between every pair of words and from the root symbol to every word. Dependency trees for x and spanning trees for G_x coincide, since both kinds of trees are required to reach all the words in the sentence. Therefore, finding the dependency tree of highest score is equivalent to finding the maximum spanning tree in G_x rooted in the root (McDonald et al., 2006).

The MATE parser used in *bRol* consists of the second-order parsing algorithm described in (Carreras, 2007), the non-projective approximation algorithm in (McDonald and Pereira, 2006) used to handle non-projective dependency trees, the passive-aggressive *SVM* algorithm and a feature extraction component. The second-order algorithm has a complexity of $O(n^4)$.

3.1 Non-projectivity

The total number of syntactic links in the training set of EPEC is 108,003 and out of these 2224 (2.06%) are non-projective. The number of sentences that contain at least one non-projective link is 1078, which constitute 15.5% of the sentences in the training set. These values are higher than the values reported for non-projectivity in, for example, the training set of English for the CoNLL-2009 shared task (0.4% of non-projective links and 7.6% sentences with at least one non-projective link).

According to (Johansson and Nugues, 2008) non-projectivity cannot be handled by span-based dynamic programming algorithms. Normally, the Chu-Liu/Edmonds algorithm (Chu and Liu, 1965) is used to find the highest scoring non-projective spanning tree in directed graphs; nevertheless, this algorithm cannot be extended to the second order (McDonald et al., 2006) and for this reason MATE uses the Non-Projective Approximation Algorithm in (McDonald and Pereira, 2006).

3.2 Features

In order to select the features for the syntactic dependency parser we took into account that Basque, on the contrary to English, Chinese, Spanish and Catalan, is a morphologically rich language (MRL) that exhibits a high degree of inflectional and derivational morphology. It is stated in (Nilsson et al., 2007) that the use of state-of-the-art parsers for non-inflecting languages like English does not reach similar performance levels when labeling MRLs like Basque. To overcome this difference, morphological information is normally used as a feature for parsing languages.

Based on the results reported in (Goenaga et al., 2013) we selected the following features from the ones annotated in EPEC: (1) declension case; (2) number; (3) type of subordinate sentence.

4 Semantic Dependency Parsing

From the sequence of five cascaded subtasks mentioned in section 1, all but the first form the semantic dependency parsing module (PI+PC+AI+AC). In addition, a post-process method is used to relabel duplicate roles.

First, verbal predicates are identified (PI) by examining every word in a sentence. Then, a certain roleset-ID is assigned to the words that have been marked as predicates (PC). Next, target arguments are discovered for the predicate(s) in a sentence (AI). Finally, the words that have been targeted as arguments are assigned a semantic role label by the default classifier (AC). Duplicated roles are relabeled using an Integer Linear Programming-based method (ILP post-process).

Classifiers: The classifiers used in the four-stage SRL pipeline of *bRol* are *Support Vector Machine* classifiers implemented using the *SVM-light* and *SVM-multiclass* packages (Joachims, 1999). The *SVM-light* package is used for binary classification (e.g. PI); the *SVM-multiclass* package, on the other hand, is used for multi-class problems (e.g. PC). The type of kernel function used is linear and the trade-off between training error and margin is computed through the $avg(x * x)^{-1}$ formula.

For the argument classification a maximum entropy classifier implemented with the MEGA package (Daumé III, 2004) is used. The specified minimum change in perplexity for the classifier is -99999 and the precision of the Gaussian prior is 1. The reason not to use a *Support Vector Machine* classifier for argument classification is motivated by the fact that standard *SVM* classifiers do not produce the posterior probability values ($P(class|input)$) that are needed, in our case, for the ILP post-process method (Platt et al., 1999).

Feature Selection: In order to select useful features for semantic dependency parsing we initially studied the features that were used by the participants in the the CoNLL-2009 Shared Task. Additionally, we also took into account the features that we proved to be useful for the classification of arguments in Basque (Salaberri et al., 2014). We then followed a Leave-One-Out (LOO) procedure to determine the impact that each individual feature had in each semantic subtask. This procedure evaluated the value of each feature that had been initially considered by iteratively removing the information relative to that feature and by then training the classifier with the rest of features.

4.1 Predicate Identification (PI)

We have treated the predicate identification subtask as a binary classification problem. Every word in a sentence is viewed as a candidate to be a predicate (punctuation marks are previously excluded from the candidates list for obvious reasons). For each candidate word a set of features is extracted. The following is the list of the features used:

WORD_Lex, WORD_Lemma, WORD_PoS, WORD_SubPoS, WORD_DepRel, HEAD_Lex, HEAD_Lemma, HEAD_PoS, HEAD_SubPoS, CHILD_DependRel_Set, CHILD_Lemma_Set, CHILD_Lex_Set.

4.2 Predicate Classification (PC)

After identifying the predicates from the list of candidate words, a roleset-ID is assigned to these predicates. For this purpose a single multiclass classifier is trained for all the predicates that have multiple senses (roleset-IDs). From the 243 different predicates in our training set 80 have multiple senses and 163 have a single sense. The following list shows the features that have been used:

PRED_Lex, PRED_Lemma, PRED_PoS, PRED_SubPoS, PRED_DepRel, PRED_DecCas, HEAD_Lex, HEAD_Lemma, HEAD_PoS, HEAD_SubPoS, CHILD_DependRel_Set, CHILD_Lemma_Set, CHILD_Lex_Set.

4.2.1 Handling "new" Predicates

We stated in section 2 that predicate-argument relations were added to the syntactic trees in the EPEC corpus using the BVI verb lexicon. The number of different verbs that can be found in EPEC is 1,242 and the number of verbs in the BVI verb lexicon is 243 as stated in section 2. These values indicate that 999 verbs in the corpus have no manually labeled predicate-argument relations. As a result *bRol*, which uses EPEC as a training corpus, would only be capable of assigning a

Characteristics	Basque	Catalan	Chinese	Czech	English	German	Japanese	Spanish
Training data size (sent.)	6941	13200	22277	38727	39279	36020	4393	14329
Training data size (tokens)	108003	390302	609060	652544	958167	648677	112555	427442
Avg. Sent length	15.56	29.6	27.3	16.8	24.4	18.0	25.6	29.8
Tokens with arguments (%)	10.75	9.6	16.9	63.5	18.7	2.7	22.8	10.3
DEPREL types	30	50	41	49	69	46	5	49
POS types	26	12	41	12	48	56	40	12
FEAT types	298	237	1	1811	1	267	302	264
FORM vocabulary size	20051	33890	40878	86332	39782	72084	36043	40964
LEMMA vocabulary size	9042	24143	40878	37580	28376	51993	30402	26926
Evaluation data size (sent)	3438	1862	2556	4213	2399	2000	500	1725
Evaluation data size (tokens)	53809	53355	73153	70348	57676	31622	13615	50630
Evaluation FORM OOV	12.41	5.40	3.92	7.98	1.58	7.93	6.07	5.63
Evaluation LEMMA OOV	6.38	4.14	3.92	3.03	1.08	5.83	5.21	3.69

Table 1: Elementary data statistics for the CoNLL-2009 Shared Task languages plus the statistics for Basque (EPEC). All evaluation data statistics are derived from the in-domain evaluation data.

DEPREL	Basque		Catalan		Chinese		Czech		English		German		Japanese		Spanish	
Labels	ncmod	0.26	sn	0.16	COMP	0.21	Atr	0.26	NMOD	0.27	NK	0.31	D	0.93	sn	0.16
	PUNC	0.15	spec	0.15	NMOD	0.14	Aux	0.10	P	0.11	PUNC	0.14	ROOT	0.04	spec	0.15
	lot	0.09	f	0.11	ADV	0.10	Adv	0.10	PMOD	0.10	MO	0.12	P	0.03	f	0.12
	auxmod	0.08	sp	0.09	UNK	0.09	Obj	0.07	SBJ	0.07	SB	0.07	A	0.00	sp	0.08
	ncsubj	0.07	suj	0.07	SBJ	0.08	Sb	0.06	OBJ	0.06	ROOT	0.06	I	0.00	suj	0.08
Total	0.65		0.58		0.62		0.59		0.61		0.70		1.00		0.59	

Table 2: Unigram probability is shown for the five most frequent DEPREL labels in the training data of the CoNLL-2009 Shared Task and in the training data from the EPEC corpus. Total is the probability mass covered by the five dependency labels shown.

APRED	Basque		Catalan		Chinese		Czech		English		German		Japanese		Spanish	
Labels	A1	0.21	arg1-pat	0.22	A1	0.30	RSTR	0.30	A1	0.37	A0	0.40	GA	0.33	arg1-pat	0.20
	A2	0.15	arg0-agt	0.18	A0	0.27	PAT	0.18	A0	0.25	A1	0.39	WO	0.15	arg0-agt	0.19
	A0	0.14	arg1-tem	0.15	ADV	0.20	ACT	0.17	A2	0.12	A2	0.12	NO	0.15	arg1-tem	0.15
	AM-TMP	0.08	argM-tmp	0.08	TMP	0.07	APP	0.06	AM-TMP	0.06	A3	0.06	NI	0.09	arg2-atr	0.08
	AM-MNR	0.07	arg2-atr	0.08	DIS	0.04	LOC	0.04	AM-MNR	0.03	A4	0.01	DE	0.06	argM-tmp	0.08
Total	0.65		0.71		0.91		0.75		0.83		0.97		0.78		0.70	
Avg.	1.97		2.25		2.26		0.88		2.20		1.97		1.71		2.26	

Table 3: Unigram probability is shown for the five most frequent APRED labels in the training data of the CoNLL-2009 Shared Task and in the training data from the EPEC corpus. Total is the probability mass covered by the five argument labels shown.

roleset-ID and consequently semantic role labels to instances of the 243 verbs in the lexicon.

We decided to add a translation component (TC) to the PC problem. The TC is used to assign a roleset-ID to instances of the 999 predicates, or any other new verb predicate, that is not mapped in BVI. By using this component we achieve an increase in number of predicate-argument relations that are labeled by *bRol*. The relations labeled as a result of the TC can not be compared to any manual annotation; therefore, the performance of the TC can not be evaluated. Nevertheless, we believe that the TC is able to correctly label many predicate-argument relations, since these relations correspond to predicates that have less than 30 occurrences in the corpus (usually, these infrequent verbs have only one roleset-ID in PropBank).

The translation component is implemented using the Basque-to-English *Elhuyar Hiztegia* dictionary and PropBank. When a word that has been targeted as a predicate at the PI stage is handed over to the PC stage, *bRol* checks whether or not this predicate is present in the lexicon. If the predicate can not be found, it is delivered to the TC.

The translation component operates in the following way: first the predicate is translated into English; then the translation is looked for in PropBank (PB). If the translation can be found as a PropBank frame, the first roleset-ID mapped for this frame is assigned to the original predicate. If

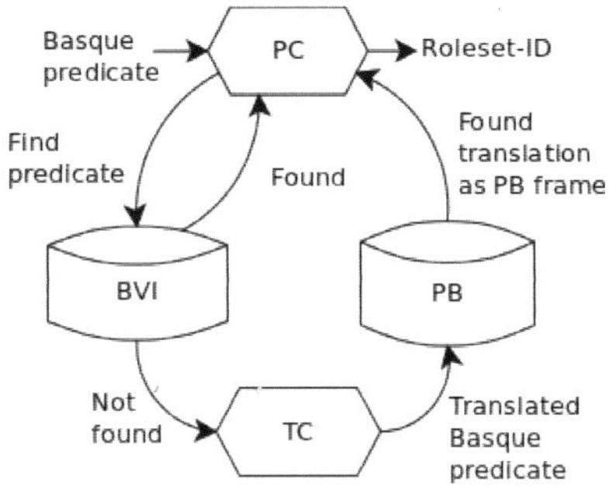

Figure 1: PC pipeline.

not, the original predicate will not be assigned a roleset-ID and consequently its arguments will not be labeled. Figure 1 illustrates the PC pipeline.

4.3 Argument Identification (AI)

After the PC subtask is completed and predicates are assigned a roleset-ID sentences are handed to the AI module. *bRol* performs argument identification based on a high precision heuristic. Every word in a sentence is treated as a candidate to be an argument for each semantic predicate (in the sentence).

Our heuristic uses information such as the predicted PoS tag, the syntactic head (HEAD) and dependency relation to the head (DEPREL) in order to determine if word w_i is an argument for predicate P_j. More precisely, if word w_i's head is predicate P_j and the dependency relation is not labeled as *auxmod* (auxiliary), *haos* (component of a multiword lexical unit), *postos* (component of a multiword postposition), *entios* (component of a multiword entity) or *PUNC* (punctuation), then, w_i is considered to be an argument of P_j but only if P_j's PoS tag is not ADK (phrasal verb). We came up with the optimal argument identification heuristic after several train-test runs.

We performed several experiments in order to determine which approach, the machine learning-based or the heuristic-based, would prove to be the best for AI. We concluded the heuristic-based approach to be the best; in addition to a slightly higher performance, the running time is reduced thanks to the fact that there is no need for a feature extraction component (these are usually the most time-consuming components in ML-based systems).

4.4 Argument Classification (AC)

When predicate argument identification by the AI component has been completed the arguments that have been identified are handed over to the AC component. Our system treats argument classification as a multi-class classification problem; the machine-learning method used in this stage is maximum entropy. The model gives every argument a probability to take each semantic role and the one with the highest value is assigned to the argument. The features used are shown in the following list:

PRED_Roleset, PRED_Lemma, ARG_Lemma, ARG_PoS, ARG_SubPoS, ARG_DependRel, ARG_DecCas.

4.5 The Post-process Method

Before the final semantic role labeling result is generated, a post-process similar to the one described in (Che et al., 2008) is performed. The arguments corresponding to the same predicate which have been labeled with the same core argument label by the AC component are relabeled through a Integer Linear Programming-based method (ILP).

In some languages, as for example English, the possibility to have duplicated roles exists. Statistics show that most roles usually appear only once for a predicate; nevertheless, some rare cases exist. Before starting with the development of *bRol* we examined the verbs in our lexicon one by one; we did not find any duplicated roles.

Our system uses the probabilities given by the maximum entropy model in the AC component in order to perform the relabeling process. For every set of arguments which have been assigned a label that is duplicated for the predicate we maximize the objective function

$$f = \sum log(p_{ir}.v_{ir})$$

where v_{ir} is a binary variable indicating whether the argument indexed i (token ID) is assigned role $r \in R$ or not (where R is the set of role labels). p_{ir}, on the other hand, denotes the probability of the argument indexed i to be labeled as label r. We establish a No Duplicated Roles constraint and when the process is finished we obtain the optimal labeling for each predicate from the assignments to v_{ir}.

Measures	Basque	Catalan	Chinese	Czech	English	German	Japanese	Spanish
Labeled Attachment Score	80.51	87.86 (2)	79.17 (5)	80.38 (2)	89.88 (1)	87.48 (1)	92.57 (3)	87.64 (2)
Semantic Labeled F_1	75.10	80.10 (4)	77.15 (3)	86.51 (3)	86.15 (4)	78.61 (3)	78.26 (3)	80.29 (4)
Macro F_1 Score	77.80	83.01 (4)	76.38 (3)	83.27 (3)	87.69 (4)	82.44 (3)	85.65 (3)	83.31 (4)

Table 4: Official results of the Joint task (in-domain, closed challenge) reported by the teams that participated in the CoNLL-2009 Shared Task plus the results of *bRol*. The results shown correspond to the systems with the best performance. Teams are denoted by the last name of the author who registered for the evaluation data [(1):Bohnet, (2):Merlo, (3):Che, (4):Chen, (5):Ren].

5 Results and Discussion

In order to evaluate the performance of *bRol* we have run the scorer function from the CoNLL-2009 Shared Task (*eval09.pl*) on our test set. As of today there is no other Basque corpus than EPEC manually annotated with syntactic and semantic dependencies. For this reason the only available test set that can be used for evaluation is the one extracted from this corpus; thus, the only evaluation that can be made is an in-domain evaluation.

Table 4 shows the results obtained by our parser and the results reported by the participants in the Joint Task of the CoNLL-2009 Shared Task (in-domain, closed challenge). The results in the table correspond to the systems that, according to the language, performed best with respect to the official evaluation measures.

5.1 Syntactic Dependency Parsing

The Labeled Attachment Score (LAS) is defined as the percentage of tokens for which a parser has predicted the correct syntactic head and dependency relation. Our parser has a LAS of 80.51 points. If we compare our score with the ones reported for the other seven languages in table 4, our LAS is more than one point better than the score reported for Chinese (79.17) and 0.13 points better than the score reported for Czech (80.38). On the opposite site, our LAS is almost twelve points lower than the score reported for Japanese (92.57), nine points lower than the score reported for English (89.88) and almost seven points lower than the scores reported for Catalan (87.86), Spanish (87.64) and German (87.48).

We believe that several linguistic and data-related factors need to be addressed in order to correctly interpret this result. Linguistically speaking, we must bear in mind that, in general, the syntactic parsing results reported for morphologically rich languages (MRL) like Basque, despite the use of morphological features, do not reach the performance levels of languages like English. In the CoNLL-2009 Shared Task, for instance (see table 4), Czech and German, which are MRLs, get worse results than English, Spanish and Catalan, which are not MRLs. In our opinion the outstanding LAS score obtained by Japanese (92.57), which has an agglutinating morphology, is the result of having a DEPREL set of just five different labels (see tables 1 and 2). Chinese, on the other hand, which has a poor morphology, presents the worst labeled attachment score (79.17); we believe this score to be a result of the typological nature of Chinese; namely, that Chinese presents an isolating morphology, e.g. that each morpheme corresponds to an independent word or semantic unit and that therefore there is hardly any overt morphology. In fact, according to (Seddah et al., 2013) languages which are typologically farthest from English, such as Semitic and Asian languages, are still among the hardest to parse, regardless of the parsing method used.

In addition to the previously mentioned, another key factor in order to correctly interpret the LAS obtained by *bRol* is the free word order displayed by Basque syntax in combination with its rich morphology. As a matter of fact, (Donelaicio et al., 2013) state that it has been observed that richly inflected languages, which often also exhibit relatively free word order, obtain lower parsing accuracy, especially compared to English.

5.2 Semantic Dependency Parsing

bRol has a Semantic Labeled F_1 score of 75.10 points. The exact definition of how the Semantic Labeled F_1 score is computed can be seen in (Hajič et al., 2009) (section 2). As may be noticed in table 4, our result is two points lower than the result reported for Chinese (77.15), which is the language with the lowest Semantic Labeled F_1 score among the ones in CoNLL-2009.

We believe that the distribution of the APRED labels in our training data (see table 3) and other characteristics such as the number of PoS types or the number of FEAT types (see table 1) do not constitute any added difficulty when compared to the distribution and the characteristics in the other languages. In our opinion the only reason for this result in Basque, which compared to the results for the other seven languages can be understood as low or at least not average, is that the size of our training set is very reduced. In fact, the number of sentences in our training set is 6,941 and the number of tokens is 108,003. If we compare these to the average sentence and token number in the rest of the training sets (24,032 sentences and 542,678 tokens) we find that the number of sentences is 71.1% smaller and the number of tokens is 80.1% smaller in our training set.

Next we present the results for *bRol* through the four-stage SRL pipeline (see table 5). For this purpose we have used standard precision, recall and F1 score metrics.

Subtask	Precision	Recall	F_1
Predicate Identification (PI)	87.00	88.00	87.50
Predicate Classification (PC)	79.41	81.29	79.82
Argument Identification (AI)	72.70	86.10	78.80
Argument Classification (AC)	77.60	77.80	77.50

Table 5: Results for the semantic subtasks

The semantic subtask with the best F_1 score is predicate identification (87.50), followed by predicate classification (79.82) and argument identification (78.80). Argument classification, on the other hand, gets the lowest F_1 score (77.50). In our opinion, these results are highly dependent on the complexity of the subtask itself. In fact, PI is a binary classification problem, whereas PC and AC are multiclass classification problems.

Another way to approach the PC subtask would be by training a separate classifier for each predicate with multiple senses, as in (Che et al., 2008). Nevertheless, we decided not to implement *bRol* using separate PC classifiers for two reasons: (1) The size of our training set is too limited for this approach to be effective: we have 11,740 predicate instances and 8,166 correspond to the 80 verbs with multiple senses (69.55%). Thus, the average number of instances available for training each separate classifier is 102. We consider this amount to be too small. (2) We consider that the *PRED_Lemma* feature used to train our single PC classifier is given enough weight by the learning algorithm when training the classifier. We understand that operations where roleset-ID A_i of predicate A is assigned to predicate B are avoided.

5.3 Overall Result

In order to compute the overall result of our parser, the syntactic and semantic measures (LAS and Semantic Labeled F_1 score) are combined into one global measure using Macro Averaging. The exact way in which this is achieved can be found in (Hajič et al., 2009) (section 2). The Macro F_1 score of *bRol* is 77.80. If we compare our score to the Macro F_1 scores reported in CoNLL-2009 (see table 4), we find out that our parser performs 1.42 points better than the result reported for Chinese. As opposed to this, *bRol* has a performance of about five Macro F_1 points lower than the results reported for Catalan, Spanish, Czech and German; eight points lower than the results reported for Japanese, and ten points lower than the results reported for English. Although the performance that our parser would have in an out-of-domain setup can not be evaluated, we believe that our results would drop in approximately 10 labeled macro F_1 points, as in the results reported for CoNLL-2005 (Carreras and Màrquez, 2005) and CoNLL-2009.

It is worth mentioning that before running *bRol* over the test set we deactivated the translation component, since the predicates and their corresponding arguments that would have been labeled as a consequence of the TC are not manually annotated in the test set. As a result, all of these would have been computed as fails although some might be correctly labeled by *bRol*.

6 Conclusions

We have presented the first fully automatic system to be developed for the parsing of syntactic and semantic dependencies in Basque. The evaluation measures we have used to evaluate our parser are the ones used in the CoNLL-2009 Shared Task, as we understand these to be the standard metrics used in order to evaluate these kind of applications. In addition, we have established a performance baseline for Basque and compared our results to the results reported for languages of different morphological and typological natures.

Acknowledgments

Haritz Salaberri holds a PhD grant from the University of the Basque Country. In addition, this work has been supported by the EXTRECM project (Grant No. TIN2013-46616-C2-1-R) and IXA Group, research group of type A (2010-2015)(IT34410).

References

Izaskun Aldezabal. 2004. *Aditz-azpikategorizazioaren azterketa sintaxi partzialetik sintaxi osorako bidean: 100 aditzen azterketa, Levin-en lana oinarri hartuta eta metodo automatikoak baliatuz*. PhD thesis, UPV-EHU, Donostia.

Izaskun Aldezabal, Maxux Aranzabe, Arantza D. Ilarraza, and Ainara Estarrona. 2010. Building the basque propbank. In *LREC*.

Izaskun Aldezabal, Maxux Aranzabe, Arantza D. Ilarraza, and Ainara Estarrona. 2013. A methodology for the semiautomatic annotation of epec-rolsem, a basque corpus labeled at predicative level following the propbank-verb net model. *UPV/EHU/LSI/TR; 01-2013*.

Bernd Bohnet. 2010. Very high accuracy and fast dependency parsing is not a contradiction. In *Proceedings of the 23rd International Conference on Computational Linguistics*, pages 89–97. Association for Computational Linguistics.

Xavier Carreras. 2007. Experiments with a higher-order projective dependency parser. In *EMNLP-CoNLL*, pages 957–961.

Xavier Carreras and Lluis Màrquez. 2005. Introduction to the conll-2005 shared task: Semantic role labeling. In *Proceedings of the Ninth Conference on Computational Natural Language Learning*, pages 152–164. Association for Computational Linguistics.

Wanxiang Che, Zhenghua Li, Yuxuan Hu, Yongqiang Li, Bing Qin, Ting Liu, and Sheng Li. 2008. A cascaded syntactic and semantic dependency parsing system. In *Proceedings of the Twelfth Conference on Computational Natural Language Learning*, pages 238–242. Association for Computational Linguistics.

Yoeng-Jin Chu and Tseng-Hong Liu. 1965. On shortest arborescence of a directed graph. *Scientia Sinica*, 14(10):1396.

Hal Daumé III. 2004. Notes on cg and lm-bfgs optimization of logistic regression. *Paper available at http://pub. hal3. name# daume04cg-bfgs, implementation available at http://hal3. name/megam*, 198:282.

Ka Donelaicio, Joakim Nivre, and Algis Krupavicius. 2013. Lithuanian dependency parsing with rich morphological features. In *Fourth Workshop on Statistical Parsing of Morphologically Rich Languages*, page 12.

Iakes Goenaga, Koldo Gojenola, and Nerea Ezeiza. 2013. Exploiting the contribution of morphological information to parsing: the basque team system in the sprml2013 shared task. In *Proceedings of the Fourth Workshop on Statistical Parsing of Morphologically-Rich Languages*, pages 61–67.

Jan Hajič, Massimiliano Ciaramita, Richard Johansson, Daisuke Kawahara, Maria Antònia Martí, Lluís Màrquez, Adam Meyers, Joakim Nivre, Sebastian Padó, Jan Štěpánek, and others. 2009. The conll-2009 shared task: Syntactic and semantic dependencies in multiple languages. In *Proceedings of the Thirteenth Conference on Computational Natural Language Learning: Shared Task*, pages 1–18. Association for Computational Linguistics.

Thorsten Joachims. 1999. Making large scale svm learning practical. *tu-dortmund.de*.

Richard Johansson and Pierre Nugues. 2008. Dependency-based syntactic-semantic analysis with propbank and nombank. In *Proceedings of the Twelfth Conference on Computational Natural Language Learning*, pages 183–187. Association for Computational Linguistics.

Ryan McDonald, Koby Crammer, and Fernando CN. Pereira. 2006. Spanning tree methods for discriminative training of dependency parsers. Technical Report MS-CIS-06-11, University of Pennsylvania, Pennsylvania.

Ryan McDonald and Fernando CN. Pereira. 2006. Online learning of approximate dependency parsing algorithms. In *EACL*.

Jens Nilsson, Sebastian Riedel, and Deniz Yuret. 2007. The conll 2007 shared task on dependency parsing. In *Proceedings of the CoNLL shared task session of EMNLP-CoNLL*, pages 915–932. sn.

Joakim Nivre. 2003. An efficient algorithm for projective dependency parsing. In *Proceedings of the 8th International Workshop on Parsing Technologies (IWPT)*. Citeseer.

John Platt and others. 1999. Probabilistic outputs for support vector machines and comparisons to regularized likelihood methods. In Advances in large margin classifiers, volume 10, number 3, pages 61–74. Cambridge, MA.

Haritz Salaberri, Olatz Arregi, and Beñat Zapirain. 2014. First approach toward Semantic Role Labeling for Basque. In *Proceedings of the 9th edition of the Language Resources Evaluation Conference (LREC)*, pages 1387–1393.

Djamé Seddah, Reut Tsarfaty, Sandra Kübler, Marie Candito, Jinho Choi, Richárd Farkas, Jennifer Foster, Iakes Goenaga, Koldo Gojenola, Yoav Goldberg, and others. 2013. Overview of the spmrl 2013 shared task: cross-framework evaluation of parsing morphologically rich languages. In *Fourth Workshop on Statistical Parsing of Morphologically Rich Languages*. Association for Computational Linguistics.

Error Analysis and Improving Speech Recognition for Latvian language

Askars Salimbajevs
Tilde, Vienibas gatve 75a, Riga, Latvia
askars.salimbajevs@tilde.lv

Jevgenijs Strigins
Tilde, Vienibas gatve 75a, Riga, Latvia
jevgenijs.strigins@tilde.lv

Abstract

Developing a large vocabulary automatic speech recognition system is a very difficult task, due to the high variations in domain and acoustic variability. This task is even more difficult for the Latvian language, which is very rich morphologically and in which one word can have dozens of surface forms. Although there is some research on speech recognition for Latvian, Latvian ASR remains behind "big" languages such as English, German etc. In order to improve the performance of Latvian ASR, it is important to understand what errors does it make and why. In this paper, the authors analyze the most common errors of Latvian ASR. Based on this, baseline system WER is improved from 30.94% to 28.43%.

1 Introduction

When developing an Automatic Speech Recognition (ASR) system it is typical to evaluate system performance by calculating quantitative measures like accuracy, F1 score, Word Error Rate (WER) etc. However, in order to improve ASR performance, it is important to understand which factors are most problematic for recognition, identify the types of errors, their main causes and how critical these errors are. This is even more important when developing ASR for a language, for which no such analysis has ever been done, because the developer might not know what problems to expect, where more effort and focus is needed and what possible solutions there are.

The Latvian language is a moderately inflected language, with complex nominal and verbal morphology. Latvian also has a selection of prefixes and suffixes that can modify nouns, adjectives, adverbs and verbs. There is no definite or indefinite article in Latvian, but definiteness can be indicated by the endings of adjectives. Because of these properties, one word in Latvian can have tens or even hundreds (in the case of verbs) of surface forms. For example, a word "cat" in English has 3 surface forms: *cat, cats* and *cat's*, but in Latvian the variation is much bigger: *kaķis, kaķa, kaķim, kaķi, kaķī, kaķu, kaķiem* etc. They all describe an animal – cat, but in the same time these are different surface forms that change the meaning of sentence.

To the best of our knowledge there has been no research conducted on analyzing misrecognized words for Latvian LVASR. In fact, there are only a few published results on speech recognition for Latvian (Oparin et al., 2013; Darģis, R., & Znotiņš, A., 2014; Salimbajevs & Pinnis, 2014), that report the best performance of WER 20.2%.

However, there are no lack of efforts on error analysis for "bigger" languages (Goldwater et al., 2010; Vasilescu et al, 2012). In many cases factors discovered in these works also apply to "smaller" languages. For example there are results for English (Fosler-Lussier & Morgan, 1999) and Japanese (Shinozaki & Furui, 2001) that show that infrequent words are more likely to be misrecognized, which is most likely to be true also for other languages.

Most studies analyze errors from the perspective of the ASR vs. human capacities in decoding spoken signals and consider ASR errors from lexical or phonetic standpoints. There are, however, also efforts that focus on morpho-syntactic structure (Goryainova, 2014).

In this paper we present an error analysis of the Latvian Large Vocabulary Automatic Speech Recognition (LVASR) system. We do not perform in-depth analysis of ASR error causes, but rather concentrate on typical surface errors to

Proceedings of Recent Advances in Natural Language Processing, pages 563–569,
Hissar, Bulgaria, Sep 7–9 2015.

produce classes of errors and find general solutions.

The remainder of the paper is organized as follows. Section 2 describes the present Latvian ASR system used in this study. Classes of errors, their effect on utterance meaning and their causes are discussed in Section 3. Section 4 describes improvements which we have made after analyzing errors and gives a short evaluation of the improved system. All results of this study are then interpreted in Section 5. Section 6 concludes the paper.

2 Latvian ASR

The present Latvian Automatic Speech Recognition system is based on an open-source Kaldi toolkit (Povey et al., 2011), which in turn is based on the Weighted Finite State Transducer (WSFT) approach. We use this system as a baseline for analyzing recognition errors and testing improvement ideas. The system's details are described in the following subsections.

A few results on Latvia

2.1 Acoustic Modelling

The acoustic model (AM) is trained on a 100 hour-long Latvian Speech Recognition Corpus (Pinnis et al., 2011). We use the following acoustic model setup:

- HMM (hidden Markov models)-DNN (deep neural network) modelling approach.
- MFCC features and LDA. These are 40-dimensional feature vectors that are calculated from audio signal, and are used in actual calculations
- 37 base phonemes.
- 1 unified filler\silence model. Fillers represent sounds that are not spoken words, such as breathing, laughing etc.
- 1 garbage model for fragmented words and other garbage. For example, if word was not fully pronounced.
- iVectors are used for speaker adaptation (Miao et al., 2014). That is, for each speaker model parameters are changed so the better fit is obtained.

2.2 Language Modelling

The baseline ASR system uses n-gram language models (LM) which are trained on a 22M sentence and 304M word text corpus, which was collected by crawling Latvian web news portals. A vocabulary of 200K units is used, selected by their frequency in the training corpus.

Two language models are used during recognition:

- A 2-gram heavily pruned model is used during first-pass.
- A full not-pruned 3-gram model is used for rescoring lattices.

3 Recognition Errors

Here we used a small (approximately 23 minutes) corpus of Latvian speech, which was obtained by recording various people reading internet web news. The corpus was divided into two equal parts:

- A development set which is used for error analysis and testing possible improvements.
- A test set which is used to evaluate an improved speech recognition system.

Division was performed by randomly dividing this Latvian speech corpus in two parts with approximately equal length and same speakers.

3.1 Types of Errors

First we classified all errors by the following criteria:

- Whether the error is in the ending of the word.
- Whether the error is in a short word (we classify a word as short if it is no longer than 3 letters)
- Whether word boundaries were misaligned e.g. when the second part of one word is recognized as a part of the next word.
- Whether the previous word was recognized incorrectly.
- Whether the correct word is substituted with other word(s).

Using this criteria ASR output was compared with the correct transcripts. A summary of analyzed data is presented in the table below:

Category	% of All Errors
Ending	41%
Short word	15%
Word boundaries	13%
Error in previous word	28%
Substitution	52%

Table 1: Error summary from analyzing transcripts.

The table shows the percentage of specific categories of errors from all errors. It is important to analyze these categories, because, endings define different inflections. Short words are hard to discriminate acoustically and often they are partially skipped or spelled incompletely during fast human speech. Incorrectly defined word boundaries and word substitutions are common errors for speech recognizers. If one word is incorrectly recognized, then wrong n-grams of language model will be used in the process of calculating the probability of word sequence, therefore an effect of wrongly recognized previous word must be measured.

As our error categories overlap the total can be more than 100%. It can be seen that because of the inflective nature of Latvian, a large amount of misrecognitions are incorrect surface forms. For example, if the correct word is *kaķis*, but recognition output is *kaķi*, then it will be treated as an error, although these are actually different inflections representing the same word.

The usual output of a speech recognition decoder is a lattice of words, containing their estimated acoustic and language model costs. We used lattices to look deeper and classify errors using the following criteria:

- Whether words preceding or succeeding the wrongly recognized word are out of vocabulary words.
- Whether the correct word is in the lattice i.e. corrected word was pruned and cannot be recovered by rescoring.
- Whether the AM cost is too high (the incorrect word or surface form has a lower cost).
- Whether the LM cost is too high.

This means that in the case of an incorrectly recognized word, we investigate whether the correct word was actually present in the lattice along the best path, and if it was we compare the acoustic and language model scores of correct and recognized words. A summary of the lattice analysis is presented in Table 2.

Category	% of All Errors
Pruned from lattice	45%
Bad AM score	67%
Bad LM score	51%

Table 2: Error summary from analyzing lattices.

It can be seen that 45% of misrecognized words were pruned from lattices. Table 2 also suggests that there are more errors with bad AM cost, but this data is not sufficient to make any conclusions.

While performing this analysis we found that none of the fractional numbers were recognized correctly because of misrecognition of the word "komats" (decimal comma). We will investigate the cause of this problem further in the next paragraphs.

3.2 Effect of Errors

Not all recognition errors are equally important. For example a user will most likely be able to understand a transcript with errors in word endings, but completely misrecognized words (especially OOV words) and numbers can significantly change the meaning of utterances. These words can carry such critical data as time, person names, places etc. There have been attempts to automatically detect errors in critical words and use different clarification strategies to resolve them (Stoyanchev et al., 2012; Pappu et al., 2014).

First we analyzed the error distribution between parts of speech (POS) and how many of these errors are in word endings.

The second column in Table 3 shows what percentage of each part of speech is not recognized correctly. It can be seen that adjectives, verbs, particles and prepositions are the most difficult to recognize. Misrecognized verbs are more critical, as they can change the meaning of utterance or make whole utterance meaningless. Misrecognized adjectives are less important, as 75% of these misrecognitions are errors in endings, which should not make utterance unintelligible. Particles and prepositions are also less important for recovering the meaning of utterance.

Although there is no inflections for particles and prepositions, these are hard to recognize because usually they are short words that are not spelled very clearly during human speech and can become part of other words.

POS	% of Misrecognitions	% of Ending Errors
Adjectives	20%	75%
Conjunctions	12%	-
Nouns	16%	34%
Numerals	13%	53%
Particles	20%	50%
Participles	12%	57%
Prepositions	20%	-
Verbs	20%	45%
Other	10%	51%

Table 3: Errors in Parts of Speech.

Next we performed a subjective evaluation of recognized utterances. In total, 56% of utterances contain one or more errors that make it very difficult or impossible to recover the original meaning, while 47% of errors were critical. This result shows that the usability of transcriptions made with the current ASR can be very limited if no audio is available to check suspicious or important places in the text.

Also, while analyzing utterances we confirmed that OOV errors are critical for recovering the meaning of utterances. 82% of OOV errors significantly changed the meaning of utterances.

3.3 Causes of Errors

Analysis of the transcripts and lattices led to a number of hypotheses about the causes of different types of errors. In this section we list and test these hypotheses.

3.3.1 Word Length

Of particular interest was whether short words are harder for ASR to recognize than long ones. Let us define the probability of ASR wrongly recognizing short and long words by *P(s)* and *P(l)* respectively. A maximum likelihood estimate for these probabilities would be

$$\tilde{P}(s) = \frac{cnt(e_s)}{cnt(sw)}; \tilde{P}(l) = \frac{cnt(e_l)}{cnt(lw)}$$

where $cnt(e_s)$ and $cnt(e_l)$ are counts of errors in short words and long words, but $cnt(sw)$ and $cnt(lw)$ are the total count of short and long words in the corpus. The estimates are compared using Welch's t test to test the following hypotheses:

$$H_0: \tilde{P}(s) = \tilde{P}(l)$$
$$H_1: \tilde{P}(s) < \tilde{P}(l)$$

The statistical test yields a p-value of 0.001956, which is strong evidence against the null hypothesis. This result appears to be quite confusing, as short words are easier for ASR to recognize than longer ones.

3.3.2 Misrecognized Previous Word

Another issue is the effect of a wrongly recognized word on the recognition of the next word. Let us define the probability of ASR wrongly recognizing the current word given that the previous word was wrongly recognized by $P_{-1}(e)$ and the probability of ASR wrongly recognizing the current word given that the previous word was recognized correctly by $P_{-1}(c)$. The maximum likelihood estimates of these probabilities would be

$$\tilde{P}_{-1}(e) = \frac{cnt(w_e w_e)}{cnt(w_e)}; \tilde{P}_{-1}(c) = \frac{cnt(w_c w_e)}{cnt(w_c)}$$

Where $cnt(w_e w_e)$ is a count of the sequences of two consecutive errors, $cnt(w_c w_e)$ is a count of the sequences of an error preceeded by a correctly recognized word and $cnt(w_e)$ $cnt(w_c)$ would be the total number of errors and correct words. Then we would test the following hypotheses:

$$H_0: \tilde{P}_{-1}(e) = \tilde{P}_{-1}(c)$$
$$H_1: \tilde{P}_{-1}(e) > \tilde{P}_{-1}(c)$$

This statistical test yields a p-value of 0.8e-6, which is strong evidence against the null hypothesis. The estimated probabilities are 28% and 12%, which means that the previously incorrectly recognized word increases the probability of recognizing the next word incorrectly by more than 2 times.

3.3.3 Weak Decoding LM

As we have already seen, the correct words were pruned from the lattices in 45% of cases. Our hypothesis was that 2-gram pruned LM used in decoding would assign the wrong costs.

To test this hypothesis we made several experiments where a bigger 3-gram LM was used in decoding. We also tried to increase the lattice beam so that fewer paths are pruned. However, despite a decrease in the percentage of pruned words, no improvement was observed.

We also made a short analysis of cases where the correct word was still present in the lattice, but had a worse LM or AM cost (Table 4). The LM and AM costs are inversely proportional to probabilities of corresponding hypothesis obtained from *Kaldi* speech recognition toolkit.

Type	%
Only LM cost	30%
Only AM cost	46%
Both	24%

Table 4: Incorrect costs in lattices.

In a majority of cases the correct word was not chosen because it had a worse acoustic score and the LM cost was not small enough for correct variant (or large enough for the incorrect variant) to compensate for this. This result shows that our hypothesis was false and improvements in both AM and LM (both decoding and rescoring) are needed.

3.3.4 Out-of-Vocabulary

If the word is not in the system's vocabulary, it cannot be recognized. Moreover, an out-of-vocabulary word is known to generate between 1.5 and 2 errors (Schwartz et al, 1994). This is an important problem for Latvian ASR, because each word in Latvian has many surface forms and all of them must be in the vocabulary.

We found out that OOV words contribute to 13% of recognition errors. Also 5% of misrecognized words preceded or succeeded OOV words.

3.3.5 Misrecognition of Word "komats"

We identified two reasons for incorrect recognition of the word "komats" (comma). The first is pronunciation. Many people pronounce "komats" as "koma" which is a different word. The second is an excessively high LM cost for numerals and "komats". LM is trained on a written text, but it is rare for numerals to be written using words, so numbers are written mostly using digits. Our baseline training procedure does not have any number to word conversion and all sentences with such numbers are filtered. Hence n-grams with numerals and "comma" are very rare, their probability is estimated as low and they can be pruned from decoding LM.

As a result both costs of word "komats" were high, so it was never chosen, instead some completely different words were chosen as the final hypothesis, making it very difficult to understand the meaning of the utterance.

4 Improving Latvian ASR

After analyzing error types, their importance and causes, the next step was to find ways to improve the current baseline system. In this section we describe our efforts to deal with some type of errors that we identified earlier.

We first tested individual improvement ideas on our development set. Then all the improvements were combined together and the improved system was evaluated on a test set.

4.1 Recognition of Word "komats"

The first step was adding the alternative pronunciation "komats = K O M A" in the grapheme-to-phoneme (G2P) dictionary. With this simple solution we achieved a 50% reduction of errors for the word "komats".

The next step was implementing a number conversion step (done with a custom python script) in our LM training procedure. Implementing such a converter for Latvian is challenging, because all word endings must be matched. Our implementation covers only basic cases. After these efforts, 25% of the remaining errors with "komats" were corrected.

4.2 Word Endings

Table 1 shows that 41% of all errors are caused by misrecognized endings. Our solution to this problem involves increasing the language model training corpus from 22M to 47M sentences, while leaving the vocabulary size at 200K units. This should help to better estimate bigrams and trigrams, which contain words with rare endings, compared to the estimate obtained using backoff and a smaller corpus.

This approach led to a decrease of word ending errors to 21%, although there was no WER improvement.

4.3 Improving Vocabulary

Analysis reveals that 13% of all errors are due to the fact that a word is out of vocabulary. The out of vocabulary problem by itself can be solved by applying language models that use sub-word units instead of whole words. Although this approach solves out of vocabulary issue, it does not yield an improvement in terms of word error rate (Salimbajevs et al., 2015.). This time authors try the more obvious solution to deal with this problem and increase the training corpus used to prepare language model. In our case the training corpus was increased up to 47 million sentences with a 2.8 million unique word vocabulary, which reduced the out of vocabulary rate to 0.7%.

This resulted in WER reduction of 0.86%, and 61% of previously out of vocabulary words were correctly recognized. However, such a large increase in language model and vocabulary size resulted in the language model perplexity increasing on testing utterances by 647 compared to 498 obtained with language model trained on 22M sentence corpus and using 200K unit vocabulary, so the WER reduction was not as great as anticipated.

4.4 Evaluation

Combining all of the above mentioned improvements resulted in an improved final ASR system, which was then evaluated in terms of WER on both development and test sets (see Table 5).

System	Dev Set	Test Set
Baseline	18.06%	30.94%
Final	15.90%	28.43%

Table 5: WER of the final system.

5 Discussion

The Latvian language is an inflective language with complex morphology. Latvian also has a selection of prefixes and suffixes that can modify nouns, adjectives, adverbs and verbs. Because of this, two big problems arise: (1) high OOV rate, (2) errors in word endings.

Our error analysis reveals that endings contribute to 41% of errors and OOV words directly or indirectly cause 18% of errors. Together these two problems cause 59% of errors. Solving these problems will be very important for the further development of Latvian ASR.

However, not all errors are equal. Our results show that only 47% of errors make utterances difficult or impossible to understand. In most cases it is easy for a human reader to recover from errors in word endings, while in cases of OOV 82% of errors significantly change the meaning of the utterance.

We also found out that adjectives and verbs are more difficult to recognize than other parts of speech (excluding prepositions and particles). This is due to fact that they have the most variants of endings.

Non-canonical pronunciation can cause significant problems for ASR. In our development set no fractional numbers were recognized correctly because the pronunciation of the word "komats" (comma) was not canonical. We managed to reduce these errors by 50% by adding an alternative pronunciation to the G2P vocabulary.

Evaluation results show that there is a big difference in WER between the development and test sets. It seems that our random splitting was not very successful and resulted in uneven distribution of utterances which are hard to recognize. Both sets should have been tested before any analysis began. It is possible that some large class of errors was not identified.

Nevertheless, the final system showed noticeable improvement and outperformed the baseline system by about 2% WER on both test sets. This shows that our improvements were effective. Also it can be concluded that "surface" analysis of errors can help to improve speech recognition

6 Conclusions

In this paper we presented a surface error analysis of the Latvian Large Vocabulary Automatic Speech Recognition system.

The results show that more than 50% of errors are OOV and misrecognized word endings. Both of these problems are caused by the inflective nature and complex morphology of Latvian. Finding solution to these problems will greatly reduce the WER of Latvian ASR.

This analysis was then used to improve the present ASR system. After the changes the system showed 2% WER improvement on both the development and test sets.

In future we plan to perform more in-depth error analysis of errors in word endings. It is also important to find effective way of dealing with OOV, instead of just continuing to increase the size of the vocabulary.

7 Acknowledgments

The research leading to these results has received funding from the research project "Information and Communication Technology Competence Centre" of EU Structural funds, contract nr. L-KC-11-0003 signed between the ICT Competence Centre (www.itkc.lv) and the Investment and Development Agency of Latvia, research No. 2.4 "Speech recognition technologies".

References

Darģis, R., & Znotiņš, A. (2014). Baseline for Keyword Spotting in Latvian Broadcast Speech. In *Human Language Technologies – The Baltic Perspective* (pp. 75–82). IOS Press.

Fosler-Lussier, E., & Morgan, N. (1999). Effects of speaking rate and word frequency on pronunciations in conversational speech. *Speech Communication, 29*, 137–158. doi:10.1016/S0167-6393(99)00035-7

Goldwater, S., Jurafsky, D., & Manning, C. D. (2010). Which words are hard to recognize? Prosodic, lexical, and disfluency factors that increase speech recognition error rates. *Speech Communication, 52*, 181–200. doi:10.1016/j.specom.2009.10.001

Goryainova, M., Grouin, C., Rosset, S., & Vasilescu, I. (2014). Morpho-Syntactic Study of Errors from Speech Recognition System. In N. C. (Conference Chair), K. Choukri, T. Declerck, H. Loftsson, B. Maegaard, J. Mariani, … S. Piperidis (Eds.), *Proceedings of the Ninth International Conference on Language Resources and Evaluation (LREC'14).* Reykjavik, Iceland: European Language Resources Association (ELRA).

Miao, Y., Zhang, H., & Metze, F. (2014). Towards speaker adaptive training of deep neural network acoustic models. *Proc. Interspeech.*

Oparin, I., Lamel, L., & Gauvain, J.-L. (2013). Rapid development of a Latvian speech-to-text system. In *Acoustics, Speech and Signal Processing (ICASSP), 2013 IEEE International Conference on* (pp. 7309–7313). doi:10.1109/ICASSP.2013.6639082

Pappu, A., Misu, T., & Gupta, R. (2014). Investigating Critical Speech Recognition Errors in Spoken Short Messages. In *Proceedings of the 5th International Workshop on Spoken Dialog Systems (IWSDS).* Napa, California.

Pinnis, M., Auziņa, I., & Goba, K. (2014). Designing the Latvian Speech Recognition Corpus. In *Proceedings of the 9th edition of the Language Resources and Evaluation Conference (LREC'14)* (pp. 1547–1553).

Povey, D., Ghoshal, A., Boulianne, G., Burget, L., Glembek, O., Goel, N., … Vesely, K. (2011). The Kaldi Speech Recognition Toolkit. In *IEEE 2011 Workshop on Automatic Speech Recognition and Understanding*. IEEE Signal Processing Society.

Salimbajevs, A., & Pinnis, M. (2014). Towards Large Vocabulary Automatic Speech Recognition for Latvian. In *Human Language Technologies – The Baltic Perspective* (pp. 236–243). IOS Press.

Schwartz, R., Nguyen, L., Kubala, F., Chou, G., Zavaliagkos, G., & Makhoul, J. (1994). On Using Written Language Training Data for Spoken Language Modeling. In *Proceedings of the Workshop on Human Language Technology* (pp. 94–98). Stroudsburg, PA, USA: Association for Computational Linguistics. doi:10.3115/1075812.1075830

Shinozaki, T., & Furui, S. (2001). Error analysis using decision trees in spontaneous presentation speech recognition. *IEEE Workshop on Automatic Speech Recognition and Understanding, 2001. ASRU '01.* doi:10.1109/ASRU.2001.1034621

Stoyanchev, S., Salletmayr, P., Yang, J., & Hirschberg, J. (2012). Localized detection of speech recognition errors. In *Spoken Language Technology Workshop (SLT), 2012 IEEE* (pp. 25–30). doi:10.1109/SLT.2012.6424164

Vasilescu, I., Adda-Decker, M., & Lamel, L. (2012). Cross-lingual studies of ASR errors: paradigms for perceptual evaluations. In N. C. (Conference Chair), K. Choukri, T. Declerck, M. U. Do?an, B. Maegaard, J. Mariani, … S. Piperidis (Eds.), *Proceedings of the Eight International Conference on Language Resources and Evaluation (LREC'12).* Istanbul, Turkey: European Language Resources Association (ELRA).

Salimbajevs, A. and Strigins, J. (2015) Using sub-word n-gram models for dealing with OOV in large vocabulary speech recognition for Latvian. In *Proceedings of the 20th Nordic Conference of Computational Linguistics*

Towards the Unsupervised Acquisition of Implicit Semantic Roles

Niko Schenk, Christian Chiarcos, Maria Sukhareva
Applied Computational Linguistics Lab
Goethe University Frankfurt am Main, Germany
{n.schenk,chiarcos,sukhareva}@em.uni-frankfurt.de

Abstract

This paper describes a novel approach to find evidence for implicit semantic roles. Our data-driven models generalize over large amounts of *explicit* annotations only, in order to acquire information about implicit roles. We establish a generic background knowledge base of probablistic predicate-role co-occurrences in an unsupervised manner, and estimate thresholds which trigger the prediction of a missing role. Our approach outperforms the state-of-the-art in terms of recognition rate and offers a more flexible alternative to rule-based solutions which rely on costly, language and domain-specific lexica.

1 Introduction

In its classical form, an automated semantic role labeling (SRL) system (Gildea and Jurafsky, 2002) detects events (verbal or nominal predicates), together with their associated participants within the local context. Semantic roles are assigned to syntactic elements, such as A0 for the *agent* of an event, A1 for the patient (i.e. the entity which undergoes the action), etc.[1] The output of SRL systems have proven to offer a good approximation to a deeper semantic modeling of natural language. However, given its inherent complexity, recent efforts for improvement have tried to extend traditional SRL from the sentence-internal context to the *surrounding discourse*. As an illustration, consider the following biomedical example from Ruppenhofer et al. (2010).

> [$_{A0}$Twenty-two month old] with history of recurrent right middle lobe infiltrate. Increased [$_{A0}\varnothing$] cough, [$_{A0}\varnothing$] tachypnea, and [$_{A0}\varnothing$] work of breathing.

In the second sentence, a standard SRL system would ideally identify *cough*, *tachypnea* and *work of breathing* as nominal predicates. However, the A0 (experiencer/agent) role of these predicates is unfilled in the current sentence, and only explicitly realized in the preceding one (cf. *twenty-two month old*). Its identification is thus beyond the scope of the traditional parser, which is restricted to an isolated per-sentence analysis.

More precisely, the agent (argument) role of *cough*, for example, is non-overt or **implicit**, i.e. locally unexpressed in the second sentence and can only be resolved from the wider context. In general, many role realizations of this sort are suppressed on the surface level. These implicit roles are also called *null instantiations* (NIs) (Fillmore, 1986; Ruppenhofer, 2005) and have been extensively studied in the literature, cf. *zero anaphora* (Levinson, 1987; Hangyo et al., 2013).

The automated detection of such implicit roles (iSRL) and their fillers is a challenging task. Yet, if uncovered, NIs provide highly beneficial 'supplementary' information: These can in turn be incorporated into practical, downstream applications in the context of Natural Language Understanding, like text summarization, recognizing textual entailment or question answering.

Current issues in iSRL Corpus data with manually annotated implicit roles is extremely sparse and hard to obtain, and annotation efforts have emerged only recently; cf. Ruppenhofer et al. (2010), Gerber and Chai (2012), and also Feizabadi and Padó (2015) for an attempt to enlarge the number of annotation instances by combination of scarce resources. As a result, most state-of-the-art iSRL systems cannot be trained in a supervised setting and thus integrate custom, rule-based components to detect NIs. (We elaborate on related work in Section 2.) To this end, a predicate's overt roles are matched against a predefined predicate-

[1]For details on the PropBank labels used in our study, see Palmer et al. (2005).

Proceedings of Recent Advances in Natural Language Processing, pages 570–578,
Hissar, Bulgaria, Sep 7–9 2015.

specific template. Informally, all roles found in the template but not in the text are regarded as null instantiations. Such pattern-based methods perform satisfactorily, yet there are drawbacks:
(1) They are inflexible and absolute according to their type, in that they assume that all candidate NIs are equally likely to be missing, which is unrealistic given the variety of different linguistic contexts in which predicates co-occur with their semantic roles.
(2) They are expensive in that they require handcrafted, idiosyncratic rules (Ruppenhofer et al., 2011) and rich background knowledge in the form of language-specific lexical resources, such as FrameNet (Baker et al., 1998), PropBank (Palmer et al., 2005) or NomBank (Meyers et al., 2004). Dictionaries providing information about each predicate and status of the individual roles (e.g., whether they can serve as implicit elements or not) are costly, and for most other languages not available to the same extent as for English.
(3) Most earlier studies heuristically restrict implicit arguments to *core* roles only,[2] but this is problematic as it ignores the fact that implicit non-core roles also provide valid and valuable information. Our approach remains agnostic regarding the role inventory, and can address both core and non-core arguments. Yet, in accordance with the limited evaluation data and in line with earlier literature, we had to restrict ourselves to evaluate NI predictions for core arguments only.

Our contribution We propose a novel, generic approach to infer information about implicit roles which does not rely on the availability of manually annotated gold data. Our focus is exclusively on *NI role identification*, i.e., per-predicate detection of the missing implicit semantic role(s) given their overtly expressed explicit role(s) (without finding filler elements) as we believe that it serves as a crucial preprocessing step and still bears great potential for improvement. We treat NI identification *separately* from the resolution of their fillers, also because not all NIs are resolvable from the context. In order to facilitate a more flexible mechanism, we propose to condition on the presence of other roles, and primarily argue that NI detection should be **probabilistic instead of rule-based**. More specifically, we predict implicit arguments using large corpora from which we build a background knowledge base of predicates, co-occurring (explicit) roles and their probabilities. With such a **memory-based** approach, we generalize over large quantities of explicit roles to find evidence for implicit information in a mildly supervised manner. Our proposed models are largely domain independent, include a sense distinction for predicates, and are not bound to a specific release of a hand-maintained dictionary. Our approach is portable across languages in that training data can be created using projected SRL annotations. Unlike most earlier approaches, we employ a generic role set which is based on PropBank/NomBank rather than FrameNet: The PropBank format comprises a relatively small role inventory which is better suited to obtain statistical generalizations than the great variety of highly specific FrameNet roles. While FrameNet roles seem to be more fine-grained, their greater number arises mostly from predicate-specific semantic roles, whose specific semantics can be recovered from PropBank annotations by pairing semantic roles with the predicate.

Yet another motivation of our work is related to the recent development of AMR parsing (Banarescu et al., 2013, Abstract Meaning Representation) which aims at modeling the semantic representation of a sentence while abstracting from syntactic idiosyncrasies. This particular appraoch makes extensive use of the PropBank-style framesets, as well, and would greatly benefit from the integration of information on implicit roles.

The paper is structured as follows: Section 2 outlines related work in which we exclusively focus on how previous research has handled the sole identification of NIs. Section 3 describes our approach to probabilistic NI detection; Section 4 presents two experiments and their evaluation in comparison with previous studies. Finally, we conclude our work in Section 5.

2 Related Work

In the context of the 2010 SemEval Shared Task on *Linking Events and Their Participants in Discourse*[3] on implicit argument resolution, Ruppenhofer et al. (2010) have released a data set of fiction novels with manual NI role annotations for diverse predicates. The data has been referred to

[2] *Core* roles are obligatory arguments of a predicate. Informally, *non-core* roles are optional arguments often realized as adjuncts or modifiers.

[3] http://semeval2.fbk.eu/semeval2.php

by various researchers in the community for direct or indirect evaluation of their results. The NIs in the data set are further subdivided into two categories: Definite NIs (DNIs) are locally unexpressed arguments which can be resolved to elements in the proceeding or following discourse; Indefinite NIs (INIs) are elements for which no antecedent can be identified in the surrounding context.[4] Also, the evaluation data comes in two flavors: a base format which is compliant with the FrameNet paradigm and a CoNLL-based PropBank format. Previous research has exclusively focused on the former.

Chen et al. (2010) present an extension of an existing FrameNet-style parser (SEMAFOR) to handle implicit elements in text. The identification of NIs is guided by the assumption that, whenever the traditional SRL parser returns the default label involved in a non-saturated analysis for a sentence, an implicit role has to be found in the context instead. Additional FrameNet-specific heuristics are employed in which, e.g., the presence of one particular role in a frame makes the identification of another implicit role redundant.[5]

Tonelli and Delmonte (2010, VENSES++) present a deep semantic approach to NI resolution whose system-specific output is mapped to FrameNet valency patterns. For the detection of NIs, they assume that these are always core arguments, i.e., non-omissible roles in the interaction with a specific predicate. It is unclear how different predicate senses are handled by their approach. Moreover, not all types of NIs can be detected, resulting in a low overall recall of identified NIs, also having drawbacks for nouns. Again using FrameNet-specific modeling assumptions, their work has been significantly refined in Tonelli and Delmonte (2011).

Despite their good performance in the overall task, Silberer and Frank (2012, S&F) give a rather vague explanation regarding NI identification in text. Using a FrameNet API, the authors restrict their analysis only to the core roles by excluding "conceptually redundant" roles without further elaboration.

Laparra and Rigau (2013) propose a deterministic algorithm to detect NIs on grounds of discourse coherence: It predicts an NI for a predicate if the corresponding role has been explicitly realized for the same predicate in the preceding discourse but is currently unfilled. Their approach is promising but ignorant of INIs.

Earlier, Laparra and Rigau (2012, L&R) introduce a statistical approach to identifying NIs similar to ours in that they rely on frequencies from overt arguments to predict implicit arguments. For each predicate template (frame), their algorithm computes all Frame Element patterns, i.e., all co-occurring overt roles and their frequencies. For NI identification a given predicate and its overtly expressed roles are matched against the most frequent pattern not violated by the explicit arguments. Roles of the pattern which are not overtly expressed in the text are predicted as missing NIs. Even though their approach outperforms all previous results in terms of NI detection, Laparra and Rigau (2012) only estimate the *raw* frequencies from a very limited training corpus, raising the question whether all patterns are actually sufficiently robust. Also, the authors disregard all the valuable less frequent patterns and limit their analysis to only a subtype of NI instances which are resolvable from the context.

Finally, Gerber and Chai (2012) describe a supervised model for implicit argument resolution on the NomBank corpus which—unlike the previous literature—follows the PropBank annotation format. However, NI detection is still done by dictionary lookup, and the analysis is limited to only a small set of predicates with only one unambiguous sense. Again limiting NIs to only core roles, the authors empirically demonstrate that this simplification accounts for 8% of the overall error rate of their system.

3 Experimental Setup

3.1 Memory-Based Learning

Memory-based learning for NLP (Daelemans and van den Bosch, 2009) is a lazy learning technique which keeps a record of training instances in the form of a background knowledge base (BKB). Classification compares new items directly to the stored items in the BKB via a distance metric. In semantics, the method has been applied by, e.g., Peñas and Hovy (2010) for semantic enrichment, and Chiarcos (2012) to infer (implicit markers for) discourse relations. Here, we adopt its methodology to identify null-instantiated argument roles in text. More precisely, we setup a BKB of probablistic predicate-role co-occurrences and estimate

[4]The average F-score annotator agreement for frame assignments is about .75 (Ruppenhofer et al., 2010).

[5]Cf. *CoreSet* and *Exludes* relationship in FrameNet.

thresholds which serve as a trigger for the prediction of an implicit role (a slight modification of the distance metric). We elaborate on this methodology in Section 4.

3.2 Data & Preprocessing

We train our model on a subset of the *WaCkypedia_EN*[6] corpus (Baroni et al., 2009). The data set provides a 2008 Wikipedia dump from which we extracted $\frac{1}{5}$ of the complete corpus ($\approx$ 10 million sentences which are tokenized already). We applied the MATE[7] parser (Björkelund et al., 2009) for the automatic detection of semantic roles to the portion of the Wikipedia dump annotating it with SRL information. MATE has been used in previous research on implicit elements in text (Roth and Frank, 2013) and provides semantic roles with a sense disambiguation for both verbal and nominal predicates. The resulting output is based on the PropBank format.

3.3 Model Generation

We build a probablistic model from annotated predicate-role co-occurrences as follows:

1. For every sentence, record all distinct predicate instances and their associated roles.
2. For every predicate instance, sort the role labels lexicographically (not the role fillers), disregarding their sequential order. (We thus obtain a normalized template of role co-occurrences for each frame instantiation.)
3. Compute the frequencies for all templates associated with the same predicate.
4. By relative frequency estimation, derive all conditional probabilities of the form:

$$P(r|R, \text{PREDICATE})$$

with $\mathcal{R}$ being the role inventory of the SRL parser, $R \subseteq \mathcal{R}$ a (sub)set of explicitly realized semantic roles, and $r \in \mathcal{R} \setminus R$ an arbitrary semantic role. When we try to gather information on null instantiated roles, r is typically an unrealized role label. The PREDICATE consists of the lemma of the corresponding verb or noun, followed by sense number (predicates are sense-disambiguated) and its part of speech (V/N), e.g., PLAY.01.N.

[6]http://wacky.sslmit.unibo.it/doku.php?id=corpora

[7]http://code.google.com/p/mate-tools/

Paradigm		#Roles			#Overt
		Overt	DNI	INI	#DNI+#INI
Train	FrameNet	2,526	303	277	4.36
	PropBank	1,027	125	101	4.52
Test	FrameNet	3,141	349	361	4.42
	PropBank	1,332	167	85	5.28

Table 1: Label distribution of the SemEval 2010 data set for overt and null instantiated arguments for both the FrameNet (all roles and parts of speech) and the PropBank version (only core roles for nouns and verbs).

3.4 Annotated Data

In accordance with previous iSRL studies, we evaluate our model on the SemEval data set (Ruppenhofer et al., 2010). However, to the best of our knowledge, this is the first study to focus on the PropBank version of this data set. It has been derived semi-automatically from the FrameNet base format using hand-crafted mapping rules (as part of the data set) for both verbs and nouns. For example, a conversion for the predicate *fear* in FrameNet's EXPERIENCER_FOCUS frame is defined as *fear.01* (its first sense) with the roles EXPERIENCER and CONTENT mapped to PropBank labels A0 and A1, respectively. In accordance with the mapping patterns, the resulting distribution of NIs varies slightly from the base format. Table 1 shows the label distribution of overt roles, DNIs, INIs for both the FrameNet and PropBank versions, respectively. Some information is lost while the general proportions remain similar to the base format. This is also due to the fact that for some parts of speech (e.g., for adjectives) no mappings are defined, even though some of them are annotated with NI information in the FrameNet version. Moreover, mapping rules exist *only for core roles* A0-A4 (agent, patient, ...). As a consequence, we restrict our analysis to these five (unique) roles, even though our models described in this work incorporate probabilistic information for *all possible roles* in $\mathcal{R}$, i.e., A0-A4, but also for *non-core* (modifier) roles, such as AM-TEMP (temporal), AM-LOC (location), etc.

4 Experiments

4.1 Experiment 1

Usually, a predicate occurs with an arbitrary number of overt arguments, and similarly the number of missing NIs varies, too. In this experiment, we introduce different data-driven variants to predict the correct set of null instantiations for any given

NI Pattern	Freq	NI Pattern	Freq
-	706	A0 A2	7
A1	86	A1 A2	6
A0	51	A3	5
A2	35	A1 A4	3
A4	18	A0 A1 A2	1
A0 A1	11		

Table 2: The 929 NI role patterns from the test set sorted by their number of occurrence. Most of the predicates are saturated and do not seek an implicit argument. Only one predicate instance has three implicit roles.

predicate and its associated explicit roles. Specifically, to tackle the problem, we take the SemEval train and test split (744 vs. 929 unrestricted frame instances of the form: any combination of overt roles vs. any combination of NI roles per predicate). In this setting, we do not draw a distinction between DNIs and INIs, but treat them generally as NIs. Table 2 shows the distribution of the different NI role patterns in the test data.

4.1.1 Task Description

Given a predicate and its overtly expressed arguments (ranging from any combination of A0 to A4 or none), predict the correct set of null instantiations (which can also be empty or contain up to five different implicit elements).

4.1.2 Predicting Null Instantiations

We distinguish two main types of classifiers: *supervised classifiers* are directly obtained from NI annotations in the SemEval training data, *mildly supervised classifiers* instead use only information about (automatically obtained) explicitly realized semantic roles in a given corpus, *hybrid classifiers* combine both sources of information. We estimated all parameters optimizing F-measure on the train section of the SemEval data set. Their performance is evaluated on its test section. We aim to demonstrate that mildly supervised classifiers are capable of predicting implicit roles, and to study whether NI annotations can be used to improve their performance.

Baseline: Given the diversity of possible patterns, it is hard to decide how a suitable and competitive baseline should be defined: predicting the majority class means not to predict anything. So, instead, we predict implicit argument roles randomly, but in a way that emulates their frequency distribution in the SemEval data (cf. Tab. 2), i.e., predict no NIs with a probability of 76.0% (706/929), A1 with 38.6% (86/929), etc. The baseline scores are averaged over 100 runs of this random 'classifier', further referred to as A.

Supervised classifier: Supervised classifiers, as understood here, are classifiers that use the information obtained from manual NI annotations. We set up *two* predictors B_1 and B_2 tuned on the SemEval training set: B_1 is obtained by counting for each predicate its *most frequent NI role pattern*. For instance, for *seem.02*—once annotated with implicit A1, but twice without implicit arguments—B_1 would predict an empty set of NIs. B_2 is similar to B_1 but conditions NI role patterns not only on the predicate, but also on its explicit arguments.[8] For prediction, these classifiers consult the most frequent NI pattern observed for a predicate (B_2: plus its overt arguments). If a test predicate is unknown (i.e., not present in the training data), we predict the majority class (empty set) for NI.

Mildly supervised classifier: Mildly supervised classifiers do not take any NI annotation into account. Instead, they rely on explicitly realized semantic roles observed in a corpus, but use explicit NI annotations only to estimate prediction thresholds. In what follows, we present eight parameter-based classification algorithms for our model trained on 10 million sentences.

We define prediction for classifier $\mathbf{C}_0$ as follows: Given a predicate PREDICATE, the role inventory $\mathcal{R} = \{A0..A4\}$, its (possibly empty) set of overt roles $R \subseteq \mathcal{R}$ and a fixed, predicate-independent threshold t_0. We start by optimizing threshold t_0 on all predicate instances with *no* given overt argument. If there is *no* overt role and an unrealized role $n_i \in \mathcal{R}$ for which it is true that $P(n_i|\text{PREDICATE}) > t_0$, then predict n_i as an implicit role. If there is an overt role $o_j \in R$ and an unrealized role $n_i \in \mathcal{R} \setminus R$ for which it is true that $P(n_i|o_j,\text{PREDICATE}) > t_0$, then predict n_i as an implicit role. Note that C_0 requires that this condition to hold for *one* o_j, not all explicit arguments of the predicate instance (logical disjunction).

We refine this classifier by introducing an additional parameter that accounts for the group of overtly realized frames with exactly *one* overt argument, i.e., $\mathbf{C}_1$ predicts n_i if $P(n_i|o_j,\text{PREDICATE}) > t_1$; for all other configu-

[8] Specifically, we extract finer-grained patterns, e.g., *evening.01*[A1] → {}=2, {A2}=3, where a predicate is associated with its overt role(s) (left side of the arrow). The corresponding implicit role patterns and their number of occurrence is shown to the right.

Classifier	A	B_1	B_2	C_0	C_1	C_2	C_3	C_4	$C_{4_{n,v}}$	$C_{4_{n,v,B1}}$	$C_{4_{n,v,B2}}$
Precision	*0.149*	0.848	**0.853**	*0.368*	*0.378*	0.398	0.400	0.400	0.423	0.561	0.582
Recall	*0.075*	*0.155*	*0.206*	**0.861**	0.851	0.837	0.837	0.837	0.782	0.615	0.814
F_1 Score	*0.100*	*0.262*	*0.332*	*0.516*	*0.523*	*0.540*	*0.541*	*0.541*	*0.549*	0.589	**0.679**

Table 3: Precision, recall and F_1 scores for all classifiers introduced in Experiment 2. Scores are compared row-wise to the best-performing classifier $C_{4_{n,v,B2}}$. A significant improvement over a cell entry with $p < .05$ is indicated in *italics*.

rations the procedure is the same as in C_0, i.e., the threshold t_0 is applied.

Classifiers $\mathbf{C}_2$, $\mathbf{C}_3$ and $\mathbf{C}_4$ extend C_1 accordingly and introduce additional thresholds t_2, t_3, t_4 for the respective number of overt arguments. For example, $\mathbf{C}_3$ predicts n_i if $P(n_i|o_{j1}, o_{j2}, o_{j3}, \text{PREDICATE}) > t_3$, for configurations with less arguments, it relies on C_2, etc. Our general intuition here is to see whether the increasing number of specialized parameters for increasingly marginal groups of frames is justified by the improvements we achieve in this way.

A final classifier $\mathbf{C}_{4_{n,v}}$ extends C_4 by distinguishing verbal and nominal predicates, yielding a total of ten parameters $t_{0_n}..t_{4_n}, t_{0_v}..t_{0_n}$.

Hybrid classifier: To explore to what extent explicit NI annotations improve the classification results, we combine the best-performing and most elaborate mildly supervised classifier $C_{4_{n,v}}$ with the supervised classifiers B_1 and B_2: For predicates encountered in the training data, $\mathbf{C}_{4_{n,v,B_1}}$ (resp., $\mathbf{C}_{4_{n,v,B_2}}$) uses B_1 (resp., B_2) to predict the most frequent pattern observed for the predicate; for unknown predicates, apply the threshold-based procedure of $C_{4_{n,v}}$.

4.1.3 Results & Evaluation

Table 3 contains the evaluation scores for the individual parameter-based classifiers. All classifiers demonstrate significant improvements over the random baseline. Also the mildly supervised classifiers outperform the supervised algorithms in terms of F_1 score and recall. However, detecting NIs by the supervised classifiers is very accurate in terms of high precision. Classifier B_2 outperforms B_1 as a result of directly incorporating additional information about the overt arguments.

Concerning our parameter-based classifiers, the main observations are: First, the overall performance (F_1 score) increases from C_0 to C_4 (yet not significantly). Secondly, with more parameters, recall decreases while precision increases. We can observe, however, that improvements from C_2 to C_4 are marginal, at best, due to the sparsity of predicates with two or more overt arguments. Similar problems related to data sparsity have been reported in Chen et al. (2010). Results for C_3 and C_4 are identical, as no predicate with more than three overt arguments occurred in the test data. Encoding the distinction between verbal and nominal predicates into the classifier again slightly increases the performance.

A combination of the high-precision supervised classifiers and the best performing mildly supervised algorithm yields a significant boost in performance (Tab. 3, last two columns). In Table 4, we report the performance of our best classifier $C_{4_{n,v,B2}}$ with detailed label scores.

Roles	A0	A1	A2	A3	A4
# Labels	70	107	49	5	21
Precision	0.675	0.578	0.432	0.400	0.791
Recall	0.800	0.897	0.653	0.400	0.905
F_1 Score	0.732	0.703	0.520	0.400	0.844

Table 4: Evaluation of $C_{4_{n,v,B2}}$ for all 252 implicit roles.

Summarizing our results, Experiment 1 has shown that combining supervised and mildly supervised strategies to NI detection achieves the best results on the SemEval test set. Concerning the mildly supervised, parameter-based classifiers, it has proven beneficial to incorporate a maximum of available information on overtly expressed arguments in order to determine implicit roles.

4.2 Experiment 2

A second experiment focuses on the comparison with previous research in which DNI and INI predictions are separately evaluated. In our setting, however, we regard this evaluation as artificial as DNI/INI classification could alternatively be decided depending on distance and availability of potential antecedents, a problem we would like to address in subsequent experiments.

System	NI recall	DNI/INI interpret. prec	
		relative	absolute
L&P	0.66	-	-
SEMAFOR	0.63	0.55	0.35
S&F	0.58	0.70	**0.40**
T&D	0.54	**0.75**	**0.40**
VENSES++	0.08	0.64	0.05
This Paper	**0.81**	0.57	0.36

Table 5: Recognition rate (recall) for all NIs, relative (based on correctly recognized) and absolute precision scores comparing the different state-of-the-art systems to our best-performing classifier $C4_{n,v,B2}$.

System	Type	Precision	Recall	F_1 Score
T&D	DNI	0.39	0.43	0.41
	INI	**0.46**	0.38	**0.42**
SEMAFOR	DNI	**0.57**	0.03	0.06
	INI	0.20	**0.61**	0.30
This paper	DNI	0.43	**0.44**	**0.43**
	INI	0.24	0.51	0.32
L&R	DNI	**0.50**	0.66	**0.57**
This paper	DNI	0.41	**0.86**	0.55

Table 6: INI vs. DNI classification compared to previous works (upper part). Silberer and Frank (2012) do not report individual NI type scores. L&R focus only on DNI detection. Our results on this subtask are shown in the last column.

4.2.1 Task Description

For every predicate, predict the set of null instantiations as in Exp. 1. Then, classify every predicted NI as DNI or INI.

4.2.2 Predicting Null Instantiations

We take the best-performing classifier $C4_{n,v,B2}$ from Exp. 1. Following Tonelli and Delmonte (2011), we then employ a rule-based classifier $C_{\text{DNI,INI}}$ to separate predicted NIs into DNIs or INIs: (a) predict INI for predicates with part of speech VBN/VBG (e.g., in passive voice); (b) predict the majority class according to DNI/INI frequencies for the predicate in the SemEval training set; (c) predict DNI if DNI/INI frequencies are equal or the predicate is missing in the SemEval training data.

4.2.3 Results

Incorporating $C_{\text{DNI,INI}}$ into the best performing NI classifier from Experiment 1 outperforms current state-of-the-art systems in terms of NI recall (Table 5) but has drawbacks in DNI/INI classification.[9]

A closer look at the individual NI types (upper part of Table 6) reveals that, overall, the performance of our predictor is competitive regarding the accuracies by the systems reported by Tonelli and Delmonte (2011, T&D) and Chen et al. (2010, SEMAFOR). More specifically, there is no single best performing system. The T&D system is generally powerful in predicting INIs, SEMAFOR has high recall and high precision for both, while we outperform the others on DNI analysis. Clearly, the best results are obtained by Laparra and Rigau (2012, L&R). However, they only report accuracies for the identification of DNIs, as INIs are beyond their scope. The last row of Table 6 gives the scores of our tool when we substitute $C_{\text{DNI,INI}}$ by predicting the majority class (DNI). Outperforming all other systems, we are able to detect 86% of all DNIs in the test set with an F_1 score only marginally worse than L&R.

[9]Note that our scores are not directly comparable as none of the other systems report precision scores for their pattern-based NI detection modules and our evaluation is based on the PropBank version of the data set whose label distribution, contrasting DNIs and INIs, is different from the FrameNet format (DNI majority class: 66.3% vs. 50.8%).

5 Summary and Outlook

We have presented a novel, statistical method to infer evidence for implicit roles from their explicit realizations in large amounts of automatically annotated SRL data. Despite its simplicity, we demonstrated the suitability of our approach: Even though our results do not outperform the state-of-the-art in F_1 score, they are still highly competitive. Our models are best in the overall recognition rate, however, still suffer in precision of the respective null instantiated arguments.

Thus, directions for future research should consider integrating additional contextual features and would benefit from the *complete* role inventory of our models (including non-core/modifier roles). Regarding this extended setting, we would like to experiment with other machine learning approaches, as well, in order to assess whether the accuracy of the detected NIs can be increased.

In addition, we plan to extend the memory-based strategy described in this paper to NI *resolution* (on top their detection), and in this context, also re-address the DNI/INI classification problem.

We conclude that—especially when annotated training data is sparse—memory-based approaches to implicit role detection seem highly promising and offer an alternative solution to static rule- or template-based methods with a much greater degree of flexibility.

References

Collin F. Baker, Charles J. Fillmore, and John B. Lowe. 1998. The Berkeley FrameNet Project. In *Proceedings of the 36th Annual Meeting of the Association for Computational Linguistics and 17th International Conference on Computational Linguistics - Volume 1*, ACL '98, pages 86–90, Stroudsburg, PA, USA. Association for Computational Linguistics.

Laura Banarescu, Claire Bonial, Shu Cai, Madalina Georgescu, Kira Griffitt, Ulf Hermjakob, Kevin Knight, Philipp Koehn, Martha Palmer, and Nathan Schneider. 2013. Abstract Meaning Representation for Sembanking. Proc. Linguistic Annotation Workshop.

Marco Baroni, Silvia Bernardini, Adriano Ferraresi, and Eros Zanchetta. 2009. The WaCky Wide Web: A Collection of Very Large Linguistically Processed Web-Crawled Corpora. *Language Resources and Evaluation*, 43(3):209–226.

Anders Björkelund, Love Hafdell, and Pierre Nugues. 2009. Multilingual Semantic Role Labeling. In *Proceedings of the Thirteenth Conference on Computational Natural Language Learning (CoNLL 2009): Shared Task*, pages 43–48, Boulder, Colorado, June. Association for Computational Linguistics.

Desai Chen, Nathan Schneider, Dipanjan Das, and Noah A. Smith. 2010. SEMAFOR: Frame Argument Resolution with Log-linear Models. In *Proceedings of the 5th International Workshop on Semantic Evaluation*, SemEval '10, pages 264–267, Stroudsburg, PA, USA. Association for Computational Linguistics.

Christian Chiarcos. 2012. Towards the Unsupervised Acquisition of Discourse Relations. In *Proceedings of the 50th Annual Meeting of the Association for Computational Linguistics: Short Papers - Volume 2*, ACL '12, pages 213–217, Stroudsburg, PA, USA. Association for Computational Linguistics.

Walter Daelemans and Antal van den Bosch. 2009. *Memory-Based Language Processing*. Cambridge University Press, New York, NY, USA, 1st edition.

Parvin Sadat Feizabadi and Sebastian Padó. 2015. Combining Seemingly Incompatible Corpora for Implicit Semantic Role Labeling. In *Proceedings of STARSEM*, pages 40–50, Denver, CO.

Charles J. Fillmore. 1986. Pragmatically Controlled Zero Anaphora. In *Proceedings of Berkeley Linguistics Society*, pages 95–107, Berkeley, CA.

Matthew Gerber and Joyce Chai. 2012. Semantic Role Labeling of Implicit Arguments for Nominal Predicates. *Comput. Linguist.*, 38(4):755–798, December.

Daniel Gildea and Daniel Jurafsky. 2002. Automatic Labeling of Semantic Roles. *Comput. Linguist.*, 28(3):245–288, September.

Masatsugu Hangyo, Daisuke Kawahara, and Sadao Kurohashi. 2013. Japanese Zero Reference Resolution Considering Exophora and Author/Reader Mentions. In *EMNLP*, pages 924–934. ACL.

Egoitz Laparra and German Rigau. 2012. Exploiting Explicit Annotations and Semantic Types for Implicit Argument Resolution. In *Sixth IEEE International Conference on Semantic Computing, ICSC 2012.*, Palermo, Italy. IEEE Computer Society.

Egoitz Laparra and German Rigau. 2013. ImpAr: A Deterministic Algorithm for Implicit Semantic Role Labelling. In *Proceedings of the 51st Annual Meeting of the Association for Computational Linguistics (Volume 1: Long Papers)*, pages 1180–1189. Association for Computational Linguistics.

Stephen C. Levinson. 1987. Pragmatics and the grammar of anaphora: A partial pragmatic reduction of Binding and Control phenomena. *Journal of Linguistics*, 23:379–434.

Adam Meyers, Ruth Reeves, Catherine Macleod, Rachel Szekely, Veronika Zielinska, Brian Young, and Ralph Grishman. 2004. The NomBank Project: An Interim Report. In A. Meyers, editor, *HLT-NAACL 2004 Workshop: Frontiers in Corpus Annotation*, pages 24–31, Boston, Massachusetts, USA, May 2 - May 7. Association for Computational Linguistics.

Martha Palmer, Daniel Gildea, and Paul Kingsbury. 2005. The Proposition Bank: An Annotated Corpus of Semantic Roles. *Comput. Linguist.*, 31(1):71–106, March.

Anselmo Peñas and Eduard Hovy. 2010. Semantic Enrichment of Text with Background Knowledge. In *Proceedings of the NAACL HLT 2010 First International Workshop on Formalisms and Methodology for Learning by Reading*, FAM-LbR '10, pages 15–23, Stroudsburg, PA, USA. Association for Computational Linguistics.

Michael Roth and Anette Frank. 2013. Automatically Identifying Implicit Arguments to Improve Argument Linking and Coherence Modeling. In *Proceedings of the Second Joint Conference on Lexical and Computational Semantics (*SEM)*, pages 306–316, Atlanta, Georgia, USA, June. Association for Computational Linguistics.

Josef Ruppenhofer, Caroline Sporleder, Roser Morante, Collin Baker, and Martha Palmer. 2010. SemEval-2010 Task 10: Linking Events and Their Participants in Discourse. In *Proceedings of the 5th International Workshop on Semantic Evaluation*, SemEval '10, pages 45–50, Stroudsburg, PA, USA. Association for Computational Linguistics.

Josef Ruppenhofer, Philip Gorinski, and Caroline Sporleder. 2011. In Search of Missing Arguments: A Linguistic Approach. In Galia Angelova, Kalina

Bontcheva, Ruslan Mitkov, and Nicolas Nicolov, editors, *RANLP*, pages 331–338. RANLP 2011 Organising Committee.

Josef Ruppenhofer. 2005. Regularities in Null Instantiation. Ms, University of Colorado.

Carina Silberer and Anette Frank. 2012. Casting Implicit Role Linking as an Anaphora Resolution Task. In *Proceedings of the First Joint Conference on Lexical and Computational Semantics - Volume 1: Proceedings of the Main Conference and the Shared Task, and Volume 2: Proceedings of the Sixth International Workshop on Semantic Evaluation*, SemEval '12, pages 1–10, Stroudsburg, PA, USA. Association for Computational Linguistics.

Sara Tonelli and Rodolfo Delmonte. 2010. VENSES++: Adapting a Deep Semantic Processing System to the Identification of Null Instantiations. In *Proceedings of the 5th International Workshop on Semantic Evaluation*, pages 296–299. Association for Computational Linguistics.

Sara Tonelli and Rodolfo Delmonte. 2011. Desperately Seeking Implicit Arguments in Text. In *Proceedings of the ACL 2011 Workshop on Relational Models of Semantics*, pages 54–62. Association for Computational Linguistics.

Evaluating the Impact of Using a Domain-specific Bilingual Lexicon on the Performance of a Hybrid Machine Translation Approach

Nasredine Semmar, Othman Zennaki, Meriama Laib
CEA, LIST, Vision and Content Engineering Laboratory
F-91191, Gif-sur-Yvette, France
{nasredine.semmar,othman.zennaki,meriama.laib}@cea.fr

Abstract

This paper describes an Example-Based Machine Translation prototype and presents an evaluation of the impact of using a domain-specific vocabulary on its performance. This prototype is based on a hybrid approach which needs only monolingual texts in the target language and consists to combine translation candidates returned by a cross-language search engine with translation hypotheses provided by a finite-state transducer. The results of this combination are evaluated against a statistical language model of the target language in order to obtain the n-best translations. To measure the performance of this hybrid approach, we achieved several experiments using corpora on two domains from the European Parliament proceedings (Europarl) and the European Medicines Agency documents (Emea). The obtained results show that the proposed approach outperforms the state-of-the-art Statistical Machine Translation system Moses when texts to translate are related to the specialized domain.

1 Introduction

Current Machine Translation (MT) technology has serious limitations: there are, on the one hand, the rule-based systems which require handcrafted linguistic rules and their manual construction is time consuming and expensive, and, on the other hand, the statistical systems which try to learn how to translate by analyzing the translation patterns found in large collections of human translations and these systems are effective only when large amounts of parallel corpora are available. However, parallel corpora are only available for a limited number of language pairs and domains. In several fields, available corpora are not sufficient to make Statistical Machine Translation (SMT) approaches operational.

We present, in this paper, an Example-Based Machine Translation (EBMT) prototype and we study the impact of using a domain-specific lexicon on its performance. The EBMT prototype is based on a hybrid approach which uses only a monolingual corpus in the target language. This corpus is considered as a textual database of a cross-language search engine. For each sentence to translate (query in natural language), the cross-language search engine is used to provide a set of sentences in the target language. These sentences are combined with translation hypotheses provided by a finite-state transducer. The result of this combination is evaluated against a statistical language model learned from the target language corpus in order to produce the n-best translations. We believe that this is the first application of cross-language information retrieval in machine translation (Semmar and Bouamor 2011; Semmar et al., 2011; Semmar et al., 2014).

The remainder of this paper is organized as follows: Section 2 describes the main approaches used in machine translation and presents previous works addressing the task of domain adaptation in statistical machine translation. Section 3 introduces the hybrid approach used to implement the EBMT prototype and presents its architecture. In section 4 we discuss results obtained after translating two types of texts in general and specialized domains. Section 5 concludes our study and presents our future work.

2 Related Work

Machine translation systems are indispensable tools in a globalizing world. In the last years, several online MT systems have been proposed and are used by millions of people every day. However, there are serious limitations to current MT technology which mainly uses two approaches: rule-based and corpus-based (Trujillo, 1999; Hutchins, 2003). The rule-based approach-

Proceedings of Recent Advances in Natural Language Processing, pages 579–587,
Hissar, Bulgaria, Sep 7–9 2015.

es regroup word-to-word translation, syntactic translation with transfer rules and interlingua. The corpus-based machine translation approaches regroup Example-based MT and statistical-based MT techniques (Somers, 2003). These two techniques have in common the use of a database containing already translated sentences. EBMT uses a process which consists in matching a new sentence against this database to extract suitable sentences which are recombined in an analogical manner to determine the correct translation. The second corpus-based strategy is the statistical approach (Brown et al., 1993) which consists in searching for a target language string that maximizes the probability that this string is the translation of a source target string (translation model) and the probability that this target language string is a valid sentence (language model). This approach uses strings co-occurrence frequency in aligned texts in order to build the translation model and strings succession (n-grams) in order to build the language model. Rule-Based MT (RBMT) approaches require manually made bilingual lexicons and linguistic rules, which can be costly, and not generalized to other languages. Corpus-based MT approaches are effective only when large amounts of parallel corpora are available. Recently, several strategies have been proposed to combine the strengths of rule-based and corpus-based MT approaches or to add deep linguistic knowledge into statistical machine translation. Examples include Part-Of-Speech and morphological information (Koehn et al., 2010), word sense disambiguation models (Carpuat and Wu, 2007) and semantic role labels (Wu and Fung, 2009). Carbonell et al. (2006) described a new paradigm for corpus based translation that does not require parallel text. They called this paradigm Context-Based Machine Translation (CBMT) which relies on a lightweight translation model utilizing a full-form bilingual lexicon and a decoder using long-range context via long n-grams and cascaded overlapping. The authors evaluated their approach in Spanish-English translation using Spanish newswire text. This approach achieves a BLEU score of 0.64. The results showed that quality increases above the reported score as the target corpus size increases and as dictionary coverage of source words and phrases becomes more complete.

As regards domain adaptation in MT, most previous works addressing this task have proven that a statistical machine translation system trained on general texts, has poor performance on specific domains. In order to adapt MT systems designed for one domain to work in another, several ideas have been explored and implemented (Bungum and Gambäck, 2011). Langlais (2002) integrated domain-specific lexicons in the translation model of a SMT engine which yields a significant reduction in word error rate. Lewis et al. (2010) developed domain specific SMT by pooling all training data into one large data pool, including as much in-domain parallel data as possible. They trained highly specific language models on "in-domain" monolingual data in order to reduce the dampening effect of heterogeneous data on quality within the domain. Hildebrand et al. (2005) used an approach which consisted essentially in performing test-set relativization (choosing training samples that look most like the test data) to improve the translation quality when changing the domain. Civera and Juan (2007), and Bertoldi and Federico (2009) used monolingual corpora and Snover et al. (2008) used comparable corpora to adapt MT systems designed for Parliament domain to work in News domain. The obtained results showed significant gains in performance. Banerjee et al. (2010) combined two separate domain models. Each model is trained from small amounts of domain-specific data. This data is gathered from a single corporate website. The authors used document filtering and classification techniques to realize the automatic domain detection. However, this work did not report the impact of generic data on domain translation accuracy. Daumé III and Jagarlamudi (2011) used dictionary mining techniques to find translations for unseen words from comparable corpora and they integrated these translations into a statistical phrase-based translation system. They reported improvements in translation quality (between 0.5 and 1.5 BLEU points) on four domains and two language pairs. Pecina et al. (2011) exploited domain-specific data acquired by domain-focused web-crawling to adapt general-domain SMT systems to new domains. They observed that even small amounts of in-domain parallel data are more important for translation quality than large amounts of in-domain monolingual data. Wang et al. (2012) used a single translation model and generalized a single-domain decoder to deal with different domains. They used this method to adapt large-scale generic SMT systems for 20 language pairs in order to translate patents. The authors reported a gain of 0.35 BLEU points for patent translation and a loss of only 0.18 BLEU points for generic translation.

The approach we propose for domain adaptation is close in spirit to the work of Langlais (2002), but assumes the integration of the domain-specific lexicon in the two components of the EBMT prototype: the cross-language search engine and the bilingual reformulator.

3 Machine Translation Based on Cross-language Information Retrieval

The hybrid approach used in the Example-Based Machine Translation prototype consists, on the one hand, in indexing a database of sentences in the target language and considering each sentence to translate as a query to that database, and on the other hand, in combining sentences returned by a cross-language search engine with translation hypotheses provided by a bilingual reformulator (Figure 1).

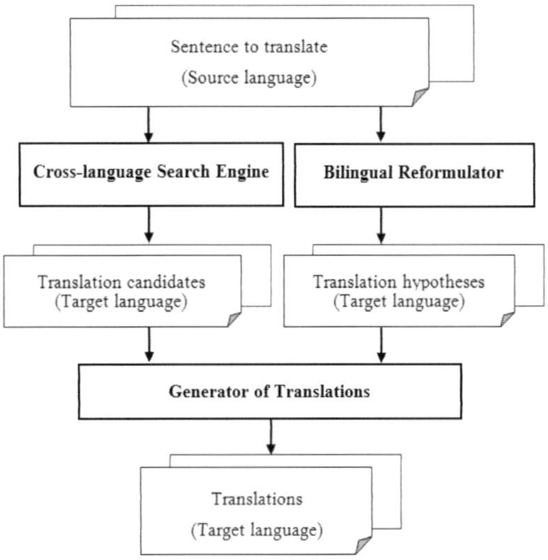

Figure 1: Architecture of the Example-Based Machine Translation prototype.

The EBMT prototype is composed of:

- A cross-language search engine to extract sentences or sub-sentences of the target language from the textual database which correspond to a total or a partial translation of the sentence to translate.
- A bilingual reformulator to transfer syntactic structures from the source language to the target language using transfer rules and bilingual lexicons.
- A generator of translations which consists in assembling the results returned by the cross-language search engine and the bilingual reformulator, and in choosing the n-best translations according to a statistical language model learned from the target language corpus.

In order to illustrate the translation process of the EBMT prototype, we indexed a textual database composed of 1127 French sentences extracted from the ARCADE II corpus[1] and we considered the input source sentence "Social security funds in Greece encourage investment in innovation." as the sentence to translate.

3.1 The Cross-language Search Engine

The purpose of Cross-Language Information Retrieval (CLIR) is to find similar or relevant documents for a given query where the documents and the query are written in different languages (Davis and Ogden, 1997; Grefenstette, 1998). In our use of CLIR in machine translation, a document corresponds to a sentence. The role of the cross-language search engine is to retrieve for each user's query (which is introduced as a sentence in natural language) translation candidates from an indexed monolingual corpus. The cross-language search engine used in the EBMT prototype is based on a deep linguistic analysis (Besançon et al., 2010) of the query and the monolingual corpus to be indexed and uses a weighted vector space model in which sentences to be indexed are grouped into classes characterized by the same set of words (Salton and McGill, 1986). This cross-language search engine (Besançon et al., 2003) is composed of a linguistic analyzer based on the open source multilingual platform LIMA[1], a statistical analyzer that attributes to each word or a compound word of the sentences to be indexed a weight by using the TF-IDF weighting, a comparator which measures the similarity between the sentence to translate (query) and the indexed sentences in the target language, a query reformulator to translate words of the query from the source language into the target language using a bilingual lexicon, and a indexer to build the inverted files of the sentences to be indexed on the basis of their linguistic analysis. The cross-language search engine provides the linguistic information (lemma, Part-Of-Speech, gender, number and syntactic dependen-

[1] http://www.technolangue.net/article.php3?id_article=201.

cy relations) of all words included both in the sentence to translate and the retrieved sentences (translation candidates). The result is a list of sentences classes ordered according to the weight of the intersection (similarity measure) between the sentence to translate and the indexed sentences. The translation candidates are represented as graphs of words and encoded with Finite-State Machines (FSMs). The nodes correspond to the states and the arcs refer to transitions. Each transition of the automaton indicates a lemma and its linguistic information which is provided by the linguistic analyzer of the cross-language search engine. Table 1 illustrates the two first translation candidates provided by the cross-language search engine for the sentence to translate "Social security funds in Greece encourage investment in innovation.".

Class n°.	Class query terms	Translation candidates
1	fund_security_social, Greece, investment	Les caisses de sécurité sociale de Grèce revendiquent l'indépendance en matière d'investissements.
2	fund_security_social	Objet: Caisses de sécurité sociale grecques.

Table 1: The two first translation candidates returned by the cross-language search engine for the query "Social security funds in Greece encourage investment in innovation.".

3.2 The Bilingual Reformulator

Because the indexed monolingual corpus does not contain the entire translation of each sentence, we added a mechanism to extend translations returned by the cross-language search engine. This is achieved by a Finite-State Transducer (FST) which consists, on the one hand, in transforming into the target language the syntactic structure of the sentence to translate, and, on the other hand, in translating its words. The transducer uses a set of linguistic rules to transform syntactic structures from the source language to the target language and the cross-language search engine bilingual lexicon to translate words of the sentence to translate. This reformulator produces translation hypotheses for the sentence to translate and proceeds in two phases: The first one (Syntactic transfer) consists in transforming syntactic structures from the source language to the target language using transfer rules. These rules built manually are based on morpho-syntactic patterns (Table 2). Expressions (phrases) corresponding to each pattern are identified by the LIMA's syntactic analyzer during the step of recognition of verbal and nominal chains. These expressions can be seen as sentences accepted by a FSM transducer whose outputs are instances of these sentences in the target language (Figure 2).

Rule n°.	Tag pattern (English)	Tag pattern (French)
1	AN	NA
2	ANN	NNA
3	NN	NN
4	AAN	NAA
5	NAN	NNA
6	NPN	NPN
7	NNN	NNN
8	ANPN	NAPN
9	NPAN	NPNA
10	TN	TN

Table 2: Frequent Part-Of-Speech tag patterns used to transform syntactic structures of the sentence to translate from English to French. In these patterns A refers to an Adjective, P to a Preposition, T to Past Participle, and N to a Noun.

For example, from the sentence to translate "Social security funds in Greece encourage investment in innovation.", two nominal chains are recognized: "Social security funds in Greece" and "investment in innovation". These nominal chains are linked with the verb "encourage". The expression "investment in innovation" is transformed using the sixth rule (Table 2) into the expression "the investment in the innovation". It is important to mention here that the linking word "the" (definite article) is added to the applied rule before each noun (investment, innovation) in order to complete the transformation.

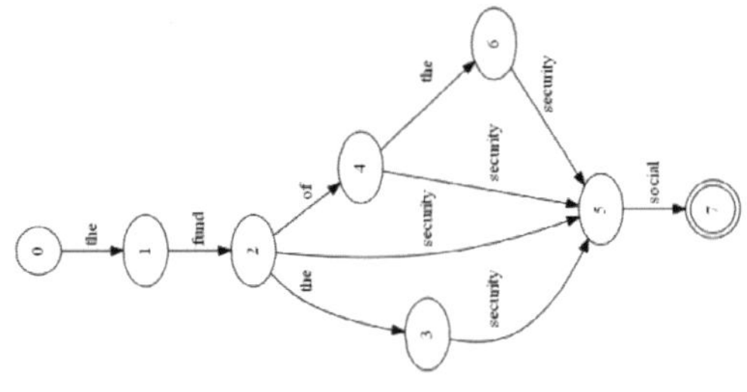

Figure 2: Example of syntactic transformation of the compound word "Social security funds".

The second phase of the bilingual reformulator (Lexical transfer) translates in the target language the lemmas of the obtained syntactic structures words using the cross-language search engine bilingual lexicon. This English-French lexicon is composed of 243539 entries[2]. These entries are represented in their normalized forms (lemmas). A lemmatization process provided by the linguistic analyzer is applied on the obtained syntactic structures words. This step could produce an important number of translation hypotheses. This is due to the combination of the syntactic transfer rules and the polysemy in the bilingual lexicon. The bilingual transducer produces a lattice of words. Each word is represented with its lemma in the lattice and is associated with its linguistic information (Part-Of-Speech, gender, number, etc.).

3.3 The Generator of Translations

The generator of translations consists in producing correct sentences in the target language by using morphological information and syntactic structures of translation candidates. Its role is to assemble in a lattice of words translation hypotheses produced by the transducer with the translation candidates returned by the cross-language search engine. The assembling process consists in composing FSMs corresponding to the translation hypotheses with FSMs corresponding to the translation candidates. Syntactic dependency relations of the translation hypotheses and the translation candidates as well as transfer rules are used to determine the FSM state where the composition is made. In our example, the verb "encourager" (encourage) which links the two patterns involved in the syntactic transformation of the sentence to translate, and the word "revendiquer" (claim) which links the two nominal chains of the first translation candidate (Table 1) determine this state. All the operations applied on the FSMs are made with the AT&T FSM Library[3] (Mohri et al., 2002). In order to find the best translation hypothesis from the lattice, a statistical model is learned with the CRF++ toolkit[4] (Lafferty et al., 2001) on the lemmatized corpus of the target language. Therefore, the n-best translations words are in their normalized forms (lemmas). To generate the n-best translations with words in inflected forms, a morphological generator (flexor) is used to transform the lemmas of the translations words into their surface forms. This flexor uses the linguistic information (Part-Of-Speech, gender, number, etc.) provided by the linguistic analyzer of the cross-language search engine for each word of the sentence to translate and the retrieved sentences. The lattice of words corresponding to the translations is enriched with the results of the flexor. This lattice is then scored with another statistical language model learned from texts of the target language containing words in inflected forms. The CRF++ toolkit is used to select the n-best translations in inflected forms. Table 3 shows the two first translations provided by the EBMT prototype for the input source sentence "Social security funds in Greece encourage investment in innovation.".

Rank	Translation
1	les caisses de la sécurité sociale en Grèce encouragent l'investissement dans l'innovation.
2	les fonds de la sécurité sociale en Grèce encouragent l'investissement en l'innovation.

Table 3: The two first translations for the English sentence "Social security funds in Greece encourage investment in innovation.".

4 Experimental Results

4.1 Data and Experimental Setup

We conducted our experiments on two English-French parallel corpora: Europarl (European Parliament Proceedings) and Emea (European Medicines Agency Documents). Both corpora were extracted from the open parallel corpus OPUS (Tiedemann, 2012). Table 4 lists corpora details.

Run n°.	Training (# sentences)	Tuning (# sentences)
1	150000 (Europarl)	3750 (Europarl)
2	150000+10000 (Europarl+Emea)	1500 (Europarl)
3	150000+20000 (Europarl+Emea)	1500 (Europarl)
4	150000+30000 (Europarl+Emea)	1500 (Europarl)

Table 4: Corpora details used to train Moses and to build the database of the cross-language search engine integrated in the EBMT prototype.

[2] http://catalog.elra.info/product_info.php?products_id=666.
[3] FSM Library is available from AT&T for non-commercial use as executable binary programs.
[4] http://wing.comp.nus.edu.sg/~forecite/services/parscit-100401/crfpp/CRF++-0.51/doc/.

The English-French training corpus is used to build Moses's translation and language models. The French sentences of this training corpus are used to create the indexed database of the cross-language search engine integrated in the EBMT prototype. We conducted four runs and two test experiments for each run: In-Domain and Out-Of-Domain. For this, we randomly extracted 500 parallel sentences from Europarl as an In-Domain corpus and 500 pairs of sentences from Emea as an Out-Of-Domain corpus. These experiments are done to show the impact of the domain vocabulary on the translation results. The domain vocabulary is represented in the case of Moses by the specialized parallel corpus (Emea) which is added to the training data (Europarl). In the case of the EBMT prototype, the domain vocabulary is identified by a bilingual lexicon which is extracted automatically from the specialized parallel corpus (Emea) using a word alignment tool (Semmar et al., 2010; Bouamor et al., 2012). This specialized bilingual lexicon is added to the English-French lexicon which is used by the cross-language search engine and the bilingual reformulator. First, both corpora have been normalized through the following preprocessing tools provided by the open source SMT toolkit Moses (Khoen et al., 2007): Tokenization, True-casing (the initial words in each sentence are converted to their most probable casing) and Cleaning (long sentences –more than 80 characters- and empty sentences are removed). To evaluate the performance of our approach, we used Moses (Koehn et al., 2007) as a baseline, and the BLEU score as an automatic evaluation metric (Papineni et al; 2002).

4.2 Results and Discussion

We measure translation quality on the two test sets for the four runs described in the previous section and calculate the BLEU score. We also consider only one reference for each test sentence. Obtained results are reported in Table 5.

Run n°.	In-Domain		Out-Of-Domain	
	Moses	EBMT	Moses	EBMT
1	34.79	30.57	13.62	24.27
2	32.62	30.10	22.96	27.80
3	33.81	29.60	23.30	28.70
4	34.25	28.70	24.55	29.50

Table 5: BLEU scores of Moses and the EBMT prototype.

The first observation is that, when the test set is In-Domain, we achieve a relatively high score BLEU for both the two systems and the score of Moses is better in all the runs. For the Out-Of-Domain test corpus, the EBMT prototype performs better than Moses in all the runs and in particular Moses has obtained a very low BLEU score in the first run. This result can be explained by the fact that the test corpus has a vocabulary which is different from the entries of the translation table. Furthermore, it seems that the English-French lexicon used by the cross-language search engine and the bilingual reformulator has had a significant impact on the result of the EBMT prototype. It improved regularly its BLEU score in all the runs. These results confirm that adding specialized parallel corpora to the training data improves the translation quality for the both MT systems in all cases but the improvement of the EBMT prototype is more significant. These results also show that the proportion of the specialized corpus in the training data has a strong impact on the performance of Moses. Indeed, in the fourth run, adding a specialized parallel corpus composed of 30000 sentences to the 150000 sentences of Europarl, reported a gain of 10.93 BLEU score. Tables 6 and 7 illustrate two examples of translations produced by our EBMT prototype and Moses drawn from texts relating to the European Parliament proceedings and the European Medicines Agency texts. Analysis of the translation results shows that for the In-Domain sentences (Example 1) the EBMT prototype and Moses provide close translations and these translations are more or less correct.

Example 1 Input: our success must be measured by our capacity to *keep* growing while ensuring solidarity and cohesion.	
Reference	nous devons mesurer notre réussite à notre capacité à *poursuivre sur la voie* de la croissance tout en garantissant la solidarité et la cohésion.
EBMT prototype	notre succès doit être mesuré à notre capacité à *garder* la croissance en garantissant la solidarité et la cohésion.
Moses	notre succès doit être mesuré par notre capacité à *maintenir* la croissance tout en assurant la solidarité et de cohésion.

Table 6: Translations produced by the EBMT prototype and Moses for an In-Domain sentence.

Example 2 Input:	there was also a small increase in *fasting blood glucose* and in *total cholesterol* in duloxetine-treated patients while those laboratory tests showed a slight decrease in the *routine care group*.
Reference	il y a eu également une faible augmentation de la *glycémie à jeun* et du *cholestérol total* dans le groupe duloxétine alors que les tests en laboratoire montrent une légère diminution de ces paramètres dans le *groupe traitement usuel*.
EBMT prototype	il y avait aussi une petite augmentation dans la *glycémie à jeun* et du *cholesterol total* chez les patients traités par la duloxétine alors que les tests en laboratoire montraient une légère diminution dans le *groupe de soins de routine*.
Moses	il y a également une légère augmentation de répréhensible *glycémie artérielle* et *cholesterol total* de patients duloxetine-treated laboratoire alors que ces tests, ont montré une diminution sensible dans les *soins standards groupe*.

Table 7: Translations produced by the EBMT prototype and Moses for an Out-Of-Domain sentence.

For the Out-Of-Domain sentences, the EBMT prototype results are clearly better and most of the translations produced by Moses are incomprehensible and ungrammatical (Example 2). This result could be due, on the one hand, to differences between the vocabulary of the test corpus and the entries of Moses's translation table, and, on the other hand, to their impact on the phrase reordering model. In the first example, the English word "keep" was identified by the morpho-syntactic analyzer as a verb and the bilingual lexicon of the EBMT prototype proposed the word "garder" as translation. Of course, this translation is correct but it is less expressive than "poursuivre sur la voie" of the translation reference. Likewise, the compound words "fasting blood glucose" and "total cholesterol" of the second example are translated correctly (glycémie à jeun, cholesterol total). On the other hand, the compound word "routine care group" is translated as "groupe de soins de routine" instead of "groupe de soins routiniers". As we can see, this translation could not be provided by the bilingual reformulator because there is no transfer rule implementing the tag pattern of this compound word which is NPNPN (Table 2). This expression corresponds to a partial translation provided by the cross-language search engine for the sentence to translate. We observed that the major issues of our EBMT prototype are related to errors from the source-language syntactic analyzer, the non-isomorphism between the syntax of the two languages and the polysemy in the bilingual lexicon. To handle the first two issues, we proposed to take into account translation candidates returned by the cross-language search engine even if these translations correspond only to a part of the sentence to translate. For the presence of the polysemy in the bilingual lexicon, the EBMT prototype has no specific treatment.

Concerning Moses's translation results for Out-Of-Domain sentences, we noted that most of errors are related to vocabulary. For example, Moses proposes the compound word "glycémie artérielle" as a translation for the expression "fasting blood glucose" which is not correct. In SMT systems such as Moses, phrase tables are the main knowledge source for the machine translation decoder. The decoder consults these tables to figure out how to translate an input sentence from the source language into the target language. These tables are built automatically using the open-source word alignment tool GIZA++[5] (Och and Ney, 2003). However, this tool could produce errors in particular when it aligns multiword expressions.

As a conclusion to this study, even if the comparison between the results of the two MT systems is not completely adequate since the EBMT prototype includes several components that require additional training data (Part-Of-Speech tagger), handwritten rules (Syntactic analyzer, Bilingual reformulator), monolingual and bilingual lexicons (Morphological analyzer, Bilingual reformulator), and Moses is trained on a small amount of the Emea corpus, the experiments show that the EBMT prototype performs better than Moses when texts to translate are related to the specialized domain in all configurations. Our preliminary results also show that the EBMT prototype continues to perform better than Moses when we increase the size of the training corpus of the specialized domain. Likewise, after analyzing qualitatively translations produced by Moses and the EBMT prototype, we observed that the good quality translation of the EBMT prototype is due to its linguistic components and in particular to the syntactic parser and the bilin-

[5] http://www.statmt.org/moses/giza/GIZA++.html.

gual lexicon which contains correct translations of most of the multiword expressions present in the Emea corpus. On the other hand, we noted that Moses fails to translate correctly several multiword expressions (which are very frequent in this corpus) as those of the Example 2, and we are not sure that increasing the training corpus size would limit these incomprehensible and ungrammatical translations.

5 Conclusion

We presented in this paper an EBMT prototype and we compared its performance to the SMT system Moses on domain-specific translation. The first results of our experiments show that, on the one hand, the EBMT prototype performs better than Moses when texts to translate are related to the specialized domain, and, on the other hand, large amounts of in-domain parallel data are necessary for Moses to obtain an acceptable translation quality. These experiments reveal the ability of the EBMT prototype to adapt better to out-domain material. In order to consolidate and improve these encouraging results, we expect to explore a number of ways. First, we will focus on using machine learning techniques to automatically extract transfer rules for the finite-state transducer from a bi-parsed and a word-aligned parallel corpus. Second, we will develop filtering techniques to be applied on these rules in order to reduce the number of translation hypotheses proposed by the bilingual reformulator. Third, we will use word sense disambiguation approaches to deal with polysemy in the extracted bilingual lexicon. In the final line of our future work, we will continue experimenting our machine translation approach on other specific domains and comparing its performance to other domain adaptation techniques.

Acknowledgments

The research leading to these results has received funding from the European Union's Seventh Framework Programme (FP7/2007-2013) under grant agreement n° 312651 – ePOOLICE.

References

Pratyush Banerjee, Jinhua Du, Baoli Li, Sudip Kr. Naskar, Andy Way, and Josef van Genabith. 2010. Combining Multi-Domain Statistical Machine Translation Models using Automatic Classifiers. In *Proceedings of the Ninth Conference of the Association for MT in the Americas, pages 141–150.*

Nicola Bertoldi and Marcello Federico. 2009. Domain adaptation for statistical machine translation with monolingual resources. In *Proceedings of the 4th Workshop on Statistical Machine Translation.*

Romaric Besançon, Gaël De Chalendar, Olivier Ferret, Christian Fluhr, Olivier Mesnard, and Hubert Naets. 2003. Concept-Based Searching and Merging for Multilingual Information Retrieval: First Experiments at CLEF 2003. In *C. Peters et al. (Ed.): CLEF 2003, Springer Verlag, Berlin, 2004.*

Romaric Besançon, Gaël De Chalendar, Olivier Ferret, Faïza Gara, Meriama Laib, Olivier Mesnard, and Nasredine Semmar. 2010. LIMA: A multilingual framework for linguistic analysis and linguistic resources development and evaluation. In *Proceedings of the seventh international conference on Language Resources and Evaluation.*

Dhouha Bouamor, Nasredine Semmar, and Pierre Zweigenbaum. 2012. Automatic Construction of a Multiword Expressions Bilingual Lexicon: A Statistical Machine Translation Evaluation Perspective. In *Proceedings of the 3rd Workshop on Cognitive Aspects of the Lexicon, COLING 2012,* India.

Peter F. Brown, Vincent J. Della Pietra, Stephen A. Della Pietra, and Robert L. Mercer. 1993. The mathematics of statistical machine translation: parameter estimation. In *Computational Linguistics - Special issue on using large corpora: II, Volume 19 Issue 2, MIT Press Cambridge, pages 263-311.*

Lars Bungum and Bjorn Gambäck. 2011. A Survey of Domain Adaptation in Machine Translation Towards a refinement of domain space. In *Proceedings of the India-Norway Workshop on Web Concepts and Technologies.*

Jaime Carbonell, Steve Klein, David Miller, Michael Steinbaum, Tomer Grassiany, and Jochen Frey. 2006. Context-Based Machine Translation. In *Proceedings of the 7th Conference of the Association for Machine Translation in the Americas.*

Marine Carpuat and Dekai Wu. 2007. Improving statistical machine translation using word sense disambiguation. In *Proceedings of the Joint Conference EMNLP-CoNLL.*

Jorge Civera and Alfons Juan. 2007. Domain adaptation in statistical machine translation with mixture modelling. In *Proceedings of the Second Workshop on Statistical Machine Translation.*

Hal Daumé III and Jagadeesh Jagarlamudi. 2011. Domain Adaptation for Machine Translation by Mining Unseen Words. In *Proceedings of the 49th Annual Meeting of the Association for Computational Linguistics: short papers, pages 407–412.*

Mark W. Davis and William C. Ogden. 1997. QUILT: Implementing a large-scale cross-language text retrieval system. In *Proceedings of SIGIR.*

Gregory Grefenstette. 1998. Cross-Language Information Retrieval. In *The Information Retrieval Series, Vol. 2, Springer.*

Almut Silja Hildebrand, Matthias Eck, Stephan Vogel, and Waibel Alex. 2005. Adaptation of the translation model for statistical machine translation based on information retrieval. In *Proceedings of the European Association for Machine Translation Conference.*

John Hutchins. 2003. Machine Translation: General Overview. In *Ruslan (Ed.), The Oxford Handbook of Computational Linguistics, Oxford: University Press, pages 501-511.*

Philipp Koehn, Hieu Hoang, Alexandra Birch, Chris Callison-Burch, Marcello Federico, Nicolas Bertoldi, Brooke Cowan, Wade Shen, Christine Moran, Richard Zens, Chris Dyer, Ondrej Bojar, Alexandra Constantin, and Evan Herbst. 2007. Moses: Open source toolkit for statistical machine translation. In *Proceedings of the Conference ACL 2007, demo session, Prague, Czech Republic.*

Philipp Koehn, Barry Haddow, Philip Williams, and Hieu Hoang. 2010. More Linguistic Annotation for Statistical Machine Translation. In *Proceedings of the Fifth Workshop on Statistical Machine Translation and Metrics.*

John Lafferty, Andrew McCallum, and Fernando C. N. Pereira. 2001. Conditional random fields: Probabilistic models for segmenting and labeling sequence data. In *Proceedings of the Eighteenth International Conference on Machine Learning.*

Philippe Langlais. 2002. Improving a general-purpose statistical translation engine by terminological lexicons. In *Proceedings of COLING: Second international workshop on computational terminology.*

William D. Lewis, Chris Wendt, and David Bullock. 2010. Achieving Domain Specificity in SMT without Overt Siloing. In *Proceedings of the 7th International Conference on Language Resources and Evaluation.*

Mehryar Mohri, Fernando Pereira, and Michael Riley. 2002. Weighted Finite-State Transducers in Speech Recognition. In *Computer Speech and Language, 16(1): pages 69-88.*

Franz Josef Och and Hermann Ney. 2003. A Systematic Comparison of Various Statistical Alignment Models. In *Computational Linguistics, Vol. 29(1).*

Kishore Papineni, Salim Roukos, Todd Ward, and Wei-Jing Zhu. 2002. BLEU: a method for automatic evaluation of machine translation. In *Proceedings of the 40th Annual meeting of the Association for Computational Linguistics, pages 311–318.*

Pavel Pecina, Antonio Toral, Andy Way, Vassilis Papavassiliou, Prokopis Prokopidis, and Maria Giagkou. 2011. Towards Using Web-Crawled Data for Domain Adaptation in Statistical Machine Translation. In *Proceedings of the 15th Conference of the European Association for Machine Translation.*

Gerard Salton and Michael J. McGill. 1986. Introduction to Modern Information Retrieval. In *McGraw-Hill, Inc.*

Nasredine Semmar and Meriama Laib. 2010. Using a Hybrid Word Alignment Approach for Automatic Construction and Updating of Arabic to French Lexicons. In *Proceedings of the Workshop on LR and HLT for Semitic Languages, LREC.*

Nasredine Semmar, Dhouha Bouamor. 2011. A New Hybrid Machine Translation Approach Using Cross-Language Information Retrieval and Only Target Text Corpora. In *Proceedings of the International Workshop on Using Linguistic Information for Hybrid Machine Translation*, Spain.

Nasredine Semmar, Christophe Servan, Dhouha Bouamor, and Ali Joua. 2011. Using Cross-Language Information Retrieval for Machine Translation. In *Proceedings of the 5th Language & Technology Conference*, Poland.

Nasredine Semmar, Othman Zennaki, and Meriama Laib. 2014. Using Cross-Language Information Retrieval and Statistical Language Modelling in Example-Based Machine Translation. In *Proceedings of the 36th Translating and the Computer conference*, England.

Matthew Snover, Bonnie Dorr, and Richard Schwartz. 2008. Language and translation model adaptation using comparable corpora. In *Proceedings of the Conference on Empirical Methods in Natural Language Processing.*

Harold Somers. 2003. Machine Translation: Latest Developments. In *Ruslan (ed.), The Oxford Handbook of Computational Linguistics, Oxford: University Press, pages 513-527.*

Jörg Tiedemann. 2012. Parallel Data, Tools and Interfaces in OPUS. In *Proceedings of the 8th International Conference on Language Resources and Evaluation.*

Arturo Trujillo. 1999. Translation Engines: Techniques for Machine Translation. In *Applied Computing, Springer.*

Wei Wang, Klaus Macherey, Wolfgang Macherey, Franz Och, and Peng Xu. 2012. Improved Domain Adaptation for Statistical Machine Translation. In *Proceedings of the Association for Machine Translation in the Americas Conference.*

Dekai Wu and Pascale Fung. 2009. Semantic Roles for SMT: A Hybrid Two-Pass Model. In *Proceedings of the Conference of the North American Chapter of the Association for Computational Linguistics: Human Language Technologies.*

Hierarchical Topic Structuring: From Dense Segmentation to Topically Focused Fragments via Burst Analysis

Anca-Roxana Simon
Université de Rennes 1
IRISA & INRIA Rennes
anca-roxana.simon@irisa.fr

Pascale Sébillot
INSA de Rennes
IRISA & INRIA Rennes
pascale.sebillot@irisa.fr

Guillaume Gravier
CNRS
IRISA & INRIA Rennes
guig@irisa.fr

Abstract

Topic segmentation traditionally relies on lexical cohesion measured through word re-occurrences to output a dense segmentation, either linear or hierarchical. In this paper, a novel organization of the topical structure of textual content is proposed. Rather than searching for topic shifts to yield dense segmentation, we propose an algorithm to extract topically focused fragments organized in a hierarchical manner. This is achieved by leveraging the temporal distribution of word re-occurrences, searching for bursts, to skirt the limits imposed by a global counting of lexical re-occurrences within segments. Comparison to a reference dense segmentation on varied datasets indicates that we can achieve a better topic focus while retrieving all of the important aspects of a text.

1 Introduction

Being aware of the topical structure of texts or automatic transcripts is known to be helpful for multiple natural language processing tasks such as summarization, question answering, etc. Various solutions have emerged to obtain such a structure, the most interesting ones being generic solutions that can be applied on any kind of textual data. These generic solutions are generally based on lexical cohesion, i.e., on identifying segments with a consistent use of vocabulary, in particular measured via word re-occurrences. Their output is a dense segmentation, i.e., contiguous segments, most of the time linear even if the structure of discourse is known to have a hierarchical form (Grosz and Sidner, 1986; Marcu, 2000).

Dense segmentation, linear or hierarchical, is however not necessarily appropriate to reflect the fact that some fragments of the data bear important ideas while others are simple fillers, i.e., they do not bring additional important information. This notion of irrelevant ideas was also mentioned in (Choi, 2000) where the author notes that skipping irrelevant fragments improves navigation. In addition, lexical re-occurrence is not sufficient for this type of segmentation, as we will demonstrate. In particular in the hierarchical case, segments get smaller as we go towards fine grain segmentation: As a consequence, there is a reduced number of words per segment and neighboring segments might refer to the same general topic and hence exhibit high lexical coherence.

To skirt these limits, we investigate a different way of organizing the topical structure of textual content. We rely on the fact that some words appear in bursts, i.e., with a frequency higher than normal at specific locations in the text. The key idea that we leverage is that the presence of lexical bursts usually indicates a strong topical focus, as we will highlight. As an alternative to dense hierarchical topic segmentation, we propose to derive a hierarchy of topically focused fragments as illustrated in Figure 1. A generic representation for classical hierarchical topic segmentation is depicted in Figure 1(a), where the main topics are divided into sub-topics, which in turn can be divided. A dense segmentation is provided at each level and the goal is to identify topic frontiers. Departing from the traditional thinking, the idea in Figure 1(b) is to spot topically focused fragments that are not necessarily contiguous and organize the fragments at various levels in a hierarchical way. Exploiting Kleinberg's algorithm (Kleinberg, 2002) to provide a hierarchy of bursty frag-

Proceedings of Recent Advances in Natural Language Processing, pages 588–595,
Hissar, Bulgaria, Sep 7–9 2015.

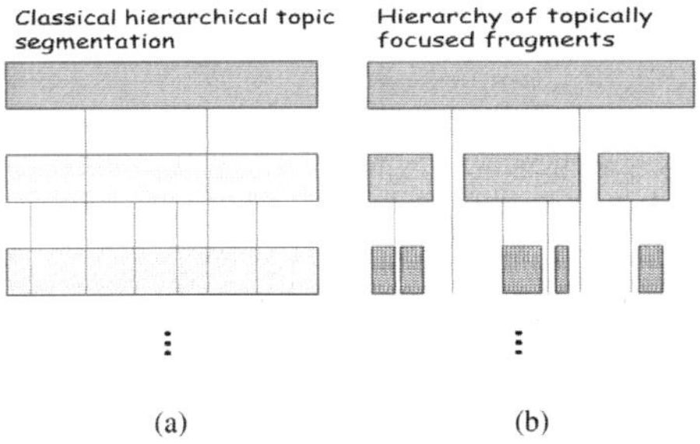

Figure 1: Generic respresentations of (a) classical dense topic segmentation vs (b) topically focused fragments. Vertical lines illustrate topic and subtopic frontiers.

ments for each word, we propose an algorithm to build a topical organization of a document such as the one in Figure 1(b). As a proof of concept, evaluations are performed by qualitative and quantitative comparison to the traditional dense segmentation for which hierarchical reference segmentation exists.

The paper is organized as follows. Section 2 presents a brief overview of existing work on hierarchical topic segmentation. Section 3 shows the limits of current hierarchical segmentation strategies relying on lexical cohesion. Section 4 analyzes the distribution of reiterations via burst analysis. Section 5 describes and evaluates the algorithm to build the hierarchy of topically focused fragments. Section 6 concludes the paper.

2 Related Work

Several studies for statistical laws in language have proposed burst detection models that analyze the distributional pattern of words (Sarkar et al., 2005a; Madsen et al., 2005). The quest for these models has been driven by various applications like: keyword extraction (Monachesi et al., 2006), style investigation (Sarkar et al., 2005b), etc. To our knowledge, burst detection hasn't been used before in the context of topic segmentation of textual data, most of the approaches exploiting lexical cohesion through words re-occurrences

In the case of hierarchical topic segmentation, a first approach is to apply a linear topic segmentation algorithm recursively (Carroll, 2010; Guinaudeau, 2011). One of the challenges is to decide when to stop. Additionally, a segmentation error at a higher level in the hierarchy can be propagated towards the lower levels. Hence, a few models have been proposed to explicitly model the hierarchical segment structure. HierBayes (Eisenstein, 2009) is an unsupervised algorithm formalized in a Bayesian probabilistic framework. The underlying principle is that each word in a text is represented by a language model estimated on a portion, more or less important, of the text. The drawback of this approach is that it cannot deal with segments of variable lengths and it needs prior information on the duration of the segments at each level in the hierarchy. In (Kazantseva and Szpakowicz, 2014), the authors propose to use the hierarchical affinity propagation graphical model introduced in (Givoni et al., 2011) to extract the hierarchical topic structure. Similar to Eisenstein, prior information on the granularity of the segmentation is required.

3 The Limits of Current Hierarchical Topic Segmentation Strategies

All of the techniques mentioned in the previous section target dense segmentation. To motivate the use of burst analysis and the introduction of a non-dense topical structure, we first show that lexical re-occurrences fail at explaining the reference hierarchical segmentation in a number of cases. We study here the behavior of two commonly-used measures of lexical cohesion on the hierarchical reference segmentation of a number of datasets.

3.1 Measures of Lexical Cohesion via Word Re-occurrences

The first measure considered is the similarity-based approach for which a cosine similarity is computed between vectors representing the content of adjacent segments. Let $\mathcal{V}$ represent the vocabulary containing each word that appears in the text to segment. For each segment S_i, the vector $\mathbf{v}_i$ contains the TF-IDF weight of each term in $\mathcal{V}$ computed over S_i, where the IDF values are computed over the entire collection for each dataset. The cosine similarity is defined as

$$C(S_{i-1}, S_i) = \frac{\sum_{v \in \mathcal{V}} \mathbf{v}_{i-1}(v)\, \mathbf{v}_i(v)}{\sqrt{\sum_{v \in \mathcal{V}} \mathbf{v}_{i-1}^2(v) \sum_{v \in \mathcal{V}} \mathbf{v}_i^2(v)}} .$$

The second measure considered is a probabilistic one where lexical cohesion for a segment S_i is computed using a Laplace law as in (Utiyama and Isahara, 2001), i.e.,

$$C(S_i) = log \prod_{j=1}^{n_i} \frac{f_i(w_j^i) + 1}{n_i + k} ,$$

where n_i is the number of word occurrences in S_i, $f_i(w_j^i)$ is the number of occurrences of the word w_j^i in segment S_i and k is the number of words in $\mathcal{V}$. The quantity $C(S_i)$ increases when words are repeated and decreases consistently when they are different. This value obtained for a segment S_i can be seen as the capacity of a language model learned on the segment to predict the words of the segment.

Note that the two measures are complementary: One considers adjacent segments to identify topic shifts, while the other intrisically measures the cohesion of a segment. Both are nevertheless independent of the segmentation method used.

3.2 Corpora

Three datasets, previously used in the context of hierarchical segmentation, are considered in this paper: a medical textbook (Eisenstein, 2009); Wikipedia articles (Carroll, 2010); manual and automatic French TV show transcripts (Guinaudeau, 2011). All the datasets are preprocessed in the same way: Words are tagged and lemmatized with TreeTagger[1] and only the nouns, non modal verbs and adjectives are retained.

The Wikipedia corpus contains 66 articles with a hierarchy of up to 4 levels. The reference segmentation is obtained from the structures given by the author of each article. Alike, the reference segmentation considered for the medical dataset is the structure created by the author when writing the book. The book is organized as follows: It has 17 parts; each part is divided into chapters, which are in turn divided into sections. This corpus was first used by (Eisenstein and Barzilay, 2008) for linear topic segmentation and the segmentation was done at the level of sections (227 chapters and 1,136 sections). The French TV show transcripts dataset is more challenging than the two others, particularly with automatic transcripts. The corpus contains seven episodes of a report show *Envoyé Spécial*. Each report has a duration of about 2 hours and was automatically transcribed with a standard ASR system. Manual transcripts for 4 reports are also available. Note that transcripts do not respect the norms of written texts: no paragraphs; structure based on utterances (i.e., sequences of words often separated by breath intakes) rather than sentences; no punctuation signs or capital letters. Additionally, ASR transcripts contain transcription errors (word error rate ca. 30 %) which may imply a lack of word repetitions. The reference segmentation has 3 levels and was obtained through manual annotation (done by an annotator). The first level has 26 frontiers, the second one 246 and the third one 722.

Throughout this paper the highest level in the hierarchy will be denoted level 0 and represents an entire Wikipedia article/part of the medical textbook/transcript of a TV show and the lowest level will correspond to level 4/2/3 respectively.

3.3 Experimental Evaluation

For the two measures, Figure 2 reports the evolution of the lexical cohesion over all segments of the second level in the reference topic hierarchy as well as global statistics for $C(S_i)$. Each row corresponds to a different dataset: First, the TV show manual transcripts (Fig. 2(a), 2(b), 2(c)) and second, the medical textbook (Fig. 2(d), 2(e), 2(f). Similar results are obtained also for the Wikipedia articles, but for brevity we do not present them here. The figures on the first column show the cohesion values obtained with the probabilistic measure for each sub-topic in the reference segmentation. The figures on the second column show general statistics (average, min and max values) for the same measure on the entire datasets. And the figures on the last column show the values obtained with the cosine similarity measure between consecutive sub-topics. For the medical textbook corpora the values on the first and last column are reported only on 4 samples for a better visibility. As it can be observed, there is a high variability in the cohesion values across sub-topics segments as well as in the similarity between consecutive segments within a document. Variability is also significantly high across documents (Fig. 2(b),2(e)), thus making it very difficult to define a threshold for segmentation purposes.

These findings point to the fact that the reference segmentation cannot be explained by the lexical cohesion measured via word re-occurrences counted globally on a segment. However, given the advantages of using lexical re-occurrences, we propose to analyze them from a different angle, by looking at the distributions of word repetitions via burst analysis. The words that are important in the process of topic segmentation are those with increased frequency for a particular segment and with insignificant appearances in the rest of the

[1] http://www.ims.uni-stuttgart.de/projekte/corplex/TreeTagger

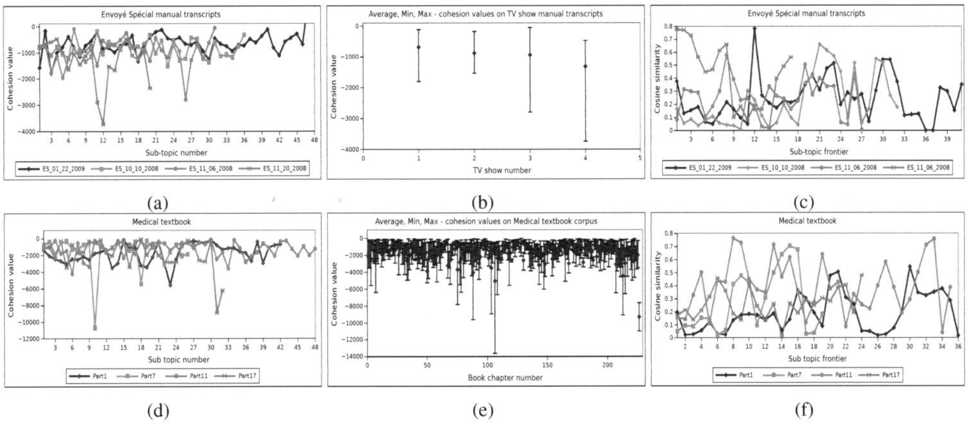

Figure 2: Lexical cohesion measures for each dataset. Each row correspond to a dataset, from top to bottom: TV shows, medical textbook. Columns correspond to, from left to right: $C(S_i)$, distribution of $C(S_i)$ per document, $C(S_{i-1}, S_i)$. Only a fraction of the results are presented for the textbook for legibility reasons.

segments. Note that the second point is usually not taken into account in existing segmentation algorithms. Such words can be captured through burst analysis. In the following sections, we thus analyze the relevance of bursts in the context of hierarchical topic segmentation.

4 Distribution of Lexical Reiterations Through Burst Analysis

The burst of a given word corresponds to a period where the word occurs with increased frequency with respect to normal behavior. Thus a burst signals both the existence of lexical disruption and of fragments of text that are cohesive: A fragment with one or more words bursts has a more consistent use of vocabulary, with concepts repeated locally in the fragment, apart from the rest of the text; also a fragment with bursty words can be differentiated from other fragments in the text since the burst of a word signals a high frequency of that word in a restricted interval and therefore increases the disruption with adjacent fragments.

4.1 Kleinberg's Algorithm

At the core of the analysis of the distribution of word re-occurrences, we rely on Kleinberg's algorithm (Kleinberg, 2002) to identify word bursts, together with the intervals where they occur[2]. The algorithm relies on an infinite-state automaton where the states $i \in \mathbb{N}^+$ correspond to the frequency at which an individual word repeats. Arbitrarily, state 0 accounts for normal behavior while increasing values of i correspond to increasing levels of burstiness. State transitions thus correspond to points in time when there is a important change in the occurrence frequency of a word. The algorithm outputs a hierarchy of burst intervals for each word, taking one word at a time, by searching for the state sequence that minimizes a cost function. For more details, see (Kleinberg, 2002). The interval of a burst at level j in the hierarchy of bursts is the maximal interval during which the optimal state sequence is in state j or higher, i.e., $k > j$, thus forming a hierarchical organization of burst intervals. In other words, a word considered bursty on a time interval $[a, b]$ with a burstiness level of i is simultaneously considered as busty at a level $i-1$ on an interval $[c, d]$, with $[a, b] \subset [c, d]$. This hierarchy is illustrated in Figure 4 for one word: The word occurs with a burstiness level of 1 on the first utterances, with an important amount of occurrences at the very beginning yielding a short interval at level 2 included in the interval at level 1. Long bursts intensifying into briefer ones can be seen as imposing a fine-grain organization within the text according to a natural tree structure.

4.2 A Case Analysis of Bursts

We conducted a case-study to assess if the concept of bursts is relevant or not to produce traditional dense segmentations. For each segment at each

[2]We use Jeff Binder's open-source implementation, available at http://cran.r-project.org/web/packages/bursts

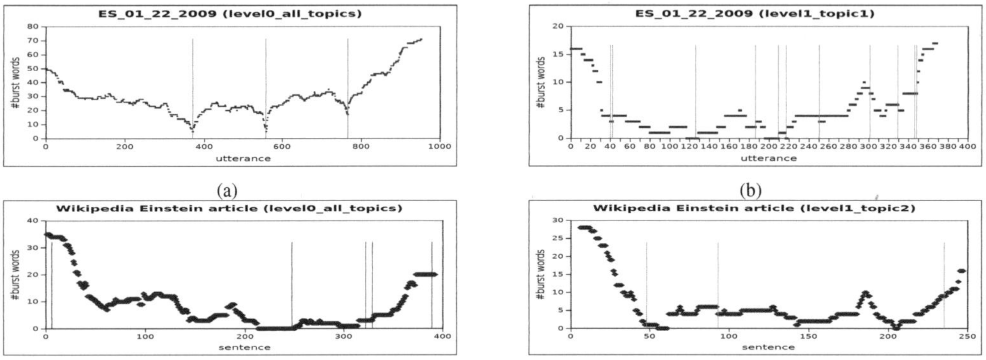

(a) (b) (c) (d)

Figure 3: Number of bursty words for each utterance on a TV show (top) and on a Wikpedia article (bottom). Burst intervals are computed either from dense topic segments taken at level 0 (left), or from the level 1 subtopics of the first level-0 topic (right). Vertical lines indicate reference segment boundaries.

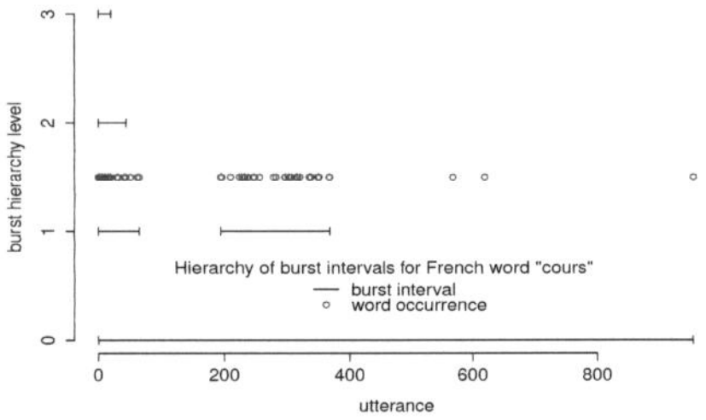

Figure 4: Sample output of Kleinberg's algorithm: The y-axis depicts the burstiness level while utterance number are on the x-axis; Circles indicate occurrences of the word considered. There are two bursts of level 1, the first one coming along with a burst of level 2 for a fraction of its time.

level of the reference dense topic segmentation, a hierarchy of burst intervals as the one illustrated in Figure 4 is computed for each word. Given the set of burst intervals, we count for each utterance the number of words within the utterance which appear as bursty at that position. Figure 3 presents the counts for bursts computed at two levels (level 0 and level 1) in the reference hierarchical topic segmentation for a sample from the TV show transcripts and one from a Wikipedia article. The reference frontiers are marked with vertical lines. For brevity, figures for the medical corpus, which are similar to those of the TV show transcripts, are not presented. We expect that local minima in the plots, i.e., utterances that contain few bursy words, are indicators of topic shifts.

Results in Figures 3(a) and 3(b) are obtained on the reference transcript of one TV show, for level 0 and level 1. Clearly, local minima in the plot for level 0 can be associated with the reference frontiers: The number of bursts shared between the utterances at these points are considerably fewer than at any other point. Thus, at this level, the topical segments can be easily identified relying on bursts information. The same analysis for level 1 shows that local minima are neither easy to identify in this case, nor do they correspond with reference frontiers (see, Figure 3(b)). Results on a Wikipedia article in Figures 3(c) and 3(d) show that in this type of documents the topic shifts are not as obvious to identify as in the case of the TV show at level 0.

By looking specifically at each segment and analyzing the bursts in the segment, two types of bursts can be distinguished: Bursts that are specific to each of the segments' sub-segments and bursts that are shared between the segments' sub-segments. The number of specific bursts for a sub-segment is given by the number of burst intervals contained between the boundaries of that sub-segment, while the number of bursts shared between sub-segments is given by the number of burst intervals crossing over the frontier between the sub-segments. For example, the French TV show has an average number of specific (resp. shared) bursts of 51 (resp. 6.75) at level 0 while the figures decrease to resp. 2.91 and 1.58 at level 1. When going to lower levels, the number of specific bursts decreases and approaches the number of bursts shared. Thus similar observations as the ones drawn from the counts of bursts (Figure 3) can be made.

This case study leads to several important observations: Frontiers can be identified when there are few bursts across a position and many before/after that position; words that are bursty at one level in the topic hierarchy (i.e., specific at this level) can become general for lower levels in the hierarchy; when going to lower levels in the topic hierarchy, the number of bursts decreases; there are segments with no bursty words. Thus burst analysis is relevant in the context of hierarchical topic segmentation, but an appropriate way to exploit it has to be proposed; we address this open issue in the following section.

5 Hierarchical Structure of Topically Focused Fragments

Burst modeling has the effect of exposing salient words (i.e., keywords) with different (burst hierarchy) levels. We propose to take advantage of this fact to spot salient topics and sub-topics. Thus, we do not focus anymore on producing a dense hierarchy of segments but instead we aim to derive a hierarchy of topically focused, i.e., salient, fragments which are not necessarily contiguous.

5.1 The Algorithm

We propose a new algorithm that generates a hierarchy of salient topics using an agglomerative clustering of burst intervals. The result is a set of nested topically focused fragments which are hierarchically organized. Note that contrary to the segments obtained with traditional topic segmentation, the fragments resulting from clustering burst intervals are not necessarily contiguous, and they have a stronger focus. Obtaining this structuring of the data brings several advantages: It is a representation of the entire document; it is highly informative since the words included are assumed to be the most informative ones in the document; the bursty words present in the resulting fragments offer an approximation of what the document is about and facilitate its understanding; relevant information is given at various levels of detail.

The clustering algorithm exploits the output of Kleinberg's burst detection algorithm which provides for each word a hierarchy of burst intervals. The key idea is to iteratively group together burst intervals from distinct words at each level of the hierarchy of bursts based on their overlaps, thus yielding a nested set of clusters. We first group the two most overlapping intervals to form a new interval (or fragment) and proceed until no more

Algorithm 1 Create a hierarchy of topically focused segments.

for each level l **do**
  Step 0. Initialize segment clusters
  for all word w **do**
    $I_{l_w} = \{I_{l_w}(1), I_{l_w}(2), ...I_{l_w}(n_{l_w})\}$
    where $I_{l_w}(i) = [S_{l_w}(i), E_{l_w}(i)]$
  end for
  Step 1. Agglomerative clustering
  repeat
    for all $I_{l_u}(i), I_{l_v}(j) \in I_{l_w}, \forall u, v, \forall i, j, i \neq j$ **do**
      if $I_{l_u}(i) \cap I_{l_v}(j) \neq \emptyset$ **then**
        $I_{l_{u,v}}(t) = [min(S_{l_u}(i), S_{l_v}(j)), max(E_{l_u}(i), E_{l_v}(j))]$
        $add(I_{l_{u,v}}(t), I_{l_w})$
        $remove(I_{l_u}(i), I_{l_w})$
        $remove(I_{l_v}(j), I_{l_w})$
      end if
    end for
  until convergence
end for
Step 2. Mapping across levels
for $l = L \rightarrow 1$ **do**
  $I_{l_w}(i)$ mapped to $I_{l-1_w}(j)$ such that $I_{l_w}(i) \subset I_{l-1_w}(j)$
end for

overlapping intervals appear. Details are given in Algorithm 1. For each level $l \in [1, L]$ in the hierarchy of bursts H, the burst intervals contained at this level for each word w form a collection of intervals I_{l_w}. Each interval $I_{l_w}(i)$ in the collection has a start $S_{l_w}(i)$ and an end $E_{l_w}(i)$ point. An exhaustive comparison between the intervals in H is done independently for each level. If two burst intervals ($I_{l_u}(i)$, $I_{l_v}(j)$) overlap, they are merged together and a new interval is obtained ($I_{l_{u,v}}(t)$) and added to the collection. This step is done until there are no more overlapping intervals. In the end the fragments corresponding to the final intervals are extracted to represent the salient fragments at level l. The hierarchy of topically focused fragments is created using a mapping across levels of the fragments obtained. An example of such a hierarchy, of two levels, is presented in Figure 5. The limits of the fragments formed are given by the starting and ending utterance/sentence positions and their content is represented by a sample of the bursty words that contributed in forming them. These fragments pertain the most relevant information in the data at various levels of detail. The solution we propose to create the hierarchy of topically focused fragments has the advantage of deriving the hierarchy directly, without any prior on the duration of fragments (segments in case of traditional segmentation) and number of levels in

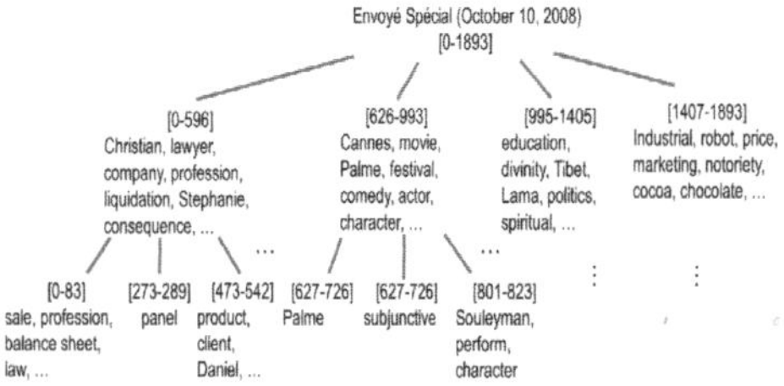

Figure 5: A two-level hierarchy of topically focused fragments obtained with a TV show. At each level, fragments are represented by their limits in terms of utterance number (in brackets) and characterized with the bursty words (translated from French) that helped form the fragments.

the hierarchy, unlike traditional hierarchical topic segmentation strategies.

5.2 Evaluation and Discussion

Currently, there is no metric to evaluate the structure resulting from the above algorithm, the measures traditionally used for hierarchical topic segmentation being inappropriate for at least two reasons: 1- The structure that our algorithm outputs is a hierarchy of topically focused fragments and not a dense hierarchy of segments (cf. Figure 1); 2- there is no groundtruth for this hierarchy of topically focused fragments, which is required for the metrics used to evaluate traditional segmentations. Moreover building such a groundtruth is not an easy task: the topically focused fragments are obtained in a data-driven, bottom-up, manner that does not necessarily reflect a prior organization as would be provided by human experts; introducing this new way of thinking is indeed the main goal pursued by the paper. In addition of being costly, annotating new data requires that clear, shared, annotation guidelines be defined first. This last point requires a good understanding and characterization of what our approach can yield, which is exactly what this paper intends to provide. Therefore, to prove the relevance of our approach and provide a good insight into the hierarchical fragments that it outputs, we believe that it is important to see how focused fragments compare with traditional dense segmentation before moving further into annotating data with this new paradigm.

We thus report a number of measures relying on existing dense annotations: At each level, fragments are compared to their counterpart in the dense segmentation, after mapping. Conversely, dense segments are mapped to topically focused

		HTFF		HierBayes	
Data-set	level	M1	M2	M1	M2
ES(manual)	1	0.75	1	0.51	1
	2	0.56	0.74	0.15	1
	3	0.47	0.17	–	–
ES(auto)	1	0.73	1	0.48	1
	2	0.46	0.62	0.1	1
	3	0.51	0.11	–	–
Wikipedia	1	0.22	0.97	0.29	1
	2	0.62	0.66	0.42	1
	3	0.69	0.29	–	–
	4	0.49	0.06	–	–

Table 1: The values obtained with M1 and M2 measures on two data sets after applying HierBayes and HTFF.

fragments. Two measures are defined: $M1$, the proportion of topically focused fragments belonging to a unique reference segment; $M2$, the percentage of reference segments which have at least one matching topically focused fragment. The values obtained with these measures both for a dense segmentation resulting from applying HierBayes and a hierarchy of topically focused fragments (HTFF) are reported in Table 1. Similar results are obtained on the medical corpus. For HierBayes we report only the results at two levels since trying to obtain more levels worsened the segmentation, resulting in the same segments at all levels. As going to lower levels with HTFF it is expected to have such a small coverage of the segments since their number is considerably high and the average number of bursts is ≈ 1. Results demonstrate that the fragments we extract in a bottom-up manner usually have an equivalent in a dense segmentation and have a stronger focus than their counterpart.

6 Conclusion

In this paper, we have investigated the relevance of bursts to organize the topical structure of textual content. We have shown that global measures of lexical re-occurrence are not adequate to detect topic shifts while the temporal distribution of word re-occurrences provides strong cues. As a consequence, we have proposed an algorithm to extract a hierarchy of topically focused fragments using agglomerative clustering of burst intervals. Comparison of this novel structure to a reference dense segmentation on several datasets has indicated that we can achieve a better topic focus than the one provided by the reference dense segmentation while retrieving the important aspects of a text.

References

Lucien Carroll. 2010. Evaluating hierarchical discourse segmentation. In *11th International Conf. of the North American Chapter of the Association for Computational Linguistics*, pages 993–1001.

Freddy Y. Y. Choi. 2000. A speech interface for rapid reading. In *Proceedings of IEE colloquium: Speech and Language Processing for Disabled and Elderly People*, pages 1–4.

Jacob Eisenstein and Regina Barzilay. 2008. Bayesian unsupervised topic segmentation. In *Proceedings of Empirical Methods in Natural Language Processing*, pages 334–343.

Jacob Eisenstein. 2009. Hierarchical text segmentation from multi-scale lexical cohesion. In *Proceedings of 10th International Conf. of the North American Chapter of the Association for Computational Linguistics*, pages 353–361.

Inmar E. Givoni, Clement Chung, and Brendan J. Frey. 2011. Hierarchical affinity propagation. In *Proceedings of the 27th Conf. on Uncertainty in Artificial Intelligence*, pages 238–246.

Barbara J. Grosz and Candace L. Sidner. 1986. Attention, intentions, and the structure of discourse. *Computational Linguistics*, 12(3):175–204.

Camille Guinaudeau. 2011. *Structuration automatique de flux télévisuels*. Ph.D. thesis, INSA de Rennes.

Anna Kazantseva and Stan Szpakowicz. 2014. Hierarchical topical segmentation with affinity propagation. In *Proceedings of the 25th International Conference on Computational Linguistics: Technical Papers*, pages 37–47.

Jon Kleinberg. 2002. Bursty and hierarchical structure in streams. In *8th ACM SIGKDD International Conf. on Knowledge Discovery and Data Mining*, pages 91–101.

Rasmus E. Madsen, David Kauchak, and Charles Elkan. 2005. Modeling word burstiness using the dirichlet distribution. In *Proceedings of the 22Nd International Conference on Machine Learning*, ICML '05, pages 545–552, New York, NY, USA. ACM.

Daniel Marcu. 2000. *The Theory and Practice of Discourse Parsing and Summarization*. MIT Press, Cambridge, MA, USA.

Paola Monachesi, Lothar Lemnitzer, and Kiril Simov. 2006. Language technology for elearning. In Wolfgang Nejdl and Klaus Tochtermann, editors, *Innovative Approaches for Learning and Knowledge Sharing*, volume 4227 of *Lecture Notes in Computer Science*, pages 667–672. Springer Berlin Heidelberg.

Avik Sarkar, Paul H. Garthwaite, and Anne De Roeck. 2005a. A bayesian mixture model for term reoccurrence and burstiness. In *Proceedings of the Ninth Conference on Computational Natural Language Learning*, CONLL '05, pages 48–55. Association for Computational Linguistics.

Avik Sarkar, Anne De Roeck, and Paul Garthwaite. 2005b. Team re-occurrence measures for analyzing style. In S. Argamon, J. Karlgren, and J.G. Shanahan, editors, *Proceedings of the SIGIR 2005 Workshop on Stylistic Analysis of Text for Information Access.*, pages 28–36. ACM Press, August.

Masao Utiyama and Hitoshi Isahara. 2001. A statistical model for domain-independent text segmentation. In *39th Annual Meeting on the Association for Computational Linguistics*, pages 499–506.

Improving Word Sense Disambiguation with Linguistic Knowledge from a Sense Annotated Treebank

Kiril Simov **Alexander Popov** **Petya Osenova**
Linguistic Modeling Department
IICT-BAS
{kivs|alex.popov|petya}@bultreebank.org

Abstract

In this paper we present an approach for the enrichment of WSD knowledge bases with data-driven relations from a gold standard corpus (annotated with word senses, valency information, syntactic analyses, etc.). We focus on Bulgarian as a use case, but our approach is scalable to other languages as well. For the purpose of exploring such methods, the Personalized Page Rank algorithm was used. The reported results show that the addition of new knowledge improves the accuracy of WSD with approximately 10.5%.

1 Introduction

Solutions to WSD-related tasks usually employ lexical databases, such as wordnets and ontologies. However, lexical databases suffer from esparseness in the availability and density of relations. One approach towards remedying this problem is the BabelNet (Navigli and Ponzetto, 2012), which relates several lexical resources — WordNet[1], DBpedia, Wiktionary, etc. Although such a setting takes into consideration the role of lexical and world knowledge, it does not incorporate contextual knowledge learned from actual texts (such as collocational patterns, for example). This happens because the knowledge sources for WSD systems usually capture only a fraction of the relations between entities in the world. Many important relations are not present in ontological resources but could be learned from texts.

One possible approach to handling this sparseness issue is the incorporation of relations from sense annotated corpora into the lexical databases. We decided to focus on this line of research, by using the Bulgarian sense annotated treebank (Sensed BulTreeBank) in order to extract semantic relations and add them into the lexical resources. The hypothesis that this enrichment would lead to better WSD for Bulgarian was tested in the context of the Personalized PageRank algorithm.

The structure of the papers is as follows: the next section discusses the related work on the topic. Section 3 presents the Bulgarian sense annotated treebank. Section 4 focuses on the Bulgarian Syntactic and Lexical Resources. Section 5 introduces the WSD experiments and results. Section 6 concludes the paper.

2 Related Work

Knowledge-based systems for WSD have proven to be a good alternative to supervised systems, which require large amounts of manually annotated training data. In contrast, knowledge-based systems require only a knowledge base and no additional corpus-dependent information. An especially popular knowledge-based disambiguation approach has been the use of popular graph-based algorithms known under the name of "Random Walk on Graph" (Agirre et al., 2014). Most approaches exploit variants of the PageRank algorithm (Brin and Page, 2012). Agirre and Soroa (2009) apply a variant of the algorithm to Word Sense Disambiguation by translating WordNet into a graph in which the synsets are represented as vertices and the relations between them are represented as edges between the nodes. The resulting graph is called a *knowledge graph* in this paper. Calculating the PageRank vector **Pr** is accomplished through solving the equation:

$$\mathbf{Pr} = cM\mathbf{Pr} + (1 - c)\mathbf{v} \quad (1)$$

where M is an $N\,x\,N$ transition probability matrix (N being the number of vertices in the graph), c is the damping factor and $\mathbf{v}$ is an $N\,x\,1$ vector. In the traditional, static version of PageRank the val-

[1] In this work we used version 3.0 of Princeton WordNet: https://wordnet.princeton.edu/.

Proceedings of Recent Advances in Natural Language Processing, pages 596–603,
Hissar, Bulgaria, Sep 7–9 2015.

ues of **v** are all equal (*1/N*), which means that in the case of a random jump each vertex is equally likely to be selected. Modifying the values of **v** effectively changes these probabilities and thus makes certain nodes more important. The version of PageRank for which the values in **v** are not uniform is called *Personalized PageRank*.

The words in the text that are to be disambiguated are inserted as nodes in the knowledge graph and are connected to their potential senses via directed edges (by default, a context window of at least 20 words is used for each disambiguation). These newly introduced nodes serve to inject initial probability mass (via the **v** vector) and thus to make their associated sense nodes especially relevant in the *knowledge graph*. Applying the Personalized PageRank algorithm iteratively over the resulting graph determines the most appropriate sense for each ambiguous word. The method has been boosted by the addition of new relations and by developing variations and optimizations of the algorithm (Agirre and Soroa, 2009). It has also been applied to the task of Named Entity Disambiguation (Agirre et al., 2015).

Montoyo et al. (2005) present a combination of knowledge-based and supervised systems for WSD, which demonstrates that the two approaches can boost one another, due to the fundamentally different types of knowledge they utilise (paradigmatic vs. syntagmatic). They explore a knowledge-based system that uses heuristics for WSD depending on the position of word potential senses in the WordNet knowledge base. In terms of supervised machine learning based on an annotated corpus, it explores a Maximum Entropy model that takes into account multiple features from the context of the to-be-disambiguated word. This earlier line of research demonstrates that combining paradigmatic and syntagmatic information is a fruitful strategy, but it does so by doing the combination in a postprocessing step, i.e. by merging the output of two separate systems; also, it still relies on manually-annotated data for the supervised disambiguation. Building on the already mentioned work on graph-based approaches, it is possible to combine paradigmatic and syntagmatic information in another way – by incorporating both into the knowledge graph. This approach is described in the current paper.

The success of knowledge-based WSD approaches apparently depends on the quality of the knowledge graph – whether the knowledge represented in terms of nodes and relations (arcs) between them is sufficient for the algorithm to pick the correct senses of ambiguous words. Several extensions of the knowledge graph constructed on the basis of WordNet have been proposed and implemented. An approach similar to the one presented here is described in Agirre and Martinez (2002), which explores the extraction of syntactically supported semantic relations from manually annotated corpora. In that piece of research, SemCor, a semantically annotated corpus, was processed with the MiniPar dependency parser and the subject-verb and object-verb relations were consequently extracted. The new relations were represented on several levels: as word-to-class and class-to-class relations. The extracted selectional relations were then added to WordNet and used in the WSD task. The chief difference with the presently described approach is that the set of relations used here is bigger (it includes also indirect-object-to-verb relations, noun-to-modifier relations, etc.). Another difference is that the new relations in the present piece of research are not added as selectional relations, but as semantic relations between the corresponding synsets. This means that the specific syntactic role of the participant is not taken into account, but only the connectedness between the participant and the event is registered in the knowledge graph.

3 The Bulgarian Sense Annotated Treebank

The sense annotation process over BulTreeBank (BTB) was organized in three layers: verb valency frames (Osenova et al., 2012); senses of verbs, nouns, adjectives and adverbs; DBpedia URIs over named entities. However, in the experiment presented here, we used mainly the annotated senses of nouns and verbs (together with the valency information), as well as the concept mappings to WordNet. For that reason we do not discuss the DBpedia annotation here. A brief outline can be found in Popov et al. (2014).

The sense annotation was organized as follows: the lemmatized words per part-of-speech (POS) from BTB received all their possible senses from the explanatory dictionary of Bulgarian and from our Core WordNet[2]. When two competing definitions came from both resources, preference was

[2] Available at http://compling.hss.ntu.edu.sg/omw/

given to the one that was mapped to the WordNet. In the ambiguous cases the correct sense was selected according to the context of usage. For the purposes of the evaluation, some of the files were independently manually checked by two individual annotators. In total, 92,000 running words have been mapped to word senses. Thus, about 43 % of all the treebank tokens have been associated with senses.

The word forms annotated with senses mapped to WordNet synsets are 69,333, consisting of nouns and verbs. From these POS, 12,792 word forms have been used for testing, and the rest have been used for relation extraction. About 20,000 word forms are now in the process of being mapped to WordNet synsets. Most of them are adjectives and adverbs. They will be included in the next round of experiments, which will result in an increase the sense density of the graph.

4 Bulgarian Lexical and Syntactic Resources: BTB-Wordnet and Valency Lexicon

The BTB-Wordnet has been compiled in several steps. Initially, the Core WordNet was created for Bulgarian, which covered 4,999 synsets. Then, nearly the same number of new synsets were added to the WordNet (now we have 9,000 synsets or so). We tried to map the Bulgarian senses to the English ones as faithfully as possible, respecting the Princeton WordNet hierarchy.

Although connectivity was very important for the experiments, we also mapped specific concepts to more general ones in both directions (English to Bulgarian and Bulgarian to English). New definitions for concepts which did not have a counterpart in the Princeton Wordnet have been introduced. In this way, we established a language specific hierarchy for Bulgarian.

The ongoing mapping of word senses in the treebank to the WordNet is thus complicated by the fact that the available resources are not directly comparable. These are: the Treebank, where words were annotated with definitions from an explanatory dictionary of Bulgarian (dictionary entries), and the Princeton WordNet, which contains whole groups of synonyms (synonym sets) unified by common definitions of the concepts. At the same time, such an approach makes it possible to easily structure the resource via the Princeton Wordnet hierarchy, and it also leaves the door open for developing a language-specific hierarchy.

The valency lexicon consists of around 18,000 verb frames extracted from the BTB. The participants in these frames have ontological constraints. At the moment, the verb senses are mapped to WordNet, but the constraints over arguments are not synchronized with the WordNet concepts in their levels of granularity and specificity. This syncronization is planned as a next step in our work, in order to further enrich the knowledge graph.

5 Experiments

5.1 Description of the WSD tool

The experiments that serve to illustrate the outlined approaches were carried out with the UKB[3] tool, which provides graph-based methods for Word Sense Disambiguation and measuring lexical similarity. The tool uses the Personalized PageRank algorithm, described in Agirre and Soroa (2009). It can be and has been used to perform Named Entity Disambiguation as well (Agirre et al., 2015). The tool builds a knowledge graph over a set of relations that can be induced from different types of resources, such as WordNet or DBPedia; then it selects a context window of open class words and runs the algorithm over the graph. There is an additional module called NAF UKB[4] that can be used to run UKB with input in the NAF format[5] and to obtain output structured in the same way, only with added word sense information. For compatibility reasons, NAF UKB was used to perform the experiments reported here; the input NAF document contains in its "term" nodes lemma and POS information, which is necessary for the running of UKB. We have used the UKB default settings, i.e. a context window of 20 words that are to be disambiguated together, 30 iterations of the Personalized PageRank algorithm.

The UKB tool requires two resource files to process the input file. One of the resources is a dictionary file with all lemmas that can be possibly linked to a sense identifier. In our case WordNet-derived relations were used for our knowledge base; consequently, the sense identifiers are WordNet IDs. For instance, a line from the dictionary extracted from WordNet looks like this:

[3] http://ixa2.si.ehu.es/ukb/

[4] https://github.com/asoroa/naf_ukb

[5] http://www.newsreader-project.eu/files/2013/01/techreport.pdf

predicate 06316813-n:0 06316626-n:0

01017222-v:0 01017001-v:0 00931232-v:0

First comes the lemma associated with the relevant word senses, after the lemma the sense identifiers are listed. Each ID consists of eight digits followed by a hyphen and a label referring to the POS category of the word. Finally, a number following a colon indicates the frequency of the word sense, calculated on the basis of a tagged corpus. When a lemma from the dictionary has occurred in the analysis of the input text, the tool assigns all associated word senses to the word form in the context and attempts to disambiguate its meaning among them. The Bulgarian dictionary comprises of all the lemmas of words annotated with WordNet senses in the BTB. It has 8,491 lemmas mapped to 6,965 unique word senses. Currently we have opted to copy over the frequencies from the English corpus, but they are not actually used in the experiments.

The second resource file required for running the tool is the set of relations that is used to construct the knowledge graph over which Personalized PageRank is run. The distribution of the tool provides data (dictionary and relation files) for WordNet 1.7 and 3.0. Since the BTB has been annotated with word senses from WordNet 3.0, the resource files for version 3.0 were used for our experiments. The distribution of UKB comes with a file containing the standard lexical relations defined in WordNet, such as hypernymy, meronymy, etc., as well as with a file containing relations derived on the basis of common words found in the synset glosses, which have been manually disambiguated. As the Bulgarian lemmas in the generated dictionary are mapped to the English WordNet and the specific Bulgarian WordNet hierarchy is not exploited in this phase, we have used the same file with the relations for English. Because the generation of gloss-based relations is a time-consuming task, we have used the relations for the English glosses, on the assumption that they should capture to a significant degree the relatedness between Bulgarian word senses as well. The WordNet ontological relations are 252,392 and the relations from the glosses are 419,387.

5.2 Additional Relations in the Knowledge Graph

In addition to these available relations, we have utilized further resources from WordNet itself and from the annotations in BTB. These additional resources are:

- Inferred hypernymy relations
- Syntactic relations from the golden corpus
- Extended syntactic relations
- Domain relations from WordNet

The phrase "inferred hypernymy relations" means the transitive closure of the hypernymy relation type. That is, if A is a hyponym of B and B is a hyponym of C, it is inferred that A is a hyponym of C. This type of inference has been done for all synset IDs that participate in hypernymy relations in the WordNet hierarchy and are found in the Bulgarian dictionary. 590,272 new relations have been generated in this way.

All relations described up until now are of a lexical nature, therefore essentially paradigmatic and providing information about an idealized model of the world. The work presented here enriches further the knowledge graph by adding syntagmatic information, i.e. contextual knowledge about words and word senses. This has been done by extracting the intersection of the syntactic dependency relations from the BTB corpus and the WordNet sense annotations in the same resource. In this way dependency relations between specific words in the text that also have attached WordNet identifiers have been transformed into graph relations of the kind described above. The targeted dependency relations are of the types: *nsubj*, *nmod*, *amod*, *iobj*, *dobj*; for more information about the Universal Dependencies set of relations that we have used, see the documentation of the UD project[6], which includes contribution from the BulTreeBank group for the Bulgarian language.

These syntactic relations have been extended in a similar way as the hypernymy relations. For example, in the case of the *nsubj* relation, the hyponyms of the dependent node have been replicated in new relations of the same kind, for all hyponyms of that particular word sense encountered in the golden corpus. Thus, the relation

u:00118523-v v:00510189-n

is derived from an *nsubj* relation, where 00118523-v stands for a sense of the Bulgarian verb "prodalzha" (continue) and is the head

[6]`http://universaldependencies.github.io/docs/`

node (the predicate in *nsubj*), and 00510189-n, corresponding to a particular word sense of "veselba" (revelry), is the dependent node (the subject). The dependent node has a number of hyponyms in the WordNet hierarchy, therefore all these (and their hyponyms, too) have been added into a relation with the node 00118523-v. For instance, 00510723-n (the synset for particular word senses of the words "binge", "bout" and "tear") has been entered analogously in the same slot as 00510189-n.

The open class word forms in the BTB are all tagged with their respective word senses, but a big portion of those senses are yet to be mapped to WordNet identifiers. Thus, only a part of the dependency relations from the corpus have been extracted for the purpose of these experiments (because both nodes in a relation must have WordNet IDs). More specifically, for 15,675 dependency relations, the numbers for the extracted relations are as follows: 1,844 *nsubj*, 3,875 *nmod*, 1,025 *amod*, 716 *iobj*, and 1,312 *dobj* relations. The numbers for the extended relations are: 372,247 *nsubj*, 1,125,823 *nmod* (note that there are two cases with *nmod*: once we extend along the chain of descendants of the dependent element, and once along the chain of those of the head), 377,577 *amod*, 114,760 *iobj*, and 292,202 *dobj* relations.

Our motivation for using the hyponyms to infer new relations is based on the intuition that these syntactic relations connect an entity to an event[7] in which the entity participates or connects two participants of an event. We assume that if a class of entities contains possible participants in an event, then the instances of all sub-classes are possible participants in the same kind of event. The original relations are trusted to be valid, because they were annotated manually in the semantically annotated treebank. Another important assumption is that the relations found in the treebank are not the most general ones, which means that there is room for generalization over the participants in these events.

Thus, in addition to the extension of the dependency relations outlined above, we did a further enrichment of the knowledge base by taking the hypernym of the node of interest in the syntactic relation and then taking all nodes beneath it in the hypernym hierarchy, and inserting them in the relevant relation attested in the golden corpus. Returning to the example from above in order to illustrate this strategy, we identify the "revelry" node ("unrestrained merrymaking") as subject of the "continue" node, then we go one level up to its hypernym, which is "merrymaking" ("a boisterous celebration; a merry festivity"), and extend the *nsubj* relation from there downwards the hierarchy. Thus, the hyponym sense "jinks" ("noisy and mischievous merrymaking") is also inserted in the *nsubj* relation with the relevant sense of the verb "continue". This extension leads to an additional significant increase in the size of the knowledge base.

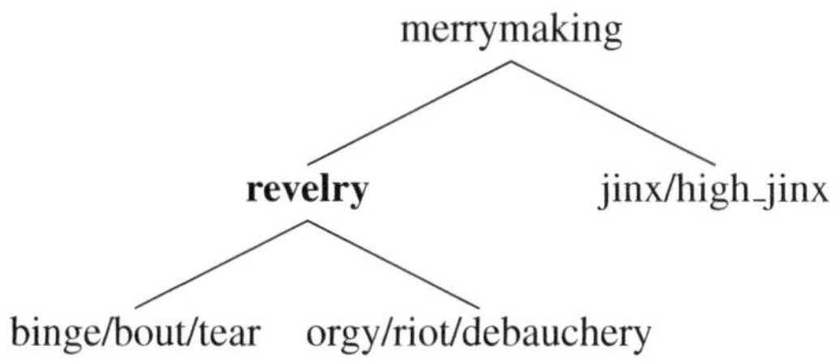

Figure 1: Traversing the hypernymy hierarchy, an example.

Figure 1 illustrates the described hierarchy as a simple tree. The bolded term ("revelry") is the node we want to use to expand the *nsubj* relation. The expanding procedure finds the hypernym of that node ("merrymaking"), then takes all the nodes below it and inserts them in the same type of relation, in place of "revelry". In this way, multiple relations can be derived from the initial *nsubj* relation.

Finally, we have used information about WordNet domains, e.g. biology, linguistics, time_period, etc. An initial experiment was run whereby all synsets in a given domain were entered in a relation with the domain. Unique WordNet-style IDs were generated for all domains and the relevant synsets were connected to those nodes. This approach yielded poor results, possibly due to the fact that in the PageRank algorithm the contribution of a node weakens the more outgoing edges it has, and the artifical domain nodes have hundreds of outgoing links. Thus, an alternative strategy was adopted of connecting all synsets within a domain to each other. In order to avoid generating many millions of new relations, only the synsets in the Bulgarian dictionary were connected in this fashion. This resulted in 132,596 new relations. The hierarchical relations between

[7] Here we interpret the concept of "event" in a wider sense that also includes states.

domains were also added to the graph, e.g. "grammar" is a hyponym of "linguistics".

5.3 Experimental Setup and Results

Several different versions of the relations graph were used in the experiments with the UKB tool. Those configurations that use relations independently of the corpus (i.e. ontological and definitional) were tested on the full corpus of 40 files. Most of the texts in the corpus are journalistic articles, but there are a number of texts from literary, academic, legal and other sources. Those configurations that include context-dependent relations were tested on a test portion of the corpus comprising of 3 large files with journalistic articles. The syntactic depedency relations and their extensions used in these configurations were extracted and constructed from the development portion of the corpus, i.e. the remaining 37 files.

This is a short description of the different configurations for the graph:

- **WN**: WordNet relations
- **WNG**: WordNet relations + relations from the glosses
- **WNI**: WordNet relations + inferred hypernymy relations
- **WNGI**: WordNet relations + relations from the glosses + inferred hypernymy relations
- **WNGID1**: WordNet relations + relations from the glosses + inferred hypernymy relations + domain relations of the kind synset-to-domain and domain hierarchy relations
- **WNGID2**: WordNet relations + relations from the glosses + inferred hypernymy relations + domain relations of the kind synset-to-synset and domain hierarchy relations
- **WNGIS**: WordNet relations + relations from the glosses + inferred hypernymy relations + dependency relations from the golden corpus
- **WNGISE**: WordNet relations + relations from the glosses + inferred hypernymy relations + dependency relations from the golden corpus + extended dependency relations
- **WNGISED1**: WordNet relations + relations from the glosses + inferred hypernymy relations + dependency relations from the golden corpus + extended dependency relations + domain relations of the kind synset-to-domain and domain hierarchy relations
- **WNGISED2**: WordNet relations + relations from the glosses + inferred hypernymy relations + dependency relations from the golden corpus + extended dependency relations + domain relations of the kind synset-to-synset and domain hierarchy relations
- **WNGISEUD2**: WordNet relations + relations from the glosses + inferred hypernymy relations + dependency relations from the golden corpus + extended dependency relations starting from one level up + domain relations of the kind synset-to-synset and domain hierarchy relations

Table 1 shows the results obtained after running the UKB tool on all texts in the corpus and only with WordNet-induced relations, while table 2 shows the results on the test set and with all relations (WordNet-induced and corpus-induced). The "Recall" column presents results according to the formula:

(CORRECT DECISIONS + INCORRECT DECISIONS) / (ALL DECISIONS + FALSE NEGATIVES)

As evidenced by the "Recall" column, about 6% of the word forms with gold senses are not tagged at all by the UKB tool (which results in the false negatives). The reasons for this are not completely clear at this moment; possible culprits could be inconsistencies between the lemmatizer and the dictionary or some option of the tool not to output decisions for words that cannot be disambiguated. We are currently working to solve this issue; the solution would possibly lead to a further increase in accuracy (e.g. decision making based on frequency counts can be used as a fall-back disambiguation mechanism).

Config	*Accuracy*	*Recall*
WN	0.516	0.942
WNG	0.542	0.942
WNI	0.537	0.942
WNGI	0.549	0.942
WNGID1	0.549	0.942
WNGID2	**0.551**	0.942

Table 1: Results on the full corpus

Config	*Accuracy*	*Recall*
WN	0.517	0.940
WNG	0.538	0.940
WNI	0.535	0.940
WNGI	0.537	0.940
WNGID1	0.538	0.940
WNGID2	0.550	0.940
WNGIS	0.565	0.941
WNGISE	0.616	0.941
WNGISED1	0.617	0.941
WNGISED2	0.624	0.941
WNGISEUD2	**0.656**	0.941

Table 2: Results on the test portion of the corpus

Several interesting facts can be observed from the two tables. With regards to just the context-independent configurations, it is evident that the inferred hypernymy relations help increase accuracy when added on top of the WordNet ontological relations alone; however, the relations derived from the glosses are more effective and the two sets of relations do not seem to complement each other, i.e. the addition to inferred hypernymies to the gloss similarity relations does not improve the results.

Secondly, the addition of domain relations does not contribute significantly when all synsets are linked to the domain nodes. Linking all synsets in a domain with each other, however, causes significant improvement, both in the case of context-independent configurations, and when combined with dependency relations (one such configuration gives the highest accuracy for all experiments).

The last and perhaps most important insight concerns the impact of syntactic information on WSD. Adding the dependency relations extracted from the golden corpus results in close to 3% improvement, while the addition of the downwards extended set adds a further improvement of 5%; extending the set by starting from one level above the original nodes in the dependency relations helps even more. Contextual information accounts for about 10% higher accuracy in the experiment done with the last configuration.

6 Conclusion

The paper demonstrates that the inclusion of additional linguistic knowledge to a graph-based experimental setting increases the accuracy of the WSD module for Bulgarian. The incorporation of additional hypernymy and domain relations from WordNet, as well as syntactic Universal Dependency relations from the BulTreeBank, improves WSD significantly. However, the algorithm performance drops in terms of speed with the addition of links to the graph, and optimization is needed in order to handle the increased space of relations.

The experiments also demonstrate that, given the availability of appropriate language resources, a graph model for one language (in our case English) can be successfully adapted to another language (in our case Bulgarian).

Our future work on WSD for Bulgarian will be focused on: adding more syntactic relations to the setting, adding the information from the mapped-to-WordNet adjectives and adverbs, adding more context related features, trying to link WordNet relations with additional resources (e.g. Wikipedia, FrameNet, etc.), experimenting with the fine options of the UKB tool.

Acknowledgements

This research has received partial support by the EC's FP7 (FP7/2007-2013) project under grant agreement number 610516: "QTLeap: Quality Translation by Deep Language Engineering Approaches" and FP7 grant 316087 AComIn "Advanced Computing for Innovation", funded by the European Commission in 20122016.

We are grateful to the three anonymous reviewers, whose remarks, comments, suggestions and encouragement helped us to improve the initial variant of the paper. All errors remain our own responsibility.

References

Eneko Agirre and David Martinez. 2002. Integrating selectional preferences in wordnet. In *Proceedings of First International WordNet Conference*.

Eneko Agirre and Aitor Soroa. 2009. Personalizing PageRank for word sense disambiguation. In *Proceedings of the 12th Conference of the European Chapter of the ACL (EACL 2009)*, pages 33–41, Athens, Greece, March. Association for Computational Linguistics.

Eneko Agirre, Oier López de Lacalle, and Aitor Soroa. 2014. Random walks for knowledge-based word sense disambiguation. *Comput. Linguist.*, 40(1):57–84, March.

Eneko Agirre, Ander Barrena, and Aitor Soroa. 2015. Studying the wikipedia hyperlink graph for relatedness and disambiguation. *arXiv preprint arXiv:1503.01655*.

Sergey Brin and Lawrence Page. 2012. Reprint of: The anatomy of a large-scale hypertextual web search engine. *Computer networks*, 56(18):3825–3833.

Andres Montoyo, Armando Suárez, German Rigau, and Manuel Palomar. 2005. Combining knowledge- and corpus-based word-sense-disambiguation methods. *J. Artif. Intell. Res.(JAIR)*, 23:299–330.

Roberto Navigli and Simone Paolo Ponzetto. 2012. BabelNet: The automatic construction, evaluation and application of a wide-coverage multilingual semantic network. *Artificial Intelligence, Elsevier*, 193:217–250.

Petya Osenova, Kiril Simov, Laska Laskova, and Stanislava Kancheva. 2012. A treebank-driven creation of an ontovalence verb lexicon for Bulgarian. In *Proceedings of the Eight International Conference on Language Resources and Evaluation (LREC'12)*, pages 2636–2640, Istanbul, Turkey. LREC 2012.

Alexander Popov, Stanislava Kancheva, Svetlomira Manova, Ivaylo Radev, Kiril Simov, and Petya Osenova. 2014. The sense annotation of bultreebank. In *Proceedings of the Thirteenth International Workshop on Treebanks and Linguistic Theories (TLT13)*, pages 127–136, Tuebingen, Germany. TLT 2014.

Learning Relationship between Authors' Activity and Sentiments: A case study of online medical forums

Marina Sokolova
IBDA and University of Ottawa
sokolova@uottawa.ca

Victoria Bobicev
Technical University of Moldova
vika@rol.md

Abstract

Our current work analyses relations between sentiments and activity of authors of online In-Vitro Fertilization forums. We focus on two types of active authors: those who start new discussions and those who post significantly more messages than other authors. By incorporating authors' activity information into a domain-specific lexical representation of messages, we were able to improve multi-class classification of sentiments by 9% for Support Vector Machines and by 15.3 % for Conditional Random Fields.

1 Introduction

User-friendly information and communications technologies and easily available access to the Internet were critical in development of Social Web, a socio-technical phenomenon that enables people to connect, support and learn from each other (Ho et al, 2014). The world-wide social media helped to create a digital resource of texts written by the general public. Those texts aggregate sentiments expressed by millions of people in relations to consumer goods, political campaigns, climate change and other matters of social importance. However, not all participants in online communities contribute equally to that resource: there are visitors who only read the posted texts, authors posting occasional messages and a small group of active authors whose online contributions significantly overweigh contributions of other authors. Those most active participants significantly influence online discussions (Tan et al., 2011; Zafarani et al., 2010).

Our current work studies relations between authors' activity levels and expressed sentiments in an online IVF forum. The forum is a public platform for discussion of In-Vitro Fertilization (IVF) treatment. It has been shown that sentiments on forums dedicated to specific health conditions dependent on the topic of discussion (Ali et al, 2013). We use a set of sentiment and factual categories tailored for on-line IVF discussions: *encouragement, gratitude, confusion, endorsement* and *facts*.

We are interested in two types of active authors: a) those who start discussions (a.k.a. first authors), b) those who post significantly more messages than other authors (a.k.a. prolific authors). The remaining authors usually post one-two messages, and their contributions are rather sporadic. We have found that distribution of sentiments appeared in text written by different types of authors differs considerably. For example, the authors who start new topics and actively post in the following discussion usually express more *gratitude*: 26% of messages posted by the first authors vs. 9% of messages for all the authors.

We wanted to confirm that information about the author's activity has practical implication and can enhance sentiment and subjectivity lexicons. We used automated prediction of sentiments, where messages were first represented through a domain-specific subjectivity lexicon and then authors' activity information was added to the representation. This enhancement helped to improve the sentiment classification up to 9 % for Support Vector Machines and up to 15.3% for Conditional Random Fields.

2 Related Work

Subjectivity, opinion and attitude classification, mood summarization, emotion and affect detection exemplify Sentiment Analysis and Opinion Mining research (Banea et al, 2012). Those studies increasingly apply to health-related issues, with drug-related sentiment studies emerging as a new sub-topic (Nikfarjam and Gonzalez, 2011). Sentiment dynamics in a health-related online community was studied by Qiu et al. (2011). The authors collected the data from the American Cancer Society Cancer Survivors Network; the data represented a 10-year time span from July

Proceedings of Recent Advances in Natural Language Processing, pages 604–610,
Hissar, Bulgaria, Sep 7–9 2015.

2000 to October 2010. The authors applied binary classification of positive and negative sentiments; e.g., My mom became resistant to carbo after 7 treatments and now the trial drug is no longer working :(, *Negative*; ID-x, I love the way you think, ..., hope is crucial and no one can deny that a cure may be right around the corner!!! *Positive*.

The results demonstrated that the initial negative posts were often followed by positive posts of the same participant. The change was attributed to interaction with other participants of the same thread. The authors hypothesized that the use of multiple categories of sentiments can improve sentiment analysis of the same data.

A predefined set of general sentiment labels may not be sufficient for emotionally charged discussions. Sentiment transition and topic influence on Twitter were studied in (Kim et al, 2011). The results showed that an extensive set of sentiment categories including teasing, complaining, sympathy, and apology provided for a more accurate sentiment prediction and classification than positive, negative and neutral sentiments or six basic emotions: *anger, disgust, joy, fear, sadness, surprise*. The authors concluded that the 'social' sentiments *sympathy*, *apology*, and *complaining* were influential in sentiment change.

Celli and Zaga (2013) demonstrated that personality traits help in a sentiment analysis task. The authors used the Big5 model (Costa, and MacCrae, 1992) which describes personality along five traits formalized as bipolar scales: extroversion (sociable or shy), neuroticism (calm or neurotic), agreeableness (friendly or uncooperative), conscientiousness (organized or careless) and openness to experience (insightful or unimaginative). Life cycles of online groups had been studied by Patil et al. (2013). The authors determined that 'prolific' members play an important role in maintaining the group stability.

Not all subjective statements are perceived equal: messages posted by frequent contributors may trigger a bigger effect than those posted by occasional authors. At the same time, few sentiment analysis studies of online health-related forums connect activity levels of authors with sentiments and opinions expressed in their messages. In the current work, we study activity characteristics of the forum authors, such as their message productivity, willingness to start new topics and maintain dialogue started by others.

3 The IVF Data Set

In this research, we have used the IVF data set introduced in (Sokolova & Bobicev, 2013). The data is available for research purposes upon request. All the messages were collected from online medical forums dedicated to infertility issues and reproductive technologies. The data set consists of 1321 messages written by 359 female authors and posted on 80 discussions. The average length of the discussion - 16.5 posts (s.t.d. = 9.6). The average number of participants in one topic - 9.5 persons (s.t.d. = 4.2). The average post had 750 characters and 5-10 sentences.

Each post was annotated by two independent annotators. They categorized a post into one category selected among three sentiment categories (encouragement, gratitude, confusion) and two factual categories (facts, endorsement). For example,

post_id_300078 "I am so so sorry for your loss, but I want to give you some hope. EXACTLY the same happened to me, only this past May gone. I was ready to give up; I didn't think I could try again. We ended up doing IVF in August and I am now 20 weeks pregnant.Take the time to take good care of yourself over the holidays and enjoy some wine... All the best to you and your dear wee family.RG" ***endorsment***
post_id_300144 Candis I am sorry about your lossHope you get well soon and have a successful cycle next yearIn the mean time take good care of your selfSam ***encouragement***
post_id_300160 Thanks so much everyone ..all your kind words have truly made my day ***gratitude***

The annotators achieved a high Fleiss Kappa = 0.791 that indicates a near-*strong* agreement[1]. There were 433 posts marked as *facts*, 310 obtained the label *encouragement*, 162 posts marked with *endorsement* and 124 as *gratitude*. 176 posts were left ambiguous as the annotators did not agree on their sentiment label.

The analyzed forum discussions are intrinsically heterogeneous. We identify three main factors contributing for the diversity:

- The authors go through different experience (successful IVF treatment vs. complications and uncertainty), exhibit conflicting personal traits (reserve vs. openness) and vary in contributing to the forum. (e.g., many authors add one or two messages per discussion).

[1] A *strong* agreement is indicated by Kappa = 0.80.

- Time delay (the last message can be posted weeks or even months after the first one) might weaken relations between messages and the expressed sentiments.
- New participants were bringing new ideas and emotions in already established discussions.

We observed that despite those diversifying factors discussions exhibited a common content flow: it could start by a participant by expressing her doubts and concerns, continued by describing a treatment and concluded by posting the results. Within discussions, the messages were coherent and related, i.e., every posted message answered to one or several previous messages, and in most cases did not diverge from the discussed topic.

To estimate divergence of sentiment categories due to discussion progress, we computed the sentiment categories in the first messages of discussions, last messages of the discussions and all the messages. The first posts of the discussions express the author's *confusion* more often than not (56% of the post) or describe the author's situation in more objective manner (*facts* – 17%). With the progress of discussions, *confusion* decreased to 9% of all the posts, and *facts* increased to 33% of all the posts. There were no discussions that started with positive sentiments, i.e. *gratitude* and en*couragement*, and only one stated with *endorsement*. Those three categories appeared in the following posts as responses to the *confusion* posts.

They eventually formed 44% of the all messages (*encouragement* – 24%; *endorsement* – 12%, *gratitude* – 9%). The first posts were more difficult for annotation than others, as 26% of the first posts were *ambiguous* whereas only 13% of all the messages were *ambiguous*.

We gathered posts from discussions marked "inactive" by the forum. Thus, we considered that the discussions have the "last" post. In most cases, discussion was perceived as completed and became inactive when participants posted a post conveying necessary information *(facts – 39%, endorsement – 8%),* or a moral support *(encouragement – 25%, gratitude - 11%).* Only one of the analyzed threads became inactive after a post labeled as *confusion.*[2] The reported results support our hypothesis that the position of the post in discussion provides additional insight about the sentiments it could contain. We used the position information in Machine Learning classification of sentiments. Figures 1- 3 visualize those results.

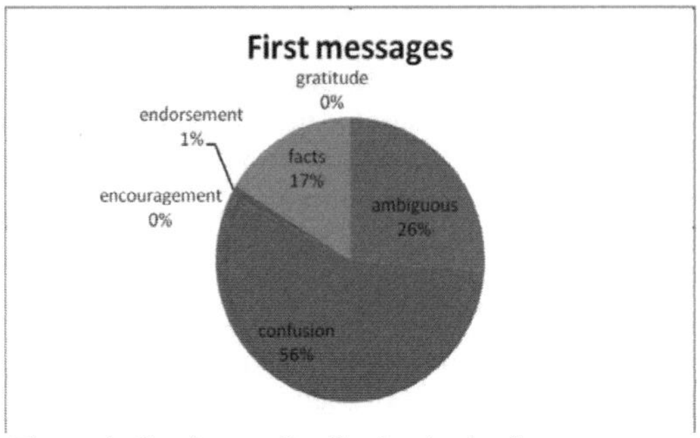

Figure 1. Sentiment distribution in the first messages.

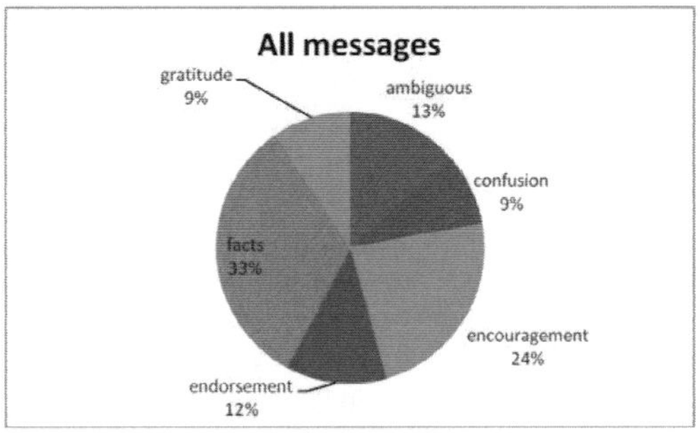

Figure 2. Sentiment distribution in all the messages.

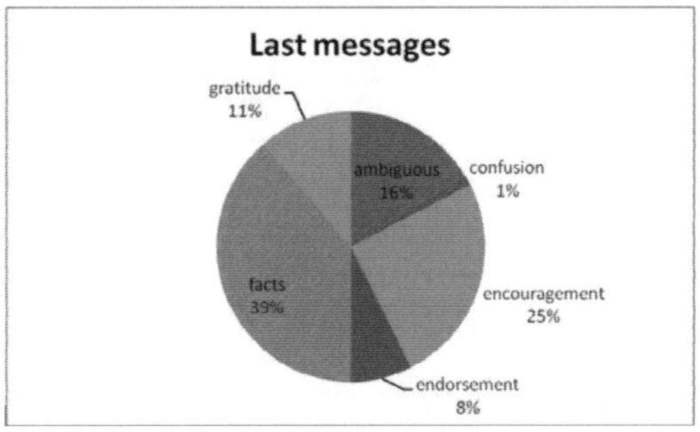

Figure 3. Sentiment distribution in the last messages.

4 Authors' Activity on the Forum

We focused on how information about the authors and their activity on the forum can help in prediction of expressed sentiments. We looked at

1) the total number of messages posted by an author;
2) initiation of new discussions; and
3) contribution to discussions initiated by other authors.

The authors who start discussions (a.k.a. first authors) actively participate in the initiated discussion and guide it in the direction they need. In only 10% of cases they posted only the first mes-

[2] This discussion has not been re-activated on the time of this paper submission.

sage in the discussion and did not respond on messages posted afterwards.

On average, 25% of messages in discussions were posted by the author of the first post. Figure 4 shows distribution of sentiments in messages of the first authors. Per cent with the posts with *confusion* is larger in comparison with the other authors. Recall that 56% of discussions started with posts marked *confusion*. However, *confusion* posts for these participants decrease considerably as discussions progress and result in 17% of all their posts. The first authors post many messages with *facts* and 26% of their posts express *gratitude* to the participants who helped them with information or moral support.

Our results support those obtained by Qiu et al. (2012) although both studies were conducted on data gathered from different health-related forums.

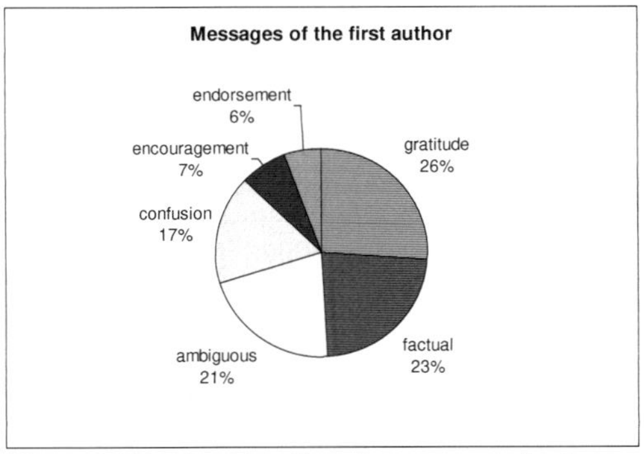

Figure 4. Distribution of sentiment categories in messages of the first authors.

We intended to explore whether the active participants have any specific characteristics regarding sentiments expressed in their posts and whether sentiments the threads they actively participated in are more predictable. We call the most active authors "prolific". We estimated "prolificness" of the authors as the ratio of the total number of author's posts to the total number of posts of the most prolific author in the studied topics (Patil et al, 2013). Thus, prolificness ranges between [0, 1] and the participant with the greatest number of posts has prolificness equal to 1. In our data, the average prolificness of the prolific authors is 0.44, while the overall prolificness is 0.06. More detailed analysis of these authors' activity can be found in (Bobicev et al., 2015b).

The prolific authors mostly conveyed *facts* and *encouragement*: 39.1% and 24.1% of their messages. In messages posted by the prolific authors, *confusion* appeared less than other sentiments: 22 posts in total, or 5.7% of their messages. *Gratitude* was the second least frequent sentiment among the authors: 6.7% of their posts marked as *gratitude*. The prolific authors showed considerably more confidence and assurance than the authors who posted only 1-2 messages on the forum. Figures 5 and 6 compare sentiments in messages of the prolific authors with sentiments of messages written by the infrequent authors.

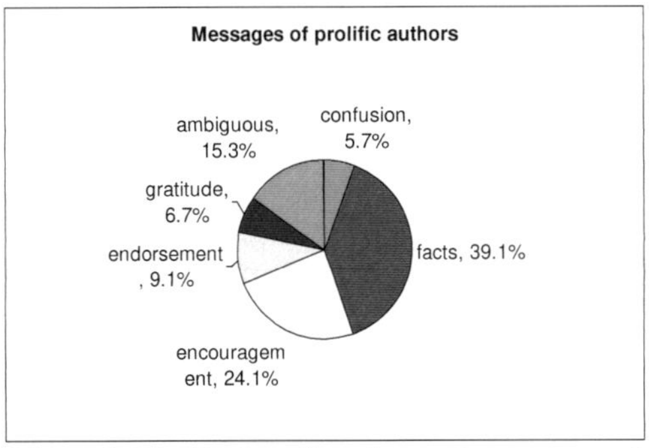

Figure 5. Distribution of sentiments in messages of the prolific authors.

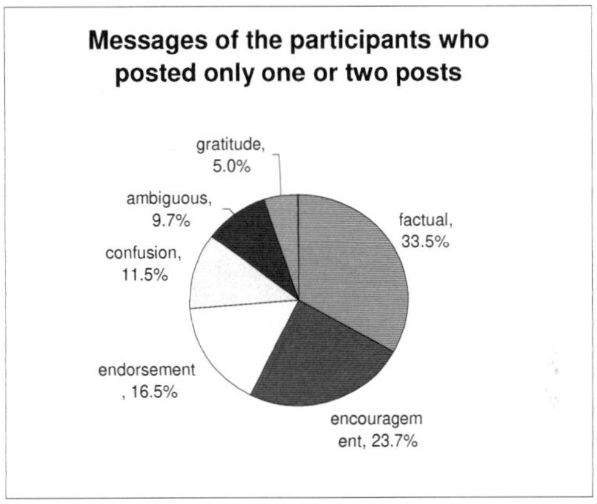

Figure 6. Distribution of sentiments in messages of the infrequent authors.

Comparing the group of the prolific participants and the group of first authors, we observed that 14 of 80 discussions were started by the prolific authors. 10 prolific authors started at least one topic, two of them started two and one started three topics. Thus, they were active not only in participating in various discussions but also in starting the new ones. On the other hand, the average prolificness of the first authors is 0.15 which means that the participants who start new topics are more active in general than in the average participant whose prolificness is 0.06.

It was much easier to predict the characteristics of the message posted by an interlocutor already involved in discussion while a message posted by a person who decided to join this thread was rather unpredictable. Thus, we pooled together messages posted by authors joining discussion for the first time (a.k.a. discussion newcomers) (Figure 7). In comparison with the sentiment distribution of all the authors, there were fewer messages with gratitude and more with confusion as many participants post the first message describing their problems. 75% of the discussion newcomer's posts contained facts or/and encouragement addressed the previous thread participants; thus they were not as much unpredictable as we expected.

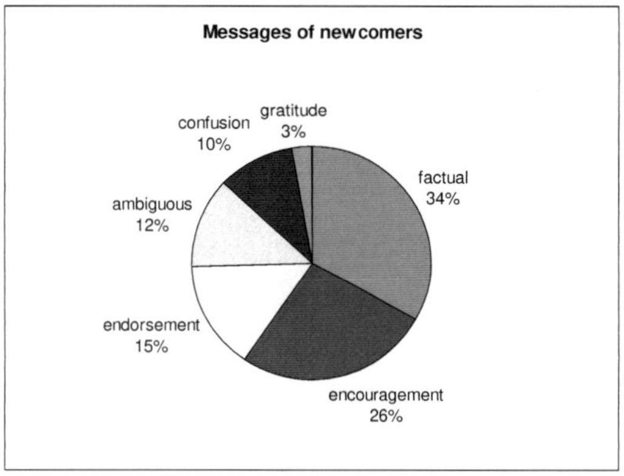

Figure 7. Distribution of sentiments in messages of discussion newcomers.

5 Sentiment Classification

Sentiment analysis of the IVF forum demonstrated that a domain-specific HealthAffect lexicon is effective in prediction of expressed sentiments. HealthAffect (HA) is built by applying Pointwise Mutual Information on a small number of training examples and candidates (unigrams, bigrams and trigrams) with occurrence > 5 in the training data. The detailed description of the HA lexicon creation can be found in (Sokolova & Bobicev, 2013). To represent the data, we used the top frequent 207 terms that appear in Health Affect (HA 207 terms).

We applied 6-class classification to classify 1321 posts into *confusion, encouragement, endorsement, gratitude, facts,* and *ambiguous*.

We used Support Vector Machines (SVM) from WEKA toolkit and Conditional Random Fields (CRF) from Mallet toolkit. SVM used the logistic model and normalized poly kernel; CRF had default settings. The best classifier was selected by 10-fold cross-validation.

We obtained the baseline classification accuracy by represented the messages through the HA 207 terms. We then reinforced the HA representation by adding information about positioning of the post in discussion and information about the author activities. We used two categorical features to represent the position of the post in discussion:

- an indicator showing that the current post holds the first, last or mid position in discussion.
- an indicator showing that the previous post holds the first, last or mid position in discussion;

We used three binary features describing author's activity:

- an indicator that the author of the post started the discussion from which the post was collected;
- an indicator whether the author of the post is a prolific author;
- an indicator that the author of the post joined the discussion from which the post was collected.

Tables 1 and 2 report the classification results for SVM and CRF respectively. For both algorithms, the access to the author information has shown to be beneficial: F-score improved up to 9% for SVM and up to 15.3% for CRF.

The aim of the next set of the sentiment classification experiments was to study what group of authors expressed sentiments in a way more predictable for automated classification. We built three sets:

- First authors: we collected 269 posts from 10 discussions which had the largest number of posts posted by the initial author;
- Prolific authors: we gathered 224 posts from 10 discussions which the largest number of posts posted by prolific authors among all the discussions;
- Discussion newcomers: we collected 130 posts from 10 discussions which had the largest number of authors joining the discussion.

The posts were represented by 207 HA terms. The results of 6-class sentiment classification in Table 3 show that SVM classifies sentiments more accurately when the initiators of discussions actively participate in following message exchange. CRF better recognizes sentiments if many new authors join the discussion.

Features	SVM		
	P	R	F
HA 207	*0.40*	*0.43*	*0.41*
HA 207 + pos of current post	0.42	0.45	0.43
HA 207 + pos of current and prev. post	0.41	0.44	0.42
HA 207 + pos of current post + if the author is the first	0.43	0.46	***0.44***
HA 207 + pos of current post + if the author is the new one	0.42	0.45	0.43
HA 207 + pos of current post + if the author is prolific	0.41	0.45	0.42
HA 207 + pos of current post + if the author is the first, new or prolific	0.44	0.47	**0.45**
HA 207 + if the author is the first, new or prolific	0.43	0.45	0.43

Table 1: 6-class sentiment classification by SVM. Baseline results are in *italic*. The best F-score is in **bold**, the 2nd best is in ***that font.***

Features	CRF		
	P	R	F
HA 207	*0.31*	*0.29*	*0.30*
HA 207 + pos of current post	0.32	0.30	0.31
HA 207 + pos of current and prev. post	0.34	0.32	0.33
HA 207 + pos of current post + if the author is the first	0.36	0.33	***0.34***
HA 207 + pos of current post + if the author is the new one	0.33	0.31	0.32
HA 207 + pos of current post + if the author is prolific	0.35	0.31	0.33
HA 207 + pos of current post + if the author is the first, new or prolific	0.35	0.31	0.33
HA 207 + if the author is the first, new or prolific	0.36	0.34	**0.35**

Table 2: 6-class sentiment classification by CRF. The best F-score is in **bold**, the 2nd best is in ***that font.***

Discussion sets	SVM			CRF		
	P	R	F	P	R	F
First authors	0.44	0.46	**0.44**	0.33	0.39	0.35
Prolific authors	0.38	0.35	0.36	0.33	0.33	0.33
Discussion newcomers	0.39	0.39	0.39	0.40	0.33	**0.37**

Table 3: Sentiment classification related to three types of the author activities.

6 Discussion and Future Work

Currently 19%-28% of Internet users participate in online health discussions (Balicco, Paganelli, 2011). Analysis of sentiments and opinions posted online can help in understanding of sentiments and opinions of the public at large. Such understanding is especially important for the development of public policies whose success greatly depends on public support, including health care (Atkinson, 2009; Eysenbach, 2009).

In this work, we have focused on relations between sentiments and authors' activity on online health-related forums. We worked with 6 sentiment and factual categories: *encouragement, gratitude, confusion, endorsement* and *facts*.

We have identified three groups of the forum authors: the most prolific authors, the authors who start new discussions, and the authors who join discussions started by other authors. We have shown that distribution of sentiments differs considerably for those categories of the authors. Annotation agreement is the strongest (Kappa = 0.806) on messages with the greatest presence of the new authors, as well as ability of CRF to identify the six sentiments (F-score = 0.37). At the same time, SVM achieved the most accurate classification on messages with the greatest contribution from the first authors (F-score = 0.44 in six-class classification). We have shown that adding the author information to a semantic representation of the messages can significantly improve sentiment recognition (up to 15.3%).

As a future work we intend to study participants' interaction in more details. In (Bobicev et al., 2015a) we analyzed message sequences and found patterns of sentiments in the consecutive posts. However, many posts were addressed to the one specific interlocutor by her name. We plan to analyze these direct communications and interaction of sentiments expressed in these sequences of posts.

Also, we plan to investigate the ambiguous messages and find a suitable solution for their sentiment annotation. One of the solutions would be to allow multiple annotations for one post. In this case we can use both labels assigned by the annotators to the ambiguous post and find a way to automate learning of multiple annotations. Taking into consideration that the messages are comparatively long (5 to 10 sentences) the other possible solution is to annotate some parts of one message with different labels. This could be done by automatically applying a sentiment lexicon.

References

Ali, T., D. Schramm, M. Sokolova and D. Inkpen. 2013. *Can I hear you? Sentiment Analysis on Medical Forums*, International Joint Conference on Natural Language Processing, pp. 667-673.

Atkinson N.L., Saperstein S.L., Pleis J. 2009. *Using the internet for health-related activities: findings from a national probability sample.* J Med Internet Res. 2009 Feb 20;11(1):e4.

L. Balicco, C. Paganelli. 2011. *Access to health information: going from professional to public practices.* SIIE'2011.

Banea, C., R. Mihalcea, and J. Wiebe. 2012. *Multilingual sentiment and subjectivity analysis, in Multilingual Natural Language Applications: From Theory to Practice.* D. Bikel and I. Zitouni (eds). Prentice-Hall. 2012.

Bobicev, V., Sokolova, M., Oakes. M. 2015a. What Goes Around Comes Around: Learning Sentiments in Online Medical Forums, *Journal of Cognitive Computation*, 2015.

Bobicev, V., Sokolova, M., Oakes. M. 2015b. *Sentiment and Factual Transitions in Online Medical Forums.* Proceedings of Canadian AI 2015 conference.

Celli, F., C. Zaga. 2013. Be *Conscientious, Express your Sentiment!* ESSEM@AI*IA 2013: 140-147.

Costa, P. T. and MacCrae, R. R. 1992. *Normal personality assessment in clinical practice: The neo personality inventory.* Psychological assessment, 4(1):5.

Eysenbach, G. 2009. Infodemiology and infoveillance: framework for an emerging set of public health informatics methods to analyze search, communication and publication behaviour on the Internet. *Journal of Medical Internet Research*, 11(1).

Ho, K., Peter Wall Workshop Participants. 2014. Harnessing the Social Web for Health and Wellness: Issues for Research and Knowledge Translation. *Journal of medical Internet research* 16.2.

Kim, S., J. Yeong Bak, Y. Jo, Alice Oh. 2011. *Do you feel what I feel? Social Aspects of Emotions in Twitter Conversations,* Workshop on Computational Social Science and the Wisdom of Crowds. NIPS.

Nikfarjam, A., and Gonzalez, G. H. 2011. *Pattern mining for extraction of mentions of adverse drug reactions from user comments.* In AMIA Annual Symposium Proceedings (Vol. 2011, p. 1019).

Qiu, B., K. Zhao, P. Mitra, D. Wu, C. Caragea, J. Yen, Greta E. Greer, K. Portier. 2011. *Get online support, feel better – sentiment analysis and dynamics in an online cancer survivor community.* Privacy, Security, Risk and Trust (PASSAT) and 2011 IEEE Third Inernational Conference on Social Computing.

Patil, A., J. Liu, J. Gao. 2013. *Predicting Group Stability in Online Social Networks.* Proceedings of the 22nd international conference on World Wide Web, , pages 1021-1030.

Sokolova, M., V. Bobicev. 2013. *What Sentiments Can Be Found in Medical Forums?* RANLP 2013: 633-639.

Tan, C., L. Lee , J. Tang , L. Jiang , M. Zhou, P. Li. 2011. *User-level sentiment analysis incorporating social networks.* The 17th ACM SIGKDD international conference on Knowledge Discovery and Data Mining, pp. 1397-1405.

Zafarani, R., W. Cole, and H. Liu. 2010 *Sentiment Propagation in Social Networks: A Case Study in LiveJournal.* Advances in Social Computing (SBP 2010), pp. 413–420.

Translating from Original to Simplified Sentences using Moses: When does it Actually Work?

Sanja Štajner
Research Group in Computational Linguistics
University of Wolverhampton, UK
SanjaStajner@wlv.ac.uk

Horacio Saggion
TALN Research Group
Universitat Pompeu Fabra, Spain
horacio.saggion@upf.edu

Abstract

In recent years, several studies have approached the Text Simplification (TS) task as a machine translation (MT) problem. They report promising results in learning how to translate from 'original' to 'simplified' language using the standard phrase-based translation model. However, our results indicate that this approach works well only when the training dataset consists mostly of those sentence pairs in which the simplified sentence is already very similar to its original. Our findings suggest that the standard phrase-based approach might not be appropriate to learn strong simplifications which are needed for certain target populations.

1 Introduction

Text Simplification (TS) aims to convert complex texts into simpler variants which are more accessible to a wider audiences, e.g. non-native speakers, children, and people diagnosed with intellectual disability, autism, aphasia, dyslexia or congenital deafness. In the last twenty years, many automatic text simplification systems have been proposed, varying from rule-based, e.g. (Brouwers et al., 2014; Saggion et al., 2015) to data-driven, e.g. (Zhu et al., 2010; Woodsend and Lapata, 2011), and hybrid (Siddharthan and Angrosh, 2014). Since 2010, there have been several attempts to approach TS as a machine translation (MT) problem (Specia, 2010; Coster and Kauchak, 2011a; Štajner, 2014). Instead of translating sentences from one language to another, the goal of text simplification is to translate sentences from 'original' to 'simplified' language.

In this paper, we seek to explore the main reasons for the success or failure of the phrase-based statistical machine translation (PB-SMT) approach to TS. The results of our translation experiments in three languages indicate that the size of the dataset might not be the key factor for the success of this approach and that the effectiveness of such systems heavily depends on the similarity between the original and manually simplified sentences in the datasets used for training and tuning.

2 Related Work

Specia (2010) achieves BLEU score of 60.75 on a small (only 4,483 sentence pairs) dataset in Brazilian Portuguese, using the standard phrase-based translation model (Koehn et al., 2003) in the Moses toolkit (Koehn et al., 2007). The dataset consists of original sentences and their corresponding manually simplified versions obtained under the PorSimples project (Aluísio and Gasperin, 2010) following specific guidelines.

Coster and Kauchak (2011a) exploit the same translation model to learn how to simplify English sentences using 137,000 sentence pairs from Wikipedia and Simple English Wikipedia. They show that those results (BLEU = 59.87) can be improved by adding phrasal deletion to the probabilistic translation model, reaching the BLEU score of 60.46. Both those approaches seem to outperform all previous non-MT approaches to TS for English.

The fact that Specia (2010) and Coster and Kauchak (2011a) achieve similar performances of the PB-SMT system in spite of large differences in size of their datasets motivates our hypothesis that the key factor for a success of such an approach to TS might not lie in the size of the datasets but rather in the nature of the sentence pairs used for training and tuning of the PB-SMT models.

3 Methodology

We apply the following methodology:

- We run MT-based text simplification exper-

Proceedings of Recent Advances in Natural Language Processing, pages 611–617,
Hissar, Bulgaria, Sep 7–9 2015.

iments on three different datasets and languages following the methods proposed in previous studies (Specia, 2010; Coster and Kauchak, 2011a).

- We perform automatic evaluation in terms of the document-wise (BLEU) and the sentence-wise BLEU score (S-BLEU).
- We conduct a manual error analysis of the output of all three translation experiments.
- We calculate sentence-wise BLEU score on the training and development datasets to further understand the differences observed in the translation experiments.

3.1 Datasets

We use three sentence-aligned TS corpora in three different languages:

1. **EsSim** – The corpus of original news texts in Spanish and their manual simplifications aimed at people with Down syndrome. Simplification was performed by trained human editors under the Simplext project (Saggion et al., 2015).
2. **PorSim** – The corpus of original news texts in Brazilian Portuguese and their manual simplifications compiled under the PorSimples project (Caseli et al., 2009). Original sentences and their corresponding 'natural' simplifications of this corpus were used for in the previous PB-SMT experiments (Specia, 2010).
3. **Wiki** – The parallel corpus of automatically aligned sentence pairs from English Wikipedia and Simple English Wikipedia, used for the PB-SMT experiments by Coster and Kauchak (2011a).[1]

In order to compare the results of translation experiments among the three corpora, we train and tune all three systems on a similar amount of data. Therefore, we focus only a subset of sentence pairs used by Specia (2010), and by Coster and Kauchak (Coster and Kauchak, 2011a). The sizes of the corpora used are shown in Table 1.

[1]http://www.cs.middlebury.edu/ dkauchak/simplification/

	EsSim	Wiki	PorSim
Training	745	800	800
Dev.	90	200	200
Test	90	100	100
Total	925	1100	1100
Selection	all	random	random

Table 1: Size of the corpora

3.2 Translation Experiments

We run three MT experiments using the standard PB-SMT models (Koehn et al., 2003) implemented in the Moses toolkit (Koehn et al., 2007) and GIZA++ (Och and Ney, 2003) to obtain the word alignment. The English experiment uses the Wiki aligned corpus for translation model (TM) and the English part of the Europarl corpora[2] for building the language model (LM). The Spanish experiment uses the EsSim dataset to build the TM and the Spanish Europarl for the LM. The Brazilian Portuguese experiment uses the PorSim dataset for the TM and the Lácio-Web corpus[3] in Brazilian Portuguese for the LM[4]. The sentence pairs for training, development and test sets are selected randomly from the initial dataset.

4 Results and Discussion

In the next three subsections, we present and discuss the results of the automatic evaluation of the translation experiments (Section 4.1), the error analysis of the translation experiments (Section 4.2), and the distribution of the S-BLEU score across the four datasets (Section 4.3).

4.1 Automatic Evaluation

The results of the translation experiments and sentence similarity metrics on the three datasets used for training the translation models are presented in Table 2. The BLEU scores achieved by translation experiments in English and Brazilian Portuguese are similar to those reported by Specia (2010) and Coster and Kauchak (2011a) in spite of our experiments having reduced the sizes of the two corpora for fair comparison with the Spanish dataset. As can be observed (Table 2), we cannot claim to

[2]http://www.statmt.org/europarl/

[3]http://www.nilc.icmc.usp.br/lacioweb/

[4]The Portuguese in the Europarl corpora belong to the different regional language variety, and thus we opted for the Lácio-Web corpus written in the same regional variety as the used TS dataset.

	EsSim	Wiki	PorSim
BLEU	10.55	53.28	65.66
t-BLEU	10.16	56.39	48.46
BP	0.59	0.87	0.93
S-BLEU	0.16	0.58	0.58

Table 2: Automatic evaluation

Modification	EsSim	PorSim	Wiki
None	4.44%	40%	65%
1 Substitution	4.44%	40%	28%
>1 Substitution	91.11%	20%	2%
Split	6.67%	14%	5%
Combined	6.67%	14%	3%

Table 3: Classification of modifications

have an equally good performance on the Spanish dataset for which we obtained a BLEU score of 10.55.

In order to understand better the differences in translation performances (BLEU) across datasets, we calculated BLEU score (t-BLEU) with brevity penalty (BP), and sentence-wise BLEU score (S-BLEU)[5] on the training datasets (EsSim, PorSim, and Wiki). The manual simplifications (or in the case of English, the Simple Wikipedia versions) were used as hypotheses and the original non-simplified versions as references. It appears that the similarity between the original and simplified sentences used for training is much higher (up to four times higher in the case of the *S-BLEU*) in the Wiki and PorSim datasets than in the third dataset (EsSim).

It can be noted that the EsSim dataset achieves significantly lower BLEU score than the other two. Additionally, the EsSim dataset has a much higher brevity penalty (BP) on the training set than the other two datasets, indicating that the sentence shortening is more commonly used simplifying operation in this dataset than in the other two. It seems that whenever MT performs well (Table 2), we actually have a dataset that is more MT-looking and complies with the underlying assumptions of the standard phrase-based model (reflected in the high BLEU score on the training data). The low BLEU score on the training dataset (t-BLEU) suggests that there are many string transformations and strong paraphrases to be learnt, and thus the standard phrase-based translation model might not be the most suitable for the task.

As it is known that the BLEU score does not give a fair comparison among systems with different architectures – or, in this case, systems trained for different languages and tested on different datasets – we do not rely on the automatic evaluation of our models. Instead, we perform a detailed manual analysis of the output of all three systems.

4.2 Error Analysis

In order to clarify doubts raised by the results of the automatic evaluation, we performed error analysis on all sentences from the three datasets (90 sentences in Spanish, 100 sentences in English, and 100 sentences in Portuguese). The classification of the test sentences based on the number and type of modifications made by the translation/simplification models is presented in Table 3.

The manual examination of the output of the translation model trained on the EsSim corpora confirmed the poor performance of the system, describing the output of the automatic simplification as barely comprehensible in most of the cases. At the same time, the manual examination of the output of the model trained on the Wiki corpus revealed that such a high performance (in terms of the BLEU score) is indeed due to the fact that the output was in most cases identical to the original sentence. The human evaluation of the automatically generated sentences in Portuguese, confirmed that the model was able to perform at least one lexical substitution in 40% of the sentences, more than one lexical substitution in 20% of the cases, and sentence splitting combined with lexical substitution(s) in 14% of the cases.

It was not possible to perform usual human evaluation of the generated sentences in terms of their grammaticality, simplicity, and meaning preservation due to: (1) 82 automatically simplified sentences in Spanish (out of 90) being severely ungrammatical (due to the multiple wrong word substitutions), to the extent that it was impossible to assess their simplicity (as they were barely comprehensible) or to compare their meaning with the meaning of the original sentence, and (2) 65 automatically simplified sentences for English being identical to their originals and another

[5]Sentence-level BLEU score (S-BLEU) differs from BLEU score only in the sense that S-BLEU will still positively score segments that do not have higher n-gram matching (n=4 in our setting) unless there is no unigram match; otherwise it is the same as BLEU.

Ex.	Original	Automatic	Reference
p1	**Porém**, ninguém pode subestimar a capacidade de mobilização de Chávez.	**Mas** ninguém pode subestimar a capacidade de mobilização de Chávez.	Mas ninguém pode *desprezar* a capacidade de mobilização de Chávez.
p2	Dom Odilo**, que** trabalhou no Vaticano entre 1994 e 2001, é tido como um religioso moderado, próximo à Cúria Romana e **alinhado** com as **diretrizes** da Santa Sé.	Dom Odilo trabalhou no Vaticano entre 1994 e 2001**. Ele** é tido como um religioso moderado, próximo à Cúria Romana e **concorda** com as **normas** da Santa Sé.	Dom Odilo trabalhou no Vaticano entre 1994 e 2001. Ele é tido como um religioso moderado, próximo à Cúria Romana e *que* concorda com as normas da Santa Sé.
p3	A segunda sugestão de modificação diz respeito **ao veto** de pesquisas com células-tronco **embrionárias humanas** e com clonagem **terapêutica**.	A segunda sugestão de modificação diz respeito **à proibição** de pesquisas com células-tronco **de embriões humanos** e com clonagem **para tratamento de doentes**.	A segunda sugestão de modificação diz respeito à proibição de pesquisas com células-tronco de embriões humanos e com clonagem para tratamento de doentes.

Table 4: Examples of the automatic simplification in Brazilian Portuguese (differences between the original sentences and their automatic simplifications are shown in bold, and the deviations of the manual simplifications from the automatic simplifications are shown in italics)

28 sentences differing from their originals by only one word. Therefore, we focused on detailed analysis of the generated sentences in all three languages, seeking to discover what are the possibilities and limitations of our simplification models.

4.2.1 Portuguese

Table 4 shows examples of the original sentences from the test dataset (*Original*), their automatic simplifications (*Automatic*), and their corresponding reference simplifications ('gold standards') manually simplified under the PorSimples project (*Reference*). As previously mentioned, 60 out of 100 original test sentences were lexically modified by the system, while 14 of them were additionally split into two sentences.

In the first example (*p1*), the system performed one lexical substitution replacing the word "Porém" (*however*) with "Mas" (*but*). The same substitution was done by human editors. However, the system only performed this one substitution, while the manual simplification encompassed one additional lexical simplification.

In the second example (*p2*), the system performed a correct sentence splitting taking the apposition in a separate sentence ("Dom Odilo trabalhou no Vaticano entre 1994 e 2001."), and two correct lexical simplifications: "alinhado" (*aligned*, *in line*) was changed into "concorda" (*agree*, *comply*) and "diretrizes" (*guidelines*) into "normas" (*standards*, *norms*). The difference between the manual and automatic simplification of this sentence was not significant (the automatically simplified sentence is still grammatical, although the manually simplified sentence might be stylistically better).

The third example (*p3*) shows a case in which the automatic simplification managed to reach the level of manual simplification by performing three corrected lexical simplifications and generating the output sentence equal to the manually simplified sentence.

4.2.2 Spanish

Table 5 shows examples of the original sentences from the test dataset (*Original*), their automatic simplifications (*Automatic*), and their corresponding reference simplifications ('gold standards') manually simplified under the Simplext project (*Reference*).

In the first example (*s1*), "UE" (*EU*) was correctly replaced with "Europa" (*Europe*), while the incorrect substitution of "sacar de la pobreza" (*get out of poverty*) with "objetivo" (*goal/aim/objective*) left the sentence meaningless. Together with the deletion of "20" (in *"20 million people"*) and "hasta 2020" (*until 2020*), and the insertion of "a" at the end of the sentence, the generated sentence is completely ungrammatical and meaningless. The original sentence *"The EU wants to get out of poverty 20 million people until 2020"* is simplified as *"The Europe wants goal to millions of people"*.

The second example (*s2*) is particularly interesting as the manual simplification ('gold standard') is identical to the original sentence. In the automatically generated sentence, however, the phrase "dimitirá como presidente" (*will quit as a president*) in the original sentence was correctly 'translated' as "deja la presidencia" (*leaves the presi-*

Ex.	Original	Automatic	Reference
s1	La **UE** quiere **sacar de la pobreza** a **20** millones de personas **hasta 2020**.	La **Europa** quiere **objetivo** a millones de personas **a**.	Europa quiere ayudar a millones de personas a dejar de ser pobres.
s2	Alex de la Iglesia **dimitirá como presidente** de la Academia de Cine.	**Cine** Alex de la Iglesia **deja la presidencia** de la Academia de Cine.	Alex de la Iglesia dimitirá como presidente de la Academia de Cine.
s3	**Por otro lado**, el informe de **"la Caixa"** sitúa en el 9,5% **del PIB** el déficit público al término de 2010 y **calcula** que el **conjunto** de las **administraciones** podrán reducirlo hasta el 6,4**%** **durante** 2011.	, el informe de **la** sitúa en el 9,5 **mitad el** el déficit público al término de 2010 y **cree** que el **literaria** de las **corridas** podrán reducirlo hasta el 6,4 **mitad en** 2011.	El informe también mostraba que una parte de la deuda en 2010 era de las administraciones públicas. El informe calcula que las administraciones públicas podrán reducir su deuda en 2011.

Table 5: Examples of the automatic simplification in Spanish (differences between the original sentences and the automatically simplified sentences are given in bold)

Ex.	Original	Automatic	Reference
e1	Parennes is a commune in the Sarthe department in the region of Pays-de-la-Loire in north-western France.	Parennes is a commune**. It is found** in the Sarthe department in the region Pays de la Loire in north-western France.	Parennes is a commune. It is found in the *region Pays de la Loire in the Sarthe department* in *the west* of France.
e2	Mated **females** will lay a clutch of 30-60 eggs in a mound of dry leaves or peat.	Mated **women** will lay a clutch of 30-60 eggs in a mound of dry leaves or peat.	Mated *females* will lay a clutch of 30-60 eggs in a mound of dry leaves or peat.
e3	Elections to the new **authorities** were held on three different Thursdays in 1973.	Elections to the new **government** were held on three different Thursdays in 1973.	Elections *were held to the new authorities* on three different Thursdays in 1973.

Table 6: Examples of the automatic simplification in English (differences between the original sentences and their automatic simplifications are shown in bold, and the deviations of the manual simplifications from the automatic simplifications are shown in italics)

dency). One could argue that the phrase used in the automatically simplified sentence is actually simpler than the corresponding phrase in the 'gold standard' (and the original), as the verb "dejar" (*to leave*) is more frequent than the verb "dimitir" (*to quit*). This complies with the common practice in text simplification to replace the infrequent and more specific terms/phrases with their more frequent synonyms. The native speakers might argue that use of the verb "dejar" (*to leave*) introduces ambiguity (as it is not clear whether Alex leaves his presidency because his mandate is over or because he is quitting), while the use of the verb "dimitir" (*quit*) does not leave any doubt about the way/reason Alex is leaving his presidency. Still, non-native speakers will definitely be familiar with the Spanish word "dejar", while (depending on their level of Spanish) may not be familiar with the Spanish word "dimitir".

The third example (*s3*) represents one of the most frequently observed cases of automatic simplification in the test dataset. In those cases, the PB-SMT system generates the output which is at the same time ungrammatical (mostly due to the incorrect deletions of various sentence parts) and meaningless (mostly due to the incorrect word substitutions, but also due to the ungrammatical sentence constructions). For instance, the word "conjunto" (*set*) is replaced with the word "literaria" (*literary*), and the word "administraciones" (*administrations*) with the word "corridas" (*runs*). In the first case, the original word was replaced with the word with a different part-of-speech (a noun replaced with an adjective). However, this example (*s3*) also shows a particularly interesting case of lexical simplification performed by the PB-SMT system, but not performed by the human editor. The word "calcula" (*calculates*) is replaced with the word "cree" (*believes*). In this sentence, the word "calcula" (*calculates*) was indeed used with the meaning "cree" (*believes*), which is not its most common meaning. Such replacements are favourable in text simplification, as stated in Web Content Accessibility Guidelines (W3C, 2008).

4.2.3 English

Table 6 contains several examples of the original sentences from the test dataset (*Original*), their automatic simplifications (*Automatic*), and their corresponding reference simplifications ('gold standards') from the Simple English Wikipedia (*Reference*). They illustrate some of the phenomena

Corpus	[0, 0.3)	[0.3, 0.4)	[0.4, 0.5)	[0.5, 0.6)	[0.6, 0.7)	[0.7, 0.8)	[0.8, 0.9)	[0.9, 1]
EsSim	85.96%	4.45%	1.62%	0.94%	0.94%	0.27%	0.40%	5.40%
PorSim	12.96%	11.20%	11.74%	18.08%	13.23%	12.82%	7.83%	12.28%
Wiki	26.86%	6.48%	9.31%	6.34%	8.37%	6.88%	6.75%	29.15%

Table 7: Distribution of the S-BLEU scores (columns represent the intervals for S-BLEU)

revealed during the manual error analysis.

Example *e1* presents one of the five correctly performed sentence splittings learned by the PB-SMT system. However, it is important to mention that all five split sentences in the test dataset share the same structure of the original sentence (*'X is a commune in...'*). In all five cases, such an original sentence is transformed into two sentences which again share the same structure (*'X is a commune. It is found in...'*). The example *e2* presents an example of a bad word substitution (lexical simplification which leads to a simpler sentence but changes the original meaning), while *e3* shows a good word substitution (lexical simplification).

It can be noted that all examples of the automatically simplified sentences are still grammatical. One or two wrongly applied word substitutions may only change the meaning of the sentence but they do not deteriorate the grammaticality of the sentence. Correctly applied word substitutions and sentence splittings preserve the original meaning and grammaticality of the sentence, and lead to a slightly simpler output.

4.3 Distribution of S-BLEU Scores

A closer examination of the S-BLEU distribution (Table 7) indicate that the cause behind the good performance of the 'translation' system trained on PorSim and Wiki datasets probably lies in the nature of the data. The Wiki corpus contains only those sentence pairs whose normalised similarity was higher than 0.5 (Coster and Kauchak, 2011b). The PorSim corpus consists only of the sentence pairs simplified by 'natural' simplification in which the most common simplifying operation is sentence splitting (Gasperin et al., 2009). EsSim corpus, on the other hand, contain a great number of deletions and strong paraphrases (combinations of lexical and syntactic transformations with deletions) as reported by Štajner *et al.* (2013). Such strong paraphrases and reordering of clauses within a sentence are very frequent in the EsSim dataset, while hardly present in the Wiki and PorSim datasets.[6] Although well-motivated and necessary for the target population in mind (people with intellectual impairments), those transformations cannot be learnt by the standard PB-SMT model.

5 Conclusions and Future Work

Text simplification has recently been treated as a statistical machine translation problem. By comparing the performance of this translation paradigm across three datasets, we have identified possible causes for the success and failure of such a simplification approach. It appears that learning how to 'translate' from original to simplified language using standard PB-SMT model works well only in some special cases, when the training data mostly consists of the sentence pairs which are already very similar.[7] Our results indicate that this approach would not be effective if we want to learn 'real', strong simplifications like those performed by trained human editors familiar with the specific needs of their target population (e.g. people with intellectual disabilities). Those simplifications involve linguistically rich transformations (e.g. paraphrase, summarisation) which cannot be modelled by standard PB-SMT systems.

We are currently investigating how to improve the translation model with the addition of synonym datasets and the language model using a large bootstrapped corpus of "simple" sentences instead of normal, non-simplified language.

Acknowledgements

The research described in this paper was partially funded by the project SKATER-UPF-TALN (TIN2012-38584-C06-03), Ministerio de Economía y Competitividad, Secretaría de Estado de Investigación, Desarrollo e Innovación, Spain,

[6]For examples from all three corpora and a more detailed discussion see (Štajner, 2015).

[7]Our recent study on PB-SMT approach to text simplification using larger datasets for English (Štajner et al., 2015) confirms these findings.

and the project ABLE-TO-INCLUDE (CIP-ICT-PSP-2013-7/621055). We would also like to thank Hannah Béchara, Wilker Aziz, and Lucia Specia for the help with the translation experiments and resources.

References

Sandra Maria Aluísio and Caroline Gasperin. 2010. Fostering digital inclusion and accessibility: The porsimples project for simplification of portuguese texts. In *Proceedings of the NAACL HLT 2010 Young Investigators Workshop on Computational Approaches to Languages of the Americas*, YIW-CALA '10, pages 46–53, Stroudsburg, PA, USA. Association for Computational Linguistics.

Laetitia Brouwers, Delphine Bernhard, Anne-Laure Ligozat, and Thomas François. 2014. Syntactic sentence simplification for french. In *Proceedings of the EACL Workshop on Predicting and Improving Text Readability for Target Reader Populations (PITR), Gothenburg, Sweden*, pages 47–56.

Helena M. Caseli, Tiago F. Pereira, Lucia Specia, Thiago A. S. Pardo, Caroline Gasperin, and Sandra M. Aluísio. 2009. Building a Brazilian Portuguese parallel corpus of original and simplified texts. In *10th Conference on Intelligent Text PRocessing and Computational Linguistics (CICLing 2009)*.

William Coster and David Kauchak. 2011a. Learning to Simplify Sentences Using Wikipedia. In *Proceedings of the 49th Annual Meeting of the Association for Computational Linguistics*, pages 1–9.

William Coster and David Kauchak. 2011b. Simple English Wikipedia: a new text simplification task. In *Proceedings of the 49th Annual Meeting of the Association for Computational Linguistics: Human Language Technologies. Portland, Oregon, USA: Association for Computational Linguistics*, pages 665–669.

Caroline Gasperin, Lucia Specia, Tiago F. Pereira, and Sandra M. Aluísio. 2009. Learning When to Simplify Sentences for Natural Text Simplification. In *Proceedings of the Encontro Nacional de Inteligncia Artificial (ENIA-2009), Bento Gonalves, Brazil.*, pages 809–818.

Philipp Koehn, Franz Josef Och, and Daniel Marcu. 2003. Statistical phrase-based translation. In *Proceedings of the 2003 Conference of the North American Chapter of the Association for Computational Linguistics on Human Language Technology - Volume 1*, NAACL '03, pages 48–54, Stroudsburg, PA, USA. Association for Computational Linguistics.

Philipp Koehn, Hieu Hoang, Alexandra Birch, Chris Callison-Burch, Marcello Federico, Nicola Bertoldi, Brooke Cowan, Wade Shen, Christine Moran, Richard Zens, Chris Dyer, Ondrej Bojar, Alexandra Constantin, and Evan Herbst. 2007. Moses: Open source toolkit for statistical machine translation. In *Proceedings of ACL*.

Franz Josef Och and Hermann Ney. 2003. A systematic comparison of various statistical alignment models. *Computational Linguistics*, 29(1):19–51.

Horacio Saggion, Sanja Štajner, Stefan Bott, Simon Mille, Luz Rello, and Biljana Drndarevic. 2015. Making It Simplext: Implementation and Evaluation of a Text SImplification System for Spanish. *ACM Transactions on Accessible Computing (TACCESS)*, 6(4).

Advaith Siddharthan and M.A. Angrosh. 2014. Hybrid text simplification using synchronous dependency grammars with hand-written and automatically harvested rules. In *Proceedings of the 14th Conference of the European Chapter of the Association for Computational Linguistics (EACL), Gothenburg, Sweden*, pages 722–731.

Lucia Specia. 2010. Translating from complex to simplified sentences. In *Proceedings of the 9th international conference on Computational Processing of the Portuguese Language*, pages 30–39, Berlin, Heidelberg.

Sanja Štajner, Biljana Drndarević, and Horacio Saggion. 2013. Corpus-based Sentence Deletion and Split Decisions for Spanish Text Simplification. *Computación y Systemas*, 17(2):251–262.

Sanja Štajner, Hannah Bechara, and Horacio Saggion. 2015. A Deeper Exploration of the Standard PB-SMT Approach to Text Simplification and its Evaluation. In *Proceedings of the 53rd Annual Meeting of the Association for Computational Linguistics and the 7th International Joint Conference on Natural Language Processing (Volume 2: Short Papers)*, pages 823–828, Beijing, China. ACL.

Sanja Štajner. 2014. Translating sentences from 'original' to 'simplified' spanish. *Procesamiento del Lenguaje Natural*, 53:61–68.

Sanja Štajner. 2015. *New Data-Driven Approaches to Text Simplification*. Ph.D. thesis, University of Wolverhampton, UK.

W3C, 2008. *Web Content Accessibility Guidelines (WCAG) 2.0*.

Kristian Woodsend and Mirella Lapata. 2011. Learning to Simplify Sentences with Quasi-Synchronous Grammar and Integer Programming. In *Proceedings of the 2011 Conference on Empirical Methods in Natural Language Processing (EMNLP)*.

Zhemin Zhu, Delphine Berndard, and Iryna Gurevych. 2010. A Monolingual Tree-based Translation Model for Sentence Simplification. In *Proceedings of the 23rd International Conference on Computational Linguistics (Coling 2010)*, pages 1353–1361.

Automatic Text Simplification for Spanish: Comparative Evaluation of Various Simplification Strategies

Sanja Štajner[1] and **Iacer Calixto**[2] and **Horacio Saggion**[3]
[1]Research Group in Computational Linguistics, University of Wolverhampton, UK
SanjaStajner@wlv.ac.uk
[2]ADAPT Centre, Dublin City University, School of Computing, Ireland
icalixto@computing.dcu.ie
[3]TALN Research Group, Universitat Pompeu Fabra, Spain
horacio.saggion@upf.edu

Abstract

In this paper, we explore statistical machine translation (SMT) approaches to automatic text simplification (ATS) for Spanish. First, we compare the performances of the standard phrase-based (PB) and hierarchical (HIERO) SMT models in this specific task. In both cases, we build two models, one using the TS corpus with "light" simplifications and the other using the TS corpus with "heavy" simplifications. Next, we compare the two best systems with the state-of-the-art text simplification system for Spanish (Simplext). Our results, based on an extensive human evaluation, show that the SMT-based systems perform equally as well as, or better than, Simplext, despite the very small datasets used for training and tuning.

1 Introduction

The goal of automatic text simplification (ATS) is to transform lexically and syntactically complex texts or sentences into their simpler variants which can be more easily understood by non-native speakers, children, and people with various language or learning impairments (e.g. people with autism, dyslexia, or intellectual disabilities). Due to the scarcity and limited sizes of parallel corpora of original and manually simplified sentences, the state-of-the-art ATS systems are still predominantly rule-based for many languages, e.g. Spanish (Drndarević et al., 2013), Basque (Aranzabe et al., 2013), and French (Brouwers et al., 2014).

Recently, several studies proposed applying the standard PB-SMT model to the text simplification task for Brazilian Portuguese (Specia, 2010), English (Coster and Kauchak, 2011), and Spanish (Štajner, 2014). None of those studies, however, performed a thorough human evaluation of the systems or directly compared their systems to the existing rule-based ATS systems for those languages. The reported automatic evaluation (using BLEU score) gives us no insights on the correctness and usefulness of those systems and how well they perform in comparison to the state-of-the-art rule-based ATS systems.

In this paper, we address the problem of ATS for Spanish, investigating the possibility of applying the standard phrase-based (PB) and hierarchical (HIERO) SMT models to the only two currently-known text simplification (TS) parallel corpora for Spanish. We perform an extensive human evaluation of the generated output which allows us to compare the systems directly. Additionally, we compare our two best systems with Simplext, the state-of-the-art text simplification system for Spanish (Saggion et al., 2015).

Our experiments make several contributions to the field of automatic text simplification by exploring the following important questions:

1. How well can PB-SMT and HIERO models perform if built using very small parallel TS corpora?

2. Do the results obtained using standard PB-SMT models differ significantly from the ones obtained using the HIERO models?

3. How do the SMT-based models for ATS perform in comparison with the state-of-the-art ATS system for Spanish?

Proceedings of Recent Advances in Natural Language Processing, pages 618–626,
Hissar, Bulgaria, Sep 7–9 2015.

To the best of our knowledge, this is the first study (for any language) which applies a HIERO model to text simplification, and the first study which directly compares performances of the SMT-based models with a state-of-the-art ATS system.

2 Related Work

With the emergence of the Simple English Wikipedia[1], which together with the "original" English Wikipedia offered a large comparable text simplification (TS) corpus (137,000 sentence pairs), the focus of the ATS for English was shifted towards data-driven approaches. Most of them applied various SMT techniques, either phrase-based (Coster and Kauchak, 2011; Wubben et al., 2012), or syntax-based (Zhu et al., 2010; Woodsend and Lapata, 2011). In other languages, TS corpora either do not exist or they are very limited in size (only up to 1,000 sentence pairs). The only known exception to this is the case of Brazilian Portuguese for which there is a parallel TS corpus with 4,483 sentence pairs, built under the PorSimples project (Aluísio and Gasperin, 2010), aimed at simplifying texts for low literacy readers. This corpus has been used to train the standard PB-SMT model for ATS (Specia, 2010), and the reported results were promising (BLEU = 60.75) despite the small size of the dataset. The recent attempt at using the standard PB-SMT models for ATS for Spanish on two TS corpora of limited size (850 sentence pairs each) indicated that: (1) the level of simplification present in the datasets ("heavy" or "light") significantly influences the results, and (2) the model built using the "light" corpora can still learn some useful simplifications despite the very small size of the dataset (Štajner, 2014).

2.1 SMT for Low-Resourced Languages

The main problems in SMT applied to low-resourced languages ("simplified" Spanish can be seen as such) are the accuracy and coverage (Irvine and Callison-Burch, 2013). The first problem is the result of the fact that the model does not have enough data to estimate good probabilities over the possible translations and therefore ensure correctness of the translation pairs. The second problem occurs when the model and its word coverage are small, which leads to a high number of out-of-vocabulary (OOV) words. Words which the model have not encountered during the training phase cannot be correctly dealt with during the test phase.

2.2 Monolingual SMT

When monolingual SMT is used for text simplification, the problem of coverage is not so much of an issue as it is in cross-lingual SMT. In our case, the source language is the "regular" Spanish, and the target language is the "simplified" Spanish. Therefore, if a word in the source language is not found in the translation table – and is, therefore, an OOV word – it will be left untranslated. This might impact the overall simplicity of the output (in the case that the OOV word was complex), but it will not necessarily deteriorate the grammaticality and meaning preservation of the output sentence (as would be the case in cross-lingual SMT).

The problem of accuracy is still present even in monolingual SMT. A small model will not have high enough probability mass to be able to generalise well all the linguistic phenomena a good translation should encompass. The translation model will suffer from a low number of examples and thus might not be able to estimate the probabilities correctly. The unsupervised alignment model implemented in Moses using GIZA++ aligner (Och and Ney, 2003) will have rough statistics for the alignment estimation if computed from a small number of parallel sentences.

2.3 State-of-the-Art ATS System for Spanish

The current state-of-the-art text simplification system for Spanish (Saggion et al., 2015) was built under the Simplext project.[2] It employs a modular approach to TS, consisting of three main modules: a rule-based syntactic and lexical simplification modules (Drndarević et al., 2013); and a synonym-based lexical simplification module (Bott et al., 2012). According to the recent evaluation of the full Simplext system (Saggion et al., 2015), the system achieved human scores for grammaticality, meaning preservation, and simplicity comparable to those of the current state-of-the-art data-driven text simplification systems for English (Wubben et al., 2012; Angrosh and Siddharthan, 2014).

3 Methodology

The corpora, translation/simplification experiments, and the evaluation procedure are presented

[1] https://simple.wikipedia.org/wiki/Main_Page

[2] www.simplext.es

Version	Example
Original	Los expertos presentarán un informe de esta misión en la próxima reunión del Comité del Patrimonio Mundial, que tendrá lugar en Bahrein en junio de 2011.
Light	Los expertos presentarán un informe de*l estudio del estado de conservación de Pompeya* en la próxima reunión del Comité del Patrimonio Mundial, que *será* en Bahrein en junio de 2011.
Heavy	Los expertos presentarán un informe *sobre Pompeya* en la próxima reunión *sobre la cultura del mundo. Esta reunión será* en junio de 2011.

Table 1: Different levels of simplification (deviations from the original sentence are shown in italics)

in the next three subsections.

3.1 Corpora

In order to test the influence of the level of simplification in TS datasets ("heavy" or "light") on the system performance, we trained the standard PB-SMT (Koehn et al., 2003) and HIERO (Chiang, 2007) models in the Moses toolkit (Koehn et al., 2007) on two TS corpora:

1. *Heavy* – The TS corpus built under the Simplext project (Saggion et al., 2011), aimed at simplifying texts for people with intellectual disabilities. The original news stories were simplified manually by trained human editors, following detailed guidelines (Anula, 2007).

2. *Light* – The TS corpus consisting of various texts (some of which present in the *Heavy* corpus) and their manual simplifications obtained using only six main simplification rules (Mitkov and Štajner, 2014).

In both corpora, the sentence-alignment was manually checked and corrected where necessary. An example of an original sentence and its corresponding manual simplifications in the two corpora is given in Table 1.

3.2 SMT Models

In order to compare the impact of different SMT models (PB vs. HIERO) on the system performance, the language model (LM) and the test set (consisting of 47 sentence pairs from each of the two corpora) were kept the same for all systems. Ideally, the LM should be trained on a large corpus of "simplified" Spanish. However, as such a corpus has not been compiled yet, we trained the LM on a subset of the Europarl v7 Spanish corpus (Koehn, 2005) using the SRILM toolkit (Stolcke, 2002). In order to reduce the complexity of the sentences used for the training of the LM, we filtered out all sentences that contain more than 15 tokens. The sizes of the datasets used in the four experiments are given in Table 2.

Corpus	Model	Training	Dev.	Test
Light	PB-SMT	659	100	94
Light	HIERO	659	100	94
Heavy	PB-SMT	725	100	94
Heavy	HIERO	725	100	94

Table 2: SMT experiments

3.3 Evaluation

In order to obtain better insights into the potential problems in the SMT-based ATS, where the models are trained on the small datasets, we opted for human evaluation of the output in addition to the automatic evaluation (using the BLEU scores). Following the standard procedure for human evaluation of TS systems used in previous studies (Coster and Kauchak, 2011; Wubben et al., 2012; Drndarević et al., 2013), we asked human evaluators to assess, on a 1–5 scale (where the higher mark always denotes better output), three aspects of the presented sentences: grammaticality (G), meaning preservation (M), and simplicity (S).

We first asked thirteen annotators (8 native and 5 non-native with advanced knowledge of Spanish) to rate 20 original sentences and their corresponding simplifications (one manual and four automatic SMT-based) in order to directly compare the performances of the PB and HIERO models on both corpora. Next, we asked the annotators to rate another 20 original sentences and their corresponding simplifications (one manual and three automatic, out of which two were produced by the two best SMT systems and the third by the Simplext system) in order to directly compare the performances of the SMT systems with the state-of-the-art (rule-based) text simplification system for Spanish (Section 2.3).

We obtained a total of 260 human scores for each aspect-system-corpora combination in each of the two evaluation phases. The 40 original sentences for human evaluation (and their corre-

System	Corpus	S-BLEU	BLEU
PB	Light	**0.3742**	0.3374
	Heavy	0.3662	0.3313
HIERO	Light	**0.3718**	0.3336
	Heavy	0.2959	0.2718
Baseline		0.3645	0.3260

Table 3: Automatic evaluation

Aspect		Heavy		Light		Manual
		PB	HIERO	PB	HIERO	
G	Mean	1.74	1.77	**4.03**	3.91	4.61
	Median	1	1	5	4	5
	Mode	1	1	5	5	5
M	Mean	1.98	1.93	**4.57**	4.40	3.62
	Median	1	1	5	5	4
	Mode	1	1	5	5	4
S	Mean	2.31	2.29	**2.99**	2.93	4.40
	Median	2	2	3	3	5
	Mode	1	1	2	2	5

Table 4: Phrase-based vs. hierarchical SMT

sponding simplified variants) were selected randomly from the test set under the criterion that they have been modified by at least two ATS systems. Every annotator was asked to rate all versions of the same original sentence (different versions of the same sentence were always shown in a random order). This allowed us to have a direct pairwise comparison of each pair of systems.

4 Results

The results of the automatic and human evaluations are presented in the next two subsections.

4.1 Automatic Evaluation

We compared the performances of the systems using two automatic MT evaluation metrics, the sentence-level BLEU score (S-BLEU)[3] and the document-level BLEU score (Papineni et al., 2002). As the baseline, we used the system which makes no changes to the input (i.e. output of the system is the original sentence). This seems as a natural baseline for this specific task (ATS), as all previous studies (Specia, 2010; Coster and Kauchak, 2011; Štajner, 2014) reported that their systems are overcautious, usually making only a few or no changes to the input sentence, and only slightly outperform this baseline. For calculating the S-BLEU and BLEU scores, we used the manual simplification ('gold standard') as the reference, and the original sentences and the outputs of the four systems as five corresponding hypotheses. The results are presented in Table 3.

The only two systems which significantly outperform the baseline in terms of the S-BLEU scores (0.05 level of significance; Wilcoxon signed rank test for repeated measures) are the systems trained and tuned on the *Light* corpus. The performance of the PB and HIERO systems trained and tuned on the *Heavy* corpus was not significantly different from the baseline.

4.2 Human Evaluation

The results of the human evaluation of the PB and HIERO systems built using each of the two corpora (*Heavy* and *Light*) are given in Table 4. For each of the three aspects (G – grammaticality, M – meaning preservation, and S – simplicity), we present the mean, median and mode calculated on the 260 entries for each system-corpus combination.

As can be seen (Table 4), the systems built using the *Light* corpus were rated higher than those built using the *Heavy* corpus on all three aspects (especially pronounced for grammaticality and meaning preservation). The performances of the PB and HIERO models built using the *Heavy* corpus achieved almost the same scores, while the PB model was rated as slightly better than HIERO in the case when the models were built using the *Light* corpus (the differences in G and M scores were statistically significant at a 0.01 level of significance[4]). It is interesting to note that the meaning preservation (M) score was higher for both SMT-models built using the *Light* corpus than for the manual simplifications. This reflects the fact that manual simplification often relies on heavy paraphrasing and sometimes does not retain all information present in the original sentence (see the example in Table 9, Section 5).

Additionally, we calculated how many times: (1) the output of the systems built using the *Light* corpus was rated better than the output of the systems built using the *Heavy* corpus on the same test sentence (Table 5), and (2) the output of the HIERO models was rated better than the output of

[3]Sentence-level BLEU score (S-BLEU) differs from BLEU score only in the sense that S-BLEU will still positively score segments that do not have higher n-gram matching (n=4 in our setting) unless there is no unigram match; otherwise it is the same as BLEU.

[4]Statistical significance was measured in SPSS using the marginal homogeneity test which represent the extension of McNemar test from binary to multinominal response for two related samples.

Comparison	HIERO	PB
G(Light) > G(Heavy)	221	228
G(Light) = G(Heavy)	36	29
G(Light) < G(Heavy)	3	3
M(Light) > M(Heavy)	225	230
M(Light) = M(Heavy)	31	28
M(Light) < M(Heavy)	4	2
S(Light) > S(Heavy)	119	119
S(Light) = S(Heavy)	88	84
S(Light) < S(Heavy)	53	57

Table 5: Impact of the corpora used

Comparison	Light	Heavy
G(HIERO) > G(PB)	12	39
G(HIERO) = G(PB)	216	182
G(HIERO) < G(PB)	32	39
M(HIERO) > M(PB)	7	36
M(HIERO) = M(PB)	217	179
M(HIERO) < M(PB)	36	45
S(HIERO) > S(PB)	22	40
S(HIERO) = S(PB)	219	171
S(HIERO) < S(PB)	19	49

Table 6: Impact of the model used

the PB models on the same test sentence (Table 6). The results of these comparisons confirmed that both models (HIERO and PB) achieve better performances if they are built using the *Light* corpus instead of using the *Heavy* corpus (Table 5). It also seems that the PB model generates more grammatical sentences and better preserves the original meaning than the HIERO model when trained the *Light* corpus, while both models lead to similar performances when trained on the *Heavy* corpus (Table 6).

5 Comparison with the State of the Art

The results of the human evaluation of 20 original sentences and their four corresponding simplified versions (Table 7) indicate that the output of the SMT-based systems is more grammatical and preserves the meaning better than the output of Simplext, at the cost of being less simple.[5] The pairwise comparison of 260 sentences (Table 8) confirmed those findings.

Aspect		PB	HIERO	Simplext	Manual
	Mean	3.68	**3.86**	3.49	4.47
G	Median	4	4	4	5
	Mode	4	4	4	5
	Mean	4.17	**4.37**	3.95	3.17
M	Median	4	5	4	3
	Mode	5	5	5	4
	Mean	2.60	2.61	**2.80**	4.42
S	Median	3	3	3	5
	Mode	3	2	3	5

Table 7: Comparison with the state of the art

Comparison	PB	HIERO
G(SMT-based) > G(Simplext)	96	104
G(SMT-based) = G(Simplext)	90	99
G(SMT-based) < G(Simplext)	76	57
M(SMT-based) > M(Simplext)	92	103
M(SMT-based) = M(Simplext)	109	113
M(SMT-based) < M(Simplext)	59	44
S(SMT-based) > S(Simplext)	59	55
S(SMT-based) = S(Simplext)	96	105
S(SMT-based) < S(Simplext)	95	100

Table 8: Comparison with Simplext

An example of an original sentence, its manual simplification ("gold standard"), and its automatic simplifications by three different systems (PB, HIERO, and Simplext) are given in Table 9. In this example, both SMT-based systems perform two lexical simplifications: (1) "galardón (*award*) is replaced with "premio" (*prize*), and (2) "concede" (*concede*) is replaced with "da" (*gives*). These lexical substitutions lead to a sentence which is simpler than the original and preserves the original meaning. In the same example, the Simplext system performs two syntactic simplifications by splitting the original sentence into three new sentences, out of which only one (the second) is grammatical and preserves the original meaning. The first of the three new sentences is grammatical but changes the original meaning, while the third one is neither grammatical, nor preserves the original meaning. Additionally, in this example, the Simplext system does not lexically simplify the original sentence. The manually simplified sentence is, as expected, the simplest and most grammatical. However, it represents a very strong paraphrase of the original sentence which does not preserve the original meaning faithfully and is, therefore, penalised with the lowest score for the meaning preservation out of all four simplification variants.

6 Error Analysis

In order to better understand the shortcomings of the SMT-based systems (and the phrase-based approach to ATS using small size corpora, in general), we performed manual error analysis of all sentences for which the SMT-based systems received lower scores than the Simplext system (on

[5] All differences, except the S score for the PB and HIERO models, are statistically significant at a 0.05 level of significance.

Version	Example	G	M	S
Original	Este galardón, dotado con 20.000 euros, lo concede el Ministerio de Cultura para distinguir una obra de autor español escrita en cualquiera de las lenguas oficiales y editada en España durante 2009.	4.77	5.00	2.84
PB/HIERO	Este *premio*, dotado con 20.000 euros, lo *da* el ministerio de cultura para distinguir una obra de autor español escrita en cualquiera de las lenguas oficiales y editada en España durante 2009.	4.15	4.77	3.15
Simplext	Este galardón lo concede el Ministerio de Cultura para distinguir una obra de autor español *durante el año 2009. El galardón está* dotado con 20.000 euros. *El autor está* escrita en cualquiera de las lenguas oficiales y editada en España.	3.54	3.77	2.92
Manual	Este premio es para un autor español que escriba en español, catalán, vasco o gallego.	4.85	3.31	4.85

Table 9: An example of an original sentence, its manual simplification, and its automatic simplifications generated by three different ATS systems (deviations from the original sentences are shown in italics; columns 'G', 'M', and 'S' contain mean value of the scores for grammaticality, meaning preservation, and simplicity obtained from all thirteen annotators)

average). In all of those cases when the SMT-based systems scored lower than the Simplext system the reason was one (or both) of the following: the system performed one wrong lexical substitution which led to a low grammaticality score; and/or the system did not perform sentence splitting and the Simplext system did. Table 10 contains three such examples.

In the first example (1), the SMT-based systems applied an incorrect lexical substitution, replacing the word "informó" (*informed*) with "gracias" (*thanks*). That led to an ungrammatical output of the system and the lower total score. The same word was correctly simplified by the Simplext system using the word "dijo" (*said*) instead. The Simplext system additionally performed a sentence splitting. During that process, the name of the university at which the writer graduated has been replaced with the name of the writer, which changed the original meaning of the sentence. However, this did not lead to an ungrammatical output (as opposed to the wrong lexical substitution performed by the SMT-based models), and the Simplext system thus obtained better scores for grammaticality (G) and simplicity (S), and a lower score for meaning preservation (M) than the SMT-based systems.

In the second example (2), the SMT-based systems performed one good lexical simplification (which was not performed by the Simplext system) by replacing the word "aseguró" (*assured*) with the word "dice" (*says*). However, our systems also applied one incorrect lexical simplification which, although it did not change the original meaning of the sentence, led to the ungrammatical output. In the same example, the Simplext system correctly split the original sentence into two shorter sentences and performed one correct lexical simplification. The changes made by the Simplext system led to a small grammatical issue ("poner le" should be written together), but this did not significantly influence grammaticality score (G).

The third example (3) illustrates the case in which the Simplext system was rated better than the SMT-based systems because it performed a sentence splitting when the SMT-based systems did not. At the same time, the SMT-based systems applied one correct lexical simplification. The same word was left unchanged by the Simplext system. However, it appears that human evaluators tend to give a higher simplicity score to the system which performs sentence splitting than to the system which performs lexical simplification (in the case that each of the systems performs only one of the two possible modifications).

7 Conclusions and Future Work

In this paper, we presented the results of the phrase-based (PB) and hierarchical (HIERO) SMT models for ATS, built using two small TS corpora. One corpus contained "heavy" simplifications, and the other "light" simplifications. The direct comparison of the systems' performances, based on an extensive human evaluation, indicated that both models (PB and HIERO) achieve similar performances if they are built using the same corpus (either *Heavy* or *Light*). The results of the human evaluation also showed that SMT-based models built using the *Light* corpus generate sentences that are more grammatical and preserve the meaning better, but are less simple than those generated

Version	Example	G	M	S
(1) Original	Castellet (Barcelona, 1926), escritor, crítico literario y editor, estudió en la Universidad de Barcelona, donde se graduó en Derecho, según informó el Ministerio de Cultura.	4.85	5.00	3.46
(1) HIERO, PB	Castellet (Barcelona, 1926), escritor, crítico literario y editor, estudió en la Universidad de Barcelona, donde se graduó en Derecho, según *gracias* el Ministerio de Cultura.	3	3.54	3.15
(1) Simplext	Castellet, escritor, crítico literario y editor, estudió en la Universidad de Barcelona. *En Castellet se licenció* en Derecho, según *dijo* el Ministerio de Cultura.	4.69	3.46	3.53
(2) Original	El presidente del Grupo Planeta, José Manuel Lara, aseguró en el Foro de la Nueva Cultura que el problema de la piratería en España es"grave" y"preocupante" y la sociedad "debe tomar conciencia para ponerle coto".	4.46	5.00	2.77
(2) HIERO, PB	El presidente del Grupo Planeta, José Manuel Lara, *dice* en el Foro de la Nueva Cultura que el problema de la piratería en España es "grave" y "preocupante" y la sociedad "*hay* tomar conciencia para ponerle coto".	3.23	4.31	2.46
(2) Simplext	El presidente del Grupo Planeta, José Manuel Lara, aseguró en el Foro de la Nueva Cultura que el problema de la piratería en España es "grave" y "preocupante". *La* sociedad "debe tomar conciencia para poner *le límite*".	4.23	4.77	3.38
(3) Original	Sin embargo, el terrorismo, que aparece en cuarto lugar (19%), registra la cota más baja de toda la serie desde 2004, experimentando una caída de 12 puntos respecto del Sociómetro de mayo.	4.38	5.00	3.15
(3) HIERO, PB	Sin *pero*, el terrorismo, que *sale* en cuarto lugar (19%), registra la cota más baja de toda la serie desde 2004, experimentando una caída de 12 puntos respecto del Sociómetro de mayo.	3.08	3.92	2.23
(3) Simplext	Sin embargo, el terrorismo,, registra la cota más baja de toda la serie desde *el año* 2004, experimentando una caída de 12 puntos respecto del Sociómetro de mayo. *Este terrorismo* aparece en cuarto lugar.	3.08	3.77	2.92

Table 10: Three examples of the original sentences and their automatic simplifications generated by our systems and the Simplext system (deviations from the original sentences are shown in italics; the columns 'G', 'M', and 'S' contain mean value of the scores for grammaticality, meaning preservation, and simplicity obtained from all thirteen annotators)

by the Simplext system.

We acknowledge that the fact that we built the language models using the Europarl corpus which is not a good representative of "simplified" language (despite our efforts to filter out complex sentences) is probably one of the main reasons why the SMT-based systems are not able to generate sentences as simple as those generated by Simplext. Our future work will thus focus on finding better strategies for filtering out complex sentences from the Europarl corpus (e.g. using just those sentences with certain simple syntactic structures, and those with simple and frequently used words).

Acknowledgements

The research described in this paper was partially funded by the project SKATER-UPF-TALN (TIN2012-38584-C06-03), Ministerio de Economía y Competitividad, Secretaría de Estado de Investigación, Desarrollo e Innovación, Spain, the project ABLE-TO-INCLUDE (CIP-ICT-PSP-2013-7/621055), and by Science Foundation Ireland through the CNGL Programme (Grant 12/CE/I2267) in the ADAPT Centre (www.adaptcentre.ie) at Dublin City University. We are also grateful to all the annotators for their evaluation efforts, and the anonymous reviewers for their constructive comments.

References

Sandra Maria Aluísio and Caroline Gasperin. 2010. Fostering Digital Inclusion and Accessibility: The PorSimples Project for Simplification of Portuguese Texts. In *Proceedings of the NAACL HLT 2010 Young Investigators Workshop on Computational Approaches to Languages of the Americas (YIW-CALA)*, pages 46–53. ACL.

M.A. Angrosh and A. Siddharthan. 2014. Text simplification using synchronous dependency grammars: Generalising automatically harvested rules. In *Proceedings of the 8th International Natural Language Generation Conference (INGL)*, pages 16–25.

Alberto Anula. 2007. Tipos de textos, complejidad lingüística y facilicitación lectora. In *Actas del Sexto Congreso de Hispanistas de Asia*, pages 45–61.

María Jesús Aranzabe, Arantza Díaz de Ilarraza, and Itziar Gonzalez-Dios. 2013. Transforming Complex Sentences using Dependency Trees for Automatic Text Simplification in Basque. *Procesamiento del Lenguaje Natural*, 50:61–68.

Stefan Bott, Luz Rello, Biljana Drndarevic, and Horacio Saggion. 2012. Can Spanish Be Simpler? LexSiS: Lexical Simplification for Spanish. In *Proceedings of COLING*, pages 357–374.

Laetitia Brouwers, Delphine Bernhard, Anne-Laure Ligozat, and Thomas François. 2014. Syntactic sentence simplification for french. In *Proceedings of the EACL Workshop on Predicting and Improving Text Readability for Target Reader Populations (PITR), Gothenburg, Sweden*, pages 47–56.

David Chiang. 2007. Hierarchical Phrase-Based Translation. *Computational Linguistics*, 33(2):201–228.

William Coster and David Kauchak. 2011. Learning to Simplify Sentences Using Wikipedia. In *Proceedings of the 49th Annual Meeting of the Association for Computational Linguistics (ACL)*, pages 1–9. ACL.

Biljana Drndarević, Sanja Štajner, Stefan Bott, Susana Bautista, and Horacio Saggion. 2013. Automatic Text Simplication in Spanish: A Comparative Evaluation of Complementing Components. In *Proceedings of the 12th International Conference on Intelligent Text Processing and Computational Linguistics (CICLing)*, pages 488–500.

Ann Irvine and Chris Callison-Burch. 2013. Combining Bilingual and Comparable Corpora for Low Resource Machine Translation. In *Proceedings of the Eighth Workshop on Statistical Machine Translation*, pages 262–270.

Philipp Koehn, Franz Josef Och, and Daniel Marcu. 2003. Statistical phrase-based translation. In *Proceedings of the Conference of the North American Chapter of the Association for Computational Linguistics on Human Language Technology (NAACL)*, volume 1, pages 48–54. ACL.

Philipp Koehn, Hieu Hoang, Alexandra Birch, Chris Callison-Burch, Marcello Federico, Nicola Bertoldi, Brooke Cowan, Wade Shen, Christine Moran, Richard Zens, Chris Dyer, Ondrej Bojar, Alexandra Constantin, and Evan Herbst. 2007. Moses: Open source toolkit for statistical machine translation. In *Proceedings of the 45th Annual Meeting of the ACL on Interactive Poster and Demonstration Sessions*, pages 177–180. ACL.

Philipp Koehn. 2005. Europarl: A Parallel Corpus for Statistical Machine Translation. In *Proceedings of the Machine Translation Summit*.

Ruslan Mitkov and Sanja Štajner. 2014. The Fewer, the Better? A Contrastive Study about Ways to Simplify. In *Proceedings of the COLING workshop on Automatic Text Simplification – Methods and Applications in the Multilingual Society (ATS-MA), Dublin, Ireland*, pages 30–40.

Franz Josef Och and Hermann Ney. 2003. A systematic comparison of various statistical alignment models. *Computational Linguistics*, 29(1):19–51.

Kishore Papineni, Salim Roukos, Todd Ward, and Wei-Jing Zhu. 2002. BLEU: a Method for Automatic Evaluation of Machine Translation. In *Proceedings of the 40th Annual Meeting of the Association for Computational Linguistics (ACL)*, pages 311–318.

Horacio Saggion, Elena Gómez Martínez, Alberto Anula, Lorena Bourg, and Esteban Etayo. 2011. Text Simplification in Simplext: Making Text More Accessible. *Revista de la Sociedad Española para el Procesamiento del Lenguaje Natural*, 47:341–342.

Horacio Saggion, Sanja Štajner, Stefan Bott, Simon Mille, Luz Rello, and Biljana Drndarevic. 2015. Making It Simplext: Implementation and Evaluation of a Text Simplification System for Spanish. *ACM Transactions on Accessible Computing*, 6(4):14:1–14:36.

Lucia Specia. 2010. Translating from complex to simplified sentences. In *Proceedings of the 9th international conference on Computational Processing of the Portuguese Language (PROPOR)*, pages 30–39. Springer-Verlag Berlin, Heidelberg.

Andreas Stolcke. 2002. SRILM - an Extensible Language Modeling Toolkit. In *Proceedings of the International Conference on Spoken Language Processing (ICSLP)*, pages 901–904.

Sanja Štajner. 2014. Translating sentences from 'original' to 'simplified' spanish. *Procesamiento del Lenguaje Natural*, 53:61–68.

Kristian Woodsend and Mirella Lapata. 2011. Learning to Simplify Sentences with Quasi-Synchronous Grammar and Integer Programming. In *Proceedings of the Conference on Empirical Methods in Natural Language Processing (EMNLP)*, pages 409–420.

Sander Wubben, Antal van den Bosch, and Emiel Krahmer. 2012. Sentence simplification by monolingual machine translation. In *Proceedings of the 50th Annual Meeting of the Association for Computational Linguistics: Long Papers*, volume 1, pages 1015–1024.

Zhemin Zhu, Delphine Berndard, and Iryna Gurevych. 2010. A Monolingual Tree-based Translation Model for Sentence Simplification. In *Proceedings of the 23rd International Conference on Computational Linguistics (COLING)*, pages 1353–1361.

Appendix A: Scoring Instructions Given to the Annotators

	Grammaticality (G)
5	Grammatically correct sentence
4	One or two typos (not capitalised first letter of the sentence, ''s' separated from the noun, missing comma, etc.)
3	One incorrect construction but the sentence still has a meaning (missing preposition in a phrasal verb, transitive instead of intransitive verb or vice versa, use of animate instead of inanimate object or vice versa, etc.)
2	A few incorrect constructions of the above type, or a combination of a typo and an incorrect construction, but the sentence is still meaningful
1	So many mistakes (or such a mistake) that the sentence is grammatically incorrect and completely meaningless
	Meaning preservation (M)
5	The two sentences have exactly the same meaning
4	The meanings of the two sentences differ just in a nuance or some minimal addition of a world knowledge
3	The two sentences do not mean exactly the same, but the main point is the same
2	The meanings of the two sentences differ, but they are not opposite
1	The meanings of the two sentences are opposite
	Simplicity (S)
5	Very simple (all words are short, frequent, and used with their most commonly used meaning)
4	Simple (a few longer words, but still frequent and used with their most commonly used meaning)
3	A few difficult words or phrases, but the overall meaning of the sentence is clear
2	Quite a few difficult words or phrases which makes it difficult to understand the main meaning of the sentence
1	Very difficult to understand (many difficult words and phrases, not used with their most commonly used meaning)

Towards Multilingual Event Extraction Evaluation: A Case Study for the Czech Language

Josef Steinberger
DCSE, NTIS Centre, FAV
University of West Bohemia
Univerzini 8, 306 14 Plzen
Czech Republic
jstein@kiv.zcu.cz

Hristo Tanev
Joint Research Centre
European Commission
via Fermi 2749, Ispra
Italy
hristo.tanev@jrc.ec.europa.eu

Abstract

This paper presents a multilingual corpus of news, annotated with event metadata information. The events in our corpus are from the domain of violence, natural and man made disasters. The main goal of the corpus is automatic evaluation of event detection and extraction systems in different languages. As a use case, we take a rule-based event extraction system, extend it to cover a new language, Czech in our case, and evaluate it on the corpus. We explain what needs to be done to cover a new language, especially learning domain-specific dictionaries and event extraction patterns. The evaluation of the Czech system can be viewed as a starting point for further research into the evaluation of multilingual event extraction systems, which is an important stage during the development of such systems. The comparison of the performance for the Czech and English systems indicates the importance for multilingual event extraction evaluation.

1 Introduction

The quantity of information on Internet has reached a critical point. Simple keyword indexing cannot satisfy any more the need for fast and accurate access to this information ocean. In this light, the development of effective methods for information extraction are of particular importance. In this paper we will discuss issues related to automatic event metadata extraction. Mainstream media and part of the social media are event-oriented, therefore development of methods for accurate identification, classification and extraction of metadata about events is of particular importance. Noteworthy, crisis events, such as natural, man-made disasters, crime and armed conflicts are the most frequent types of events, described in online news and often referred to in social media.

Due to the complexity of the event extraction task, preparing a gold standard and evaluation of event extraction systems is not straightforward. Event annotation can be done in many different ways. Different taxonomies of event types can be used, as well as different event properties may be annotated. Moreover, one cannot give a single accuracy number, which characterizes an event extraction system performance. Rather than that, the accuracy for the extraction of each event property is measured separately. Even measuring the overlap between the gold standard and the output, produced by a system, can be done in different ways. Similarly, evaluating the similarity between event types, such as *bombing* and *terrorist attack* requires investigating into the nature of the events and the goals of the evaluation schema.

In this paper we make a small step into the infinite field of problems and solutions which the evaluation of event extraction system poses in front of the researchers in the field of information extraction.

We propose an event annotation model which consists of a taxonomy for classification of crisis events, as well as a template model with their most important slots. Then, we present a multilingual corpus annotated according to this model. Finally, we describe semi-automatic acquisition of lingistic resources for event extraction in Czech language. We plug these resources into a state-of-the-art event metadata extraction system and then we evaluate the performance of the system, using the annotated event corpus. Clearly, our solution is just an island in the sea of possible annotation and evaluation schemas.

The rest of the paper is structured as follows: Section 2 reports about related work. Section 3 describes the event annotation model. Section 4 is about the creation of the corpus. Section 5 de-

Proceedings of Recent Advances in Natural Language Processing, pages 627–635,
Hissar, Bulgaria, Sep 7–9 2015.

scribes the creation of event extraction resources for the Czech language. Finally, we discuss the results of our case study evaluation.

2 Related work

Recently, there is a significant amount of work, regarding automatic event detection from traditional and social media. However, few systems extract event metadata. Similarly, there are not many corpora, annotated with such metadata. In (Kim et al., 2008) annotation of event corpus from the biomedical domain is presented. The annotation is carried out according to event ontology, which partially overlaps with the GENIA ontology. A similar corpus is presented also in (Vincze et al., 2008).

FactBank (Saurí and Pustejovsky, 2009) is a corpus annotated with factuality information about news events. The GDELT database (Leetaru and Schrodt, 2013) contains automatically extracted metadata for politically-motivated events.

Most of the existing corpora are in English. The only multilingual corpus annotated with event metadata was created in the framework of the News Reader project (NewsReader et al., 2014). However, the corpus was annotated automatically in this project. Most of other event corpora are in the biomedical domain and few represent the domain of generic news discussed in the media.

Regarding automatic acquisition of event extraction resources, one of the first system for learning of event extraction lexicon and patterns is AutoSlog (Riloff and others, 1993). Other systems are presented in (Yangarber et al., 2000) and (Du and Yangarber, 2015). The problem with these and the other learning systems is that they rely on language-specific resources and consequently work only for the English language.

There are different event-extraction systems, presented in the literature: the KEDS/TABARI project (Schrodt, 2001), whose purpose is automatic detection and extraction of event metadata for political events, the Proteus system (Yangarber and Grishman, 1998) and others. There are two main classification schemas for political events: CAMEO (Gerner et al., 2002), developed inside the KEDS project and IDEA (Bond et al., 2003).

3 Event annotation model

The model we use for annotating events consists of two parts: a taxonomy of event classes and a template, whose slots represent the properties of the events. As a matter of fact, both parts of this model can be united into an ontology, where the taxonomy represents the is-a relations and the template slots are represented as ontological properties.

3.1 Event taxonomy

The event taxonomy is inspired by the one used in the NEXUS event extraction system (Tanev et al., 2008). We tried to create classes which correspond to the main crisis event types, mentioned in the news and social media. Definitely, more detailed event classification can be done. On the other hand, going for a very fine grained classification, would result in annotations which are difficult to be matched by event extraction systems. The crisis events in our taxonomy fall mainly in one of the two big top classes: *Disaster* and *Violence-related event*. The third group of events modeled in our taxonomy is related to the violent events: the class *Juridical event*. Juridical event is the smallest cluster, it contains arrests, trials, detentions, executions and raids of security forces. The category *Violence-related event* encompasses mainly events in which there is violence or attempt for violence against people, such as armed conflicts, crime, terrorism etc., as well as events, which can turn violent, such as demonstrations and strikes. We consider also the class *Sabotage* to be under *Violence-related event*, even if it does not include violence against people, it implies intentional damage of infrastructure and machines. Similarly, *Asylum/Fleeing a country for political reason* is considered to be *Violence-related*, since when people flee a country for political reason, their life and liberties are most likely threatened.

The category *Disaster* has two main sub classes - *Natural disaster* and *Man made disaster*. Natural disasters are storms, quakes, floodings, forest fires and others. Man made disasters are divided in extraordinary, like industrial accidents and explosions, as well as ordinary ones, which include traffic and aircraft accidents.

The category *Violence* is divided in three subcategories: *Politcally-motivated violence*, which includes differen types of armed conflicts and terrorist attacks, *Crime*, and *Socio-political event*, which includes different forms of protest actions: demonstrations, riots, sabotages, etc.

The event classes in our taxonomy reflect the nature of the event - its dynamics and the means,

Violence-related event (upper level subclasses)		
	Politically motivated	
		Political execution
		Armed conflict
		Terrorist attack
		Anti-terrorist operation
		Assassination
		Kidnapping/Hostage taking (political)
		Hostage release (political)
		Military movements
		Asylum/Fleeing a country for political reason
	Criminal	
		Robbery
		Kidnapping/Hostage taking (criminal)
		Hostage release (criminal)
		Shooting (criminal)
		Stabbing
		Abusing/offending people
		Physical attack
		Drug trade
		Vandalism
		Arson/Firebombing
		Piracy
		Cyber attack
		Prison break
	Socio-political	
		Boycott/Strike
		Public demonstration
		Riot
		Sabotage
		Mutiny
	Juridical	
		Arrest
		Charging
		Trial
		Execution
		Raid

Table 1: A part of the event taxonomy - violence-related events.

which were used, but also the motivation behind it and its context. While some event types may look similar, like *Shooting* as a subtype of *Armed conflict* and *Shooting* as a criminal event, in our taxonomy they are two different event classes, since the context and the motivation behind these actions are different. In the armed conflict shooting, the action is carried out by troops which serve their country, while in the criminal shooting, the main actors are criminals, whose motivation is to rob, to defend themselves from the police, etc. In the same way, we make difference between politically-motivated executions, executions by terrorists, and normal executions ordered by the court, without political motivations. Consideration of the motivation and the context is important, since they can give birth to different participants, means in use and consequences from the events. On the other hand, it is difficult for an event extraction system to draw the line between similar event classes. In order to overcome this last issue, during our experiments, we allowed for mapping of one class of the event extraction output to several classes from our model. For example, the event extraction system type *Execution* is considered a correct match for any of the execution classes used in our model.

Clearly, a taxonomy is not a complete knowledge representation model, since it does not represent relations other than *is-a* relation between event classes. In order to have more comprehensive knowledge-representation schema, the event taxonomy should be transformed into ontology. The structure of a crisis event is usually complicated: One event encompasses many subevents, which are related via causal relations. For example, event of type *Piracy* may include as subevents *Shooting* and *Kidnapping/Hostage taking*, which on its own may trigger event *Raid* by security forces to free the hijacked ship which can trigger event of type *HostageRelease*. In order to model this type of relations, the event ontology should encompass different types of relations, such as *causes* and *subevent-of*. The upper level violence-related classes of our taxonomy are shown in table 1.

3.2 Event properties

The properties of the event types in our model are represented through a unified template, which features the union of the properties of all event types. This is a simplification, since in reality the three big event classes: *Violent event*, *Natural disaster* and *Juridical event* have different properties. Properties related to the participants of the events: dead, wounded, kidnapped, arrested, etc. are actually pairs - specification of the participants, e.g. *five people* and their number, e.g. *5*. The properties template is shown on table 2.

Property
Time
Location
Dead count and specification
Missing count and specification
Wounded count and specification
Perpetrator count and specification
Kidnapped count and specification
Arrested count and specification
Weapons used

Table 2: The event properties template.

In addition, the model includes quantifiers where it is applicable. Examples:

- at least 20 people died (or not more than 20) = 20-
- over 20 dead = 20+
- hudreds of injured = 100x
- around 100 people = 100˜

4 Creating multilingual corpus with annotated events

Annotating articles about same events in multiple languages gives us a possibility to evaluate a multilingual event extraction system and the results are then directly comparable among languages. By comparing the results among languages, one could analyse how different language properties affect the quality of template extraction. As we want to make our corpus available to the community, we selected Wikinews as the source of event-related articles, since its licence allows us to share the news.

As a first application of the multilingual corpus, we wanted to evaluate our system in a newly supported language, namely Czech. Because of that, our starting page was the Czech Wikinews site. We manually selected event-related articles. We selected only articles which were available for more languages (visible in the left bar of the Wikinews site).

As the coverage of Czech Wikinews is not that high we included articles from the Multiling'13 corpus[1]. For now, we included only Czech, English and Spanish variants from the Multiling corpus.

An example of an event topic with English and Czech data and annotation can be found in table 3.

There are 109 topics in the corpus. Altogether, it includes 344 articles in 14 langauges. Distribution of between languages is given in table 4.

Language	Articles
cs	109
en	96
es	39
fr	34
de	18
it	13
ru	11
pt	6
pl	6
bg	3
ar	3
fi	2
no	1
gr	1

Table 4: Topics per language counts.

Most of the annotated news articles were available both in Czech and English languages.

4.1 Statistics about event roles

Regarding the event slots, which are represented in the corpus, the predominant event-specific role

[1]A corpus created by the summarization community: http://multiling.iit.demokritos.gr/pages/view/662/multiling-2013

topic metadata	event type	violence - criminal - shooting
	date	September 23, 2008
en	article title	School shooting in Kauhajoki, Finland kills eleven
	article perex	At approximately 11:00 a.m. Central European Summer Time, a man in his twenties entered the Kauhajoen vocational school in Kauhajoki, Finland with a gun and began to open fire, killing 11 people.
	perpetrator count	1
	perpetrator specification	a man in his twenties
	victim count	11
	victim specification	eleven; 11 people
cs	article title	Střelba ve finské škole
	article perex	Ve finském městě Kauhajoki na severozápadu země došlo ke střelbě. Na zdejší ekonomické škole jeden ze studentů vypálil po svých spolužácích, policie se obává, že incident si vyžádal několik obětí. Útočník se nachází ještě stále v budově školy.
	perpetrator count	1
	perpetrator specification	jeden ze studentů
	victim count	—
	victim specification	svých spolužácích

Table 3: An example of an annotated event topic.

for all the languages was found to be: *victim*, which includes dead, injured and kidnapped people. There are around 600 victims mentions (usually they are mentioned in both title and the first paragraph). For Czech only we have found more than 110 victim mentions. 15 weapons mentioned - too little to provide a proper basis for evaluation; 73 perpetrator mentions; 64 arrested people mentions; 37 sentenced people mentions.

We plan to extend the corpus with articles from English Wikinews and translate them to other languages. [2]

5 Event extraction system and semi automatic acquisition of dictionaries for it

We created Czech dictionaries and a cascaded grammar for analysis of crisis events, as well as boolean combination of keywords for recognition of event types, which was then used in the multilingual event extraction system – NEXUS (Tanev et al., 2008).

5.1 NEXUS

NEXUS is a multilingual rule-based event extraction system, developed at the Joint Research Centre, EC, which extracts event metainformation from online news in several languages. NEXUS essentially performs two types of tasks: first, using semantic grammar rules, backed up by domain specific dictionaries, it identifies in the text a set of noun phrases, which are assigned certain semantic roles. For example, in the text *The prime minister was kidnapped by masked gunmen*, the system will extract *the prime minister* as kidnapped victim and *masked gunmen* as perpetrators. Moreover, the system classifies the events, based on combinations of keywords. In the previously mentioned text *gunmen* and *kidnapped* will trigger the event type *kidnapping*. In order to plug in a new language in our event extraction system, we implement new domain specific dictionaries, as well as keyword combinations for event classifications. The grammars in use are also changed, although between similar languages, the change is small. This is due to the fact that the linguistic knowledge is mostly encoded in the domain-specific dictionaries: for example, for English we have all the possible patterns for *kill*: *was killed*, *have been killed*, *murdered*, *murdered by*, etc. This solution puts a stress on the domain-specific dictionaries, which are usually large and therefore we use semi-automatic methods, in order to learn them.

5.2 Learning dictionaries and linguistic patterns

The dictionaries used by NEXUS are developed following a semi-automatic procedure described in (Tanev et al., 2009). For each dictionary, the following steps are performed:

1. The user provides manually a seed set of entries

[2]The corpus will be available for download at http://nlp.kiv.zcu.cz.

2. It runs the LexiClass multilingual dictionary expansion tool which suggests more words and multiwords, distributionally similar to the seed set, ordered by their l similarity

3. The expanded dictionary is cleaned manually by looking at its top elements (which are most similar to the seed set)

For example, if the seed set are the English words: *soldiers*, *policemen*, *security forces*, the top elements from the expanded dictionary are *troops*, *civilians*, *officers*, *personnel*, *militants*, *peacekeepers*. A better description of the algorithm is provided in (Tanev et al., 2009) , where the precision of the algorithm for Portuguese was found to be 51% and for Spanish 71%. The algorithm is described also in (Tanev and Zavarella, 2013). Following the above-mentioned algorithm. we created the following Czech dictionaries, which are used by NEXUS: dictionary of noun phrases, referring to people and a dictionary of modifiers of these noun phrases. Moreover, we manually created a list of Czech numerals. These three resources were used in the first layer of the event-slot extraction grammar, which is responsible for detection of references to people.

The second layer of the grammar detects patterns, which co-occur with the person references, found on the first level. These patterns express different semantic roles which people take in the crisis event contexts: *dead* or *wounded victim*, *perpetrator*, etc. In order to discover the patterns, first we used the previously-described procedure to learn verbs and nouns, which introduce the considered semantic roles. Then, we searched automatically in a corpus co-occurrence patterns between these role-expressing words and references to people. A detailed description of the algorithm is provided in (Tanev et al., 2009). As an example, the output of the algorithm for English language for the semantic role *dead victim* will be patterns like *killed [PERSON]*, *[PERSON] was murdered*, etc.

Using these algorithms, we acquired 270 person-referring nouns, 600 person modifiers and 250 patterns for dead, wounded, arrested, kidnapped and perpetrators.

5.3 Providing keyword combinations for event type detection

In our event extraction system, the event class, e.g. *armed conflict*, *robbery*, etc., are detected through boolean combinations of keywords. We created these keyword combination mostly manually, using in some cases the LexiCLass system.

6 Evaluation

6.1 Methodology

We have run the NEXUS event extraction system on the news from our annotated corpus and evaluated the results. As NEXUS can currently detect only part of the event types in the corpus, we run the system only on the events, whose types are detectable by the system.

It is an important issue in the event extraction evaluation that the annotated event types and the detected by the system can differ in their specificity. For example, if the annotation is *suicide bombing* and the system says *terrorist attack*, is that a correct match? Probably, it is appropriate to consider this as a correct hit. However, if the system says that the type is *terrorist executing hostages* and the annotation is *suicide bombing*, then the match should not be considered correct.

In our experiments, we adopted a simple solution, which even if not perfect, provides a basis for evaluation of the event class detection. We simply mapped both annotated event types and the detected ones to event types, which were found to be specific enough, but not too specific, i.e. their taxonomy depth is somewhere in the middle. For example, all the daughter nodes of *socio-political* were mapped to this event type, the same for *terrorist attack*. Apart from the event type, we evaluated the following event participant properties:

- dead victim specification
- dead victim count
- wounded victim specification
- wounded victim count
- perpetrator spectification
- arrested spectification

Another problem in evaluating the performance of an event extraction system is the difference in the span of the annotated and detected slot fillers. For example, an event extraction system may detect as victims *Chinese*, while the annotation may be seven Chinese businessmen from Beijing. Our solution to this problem was that we used partial matching, i.e. if the system finds a part of the specification, it counts as a correct match. The obvious disadvantage is that we do not evaluate the completeness of the phrase detection, however from a practical point of view, event a partial match is useful.

Another problem in front of evaluation of event extraction systems is matching the numbers of victims. In some cases, the system may detect a number which is close to the annotated number. For example, if in the text there is the phrase *more than 100 died*, the event extraction system may suggest *100* as number of dead. This is not correct, but again, from a practical point of view, it is better to have a rough estimation of the death toll, rather than having no estimation. In such cases, we consider the system output as correct.

6.2 Event type detection

75% of the events in the corpus could be mapped to NEXUS event types. The system classifies the event type with .38 precision and .60 recall (F is .46).

The easiest type is Shooting, the system correctly classified all events. On the other side is Suicide bombing (a terrorist attack), which was most of the times wrongly classified as Explosion (a man-made disaster). The solution will be to make more complex patterns which would distinguish these lexically similar event types.

A large corpus and a trainable classifier would be a good solution for event type detection, although distinguishing close event types would require a very large number of countersamples.

6.3 Event roles detection

The system predicts an event property with .49 recall and .85 precision (F is .63). It performs the best on predicting dead victim specifications (F is .80), the most difficult is perpetrator specification (F is .42). Counts of dead and wouded victims are predicted with F=.57 and F=.62. The complete results are given in table 5.

6.4 Discussion

In 56% of the wrong predictions, the problem was in the grammar. An example:

CZ: Ozbrojenci se dostali do nigerijské věznice tím, že odpálili nálože a zabili při přestřelce jednoho strážce.

EN: Gunmen entered a Nigerian prison by bombing their way inside and killing a guard during a shootout.

Property	R	P	F
dead victim specification	.67	1	.80
dead victim count	.48	.71	.57
wounded victim specification	.63	1	.77
wounded victim count	.50	.80	.62
perpetrator specification	.29	.80	.42
arrested specification	.33	.75	.46
all	.49	.85	.63

Table 5: Results of event roles detection for Czech.

The lexical resources contain both *ozbrojenci = gunmen* as a possible actor, *zabili = killed* as a pattern and *jednoho strážce = a guard* as another possible actor. The perpetrator patterns contain '[perpetrator-group] zabili [dead-group]', however, the word spans between the pattern items does not allow to catch the pattern. A solution could be to allow larger gaps between the pattern items, but this can result in a lower precision.

In 44% of the wrong predictions, the lexical resources were missing the specification. Examples of missing complex person groups:

CZ-1: militantní skupina al-Šabab spojená s al Káidou

EN-1: the militant group al-Shabab associated with al Qaeda

CZ-2: programátor otevřeného software

EN-2: programmer of open software

The are several challenges connected to a rule-based approach and dealing with the Czech language. First, Czech has a free word order. The grammar patterns would need to capture all the following statements. In the following example, all the four sentences could be found in news:

CZ-1: Bombový útok zabil v lednu na moskevském letišti Domodědovo 36 lidí.

CZ-2: Bombový útok zabil na moskevském letišti Domodědovo v lednu 36 lidí.

CZ-3: Bombový útok zabil 36 lidí na moskevském letišti Domodědovo v lednu.

CZ-4: 36 lidí zabil bombový útok v lednu na moskevském letišti Domodědovo.

EN: The suicide bombing killed 36 people at the Moscow's Domodedovo airport in January.

Then, an object can preseed a subject and a lexical form of the nouns cannot distinguish them. The system can thus wrongly exchange a victim and a perpetrator. In the following example, the following sentences are equal and the roles can be distiguished only by their case, not by the position.

CZ-1: Sebevražedný atentátník zabil osm desítek Pákistánců

CZ-2: osm desítek Pákistánců zabil Sebevražedný atentátník
EN: a suicide bomber killed eighty Pakistanians.

As the corpus includes only violent event texts, we cannot see to what extent the system detects false positives (wrongly detects a violent event in a non-event article). We ran the system on 944 general news articles and found only 3 cases of non-violent events captured (0.3%). As an example, the following was classified as an armed conflict, which is not correct as the conflict not happened yet.

CZ: Turci před pár týdny poslali k hranici s Irákem sto tisíc vojáků.
EN: Turks sent to the border with Iraq hundred thousand soldiers a few weeks ago.

We compared the performance of the Czech system to English, which is already well covered in the corpus. The event types in English were recognized better by .16 in F-score and event roles by .17. This can roughly quantify the difference in difficulty between the event extraction task done in these languages.

7 Conclusion

We describe our work towards multilingual evaluation of event extraction systems. Namely, creation of a multilingual event metadata corpus and evaluation of event extraction for the Czech language.

There are many opened issues. First, we plan to extend the evaluation resources. This would make possible training and testing of supervised algorithms for event extraction. As the language coverage of in the corpus differs, the next task is to translate each topic to all the languages. In this way cross-language performance will be more comparable. When working on the event extraction itself, one research direction is machine learning. In the case of event type classification, we need a very large traning corpus to be able to distinguish lexically close event types. For learning of event-role detection features and their frequency by supervised approaches, a large corpus is necessary as well, especially in the case of free-word order languages like Czech. When using a rule-based approach and automatic resource acquision, there are difficulties to cover all the necessary patterns and rules. The current grammars can be further improved by adding some language-specific elements in the rules. The partial coverage of the Czech resources leads to a lower recall. We can improve further the dictionaries by adding the different morphological forms for the words.

Acknowledgments

This work was supported by project MediaGist, EU's FP7 People Programme (Marie Curie Actions), no. 630786.

References

Doug Bond, Joe Bond, Churl Oh, J Craig Jenkins, and Charles Lewis Taylor. 2003. Integrated data for events analysis (idea): An event typology for automated events data development. *Journal of Peace Research*, 40(6):733–745.

Mian Du and Roman Yangarber. 2015. Acquisition of domain-specific patterns for single document summarization and information extraction. In *The Second International Conference on Artificial Intelligence and Pattern Recognition (AIPR2015)*, page 30.

Deborah J Gerner, Philip A Schrodt, Omur Yilmaz, and Rajaa Abu-Jabr. 2002. The creation of cameo (conflict and mediation event observations): An event data framework for a post cold war world. In *annual meeting of the American Political Science Association*, volume 29.

Jin-Dong Kim, Tomoko Ohta, and Jun'ichi Tsujii. 2008. Corpus annotation for mining biomedical events from literature. *BMC bioinformatics*, 9(1):10.

Kalev Leetaru and Philip A Schrodt. 2013. Gdelt: Global data on events, location, and tone, 1979–2012. In *ISA Annual Convention*, volume 2, page 4.

Proyecto NewsReader, Rodrigo Agerri, Eneko Agirre, Itziar Aldabe, Begona Altuna, Zuhaitz Beloki, Egoitz Laparra, Maddalen López de Lacalle, German Rigau, Aitor Soroa, et al. 2014. Newsreader project. *Procesamiento del Lenguaje Natural*, 53:155–158.

Ellen Riloff et al. 1993. Automatically constructing a dictionary for information extraction tasks. In *AAAI*, pages 811–816.

Roser Saurí and James Pustejovsky. 2009. Factbank: A corpus annotated with event factuality. *Language resources and evaluation*, 43(3):227–268.

Philip A Schrodt. 2001. Automated coding of international event data using sparse parsing techniques. In *annual meeting of the International Studies Association, Chicago*.

H Tanev and V Zavarella. 2013. Multilingual learning and population of event ontologies. a case study for social media. *Towards Multilingual Semantic Web (Springer, Berlin & New York*.

Hristo Tanev, Jakub Piskorski, and Martin Atkinson. 2008. Real-time news event extraction for global crisis monitoring. In *Natural Language and Information Systems*, pages 207–218. Springer.

Hristo Tanev, Vanni Zavarella, Jens Linge, Mijail Kabadjov, Jakub Piskorski, Martin Atkinson, and Ralf Steinberger. 2009. Exploiting machine learning techniques to build an event extraction system for portuguese and spanish. *Linguamática*, 1(2):55–66.

Veronika Vincze, György Szarvas, Richárd Farkas, György Móra, and János Csirik. 2008. The bioscope corpus: biomedical texts annotated for uncertainty, negation and their scopes. *BMC bioinformatics*, 9(Suppl 11):S9.

Roman Yangarber and Ralph Grishman. 1998. Nyu: Description of the proteus/pet system as used for muc-7. In *In Proceedings of the Seventh Message Understanding Conference (MUC-7*. Citeseer.

Roman Yangarber, Ralph Grishman, Pasi Tapanainen, and Silja Huttunen. 2000. Automatic acquisition of domain knowledge for information extraction. In *Proceedings of the 18th conference on Computational linguistics-Volume 2*, pages 940–946. Association for Computational Linguistics.

A VSM-based Statistical Model for the Semantic Relation Interpretation of Noun-Modifier Pairs

Nitesh Surtani
IIIT Hyderabad
nitesh.surtani0606@gmail.com

Soma Paul
IIIT Hyderabad
soma@iiit.ac.in

Abstract

The paper addresses the task of automatic interpretation of semantic relation in noun compounds. The problem has been attempted with both Ontology-based and Statistical approaches, but both approaches having their own limitations. We present a novel VSM-based statistical model which represents each relation with a weighted vector of prepositional and verbal paraphrases. The model ranks the paraphrases on their relevance and assigns higher weights to more relevant paraphrases. The performance of the model is compared with the Ontology model and the results are quite encouraging. We finally propose a Hybrid of the two models which compares on par with the best performing systems on Nastase and Szpakowicz (2003) dataset.

1 Introduction

There has been an increased interest in discovering the semantics of Noun Compounds (NCs[1]). There are two reasons that make this task quite essential and interesting in text understanding: **(i) their implicit nature**, for instance the NC *'monday meeting'* is the *meeting scheduled on monday* (Temporal), *'teacher meeting'* is the *meeting organized for teachers* (Participant) and *'NLP meeting'* is the *meeting to discuss NLP topics* (Quality-Topic); and **(ii) their frequent and compounding behavior**. NCs are very frequent in english and comprise of 3.9% and 2.6% of all tokens in the Reuters corpus and the British National Corpus (BNC) respectively (Baldwin and Tanaka, 2004). New NCs are very frequently constructed *eg. website design, internet usage, orange juice* etc., and sometimes combine with other words to form longer compounds, e.g., *orange juice company, orange juice company homepage* etc.

[1]A noun compound (NC) is a sequence of nouns which act as a single noun (Downing, 1977), *eg. sunday morning*

The frequency spectrum of NCs follows a Zipfian distribution (Séaghdha, 2008), where many NC tokens belong to a *long tail* of low-frequency types. Over half of the *two-type* compounds in BNC occur just once (Kim and Baldwin, 2006).

The research focusing on the semantic interpretation of NCs has followed two directions: (i) Identifying the underlying semantic relation (Girju et al., 2005; Tratz and Hovy, 2010); and (ii) Paraphrasing the NC (Nakov, 2008; Butnariu and Veale, 2008; Butnariu et al., 2010). Consider the text:

> "A **large student protest** was *carried out during* **monday evening** by various **engineering colleges** to raise funds for research. This **London protest** saw tremendous participation by students from 14 colleges, seeing to which R&D dept. agreed to increase the **college funds** to 10,000,000 GBP. "

The sequences marked in bold in the above example are Noun compounds (NCs). In the above text, some NCs are interpretable via paraphrasing: **protest** was *carried out during* **evening**, where *'during'* defines the temporality of the protest. On the other hand, some NCs are not explicit: **student protest** meaning that the *'protest was done by the students'* (Agent), **London protest** meaning *'protest was held in London'* (Spatial), **monday evening** meaning *'evening of monday'* (Part-Of), **engineering colleges** meaning the *'colleges that specialize in engineering course'* (Purpose), **college funds** are the *'funds allocated for the college'* (Beneficiary). The goal of this paper is to discover the underlying semantic relation of the NCs *via paraphrasing*. The knowledge of semantic relation in the above NCs can help in answering questions like: *Where was the protest held? Who led the protest? etc.* The tasks has applications in many subfields of NLP, including Question Answering (Girju et al., 2006), Knowledge Base acquisition (Hearst, 1998) and others.

The task of semantic relation classification of NCs has been attempted in two directions: (i) using

Proceedings of Recent Advances in Natural Language Processing, pages 636–645,
Hissar, Bulgaria, Sep 7–9 2015.

a *knowledge-intensive ontology* and (ii) *extracting paraphrases from a large corpus*. We discuss two existing WordNet-based ontology models: SemScat 1 (by Moldovan et al. (2004)) and SemScat 2 (by Beamer et al. (2008)), which uses the WordNet's noun Hypernym (IS-A) hierarchy to find semantic similarity between two Noun-Noun pairs. The main focus (and contribution) of this paper is towards developing a Statistical model which uses Prepositional (*eg. 'benefit for consumer'*), Verbal (*eg. 'benefit involving consumer'*) and Verb+Prep (*eg. 'benefit received by consumer'*) paraphrases of the NC (*eg. 'consumer benefit'*) for identifying its relation.

The paper is organized as follows: **Section 2 (Related Works)** describes previous works on Ontology and Statistical models; **Section 3 (Data Analysis and Specification)** describes the dataset used for experiments, **Section 4 (Ontology-Based Model)** and **Section 5 (Corpus-Based Model)** discusses, experiments and provide insights on these two models. **Section 6 (Integrated Model)** develops a hybrid of the two models and **Section 7** concludes the paper.

2 Related Works

Ontology-based Approach: Nastase et al. (2006) explores both WordNet and Roget's Theasaurus for forming the classification features and find WordNet ontology to be more suitable for the task. Girju et al. (2003), Moldovan et al. (2004) and Beamer et al. (2008) propose *Iterative semantic specialization (ISS), SemScat 1 and SemScat 2 models* respectively, which utilize WordNet's Hypernym hierarchy and specialize the synsets from general to specific level. *ISS* employs *Decision Tree (C4.5)* for modelling a single *Part-Whole* relation. *SemScat 1* and *SemScat 2* are designed as multi-class classifiers for modelling a set of 35 relations (Moldovan et al., 2004) and 7 relations (Girju et al., 2007) respectively.

Statistical Approach: Nakov and Hearst (2006) suggests that the semantics of noun compounds is best expressible using multiple paraphrases involving verbs and prepositions. For example, *bronze statue* is a statue that is *made of, is composed of, consists of, contains, is of, is, is handcrafted from, is dipped in, looks like* bronze. Nastase et al. (2006) makes an assumption that senses of NCs can be derived through collocated words learned from large corpus and use a sparse vector of collocated words as features (approx 10,000 features). Their system performs with low accuracy and is outperformed by their WordNet model of sparse Hypernym synset feature vector. Nulty (2007) extracts 28 prepositional paraphrases by forming simple *'N2 prep N1'* or *'N2 prep the Y'* templates and querying the web. He shows that the less frequent prepositions achieve higher accuracy than the more frequent ones in classifying the relation. This observation aligns with ours and we employ a TF/IDF (modified) scheme to assign higher weights to such paraphrases. Turney (2006b) introduces a *Latent Relational Analysis (or LRA)* model. The model extracts all possible synonyms for the modifier and the head using a thesaurus and uses a list of 64 joining terms, J such as *'of'*, *'for'* and *'to'* to form 128 phrases (i.e. $M\ J\ H$ and $H\ J\ M$). From the set of extracted paraphrases, top few thousands selected paraphrases are used to build an incidence matrix, whose dimensionality is reduced using singular value decomposition (SVD). Nastase et al. (2006), Turney and Littman (2005), Turney (2006a), Turney (2006b) and Nulty (2007) compare their systems on Nastase dataset, where Turney (2006b) outperforms others achieving a accuracy of 58% and 54.6% macro-averaged f-score[2].

3 Data Specification

We work with two datasets: (i) Nastase and Szpakowicz (2003) dataset of noun-modifier pairs (referred as Nastase dataset in the paper); and (ii) Butnariu et al. (2013) SemEval-13 Task 4 gold-paraphrased dataset (referred as SemEval dataset). Nastase dataset uses a two-level taxonomy of 5 coarse-grained and 30 fined-grained relations and comprises of 600 Noun-Modifier pairs consisting of a head noun and a modifier which can either be noun, adjective or adverb. The data is annotated with *semantic relation* of the NC and *POS tag* and *WordNet senses* of the modifier & head. This data has some issues: there are 4 cases of repetition and 3 compounds contain multi-word modifier (eg.- *'test tube' baby*), which have been pruned out. In the remaining 593 NCs, there are 326 instances of noun (55%), 260 instances of adjectives (44%) and 7 instances of adverbs (1%) modifier. The SemEval dataset consists of 355 Noun-Noun compounds which are manually paraphrased by *approx.* 30 annotators, with a total of 12,471 paraphrases. Each paraphrase is assigned a frequency, which is number of annotators who have marked that paraphrase for the given NC. We have annotated the NCs with *semantic relations* and modifier & head *WordNet senses* following the guidelines from Nastase and Szpakowicz (2003). The experiments on

[2]Macroaveraged f-score is the overall mean of f-scores of individual classes.

RELATION	Nastase (2003)	SemEval (2013)
Causal	85 (14.33%)	95(26.9)
Participant	259 (43.67%)	108 (30.5)
Quality	144 (24.28%)	107 (30.2)
Spatial	54 (9.1%)	32 (9.1)
Temporal	51 (8.6%)	13 (3.3)
Total	593 (100%)	355 (100%)

Table 1: Distribution of Relations in Datasets

the SemEval dataset of gold paraphrases helps us in harnessing the full potential of the Statistical model which is not possible with Nastase dataset, as the quality of extracted paraphrases is nowhere close to manually annotated paraphrases. On the Nastase dataset, we compare the performance of our Hybrid model with other models evaluated on this dataset.

The ontology and corpus models are designed to handle only Noun-Noun compounds (Beamer et al., 2008; Turney, 2006b). We extend the ontology model to work with adjective and adverb modifiers but such adaptation is not possible for the corpus model. The ontology model uses the Noun Hypernymy hierarchy, which is extended to adjectives and adverbs by linking them to their corresponding noun synsets, through following WordNet relations: *derivationally_related_form, pertainym, attributes_to* and *similar_to* (eg. *electric#a#1* $\rightarrow$ *electricity#n#1*). The corpus model always yields similar paraphrases with adjective or adverb modifiers, making such paraphrases irrelevant for classification. Thus, the corpus model works with only 326 Noun-Noun compounds in Nastase dataset.

4 Ontology-Based Approach

We experiment with two WordNet-based models: *SemScat 1* by Moldovan et al. (2004) and *SemScat 2* by Beamer et al. (2008). The model works on the principle that two NCs having similar concepts in the Hypernym hierarchy encode same relation.

4.1 Model Formulation

Let L be the set of all the hypernym entity types (or synsets). Let the training set of n instances $T = ((x_1r_1)....(x_nr_n))$, where $x_1....x_n$ represent the NCs annotated with semantic relations $r_1....r_n$ respectively, where $r_i \in$ relation set R. The input x_k is represented in terms of modifier and head features $< f_i^m, f_j^h >$, where f_i^m, $f_j^h \in L$ represent synsets at level i and j in the hypernym hierarchy, combinedly represented as f_{ij}. Therefore, the goal is to model the prediction function $F : (L \times L) \rightarrow R$.

The SemScat models strives to learn generalized sets of Hypernym synsets, known as Boundary, G. For instance - $G_1 = \{entity\}$ and $G_2 = \{physical - entity, abstract - entity, thing\}$ are two boundaries where G_2 is hyponym of G_1. The algorithm starts by creating the most general boundary $G_1 = \{entity\}$ and all the training examples are mapped to this boundary by forming $< Modifier-Head >$ feature $f_{11} = \{entity-entity\}$. Then, the model computes the probability of each relation r for every feature formed in this new boundary. Next, the model identifies the most ambiguous feature (the one having the highest entropy) using the weighted entropy measure (Beamer et al., 2008) and specializes its modifier & head synsets by their hyponyms. The algorithm again computes the statistics on this new boundary and the process is repeated.

Key Differences- SemScat 1 and SemScat 2: The main difference between the two models is the manner in which they store their boundary. SemScat1 strives to discover a single optimal boundary G^*, at which all the features map uniquely to a relation. But practically, the boundary G^* is overspecialized and therefore, the model finds a boundary G_k which generalizes well over the test set by using a *development set*. The SemScat 1 terminates the further specialization of the boundary when the performance of the model drops on the development set (i.e. the model starts to over-specialize). It also uses a Threshold parameter (T) to restricts the over-specialization of the features f_{ij}, by treating it as disambiguated if the most probable relation corresponding to feature f_{ij} has the probability greater than T. On the other hand, the SemScat 2 model keeps track of all the boundaries ranging from the most general to most specific boundary (G^*), $G = \{G_1, ..., G^*\}$ and terminates the training after discovering the boundary G^*. Given an unseen instance (with feature f_{ij}), SemScat 1 searches for this feature in the stored boundary G_k, and if the feature is matched at this boundary, it assigns the most probable relation corresponding to the feature f_{ij}, otherwise the instance is considered as missed and no relation is assigned; while SemScat 2 starts the search for the feature f_{ij} from the most specific boundary G^* and moves towards more general boundaries, and assigns the relation corresponding to the most specific feature matched.

4.2 Experiments

We perform two progressive experiments with ontology model. The experimental setup, results and insights gained are presented for each experiment separately. This section discusses the results of experiments on ***ONLY*** Nastase dataset. The results on SemEval dataset are presented in Section 6.

Experiment I: Comparison of SemScat 1 and SemScat 2: In this experiment, we compare the performance of the two models on the Nastase dataset. We perform k-fold cross-validation to evaluate the performance of the model over the complete dataset. The value of k is varied as: k = 5, 7, 10, 15, 30, 50, $N - 1$ (Leave-one-out [3]). The data is divided into training, development and testing set for SemScat 1, while into training and testing set for SemScat2. The development set used in SemScat 1 comprises of 20% data from the training set. The Threshold factor (T) is varied from 0.6 to 0.9 in steps of 0.05.

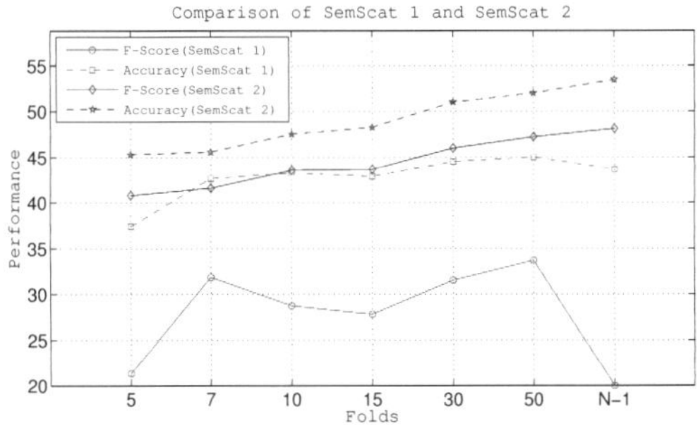

Figure 1: Performance comparison of SemScat 1 and SemScat 2 on Nastase dataset at varying k folds

SemScat 2 outperforms SemScat 1 on each fold achieving the optimal performance at $k = N - 1$ with the 53.46% accuracy (baseline 43.67%) and 48.13% f-score. SemScat 1 performs just above the baseline with accuracy and f-score of 45.02% and 33.70% respectively at $k = 50$ and $T = 0.7$, classifying most of the instances with the majority relation *Participant*. We find that the boundary G^* is quite specific (ranging from *level 6-8* on Nastase dataset) while the boundary generally selected by SemScat 1 ranges from *level 3-4* in the experiments. This reveals that SemScat 1 fails in achieving the goal of finding its optimal boundary that is the closest approximation of the boundary G^* and thus, misses out knowledge that would be useful for classification. The huge performance gap between the model using single boundary and the model storing multiple boundaries motivates us to investigate the authenticity of each boundary in attesting the relation.
Experiment II: Performance of Different Boundary Levels in SemScat 2: This experiment evaluates and compares the performance of multiple boundaries stored by the SemScat 2 model. The model is trained on optimal parameters $k = N - 1$ and the accuracy of each level is computed.

[3]In Leave-one-out, one instance is tested at a time while rest $N - 1$ instances are used for training

Level	Total	Correct	Accuracy
2	17	5	29.41
3	162	65	40.12
4	198	107	54.04
5	152	104	68.42
6	36	17	47.22
7	23	18	78.26

Table 2: Performance of SemScat 2 at different levels

The results presented in Table 2 show that the confidence of the model in assigning the relation improves significantly with each level (except for *level 6*). The model performs with accuracy of only 29% at boundary *level 2* which shoots up to 78% at *level 7*. Most of the test instances are mapped at *level 4 and 5*, achieving accuracy of 54% and 68% respectively. This indicates that the NCs are classified accurately when matched with more specific knowledge. We capitalize of this useful insight in the Hybrid model. Further, we observe that the ontology model faces difficulty in disambiguating between certain set of relations, eg. *Student Protest* (Agent) and *Student Discount* (Beneficiary) are represented with very similar concepts in the Hypernym hierarchy and therefore, the model fails to classify the NCs correctly. On the other hand, the corpus model easily classifies these NCs, since *'protest **(led_by, organized_by)** students'* clearly points to **Agent** relation whereas *'discount **(for, given_to)** students'* suggest that modifier is the **Beneficiary** of the action. This complementing behavior of two models establishes the ground for integrating them.

5 Statistical Approach

The statistical model captures the meaning of the NC using *Prepositional, Verbal* and *Verb+Prepositional* paraphrases and uses them to identify the underlying semantic relation. For instance, *student protest* **(Participant)** is paraphrased as *'protest **(by, of, led_by, involving, started_by)** students'*, *London protest* **(Spatial)** as *'protest **(in, at, of, held_at)** London'* and *evening protest* **(Temporal)** as *'protest **(during, of, held_during)** evening'*. In the above examples, the preposition ***'by'*** clearly points to **Participant** relation, ***'in'*** and ***'at'*** to **Spatial** relation and ***'during'*** to Temporal relation. Similarly, verbal paraphrases ***'involving'*** and ***'started_by'*** indicate **Participant** while paraphrases ***'held_at'*** and ***'held_during'*** indicate **Spatial** and **Temporal** relations respectively. Prepositions are polysemous in nature and the same preposition can indicate different semantic relation, as also observed by (Srikumar and Roth, 2013), *for eg.* the preposition ***'from'*** occurs in: *'death*

from** cancer'* (Causal-Cause), *'excerpt **from** the book'* (Participant-Source), *'protest **from** evening'* (Temporal) etc. But the degree of polysemity varies with prepositions, *for eg.* the preposition ***'of' in the above 3 NCs maps to 3 different relations but the prepositions ***'by', 'at'*** and ***'during'*** occur specifically with *Participant, Spatial* and *Temporal* relations respectively. Prepositions that map to a single or fewer relations are more relevant for the task than the ones which frequently occur with different relations and thus, are weighted higher. Furthermore, we observe that the verb+prep paraphrases are quite significant, as such verbs are mostly accompanied with relevant prepositions, *for eg.* the paraphrase *'Protest held during evening'* is plausible but *'Protest held of evening'* is not. Therefore, the preposition & verb in such paraphrases are given more relevance using a Strength parameter.

The statistical model represents each NC as a pair of vector of prepositional and verbal paraphrases. With the relation of the NC known (*i.e. supervised learning*), we transform the NC vectors into Relation Vectors, which represent the complete semantic class with a single pair of prepositional and verbal vector. The *Vector Space Model (VSM)* with *Nearest Neighbour* classifier employed by the model computes the cosine similarity of the test vector with each Relation vector and assigns it the relation with the highest similarity. The next sections describe the two most important modules of this model: Paraphrase Extraction and Vector Formation module.

5.1 Paraphrase Extraction Module

The goal of this system is to take an NC as input and provide the set of *prepositional, verbal and verb+prep* paraphrases for it. It consists of three submodules: former dealing with extraction while latter two perform cleaning of paraphrases.

Module 1: Paraphrase Extraction: We have relied mainly on the Google N-gram Corpus for extracting the paraphrases. Google has publicly released their web data as n-grams, also known as Web-1T corpus (Brants and Franz, 2006). The corpus contains 2-, 3-, 4- and 5-grams sequences and returns n-gram matches that occur more than 40 times. The templates for extraction with few (*correct and incorrect*) selected paraphrases for NC *Copper Coin* are presented in Table 3 and 4 respectively. Among incorrect paraphrases, the first two are syntactically illegitimate while the last two are syntactically sound but semantically illegitimate. *'coins are copper'* is part of *'one cent **coins are copper** or not'* while *'coins in copper'* is part of **'coins in copper** *bowl'*.

coin [s|p] <*>copper [s|p]	coin of copper
coin [s|p] <*><*>copper [s|p]	coins made from copper
coin [s|p] <*><*><*>copper [s|p]	coin is made of copper

Table 3: Extraction Templates with Examples

Correct Paraphrase	Incorrect Paraphrase
coin of copper 63	coin : copper 91
coins made from copper 108	coin jewelry copper 51
coins made of copper 49	coins are copper 91
coin is made of copper 146	coins in copper 55

Table 4: Paraphrases Extracted from Google N-Gram

Module 2: Syntactic Cleaning: To handle the syntactically ill-formed paraphrases, we prepare a set of plausible syntactic templates. The paraphrases for 60 NCs (*with total of 5716 paraphrases*) are manually marked as incorrect or correct (0 or 1 respectively) by two annotators, with high agreement of annotation, since the complexity of the task is **EASY**. The correct paraphrases are POS tagged using the *CMU ark-tweet POS-tagger* (more efficient in tagging 3- & 4-grams than the Stanford POS-tagger) and POS templates are extracted. The data is divided equally into training and testing sets of 30 NCs each. Table 5 shows that the syntactic templates, although learnt from considerably small training data, are exhaustive and achieve good coverage of 91.4% on the test set, but low precision of 56.7% as many semantically illegitimate paraphrases are matched by these templates.

	Recall	Precision	F-Score
[Without Constraints]	91.4	56.68	69.97
[With Constraints]	91.4	72.9	81.11

Table 5: Comparison of Syntactic Templates *before* and *after* applying Semantic Constraints

Module 3: Semantic Cleaning: The syntactic templates are unable to filter out semantically illegitimate paraphrases. Such paraphrases are cleaned by looking at their context, extracted from extended paraphrases: *coins in copper* $< * >< * >$.

> **Constraint:** *If the modifier of a given NC is part of a NP chunk having another noun as head, then it is not a legitimate paraphrase.*

eg: (NP (NNS **coins***)) (PP (IN* **in***) (NP (NN* **copper***) (NN bowl)))*

which means *'coins kept in bowl made of copper'*. Applying this constraint shows significant improvement in precision, with f-score reaching ~81%. There are still few paraphrases which are not filtered out by this module. For eg. ***'party after class** gets over'* for NC *'class party'*. The verb+prep paraphrases (eg. *'make_of: 242'*) are splitted into verb (eg. *'make: 242'*) and preposition (eg. *'of: 242'*) and contribute to respective vectors with Strength parameter S_p and S_v, as discussed in Experiment II.

5.2 Model Formulation

Let the training set of n instances $T = ((x_1 r_1)...(x_n r_n))$, where $x_1...x_n$ are the NCs' and $r_1...r_n \in R$ are their corresponding relations. Each instance x_i is represented by two vectors: a prepositional and a verbal vector. The prepositional vector consists of $m = 30$ prepositions, $P =< p_1, ..., p_m >$ and the verbal vector consisting of top-k frequent verbs represented as, $V =< v_1, ..., v_k >$. The input x_i is mapped to the prepositional vector, $x_i^p =< p_1^i, ..., p_m^i >$ and verb vector $x_i^v =< v_1^i, ..., v_k^i >$, where p_j^i represents the weight of the feature j in prepositional vector. The NC vectors are transformed into Relation vectors, where each relation $r_i \in R$ is represented by a single pair of prepositional and verbal vectors, $R_i^p =< p_1^i, ..., p_m^i >$ and $R_i^v =< v_1^i, ..., v_k^i >$ respectively. The VSM computes the cosine similarity between the two vectors, where higher value of cosine similarity means that two vectors are more similar to each other.

$$\cos(\theta) = \frac{\sum_{i=1}^{n} \vec{r_{1i}}.\vec{r_{2i}}}{\sqrt{\sum_{i=1}^{n}(\vec{r_{1i}})^2 . \sum_{j=1}^{n}(\vec{r_{2j}})^2}} = \frac{\vec{r_1}.\vec{r_2}}{\| \vec{r_1}.\vec{r_2} \|} \quad (1)$$

where $\vec{r_1}$ is the training vector and $\vec{r_2}$ is the test vector. We modify the VSM algorithm in case of computing similarity with Relation vectors, in order to allow them to handle the distribution of relations. Therefore, the Relation vectors are not converted to unit vector and thus, the VSM computes $\vec{r_1}\cos(\theta)$.

5.3 Vector Formation

In this module, we discuss the transformation of NC vector to Relation vector and describe the (modified) TF/IDF scheme used for weighting the vectors.

Forming Relation vector: A relation vector is a single pair of prepositional and verbal vector that captures the behavior of the entire relation and also incorporates the distribution of each relation in training data. The Relation vector (of relation r) is formed by the vector addition of all NC vectors in the training set that belong to relation r:

$$\langle R^r \rangle = \sum_{x \in T} \langle x^r \rangle \quad (2)$$

where T is the training set and x^r are the NCs in T with relation r.

Weighting Scheme: By weighting the vectors, we want to assign higher weights to more relevant paraphrase features. For our model, the paraphrases that map to a single or fewer relations are more relevant than the ones mapping to many relations. We use the *TF/IDF weighting function* but modify it with necessary variations. First, our *TF* function takes usual logarithmically scaled frequency but is normalized to ensure the equality in document length, since the frequency of paraphrases extracted for different NCs vary significantly. For calculating the *IDF*, we take into account the relative weights of each paraphrases (or features) rather than their occurrence (0 or 1) with the NC. This modification is essential, since the Vocabulary size $|V|$ = *Number of prepositions (or verbs)* in our model is relatively very small, and doing this ensures that the noisy extracted paraphrases (with low frequencies) do not harm the model.

$$TF_i^x = \frac{log(f_i)^x}{\sum_i log(f_i^x)}; \; IDF_j = \frac{1}{\sum_{x \in T}(TF_j^x)} \quad (3)$$

5.4 Integration of Prep and Verb models

The employ two strategies to integrate the models using prepositional and the verb vector:

(i) Concatenation Model concatenates the features of preposition and verb vectors to form a single Prep+Verb vector of $m + k$ features. The relevance of verb and preposition vector features are weighted with a contribution factor f.

$$\langle Verb{+}Prep \rangle = \langle Prep \rangle \oplus f * \langle Verb \rangle \quad (4)$$

where $\oplus$ denotes concatenation of two vectors.

(ii) Best Selection Model employs Best-Selection strategy by selecting the more confident of two models for classification in a given situation. This model separately evaluates for preposition and verb model the performance (i.e. $f - score$) of classifying each relation. Given a unseen instance, the two models predict the relation of NC independently but the model which assigns the relation with higher f-score is ultimately selected for classification.

5.5 Experiments

We perform *three* progressive experiments on the Statistical model on the SemEval dataset:

Experiment I: Comparing models on different parameters: In this experiment, we introduce 6 models on *three* varying parameters and compare their performance: NC vector (**-R**) vs Relation vector (**+R**), Weighted vector (**+W**) vs Unweighted vector (**-W**), Prior Probability (**+P**) vs Unit vector (**-P**). The experiments are conducted separately on prepositional and verbal vectors. The data is divided into training and testing set with *k-fold cross-validation*, k varying as, $k = 5, 7, 10, 15, 30, 50$ and $N - 1$.

Model	F	A	Model	F	A
1: [-R -W -P]	35.23	36.21	**4: [+R +W -P]**	35.77	38.54
2: [-R +W -P]	36.33	38.18	**5: [+R -W +P]**	37.97	39.34
3: [+R -W -P]	24.41	35.9	**6: [+R +W +P]**	38.82	40.72

Table 6: Performance of Models on Prepositional vector

The description of the models with their performance on prepositional vector is presented in Table 6. The **Model 6 [+R +W +P]** (i.e. *Model using weighted prior probability Relation vectors*) outperforms other models on both preposition and verb vectors. This model achieves an accuracy of 40.72% (baseline 30.55%) and f-score of 38.82% with prepositional vector and (Acc, F) of (34.93%, 35.78%) with verb vector at $k = N - 1$. Therefore, Model 6 is selected for the next two experiments.

Experiment II: Investigating the relevance of Verb+Prep paraphrases: This experiment investigates the relevance of verb+prep paraphrases (e.g. *'held during'*) over preposition and verb paraphrases. We have discussed that these paraphrases are splitted into preposition (i.e. *'during'*) and verb (*'hold'*) and contribute to the frequencies of corresponding features in preposition and verb vector, with respective weighting factors S_p and S_v, referred as the Strength parameters. Thus, a higher value of S_p and S_v means greater contribution of verb+preposition paraphrases in the classification model. The Strength parameters in Experiment I were fixed to $S_p = 1$ and $S_v = 1$ but are varied in this experiment from values 1 to 15.

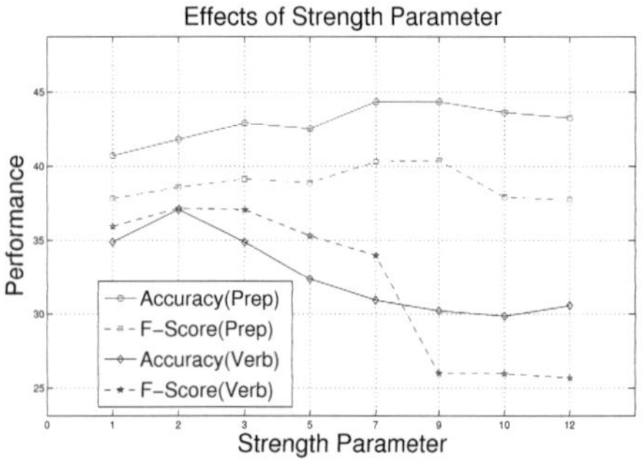

Figure 2: Performance of Preposition and Verb models on varying the Strength parameters S_p and S_v

The effects of Strength parameter on the preposition and the verb models on SemEval dataset are shown in Figure 2. The performance of prepositional model improves drastically (Acc, F) from (40.72%, 38.82%) to (44.36%, 40.39%) between values 1 to 9 (~4% improvement in accuracy and ~2.5% in f-score) and then drops down. The verb vector achieves best results at $S_v = 2$. This proves two things: First, verb+prep paraphrases have crucial contribution in the model and thus, finding such paraphrases in corpus is important, and secondly, the high value of $S_p = 9$ reveals that prepositions in verb+prep paraphrases are in fact quite relevant.

Experiment III: Integrating the Preposition and Verb models: In this experiment, we compare the Concatenation model and Best-Selection model for integrating the Prepositional and Verbal models. The experiment is performed on optimal parameters learnt from previous experiments, i.e. *Model 6* with $S_p = 9$ and $S_v = 2$ at $k = N - 1$. The Concatenation model concatenates the preposition and the verb feature vectors to form a single vector, with Contribution factor f varying from 0 to 2 in steps of 0.2. The Best-Selection model evaluates the performance of each relation on both the models and given a unseen instance, selects the model which classifies the relation with higher $f - score$.

The concatenation of prepositional and verbal features in the Concatenation model degrades the performance at every contribution factor f, achieving the best accuracy of only 36.72% with 35.16% f-score when both vectors are equally weighted at $f = 1$, shown in Figure 3. This shows that the significance of preposition features is diluted by the less significant verb features. On the other hand, the performance with Best-Selection model shoots up, which achieves accuracy of 46% with drastic improvement of ~ 7 in f-score, reaching 47.19%.

5.6 Observations

The Best-Selection model integrating the prepositional model and verbal model is selected as the best Statistical model, with optimal parameters $S_p = 9$ and $S_v = 2$ at fold $k = N - 1$. It uses Weighted Relation vector incorporating Prior probability [+R +W +P] for both preposition and verb feature vectors. This model achieves 46.04% accuracy (baseline 30.5%) and 47.19% f-score on SemEval dataset and hugely outperforms the ontology model, which performs just above the baseline achieving accuracy of only 34.53% and f-score of 36.56%.

The corpus model performs below the expectations on Nastase dataset, with performance subpar to the ontology model, achieving accuracy of 52.3% (~2% less than ontology model) with low f-score of 35.1%. The main reason for this is the insuffi-

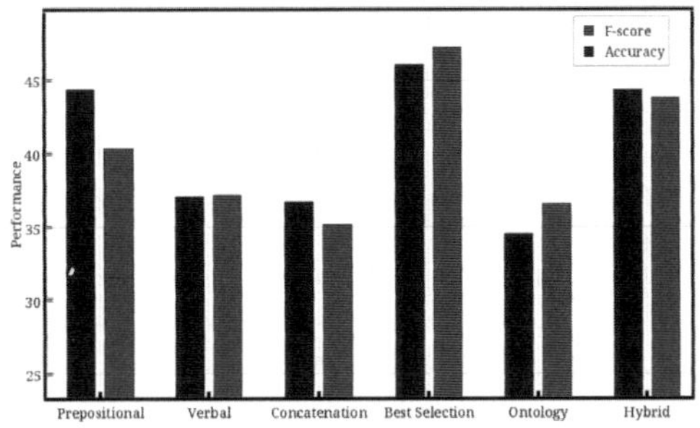

Figure 3: Comparison of All Models on SemEval Data

cient and poor quality of paraphrases obtained from the corpus, mainly verb and verb+preposition paraphrases, which are nowhere close to the human annotated paraphrases. We have selected only those NCs for the experiments for which atleast 3 paraphrases are found. Thus, experiment is performed with 241 NCs (out of 326 Noun-Noun pairs) for which this criteria is satisfied. An interesting property of the Relation vector is that it maps the lexical terms (*i.e. prepositions and verbs*) to semantic relations, and ranks them in decreasing order of their co-occurence with the relation. Table 7 presents the *five* top weighted prepositions for each relation.

Relation	Examples	Top-5 Prepositions
Causal	*advertisement agency, cancer death*	for, with, against, from, on
Quality	*trade statistics, wafer buscuit*	like, about, as, of, on
Spatial	*garden party, village school*	towards, near, at, in, around
Temporal	*spring weather, summer meeting*	during, after, in, at, from
Participant	*army coup, class party*	by, from, of, in, for

Table 7: Top-5 Relevant prepositions for each relation

6 Hybrid Model

The goal of the Hybrid model is to integrate knowledge of two very different models: one using the knowledge from a ontology while other deriving it from a corpus. The model employs a Best-Selection strategy which does nothing more than selecting the more suitable model for classification for any given test instance. Therefore, for the model to be efficient, it must satisfy two conditions:

a) The constituent models must be complimenting.

b) The model must have a selection criteria that works efficient in different circumstances. We find the two models to be complementing as the statistical model identifies some relations more accurately than ontology model and vice-versa, as discussed in Section 4.2. Further, we find that the performance of ontology model improves with each level of specialization (in Table 2). This insight is useful in implementing the selection criteria. The model computes a *Preference Score, P* for each model and selects the model with higher score for classifying the unseen instance. For ontology model, the *f-score* of each relation, r_i at each boundary level G_k is evaluated. Similarly, the *f-score* of each relation, r_i is evaluated for corpus model. Now, given a unseen instance, the following decision is taken:

$$P^{Ont}(r_1)^X > P^{Cor}(r_2), \quad then\ R^* = r_1; \quad else\ R^* = r_2 \tag{5}$$

where $P^{Ont}(r_1)^{G_k}$ is the f-score of relation r_1 at boundary level G_k and R^* is the assigned relation.

The Hybrid model on the data of 241 NCs (on which corpus model is evaluated) performs quite well and outperforms the ontology and corpus models by 4.5% and 6.5% respectively, as shown in Table 8. These results are slightly better than the state-of-the-art system tested on this dataset (Turney, 2006b) but are below when compared on complete dataset of 593 NCs (out of which 352 NCs use only ontology model). The overall performance on Nastase dataset of 593 NCs achieves 55.31% accuracy with 49.47% f-score. On SemEval dataset, the performance of statistical model drops by ~2% when integrated with ontology model, which performs poorly on this dataset, as shown in Figure 3.

Relation	Ontology (593 NC)	Corpus (241 NC)	Hybrid (241 NC)	Hybrid (593 NC)
Quality	45	39.18	49.59	49.59
Temporal	78.26	55.81	75	75
Spatial	29.41	14.81	35.71	35.71
Participant	64.6	65.72	67.78	67.78
Causal	29.09	0	34.78	34.78
Macro-Avg F	49.27	35.11	52.57	52.57
Accuracy	54.35	52.28	58.92	55.31

Table 8: Comparison of Models on Nastase Dataset

7 Conclusion

This paper presents a Statistical VSM-based model which represents each relation with a vector of prepositional and verbal paraphrases. The statistical model needs to solve two problems: **(i)** Identifying which paraphrases are relevant in disambiguating the relations, which is challenging (Nastase et al., 2006; Nulty, 2007); and **(ii)** Finding those paraphrases in corpus for given NC is hard (Surtani et al., 2013). We work extensively to improve on the first part of the problem, but we fail in finding good set of paraphrases from the corpus. The statistical model has shown huge potential over the ontology model (which also requires WordNet senses of modifier & head, a challenging task (WSD)). The future task is to achieve a better Paraphrase Extraction system.

References

Barbara Rosario and Marti Hearst. 2001. *Classifying the semantic relations in noun compounds via a domain-specific lexical hierarchy*. In Proceedings of the 2001 Conference on Empirical Methods in Natural Language Processing (EMNLP-01).

Brandon Beamer, Alla Rozovskaya and Roxana Girju. 2008. *Automatic Semantic Relation Extraction with Multiple Boundary Generation*. In AAAI (pp 824-829).

Cristina Butnariu and Tony Veale. 2008. *A concept-centered approach to noun-compound interpretation*. Proceedings of the 22nd International Conference on Computational Linguistics-Volume 1. Association for Computational Linguistics.

Cristina Butnariu, Su Nam Kim, Preslav Nakov, Diarmuid O Séaghdha, Stan Szpakowicz and Tony Veale. 2010. *Semeval-2 task 9: The interpretation of noun compounds using paraphrasing verbs and prepositions*. In Proceedings of the 5th SIGLEX Workshop on Semantic Evaluation.

Cristina Butnariu, Su Nam Kim, Preslav Nakov, Diarmuid O Séaghdha, Stan Szpakowicz and Tony Veale. 2013. *Semeval-13 task 4: Free Paraphrases of Noun Compounds*. In Proceedings of the International Workshop on Semantic Evaluation, Atlanta, Georgia.

Dan Moldovan, Adriana Badulescu, Marta Tatu, Daniel Antohe and Roxana Girju. 2004. *Models for the Semantic Classification of Noun Phrases*. In the proceedings of the HLT/NAACL Workshop on Computational Lexical Semantics . Boston, MA.

Diarmuid O Séaghdha. 2008. *Learning compound noun semantics*. University of Cambridge, Cambridge, UK.

Marti Hearst. 1998. *Automated discovery of WordNet relations*. WordNet: an electronic lexical database, 131-151.

Nitesh Surtani, Arpita Batra, Urmi Ghosh and Soma Paul. 2013. *IIITH: A Corpus-Driven Co-occurrence Based Probabilistic Model for Noun Compound Paraphrasing*. In Proceedings of the International Workshop on Semantic Evaluation, Atlanta, Georgia.

Olutobi Owoputi, Brendan O Connor, Chris Dyer, Kevin Gimpel, Nathan Schneider and Noah A. Smith 2013. *Improved Part-of-Speech Tagging for Online Conversational Text with Word Clusters*. HLT-NAACL.

Pamela Downing. 1977. On the creation and use of English noun compounds. *Language*, 53(4): 810-842.

Paul Nulty. 2007. *Semantic classification of noun phrases using web counts and learning algorithms*. In Proceedings of the ACL 2007 Student Research Workshop (ACL-07), pages 79-84.

Peter D Turney and Michael L. Littman. 2005. *Corpus-based learning of analogies and semantic relations*. Machine Learning, 60(1-3):251-278.

Peter D Turney. 2006. *Expressing implicit semantic relations without supervision*. In Proceedings of the 21st International Conference on Computational Linguistics and 44th Annual Meeting of the Association for Computational Linguistics (Coling/ACL-06), Sydney, Australia.

Peter D Turney. 2006. *Similarity of semantic relations*. Computational Linguistics, 32 (3), 379-416.

Preslav Nakov and and Marti Hearst. 2006. *Using verbs to characterize noun-noun relations*. Artificial Intelligence: Methodology, Systems, and Applications. Springer Berlin Heidelberg.

Preslav Nakov. 2008. *Noun compound interpretation using paraphrasing verbs: Feasibility study*. Artificial Intelligence: Methodology, Systems, and Applications. Springer Berlin Heidelberg, 2008. 103-117.

Roxana Girju, Adriana Badulescu and Dan Moldovan. 2003. *Learning Semantic Constraints for the Automatic Discovery of Part-Whole Relations*. Proceedings of the 2003 Conference of the North American Chapter of the Association for Computational Linguistics on Human Language Technology-Volume 1. Association for Computational Linguistics.

Roxana Girju, Dan Moldovan, Marta Tatu and Daniel Antohe. 2005. *On the semantics of noun compounds*. Computer, Speech and Language 19(4):479-496.

Roxana Girju, Adriana Badulescu and Dan Moldovan. 2006. *Automatic Discovery of Part-Whole Relations*. In Computational Linguistics.

Roxana Girju, Preslav Nakov, Vivi Nastase, Stan Szpakowicz, Peter D. Turney, Deniz Yuret. 2007. *Semeval-2007 task 04: Classification of semantic relations between nominals.*. In Proceedings of the 4th International Workshop on Semantic Evaluations (pp. 13-18). Association for Computational Linguistics.

Satanjeev Banerjee, Ted Pedersen. 2002. *An Adapted Lesk Algorithm for Word Sense Disambiguation using WordNet - In the Proceedings of the Third International Conference on Intelligent Text Processing and Computational Linguistics, pp.* 136-145, Mexico City.

Su Nam Kim and Timothy Baldwin. 2006. *Interpreting semantic relations in noun compounds via verb semantics*. Proc. ACL-06 Main Conference Poster Session, Sydney, Australia, 491-498.

Stephen Tratz and Eduard Hovy. 2010. *A taxonomy, dataset, and classifier for automatic noun compound interpretation*. In Proceedings of the 48th Annual Meeting of the Association for Computational Linguistics. Association for Computational Linguistics.

Thorsten Brants, Alex Franz. 2006. *Web 1T 5-gram Version1*. Linguistic Data Consortium.

Timothy Baldwin and Takaaki Tanaka. 2004. *Translation by machine of compound nominals: Getting it right*. In Proceedings of ACL-2004 Workshop on Multiword Expressions: Integrating Processing.

Vivek Srikumar and Dan Roth. 2013. *Modeling semantic relations expressed by prepositions*. Transactions of Association of Computational Linguistics.

Vivi Nastase and Stan Szpakowicz. 2003. *Exploring noun-modifier semantic relations*. In Fifth International Workshop on Computational Semantics (IWCS-5), pages 285-301, Tilburg, The Netherlands.

Vivi Nastase, Jelber Sayyad Shirabad, Marina Sokolova and Stan Szpakowicz. 2006. *Learning noun-modifier semantic relations with corpus-based and Wordnet-based features*. In Proceedings of the 21st National Conference on Artificial Intelligence (AAAI-06), pages 781-787.

Vivi Nastase, Preslav Nakov, Diarmuid O Séaghdha and Stan Szpakowicz. 2014. *Semantic Relations between Nominals*.

An LDA-based Topic Selection Approach to Language Model Adaptation for Handwritten Text Recognition

Jafar Tanha, Jesse de Does and Katrien Depuydt
Institute for Dutch Lexicology (INL)
jafar.tanha.pnu@gmail.com, {jesse.dedoes, katrien.depuydt}@inl.nl

Abstract

Typically, only a very limited amount of in-domain data is available for training the language model component of an Handwritten Text Recognition (HTR) system for historical data. One has to rely on a combination of in-domain and out-of-domain data to develop language models. Accordingly, domain adaptation is a central issue in language modeling for HTR. We pursue a topic modeling approach to handle this issue, and propose two algorithms based on this approach. The first algorithm relies on posterior inference for topic modeling to construct a language model adapted to the development set, and the second algorithm proceeds by iterative selection, using a new ranking criterion, of topic-dependent language models. Our experimental results show that both approaches clearly outperform a strong baseline method.

1 Introduction

Huge amounts of handwritten historical documents are nowadays being published by on-line digital libraries as document images. The content of these documents is of great interest to historians, linguists and literary scholars alike. However, if the transcription of the documents is not available for information retrieval, we can hardly consider this content to be accessible for research. Full manual transcription is slow and costly, but the development of efficient and cost-effective approaches for the indexing, search and full transcription of historical handwritten document images can benefit from modern Handwritten Text Recognition (HTR) technology (Sánchez et al., 2013).

An indispensable component of state-of-the-art HTR is language modeling (Plötz and Fink, 2009) (Espana-Boquera et al., 2011), which is necessary to guide the decoding process by ranking and constraining the possible recognition hypotheses. Language modeling has proven extremely successful in improving results of Automatic Speech Recognition (Chelba et al., 2012), which is a very similar task from the technical point of view. Highly effective language models in this field have been developed from huge language corpora. cf. for instance (Chelba et al., 2012). Language models are usually constructed from large text corpora which – ideally – are *in-domain*, linguistically close to the language of the document collection which is being processed. However, for HTR of historical documents, obtaining effective models is much less straightforward: models built from the strictly in-domain data are generally unsatisfactory because not enough data can be obtained to avoid overfitting, and in order to exploit the larger pool of out-domain data one has to surmount two difficulties: (1) indiscriminate use of *out-of-domain* data may not benefit, in fact even deteriorate system performance and (2) the use of the complete out-domain data for training may increase the complexity of the system, making the decoding process almost untractable (Axelrod et al., 2011; Tanha et al., 2014).

The above-mentioned issues are typically dealt with by using *domain adaptation* techniques (Axelrod et al., 2011) (Foster et al., 2010) (Jiang and Zhai, 2007), which aim to leverage the knowledge that can be obtained from the out-of-domain data by tuning it to the in-domain data.

In this paper, we study the application of topic modeling-based approaches to the task of improving the language modeling component of the HTR system by domain adaptation. Our approach is characterized by the combination of the topic modeling approach with *intelligent sample selection* methods. We first propose a Latent Dirichlet Allocation (LDA)-based language model adap-

Proceedings of Recent Advances in Natural Language Processing, pages 646–653,
Hissar, Bulgaria, Sep 7–9 2015.

tation framework (Blei et al., 2003). We then develop an algorithm for language model adaptation using the result of topic modeling and a new language model ranking criterion to select the most relevant topics. In our experiments, we use the TRANSCRIPTORIUM HTR engine described in (Sánchez et al., 2013) on a set of digitised images of manuscripts written by the 18th and early 19th-century British philosopher Jeremy Bentham[1]. We show that our techniques improve the performance of the HTR system. Besides producing an adapted language model, the proposed methods also reduce the computational resources needed to exploit a large amount of out-domain data in the decoding process of the HTR system.

The rest of the paper is organised as follows. We refer the reader to related work in section 2. Our approaches to sample selection are described in detail in section 3 and evaluated in section 4. Results are reported in section 5. Section 6 addresses the discussion and conclusion.

2 Related Work

Statistical language models assign probabilities to sequences of words. Typically, the probability of a word is estimated on the basis of a limited history, consisting of some fixed number n of preceding words. This has the drawback that long-range dependencies cannot be exploited. Several approaches have been proposed to overcome this problem, such as Cache-based (Kuhn and De Mori, 1990) or Trigger-based (Lau et al., 1993) language models.

Taking into account that a language model built for domain-specific data can give low perplexity, topic modeling can be a promising approach for language model adaptation. A language model training corpus may contain many topics. As a result, the corpus can be divided into topic-specific subcorpora. The distribution of topics in the corpus may be determined manually, or by automatic, unsupervised techniques. A practical approach to language modeling will have to rely on the latter approach.

The leading paradigm in unsupervised topic modeling is Latent Dirichlet Allocation (LDA) (Blei et al., 2003). LDA and similar approaches can be used for the language model adaptation problem. There are several studies for language model adaptation using LDA models. In (Liu and Liu, 2008) a new mixture topic model is proposed for LDA based language model adaptation. Hsu *et al.* (2006) proposed a method for adaptation using hidden Markov model with LDA model. In (Eidelman et al., 2012) LDA model is used to compute topic-dependent lexical weighting probabilities for domain adaptation. Iyer *et al.* (1996) used a clustering approach to build topic clusters for language model adaptation. In (Bellegarda, 2000) Latent Semantic Analysis is applied to map documents into a topic space for language model adaptation. Gildea *et al.* (1999) proposed a language model adaptation approach using the probabilistic extension of LSA (pLSA). In (Tam and Schultz, 2005), an LDA model is applied to language model adaptation. This method interpolates the background language model with the dynamic unigram language model generated by the LDA model. Heidel *et al.* (2007) applied an LDA-based topic inference approach to language model adaptation.

As mentioned in the introduction, the main characteristic of our approach is that we use topic modeling in conjunction with *Intelligent sample selection* techniques. Unlike current approaches, like (Liu and Liu, 2008) (Eidelman et al., 2012), which use all documents of each topic for adaptation, we select the most relevant resources. In this way, language model adaptation yields a model that matches better to the domain, but also reduces the computational complexity of the HTR system by producing more compact language models.

More specifically, we propose an iterative approach to language model adaptation using LDA modeling. Since perplexity does not always correlate well to the recognition accuracy of the HTR system, we use a new criterion for related topic selection using the combination of the perplexity and the size of out of vocabulary of the documents. We then use a topic mixture approach for language model adaptation.

3 Topic Modeling for Language Model Adaptation

We first briefly review the Latent Dirichlet Allocation (LDA) framework. We then formulate the problem and introduce the proposed methods to language model adaption for improving the performance of the HTR system.

[1]Images and transcriptions have been produced in the *Transcribe Bentham* project (Moyle et al., 2011), http://www.ucl.ac.uk/transcribe-bentham

3.1 LDA Models and Language Model Adaptation

The frequency distribution of words in text is highly dependent on the "topic" of the text. A topic model captures this intuition in a mathematical framework, and allows discovering a set of topics from a collection of documents. Blei *et al.* (2003) introduced a new approach, Latent Dirichlet Allocation (LDA). LDA is a generative approach characterized by the topic-word distribution ϕ and the topic distribution θ for each document. This method imposes a Dirichlet distribution on the topic mixture weights corresponding to the documents in the corpus. Figure 1 shows the graphical representation of the LDA model, where α is the parameter of the Dirichlet prior on the per-document topic distribution, D is the number of documents, β is the parameter of the Dirichlet prior on the per-topic word distribution, θ_d is the topic distribution for document d, N is the number of words in document d $z_{d,n}$ is the topic for the dth word in document n, and $w_{d,n}$ is the specific word.

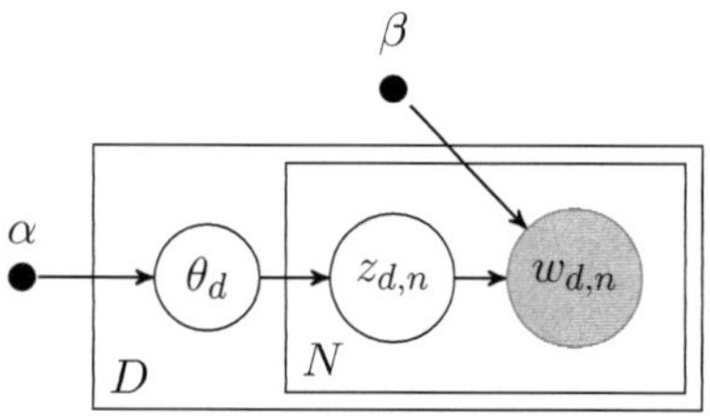

Figure 1: The graphical representation of LDA.

In order to apply topic-based language modeling, we need to be able to determine the topic distribution for an unseen document (topic inference). We use the collapsed variational inference method (CVB) for LDA (Mukherjee and Blei, 2009) in our experiments.

3.2 Problem Formulation

In this paper, we use topic modeling to identify relevant resources for language model adaptation. We assume a partition ($\mathcal{B}_0$, $\mathcal{B}_1$) of the in-domain corpus $\mathcal{B}$, see Figure 2. In the setting of handwritten text recognition, $\mathcal{B}_0$ could for instance be the HTR training set or some other portion of a transcribed corpus, and $\mathcal{B}_1$ is the rest of the text. We then use $\mathcal{E}$ corpus as a general large out-of-domain corpus. Our goal here is to find an informative subset $\mathcal{E}_1$ of resources from the $\mathcal{E}$ corpus, which is relevant to the $\mathcal{B}_0$ collection, and to exploit this for domain adaptation.

The adapted language model can be then obtained as follows: for a word sequence W, let

$$P(W) = \lambda_{\mathcal{B}_0} P_{\mathcal{B}_0}(W) + \lambda_{\mathcal{B}_1} P_{\mathcal{B}_1}(W) + \lambda_{\mathcal{E}_1} P_{\mathcal{E}_1}(W) \quad (1)$$

where $\lambda_{\mathcal{B}_0}$, $\lambda_{\mathcal{B}_1}$ and $\lambda_{\mathcal{E}_1}$ are interpolation weights. We use the *SRILM* toolkit (Stolcke et al., 2011) to find the optimal values for the weights in equation (1).

In (1) the third term is the resulting adapted language model, which we formulate as:

$$P_{\mathcal{E}_1}(W) = \Sigma_{i=1}^{K'} \gamma_i P_{z_j}(w_i | w_{i-1}^{i-n+1}) \quad (2)$$

where γ_i is the mixture weight and K' is the number of relevant topics to the domain ($K' \ll K$). Based on this formulation, we propose two algorithms to handle the equation (2).

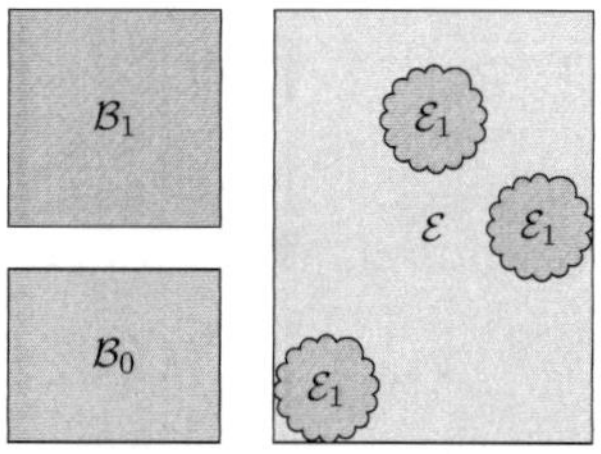

Figure 2: Resource situation consisting of in-domain corpora $\mathcal{B}_0$ and $\mathcal{B}_1$ and out-of-domain corpus $\mathcal{E}$. The aim of intelligent sample selection is to pick out the informative bits $\mathcal{E}_1$ from $\mathcal{E}$.

3.3 LDA Inference for LM Adaptation

We first introduce an unsupervised language model adaptation method using posterior inference for LDA, which we call *Inference-Based Topic Selection*. In accordance with the sample selection approach, the goal is to pick the most relevant documents to in-domain data from the out-of-domain corpus. We start by applying LDA to the $\mathcal{E}$ corpus to construct a model with N topics, and we select, for each topic found, the set of most relevant (high-confidence) documents from $\mathcal{E}$. Next, the topic model is used to inference the topic distribution of the development set ($\mathcal{B}_0$). Finally, based on the distribution found in the development set, the algorithm selects the most relevant topics. The sets of all high-confidence documents from the selected topics are then used to train language models, and the interpolation of the resulting language models will be the output of the proposed algorithm. The pseudo-code of the Inference-Based Topic-Selection algorithm is presented in Algorithm 1. In the experiment section, we will describe the tuning parameters of the algorithm for improving the HTR system.

Algorithm 1 Inference-Based Topic-Selection

```
Initialize:
ℰ: out-domain data; conf ← 0; // A pre-defined threshold for confidence measure;
θ ← Threshold for Topic Selection; N ← Identify maximum number of topics;
TopicModel ← {Make a topic model with N topics for ℰ resources using LDA model };
for each T_i ∈ TopicModel do
    if ( probability of d_j ∈ T_i is greater than conf ) then
        D_i ← D_i + d_j;
    end if
end for
DocSet ← {D_i | D_i is more relevant document for topic T_i }
DevelopmentSetTopics ← Infer Topics for Development set using the resulting TopicModel;
for each t_i ∈ DevelopmentSetTopics do
    if probability of t_i is greater than θ then
        BestTopicSet ← BestTopicSet + {t_i ∈ TopicModel};
    end if
end for
Build LM_i for each t_i ∈ BestTopicSet;
InterpolatedLMs ← Σ_i λ_i LM_i;
Output:
    InterpolatedLMs and BestTopicSet;
```

3.4 Iterative Topic Selection for Language Model Adaptation

We present an iterative algorithm, *Iterative Topic-Selection*, for topic selection based on a new ranking criterion. As described in Section 3.3, first the algorithm builds a topic model for the $\mathcal{E}$ corpus. Then for each topic, we construct a language model. The resulting language models are evaluated against the development dataset. Since comparing and ranking different resources by the usual perplexity-related criteria alone is much less appropriate (Moore and Lewis, 2010; Axelrod et al., 2011; Tanha et al., 2014), we use a new criterion for related topic selection in terms of the perplexity and out-of-vocabulary (OOV) word rate in the following section. Note that, as mentioned in Section 3.3, we do not use all topics for language model adaptation, but only the most relevant ones.

Next, the algorithm ranks the resulting language model of each topic using the new criterion. The language models of the related topics are then interpolated until some stopping condition is reached. Algorithm 2 shows the pseudo-code of the proposed algorithm. Finally, the interpolated language model is returned as the adapted language model, which can be used in (1).

Algorithm 2 Iterative Topic-Selection

```
Initialize:
ℰ: out-domain data; conf ← 0; // A pre-defined threshold for confidence measure;
θ ← Threshold for Topic Selection; N ← Identify maximum number of topics;
TopicModel ← {Make a topic model with N topics for ℰ resources using LDA model };
for each T_i ∈ TopicModel do
    if ( probability of d_j ∈ T_i is greater than conf ) then
        D_i ← D_i + d_j;
    end if
end for
DocSet ← {D_i | D_i is more relevant document for topic T_i }
for each D_i ∈ DocSet do
    LM_i ← Train a Language Model for D_i;
    EvalSet_i ← Evaluate LM_i using a development set;
    RankSet_i ← Assign ranks to the evaluated sets using (3);
end for
BestRank ← Find the best rank based on the ranking criterion;
BestTopicSet ← Find the best topic based on the ranking criterion;
while ( TopicSet ) do
    Interpolate the related LMs T_i and T_BestRank, where T_i is the second best related topic;
    New_rank ← Compute new rank for the interpolated LM;
    if (New_rank < BestRank) then
        BestTopicSet ← BestTopicSet + T_i;
        BestRank ← New_rank;
    else
        Break;
    end if
end while
Output:
    Adapted Language model and RelatedTopics;
```

3.5 Ranking based on Out-of-vocabulary and Perplexity

Algorithm 2 first builds a language model for each topic, and subsequently assumes that the resulting language models can to be ranked in an appropriate way. Current approaches to rank language models use perplexity as a criterion (Moore and Lewis, 2010). However, perplexity as a criterion is unreliable when the text contains more than a small portion of OOV words (Tanha et al., 2014).

Let $|\mathcal{V}|$ be the number of running words (i.e. tokens) of in the evaluation data, $|OOV|$ be the number of running out-of-vocabulary words, and PPL denote the perplexity. We use the following ranking function combining OOV rate and perplexity:

$$Rank(LM_i) = \log PPL \times \frac{|OOV|}{|\mathcal{V}|} \quad (3)$$

We apply this *Multiplicative* ranking function to rank resources for sample selection in algorithm 2.

4 Experiments

In this section we perform several experiments on linguistic resources to show the effect of the proposed methods for language model adaption on the HTR system. In order to evaluate the proposed methods, it is important to compare them to a strong baseline, in our case a well-tuned linear interpolation of in-domain and out-of-domain language models.

4.1 Dataset

We make use of the English-language data processed in the TRANSCRIPTORIUM (Sánchez et al., 2013) project for the evaluation of HTR performance. This collection consists of a set of images and with ground truth transcriptions of Bentham manuscripts. Part of the ground truth transcriptions is used for language modeling, a held-out set is used for testing HTR. In addition to this, we use the corpus of all transcribed Bentham manuscripts (about 15.000 pages and 5m words), as obtained from the *Transcribe Bentham* project (Moyle et al., 2011), and the public part of the ECCO (*Eighteenth Century Collections Online*[2]), about 70m words.

With these two corpora, we make a two-level in-domain/out-domain distinction: The ECCO corpus is considered as a general out-of-domain resource. Within the set of Bentham transcriptions, we distinguish the set of *Batch 1 ground truth transcriptions* as an in-domain resource and the rest of the available transcriptions as Bentham out-of-domain.

In the experiments, we use a separate development set for tuning parameters of the proposed methods and a separate test set for evaluating the HTR system, consisting of the held-out data from the "Batch 1" set.

4.2 Experimental Setup

We perform the following experiments to evaluate the baseline methods and the proposed Inference-Based Topic-Selection and Iterative Topic-Selection algorithms.

[2]http://www.textcreationpartnership.org/tcp-ecco/

Baseline: Language model interpolation Our first set of experiments is about finding an optimal way to combine in-domain and out-of domain resources by language model interpolation. We explore the effect of tuning language model interpolation parameters and HTR dictionary selection settings on the performance of the HTR system. We have applied the following scenarios in our experiments:

1. Combining two Bentham resources ($\mathcal{B}_0$ and $\mathcal{B}_1$) and using a dictionary from the merged data to train the language model (*Merged-InOut-Dic-InOut*).
2. Interpolating Bentham $\mathcal{B}_0$ and $\mathcal{B}_1$ resources using a HTR dictionary from both $\mathcal{B}_0$ and $\mathcal{B}_1$ domain data (*Inter-InOut-Dic-InOut*).
3. Interpolating Bentham $\mathcal{B}_0$ and $\mathcal{B}_1$ resources with the ECCO collection using the dictionary from Bentham $\mathcal{B}_0$ and $\mathcal{B}_1$ data (*Inter-InOutECCO-Dic-InOut*).
4. Interpolating the Bentham $\mathcal{B}_0$ and $\mathcal{B}_1$ resources with ECCO collection using dictionary from all of them (*Inter-InOutECCO-Dic-InOutECCO*).

Inference-Based Topic-Selection We perform several experiments with different numbers of topics and different values for the θ threshold.

Iterative Topic-Selection The following scenarios are used for the Iterative Topic-Selection algorithm:

Single Iteration (Best Topic): In this scenario, a single iteration of the algorithm is used to select the most relevant topic. The selected set is then used to build a language model. We vary the number of topics and the threshold for document selection.

Multiple Iterations: In this scenario, the algorithms perform several iterations. At each iteration the resulting best-fitted language model is interpolated with the last language model.

5 Results

We have considered three main evaluation criteria for each experiment, the general word error rate (WER), the word error rate without taking the first word of each line into account[3], and the character error rate (CER).

[3]Current HTR is line-based, which means that language modeling fails at the line boundaries, most notably for hyphenated words.

Method	WER %	WER without first word	CER %	OOV %	Size of model (1-grams,2-grams)
Initial model using only Batch 1 training set	34.5	34.3	19.9	9.44	(1894 , 6641)
Merged-InOut-Dic-InOut	34.01	-	-	-	(13211 , 808724)
Inter-InOut-Dic-InOut	30.02	24.57	-	-	(12966, 795029)
Inter-In+OutECCO-Dic-InOutECCO	31.7	26	16.5	-	(12966 , 2817124)
Inter-InOutECCO-Dic-InOut	30.7	25.3	15.9	-	(12966, 2833622)
Inter-InOutECCO-Dic-InOutECCO	**28.3**	22.7	14.7	5.4	**(64416, 5811657)**

Table 1: The results of the baseline methods for HTR system

Number of Topics			WER%	WER without first word	CER%	Size of model (1-grams,2-grams)
#Topics	Threshold for document selection	θ				
30	0.3	0.2	27.4	22.0	14.4	(51682, 1281779)
30	0.8	0.2	27.4	22.0	-	(40010, 984660)
40	0.4	0.1	**27.3**	22.0	14.4	**(55054, 1073172)**
50	0.7	0.2	27.5	22.1	-	(41091, 996482)
70	0.2	0.2	27.4	22.1	-	(41476, 1005868)
70	0.2	0.1	27.4	22.1	-	(49755, 132526)
100	0.2	0.1	27.3	22.0	-	(56533, 1312630)

Table 2: The results of Inference Best-Topic approach

Number of Topics		WER %	WER without first word	CER%	Size of model (1-grams,2-grams)
#Topics	Threshold for document selection				
10	0.5	27.2	21.9	14.3	(63379, 1595014)
10	0.8	27.2	21.7	-	(47839, 1345021)
20	0.3	27.5	22.1	-	(54626, 1355764)
40	0.3	27.3	21.9	-	(46880, 1164894)
40	0.4	**27.2**	21.8	14.3	**(46227, 1180713)**
50	0.3	27.3	22.0	-	(49517, 1286652)
50	0.4	27.3	21.9	-	(53761, 1187976)
100	0.3	27.6	22.2	-	(51512, 1457114)

Table 3: The results of the Best-Topic approach

Number of Topics		WER %	WER without first word	CER%	Size of model
#Topics	Threshold for document selection				
10	0.9	27.3	22.0	14.4	(64034, 1439691)
15	0.9	27.8	22.5	-	(53159, 1605800)
20	0.9	27.3	22.0	-	(63113, 1355451)
30	0.9	27.4	22.0	-	(58891, 1235159)
40	0.9	27.4	22.0	-	(48768, 1078245)
50	0.5	**27.2**	21.9	14.3	**(61682, 1567515)**
50	0.9	27.3	21.9	-	(56580, 1100616)
70	0.8	27.4	22.0	-	(52146, 1154698)
100	0.3	27.6	22.2	-	(65343, 1455298)

Table 4: The results of the Iterative Best-Topic approach

In the first experiment we also include the size of OOV sets. In each table the best results have been boldfaced.

Table 1 shows the results of interpolating the language model from Bentham in-domain data with the language models from the Bentham out-of-domain and ECCO resources. This procedure improves the performance of the HTR system by 6.2%. In other words, these results emphasize that the out-of-domain data contains useful information.

Table 2 shows the performance of the HTR system using the proposed Inference Best-Topic algorithm. In Table 2 the first column shows the number of topics identified. The second and third columns are the threshold for document selection for each topic and the threshold for the related topic selection respectively. The Inference Best-Topic algorithm performs better than the baseline methods in most of the cases. Furthermore, the resulting language model is much more compact than the baseline model.

We continue with the experiments for the *Iterative Topic-Selection* algorithm. In the first experiment, the *Iterative Topic-Selection* algorithm (single iteration) finds the most relevant language model for adaptation. Table 3 shows the results of this experiment.

The Iterative Topic-Selection algorithm (multiple iterations) deploys the interpolation of the most relevant language models. The results have been reported in Table 4. The results of both experiments emphasize that the proposed methods for language model adaptation outperform the baseline and produce a more domain-specific language model.

6 Conclusion

We have studied and tested several ways in which domain adapted language modeling can improve hand-written text recognition results, when the resulting language models are deployed in the TRANSCRIPTORIUM HTR system. Our methods for the combination of in-domain and out-of domain data have been shown to yield improvement in HTR results, both using established techniques (model interpolation) and novel approaches for language model adaptation. Consistent to our hypothesis, the proposed methods outperform the baseline, both in terms of HTR accuracy and in terms of model complexity. The experimental results show that our proposed approaches for domain adaptation can effectively exploit informative data from the out of domain data and improve the recognition performance of the HTR system significantly.

Acknowledgment

The research leading to these results has received funding from the European Union's Seventh Framework Programme (FP7/2007-2013) under grant agreement no. 600707 - tranScriptorium.

References

Amittai Axelrod, Xiaodong He, and Jianfeng Gao. 2011. Domain adaptation via pseudo in-domain data selection. In *Proceedings of the Conference on Empirical Methods in Natural Language Processing*, pages 355–362. ACL.

J.R. Bellegarda. 2000. Exploiting latent semantic information in statistical language modeling. *Proceedings of the IEEE*, 88(8):1279–1296, Aug.

David M Blei, Andrew Y Ng, and Michael I Jordan. 2003. Latent dirichlet allocation. *the Journal of machine Learning research*, 3:993–1022.

Ciprian Chelba, Dan Bikel, Maria Shugrina, Patrick Nguyen, and Shankar Kumar. 2012. Large scale language modeling in automatic speech recognition. Technical report, Google.

Vladimir Eidelman, Jordan Boyd-Graber, and Philip Resnik. 2012. Topic models for dynamic translation model adaptation. In *Proceedings of the 50th Annual Meeting of the ACL: Short Papers-Volume 2*, pages 115–119. ACL.

Salvador Espana-Boquera, Maria Jose Castro-Bleda, Jorge Gorbe-Moya, and Francisco Zamora-Martinez. 2011. Improving offline handwritten text recognition with hybrid hmm/ann models. *PAMI, IEEE Transactions on*, 33(4):767–779.

George Foster, Cyril Goutte, and Roland Kuhn. 2010. Discriminative instance weighting for domain adaptation in statistical machine translation. In *Proceedings of the 2010 Conference on EMNLP*, pages 451–459.

Jing Jiang and ChengXiang Zhai. 2007. Instance weighting for domain adaptation in nlp. In *ACL*, volume 2007, page 22.

R. Kuhn and R. De Mori. 1990. A cache-based natural language model for speech recognition. *IEEE Trans. PAMI*, 12(6):570–583, June.

R. Lau, R. Rosenfeld, and S. Roukos. 1993. Trigger-based language models: A maximum entropy approach. In *Proceedings IEEE International Conference on Acoustics, Speech and Signal Processing*, volume 2, pages 45–48, Minneapolis MN.

Yang Liu and Feifan Liu. 2008. Unsupervised language model adaptation via topic modeling based on named entity hypotheses. In *Acoustics, Speech and Signal Processing, ICASSP*, pages 4921–4924. IEEE.

Robert C Moore and William Lewis. 2010. Intelligent selection of language model training data. In *Proceedings of the ACL 2010 Conference Short Papers*, pages 220–224. Association for Computational Linguistics.

Martin Moyle, Justin Tonra, and Valerie Wallace. 2011. Manuscript transcription by crowdsourcing: Transcribe bentham. *LIBER Quarterly*, 20(3).

Indraneel Mukherjee and David M Blei. 2009. Relative performance guarantees for approximate inference in latent dirichlet allocation. In *NIPS*, pages 1129–1136.

Thomas Plötz and Gernot A Fink. 2009. Markov models for offline handwriting recognition: a survey. *Journal on Document Analysis and Recognition*, 12(4):269–298.

Joan Andreu Sánchez, Günter Mühlberger, Basilis Gatos, Philip Schofield, Katrien Depuydt, Richard M Davis, Enrique Vidal, and Jesse de Does. 2013. transcriptorium: a european project on handwritten text recognition. In *Proceedings of the 2013 ACM symposium on Document engineering*, pages 227–228. ACM.

Andreas Stolcke, Jing Zheng, Wen Wang, and Victor Abrash. 2011. Srilm at sixteen: Update and outlook. In *Proceedings of IEEE Automatic Speech Recognition and Understanding Workshop*, page 5.

Yik-Cheung Tam and Tanja Schultz. 2005. Dynamic language model adaptation using variational bayes inference. In *INTERSPEECH*, pages 5–8. Citeseer.

Jafar Tanha, Jesse de Does, and Katrien Depuydt. 2014. An intelligent sample selection approach to language model adaptation for hand-written text recognition. *Proceedings of the 2014 ICFHR conference*, pages 349–355.

Training Automatic Transliteration Models on DBpedia Data

Velislava Todorova
Linguistic Modeling Department
IICT-BAS
slava@bultreebank.org

Kiril Simov
Linguistic Modeling Department
IICT-BAS
kivs@bultreebank.org

Abstract

Our goal is to facilitate named entity recognition in Bulgarian texts by extending the coverage of DBpedia (http://www.dbpedia.org/) for Bulgarian. For this task we have trained translation Moses models to transliterate foreign names to Bulgarian. The training sets were obtained by extracting the names of all people, places and organizations from DBpedia and its extension Airpedia (http://www.airpedia.org/). Our approach is extendable to other languages with small DBpedia coverage.

1 Introduction

DBpedia Linked Open Dataset[1] provides the wealth of Wikipedia in a formalized way via the ontological language in which DBpedia statements are represented. Still DBpedia reflects the multilingual nature of WikiPedia. But if a user needs to access the huge number of instances extracted from the English version of WikiPedia, for example, in a different language (in our case Bulgarian) he/she will not be able to do so, because the DBpedia in the other language will not provide appropriate Uniform Resource Identifiers (URIs) for many of the instances in the English DBpedia. In this paper we describe an approach to the problem. It generates appropriate names in Bulgarian from DBpedia URIs in other languages. These new names are used in two ways: (1) to form gazetteers for annotation of DBpedia instances in Bulgarian texts; and (2) they refer back to the DBpedia URIs from which they have been created and in this way provide access to all RDF statements about the original URIs.

The paper presents several transliteration models and their evaluation. Their evaluation is done over 100 examples, transliterated manually by two people, independently from each other. The discrepancies between the two human transliterations demonstrate the complexity of the task.

The structure of the paper is as follows: in section 2 we describe the problem in more detail; in section 3 we present some related approaches; section 4 reports on the preliminary experiments; section 5 describes how the training data is extended on the basis of the results from the preliminary models and new models are trained; section 6 provides some heuristic rules for combining transliteration and translation of names' parts; section 7 describes the evaluation of the models; the last section concludes the paper and presents some directions for future work.

2 Challenges

The transliteration of proper names presents many and quite challenging difficulties not only to automatic systems, but also to humans. A lot of information is needed to perform the task: the language of origin to determine the pronunciation; some real world facts like how this name was/is actually pronounced by the person it belongs or belonged to (in case of personal names) or by the locals (in case of toponyms) and so on; and also the tradition in transliterating names from this particular language into the given target language. Even if all of this information is gathered and if it is consistent (which is not always the case), there are still decisions to be made – the task of finding a phonetic equivalent of one language's phoneme into another is not trivial; in

[1] http://wiki.dbpedia.org/

Proceedings of Recent Advances in Natural Language Processing, pages 654–662,
Hissar, Bulgaria, Sep 7–9 2015.

some cases the name or parts of it are meaningful words in the source language and it might not be obvious which is more appropriate – translation or transliteration; and sometimes it might be better to leave the name in its original script.

In their survey on machine transliteration (Karimi et al., 2011) give a list of five main challenges for an automated approach to the task: *1)* script specifications, *2)* language of origin, *3)* missing sounds, *4)* deciding on whether or not to translate or transliterate a name (or part of it), and *5)* transliteration variants.

Fortunately, *1)* does not present great difficulties when dealing with European languages only, as the direction of writing is the same and the characters do not undergo changes in shape due to the phonetic environment. The only problem related to the script (apart from the minor one of choosing appropriate encoding) is the letter case. We decided to leave the upper and lower case characters in our training data, trading overcomplication of the statistical models for a result that does not need additional postprocessing.

On the other hand, *2)* is a very hard challenge and we decided to leave it aside for now. When we extract names from Wikipedia, we know the language they are written in, but there are no straightforward ways to figure out the language they came from.

3) is the challenge of finding a phonetic match for a sound that does not exist in the target language. Human translators need to make a decision which of the phonemes at hand is most appropriate in the particular case, and *appropriate* does not necessarily mean *phonetically close*, as orthography and etymology could also be considered important. We hope to overcome this difficulty by training machine translation Moses models on parallel lists of names where the decisions about sound mapping have already been made by humans.

Challenge *4)* is related to the fact that transferring a name from one language to another can happen not only through transliteration, but also via translation (for example, until 1986, the French name *Côte d'Ivoire* has been translated, not transliterated in Bulgarian as *Бряг на слоновата кост*) or direct adoption (like many music band names).[2] To distinguish the cases where transliteration is needed from those where direct adoption or translation is more appropriate, we use some heuristics that involve the combination of several different models and are described in more details in section 6.

Problem *5)* is very peculiar. It looks similar to the variation in translation, but is different in its 'abnormality'. One would accept as normal different translations of a single sentence and we know that even in the source language the meaning of this sentence can be expressed in other ways. Transliteration, on the other hand, is expected to produce one single result for each name, just as this name is an unvaried reference to an entity. However, there are often multiple transliterations of the same name. Our models do not attempt to generate all the acceptable variants, but we calculate how different our results are from manually generated transliterations and we expect this estimation to be useful to determine if an expression is likely to be a transliteration of a certain name.

3 Related Works

(Matthews, 2007) approaches transliteration very similarly to the way we do. Like us, he trains machine translation Moses models on parallel lists of proper names. The language pairs for which he obtains transliteration and backtransliteration models are English and Arabic, and English and Chinese. Unlike him, we are only interested in forward transliteration to Bulgarian. And our approach differs from his in several other aspects. First, we do not lowercase our training data. Second, we explore not only unigram models, but also bigram ones. And finally, we employ heuristics to decide whether to transliterate or not.

The construction of our models was inspired by (Nakov and Tiedemann, 2012). They train the only transliteration models for Bulgarian known to us. They use automatic transliteration as a substitution for machine transla-

[2] Or it might be a combination of the three. Here we will not deal with mixed cases as such. We will consider as cases of direct adoption only those where the whole name has been directly adopted. We will treat as translation cases all cases where at least some part of the name has been translated, and we will take the rest to be transliteration ones.

tion between very closely related languages, namely Bulgarian and Macedonian. Their models are of several different types – unigram, bigram, trigram – and their results show that bigrams perform best, because they are "a good compromise between generality and contextual specificity" (Nakov and Tiedemann, 2012, p. 302). We have also trained and compared unigram and bigram models (see Sections 4 and 5), however we left the trigrams out because of the specificity problem (a trigram generally occurs much less often than a unigram, for example), which gets even worse with proper names coming from many different languages with very diverse letter sequence patterns.[3]

Here we will not give a full overview of the automatic transliteration techniques, instead we will reference (Karimi et al., 2011), which is a detailed survey on the topic, and (Choi et al., 2011), where the main approaches to the task are explained and compared.

4 Preliminary Transliteration Models

We have trained several machine translation Moses[4] models. We have used standard settings for Moses baseline models for this purpose. The language models have been trained on the Bulgarian part of the English – Bulgarian parallel list of names. The translation models were obtained in two steps. The first step was to train models on the data we had, cleaned and tidied as much as possible (details are given in section 4.1).

The second step was to apply the first models on the data to further clean and tidy it up (details are given in section 5.1), so that a second, better series of models is obtained. In this section, we describe the first models, and the next section deals with the ones that were the product of the second step.

4.1 Training Data

The parallel lists of names on which we have trained our models have been extracted from DBpedia. We have used the instance type feature to select the URLs of all people, places and organizations in seven languages: Bulgarian, English, German, French, Russian, Italian and Spanish. Then we have mapped the Bulgarian names to the corresponding foreign names via the interlanguage links in DBpedia. We have further enlarged the lists by adding Airpedia[5] entries with assumed types 'Person', 'Place' or 'Organization' that were not present in DBpedia.

The obtained parallel lists have been cleaned from potential noise. Bulgarian entries that did not contain any Cyrillic letters were removed, as these are not cases of transliteration, but rather adoption of a foreign spelling. We used a Bulgarian word form dictionary (Popov et al., 2003) to detect and exclude probable translation cases.[6] We have also removed name pairs with mismatching number of words to avoid confusing the model if two names of a person are given in one language and only one in the other.

At the end, for each language paired with Bulgarian we had name lists with the following lengths:

English	38,360	German	30,899
Frinch	30,446	Italian	27,369
Spanish	25,312	Russian	21,256

[3]We have trained several trigram models, but they performed poorly in our development tests, which was strong enough reason for us to drop them. The following table shows the BLEU scores that the different models obtained for each source language they were applied on. (The abbreviations representing the model names are clarified in section 5, here 'T' stands for 'trigram'.)

	en	**fr**	**de**	**it**	**ru**	**es**
PUM	86.31	85.63	86.84	86.36	90.01	86.25
PBM	81.94	81.45	83.30	82.02	86.37	82.25
PTM	73.79	73.79	76.94	74.56	81.22	74.39
UUM	88.63	88.56	88.77	87.76	87.24	87.80
UBM	83.76	85.02	85.77	84.47	83.30	84.46
UTM	76.76	77.52	78.77	77.80	78.71	77.01
BUM	88.29	88.12	88.67	88.11	87.65	88.07
BBM	84.50	85.32	85.54	84.73	84.04	84.52
BTM	76.78	77.52	78.77	77.80	77.71	77.01
TUM	88.17	88.40	88.79	87.86	87.31	87.94
TBM	84.42	84.72	85.44	84.62	83.34	84.48
TTM	77.41	77.69	78.82	77.70	78.97	77.09

[4]http://www.statmt.org/moses/

[5]http://www.airpedia.org/, this is an automatically generated extension of DBpedia.

[6]A minor problem here is that some foreign names look like a Bulgarian word when transliterated. We extracted the 100 most frequent meaningful word forms from the lists of Wikipedia articles we had and we filtered 20 of them that are more likely to have been obtained via transliteration, not translation. These 20 words were not treated as meaningful ones and the names containing them were not excluded from our lists.

4.2 Models Trained

The data was divided into training (80%), tuning and development sets (10% each). We have trained 12 preliminary transliteration models – two for each source language: one unigram model and one bigram model. The names in the training sets for the unigram models looked like this:

$$(E\ l\ v\ i\ s\ )$$

The training data for the bigram model looked like this:

$$(E\ El\ lv\ vi\ is\ s)$$

The opening bracket indicates the beginning of the word and the closing bracket indicates the end of the word.

5 Main Transliteration Models

5.1 Training Data

Before the training of the preliminary models, the data was cleaned from all name pairs with mismatching number of words. After obtaining the first transliteration models, we were able to put back these parts of the names that were present in both languages. We detected which word corresponds to which by transliterating (with the preliminary models) the foreign name to Bulgarian and comparing this transliteration to the original Bulgarian name. The words that were similar enough (were at NLD less than 0.1[7]) were considered as an indication that the source word and the Bulgarian word correspond to each other, and thus were retained. For example, the English name *A. J. Kronin* and the Bulgarian counterpart *Арчибалд Кронин* both contain the family name of the person, but in Bulgarian the first name is given in its full form, and in English it is abbreviated as well as the second and they would only confuse the models if they are present in the training data.

Another problem that we were able to solve with the help of the preliminary models were the swapped names (some languages prefer to put the given name before the family name, other not). We again calculated the similarity between each word in the transliteration and in the original Bulgarian name, to determine if rearrangement is needed and to perform it.

As we have two preliminary models – unigram and bigram – we obtained two new data sets – one enhanced by the unigram models, and one enhanced by the bigram models.

The application of the unigram models on the name lists lead to the following, larger data sets:

English	43,673	German	34,014
French	33,807	Italian	31,619
Spanish	29,579	Russian	27,980

The application of the bigram models also enlarged the initial data sets with similar success:

English	43,608	German	34,004
French	33,944	Italian	31,620
Spanish	29,520	Russian	27,994

5.2 Models Trained

On each of the new enhanced data sets we have trained 12 new models, altogether 24. The models that we used to improve the training sets will be called from now on preliminary unigram and preliminary bigram model (PUM and PBM). The unigram models trained on the data, amended with the help of the preliminary unigram models, will be called unigram enhanced unigram models or UUM for short. Similarly, we will have bigram enhanced unigram models (BUM), unigram enhanced bigram models (UBM), and bigram enhanced bigram models (BBM).

6 Ensemble Approach

What we train our models, for is *how* to transliterate. To decide *if* transliteration is needed, we do not employ statistical approach, but the following heuristics.

6.1 First Heuristic

We use this heuristic to resolve the *direct addoption vs. trasnliteration* problem. When one name is the same in all source languages, we assume that this name should stay as it is in Bulgarian too, and not be transliterated.[8] One example would be the band name *Skazi* that

[7] Normalized Levenshtein Distance, see Section 7 for an explanation of the metric.

[8] It is very important here that we have Russian, a language using Cyrillic script among our languages. Languages that use the same alphabet are more likely to directly adopt each other's proper names and if we only relied on Latin script, we would have concluded that direct addoption in Bulgarian is more appropriate in most cases, which is not desirable.

our heuristics leave in Latin script, because it is given like this in all of the source languages.

6.2 Second Heuristic

We use this heuristic to resolve the *translia-tion vs. trasnliteration* problem. If the results we got from all models are all different, then we assume that this name has been translated, not transliterated in our source languages and needs a translation in the target language too. An example from our evaluation set would be the *Romanian Television*, whose name is always transliterated differently by our models depending on the language it comes from.[9]

6.3 Voting

We assume that in the rest of the cases, trasnliteration is the appropriate method to transfer a name to Bulgarian. We apply voting to decide which transliteration (the one from which source language) to take. In case of a tie, a random choice is made.

7 Evaluation

We have evaluated the transliteration models on a small set of 100 names. The names were taken from the English DBpedia and we made sure that there are DBpedia entries for these entities in the other five languages too. We asked volunteers to transfer the names to Bulgarian by whatever method they find more appropriate: transliteration, translation or direct adoption of the foreign name. The 100 names were divided in portions of 10 and each portion was transliterated by two different volunteers.[10] In this way, we obtained two different references to compare the automatically generated transliterations to. From now on, we will refer to these two references as REF1 and REF2.

7.1 General Evaluation

The measure we use is normalized (by the length of the longer name) Levenshtein distance (NLD). We have chosen it because it is very intuitive – a 0-distance means that the two names are absolutely the same, 1 means that they are completely different and all the values in between can be interpreted as the proportion of errors. 0.1 for example means that there is one error (a letter that needs to be removed, inserted or substituted to obtain the correct name) for each ten letters. This measure is also fair to long names, unlike the simple Levenshtein distance.[11]

If our models have chosen wrongly whether transliteration is needed or not for a particular name, they get NLD score 1 for it. Further down in this section we present a separate evaluation of the heuristics that detect translation or direct adoption cases. So, for each name the distance between the automatic and the human generated transliteration is calculated as follows:

$$NLD = \begin{cases} \frac{LD(w_{aut}, w_{ref})}{|max(w_{aut}, w_{ref})|}, & \text{for correct decision to transliterate} \\ 0, & \text{for correct decision to translate/adopt} \\ 1, & \text{for wrong decision.} \end{cases}$$

where $LD(w_{aut}, w_{ref})$ is the well known Levenshtein distance between the words w_{aut} (which is the automatic generated transliteration) and w_{ref} (the human generated reference), i.e. the minimal number of edit operations (deletions, insertions and substitutions) that can transform w_{aut} into w_{ref}.

In our evaluation we present mean NLD for all the 100 names, the percentage of the names that received NLD score exactly 0, as well as the percentage of those that received score less than 0.1.

Table 1 shows how different from each other the two sets of manual transliterations are.

[9]With this heuristic we aim at detecting cases of at least partial translation and we do not attempt to identify which parts of the name are translated and which are not.

[10]This division of the data in portions is not relevant to our evaluation method, it is only a way to speed up the gathering of human input. Transliteration is one of the most time consuming subtasks of translation and together with the research it takes quite a lot time and effort, which we opted to bring to a minimum for our volunteers.

[11]The measures we use are very similar to the ones chosen by (Matthews, 2007, pp. 29-46) with the only difference that we normalize the Levenshtein distance. Other measures exist too, for example the ones recommended for the shared transliteration task in 2012 (Zhang et al., 2012, pp. 4-5).
We feel free to refine the measure we use and not stick to one that has been previously employed, because there are no other proper name transliteration systems for Bulgarian, to which we could compare our results anyway.

mean NLD	zeroes	less than 0.1
0.173	57%	68%

Table 1: Comparison of REF1 and REF2.

model	mean NLD	zeroes	< 0.1
PUM	0.256	39%	51%
PBM	0.234	42%	**57%**
UUM	0.242	41%	53%
UBM	0.270	36%	51%
BUM	0.286	37%	51%
BBM	**0.222**	**43%**	54%

Table 2: Comparison of the performance of the automatic models to REF1.

'Mean NLD' is the mean normalized Levenshtein distance for the 100 names, 'zeros' is the percentage of name pairs with NLD equal to zero, and 'less than 0.1' is the percentage of pairs for which NLD is less or equal to 0.1.

It is to note that only 57% of the name pairs in the two reference sets are absolutely the same (NLD=0). This is due to the 'abnormal' variation of transliterations that was mentioned as one peculiar challenge in Section 2.

We have compared the results of our automatic ensemble approach to each of the two references. Tables 2 and 3 present how different the machine transliteration is from respectively REF1 and REF2.

Generally, the automatic transliterations are not more different from the references than the references are from each other. From Table 2 it seems that BBM performs best, as it has lowest mean NLD and a greater percentage of exact matches. However, the models that are closest to the second reference are different. It is not clear if the enhanced models are altogether better or worse than the preliminary ones, but in most cases the best result is presented by one of the enhanced models.

model	mean NLD	zeroes	< 0.1
PUM	0.226	41%	56%
PBM	0.184	43%	57%
UUM	0.225	37%	55%
UBM	0.184	**46%**	59%
BUM	**0.180**	44%	**60%**
BBM	0.188	44%	58%

Table 3: Comparison of the performance of the automatic models to REF2.

model	F_{ref1}	F_{ref2}
PUM	0.64	0.67
PBM	0.56	0.50
UUM	0.79	0.67
UBM	0.71	0.68
BUM	0.69	0.64
BBM	0.55	0.50

Table 4: Evaluation of the 'translation vs. transliteration' heuristic

7.2 Evaluation of the Heuristics

The tables above present an overall evaluation of our approach. It might be interesting, though, to look into the performance of our heuristics separately.

The first heuristic detects cases where direct adoption is to be preferred over transliteration. It relies solely on the input in the source languages, so it produces the same results for all models.

Against the first reference we have calculated F score $F_{ref1} = 0$, and against the second reference we obtained $F_{ref2} = 0.75$. This result is more odd than bad, which can be explained quite well by the absent inter-annotator agreement for this task ($\kappa = -0.03$).[12]

The second heuristic resolves the 'translation or transliteration' problem and it is dependent on the output of the transliteration models, which is why we present F scores for each model separately in Table 4 (again there are two F scores, because there are two references). The inter-annotator agreement for this task is almost perfect, $\kappa = 0.89$.

It is worth noticing that BBM, which seemed to be performing best of all models, is the worst one in this task.

7.3 Evaluation of the Transliteration Models Alone

The names from the evaluation list which were considered by both human transliterators to

[12]There is not a single case in which the two human transliterators both think that a name should be left in its original script. This reveals that there is an ongoing process in Bulgarian to establish when direct adoption is more appropriate than transliteration.

mean NLD	zeroes	less than 0.1
0.107	57.7%	71.8%

Table 5: Comparison of the two manually generated transliterations for the 78 pure transliteration cases.

need pure transliteration, were 78. On them we have calculated mean NLD, percent of zero scores and percent of low scores (< 0.1), as in the general evaluation of our approach, to be able to present this time an evaluation of the transliteration models without the impact of the heuristics. Table 5 shows how close the two references are to each other for the pure transliteration cases only, Tables 6 and 7 present the transliterations of the automatic models compared to REF1 and REF2 respectively. There are six models of a kind, one for each of the six different source languages.

Generally, all models seem to perform better when they only need to transliterate, not to decide whether to transliterate. The gap between the references is also narrower. REF2 is again more similar to the automatic transliterations than REF1. It is interesting that REF2 is in average closer to the automatic models than to REF1 for English (all models) and German (almost all models).

All the models perform best when applied to English as source language. This might be due to the fact that the training data for English is more than for any of the other languages. Another reason for this result might be that the list of names, that was presented to the human transliterators, was extracted from the English DBpedia. Even though the volunteers were encouraged to use Wikipedia as resource also in the other five languages, they might have had somewhat of an inclination towards a more English sounding transliteration.

It is not very easy to explain why Russian as source language challenges the automatic models so much. One would expect that transliteration between two languages using the same alphabet would be easier, but it is exactly the opposite here. The two languages have very different pronunciation rules and even use quite different sets of phonemes, which is one possible reason why a name is transliterated with one sequence of letters in Russian and a different one in Bulgarian.

Now, when we have the evaluation of the different models for each source language, we can start working on a weighted version of the voting in our ensemble approach. It would be interesting to see, if giving more weight to the English and German models, and less to the Russian ones would contribute significantly to the final results.

8 Conclusion and Future Work

We have presented an approach to machine transliteration that makes use of machine translation Moses models and some simple heuristics to detect if transliteration is appropriate, and to perform it if it is. This approach can help closing the gap between well and not so well represented languages in DBpedia. Even though the transliterations generated by our models would be somewhat different than manual transliteration, one could still make use of them. For example, in an information retrieval task, one could search not for exact matches of the name, but for words that are very similar. (Our evaluation can serve as a guide to what similarity should be taken as being enough. It would be nice to have at some point a larger set of human generated references for a sounder result.) Besides, if integrated in a machine translation system, our transliteration approach would give a (close to) acceptable result, improving in this way the performance of the whole machine translation system.

One problem that we have not tackled yet is determining the language of origin for each name. When we do, we could train different models according to this information and see if automatic transliteration benefits from it as much as a human transliterator does.

Another improvement would be to train models for more languages to extend the coverage of our approach. It is also interesting to experiment with different groups of languages and see how the number and kind of the source languages influences the results of our ensemble approach. Experiments with weighted voting for our ensemble approach would also be beneficial.

model		mean NLD	zeroes	< 0.1
PUM	de	0.131	39.5%	56.6%
	en	**0.114**	**44.7%**	**57.9%**
	es	0.156	36.8%	44.7%
	fr	0.142	34.2%	55.3%
	it	0.162	32.9%	48.7%
	ru	0.412	22.4%	27.7%
PBM	de	0.132	36.8%	53.9
	en	**0.114**	**39.5%**	**59.2%**
	es	0.157	34.2%	48.7%
	fr	0.134	**39.5%**	56.6%
	it	0.167	30.2%	48.7%
	ru	0.407	26.3%	31.6%
UUM	de	**0.120**	42.1%	**57.9%**
	en	0.126	**43.4%**	56.6%
	es	0.150	36.8%	48.7%
	fr	0.139	39.5%	51.3%
	it	0.158	38.1%	50.0%
	ru	0.411	17.1%	22.4%
UBM	de	0.122	39.5%	56.6%
	en	**0.116**	**43.4%**	53.2%
	es	0.147	34.2%	48.7%
	fr	0.135	38.3%	**57.9%**
	it	0.156	34.2%	55.3%
	ru	0.403	23.7%	27.6%
BUM	de	0.128	40.8%	58.9%
	en	**0.123**	**43.4%**	**59.2%**
	es	0.158	34.2%	43.4%
	fr	0.132	43.4%	57.9%
	it	0.160	36.8%	47.4%
	ru	0.405	19.7%	27.6%
BBM	de	0.125	39.5%	**60.5%**
	en	**0.120**	**44.7%**	59.2%
	es	0.156	32.9%	59.2%
	fr	0.135	38.1%	55.3%
	it	0.172	31.6%	48.7%
	ru	0.392	26.3%	30.3%

Table 6: Comparison of the performance of the automatic models to REF1 for the pure transliteration cases.

model		mean NLD	zeroes	< 0.1
PUM	de	0.103	38.2%	57.9%
	en	**0.096**	**42.1%**	**60.5%**
	es	0.124	38.2%	51.3%
	fr	0.117	35.5%	51.3%
	it	0.141	31.6%	50.0%
	ru	0.400	21.1%	26.3%
PBM	de	0.109	34.2%	53.9
	en	**0.098**	**36.8%**	**57.9%**
	es	0.134	32.9%	53.9%
	fr	0.119	**36.8%**	53.9%
	it	0.142	27.6%	50.0%
	ru	0.402	23.7%	26.3%
UUM	de	**0.097**	40.8%	59.2%
	en	0.103	**42.1%**	**60.5%**
	es	0.121	39.5%	52.6%
	fr	0.109	39.5%	53.9%
	it	0.140	34.2%	48.7%
	ru	0.398	18.4%	21.1%
UBM	de	0.102	36.8%	59.2%
	en	**0.098**	**42.1%**	**61.8%**
	es	0.121	35.5%	50.0%
	fr	0.117	35.5%	56.6%
	it	0.133	32.9%	56.3%
	ru	0.394	25%	27.6%
BUM	de	0.108	36.8%	57.9%
	en	**0.103**	**40.8%**	**59.2%**
	es	0.127	35.5%	48.7%
	fr	0.108	34.4%	55.3%
	it	0.139	34.2%	48.7%
	ru	0.392	22.4%	25.0%
BBM	de	**0.101**	36.8%	**60.5%**
	en	0.105	**40.8%**	57.9%
	es	0.129	32.9%	47.4%
	fr	0.117	36.8%	55.6%
	it	0.154	28.9%	44.7%
	ru	0.379	26.3%	30.3%

Table 7: Comparison of the performance of the automatic models to REF2 for the pure transliteration cases.

Acknowledgments

This research has received partial support by the EC's FP7 (FP7/2007-2013) project under grant agreement number 610516: "QTLeap: Quality Translation by Deep Language Engineering Approaches" and FP7 grant 316087 AComIn "Advanced Computing for Innovation", funded by the European Commission in 2012–2016.

We are grateful to all the volunteers for their input, also to Petya Ossenova and Hristo Todorov for revising an early draft of this paper.

We thank the three anonymous reviewers, whose remarks, comments, suggestions and encouragement helped us to improve the initial version of the paper. All errors remain our own responsibility.

References

Key-Sun Choi, Hitoshi Isahara, and Jong-Hoon Oh. 2011. A comparison of different machine transliteration models. *CoRR*, abs/1110.1391.

Sarvnaz Karimi, Falk Scholer, and Andrew Turpin. 2011. Machine transliteration survey. *ACM Comput. Surv.*, 43(3):17:1–17:46, April.

David Matthews. 2007. Machine transliteration of proper names. Master's thesis, School of Informatics, University of Edinburgh.

Preslav Nakov and Jörg Tiedemann. 2012. Combining word-level and character-level models for machine translation between closely-related languages. In *Proceedings of the 50th Annual Meeting of the Association for Computational Linguistics: Short Papers - Volume 2*, ACL '12, pages 301–305, Stroudsburg, PA, USA. Association for Computational Linguistics.

Dimityr Popov, Kiril Simov, Svetlomira Vidinska, and Petya Osenova. 2003. *Spelling Dictionary of Bulgarian.* Nauka i izkustvo, Sofia, Bulgaria.

Min Zhang, Haizhou Li, Ming Liu, and A Kumaran. 2012. Whitepaper of news 2012 shared task on machine transliteration. In *Proceedings of the 4th Named Entity Workshop*, NEWS '12, pages 1–9, Stroudsburg, PA, USA. Association for Computational Linguistics.

Arabic-English Semantic Class Alignment to Improve Statistical Machine Translation

Ines Turki Khemakhem
MIRACL Laboratory,
University of Sfax-TUNISIA
ines_turki@yahoo.fr

Salma Jamoussi
MIRACL Laboratory,
University of Sfax-TUNISIA
salma.jamoussi@isimsf.rnu.tn

Abdelmajid Ben Hamadou
MIRACL Laboratory,
University of Sfax-TUNISIA
abdelmajid.benhamadou@isimsf.rnu.tn

Abstract

Clustering words is a widely used technique in statistical natural language processing. It requires syntactic, semantic, and contextual features. Especially, semantic clustering is gaining a lot of interest. It consists in grouping a set of words expressing the same idea or sharing the same semantic properties.

In this paper, we present a new method to integrate semantic classes in a Statistical Machine Translation (SMT) context to improve the Arabic-English translation quality.

In our method, we first apply a semantic word clustering algorithm for English. We then project the obtained semantic word classes from the English side to the Arabic side. This projection is based on available word alignments provided by the alignment step using GIZA++ tool. Finally, we apply a new process to incorporate semantic classes in order to improve the SMT quality. The experimental results show that introducing semantic word classes achieves 4 % of relative improvement on the BLEU score for the Arabic → English translation task.

1 Introduction

In the past decade, statistical machine translation (SMT) has been advanced from word based SMT to phrase and syntax based SMT. Although this advancement produces major improvements in BLEU scores, important meaning errors still harm the quality of SMT translations.

More recently, research in statistical machine translation has witnessed many attempts to integrate semantic feature into SMT models, to generate not only grammatical but also meaning preserved translations.

Integrating semantic features into SMT tasks aims at improving translation adequacy. In a bilingual corpus, different senses of words in the source language can have different translations in the target language, as the context in which they appear.

This motivates the introduction of semantic word classes in statistical machine translation.

A semantic word class is represented by a set of words expressing the same idea and sharing the same semantic properties. For example, the words plane, train, boat, bus can all correspond to the semantic class "transport".

Semantic word clustering is a technique for partitioning sets of words into subsets of semantically similar words. It is increasingly becoming a major technique used in SMT task.

Furthermore, most of the SMT system well suited for processing English and other languages with a relatively rigid word order, while languages with complicated morphological paradigms still pose difficulties as Arabic.

In this paper, we present a new method to integrate the underlined semantic classes in a SMT context to improve the Arabic-English translation quality.

We first describe the semantic word clustering algorithm for English and we proceed to directly project the obtained semantic word classes from English side into Arabic side. This projection is based on available word-alignments provided by

Proceedings of Recent Advances in Natural Language Processing, pages 663–671,
Hissar, Bulgaria, Sep 7–9 2015.

the alignment step using GIZA++ tool. The rest of the paper is organized as follows.

Section 2 presents an overview of some recent approaches attempting to introduce semantic features into the statistical machine translation framework. In Section 3, we describe our method to improve the Arabic-English translation quality. In this section, we first give an overview of the baseline SMT. Then, we present the semantic word clustering algorithm for English and we proceed to directly project the obtained semantic word classes from English side into Arabic side. Finally, we introduce the proposed method to incorporate semantic word classes in SMT. Section 4 describes the experimental settings and results, which are discussed in the remainder of this Section. Finally, section 5 presents the most relevant conclusions of this work and suggest possible directions for future work.

2 Related Work

Several attempts to integrate semantic features into the statistical machine translation framework have been reported in the majority of previous works (Kevin and Smith, 2008). We provide a brief overview of some of the most recent work within this area which are relevant to the phrase based statistical machine translation approach.

Vickrey et al. (2005) build word sense disambiguation inspired classifiers to fill in blanks in partially completed translations.

Stroppa et al. (2007) add source-side contextual features into a phrase based SMT system by integrating context dependent phrasal translation probabilities learned using a decision-tree classifier. Authors obtain significant improvements on Italian-to-English and Chinese-to-English IWSLT tasks.

In Carpuat et Wu (2007), word sense disambiguation techniques are introduced into statistical machine translation; and in Carpuat et Wu (2008), authors show that dynamically-built context-dependant phrasal translation lexicons are more useful resources for phrase-based machine translation than conventional static phrasal translation lexicons, which ignore all contextual information.

Some work has been reported to improve translation quality with word classes, by using syntactic and semantic information for the SMT decoding in Baker et al. (2010).

In a previous work (Turki Khemakhem I. et al, 2010), a solution for disambiguation of the output of the Arabic morphological analyzer was presented. This method was used to help in selecting the proper word tags for translation purposes via word-aligned bitext.

In Banchs et Costa-jussà (2011), a semantic feature for statistical machine translation, based on Latent Semantic Indexing, is proposed and evaluated. The objective of this feature is to account for the degree of similarity between a given input sentence and each individual sentence in the training dataset. This similarity is computed in a reduced vector-space constructed by means of the Latent Semantic Indexing decomposition. The computed similarity values are used as an additional feature in the log-linear model combination approach to statistical machine translation. Authors obtain significant improvements on a Spanish-to-English translation task.

The system, presented in Costa-jussà et al. (2014), is Moses-based with an additional feature function based on deep learning. This feature function introduces source-context information in the standard Moses system by adding the information of how similar is the input sentence to the different training sentences. Significant improvements are reported in the task from English to Hindi.

On the other hand, there are approaches which use machine learning techniques. In Haque et al. (2009), authors have proposed syntactic and lexical context features, for integrating information about the neighboring words into a phrase-based SMT system ; and in España-Bonet et al.(2009), authors implements a standard Phrase-Based SMT architecture, extended by incorporating a local discriminative phrase selection model to address the semantic ambiguity of Arabic. Local classifiers are trained, using linguistic and context information, to translate a phrase.

3 Proposed Method

3.1 Phrase-Based Machine Translation

SMT methods have evolved from using the simple word based models (Brown et al,1993) to phrase based models (Marcu and Wong, 2002; Koehn P, 2004; Och and Ney, 2004). It has been formulated as a noisy channel model in which the target language sentence, *s* is seen as distorted by the channel into the foreign language *t*. In that, we try to find the sentence *t* which maximizes the *P(t/s)* probability:

$$argmax_t P(t|s) = argmax_t P(s|t)P(t) \quad (1)$$

here $P(t)$ is the language model and $P(s|t)$ is the translation model. We can get the language model from a monolingual corpus (in the target language). The translation model is obtained by using an aligned bilingual corpus.

The translation model is combined together with the following six additional feature models: the target language model, the word and the phrase penalty and the source-to-target and target-to-source lexicon model and the reordering model. These models are optimized by the decoder[1]. In our case, we use the open source Moses decoder described in (Koehn et al, 2007).

3.2 Pre-processing Step

Arabic is a morphologically complex language. In Arabic, various clitics such as pronouns, conjunctions and articles appear concatenated to content words such as nouns and verbs (Example: the Arabic word "أتتذكروننا" corresponds in English to the sentence: "Do you remember us"). This can cause data sparseness issues. Thus clitics are typically segmented in a preprocessing step.

The aim of a preprocessing step is to recognize word composition and to provide specific morphological information about it. For Example: the word "سيخبرهم" (in English: he will notify them) is the result of the concatenation of the proclitic "س" indicating the future, enclitic "هم" (for the masculine plural possession pronoun) and the rest of the word "يخبر" (verb).

In our proposed method, each Arabic word, from the target Arabic training data, is replaced by the reduced word (obtained by removing its clitics), where clitic are featured with their morphological classes (e.g. proclitic and prefix). For example, the verbal form "سيخبرهم" can be decomposed as follows:

"enclitic _هم   يخبر   proclitic _س"

3.3 Extraction of English Concepts Using Clustering Methods

Our aim is to cluster input set of words $W = \{w_1, \ldots, w_n\}$ into disjoint groups containing words sharing similar meaning $C = \{C_1, \ldots, C_k\}$ (C forms a partition of W).

In the context of this work it is assumed that there is a semantic affinity between two words if they are topically related. For example $C_i = \{w_1, w_2, w_3, w_4, w_5\}$ = {baseball, game, football, pitch, hit} would be a cluster of semantically related words.

The aim of this step is to identify the semantic concepts of the English side of the parallel corpus. The manual determination of these concepts is a very heavy task, so we should find an automatic method to achieve such a work.

To build up the appropriate concepts, the corpus words have to be gathered in several classes.

To reach our goal we used an unsupervised classification technique proposed in (Jamoussi et al., 2009). In the later, a new method to automatically extract semantic concepts for automatic speech understanding was suggested. This method gives good results. In (Jamoussi et al., 2009), authors use the average mutual information measure to compute similarities between words. They then associate to each word a vector with M elements, where M is the size of the lexicon. The jth element of this vector represents the average mutual information between the word j of the lexicon and the word to be represented.

$$w_i = \begin{bmatrix} I(w_1 : w_i) \\ I(w_2 : w_i) \\ \vdots \\ I(w_j : w_i) \\ \vdots \\ I(w_M : w_i) \end{bmatrix}$$

Where

$$I(w_i : w_j) = P(w_i, w_j)log\frac{P(w_i|w_j)}{P(w_i)P(w_j)} + P(\overline{w_i}, w_j)log\frac{P(\overline{w_i}|w_j)}{P(\overline{w_i})P(w_j)} +$$

$$P(w_i, \overline{w_j})log\frac{P(w_i|\overline{w_j})}{P(w_i)P(\overline{w_j})} + P(\overline{w_i}, \overline{w_j})log\frac{P(\overline{w_i}|\overline{w_j})}{P(\overline{w_i})P(\overline{w_j})}$$

$P(w_i,w_j)$ is the probability to find w_i and w_j in the same sentence, $P(w_i|w_j)$ is the probability to find w_i knowing that we already met w_j, $P(w_i)$ is the probability of w_i and $P(\overline{w_i})$ is the probability of any other word except w_i.

To combine context and mutual information vector, (Jamoussi et al., 2009) represent each word by a matrix M×3 of average mutual information measures. The first column of this matrix corresponds to a vector of average mutual information, the second column represents the average mutual information measures between the vocabulary words and the left context of the represented word. The third column is determined in the same manner but it concerns

[1] http://www.statmt.org/moses/

the right context. The jth value of the second column is the weighted average mutual information between the jth word of the vocabulary and the vector constituting the left context of the word W_i. It is calculated as follows:

$$IMM_j(C_l^i) = \frac{\sum_{w_l \in L_{w_i}} I(w_j : w_l) * K_{wl}}{\sum_{w_l \in L_{w_i}} K_{wl}}$$

Where $IMM_j(C_l^i)$ is the average mutual information between the word w_j of the lexicon and the left context of the word W_i. L_{Wi} is a set of words belonging to the left context of W_i. $I(w_j{:}w_l)$ represents the average mutual information between the word j of the lexicon and the word w_l belonging to the left context of W_i. K_{wl} is the occurrence number of the word w_l found in the left context of W_i. The word W_i is thus represented by the matrix shown in the figure 1.

$$w_i = \begin{bmatrix} I(w_1 : w_i) & IMM_1(C_l^i) & IMM_1(C_r^i) \\ I(w_2 : w_i) & IMM_2(C_l^i) & IMM_2(C_r^i) \\ \vdots & \vdots & \vdots \\ I(w_j : w_i) & IMM_j(C_l^i) & IMM_j(C_r^i) \\ \vdots & \vdots & \vdots \\ I(w_M : w_i) & IMM_M(C_r^i) & IMM_M(C_l^i) \end{bmatrix}$$

Figure 1: The matrix representation of the word W_i

The matrix representation of words as described previously, exploits a maximum of information related to a given word. It considers its context and its similarity to all the other words in the corpus. We use then the PAM method, proposed by (Kaufman and Rousseeuw, 1990), for classification of words in the corpus. We obtain a coherent list of concepts that will be used in our statistical translation system.

3.4 Projection of English Concepts to Arabic

After extracting English concepts, we proceed to directly project those concepts from English side into Arabic side. This projection is based on available word-alignments provided by the alignment step using GIZA++ tool. This projection is performed in three main steps:

- Each English word of the parallel corpus is combined with its respective semantic class. In the other side, Arabic words are kept unchanged.
- This obtained bilingual corpus is automatically word aligned by the alignment toolkit.

Arabic-English sentence alignment is illustrated in Figure 2, where each Arabic morpheme is aligned to one or zero English word and its semantic classes.

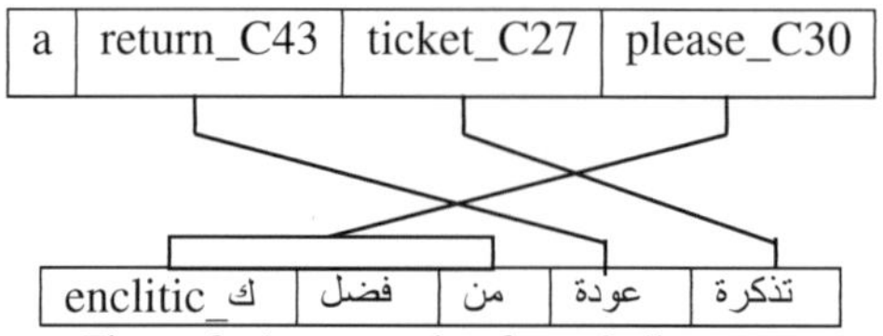

Figure 2. An example of word alignment

The alignment model was trained with the popular toolkit GIZA++ (Och and Ney, 2003), which implements the most typical IBM and HMM alignment models for translation. The alignment models used in our case are IBM-1, HMM, IBM-3 and IBM-4.

After this alignment step we obtain one model table containing English words and its respective semantic classes, aligned with Arabic words with an alignment probability.

- The obtained table is sorted and the probability that correspond to the same Arabic word and the same semantic class is added. Then the resulting probabilities are sorted, and the semantic class that corresponds to the maximum probability is selected.

Finally a matching table is got, where each line from this table refers to the corresponding Arabic word in the training corpus and its semantic class projected from the English word.

your_C9 0,0124172 أمتعة baggages_C27 0,5000000 أمتعة baggage_C27 0,2914286 أمتعة luggage_C27 0,4179104 أمتعة my_C32 0,0282752 أمتعة out_C8 0,0024038 أمتعة things_C49 0,0208333 أمتعة	1. English words and its respective semantic classes, aligned with Arabic words with an alignment probability
C9 0,0124172 أمتعة C27 1,209339 أمتعة C32 0,0282752 أمتعة C8 0,0024038 أمتعة C49 0,0208333 أمتعة	2. Probabilities corresponding to the same Arabic word and the same semantic class are added
C27 1,209339 أمتعة C32 0,0282752 أمتعة C49 0,0208333 أمتعة C9 0,0124172 أمتعة C8 0,0024038 أمتعة	3. Semantic class which correspond to the maximum probability is selected.

Figure 3. An example of projection of English concepts to Arabic

3.5 SMT Using Semantic Word Classes

The translation model of most phrase-based SMT systems is parameterized by two phrasal and two lexical channel models (Koehn et al., 2003) which are estimated as relative frequencies. Their counts are extracted heuristically from a word aligned bilingual training corpus.

Our phrase-based baseline system is built upon the open-source MT toolkit Moses (Koehn et al, 2007). Phrase pairs are extracted from word alignments generated by GIZA++ (Och and Ney, 2003). The phrase-based translation model provides direct and inverted frequency-based and lexical-based probabilities for each phrase pair. The English side of the training corpora was used to generate 3-gram target language model for the translation task. For this purpose, the SRI language modeling toolkit (Stolcke, 2002) was used.

To incorporate semantic word classes in our SMT process, we first proceed to run the semantic word clustering algorithm for English side of the bilingual training data, as already described in section 3.3, to cluster the vocabulary into semantic classes. The obtained classes are directly projected from English side into Arabic side.
Then, we replace each word on both source and target side of the training data with their respective semantic word classes.

By considering the same training procedure as usual, we can easily train the standard models conditioned on word classes.
We obtain finally two phrase tables, the first one with word identities and the second with semantic word classes.

By considering both sorted tables simultaneously, we can select the translation for Arabic word in input test. However, each Arabic word (s_i) in the test corpus is mapped to a single semantic class c_i. We can first uses the phrase table based on word classes to select the translation for this semantic class (c_i'). The translation of the source word (s_i) is among the words of the class (c_i'). Then, to generate the target word e_i (translation of s_i), we uses the generated phrase table based on word identities. Our approach is shown in Figure 4.

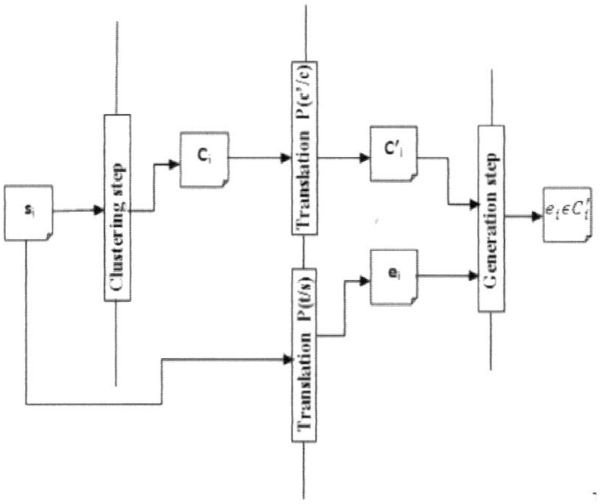

Figure4. The proposed approach: SMT using semantic word classes

Our approach to integrate semantic word classes in SMT process is performed in four main steps:

- Clustering step: (Input: word s_i , output: semantic class c_i)
Each word on source side of the test corpus s_i is replaced by their respective semantic word classes c_i.

- Translation P(t/s): (Input : word s_i ,output: E_i: list of translation of s_i)
The phrase table based on word identities is used to select the list of the translation of the word s_i .

- Translation P(c'/c): (Input : class c_i ,output semantic class c_i')
The phrase table based on word classes is used to select the translation for the semantic class c_i (c_i')

- Generation step: (Input: E_i: list of translation of s_i, semantic class c_i'; output: e_i (translation of s_i) $\in c_i'$)
The target word e_i (translation of s_i), witch is among the words of the class (c_i'), is generated.

4 Experiments

This section describes the experimental work conducted to evaluate the incidence of the proposed method to integrate semantic classes in a SMT context on translation quality. First, subsection 4.1 describes the used dataset. Then, subsection 4.2 presents and discusses the results.

4.1 Used Resources

Our experiments are performed on an Arabic → English task. We train the system on the data provided for the evaluation campaign of the International Workshop on Spoken Language Translation (IWSLT 2010) task[2].

The test set is made up of 507 sentences, which corresponds to the IWSLT08 data (there were 16 English reference translations for each Arabic sentence).

To confirm our results we also run experiments on the Arabic → English task of the IWSLT 2014 evaluation campaign[3].
Table 1 presents the main statistics related to the used data.

		Arabic	English
Train (IWSLT 2010)	sentences	19972	
	words	18149	7296
Test (IWSLT 2008)	sentences	507	
	words	459	184
Train (IWSLT 2014)	sentences	155047	
	words	162148	65774
Test (tst 2010)	sentences	3138	
	words	8101	5733

Table 1: Corpus description of the Arabic→English translation tasks.

4.2 Experimental Results

The proposed method is evaluated on the Arabic-to-English translation task, using the MOSES framework as baseline phrase-based statistical machine translation system (Koehn et al., 2007). The performances reported in this paper were measured using the BLEU score (Papineni et al., 2002).

a- Pre-processing Step:

The Arabic part of the bitext was systematically segmented to train the phrase tables.
Thus each Arabic word of the training corpus is replaced by its segmentation according to the "proclitic stem enclitic" form, as described in section 3.2.

[2] Basic Travel Expression Corpus (BTEC) 2010
[3] Basic Travel Expression Corpus (BTEC) 2014

To perform morphological decomposition of the Arabic source, we use the morphological analyzer MADA (Habash et al, 2009).

MADA is a system for Morphological Analysis and Disambiguation for Arabic. MADA produces for each input word a list of analyses specifying every possible morphological interpretation of that word, covering all morphological features of the word (diacritization, POS, lemma, and 13 inflectional and clitic features). MADA then uses SVM-based classifiers for features (such as POS, number and gender, etc.) to choose among the different analyses of a given word in context.

The resulting corpus was paired with the word-based English corpus to train the translation model. The translation table was trained using the so obtained parallel data (no change was made on the English side). In decoding, the same segmentation form was also applied to the test input.

b- SMT Using Semantic Word Classes:

In this section, we investigated to incorporate semantic word classes in Arabic-English SMT task.
We first proceed by running the semantic word clustering algorithm for English side of the bilingual training data to cluster the vocabulary into 100 classes each. The obtained classes are directly projected from English side into Arabic side.

We train the models conditioned on word classes as described above. We also train the models based on word identity, by using the same training data.
Table 2 presents the score BLEU, measured over the test sets, for three different Arabic → English SMT systems : the baseline system, a second system using the pre-processing step (pp-SMT), and a third system integrating the semantic word class in the SMT process (swc-SMT)

System	Test (IWSLT 2008)	Test 2010
Baseline	40.69	21.42
pp-SMT	42.15	22.59
Swc-SMT	43.75	23.77

Table 2: Comparison of the Arabic-English translation systems

As seen from the table, the system implementing the semantic word classes outperforms the pp-SMT system by almost 1.4 absolute BLEU point.

To confirm our results we also run experiments on the English → Arabic task of the IWSLT evaluation campaign. In this case, both training and decoding phases use Arabic segmented words. The final output of the decoder will be also composed of segmented words. Therefore these words must be recombined into their surface forms. Therefore we apply reconstruction of the Arabic segmented words just by agglutinating the morphological segments in the following order:

Proclitic + stem + enclitic.

For example: in the segmented words:
"سلمت ك ذلك ال كتاب"

The clitic "ك" can be recombined with the previous word ("ك": enclitic).

So the segmented words "سلمت ك ذلك ال كتاب" cans be recombined to "سلمتك ذلك ال كتاب", in English: "I gave this book". The clitic "ك" can be recombined also with the following word ("ك": proclitic), in this case, the segmented words "سلمت ك ذلك ال كتاب" can be recombined to "سلمت كذلك ال كتاب", in English: "I also gave the book".

Those two sentences have the same segmented form, but they have different meanings. By introducing morphological features (e.g. proclitic and enclitic) for each segment, we may remove this ambiguity.

The English-Arabic translation performance of this English-Arabic SMT system is reported in table 3. We show that the swc-SMT yields 0.8% BLEU.

System	Test (IWSLT 2008)	Test 2010
Baseline	12.86	9.3
pp-SMT	13.14	10.1
Swc-SMT	14.07	10.91

Table 3: Comparison of the English-Arabic translation systems

4.3 Discussion

Experimental results on an Arabic-to-English translation task on the corpus showed significant improvements. In this work, we integrate semantic word classes in Arabic to English SMT context for improving machine translation quality. With this, we expect to reduce the noise resulting from data sparseness problems.

To better illustrate the concepts discussed here, let us consider the Arabic word "أم" and the corresponding English translations for its two senses: "mother" and "or". Both translations can be automatically inferred from training data; and Table 4 illustrates the resulting probability values derived for both senses of the Arabic word "أم" from the actual training dataset used in this work.

phrase	φ(f|e)	lex(f|e)	φ(e|f)	lex(e|f)
{أم|||or}	0.5652096	0.720501	0.284662	0.318320
{أم|||mother}	0.264679	0.120287	0.407367	0.435377

Table4. Actual probability values for the two possible translations of the Arabic word "أم".

Notice from the table, how in general the most probable sense of "أم" in our considered dataset is "or". This actually happens because the English word "or" is always related to the Arabic word "أم". Whereas by integrating semantic word classes in the SMT system, the English word "mother" can refer to the Arabic word "أم".

5 Conclusion

We have presented a method to integrate semantic word classes in a Arabic to English SMT context for improving machine translation quality. In our method, we first have applied a semantic word clustering algorithm for English. Then, we have projected the obtained semantic word classes from the English side to the Arabic side. This projection is based on available word alignments provided by the alignment step using GIZA++ tool. Finally, we have applied a new process to incorporate semantic classes in order to improve the SMT quality.

We have shown the efficiency of this method on Arabic to English translation tasks. To confirm our results we have also run experiments on the English → Arabic task.
In our experiments, the baseline is improved by 1.4% BLEU on the Arabic → English task and by 0.3% BLEU on the English → Arabic task.
In future work we plan to apply our method to a wider range of languages.

References

Baker K., Bethard S., Blodgood M., Brown R., Callison-Burch C., Copper-smith G., Dorr B., Filardo W., Giles K. (2009). *Semantically Informed Machine Translation.* Final report of the 2010 Summer Camp for Advanced Language Exploration (SCALE).

Banchs R. and Costa-jussà M. (2011). *A semantic feature for statistical machine translation.* In proceedings of SSST-5, Fifth Workshop on Syntax, Semantics and Structure in Statistical Translation, ACL HLT 2011, Portland, Oregon, USA, 126-134.

Brown. P., Della Pietra V., Della Pietra S., and Mercer R. 1993. *The mathematics of statistical machine translation: parameter estimation,* Computational Linguistics, 19(1): 263–311.

Carpuat, M., Wu, D. (2007) *How Phrase Sense Disambiguation Outperforms Word Sense Disambiguation for Statistical Machine Translation.* In: 11th International Conference on Theoretical and Methodological Issues in Machine Translation. Skovde

Carpuat, M., Wu, D. (2008). *Evaluation of Context-Dependent Phrasal Translation Lexicons for Statistical Machine Translation.* In: 6th International Conference on Language Resources and Evaluation (LREC). Marrakech.

Costa-jussà M., Gupta P., Banchs R. and Rosso P. (2014). *English-to-Hindi system description for WMT 2014: Deep Source-Context Features for Moses.* In proceedings of the Ninth Workshop on Statistical Machine Translation, Baltimore, Maryland USA, 79–83.

España-Bonet C., Gimenez J., Marquez L. (2009). *Discriminative Phrase-Based Models for Arabic Machine Translation.* ACM Transactions on Asian Language Information Processing Journal (Special Issue on Arabic Natural Language Processing)

Habash, N., Rambow, O., and Roth, R. 2009. *MADA+TOKAN: A toolkit for Arabic tokenization, diacritization, morphological disambiguation, POS tagging, stemming and lemmatization,* Proceedings of the Second International Conference on Arabic Language Resources and Tools.

Haque R., Naskar S. K., Ma Y., Way A. (2009). *Using Supertags as Source Language Context in SMT.* In 13th Annual Conference of the European Association for Machine Translation, pp. 234--241. Barcelona

Jamoussi S. (2009). *New Word Vector Representation for Semantic Clustering.* TAL 50(3): 23-57.

Kaufman L. et Rousseeuw P. J. (1990). *Finding groups in data : An introduction tocluster analysis.* John Wiley & Sons (New York), 19-20.

Kevin G. and Smith N. A. (2008). *Rich Source-Side Context for Statistical Machine Translation.* In Proceedings of the Third Workshop on Statistical Machine Translation

Koehn P. 2004. *Pharaoh: A Beam Search Decoder for phrase-based Statistical Machine Translation Models.* In R. Frederking & K. Taylor (eds.) Machine Translation: From Real Users to Research; 6th Conference of the Association for Machine Translation in the Americas, AMTA, Berlin/Heidelberg, Germany: Springer Verlag, 115–124.

Koehn P., Hoang H., Birch A., Callison-Burch C., Federico M., Bertoldi N., Cowa B., Shen W., Moran C., Zens R., Dyer C., Bojar O., Constantin A., and Herbst E., 2007. *Moses: Open source toolkit for statistical machine translation.* In Proceedings of the ACL Demoand Poster Sessions, Prague, Czeck Republic, 177–180.

Marcu D. and Wong W. 2002. *A Phrase-Based, Joint Probability Model for Statistical Machine Translation.* Proceedings of the Conference on Empirical Methods in Natural Language Processing, Philadelphia, PA, 133-139.

Och F. J., and Ney H., 2003. *A Systematic comparison of various statistical alignment models.* Computational Linguistics, 29(1): 19-51.

Och F. J., Ney H. 2004. *The alignment template approach to statistical machine translation.* Computational Linguistics, 30(4): 417-449.

Papineni K. A., Roukos S., Ward T., and Zhu W.J., 2002. *Bleu: a method for automatic evaluation of machine translation.* The Proc. of the 40th Annual Meeting of the Association for Computational Linguistics, Philadelphia, 311–318.

Stolcke A., 2002. *SRILM an Extensible Language Modeling Toolkit.* The Proc. of the Intl. Conf. on Spoken Language Processing, Denver, CO, USA, 901–904.

Stroppa N., van den Bosch A., and Way A. (2007). *Exploiting source similarity for SMT using context-informed features.* In Proc. of TMI.

Turki Khemakhem I., Jamoussi S., and Ben Hamadou A. (2010). *Arabic morpho-syntactic feature disambiguation in a translation context.* In Proceedings of SSST-4, Fourth Workshop on Syntax and Structure in Statistical Translation, COLING, Beijing, 61-65.

Vickrey D. ,Biewald L., Teyssier M. and Koller D. (2005). *Word-sense disambiguation for machine translation*. In Proc. of HLT-EMNLP.

Detection and Fine-Grained Classification of Cyberbullying Events

Cynthia Van Hee*, **Els Lefever***, **Ben Verhoeven**†, **Julie Mennes***, **Bart Desmet***
Guy De Pauw†, **Walter Daelemans**† **and Véronique Hoste***

* LT3 - Language and Translation Technology Team, Ghent University
Groot-Brittanniëlaan 45, 9000 Ghent, Belgium
firstname.lastname@ugent.be
† CLiPS - Computational Linguistics Group, University of Antwerp
Prinsstraat 13, 2000 Antwerp, Belgium
firstname.lastname@uantwerpen.be

Abstract

In the current era of online interactions, both positive and negative experiences are abundant on the Web. As in real life, negative experiences can have a serious impact on youngsters. Recent studies have reported cybervictimization rates among teenagers that vary between 20% and 40%. In this paper, we focus on cyberbullying as a particular form of cybervictimization and explore its automatic detection and fine-grained classification. Data containing cyberbullying was collected from the social networking site Ask.fm. We developed and applied a new scheme for cyberbullying annotation, which describes the presence and severity of cyberbullying, a post author's role (harasser, victim or bystander) and a number of fine-grained categories related to cyberbullying, such as insults and threats. We present experimental results on the automatic detection of cyberbullying and explore the feasibility of detecting the more fine-grained cyberbullying categories in online posts. For the first task, an F-score of 55.39% is obtained. We observe that the detection of the fine-grained categories (e.g. threats) is more challenging, presumably due to data sparsity, and because they are often expressed in a subtle and implicit way.

1 Introduction

Young people are gaining more frequent and rapid access to online, mobile and networked media. Although most of the time, children's Internet use is harmless, there are some risks associated with the online activity, such as the use of social networking sites (e.g. Facebook). The anonymity and freedom provided by social networks makes children vulnerable to threatening situations on the Web, such as grooming by paedophiles or cyberbullying. According to Smith et al. (2008), cyberbullying is defined as *an aggressive, intentional act carried out by a group or individual, using electronic forms of contact, repeatedly and over time against a victim who cannot easily defend him or herself.* Their definition is based on three criteria (repetitiveness, intentionality, and an imbalance of power between the harasser and the victim) that are recognized as inherent characteristics of bullying by Olweus (1996). Some doubt exists, nevertheless, as to whether all three criteria are necessary conditions for cyberbullying. For example Dooley and Cross (2010) and Grigg (2010) stress that online posts are persistent, a single aggressive act can result in continued and widespread ridicule for the victim. Furthermore, it is hard to decide upon intentionality since online communication is prone to misinterpretation (Kiesler et al., 1984; Vandebosch et al., 2006). Finally, the assessment of a power imbalance is complicated in online bullying as it may be related to ICT proficiency, anonymity or the inability of victims to get away (Dooley and Cross, 2010). In general, when working with social media data, the available context is often limited. This makes it hard to decide upon the repetitive character of a cyberbullying incident, to determine whether the victim of an aggressive act is able to defend himself or to decide whether the bully is acting intentionally. Considering these limitations, we restrict the scope of our research to the detection of textual content that is published online by an individual and that is aggressive or hurtful against a victim.

Proceedings of Recent Advances in Natural Language Processing, pages 672–680,
Hissar, Bulgaria, Sep 7–9 2015.

Tokunaga (2010) analyzed a body of quantitative research on cyberbullying and found that cybervictimization rates vary between 20% and 40% on average (Dehue et al., 2006; Hinduja and Patchin, 2006; Li, 2007; Smith et al., 2008; Ybarra and Mitchell, 2008). The rate varies among different studies depending on location, interval and the conceptualisations researchers use in describing cyberbullying. Indeed, according to The EU Kids Online Report (2014), 17% of 9- to 16-year-olds had been bothered or upset by something online in the past year, whereas Juvonen et al. (2008) found that no less than 72% of 12- to 17-year-olds had encountered cyberbullying at least once within the year preceding the questionnaire. According to a recent study by Van Cleemput et al. (2013), 11% of 2,000 Flemish secondary school students had been bullied online at least once in the six months preceding the survey. These figures demonstrate that cyberbullying is not a rare phenomenon. Evidently, it can have a serious impact on children's and youngsters' well-being. This is shown by a number of studies that link cyberbullying to depression, school problems, low self-esteem and even self-harm (Price and Dalgleish, 2010; Šléglová and Černá, 2011; Vandebosch et al., 2006). It is therefore of key importance to identify possibly threatening situations on the Web before they can cause harm.

As it is unfeasible for humans to keep track of all conversations produced online, researchers have started to explore automatic procedures for signalling harmful content. This would allow for large-scale social media monitoring and early detection of harmful situations including cyberbullying. Research has also focused on the desirability of such automatic systems. Van Royen et al. (2015), for example, found that a major part of their respondents favoured automatic monitoring, provided that effective follow-up strategies are included and that privacy and autonomy are guaranteed. Reynolds et al. (2011), Dinakar et al. (2012), and Dadvar et al. (2014) describe some of the first forays into the automatic detection of cyberbullying. However, to the best of our knowledge, we present the first study on recognizing cyberbullying events in social media content by means of a fine-grained textual annotation of the corpus, rather than implementing a binary annotation (i.e. cyberbullying versus non-cyberbullying). For the annotation of the data, we consider fine-grained categories related to cyberbullying such as insults and threats. Implementing this fine-grained distinction allows for insight into various types of cyberbullying and the degree to which they are alarming (e.g. a threat could be considered more alarming than a single insult). Additionally, the annotation scheme allows to identify, for each cyberbullying post, the role of the author (i.e. bully, victim, bystander) and the harmfulness. The idea is that this information allows a more detailed reconstruction of cyberbullying *events*, which can be used to enhance the detection process.

We present experiments on the identification of cyberbullying events and the classification of online posts in fine-grained categories related to cyberbullying. The focus of our experiments is on a Dutch dataset, but the technique is language-independent, provided there is annotated data available in the target language.

2 Related Research

Cyberbullying is a widely covered research topic in the realm of social sciences and psychology. A fair amount of research has been done on the definition and occurrence of the phenomenon (Livingstone et al., 2010; Hinduja and Patchin, 2012; Slonje and Smith, 2008), the identification of different forms of cyberbullying (O'Sullivan and Flanagin, 2003; Vandebosch and Cleemput, 2009; Willard, 2007) and the consequences of cyberbullying (Cowie, 2013; Price and Dalgleish, 2010; Smith et al., 2008). By contrast, the number of studies that focus on the annotation and automatic detection of cyberbullying is limited.

Yin et al. (2009) applied a supervised machine learning approach to the automatic detection of cyberharassment by representing each post in their corpus by local tf-idf features, sentiment features and features capturing the similarity between posts, assuming that posts which are significantly different from their neighbors are more likely to contain cyberbullying. By combining all features, they obtain an F-score of 0.44. Dinakar et al. (2012) conducted text classification experiments on YouTube data. They adopted a bag-of-words supervised machine learning classification approach to identify the sensitive topic for a cyberbullying post (i.e. sexuality, intelligence or race and culture) and report an averaged F-score of 0.63. Reynolds et al. (2011) compared a rule-based model to a bag-of-words model for detecting cyberbullying posts and found that rule-based learning with a number of lexical features (e.g. the number of curse words in a post) outperformed the bag-of-words model. Dadvar et al. (2014) combined the potential of machine learning algorithms with information from social studies for the automatic recognition of cyberbullying. User information and expert views were used in addition to textual features, which resulted in a classification performance of F = 0.64. Nahar et al. (2014) applied a fuzzy SVM algorithm for cyberbullying detection. They implemented a number of lexical features (e.g. the number of swear-words and capitalized words), sentiment features and features based on metadata (e.g. the user's age and gender) and report an F-score of 47%. In all of the aforementioned studies, cyberbullying detection was approached as a binary classification task (cyberbullying versus non-cyberbullying). In this paper, specific forms of cyberbullying like threats and insults are taken into account as fine-grained categories. Moreover, we aim to detect cyberbullying events and therefore consider posts from harassers as well as from victims and bystanders. We present two sets of experiments in which we explore 1) the detection of cyberbullying posts regardless of the author's role (i.e. *cyberbullying events*) and 2) the identification of fine-grained text categories related to cyberbullying.

The remainder of this paper is organized as follows: Section 3 describes our experimental corpus as well as the data collection and annotation. Section 4 gives an overview of the experimental setup. The results are discussed in Section 5 and we formulate conclusions and directions for future research in Section 6.

3 Dataset Construction and Annotation

3.1 Data Collection

The data was collected from Ask.fm[1], a social networking site where users can ask and answer questions to each other, with the option of doing so anonymously. Typically, Ask.fm data consists of question-answer pairs published on a user's profile. We retrieved the data using GNU Wget[2] and crawled a number of randomly chosen seed sites. Although the seed profiles were chosen to be of a user with Dutch as mother-tongue, the crawled data contained a fair amount of non-Dutch data (12,954 posts). The non-Dutch posts were filtered out, which resulted in our experimental corpus containing 85,485 Dutch posts.

3.2 Data Annotation

To operationalize the task of automatic cyberbullying detection, we developed and tested a fine-grained annotation scheme detailed in Van Hee et al. (2015), and applied it to our corpus. To provide the annotators with some context, all posts were presented within their original conversation when possible. The annotation scheme describes two levels of annotation. Firstly, the annotators were asked to indicate, at the post level, whether a post is part of a cyberbullying event. This was done with a harmfulness score on a three-point scale, with 0 signifying that the post does not contain indications of cyberbullying, 1 that the post contains indications of cyberbullying, although they are not severe, and 2 that the post contains serious indications of cyberbullying (e.g. physical threats or incitements to commit suicide). When a post is considered to be part of a cyberbullying event (i.e. its score is 1 or 2), annotators identify the author's role (i.e. harasser, victim or bystander). Two types of bystanders are distinguished in this annotation scheme: 1) bystanders who help the victim and discourage the harasser from continuing his actions (i.e. *bystander-defender*) and 2) bystanders who do not initiate, but take part in the actions of the harasser (i.e. *bystander-assistant*).

Secondly, at the subsentence level, the annotators were tasked with the identification of fine-grained text categories related to cyberbullying. More concretely, they identified all text spans corresponding to one of the categories described in the annotation scheme. For our experiments we focused on the cyberbullying-related text categories that are described below.

- **Threat/Blackmail:** expressions containing physical or psychological threats or indications of blackmail (e.g. *My fist is itching to punch you so hard in the face*).
- **Insult:** expressions containing abusive, degrading or offensive language that are meant to insult the addressee (e.g. *You're a sad little fuck*).
- **Curse/Exclusion:** expressions of a wish that some form of adversity or misfortune will befall the victim and expressions that exclude

[1]http://ask.fm

[2]https://www.gnu.org/software/wget

the victim from a conversation or a social group (e.g. *Just kill yourself*).

- **Defamation:** expressions that reveal confident or defamatory information about the victim to a large public (e.g. *She's a whore and she'll influence you to be one too*).
- **Sexual talk:** expressions with a sexual meaning that are possibly harmful (e.g. *Post a naked pic, now!!*).
- **Defense:** expressions in support of the victim, expressed by the victim himself or by a bystander (e.g. *Shut up about my sister, she is not a slut!*)
- **Encouragement to the harasser:** expressions in support of the harasser (e.g. *Haha, you're so right, he's a nobody*)

We refer to our technical report for a complete overview of the annotation guidelines, including practical remarks and notes. All annotations were done using the brat rapid annotation tool (Stenetorp et al., 2012). Below are given some annotation examples from our dataset.

As shown in the annotation examples, the author's role and harmfulness score are indicated on the pilcrow sign preceding each post. The example posts contain a general insult (*Ge zijt fucking dik*, "you are fucking fat"), a defense (*Vind je jezelf nu beter dan mij nu je dit allemaal zegt? Zoek een leven*, "Do you think that saying this makes you a better person than I am? Get a life"), a threat (*Ik maak u kapot*, "I will destroy you") and a curse (*Pleeg gew zelfmoord*, "Just kill yourself").

In total, 85,485 Dutch posts were annotated by two annotators. To demonstrate the validity of our guidelines, inter-annotator agreement scores were calculated using Kappa (Cohen, 1960) and F-score[3] on a subset of the corpus (~6,500 posts). Kappa scores for the fine-grained categories range from substantial (0.69) to moderate (0.19), except for the category *Defamation*, whose identification seems to be rather difficult.

Annotation	**Kappa**	**F-score**
Cyberbullying -vs- non-cyberbullying	0.69	0.69
Author's role	0.65	0.63
Threat/Blackmail	0.52	0.53
Insult	0.66	0.68
Curse/Exclusion	0.19	0.20
Defamation	0	0
Sexual Talk	0.53	0.54
Defense	0.57	0.58
Encouragement to the harasser	0.21	0.21

Table 1: Inter-annotator agreement scores for the annotation of cyberbullying events, the author's role, and the fine-grained categories.

3.3 Experimental Corpus

The resulting experimental corpus of 85,485 Dutch posts features a skewed class distribution with the large majority of posts not referring to any cyberbullying event. In total, there were 5,685 cyberbullying events (i.e. posts containing at least one of the categories mentioned below), which corresponds to the ratio 1:15. As a cyberbullying event are considered all posts that are given a harmfulness score of 1 or 2.

Category	**# Positive posts**	**Ratio**
Threat/Blackmail	204	~1:418
Insult	4,276	~1:19
Curse/Exclusion	1,110	~1:76
Defamation	162	~1:527
Sexual talk	498	~1:171
Defense	2,218	~1:37
Encouragements to the harasser	42	~1:2,034

Table 2: Data distribution for the fine-grained text categories related to cyberbullying.

In what relates to the fine-grained cyberbullying categories, we can infer from Table 2 that insults are the most frequent type of cyberbullying activity in our data, followed by defense statements and

[3]F-score is an evaluation measure that is the weighted average of precision and recall.

curse/exclusion posts. *Encouragements to the harasser* is the least represented category, with a ratio of 1:2,034. It should be noted that in case the annotators had too little context at their disposal to discern encouragements by bystanders from bullying acts by bullies, they annotated the post as a bullying act.

Table 3 presents the different roles in the annotated bullying posts: the role of bully features in more than half of the annotated posts, followed by the victim role in about 30% of the posts. The bystander role in its two different subroles accounts for about 10% of the experimental corpus.

Author's role	Harmfulness	# Posts
Harasser	1	3085
Harasser	2	181
Victim	1	1671
Victim	2	129
Bystander-defender	1	546
Bystander-defender	2	23
Bystander-assistant	1	49
Bystander-assistant	2	1

Table 3: Data distribution for the different author roles in cyberbullying events.

4 Experiments

This section describes the experiments that were conducted to gain insight into the detection and fine-grained classification of cyberbullying events.

4.1 Experimental Setup

Two sets of experiments were conducted. Firstly, we explored the detection of cyberbullying posts regardless of the harmfulness score (i.e. we considered posts that were given a score of 1 or 2) and the author's role. The second set of experiments focuses on a more complex task, the identification of fine-grained text categories related to cyberbullying (see Section 3.2). To this end, a binary classifier was built for each category. Evaluation was done using 10-fold cross-validation. We used Support Vector Machines (SVM) as the classification algorithm since they have proven to work well for high-skew text classification tasks similar to the ones under investigation (Desmet and Hoste, 2014). We used linear kernels and experimentally determined the optimal cost value c to be 1. All experiments were carried out using Pattern (De Smedt and Daelemans, 2012a), a Python package for data mining, natural language processing and machine learning. As preprocessing steps, we applied tokenization, PoS-tagging and lemmatization to the data using the LeTs Preprocess Toolkit (van de Kauter et al., 2013).

4.2 Features

We experimentally tested whether cyberbullying events and fine-grained categories related to cyberbullying can be recognized by lexical markers in a post. To this end, all posts were represented by a number of standard NLP features including bag-of-words features and sentiment lexicon features:

- **Word n-gram bags-of-words:** binary features indicating the presence of word unigrams and bigrams.
- **Character n-gram bag-of-words:** binary features indicating the presence of character trigrams (without crossing word boundaries), to provide some abstraction from the word level.
- **Sentiment lexicon features:** four numeric features representing the number of positive, negative, and neutral lexicon words (averaged over text length) and the overall post polarity (i.e. the sum of the values of identified sentiment words averaged over text length)[4]. The features were calculated based on existing sentiment lexicons for Dutch (De Smedt and Daelemans, 2012b; Jijkoun and Hofmann, 2009).

5 Results

We implemented different experimental set-ups with various feature groups and hence determined the informativeness of each feature group for the current classification tasks. We explored the contributiveness of the following feature groups in isolation: word unigram bag-of-words (which can be considered as the baseline approach), word bigram bag-of-words, character trigram bag-of-words, and sentiment lexicon features. In addition, all feature groups were combined (*full system*). The results obtained for the cyberbullying event detection and the more fine-grained classification task are described in Section 5.1 and Section 5.2, respectively. A general discussion of the results can be found in Section 5.3.

[4]To increase the lexicon coverage, lemmas were taken into account.

	Word unigrams	Word bigrams	Character trigrams	Sentiment lexicon	Full system
Cyberbully event	47.94	24.31	33.18	6.35	**55.39**

Table 4: F-scores (percentages) obtained for the identification of cyberbullying events when using the feature groups in isolation and combined *(full system)*.

	Word unigrams	Word bigrams	Character trigrams	Sentiment lexicon	Full system
Threat/blackmail	5.42	0.78	2.48	0.14	**19.84**
Sexual talk	15.42	2.40	10.32	0.91	**35.18**
Insult	47.62	19.44	32.13	4.91	**56.32**
Curse/exclusion	20.06	4.76	9.68	0.96	**33.46**
Defense	22.45	8.17	10.38	2.01	**35.09**
Defamation	1.05	0.36	0.23	0.10	**7.41**
Encouragement	**0.12**	0.10	0.07	0.01	0.00

Table 5: F-scores (percentages) obtained for the classification of fine-grained text categories related to cyberbullying when using the feature groups in isolation and combined *(full system)*.

5.1 Cyberbullying Event Classification

For the detection of cyberbullying events, the best results are obtained by combining all features groups (F = 55.39%). Considering the scores of the separate feature groups, we find that word unigram bag-of-words *(b-o-w)* features are the most contributive features, followed by character trigram b-o-w features. Sentiment lexicon features perform the least well for this task. As shown in Table 6, the system performs better in terms of precision than recall.

5.2 Fine-Grained Classification

In line with the cyberbullying event classification, the performance of the fine-grained classifiers benefits from combining all feature groups. F-scores for the fine-grained classification vary rather strongly, reaching up to 56.32% for the *Insult* category. Just as for the cyberbullying event detection, the most contributive feature groups are the word unigram and character trigram b-o-w features, whereas the sentiment lexicon features are the least informative for the classifier. Table 5 shows that the classification of some fine-grained categories related to cyberbullying is more difficult than that of others: the insults classifier obtains an F-score of 56.32%, whereas the best classification performance for *Encouragement* and *Defamation* remains at 0.12% and 7.41%, respectively. In addition to data scarcity (e.g. only 42 positive posts for the *Encouragement* category), the large discrepancies in performance are presumably due to the extent to which a category is lexicalized. Except for these last two groups, most fine-grained categories also show a good balance between precision and recall (see Table 6).

	Recall	Precision
Cyberbully event classification		
Cyberbully event	51.46	59.96
Fine-grained classification		
Threat/Blackmail	25.00	16.45
Sexual talk	36.35	34.09
Insult	53.60	59.33
Curse/Exclusion	32.34	34.65
Defense	31.74	39.22
Defamation	9.88	5.93
Encouragement	0	0

Table 6: Full system performance by means of recall and precision.

5.3 General Discussion

As can be inferred from Tables 4 and 5, using the feature groups in isolation is insufficient for cyberbullying detection. This is especially clear from the sentiment lexicon features. The poor performance of sentiment features in isolation is in line with the findings of Yin et al. (2009). They argue that the sentiment word coverage is limited by the occurrence of spelling errors in social media content. Furthermore, some cyberbullying posts are hurtful even when they do not contain explicit negative language. Inversely, a post may be very negative while devoid of any form of cyberbullying. Although our experiments show that sentiment lexicon features are not very informative when used in isolation, we believe that they should not be discarded for future work as they may be beneficial to the classification performance when used in a combined feature set.

In this paper, we mainly focused on lexical (bag-of-words) features. A major limitation of bag-of-words features is that they often result in sparse feature vectors: a large part of the n-grams in the training data only occur in one or two posts. To reduce feature sparseness, we explored the effect of filtering the n-gram features based on their PoS-tags. Hence we only considered nouns, verbs, adjectives and adverbs for the extraction of word unigram and bigram bag-of-word features. However, this filtering decreased the classification performance by 10% on average. The insults classifier suffered the largest drop (16%). A plausible explanation for this drop is that, by considering only words with simplified PoS-tags, pronouns (e.g. *you*), interjections (e.g. *haha*), foreign words (e.g. *putain*), and misspelled words (e.g. *uglyy*) are discarded although they might be relevant for distinguishing between cyberbullying and non-cyberbullying posts. Although our results show that there is room for improvement, the scores obtained for the binary distinction between cyberbullying and non-cyberbullying are in line with state-of-the-art approaches to automatic cyberbullying detection (e.g. Dadvar et al., 2014; Dinakar et al., 2012). Reynolds et al. (2011) worked with data that is similar to ours (i.e. question-answer pairs) and made use of lexical features including the number of 'bad' words in a post. They obtained an accuracy of 78.5% when the positive posts were overrepresented (their actual presence multiplied by 10) in the training corpus. When the normal distribution was kept, however, the accuracy remained at 53.82%.

Nevertheless, all of the above-mentioned studies mainly focus on the detection of cyberbullying posts that contain insults or curses. The focus of our work is on the detection of cyberbullying events (i.e. posts from victims and bystanders as well as posts from the harasser). Moreover, we aim to detect fine-grained categories related to cyberbullying.

6 Conclusions and Future Work

As cyberbullying often has an implicit and subtle nature, its detection is not a trivial task. We show promising initial results for the identification of cyberbullying events and the fine-grained classification of insults. For the experiments presented in this paper, we relied on lexical features to gain insight into the difficulty and learnability of the detection and fine-grained classification of cyberbullying. We conclude that especially this fine-grained classification is a very challenging task, which is hindered by data sparseness on the one hand and by the degree to which the categories are lexicalized on the other hand.

The ultimate goal of automatic cyberbullying detection is to reduce manual monitoring efforts on social media. As we want to send as much online threats as possible to the moderator of the network, recall optimization will be a prior focus for further research. We will also explore to what extent author role information can be used to enhance the detection of cyberbullying events. Moreover, implicit realizations of cyberbullying are hard to recognize as they are devoid of lexical cues including profanity. Therefore, we will explore the use of more advanced features (e.g. syntactic patterns, semantic information) in addition to lexical features. Additionally, we will examine feature selection techniques to decrease vector sparseness and hence avoid the introduction of noise. Finally, social media texts tend to deviate from the linguistic norm, which reduces the effectiveness of more complex features. Another direction for future work will therefore be orthographic normalization of the data as a preprocessing step.

All experiments in this paper were conducted on a Dutch dataset. Nevertheless, a set of similar experiments will be carried out on an English dataset that is currently under construction.

Acknowledgments

The work presented in this paper was carried out in the framework of the AMiCA (IWT SBO-project 120007) project, funded by the government agency for Innovation by Science and Technology (IWT).

References

Jacob Cohen. 1960. A coefficient of agreement for nominal scales. *Educational and Psychological Measurement*, 20(1):37–46.

Helen Cowie. 2013. Cyberbullying and its impact on young people's emotional health and well-being. *The Psychiatrist*, 37(5):167–170.

Maral Dadvar, Dolf Trieschnigg, and Franciska de Jong. 2014. Experts and Machines against Bullies: A Hybrid Approach to Detect Cyberbullies. In *Advances in Artificial Intelligence*, pages 275–281. Springer International Publishing.

Tom De Smedt and Walter Daelemans. 2012a. Pattern for Python. *Journal of Machine Learning Research*, 13:2063–2067.

Tom De Smedt and Walter Daelemans. 2012b. "Vreselijk mooi!" ("Terribly Beautiful!"): A Subjectivity Lexicon for Dutch Adjectives. In *Proceedings of the Eight International Conference on Language Resources and Evaluation (LREC'12)*, pages 3568–3572, Istanbul, Turkey.

Francine Dehue, Catherine Bolman, and Trijntje Vollink. 2006. Cyberbullying: Youngster's Experiences and Parental Perception. *CyberPsychology*, 4(2):148–169.

Bart Desmet and Véronique Hoste. 2014. Recognising suicidal messages in Dutch social media. In *Proceedings of the Ninth International Conference on Language Resources and Evaluation (LREC)*, pages 830–835, Reykjavik, Iceland.

Karthik Dinakar, Birago Jones, Catherine Havasi, Henry Lieberman, and Rosalind Picard. 2012. Common Sense Reasoning for Detection, Prevention, and Mitigation of Cyberbullying. *ACM Transactions on Interactive Intelligent Systems*, 2(3):18:1–18:30.

Julian J. Dooley and Donna Cross. 2010. Cyberbullying versus face-to-face bullying: A review of the similarities and differences. *Journal of Psychology*, 217:182–188.

Dorothy Wunmi Grigg. 2010. Cyber-Aggression: Definition and Concept of Cyberbullying. *Australian Journal of Guidance and Counselling*, 20:143–156, 12.

Sameer Hinduja and Justin W. Patchin. 2006. Bullies Move Beyond the Schoolyard: A Preliminary Look at Cyberbullying. *Youth Violence And Juvenile Justice*, 4(2):148–169.

Sameer Hinduja and Justin W. Patchin. 2012. Cyberbullying: Neither an epidemic nor a rarity. *European Journal of Developmental Psychology*, 9(5):539–543.

Valentin Jijkoun and Katja Hofmann. 2009. Generating a Non-English Subjectivity Lexicon: Relations That Matter. In *Proceedings of the 12th Conference of the European Chapter of the Association for Computational Linguistics*, pages 398–405, Stroudsburg, PA, USA.

Jaana Juvonen and Elisheva F. Gross. 2008. Extending the school grounds?-Bullying experiences in cyberspace. *Journal of School Health*, 78(9):496–505.

Sara Kiesler, Jane Sigel, and W.Timothy McGuire. 1984. Social psychological aspects of computer-mediated communication. *American Psychologist*, 39(10):1123–1134.

Qing Li. 2007. New Bottle but Old Wine: A Research of Cyberbullying in Schools. *Computers in Human Behavior*, 23(4):1777–1791.

Sonia Livingstone, Leslie Haddon, Anke Görzig, and Kjartan Ólafsson. 2010. Risks and safety on the internet: The perspective of European children. Initial Findings.

Vinita Nahar, Sanad Al-Maskari, Xue Li, and Chaoyi Pang. 2014. Semi-supervised Learning for Cyberbullying Detection in Social Networks. In *ADC.Databases Theory and Applications*, pages 160–171. Springer International Publishing.

Dan Olweus. 1996. Bullying at School: Knowledge Base and an Effective Intervention Program. *Annals of the New York Academy of Sciences*, 794:265–276.

EU Kids Online. 2014. EU Kids Online: findings, methods, recommendations. EU Kids Online, LSE, London, UK. http://eprints.lse.ac.uk/60512/.

Patrick B. O'Sullivan and Andrew J. Flanagin. 2003. Reconceptualizing 'flaming' and other problematic messages. *New Media & Society*, 5(1):69–94.

Megan Price and John Dalgleish. 2010. Cyberbullying: Experiences, Impacts and Coping Strategies as Described by Australian Young People. *Youth Studies Australia*, 29(2):51–59.

Kelly Reynolds, April Kontostathis, and Lynne Edwards. 2011. Using Machine Learning to Detect Cyberbullying. In *Proceedings of the 2011 10th International Conference on Machine Learning and Applications and Workshops*, ICMLA '11, pages 241–244, Washington, DC, USA. IEEE Computer Society.

Robert Slonje and Peter K. Smith. 2008. Cyberbullying: Another main type of bullying? *Scandinavian Journal of Psychology*, 49(2):147–154.

Peter K. Smith, Jess Mahdavi, Manuel Carvalho, Sonja Fisher, Shanette Russell, and Neil Tippett. 2008. Cyberbullying: its nature and impact in secondary school pupils. *Journal of Child Psychology and Psychiatry*, 49(4):376–385.

Pontus Stenetorp, Sampo Pyysalo, Goran Topić, Tomoko Ohta, Sophia Ananiadou, and Jun'ichi Tsujii. 2012. brat: a Web-based Tool for NLP-Assisted Text Annotation. In *Proceedings of the Demonstrations Session at EACL 2012*, pages 102–107, Avignon, France.

Robert S. Tokunaga. 2010. Following You Home from School: A Critical Review and Synthesis of Research on Cyberbullying Victimization. *Computers in Human Behavior*, 26(3):277–287.

Katrien Van Cleemput, Sara Bastiaensens, Heidi Vandebosch, Karolien Poels, Gie Deboutte, Ann DeSmet, and Ilse De Bourdeaudhuij. 2013. Zes jaar onderzoek naar cyberpesten in Vlaanderen, België en daarbuiten: een overzicht van de bevindingen. (Six years of research on cyberbullying in Flanders, Belgium and beyond: an overview of the findings.) (White Paper). Technical report, University of Antwerp & Ghent University.

Marjan van de Kauter, Geert Coorman, Els Lefever, Bart Desmet, Lieve Macken, and Véronique Hoste. 2013. LeTs Preprocess: The multilingual LT3 linguistic preprocessing toolkit. *Computational Linguistics in the Netherlands Journal*, 3:103–120.

Cynthia Van Hee, Ben Verhoeven, Els Lefever, Guy De Pauw, Walter Daelemans, and Véronique Hoste. 2015. Guidelines for the Fine-Grained Analysis of Cyberbullying, version 1.0. Technical Report LT3 15-01, LT3, Language and Translation Technology Team–Ghent University.

Kathleen Van Royen, Karolien Poels, Walter Daelemans, and Heidi Vandebosch. 2015. Automatic monitoring of cyberbullying on social networking sites: From technological feasibility to desirability. *Telematics and Informatics*, 32(1):89–97.

Heidi Vandebosch and Katrien Van Cleemput. 2009. Cyberbullying among youngsters: profiles of bullies and victims. *New Media & Society*, 11(8):1349–1371.

Heidi Vandebosch, Katrien Van Cleemput, Dimitri Mortelmans, and Michel Walrave. 2006. Cyberpesten bij jongeren in Vlaanderen: Een studie in opdracht van het viWTA (Cyberbullying among youngsters in Flanders: a study commissoned by the viWTA). Brussels: viWTA.

Veronika Šléglová and Alena Černá. 2011. Cyberbullying in Adolescent Victims: Perception and Coping. *Cyberpsychology: Journal of Psychosocial Research on Cyberspace*, 5(2).

Nancy E. Willard. 2007. *Cyberbullying and Cyberthreats: Responding to the Challenge of Online Social Aggression, Threats, and Distress*. Research Publishers LLC, 2nd edition.

Michele L. Ybarra and Kimberly J. Mitchell. 2008. How Risky are Social Networking Sites? A Comparison of Places Online Where Youth Sexual Soliciation and Harassment Occurs. *Paediatrics*, 121:350–357.

Dawei Yin, Brian D. Davison, Zhenzhen Xue, Liangjie Hong, April Kontostathis, and Lynne Edwards. 2009. Detection of Harassment on Web 2.0. In *Proceedings of the Content Analysis in the Web 2.0 (CAW2.0)*, Madrid, Spain.

A New Approach for Idiom Identification Using Meanings and the Web*

Rakesh Verma
Computer Science Dept.
University of Houston
Houston, TX, 77204, USA
rverma@uh.edu

Vasanthi Vuppuluri
Computer Science Dept.
University of Houston
Houston, TX, 77204, USA
vvuppuluri@uh.edu

Abstract

There is a great deal of knowledge available on the Web, which represents a great opportunity for automatic, intelligent text processing and understanding, but the major problems are finding the legitimate sources of information and the fact that search engines provide page statistics not occurrences. This paper presents a new, domain independent, general-purpose idiom identification approach. Our approach combines the knowledge of the Web with the knowledge extracted from dictionaries. This method can overcome the limitations of current techniques that rely on linguistic knowledge or statistics. It can recognize idioms even when the complete sentence is not present, and without the need for domain knowledge. It is currently designed to work with text in English but can be extended to other languages.

1 Introduction

Automatically extracting phrases from the documents, be they structured, un-structured or semistructured has always been an important yet challenging task. The overall goal is to create a easily machine-readable text to process the sentences. In this paper we focus on identifying idioms from text. An idiom is a phrase made up of a sequence of two or more words that has properties that are not predictable from the properties of the individual words or their normal mode of combination. Recognition of idioms is a challenging problem with wide applications. Some examples of idioms are 'yellow journalism,' 'kick the bucket,' and 'quick fix'. For example, the meaning of 'yellow journalism' cannot be derived from the meanings of 'yellow' and 'journalism.'

*Research supported in part by NSF grants CNS 1319212, DUE 1241772 and DGE1433817

Idioms play an important role in Natural Language Processing (NLP). They exist in almost all languages and are hard to extract as there is no algorithm that can precisely outline the structure of an idiom. Idioms are important for natural language generation, parsing, and significantly influence machine translation and semantic tagging. Idioms could be also useful in document indexing, information retrieval, and in text summarization or question-answering approaches that rely on extracting key words or phrases from the document to be summarized, e.g., (Barrera and Verma, 2011; Barrera and Verma, 2012; Barrera et al., 2011). Efficiently extracting idioms significantly improves many areas of NLP. But most of the idiom extraction techniques are biased in a way that they focus on a specific domain or make use of statistical techniques alone, which results in poor performance. The technique in this paper makes use of knowledge from the Web combined with knowledge from dictionaries in deciding if a phrase is a idiom rather than solely depending on frequency measures or following rules of a specific domain. The Web has been attractive to NLP researchers because it can solve the sparsity issue and also its update latency is lower than for dictionaries, but its disadvantages are noise, lack of a good method for finding reliable sources and the coarseness of page statistics. Dictionaries are more reliable but they have higher update latency. Our work tries to minimize the disadvantages and maximize the advantages when combining these resources.

1.1 Contribution

This paper proposes a new idiom identification technique, which is general, domain independent and unsupervised in the sense that it requires no labeled datasets of idioms. The major problem with existing approaches is that most of them are supervised, requiring manually annotated data,

Proceedings of Recent Advances in Natural Language Processing, pages 681–687,
Hissar, Bulgaria, Sep 7–9 2015.

and many of them impose syntactic restrictions, e.g., verb-particle, noun-verb, etc. Our technique makes use of carefully extracted reliable knowledge from the Web and dictionaries. Moreover, our technique can be extended to languages other than English, provided similar resources are available. Although our approach uses meanings, with the advancement of the web, more and more phrase definitions are becoming available on the web and thus the reliance on dictionaries can be reduced or even eliminated. However, in many cases, even though the definition of a phrase may be available, the phrase itself is not necessarily labeled as an idiom so we cannot just do a simple lookup of a phrase and mark it as an idiom.

The rest of the paper is organized as follows. Section 2 presents previous work on idiom extraction and classification. In Section 3 we present our approach in detail. Section 4 presents the datasets and in Section 5 we present the experiments and comparisons. We conclude in Section 6.

2 Related Work

There is considerable work on extracting multiword expressions (MWEs), a superclass of idioms, e.g., (Zhang et al., 2006); (Villavicencio et al., 2007); (Li et al., 2008); (Spence et al., 2013); (Ramisch, 2014); (Marie and Constant., 2014); (Schneider et al., 2014); (Kordoni and Simova, 2014); (Yulia and Wintner, 2014). We do not cover this work here since our focus is on idioms.

Because of its importance, several researchers have investigated idiom identification. As mentioned in (Muzny and Zettlemoyer, 2013), prior work on this topic can be categorized into two streams: *phrase classification* in which a phrase is always idiomatic or literal, e.g., (Gedigian et al., 2006); (Shutova et al., 2010), or *token classification* in which each occurrence of a phrase is classified as either idiomatic or literal, e.g., (Birke et al., 2006); (Katz and Eugenie, 2006); (Li and Sporleder, 2009); (Fabienne et al., 2010); (Caroline et al., 2010); (Peng et al., 2014). Most work on the phrase classification stream imposes syntactic restrictions. Verb/Noun restriction is imposed in (Fazly et al., 2009) and (Diab and Pravin, 2009); subject/verb and verb/direct-object restrictions are imposed in (Shutova et al., 2010) and verb-particle restriction is imposed in (Ramisch et al., 2008). Portions of the American National Corpus were tagged for idioms composed of verb-noun constructions, prepositional phrases, and subordinate clauses in (Laura et al., 2010).

To our knowledge, there are only a few general approaches for idiom identification in the phrase classification stream (Muzny and Zettlemoyer, 2013); (Feldman and Peng, 2013) and most of the techniques are supervised. A supervised technique for automatically identifying idiomatic dictionary entries with the help of online resources like Wiktionary is discussed in (Muzny and Zettlemoyer, 2013). There are three lexical features and five graph-based features in this technique, which model whether phrase meanings are constructed compositionally. The dataset consists of phrases, definitions, and example sentences from the English-language Wiktionary dump from November 13th, 2012. The lexical and graph-based features when used together yield F-scores of 40.1% and 62.0% when tested on the same dataset, once without annotating the idiom labels and once after providing the annotated labels. This approach when combined with the Lesk word sense disambiguation algorithm and a Wiktionary label default rule, yields an F-score of 83.8%.

An unsupervised idiom extraction technique using Principal Component Analysis (PCA) treating idioms as semantic outliers and a supervised technique based on Linear Discriminant Analysis (LDA) was described by (Feldman and Peng, 2013). The idea of treating idioms as outliers was tested on 99 sentences extracted from the British National Corpus (BNC) social science (non-fiction) section, containing 12 idioms, 22 dead metaphors and 2 living metaphors. The idea of idiom detection based on LDA was tested on 2,984 Verb-Noun Combination (VNC) tokens extracted from BNC described in (Fazly et al., 2009). These 2,984 tokens are translated into 2,550 sentences of which 2,013 are idiomatic sentences and 537 are literal sentences. A variety of results were presented for PCA for different false positive rates ranging from 1 to 10% (one Table with rates of 16-20%). For idioms only, the detection rates range from 44% at 1% false positive rate to 89% at 10% false positive rate.

Some of the work in the token classification stream, e.g., (Peng et al., 2014), relies on a list of potentially idiomatic expressions. Such a list can be generated using our technique.

3 Idiom Extraction Model

We now present the details of our approach for extracting idioms, which is implemented in Python and called IdiomExtractor. We focus on the meaning of the word *idiom*, i.e., *"properties of individual words in a phrase differ from the properties of the phrase in itself."* Hence, we look at what individual words in a phrase mean and what the phrase means as a whole. If the meaning of phrase is different from what the individual words in the phrase try to convey then by definition of the word *idiom*, that phrase is a idiom.

Steps involved in the process of idiom extraction are as follows:

3.1 Definition Extraction

This step is the most important step in determining if a phrase is a idiom. The definitions of the phrase (D_p) and individual words as per the Part-of-Speech (POS) *whenever possible*, in the phrase are obtained, $\{D_{W1}, D_{W2}, ..., D_{Wj}\}$. In some case a dictionary may not have definitions for a word for the given POS, in which case definition of the word is obtained without taking POS into consideration. For obtaining definitions, we use WordNet, WordNik dictionary API and Bing search API. Here,

$D_p = \{D_1, D_2, D_3, ..., D_k\}$

$D_{W1} = \{D_{11}, D_{12}, D_{13}, ..., D_{1n}\}$

$D_{W2} = \{D_{21}, D_{22}, D_{23}, ..., D_{2m}\}$, and so on.

3.2 Recreating Definitions

Once we have the definitions of each word and those of the phrase, each of the definition is POS tagged using the NLTK POS tagger and only the words whose POS tag is from {noun, verb} are considered and the definitions are recreated after stemming the words using the Snowball Stemmer[1] as, RD_p and $\{RD_{W1}, RD_{W2}, ..., RD_{Wn}\}$ with only those words present. This constraint stems from our observations of several idioms, which showed that idioms in general have at least one of the mentioned POS tags in-order for the phrase to have a meaning. Here,

$RD_p = \{RD_1, RD_2, RD_3, ..., RD_k\}$

$RD_{W1} = \{RD_{11}, RD_{12}, RD_{13}, ..., RD_{1n}\}$

$RD_{W2} = \{RD_{21}, RD_{22}, RD_{23}, ..., RD_{2m}\}$, and so on.

Now, each of the word in the original phrase is replaced with its definitions which results in a set of new phrases P as follows:

$P = \{RD_{11}RD_{12}...RD_{j1}, RD_{12}RD_{21}...RD_{j1}, RD_{1n}RD_{2m}...RD_{jl}\}$

To avoid any confusion regarding how the procedure is implemented an example is provided below.

3.3 Subtraction

Each of the phrases present in P is subtracted from each of the recreated definition in RD_p and the result is stored in set S.

3.4 Idiom Result

There are two options the user can choose in deciding if a phrase is a idiom. They are:

- By Union
- By Intersection

By Union: This is a lenient way of deciding if a phrase is a idiom. Here, if at least one word survives the subtraction step above, then that phrase is declared to be a idiom.

By Intersection: This is a stricter way of deciding if a phrase is a idiom. Here, a phrase is a idiom if and only if at least one word survives all of the subtraction operations.

Example - Definition extraction

D_p = Definition of 'forty winks' = {sleeping for a short period of time (usually not in bed)}

D_{W1} = Definitions of 'forty' as a 'Noun' = {the cardinal number that is the product of ten and four}

D_{W2} = Definitions of 'winks' as a 'Noun' = {a very short time (as the time it takes the eye to blink or the heart to beat), closing one eye quickly as a signal, a reflex that closes and opens the eyes rapidly}

Example - Recreating definitions

RD_p = {sleep period time bed}

RD_{W1} = {number product ten}

RD_{W2} = {time time eye blink heart beat, eye signal, reflex}

P = {number product ten time time eye blink heart beat, number product ten eye signal, number product ten reflex}. Note that we do not eliminate duplicate words such as the word "time" in RD_{W2}, since they really do not affect the idiom extraction,

[1] `http://snowball.tartarus.org/download.php`

procedure IDIOM EXTRACTION
  for *phrase* p in *phrases* extracted **do**
    D_p = Definition of phrase p
    RD_p = Recreated definitions of phrase p
    for _word in phrase **do**
      D_{wi} = Definition of the _word
      RD_{wi} = Recreated definitions of the _word
    Recreating definition phrases, P
    $P = \{RD_{11}RD_{12}...RD_{j1}, RD_{12}RD_{21}...RD_{j1}, RD_{1n}RD_{2m}...RD_{jl}\}$
    Subtraction. $S = RD_p - P$
    idiom result: by Union.
    if S is non-empty **then**
      phrase p is an idiom
    idiom result: by Intersection
    if at least one word survives all subtractions **then**
      phrase p is an idiom

Figure 1: Idiom Extraction Algorithm

but future versions of the software will optimize this aspect.

Example - Subtraction

S = {sleep period time bed} - {number product ten time time eye blink heart beat, number product ten eye signal, number product ten reflex}
= {sleep period bed, sleep period time bed, sleep period time bed}

Count of each word that after subtraction = {sleep: 3, period: 3, time: 2, bed: 3}

The idiom extraction steps can easily be understood with an example as follows:

Example - idiom Result
By Union: Since S is a non-empty set, the phrase 'forty winks' is a idiom
By Intersection: At least one word in S is present as many times as those of recreated definitions. Hence 'forty winks' is a idiom.

4 Datasets

For the experiments in this paper, we used different datasets extracted from englishclub.com and Oxford Dictionary of Idioms and VNC corpus. The datasets and their extraction process is explained here.

4.1 Idiom Example Sentences Dataset

Dataset-1: An idiom dataset is obtained from englishclub.com[2]. From the website, 198 idioms are randomly chosen and 198 example sentences that exemplify those 198 idioms are used. These 198 example sentences that are manually extracted serve as our dataset. This dataset facilitates the evaluation of false positive rate of our technique.

4.2 Oxford Dictionary of Idioms Dataset

Dataset-2: This dataset is a collection of idioms obtained from the Oxford Dictionary of idioms. The text file consisting of 176 idioms is the input for IdiomExtractor. This dataset facilitates the evaluation of recall and false negative rate of our approach.
Preprocessing and Sanitization:
PDFMiner[3] was used to extract text as XML from the PDF version of Oxford Dictionary of Idioms and then a Python script was used to extract idioms from the .xml file into a text file. Also, any non-ASCII characters are ignored while writing the idioms to the text file.

4.3 VNC Dataset

Dataset-3: VNC-tokens are obtained from (Fazly et al., 2009). This dataset consists of 53 unique

[2] `https://www.englishclub.com/ref/Idioms/` (02/23/2015)
[3] `http://www.unixuser.org/~euske/python/pdfminer/` (11/28/2014)

(%)	IdiomExtractor (Union)	IdiomExtractor (Intersection)	AMALGr	Expected maximum
Recall	82.30	67.17	31.50	100.00
Precision	65.90	95.50	14.82	100.00
F-score	73.25	78.69	20.16	100.00

Table 1: Idiom extraction: IdiomExtractor Vs. AMALGr on Dataset-1

(%)	IdiomExtractor (Union)	IdiomExtractor (Intersection)	AMALGr	Expected maximum
Recall	100.00	90.90	67.61	100.00
Precision	100.00	100.00	67.23	100.00
F-score	100.00	95.23	67.42	100.00

Table 2: Idiom extraction: IdiomExtractor Vs. AMALGr on Dataset-2

tokens which were tagged as idiomatic or literal. Irrespective of what the tag was we considered all the tokens as input for our software. We evaluate the recall and false negative rate of our software with the help of this dataset.

5 Performance Evaluation

5.1 IdiomExtractor's Performance

Depending on the number of idioms whose definitions were obtained, the maximum possible recall, precision and F-score are calculated for each of three datasets and the values are tabulated under the 'Expected maximum' column.

On Dataset-1: IdiomExtractor has an F-score of 73.25% by Union approach and 78.69% by Intersection approach. Recall and Precision is documented in Table 3.4. Definitions of all 198 idioms in this dataset are obtained from englishclub.com.

On Dataset-2: IdiomExtractor has an F-score of 95.23% by Intersection approach and 100.00% by Union approach. Recall and Precision is documented in the Table 3.4. For this experiment, we used Oxford Dictionary of Idioms to obtain definitions of 176 idioms.

On Dataset-3: IdiomExtractor has an F-score of of 90.72% by Intersection approach and an F-score of 95.04% by Union approach. In this experiment, we used idiom definitions obtained from two Internet sources[4,5] and individual word definitions are obtained from WordNet dictionary.

5.2 IdiomExtractor Vs. AMALGr

We compare our idiom extraction module with AMALGr from (Schneider et al., 2014) since their definition of MWE "lexicalized combinations of two or more words that are exceptional enough to be considered as single units in the lexicon" aligns with our definition of a idiom and since the authors kindly made their software available.[6] AMALGr requires SAID[7] corpus to be purchased from Linguistic Data Consortium (LDC) (which we purchased) to train the software along with other training data sets. AMALGr requires input text to be represented as two tab separated tokens per line, with the first token being a word from the input and the second token being the part of speech of the word, followed by an empty line when the sentence ends.

When tested on Dataset-1, F-score of IdiomExtractor is 50% more when compared to the F-score of AMALGr. We believe that IdiomExtractor's performance can further be improved if efficient phrasal dictionaries were available for research purposes. Results are documented in Table 3.4.

Reason for low precision of AMALGr: AMALGr joins individual words of MWEs either with an underscore (strong MWE) or tilde (weak MWE). In certain cases, not all words of all the idioms are joined together with either of the special characters and parts of idioms were tagged as MWEs. For example, 'ugly duckling', 'settle a score' weren't tagged as MWEs. An example where part of an idiom is tagged as a MWE is "punch someones lights out." These are declared

[4] `http://idioms.thefreedictionary.com/`
[5] `http://dictionary.reference.com/`

[6] Not everyone we contacted was willing to share idiom extraction software.
[7] `https://catalog.ldc.upenn.edu/LDC2003T10` (02/03/2015)

(%)	IdiomExtractor (Union)	IdiomExtractor (Intersection)	AMALGr	Expected maximum
Recall	90.56	83.01	54.71	90.56
Precision	100.00	100.00	100.00	100.00
F-score	95.04	90.72	70.73	95.04

Table 3: Idiom extraction: IdiomExtractor Vs. AMALGr on Dataset-3

as false positives since we were looking for an exact match for the idiom. This caused a drop in the precision.

When tested on Dataset-2, out of 176 idioms, 119 are tagged as idioms by AMALGr (including both strong and weak idioms as described in (Schneider et al., 2014)) with Recall = 67.61%, Precision = 67.23%, F-score = 67.42%, which, when compared to the performance of IdiomExtractor's Union approach is 32.39% less. Results are documented in Table 3.4.

When tested on Dataset-3, out of 55 VNC-tokens, 29 are tagged as MWEs (strong MWEs and weak MWEs combined). In comparison with IdiomExtractor, the recall from AMALGr is 28.30% less than that of IdiomExtractor, which is 83.01%. IdiomExtractor failed to catch 5 VNC-tokens whose definitions were not provided.

6 Conclusion

In this paper we have presented a new approach for idiom extraction that is both domain and language independent, and does not require labeling of idioms. Our approach is effective as demonstrated on two datasets and in a direct comparison with the supervised approach AMALGr.

One problem with our approach is that the current resources available to us do not contain meanings of all of the idiom phrases. However, we believe that with advancement in technology we would be able to do a much better job of obtaining the phrase definitions in the near future.

One direction for future work is to compare with the set {noun, verb, adjective, adverb} when recreating definitions.

References

Araly Barrera and Rakesh Verma, *Combining Syntax and Semantics for Automatic Extractive Single-document Summarization*, ACM SAC, Document Engineering Track, 2011, Taiwan.

Araly Barrera and Rakesh Verma, *Combining Syntax and Semantics for Automatic Extractive Single-document Summarization*, CICLING, LNCS 7182, 366-377, 2012, New Delhi, India.

Araly Barrera, Rakesh Verma and Ryan Vincent, *SemQuest: University of Houston's Semantics-based Question Answering System*, Text Analysis Conference, 2011.

Julia Birke and Anoop Sarkar. *A Clustering Approach for Nearly Unsupervised Recognition of Nonliteral Language.* EACL 2006, 11st Conference of the European Chapter of the Association for Computational Linguistics, Proceedings of the Conference, April 3-7, 2006, Trento, Italy.

Marie Candito and Matthieu Constant. *Strategies for Contiguous Multiword Expression Analysis and Dependency Parsing.* Proceedings of the 52nd Annual Meeting of the Association for Computational Linguistics, ACL 2014, June 22-27, 2014, Baltimore, MD, USA, Volume 1: Long Papers : 743-753.

Mona T. Diab and Pravin Bhutada. *Verb noun construction MWE token supervised classification.* In Proceedings of the Workshop on Multiword Expressions: Identification, Interpretation, Disambiguation and Applications, pp. 17-22. Association for Computational Linguistics, 2009.

Afsaneh Fazly, Paul Cook and Suzanne Stevenson. *Unsupervised Type and Token Identification of Idiomatic Expressions.* Computational Linguistics 35, no. 1 (2009): 61-103.

Anna Feldman and Jing Peng. *Automatic detection of idiomatic clauses.* Computational Linguistics and Intelligent Text Processing - 14th International Conference, CICLing 2013, Samos, Greece, March 24-30, 2013, Proceedings, Part I.

Fabienne Fritzinger, Marion Weller and Ulrich Heid. *A Survey of Idiomatic Preposition-Noun-Verb Triples on Token Level.* Proceedings of the International Conference on Language Resources and Evaluation, LREC 2010, 17-23 May 2010, Valletta, Malta.

Matt Gedigian, John Bryant, Srini Narayanan and Branimir Ciric. *Catching metaphors.* In Proceedings of the Third Workshop on Scalable Natural Language Understanding, pp. 41-48. Association for Computational Linguistics, 2006.

Spence Green, Marie-Catherine de Marneffe and Christopher D. Manning. *Parsing models for identifying multiword expressions.* Computational Linguistics 39.1 (2013): 195-227.

Graham Katz and Eugenie Giesbrecht. *Automatic identification of non-compositional multi-word expressions using latent semantic analysis.* In Proceedings of the Workshop on Multiword Expressions: Identifying and Exploiting Underlying Properties, pp. 12-19. Association for Computational Linguistics, 2006.

Valia Kordoni and Iliana Simova. *Multiword Expressions in Machine Translation.* Proceedings of the Ninth International Conference on Language Resources and Evaluation (LREC-2014), Reykjavik, Iceland, May 26-31, 2014.

Street Laura, Nathan Michalov, Rachel Silverstein, Michael Reynolds, Lurdes Ruela, Felicia Flowers, Angela Talucci, Priscilla Pereira, Gabriella Morgon, Samantha Siegel, Marci Barousse, Antequa Anderson, Tashom Carroll and Anna Feldman. *Like Finding a Needle in a Haystack: Annotating the American National Corpus for Idiomatic Expressions.* Proceedings of the International Conference on Language Resources and Evaluation, LREC 2010, 17-23 May 2010, Valletta, Malta.

Linlin Li and Caroline Sporleder. *Classifier combination for contextual idiom detection without labeled data.* Proceedings of the 2009 Conference on Empirical Methods in Natural Language Processing, EMNLP 2009, 6-7 August 2009, Singapore, A meeting of SIGDAT, a Special Interest Group of the ACL.

Linlin Li and Caroline Sporleder. *Linguistic Cues for Distinguishing Literal and Non-Literal Usages.* COLING 2010, 23rd International Conference on Computational Linguistics, Posters Volume, 23-27 August 2010, Beijing, China.

Ru Li, Lijun Zhong and Jianyong Duan. *Multiword Expression Recognition Using Multiple Sequence Alignment.* ALPIT 2008, Proceedings of The Seventh International Conference on Advanced Language Processing and Web Information Technology, Dalian University of Technology, Liaoning, China, 23-25 July 2008.

Grace Muzny and Luke S. Zettlemoyer *Automatic Idiom Identification in Wiktionary.* Proceedings of the 2013 Conference on Empirical Methods in Natural Language Processing, EMNLP 2013, 18-21 October 2013, Grand Hyatt Seattle, Seattle, Washington, USA, A meeting of SIGDAT, a Special Interest Group of the ACL.

Jing Peng, Anna Feldman and Ekaterina Vylomova. *Classifying Idiomatic and Literal Expressions Using Topic Models and Intensity of Emotions.* Proceedings of the 2014 Conference on Empirical Methods in Natural Language Processing, EMNLP 2014, October 25-29, 2014, Doha, Qatar, A meeting of SIGDAT, a Special Interest Group of the ACL.

Carlos Ramisch, Aline Villavicencio, Leonardo Moura and Marco Idiart. *Picking them up and figuring them out: Verb-particle constructions, noise and idiomaticity.* Proceedings of the Twelfth Conference on Computational Natural Language Learning, CoNLL 2008, Manchester, UK, August 16-17, 2008: 49-56.

Carlos Ramisch. *Multiword Expressions Acquisition: A Generic and Open Framework.* Theory and Applications of Natural Language Processing. Springer. 2015.

Nathan Schneider, Emily Danchik, Chris Dyer and Noah A. Smith. *Discriminative lexical semantic segmentation with gaps: running the MWE gamut.* Transactions of the Association for Computational Linguistics 2 (2014): 193-206.

Ekaterina Shutova, Sun Lin and Anna Korhonen. *Metaphor Identification Using Verb and Noun Clustering.* COLING 2010, 23rd International Conference on Computational Linguistics, Proceedings of the Conference, 23-27 August 2010, Beijing, China 1002–1010, 2010.

Caroline Sporleder, Linlin Li, Philip Gorinski and Xaver Koch. *Idioms in Context: The IDIX Corpus* Proceedings of the International Conference on Language Resources and Evaluation, LREC 2010, 17-23 May 2010, Valletta, Malta.

Yulia Tsvetkov and Shuly Wintner. *Identification of multiword expressions by combining multiple linguistic information sources.* Computational Linguistics 40, no. 2 (2014): 449-468.

Aline Villavicencio, Valia Kordoni, Yi Zhang, Marco Idiart and Carlos Ramisch. *Validation and Evaluation of Automatically Acquired Multiword Expressions for Grammar Engineering.* EMNLP-CoNLL 2007, Proceedings of the 2007 Joint Conference on Empirical Methods in Natural Language Processing and Computational Natural Language Learning, June 28-30, 2007, Prague, Czech Republic.

Yi Zhang, Valia Kordoni, Aline Villavicencio and Marco Idiart. *Automated multiword expression prediction for grammar engineering.* In Proceedings of the Workshop on Multiword Expressions: Identifying and Exploiting Underlying Properties, pp. 36-44. Association for Computational Linguistics, 2006.

Learning the Impact and Behavior of Syntactic Structure: A Case Study in Semantic Textual Similarity

Ngoc Phuoc An Vo
University of Trento,
Fondazione Bruno Kessler
Trento, Italy
ngoc@fbk.eu

Octavian Popescu
IBM Research, T.J. Watson
Yorktown, US
o.popescu@us.ibm.com

Abstract

We present a case study on the role of syntactic structures towards resolving the Semantic Textual Similarity (STS) task. Although various approaches have been proposed, the research of using syntactic information to determine the semantic similarity is a relatively under-researched area. At the level of syntactic structure, it is not clear how significant the syntactic structure contributes to the overall accuracy of the task. In this paper, we analyze the impact of syntactic structure towards the overall performance and its behavior in different score ranges of the STS semantic scale.

1 Introduction

The task Semantic Textual Similarity (STS) has become a noticed trend in the Natural Language Processing (NLP) community since the SemEval 2012 with a large number of participating systems.[1] The participating systems should be able to determine the degree of similarity for pair of short pieces of text, like sentences, where the similarity score is normally obtained by averaging the opinion of several annotators. A semantic similarity score is usually a real number in a semantic scale [0-5], from *no relevance* to *semantic equivalence*. Some examples from the STS 2012 dataset with associated similarity scores (by human judgment) are as below:

_ *In May 2010, the troops attempted to invade Kabul.* vs. *The US army invaded Kabul on May 7th last year, 2010.* (score = 4.0)

_ *Vivendi shares closed 3.8 percent up in Paris at 15.78 euros.* vs. *Vivendi shares were 0.3 percent up at 15.62 euros in Paris at 0841 GMT.* (score = 2.6)

_ *The woman is playing the violin.* vs. *The young lady enjoys listening to the guitar.* (score = 1.0)

The literature (Agirre et al., 2012; Agirre et al., 2013; Agirre et al., 2014) shows that in order to compute the semantic similarity, most STS systems rely on pairwise similarity, either using taxonomies (WordNet (Fellbaum, 1998)) or distributional semantic models LDA (Blei et al., 2003), LSA (Landauer et al., 1998), ESA (Gabrilovich and Markovitch, 2007), and word/n-grams overlap as main features to train supervised models, or deploy unsupervised word-alignment metrics to align two given texts.

In common sense, syntactic structure may keep a crucial part for human being to understand the meaning of a given text. Thus, it also may help to identify the semantic equivalence between two given texts. However, in the STS task, very few systems provide evidence of the contribution of syntactic structure in its overall performance. Following the work in the literature (Vo and Popescu, 2015), we would like to make a deeper study and analysis whose contribution consists of two folds, on the STS 2012, 2013, and 2014 datasets (1) we assess the impact of syntactic structure towards the overall performance, and (2) analyze the behavior of syntactic structure in each score range of STS semantic scale. We consider three methods reported to perform efficiently and effectively on processing syntactic trees using three proposed approaches Syntactic Tree Kernel (Moschitti, 2006), Syntactic Generalization (Galitsky, 2013) and Distributed Tree Kernel (Zanzotto and Dell'Arciprete, 2012). The reason for this selection consists of two folds: (1) all these approaches use the syntactic parsing as a source for learning syntactic struc-

[1] http://www.cs.york.ac.uk/semeval-2012/task6

Proceedings of Recent Advances in Natural Language Processing, pages 688–696,
Hissar, Bulgaria, Sep 7–9 2015.

ture and information, (2) we compare two well-known groups of method for learning syntactic structure: tree kernel and generalization.

The remainder of the paper is as follows: Section 2 introduces three approaches to exploit the syntactic structure in STS task, Section 3 describes Experimental Settings, Section 4 discusses about the Evaluations and Discussion, Section 5 is the Related Work, and Section 6 is the Conclusions and Future Work.

2 Three Approaches for Learning the Syntactic Structure

In this section, we describe three approaches exploiting the syntactic structure to be used in the STS task: **Syntactic Tree Kernel** (Moschitti, 2006), **Syntactic Generalization** (Galitsky, 2013), and **Distributed Tree Kernel** (Zanzotto and Dell'Arciprete, 2012). They learn the syntactic information either from the dependency or constituency parse trees. Table 1 shows a side-by-side comparison between three approaches for learning syntactic structures.

2.1 Syntactic Tree Kernel (STK)

Given two trees T1 and T2, the functionality of tree kernels is to compare two tree structures by computing the number of common substructures between T1 and T2 without explicitly considering the whole fragment space. According to the literature (Moschitti, 2006), there are three types of fragments described as the subtrees (STs), the subset trees (SSTs) and the partial trees (PTs). A subtree (ST) is a node and all its children, but terminals are not STs. A subset tree (SST) is a more general structure since its leaves need not be terminals. The SSTs satisfy the constraint that grammatical rules cannot be broken. When this constraint is relaxed, a more general form of substructures is obtained and defined as partial trees (PTs).

Syntactic Tree Kernel (Moschitti, 2006) is a tree kernels approach to learn the syntactic structure from syntactic parsing information, particularly, the Partial Tree (PT) kernel is proposed as a new convolution kernel to fully exploit dependency trees. The evaluation of the common PTs rooted in nodes n1 and n2 requires the selection of the shared child subsets of the two nodes, e.g. [S [DT JJ N]] and [S [DT N N]] have [S [N]] (2 times) and [S [DT N]] in common.

In order to learn the similarity of syntactic structure, we seek for a corpus which should fulfill the two requirements, (1) sentence-pairs contain similar syntactic structure, and with (2) a variety of their syntactic structure representations (in their parsing trees). However, the STS corpus does not seem suitable. As the STS corpus contains several different datasets derived from different sources (see Table 2) which carry a large variety of syntactic structure representations, but lack of learning examples from sentence pairs due to different sentence structures. Hence, having assumed that paraphrased pairs would share the same content and similar syntactic structures, we decide to choose the Microsoft Research Paraphrasing Corpus (Dolan et al., 2005) which contains 5,800 sentence pairs extracted from news sources on the web, along with human annotations indicating whether each pair captures a paraphrase/semantic equivalence relationship.[2] This corpus is split into Training set (4,076 pairs) and Testing set (1,725 pairs).

We use Stanford Parser[3] to obtain the dependency parsing from sentence pairs. Then we use the machine learning tool svm-light-tk 1.5 which uses Tree Kernel approach to learn the similarity of syntactic structure to build a binary classifying model on the Train dataset.[4] According to the assumption above, we label paraphrased pairs as 1, -1 otherwise. We test this model on the Test dataset and obtain the Accuracy of 69.16%, with Precision/Recall is: 69.04%/97.21%.

We evaluate this model on the STS data to predict the semantic similarity between sentence pairs. The output predictions are probability confidence scores in [-1,1], corresponds to the probability of the label to be positive.

2.2 Syntactic Generalization (SG)

Given a pair of parse trees, the Syntactic Generalization (SG) (Galitsky, 2013) finds a set of maximal common subtrees. Though generalization operation is a formal operation on abstract trees, it yields semantics information from commonalities between sentences. Instead of only extracting common keywords from two sentences, the generalization operation produces a syntactic expression. This expression maybe semantically interpreted as a common meaning held by

[2] http://research.microsoft.com/en-us/downloads/607d14d9-20cd-47e3-85bc-a2f65cd28042

[3] http://nlp.stanford.edu/software/lex-parser.shtml

[4] http://disi.unitn.it/moschitti/SIGIR-tutorial.htm

Properties	STK	SG	DTK
Method	- tree kernel	- least general generalization	- distributed tree kernel
Parsing	- dependency parse	- constituency parse	- dependency parse
Function	- computes the number of common partial trees between trees T1 & T2	- computes the most specific generalization between two expressions	- uses a linear complexity algorithm to compute vectors for trees

Table 1: Methods Comparison.

both sentences. This syntactic parse tree generalization learns the semantic information differently from the kernel methods which compute a kernel function between data instances, whereas a kernel function is considered as a similarity measure.

SG uses least general generalization (also called anti-unification) (Plotkin, 1970) to anti-unify texts. Given two terms E_1 and E_2, it produces a more general one E that covers both rather than a more specific one as in unification. Term E is a generalization of E_1 and E_2 if there exist two substitutions σ_1 and σ_2 such that $\sigma_1(E) = E_1$ and $\sigma_2(E) = E_2$. The most specific generalization of E_1 and E_2 is called anti-unifier. Technically, two words of the same Part-of-Speech (POS) may have their generalization which is the same word with POS. If lemmas are different but POS is the same, POS stays in the result. If lemmas are the same but POS is different, lemma stays in the result. The example for finding a commonality between two expressions as below:

- camera with digital zoom.
- camera with zoom for beginners.

Then, we can use logic predicates to express the meanings as:

- *camera(zoom(digital), AnyUser)*
- *camera(zoom(AnyZoom), beginner)*

where variables (empty values, not specified in the expressions) are capitalized. Given the above pair of formulas, the unification computes their most general specialization *camera(zoom(digital), beginner)*, while the anti-unification computes their most specific generalization, *camera(zoom(AnyZoom), AnyUser)*.

At syntactic level, we have generalization of two noun phrases as: *{NN-camera, PRP-with, [digital], NN-zoom [for beginners]}*. Then, the expressions in square brackets are eliminated since they occur in one expression and do not occur in another. As a result, we obtain *{NN-camera, PRP-with, NN-zoom]}*, which is a syntactic analog as the semantic generalization above.

We use the toolkit "relevance-based-on-parse-trees" to measure the similarity between two sentences by finding a set of maximal common subtrees, using representation of constituency parse trees via chunking.[5]

2.3 Distributed Tree Kernel (DTK)

Distributed Tree Kernel (DTK) (Zanzotto and Dell'Arciprete, 2012) is a tree kernels method using a linear complexity algorithm to compute vectors for trees by embedding feature spaces of tree fragments in low-dimensional spaces. Then a recursive algorithm is proposed with linear complexity to compute reduced vectors for trees. The dot product among reduced vectors is used to approximate the original tree kernel when a vector composition function with specific ideal properties is used. We extract the parsing by the Stanford Parser and use the software "distributed-tree-kernels" to produce the distributed trees.[6] Then, we compute the Cosine similarity between the vectors of distributed trees of each sentence pair.

3 Experiments

In this section, we describe the STS datasets that we experiment with several different settings in order to evaluate the impact of each syntactic structure approach and in combination with other features in our baseline system.

3.1 Datasets

The STS dataset (English STS) consists of several datasets in STS 2012, 2013 and 2014 (Agirre et al., 2012; Agirre et al., 2013; Agirre et al., 2014). Each sentence pair is annotated the semantic similarity score in the scale [0-5]. Table 2 shows the

[5] https://code.google.com/p/relevance-based-on-parse-trees

[6] https://code.google.com/p/distributed-tree-kernels

year	dataset	pairs	source
2012	MSRpar	1500	newswire
2012	MSRvid	1500	video descriptions
2012	OnWN	750	OntoNotes, WordNet glosses
2012	SMTnews	750	Machine Translation evaluation
2012	SMTeuroparl	750	Machine Translation evaluation
2013	headlines	750	newswire headlines
2013	FNWN	189	FrameNet, WordNet glosses
2013	OnWN	561	OntoNotes, WordNet glosses
2013	SMT	750	Machine Translation evaluation
2014	headlines	750	newswire headlines
2014	OnWN	750	OntoNotes, WordNet glosses
2014	Deft-forum	450	forum posts
2014	Deft-news	300	news summary
2014	Images	750	image descriptions
2014	Tweet-news	750	tweet-news pairs

Table 2: Summary of STS datasets in 2012, 2013, and 2014.

summary of STS datasets and sources over the years. We use four settings for training and evaluation as below:

- Setting 1: train on STS 2012 Train datasets, and evaluate on STS 2012 Test datasets.
- Setting 2: train on all STS 2012 datasets, and evaluate on STS 2013 datasets.
- Setting 3: train on all STS 2012 and 2013 datasets, and evaluate on STS 2014 datasets.
- Setting 4: to avoid the fact that STS provides train and test data derived from different sources, which may requires domain adaptation technique, we performs 10-fold cross validation on each year datasets in 2012, 2013 and 2014; and on all STS datasets together, to speculate the behavior of syntactic structure on each score range of STS, i.e [0-1], [1-2], [2-3], [3-4], and [4-5].

3.2 Baseline

In order to assess the impact of syntactic structure in the STS task, we not only examine the syntactic structure alone, but also combine it with features learned from the most common approach, bag-of-words. Therefore, we use a bag-of-word baseline to evaluate the performance of syntactic approaches. This baseline is the basic one used for evaluation in the STS task, namely **tokencos**. It represents each sentence as a vector in the multidimensional token space (each dimension has 1 if the token is present in the sentence, 0 otherwise) and computes the cosine similarity between vectors.

3.3 Settings

In this section, we present other eight different settings for experimenting the contribution of syntactic structure individually and in combination with typical similarity features to the overall performance of computing similarity score on STS datasets, as follows:

- The STK (2), SG (3), and DTK (4) assess the individual contribution of Syntactic Tree Kernel, Syntactic Generalization and Distributed Tree Kernel approaches, respectively.
- The (2), (3) & (4), assesses the overall contribution of syntactic structure of three approaches.
- The (1) & (2), (1) & (3), and (1) & (4), examine the contribution of each syntactic approach with feature learned from bag-of-words approach in the baseline tokencos.
- The (1), (2), (3) & (4), is the combination of all three approaches with the baseline tokencos.

The output of each approach is normalized to the standard semantic scale [0-5] of STS task to evaluate its standalone performance, or combined with result from other approaches using a simple Linear Regression model in WEKA machine learning tool (Hall et al., 2009) with default configurations and parameters.

4 Evaluations and Discussion

The results reported here are obtained by Pearson correlation, which is the official measure used in STS task.[7]

4.1 Evaluation on STS 2012

Only STS 2012 datasets consists of several of test datasets which have designated training data. Table 3 shows that each method behaves differently on different dataset and results in both positive and negative correlation to human judgment. Only the STK and SG outperform the baseline on *MSRpar* and *MSRvid* by large margins of 16% and 13%, respectively. All methods perform lower than the baseline on most of the datasets, even negative results.

The combination of three approaches does not improve the overall performance on each dataset

[7]http://en.wikipedia.org/wiki/Pearson_product-moment_correlation_coefficient

Settings	MSRpar	MSRvid	SMTeuroparl	OnWN	SMTnews	Mean
Baseline (1)	0.4334	0.2996	0.4542	0.5864	0.3908	0.4329
STK (2)	**0.5988**	0.0916	*-0.1647*	0.0621	0.0986	0.1373
SG (3)	*-0.08*	**0.5354**	0.2095	0.4738	0.3395	0.2956
DTK (4)	0.0205	0.1139	*-0.3427*	*-0.2466*	*-0.1217*	*-0.1153*
(2), (3) & (4)	**0.5832**	0.2339	*-0.0895*	0.2625	0.1897	0.236
(1) & (2)	**0.6546**	0.285	0.2615	0.4687	0.323	0.3986
(1) & (3)	0.1812	**0.3889**	0.4539	**0.5964**	**0.436**	0.4113
(1) & (4)	0.4326	**0.4421**	0.044	0.4986	0.3074	0.3449
(1), (2), (3) & (4)	**0.6447**	**0.4072**	0.0614	0.4799	0.3159	0.3818

Table 3: Results on STS 2012 datasets (represent Pearson correlation with human judgments).

Settings	FNWN	headlines	OnWN	SMT	Mean
Baseline (1)	0.2146	0.5399	0.2828	0.2861	0.3309
STK (2)	0.0458	0.0286	0.0365	*-0.0329*	0.0195
SG (3)	**0.2154**	0.4434	**0.4558**	0.2675	**0.3455**
DTK (4)	*-0.0516*	*-0.1241*	0.1247	*-0.2577*	*-0.0772*
(2), (3) & (4)	0.0991	0.2981	0.2585	0.2096	0.2163
(1) & (2)	0.1398	0.4937	0.2634	0.2321	0.2823
(1) & (3)	**0.2307**	**0.5676**	**0.3617**	**0.3091**	**0.3673**
(1) & (4)	0.2005	**0.547**	**0.3541**	0.181	0.3207
(1), (2), (3) & (4)	0.1651	0.5355	**0.3585**	0.2145	0.3184

Table 4: Results on STS 2013 datasets (represent Pearson correlation with human judgments).

Settings	deft-forum	deft-news	headlines	images	OnWN	tweet-news	Mean
Baseline (1)	0.3531	0.5957	0.5104	0.5134	0.4058	0.6539	0.5054
STK (2)	0.1163	0.2369	0.0374	*-0.1125*	0.0865	*-0.0296*	0.0558
SG (3)	0.2816	0.3808	0.4078	0.4449	**0.4934**	0.5487	0.4262
DTK (4)	0.0171	0.1	*-0.0336*	*-0.109*	0.0359	*-0.0986*	*-0.0147*
(2), (3) & (4)	0.2402	0.3886	0.3233	0.2419	**0.4066**	0.4489	0.3416
(1) & (2)	0.3408	0.5738	0.4817	0.4184	0.4029	0.6016	0.4699
(1) & (3)	**0.3735**	0.5608	**0.5367**	**0.5432**	**0.4813**	**0.6736**	**0.5282**
(1) & (4)	**0.3795**	**0.6343**	**0.5399**	0.5096	**0.4504**	**0.6539**	**0.5279**
(1), (2), (3) & (4)	**0.3662**	0.5867	**0.5265**	0.464	**0.4758**	0.6407	**0.51**

Table 5: Results on STS 2014 datasets (represent Pearson correlation with human judgments).

or overall result. However, it partially covers the weakness of each method on each dataset.

The combination of each method with the bag-of-word approach returns both increase and decrease results. However, this combination obtains the best performance on the dataset *MSRvid* whereas two settings outperform the baseline and another is very close to the baseline. Among the three methods, SG seems to integrate well with the bag-of-word approach in which its combinations outperform the baseline on three datasets *MSRvid, OnWN*, and *SMTnews*. However, none of these settings equals to the baseline in overall result.

4.2 Evaluation on STS 2013

Table 4 shows that none of the approach individually equals to the baseline on any dataset, except the SG is slightly better than the baseline

Settings	**STS 2012**	**STS 2013**	**STS 2014**	**STS 2012-2013-2014**
Baseline (1)	0.3147	0.3541	0.4353	0.3826
STK (2)	**0.3267**	0.2652	0.0019	0.2335
SG (3)	0.2613	**0.429**	0.4268	0.3583
DTK (4)	0.0842	*-0.0543*	*-0.0428*	0.0184
(2), (3) & (4)	**0.3954**	**0.4662**	0.4271	**0.4041**
(1) & (2)	**0.4316**	**0.452**	0.4346	**0.4361**
(1) & (3)	**0.3544**	**0.4498**	**0.4921**	**0.4353**
(1) & (4)	**0.3905**	**0.3754**	**0.4617**	**0.4223**
(1), (2), (3) & (4)	**0.4634**	**0.5**	**0.5082**	**0.4796**

Table 6: Cross Validation Results on STS datasets (represent Pearson correlation with human judgments).

on *FNWN*. The DTK the returns the worst performance (negative results) on three datasets *FNWN*, *headlines* and *SMT*.

The combination of three approaches brings no improvement over the baseline, but it covers the weakness from DTK on all datasets.

The combination between each method with the bag-of-word approach covers the weakness of each method itself (no more negative result appears). This combination especially works very well on the datasets *headlines* and *OnWN* with two times outperform the baseline. SG proves to be the best method integrate with the bag-of-word approach by obtaining 3% better than the baseline.

4.3 Evaluation on STS 2014

Table 5 shows that none of these three methods equals to the baseline. Though the STK and DTK both use the tree kernel approach, just different representations, in overall, the STK performs better than DTK on most of datasets. STK and DTK return negative results on the datasets images and tweet-news whereas the SG obtains quite good result.

The combination of three approaches does not collaborate well on STS datasets, it even decreases the overall performance of the best method SG by a large margin of 8%. Finally, this combination does not make any improvement over the baseline. Thus, this combination of syntactic approaches cannot solve the STS task.

The combination of syntactic information and bag-of-word approach improves the performance on many datasets over the baseline. On STS, SG and DTK are benefited from the combination by outperforming the baseline around 2%. SG is the best method to integrate with the bag-of-word on all STS datasets. The combination of three methods with the bag-of-word returns 0.5% and 2% better results than the baseline.

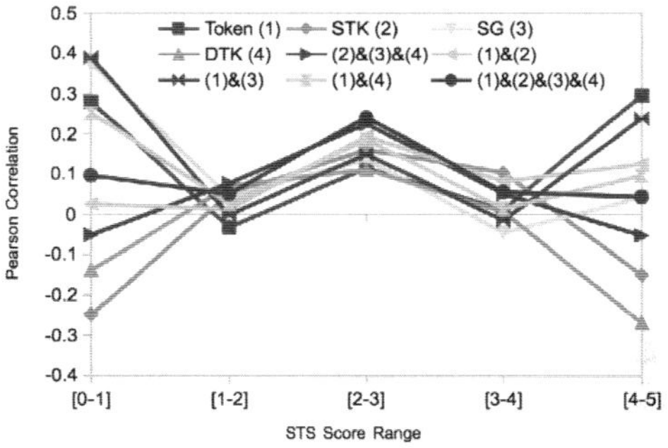

Figure 1: STS2012 Cross-Validation Analysis.

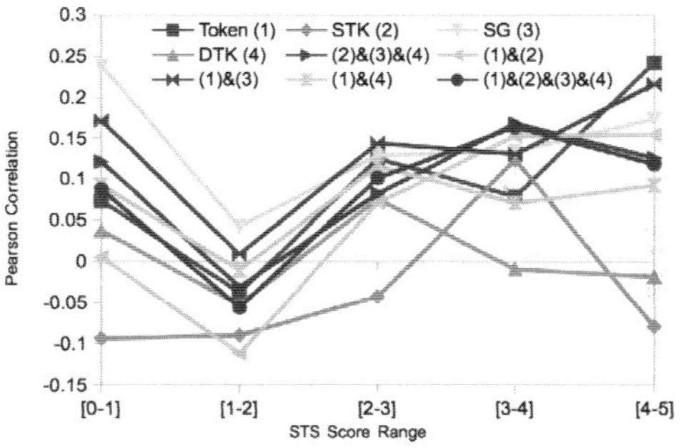

Figure 2: STS2013 Cross-Validation Analysis.

4.4 Evaluation by Cross-Validation

Table 6 shows that each approach usually performs lower than the baseline, but its combinations with baseline outperform the baseline itself in most of cases. In the semantic scale from 0 (dissimilar) to 5 (completely equivalent), we speculate the behavior of syntactic structure and its impact to predicting correct semantic similarity scores in STS.

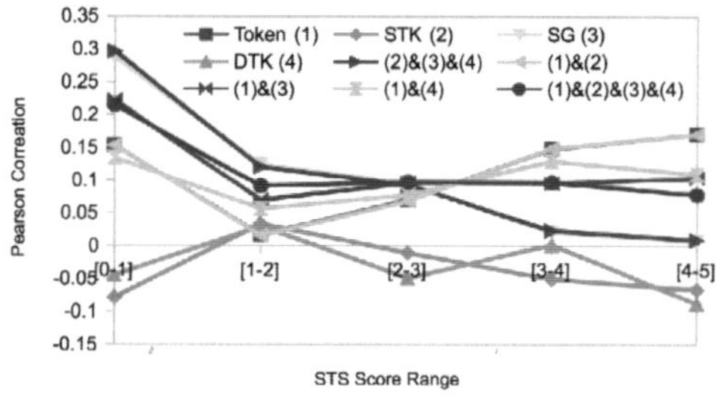

Figure 3: STS2014 Cross-Validation Analysis.

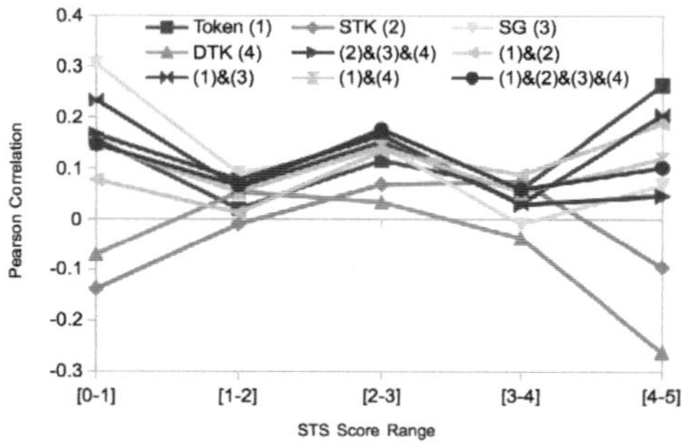

Figure 4: STS2012, 2013, and 2014 Cross-Validation Analysis.

Cross-validation on STS 2012. Figure 1 shows that syntactic structure in different settings results high correlation (either positive or negative) mostly in three score ranges [0-1] (dissimilar, or not equivalent but same topic), [2-3] (not equivalent but share some detailes, or roughly equivalent but some important information missing), and [4-5] (mostly equivalent, or completely equivalent).

Cross-validation on STS 2013. Similar to STS 2012, Figure 2 shows that syntactic structure obtains high correlation (both positive and negative) mostly in three score ranges [0-1], [2-3], [4-5], and also [3-4] (roughly equivalent, or mostly equivalent).

Cross-validation on STS 2014. Figure 3 shows that the impact of syntactic structure presents most significantly in the range [0-1], and almost equivalently in other ranges [1-2], [2-3], [3-4], and [4-5].

Cross-validation on the combination of STS 2012, 2013 and 2014. In overall, Figure 4 confirms the significance of syntactic structure mostly in three score ranges [0-1], [2-3], and [4-5].

All the cross-validation results reveal some interesting behaviors of syntactic structure on STS datasets:

- The bag-of-word approach mostly has positive correlation in all ranges, but highest in [0-1] and [4-5].
- STK always obtains highly negative correlation on STS datasets in the ranges [0-1] and [4-5], but it results unpredictable correlation (both positive and negative) in other ranges.
- DTK seems to have similar behavior to STK but more fluctuate. This confirms that since these two approaches use the same method (tree kernel), they tend to have similar behaviors.
- In contrast, SG always returns positive correlation in all ranges (except the a very slightly negative correlation in range [3-4] on STS 2012), but highest in [0-1] and [4-5]. The trends confirm that SG usually has highest correlation in [0-1], [1-2], and [2-3].
- The combination of three approaches tends to correlate closely to the trend of SG.
- The combination of three approaches with bag-of-word behaves similarly to the bag-of-word itself, but sometimes slightly turns down in ranges [0-1] and [4-5]. This setting usually helps to improve the overall performance in ranges [1-2], [2-3], and [3-4].
- The combination of each approach with the bag-of-word returns similar behavior to the bag-of-word itself. Sometimes, this setting slightly improves the performance of bag-of-word in different ranges.

In conclusion, despite the fact that we experiment different methods to exploit syntactic information on different datasets derived from various data sources, the results confirm the positive impact of syntactic structure in the overall performance on STS task. However, syntactic structure does not always work well and effectively on any dataset, it requires a certain level of syntactic presentation in the corpus to exploit. In some cases, applying syntactic structure on poor-structured data may cause negative effect to the overall performance. Among these three methods, the SG shows to be the most effective one to exploit syntactic and semantic information individually or collaboratively with the bag-of-word approach. Moreover, the experiment results show that the bag-of-word approach is still a very strong and effective method to learn the semantic information in the STS task; and its combination with syntactic approaches returns improvement in the overall performance.

5 Related Work

Complex logical representations are usually used for semantic inference tasks. Nevertheless, due to the high cost of constructing complex logical representations, practical applications usually support shallower level of lexical or lexical-syntactic representations. The literature (Bar-Haim et al., 2007) proposed an approach operating on syntactic trees directly. Basically, entailment rules are used to infer new trees and provide unified representation for various inference types. Manual and automatic methods are used to generate rules and cover generic linguistic structures as well as specific lexical-based inferences. However, current works focus on syntactic tree transformation in graph learning framework (Chakrabarti and Faloutsos, 2006), (Kapoor and Ramesh, 1995), treating various phrasings for the same meaning in a more unified and automated manner.

In the STS task, several attempts are made to exploit the syntactic structure to solve the task. In the literature (Islam and Inkpen, 2008), a simple method is deployed to examine the shallow syntactic relation between two given sentences towards computing their semantic similarity, namely, Common Word Order Similarity between Sentences. The basic idea is that if the two texts have some words in common, we can measure how similar the order of the common-words is in the two texts (if these words appear in the same order, or almost the same order, or very different order). This similarity is determined by the normalized difference of common-word order.

The Takelab system (Šarić et al., 2012) which is ranked 2nd at STS 2012 used two methods to learn the syntactic structure for computing the semantic similarity between given sentences. (1) Syntactic Roles Similarity uses dependency parsing to identify the lemmas with the corresponding syntactic roles in the two sentences. Given two sentences, the similarity of words or phrases that have the same syntactic roles may indicate their overall semantic similarity (Oliva et al., 2011). (2) Syntactic Dependencies Overlap computes the overlap of the dependency relations between two given sentences. A similar measure has been proposed in (Wan et al., 2006) in which if two syntactic dependencies share the same dependency type, governing lemma and dependent lemma, they are considered equal.

At STS 2013, the iKernels system (Severyn et al., 2013) proposed the idea of using relational structures to jointly model text pairs. They defined two new relational structures based on constituency and dependency trees. In constituency tree, each sentence is represented by its constituency parse tree. Then a special REL tag is used to link the related structures and encode the structural relationships between two sentences. In contrast, the dependency relations between words are used to derive an alternative structural representation in which words are linked in a way that words are always at the leaf level. The part-of-speech tags between the word nodes and nodes carrying their grammatical role are also plugged in. Then the REL tag is used to establish relations between tree fragments. Finally, the Partial Tree Kernel is used to compute the number of common substructures.

6 Conclusions and Future Work

In this paper, we deploy three different approaches to exploit and evaluate the impact of syntactic structure in the STS task. We use a bag-of-word baseline which is the official baseline of STS task for the evaluation. We also evaluate the contribution of each syntactic structure approach integrated with the bag-of-word approach in the baseline. From our observation, for the time being with recent proposed approaches, the results in Tables 3, 4, and 5 shows that the syntactic structure does contribute and play a part individually and together with typical similarity approaches for computing the semantic similarity scores between given sentence pairs. However, compared to the baseline, the contribution of syntactic structure is not significant to the overall performance. For future works, we may expect to see more effective ways for exploiting and learning syntactic structure to have better contribution into the overall performance in the STS task.

References

Eneko Agirre, Mona Diab, Daniel Cer, and Aitor Gonzalez-Agirre. 2012. Semeval-2012 task 6: A pilot on semantic textual similarity. In *Proceedings of the First Joint Conference on Lexical and Computational Semantics-Volume 1: Proceedings of the main conference and the shared task, and Volume 2: Proceedings of the Sixth International Workshop on Semantic Evaluation*, pages 385–393. Association for Computational Linguistics.

Eneko Agirre, Daniel Cer, Mona Diab, Aitor Gonzalez-Agirre, and Weiwei Guo. 2013. sem 2013 shared task: Semantic textual similarity, including a pilot on typed-similarity. In *Proceedings of the *SEM 2013: The Second Joint Conference on Lexical and Computational Semantics. Association for Computational Linguistics*. Citeseer.

Eneko Agirre, Carmen Baneab, Claire Cardiec, Daniel Cerd, Mona Diabe, Aitor Gonzalez-Agirrea, Weiwei Guof, Rada Mihalceab, German Rigaua, and Janyce Wiebeg. 2014. Semeval-2014 task 10: Multilingual semantic textual similarity. *SemEval 2014*, page 81.

Roy Bar-Haim, Ido Dagan, Iddo Greental, and Eyal Shnarch. 2007. Semantic inference at the lexical-syntactic level. In *Proceedings of the National Conference on Artificial Intelligence*, volume 22, page 871. Menlo Park, CA; Cambridge, MA; London; AAAI Press; MIT Press; 1999.

David M Blei, Andrew Y Ng, and Michael I Jordan. 2003. Latent dirichlet allocation. *the Journal of machine Learning research*, 3:993–1022.

Deepayan Chakrabarti and Christos Faloutsos. 2006. Graph mining: Laws, generators, and algorithms. *ACM Computing Surveys (CSUR)*, 38(1):2.

Bill Dolan, Chris Brockett, and Chris Quirk. 2005. Microsoft research paraphrase corpus. *Retrieved March*, 29:2008.

Christiane Fellbaum. 1998. *WordNet*. Wiley Online Library.

Evgeniy Gabrilovich and Shaul Markovitch. 2007. Computing semantic relatedness using wikipedia-based explicit semantic analysis. In *IJCAI*, volume 7, pages 1606–1611.

Boris Galitsky. 2013. Machine learning of syntactic parse trees for search and classification of text. *Engineering Applications of Artificial Intelligence*, 26(3):1072–1091.

Mark Hall, Eibe Frank, Geoffrey Holmes, Bernhard Pfahringer, Peter Reutemann, and Ian H Witten. 2009. The weka data mining software: an update. *ACM SIGKDD explorations newsletter*, 11(1):10–18.

Aminul Islam and Diana Inkpen. 2008. Semantic text similarity using corpus-based word similarity and string similarity. *ACM Transactions on Knowledge Discovery from Data (TKDD)*, 2(2):10.

Sanjiv Kapoor and Hariharan Ramesh. 1995. Algorithms for enumerating all spanning trees of undirected and weighted graphs. *SIAM Journal on Computing*, 24(2):247–265.

Thomas K Landauer, Peter W Foltz, and Darrell Laham. 1998. An introduction to latent semantic analysis. *Discourse processes*, 25(2-3):259–284.

Alessandro Moschitti. 2006. Efficient convolution kernels for dependency and constituent syntactic trees. In *Machine Learning: ECML 2006*, pages 318–329. Springer.

Jesús Oliva, José Ignacio Serrano, María Dolores del Castillo, and Ángel Iglesias. 2011. Symss: A syntax-based measure for short-text semantic similarity. *Data & Knowledge Engineering*, 70(4):390–405.

Gordon D Plotkin. 1970. A note on inductive generalization. *Machine intelligence*, 5(1):153–163.

Frane Šarić, Goran Glavaš, Mladen Karan, Jan Šnajder, and Bojana Dalbelo Bašić. 2012. Takelab: Systems for measuring semantic text similarity. In *Proceedings of the First Joint Conference on Lexical and Computational Semantics-Volume 1: Proceedings of the main conference and the shared task, and Volume 2: Proceedings of the Sixth International Workshop on Semantic Evaluation*, pages 441–448. Association for Computational Linguistics.

Aliaksei Severyn, Massimo Nicosia, and Alessandro Moschitti. 2013. ikernels-core: Tree kernel learning for textual similarity. In *Proceedings of the Second Joint Conference on Lexical and Computational Semantics*, volume 1, pages 53–58. Citeseer.

Ngoc Phuoc An Vo and Octavian Popescu. 2015. A preliminary evaluation of the impact of syntactic structure in semantic textual similarity and semantic relatedness tasks. In *NAACL-HLT 2015 Student Research Workshop (SRW)*, page 64.

Stephen Wan, Mark Dras, Robert Dale, and Cécile Paris. 2006. Using dependency-based features to take the "para-farce" out of paraphrase. In *Proceedings of the Australasian Language Technology Workshop*, volume 2006.

Fabio Massimo Zanzotto and Lorenzo Dell'Arciprete. 2012. Distributed tree kernels. In *Proceedings of the 29th International Conference on Machine Learning (ICML-12)*.

Six Good Predictors of Autistic Text Comprehension

Victoria Yaneva
Research Group in Computational Linguistics
University of Wolverhampton
V.Yaneva@wlv.ac.uk

Richard Evans
Research Group in Computational Linguistics
University of Wolverhampton
R.J.Evans@wlv.ac.uk

Abstract

This paper presents our investigation of the ability of 33 readability indices to account for the reading comprehension difficulty posed by texts for people with autism. The evaluation by autistic readers of 16 text passages is described, a process which led to the production of the first text collection for which readability has been evaluated by people with autism. We present the findings of a study to determine which of the 33 indices can successfully discriminate between the difficulty levels of the text passages, as determined by our reading experiment involving autistic participants. The discriminatory power of the indices is further assessed through their application to the FIRST corpus which consists of 25 texts presented in their original form and in a manually simplified form (50 texts in total), produced specifically for readers with autism.

1 Introduction

Autism Spectrum Disorder (ASD) is a developmental disorder of neural origin, characterised by impairment in communication and social interaction and stereotyped repetitive behaviour (American Psychiatric Association, 2013). Currently about 1 in 100 people in the UK are diagnosed with this condition (Brugha et al., 2012), and there are assumed to be two undiagnosed cases for every three diagnosed (Baron-Cohen et al., 2009). In many countries there are no official statistics about the number of affected individuals, but with rising awareness of the condition, this number has been continually increasing to the extent that it is now referred to as an autism epidemic (Wazana, 2007).

One of the central characteristics of autism is impairment in communication both in terms of language comprehension and social interaction. Depending on the severity with which the condition affects individuals, they may be low-functioning and often non-verbal or medium and high-functioning, requiring help with only the social aspects of language use. While most medium- and high-functioning autistic people have a high level of word decoding skills when reading, they struggle at semantic, syntactic and most of all, pragmatic levels of understanding. For example it may be challenging for autistic readers to access the meaning of some words if they are very abstract or are too long; they may have difficulty in processing long and complex sentences due to the cognitive load that these impose on the reader and the comparatively short working memory span that people with autism may have (Bennetto et al., 1996). However, the area of utmost difficulty for autistic individuals, which differentiates them from non-autistic readers in the way that they read, is their inability to "refer to the whole", to struggle to infer meaning from both the semantic and the social context of a text (Frith and Snowling, 1983; Happé, 1997). These characteristics of their reading can be illustrated by the ability of autistic readers to use syntactic context but not semantic context to disambiguate homophones (Happé, 1997) and by their reduced ability to understand non-literal language, sarcasm, irony and authors' intentions (O'Connor and Klein, 2004; MacKay and Shaw, 2004).

There are a number of software tools designed to assist people with autism in their use of language, including automatic text simplification tools (Section 2.1). The emergence of such software entails a need, at the very least, to assess the accessibility of instruction manuals provided for users with autism. In the case of text simplification software, it is necessary to assess (1) the extent to which texts require conversion to a more accessible form, (2) the types of conversion oper-

Proceedings of Recent Advances in Natural Language Processing, pages 697–706,
Hissar, Bulgaria, Sep 7–9 2015.

ations that are required, and (3) the suitability of the converted output for readers with autism. It is expected that people working to improve the accessibility of a given text, both in automatic and manual text conversion, will benefit from relevant feedback concerning the effects of different conversion operations and the extent to which different versions of a text meet the particular requirements of intended readers. So far the only way to perform such evaluation has been to conduct time-consuming and expensive user-focused evaluation studies. Automatic methods to assess the readability of texts for people with autism have proven useful in the process of automatic text simplification but these have not been applied to user-evaluated texts and thus their merit is unknown. In this paper, the term *user-evaluated texts* is used to denote texts whose readability has been evaluated via reading comprehension testing and recording of the reading times of people with autism. So far, their scarcity has meant that user-evaluated texts have not been exploited in the development of language technology intended to provide reading support. (Section 2.2). There has also been no user-focused research on readability in autism.

The research described in the current paper includes:

- the production of reading passages at different readability levels evaluated by 20 participants with autism with no developmental delay.

- evaluation of the effectiveness of 33 automatically computed readability indices to discriminate between texts classified by the users as easy or difficult. Some of these indices have been used in the past to account for reading difficulties in autism but this is the first time that their effectiveness has been tested on text passages evaluated by users.

- evaluation of the indices on the FIRST corpus which consists of 25 texts presented in their orginal form and in a more accessible form, converted by experts working with people with autism and following ASD-specific text simplification guidelines (Jordanova et al., 2013).

These are contributions toward a better understanding of text readability from the perspective of people with autism.

2 Related Work

2.1 Assistive Language Technology for People with Autism

Assistive software and technologies have repeatedly been reported to be well-received among autistic individuals for various reasons, including their demand for structure and uniformity, the ability of automatic tools to repeat the same action or instruction multiple times and the ability of these tools to reduce the complexity of social situations (Bosseler and Massaro, 2003; Putnam and Chong, 2008). As the need of autistic individuals for assistance with language-related tasks is well-known, a number of software tools have been developed to assist the language development of autistic individuals of various age groups and at various levels of ability.

A suitable tool for people with ASD who are severely impaired and who may remain completely or partially non-verbal, are the various types of picture exchange communication systems (PECS), which allow them to produce sentences by combining images and words on a tablet screen or PDA (Charlop-Christy et al., 2002). For those who are not so severely impaired as to remain non-verbal but are still in the process of acquiring verbal skills, the *VAST-Autism* app[1] combines videos with written words and auditory cues to help autistic and apraxic individuals acquire certain words, phrases or sentences. *Stories About Me*,[2] is another iPad application, which helps autistic users produce stories by combining photographs with text and voice recordings.

For autistic individuals who are fairly able, the *OpenBook* tool[3] provides semi-automatic conversion of text documents by reducing syntactic complexity and disambiguating meaning by resolving pronominal reference, performing word sense disambiguation and detecting conventional metaphors. The output is an accessible version of the original document supplemented with additional elements such as glossaries, illustrative images, and document summaries. The system is deployed as an editing tool for healthcare and educational service providers.

Systems such as *OpenBook* can benefit from ad-

[1]https://itunes.apple.com/us/app/vast-autism-1-core/id426041133?mt=8, last accessed May 2015.

[2]https://itunes.apple.com/us/app/stories-about-me/id531603747?mt=8, last accessed May 2015.

[3]http://openbooktool.net, last accessed May 2015.

vances in autism-specific automatic readability assessment, as this process can be used to evaluate each conversion operation applied.

2.2 Readability Assessment

Readability assessment has been used to match intended readers to texts with a view to the specific purpose of reading (Chall and Dale, 1995). Classic readability formulae typically exploit textual features such as sentence length, word length, and the average number of syllables per word, or make use of word lists such as Dale and Chall's list of 3 000 EasyWords (Dale and Chall, 1948). Dubay (2004) provides information on a large number of readability formulae. More sophisticated systems, such as the *Coh-Metrix* system (Graesser et al., 2004) and the Lexile Framework (Smith et al., 1989), are based on surface features, cognitively-motivated features and features of cohesion and syntactic complexity, exploiting human-evaluated databases such as the Colorado Norms for word familiarity, and age of acquisition and concreteness indices, among others (Smith et al., 1989; McNamara et al., 2010).

Readability formulae are developed with particular target populations and text types in mind (Siddharthan, 2004; Benjamin, 2012; Bruce et al., 1981), which is why readability features relevant specifically to people with special needs have also been explored. For example, people with intellectual disability have been found to have decreased working memory capacity (a characteristic they share with some people with autism), which results in their difficulty in remembering relations within and between sentences (Jansche et al., 2010). Thus, features developed for and evaluated on this reader population include entity density (counts of entities such as person, location and organisation per sentence) and lexical chains (synonymy or hyponymy relations between nouns) (Jansche et al., 2010; Feng et al., 2010; Huenerfauth et al., 2009). Word frequency and word length have been found to affect readability for Spanish readers with dyslexia based on data from eye tracking techniques and comprehension questions (Rello et al., 2012a; Rello et al., 2012b).

Previous assessments of the readabiliy of texts to be read by people with autism have explored features hypothesised to be related to those aspects of language known to pose reading comprehension difficulties for this population (Martos et al., 2013; Štajner et al., 2012; Štajner et al., 2014).[4] In previous research, a set consisting of three groups of readability indices, used to estimate syntactic complexity and ambiguity in meaning, together with several other exisiting readability formulae were used to assess the readability of texts of the registers of news, health, and fiction. The scores obtained were compared with those obtained when estimating the readability of texts from Simple Wikipedia, which were assumed to be a gold standard of readability. This assumption is disputed (Štajner et al., 2012) but at the time of their experiments, no user-evaluated text resources were available. Readability indices such as the number of metaphors or passive verb constructions per text have been considered (Jordanova et al., 2013) but their discriminative power has not previously been evaluated on texts whose difficulty for autistic readers is known. The research presented in this paper builds upon these previous studies by evaluating text passages with respect to 20 participants with autism and testing the effectiveness of various readability indices, including those developed by Jordanova et al. (2013), to discriminate between the levels of difficulty of the passages.

3 Production of User-Evaluated Text Passages

This section presents the experimental design and procedure for evaluating the difficulty of 16 text passages by 20 participants diagnosed with autism spectrum disorder.

3.1 Design and Materials

The participants were asked to read text passages and answer three multiple choice questions (MCQs) per passage. Evaluation of the difficulty of the texts is then based on their answers to the questions and their reading time scores, produced by dividing the amount of time a participant spends reading the text (measured in seconds) by the number of words in the text to control for the differences in length between the texts.

3.1.1 Text Passages

To avoid bias, the study included a total of 16 text passages from miscellaneous domains and registers (3 newspaper articles, 3 educational articles, 3 general informational texts obtained from the web,

[4] Hypotheses that were not formally tested.

and 7 easy-read documents, which are simple documents developed specifically for people with disabilities) (Table 1).The presented texts vary in difficulty and avoid potentially sensitive topics such as religion, sexuality, and disabilities.

One of the biggest challenges in the design of this study and the selection of materials was the fact that people with autism are prone to experience difficulties with concentration and attention, resulting in fatigue (Happé and Frith, 2006; Lai et al., 2014). For this reason, the evaluation by a single participant of a large set of long text passages is not feasible. The length of each text and the number of texts presented to each participant were selected with a view to avoid fatigue and to comply with ethical considerations. Table 1 summarises some of the characteristics of the texts included in this study.

Text Number	Register	#Words	Flesch-Kincaid Grade Level[5]	Flesh Reading Ease Score[6]
1	Informational	163	4.93	79.548
2	Educational	178	4.671	80.22
3	Educational	206	7.577	65.437
4	Educational	189	9.276	56.758
5	Newspaper	226	11.983	40.658
6	Newspaper	160	8.866	59.82
7	Informational	163	8.765	66.657
8	Informational	185	14.678	45.34
9	Newspaper	188	9.823	58.298
10	Easy-Read	77	8.16	60.11
11	Easy-Read	96	6.73	67.33
12	Easy-Read	74	2.71	92.54
13	Easy-Read	178	5.52	75.33
14	Easy-Read	77	5.79	70.67
15	Easy-Read	121	1.75	95
16	Easy-Read	58	6.63	68.16

Table 1: Characteristics of the 16 texts included in the study.

3.1.2 Questions

Three multiple choice questions (MCQs) with four possible answers were developed for each text. Three different types of MCQs were presented to assess different types of reading comprehension:

1. Literal MCQs, examining literal understanding of the texts;

2. Reorganisation MCQs, examining the ability of participants to combine information from different parts of the text. One characteristic of autistic readers is that they make little use of context (Oliver, 1998; O'Connor and Klein, 2004), which is crucial for performing the task of reorganisation;

3. Gap Inference MCQs, examining participants' abilities to use two or more pieces of information from a text in order to arrive at a third piece of information that is implicit (Kispal, 2008). Since this type of question is based on literal understanding, they evaluate the role of context and structure of the text. Inferences involve both literal understanding and general knowledge, intuition, and pragmatic understanding of the text (Day and Park, 2005), which is a central area of impairment in ASD.

In the case of the easy-read documents, only literal questions were presented due to the simplicity of the information contained in the text. All MCQs developed for the 16 texts used simple language with highly frequent words combined in sentences containing a maximum of three clauses.

3.2 Participants

Participants in the study were 20 adults (7 female, 13 male) with a confirmed diagnosis of autism recruited through 4 local charity organisations. None of the 20 participants had comorbid conditions affecting reading (e.g. dyslexia, learning difficulties, aphasia etc.). Mean age (m) for the group in years was m=30.75, with standard deviation SD=8.23, while years spent in education, as a factor influencing reading skills, were m=15.31, with SD=2.9. None of the participants had been diagnosed with a learning disability or developmental delay. All participants were native speakers of English.

3.3 Apparatus and Procedure

The texts were displayed on a 19" LCD monitor via software specifically designed following analysis of the requirements of people with ASD (Martos et al., 2013): there were no bright colours, complex navigation systems or distracting logos or images. Reading time was measured in seconds using the software, which also randomised both the order of presentation of the texts and the

[5]*Flesch-Kincaid Grade Level* is inversely proportional to text readability. For text passages of less than 100 words, the Flesch-Kincaid Grade Level and the Flesch Score have been computed for whole documents rather than selected text snippets, due to the fact that these formulae are not recommended for texts shorter than 100 words (Dubay, 2004).

[6]*Flesch Reading Ease Score* is proportional to text readability.

questions pertaining to texts for each participant, to avoid bias. Each session lasted between 40 and 70 minutes. Informed consent was first obtained and demographic information about diagnoses, age and level of education collected. Participants then read all texts and answered all questions, taking as many breaks as they requested. At the end of the experiment, participants were debriefed.

3.4 Results from the Reading Comprehension Experiment

A Shapiro-Wilk test showed that the answers to reading comprehension questions based on the texts are non-normally distributed. A Friedman test was performed, confirming that there are significant differences between scores obtained for different texts ($\chi^2(12) = 39.698$, $p < 0.001$). A post-hoc Wilcoxon Signed Rank test with Bonferroni adjustment of the significance level identified the differences between the particular texts and on this basis, they were divided into two groups: *easy* and *difficult*. All easy-read texts (10 to 16) and texts 1 to 4 were classified as *easy*, with only text 1 being significantly easier than the other texts in this group (text 2 and text 1: $p = 0.008$). Texts 5 to 9 varied in difficulty but were classified as significantly more difficult than the first 4 texts and the easy-read texts. Therefore they were assigned to a separate class: *difficult* (text 5 and text 4: $p = 0.012$; text 6 and text 5: $p = 0.083$; text 7 and text 6: $p = 0.034$; text 8 and text 7: $p = 0.037$; text 9 and text 8: $p = 0.021$).

These differences in the level of difficulty of the texts were also confirmed by the reading time score. The data from the reading time scores was also non-normally distributed according to the Shapiro-Wilk test and a Friedman test identified significant differences between the 9 texts ($\chi^2(12) = 45.060$, $p < 0.001$). A post-hoc Wilcoxon Signed Rank test with Bonferroni adjustment confirmed that texts 5 to 9 were to be considered more difficult than texts 1 to 4 (text 5 and text 4: $p = 0.001$), with no significant differences in the reading time scores between texts 5 and 6 (text 6 and text 5: $p = 0.409$; text 7 and text 6: $p = 0.683$; text 8 and text 7: $p = 0.331$; text 9 and text 8: $p = 0.601$).

Both measures, *question answers* and *reading time scores*, classified texts 1 to 4 and texts 10 to 16 as *easy*, while texts 5 to 9 were significantly more complex and were thus classified as *difficult*. The next section describes the readability indices applied to these two classes of text in order to find the most suitable indices for predicting reading difficulty for people with autism.

4 Readability Indices

Four groups of readability metrics, comprising 33 indices overall, were selected on the basis of their relationship to the types of difficulties that readers with autism face. All of the selected metrics were automatically computed with the exception of the *metaphor index*, which required manual counting of metaphors, due to the scarcity of accurate systems for automatic figurative language detection. The sets of syntactic and cognitively-motivated lexical features were computed using the *Coh_Metrix 3.0* tool (McNamara et al., 2010), which exploits the Charniak parser (Charniak, 2000).

4.1 Indices Previously Used to Assess Text Difficulty for Readers with ASD

The indices described in this section were proposed during the development of the OpenBook tool and are based on a user study identifying 43 user requirements (Jordanova et al., 2013; Martos et al., 2013). Indices (1), (2), (3) and (7) relate to features of syntactic and lexical complexity, while (4), (5) and (8) are intended to measure ambiguity in meaning. Index (6), the only index whose evaluation requires human input, estimates the difficulty posed by texts to autistic readers due to their difficulties in understanding metaphor and figurative language.

Definitions:

(1) **Comma index (C)** is proportional to the ratio of commas to words in the text. It indicates the average syntactic complexity of the sentences occurring in the text.

(2) **Index of words with three or more syllables (MSW)** is proprotional to the ratio of the number of words in the text with three or more syllables to the number of words in the text.

(3) **Index of words per sentence (WPS)** is the ratio of words to sentences in the text.

(4) The **Index of word diversity (WD)** is the type-token ratio of the text. The greater the number of word types occurring, the greater the likelihood that one or more of them will be semantically ambiguous.

(5) **Pronoun index (P)** is proportional to the ratio of the number of pronouns in the text to the number of words in the text. This index is relevant to the difficulty some autistic readers have in resolving anaphors (Martos et al., 2013).
(6) **Metaphor index (M)** is proportional to the ratio of the number of phraseological units and non-lexicalised metaphors in the text to the number of sentences in the text.
(7) **Passive verb index (PV)** is proportional to the ratio of passive verbs in the text to the number of sentences in the text. LT was developed to detect the occurrence of passive verbs in English on the basis of part-of-speech patterns, exploiting the LT TTT package (Grover et al.,).
(8) **Polysemic word index (PW)** is proportional to the ratio of the number of words in the text that belong to more that one synset in a language-specific ontology to the number of words in the text.

4.2 Syntactic Complexity Features

Syntactic complexity features account for the difficulties readers with ASD may experience in processing long and complex sentences. For example, the metric *Words Before Main Verb* estimates the working memory load imposed by a sentence (McNamara et al., 2010), and is particularly relevant to autism, as some autistic individuals have been shown to have decreased working memory capacity (Bennetto et al., 1996).

The set of 12 syntactic complexity features includes *Words before Main Verb* (the mean number of words occurring before the main verb of the main clause in each sentence), *Mean Number of Modifiers per Noun-Phrase*; *Syntactic Structure Similarity (Adjacent)* (proportional to the number of nodes in syntactic sub-trees shared by adjacent sentences, averaged over all pairs of adjacent sentences), *Syntactic Structure Similarity (All)* (computed in a similar way, but between all pairs of sentences in the text, not just adjacent ones), and *incidence scores* of *nouns*, *verbs*, *adverbial and prepositional phrases*, *passive voice forms*, *negation expressions*, *gerunds* and *infinitives*.

4.3 Cognitively Motivated Lexical Features

Cognitively-motivated readability features evaluate various phenomena relevant to autistic readers such as references to highly abstract concepts, which some readers with ASD may be unable to understand, and unfamiliar words that may pose difficulties because some readers are unable to exploit context to comprehend them. A set of 5 cognitively-motivated indices, based on word norms from the MRC psycholinguistic database (Gilhooly and Logie, 1980) and obtained using the *Coh_Metrix 3.0* system, were included in the study: *Frequency of Words*, *Age of Acquisition*, *Familiarity*, *Concreteness*, and *Imagability*.

4.4 Readability Formulae

Readability formulae included in the study were *Flesch Reading Ease* (Flesch, 1948), *Flesch-Kincaid Grade Level* (Kincaid et al., 1975; Kincaid et al., 1981), *Army's Readability Index (ARI)* (Senter and Smith, 1967), *Fog Index* (Gunning, 1952), *Lix* (Björnsson, 1968); and *SMOG* (McLaughlin, 1969).

5 Data Analysis and Results

A Shapiro-Wilk test showed that some of the datasets were normally distributed, while others were not. A paired samples t-test with corrections for outliers and a Wilcoxon signed rank test were both applied, showing consistent results.[7]

A paired samples t-test was used to evaluate whether each of the readability indices described in Section 4 could discriminate significantly between the two classes of easy and difficult texts. After that, a bootstrap for the paired samples test was used to calculate 95% confidence intervals (CI) based on 1 000 bootstrap samples of each measure. Table 2 presents values of p, t-test results, and the 95% CI endpoints of each of the three discriminative sets of readability features. Of the set of readability indices developed to evaluate texts for readers with ASD, statistical analysis indicates that a two-tailed significant difference was yielded by two indices: *words in sentences* and *metaphor index*. Of the syntactic set, significant results were yielded by the *Words Before Main Verb* measure of cognitive load and the *Syntactic Structure Similarity (Adjacent)* measure. *Syntactic Structure Similarity (All)* did show significance at the t-test ($t = 2.932$, $p < 0.05$ with 95% CI (0.01 800, 0.08 540)) but the p value after bootstrapping increased to $p = 0.086$, indicating that it is not a significant discriminator. The third set of cognitively motivated features failed to discriminate between the two classes, while the only readability formula of the fourth set which

[7]For brevity, only the t-test results are reported in this paper.

Index	t	p	*95% CI Endpoints*	
			Lower	*Upper*
ASD-Specific				
Words in Sentences	−6.514	< 0.05	−8.75 421	−511 480
Metaphor Index	−3.723	< 0.05	−0.66 997	−0.26 537
Syntactic				
Words Before Main Verb	−3.264	< 0.05	−3.21 221	−1.05 580
Syntactic Structure Similarity (Adjacent)	3.510	< 0.05	0.03 080	0.09 540
Readability				
Flesch-Kincaid Reading Ease	−3.362	0.028	−7.02 138	−0.66 982
ARI	−3.706	< 0.05	−5.46 000	−2.12 000

Table 2: Six features discriminative between *easy* and *difficult* texts.

managed to do so was *Flesch-Kincaid Reading Ease*. The t-test indicated significance of the *Lix* measure in discriminating between *easy* and *difficult* texts ($t = -2.824$, $p < 0.05$, with 95% CI ($-16.5\,800$, $-3.78\,000$)), but bootstrapping contradicted this ($p = 0.090$).

6 Application to Manual Text Simplification Evaluation

6.1 Materials

The effectiveness of the readability indices described in Section 4 was assessed over a larger set of texts specifically designed for people with autism. They were applied to the FIRST corpus, which consists of 25 documents of the registers of popular science and literature (13 texts) and newspaper articles (12 texts) (Jordanova et al., 2013). These texts were presented in both their original form and in a form intended to facilitate reading comprehension, so that the corpus contains 25 paired original and simplified documents (50 documents in total). The simplification was performed by 5 experts working with autistic people, who were given ASD-specific text simplification guidelines, specified by Jordanova et al. (2013), which contains full details of the simplification procedure and the characteristics of the corpus. It is important to note that no user-based evaluation of those texts has been conducted. Evaluating the readability indices on the FIRST corpus would test their efficacy in discriminating between original and manually simplified versions of texts.

6.2 Results

All readability indices that successfully discriminated between *easy* and *difficult* user-evaluated texts and all 7 readability formulae discriminated successfully between the original and simplified versions of texts with $p < 0.0001$. Other indices from the first set of ASD-specific features that performed well were the *Comma Index*, *Syllables in Long Words*, *Word Diversity*, and *Pronoun Index*. Successful discriminators from the cognitive set were the features *Average Word Length in Syllables*, *word frequency*, *Age of Acquisition*, *Familiarity*, and *Polysemy*. Finally, of the syntactic set, *Mean Number of Modifiers per NP*, *incidence score of preposition phrases*, and *gerunds* were significant discriminators. Table 3 displays p-values and t-test results of each of these features.

Index	t	p
ASD-Specific		
Comma index	−8.077	0.0001
Syllables in long words	−3.006	0.0001
Word Diversity	−5.840	0.0001
Pronoun Index	4.211	0.0001
Cognitive		
Average word length (syllables)	−2.500	0.016
Word frequency	4.727	0.0001
Age of Acquisition	−3.438	0.002
Familiarity	4.426	0.001
Polysemy	3.048	0.006
Syntactic		
Mean number of modifiers per NP	−3.934	0.001
Incidence Score of Prepositional Phrases	−2.446	0.022
Incidence Score of Gerunds	−3.544	0.002

Table 3: Features discriminative between original and manually simplified versions of texts.

7 Discussion

The study shows that the main differences between the *easy* and *difficult* texts evaluated by autistic users were that, unsurprisingly, the easy texts contain shorter words and sentences. However, an even more marked characteristic of the easier texts is the fact that they contain fewer metaphors. The *metaphor index* was far more predictive than commonly used readability features such as modifiers per noun phrase, type-token ratio, or instances of passive voice. This feature is directly related to the inability of even some of the highly skilled readers with autism to comprehend figurative constructions. One limitation is that the *metaphor index* needs to be derived manually and that manual annotation of metaphors can be an onerous and unreliable process. However, we argue that, in the case of readability assessment for autism, a very detailed annotation scheme encoding fine-grained distinctions is unnecessary and that a less detailed approach would be sufficient. In due course, advances in NLP may make the automatic tagging of metaphors a feasible option.

One feature, whose use is relatively uncommon in the metrics used to assess readability for other populations, is the occurrence of fewer words before the main verb in a sentence, which has proven effective due to the decreased working memory capacity of people with autism. That is, the closer that main verbs are to the starts of sentences, the more comprehensible the text is for readers with autism. Consistency of syntactic structure was also found to be a highly-discriminative measure, meaning that sentences in *easy* texts have greater uniformity of syntactic structure. Furthermore, the results indicate that it is more important for autistic readers that syntactic structure is similar in adjacent sentences rather than over whole documents, as the latter index was insignificant after bootstrapping. One possible explanation for the significance of this index is that the syntactic structure of texts of the register of news is quite diverse, possibly due to the variety of sources, including reported speech and reportage, included in news articles. It would be interesting to investigate whether this index is as discriminative when applied only to educational texts. Finally, *Flesch-Kincaid Grade Level* and *ARI* were found to be suitable formulae for assessing the readability of texts for autistic readers. This may be due to the sensitivity of autistic readers to sentence length, a feature which is weighted more heavily in the *Flesch-Kincaid* formula than in others, such as the original *Flesch* formula (Dubay, 2004). The occurrence of passive verbs and the frequent use of pronouns, which were previously thought to increase reading difficulty for people with autism, did not prove to be significant in our experiments.

All indices which successfully discriminated between the user-evaluated texts retained their significance when applied to the FIRST corpus with $p < 0.0001$, showing that they are suitable for use in text simplification tasks. Due to the considerable number of simplification operations applied in the FIRST corpus, which resulted in larger differences between the two classes of texts than between texts included in the user-evaluated materials, many other indices were also discriminative.

8 Conclusions and Future Work

The study identified six readability indices as being highly-discriminative of text complexity for readers with autism: the *number of words per sentence*, the *number of metaphors per text*, the *average number of words occurring before the main verb in a sentence*, *syntactic structure similarity for adjacent sentences*, *Flesch-Kincaid Grade Level*, and the *Automated Readability Index*. These indices discriminated successfully both between texts evaluated as *easy* or *difficult* by reference to comprehension testing and reading times of participants with ASD and between texts in the FIRST corpus in original and simplified forms.

An additional set of autism-specific, syntactic and cognitively-based readability indices and readability formulae discriminated successfully between original and simplified texts of the FIRST corpus, but this is most likely explained by the considerable number of simplification operations applied to it. On the assumption that this corpus of simplified texts is more accessible for readers with autism, this extended set of indices could be considered suitable for this target population.

This study shares the limitations of all research involving participants with autism: small sample sizes and strict limits on the demands that can be placed on participants, due to their condition. The results should therefore be applied with caution and not necessarily generalised to children, people at the lower ends of the autism spectrum, or people with other types of disabilities. Future work would include evaluation of a larger set of texts by a larger group of particpants and the exploration of new readability indices tailored to the specific reading difficulties of autistic individuals.

9 Acknowledgments

The authors gratefully acknowledge the volunteers who took part in this study, the charity organisations which facilitated their recruitment, and the three anonymous reviewers for their valuable comments.

References

American Psychiatric Association. 2013. Diagnostic and Statistical Manual of Mental Disorders (5th ed.).

Rebekah George Benjamin. 2012. Reconstructing readability: Recent developments and recommendations in the analysis of text difficulty. *Educational Psychology Review*, 24:1–26.

Loisa Bennetto, Bruce F. Pennington, and Sally J. Rogers. 1996. Intact and Impaired Memory Functions in Autism. *Child Development*, 67(4):1816–1835.

Carl-Hugo Björnsson. 1968. *Läsbarhet*. Liber, Stockholm.

Alexis Bosseler and Dominic W. Massaro. 2003. Development and evaluation of computer-animated tutor for vocabulary and language learning in children with autism. *Journal of autism and developmental disorders*, 33(6):553–567.

Bertram C. Bruce, Ann D. Rubin, and Kathleen S. Starr. 1981. Why readability formulas fail. *IEEE Transactions on Professional Communication*, PC-24:50–52.

Terry S. Brugha, Sally Anne Cooper, and Sally McManus. 2012. Estimating the Prevalence of Autism Spectrum Conditions in Adults: Extending the 2007 Adult Psychiatric Morbidity Survey. Technical report, NHS, The Health and Social Care Information Centre., London.

Jeanne S. Chall and Edgar Dale. 1995. *Readability Revisited: the new Dale-Chall readability formula*. Brookline Books, Cambridge, Massachusetts.

Marjorie H. Charlop-Christy, Michael Carpenter, Loc Le, Linda A. LeBlanc, and Kristen Kellet. 2002. Using the picture exchange communication system (pecs) with children with autism: assessment of pecs acquisition, speech, social-communicative behavior, and problem behaviour. *JOURNAL OF APPLIED BEHAVIOR ANALYSIS*, 3(3):213–231.

Eugene Charniak. 2000. A maximum-entropy-inspired parser. In *Proceedings of the First Conference on North American Chapter of the Association for Computational Linguistics*, pages 132–139, San Francisco.

Edgar Dale and Jeanne S. Chall. 1948. A formula for predicting readability: Instructions. *Educational Research Bulletin*, 27(2):37–54.

Richard R. Day and Jeong-Suk Park. 2005. Developing Reading Comprehension Questions. *Reading in a Foreign Language*, 17(1).

William H. Dubay. 2004. *The Principles of Readability*. Impact Information.

Lijun Feng, Martin Jansche, Matt Huenerfauth, and Noémie Elhadad. 2010. A comparison of features for automatic readability assessment. In *Proceedings of the 23rd International Conference on Computational Linguistics: Posters*, COLING '10, pages 276–284, Stroudsburg, PA, USA. Association for Computational Linguistics.

Rudolf Flesch. 1948. A new readability yardstick. *Journal of applied psychology*, 32(3):221–233.

Uta Frith and Maggie Snowling. 1983. Reading for meaning and reading for sound in autistic and dyslexic children. *Journal of Developmental Psychology*, 1:329–342.

Ken J. Gilhooly and Robert H. Logie. 1980. Age-of-acquisition, imagery, concreteness, familiarity, and ambiguity measures for 1,944 words. *Behavior Research Methods & Instrumentation*, 12(4):395–427.

Arthur C. Graesser, Danielle S. McNamara, Max M. Louwerse, and Zhiqiang Cai. 2004. Coh-metrix: Analysis of text on cohesion and language. *Behavioral Research Methods, Instruments, and Computers*, 36:193–202.

Claire Grover, Colin Matheson, Andrei Mikheev, and Marc Moens. LT TTT - a flexible tokenisation tool.

Robert Gunning. 1952. *The technique of clear writing*. McGraw-Hill, New York.

Francesca Happé and Uta Frith. 2006. The weak coherence account: Detail focused cognitive style in autism spectrum disorder. *Journal of Autism and Developmental Disorders*, 36:5–25.

Francesca Happé. 1997. Central coherence and theory of mind in autism: Reading homographs in context. *British Journal of Developmental Psychology*, 15:1–12.

Matt Huenerfauth, Lijun Feng, and Noémie Elhadad. 2009. Comparing evaluation techniques for text readability software for adults with intellectual disabilities. In *Proceedings of the 11th International ACM SIGACCESS Conference on Computers and Accessibility*, Assets '09, pages 3–10, New York, NY, USA. ACM.

Martin Jansche, Lijun Feng, and Matt Huenerfauth. 2010. Reading difficulty in adults with intellectual disabilities: Analysis with a hierarchical latent trait model. In *Proceedings of the 12th International ACM SIGACCESS Conference on Computers and Accessibility*, ASSETS '10, pages 277–278, New York, NY, USA. ACM.

Vesna Jordanova, Richard Evans, and Arlinda Cerga-Pashoja. 2013. FIRST Deliverable - Benchmark report (result of piloting task). Technical Report D7.2, Central and Northwest London NHS Foundation Trust, London, UK.

J. Peter Kincaid, Robert P. Fishburne, Richard L. Rogers, and Brad S. Chissom. 1975. *Derivation of new readability formulas (Automatic Readability Index, Fog Count and Flesch Reading Ease Formula) for Navy enlisted personnel*. CNTECHTRA, 8-75 edition.

J. Peter Kincaid, James A. Aagard, John W. O'Hara, and Larry K. Cottrell. 1981. Computer readability editing system. *IEEE transactions on professional communications*.

Anne Kispal. 2008. Effective Teaching of Inference Skills for Reading. Literature Review.

Meng-Chuan Lai, Michael V. Lombardo, and Simon Baron-Cohen. 2014. Autism. *Lancet*, 383(9920):896–910.

Gilbert MacKay and Adrienne Shaw. 2004. A comparative study of figurative language in children with autistic spectrum disorders. *Child Language Teaching and Therapy*, 20(13).

Juan Martos, Sandra Freire, Ana González, David Gil, Richard Evans, Vesna Jordanova, Arlinda Cerga, Antoneta Shishkova, and Constantin Orasan. 2013. FIRST Deliverable - User preferences: Updated. Technical Report D2.2, Deletrea, Madrid, Spain.

Harry G. McLaughlin. 1969. SMOG grading - a new readability formula. *Journal of Reading*, pages 639–646, May.

Danielle S. McNamara, Max M. Louwerse, Philip M. McCarthy, and Arthur C. Graesser. 2010. Coh-Metrix: Capturing Linguistic Features of Cohesion, May.

Irene M. O'Connor and Perry D. Klein. 2004. Exploration of strategies for facilitating the reading comprehension of high-functioning students with autism spectrum disorders. *Journal of Autism and Developmental Disorders*, 34:2:115–127.

Stephen Oliver. 1998. *Understanding Autism*. Oxford Brookes University, UK.

Cynthia Putnam and Lorna Chong. 2008. Software and technologies designed for people with autism: What do users want? In *Proceedings of the 10th International ACM SIGACCESS Conference on Computers and Accessibility*, Assets '08, pages 3–10, New York, NY, USA. ACM.

Luz Rello, Ricardo Baeza-yates, Laura Dempere-marco, and Horacio Saggion. 2012a. Frequent Words Improve Readability and Shorter Words Improve Understandability for People with Dyslexia. (1):22–24.

Luz Rello, Clara Bayarri, and Azuki Gorriz. 2012b. What is wrong with this word? dyseggxia: A game for children with dyslexia. In *Proceedings of the 14th International ACM SIGACCESS Conference on Computers and Accessibility*, ASSETS '12, pages 219–220, New York, NY, USA. ACM.

R. J. Senter and E. A. Smith. 1967. Automated Readability Index. Technical Report AMRL-TR-6620, Wright-Patterson Air Force Base.

Advaith Siddharthan. 2004. *Syntactic Simplification and Text Cohesion*. Ph.D. thesis, University of Cambridge.

Dean R. Smith, A. Jackson Stenner, Ivan Horabin, and III Malbert Smith. 1989. The lexile scale in theory and practice: Final report. Technical report, MetaMetrics (ERIC Document Reproduction Service No. ED307577)., Washington, DC:.

Sanja Štajner, Richard Evans, Constantin Orasan, and Ruslan Mitkov. 2012. What can readability measures really tell us about text complexity? In Luz Rello and Horacio Saggion, editors, *Proceedings of the LREC'12 Workshop: Natural Language Processing for Improving Textual Accessibility (NLP4ITA)*, Istanbul, Turkey, may. European Language Resources Association (ELRA).

Sanja Štajner, Ruslan Mitkov, and Gloria Corpas Pastor, 2014. *Simple or not simple? A readability question*. Springer-Verlag, Berlin.

Ashley Wazana. 2007. The Autism Epidemic: Fact or Artifact? *Journal of the American Academy of Child & Adolescent Psychiatry*, 46(6):721 – 730.

User Name Disambiguation in Community Question Answering

Baoguo Yang
Department of Computer Science
University of York, UK
by550@york.ac.uk

Suresh Manandhar
Department of Computer Science
University of York, UK
suresh@cs.york.ac.uk

Abstract

Community question answering sites provide us convenient and interactive platforms for problem solving and knowledge sharing, which are attracting an increasing number of users. Accordingly, it will be very common that different people have the same user name. When a query question is given, some potential answer providers would be recommended to the asker in the form of user name. However, some user names are ambiguous and not unique in the community. To help question askers match the ambiguous user names with the right people, in this paper, we propose to disambiguate same-name users by ranking their tag-based relevance to a query question. Empirical studies on three community question answering datasets demonstrate that our method is effective for disambiguating user names in community question answering.

1 Introduction

In recent years, community-based question answering (CQA) sites like StackOverflow[1], Quora[2] and Yahoo!Answers[3], have achieved great success and attracted a huge number of users. It is not uncommon that some people in the CQA services share the same user names. Figure 1(a), Figure 1(b) and Figure 1(c) show three lists of user names from three different CQA communities: Travel[4], Webapps (Web Applications)[5], and Cooking[6], where each user name is shared by multiple users. In Figure 1(b), "David" is the most common and ambiguous user name related to 57 users.

In some cases, an off-line person asks people around a difficult question verbally, then he/she may be recommended by word of mouth to visit the CQA homepages of some potential answer providers. However, the links to their homepages are not provided sometimes, then the asker has to search them according to the provided user names. Some user names are unique, and they can easily access the historical QA records of these potential answer providers. However, some are very common and ambiguous, accordingly, many users with the same user name will be displayed.

Motivated by the above scenario, it is very necessary to help askers disambiguate these users, which can release them from wondering which user should be the right one. Moreover, if the user name is not clearly given, the askers will waste a lot of valuable time on searching and visiting irrelevant users, which can cause misunderstanding and misleading. Then the asker will get puzzled.

In CQA, given a new question, the related research studies mainly fall into three areas: 1) Answer recommendation (Zhou et al., 2012b; Tian et al., 2013); 2) Similar question retrieval (Cao et al., 2010; Zhang et al., 2014b); 3) Expert user recommendation (Pal and Konstan, 2010; Liu et al., 2011; Zhou et al., 2012a). As for user recommendation, when some user names are ambiguous, the askers will be thrown into another dilemma.

To our knowledge, this is the first work on user name disambiguation in community question answering. Although there have been some studies on user name disambiguation in bibliographic citation records (Han et al., 2005; Treeratpituk and Giles, 2009; Ferreira et al., 2010), the related methods are not directly applicable to our work. In this paper, to disambiguate the same-name users, we present a simple vector-style tag-based method, *relTagVec*, to learn the relevance

[1] http://www.stackoverflow.com/
[2] https://www.quora.com/
[3] http://answers.yahoo.com/
[4] http://travel.stackexchange.com/
[5] http://webapps.stackexchange.com/
[6] http://cooking.stackexchange.com/

Proceedings of Recent Advances in Natural Language Processing, pages 707–713,
Hissar, Bulgaria, Sep 7–9 2015.

displayname	num
Chris	10
David	10
Matt	9
John	8
Michael	8
Paul	8
Ben	8
alex	7
Kevin	7
Dan	6
Richard	6
Daniel	6
Simon	6
Phil	5
Ryan	5
Brian	5
steve	5

(a) Travel community

displayname	num
David	57
Matt	45
Chris	45
Alex	36
Tom	34
Sam	32
Mike	31
James	30
Ben	30
John	27
mark	27
Nick	26
Dan	26
Daniel	25
Michael	24
Dave	23
Jason	23

(b) Webapps community

displayname	num
Chris	24
John	23
Matt	19
Mike	18
Michael	18
Joe	18
Dave	17
Jason	16
Nick	16
Dan	15
steve	14
Tim	14
James	13
Scott	13
Alex	13
eric	13
Richard	12

(c) Cooking community

Figure 1: Example of lists of most ambiguous user names in some CQA communities (all the lists are not shown completely, Figure 1(a) is based on the data between 2011-06-21 and 2013-05-09, Figure 1(b) is based on the data between 2009-07-15 and 2013-03-10, and Figure 1(c) is based on the data before 2013-03-10).

between each user and the question by comparing their tag lists, where each tag is represented by a vector. Then the one who has the highest relevance score will be the right person to recommend. Experimental results on three CQA datasets from StackExchange[7] network demonstrate that our method is very effective, and performs much better than the baseline methods.

The remainder of this paper is organized as follows. Section 2 presents the related work. Then we introduce the framework of our method in Section 3. Section 4 reports the empirical studies on real CQA datasets. Finally, we conclude this paper in Section 5.

2 Related Work

In this section, we briefly review the work that is related to some extent.

User Name Disambiguation. Han et al. (2005) present a K-way spectral clustering approach to disambiguate users in citations. In (Treeratpituk and Giles, 2009), a random forests based machine learning algorithm is introduced for pairwise user name disambiguation. A novel approach, Self-training Associative Name Disambiguator (Ferreira et al., 2010), is proposed for author name disambiguation through two steps. Recently, another method has been presented in (Zhang et al., 2014a) by exploring the link information in collaboration networks for disambiguating user names. Nevertheless, these disambiguation methods cannot be directly used for user name disambiguation in C-QA.

Expert Learning. Zhang et al. (2007) propose to use network-based ranking algorithms to find authoritative users. In (Guo et al., 2008), to recommend answer providers, a two-step method is introduced and the user profiles are also explored. Liu et al. (2011) present a pairwise competition based method for estimating user expertise scores. In (Zhou et al., 2012a), both link analysis and topical similarity are combined in a probabilistic model for experts finding in CQA. In (Yang and Manandhar, 2014), the descriptive ability of users is also studied.

3 Framework of Our Method

In this section, the concrete steps of our *relTagVec* method are presented and explained.

3.1 Computing user relevance to the questions

For each user u, we can get a list of tags, T_u, from the questions to which he/she has recently answered. For each question q, the corresponding tag list can be represented as T_q. We use word2vec (Mikolov et al., 2013) technique to compute the

[7] http://stackexchange.com/

vector representation of all the tags. And then the relevance value $relevance(u, q)$ of user u over q can be represented as follows.

$$relevance(u, q) = \frac{1}{|T_q|} \sum_{i=1}^{|T_q|} \max_{j=1,2,\ldots,|T_u|} (sim(\mathbf{v}_i^{T_q}, \mathbf{v}_j^{T_u}) \cdot w_j^{T_u}), \quad (1)$$

where $\mathbf{v}_i^{T_q}$ is the vector representation for the i-th tag in the tag list of question q. Accordingly, $\mathbf{v}_j^{T_u}$ is the vector for the j-th tag in the tag list of user u. Here $sim(\mathbf{v}_i^{T_q}, \mathbf{v}_j^{T_u})$ denotes the cosine similarity between $\mathbf{v}_i^{T_q}$ and $\mathbf{v}_j^{T_u}$. In addition, $w_j^{T_u}$ is the weight of j-th tag in the tag list of user u, which can be represented as $w_j^{T_u} = 1/(1+\exp(-N_j^{T_u}))$. Here, $N_j^{T_u}$ is the number of times the j-th tag of user u appearing in the questions to which the user u has answered.

3.2 Selecting the user with highest relevance value

When we get each relevance value $relevance(u, q)$ of candidate users to the query question q, the user with highest relevance value will be considered as the right person to recommend. Here we use $u^q_{predicted}(username)$ to denote the predicted user with the name "username" for recommendation over question q.

3.3 Recommending ranked user list

In many cases, a considerable number of users share the same user name, then the prediction to the target person is getting difficult based on insufficient historical data, and the prediction accuracy will be low. It is very necessary to provide a ranking list to the asker.

For a query question q, we rank the candidate users to generate a ranking list based on relevance scores $relevance(u, q)$ in descending order. Then the askers just need to check the top-ranking users, which is time-saving.

4 Experimental Analysis

In this paper, two types of user names are considered.

Type 1: Each provided ambiguous user name is exactly the *DisplayName* of the target user.

Type 2: The recommendation is only given in the form of each target user's first name. For example, a user named "Tom Smith" is mentioned in the name of "Tom" instead. However, there are many members named "Tom" in the community.

4.1 Datasets and Settings

In our experiments, three Data Dumps[8] from Travel[9], Seasoned Advice (Cooking)[10] and MathOverflow communities are used to evaluate our method. Note that all the user names are case insensitive in our experiments.

Travel: We use a Travel Data Dump ranging from June 2011 to September 2014. First, the dataset is divided into two parts, the data before 2013-05-09 is viewed as historical data, while the remainder is used for evaluation.

For Type 1, firstly, from the historical set we select all the user names associated with at least two different users. Then the userIds of all the users who share the same user name will be selected, and then we collect all their previous Q&A records (833 posts associated with 231 different users). Based on the userIds of these historical Q&A records, the questions answered by the corresponding users are selected from the initial evaluation dataset. Then we build the final evaluation data in the form of triples (question, user name, userId). Here the user name is ambiguous, and the user with this userId is a **gold standard** answer provider for this question. The final evaluation dataset contains 298 (question, user name, userId) records. For each ambiguous user name, the associated users with this name form the candidates. Note that each gold standard userId is known in evaluation set without manual annotation.

As for Type 2, we first select all the one-word user names from historical set, then all the user names containing these given names are selected. And then the userIds associated with these given names are collected from historical set, the remainder steps are similar to Type 1.

Cooking: The Seasoned Advice (Cooking) Data Dump is dated from July 2010 to September 2014. For Type 1, we preprocess it in the same way as that for Travel Data Dump. Here the historical set is composed of the data before 2013-03-10, and the rest are used for evaluation. For historical set, we collect 3306 Q&A posts from 982 different users. And we get 284 (question, user name,

[8] https://archive.org/details/stackexchange
[9] http://travel.stackexchange.com/
[10] http://cooking.stackexchange.com/

Methods	User Predicting	User Ranking			
	Accuracy	avgR	MRR	CDR@2	CDR@5
random	0.4536	1.8944	0.6892	0.8284	0.9883
relTitle-Avg	0.6472	1.6296	0.7931	0.8607	0.9894
relTitle-Max	0.6986	1.5790	0.8185	0.8592	0.9894
relTagVec	0.8625	1.2747	0.9148	0.9296	0.9978

(a) MathOverflow

Methods	User Predicting	User Ranking			
	Accuracy	avgR	MRR	CDR@2	CDR@5
random	0.2226	4.7102	0.4179	0.3957	0.6360
relTitle-Avg	0.6360	1.7138	0.7824	0.8304	0.9859
relTitle-Max	0.8551	1.3887	0.9078	0.9152	0.9859
relTagVec	0.9329	1.1166	0.9609	0.9753	0.9965

(b) Cooking

Methods	User Predicting	User Ranking			
	Accuracy	avgR	MRR	CDR@2	CDR@5
random	0.5235	1.5336	0.7535	0.9564	1.0
relTitle-Avg	0.8993	1.1376	0.9435	0.9631	1.0
relTitle-Max	0.9262	1.1107	0.9569	0.9631	1.0
relTagVec	0.9698	1.0335	0.9843	0.9966	1.0

(c) Travel

Table 1: Performance under Type 1.

userId) records for the evaluation set. The preprocessing for Type 2 is similar to that in Travel set.

MathOverflow: The Data Dump for MathOverflow ranging from September 2009 to September 2014 is also publicly available. Here the data before 2011-02-05 is formed as historical data. For Type 1, we finally collect 2770 (question, user name, userId) records for evaluation. All the preprocessing steps for both types are the same as those for Travel Data Dump.

All the experiments are performed on a PC with Pentium Dual-core 2.3 GHz CPU and 4.0 GB RAM. For the tag vector representation, word2vec continuous bag of words (CBOW) model (Mikolov et al., 2013) is used, and the vectors are got based on the question tags from the whole dataset. We set the dimension of each vector as 50, and the training is executed for 10 iterations.

4.2 Experiments on user name disambiguation in CQA

We compare our *relTagVec* method with the following three baseline methods on *Travel*, *MathOverflow* and *Cooking* datasets under Type 1 and Type 2 separately. For each type and each dataset, all the methods are run 10 times, then the averaged results are reported.

Baselines:

- *Random*: A predictor generates random ranking of candidate answer providers for each question.
- *relTitle-Avg*: Given the title $Title_q$ of a query question q, the titles $\{Title_{q_i \in Q_u}\}_{i=1}^{|Q_u|}$ of the previously asked and answered questions Q_u from each candidate user u are collected, then we compute the Jaccard similarity coefficient between $Title_q$ and each $\{Title_{q_i \in Q_u}\}_{i=1}^{|Q_u|}$, and then the averaged similarity value is calculated, which is considered as the relevance score of user u to question q.
- *relTitle-Max*: Different from *relTitle-Avg*, in *relTitle-Max*, the maximum Jaccard similarity value is computed instead of the averaged similarity value.

Metrics: We use accuracy as the metric for the most likely user prediction evaluation. The repre-

Methods	User Predicting	User Ranking			
	Accuracy	avgR	MRR	CDR@2	CDR@5
random	0.1646	9.4405	0.3408	0.3072	0.5505
relTitle-Avg	0.3648	4.8563	0.5509	0.5669	0.8084
relTitle-Max	0.4910	4.4630	0.6359	0.6504	0.8354
relTagVec	0.6947	2.1003	0.7991	0.8250	0.9413

(a) MathOverflow

Methods	User Predicting	User Ranking			
	Accuracy	avgR	MRR	CDR@2	CDR@5
random	0.1731	8.0061	0.3375	0.2933	0.5030
relTitle-Avg	0.4562	3.6558	0.6147	0.6191	0.8228
relTitle-Max	0.6680	3.1181	0.7569	0.7719	0.8391
relTagVec	0.7719	2.2546	0.8459	0.8717	0.9369

(b) Cooking

Methods	User Predicting	User Ranking			
	Accuracy	avgR	MRR	CDR@2	CDR@5
random	0.3199	3.6919	0.5230	0.5446	0.7609
relTitle-Avg	0.6987	1.6355	0.8221	0.8956	0.9646
relTitle-Max	0.8476	1.4200	0.9046	0.9326	0.9697
relTagVec	0.9217	1.1700	0.9535	0.9731	0.9899

(c) Travel

Table 2: Performance under Type 2.

sentation of accuracy is shown as follows.

$$Accuracy = \frac{N_{(u_{predicted}==u_{true})}}{N_{records}},$$

where $N_{records}$ denotes the number of (question, user name, userId) records in the evaluation set, and $N_{(u_{predicted}==u_{true})}$ is the number of records whose answer providers have been correctly matched. Here $u_{predicted}$ denotes the predicted userId, and u_{true} is the ground-truth userId of a user name for a record. The higher accuracy, the better performance is.

Because some user names are shared by many users, we also evaluate the predicted ranking of the ground-truth[11] user by our method and baselines in terms of the following metrics.

- The average rank of ground-truth users (*avgR*): the average rank of ground-truth users among the candidate users for the query questions.

- Mean reciprocal rank (*MRR*): the average of the reciprocal ranks of ground-truth users for the query questions.

[11]The real ranking for ground-truth user should be 1.

- Cumulative distribution of ranks (*CDR*): *CDR@m* is the percentage of query questions whose ground-truth answer providers are in the top m of the ranking list of candidate users.

The mathematical expressions for *avgR*, *MRR* and *CDR@m* are shown as follows.

$$AvgR = \frac{1}{|Q|}\sum_{q \in Q} r^q_{u_{true}}$$

$$MRR = \frac{1}{|Q|}\sum_{q \in Q} \frac{1}{r^q_{u_{true}}}$$

$$CDR@m = \frac{|\{q \in Q | r^q_{u_{true}} \leq m\}|}{|Q|}$$

Here, q is the query question from the question set Q. The expression $r^q_{u_{true}}$ denotes the rank of the ground-truth user u_{true} among the candidate users for question q.

The higher the values of *MRR* and *CDR*, the better the performance is, while it is contrary for *avgR*.

4.2.1 Performance under Type 1

In Type 1, the candidate users share the same names. Table 1(a) shows the results for all the methods on *MathOverflow* dataset, as for the most likely user prediction, *relTagVec* method performs best with promising accuracy value 0.8625, which is much more competitive than the baselines. For the performance on the ranking of ground-truth users, *relTagVec* is still superior to others in terms of avgR, MRR, CDR@2 and CDR@5. In addition, both *relTitle-Max* and *relTitle-Avg* methods perform better than *random* method. And *relTitle-Max* method can yield more accurate results than *relTitle-Avg*.

In Table 1(b), we can observe that *relTagVec* method still performs better than the baselines on *Cooking* dataset, and *random* method is the worst choice again. As for Title-based methods, *relTitle-Max* is still superior to *relTitle-Avg* especially on accuracy.

As for the performance on *Travel* dataset shown in Table 1(c), it can be seen that *relTagVec* method still yields superior results in terms of all the metrics. By contrast, *random* is less competitive. Note that their CDR@5 values are all 1, which means that all the questions whose ground-truth answer providers are in the top 5 of the candidate list.

It is obvious from Table 1 that *relTagVec*, *relTitle-Max* and *relTitle-Avg* can effectively disambiguate the user names given the query question with regard to different evaluation metrics. By contrast, *relTagVec* performs best in Type 1.

4.2.2 Performance under Type 2

Different from Type 1, given a question, under Type 2, the querying user name only contains one word, which is usually viewed as the first name of a user. In such case, the candidate set is composed of all the users with the same first name. Accordingly, the user name will be more ambiguous with larger candidate set.

As can be seen from Table 2(a) that our *relTagVec* method still shows very promising performance, which outperforms the baseline methods in terms of all the listed evaluation metrics on MathOverflow dataset. Among the baselines, *random* method yields very low accuracy. As for the two title-based methods, *relTitle-Max* is still better than *relTitle-Avg*.

From Table 2(b) and Table 2(c), it tends to the similar conclusion that our *relTagVec* method performs better than the baselines on both *Cooking* and *Travel* datasets with acceptable performance.

Overall, *relTagVec* outperforms baseline methods under both types. Comparing Table 1 with Table 2 on each dataset, we can easily notice that the performance under Type 2 is reduced on each dataset with regard to nearly all the metrics, which is in accord with the fact that the user names (only given names) are more ambiguous. Moreover, the performance on Travel dataset is better than that on Cooking set in both types, which can be partly explained by Figure 1(a) and Figure 1(c), where the user names are less ambiguous in Travel community than Cooking Community, hence the performance is better on Travel dataset.

Error Analysis: We perform error analysis for *relTagVec* method and find that some candidate users share very similar values of $relevance(u, q)$, which can increase error rate and the difficulty in identifying target users.

5 Conclusions

The rapid growth of social question answering services comes with the contributions from the increasing number of registered members. Accordingly, the phenomenon about users with the same user names is getting more and more prevalent. If a user name is shared by many people in the community, once you input the user name, the system will display all the related users, in this case, it will get difficult to find out the target user. In this paper, given a question, we focus on the user name disambiguation of potential answer providers in CQA. We utilize the tag information of both users and the query question to compute the relevance values. Then the user with highest relevance is viewed as the target user. We also recommend the possible ranked user list when there are a great number of candidates. In addition, the title-based methods are introduced in evaluation. Experimental analysis on three CQA datasets show that our *relTagVec* method is simple but very effective in user name disambiguation.

There are some directions needing further investigation. First, there are other kinds of ambiguous types to consider, like misspelling. Second, it is interesting to try other ways to compute the relevance between a user and a question.

References

Xin Cao, Gao Cong, Bin Cui, and Christian S Jensen. 2010. A generalized framework of exploring category information for question retrieval in community question answer archives. In *Proceedings of the 19th international conference on World wide web*, pages 201–210. ACM.

Anderson A Ferreira, Adriano Veloso, Marcos André Gonçalves, and Alberto HF Laender. 2010. Effective self-training author name disambiguation in scholarly digital libraries. In *Proceedings of the 10th annual joint conference on Digital libraries*, pages 39–48. ACM.

Jinwen Guo, Shengliang Xu, Shenghua Bao, and Yong Yu. 2008. Tapping on the potential of q&a community by recommending answer providers. In *Proceedings of the 17th ACM conference on Information and knowledge management*, pages 921–930. ACM.

Hui Han, Hongyuan Zha, et al. 2005. Name disambiguation in author citations using a k-way spectral clustering method. In *Proceedings of the 5th ACM/IEEE-CS Joint Conference on Digital Libraries (JCDL'05)*, pages 334–343.

Jing Liu, Young-In Song, and Chin-Yew Lin. 2011. Competition-based user expertise score estimation. In *Proceedings of the 34th international ACM SIGIR conference on Research and development in Information Retrieval*, pages 425–434. ACM.

Tomas Mikolov, Kai Chen, Greg Corrado, and Jeffrey Dean. 2013. Efficient estimation of word representations in vector space. *arXiv preprint arXiv:1301.3781*.

Aditya Pal and Joseph A Konstan. 2010. Expert identification in community question answering: exploring question selection bias. In *Proceedings of the 19th ACM international conference on Information and knowledge management*, pages 1505–1508. ACM.

Qiongjie Tian, Peng Zhang, and Baoxin Li. 2013. Towards predicting the best answers in community-based question-answering services. In *Seventh International AAAI Conference on Weblogs and Social Media*, pages 725–728.

Pucktada Treeratpituk and C Lee Giles. 2009. Disambiguating authors in academic publications using random forests. In *Proceedings of the 9th ACM/IEEE-CS joint conference on Digital libraries*, pages 39–48. ACM.

Baoguo Yang and Suresh Manandhar. 2014. Exploring user expertise and descriptive ability in community question answering. In *Proceedings of 2014 IEEE/ACM International Conference on Advances in Social Networks Analysis and Mining*, pages 320–327. IEEE.

Jun Zhang, Mark S Ackerman, and Lada Adamic. 2007. Expertise networks in online communities: structure and algorithms. In *Proceedings of the 16th international conference on World Wide Web*, pages 221–230. ACM.

Baichuan Zhang, Tanay Kumar Saha, and Mohammad Al Hasan. 2014a. Name disambiguation from link data in a collaboration graph. In *2014 IEEE/ACM International Conference on Advances in Social Networks Analysis and Mining (ASONAM)*, pages 81–84. IEEE.

Kai Zhang, Wei Wu, Haocheng Wu, Zhoujun Li, and Ming Zhou. 2014b. Question retrieval with high quality answers in community question answering. In *Proceedings of the 23rd ACM International Conference on Information and Knowledge Management*, pages 371–380. ACM.

Guangyou Zhou, Siwei Lai, Kang Liu, and Jun Zhao. 2012a. Topic-sensitive probabilistic model for expert finding in question answer communities. In *Proceedings of the 21st ACM international conference on Information and knowledge management*, pages 1662–1666. ACM.

Zhi-Min Zhou, Man Lan, Zheng-Yu Niu, and Yue Lu. 2012b. Exploiting user profile information for answer ranking in cqa. In *Proceedings of the 21st international conference companion on World Wide Web*, pages 767–774. ACM.

Discovering Causal Relations in Textual Instructions

Kristina Yordanova
University of Rostock
kristina.yordanova@uni-rostock.de

Abstract

One aspect of ontology learning methods is the discovery of relations in textual data. One kind of such relations are causal relations. Our aim is to discover causations described in texts such as recipes and manuals. There is a lot of research on causal relations discovery that is based on grammatical patterns. These patterns are, however, rarely discovered in textual instructions (such as recipes) with short and simple sentence structure. Therefore we propose an approach that makes use of time series to discover causal relations. We distinguish causal relations from correlation by assuming that one word causes another only if it precedes the second word temporally. To test the approach, we compared the discovered by our approach causal relations to those obtained through grammatical patterns in 20 textual instructions. The results showed that our approach has an average recall of 41% compared to 13% obtained with the grammatical patterns. Furthermore the discovered by the two approaches causal relations are usually disjoint. This indicates that the approach can be combined with grammatical patterns in order to increase the number of causal relations discovered in textual instructions.

1 Introduction and Motivation

There is an increasing number of approaches and systems for ontology learning based on textual data partially because of the availability of web resources that are easily accessible on the internet (Wong et al., 2012). One problem these approaches face is the discovery of relations in the data (Wong et al., 2012). One type of relations are the causal relations between text elements, that is, whether one word or phrase causes another. Most of the research regarding causal relations is centred on the discovery of causal relations between topics (Radinsky et al., 2011; Kim et al., 2012; Li et al., 2010) or based on a large amount of textual data (Silverstein et al., 2000; Mani and Cooper, 2000; Girju, 2003). Moreover, the works usually focus on the discovery of causal relations in rich textual data with complex sentence structure (Silverstein et al., 2000; Mani and Cooper, 2000; Girju, 2003). There is however little research on discovering causal relations in textual instructions that have short sentence length and simple structure (Zhang et al., 2012). This can be explained with the fact that short sentences often do not contain any grammatical causal patterns, rather the relations are implicitly inferred by the reader. There is a large amount of web instructions available in the form of recipes, manuals, and tutorials[1] that contain such simple structures. For example, in the sentence *"Add the pork pieces, fry them for 2 minutes."* there is no explicit causal relation between *add* and *fry*. However, we implicitly know, that without adding the pork pieces, we cannot fry them. This means that when attempting to learn an ontology representing the domain knowledge of such domain, it is difficult to discover causal relations between the ontology elements. For example, when attempting to learn the ontology structure of our experimental data with a state of the art tool (Cimiano and Völker, 2005), it is able to identify *is-a* relations, but no similarity or causal relations in the text. To address the problem of identifying causal relations in textual data, in this paper we discuss an approach that utilises time series in order to find temporally dependent elements in the text. We concentrate on the discov-

[1] For example, *BBC Food Recipes* provides currently 12 385 recipes (BBC, 2015).

Proceedings of Recent Advances in Natural Language Processing, pages 714–720,
Hissar, Bulgaria, Sep 7–9 2015.

ery of relations between events[2], and on the relation between events and the words that describe the changes these events cause.

The work is structured as follows. In Section 2 we discuss the related work on causal relations discovery. In Section 3 we present our approach to causality discovery. The experimental setup to test our approach is described in Section 4. Later, we discuss the results in Section 5 and we conclude the work with a discussion about the advantages and limitations of the approach (Section 6).

2 Related Work

There is a lot of research on discovery of causal relations in textual data. Most of it is centred on applying grammatical patterns in order to identify the relations. Khoo et al. (Khoo et al., 1998) propose five ways of explicitly identifying cause-effect pairs, and based on them construct patterns for discovering them. The patterns employ causal links between two phrases or clauses (e.g. *hence*, *therefore*), causative verbs (e.g. *cause*, *break*), resultative constructions (verb-noun-adjective constructions), conditionals (e.g. *if-then*), and causative adverbs and adjectives (e.g. *fatally*). Khoo et al. also provide an extensive catalogue of causative words and phrases. Based on this concept other works search for causal relations for different applications. For example, Li et al. attempt to generate attack plans based on newspaper data (Li et al., 2010); Girju et al. utilise grammatical patterns in order to analyse cause-effect questions in question answering system (Girju, 2003); Cole et al. apply grammatical patterns to textual data in order to obtain Bayesian network fragments (Cole et al., 2006); and Radinsky et al. mine web articles to identify causal relations (Radinsky et al., 2011).

Other approaches combine grammatical patterns with machine learning in order to extract preconditions and effects from textual data. For example, Sill et al. train a support vector machine with a large annotated textual corpus in order to be able to identify preconditions and effects, and to build STRIPS representations of actions and events (Sil and Yates, 2011).

Alternative approaches rely on the Markov condition to identify causal relations between documents. They utilise the LCD algorithm that tests variables for dependence, independence, and conditional independence to restrict the possible causal relations (Cooper, 1997). Based on this algorithm Silverstein et al. were able to discover causal relations between words by representing each article as a sample with the n most frequent words (Silverstein et al., 2000). Similarly, Mani et al. apply the LCD algorithm to identify causal relations in medical data (Mani and Cooper, 2000).

All of the above methods are applied to large amounts of data, usually with rich textual descriptions. There is, however, no much research on finding the causal relations within a textual instructions document, where the sentences are short and simple. Zahng et al. attempt to extract procedural knowledge from textual instructions (manuals and recipes) in order to build a procedural model of the instruction (Zhang et al., 2012). By applying grammatical patterns they are able to build a procedural model of each sentence. They, however, do not discuss the relations between the identified procedures, thus, do not identify any causal relations between the sentences.

In our work we identify implicit causal relations within and between sentences in a document. To do that we adapt the approach proposed by Kim et al. (Kim et al., 2012; Kim et al., 2013), where they search for causally related topics by representing each topic as a time series where each time stamp is represented by a document from the corresponding topic. In the following we explain how the approach can be adapted to identify causal relations within a textual document.

3 Discovering Causal Relations using Time Series

Textual instructions such as recipes and manuals have a simple sentence structure that does not contain many grammatical patterns, indicating explicit causal relations. On the other hand, we as humans are able to detect implicit relations, e.g. that one instruction can be executed only after another was already executed. In that case, we can either assume that the causal relation between events follows the temporal relation (i.e. each event causes the next), or we can attempt to identify only those events that are causally related. Similarly, to identify the effects one event has on the object, or the state of the object that allows the occurrence of the event, one can search for grammatical patterns. That will however only

[2] By *event* we mean the verb describing the action that has to be executed in an instruction.

identify relations within the sentence but not between sentences (unless they are connected with a causal link). For example, in the sentences *"Simmer (the sauce) until thickened. Add the pork, mix well for one minute."* using a grammatical pattern we will discover that *simmer* causes *thickened* (through the causal link *until*). However, it will not discover that the sauce has to *thicken*, in order to *add* the pork. A grammatical pattern will also not discover the relation between *add* and *mix*, as there is no causal link between them. To discover such implicit relations, we treat each word in textual instructions as a time series. Then we apply causality test on the pairs of words we are interested in to identify whether they are causally related or not.

We concentrate on three types of causal relations. These are discovering causal relation (1) between two events; (2) between an event and its effect on the state of object over which the event is executed; (3) between the state of the object before an event can be executed over it. By state of the object we mean the phrase that serves as an adjectival modifier or a nominal subject.

We consider a text to be a sequences of sentences divided by a sentence separator.

Definition 1 ***(Text)*** *A text I is a set of tuples $(S, C) = \{(s_1, c_1), (s_2, c_2), ..., (s_n, c_n)\}$ where S represents the sentence and C the sentence separator, with n being the length of the text.*

Each sentence in the text is then represented by a sequence of words, where each word has a tag describing its part of speech (POS) meaning.

Definition 2 ***(Sentence)*** *A sentence S is a set of tuples $(W, T) = \{(w_1, t_1), ..., (w_m, t_m)\}$ where W represents the words in the sentence, and T the corresponding POS tag assigned to the words. The sentence is m words long.*

In a text we have different types of words. We are most interested in verbs as they describe the events that cause other events or changes. More precisely, a verb $v \in W$ is a word where for the tuple (v, t) holds that $t = verb$. We denote the set of verbs with V. The events are then verbs in their infinitive form or in present tense, as textual instructions are usually described in imperative form with a missing agent.

Definition 3 ***(Event)*** *An event $e \in V$ is a verb where for the tuple (e, t) holds that $t = verb\_infinitive\ OR\ verb\_present$. For short we say $t = event$.*

We are also interested in those nouns that are the direct (accusative) objects of the verb. A noun $n \in W$ is a word where for the tuple (n, t) holds that $t = noun$. We denote the set of nouns with N. Then we define the object in the following manner.

Definition 4 ***(Object)*** *An object $o \in N$ of a verb v is the accusative object of v. We denote the relation between o and v as $dobj(v, o)$, and any direct object-verb in a sentence s_n as a tuple $(v, o)_n$.*

We define the state of an object as the adjectival modifier or the nominal subject of an object.

Definition 5 ***(State)*** *A state $c \in W$ of an object o is a word that has one of the following relations with the object: $amod(c, o)$, denoting the adjectival modifier or $nsubj(c, o)$, denoting the nominal subject. We denote such tuple as $(c, o)_n$, where n is the sentence number.*

As in textual instructions the object is often omitted (e.g. *"Simmer (the sauce) until thickened."*), we also investigate the relation between an event and past tense verbs or adjectives that do not belong to an adjectival modifier or to nominal subject, but that might still describe this relation.

3.1 Generating time series

Given the definitions above, we can now describe each unique word in a text as a time series. Each element in the series is a tuple consisting of the number of the sentence in the text, and the number of occurrences of the word in the sentence.

Definition 6 ***(Time series)*** *A time series of a word w is a sequence of tuples $(D, F)_w = \{(1, f_1)_w, (2, f_2)_w, ..., (n, f_n)_w\}$ where $D = \{1, ..., n\}$ is the timestamp, and F is the number of occurrences of a word at the given timestamp. Here n corresponds to the sentence number in the text.*

Algorithm 1 Generate time series for a given object and the events applied on it.

```
Require: (V, O)                                          ▷ all event-object pairs in I
Require: m ∈ O                                           ▷ a unique object
for S_n in I do                                          ▷ for each sentence in a text
    V_n ← [w | t == event, (w, t) ← S_n]                 ▷ extract the events
end for
U ← unique(V)                                            ▷ returns all unique events in I
N ← [unique(o) | (v, o) ← (V, O)]                        ▷ collect the unique objects in I
for u in U do                                            ▷ for each unique event in I
    i ← 1
    while i ≤ length(I) do
        for (v, o) in (V, O)_i do                        ▷ for each event-object pair in S_i
            (D, F)_{u,i} ← (i, count((v == u, o == m)))  ▷ calculate the number of occurrences of (u, m) for each sentence
            i ← i + 1
        end for
    end while
end for
return (D, F)_m                                          ▷ return the time series for all events w.r.t. an object
```

Generally, we can generate a time series for each kind of word in the corpus, as well as for each tuple of words. Here we concentrate on those describing or causing change in a state. That means we generate time series for all events and for all states that change an object. To generate time series for the events we distinguish two cases. The first is of events that are applied to objects (e.g. *"simmer the sauce"*). In that case, for each unique object o in the corpus we generate a time series that describes how often this object had a direct object relation with a verb v, namely we are looking for the number of occurrences of $(v, o)_n$ in each sentence s_n (see Algorithm 1).

Apart from the events that are applied to an object, there are such that do not have a direct object relation, or where the relation is not explicitly described (e.g. *"Mix (the pork) well for one minute."*). In that case, we also search for causal relations in events without considering their direct objects (see Algorithm 2).

Algorithm 2 Generate time series representing the events in a textual corpus

Require: U ▷ all unique events in I
Require: V_n ▷ all unique events in each sentence S_n
for u in U **do** ▷ for each unique event in I
  $i \leftarrow 1$
  while $i \leq length(I)$ **do**
    for v in V_i **do** ▷ for each event in S_i
      $(D, F)_{u,i} \leftarrow (i, count(v == u))$ ▷ calculate the number of occurrences of u for S_i
      $i \leftarrow i + 1$
    end for
  end while
end for
return (D, F) ▷ return the time series for all events

To investigate the causal relation between a state of the object and an event, we also generate time series describing the state. This is done by following the procedure described in Algorithm 1 where the (O, V) pair is replaced with (C, O) pair, and where we no longer extract events but rather states c. In order to include all states where the object is omitted, we also generate time series for each adjective or verb in past tense that could potentially describe a state. To do that we follow the procedure in Algorithm 2, where instead of events we search for adjectives or past tense verbs.

3.2 Searching for causality

In order to discover causal relations based on the generated time series, we make use of the Granger causality test. It is a statistical test for determining whether one time series is useful for forecasting another. More precisely, Granger testing performs statistical significance test for one time series, "causing" the other time series with different time lags using auto-regression (Granger, 1969). The causality relationship is based on two principles. The first is that the cause happens prior to the effect, while the second states that the cause has a unique information about the future values of its effect (Granger, 2001). Based on these assumptions, given two sets of time series x_t and y_t, we can test whether x_t Granger causes y_t with a maximum p time lag. To do that, we estimate the regression $y_t = a_o + a_1 y_{t-1} + ... + a_p y_{t-p} + b_1 x_{t-1} + ... + b_p x_{t-p}$. An F-test is then used to determine whether the lagged x terms are significant.

Algorithm 3 Identify causal relation between two words

Require: (D, F) ▷ all time series describing words of interest in a corpus
Require: L ▷ the lag in the Granger causality test
Require: Th ▷ significance threshold
Require: $u \in W$ ▷ a word which causal relation w.r.t. the rest of the words is tested
for w in W, $w \neq u$ **do** ▷ for each unique time series
  $C_{u,w} \leftarrow granger.Causality(((D, F)_u, (D, F)_w), L)$ ▷ calculate the causality between w and u
  if $p.value(C_{u,w}) \leq Th$ **then** ▷ the relation is significant
    $R_{u,w} \leftarrow C_{u,w}$ ▷ u causes w
  end if
end for
return R_u ▷ return the list of words with which u is causally related

We use the Granger causality test to search for causal relations between the generated time series (see Algorithm 3). Generally, for each two time series of interest, we perform Granger test, and if the p value of the result is under the significance threshold, we conclude that the first time series causes the second, hence the first word causes the second. The Granger causality test can be applied only on stationary time series. Otherwise, they have to be converted into stationary time series before applying the test (e.g. by taking the difference of every two elements in the series).

4 Experimental Setup

To test our approach, we selected 20 different instructions: 10 recipes from BBC Food Recipes[3], 3 washing machine instructions[4], 3 coffee machine instructions[5], 3 kitchen experiment instructions describing the experiments from the CMU Grand challenge dataset[6], and one description of a cooking task experiment[7]. The shortest instruction is 5 lines (each line being a sentence with a

[3] http://www.bbc.co.uk/food/recipes/
[4] http://www.miele.co.uk/Resources/OperatingInstructions/W%203923%20WPS.pdf
[5] http://www.cn.jura.com/service_support/download_manual_jura_impressa_e10_e20_e25_english.pdf
[6] http://kitchen.cs.cmu.edu/
[7] Source not shown due to blind reviewing.

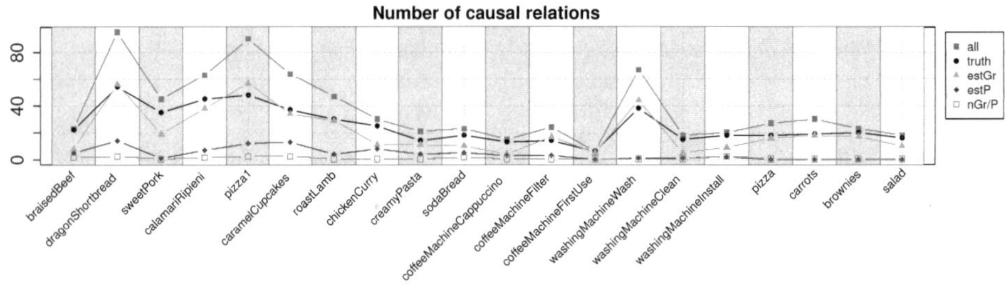

Figure 1: Number of causal relations discovered by a human expert (circle), Granger causality (triangle), part of speech patterns (rhombus), and all discovered relations (solid square). The square without fill shows the causal relations that have been discovered by both Granger causality and grammatical patterns.

full stop at the end), the longest is 111 lines, with a mean length of 31 lines. The average sentence length in an instruction text is 11.2 words, with the shortest text having an average of 5.7 words per sentence, and the longest an average of 17.4 words per sentence. The average number of events per sentence is 1.6, with the minimum average of 1 event per sentence in a text, and the average maximum of 2.23 events per sentence.

A human expert was asked to search for causal relations in the text, concentrating on relations between events or between states and events. This was later used as the ground truth against which the discovered relations were compared.

Later, each of the instructions was parsed by the Stanford NLP Parser[8] in order to obtain the part of speech tags and the dependencies between the words. This was then used as an input for generating the time series. We considered as a sentence separator a full stop and a comma, as in this type of instructions it divides sequentially executed events in one sentence. The time series were then tested for stationarity by using the Augmented Dickey–Fuller (ADF) t-statistic test. It showed that the series are already stationary.

We search for causal relations between events without considering the object, between events given the object, and between events and states. For the case of events given the object we performed Granger causality test with a lag from 1 to 5 as the shortest instructions text has 5 sentences. For identifying relations between events and states we used a lag of 1, as the event and the change of state are usually described in the same sentence or in following sentences. For identifying relations between events without considering the object, we also took a lag of 1, because in texts with longer sentences, the test tends to discover false positives when applied with a longer lag. Furthermore, to reduce the familywise error rate during the multiple comparisons, we decreased the significance threshold by applying the Bonferroni correction.

To compare the approach with that of using grammatical patterns, we implemented patterns with a causal link that contain words such as *until*, *because*, *before*, etc. We also added the conjunction *and* to the causal links, as it was often used in the recipes to describe a sequence of events. We also implemented a verb-noun-adjective pattern to search for the relation between events and states, and a verb(present)-noun-verb(past) pattern to search for relations between events and states. Finally, we implemented a conditional pattern (e.g. the *if-then* construction). As an input for these patterns we used once again the text instructions with POS tags from the Stanford Parser.

5 Results

The human expert discovered an average of 25.25 causal relations per text document. Using the grammatical patterns, an average of 4.15 causal relations per text document were discovered. Using the time series approach, an average of 20.9 causal relations per document were discovered.

The number of causal relations discovered in each text document can be seen in Figure 1. It shows that the number of discovered relations is lower in texts with short sentences.

Furthermore, the recall for each textual instruction is shown in Figure 2. The recall increases with decreasing the sentence length, while the false discovery rate (FDR) decreases.

On the other hand, the recall for the grammatical patterns is low for all instructions. However, in

[8] http://nlp.stanford.edu/software/lex-parser.shtml

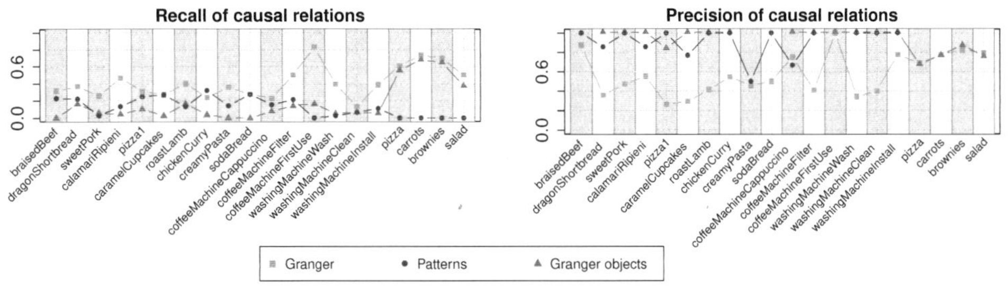

Figure 2: Recall and precision of the discovered causal relations for each dataset. Square indicates Granger causality, circle grammatical patterns, triangle Granger causality when using only the event-object pairs.

difference to the time series approach, the grammatical patterns have a high precision.

The precision and recall of the time series when using only the event-object pairs (Algorithm 1) show that the precision for the event-object pairs is very high in comparison to the overall time series precision (Figure 2).

Finally, we tested whether there is a significant correlation between the performance of the approaches and the type of textual instruction. We applied a two sided correlation test that uses the Pearson's product moment correlation coefficient. The results showed that in the approach using time series and the Granger causality test, the performance is inversely proportional to the sentence length and the number of events in the sentence. On the other hand, the approach using the grammatical patterns is proportional to the sentence length and the number of events.

6 Discussion

In this work we presented an approach that relies on time series to discover causal relations in textual descriptions such as manuals and recipes.

Among the advantages of the approach are the following. The approach allows the discovery of implicit causal relations in texts where explicit causal relations are not discoverable through grammatical patterns. It does not require a training phase (assuming the text has POS tags), or explicit modelling of grammatical patterns. This makes the approach more context independent. It discovers relations different from those discovered with grammatical patterns, and can detect causal relations between elements that are several sentences apart. This indicates that both approaches can be combined to provide better performance.

Apart from the advantages, there are several shortcomings to the approach. The approach is not suitable for texts with complex sentence structure and many events in one sentence, as this generates false positive relations. The cause for this is that when we have several words we want to test in the same sentence, they will also have the same time stamp. To solve this problem, one can introduce additional sentence separators.

Another characteristic of textual instructions is that they often omit the direct object. On the other hand, as the results showed, the usage of objects reduces the generation of false positives. To make use of this, we can introduce a preprocessing phase, where verbs that are in conjunction all receive the same direct object.

Another problem is the lag size in the Granger causality test. The test is very sensitive to the lag size in the case when it is applied to events that do not have direct objects. On the other hand, the approach is less sensitive to the lag when the sentence length is reduced, and it is robust when direct object is used.

Another problem associated with the Granger causality test is whether it discovers causality or simply correlation. As the approach does not rely on contextual information, apart from the causes, it also discovers any number of correlations in the time series. To that end, Granger causality is probably not the best tool for searching for causal relations in textual instructions, but it produces results in situations where the grammatical patterns are not able to yield any results.

As a conclusion, the usage of time series in textual instructions allows the discovery of implicit causal relations that are usually not discoverable when using grammatical patterns. This can potentially improve the learned semantic structure of ontologies representing the knowledge embedded in textual instructions.

References

BBC (2015). BBC Food Recipes. Retrieved: 22.04.2015 from http://www.bbc.co.uk/food/recipes/.

Cimiano, P. and Völker, J. (2005). Text2onto. In Montoyo, A., Muńoz, R., and Métais, E., editors, *Natural Language Processing and Information Systems*, volume 3513 of *Lecture Notes in Computer Science*, pages 227–238. Springer Berlin Heidelberg.

Cole, S., Royal, M., Valtorta, M., Huhns, M., and Bowles, J. (2006). A lightweight tool for automatically extracting causal relationships from text. In *SoutheastCon, 2006. Proceedings of the IEEE*, pages 125–129.

Cooper, G. (1997). A simple constraint-based algorithm for efficiently mining observational databases for causal relationships. *Data Mining and Knowledge Discovery*, 1(2):203–224.

Girju, R. (2003). Automatic detection of causal relations for question answering. In *Proceedings of the ACL 2003 Workshop on Multilingual Summarization and Question Answering - Volume 12*, MultiSumQA '03, pages 76–83, Stroudsburg, PA, USA. Association for Computational Linguistics.

Granger, C. W. J. (1969). Investigating Causal Relations by Econometric Models and Cross-spectral Methods. *Econometrica*, 37(3):424–438.

Granger, C. W. J. (2001). Testing for causality: A personal viewpoint. In Ghysels, E., Swanson, N. R., and Watson, M. W., editors, *Essays in Econometrics*, pages 48–70. Harvard University Press, Cambridge, MA, USA.

Khoo, C. S., Kornfilt, J., Myaeng, S. H., and Oddy, R. N. (1998). Automatic extraction of cause-effect information from newspaper text without knowledge-based inferencing. *Literature and Linguist Computing*, 13(4):177–186.

Kim, H. D., Castellanos, M., Hsu, M., Zhai, C., Rietz, T., and Diermeier, D. (2013). Mining causal topics in text data: iterative topic modeling with time series feedback. In *Proceedings of the 22nd ACM international conference on Conference on information & knowledge management*, CIKM '13, pages 885–890, New York, NY, USA. ACM.

Kim, H. D., Zhai, C., Rietz, T. A., Diermeier, D., Hsu, M., Castellanos, M., and Ceja Limon, C. A. (2012). Incatomi: Integrative causal topic miner between textual and non-textual time series data. In *Proceedings of the 21st ACM International Conference on Information and Knowledge Management*, CIKM '12, pages 2689–2691, New York, NY, USA. ACM.

Li, X., Mao, W., Zeng, D., and Wang, F.-Y. (2010). Automatic construction of domain theory for attack planning. In *IEEE International Conference on Intelligence and Security Informatics (ISI), 2010*, pages 65–70.

Mani, S. and Cooper, G. F. (2000). Causal discovery from medical textual data. In *Proceedings of the AMIA annual fall symposium 2000, Hanley and Belfus Publishers*, pages 542–546.

Radinsky, K., Davidovich, S., and Markovitch, S. (2011). Learning causality from textual data. In *Proceedings of the IJCAI Workshop on Learning by Reading and its Applications in Intelligent Question-Answering*, pages 363–367, Barcelona, Spain.

Sil, A. and Yates, E. (2011). Extracting strips representations of actions and events. In *Recent Advances in Natural Language Processing*, pages 1–8.

Silverstein, C., Brin, S., Motwani, R., and Ullman, J. (2000). Scalable techniques for mining causal structures. *Data Min. Knowl. Discov.*, 4(2-3):163–192.

Wong, W., Liu, W., and Bennamoun, M. (2012). Ontology learning from text: A look back and into the future. *ACM Comput. Surv.*, 44(4):20:1–20:36.

Zhang, Z., Webster, P., Uren, V., Varga, A., and Ciravegna, F. (2012). Automatically extracting procedural knowledge from instructional texts using natural language processing. In Chair), N. C. C., Choukri, K., Declerck, T., Doğan, M. U., Maegaard, B., Mariani, J., Moreno, A., Odijk, J., and Piperidis, S., editors, *Proceedings of the Eight International Conference on Language Resources and Evaluation (LREC'12)*, Istanbul, Turkey. European Language Resources Association (ELRA).

A Large Wordnet-based Sentiment Lexicon for Polish

Monika Zaśko-Zielińska
University of Wrocław
Wrocław, Poland
monika.zasko-zielinska@uwr.edu.pl

Maciej Piasecki
Wrocław University of Technology
Wrocław, Poland
maciej.piasecki@pwr.edu.pl

Stan Szpakowicz
University of Ottawa
Ottawa, Ontario, Canada
szpak@eecs.uottawa.ca

Abstract

The applications of plWordNet, a very large wordnet for Polish, do not yet include work on sentiment and emotions. We present a pilot project to annotate plWordNet manually with sentiment polarity values and basic emotion values. We work with lexical units, plWordNet's basic building blocks.[1] So far, we have annotated about 30,000 nominal and adjectival LUs. The resulting lexicon is already one of the largest sentiment and emotion resources, in particular among those based on wordnets. We opted for manual annotation to ensure high accuracy, and to provide a reliable starting point for future semi-automated expansion. The paper lists the principal assumptions, outlines the annotation process, and introduces the resulting resource, plWordNet-emo. We discuss the selection of the material for the pilot study, show the distribution of annotations across the wordnet, and consider the statistics, including inter-annotator agreement and the resolution of disagreement.

1 Introduction

The Polish wordnet, plWordNet (Piasecki et al., 2009; Maziarz et al., 2013), is very large and comprehensive, with well over 150,000 synsets and 200,000 LUs at the time of writing. It has many applications, *e.g.,* text similarity (Siemiński, 2012), terminology extraction and clustering (Mykowiecka and Marciniak, 2012), extraction of opinion attributes from product descriptions (Wawer and Gołuchowski, 2012), addition of features for text mining (Maciołek and Dobrowolski, 2013), or a mapping between a lexicon and an ontology (Wróblewska et al., 2013). It is fast becoming a go-to resource in Polish lexical semantics. So far, however, it has not supported applications in the crucially important area of sentiment analysis and opinion mining. That area requires annotation: a word or word sense either does or does not carry sentiment, emotion or affect. That is why we have recently set out to annotate plWordNet with sentiment polarity and basic emotions.

Automatic annotation of lexical material is not a viable option. Wordnets are reference resources, relied upon for the absence of lexical errors. In fact, all widely published sentiment-marked and emotion-marked lists of lexical items have been created manually, sometimes by crowdsourcing. Now, plWordNet is much too large for complete, *affordable* manual annotation, but a reliable core of as little as 10% of the wordnet annotated makes it entirely possible to continue with semi-automatic expansion. Our pilot project manually annotated around 30,000 LUs (15% of plWordNet)[2] with sentiment and basic emotions, so we have ample material to also compare fully manual and semi-automatic annotation.

[1] The term *lexical unit* will be abbreviated to *LU* throughout this paper.

[2] This annotation is already on a scale several times larger than SentiWordNet (Esuli and Sebastiani, 2006).

Proceedings of Recent Advances in Natural Language Processing, pages 721–730,
Hissar, Bulgaria, Sep 7–9 2015.

2 Sentiment and Affect Annotations in Wordnets

Several sentiment lexicons are available for English, but hardly any for most other languages. Chen and Skiena (2014) have found 12 publicly available sentiment lexicons for 5 languages; there are none for Polish. Some sentiment lexicons have been built upon Princeton WordNet,[3] a natural starting point because of its comprehensive coverage and its numerous applications. The lexicons not based on PWN consider lemmas rather than lexical meanings or concepts.

WordNet-Affect is a selection of synsets very likely to represent "affective concepts" (Strapparava and Valitutti, 2004). A small core of 1903 lemmas was selected and described manually with "affective labels". Next, a set of rules based on wordnet relation semantics drove the transfer of the sentiment description onto the synsets connected to the core by wordnet relations. This produced 2874 synsets and 4787 lemmas.

SentiWordNet (Esuli and Sebastiani, 2006) annotates a synset with three values from the interval $\langle 0, 1 \rangle$. They describe "how objective, positive, and negative the terms contained in the synset are". About 10% of the adjectives were manually annotated, each by 3-5 annotators (Baccianella et al., 2010). In SentiWordNet 3.0, the automated annotation process starts with all the synsets which include 7 "paradigmatically positive" and 7 "paradigmatically negative" lemmas.[4] In the end, SentiWordNet 3.0 added automatic sentiment annotation to all of PWN 3.0.

SentiSense (Carrillo de Albornoz et al., 2012) is also a concept-based affective lexicon, with emotion categories assigned to PWN synsets. The initial list of 20 categories, a sum of several sets including WordNet-Affect, was reduced to 14 after some work with annotators. The authors write: "the manual labelling techniques generate resources with very low coverage but very high precision", but note that such precision can be only achieved for specific domains. The construction of SentiSense began with a manual annotation of only 1200 synsets with 14 emotions. Annotation was transferred onto other synsets using wordnet relations. The authors' visualisation and editing tools, designed to allow relatively easy expansion and adaptation, did not add much to the resource, so every user must enlarge it further to make it really applicable.

To sum up, a wordnet may be a good starting point for the construction of a sentiment lexicon: annotation can be done at the level of lexical meanings (concepts) or lemmas. PWN appears to be a good choice due to its sense-based model and large coverage. All large wordnet-based sentiment lexicons have been built by giving very limited manual annotation to algorithms for automated expansion onto other synsets. This, however, seems to have to result in lower precision, as noted, *e.g.*, by Poria et al. (2012): "Currently available lexical resources for opinion polarity and affect recognition such as SentiWordNet (Esuli and Sebastiani, 2006) or WordNet-Affect are known to be rather noisy and limited."

No large wordnets are available for most languages other than English. Many sentiment lexicons were created by translating sentiment-annotated PWN, *e.g.*, Bengali WordNet-Affect (Das and Bandyopadhyay, 2010), Japanese WordNet-Affect (Torii et al., 2011) and Chinese Emotion Lexicon (Xu et al., 2013). It is not clear how well annotations of that kind can be transferred across the language barrier. Moreover, as we discuss it in section 3.1, plWordNet's model differs slightly from that of PWN.

Crowdsourcing has also been used to develop sentiment lexicons (Mohammad and Turney, 2013). It *can* outdo automated annotation (or automatic expansion of a manually annotated part), but the consistency of the result is low compared to manual description by trained annotators.

Unlike most of the existing methods, our aim is a manual annotation of a substantial part of plWordNet by a team of linguists and psychologists. The manually annotated part – several times larger than other known manually created sentiment lexicons – can be an important resource on its own. It can also be a solid basis for the development of automated sentiment annotation methods for more lexical material in a wordnet. We have adopted a rich annotation model in which sentiment polarity description is combined with emotion categories.

[3] *Princeton WordNet* will be abbreviated to PWN throughout this paper.

[4] good, nice, excellent, positive, fortunate, correct, superior; bad, nasty, poor, negative, unfortunate, wrong, inferior (Turney and Littman, 2003)

3 An Annotation Model for plWordNet

3.1 The Principles

In contrast with most wordnet-building projects, plWordNet is not based on PWN. It also has a slightly, but significantly different model of word sense description. Its main building block is an LU understood as a pair: lemma plus sense number. LUs are grouped into a synset when they share constitutive lexico-semantic relations (hyponymy/hypernymy, meronymy/holonymy etc.) (Maziarz et al., 2013) Synsets are a notational shorthand for LUs which share their relations, so that all plWordNet relations recorded at the level of synsets can also be expressed at the level of LUs. More than half of relation instances in plWordNet are defined for LUs, because they are LU-specific, among them antonymy and relations signalled derivationally. Glosses and use examples in plWordNet are also assigned to LUs. LUs, then, seem to be a natural place to represent information related to sentiment polarity and emotions.

Sentiment polarity of an utterance is the result of a complex process influenced by word sense, language structure, communication and interpretation. It is difficult to describe sentiment polarity of a word sense in isolation from the context, but a "context-agnostic" sentiment lexicon can be a useful approximation for many applications. Too many factors govern sentiment perception from the point of view of the hearer (receiver) of the utterance. That is why we have assumed that the description from the point of view of the speaker would let us concentrate on the word sense typically intended by the speaker and its sentiment polarity included in that sense. We wanted to abstract away any further interpretation process and concentrate on the core of a word sense, which can be understood with no information about the context of interpretation.

Sentiment polarity appears to be associated with emotions which typify the source of the polarity in question. It can also be characterised by the fundamental human values associated with a given type of polarity (Puzynina, 1992) – more on that in section 3.3, step 2.

All in all, we have annotated LUs, plWordNet's basic building blocks, as completely as possible. We encode the sign of polarity (positive, negative, ambiguous), its intensity (strong, weak), as well as emotions and fundamental values.

3.2 The Pilot Project

The pilot sentiment annotation has been designed to add annotations to plWordNet manually. This is not what other wordnet annotation projects did – see section 2. Manual annotation on a larger scale does not only allow a broader vocabulary annotated with higher accuracy, often negotiated between annotators, but also becomes a much more reliable basis for *semi*-automatic expansion. We also wanted to test on a suitable scale the annotation guidelines we had adopted. Finally, we wanted to investigate how sentiment values and other related values are distributed over the various plWordNet relations and over synsets. It was not clear if LUs in a synsets must all have the same sentiment description. To avoid any bias, all that work was entrusted to a new group of linguists, separate from the main plWordNet team. A fresh look was also to be an independent diagnostic test for a sizeable part of the contents of plWordNet.

A manual analysis of the first sample of plWordNet LUs showed that even synsets with no positively or no negatively marked LUs can include LUs neutral in relation to sentiment, *e.g.*, {*mańkut* 1 '*coll.* left-hander' -weak, *leworęczny* 1 'left-handed' neutral, *szmaja* 1 '≈southpaw' -weak} or {*bliźni* 1 'neighbour [biblical]' +weak, *brat* 2 'brother' +weak, *drugi* 2 'the other' neutral}. Mixed-sentiment synsets rarely include positive, negative and ambiguous LUs, but they do occur, *e.g.*, {*pożądanie* 3 'desire' +strong, *pociąg fizyczny* 1 'physical attraction' +strong, *chuć* 1 '*coll.* sexual attraction, lust' -strong, *pożądliwość* 1 'lust' ambiguous}.

Notwithstanding, such synsets are well formed according to the general plWordNet guidelines. We also noted that LUs which share a derivational basis do not necessarily share their sentiment marking. There are marked bases with neutral derivatives, *e.g.*, *gadać* 'to chatter' → *pogadanka* 'a chat', or *łazić* 'to tramp' → *łazik* 'a jeep' (Burkacka, 2003, p. 127). Derivational semantic relations, then, cannot be treated as copying the sentiment values to the derivatives.[5]

The sentiment of an LU x was determined in five main steps.

1. Decide if x is marked with respect to senti-

[5]Derivational semantic relations originate from a formal derivation relation and are mostly represented by a derivational link, but they are semantic in nature. They are suitably defined in the plWordNet model (Maziarz et al., 2013).

ment polarity, or neutral; if x is neutral, skip the remaining steps.

2. Assign the basic emotions and fundamental human values which appear to be associated with x.
3. Mark x as negative, positive or ambiguous.
4. Evaluate the intensity of x's sentiment polarity: strong or weak.
5. Give example sentences: one for x with a positive or negative polarity, two for an ambiguous x.

3.3 The Steps

Step 1 identifies noun LUs marked by non-neutral sentiment polarity. We have adopted two linguistic test procedures.

The first procedure is based on the method introduced by Markowski (1992) for the recognition of the lexis common to different genres, *i.e.,* nouns which are unmarked, non-erudite, and not terminological. A marked LU's expressivity can be implicit (*e.g.,* names of emotional states) or explicit (motivated by form or meaning) (Grabias, 1981, p. 40). The former are relatively easily spotted: they are established in language and occur in all genres (Zaśko-Zielińska and Piasecki, 2015), and their emotional markedness can be recognised without referring to context. The latter require the language user to check how she or other language users deploy it. For example, *troll* is either a Norse mythical creature or a person whose sole purpose in life is to seek out people to argue with on the internet over extremely trivial issues.[6]

For each LU analysed, we tested corpora for its occurrences together with deictic and possessive pronouns and operators which specify markedness.[7] Consider examples of the form *proszę pomyśleć o...* 'please think of...': *krześle* 'a chair' – acceptable; *tym krześle* 'this chair' – acceptable; *starociu* 'a relic' – unacceptable (this cannot be left unspecific); *tym naszym starociu* 'this relic of ours' – acceptable.

This method was applied earlier in research on Polish expressive lexis: expressivity is confirmed in context, and signalled (among others) by concretisation due to the use of pronouns (Rejter, 2006, pp. 88-90). For the recognition of marked LUs, we also used a concreteness test (Markowski, 1992): whether the LU can be modified by the pronouns *ten* 'this, the', *taki* 'such, such as', *twój* 'your$_{possessive}$' and *jakiś* 'some, a$_{referential}$, one'. The verdict was based on corpus search and the linguist's intuition.

We had to distinguish between neutral and marked adjectives. As in the analysis of nouns, we took into account such interrelated factors as meaning, word formation and context. Adjectives participate in the construction of expressive contexts in a sentence. Alongside such language mechanisms as the already noted deictic and possessive pronouns, adjectives are responsible for the semantic consistency of an utterance (Rejter, 2006, p. 76). That is why we placed a strong emphasis on the analysis of contexts in which adjectives occur.

The second test procedure in step 1 is based on checking the presence of pragmatic elements in the wordnet glosses for the analysed LUs and in their definitions in various dictionaries. We also tested the presence of qualifiers for genres—posp. (*pospolity* 'common'), pot. (*potoczny* 'colloquial'), wulg. (*wulgarny* 'vulgar') and książk. (*książkowy* 'bookish, literary')[8]—in the wordnet glosses of the analysed LUs.

The recognition of marked words is aimed not only at determining which LUs go through the subsequent steps of emotion analysis, but also at collecting neutral LUs (those not carrying polarity or emotion). Such LUs can play a role in automatic methods of emotional markedness recognition, see, *e.g.,* (Koppel and Schler, 2006).

Step 2 assigns emotions and values to LUs. We initially intended only to use the set of basic emotions which Plutchik (1980) identified in his Wheel of Emotions: joy, trust, fear, surprise, sadness, disgust, anger, anticipation. This set had figured in many later publications, *e.g.,* in (Ekman, 1992), and a number of resources and projects, including the NRC emotion lexicon (Mohammad and Turney, 2013) and the SentiSense Affective Lexicon (Carrillo de Albornoz et al., 2012).

In the Polish linguistic tradition, however, the description of the basic emotions is often associated with references to the fundamental values, like *użyteczność* 'utility', *dobro drugiego*

[6] http://www.urbandictionary.com/

[7] The corpora and other sources include:
http://tinyurl.com/kpwrl
http://www.nkjp.uni.lodz.pl/
http://www.nowewyrazy.uw.edu.pl/
http://www.miejski.pl/

[8] The term "książkowy" suggests *podniosły/uroczysty* 'solemn' as well as 'formal'.

człowieka 'another's good', *prawda* 'truth', *wiedza* 'knowledge', *piękno* 'beauty', *szczęście* 'happiness' (all of them positive), *nieużyteczność* ''futility', *krzywda* 'harm', *niewiedza* 'ignorance', *błąd* 'error', *brzydota* 'ugliness', *nieszczęście* 'misfortune' (all negative) (Puzynina, 1992). This set of fundamental values was proposed as a tool of linguistic analysis in the research on the language of values. We used it in our annotations. Kaproń-Charzyńska (2014, pp. 134-137) argues that expressions of emotions and values are usually associated in language expressions, and that it is difficult to separate them.

Evidence from psychological research, *e.g.,* (Barrett, 2006), and from linguistic research, *e.g.,* (Fries, 1992), shows that evaluation in terms of values is tightly connected with the feeling of emotions. Values can have different status in the description of lexical meaning: from included in the central aspects to peripheral. That is compatible with the semantics of prototypes, *e.g.,* (Mikołajczuk, 2000, p. 120).

To account for fundamental human values, then, the annotators could select labels from a predefined list, but they also could omit this sub-step.

The assignment of the emotion value helps annotators decide on the sentiment polarity of an LU. If the annotator selects, *e.g., wiedza* 'knowledge' and *piękno* 'beauty', *szczęście*, then we can assume that the given LU has a positive sentiment. If there are only negative emotions in the assigned set, *i.e.,* fear, surprise, sadness, anger, and disgust, and the values are only negative, then we can be sure that the LU has a negative sentiment. The presence of positive and negative emotions or values in the annotation of the given LU is a strong signal in favour of its ambiguity in relation to sentiment polarity.

We initially assumed that in some cases only emotions or values can be assigned to an LU. We observed, however, that only rarely did the annotator refrain from an assignment. Here is a likely reason: the annotators, while using combinations of basic emotions, tried to express complex emotions for which association with fundamental human values was much less straightforward. A mechanism for constructing complex emotions from basic ones (*e.g.,* disgust + anger = hostility) has been already described by Plutchik (2001, p. 349). That is why LUs marked by sentiment polarity and given some fundamental value had at least two or three basic emotions assigned.

The annotation with emotions and fundamental values was treated as supplementary to the primary annotation with sentiment polarity. We did not require perfect agreement in the assignment of basic emotions and fundamental values. High inter-annotator agreement was expected in the case of sentiment polarity, where the third annotator, the supervisor, arbitrated any disagreement. (See section 4 for more on team organisation.) The practice has shown, hovewer, that there is very high overlap between the sets assigned by two annotators. One set is mostly a subset of the other, which adds only one or two emotions or values. Consider *antytalent* 2 'a person who exhibits lack of skill in some area':

A1: {*smutek* 'sadness', *wstręt* 'disgust'}; {*nieużyteczność* 'futility', *niewiedza* 'ignorance'}
A2: {*smutek* 'sadness', <u>*złość* 'anger'</u>, *wstręt* 'disgust'}; {*nieużyteczność* 'futility', *niewiedza* 'ignorance'}

The evaluation of the sentiment polarity in **step 3** was based on several tests applied in parallel:

- a congruence test,
- a discord test,
- a test of collocations,
- a test of dictionary definitions.

The ongruence test requires all occurrences of the given LU x (not a lemma/word) in the usage examples to have the same sentiment polarity as that considered for x. The co-occurring adjectives, nouns and verbs do not change the polarity value, but support the polarity value considered for the given LU. For example:

- ***Przyjaźń*** *to lojalność, wierność i bezgraniczne oddanie.* 'Friendship is loyalty, faithfulness and all-embracing devotion.'
  This supports the positive sentiment polarity for *przyjaźń* 1 'friendship'.
- *I że dolega mu jakiś* ***niepokój****, gorycz lub zgoła rozczarowanie.* 'And that he feels some restlessness, bitterness or even disappointment.'
  This supports the negative polarity for *niepokój* 1 'restlessness'.

The congruence test can be also applied to LUs suspected of having ambiguous sentiment polarity. In such cases, we expect to find diverse usage examples supported by the sentiment polarity of words co-occurring with the LU under analysis.

The discord test refers to plWordNet (or a wordnet in a more general setting). It checks the presence of the proper antonymy link between the LU considered and some other LUs with clear sentiment polarity. We assume that proper antonyms have opposite sentiment polarity values, *e.g.*, the relation *skłonność* 'inclination' – *niechęć* 'aversion' [negative] suggests the positive value for *skłonność* , and *nadzieja* 'hope' [positive] – *rozczarowanie* 'disappointment' suggests the negative value for *rozczarowanie*.

In the collocation test, words included in collocations for the given LUs are examined with respect to their sentiment polarity. In the ideal case, a positive LU is associated only with the positive words, and a negative one with the negative words. Such perfect association happens rarely, but the strength of the observed tendency supplies evidence for the annotator's decision about x.

Finally, annotators search through dictionary definitions for the given LU in order to check if all components of the definition (definition parts) are clearly positive, negative or mixed. Examples:

1. *szatan* 'devil' – *z* ***podziwem*** *o człowieku bardzo* ***zdolnym****, sprytnym,* ***odważnym*** '**admiringly** about someone very **capable**, canny, **courageous**' [plWordNet gloss]. This suggests positive polarity.
2. *bubek* 'a kind of ass and upstart' – *z niechęcią o mężczyźnie* ***mało wartym****, ale mającym* ***wygórowane*** *mniemanie o sobie* 'with dislike about a man **worth little** but with an **excessively high** opinion of himself'. This suggests negative polarity.
3. *zlewka* 3 '*coll.* ≈ funny situation' – *ubaw, dużo śmiechu, śmieszna sytuacja, ale bardziej w znaczeniu wyśmiewania się z kogoś* 'hilarity, much laughter, an amusing situation, but more in the sense of mocking somone'. This suggests both positive and negative polarity. Both annotators assigned contradictory annotations: +weak and - weak. The coordinator described the LU as ambiguous, with examples for either polarity.

We have developed several heuristics for **step 4** to evaluate the strength of polarity.

1. Given the basic emotions and fundamental values assigned to an LU, we can examine how close it is to them on some intensity scale, such as strong versus weak polarity. If, *e.g., smutek* 'saddness' and *złość* 'pique' are assigned to the LU *niezadowolenie* 'dissatisfaction', then we can consider whether they fully describe the state of dissatisfaction.
2. We can compare an LU with another, similar in meaning. If that LU is evidently more marked, the given one gets weak polarity.
3. If the given LU seems to have negative polarity but it is used to characterise a child humorously, we assign it weak polarity.[9]

It must also be noted that, for the common genre of Polish, the expressiveness and strength of markedness (including polarity) decreases in time. Very often, then, new marked words replace older less marked ones. For the native speakers today, old words do not have so clear a character and do not have the full strength of polarity, In the pilot project, we try to evaluate only the contemporary state and the contemporary polarity of LUs.

Examples added in **step 5** play a double role: they illustrate the annotations and the related aspects of the LU's meaning, and they verify the earlier decisions. Concerning the first role, it is especially important for the LUs considered ambiguous with respect to sentiment polarity.

The selection or creation of an example by the annotator is also the moment of the verification of the annotation decisions made so far. The example sentence should include frequent collocations of the LU under consideration. The sentence should show that the selected sentiment polarity does not result from the annotator's individual experience, but is also supported by the observed connectivity of the LU. So, all examples which the annotators create contain collocations found in corpora or other sources.

The language material stored in the examples is very interesting from the linguistic point of view. It often shows language use in unofficial situations. Examples also include also samples of transcribed speech. Such illustrations are not frequent in dictionaries. The corpus-based material needed careful selection and finding examples to match the given LU and its meaning, as well as illustrating the polarity value.

[9]For example, *ty draniu* 'you son of a gun' directed to a child is neither offensive nor angry. Related words *łobuziak, psotnik, urwipołeć* 'scamp, prankster, rascal' in the same usage serve to point out improper, but not harmful, behaviour.

4 The Annotation Process

The project team consisted of six annotators, coordinated by a "super-annotator". We had to find a balance between the available funds and the future practical value of the resource. We decided to aim at two annotations per LU. Everyone worked half of their time as the first annotator, *i.e.,* the one who assigns basic emotions, fundamental values, sentiment polarity values and examples.[10] The second annotator processed the same LU independently but, right after having recorded the result in plWordNet, could see what the first annotator did and then perhaps adjust the decision.

If the second annotator disagreed, a report went to the coordinator. Also, if the coordinator found an annotator's error, a re-analysis was requested. Practically the only cause was a wrong interpretation of the LU's meaning description in plWordNet.[11] Annotators occasionally discovered likely errors in plWordNet's structure. In such cases, the analysis was postponed until the main plWordNet team has intervened.

We selected several areas of plWordNet for the annotation project. In the first phase, we worked only with nouns, in the second phase – also with adjectives. Proper names were omitted in both phases. To start with nouns may be uncommon: the WordNet-Affect project, *e.g.,* started from adjectives (Strapparava and Valitutti, 2004). We had a good practical reason. The adjectival part of plWordNet was undergoing major expansion, but the annotation project had to go ahead, not to mention the fact that the main team could inadvertently undo annotation decisions.

There also was a serious reason. Annotation turned out to be simpler for nouns, so we gained experience before taking upon the more difficult area: adjectives. To assign sentiment polarity and other elements of the annotation is not harder. The main difference is in the proper interpretation of the description of an LU's meaning – in the linking of sentiment polarity evaluation with particular meanings of individual nominal and adjectival LUs. The work with use examples requires permanent word sense disambiguation – see (Mohammad and Turney, 2013). The adjectival meaning is often revealed in combination with nouns, so practice with nouns was very helpful for annotators.

We record in plWordNet fine-grained lexical meanings, linguistically well motivated. Nouns are described by the hypernymy hierarchy. Adjectives have a much shallower hierarchy and a lower density of relations (per one LU). So, there is more effort in understanding the meaning of an adjectival LU. Adjective lemmas are also on average more semantically ambiguous, *e.g.,* the average polysemy rate per lemma is higher for adjectives.[12] We started on adjectives when the adjective database reorganisation was already well advanced, so we effectively "played catch-up". An added advantage was the possibility of a close cooperation with the main plWordNet team.

In the case of nouns, we selected several domains, represented by hypernymy subgraphs, as more significant for sentiment polarity:

- the hypernymy sub-hierarchies for affect, feelings and emotions – the domain 'czuj' in plWordNet;
- noun sub-hierarchies describing people, *e.g.,* those dominated by non-lexical ("artificial") LUs *a person characterised by personality – age – physical properties – financial status – qualifications – positivity – negativity*;
- features of people and animals ('cech'),
- events ('zdarz'), *e.g.,* the sub-hierarchy of the artificial LU *events rated negatively, evaluated as negative* and the sub-hierarchy of *entertainment.*

5 The End Product: plWordNet-emo

Table 1 shows the number of LUs eventually annotated in the pilot project. The numbers refer to LUs which received the same sentiment polarity and strength from two annotators or whose sentiment label was decided by the coordinator. The project has annotated over 27% of adjectival LUs, but only around 12% of noun LUs from plWordNet 2.3. 12% is not high, but the processed portion covers the domains most likely to include LUs with non-neutral sentiment polarity. The manual annotations should be of high quality, and thus facilitate automated propagation of sentiment polarity to the remaining parts of plWordNet 2.3.

As noted in section 4, the second annotator did not look at the first annotator's decision before

[10] The pairing of annotators, and their first/second status changed regularly.

[11] Wordnets describe lexical meaning in terms of networks of relations. Not all LUs in plWordNet have glosses.

[12] `plwordnet.pwr.wroc.pl/wordnet/stats`

PoS	#	-s	-w	n	+w	+s	amb
N	19,625	11.29	8.78	69.06	3.24	2.88	4.74
Adj	11,573	9.89	11.22	58.85	9.21	5.60	5.24
Both	31,198	10.77	9.69	65.27	5.46	3.89	4.92

Table 1: Experimental sentiment annotation of plWordNet 2.3 in numbers; -s, -w, n, +w, +s, amb (negative strong/weak, neutral, positive weak/strong, ambiguous) are shown in percentage points.

PoS	#	-s	-w	n	+w	+s	amb
N	19,625	0.961	0.915	0.976	0.864	0.930	0.868
Adj	11,573	0.958	0.935	0.960	0.919	0.976	0.935

Table 2: Inter-annotator agreement, measured in Fleiss' κ, for different types of sentiment polarity: -s, -w, n, +w, +s, amb (negative strong/weak, neutral, positive weak/strong, ambiguous).

having made her own. Only in the case of evident errors did the coordinator ask the annotators to analyse the meaning of the given LU and to rethink the decision. We store all final decisions of the two annotators for every LU, so it is natural to measure inter-annotator agreement.

For nouns, the value of Fleiss' κ (Fleiss, 1971) – calculated for the two annotators and all decisions – is 0.943: very high agreement, even if we allow that the second annotator could sometimes change the decision after seeing the work of the first annotator. A very similar Fleiss' κ value of 0.95 was calculated for all annotators' decisions on adjectives. A detailed picture of inter-annotator agreement for all types of polarity appears in Table 2.[13]

A little surprisingly, the agreement for adjectives is higher than for nouns, and it is relatively equal across different types of polarity. A possible explanation: it is harder to read the meaning of adjectival LUs from plWordNet, and the annotators were more careful in reading the wordnet structures exactly.

6 Conclusions

The resource we have constructed is a first, important step towards sentiment annotation of the whole plWordNet. That is because the achieved size is very high in comparison to other manual annotation projects. We plan to expand the annotation to other LUs by means of algorithms based on sentiment polarity propagation along the wordnet graph.

The development of plWordNet has been independent of PWN, and the amount of sentiment annotation in our pilot project exceeds that in SentiWordNet and WordNet-Affect. It might therefore be interesting to compare our annotation with the automatic annotation in those wordnets, using the manual mapping of plWordNet onto PWN (Rudnicka et al., 2012).

Acknowledgments

Work financed by the Polish Ministry of Science and Higher Education, a program in support of scientific units involved in the development of a European research infrastructure for the humanities and social sciences in the scope of the consortia CLARIN ERIC and ESS-ERIC, 2015-2016.

Heartfelt thanks to our annotators: Ada Zajączkowska, Anna Nizińska, Kamil Wabnic, Monika Górka, Amelia Kiełbawska and Joanna Wieczorek.

[13]The κ values would have probably decreased a little if we calculated them for the second annotator's initial answer, before "reconciliation" with the first annotator's verdict. There are low-level technical reasons why we did not record that initial answer: the interface had been designed to streamline the annotators' task, and we decided to leave out clerical steps deemed *a priori* to be inessential.

References

Stefano Baccianella, Andrea Esuli, and Fabrizio Sebastiani. 2010. Sentiwordnet 3.0: An enhanced lexical resource for sentiment analysis and opinion mining. In *Proceedings of the 7th Conference on Language Resources and Evaluation (LREC 2010), Valletta, MT,*, pages 2200–2204. ELRA.

Lisa Feldman Barrett. 2006. Valence is a basic building block of emotional life. *Journal of Research in Personality*, 40:35–55.

Iwona Burkacka. 2003. Aspekt stylistyczny opisu gniazdowego [The stylistic aspect of nests description]. In Mirosław Skarżyński, editor, *Słowotwórstwo gniazdowe. Historia, metoda, zastosowania [Nests derivation. History, method, applications]*, pages 114–136. Księgarnia Akademicka, Kraków.

Jorge Carrillo de Albornoz, Laura Plaza, and Pablo Gervás. 2012. SentiSense: An easily scalable concept-based affective lexicon for sentiment analysis. In *Proceedings of the Eighth International Conference on Language Resources and Evaluation (LREC-2012)*. `http://www.lrec-conf.org/proceedings/lrec2012/pdf/236_Paper.pdf`.

Yanqing Chen and Steven Skiena. 2014. Building sentiment lexicons for all major languages. In *Proceedings of the 52nd Annual Meeting of the Association for Computational Linguistics (Short Papers)*, pages 383–389, Baltimore, Maryland, USA, June 23-25 2014. ACL.

Amitava Das and Sivaji Bandyopadhyay. 2010. SentiWordNet for Indian Languages. In *Proceedings of the Eighth Workshop on Asian Language Resources*, pages 56–63.

Paul Ekman. 1992. An argument for basic emotions. *Cognition & Emotion*, 6(3):169–200.

Andrea Esuli and Fabrizio Sebastiani. 2006. SentiWordNet: A Publicly Available Lexical Resource for Opinion Mining. In *Proceedings of 5th Conference on Language Resources and Evaluation LREC 2006*, pages 417–422.

Joseph L. Fleiss. 1971. Measuring nominal scale agreement among many raters. *Psychological Bulletin*, 75(5):378–382.

Norbert Fries. 1992. Wartościowanie. Aspekty językowe i pojęciowe [Valuation. Linguistic and conceptual aspects]. In Gabriel Falkenberg, Norbert Fries, and Jadwiga Puzynina, editors, *Sprachliche Bewertung (polnisch und deutsch) [Valuation in language and text (on Polish and German material)]*, pages 25–44. University of Warsaw Press, Warszawa.

Stanisław Grabias. 1981. *O ekspresywności języka: ekspresja a słowotwórstwo [On the expressiveness of language: expression versus word formation]*. Wydawnictwo Lubelskie, Lublin.

Iwona Kaproń-Charzyńska. 2014. *Pragmatyczne aspekty słowotwórstwa. Funkcja ekspresywna i poetycka [The pragmatic aspects of word formation. The expressive and poetic function]*. Mikołaj Kopernik University Press, Toruń.

Moshe Koppel and Jonathan Schler. 2006. The Importance of Neutral Examples in Learning Sentiment. *Computational Intelligence*, 22(2):100–109.

Przemysław Maciołek and Grzegorz Dobrowolski. 2013. CLUO: Web-Scale Text Mining System for Open Source Intelligence Purposes. *Computer Science*, 14(1):45–62.

Andrzej Markowski. 1992. *Leksyka wspólna różnym odmianom polszczyzny, vol. 1-2 [Lexicon common to variations of the Polish language]*. Wydawnictwo "Wiedza o Kulturze", Wrocław.

Marek Maziarz, Maciej Piasecki, and Stanisław Szpakowicz. 2013. The chicken-and-egg problem in wordnet design: synonymy, synsets and constitutive relations. *Language Resources and Evaluation*, 47(3):769–796.

Agnieszka Mikołajczuk. 2000. Problem ocen w analizie wybranych polskich nazw uczuć z klasy semantycznej GNIEWU [The problem of evaluation in the analysis of selected Polish emotion names from the class ANGER]. *Język a Kultura [Language and Culture]*, 14:117–134.

Saif M. Mohammad and Peter D. Turney. 2013. Crowdsourcing a Word-Emotion Association Lexicon. *Computational Intelligence*, 29(3):436–465.

Agnieszka Mykowiecka and Małgorzata Marciniak. 2012. Combining Wordnet and Morphosyntactic Information in Terminology Clustering. In *Proceedings of COLING 2012: Technical Papers*, pages 1951–1962.

Maciej Piasecki, Stanisław Szpakowicz, and Bartosz Broda. 2009. *A Wordnet from the Ground Up*. Wrocław University of Technology Press.

Robert Plutchik. 1980. *EMOTION: A Psychoevolutionary Synthesis*. Harper & Row.

Robert Plutchik. 2001. The Nature of Emotions. *American Scientist*, 89(4):344.

Soujanya Poria, Alexander Gelbukh, Erik Cambria, Peipei Yang, Amir Hussain, and Tariq Durrani. 2012. Merging SenticNet and WordNet-Affect emotion lists for sentiment analysis. In *IEEE 11th International Conference on Signal Processing (ICSP), 2012*, volume 2, pages 1251–1255, Beijing.

Jadwiga Puzynina. 1992. *Język wartości [The language of values]*. Scientific Publishers PWN.

Artur Rejter. 2006. *Leksyka ekspresywna w historii języka polskiego. Kulturowo-komunikacyjne konteksty potoczności [Expressive lexicon in the history of*

Polish language. Cultural and communicative contexts of colloquialism]. University of Silesia Press, Katowice.

Ewa Rudnicka, Marek Maziarz, Maciej Piasecki, and Stan Szpakowicz. 2012. A strategy of mapping Polish WordNet onto Princeton WordNet. In *Proceedings of the 24th International Conference on Computational Linguistics COLING*, pages 1039–1048.

Andrzej Siemiński. 2012. Fast algorithm for assessing semantic similarity of texts. *International Journal of Intelligent Information and Database Systems*, 6(5):495–512.

Carlo Strapparava and Alessandro Valitutti. 2004. WordNet-Affect: An affective extension of WordNet. In *Proceedings of the 4th International Conference on Language Resources and Evaluation*, pages 1083–1086.

Yoshimitsu Torii, Dipankar Das, Sivaji Bandyopadhyay, and Manabu Okumura. 2011. A Developing Japanese WordNet Affect for Analyzing Emotions. In *Proceedings of the 2nd Workshop on Computational Approaches to Subjectivity and Sentiment Analysis (WASSA 2011), 49th Annual Meeting of the Association for Computational Linguistics: Human Language Technologies (ACL-HLT 2011)*, pages 80–86.

Peter D. Turney and Michael L. Littman. 2003. Measuring Praise and Criticism: Inference of Semantic Orientation from Association. *ACM Transactions on Information Systems*, 21(4):315–346.

Aleksander Wawer and Konrad Gołuchowski. 2012. Expanding Opinion Attribute Lexicons. In *Proceedings of Text, Speech and Dialogue, TSD 2012*, volume 7499 of *Lecture Notes in Computer Science*, pages 72–80. Springer.

Anna Wróblewska, Grzegorz Protaziuk, Robert Bembenik, and Teresa Podsiadły-Marczykowska. 2013. Associations between Texts and Ontology. In *Intelligent Tools for Building a Scientific Information Platform*, volume 467 of *Studies in Computational Intelligence*, pages 305–321. Springer.

Jun Xu, Ruifeng Xu, Yanzhen Zheng, Qin Lu, Kam-Fai Wong, and Xiaolong Wang. 2013. Chinese Emotion Lexicon Developing via Multi-lingual Lexical Resources Integration. In *Proceedings of 14th International Conference on Intelligent Text Processing and Computational Linguistics CICLing 2013*, pages 174–182.

Monika Zaśko-Zielińska and Maciej Piasecki. 2015. Lexical Means in Communicating Emotion in Suicide Notes – On the Basis of the Polish Corpus of Suicide Notes. *Cognitive Studies | Études Cognitives, to appear.*

Named Entity Recognition of Persons' Names in Arabic Tweets

Omnia H. Zayed
Center of Informatics Science
Nile University
Giza, Egypt
omnia.zayed@gmail.com

Samhaa R. El-Beltagy
Center of Informatics Science
Nile University
Giza, Egypt
samhaa@computer.org

Abstract

The rise in Arabic usage within various social media platforms, and notably in Twitter, has led to a growing interest in building Arabic Natural Language Processing (NLP) applications capable of dealing with informal colloquial Arabic, as it is the most commonly used form of Arabic in social media. The unique characteristics of the Arabic language make the extraction of Arabic named entities a challenging task, to which, the nature of tweets adds new dimensions. The majority of previous research done on Arabic NER focused on extracting entities from the formal language, namely Modern Standard Arabic (MSA). However, the unstructured nature of the colloquial language used in tweets degrades the performance of NER systems developed to support formal MSA text. In this paper, we focus on the task of Arabic persons' names recognition. Specifically, we introduce an approach to extract Arabic persons' names from tweets without employing any morphological analysis or language-dependent features. The proposed approach adopts a rule-based model combined with a statistical one. This approach uses unsupervised learning of patterns and clustered dictionaries as constrains to identify a person's name and resolve its ambiguity. Our approach outperforms the best reported result in the literature on the same test set by an increase of 19.6% in the F-score.

1 Introduction

Named Entity Recognition (NER) is the task of identifying certain types of named expressions in unstructured text and classifying them into a predefined set of categories. These expressions can be personal and geographic named expressions, as well as temporal and numeric ones. NER is a crucial constituent of many Natural Language Processing (NLP) applications (Jurafsky and Martin, 2009). Examples of these applications include Machine Translation, Text Summarization, Opinion Mining, and Semantic Web Searching (Benajiba et al., 2009).

The advent of Twitter has offered people a significant new way of communication that enables them to share their ideas, thoughts, and real-time news, an example of which was the D.C. earthquake[1], which was reported on Twitter as it was unfolding. In addition, Twitter can be used by government services to reach large audiences in real time in order to send awareness messages to citizens. The sheer amount of regularly generated tweets and their ubiquitous nature are among the factors that have encouraged researchers in many fields to analyse such content automatically for event detection and opinion mining. The informal nature of messages exchanged within this platform poses new challenges for NLP applications, as their content tends to be short, noisy and to deviate from known grammatical rules (Zayed and El-Beltagy, 2015).

When it comes to automatic text analysis, the Arabic language is challenging not only due to its inflective nature but also due to its complex linguistic structure, its rich morphology, (Farghaly and Shaalan, 2009) as well as its inherent ambiguity. Ambiguity is in fact, one of the major challenges in detecting Arabic persons' names (Zayed and El-Beltagy, 2015).

Research in the area of Arabic NER is still in its early phases compared to that of English NER (Shaalan, 2014), with the focus of most of the research being done in this area being on MSA. The language being used on most social media platforms however is colloquial Arabic introducing a new set of complications with the multitude of dialects being employed. With the rapid increase in online social media usage by Arabic speakers, it is important to build Arabic NER

[1] http://socialmediasun.com/impact-of-social-media-on-society/

Proceedings of Recent Advances in Natural Language Processing, pages 731–738,
Hissar, Bulgaria, Sep 7–9 2015.

systems capable of dealing with both colloquial Arabic and MSA text.

The aim of this work is to extract Arabic persons' names, the most challenging Arabic named entity as discussed in Section 2, from tweets. Previous approaches that have tackled the problem of Arabic NER relied heavily on complex linguistic processing in terms of parsing and morphological analysis to solve the ambiguity problem. While these approaches are applicable to MSA text, they cannot handle colloquial Arabic with an acceptable precision. The unstructured nature of the colloquial language used in tweets degrades the performance of NER systems that are trained on the formal language style used in news contexts for example. This fact was proved by experimental results as presented in (Darwish, 2013) on Arabic tweets and in (Ritter et al., 2011) on English ones.

Our proposed approach adopts a rule-based model combined with a statistical model. The statistical model is based on association rules and is built by employing unsupervised learning of context patterns that indicate the presence of a person's name. This approach makes use of a limited set of dictionaries augmented with a name-clustering module, coupled with a set of rules to identify a person's name and resolve its ambiguity.

The main contributions of this work can be summarized as follows:

1. Introduces a "text style" independent approach to recognise persons' names that can be easily ported to other languages, text styles/genres and domains.

2. Overcomes the ambiguity problem of persons' names without using language-dependent resources such as parsers, taggers and/or morphological analysers. The only resource required by the system is a list of persons' names which can be easily obtained from publicly available resources such as Wikipedia[2].

The rest of the paper is organised as follows: Section 2 highlights some of the unique characteristics of the Arabic language with respect to the task of persons' names extraction. Section 3 reviews previous work done on Arabic NER with focus on Arabic NER from social media contexts. The proposed approach is discussed in Section 4. In Section 5, the conducted experiments to evaluate the system's performance are described. Finally, the conclusion and future work are presented in Section 6.

2 The Effect of Arabic Specific Challenges on NER

Arabic is a widely used language spoken by over 300 million people, and one of the official languages used at the United Nations (UN). The very special characteristics of the Arabic language step up the challenges faced by researchers when developing an Arabic NLP application (Farghaly and Shaalan, 2009). Among the challenging characteristics are a rich morphology, complex orthography, and the different levels of ambiguity. Additionally, tweets are usually written in colloquial Arabic, with dialects from all over the Arab World being represented, which complicates the problem of Arabic NER (Zayed and El-Beltagy, 2015). This problem is more formally referred to as diglossia. Many researchers, (Shaalan, 2014; Farghaly and Shaalan, 2009; Zayed et al., 2013; Zayed and El-Beltagy, 2015), examined the unique characteristics of Arabic extensively. The coming sub-sections will highlight these characteristics briefly and explain their effects on the extraction of persons' names, which is the focus of this paper.

2.1 Diglossia

One of the major linguistic features that characterise the Arabic language is its diglossia, which refers to the existence of two forms of the language: formal and informal. The formal language, namely Modern Standard Arabic (MSA), is used for most written and formal spoken purposes but is not used for daily communication, whereas the informal language, namely colloquial Arabic, is used for daily communication and may differ geographically (Farghaly and Shaalan, 2009). Colloquial Arabic is comprised of multiple spoken Arabic dialects used for daily communication in different Arab countries. It varies regionally from one Arabic speaking country to another. Colloquial Arabic is very commonly used within all social media platforms. There are significant differences between Arabic dialects regarding various linguistic features. These differences also exist between these dialects and MSA (Habash, 2010). As mentioned earlier, colloquial Arabic adds challenges to NER due to its unstructured and informal nature.

The usage of colloquial Arabic as a written language on social media platforms adds extra

[2] https://www.wikipedia.org/

complexity to an already difficult problem, as discussed in sub-section 2.4.

2.2 Complex Orthography

Arabic has no capital letters which is a distinctive feature when it comes to NER. Besides, it has no letters dedicated for short vowels. Special marks placed above or below the letters, namely diacritics, are used to compensate for the absence of short vowels. However, these diacritics are rarely used in contemporary writings; yet, it is possible for a native speaker to infer the missing diacritics (Farghaly and Shaalan, 2009).

The absence of diacritics causes structural and lexical ambiguity in which a word may belong to more than one part of speech with different meanings. For example, the word "يحيي" without diacritics can imply the male name "Yahya", or the verb (greets) or the verb (gives life back) (Farghaly and Shaalan, 2009; Zayed and El-Beltagy, 2015; Zayed et al., 2013).

2.3 Rich Morphology

The Arabic Language has an agglutinative and inflective nature in which suffixes, infixes, and prefixes can be attached to the root of a word.

This aspect creates semantic ambiguity in which one word could imply different meanings. A lot of examples can be found frequently in tweets such as, the word "مني" which may imply the colloquial phrase (from me), or the female name "Mona". This problem will be complicated by adding a conjunction such as (and) at the beginning of the word to have a new word "ومني" which may imply (and from me) or (and Mona). The attachment of clitics such as conjunctions, particles and invocation letters to any given word only serves to complicate the task of extracting Arabic persons' names. This problem is not confined to the example above, but extends to cases where invocation particles attach directly (without a white space separation) to Arabic named entities due to the limited number of characters allowed in twitter messages. For example, the invocation particle "يا" (O) can be found frequently in tweets attached directly to a name such as in "يامني" (O Mona) (Zayed et al., 2013; Zayed and El-Beltagy, 2015).

2.4 Ambiguity

The different levels of ambiguity in Arabic text is among the major challenges in detecting Arabic persons' names (Zayed et al., 2013; Shaalan, 2014; Farghaly and Shaalan, 2009; Zayed and El-Beltagy, 2015). Many persons' names are either derived from adjectives or can be confused with other nouns sharing the same surface form. Moreover, some Arabic persons' names match with verbs or prepositions. In addition, some foreign persons' names transliterated to Arabic may be confused with prepositions or pronouns. Examples of some ambiguous names are [Ahlam, Al-Asad, Tourk, Ann, Lee] which may confused with [dreams, the lion, he left, that, me/mine]. Some colloquial words may match with foreign persons' names such as [Wayen/Wein, Mo, and Abby] which are polysemies of [Where, Not, and I want] in the Algerian/Tunisian, Saudi and Kuwaiti dialects, respectively. A variety of other examples can be found in (Zayed et al., 2013; Zayed and El-Beltagy, 2015).

Because of these factors, Arabic persons' names are the most challenging Arabic named entities to be extracted without any morphological processing. Ignoring name ambiguity and employing a rule-based system that depends on straightforward matching using dictionaries, will result in an NER system that performs poorly (Shihadeh and Neumann, 2012; Darwish, 2013). On the other hand, the nature of colloquial Arabic will not allow the application of parsers and morphological analysers (the traditional solution for these challenges), as these tools have yet to perform at an acceptable level of accuracy on colloquial text (Zayed and El-Beltagy, 2015; Zayed et al., 2013). In this paper, the ambiguity of Arabic persons' names is resolved by using scored patterns, learned in an unsupervised manner, and clustered dictionaries, as will be explained in detail in section 4.

3 Related Work

Shaalan (2014) surveyed the work done on Arabic NER. The majority of the previous work pertained to the formal MSA language style used in the news domain. A list of numerous works are reviewed extensively in this survey.

In this section, we will focus on the work done to extract Arabic named entities from social media contexts.

An attempt to extract Arabic named entities from tweets is introduced in (Darwish and Gao, 2014). In this work, a Conditional Random Field (CRF) classifier was utilized to extract persons', locations', and organizations' names depending on "language-independent" features. The authors used a set of tweets that was collected and annotated in previous work by the authors, (Darwish,

2013), as a test set. The overall system achieved an F-score, on this test set, of 65.2%.

Prior to this work, Darwish (2013) applied a system which was trained on news to extract named entities from Arabic tweets. The system utilized cross-lingual features and knowledge bases (KBs) from English using cross-lingual links to train a CRF classifier. The system obtained an overall F-score of 39.9% on the tweets set used to test it. As mentioned previously, this same test set was used for the evaluation of the system presented in (Darwish and Gao, 2014).

A recent attempt to extract Arabic persons' names from tweets is presented in (Zayed and El-Beltagy, 2015). In this work, the authors present a hybrid approach that exploits context bigrams to train a Naïve Bayes classifier, which in turn, is plugged into a rule based model. The system performance was tested on a set of tweets used in Darwish (2013) and (Darwish and Gao, 2014). The F-score of this system on this set was: 59.59%. This same set of tweets was used to evaluate the proposed approach and the result is presented in Section 5.

A system introduced in (Zirikly and Diab, 2014) utilized morphological analysis and gazetteers among other lexical and contextual features to train a CRF classifier in order to extract persons' and locations' names from micro-blogs. The system was tested on a manually annotated portion of an Egyptian dialect corpus collected and provided by the LDC[3] from web blogs. The system obtained an F-score of 49.18% for the task of persons' names recognition. A performance comparison between our system and this system is not possible as the dataset used for evaluation the former, is not publically available.

In (Zayed et al., 2013), a similar system to the one discussed in this paper is presented. However, the presented system was applied to formal MSA text. In this paper, we extend the work carried out in (Zayed et al., 2013) to extract persons' names from Arabic tweets.

4 Overview of the Proposed Approach

In this work, we introduce a novel approach to extract persons' names and resolve their ambiguity from Arabic tweets. In this approach, a rule-based model combined with a statistical model, is adopted. The approach is suitable for both MSA, as proved previously in (Zayed et al., 2013), and colloquial Arabic as illustrated in this paper. Our approach tries to overcome two of the major shortcomings of using rule-based techniques which are the difficulty of modifying a rule-based approach for new domains and the necessity of using huge sets of gazetteers. The approach depends on unsupervised learning of patterns and clustered dictionaries as constrains to identify a person's name and resolve its ambiguity. Moreover, the approach does not require complex linguistic pre-processing or language-dependent features.

4.1 General Architecture

The presented approach makes use of unsupervised learning of patterns and clustered dictionaries as combinatory constraints plugged into a rule-based model to extract persons' names and resolve their ambiguity.

This idea was initially introduced by Zayed et al. (2013). The authors' experiments, in the context of formal MSA used in news articles, proved that this approach can be used to overcome the ambiguity problem of Arabic persons' names without using morphological analysis. In this paper, we apply the same methodology to extract persons' names and resolve their ambiguity from Arabic tweets.

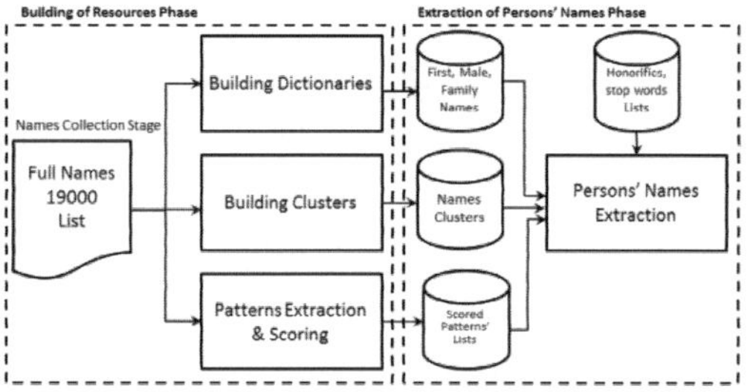

Figure 1: System's General Architecture

The approach is composed of two phases, as shown in Figure 1. In the first phase, "The building of resources phase", persons' names are clustered, in addition, 'name' indicating patterns are extracted. In the second phase, "Extraction of persons' names phase", name patterns and clusters are used to extract persons' names from input text. Both of these phases are described in depth, in the following sub-sections.

4.2 The Building of Resources Phase

This phase utilizes a list of persons' full names gathered from publicly available resources. This collected list is processed to build dictionaries of first, middle and family persons' names as well as to create clusters of persons' names. Middle names are further used to build a list of male

[3] Linguistic Data Consortium (LDC2012T09: GALE Arabic-Dialect/English Parallel Text)

names. Finally, the list is used to build a statistical model of name indicating patterns. This process was previously introduced in (Zayed et al., 2013). We revisit this process in brief in the following sub-sections.

4.2.1 Names Gathering and Building of Dictionaries

The system depends on persons' names dictionaries that were collected by Zayed et al. (2013) and which are available online[4]. The authors employed both Wikipedia's people category[5] and Kooora[6] Arabic sports website to collect a list of nearly 19K full persons' names ("full_names_19000_list"). This list, was then processed and refined to build lists of first, male/middle and family persons' names automatically. These lists were necessary, since the aim of this work is not just to recognize names of famous people, but instead to identify the name of any person even if it does not appear in the collected lists. The technique followed in gathering the names and building these lists is described in (Zayed et al., 2013).

4.2.2 Building of Names' Clusters

The inherent ambiguity of the Arabic language degrades the performance of a system based on straightforward matching using dictionaries to extract previously unseen person's name as shown by experimentation on news articles (Shihadeh and Neumann, 2012) and on tweets (Darwish, 2013).

One of the common problems when extracting names, is the possibility of incorrectly extracting a name that is a combination of an Arabic name and a foreign name. For example, given the tweet "عوده تشافي وراكتيش في الوسط..." (the return of Xavi and Rakitić in the middle...), using a simple matching approach would result in the extraction of the full name "عوده تشافي" "Ouda Xavi", which is wrong. The problem could be encountered in various contexts, which all have a common factor: one part of the name is Arabic and the other part of the name matches with a transliteration of a foreign name. To overcome the incorrect extraction of entities like this, the observation that it is highly unlikely that an Arabic person's name will appear beside a foreign person's name can be utilized. However, name lists do not contain information regarding the origin of a name.

A workaround this lack of information was presented in (Zayed et al., 2013) in the form of name clusters. In this solution, name clusters were constructed by considering each single name a node. Since a full name, is made up of multiple names, names in a full name, are connected via links. Names are then clustered into communities using a graph clustering criterion (Blondel et al., 2008). As illustrated in Figure 2, culturally similar names are grouped together.

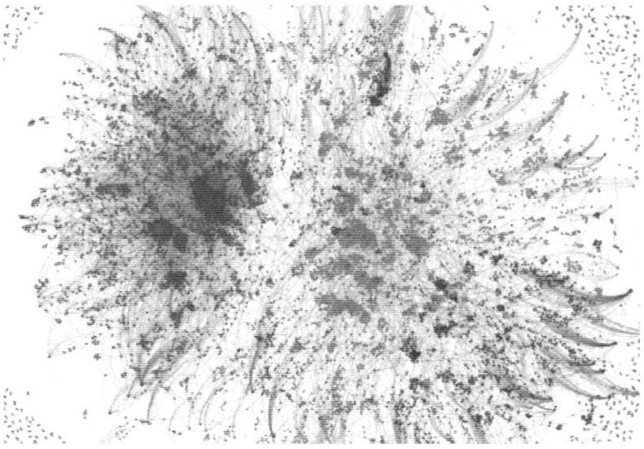

Figure 2: visualization of graph clustering of 19K persons' names

To overcome the above mentioned problem, only names in the same cluster can be combined together to form a name.

4.2.3 Extracting Scored Patterns

The goal of this phase is to build lists of patterns indicating the occurrence of a person's name in an unsupervised way. These patterns are scored using the support score to build a statistical model. After that, the statistical model is integrated with a set of rules, dictionaries and clusters to extract Arabic persons' names and resolve their ambiguity. This procedure is divided into 4 steps, as shown in Figure 3.

The initial two steps are carried out to create and pre-process the dataset used for learning the scored patterns. Since our target is to identify persons' names from Arabic tweets, we had to create our own dataset of tweets. To our knowledge, no similar dataset is currently available for NER research.

[4] http://bit.ly/NileAPgazet

[5] http://ar.wikipedia.org/wiki/تراجم:تصنيف

[6] http://www.kooora.com/default.aspx?showplayers=true

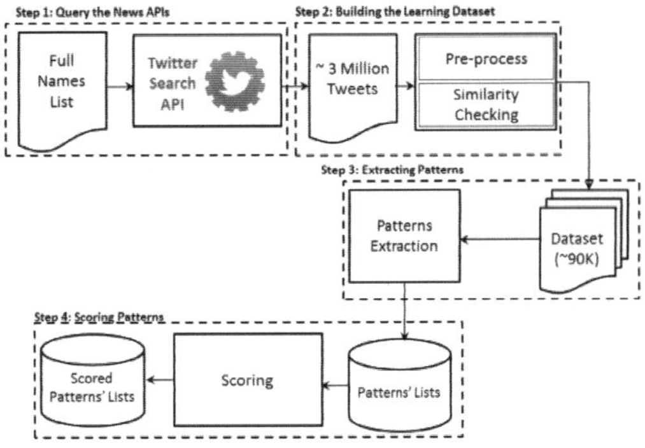

Figure 3: Building lists of patterns with score form Twitter context

The Twitter Search API was utilized to download Arabic tweets by using a random set of name selected from the aforementioned list of persons' names, as query terms. Since we are interested in getting tweets written in Egyptian Colloquial the queries were restricted to using the geo-code parameter "*30.0500, 31.2333, 500km*". This geo-code specifies the location of the retrieved tweets to be Cairo with a radius of 500km. Using this geo-code allows us to get the majority of tweets from Egypt and a small amount from Saudi Arabia, Jordan and Palestine. The language parameter was also set to Arabic ("lang: ar").

After tweets retrieval, using the Twitter Search API as mention earlier, normalization and preprocessing steps are carried out to omit unwanted features such as diacritics, hyperlinks and English words. It was also necessary to eliminate redundant tweets, due to re-tweets. To carry out this step, a similarity check was performed by employing the cosine similarity technique (Singhal, 2001) with a threshold value of 0.72. The final dataset consisted of around 100 thousand unique tweets.

Following these steps, unigram patterns around each name are extracted to form three lists of patterns. A list to keep unigram patterns before a name, and another one to keep unigram patterns after a name. Finally, a complete pattern list is created to keep set of complete patterns around the name. An example of a tweet that appears in the learning dataset is " لما استاذ ابراهيم عبد المجيد بيعملي فيفوريت" (when Mr. Ibrahim Abd El-Meguid is tagging me). The unigram patterns around the person's name "ابراهيم عبد المجيد" "Ibrahim Abd El-Meguid" are extracted as follows: the word "لما" (when) is added in the "before" list, the word "بيعملي" (is tagging) is added in the "after" list, and finally the set <when><name><is tagging> is added in the "complete pattern" list.

The final step is to score these patterns according to their significance in indicating the occurrence of a person's name. Therefore, each pattern in the three lists is scored using association rules support measure (Agrawal et al., 1993). Support is calculated as the ratio of the count of a pattern followed by a name over the total count of all patterns followed by a name. The three newly created lists of scored patterns are saved descendingly according to the value of the score.

4.3 Extraction of Persons' Names Phase

In this phase, the name extractor is created and used. The name extractor is composed of the scored patterns which are combined with rules to extract persons' names from tweets and resolve their ambiguity. Clustered dictionaries are used within the rules to ensure that all candidate portions of a name fall in the same cluster. Thus, the aforementioned problems of straight forward matching of names using dictionaries are avoided.

The baseline rule assumes that any full name consists of a first name followed by one or more male names followed by zero or one family name. Unigram patterns, honorifics, punctuations and titles that appear before and after a person's name are used to detect the name boundaries.

Examples of one of the employed rules include:

وفاه الطفل ماجد مدحت **برصاص...**
The death of the child Maged Medhat, who was shot by...

The use of scored patterns is crucial to avoid straight forward matching mistakes such as the extraction of "يمن سعيد" (Youmn Saied) which means here (Happy Yemen) in the phrase below.

باذن الله ترجع يمن سعيد
God willing, happy Yemen will return

Additionally, the use of clusters as a combinatory constraint eliminates false positives such as the extraction of "بشر بان" (Beshr Ban) which means here (bode that), as the Arabic name (Beshr) which means here (bode) and the transliterated foreign name (Ban) which means here (that) are not in the same cluster.

او بشر بان المسلمين...
Or bode that Muslims...

5 System Evaluation

System		Precision	Recall	F-score
Cross-Lingual Resources approach trained on news presented in (Darwish, 2013)		40.5%	39.2%	39.8%
Supervised ML approach presented in (Darwish and Gao, 2014)		67.1%	47.8%	55.8%
E1: (mistakes + English Entities)	Hybrid (Zayed and El-Beltagy, 2015)	67.20%	53.53%	59.59%
	Our Proposed Approach	***81.93%***	***56.32%***	***66.75%***
E2: (**no** mistakes + English Entities)	Hybrid (Zayed and El-Beltagy, 2015)	71.24%	57.24%	63.47%
	Our Proposed Approach	**85.36%**	**59.31%**	**69.99%**
E3: (mistakes + **no** English Entities)	Hybrid (Zayed and El-Beltagy, 2015)	66.49%	58.74%	62.38%
	Our Proposed Approach	**81.99%**	**61.54%**	**70.31%**
E4: (**no** mistakes + **no** English Entities)	Hybrid (Zayed and El-Beltagy, 2015)	69.92%	64.15%	66.91%
	Our Proposed Approach	**85.40%**	**65.17%**	**73.92%**

Table 1: Evaluation results of our approach in comparison to other systems' for illustration

5.1 Evaluation setups

Evaluating the performance of the proposed approach was done using CoNLL's standard evaluation script[7]. CoNLL's evaluation methods are aggressive methods, which means that no partial credit will be assigned for a partially extracted named entity (Shaalan, 2014). The results are given in terms of the standard measures for NER evaluation (De Sitter et al., 2004) which are precision, recall and F-score for each NER class; in our case, there is only a single class, which is "persons' names".

Evaluation was conducted on a test dataset of 1,423 tweets with nearly 26k tokens, used by the authors of (Darwish and Gao, 2014; Darwish, 2013). Arabic and English named entities are both tagged in this test set. This test set is referred to here as Darwish's test set. Details on Darwish's test set are provided in (Darwish and Gao, 2014). Statistical analysis of the test set can be found in (Zayed and El-Beltagy, 2015). It is worth noting that this dataset contains tweets written in Egyptian, Levantine, and Gulf Arabic dialects.

5.2 Experiments

The purpose of this evaluation was to determine the ability of the proposed approach to deal with colloquial Arabic text used on Twitter.

Similar to (Zayed and El-Beltagy, 2015), we carried out four different experiments to test the performance of our system. The first experiment was done using the dataset without any preprocessing or modification. The next experiment was done after fixing some annotation mistakes discovered in the dataset. Two final experiments were conducted to test the effect of removing English entities as a part of our pre-processing steps with and without the correction of the annotation mistakes. Since our system does not address the extraction of English entities, it is not entirely fair to include those when evaluating it.

The results obtained by our system are presented in Table 1. The table also compares the result of our proposed approach to the most recent hybrid approach proposed in (Zayed and El-Beltagy, 2015), in addition to the results obtained from the supervised Machine Learning (ML) systems presented in (Darwish and Gao, 2014; Darwish, 2013) which are used to extract named entities from tweets. We are not sure if (Darwish and Gao, 2014; Darwish, 2013) followed the same aggressive evaluation methodology as we and (Zayed and El-Beltagy, 2015) did.

It can be seen from the results that even without addressing annotation mistakes or the removal of English entities the presented approach achieves an increase of 12.01% in F-score over the one presented in (Zayed and El-Beltagy, 2015), and an increase of 19.6% over the work of (Darwish and Gao, 2014). Moreover, the F-score of our approach shows an increase of 67.7% over the one presented in (Darwish, 2013). Fixing the annotation mistakes improved the results by around 4.85%. Excluding the English entities improved the recall by 5.89%.

6 Conclusion and Future Work

This paper presented an approach for extracting Arabic persons' names and resolving their ambiguity. Our main intention while developing this approach is to attempt to resolve the inherent

[7] http://www.cnts.ua.ac.be/conll2000/chunking/conlleval.txt

ambiguity of Arabic persons' names without using "language-dependent" resources or depending on extensive lexical resources. The main goal is to be able to port the system to other domains, languages and text genres. This approach integrated name dictionaries and name clusters with a statistical model for extracting context unigram patterns in an unsupervised way, which are used to indicate the occurrence of persons' names. The main idea of this approach is to learn combinatory constraints via clustering of names and scored patterns. The approach exploited a list of full names, gathered from publicly available resources. Evaluation of the presented approach shows that it outperforms all recent attempts to extract Arabic named entities from tweets.

For the future, we plan to extend this approach to extract other named entities such as locations and organizations.

References

Rakesh Agrawal, Tomasz Imieliński, and Arun Swami. 1993. Mining association rules between sets of items in large databases. In Proceedings of the 1993 ACM SIGMOD international conference on Management of data, SIGMOD 1993, number May, pages 207–216, New York, USA. ACM Press.

Yassine Benajiba, Mona Diab, and Paolo Rosso. 2009. Arabic Named Entity Recognition: A Feature-Driven Study. IEEE Transactions on Audio, Speech, and Language Processing, 17(5):926–934, July.

Vincent D Blondel, Jean-Loup Guillaume, Renaud Lambiotte, and Etienne Lefebvre. 2008. Fast unfolding of communities in large networks. Journal of Statistical Mechanics: Theory and Experiment, 2008(10):P10008, October.

Kareem Darwish. 2013. Named Entity Recognition using Cross-lingual Resources: Arabic as an Example. In Proceedings of the 51st Annual Meeting of the Association for Computational Linguistics, volume 1, pages 1558–1567, Sofia, Bulgaria. Association for Computational Linguistics.

Kareem Darwish and Wei Gao. 2014. Simple Effective Microblog Named Entity Recognition: Arabic as an Example. In Proceedings of the Ninth International Conference on Language Resources and Evaluation (LREC 2014), pages 2513–2517, Reykjavik, Iceland, May. European Language Resources Association (ELRA).

A De Sitter, T Calders, and Walter Daelemans. 2004. A formal framework for evaluation of information extraction. Technical report, Antwerp.

A Farghaly and K Shaalan. 2009. Arabic natural language processing: Challenges and solutions. ACM Transactions on Asian Language Information Processing (TALIP), 8(4):1–22.

Nizar Y. Habash. 2010. Introduction to Arabic Natural Language Processing. Mogran & Claypool.

Daniel Jurafsky and James H. Martin. 2009. Information Extraction. In Speech and Language Processing: An Introduction to Natural Language Processing, Computational Linguistics, and Speech Recognition., chapter 22, pages 725–743. Prentice Hall, 2nd edition.

Alan Ritter, Sam Clark, and Oren Etzioni. 2011. Named Entity Recognition in Tweets : An Experimental Study. In Conference on Empirical Methods in Natural Language Processing, pages 1524–1534.

Khaled Shaalan. 2014. A survey of arabic named entity recognition and classification. Computational Linguistics, 40(2):469–510, June.

Carolin Shihadeh and Günter Neumann. 2012. ARNE: A tool for namend entity recognition from Arabic text. In Fourth Workshop on Computational Approaches to Arabic Script-based Languages (CAASL4), San Diego, CA, USA.

Amit Singhal. 2001. Modern Information Retrieval: A Brief Overview. Bulletin of the IEEE Computer Society Technical Committee on Data Engineering, 24(4):35–43.

Omnia Zayed, Samhaa El-Beltagy, and Osama Haggag. 2013. An approach for extracting and disambiguating arabic persons' names using clustered dictionaries and scored patterns. In Elisabeth Métais, Farid Meziane, Mohamad Saraee, Vijayan Sugumaran, and Sunil Vadera, editors, NLDB 2013, LNCS, volume 7934, pages 201–212. Springer Berlin Heidelberg.

Omnia H. Zayed and Samhaa R. El-Beltagy. 2015. A Hybrid Approach for Extracting Arabic Persons' Names and Resolving their Ambiguity from Twitter. In 20th International Conference on Application of Natural Language to Information Systems (NLDB 2015), Passau, Germany, June. Springer.

Ayah Zirikly and Mona Diab. 2014. Named Entity Recognition System for Dialectal Arabic. In Proceedings of the EMNLP 2014 Workshop on Arabic Natural Language Processing (ANLP), pages 78–86, Doha, Qatar, October. Association for Computational Linguistics.

One Tree is not Enough: Cross-lingual Accumulative Structure Transfer for Semantic Indeterminacy

Patrick Ziering
Institute for Natural Language Processing
University of Stuttgart, Germany
Patrick.Ziering
@ims.uni-stuttgart.de

Lonneke van der Plas
Institute of Linguistics
University of Malta, Malta
Lonneke.vanderPlas@um.edu.mt

Abstract

We address the task of parsing semantically indeterminate expressions, for which several correct structures exist that do not lead to differences in meaning. We present a novel non-deterministic structure transfer method that accumulates all structural information based on cross-lingual word distance derived from parallel corpora. Our system's output is a ranked list of trees. To evaluate our system, we adopted common IR metrics. We show that our system outperforms previous cross-lingual structure transfer methods significantly. In addition, we illustrate that tree accumulation can be used to combine partial evidence across languages to form a single structure, thereby making use of sparse parallel data in an optimal way.

1 Introduction

Parsing linguistic expressions (e.g., noun phrases (NPs)) is a fundamental component in many natural language processing (NLP) tasks like machine translation (MT) or information retrieval (IR) and indispensable for understanding the meaning of complex units. For example, while [*natural language*] *processing* means the (machine) processing of natural languages, *natural* [*language processing*] denotes the natural processing of (any) languages.

As previous work has shown, multilingual data can help resolving various kinds of structural ambiguity such as prepositional phrase (PP) attachment (Schwartz et al., 2003; Fossum and Knight, 2008), subject/object distinction (Schwarck et al., 2010) or coordination ellipsis (Bergsma et al., 2011). Parallel sentences have been jointly parsed supported by word alignment features (Smith and Smith, 2004; Burkett and Klein, 2008). Yarowsky and Ngai (2001) project part-of-speech (PoS) tags and basic NP structures across languages. Hwa et al., (2005) use projected tree structures for bootstrapping new non-English parsers. Unsupervised multilingual grammar induction has been performed on parallel corpora (Snyder et al., 2009) and on non-parallel data (Berg-Kirkpatrick and Klein, 2010; Iwata et al., 2010).

In addition to previous work focused on disambiguation, we show that multilingual data can be used to point to semantic indeterminacy. Syntactic structures are usually understood deterministically in that for every structure there exists conditions that can have no other structure. However, previous work in NLP shows that such a deterministic take might not always be suitable. Hindle and Rooth (1993) were the first to discuss the phenomenon of **semantic indeterminacy** in PP attachment, e.g., in the sentence *They mined the roads along the coast*, the PP *along the coast* may be attached to both the verb or the object without changing the meaning. On the NP level, Lauer (1995) observed 12.54% semantically indeterminate three-noun compounds (3NCs) in his dataset, e.g., in 'Most advanced aircraft have *precision navigation systems*', both *precision navigation* and *navigation system* can be bracketed leading to the same meaning. We found more striking evidence from parallel corpora, where the multiple translations found for a given NP reflect large differences in structure. While *tobacco advertising ban* is translated to German as *Werbeverbot für Tabakerzeugnisse* (advertising ban for tobacco products), the Danish equivalent is *forbuddet mod tobaksreklamer* (ban of tobacco advertising). Similarly, *animal welfare standards* is once translated to Dutch as *normen op het gebied van dierenwelzijn* (standards in the field of animal welfare) and to German as *Wohlfahrtsstandards für Tiere* (welfare standards for animals).

Despite the fact that previous work discussed

Proceedings of Recent Advances in Natural Language Processing, pages 739–746,
Hissar, Bulgaria, Sep 7–9 2015.

semantic indeterminacy, to the best of our knowledge, no attempt has been made to include this phenomenon in syntactic analysis. Vadas (2009) argues that in most cases the intended structure is unambiguous[1] and therefore chooses not to include semantic indeterminacy in his NP annotation of the Penn Treebank (Marcus et al., 1993). We believe that it is important to include semantic indeterminacy in NLP, e.g., an anaphora resolver needs to know the structural equivalence for finding all possible nested antecedents, e.g., both *animal welfare* and *welfare standards*.

This work aims at capturing semantic indeterminacy within a structural analysis. We exploit cross-linguality for this task because structural variation for semantic indeterminacy is visible in particular across languages. In a monolingual approach, we expect less variation, due to conventional language use. As a result, parse forests resulting from monolingual data would therefore be less rich in variation. We transfer syntactic structure from cross-lingual surface variation directly, without inducing grammars or annotating the source language. We coin the term **cross-lingual structure transfer** (CST) for this method.

Our system is inspired by Ziering and Van der Plas (2015), who exploit cross-lingual surface variation for bracketing 3NCs. There are various ways of translating English noun compounds. Germanic languages such as Swedish frequently use closed compounds (i.e., single nouns), whereas Romance languages such as French use open compounds (i.e., lexemes composed of several words). Paraphrased translations (e.g., *human rights abuse* aligned to the partially closed German *Verletzung der Menschenrechte* (abuse of human rights)) can reveal the internal structure of a compound. While Ziering and Van der Plas (2015) follow the deterministic take by producing a single tree output, we gather all structural information and produce a ranked list of plausible trees, where similarly-ranked trees indicate semantic indeterminacy.

Our contributions are as follows: we develop a non-deterministic cross-lingual structure transfer method which is suitable for dealing with semantic indeterminacy. We present two models that differ in granularity. The coarse-grained model restricts to full structures acquired from various languages. The fine-grained model also includes substructures, which makes it more robust against word alignment errors, and points to an intended structure. Inspired by IR metrics, we treat CST as a kind of structure retrieval and propose an evaluation method that measures quality and quantity of retrieved structures. In a case study, we present results on processing 3NCs and 4NCs. Finally, we illustrate how our methods can be used to combine partial evidence across languages to form a single structure, where individual languages fail. This way, we are able to exploit more data from sparse parallel corpora than previous work.

[1] As example, Vadas (2009) mentions *American President George Bush*, where the intended structure is [*American President*] *George Bush*, because Bush's nationality is not relevant but his political function.

2 Cross-lingual Structure Transfer

Linguistic expressions, such as kNCs, occurring in parallel data have been processed in previous work using cross-lingual aligned word distance:

$$\text{AWD}(c_i, c_j) = \min_{x \in AW_i, y \in AW_j} |pos(x) - pos(y)|$$

where AW_n is the set of aligned content words of a constituent c_n and $pos(\alpha)$ is the position of a word α in an aligned sentence. Inspired by Behaghel's (1909) First Law saying that elements which belong close together intellectually will also be placed close together, the AWD of constituents functions as indicator for the semantic cohesion. For example, the 3NC *human rights violations* being aligned to the Italian *le* ***violazioni*** *gravi e sistematiche dei* ***diritti umani*** indicates that *human rights* (*diritti umani*) has a stronger cohesion than *rights violations* (*violazioni ... diritti*), which points to a left-branched structure in English. Ziering and Van der Plas (2015) developed an AWD-based bracketing system applied on English kNCs in a parallel corpus. For each aligned language, they start bottom-up with one constituent per noun. They compare the AWDs between all adjacent constituents and iteratively merge the constituent pair with the smallest AWD until there is only one constituent left. If there is a tie among the possible AWDs, the system does not produce a tree structure. For the final decision, Ziering and Van der Plas (2015) use the majority vote across all aligned languages. If this number is not unique, the system is undecided. The main limitation of this system is that it provides a deterministic result both for each individual language and for the majority vote. As a consequence, the system neither allows several structures for a semantically indeterminate target nor combines partial results from several languages to a final structure. Subsequently, we will refer to Ziering and Van der Plas' (2015) **l**anguage-**i**solated **d**eterministic **s**tructure **t**ransfer as LIDST.

2.1 Full Tree Accumulation Structure Transfer

In the **f**ull tree **a**ccumulation **s**tructure **t**ransfer system (FAST), we consider all possible binary tree structures of an expression. Among those, there are demoted structures for a given language, because they combine constituents that have a stronger semantic cohesion than their subparts. For example, *air [traffic control]* is demoted for the Dutch paraphrase *controle van het luchtvaartverkeer* (control of air traffic), because *air traffic* has the strongest cohesion (as being aligned to a closed compound). For a given English expression Ψ, FAST is applied to each aligned language, as shown in Figure 1.

```
1: Trees ⇐ create all binary tree structures
2: for t in Trees do
3:    annotate all nodes N in t with AWD
4:    if ∃N[N.AWD > mother(N).AWD] then
5:       t.invalid ⇐ TRUE
6:    end if
7: end for
8: return {t ∈ Trees | not t.invalid }
```

Figure 1: FAST algorithm

We first create all possible binary trees for Ψ (line 1). The number of possible binary trees increases with the Catalan numbers (Church and Patil, 1982), e.g., 3NCs have two possible trees (i.e., left- or right-branched), 4NCs have five possible trees and kNCs have C_{k-1} possible trees, where C_n is the n-th Catalan number as given in (1).

$$C_n = \frac{(2n)!}{(n+1)! \cdot n!} \quad (1)$$

All tree nodes N_i in these trees are annotated with AWD numbers (line 3) according to (2), i.e., leaf nodes get zero AWD and other nodes are annotated with the AWD between their left and right children's constituent.

$$N_i.AWD = \begin{cases} \text{leaf}(N_i) & \mapsto 0 \\ \text{else} & \mapsto AWD(N_i.\text{L}, N_i.\text{R}) \end{cases} \quad (2)$$

In the next step, all annotated trees are validated (lines 4-6). A tree is **valid**, if its AWD annotation is monotonically decreasing when traversing the tree top down. If there is a node N whose AWD is larger than the AWD of its mother node, the tree is marked as invalid. Finally, we return the set of tree structures which are not marked as invalid (line 8).

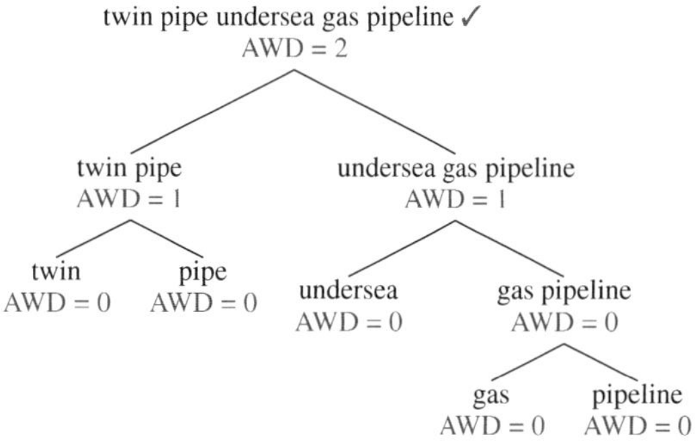

Figure 2: A valid FAST tree structure

Figure 2 shows an example of a valid AWD-annotated tree structure of the 5NC *twin pipe undersea gas pipeline* aligned to the Dutch paraphrase *onderzeese gaspijpleiding met dubbele pijp* (undersea {gas pipeline} with twin pipes).

In the final step, we put all valid trees from all languages into a tree accumulation (TA) and rank them by frequency (i.e., trees being valid in most cases are ranked first). For example, for the semantically indeterminate *air traffic control centres*, FAST assigns the same top rank to the semantically equivalent structures as shown in Table 1.

Rank	Structure	TA
1	[*air traffic*] [*control centres*]	13
1	[[*air traffic*] *control*] *centres*	13
2	[*air* [*traffic control*]] *centres*	10

Table 1: FAST top-ranking for *air traffic control centres*

In addition to a token-based setting, FAST can also be applied on expression types. In this case, we put all valid trees from all aligned languages of all instances of Ψ into the TA.

2.2 Subtree Accumulation Structure Transfer

In some cases, an invalid full tree ($✗_{ft}$) still contains an informative valid[2] subtree[3] ($✓_{st}$) as shown

[2]We use the same validity conditions as for FAST.

[3]A subtree st of a full tree ft is a tree consisting of a node in ft and all of its descendants.

in Figure 3 for the 4NC *church development aid projects* being aligned to the Italian ***progetti ecclesiastici*** *di* ***aiuti*** *allo* ***sviluppo*** (lit.: projects ecclesiastical of aid to development).

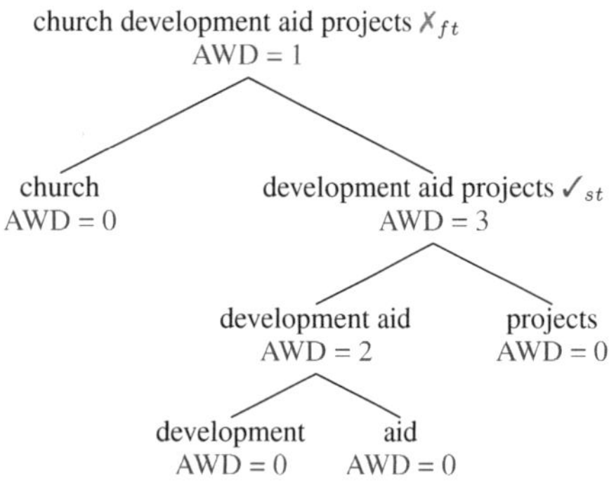

Figure 3: Invalid FAST full tree with valid subtree

The Italian translation does not provide any valid full tree, because the smallest AWD is between c_1, *church* (ecclesiastici), and c_4, *projects* (progetti). Thus, the AWD-annotation of the root node is always 1, which is smaller than any annotations below.

For exploiting as much evidence as possible from sparse parallel data, the **s**ubtree **a**ccumulation **s**tructure **t**ransfer system (SAST) takes into account all valid subtrees from both valid and invalid full trees. After gathering all valid subtrees among all full trees for an expression Ψ in all aligned languages $l \in L$, each subtree gets a subtree score (sts) according to (3), where $freq(st)$ is the number of aligned languages, $|L|$, multiplied by the Δ-th Catalan number, where Δ is the difference in the number of leaf nodes between ft and st.

$$sts(st) = \frac{freq(st.\text{valid})}{freq(st)} = \frac{freq(st.\text{valid})}{|L| \cdot C_\Delta} \quad (3)$$

A full tree gets a full tree score (fts), which is the product[4] of all its subtree scores (4).

$$fts(ft) = \prod_{st \in ft} sts(st) \quad (4)$$

In the last step, we rank all full trees according to their fts (i.e., the tree that has the highest fts is ranked first).

[4]While the product performs better in our setup, the sum would be an alternative for cases where no language provides any valid full tree (i.e., the largest subtree).

In contrast to FAST, SAST produces a more fine-grained scoring by exploiting more data. While this approach is more robust to word alignment errors, it also points to an intended structure, e.g., *air traffic control centres* gets a single top-ranked structure as shown in Table 2.

Rank	Structure	fts
1	[[*air traffic*] [*control centres*]]	1.66
2	[[[*air traffic*] *control*] *centres*]	1.35

Table 2: SAST top-ranking for *air traffic control centres*

For our initial example, Figure 4 shows two full tree structures for *church development aid projects* annotated with fts and sts information in SAST applied on a language ensemble including German, French and Italian. While FAST would give both trees the same rank (not shown), SAST exploits the higher prominence of the valid subtree in Figure 3 and thus ranks the tree in Figure 4.1 highest.

In analogy with FAST, SAST can also be applied type-based. In this case, we sum up all full tree scores from all instances of Ψ and rank the structures according to this sum.

3 Experiments

3.1 Dataset

We extracted 3NCs and 4NCs from the initial version (basic dataset) of the Europarl[5] compound database[6] (Ziering and van der Plas, 2014), compiled from the OPUS[7] corpus (Tiedemann, 2012). The database contains 10 European languages in three language families: Germanic (English, Danish, Dutch, German and Swedish), Romance (French, Italian, Portuguese and Spanish) and Hellenic (Greek). The kNCs are extracted using PoS patterns conforming a sequence of k adjacent nouns. The dataset contains 24,848 3NC tokens (16,565 types) and 1468 4NC tokens (1257 types).

3.2 Gold Standard

We use the 3NC test set[8] created by Ziering and Van der Plas (2015), which contains 278 left- or right-branched and 120 semantically indeterminate 3NC tokens. For keeping the ratio of 3NCs

[5]statmt.org/europarl

[6]ims.unistuttgart.de/data/NCDatabase.html

[7]opus.lingfil.uu.se

[8]ims.uni-stuttgart.de/data/AWDB.data.tgz

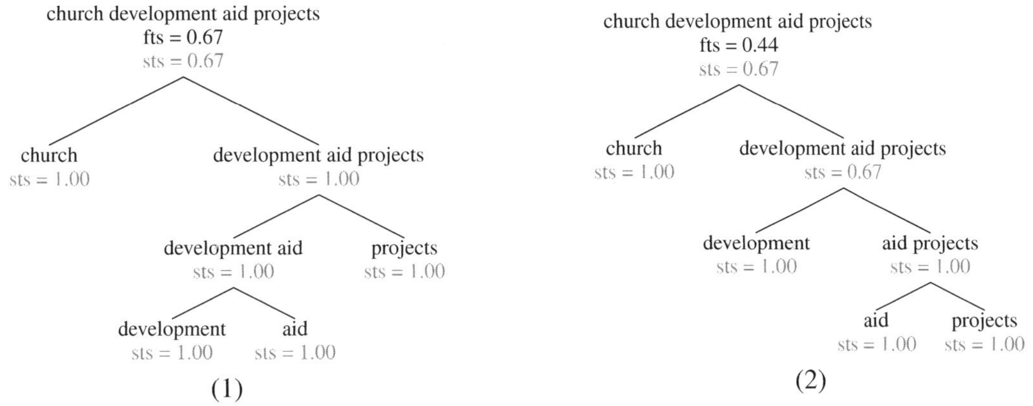

Figure 4: SAST trees for *church development aid projects* on first and second position

to 4NCs as reflected in the token numbers of our dataset, we decided on a random set of 50 4NC samples to be labeled by two trained independent annotators. We adopted the annotation guidelines described in Vadas (2009) and use the following labels for annotating 4NCs: 1, ..., 5 (referring to the five possible 4NC structures), EXTRACTION (for extraction errors, i.e., incomplete NCs or fragments of incomplete constituents as in *climate change target* ***cannot***), UNDECIDED[i; . . . ; j] (for cases in which the context cannot help to disambiguate between the distinctive structures i, . . . , j), FLAT (for expressions showing no internal structure (e.g., *John A. Smith*)) and SEMANTIC INDETERMINACY[i; . . . ; j] (for expressions with the equivalent structures i; . . . ; j). For addressing semantic indeterminacy, we take the union of single structure labels and semantic indeterminacy labels from both annotators to a test set comprising 33 4NC tokens and discard 17 tokens, which have been tagged as extraction error.

Structure pattern	Frequency									
	13	6	5	2		1				
A [B [C D]]		*					*	*	*	
A [[B C] D]				*				*	*	*
[A B] [C D]	*		*			*	*	*		
[A [B C]] D						*				*
[[A B] C] D	*				*	*				

Table 3: Frequency distribution of structures in the 4NC test set

Table 3 shows the frequency distribution of 4NC structures in the test set, where structures are represented as structure patterns[9]. Analogously to the majority class LEFT for 3NCs, the structure combination having the two left-most nouns grouped as a constituent is annotated most often.

3.3 Structure Retrieval

Our system's output is a ranked list of tree structures. Inspired by IR models, we treat CST as a kind of structure retrieval and measure how well a ranking fits to the set of gold trees. Therefore, we adapt the R-Precision score (Buckley and Voorhees, 2000) as given in (5):

$$\text{R-Prec}(k\text{NC}) = \frac{|\text{top-R}(sys\ trees) \cap gold\ trees|}{|\text{top-R}(sys\ trees)|} \quad (5)$$

where R is the number of gold trees and top-R($sys\ trees$) refers to the R highest-ranked system trees. For trees having the same rank, we choose a random order. If there are less than R system trees, the ranking is randomly complemented. Observing that this random process lead to unstable numbers, we apply it 1000 times and take the average of the resulting scores. The mean R-Precision takes the macro average of the R-Precision scores as given in (6)

$$\text{MRP} = \frac{\sum_{\Psi \in \Omega} \text{R-Prec}(\Psi)}{|\Omega|} \quad (6)$$

where Ω is the set of all expressions. In addition, we measure precision at k ($P@k$) and recall at k ($R@k$) as given in (7) and (8). We present the macro average for $P@k$ as $MP@k$ and for $R@k$ as $MR@k$. Macro F1 at k is the harmonic mean of $MP@k$ and $MR@k$. Since semantically indeterminate kNCs have about two gold trees, we evaluate the systems for $1 \leq k \leq 2$.

[9]Structure patterns are generalized structures such as [A B] [C D] for [*air traffic*] [*control centres*].

System	MRP	MP@1	MR@1	MF1@1	MP@2	MR@2	MF1@2
FAST	**70.0%**	**72.7%**	**47.5%**	**57.5%**	60.6%	74.2%	66.7%
SAST	69.5%	69.7%	44.4 %	54.2%	**63.6%**	**78.8%**	**70.4%**
LIDST	54.5%‡	69.7%	44.4%	54.2%	47.0% ‡	59.1% ‡	52.4%‡
LINDST	62.9%‡	69.7%	44.4%	54.2%	54.5% †	66.7% †	60.0 %†
UPPER	86.0%	96.7%	67.2%	79.3%	70.0%	87.8%	77.9%
FREQ	60.1%	63.6%	38.4%	47.9%	56.1%	65.2%	60.3%
CHANCE	32.0%	39.4%	23.7%	29.6%	33.3 %	42.4 %	37.3%

Table 4: Results on CST of 4NCs; ‡ means significantly outperformed by FAST and SAST; † means significantly outperformed by FAST or SAST

$$P@k = \frac{|\text{top-}k(sys\ trees) \cap gold\ trees|}{|\text{top-}k(sys\ trees)|} \quad (7)$$

$$R@k = \frac{|\text{top-}k(sys\ trees) \cap gold\ trees|}{|gold\ trees|} \quad (8)$$

3.4 Models in Comparison

We compare FAST and SAST against LIDST. While this system uses the majority vote as deterministic output, we add a further system by ranking all trees by vote frequency and evaluate this ranking as the **l**anguage-**i**solated **n**on-**d**eterministic **s**tructure **t**ransfer, LINDST. As baselines, we use the random baseline, CHANCE, that creates an arbitrary tree ranking, and the frequency baseline, FREQ, that creates a tree ranking according to the structure pattern frequencies in the test set (i.e., the tree with the most frequent structure pattern is ranked first), e.g., [A B] [C D] is most often annotated as shown in Table 3. To calculate an upper bound, one of the authors provided an additional annotation of the 4NC test set, UPPER. Since Ziering and Van der Plas (2015) showed that CST on kNCs works best in a type-based setting, we evaluate all models on types.

3.5 Results and Discussion

Table 5 shows the results of the mean R-Precision (MRP) on the test set of 3NCs and 4NCs. All CST systems outperform the baselines. Moreover, FAST and SAST outperform LIDST and LINDST, but differences are small.

Because the annotations suggest that 4NCs contain more semantically indeterminate structures, we expect to find larger differences between deterministic and non-deterministic CST when evaluating on 4NCs separately.

System	MRP
FAST	93.7%
SAST	**94.0%**
LIDST	92.6%
LINDST	92.0%
FREQ	84.6%
CHANCE	62.5%

Table 5: MRP results on CST of 3NC/4NCs

Table 4 shows the results on CST of 4NCs. For the mean R-Precision, FAST and SAST significantly[10] outperform LIDST and LINDST. Precision and Recall at 1 are similar for all CST methods, i.e., the top position of the systems' rankings hardly differ. For Precision and Recall at 2, FAST and SAST significantly outperform deterministic CST. Furthermore, SAST outperforms the non-deterministic LINDST significantly in MRP and Precision/Recall at 2. Beside the benefit of a non-deterministic approach for dealing with semantic indeterminacy, the global perspective of FAST and SAST makes the process more robust to word alignment errors: while the monolingually deterministic approaches merge adjacent constituent pairs on each tree level in isolation, FAST and SAST validate trees according to AWD annotations across all levels of the tree. This way, unwanted trees are demoted.

As an example, Table 6 shows the different rankings for the semantically indeterminate expression *harmful business tax regimes*, which has the two gold structures *harmful* [*business* [*tax regimes*]] and *harmful* [[*business tax*] *regimes*]. While FAST ranks both correct structures on first position (rows 1-2) and the false structure [*harmful business*] [*tax regimes*] on the second position,

[10] Approximate randomization test (Yeh, 2000), $p < 5\%$

the deterministic LIDST has decided for the false structure and the non-deterministic LINDST has at least one correct tree among the top 2 structures.

Structure Pattern	FAST	LIDST	LINDST
A [B [C D]]	1	–	2
A [[B C] D]	1	–	–
[A B] [C D]	2	1	1

Table 6: Ranking for *harmful business tax regimes*

4 Tree Accumulation for Deterministic Structure Transfer

Beside the non-deterministic structure transfer motivated by semantic indeterminacy, accumulative CST also represents a way for combining partial structure evidence from several languages into a deterministic output, where each individual language cannot provide a single structure.

For example, the determinate 4NC *energy efficiency action plan* has only one gold structure: [*energy efficiency*] [*action plan*]. A Spanish translation is ***plan** de **acción** de **eficiencia energética*** (plan of action of efficiency energy$_{ADJ}$). Since AWD(*energy efficiency*, *action*) equals AWD(*action*, *plan*), Spanish provides two possible structures: [[*energy efficiency*] *action*] *plan* and [*energy efficiency*] [*action plan*]. A German translation is ***Aktionsplan** zur **Effizienz** von **Energie*** (action plan {for the} efficiency of energy). According to German, AWD(*energy*, *efficiency*) equals AWD(*efficiency*, *action plan*). This leads to the two structures *energy* [*efficiency* [*action plan*]] and [*energy efficiency*] [*action plan*]. Since no language provides a single structure, LIDST cannot produce a deterministic output. In contrast, using tree accumulation we can combine the fact that the Spanish translation groups *energy* and *efficiency* closest together with the fact that the German equivalent puts *action* and *plan* into a closed compound. This results in the top-ranked structure: [*energy efficiency*] [*action plan*].

In an alternative scenario, the determinate 4NC *air transport industry representatives* having the gold structure [[*air transport*] *industry*] *representatives* is translated to Dutch as *vertegenwoordigers van de luchtvervoersector* (representatives of the air transport sector) and to Italian as *rappresentanti del settore del trasporto aereo* (representatives of the sector of the transport air$_{ADJ}$). Since the closed Dutch compound *luchtvervoersector* (air transport sector) hides the internal structure and the Italian paraphrase leads to AWD(*air transport*, *industry*) being equal to AWD(*industry*, *representatives*), both individual languages cannot be used for producing a single structure. However, the Dutch translation provides the information that *representatives* has to be separated from the rest and the Italian translation provides evidence for *air transport* having the strongest semantic cohesion. Accumulating all valid trees from Dutch and Italian, we get the single top-ranked structure: [[*air transport*] *industry*] *representatives*.

5 Conclusion

We have addressed semantic indeterminacy in NPs, a phenomenon often discussed, but usually discarded in previous work. We presented two models of cross-lingual structure transfer that output a ranked list of possible tree structures accumulated from parallel data. Having observed that structural variation for semantic indeterminacy is encountered in particular across languages, we applied our cross-lingual tree ranking for capturing semantically equivalent structures. To be able to evaluate our systems, we use common IR metrics. In an experiment on 3NCs and 4NCs, we showed that our methods outperform previous work significantly. Finally, we showed how tree accumulation can be used for combining partial structure evidence from various languages to form a deterministic structure output.

In future work, we will further investigate the nature of semantic indeterminacy and try to model this phenomenon using distributional semantics. Along with this paper, we publish[11] our 4NC test set, which can be used as training and test data for supervised learners.

Acknowledgments

We thank the anonymous reviewers for their helpful feedback. This research was funded by the German Research Foundation (Collaborative Research Centre 732, Project D11).

References

Otto Behaghel. 1909. Beziehungen zwischen Umfang und Reihenfolge von Satzgliedern. *Indogermanische Forschungen*.

[11] ims.uni-stuttgart.de/data/4NC.TestSet.tgz

Taylor Berg-Kirkpatrick and Dan Klein. 2010. Phylogenetic Grammar Induction. In *ACL 2010*.

Shane Bergsma, David Yarowsky, and Kenneth Church. 2011. Using Large Monolingual and Bilingual Corpora to Improve Coordination Disambiguation. In *ACL-HLT 2011*.

Chris Buckley and Ellen M. Voorhees. 2000. Evaluating Evaluation Measure Stability. In *SIGIR 2000*.

David Burkett and Dan Klein. 2008. Two Languages are Better than One (for Syntactic Parsing). In *EMNLP 2008*.

Kenneth Church and Ramesh Patil. 1982. Coping with Syntactic Ambiguity or How to Put the Block in the Box on the Table. *Computational Linguistics*.

Victoria Fossum and Kevin Knight. 2008. Using bilingual Chinese-English word alignments to resolve PPattachment ambiguity in English. In *AMTA Student Workshop 2008*.

Donald Hindle and Mats Rooth. 1993. Structural Ambiguity and Lexical Relations. *Computational Linguistics*.

Rebecca Hwa, Philip Resnik, Amy Weinberg, Clara Cabezas, and Okan Kolak. 2005. Bootstrapping Parsers via Syntactic Projection Across Parallel Texts. *Natural Language Engineering*.

Tomoharu Iwata, Daichi Mochihashi, and Hiroshi Sawada. 2010. Learning Common Grammar from Multilingual Corpus. In *ACL 2010*.

Mark Lauer. 1995. *Designing Statistical Language Learners: Experiments on Noun Compounds*. Ph.D. thesis, Macquarie University.

Mitchell P. Marcus, Mary Ann Marcinkiewicz, and Beatrice Santorini. 1993. Building a Large Annotated Corpus of English: The Penn Treebank. *Computational Linguistics*.

Florian Schwarck, Alexander Fraser, and Hinrich Schütze. 2010. Bitext-Based Resolution of German Subject-Object Ambiguities. In *NAACL-HLT 2010*.

Lee Schwartz, Takako Aikawa, and Chris Quirk. 2003. Disambiguation of English PP Attachment using Multilingual Aligned Data. In *MT Summit IX*.

David A. Smith and Noah A. Smith. 2004. Bilingual Parsing with Factored Estimation: Using English to Parse Korean. In *EMNLP 2004*.

Benjamin Snyder, Tahira Naseem, and Regina Barzilay. 2009. Unsupervised Multilingual Grammar Induction. In *ACL-IJCNLP 2009*.

Jörg Tiedemann. 2012. Parallel Data, Tools and Interfaces in OPUS. In *LREC 2012*.

David Vadas. 2009. *Statistical Parsing of Noun Phrase Structure*. Ph.D. thesis.

David Yarowsky and Grace Ngai. 2001. Inducing Multilingual POS Taggers and NP Bracketers via Robust Projection Across Aligned Corpora. In *NAACL 2001*.

Alexander Yeh. 2000. More Accurate Tests for the Statistical Significance of Result Differences. In *COLING 2000*.

Patrick Ziering and Lonneke van der Plas. 2014. What good are 'Nominalkomposita' for 'noun compounds': Multilingual Extraction and Structure Analysis of Nominal Compositions using Linguistic Restrictors. In *COLING 2014*.

Patrick Ziering and Lonneke van der Plas. 2015. From a Distance: Using Cross-lingual Word Alignments for Noun Compound Bracketing. In *IWCS 2015*.

Lost in Discussion? – Tracking Opinion Groups in Complex Political Discussions by the Example of the FOMC Meeting Transcriptions

Cäcilia Zirn, Robert Meusel and Heiner Stuckenschmidt
{caecilia, robert, heiner}@informatik.uni-mannheim.de
Data and Web Science Group
University of Mannheim
Germany

Abstract

The Federal Open Market Committee (FOMC) is a committee within the central banking system of the US and decides on the target rate. Analyzing the positions of its members is a challenge even for experts with a deep knowledge of the financial domain. In our work, we aim at automatically determining opinion groups in transcriptions of the FOMC discussions. We face two main challenges: first, the positions of the members are more complex as in common opinion mining tasks because they have more dimensions than *pro* or *contra*. Second, they cannot be learned as there is no labeled data available. We address the challenge using graph clustering methods to group the members, including the similarity of their speeches as well as agreement and disagreement they show towards each other in discussions. We show that our approach produces stable opinion clusters throughout successive meetings and correlates with positions of speakers on a dove-hawk scale estimated by experts.

1 Introduction

In many discussions, participants can easily be divided into two opposing groups, for example people who support democrats versus people who support republicans, or people who are *pro* or *contra* towards the discussed topic.

Having a closer look at the argumentation why people support or defend something however might reveal various stances even within one such group. People might have different opinions and reasons why they support or oppose something.

Some discussions have a subject so complex that participants cannot be simply divided in a supporting and an opposing group, like the discussion whether abortion should be legal and if yes, up to which status of the pregnancy. In that case the discussants should be grouped by similar positions rather than into *pro* or *contra* partitions.

In this paper, we are analyzing the discussions of the Federal Open Market Committee (FOMC). The FOMC is a committee within the central banking system of the US and decides on the target rate. The committee meetings are not public, however their transcriptions are released five years later. Understanding the several hundred pages long transcriptions requires a deep knowledge of the financial ecosystem. Apparently even for experts the analysis of those documents is intricate and time-consuming.

Our goal is to develop a robust approach to reveal the opinion groups present in discussions where positions are complex to detect and the content is difficult to understand for non-experts. Furthermore, we want to assist human readers with a fast automatic system to avoid reading those immense amounts of text.

There are two major reasons that make it difficult to directly learn a model for the different opinion groups hidden in the discussions. First, the data is not labeled. This is mainly due to the small number of people having sufficient knowledge of this particular domain. In order to overcome this issue, the votes at the end of each meeting, where the discussion members finally decide on the target rate, seem to be a valid starting point to serve as labels. Those votes, however, do not reveal the position of the individual speakers, as they agree on consenting votes. Thus the voting records cannot serve to learn the opinions of the committee's members. The second issue is that topics discussed in the meetings might vary. To address those issues, we choose to cluster opinion groups in each discussion dynamically, using an unsupervised approach.

There are some experts analyzing the FOMC's

Proceedings of Recent Advances in Natural Language Processing, pages 747–753,
Hissar, Bulgaria, Sep 7–9 2015.

members and discussions. They usually place the discussants on a scale between *doves* and *hawks*. Doves aim at higher employment, whereas hawks focus on a low inflation rate. However, this classification might not be appropriate to capture opinion groups: although two people might tend to behave rather hawkish, they still can have different views on how the discussed problem should be solved. We also have to keep in mind that political positions are not limited to one dimension only, but span over several ones, like left-right or liberal-conservative, to mention only a few.

To find opinion groups, we focus on two things: First, we compare the terms used to express a position among the speakers. According to political science, if speakers use the same terms, they share a similar position, as described by Laver et al. (Laver et al., 2003) and also Slapin et al. (Slapin and Proksch, 2008), among others. We will hence analyze the pairwise overlap of the speakers' vocabulary. Second, we investigate how they address each other throughout the discussion. Do speakers agree to their predecessor? Do they disagree and argue against each other's arguments?

In the rest of the paper, we will present our method to cluster positions of speakers in complex political discussions when neither labels are provided nor the underlying opinion groups are known in advance.

2 FOMC Data

The FOMC is a committee within the central banking system of the United States and decides on the target rate. The committee consists of members of the Federal Reserve Board and Federal Reserve Bank presidents. Twelve of the members have voting rights, while the rest is only allowed to attend and participate in the discussions. The meetings are non-public and the members know each other well, which allows an open and direct dialogue. As described by Havrilesky and Gildea in (Havrilesky and Gildea, 1991) and also by Adolph in (Adolph, 2013), the committee decides with consenting votes – dissenting votes appear rarely, although the members do have different goals and positions.

The transcriptions of the meetings are only released after five years and comprise several hundred pages in PDF format. In our work, we analyze the transcriptions of the FOMC meetings between 2005 and 2008. This includes 41 meetings, each containing 43 600 words and 24 speakers on average. The total number of different speakers for the selected meetings is 96.

FOMC members are considered to act *dovish* or *hawkish*. Doves aim at higher employment, whereas hawks focus on a low inflation. Domain experts thus classify the FOMC members into *doves*, *moderate doves*, *centers*, *moderate hawks* and *hawks*. We were able to retrieve this classification for 19 members only, as we could not find information dating back earlier than 2009. We collected estimations from various sources we found on the Web[1]

3 Distinguishing Statements from Discussion Elements

Browsing through the transcriptions, we figured out that there are two types of contributions - in the following called turns - to the discussion. In the first type of turns, the speakers elaborate on their opinion. Presumably they have prepared their argumentation in advance. Following those statements, other speakers ask questions or comment on the speaker's statement; discussions might arise. The contributions to those discussions are shorter and seem to be of a more spontaneous nature. We consider those turns as the second type. We think that the content of those two types of turns – **statements** and **discussion elements** – need to be analyzed with different techniques. **Statements** are prepared and reflect the general position of the speaker. According to research in political science, the political position of a speaker is determined by the topics he speaks about (Grimmer and Stewart, 2013; Hillard et al., 2008; Laver et al., 2003). The speaker will expand on the topics he considers important.

The shorter **discussion elements** are spontaneous reactions to the previous statement. They contain an attitude towards previous turns: the

[1] http://graphics.thomsonreuters.com/F/10/US_HAWKOMETER1010.html,
http://graphics.thomsonreuters.com/F/10/scale.swf
http://cib.natixis.com/flushdoc.aspx?id=54743,
http://www.mauldineconomics.com/editorial/outside-the-box-musical-chairs\\-at-the-fomc/
http://www.ritholtz.com/blog/2009/11/fed-hawks-vs-doves/
http://blogs.wsj.com/economics/2010/09/30/balancing-the-feds-hawks-doves/

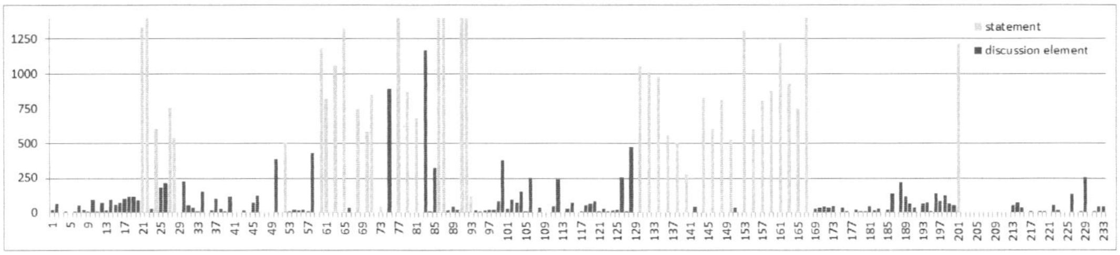

Figure 1: Manually annotated discourse contributions and their lengths (word count).

speaker often expresses agreement or disagreement, as in *"I can see why you assume that, but ..."* or *"To be honest, I don't think ..."*.

We manually annotated one meeting, classifying each discourse contribution either as statement or as discussion element. The sequence of those contributions and their word length together with their assigned class is shown in Figure 1.

From the diagram, we can see that the threshold between the statements and the discussion elements is around five hundred words. We use this number as a shallow heuristic to automatically classify the discourse contributions into statements and discussion elements. Using this straightforward approach, we correctly label 98% of the speaker turns.

3.1 Analyzing Statements

As mentioned before, the positions are expressed through the topics mentioned in the speeches, which are mainly determined by nouns. We conclude that if two speakers share similar views, they are likely to use the same vocabulary. Therefore, we access the closeness of speakers by calculating the similarities between their speeches.

As observed in Section 3, the speakers' positions are represented by the longer statements rather then the short discussion elements, so we only use the former to compare positions. In the spontaneous discussion elements, speakers tend to repeat the vocabulary of their previous speakers, for example by phrases like *"I do not agree with your view on unemployment."*, which would influence our similarity calculation. In natural language, topics are mainly determined by nouns. So we keep nouns only, lemmatize them and represent every speaker for each meeting as a word vector. Then we pairwise compare the vectors of each meeting using cosine similarity.

As we do not have a gold standard to evaluate the similarity calculation, we investigate whether the similarity between two speakers is pertained across all meetings. Two speakers having close positions in one meeting should have close ones in further meetings, too, as they are not likely to change their position while being on the committee. For each speaker pair, we calculate the standard deviation of the similarities across all meetings they both attended. It ranges from 0 to 0.37 (0.08 on average). For two thirds of the speaker pairs the standard deviation is below 0.1. Hence, this approach can be considered as being very robust.

To evaluate our hypothesis that the longer statements are more relevant for determining the speakers' positions, we compare the above described results to the similarities calculated using all utterances of a speaker including spontaneous discussion elements. The standard deviations range up to 0.46 with an average of 0.1. For better comparability, we plotted the standard deviations for all meetings of both experiments in Figure 2 sorted in descending order. We can clearly see that the standard deviations for the similarities calculated using statements only is continuously below the standard deviations based on both utterance types.

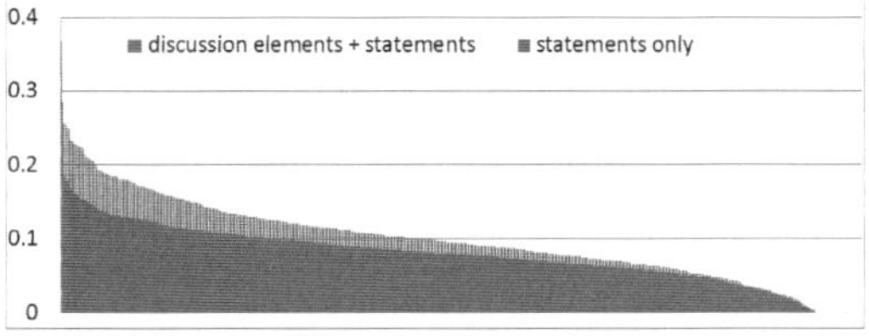

Figure 2: Comparison of the standard deviations of similarities for each speaker pair sorted in descending order calculated on the long statements only vs. calculated on both statements and discussion elements.

3.2 Analyzing Discussion Elements

While we used statements for similarity analyses, we are interested in agreement and disagreement among the speakers within discussion elements. In

(Misra and Walker, 2013), Misra and Walker analyze disagreement and rejection in dialog. They generate a set of cue phrases like *has always been, you don't understand* or *yeah, correct* to classify types of agreement and disagreement and achieve 66% accuracy. We use their cue phrases to detect (dis)agreement within discussion elements. Whenever we find a cue of (dis)agreement within a turn, we consider this as a (dis)agreement of the speaker with his predecessor. We have to consider one special case: discussions are moderated by a **Chairman**. He gives the speakers the floor, like in: "*Other questions for Mr. Kos? President Minehan.*" or "*Thank you. President Moskow.*". So if the predecessor of a turn is the Chairman, the (dis)agreement might actually be towards the Chairman's predecessor. Considering the Chairman only as the moderator is not quite appropriate, however, as he is also a participating member of the committee and thus representing his own position, too. To find the correct predecessor of a disagreement statement, we therefore have to distinguish between a call for the next speaker or the Chairman's personal contribution. We use a simple heuristic: if the Chairman mentions the following speaker's name, he is considered as moderator. We then treat his predecessor as the aim of the (dis)agreement and ignore the Chairman's turn.

4 Clustering Opinion Groups

In Subsection 3.1, we explained how we calculated the similarity between two speakers' positions based on their statements. In Subsection 3.2, we described how we detect agreement and disagreement among the speakers. To determine opinion groups in the FOMC discussions, we make use of both properties. The interactions and similarities describe the relations between the speakers. Hence it seems reasonable to model the speakers as nodes in a graph with their relations constituting the edges.

4.1 Graph Clustering

Blondel et al. (Blondel et al., 2008) introduced a novel fast and efficient community detection method for large graphs – called *Louvain Clustering* – which outperforms existing community detection methods. This method is based on optimization of the so called modularity of a network as described by Newman (Newman, 2006). The modularity of a graph or network is a measure of its structure and measures the degree of division of the network into clusters. Networks with a high modularity haven dense clusters with a minimal number of links between the clusters. The method of Blondel et al. works in a two step approach. Within the first phase all nodes are assigned to different communities and the possible gain of modularity is calculated for each node under the premise that it is removed from its own community and assigned to the community of one of its neighbors. Then, the community with the maximal, positive gain is chosen. The phase stops, when a local maximum is reached an no node can be assigned to another community to increase the modularity. In the second phase, a new network is built where a node represents a single community of the original network after phase one. The weights of the links between the new nodes are calculated by summing up all existing weights of links of old nodes between those two communities. After phase two has finished it is possible to reapply phase one until the network does not change any more.

An alternative for community detection is the *VOS Clustering* introduced by Waltman et al. (Waltman et al., 2010). This technique combines VOS mapping with a weighted and parametrized variant of the modularity function of Newman and Girvan (Girvan and Newman, 2002).

4.2 Graph Construction Methodology

We cluster the discussants of every FOMC meeting between 2006 and 2008. For each meeting, we create one graph with the speakers constituting the vertices and the relations between them constituting the edges.

Similarity. Similarity is modeled as undirected edges between two speakers s_1 and s_2 using their cosine similarity, normalized between -1 and 1:

$$sim(s_1, s_2) = norm_{-1,1}(cos(s_1, s_2)) \quad (1)$$

Agreement / Disagreement. Agreement and disagreement are in the first place directed relations: one speaker (dis)agrees with his predecessor. However, we can make the assumption that if a speaker disagrees with his predecessor, the predecessor also disagrees with him. For this reason, we will experiment with directed and undirected (dis)agreement. In order to measure the agreement or disagreement we first count the number of agreements $c_{ag,dir}(s_1, s_2)$ and disagreements $c_{disag,dir}(s_1, s_2)$ of a speaker s_1 towards his predecessor s_2. For the undirected case this count is calculated as shown in the following two equations:

$$c_{ag,undir}(s_1, s_2) = c_{ag,undir}(s_2, s_1) \\ = c_{ag,dir}(s_1, s_2) + c_{ag,dir}(s_2, s_1) \quad (2)$$

$$c_{dis,undir}(s_1, s_2) = c_{dis,undir}(s_2, s_1) \\ = c_{dis,dir}(s_1, s_2) + c_{dis,dir}(s_2, s_1) \quad (3)$$

We than flatten the total counts by using their square roots which we further scale between 0 and 1 as formalized in the following two equations:

$$ag(s_1, s_2) = norm_{0,1}(\sqrt{c_{ag}(s_1, s_2)}) \quad (4)$$

$$dis(s_1, s_2) = norm_{0,1}(\sqrt{c_{dis}(s_1, s_2)}) \quad (5)$$

We merge agreement and disagreement between speakers by subtracting disagreement from their agreement:

$$agDis(s_1, s_2) = ag(s_1, s_2) - dis(s_1, s_2) \quad (6)$$

This results in $agDis$ being scaled between -1 and 1.

4.3 Experiments

We assess the quality of our results in two ways. First, we want to track the robustness of our clusters. We expect opinion groups in one meeting to be retained in the next meeting, as the topics of the meetings are not supposed to have changed completely, neither should the opinions of a speaker have changed so fast. By pairwise comparing the clusters of one meeting to the clusters of the following one, we use the *Rand index* ri introduced by Rand in (Rand, 1971). It is a measure for the similarity between two clusterings of a set of elements, in our case the speakers:

$$ri = \frac{a + b}{a + b + c + d} \quad (7)$$

where a refers to the amount of speaker pairs being within the same cluster in both meetings (*true positives*), b refers to the amount of speaker pairs belonging to different clusters in both meetings (*true negatives*), c refers to the amount of speaker pairs who belong to the same cluster in the first meeting, but not in the second (*false positives*), and d refers to the amount of speakers who belong to different clusters in the first meeting, but to the same cluster in the second meeting (*false negatives*). The Rand index can be interpreted as the accuracy of the clustering.

Edges	Rand index
Similarity	0.634
(Dis-)Agreem. (dir.)	0.701
(Dis-)Agreem. (undir.)	**0.742**
Similarity + (Dis-)Agreem. (undir.)	0.625

Table 1: Louvain Clustering

Edges	Rand index
Similarity	0.621
(Dis-)Agreem. (dir.)	0.783
(Dis-)Agreem. (undir.)	**0.839**
Similarity + (Dis-)Agreem. (undir.)	0.651

Table 2: VOS Clustering

The list of average Rand indexes comparing all pairs of successive meetings is shown in Table 1 (applying Louvain Clustering) and in Table 2 (applying VOS Clustering). Clustering speakers based on similarity edges only, both algorithms reach a Rand index of about 0.6. The results are more stable throughout the meetings when clustering based on the directed (dis-)agreement relations only (0.7 for Louvain, 0.78 for VOS) and even improve using undirected (dis-)agreement, achieving a Rand index of 0.74 for Louvain and 0.84 for VOS. If we combine both edge types, we do not gain stability: With 0.62 and 0.65 respectively the results are worse than using one of the edges types only. It is remarkably however that both edge types being based on completely independent dialog parts and approaches still achieve comparable performance.

In a second experiment we want to verify whether our hypothesis holds that speakers in the same opinion group should have a similar position on the dove-hawk scale. We compare the opinion group clusters to the clustering of the speakers given their dove-hawk labels (*dove, moderate dove, center, moderate hawk, hawk*) calculating the Rand index. The results for Louvain are shown in Table 3, for VOS in Table 4. The results range between 0.62 and 0.77. Like in the pairwise meeting comparison, there is only little difference between directed and undirected (dis-)agreement, the differences spanning from 0.001 to 0.05 only. Again, using one type of edges only outperforms their combination. Instead of increasing perfor-

Edges	Rand index
Similarity	**0.711**
(Dis-)Agreem. (dir.)	0.651
(Dis-)Agreem. (undir.)	0.656
Similarity + (Dis-)Agreem. (undir.)	0.628

Table 3: Louvain Clustering

Edges	Rand index
Similarity	0.666
(Dis-)Agreem. (dir.)	0.743
(Dis-)Agreem. (undir.)	**0.768**
Similarity + (Dis-)Agreem. (undir.)	0.675

Table 4: VOS Clustering

mance, we receive the average performance of both information sources – the algorithm seems to suffer from contradictory information. We will further investigate how to combine information sources in an appropriate way. In general, the results show that the dove-hawk positions are correlated with the opinion groups we derive.

5 Related Work

Common approaches for position analysis in political science scale texts based on word frequencies and co-occurrences as described by Grimmer (Grimmer, 2010), by Quinn et al. (Quinn et al., 2010), and by Gerrish and Blei (Gerrish and Blei, 2011). Approaches developed in the field of computational linguistics usually classify speakers or texts as *pro* and *contra* towards discussed topic. Anand et al. (Anand et al., 2011), Somasundaran and Wiebe (Somasundaran and Wiebe, 2009), and Walker et al. (Walker et al., 2012) all classify stance in on-line debates. While Anand et al. use a supervised learning approach, Somasundaran and Wiebe mine opinions and opinion targets from the web. Then, they combine the thereby learned stance with discourse information formulating an Integer Linear Programming problem. The approach of Walker et al. makes use of *same author* links and *rebuttal* links to model posts as a graph, cutting it into two parts (*pro* and *contra*) with *MaxCut*. These methods are hardly applicable to our complex discussion data for reasons we elaborated in Section 1.

A similar idea to our approach is described by Thomas et al. (Thomas et al., 2006). Their goal is to label congressional floor-debate speeches as supporting or opposing the discussed topic. In contrast to our approach, where speakers are the nodes, they model speech turns as nodes connected by *same label* relations. They then find minimum cuts in the resulting graph.

Abu-Jbara et al. (Abu-Jbara et al., 2012) explore the dialog structure in on-line debates with the goal of subgroup detection. They represent each discussion participant as a vector consisting of the polarity and the target of their opinionated phrases, combining it with the information about who replies to whom. In a final step, they cluster the vectors. They point out that the reply feature needs further investigation since they cannot tell whether speakers tend to agree or disagree when they answer each other.

6 Conclusion

We presented a completely unsupervised approach to cluster opinion groups in the complex political discussions of the FOMC using two independent types of information. On the one side, we made use of the similarity between the speakers' statements, on the other hand we integrated their behavior towards each other within discussions. For this, we detected agreement and disagreement using cue phrases. Both types of information turned out to be comparably useful for clustering the speakers. Our simple strategy to distinguish between statements and discussion elements - the two sources of information - is straightforward and effective. We showed that the results are stable throughout successive meetings and correlate with the dove-hawk positions for speakers estimated by experts.

Regarding further challenges, we have to investigate how we can improve the combination of various information sources, e.g. by weighting them. In addition, we plan to add further sources like political party adherence, background of a speaker or their function in the FOMC, such as member of the Federal Reserve Board or Federal Reserve Bank president.

References

Amjad Abu-Jbara, Mona Diab, Pradeep Dasigi, and Dragomir Radev. 2012. Subgroup detection in ideological discussions. In *Proceedings of the 50th Annual Meeting of the Association for Computational Linguistics: Long Papers - Volume 1*, ACL '12, pages 399–409, Stroudsburg, PA, USA. Association for Computational Linguistics.

Christopher Adolph. 2013. *Bankers, Bureaucrats, and Central Bank Politics: The Myth of Neutrality*. Cambridge University Press.

Pranav Anand, Marilyn Walker, Rob Abbott, Jean E. Fox Tree, Robeson Bowmani, and Michael Minor. 2011. Cats rule and dogs drool!: Classifying stance in online debate. In *Proceedings of the 2Nd Workshop on Computational Approaches to Subjectivity and Sentiment Analysis*, WASSA '11, pages 1–9, Stroudsburg, PA, USA. Association for Computational Linguistics.

Vincent D. Blondel, Jean-Loup Guillaume, Renaud Lambiotte, and Etienne Lefebvre. 2008. Fast unfolding of communities in large networks. *Journal of Statistical Mechanics: Theory and Experiment*, 2008(10):P10008.

Sean Gerrish and David M. Blei. 2011. Predicting legislative roll calls from text. In *Proceedings of the 28th International Conference on Machine Learning (ICML-11)*, pages 489–496.

Michelle Girvan and M. E. J. Newman. 2002. Community structure in social and biological networks. *Proceedings of the National Academy of Sciences*, 99(12):7821–7826, June.

Justin Grimmer and Brandon M. Stewart. 2013. Text as data: The promise and pitfalls of automatic content analysis methods for political texts. *Political Analysis*.

Justin Grimmer. 2010. A bayesian hierarchical topic model for political texts: Measuring expressed agendas in senate press releases. *Political Analysis*, 18(1):1–35.

Thomas Havrilesky and John Gildea. 1991. The policy preferences of fomc members as revealed by dissenting votes: Comment. *Journal of Money, Credit and Banking*, 1:130–138.

Dustin Hillard, Stephen Purpura, and John Wilkerson. 2008. Computer assisted topic classification for mixed methods social science research. *Journal of Information Technology and Politics*.

Michael Laver, Kenneth Benoit, and John Garry. 2003. Extracting policy positions from political texts using words as data. *American Political Science Review*, 97(02):311–331.

Amita Misra and Marilyn A. Walker. 2013. Topic independent identification of agreement and disagreement in social media dialogue. In *Conference of the Special Interest Group on Discourse and Dialogue*, page 920.

M. E. J. Newman. 2006. Modularity and community structure in networks. *Proceedings of the National Academy of Sciences*, 103(23):8577–8582.

Kevin M. Quinn, Burt L. Monroe, Michael Colaresi, Michael H. Crespin, and Dragomir R. Radev. 2010. How to analyze political attention with minimal assumptions and costs. *American Journal of Political Science*, 54(1):209–228, January.

W.M. Rand. 1971. Objective criteria for the evaluation of clustering methods. *Journal of the American Statistical Association*, 66(336):846–850.

Jonathan B. Slapin and Sven-Oliver Proksch. 2008. A Scaling Model for Estimating Time-Series Party Positions from Texts. *American Journal of Political Science*, 52(3):705–722, July.

Swapna Somasundaran and Janyce Wiebe. 2009. Recognizing stances in online debates. In *Proceedings of the Joint Conference of the 47th Annual Meeting of the ACL and the 4th International Joint Conference on Natural Language Processing of the AFNLP: Volume 1 - Volume 1*, ACL '09, pages 226–234, Stroudsburg, PA, USA. Association for Computational Linguistics.

Matt Thomas, Bo Pang, and Lillian Lee. 2006. Get out the vote: Determining support or opposition from congressional floor-debate transcripts. In *Proceedings of the 2006 Conference on Empirical Methods in Natural Language Processing*, EMNLP '06, pages 327–335, Stroudsburg, PA, USA. Association for Computational Linguistics.

Marilyn A. Walker, Pranav Anand, Robert Abbott, and Ricky Grant. 2012. Stance classification using dialogic properties of persuasion. In *Proceedings of the 2012 Conference of the North American Chapter of the Association for Computational Linguistics: Human Language Technologies*, pages 592–596. Association for Computational Linguistics.

Ludo Waltman, Nees Jan van Eck, and Ed C.M. Noyons. 2010. A unified approach to mapping and clustering of bibliometric networks. *Journal of Informetrics*, 4(4):629 – 635.